Best American Plays

Eighth Series
1974-1982

Best American Plays

Eighth Series

1974-1982

Edited by

Clive Barnes

Introduction and biographies of Neil Simon,
Tennessee Williams, Lanford Wilson, and
David Rabe by Clive Barnes

Other biographies by Lori Weinless

Crown Publishers, Inc.
New York

Acknowledgment is due to the following for their cooperation in the preparation of this volume: Atheneum Publishers; The Dial Press; Dodd, Mead, & Co.; Farrar, Straus, and Giroux, Inc.; Samuel French, Inc.; Graham Agency; Grove Press; JCA Literary Agency; The Lantz Office, Inc.; Macmillan Publishing Co., Inc.; William Morris Agency; Ellen Neuwald, Inc.; New Directions Publishing Corp.; Random House, Inc.; Howard Rosenstone and Co., Inc.; Urizen Books, Inc.; Viking-Penguin, Inc.

Inquiries should be addressed to Crown Publishers, Inc., One Park Avenue, New York, New York 10016

Printed in the United States of America

Published simultaneously in Canada by General Publishing Company Limited

Library of Congress Catalog Card Number: 57-12830

ISBN: 0-517-54480-6

10 9 8 7 6 5 4 3 2 1

First Edition

Contents

Introduction

by Clive Barnes

It is only the editors of newspapers and magazines, together with a few professional cultural pundits, who believe that trends in the arts happen overnight and can, at least, be detected every three months or so. In fact, artistic trends are very slow-moving currents in the general stream. And expectedly so. So many factors are present in the birth of any artistic movement. Obviously there might well be the vision of one great artist, or a group of artists. Then there are economic factors: Is the economy fat or lean? What are people spending money on? What is governmental, as opposed to private, spending? There are also sociological factors: developments in technology, changes in fashion and function in the other arts, the state of education, and the whole pattern of the way people live and work. Finally, there is recognition and public acceptance.

The arts are not like fashion, where each year the fashion avatars and merchandising moguls declare that hemlines and necklines will go up or down. There is little that is arbitrary about art, and to treat it as if it were a creature of chance rather than circumstance is to do it a grave disservice.

It is just about nine years since the last John Gassner *Best American Plays* series appeared, and during these nine years almost nothing has happened. At least in the theatre. In fairness, even this is not precisely true. Of course, a great deal has happened. Plays have been written. Sometimes even produced. And when produced they have bombed or blossomed. Money has been made. Once in a while art has been created. The theatre continues, much as before, when seen through the historical perspective of a nine-year sprint. Movements are in quarter- or half-centuries. Nine years only make a ripple.

So the theatre is more or less where it was nine years ago. More or less—but, of course (for such must be the trend of history) in even nine years it will be more more and less less.

Nine years ago—even twenty years ago, if you had good eyesight—it was apparent that the general trend of the American theatre was a movement away from the private toward the public sector. And, of course, this would naturally have a marked, possibly profound, effect on the plays written and, even more, the plays produced. What do I mean by the private and public sectors? A good, fair, but difficult question.

Traditionally the American theatre, unlike, say, the American symphony, was exclusively a matter of private enterprise. The theatre was intended to make money. To make money, naturally enough, for the playwright, actors and stage staff, as this was their livelihood, but also to make money for a fairly mysterious, and sometimes even shady, entrepreneur called the producer. At first the entrepreneur put up the money, paid the bills and either reaped the profits or absorbed the loss.

Occasionally the producer might seek the financial assistance of backers, sometimes because he believed in art, more often because he was conned into thinking the Great White Way was paved with platinum, or occasionally, because he wanted to keep warm his acquaintanceship with the leading lady or, perish the thought, the leading man. During the 1920s a slightly more sophisticated system arose; numerous investors—or ''angels'' as they were piously called—would provide the hard cash needed for a show's production. Always excepting any ulterior motives, profit was the goal.

This was the American theatre in its private sector. There was no public money in question; according to the varying laws of the day, however, tax losses might be involved. The investment was almost as simple, although gratifyingly not quite so simple, as a fling on a horse or a joust on the Stock Exchange. In those days Broadway was a basic commercial enterprise. But Broadway was also the heart of the American theatre, its heart and also its soul. It was on Broadway that theatrical experiments could be made. Possibly Broadway, at that time, cared little for the past of the American theatre, but its present undeniably projected its future.

This private sector of the American theatre flourished through money, and it perished through money. But only artistically. The simple cost of production rose and rose. At the present, a lavish musical can cost slightly more than $2 million. A play comes in at about $400,000 to $800,000. The climate is not conducive to experiment; it is scarcely even conductive to gambling. Our private sector—our so-called commercial theatre—had to think again. As it happened, it was not a difficult thought. Indeed, the private sector, with its ''angels'' and its deals, was allowed to survive intact so far as money went, but not in function. Here there were to be changes.

Happily, Broadway's function was already being carefully unsurped by theatrical moves and motions beginning soon after World War II. First, remember that prior to, say, 1950, the American theatre was totally and absolutely Broadway. This dominance was maintained over forty or fifty years, and finally, the last significant indigenous theatres across the country gave way first to the movies, and later to television. It was an impossible fight, and for years the only live regional theatre available, apart from amateur theatre at all levels, was provided by Broadway itself—either shows being tested on the road, before they reached Broadway, or touring versions, in various states of disrepair on their often-tattered path away from Broadway. The road company. Even the bus and truck tour.

Finally the theatre fought back. Since World War II resident professional theatres have sprung up all over the country. Incidentally, a few years ago Actors' Equity announced that more of its members were employed outside New York than inside. This is a very welcome and totally irreversible trend.

In the post–World War II era, the American theatre has been disseminated across the country and made manifold in its possibilities. This new resident theatre has represented, to the last, a new concept in our dramatic thinking. And a very dramatic concept it was. Nonprofit.

Think of it. Since Western civilization, such as it was, first landed on our shores, it needed entertainment. Part of that entertainment soon became the theatre. But, from the beginning, this was the entrepreneurial theatre. No one could have imagined a nonprofit theatre—or, for that matter, any elitist art intended for the good of the few, but ultimately providing a benefit for the many.

So Broadway was the private sector, functioning for money to be sure, but still the ultimate focus of the Anglo-American theatre, the place where English-speaking playwrights wanted to hawk their wares, and the actors wanted to strut their stuff. Yet imagine the plight of the poor producer. How could this lily-livered hero take risks? Fear not. The Broadway producer—ingenious to a fault, even if ingenuous to a legend—magnificently found a way.

Broadway decided to go on just the way it had been going. With a few smart changes. It took account of America's new public theatre. This was a theatre, all across the country (and increasingly powerful in New York itself), that was not meant to make money but to make art. This was a new concept. Broadway took it to its bosom and, very reasonably, decided to make a profit out of it. I love it. You couldn't have a more potent or expressive example of an urban cultural form adapting itself to the socioeconomic difficulties of a new world.

Without batting an eyelid, Broadway resigned. The resignation was so sleek you couldn't even put a decade to it, during the event. With the exception of musicals—almost always a pure Broadway product—and one or two comedies, Broadway accepted the concept that most of its product would derive from elsewhere. To be precise, it would derive from the regional theatre across the country, New York's new institutional, nonprofit theatre, such as: Joseph Papp's New York Shakespeare Festival, the Manhattan Theatre Club, New York's Off Broadway and Off-Off-Broadway (the terms have to do with union deals rather than geography), and finally, the London theatre, whose function, even in relationship to Broadway, is far too complex to describe with confidence or even honesty.

But Broadway is certainly still producing plays. Indeed, Broadway has never in its history been in a better financial position. Broadway is making a fortune. And good luck to it. This is the way we, as Americans, obviously want our theatre to function. There isn't much in the way of experiment you can handle on Broadway. Once in a while you will come upon some unexpectedly blinding experience, which actually had the chutzpah to start on Broadway, such as *Sweeney Todd*. But these, however magnificent, are few and far between.

Broadway has not changed its attitude, or, for that matter, its crap-table view of financing. But the times have changed. Nowadays it does not see itself as the melting furnace of our theatre's creativity. More modestly it sees itself as a shop window. Aesthetically, it has moved from a Picasso to an Yves St. Laurent, with all the possibilities both choices offer.

The strange thing is that Broadway, being aware of its new situation, and carefully testing its consumer projects farther and farther away from the final steeling furnace, seems to be doing extraordinarily well. Financially it has not changed its process. Its backers are out for a buck—or maybe even more than a buck. The public theatre—financed by federal, state, municipal and foundation funds, much benefited by corporate industrial grants, rich patrons and (this is essential) the massive support of small and loving contributors—is wonderfully open for experiment. And Broadway lies in wait.

This, indeed, is unfair. Broadway and the rest of the theatre (one might almost say the creative theatre) have a fine symbiotic relationship. Broadway works closely with its sources. So, Broadway's laboratory is as dead as escalating prices and craft union pressures can make it. Yet by offering the best of the new theatre—which is primarily what it does—the private sector of Broadway has gotten together with the odd, public theatre and the curiously designed art theatre across the country.

Selecting anything on an objective scale of merit is frankly one of the most futile efforts of mankind. As a critic in modestly good standing, I find myself being forever questioned about the best of this or the best of that. Rubbish! Nothing is best or worst. And democratic process has nothing to do with art. Opinions must be subjective. This present selection of plays is a good and eloquent representation of its period. We have seventeen plays. They were chosen by myself and my friend and editor, Herb Michelman. I had the final choice—editors always do that to make one feel guilty—or (sometimes) to permit one to take the glory.

Seventeen plays. Most of them (not all) made it to Broadway. Most however, such as *Talley's Folly, The Ritz, American Buffalo, Wings* and *for colored girls,* hit Broadway only after a ricochet course in our present amusement arcade of strange pinball machines.

The quality of plays is getting better. For its hits and misses syndrome, Broadway has found some kind of balance. It is able today to purchase rather than initially create and often, having purchased a property (some of us still call it a play), can provide it with a cast and director, together with the right financial backing, that the nonprofit theatre could scarcely dream of. During the past few years Broadway and the institutional theatre, with all of their funding possibilities, have gotten together almost dangerously well.

With any list of best plays one is going to appear idiosyncratic after ten years, intriguingly positive after twenty-five, and plain damn foolish after a half-century. Criticism is not soothsaying. And when I am faced with the theatre's future, I bring skepticism to new and handsome heights. However, these plays do, I believe, provide an overview of this particular dramatic territory. I have recommended the selection to my son and daughter; anyone capable of taking such a crazy risk deserves consideration, if not a medal.

We try, in this series, to get what we want. I am the successor, in choosing these plays, of a great academic, John Gassner. And, in terms of plays, he knew what he wanted, even if he didn't always get it. In this spirit, I wish to acknowledge a play I tried (and failed) to get from its publisher. The management, unfortunately, did not let us have Michael Bennett's sumptuous—but I underestimate—staging of *A Chorus Line.*

A Chorus Line, however, represents something typical of the contemporary Broadway scene, not especially in its quality, but essentially in how it came to be on Broadway. *A Chorus Line* (after the final figures are in) may be the most successful musical, financially that is, since the beginning of the Broadway musical. Yet, fascinatingly, it did not start, or even end on Broadway. It began as an idea from director/choreographer Michael Bennett, who worked out that idea in a workshop at Joseph Papp's New York Shakespeare Festival Public Theater. It started life at the Public, and, indeed, was an underground hit before it ever reached Broadway. This is a new way to stage a Broadway hit. No longer do you mess around with Philadelphia, Boston and all those legendary try-out towns; instead, you go straight to the source.

Included in the present collection, is another example of this new phenomenon. Pomerance's *The Elephant Man* provides a type history of a certain kind of Broadway success. Pomerance is an American-born author living in London. He wrote his play, and it had a modest London reception. However, it was picked up by a New York management, slightly amended and staged very successfully Off Broadway. This production, with its original cast, was moved to Broadway, where it won a Tony for the Best Play of 1979.

It justifiably sold out for about a year; eventually sales flagged. An adroit management put the British pop rock star, David Bowie, in the leading role, and instantly the box-office figures climbed to capacity. *The Elephant Man,* a most rewarding play, has been made typical of the new Broadway system of presentation. It does not, of course, lessen the value of the play. But it does call attention to the system that supports it.

Yet this is a cynical approach to our theatre. For the expansion of our theatrical horizons, the possibility of our dramatists doing big things in small places (released from the essential pressure of a Broadway audience) has played an essential part in the ongoing history of our theatre.

In this present list of best plays—and once again remember best is relative!—there are a number of perfectly conventional, but, I hope, perfectly marvelous scripts. Neil Simon is not going to make history; he is only going to write plays. Yet his plays, I think, will stand that particularly corrosive test of time. He has a comedian's style that unexpectedly survives, as in the cases of Noël Coward or Philip Barry. This kind of playwright has to die to achieve fame—luckily he is terribly well paid while alive. I find Simon's *Chapter Two* a poignantly eloquent testimony to the way we survive as children and as other animals.

Realism has consistently been a force in the American theatre. Realism? One might well tag it naturalism. During the period of the Group Theatre, and later, when the American theatre first came alive, this realism/naturalism bent ran breathlessly parallel to the better equipped movie camera carrying a great deal before it. Indeed, while the rest of the world had started to wait for Godot, we in America were still waiting for Lefty. Yet the tradition of realism has persisted as a viable dramatic position. Call it, if you like, a hyperrealization of a TV drama.

Take, for example, Jason Miller's *That Championship Season,* or, with certain symbolic overtones, Joseph A. Walker's *The River Niger.* In comedy one could quote, as we have here, the Canadian author Bernard Slade's buoyant situation continuum, *Same Time, Next Year,* and Terrence McNally's naughtily riotous *The Ritz.*

But all these plays, and many others, could have been written way past the present minute. We have to be particularly fascinated by the Broadway musical and its struggle to find its own way into a conceptualized theatre, considering that its music bears very scant relationship to contemporary pop forms. Hugh Wheeler's book for the musical *A Little Night Music* beautifully supports Stephen Sondheim's music and lyrics, and possibly points out the blind-searching way for the new concept musical that, even with a genius such as Sondheim, is still bereft of the popular musical roots that once sustained it.

Most of the plays we have selected for this anthology are probably less complex in reasoning—at least in the reasoning as to why they were selected—and more complex in structure and texture. In a very real way, these plays represent the new drama. The new drama? No drama is new. Perhaps what most of these plays represent is a new realization of the role of the dramatist.

In the past, the dramatist's role had always been comparatively straightforward. After the madness of the Greeks and the heaven-sent poetry of Shakespeare, people pretty well knew what plays were about. They represented human life. They were a mirror held up to nature—with either the warts taken out or the warts left in.

There is a comparison, valid here, regarding nineteenth-century painting and the new art of photography. Right through the middle of the past century, and even beyond, painters fundamantally believed in the naturalism of their image. Be it a portrait, a still life or a landscape, it was seen as an image of reality portrayed—filtered, if you like—through the artist's technique. But, of course, the artist ran into competition from the photographer. Eventually, it became apparent—especially as the camera enlisted its own artists to its cause—that the natural image was the territory of the photographer. The painter had to move into different areas if only to exist. The result? Cézanne and all who have followed him from every "ism" in the book, each "ism" defining a new territory for art, have always found a new independence from that threatening camera.

Once change in theatre and playwriting did take place with the advent of motion pictures. Again that threatening camera. The painters caught up to it late. And so, in a different generation, did the playwrights. The movie camera was to the theatre almost precisely what the still camera had been to the easel view of life. Films, and then, with promiscuous immediacy, television, left the dramatist with his pants down, on the shore of a strange river.

Had you been watching closely there must have been one night—one mystical, horrendous night—when the past, present and future of the theatre was changed, irrevocably. To use Shakespeare's most famous stage direction: "Exit, pursued by a bear." Yet the theatre had to fight back; otherwise, it could scarcely continue to exist.

What has happened is fairly simple. Much of the theatre has done, as it were, a Cézanne. Playwrights have looked at the landscape and found a different realism.

The history of all the arts during the twentieth century has been a journey to abstraction. Yet the arts have also been coping with the effect of mass education that has demanded a kind of participation in the artistic experience. It is art that wants the missing link, the lost and final piece of the jigsaw puzzle, the person, the psyche, the cultural vote. We need to be puzzled by Harold Pinter, because Pinter gives our mind and glands a workout. We may read trash for mindless recreation, but we also want and need a new world of theatre. This is the world that sees itself as it is, but has the courage to break through and find the possibility of another reality beyond its torn curtain of conventionality.

In these special circumstances there has arisen in the United States a new kind of theatrical style I have dubbed symbolic realism. You can see it at its gentlest in Michael Weller's *Loose Ends,* where the story conveys its own simple, but serious message, and, for that matter you can see it in *Creve Coeur,* a recent work by a man who was, theatrically, the Big Daddy of us all—Tennessee Williams.

However the major emphasis of symbolic realism is scarcely a matter of reverberating mirror images offering an invitation to one's own fantasy, although such an approach— viz *Loose Ends*—can be totally valid. But what symbolic realism does—as seen in the work of such exponents as Sam Shepard, David Rabe, Thomas Babe, Ntozake Shange, David Mamet and even Arthur Kopit in *Wings*—is somewhat more oblique.

The discernible method is to take a situation—usually fairly simple—and illuminate it first with language, and then to inform it with a special, symbolic ambiguity of meaning. Presumably this method, or perhaps better, this style, evolved from Samuel Beckett and Harold Pinter, even though many of its practiners may know little or nothing of either playwright. No matter—the style's the thing.

There are many wonderful American plays in this volume and, like its predecessors, it is filled with contrasts. Compare, for example, Arthur Kopit's supremely evocative *Wings*—a play about a woman who has had a stroke—with the tougher texture of Rabe's *Streamers.* Compare these again with the elegaic poems on women, death and transfiguration by Ntozake Shange in *for colored girls.* For that matter compare the ever wayward poetry of Tennessee Williams in *Creve Coeur* with nothing, but then again perhaps with everything in this volume.

What our new playwrights seem to have in common—whether the seemingly Tweedledum and Tweedledee duo of Babe and Rabe (from Joseph Papp's Public Theater), Sam Shepard, David Mamet (with his almost mystic love of language), Arthur Kopit or Ntozake Shange—is a regard for the vernacular. They are certainly seeking truth through their own poetic version.

Any collection of plays, even taken at random, always reveals a great deal of the life and thought of its people, time and period, and this selection certainly does no less. But with today's particular dramatic techniques—its concern with the nuance and underlying, almost musical, truth of everyday speech—this present grouping will tell future generations pretty much how we spoke. Our playwrights, here and now, happen to have turned on to the common or garden poetry of the way we sound.

Isadora Duncan once declared she saw a vision of America dancing. Read this book and you will get a no less poetically impressionistic picture of America speaking. And how better can a people speak than through its playwrights?

Chapter Two

Neil Simon

FOR MARSHA

First presented by Emanuel Azenberg at the Imperial Theatre in New York City on December 4, 1977, with the following cast:

(*in order of appearance*)

GEORGE SCHNEIDER	Judd Hirsch
LEO SCHNEIDER	Cliff Gorman
JENNIE MALONE	Anita Gillette
FAYE MEDWICK	Ann Wedgeworth

Directed by Herbert Ross
Scenery by William Ritman
Costumes by Noel Taylor
Lighting by Tharon Musser

THE SCENE: The action of *Chapter Two* takes place in Jennifer Malone's upper East Side apartment and George Schneider's lower Central Park West apartment. The play begins on a late February afternoon and continues through to midspring.

In many respects Neil Simon must be the most remarkably successful playwright America has ever known. He has written a succession of hit plays, musicals, films, and television shows. Everything he touches turns to laughter and to gold. Yet if ever a man has struggled against his own success it is Neil Simon—who is not only the most successful contemporary playwright in the United States, he is also the most underestimated.

He was born on July 4, 1927. He began by writing revue sketches with his brother, Danny, and was soon remarkably successful in providing material for Sid Caesar's TV series "The Show of Shows." Working with some of the best TV gag writers in the world, and all of them masters of situation comedy, Mr. Simon soon won his spurs and his nickname, "Doc." He went on to write scripts for Phil Silvers in his "Sergeant Bilko" series. Simon later recalled that this was great training for a comedy writer, "because Phil talks so fast that you need to write a three-quarters-of-an-hour script for a half-hour show."

His first play, *Come Blow Your Horn,* was produced in 1961. It was a success in New York, London, and the movies. Mr. Simon's remarkable reign as the King of Broadway was beginning. In the years to come Mr. Simon would always have one show playing on Broadway, often two, and occasionally three. He was to buy his own theatre—the Eugene O'Neill—and to regard anything less than a two-year run as something of a failure.

Early success not infrequently spoils popular writers. Simon set out quite frankly just to make people laugh, and he was perhaps the first important comedy writer to serve his apprenticeship in television comedy. The results of this on his later work, and people's assessment of that work, have significance. He came to comedy with an instinctive sense for what made the mass audience laugh—and he had the TV ratings to prove it.

At first he was a master of the wisecrack—the sparkling one-liner that careened across the stage like a firecracker. But there was always more to Mr. Simon than that: it should be remembered that he was scriptwriter to Sid Caesar, not Bob Hope. Essential even to Mr. Simon's earliest comedies was a feel for life and a natural gift for dialogue. He has often been called a "laugh machine," and in the sense that the laughs have been consistently produced there is some justice in it. But the laughter itself is never mechanical; indeed, his very best jokes are rarely funny out of context. This is the acid test that draws the lines between a playwright who is merely a wisecracker and a playwright who is a comedian.

On the other hand, Mr. Simon's television experience was not always to the good. It has given him a tendency to play for the easy laugh, to go for a caricature rather than a character, and to pull back from anything that might be offensive to his audience. Perhaps this is it: most of the time Mr. Simon measures up his audience a shade too self-consciously. There is nothing wrong with high ratings and good box-office returns, but these should be by-products; there are times when Mr. Simon seems to confuse them with ends.

Mr. Simon's situations are largely autobiographical or, more often, biographical. More than most writers, he feeds on life—his own life and the life of his friends. But, of course, having fed, he digests and, to change a metaphor rapidly getting out of hand, he embroiders. In his plays it is clear that he is becoming increasingly serious. (His musical books, however, such as *Little Me* or *Promises, Promises,* continue to run along happily enough!) Perhaps the first hint of seriousness arrived in 1965 with *The Odd Couple.* This story of two men separated from their wives and setting up house together was both amusing and touching.

From this time on, Mr. Simon has consciously—or so it seems—tried to find a new depth in his comedy. Most comedy deals with losers rather than winners, but increasingly Mr. Simon's losers have been the victims of urban blight, middle-age menopause, and middle-class frustration. To an extent Mr. Simon has been holding up a mirror to his typical Broadway audience, but has taken care to ensure that the lighting is never too harsh.

In the first episode of *Plaza Suite,* for example, we see a man, his wife, and his secretary, and the complications such arrangements occasionally provide. These people are lonely and unfulfilled. Equally lonely is Barney, the fish-restaurateur hero of *The Last of the Red Hot Lovers,* where a married man, feeling desperately as if the sexual revolution has bypassed him at great speed, is desperate to have an affair with another woman. And any "another" woman will do.

With *The Gingerbread Lady,* Mr. Simon perhaps went too far for most of his audience. It tells of the trials and tribulations of a possibly reformed alcoholic, with all her jokes and her miseries. It is a finely written play, but unfortunately audiences failed to respond to anything quite so outside the typecasting they had imposed on Simon. Yet the playwright persevered in his quest for serious urban comedy rooted in the the New York experience. The results were *The Prisoner of Second Avenue* and *The Sunshine Boys*.

Chapter Two is concerned with New York as well, but, more important, it focuses on relationships. Actually, one relationship in particular: George and Jenny. Here we have Simon returning to his earlier autobiographical mode—it is no coincidence that *Chapter Two* is dedicated to Simon's wife Marsha. The terrors and joys of letting someone new into your life, while at the same time letting go of the ghosts from the past, form the core of this play. Its craftsmanship is intuitive rather than classic, yet there is great quality to the writing and a mixture of fun and compassion that raises it from farce to comedy. We have known these people—and not just on television.

ACT ONE

SCENE ONE

*The set consists of two separate apartments on opposite sides of Manhattan—*GEORGE SCHNEIDER *lives in one;* JENNIE MALONE, *in the other.*

His apartment, stage left, is located in the mid-seventies on Central Park West. It is one of New York's older buildings, and the ceilings and rooms are higher and larger than the smaller, flatter, uninteresting boxes they build today.

Hers is one of the smaller, flatter, uninteresting boxes they build today. It is in the upper eighties off Third Avenue.

His is decorated in a traditional, comfortable style—large inviting armchairs and sofa, bookcases from floor to ceiling, lots of personal photographs of him and his wife.

Hers is modern, bright, attractive and cheerful. That's because she is.

We see the living rooms of both apartments plus the entrance doors. His apartment has a kitchen and an archway that leads into four other rooms. Hers has a small kitchen and single bedroom.

It's about 10:30 P.M. in his apartment. The doors opens and GEORGE SCHNEIDER *enters. He wears a coat and scarf and carries a large fully packed leather suitcase and an attaché case. He turns on the lights.* GEORGE *is forty-two years old, an attractive, intelligent man who at this moment seems tired and drawn. He puts down his bags, looks around the room, and goes over to a table where his mail has been placed. A large number of letters have piled up. He goes through them, throwing every second and third piece into the wastebasket; the rest he takes with him to a chair, where he sits and starts to look through them.*

LEO SCHNEIDER *appears, carrying* GEORGE'S *other matching suitcase.* LEO *is about forty. He is wearing a suede sheepskin coat, scarf and gloves.*

———

LEO *(Coming through the door)*. George, you're not going to believe this! I found a place to park right in front of the building. First time in four years . . . I think I'll buy an apartment here—I don't want to give up that space. *(Puts the suitcase down)* Christ Almighty, it's four degrees in here. Whooo! Whyn't you rent it out for the winter Olympics, pay your ex-penses. Where to you turn your heat on? *(*GEORGE *is reading his mail.)* I smell gas. Do you smell gas, George?

GEORGE *(Looks up)*. What?

LEO. *Gas*, for Chrissakes! *(He runs into the kitchen, to the stove.* GEORGE *continues to read his mail.* LEO *comes out.)*

It was on. Didn't you check it before you left? Thank God I didn't have a cigar on me. One match, we'd *both* be back in Italy. *(Turns on the desk lamp)* Where do you turn the heat on? . . . *George?*

GEORGE. What?

LEO. Where is the heater?

GEORGE. The heater? It's, uh . . .

LEO. Take your time. Accuracy is important.

GEORGE. I'm sorry . . . The thermostat's on the wall as you come in the bedroom.

LEO *(Looks at him)*. Are you all right?

GEORGE. No. Am I supposed to be?

LEO. You lost weight, didn't you?

GEORGE. I don't know. A couple of pounds.

LEO. Sure. Who could eat that lousy food in Paris and Rome?

GEORGE. Do you smell gas?

LEO. What?

GEORGE. I smell gas.

LEO. I think your nose is having jet lag, George.

(He goes into the bedroom)

GEORGE. I was going to stay another week in Rome. Then I said, "No, I have to get back. I'm really anxious to be home." *(He looks around)* I wonder why I thought that.

LEO *(Reentering)*. Come on. You walk into Ice Station Zebra with gas leaking in the kitchen and no fresh air in here for four and a half weeks. I mean, this is February and we're standing here breathing January . . . Why don't you make some popcorn, see what's on TV.

(He takes the suitcases into the bedroom. GEORGE *shakes his head)*

GEORGE. God!

LEO *(Enters)*. You've got to see the bathroom. You left the shower dripping with the little window wide open. There are icicles hanging everywhere. It's beautiful. It looks like the john in *Doctor Zhivago* . . . What are you reading?

GEORGE. My mail.

LEO. Anything interesting?

GEORGE. Not unless you like letters of condolence. I thought I answered my last one when I left . . . Do we have an Aunt Henry?

LEO *(Offstage)*. Aunt Henry? We have an *Uncle* Henry. In Kingston, New York.

GEORGE. This is signed "Aunt Henry."

LEO *(Offstage)*. Uncle Henry's about sixty-three—maybe he's going through a change of life.

GEORGE *(Reading)*. " 'Sorry to hear about your loss. With deepest sincerity, Aunt Henry.' "

LEO *(Comes out of the kitchen; holding up the food)*. You want to see sour milk? You want to see white bread that's turned into pumpernickel all by itself? You want to see a dish of grapes that have dried into raisins?

GEORGE *(Looking at another letter)*. You want to listen to something, Leo?

LEO *(Trying to avoid the past)*. George, you just got home. You're tired. Why don't you defrost the bathroom, take a bath?

GEORGE. Just one letter: "Dear Mr. Schneider, My name is Mary Ann Patterson. We've never met, but I did know your late wife, Barbara, casually. I work at Sabrina's, where she used to come to have her hair cut. She was so beautiful and one of the warmest people I've ever met. It seems I always used to tell her my troubles, and she always found some terrific thing to say to cheer me up. I will miss her smiling face and the way she used to come bouncing into the shop like a little girl. I feel lucky to have known her. I just wanted to return a little of her good cheer. God bless you and keep you. Mary Ann Patterson." *(He puts down the letter.* LEO *looks at him, knowing not to intrude on this moment)* What the hell did I read *that* for?

LEO. It's very nice. It's a sweet letter, George.

GEORGE. Barbara knew a whole world of people I never knew . . . She knew that Ricco, the mailman, was a birdwatcher in Central Park, and that Vince, the butcher in Gristede's, painted miniature portraits of cats every weekend in his basement on Staten Island . . . She talked to people all year long that I said hello to on Christmas.

LEO *(Looks at him)*. I think you could have used another month in Europe.

GEORGE. You mean, I was supposed to come home and forget I had a wife for twelve years? It doesn't work that way, Leo. It was, perhaps, the dumbest trip I ever took in my whole life. London was bankrupt, Italy was on strike, France hated me, Spain was still mourning for Franco . . . Why do Americans go to grief-stricken Europe when they're trying to get over being stricken with grief?

LEO. Beats me. I always thought you could have just as rotten a time here in America.

GEORGE. What am I going to do about this apartment, Leo?

LEO. My advice? Move. Find a new place for yourself.

GEORGE. It was spooky in London . . . I kept walking around the streets looking for Barbara—Harrod's, King's Road, Portobello . . . Sales clerks would say, "See what you want, sir?" and I'd say, "No, she's not here." I know it's crazy, Leo, but I really thought to myself, It's a joke. She's not dead. She's in London waiting for me. She's just playing out this romantic fantasy: The whole world thinks she's gone, but we meet clandestinely in London, move into a flat, disappear from everyone and live out our lives in secret! . . . She would have thought of something like that, you know.

LEO. But she didn't. *You* did.

GEORGE. In Rome I got sore at her—I mean *really* mad. How dare she do a thing like this to me? I would *never* do a thing like that to her. Never! Like a nut, walking up the Via Veneto one night, cursing my dead wife.

LEO. In Italy, they probably didn't pay attention.

GEORGE. In Italy, they agree with you. *(He shrugs)* Okay, Leo, my sweet baby brother, I'm back . . . Chapter Two in the life of George Schneider. Where the hell do I begin?

LEO. I don't know. You want to go to a dance?

GEORGE. You know, you're cute. Does Marilyn think you're cute?

LEO. Yeah. It's not enough. I want *all* the women to think so.

GEORGE. Everything okay at home?

LEO. Couldn't be better.

GEORGE. You sure?

LEO. Never ask a question like that twice. I gotta go. *(He buttons his coat)* How about poker on Thursday?

GEORGE. I'll let you know.

LEO. Want me to get tickets for the Knicks game Saturday?

GEORGE. We'll talk about it.

LEO. How about dinner on Sunday? Monday? Maybe Tuesday will be my good news day? *(Imitates a trombone playing "The Man I Love."* GEORGE *doesn't respond)* Hey! Hey, Georgie . . .

GEORGE. I'm okay, Leo. I promise. Just give me a little time, okay?

LEO. I don't know what to do for you . . . I feel so goddamn helpless.

GEORGE. Well . . . Maybe you can come by

tomorrow and show me how to open up tuna fish.

LEO *(Looks at* GEORGE*).* Now *I'm* mad. I think it stinks, too. I'm not going to forgive her for a long time, George. (LEO *goes over and embraces* GEORGE. *Tears well up in* LEO's *eyes. He pulls away and heads for the door)* I'm coming back next week and the two of us are getting bombed, you understand? I mean, I want you *disgusting!* Then we'll drive up to Kingston and check out this Aunt Henry. If he's got money, he might be a nice catch for you.

(He turns and goes quickly. GEORGE *turns and looks at the apartment, then picks up his attache case)*

GEORGE *(He takes in a deep breath).* Okay, let's take it one night at a time, folks.

(He heads for the bedroom. The lights come down slowly)

SCENE TWO

Her apartment. It is mid-February, about four-thirty on a bitter-cold afternoon. The light of a winter's day is fading fast.

The door opens and JENNIE MALONE *enters and switches on the lights. She is an attractive woman, about thirty-two. She wears a camel's-hair coat, leather boots and a woolen hat. She puts down a valise and carries a heavily loaded shoulder bag. She looks around and exhales a deep sigh.*

Right behind her is FAYE MEDWICK, *about thirty- ve.* FAYE *dresses a bit more suburban— not chic, but right for the weather. She carries in* JENNIE's *make-up case.*

FAYE. I don't care *how* much traffic there was, no way is it twenty-six dollars from Kennedy Airport to Eighty-fourth Street. *(She closes the door)* It's one thing to pay for his gas, it's another to put his daughter through college. (JENNIE *takes off her coat)* Remember that cabbie last year? Picked up this sweet Mexican family at the airport, drove them into the city and charged them *a hundred and sixty dollars?* He told them in America the cab fare starts from the time you get on the plane. I could kill sometimes . . . It's nice and warm in here. You left the heat on for two weeks?

JENNIE. I told the doorman I was coming back today. He probably turned it on this morning.

FAYE. Organized. You're so damn organized. I'd give anything to be like you. I'm hungry. We should have stopped off at the grocery.

(She enters the kitchen)

JENNIE. I dropped an order off with them before I left. They may have delivered it this morning.

FAYE *(Opens the fridge, looks in).* It's all there! Jesus! You fly two thousand miles to get a divorce and you remember to leave a grocery order?

JENNIE *(Dials the phone).* It's that Catholic upbringing. I majored in Discipline.

FAYE. Milk, cheese, butter, eggs, bread . . . Listen, would you like a job in my house? Your own room with color TV?

JENNIE. A perfect person. The nuns loved it, but it was murder on a marriage. *(Into the phone)* Four-six-two, please.

FAYE. Your plants look nice too. Had them watered, right?

JENNIE. Three times a week. *(Into the phone)* Yes?

FAYE. You have the nerve to tell that to a woman with a dead lawn and two fallen trees?

JENN *(Into the phone).* Thank you. *(Hangs up)* I'm going to change my answering service. I get such boring messages.

FAYE. Is there *anything* you forgot?

JENNIE. Nothing. I've got everything planned up until five o'clock. Starting at 5:01—help! If it's so warm in here, why am I shivering?

FAYE. You just cut off six years of your life. Giggling would be inappropriate.

JENNIE. I can still smell the ghost of Gus's cigar. God, what a cheap thing to be haunted by . . . He probably came by to pick up the rest of his clothes.

FAYE. Sidney's been complaining the dry cleaner I use does terrible work. I haven't got the nerve to tell him I keep forgetting to send it out.

JENNIE. Y'know, I never realized I had so many books I never read . . . Okay, *Catch-22,* we're going to try it one more time.

FAYE. You see, I think that's wrong. To tackle heavyweight material is not what you should be doing now. I would read filth.

JENNIE. Listen, you're not going to hang around till I've readjusted, are you, Faye?

FAYE. Well, you've got to go slowly. I don't want you to get the bends. *(Looking out the window)* Oh, God!

JENNIE. What?

FAYE. I'm watching the most gorgeous naked person across the street.

JENNIE. Man or woman?

FAYE. Can't tell. It's a rear view.

JENNIE. That's probably Lupe, the Spanish dancer. Beautiful body.

FAYE. Fantastic. Women are really terrific. No wonder we drive men crazy . . . some of us . . . Did you ever fantasize making love to a beautiful woman?

JENNIE. You're not going to make any advances, are you, Faye? I'm really very tired.

FAYE. It's just that sometimes I watch Sidney drooling over those Dallas Cowboy cheerleaders, and I was wondering what I was missing in life . . . Maybe I never should have left Texas.

JENNIE. What's wrong this week?

FAYE. Sidney and I had dinner with friends last week. A couple married twenty years, the man never stopped fondling his wife for a minute. They both said it was the best time of their lives—that they really never knew how to enjoy each other till now. And I thought to myself, "Shit. Twelve more years to go until the good times."

JENNIE. Did you tell that to Sidney?

FAYE *(Putting on her coat)*. Not yet. I can't get an appointment with his secretary.

JENNIE. I don't understand you. I know more about what's wrong with your married life than Sidney does. Why don't you speak up? What are you afraid of? What do you think would happen to you if you told him what you tell *me* in the privacy of this room?

FAYE. That next time you'd be picking *me* up at the airport.

JENNIE. Oh, God, that infuriates me. Why are we so intimidated? I wasted five lousy years living with Gus trying to justify the one good year I had with him . . . because I wouldn't take responsibility for my own life. Dumb! You're dumb, Jennie Malone! *All* of us . . . We shouldn't get alimony, we should get the *years* back. Wouldn't it be great if just once the judge said, "I award you six years, three months, two days and custody of your former youthful body and fresh glowing skin"!

FAYE. I would be in such terrific shape if you were my mother.

JENNIE. Don't give me too much credit. I *talk* a terrific life . . . Now, go on home. I want to crawl into bed and try to remember what my maiden name was.

FAYE. Are you sure you'll be all right? All alone?

JENNIE. No. But I want to be.

(They embrace)

FAYE. You can call me in the middle of the night. Sidney and I aren't doing anything.

(FAYE leaves. JENNIE takes her suitcase into the bedroom)

SCENE THREE

His apartment. It is the next night, about 5:00 P.M. GEORGE is obviously having dif culty concentrating at the typewriter. He is wearing slacks, an open-neck shirt, woolen cardigan and slippers. The phone rings as he is typing.

GEORGE *(Into the phone)*. Hello . . . Yes . . . Who's this? . . . Leona Zorn . . . Oh, yes. Yes, I received your note. I was very dismayed to hear that you and Harvey broke up . . . Well, I wouldn't say we were close friends. He's a wonderful chiropractor . . . Dinner on Thursday? Thursday . . . Thursday . . . Ah, nuts, I have something on for Thursday . . . The following Thursday? *(The doorbell rings)* Gee, I think I have something on for that night, too . . . Uh, Mrs. Zorn, will you just hold on? I want to get my doorbell. *(He lays the receiver down; under his breath)* Oh, Jesus!

(He opens the door. LEO enters)

LEO. Sit down. I have to talk to you.

GEORGE. Just a minute, Leo, I'm on the phone. *(Into the phone)* Mrs. Zorn? . . . You said the following Thursday? . . . I think I have something on for that night, but let me check my diary. I'll be right back. *(He puts the receiver down and goes over to LEO. GEORGE beckons, gesturing that phone is "open")* Leo, there's a woman on the phone asking me for a date.

LEO. Yeah? . . . So?

GEORGE *(Whispers)*. Her husband was my chiropractor.

LEO. So what?

GEORGE. He left her for an ice-skater in Las Vegas.

LEO. What does she look like?

GEORGE. Like someone you would leave for an ice-skater in Las Vegas.

LEO. So what's your problem?

GEORGE *(Annoyed)*. What do you mean, what's my problem? I don't want to have dinner with her.

LEO. What *do* you want to have?

GEORGE. *Nothing!* I want her to hang up. I don't want her to call me. Look, she's probably a very nice woman. I don't want to be cruel to her, but I don't want to have dinner with her.

LEO. Would you feel better if *I* took her out? What's her name? I'll talk to her.

(GEORGE *stops him*)

GEORGE. Leo! Please! *(Back into the phone)* Mrs. Zorn? . . . I'm sorry to keep you waiting . . . Uh, Mrs. Zorn, I've always found it better to be completely honest . . . and . . . I'm really not all that anxious to go out at this particular time . . . Well, I've tried it a few times and it wasn't all that successful . . . I just don't think I'm psychologically ready . . . Well, I don't think I can give an exact date when I *would* be ready . . . (LEO *does push-ups on the oor*) Well, yes, in a manner of speaking, we *are* in the same boat . . . But we don't necessarily have to paddle together . . . I think we have to go up our own streams.

LEO. Jesus!

GEORGE. Well, yes, it *is* possible we could meet upriver one day, I don't rule that out.

LEO. Is that from *The African Queen?*

(GEORGE *pulls the receiver away so* LEO's *remark will not be heard*)

GEORGE. Leo, please! *(Into the phone)* Yes . . . Yes . . . Well, you sound charming too . . . Well, if I *do* reconsider, I *will* call . . . yes. Goodbye. *(He hangs up)* Christ! The guy leaves me with a bad back and *his* wife!

LEO *(Gets up)*. There just aren't enough men to go around. I *want* to help out, but Marilyn doesn't understand.

GEORGE. Women call me up, Leo. *Women!* They call me up on the *phone*.

LEO. What else would they call you up on?

GEORGE. But they're so *frank* about it. So open. They just come right out with it. "How do you do. I've been recently widowed myself." Or, "Hi! I'm a divorcee." "I'm legally separated." "I'm *il*legally separated." One woman called, I swear to God, I think her husband was just on vacation.

LEO. It's a competitive world, George. The woman who sits waiting by the phone sits waiting by the phone.

GEORGE. Do you know I've been invited to three class reunions at schools I never even went to?

LEO. Listen, George, next to Christmas, loneliness is the biggest business in America.

GEORGE. Do you realize how much courage it must have taken for that woman to call me up just now?

LEO. And you think you were the first and only one she's called? She probably has her husband's entire list of clients. If she called you, she's only up to the "Georges."

GEORGE. And you don't find that sad?

LEO. Certainly I find it sad. That's why they have game shows on TV . . . Now, if you want to feel sorry for yourself and everyone else in the world who's suffered a loss, that's your concern. It is *my* job to brighten up the place. I am God's interior decorator, and he has sent me to paint you two coats of happiness.

GEORGE. Leo, don't do this to me again!

LEO. This is different. This girl requires a serious discussion. I think I found buried treasure, George. Hear me out.

GEORGE. I haven't recovered from *last* week's buried treasure . . . All right, it's my own fault. I should have known in that first phone conversation with her. Three "honeys," two "sugars" and one "babe" was a sure tip-off . . . I'm very busy, Leo. I've written three hundred pages of my new book and I haven't thought of a story yet.

LEO. All right, I apologize. I misunderstood. I just thought you wanted someone to have a good time with.

GEORGE. Look at me, Leo. I'm a nice, plain, regular person who eats fruit and wears slippers. What makes you think I'm going to like a jazzy blonde who dyes a zigzag streak of dark-blue in her hair? She looked like the cover of a record album.

LEO. But a terrific body. You've got to admit that body was put together by someone who's very close to God.

GEORGE. I booked a table in one of the finest French restaurants in New York. I put on a nice blue suit, rang her doorbell and this creature from *Star Wars* says hello. You know what kind of a dress she was wearing? Electric! I didn't see where it was plugged in *but this was an electric dress!* I swear to God, we got in and the cab driver got static on his radio. In the restaurant I *prayed* for another blackout.

LEO. Did I tell you to take her someplace nice? Putz! You take her to the Rainbow Room, somewhere that only out-of-towners go. But you had a good time, right? Right, George? C'mon, will ya. I went to a lot of trouble. Tell me you had a good time.

GEORGE. What do you mean, I had a good time? A thunderstorm came up, and I'm sitting there with a lightning rod. I did not have a good time. She ordered a nine-dollar goose-liver pâté and made a hero sandwich out of it . . . Go home, Leo.

LEO. George, I have set that girl up with

some very heavy clients from Hollywood, and they've been very nice to me every Christmas.

GEORGE. Are you telling me she's a hooker? Are you telling me that outlet from Con Edison is a pro?

LEO. Would I do that to you? My brother? Bambi's a terrific girl. A little flashy on the exterior, yes. A little Art Deco around the wardrobe, yes. But no hooker . . . Why? Did she charge you anything?

GEORGE. For what? I was wet, I was afraid to touch her.

LEO. Bad move on my part, okay? Some like 'em hot, some like 'em milk and cookies. I know better now. But if you're telling me you're ready for a serious woman, George, I met her last night at "21."

GEORGE. Close the door on your way out, Leo.

LEO. I have a feeling about this, George. Don't deny me my feelings.

GEORGE (*Starting into the bedroom*). Leo, *please!* I have my work. I have my friends. I have the Knicks, the Giants and the Mets. I have jogging and I have watercolors. My life is full. There are no more Barbaras left in the world. If you meet them *once* in your life, God has been more than good to you . . . I *will* go out. I *will* meet people. But I have to find them in my own time, in my own way. I love you for what you're doing . . . but don't do it anymore.

LEO. At least let me describe her—a nose, a couple of eyes, one or two ears! (*Following* GEORGE *into the bedroom*) Let me leave her number. You don't have to call her right away. Whenever you feel like it!

(*Dimout*)

SCENE FOUR

Her apartment. A suitcase is on the sofa; JENNIE *is packing. The phone rings. She answers it.*

_____

JENNIE. Hello? . . . Well, what a surprise. How are you, Gus? . . . Fine . . . And how does it feel to be an ex-husband? . . . It's been a long time since I heard your "bachelor" voice. You got your old *pizzazz* back . . . Oh, I found an old pair of your basketball sneakers in the closet, did you want them? . . . Thanks, I can wear them to go shopping . . . *I* sound *down?* . . . Oh, I guess a combination of post-divorce blues and the Mexican water . . . I'm

not sure. I've got three more weeks on the soap. I've got an offer to go to Washington and do a year of rep at the Arena Theatre . . . And you? . . . Well, hang in, you always come up with something . . . It was very sweet of you to call, Gus . . . Well, I wish you every happiness, too. This has been the nicest talk we've had in a long time . . . I will . . . *Gus!* . . . I just wanted to say—I'm sorry!

(*On the verge of tears, she hangs up. The doorbell rings; she answers it. It is* FAYE)

FAYE. Do you believe in miracles?

JENNIE. Do you believe in saying hello?

FAYE. Well, two miracles happened last night at "21." The producer of *As the World Turns* saw me at our table, called me today and offered me a part—

JENNIE. Congratulations! Oh, Faye, that's fantastic! Well, what's the part?

FAYE. Her name is Jarlene Indigo.

JENNIE. Jarlene Indigo?

FAYE. She's the new cellist with the Boston Symphony.

JENNIE. I love it. Will you have to learn to play?

FAYE. By Monday.

JENNIE (*Continues her packing*). What's the second miracle?

FAYE. Do you remember that fellow Leo Schneider who came over to our table to say hello? Sidney doesn't know, but I used to date Leo when I first got to New York. Anyway, he's got this brother, George. He's recently widowed, about forty-two, forty-three years old I think . . . You're not listening. What are you doing?

JENNIE. I am packing. If you don't know this is packing, how will you learn to play a cello?

FAYE. Where are you going?

JENNIE. Home. To Cleveland. I just have an overwhelming desire to sleep in my old, tiny bed.

FAYE. How long will you be gone?

JENNIE. A couple of days—maybe a couple of weeks.

FAYE. In Cleveland a couple of days are a couple of weeks. Can't you postpone it? Leo was going to try to get George Schneider to call this week.

JENNIE. Faye, how many times must I tell you? I don't feel like dating right now.

FAYE. Well, that's perfect. Neither does George Schneider. At least you have something in common.

JENNIE. I wonder what it is that holds our

friendship together.

FAYE. He's a writer. A novelist, I think. I met him once a few years ago. Not gorgeous, but sweet-looking. With a very intelligent face.

JENNIE. Faye, please stop. I appreciate what you're doing. You and Sidney have been wonderful. I loved the dinner at "21," and the date you fixed me up with was unusual but charming.

FAYE. It's all right. I know you didn't like him.

JENNIE. It's not that I didn't like him. I couldn't *see* him. The man was six feet eight inches tall. All I could think of at dinner was what if we got married and I had a baby? I'd be giving birth for days.

FAYE. If you're going to look for things, you can find fault with everyone.

JENNIE. I don't think being uncomfortable with a man who was taller than the waiter *sitting down* is looking to find fault.

FAYE. I'm talking about everyone you go out with. You sit there and scrutinize them.

JENNIE. I scrutinize?

FAYE. Your eyes burn little holes in them. That poor fellow last night kept checking to see if his fly was open.

JENNIE. All right. I won't scrutinize if you'll stop arranging my social life for me. I told you it's not important to me—why do you do it?

FAYE. I don't do it for you. I do it for me.

JENNIE. What?

FAYE. I have visions of arranging the perfect romance for you. Someone with a dark tragic background—Jay Gatsby . . . Irving Thalberg . . . Leon Trotsky . . .

JENNIE. Jesus, do I have to live out my life with *your* fantasy?

FAYE. What the hell, I'm arranging it, I might as well pick who I like . . . I don't understand, Jennie. Are you telling me you're never dating again?

JENNIE *(Putting on her coat)*. Yes. YES! I have dated and I have gone to parties and I have had it. If one more man greets me at the door with his silk shirt unbuttoned to his tanned navel, his chest hair neatly combed, and wearing more jewelry around his neck than me, I am turning celibate. . . . I am going to spend the rest of my life doing good work in the theatre. I am going to read all the classics starting with *Agamemnon* . . . I'll work out my sex life the best I can. And don't think I'm not worried. Sometimes I lie in bed thinking, Is it physically possible if you don't have sex for a long, long time, you can go back to being

a virgin? Well, I'll find out. But first I'll find out in Cleveland.

(She grabs her suitcase and starts out. The phone rings)

FAYE. Oh, my God, maybe that's George Schneider.

JENNIE. It's *your* fantasy, *you* answer it.

(She goes. FAYE *runs after her)*

FAYE *(Yells). I'll give you two hundred dollars if you answer that phone!*

(But JENNIE *is gone.* FAYE *closes the door and goes)*

SCENE FIVE

His apartment. It is two weeks later, about 9 P.M. GEORGE *walks into the living room, carrying a reference book. He looks for something at the desk and around the sofa, then goes to the phone and dials, still looking about him.*

————

GEORGE *(Into the phone)*. Marilyn? . . . George . . . Is Leo there? . . . No, you can just yell into the bathroom . . . Ask him if he remembers where he left the phone number for a Mrs. Jenkins, or Jergins, or something like that. He wrote it down and left it for me somewhere in here last week . . . Jenkins, Jergins . . . *(Looking through some papers)* She's the old woman he told me about who used to work for the Harvard University Library about forty years ago . . . No. It's research for the book . . . Would you? *(Spots a paper under the kitchen phone)* Wait a minute, Marilyn, I'm gonna put you on hold. Just a second. *(Pushes the "hold" button, gets the paper from under the kitchen phone and picks up that receiver)* Marilyn, I found it. It was right under the other phone . . . Yeah . . . Give Tina a kiss for me. Goodbye.

(He hangs up both phones and looks at the paper. He dials again . . . And the phone rings in her empty apartment. Just then we hear the key in the door and JENNIE *enters. She turns on the lights. The phone rings again. She puts down her suitcase and picks up the receiver)*

JENNIE. Hello?

GEORGE. Hello? Is this, uh . . . I'm sorry. I'm not sure I have your name right . . . This is George Schneider—Leo Schneider's brother? I believe he told me I would be calling you.

JENNIE. George Schneider?

GEORGE. The writer.

JENNIE. Oh . . . God! Yes . . . George

Schneider. It seemed so long ago . . . I'm sorry, you caught me at a bad time. I just got off a plane and walked in the door.

GEORGE. Oh, I didn't know. I'm sorry. Can I call you back?

JENNIE. Well . . . Yes, I suppose so but, er . . . I'll be very honest with you, Mr. Schneider. I'm going through sort of a transition period right now, and I'm not planning to date for a while.

GEORGE. *Date?* Did Leo say I was going to call you for a date?

JENNIE. Well, he said you were going to call, so I assumed—

GEORGE. No, no. This wasn't a date call. I'm very surprised at Leo, Miss, er . . . Is it Jenkins or Jergins?

JENNIE. Is what?

GEORGE. Your name.

JENNIE. It's Malone. Jennifer Malone.

GEORGE *(Confused, looks at the paper).* Jennifer Malone? . . . No, that's wrong.

JENNIE. I could show you my driver's license.

GEORGE. That's not the name he gave me . . . *(He looks on the back of the paper)* Oh, geez, it's on the other side. I couldn't read his writing. Serene Jurgens was the one I wanted. She's an elderly woman, about eighty-five years old.

JENNIE. Well, you know what you want better than I do.

GEORGE. Look, I am so embarrassed. I really was going to call you socially. At another time. I mean, I really was.

JENNIE. Well, let's see how it goes with Serene first. Okay? Goodbye.

(She hangs up)

GEORGE *(Looks at the scrap of paper).* God damn you, Leo, get your women straight, will ya?

(JENNIE *takes her suitcase to the bedroom.* GEORGE *thinks a moment about what to do, then looks at the paper and dials again. The phone rings in her bedroom)*

JENNIE *(Answering it).* Hello?

GEORGE. It's me. I'm back.

JENNIE. You and the old lady didn't hit it off?

GEORGE. *Now* I know who you are. The girl Leo met at "21." Jennie Malone.

JENNIE. That sounds right to me.

GEORGE. Anyway, I'm calling back because I wanted you to know what I got the phone numbers mixed up, and I didn't want you to think I wasn't calling you. I *was.* I mean, I wasn't *then.* I am *now.*

JENNIE. For a date?

GEORGE. No. Not yet. I thought I'd wait and explain the *last* call before I went ahead with the *next* call.

JENNIE. I'm a little slow. Which call are we on now?

GEORGE. This is the call back to explain the dumb call. The charming call comes after we hang up from this one.

JENNIE. I'm so glad I'm home. If I got this message on my answering service, I'd need a private detective.

GEORGE. I'll tell you the absolute truth. I haven't made a call to a nice single girl in fourteen years. I wasn't even good at it then. If I seem inept, please bear with me.

JENNIE. You seem ept enough. The point is, Mister . . . er . . .

GEORGE. George Schneider. I got it here on 264the paper.

JENNIE. The point is, Mr. Schneider, as I told Faye to tell Leo to tell you, I really have to get my head together right now, and that's what I was going to do for the next few weeks.

GEORGE. Oh, I understand that. As a matter of fact, I was doing the same thing. I just didn't want to leave you with the image of some retarded romantic walking around town with your number and a handful of dimes.

JENNIE. Knowing that, I will sleep better . . . It was very nice talking to you, George. Goodbye.

(She hangs up. He hangs up. She turns and goes into the kitchen. He thinks a moment, then looks at the paper and dials again. The phone rings in her apartment. She comes out of the kitchen, a little annoyed, and answers it) Hello?

GEORGE. This is the charming call.

JENNIE. I think I have a problem on my hands.

GEORGE. You don't. I promise. This is definitely our last conversation.

JENNIE. Then why did you call back?

GEORGE. I couldn't resist saying, "This is the charming call" . . . Seriously, I'm sorry if I intruded on your privacy. I know very much how you feel. And I liked the sound of your voice, and I also wanted to say, "I hope you get your head together in good health." This is now the end of the charming call. Goodbye.

(He hangs up. Caught off-guard, she looks at the phone, then hangs up. His call stops her halfway to her kitchen)

JENNIE *(Returns to the phone).* Hello?

(A laugh bubbles out of her)

GEORGE. I was just trying to place your voice.

California girl, right? U.C.L.A.?

JENNIE. Born in Cleveland and I went to Bennington in Vermont.

GEORGE. How about that? I was *so* close.

JENNIE. That's where I've just come from.

GEORGE. Bennington?

JENNIE. Cleveland. I was visiting family.

GEORGE. Aha.

JENNIE. Aha what?

GEORGE. Just aha. Acknowledgment. Comprehension. I understand.

JENNIE. Oh. Well, aha to you, too.

GEORGE. Leo told me what you did but I didn't pay any attention.

JENNIE. Why not?

GEORGE. His previous social arrangements for me all ended like the *Andrea Doria*.

JENNIE. And yet here you are calling me.

GEORGE. Only by mistake.

JENNIE. No, no. The first call was a mistake, and the second one was a call back explaining the mistake. The charming call was yours.

GEORGE. That's true. You have a very good mind, Jennie Malone. Now you see why you got the charming call.

JENNIE. You're a writer, that's for sure. I took English Lit. This is what they call "repartee," isn't it?

GEORGE. No. This is what they call "amusing telephone conversation under duress" . . . So what is it you do?

JENNIE. I'm an actress. (*He doesn't respond*) No "aha"?

GEORGE. Leo didn't tell me you were an actress.

JENNIE. I'm sorry. Wrong career?

GEORGE. No. No. Actresses can be, uh, very nice.

JENNIE. Well, that's an overstatement but I appreciate your open-mindedness.

GEORGE. Wait a minute, I'm not extricating my mouth from my foot . . . There, that's better. So you're an actress and I'm a writer. I'm also a widower.

JENNIE. Yes. Faye told me.

GEORGE. Faye?

JENNIE. Fay Medwick. She's the one pushing from my side.

GEORGE. Leo is getting up a brochure on me. We'll send you one when they come in . . . I understand you're recently divorced?

JENNIE. Yes . . . How deeply do you intend going into this?

GEORGE. Sorry. Occupational hazard. I pry incessantly.

JENNIE. That's okay. I scrutinize.

GEORGE. Well, prying is second cousin to scrutiny.

JENNIE. Wouldn't you know it? It turns out we're related.

GEORGE. I don't know if you've noticed but we also talk in the same rhythm.

JENNIE. Hmmm.

GEORGE. Hmmm? What is "hmmm"?

JENNIE. It's second cousin to aha! . . . You're a very interesting telephone person, Mr. Schneider. However, I have literally just walked in the door, and I haven't eaten since breakfast. It was really nice talking to you. Goodbye. (*She hangs up, waits right there expectantly*) *He hurriedly dials. Her phone rings; she picks it up*) As you were saying?

GEORGE. Listen, uh, can I be practical for a second?

JENNIE. For a second? Yes.

GEORGE. They're not going to let up, you know.

JENNIE. Who?

GEORGE. The Pushers. Leo and Faye. They will persist and push and prod and leave telephone numbers under books until eventually we have the inevitable date.

JENNIE. Nothing is inevitable. Dates are manmade.

GEORGE. Whatever . . . The point is, I assume you have an active career. I'm a very busy man who needs quiet and few distractions. So let me propose, in the interest of moving on with our lives, that we get this meeting over with just as soon as possible.

JENNIE. Surely you jest.

GEORGE. I'm not asking for a date. Blind dates are the nation's third leading cause of skin rash.

JENNIE. Then what are you suggesting?

GEORGE. Just hear me out. What if we were to meet for just five minutes? We could say hello, look each other over, part company and tell Leo and Faye that they have fulfilled their noble mission in life.

JENNIE. That's very funny.

GEORGE. And yet I hear no laughter.

JENNIE. Because it's not *funny* funny. It's stupid funny.

GEORGE. You think it's smart to suffer an entire evening rather than a quick five-minute "hello and goodbye"?

JENNIE. Because it's demeaning. It's like shopping. And I don't like being shopped.

GEORGE. Do you prefer window-shopping? I could stand across the street, look up and wave.

JENNIE. Am I talking to a serious person?

GEORGE. My friends tell me I have a certain charm. It's like gold, though. You have to pan for it.

JENNIE. And what if during these five minutes we took a liking to each other?

GEORGE. Then we take a shot at six minutes.

JENNIE. *But* if you take a fancy to me and I don't to you—or, God forbid, vice versa—what then?

GEORGE. It's a new system. We don't have all the bugs out yet.

JENNIE. I can't believe this conversation.

GEORGE. Look, if five minutes is too exhausting, we could have two-and-a-half-minute halves with an intermission.

JENNIE. Why am I intrigued by this? . . . When would you like this momentous occasion to take place?

GEORGE. How about right now?

JENNIE. Right now? That's crazy.

GEORGE. You mean, not possible?

JENNIE. Oh, it's possible. It's just crazy.

GEORGE. Why not? I'm having trouble working anyway. And next week could be too late. Mrs. Jurgens and I could be a hot item.

JENNIE. But I just got off a plane. I look terrible.

GEORGE. So do I, and I got off one two months ago. And besides, fixing yurself up is illegal. That's a date. This is just a quick look for Leo and Faye.

JENNIE. For Leo and Faye, huh? . . . Oh, what the hell, let's give it a shot.

GEORGE. Hey, terrific! Where would you like to meet?

JENNIE. How does Paris strike you?

GEORGE. Outside is no good. Then it gets down to who says goodbye and who leaves first. Very messy . . . How about your place?

JENNIE. That's out of the question.

GEORGE. Why?

JENNIE. I don't *know* why . . . 386 East Eighty-fourth Street, apartment 12F.

GEORGE. Got it.

JENNIE. Write it down. You have a bad history with numbers.

GEORGE. I'll be there in eight minutes.

JENNIE. And you don't think this is a bizarre thing to do?

GEORGE. It is the weirdest thing I've ever come up with. But we may be blazing the trail for millions of others.

JENNIE. And neither of us will be disappointed if we're disappointed, right?

GEORGE. Please. Let's not build down our hopes too much. See you. Goodbye.

JENNIE. Goodbye.

(He hangs up. She hangs up)

GEORGE. Smart! Smart move, George!

JENNIE. Dumb! You're a dumb lady, Jennie Malone!

(They head in opposite directions)

SCENE SIX

Her apartment. Twenty minutes later. The phone rings. JENNIE *comes out of the bedroom. She has taken off her blouse and is buttoning a new one. She goes to the phone quickly.*

JENNIE *(Into the phone)*. Hello? . . . Faye, I can't talk to you now . . . He's on his way over . . . George Schneider . . . Yes, *your* George Schneider . . . It's not a date. It's a look! He looks at me and I look at him and then you don't bother us anymore . . . Faye, I can't talk to you now. I'll call you back when he leaves in five minutes . . . Because that's all it takes. *(The doorbell rings)* Dammit, he's here . . . I hate you. Goodbye.

(She hangs up, tucks her blouse into her skirt, looks in the mirror, does a last-minute brush job, then goes to the door. She takes in a deep breath, and then opens it. GEORGE *stands there, arm extended, leaning against the doorframe. They look at each other . . . Finally he smiles and nods his head)*

GEORGE. Yeah! Okayyyyyy!

JENNIE. Is that a review?

GEORGE. No. Just a response . . . Hello.

JENNIE *(Smiles)*. Hello.

(They are both suddenly very embarrassed and don't quite know what to say or how to handle this situation)

GEORGE *(Good-naturedly)*. This was a dumb idea, wasn't it?

JENNIE. Extremely.

GEORGE *(Nods in agreement)*. I think I've put undue pressure on these next five minutes.

JENNIE. You could cut it with a knife.

GEORGE. I think if I came in, it would lessen the tension.

JENNIE. Oh, I'm sorry. Please, yes.

(He steps in. She closes the door behind her)

GEORGE *(Looks around the room and nods)*. Aha!

JENNIE. Does that mean you comprehend my apartment?

GEORGE. No. It means I like it. "Aha" can be used in many situations, this being one of them.

JENNIE. Can I get you anything to drink?

GEORGE. No, thanks. I don't drink.

JENNIE. Oh, neither do I.

(There is an awkward pause)

GEORGE. Although I'd love a glass of white wine.

JENNIE. So would I. *(She goes to the kitchen)* Please, sit down.

GEORGE. Thank you. *(But he doesn't. He wanders around the room looking at things. She brings in an opened bottle of white wine in an ice bucket set on a tray with two glasses. He spots a framed photograph of a football player in action)* Is all right if I pry?

JENNIE. Sure.

GEORGE. You can scrutinize later. *(He examines the picture)* Oh, are you a football fan?

JENNIE. That's my ex-husband. He was a wide receiver for the New York Giants.

GEORGE. No kidding! What's his name?

JENNIE. Gus Hendricks.

GEORGE *(Looks at picture again)*. Gus Hendricks? . . . Funny, I can't remember him. How wide a receiver was he?

JENNIE. He was cut the beginning of his second year. Bad hands, I think they call it. Couldn't hold on to the football.

GEORGE. Well, some coaches are very demanding. What does he do now?

JENNIE. Well, he was in mutual funds, he was in the saloon business, he was in broadcasting, he was in sports promotion—

GEORGE. Very ambitious.

JENNIE. He did all those in three months. He has some problems to work out.

(She pours the two glasses of wine)

GEORGE. Who doesn't?

JENNIE. True enough.

(She hands him a glass)

GEORGE. Thank you.

JENNIE. Here's to working out problems.

(They both drink. He looks at her)

GEORGE. Leo was right. You're very attractive.

JENNIE. Thank you.

GEORGE. I'm curious. You don't have to answer this . . . How was *I* described?

JENNIE. "Not gorgeous, but an intelligent face."

GEORGE *(Smiles)*. That's true. I have. You can ask my face anything. (JENNIE *sits.* GEORGE *is still standing)* No matter how old or experienced you are, the process never seems to get any easier, does it?

JENNIE. What process?

GEORGE. Mating.

JENNIE. *Mating?* My God, is *that* what we're doing?

GEORGE *(Sits next to her on the sofa)*. Haven't you noticed? First thing I did as I passed you, I inhaled. Got a little whiff of your fragrance. In our particular species, the sense of smell is a determining factor in sexual attraction.

JENNIE. This is just a guess. Do you write for *Field and Stream?*

GEORGE *(Laughs)*. Please, give me a break, will you? I haven't done this in fourteen years. If you're patient, I get interesting with a little kindness.

JENNIE. You're not uninteresting now.

GEORGE. I'll tell you the truth. You're not the first girl Leo's introduced me to. There were three others . . . All ranked with such disasters as the *Hindenburg* and Pearl Harbor.

JENNIE. *Now* I see. That's when the Five-Minute Plan was born.

GEORGE. Necessity is the Mother of Calamity.

JENNIE. Tell me about them.

GEORGE. Oh, they defy description.

JENNIE. Please. Defy it.

GEORGE. All right. Let's see. First there was Bambi. Her name tells you everything.

JENNIE. I got the picture.

GEORGE. Then there was Vilma. A dynamite girl.

JENNIE. Really?

GEORGE. Spent three years in a Turkish prison for carrying dynamite . . . Need I go on?

JENNIE. No, I think I've had enough.

GEORGE. Since then I've decided to take everything Leo says with a grain of panic . . . And now I feel rather foolish because I was very flippant with you on the phone, and now I find myself with an attractive, intelligent and what appears to be a very nice girl.

JENNIE. You won't get a fight from me on that.

GEORGE. With an appealing sense of adventure.

JENNIE. You think so?

GEORGE. It's your five minutes, too.

JENNIE. I was wondering why I said yes. I think it's because I really enjoyed talking to you on the phone. You're very bright, and I found I had to keep on my toes to keep up with you.

GEORGE. Oh. And is that unusual?

JENNIE. I haven't been off my heels in years . . . What kind of books do you write?

GEORGE. Ah, we're moving into heavy territory. What kind of books do I write? For a living, I write spy novels. For posterity, I write good novels. I make a good living, but my posterity had a bad year.

JENNIE. Name some books.

GEORGE. From column A or column B?

JENNIE. Both.

GEORGE. Well, the spy novels I write under the name of Kenneth Blakely Hyphen Hill.

JENNIE. Hyphen Hill?

GEORGE. You don't say the hyphen. You just put it in.

JENNIE. Oh, God, yes. Of course. I've seen it. Drugstores, airports . . .

GEORGE. Unfortunately, not libraries.

JENNIE. Who picked the name?

GEORGE. My wife. You see, my publisher said spy novels sell better when they sound like they were written in England. We spent our honeymoon in London, and we stayed at the Blakely Hotel, and it was on a hill and the hall porter's name was Kenneth . . . If we had money in those days, my name might have been Kenneth Savoy Grill.

JENNIE. And from column B?

GEORGE. I only had two published. They were a modest failure. That means "Bring us more but not too soon."

JENNIE. I'd like to read them someday.

GEORGE. I'll send you a couple of cartons of them. *(They both sip their wine. He looks around, then back at her)* I'm forty-two years old.

JENNIE. Today?

GEORGE. No. In general.

JENNIE. Oh. Is that statement of some historic importance?

GEORGE. No. I just wanted you to know, because you look to be about twenty-four and right now I feel like a rather inept seventeen, and I didn't want you to think I was too young for you.

JENNIE. I'm thirty-two.

(They look at each other. It's the first time their gaze really holds)

GEORGE. Well. That was very nice wasn't it? I mean, looking at each other like that.

JENNIE. I wasn't scrutinizing.

GEORGE. That's okay, I wasn't prying.

JENNIE. My hunch is that you're a very interesting man, George.

GEORGE. Well, my advice is—play your hunches.

JENNIE. Can I get you some more wine?

GEORGE. No thanks. I think I'd better be going.

JENNIE. *Oh?* . . . Okay.

(They rise)

GEORGE. Not that I wouldn't like to stay.

JENNIE. Not that you're not welcome, but I understand.

GEORGE. I think we've hit off very well, if you've noticed.

JENNIE. I've noticed.

GEORGE. Therefore, I would like to make a regulation date. Seven to twelve, your basic normal hours.

JENNIE. Aha! With grown-up clothes and make-up?

GEORGE. Bath, shower—everything.

JENNIE. Sounds good. Let's make it.

GEORGE. You mean now?

JENNIE. Would you rather go home and do it on the phone?

GEORGE. No, no. Dangerous. I could get the wrong number and wind up with Mrs. Jurgens . . . Let's see, what is this?

JENNIE. Tuesday.

GEORGE. How about Wednesday?

JENNIE. Wednesday works out well.

GEORGE. You could play hard to get and make it Thursday.

JENNIE. No. Let's stick with Wednesday and I'll keep you waiting half an hour.

GEORGE *(At the door)*. Fair enough. This was nice. I'm very glad we met, Jennie.

JENNIE. So am I, George.

GEORGE. I can't believe you're from the same man who gave us Bambi and Vilma.

(He goes. She closes the door, smiles and heads for her bedroom. The lights fade)

Scene Seven

Her apartment. It is a week later, about 6:30 P.M. FAYE is staring out the window through binoculars, a cigarette in her hand. She is looking a little glum.

FAYE. She's putting on weight.

JENNIE *(Offstage)*. Who?

FAYE. Lupe, across the street. Sagging a little, too. Another six pounds, she'll start pulling down her shades.

JENNIE *(Offstage)*. You sound terrible. Is anything wrong?

FAYE. We're not going away for Easter. Sidney's ear infection still hasn't cleared up. He's lost his sense of balance. he keeps rolling away from me in bed. It's a very sad state of affairs when things are worse at home than they are on the soap . . . They tell me you're coming back to work on Monday.

JENNIE *(Offstage).* Maybe. We'll see.

FAYE. You haven't given me a straight answer in a week. What's all the mystery about? . . . Can I come in now? Jennie? I'm alone enough at nights.

JENNIE *(Offstage).* Give me ten more seconds.

FAYE. Four nights in one week, he's got to be someone special. Who is he, Jennie? Have I met him? Oh, God, I hate it when I'm left out of things! *(JENNIE comes out, shows off her new backless dress)* It's gorgeous. I love everything but the price tag.

(They remove it)

JENNIE. Oh, damn, I'm a basket case. I haven't worried about looking good for someone in such a long time.

FAYE. What is going on, my angel?

JENNIE. I don't know. I've been on a six-day high and I've had nothing stronger than a Diet Pepsi.

FAYE. My God, it's George Schneider, isn't it? *(JENNIE nods)* Why didn't you tell me?

JENNIE. I was afraid to.

FAYE. Why?

JENNIE. Because after six days I think I'm nuts about him, and I was afraid if I told anyone they'd have me put in the Home for the Over-Emotional. Come on, I'm going to be late.

FAYE *(Going into the corridor).* Well, tell me about him. What's he like?

JENNIE. Well, he's everything you've always wanted . . . *(She closes the door, and they are gone)*

SCENE EIGHT

His apartment, later that night.

JENNIE *(Outside his door).* Don't worry, I paid for the cab. *(She opens the door)* Where are the lights, George?

GEORGE *(In the corridor).* I don't want you to look at me.

JENNIE. George, where are the lights?

(She finds them, turns them on)

GEORGE *(Entering, puts his hand to his eyes).* Oh, God, that hurts.

JENNIE. Do you want to lie down, George?

GEORGE. I'm so embarrassed. Just let me sit a few minutes. I'll be all right.

JENNIE. Just keep taking deep breaths.

GEORGE *(Dizzy, sitting on the sofa).* That's the closest I've ever come to passing out.

JENNIE. Loosen your collar. I'll take your shoes off.

(She kneels, starts to untie his laces as he loosens his tie and wipes his brow)

GEORGE. First I thought it was the wine. Then I thought it was the fish. Then I figured it was the bill.

JENNIE. You don't know where they get the fish from anymore. *(She has his shoes off, massages his feet)* You read about tankers breaking up every day, oil spilling all over. For all we know, we just ate a gallon of Texaco.

GEORGE. Ohh. Ohh. Careful.

JENNIE. What?

GEORGE. I have very sensitive feet.

JENNIE. I'm sorry.

GEORGE. That's the weakest part of my system. Even baby powder hurts.

JENNIE. You're perspiring all over. Let me get you a cold towel.

(She gets up, looks around, goes to the kitchen)

GEORGE. You mean my feet were sweaty? Oh, God! Is it over between us, Jennie?

JENNIE *(Coming back in with a wet cloth).* Oh, shut up. I've rubbed sweaty feet before.

GEORGE. You have? You've really been around, haven't you . . . I don't want you to think this is a regular thing, passing out on dates. I mean, I played varsity football at Hofstra.

JENNIE. I faint all the time. It's the only thing that relaxes me.

(She puts the cloth on his forehead)

GEORGE. Jesus! You paid for the taxi. How humiliating! I don't want to live anymore.

JENNIE. You're not taking in enough air.

(She starts to unbuckle his belt and the top button of his pants)

GEORGE. Hey! What are you doing?

JENNIE. Oh, stop. I'm just unbuttoning your pants.

GEORGE. Please! No premarital unbuckling! I'm all right, Jennie, really.

JENNIE *(She kneels down beside him).* You look about twelve years old right now.

GEORGE. Seventeen last week, twelve this week—I'll be back in the womb by the end of the month. *(She kisses the back of his hand, then caresses it with her cheek. He touches her hair with his other hand)* You are the sweetest girl.

JENNIE *(Looks up at his face, smiles).* Thank you.

(He leans over and kisses her gently on the mouth)

GEORGE. I can't believe it's just a week. I feel like we're into our fourth year or something.

JENNIE. Have you felt that, too? As though it's not a new relationship at all. I feel like we're picking up in the middle somewhere . . . of something that started a long, long time ago.

GEORGE. That's exactly how it was when I walked in your door that night last week. I didn't say to myself, "Oh, how pretty. How interesting. I wonder what she's like." I said, "Of course. It's Jennie. I know her. I never met her but I know her. How terrific to find her again."

JENNIE. It's nice bumping into you again for the first time, George. *(They smile and kiss again. She looks up at him. He seems to have a pained expression on his face)* What is it? . . . Is it the pain again? *(He shakes his head "no," then turns away to hide the tears. He takes out a handkerchief to wipe his eyes)* George! Oh, George, sweetheart, what? Tell me.

(She cradles his head in her arms as he tries to ght back his emotions)

GEORGE. I don't know, Jennie.

JENNIE. It's all right . . . Whatever you're feeling, it's all right.

GEORGE. I keep trying to push Barbara out of my mind . . . I can't do it. I've tried, Jennie.

JENNIE. I know.

GEORGE. I don't really want to. I'm so afraid of losing her forever.

JENNIE. I understand and it's all right.

GEORGE. I know I'll never stop loving Barbara, but I feel so good about you . . . and I can't get the two things together in my mind.

JENNIE. It all happened so fast, George. You expect so much of yourself so soon.

GEORGE. On the way over the in the cab tonight, I'm yelling at the cab driver, "Can't you get there faster?" . . . And then some nights I wake up saying, "I'm never going to see Barbara again and I hope to God it's just a dream."

JENNIE. I love you, George . . . I want you to know that.

GEORGE. Give me a little time, Jennie. Stay next to me. Be with me. Just give me the time to tell you how happy you make me feel.

JENNIE. I'm not going anywhere, George. You can't lose me. I know a good thing when I see it.

GEORGE *(Managing a smile)*. Jeez! I thought I had food poisoning and it's just a mild case of ecstasy.

JENNIE *(Embraces him)*. I just want you to be happy. I want you to have room for all your feelings. I'll share whatever you want to share with me. I'm very strong, George. I can work a sixteen-hour day on a baloney sandwich and a milk shake. I have enough for both of us. Use it, George. Please. Use me . . .

GEORGE *(Wipes his eyes, puts the hanky down)*. Really? Would you knit me a camel's-hair overcoat?

JENNIE. With or without humps? *(Touches his hand)* Why did it scare you so, George? We were sitting there touching hands, and you suddenly broke into a cold sweat.

GEORGE. Because it's not supposed to happen twice in your life.

JENNIE. Who said so?

GEORGE. Don't ask intelligent questions. You're talking to a man who just swooned into his butter plate. *(He rises)* Come on. I'll show you the house that Kenneth Blakely-Hill built.

JENNIE. And don't forget to give me those books tonight.

GEORGE. They're four ninety-five each, but we can talk business later. *(Puts his arm around her waist)* Now, then . . . This is the living room. That's the hallway that leads to the bedroom. And this is the rug that lies on the floor that covers the wood of the house that Kenneth Hyphen built.

JENNIE. I want to see everything.

GEORGE. Shall we start with the bedroom?

JENNIE. Okay.

GEORGE. If we start with the bedroom, we may *end* with the bedroom.

JENNIE. Endings are just beginnings backwards.

GEORGE. It's going to be one of those fortune cookie romances, huh? Okay, my dear . . . *(They head toward the bedroom)* Trust me.

JENNIE. I do.

GEORGE. Sure. I pass out at fish. What have *you* got to be afraid of?

(They enter the bedroom as the lights fade)

SCENE NINE

His apartment. It is three days later, mid-afternoon. LEO *paces in* GEORGE's *living room, takes some Valium from his attache case and swallows one with club soda.*

_____

LEO. George, will you let somebody else in New York use the phone?

GEORGE *(Enters from the bedroom, wearing a sweater over an open-necked shirt).* I'm sorry, Leo. It was an important call. I had to take it.

LEO. Are you all right?

GEORGE. I'm wonderful! I'm terrific! I haven't felt this good in such a long time . . . Listen, Leo, I'm glad you dropped by.

LEO. You look tired. You don't have good color in your face.

GEORGE. I'll have a painter come in Tuesday, he'll show me some swatches. Leo, will you stop worrying about me? I want to talk to you.

LEO. I called you one o'clock in the morning last night, you weren't in.

GEORGE. I'm glad I wasn't. Why did you call me at one o'clock in the morning?

LEO. I couldn't sleep. I wanted to talk to you.

GEORGE *(Impatient). Leo!* I am *ne!* Everything is *wonderful!*

LEO. I wanted to talk about *me* . . . I'm in trouble, George.

GEORGE. What?

LEO *(Nods).* Marilyn wants to leave me.

GEORGE *(Looks at him).* Oh, come on.

LEO. What is that, a joke? My wife wants to leave me.

GEORGE. Why?

LEO. She's got a list. Ask her, she'll show it to you . . . She doesn't like my lifestyle, she doesn't like the hours I keep, my business, my friends, my indifference, my attitude, my coldness—and our marriage. Otherwise we're in good shape. Christ! I said to her, "Marilyn, show me a press agent who comes home at six o'clock and I'll show you a man who can't get Jimmy Carter's name in the newspapers." I'm in the theater. Life begins at eight o'clock. The world isn't just matinees.

GEORGE. She's not going to leave you, Leo. This has been going on for years.

LEO. I took on two extra shows this season. The money was good, we needed it. I can't tell what the future is. I've got to make it *now!* I've got two kids. I could be dead tomorrow.

GEORGE *(Nods).* That's possible. I guess she just wants to enjoy you while you're still alive.

LEO *(Referring to* GEORGE's *wife).* I'm sorry, George.

GEORGE. Oh, come on, Leo. I know how you feel. You'll work it out. You always have.

LEO. Not this time . . . She's leaving me the morning after *Pinocchio.*

GEORGE. *Pinocchio?* What's that?

LEO. Tina is doing *Pinocchio* at school.

Marilyn doesn't want to upset her until it's over. The kid isn't even playing the lead. She's a herring that gets swallowed by the whale.

GEORGE. When is the show?

LEO. The show is Thursday night. The only chance I have to keep her is if the play runs four years! I don't know what the hell I'm holding on to, anyway. I swear to God, I'll never get married again. You spend half your married life fighting to get back the feeling you had just before you got married.

GEORGE. Come on, Leo. You've got a good marriage—I *know.*

LEO. Really? I'll invite you to sleep in our bedroom one night, you can listen. I'll tell you, George. The trouble with marriage is that it's relentless. Every morning when you wake up, it's still there. If I could just get a leave of absence every once in a while. A two-week leave of absence. I used to get them all the time in the Army, and I always came back . . . I don't know. I think it was different for you and Barbara. I'll tell you the truth, I always thought the two of you were a little crazy. But that's what made it work for you. You had a real bond of lunacy between you . . . Marilyn has no craziness. No fantasies. No uncharted territories to explore. I'm sitting there with maps for places in my mind I've never been, and she won't even pack an overnight bag. In eleven years she never once let me make love to her with the lights on. I said to her, "Marilyn, come on, trust me, I won't tell anybody." So we stop growing, stop changing. And we stagnate . . . in our comfortable little house in the country . . . Oh, well, another thirty, thirty-five years and it'll be over, right? *(He sits back)* All right, I've told someone. I feel better . . . Now, what the hell is it you feel so wonderful about?

GEORGE *(Smiles).* You're an interesting man, Leo. Someday I'll have to get to know you . . . In the meantime there's this girl I've met—

LEO. You've gone out with her? You like her?

GEORGE. I like her, Leo. She's extraordinary.

LEO *(Pleased).* Isn't that wonderful! You see, I knew you'd like her. I only spoke to her for ten minutes, but I saw she had a vitality, a sparkle about her—I knew she would interest you.

GEORGE. She more than interests me, Leo. I'm crazy about her.

LEO. Listen, I don't blame you. If I wasn't married, I'd have beaten you to the punch. Isn't that terrific! Terrific! Well, I knew once you left yourself open, you'd start to meet some women you can relate to—

GEORGE. I'm in love with her, Leo—I mean, crazy in love with her.

LEO. Well, we'll see. The point is, you enjoy being with her and that's very important for you at this time.

GEORGE. Leo, you don't hear what I'm saying . . . I'm going to marry her.

LEO. Look, it's possible. *I* hope so. She seems very sweet. Very bright. Faye tells me there isn't a person who ever met her who doesn't like her. She could be wonderful for you. When things calm down, when you get to be your old self again, I would *love* to see it happen.

GEORGE. We're getting married on Monday. (LEO *looks at him*)

LEO. Monday's a terrific day to get married. You miss the weekend traffic. Seriously, George, I'm glad you like the girl.

GEORGE. We took the blood test. I got the license. It's Monday morning, ten o'clock, Judge Ira Markowitz's chambers. I'd like you and Marilyn to be there.

LEO. To be where?

GEORGE *(Annoyed)*. Come on, Leo, you heard me. Jennie and I are getting married on Monday morning.

LEO. Wait a minute, wait a minute, back up! Play that again. What are you telling me? You mean on Monday morning you're marrying a girl I met for twelve seconds in a restaurant?

GEORGE. I'm marrying Jennie! *Jennie Malone!*

LEO. Oh, good. You know both names. So you must have had a chance to talk to her.

GEORGE. I've lived with her twenty hours a day for the last two weeks, and I know everything I want to know about her.

LEO. Two weeks? You've known her two weeks? I eat eggs that are *boiled* for two weeks—what the hell is *two* weeks?

GEORGE. Wait a minute. What happened to "how interesting she is"? What happened to her vitality, her sparkle?

LEO. Can't you wait to see if she's still sparkling in six months?

GEORGE. Six days, six months—what the hell difference does it make? I only knew Barbara eight weeks, and the marriage lasted twelve years.

LEO. George, you're vulnerable now. You're in no shape to make a decision like this.

GEORGE. Wait a minute. You know me, Leo.

I'm not self-destructive. I wouldn't do something to hurt me *and* Jennie just to satisfy a whim. I love her. I want to be with her. I want to make this commitment.

LEO. It's my fault, George. I never should have introduced you to Bambi. After Bambi you were ready for anything.

GEORGE. Leo, it was the same thing when I met Barbara. I could have married her after the third date. I knew then she was the most special girl in the world. Well, it's twelve years later and Barbara is gone. And suddenly, miraculously, this incredible person comes into my life—a sensitive, intelligent, warm, absolutely terrific human being. I don't know. Maybe it *is* crazy. You always said I was. But I'm miserable every minute I'm away from her, and she feels the same way. I think marrying her is a Class-A idea, Leo.

LEO. Okay, okay. But what is she—Cinderella? She's leaving at twelve o'clock? Wait! You'd wait six week for a dentist appointment, and that's with *pain* in your mouth.

GEORGE. Have dinner with us tonight. You and Marilyn.

LEO. I really don't think a couple breaking up is the best company for a couple starting out.

GEORGE. Call Marilyn. Tell her. Maybe being around us will give you both a chance to work things out.

LEO *(Annoyed)*. Why can't you accept the fact that Marilyn and I are separating?

GEORGE. Why can't you accept the fact that Jennie and I are getting married?

LEO. Because my separation makes sense. Your getting married is crazy!

GEORGE. Have it your own way. But I would still like you both to be there on Monday.

LEO. George, you've always been a lot smarter than me in a lot of ways. You have the talent and the discipline I've always admired. I'm very proud of you. But once in a while I've steered you straight, and I don't think you've ever regretted it . . . Wait a couple of months. Let her move in here with you. Is she against that? She's not a Mormon or anything, is she?

GEORGE. What's the point of delaying what's inevitable? She'll wait if I ask her.

LEO. Ask her.

GEORGE. She'll move in if I ask her.

LEO. Ask her. Please, George, ask her.

GEORGE. Monday morning, Criminal Courts building. I'm wearing a blue suit.

LEO. Wait a month. Wait a month for *me*.

GEORGE. I'm not marrying *you!*

LEO. Wait a month for me, and I'll wait a month for you. I'll try to work things out with Marilyn. I'll keep us together somehow, for a month, if you and Jennie will do the same for me.

GEORGE. Leo, we're not trading baseball cards now. This is my life, that's your marriage. Save it for you and Marilyn, not for me.

LEO. George, I realize I'm not the best marriage counselor you could go to—the toll-taker in the Lincoln Tunnel is more qualified than me—all I'm saying is take the time to catch your breath. Sleep on it. Take twelve Valiums and wake up in a month.

GEORGE. We're wasting a lot of time, you know that, Leo? This conversation used up my entire engagement period.

LEO. Would you mind if I talked to her?

GEORGE. Jennie?

LEO. Yes. Would you mind if I met with her, alone, and told her how I feel about all this?

GEORGE. Yes, I certainly would. She doesn't need an interview to get into this family.

LEO. Are you afraid she might agree with me?

GEORGE. Leo, I was always bigger than you . . . and you always beat up the kids who picked on me. What Pop didn't do for me, you did. I was the only kid on the block who had to buy *two* Father's Day presents . . . All right. Look, you want to protect me? Go ahead. You want to talk to Jennie, talk to her. But I promise you—a half-hour with her and you'll come back wondering why I'm waiting so long.

LEO. Thank you. I'll call Jennie tonight.

GEORGE. Would you like me to talk with Marilyn? I could wrap up the four of us in one night.

LEO. Listen, I could be wrong. I've been wrong before.

GEORGE. When?

LEO. I can't remember when, but I must have been . . . *(Goes to the door)* I don't know what the hell I'm doing in publicity. I was born to be a Jewish mother.

(He leaves. GEORGE thinks a moment, then goes to the phone and dials. In JENNIE's apartment the phone rings. She's been reading Catch-22*)*

JENNIE *(Answering the phone),* Hello?

GEORGE. I love you. Do you love me?

JENNIE. Of course I do . . . Who is this?

GEORGE. You're going to get a call from my brother. He thinks we're crazy.

JENNIE. Of course we are. What else is new?

GEORGE. Jennie, I've been thinking . . . Let's call it off. Let's wait a month. Maybe a couple of months.

JENNIE. All right . . . Whatever you say.

GEORGE. And I'd like you to move in here with me. Until we decide what to do.

JENNIE. I'll move in whenever you want.

GEORGE. I'm crazy about you.

JENNIE. I feel the same way.

GEORGE. Then forget what I said. It's still on for Monday morning.

JENNIE. I'll be there with my little bouquet!

(They hang up. JENNIE *looks thoughtful.* GEORGE's *gaze is drawn to a framed photo of Barbara)*

Curtain

ACT TWO

SCENE ONE

His apartment. It's the next afternoon. GEORGE *is stretched out on his sofa, the phone to his ear. He is in the midst of a dif cult conversation.*

_____

GEORGE. Of course I am . . . Yes . . . An incredible girl . . . Mom, why would I marry her if I wasn't? . . . Her father sells insurance in Cleveland . . . Yes, he also lives there, that's why he works there. *(He holds the receiver aside and emits a deep sigh of exasperation. Then he puts the phone back to his ear) . . .* I just told you. Monday morning. In a judge's office . . . How can it be, Mom? How can it be a big wedding in a judge's office? . . . You'll meet her when you come up from Florida. *(Another deep sigh. The doorbell rings)* Hold it a second, Mom, the doorbell's ringing . . . No. *Mine!*

(He shakes his head, puts down the phone, opens the door. JENNIE *stands there, beaming)*

JENNIE. I'm so crazy about you, it's ridiculous. *(She throws her arms around him and kisses him)* You're the most perfect man who ever lived on the face of the earth.

GEORGE. Jeez, if I hear that one more time today . . . What are you doing here?

JENNIE. I just had a physical, a facial and a dental. I don't want to get returned because of an imperfection. And I bought you a present.

(She takes a package from her purse and

hands it to him)

GEORGE. What is it?

JENNIE. Open it. *(He does. It is two books bound in ne leather)* Two from column B. I bought them at Doubleday's. They had to order them from the publisher.

GEORGE *(Overwhelmed)*. You had them bound? In leather?

JENNIE. Guaranteed to last as long as Dickens and Twain.

GEORGE. I'm speechless. I'm so thrilled, I don't know what to say . . . I mean, the leather binding is beautiful—but to think I sold two more books! *(He hugs her)* Hey! I left my mother on the phone.

JENNIE. In Florida? I want to speak to her.

GEORGE. Mom? . . . The next voice you are about to hear is that of Jennie Malone, a girl who brings dignity and respect to the often maligned phrase, "future daughter-in-law"!

JENNIE *(Into the phone)*. Mrs. Schneider? . . . Hello . . . I'm very happy to meet you . . . Oh, how nice . . . Well, I am too . . . I hope you know you have a special and wonderful son.

GEORGE. She knows, she knows.

JENNIE. No . . . No, it's not going to be a big wedding. It's going to be in a judge's office.

GEORGE *(Into the phone extension)*. She drinks, Mom . . . And she's a jockey at Belmont.

(He hangs up)

JENNIE. All right, I will . . . Yes . . . As soon as we get back from Barbados . . . God bless you, too.

(JENNIE, *suddenly taken with tears, hands the phone to* GEORGE)

GEORGE *(Into the phone)*. Mom, I'll be right with you. Hang on. Watch Merv Griffin. *(He lays the phone down and embraces* JENNIE*)* She can drive you completely nuts and then say something that just wipes you out.

JENNIE. Listen, I'll let you work. Don't be late tonight. I'm making spaghetti with fresh basil sauce.

GEORGE. Wait a minute. I bought you a present too. *(He goes to a drawer, opens it and takes out a ring box)* I was going to wait until after dinner, but I think I'm going to be eating a long time.

(He hands it to her. She is excited, knowing full well what it probably is)

JENNIE *(Beside herself)*. Oh, George, George, what have you done?

GEORGE. It's a car.

JENNIE *(Taking out a small diamond ring)*. Oh, George . . .

GEORGE. It's no big deal. It's just a wholesale engagement ring.

JENNIE. But we'll only be engaged for two more days.

GEORGE. Well, what I paid, that's all it's going to last.

JENNIE. This is too much emotion for me in one day. Come a half-hour late—I need more time to cry. *(And she rushes to the door, stops and goes back to the phone)* Hello, Mom, he gave me a ring.

(She runs out, and into her own apartment)

GEORGE *(Into the phone)*. Mom? . . . No, she left . . . Thank you . . . Of course she knows about Barbara . . . Well, in *my* day we discuss things, Mom . . . What else am I doing? You mean besides getting married? . . . Well, I bought a new sports jacket . . . Gray . . . You can never have too much gray, Mom . . .

(Dimout)

SCENE TWO

Her apartment. The doorbell rings. JENNIE *goes over to it.*

The lights come up on his apartment. GEORGE, *having nished his long conversation with his mother, dials the phone, sitting up.* JENNIE *opens the door.* FAYE *stands there, her hair in curlers, covered with a scarf.*

———

JENNIE. I thought you were taping two shows today.

FAYE. We're on a lunch break. If I asked you for an enormous favor, would you say yes and not ask any questions?

JENNIE. Yes.

FAYE. How long are you keeping this apartment?

(The phone rings)

JENNIE. My lease is up in two months. Why?

FAYE. Would you let me have the key?

(JENNIE *looks at her. The phone rings again. She picks it up. It is* GEORGE)

JENNIE. Hello?

GEORGE. My mother said no. I'm awfully sorry.

JENNIE. I am too.

GEORGE. I think we could have made a go of it, but this is too great an obstacle.

JENNIE. Don't worry about it. I have other things to do.

GEORGE. She found someone else for me. But good news: You're invited to the reception.

JENNIE. So we can still see each other.

GEORGE. Certainly. We can chat over an hors d'oeuvre . . . I'm going to take a bath now. I know you like to follow my schedule.

JENNIE. I read it. It was in the *Times*.

GEORGE. Then there's no point in talking. Goodbye.

JENNIE. 'Bye! (*They both hang up. He turns and heads for his bathroom as the lights go down on his apartment.* JENNIE *turns to* FAYE) Why do you want the key?

FAYE. You promised no questions.

JENNIE. That's before I knew the favor.

FAYE. Please.

(JENNIE *sees that* FAYE *is serious. She crosses to her dresser, takes out a spare key, goes to* FAYE *and hands it to her*)

JENNIE. I don't want to know, Faye, but if it's something stupid, please don't do it.

FAYE. Then take the key back, because I don't know a smart way to have an affair.

JENNIE. Ohhh, Christ! What have you done?

FAYE. Everything but consummation. That's why I need the key.

JENNIE. When did all this happen?

FAYE. All what? So far it's only ten percent cocktail talk . . . But I'm leaning toward "happening."

JENNIE. I don't want to know who it is.

FAYE. It's a secret I'll keep to my grave.

JENNIE. Why won't you tell me?

FAYE. Because it's not important who it is. It's only important that I want to do it. Don't you understand, Jennie? If I don't have something like an affair, I'll scream.

JENNIE. Then scream!

FAYE. Well, I thought I'd try this first.

JENNIE. Listen, maybe you're right. You're a grown lady, you know what you're doing.

FAYE. The hell I do.

JENNIE. Then why are you doing it?

FAYE. You tell me. Why are you getting married to a man you've known two and a half weeks who was married to a woman he idolized for twelve years? Because yesterday was lousy and it seems right today. I'll worry about tomorrow the day after.

JENNIE. "The Wit and Wisdom of Women in Trouble." Someday we'll collaborate on it . . . Is there anything I can do to help?

FAYE. Just leave me a map of all quick exits from the apartment . . . I've got to get back to making America cry. (*Holding up the key*) Listen, I may never use this, but you're the best friend I ever had.

JENNIE. When is this—*thing* going to take place?

FAYE. Oh, not for a few days. I have to be hypnotized first.

(*She exits. The phone rings;* JENNIE *answers it*)

JENNIE. Hello? . . . Hello, my angel . . . I thought you were taking a bath . . . Oh, you are! . . . No, I do *not* want to hear you blow bubbles . . . I do not want to hear your rubber duck. You're down to three years old, George, and sinking fast. (*The doorbell rings*) Oh, I think that's Leo . . . I'll see you for dinner . . . Well, I'm having spaghetti and you're having baby food. 'Bye!

(*She hangs up and opens the door*)

LEO. Hello, Jennie.

JENNIE. Leo—come on in. (*He enters*) I really enjoyed dinner the other night. Marilyn is a very sweet girl.

LEO. Thank you. We'll have to have you out to the house when you two get settled.

JENNIE. I'd love it . . . Would you like some coffee and stale cookies? I'm trying to clean out the kitchen.

LEO. A few minutes. That's all I'm staying. I just wanted to state my case and leave.

JENNIE. Oh? That sounds serious . . . All right. Please sit.

LEO (*Decides to stand*). This is none of my business, you know. I have no right coming up here.

JENNIE. I think loving your brother is very much your business.

LEO. I'm glad you feel that way. Because I do. The reason I wanted to talk to you, Jennie—and if I'm out of line here, tell me . . . the reason I came up here today . . . The foundation for my thoughts . . . The . . . the structure for my desire to . . . to delineate the . . . What the hell am I saying? The structure to delineate—what is that?

JENNIE. You think George and I are going too fast.

LEO. Exactly. Thank you! Christ! I thought that sentence would take me right into middle age.

JENNIE. Two weeks *is* very fast.

LEO. In some circles it's greased lightning . . . Be that as it may—and I hasten to add that I have never used expressions like "Be that as it may" or "I hasten to add"—but I'm having trouble. This is delicate territory, and I'm dealing with someone I care very much about.

JENNIE. Leo, I told George I'd wait as long as he wanted. Two weeks, two months—I don't care how long. He said, "No. It's got to be Monday, the twenty-third. It's all arranged" . . . What is it you're afraid will happen, Leo?

LEO *(Takes a news clipping from his wallet)*. I don't know . . . I'm not sure. Listen, I once did some work for an insurance company and they published these statistics—it was in every national magazine . . . *(Reads)* "The greatest loss that can happen to a man or woman, in terms of traumatic impact to the survivor, is the death of a spouse. The loss of a parent, a child, a job, a house—any catastrophe—is not deemed as devastating as the death of a husband or wife." In time, thank God and the laws of nature, most people work through it. But it needs the time . . . And I wouldn't want you and George to be hurt because that time was denied to him—to both of you.

JENNIE. I see . . . Have you and George talked about this?

LEO. I can't always read George's mind. He keeps so much bottled up. Maybe he spills it all out when he's alone—at the typewriter. I don't know.

JENNIE. Can I ask you a question?

LEO. What?

JENNIE. What was it like when Barbara died?

LEO. Ohhh . . . I don't think you want to go through that, Jennie.

JENNIE. No, I don't . . . But you just made it clear how important it is that I do. Tell me, Leo.

LEO *(Thinks, takes his time)*. All right . . . They were very close. I mean, as close as any couple I've ever seen. After ten years, they still held hands in a restaurant. I'm married eleven years and I don't pass the salt to my wife . . . When George first found out how ill Barbara was, he just refused to accept it. He knew it was serious, but there was no way she was not going to beat it. He just couldn't conceive it. And Barbara never let on to a soul that anything was ever wrong. Her best friend, at the funeral, said to George, "I just didn't know" . . . She was beautiful, Jennie, in every way. And then in the last few months you could see she was beginning to slip. George would go out to dinner or a party and leave early, trying not to let on that anything was wrong— and especially not letting on to themselves . . . And then one morning George called me from the hospital, and he said very quietly and simply, "She's gone, Leo." And it surprised me because I thought when it was finally over, George would go to pieces. I mean, I expected a full crackup, and it worried me that he was

so held together . . . I saw him as often as I could, called him all the time, and then suddenly I didn't hear from him for about five days. He didn't answer the phone. I called the building. They said they didn't see him go in or go out, and I got plenty scared. I went up there—they let me in with the passkey—and I found him in the bedroom sitting in front of the television set, with the picture on and no sound. He was in filthy pajamas, drenched in perspiration. There was a container of milk on the floor next to him that had gone sour. He must have dropped eight or nine pounds. And I said to him, "Hey, George, why don't you answer your phone? Are you okay?" And he said, "Fine. I'm fine, Leo." Then he reached over and touched my hand, and for the first time in a year and a half, the real tears started to flow. He cried for hours—through that whole night. I still couldn't get him to eat, so the next morning I got our doctor to come over, and he checked him into Mount Sinai. He was there for ten days. And he was in terrible shape. His greatest fear was that I was going to commit him someplace. When he came out, he stayed with me about a week. I couldn't even get him to take a walk. He had this panic, this fear he'd never make it back into the house. I finally got him to walk down to the corner, and he never let go of my arm for a second. We started across the street and he stopped and said, "No, it's too far. Take me back, Leo." A few weeks later he went into therapy. A really good doctor. He was there about a month, and then suddenly he decided he wasn't going back. He wouldn't explain why. I called the doctor and he explained to me that George was making a very determined effort not to get better. Because getting better meant he was ready to let go of Barbara, and there was no way he was going to let that happen. And then one day, bang, he took off for Europe. But not new places. Only the ones he'd visited with Barbara before. When he came back he looked better, seemed more cheerful. So in my usual dumb, impulsive way, I figured he would want what I would want if I were in his place— companionship. Well, companionship to him and me, I found out, were two different things. But he has good instincts. He knows what's right for him. And God knows what I offered wasn't right . . . until the night I saw you sitting there with Faye and I said, "Oh yeah, that's for George." I swear to you, Jennie, you are the best thing that could happen to that man. I was just hoping it would happen a little later . . . I'm sorry. No matter how I say all this, it doesn't seem to come out right. But you wanted to hear it. I just felt I had an obligation to say it. I hope you understand that, Jennie.

JENNIE. I'm trying hard to.

LEO. In other words, I think the smart thing to do is wait . . . to get one thing over with before you start something new. Is it unfair of me to say that?

JENNIE. Maybe it was your timing that was wrong. It was the most detailed, descriptive, harrowing story any women who's just about to get married ever heard.

LEO. I'm sorry. The bluntness comes from twenty-one years in the newspaper business.

JENNIE. Jesus God, what a thing to hear. I know you're concerned about your brother—maybe you should have given a little consideration to your future sister-in-law.

LEO. Jennie, please . . .

JENNIE. Forgive me. I'm sorry. But just let me get angry a second, because I think I deserve it.

LEO. I came here to talk, I didn't come here to fight.

JENNIE. No, maybe you're right, Leo. Maybe George really hasn't dealt with Barbara's death yet. And maybe I haven't asked enough questions. I can only deal with one thing at a time. Let me experience my happiness before I start dealing with the tragedies . . . Even if there were no Barbara to deal with, this is scary enough. And I'm goddamned petrified!

LEO. Well, you shouldn't be.

JENNIE. What do you mean, I shouldn't be? The thing I was most frightened to hear, you just sat there and told me.

LEO. That he loved her?

JENNIE. Yes!

LEO. That he was miserable when she died?

JENNIE. Yes! Yes! Of course I know it, but I don't want to hear it. Not now. Not today. My God, I'm moving into the woman's house Monday afternoon.

LEO. That's my point.

JENNIE. I'll wait as long as he wants. But it was his choice. He picked the date. And if that's not the sign of a man who wants to get healthy quickly, I don't know what is . . . Who picked me out as the stable one, Leo? I've just come from five years of analysis and a busted marriage. I couldn't believe how *lucky* I was when George came into my life . . . that he was going to make everything all right. And look at me . . . I'm so damned nervous everything might fall apart. It all feels like it's hanging by a string, and this sharp pair of scissors is coming towards me—snapping away.

LEO. Jennie, I swear to you, the only reason I brought it up at all is because I feel so responsible. I'm the one who made this match.

JENNIE. Well, let me put your mind at rest. There are powers even higher than matchmakers. I promise you, Leo, even if what we're doing is not right, I'll *make* it right.

LEO *(After a pause)*. Okay, I'll buy that. *(Shakes her hand, smiles)* I'll see you Monday, kid.

(He starts out)

JENNIE. Leo, do me a favor. Don't tell George what we talked about. Give us time to get to that ourselves.

LEO. I'm not even talking to George. I can't understand why he waited this long.

(He opens door and leaves. She heads for the bedroom)

SCENE THREE

His apartment. Monday morning, about 9:00 A.M. GEORGE, dressed in a neat blue suit, is looking in the mirror at the tissue covering a shaving cut on his jaw. He glances at his watch; he is very nervous. He goes over to the phone and dials.

———

GEORGE *(He listens for a minute, then speaks distinctly into the phone)*. Doctor Ornstein . . . It's George Schneider again . . . I don't think I can wait any longer for you to get out of your session . . . I know this is a weird message to be leaving on a recording . . . I realize I should have called you sooner, but frankly I was nervous about it . . . I'm getting married in about forty-five minutes and . . . She's a wonderful girl and I know I'm doing the right thing . . . I'll be at 273-4681, extension 1174, Judge Markowitz's chambers, in case you have to tell me something of the utmost importance, uh . . . Goodbye. *(He hangs up and wipes his brow with a hanky, realizes he's wearing slippers, runs toward the bedroom. The doorbell rings. He yells out)* It's open!

(The door opens and LEO comes in wearing a dark-blue suit and a white carnation in his lapel)

LEO. I've been waiting downstairs fifteen minutes. I watered my carnation three times. Are we getting married today or not?

GEORGE *(Returning, shoes in hand)*. I cut myself shaving. I can't stop bleeding. Was there any royalty in our family?

LEO. Yeah. King Irving from White Plains. Come on. The cab is going to cost you more than the honeymoon.

GEORGE. I slept twelve minutes—and I woke up *twice* during the twelve minutes.

LEO. Let's go, George. The judge has a lot of murderers to convict today.

GEORGE *(Looks at him)*. Who is she, Leo? I'm marrying a girl, I don't know who she is.

LEO. Don't start with me! Don't give me trouble, George! You drove me and all your friends half-crazy and now suddenly you want information?

GEORGE. I can't breathe. What a day I pick not to be able to breathe. What should I do, Leo?

LEO. I'll buy you a balloon, you can suck on it! George, I've got to know. Are you calling this off? Because if you are, I can still catch a workout at the gym.

GEORGE *(Yells, annoyed)*. Will you have a little goddamn compassion! I can't even get my ex-analyst on the phone. A lot *they* care. Fifty dollars an hour and all they do is protect you from doing neurotic things in *their* office. *(Gets a boxed carnation from the refrigerator)* Listen, if you're too busy, run along. Take the cab. I don't want you at my wedding anyway. You're going to stand there and make funny faces. You do it all the time.

LEO. I did it at *my* wedding, never at yours. *(Sees* GEORGE *fumbling hopelessly with the cellophane wrapping of the carnation)* What are you doing? What is that, a forest fire? Hold it, hold it, *hold it!*

(He pins the carnation on GEORGE's *lapel)*

GEORGE. You never told me what you and Jennie talked about.

LEO. She wasn't home.

GEORGE. She told me I'm very lucky to have such a concerned brother.

LEO. And she told me *I'm* the one she really wants. She's just marrying you to make me jealous. Let's go, George *(Starts to push* GEORGE *to the door)* If you're late, this judge fines you.

*(*LEO *ushers* GEORGE *almost all the way out. He balks at the door)*

GEORGE. You were right, Leo. It's all too soon. I should have waited until eleven, eleven-thirty. Ten o'clock is too soon.

LEO. Will you *come on?*

GEORGE. I didn't even have breakfast!

LEO. I'll buy you an Egg McMuffin at McDonalds!

*(*LEO *hustles* GEORGE *out)*

SCENE FOUR

Her apartment. FAYE *comes out of the bedroom in a sexy black negligee, wearing dark glasses, nervously smoking a cigarette, brushing her hair. She takes perfume from her bag, sprays it all over. Music plays on the radio. She goes to the door, looks out furtively.*

His apartment. A key opens the door. LEO *rushes to the phone, dials a number, takes the phone with him as he searches through desk drawers in a slight panic. The phone rings in* JENNIE's *apartment.* FAYE *is startled, looks at it. It rings again as* LEO *mutters, "Answer it, come on!" Finally she turns off the music and answers the phone.*

FAYE. Yes?

LEO. Faye?

FAYE. What number did you want, please?

LEO. It's all right, Faye. It's me, Leo.

FAYE. Leo who?

LEO. Faye, I haven't got time to play espionage! I can't meet you now. I've got to rush back out to the airport. George forgot the airline tickets and his traveler's checks, the limousine had a flat on the Long Island Expressway, and Jennie's got the heaves . . . Can we do it tomorrow?

FAYE. No. Tomorrow's no good. Sidney and I are going to the marriage counselor.

LEO. What time do you get through?

FAYE. I'm going *there* so I don't have to come *here!*

LEO. Cool it, cool it! Let's not get untracked before the train gets started—

FAYE. Leo, please. Let's forget it. I can't go through with it.

LEO. Why?

FAYE. I was seen by two little girls in the elevator.

LEO. Faye, please stop treating this like it's the Watergate break-in. You think we're the only one doing this? What do you think they have lunch hours for? . . . I've got to run. There are two people about to leave for their honeymoon who aren't talking to each other. I'll call you later.

FAYE. No, Leo—

LEO. I'm hungry for you . . . hot, steaming, roasting, burning hungry with desire. *(Kissing and hissing sounds)* 'Bye. *(Hangs up, looks as his watch)* Oh, shit!

(He rushes out of the apartment. FAYE *hangs up and sits there glumly)*

FAYE. This is definitely my last affair.

(She goes into the bedroom. Dimout)

SCENE FIVE

His apartment. It is a week later, about 8:00 P.M. We hear the sound of thunder, then of rain. The door opens. GEORGE *enters, carrying straw bags and suitcases. He looks rather bedraggled.* JENNIE *follows him in, carrying suitcases and her shoulder bag, along with a large straw hat and bongo drums—bought in the tropics, no doubt. She drops them with a thud, then goes over to the sofa and falls into it, exhausted, her legs outstretched*

GEORGE *picks up his mail, which was tied with a rubber band and left inside his door. He closes the door, and stands there going through the letters meticulously. Both are silent and there is some degree of tension between them.*

_____

JENNIE *(Looks up at the ceiling, mournfully).* That was fun! Three days of rain and two days of diarrhea. We should have taken out honeymoon insurance.

GEORGE *(Without looking up).* Don't forget to put your watch back an hour.

JENNIE. I don't want the hour. Let 'em keep it! . . . Any mail for me?

(He opens and reads a letter)

GEORGE *(Looks at her).* You've only been *living* here thirty-eight seconds.

JENNIE. Are you going to read your mail *now?*

GEORGE. It's from my publisher. He wants some revisions.

JENNIE. Again? You "revised" in Barbados . . . Is there anything soft to drink?

GEORGE *(Testy).* I think there's some beer. I could strain it if you like.

JENNIE. No, thanks. We have all the "strain" we can handle. *(She crosses to the fridge)* I read somewhere you can tell everything about a person by looking inside his refrigerator. *(She opens it)* Oh, God! Is this the man I married? Cold and empty, with a little yogurt!

GEORGE. I'll call the grocer in the morning and have him fill up my personality.

JENNIE *(Takes out a half-empty bottle of Coke with no cap on it).* You want to share a half a bottle of opened Coke? None of that annoy-

ing fizz to worry about.

(She takes a swig)

GEORGE *(Looks at her, not amused).* How many glasses of wine did you have on the plane?

JENNIE. Two.

GEORGE. How many?

JENNIE. Four.

GEORGE. You had seven.

JENNIE. I had six.

GEORGE. And two at the airport. That's *eight.*

JENNIE. All right, it was eight. But it wasn't seven. Don't accuse me of having seven.

GEORGE *(Gets up).* You're tight, Jennie.

(He picks up the suitcases and coats)

JENNIE. Ohhh, is that what's been bothering you all day, George? That I drank too much? I can't help it: I don't like flying. I asked you to hold my hand, but you wouldn't do it. So I drank some wine instead.

GEORGE *(Starts for the bedroom with the bags).* I *did* hold your hand. And while I was holding it, you drank my wine.

(He goes into the bedroom)

JENNIE. All right, George. Get it all out. You're angry because I ate your macadamia nuts, too, aren't you? And your package of Trident chewing gum. And I read the *Time* magazine you bought *before* you. You're sore because I knew what happened to "People in the News" ahead of you.

(She glances through the mail)

GEORGE. Don't mix up my mail, please.

JENNIE *(Puts it back).* Pardonnez-moi. I'll "revise" it later. *(He takes off his jacket. She tries to be more cheerful)* It's a little glum in here . . . We need plants. Lots of plants, from the floor to the ceiling. And sunshine. How do we get some sunshine in here?

GEORGE. I think our best bet is to wait for the morning.

(He picks up her bags)

JENNIE. Oh, God! Humor! At last, humor!

GEORGE. Look, it's been a lousy day. And because of the time difference, we get an extra hour of lousy. Why don't we just write it off and go to bed.

JENNIE. I'm hungry.

GEORGE *(Starts to unpack some tropical souvenirs).* You just had dinner on the plane.

JENNIE. Airplane food is not dinner. It's survival. Come on, let's get a chili-burger.

GEORGE. I don't want one.

JENNIE. Don't be ridiculous. *Everybody* wants a chili-burger. Come on, George, a big, greasy, nongovernment-inspected burger dripping with illegal Mexican chili.

(She gooses him with the Coke bottle)

GEORGE *(Pulls away angrily). Cut it out, dammit!*

JENNIE *(Startled by his sudden hostility).* I'm sorry.

GEORGE. How many times do I have to tell you? I don't want a goddamn chili hamburger!

JENNIE. Chili-*burger*. The ham is silent, like Hyphen Hill.

GEORGE. Oh, very good. Give the girl two gallons of wine and the repartee really gets quick.

JENNIE. Well, never as quick as you, George. Ah'm jes a dumb ole country girl from Cleveland.

GEORGE. I noticed. Sitting on the place with pen poised over the *New York Times* crossword puzzle for three and a half hours without ink ever *once* touching paper.

JENNIE. I'm sorry, George. Am I not "literary" enough for you? How's this? "Up your syntax!"

GEORGE. Swell. I'll try it tonight. I've been looking for a thrill.

(He goes into the kitchen. She sits, angry now, trying to figure out how to handle all this. GEORGE *comes back in with a glass of water)*

JENNIE. I've tried everything, including my funniest faces, to get a smile out of you since eight o'clock this morning.

GEORGE. Why don't you try an hour of quiet?

(He pops a Tylenol)

JENNIE. I tried it in Barbados and it turned into twenty-four hours of gloom.

GEORGE. Listen, I'm walking a very fine line tonight. There are a lot of things I would like to say that would just get us both in trouble. I don't want to deal with it now. Let's just go to bed and hope that two extra-strength Tylenol can do all they claim to do. Okay?

(He starts to cross back into the bedroom)

JENNIE. I'd just as soon hear what you had to say.

GEORGE. I don't think you would.

JENNIE. Why don't you be in charge of saying it and I'll be responsible for not wanting to hear it.

(He looks at her, nods, then looks around and decides to sit opposite her. She looks at him. He stares at the floor)

GEORGE. As honeymoons go, I don't think you got much of a break.

JENNIE. Really? I'm sorry if you felt that way. *I* had an intermittently wonderful time.

GEORGE. Well, I don't know what you experienced in the past. I'm not a honeymoon expert, but personally I found me unbearably moody.

JENNIE. Two days in seven isn't much of a complaint—which I never did. And I think we ought to limit this conversation to present honeymoons.

GEORGE. Why?

JENNIE. Because that's where we're living.

GEORGE. You can't get to the present without going through the past.

JENNIE. Jesus, George, is that what you did in Barbados? Compare honeymoons?

GEORGE *(Stares at her).* Why don't you ever ask me questions, Jennie? Why do you treat our lives as though there never was a day that happened before we met?

JENNIE. I'm not overly curious, George. If there are things you want to tell me, then tell me . . . but *Christ,* does it have to be our first night in this house?

GEORGE. Jesus, I was wondering when that perfectly calm exterior was going to crack. Thank God for a little antagonism.

JENNIE. Antagonism, hell. That's pure fear. We haven't even started this conversation yet and I'm scared to death.

GEORGE. Why?

JENNIE. I have terrific animal instincts. I know when my life is about to be threatened.

GEORGE. Aren't you even curious to know who the hell we are? I mean, I think you've got some goddamn romantic image of this man with a tragic past right out of *Jane Eyre.*

JENNIE. You're the one with the writer's imagination, not me.

GEORGE. All right, I'll start. Who is Gus? I would appreciate some biographical information on the man you spent a few important years of your life on. I mean, he's got to be more than a comic figure in a football jersey who pops up in a conversation every time we need a laugh.

JENNIE. I never thought of him as comic.

GEORGE. Really? Well, anyone who's described as pulling the wine cork out of the bottle with his teeth didn't seem like heavyweight material to me.

JENNIE. I wish to hell I knew what you're trying to get at.

GEORGE. Oh, come on, Jennie. Tell me *some*thing—anything . . . What was your honeymoon like? Would you say your sex life was A) good; B) bad; or C) good and bad. Pick one!

JENNIE. Why are you doing this to me? I don't understand. Do you expect me to stand there and give a detailed description of what it was like in bed with him? Is that what you want to hear?

GEORGE. Okay, Jennie, forget it.

JENNIE. If you want the truth, I don't think I ever knew the first damn thing about sex, because what happened to you and me in Barbados was something I never dreamed was possible. I hope you felt the same way, George. You never gave me any cause to doubt it . . . I'm sorry. This is very painful for me to talk about . . . But I'll try, George, I'll try anything that's going to make us move closer to each other.

GEORGE. I said forget it.

JENNIE *(Yells)*. No, *goddammit!* You're not going to open me up and walk away from it. I went through one marriage ignorant as hell. At least let me learn from *this* one. What else? *Ask me!*

GEORGE. You're doing fine on your own.

JENNIE. Please, George. I'm not going to blow five years of analysis in one night because you haven't got the nerve to finish what you've started. I've always had problems with confrontations. If my father just looked at me with a curve in his eyebrow I fell apart. But I swear to God, I'm going to get through this one. *(He tries to leave the room; she blocks his way)* No other questions? *(He doesn't answer)* Then can I ask you a few?

GEORGE. Why not?

JENNIE. Tell me about Barbara.

GEORGE *(Looks at her)*. She was terrific.

JENNIE. Oh, I know she was pretty. I see enough pictures of her around here. Tell me about your honeymoon. You went to Europe, didn't you?

GEORGE. Paris, London and Rome. And if you want a romantic description, it was a knockout.

JENNIE. I got the adjectives, George, what about the details? Big room? small room? view of the park? overlooking the Seine? fourposter bed? What was the wallpaper like?

GEORGE. Stop it, Jennie!

JENNIE. Why? What's wrong? Would you rather make out a list? What's safe to talk about and what's hands-off?

GEORGE *(A deep breath)*. Jesus, I don't have the strength for this kind of thing anymore.

JENNIE. You were doing fine two minutes ago.

GEORGE *(Looks at his hands)*. Sweating like crazy . . . I'm sorry, Jennie, I don't think I'm up to this tonight.

JENNIE. Why, George? Why is it so painful? What are you feeling now? Do you think that I'm expecting you to behave a certain way?

GEORGE. No. *I* expect it. I expect a full commitment from myself . . . I did it twelve years ago . . . But I can't do it now.

JENNIE. I'm in no hurry. What you're giving now is enough for me. I know the rest will come.

GEORGE. *How* do you know? How the hell did you become so wise and smart? Stop being so goddamn understanding, will you? It bores the crap out of me.

JENNIE. Then what *do* you want? Bitterness? Anger? Fury? You want me to stand toe to toe with you like Barbara did? Well, I'm not Barbara. And I'll be damned if I'm going to re-create *her* life, just to make *my* life work with you. This is *our* life now, George, and the sooner we start accepting that, the sooner we can get on with this marriage.

GEORGE. No, you're not Barbara. That's clear enough.

JENNIE *(Devastated)*. Oh, Jesus, George. If you want to hurt me, you don't have to work that hard.

GEORGE. Sorry, but you give me so much room to be cruel, I don't know when to stop.

JENNIE. I never realized that was a *fault* until now.

GEORGE. I guess it's one of the minor little adjustments you have to make. But I have no worry—you'll make them.

JENNIE. And you resent me for that?

GEORGE. I resent you for *everything!*

JENNIE *(Perplexed)*. Why, George? *Why?*

GEORGE. Because I don't feel like making you happy tonight! I don't feel like having a wonderful time. I don't think I *wanted* a "terrifically wonderful" honeymoon! You want happiness, Jennie, find yourself another football player, will ya? I resent everything you want out of marriage that I've already had. And for making me reach so deep inside to give it to you again. I resent being at L or M and having to go back to A! And most of all, I resent not being able to say in front of you . . . that I miss Barbara so much.

(He covers his eyes, crying silently. JENNIE *has been cut so deeply, she can hardly react. She just sits there, fighting back her tears)* Oh, Christ, Jennie, I'm sorry . . . I think I need a little outside assistance.

JENNIE *(Nods)*. What do you want to do?

GEORGE *(Shrugs)*. I don't know . . . I don't want to make any promises I can't keep.

JENNIE. Whatever you want.

GEORGE. We got, as they say in the trade, problems, kid.

(He goes to her, embraces her head, then goes into the bedroom, leaving her stunned and alone.)

Dimout

SCENE SIX

Her apartment. It is two days later, about three o'clock on a sunny afternoon. The living room is empty.

FAYE *comes in from the bedroom, wearing a sheet—and apparently nothing else. Her hair is disheveled. She is distraught.*

LEO SCHNEIDER *comes out of the bedroom, zipping up his pants. He is nude from the waist up.*

_____

LEO. I'm sorry.

FAYE. Forget it.

LEO. Don't be like that.

FAYE. What *should* I be like?

LEO. It was an important phone call. I *had* to take it.

FAYE. It's not taking it that bothered me. It's *when* you took it I felt was badly timed.

LEO. Half of my year's gross income depended on that call. He's my biggest client. Come on back . . . Faye? What do you say? They won't call again.

FAYE. You mean you actually left this number? I changed taxis three times and walked with a limp into the building and you gave out this number?

LEO. It's just a number. It could be a luncheonette. He doesn't know. Faye, that phone call meant thirty thousand dollars to me.

FAYE. Jesus—I'm worried I'm going to be emotionally scarred for life, and you're getting rich.

LEO. You're so tense, Faye. You've been tense since I walked in the door. I knew when I came in and we shook hands, things weren't going to be relaxed.

FAYE. I'm no good at this, Leo. I'm nervous and I'm clumsy.

LEO. Don't be silly. You've been wonderful.

FAYE. I'm sorry about your shoes.

LEO. It's just a little red wine. They're practically dry.

FAYE. Your socks too?

LEO. Don't worry about it . . . Hey, Faye— Faysie! Have I offended you in some way? Have I been inconsiderate? Insensitive?

FAYE. Aside from adultery, you've been a perfect gentleman. I don't know . . . I just didn't think it would be so complicated. So noisy.

LEO. Noisy? What noise?

FAYE. My heart. It's pounding like a cannon. They must hear it all over the building.

LEO. I'll turn on the radio, they'll think it's the rhythm section . . . Hey! Would you like to dance?

FAYE. Are you serious?

LEO. Absolutely! You think it's corny? Well, I happen to be a very corny guy. Come on. Come dance with me.

FAYE. With red wine in your shoes? You'll squeak.

LEO *(Pulling FAYE to her feet)*. C'mon. *(Singing)*

Flamingo . . .

Like a flame in the sky . . .

Flying over the island . . .

(Taking over cigarette) Gimme that. *(Singing)*

To my lover nearby . . .

(Sings a scat phrase, starts dancing with FAYE*)*

Hey, Flamingo . . .

In your tropical hue . . .

FAYE. You're crazy, Leo.

LEO.

Words of passion and romance . . .

FAYE. You're embarrassing me.

LEO.

And my love for you . . .

(Sings a scat phrase)

One dip. Just give me one old-fashioned dip. *(He dips her)*

FAYE. Let me up, Leo. I'm in no mood to be dipped!

(She slips a little and they slide to the oor)

LEO. Jesus, you're pretty.

FAY. I'm not.

LEO. Don't tell me you're not. I'm telling you you're pretty.

FAYE. All right, I'm pretty. I don't want to argue.

LEO. You're pretty and you're sweet and you've got the softest face.

FAYE. You've done this a lot, haven't you, Leo?

LEO. You get some particular thrill in dousing me with ice water?

FAYE. You're so good at it. I admire your professionalism. It's all so well-crafted. Like a really well-built cabinet.

LEO. Where do you find a parallel between my lovemaking and woodwork?

FAYE. I may be new at this, Leo, but I'm not naïve. You've had affairs with married women before, haven't you?

LEO. No . . .

FAYE. Leo . . .

LEO. There was one woman, but she was waiting for her divorce to come through.

FAYE. A lot?

LEO. Maybe one other.

FAYE. You've done it a lot.

LEO. A few times, I swear.

FAYE. A lot.

LEO. Yes, a lot. But they were never important to me. *Today* is important to me. *(Trying to caress her, he struggles with the sheet)* What is this tent you're wearing?

FAYE *(She gets up, moves away)*. Please, Leo. A lot of meaningless affairs does not raise my appreciation of what we're doing.

LEO. It's not just the phone call that's bothering you. It's something else. You know what the problem is? You don't have a good enough reason to be here.

FAYE. That's a funny thing to say to a woman who shopped in twelve stores for the right underwear.

LEO. Well, then, maybe we rushed it. *I* rushed it, okay? Maybe this isn't the right time for you, Faye.

FAYE. What do *you* know about it? A couple of lousy affairs and you're suddenly Margaret Mead? Listen, when Jennie began having trouble with Gus, she decided to see an analyst. And I asked her, "When was the day you finally realized you needed one?" And she said, "It was the day I found myself in his office." Well, I'm *here* in your office . . . and I need something in my life. I already tried Transcendental Meditation, health foods and jogging. And I am now serenely, tranquilly and more robustly unhappy that I have ever been before . . . So don't tell me this isn't the right time, Sidney!

LEO. Leo.

FAYE. *Leo!* Oh, shit!

LEO. Oh, Faye, sweet Faye . . . You are so much more interesting-looking than you were twelve years ago. You've got so damn much character in your face.

FAYE. Why does that not overjoy me? Why is life going by so fast, Leo? First I was pretty.

Now I'm interesting-looking with character! Soon I'll be handsome followed by stately and finally, worst of all, remarkable for her age.

LEO. Gloomy! You're taking a gloomy perspective, Faye. Gloom is the enemy of a good time.

FAYE. You were right before, Leo. I don't have a good enough reason to be here. Because what I want, I can't have. I want what Jennie has: the excitement of being in love again. I'm so much smarter now, I could handle everything so much better. I am so jealous of her I could scream. I did for her what I wish I could have done for myself. And in return I got her apartment to do exactly what I swore, when I was young and pretty, I would never end up doing when I became interesting-looking with character.

LEO. I think you're a very confused person, Faye.

FAYE. I've noticed that . . . I think you'd better leave first, Leo. I have to stay for a while and practice my limp.

LEO. I was crazy about you, Faysie . . . Never stopped thinking about you all through the years. I used to skim through the trades to see if you were working or not—

FAYE. Why didn't you ever try to get in touch with me?

LEO. I heard you were happily married.

FAYE. I heard you were, too.

LEO. Go trust people.

FAYE. I never told you this, but my mother didn't like you.

LEO. I never met her.

FAYE. I know, but I used to tell her about you. She said, "I know his type. He's the kind that needs lots of women." I could call her and say, "You were right, Mom"—but how do I explain how I found out?

LEO. I wonder what would have happened if we had married each other?

FAYE. Well, I would hope a hell of a lot more than happened today . . . What's your opinion?

LEO. I think we'd have turned out swell.

FAYE. You don't really believe that, do you?

LEO. No.

FAYE. Then why did you say it?

LEO. I thought it would make you happy.

FAYE. You're awful.

LEO. Why? Because I want to please you? Are we better off deluding ourselves that ours would have been one of the great love affairs of midtown Manhattan? I know what it is and *you* know what it is—why do we have to call it something we both know it isn't?

FAYE. Because a woman *needs* delusion.

LEO *(Putting on the rest of his clothes)*. Not me. I need something new. It's why I like show business. There's another opening every three weeks. I can't be monogamous, Faye. What can I do, take shots for it? But in our system I'm put down as a social criminal. I can't be faithful to my wife, and I hate the guilt that comes with playing around. So I compromise. I have lots of unpleasurable affairs. And what makes it worse—I really do care for Marilyn. I can't stop, and I don't expect her to understand. So we end up hurting each other. I don't like it, Faye. I don't like crawling into bed at two o'clock in the morning and feeling the back of a cold, angry woman. And I don't like you coming up here under any false pretenses. I would love to make love to you, but that's the end of the sentence. I don't want a fine romance. I don't want to dance on the ceiling or have my heart stand still when "she" walks in the door. Because I really don't want to hurt anyone anymore. All I want is a little dispassionate passion . . . Let George and Jennie handle all the romance for the East Coast. The man is half-crazed right now, and he's welcome to it . . . I'll tell you what I *do* want, Faye. I want a woman who looks exactly like you and feels like you and thinks exactly like me.

FAYE. Boy, did I ever come to the wrong store to shop.

LEO. So what have we got here? We got one romantic unhappy woman, one indifferent frustrated man and one available and unused bedroom . . . is what we got here.

FAYE. It's too bad. You finally got me in the mood, and your honesty got me right out of it.

LEO. Anyway, I like you too much. Making love to people you like is very dangerous.

FAYE. Good. Save it for your enemies.

LEO *(Looks at his watch)*. Well, I can still get some work done. Can I drop you downtown?

FAYE. You mean, leave together? Suppose someone sees us?

LEO. Listen, they could have seen us in bed and never suspected anything. Come on, get dressed.

FAYE. Leo, as a lover, you make a terrific friend. Would you mind giving me one warm, passionate and very sincere kiss? I'll be goddamned if I'm going home empty-handed.

LEO *(Steps toward her)*. Hold on to your sheet, kid, kissing is my main thing.

(He gently puts his arms around her and gives her a soft, warm kiss on the lips. She pulls back, looks at him, and then suddenly feeling very safe, she leans forward again and they kiss deeply and passionately. His hands start to roam over her back. He gently puts her down on the sofa and begins to kiss her neck and her face as . . . the door opens and JENNIE *walks in. She sees them and freezes)*

JENNIE. Oh, God! I *am* sorry!

(They both jump up. LEO *backs away)*

FAYE. Oh, Jesus!

LEO. Oh, Christ!

JENNIE. I should have called. I didn't think—

LEO. It's all right. It's okay. No harm done. We're all adults. It's a grown-up world. These things happen. We have to be mature—

FAYE. Oh, shut up, Leo.

JENNIE. I just came by to pick up the rest of my summer clothes. I can do it later. I'm so sorry.

(She backs up toward the door)

FAYE. Don't think, Jennie. Don't think until I talk to you tonight. Promise me you won't think.

JENNIE. I won't. I promise . . . Goodbye, Leo. Say hello to Maril—! Goodbye, Leo!

(She turns and goes out, closing the door)

FAYE. This is one of those situations in life that a lot of people find humor in—I don't!

(She goes into the bedroom)

LEO. That's a first for me. That has never happened before. Never caught by a sister-in-law. *Never!*

(He leaves, slamming the front door)

SCENE SEVEN

His apartment, about an hour later. GEORGE *comes out of the bedroom, wearing a sports jacket and carrying a raincoat and fully packed suitcase and attache case. He puts a note on the desk and starts for the door.*

JENNIE *enters, looking a little glum, sees* GEORGE *and his luggage.*

GEORGE. Hi.

JENNIE. Hi.

GEORGE. You had some messages. *(Takes the piece of notepaper from the desk)* I was going to leave this for you. I don't know if you can read my writing . . . Jill James at CBS called and said you start shooting again on Monday. They'll send the pages over tonight. Also, Helen Franklyn called and said you have a reading for the new Tom Stoppard play Monday at ten. And Faye called a few minutes ago, said it was urgent she talk to you and can you have lunch with her on Tuesday, Wednesday, Thursday and Friday . . . And that was it.

JENNIE *(Stunned; doesn't respond immediately)*. I'm sorry, I wasn't listening . . . I couldn't take my eyes off your suitcase.

GEORGE. I tried to explain everything in a letter. I left it on the bed.

JENNIE. Good. I was worried that I wasn't getting any mail . . . Where are you going?

GEORGE. Los Angeles. Someone at Paramount is interested in *The Duchess of Limehouse* as a film.

JENNIE. When did this come up?

GEORGE. Two weeks ago.

JENNIE. Why didn't you tell me?

GEORGE. I had no reason to go two weeks ago.

JENNIE. Leave it to you to make a point clear. How long will you be gone?

GEORGE. I don't know.

JENNIE. Where will you stay?

GEORGE. I don't know.

JENNIE. Just going to circle the airport for a few days?

GEORGE. You never lose your equilibrium, do you?

JENNIE. You think not? I'd hate to see an X-ray of my stomach right now.

GEORGE. I don't think being apart for a while is going to do us any damage.

JENNIE. Probably no worse than being together the past few days.

GEORGE. But if it's really important to get in touch with me, Leo will know where I am.

JENNIE. And I'll know where Leo is.

GOERGE *(Goes to the door, turns back uncomfortably)*. I don't think I have anything else to say. How about you?

JENNIE *(Shrugs)*. I have no statement to make at this time.

GEORGE. I'm glad a lot of work is coming your way. I know it's important to you. It's what you want.

JENNIE. I'm glad you know what I want, George . . . If you told me five years ago, I could have saved a lot of doctor money.

GEORGE. I was busy five years ago.

JENNIE. You don't have to remind me. Interesting how this all worked out. You pack up and go and leave *me* with all your memories.

GEORGE. I'm sorry, but you can't get a five-room apartment in the overhead rack.

JENNIE. Is there anything you want me to take care of while you're gone?

GEORGE. You seem to be taking care of it fine right now.

JENNIE. Oh, I tripped over the wire and set off the trap, didn't I? . . . Everything I say can be so cleverly twisted around by you that you always end up the victim and I'm the perpetrator. God forbid I'm not as fast with a thought or a phrase as you, and you pounce on it like a fat cat.

GEORGE. Fat cats are very slow on the pounce because they're fat, but I got your point.

JENNIE *(Very angry)*. Oh, go on, get the hell out of here, will you! If you're going to leave, leave! Go! Your Mystery Plane is waiting to take you, shrouded in secrecy, to your Phantom Hotel on the intriguing West Coast. Even your life is turning into a goddamn spy novel—

GEORGE *(Puts down the valise)*. I've got a few minutes. I don't want to miss what promises to be our most stimulating conversation since I thought you were an eighty-five-year-old woman on the phone.

JENNIE. Isn't it amazing the minute I get angry and abusive, it's one of the few times I can really hold your attention . . . What can I say that will really hurt you, George? I want to send you off happy.

(She swarms over him, punching him. He throws her onto the sofa)

GEORGE. Just going is reward enough.

(He starts out. She runs ahead of him and grabs the suitcase to ing it out. He throws her to the oor)

JENNIE. You know what you want better than me, George . . . I don't know what you expect to find out there, except a larger audience for your two shows a day of suffering . . . I know I'm not as smart as you. Maybe I can't analyze and theorize and speculate on why we behave as we do and react as we do and suffer guilt and love and hate. You read all those books, not me . . . But there's one thing I *do* know. I know how I *feel*. I know I can stand here watching you try to destroy everything I've ever wanted in my life, wanting to smash your face with my fists because you won't even make the slightest effort to opt for happiness—and still know that I love you. That's always so clear to me. It's the one place I get all my strength from . . . You mean so much to me that I am willing to take all your abuse and insults and insensitivity—because that's what you need to do to prove I'm not going to leave you. I can't promise I'm not going to die, George, that's asking too much.

But if you want to test me, go ahead and test me. You want to leave, leave! But *I'm* not the one who's going to walk away. I don't know if I can take it forever, but I can take it for tonight and I can take it next week. Next month I may be a little shaky. . . . But I'll tell you something, George. No matter what you say about me, I feel so good about myself—better than I felt when I ran from Cleveland and was frightened to death of New York. Better than I felt when Gus was coming home at two o'clock in the morning just to change his clothes. Better than I felt when I thought there was no one in the world out there for me, and better than I felt the night before we got married and I thought that I wasn't good enough for you . . . Well, I am! I'm wonderful! I'm nuts about me! And if you're stupid enough to throw someone sensational like me aside, then you don't deserve as good as you've got! I am sick and tired of running from places and people and relationships . . . And don't tell me what I want because *I'll* tell you what I want. I want a home and I want a family—and I want a career, too. And I want a dog and I want a cat and I want three goldfish. I want *everything!* There's no harm in wanting it, George, because there's not a chance in hell we're going to get it all, anyway. But if you don't *want* it, you've got even less chance than that . . . Everyone's out there looking for easy answers. And if you don't find it at home, hop into another bed and maybe you'll come up lucky. *Maybe!* You'd be just as surprised as me at some of the "maybe's" I've seen out there lately. Well, none of that for me, George . . . You want me, then fight for me, because I'm fighting like hell for you. I think we're both worth it. I will admit, however, that I *do* have one fault. One glaring, major, monumental fault . . . Sometimes I don't know when to stop talking. For that I'm sorry, George, and I apologize. I am now through!

(She sits back on the sofa, exhausted)

GEORGE *(Looks at her for a long time, then says warmly).* I'll tell you one thing—I'm glad you're on *my* side.

JENNIE *(Looks over at him).* Do you mean it, George?

GEORGE. I didn't hear half of what you said because I was so mesmerized by your conviction. I'm not a doctor, Jennie, but I can tell you right now, you're one of the healthiest people I ever met in my life.

JENNIE *(Smiles).* Funny, I don't look it.

GEORGE. I am crazy about you. I want you to know that.

JENNIE. I know that.

GEORGE. No. You don't know that I'm absolutely crazy nuts for you.

JENNIE. Oh. No, I didn't know that. You're right.

GEORGE. I want to walk over now and take you in my arms and say, "Okay, we're finished with the bad part. Now, what's for dinner?" But I'm stuck, Jennie . . . I'm just stuck someplace in my mind and it's driving me crazy. Something is keeping me here, glued to this spot like a big, dumb, overstuffed chair.

JENNIE. I could rearrange the furniture.

GEORGE. Don't make it so easy for me. I'm fighting to hold on to self-pity, and just my luck I run into the most understanding girl in the world.

JENNIE. I'm not so understanding.

GEORGE. Yes, you are. You just said so yourself. And I swear to God, Jennie, I can't find a thing I would want to change about you . . . So let me go to Los Angeles. Let me try to get unstuck . . . I'll be at the Chateau Marmont Hotel. I'll be in my room unsticking like crazy.

JENNIE. Couldn't I go with you? I wouldn't bother you. I would just watch.

GEORGE. Then the people next door would want to watch, and pretty soon we'd have a crowd. *(He picks up his suitcase)* Take care of yourself.

JENNIE. George! *(He stops, looks at her)* Would you mind very much if I slept in my apartment while you're gone? I feel funny about staying in this place alone.

GEORGE *(Nods).* I understand . . .

JENNIE. If you don't call me, can I call you?

GEORGE *(A pause).* You know, we may have one of the most beautiful marriages that was ever in trouble.

(He goes out. She goes to the door, watches him go, then comes in and closes the door.)

Dimout

SCENE EIGHT

Her apartment. The next day. The doorbell rings. FAYE *opens the door. It is* LEO.

LEO. Oh? Hello! Do I look as surprised as you?

FAYE. What are you doing here?

LEO. I just dropped by.

FAYE. To see me?

LEO. No.

FAYE. Thank God. I was afraid it was one of those habits you can't break.

LEO. Is Jennie home?

FAYE. She's in the shower. She moved back last night . . . So much for our matchmaking business.

LEO. Actually I came back hoping to find my wallet. I think I dropped it in the bedroom yesterday during the mass exodus.

FAYE. Jennie found it. She woke up in the middle of the night with a credit card lump under her head.

(She gives him a small Manila envelope, held with a rubber band. He looks at it)

LEO. She didn't have to put my name on it. It's humiliating enough. Did she say anything about us?

FAYE. That's not her style . . . I was prepared to tell her I'd been drugged. You don't mind, do you?

LEO. Look, why don't we just write off yesterday? Even my horoscope said, "Stay outdoors."

FAYE. I'm in the process of forgetting about it. I'm seeing Jennie's old doctor on Monday.

LEO. That's terrific. I'm glad you're doing something constructive about your problems.

FAYE. And what about you, Leo? What are you doing?

LEO *(Shrugs)*. Nothing! I have no intention of changing. So why should I pay some doctor to make me feel guilty about it?

FAYE. And what about you and Marilyn? Are you going to separate?

LEO. Yes. But not this year. We have too many dinner dates . . . *(He stands)* Well, I'll see you around, kid.

FAYE. Every place but here.

LEO. Keep your options open. It makes life more interesting.

FAYE. Why is it the more you say things I don't like, the more attractive you get?

LEO. That's what's going to cost you fifty buck an hour to find out . . . We never did finish that warm, passionate, friendly kiss.

FAYE. You know what? I think I'm just crazy enough to do it.

(They kiss. JENNIE walks in from the bedroom in a bathrobe, drying her hair with a towel)

JENNIE. Faye, was that the phone I heard befo—? *(She stops, seeing them. They break apart)* Jesus, is that the same kiss from yesterday?

LEO. My regiment was just called up and

I'm trying to say goodbye to everybody . . . Maybe next week the three of us can meet in a restaurant, because I'd like to explain this whole silly business. We'll all wear hoods, of course.

JENNIE. Leo . . . Have you heard from George?

LEO. No . . . but give him a couple of days, Jen. He'll figure it out. *(Kisses her, starts out, stops)* Jesus, life was so simple when we were kids. No matter how much trouble you got into outside, when you got home you always got a cupcake.

(He leaves)

FAYE *(Looks sheepishly at JENNIE)*. I feel so foolish. Do you hate me?

JENNIE *(Smiles)*. I could never hate you.

FAYE. Well, I have another confession to make to you . . . Leo was never the one I wanted to have an affair with.

JENNIE. Who was?

FAYE. A certain ex-wide receiver from the New York Giants.

JENNIE. *Gus?*

FAYE. I lusted for that man in more places than my heart.

JENNIE. Then why did you pick Leo?

FAYE. Because I was intimate with him before I met Sidney . . . I just wanted to practice with someone I already knew.

JENNIE. You have a peculiar bookkeeping system.

FAYE. Anyway, Sidney and I are going to an adult motel in New Jersey this weekend. From now on, I'm only cheating with the immediate family . . . I've got to go. Are you sure you'll be all right? I mean, staying here all alone?

JENNIE. Wait a minute. Am I having a déjà vu or have we played this scene before?

FAYE. The dialogue *does* seem awfully familiar. I remember saying, "Shit. Twelve more years to go until the good times" and then falling in love with the girl across the street.

JENNIE. Oh, God. Our life is on a loop. Does this mean I have to go out with the giant from Chicago again?

FAYE. I'd better go before Leo comes in with a bottle of red wine. *(She crosses to the door, opens it, then turns back)* There's a lesson to be learned from all this . . . I wonder what the hell it is.

(She leaves.)

Fadeout

SCENE NINE

His apartment. The door opens. GEORGE *enters and turns on the lights. He looks a little travel-weary.*

———

GEORGE *(Putting down his suitcase).* Jennie? Jennie?

(He looks around, then goes into the bedroom. It's apparent no one is home. He comes back into the living room. In her apartment, JENNIE *goes to the refrigerator, takes out an apple, then goes to the sofa and sits.* GEORGE *picks up the phone, and starts to dial just as* JENNIE *picks up the receiver. She dials 213-555-1212. He finishes dialing and gets a busy signal. He hangs up, taking a manuscript from his attaché case)*

JENNIE *(Into the phone).* Los Angeles . . . I'd like the number of the Chateau Marmont Hotel . . . Yes, I think it *is* West Hollywood . . . *(She waits. He paces)* 656-1010 Thank you. *(She disconnects with her finger, then starts to dial just as he goes back to the phone, picks it up and starts to dial. She gets halfway through the number when she suddenly hangs up)* Patience, Jennie! Don't pressure him. *(She sits back just as he complete his dial. Her phone rings. She jumps and clutches her bosom)* Oh, God, I'm so smart! *(She reaches over and picks up the phone)* Hello?

GEORGE. Serene?

JENNIE. Who?

GEORGE. Is this Serene Jurgens? . . . It's George Schneider, Leo's brother . . . I just arrived on the Coast, darling. At last, I'm free.

JENNIE *(Near tears).* Tell me you're joking, George. Right now I wouldn't know humor if it hit me with a truck.

GEORGE. Oh. Well, then you'd better pull off the highway . . . How are you? What have you been doing?

JENNIE. Watching the telephone. Nothing good on until now . . . How's the weather there?

GEORGE *(Looks around).* Oh, about eighty-four degrees. A little humid.

JENNIE. Same here . . . How are you, George?

GEORGE. Dumb. Dummy Dumbo.

JENNIE. Why?

GEORGE. Well, when Barbara and I had a fight, I'd walk around the block and come back twenty minutes later feeling terrific . . . At the airport I said to myself, "Of course. That's

what I should do." And that's what I did.

JENNIE. I can't believe it. You mean, you just walked around the block?

GEORGE. Yes.

JENNIE. What's so dumb about that?

GEORGE. I was in the Los Angeles airport when I thought of it.

JENNIE. Well, where are you? Here or there?

GEORGE. Wait, I'll look. *(He looks around)* Looks like here.

JENNIE. You're back! You're in New York!

GEORGE. I never even checked into the Chateau Marmont . . . I got unstuck in the TWA lounge.

JENNIE. Oh, George . . .

GEORGE. I sat there drinking my complimentary Fresca, and I suddenly remembered a question Dr. Ornstein told me to ask myself whenever I felt trouble coming on. The question is "What is it you're most afraid would happen *if?"*

JENNIE. I'm listening.

GEORGE. So I said to myself, "George, what is it you're most afraid would happen—*if* you went back to New York . . . to Jennie . . . and started your life all over again?" And the answer was so simple . . . I would be happy! I have stared happiness in the face, Jennie— and I embrace it.

JENNIE *(Tearfully).* Oh, George. You got any left to embrace me?

GEORGE. From here? No. You need one of those long-armed fellas for that.

JENNIE. Well, wht are we waiting for? Your place or mine?

GEORGE. Neither. I think we have to find a new one called "Ours."

JENNIE. Thank you, George. I was hoping we would.

GEORGE. Thus, feeling every bit as good about me as you do about you, I finished the last chapter of the new book on the plane. *(He takes up the manuscript. The last few pages are handwritten)* I've got it with me. You want to hear it?

JENNIE. The last chapter?

GEORGE. No. The whole book.

JENNIE. Of course. I'll be right over.

GEORGE. No, I'll read it to you. I don't want to lose my momentum. *(He opens the manuscript folder, settles back; so does she. He reads)* You ready? . . . *Falling Into Place,* by George Schneider. Dedication: "To Jennie . . . A nice girl to spend the rest of your life with . . ." *(He turns the page)* Chapter One . . . "Walter Maslanski looked in the mirror and saw what he feared most . . . Walter Maslanski . . ." *(The curtain begins to fall)* "Not that Walter's features were awesome by any means . . . He had the sort of powder-puff eyes that could be stared down in an abbreviated battle by a one-eyed senior-citizen canary . . ."

Curtain

Same Time, Next Year

Bernard Slade

First presented by Morton Gottlieb at the Brooks Atkinson Theatre in New York City on March 13, 1975, with the following cast:

(*in order of appearance*)
GEORGE   Charles Grodin
DORIS   Ellen Burstyn

Directed by Gene Saks
Scenery by William Ritman
Costumes by Jane Greenwood
Lighting by Tharon Musser

THE SCENE: The entire action of the play takes place in a room in a traditional country-style inn, two hundred miles north of San Francisco.

ACT ONE: Scene 1: A day in February 1951. Scene 2: A day in February 1956. Scene 3: A day in February 1961.

ACT TWO: Scene 1: A day in February 1965. Scene 2: A day in February 1970. Scene 3: A day in February 1975.

Same Time, Next Year, Bernard Slade's first Broadway play, was a triumphant success at the Brooks Atkinson Theatre, where it opened on March 13, 1975. It played until June 1978 when it moved to the Ambassador Theatre and remained a box office hit for four years.

"It's trite, I know," states Slade, "but success here is a dream come true. Broadway success make the difference. In a strange way, I felt my first two hits were just an audition . . . I [now] feel I have the job . . . to me Broadway is still the Big Time. The success of *Same Time* was like a dream. It was all those stories I'd been raised on—writing a Broadway hit, lines at the box office . . . a childhood fantasy come true."

Same Time, Next Year is a play about a man (George) and a woman (Doris) who are married, but not to each other. They rendezvous in the same motel once a year for twenty-five years. Doris and George share each other's embarrassment, guilt, failure, success and the birth of a child, as well as the same bed. Eventually they seem to be more husband and wife than lovers. *Same Time, Next Year* chronicles a long unthreatening relationship that combines continuity with novelty. The playwright states, "At the end of the play, even though Doris and George have known each other for twenty-five years, they've been together for only five weeks."

Doris and George become lovers for what initially looks like a single weekend, but they continue to meet one weekend every year. The audience sees them grow and change as they come to know each other intimately. The play is structured in two acts with six scenes set at five-year intervals between 1951 and 1975. During this time both people go through deep philosophical and emotional changes. The play also dwells on the many surprises that each has in store for the other after each absence. *Same Time, Next Year* depicts a casual encounter that grows into a deep and understanding love. It reflects the social and political trends of the passing years through Doris and George's attitudes and appearance.

The idea for the play came from a holiday Slade and his wife, Jill, took near Mendocino, California. "Because of its remoteness, we started to talk to each other in a new way and I got the idea of doing a two-character play in which a man and a woman are together in a hotel room and only at the end do you find out that they are married." He later rejected this plot when he found out that Harold Pinter had already done it, but he never gave up his plan ". . . to write a two-character play that would make people laugh and touch each other."

The opportunity came when he had an "artistic and contractual disagreement" with Screen Gems (Columbia Pictures) and found himself on a plane bound for Hawaii. By the time the plane landed, Slade had an outline and a rough draft for the first scene. Six weeks later he had a finished script. "Nothing ever writes itself, but this came as close as possible . . . [I] . . . kept writing right through vacation. . . ."

Same Time, Next Year is not autobiographical, but it does have some elements in it that are derived from Slade's family and friends. "I put myself into it—every author is in his work to a degree—but I don't feel I'm really like George. . . . I've embellished things that have happened to me, my wife and the people we know. My wife, for example, did go back to UCLA as a thirty-eight-year-old freshman, and I warned some of our friends that they'd spot recognizable incidents. . . . The line in the play when Doris goes back to school, 'Listen, it's not easy being the only one in the class with clear skin' was really Jill's line. . . . I'm starting to get letters from people who have had relationships exactly like that. One couple wrote to say that they meet more often than George and Doris do in the play and they want to take me out to dinner the next time they're in New York together. *Their* affair has lasted twenty-six years."

Bernard Slade was born on May 2, 1930, in St. Catharines, Ontario, a city near Niagara Falls. "My father was moved around a lot: North Wales, Brighton, Nottingham, the outskirts of London. I never lived in the same house two years in a row until I was married, and went to thirteen changes of high school; some I hit three times." In 1948 the family returned to Canada and Slade got a job with Customs in Toronto. "But in England there'd been repertory companies, one almost in every town. I was bitten by the acting bug and now I started acting in summer stock . . . doing a play a week for fifty weeks a year. We did plays by Behrman, Van Druten, Coward. . . . In these days, I'd have paid them to let me act. . . ,"

Slade worked as an actor in Canada for the next six years and in 1953, he met and married Jill Foster when they were appeared together in a stock production of *You Can't Take It with You.* "The two of us, Jill and I with the absolute confidence and ignorance of youth, opened our own theatre, the Garden Center Theatre, in Vineland, Canada . . . twenty-five actors, twenty-five plays in twenty-five weeks—and I lost twenty-five pounds . . . I guess I grew up in that season . . . We started it on $700 and six weeks into the season were $20,000 in debt. I had never even *heard* of $20,000. We actually thought we were going to get rich. We broke even.''

In 1957 Slade wrote his first play while acting in one. His part called for appearance in only the first and third acts. So, while offstage during the second act, he wrote *The Prizewinner,* which was purchased by NBC television. This was followed by *The Long Long Laugh* that was performed on ''The United States Steel Hour Presentation'' with Arthur Hill and Teresa Wright in the leading roles. Thus began regular employment as a television writer. He wrote ''about twenty more'' hour-long television plays, in addition to two stage plays, *A Very Close Family* and *Simon Says Get Married,* both of which were produced in Canada. *A Very Close Family* was also presented by the Canadian Broadcasting Corporation as a television play.

''This is 1957–63, on up until the tail of live television in New York. In 1964 we moved to Los Angeles, where I was put under contract by Columbia Pictures, doing mostly television.'' Slade became the story editor and authored ''Bewitched,'' ''The Partridge Family,'' ''The Flying Nun,'' ''Mr. Deeds Goes to Town,'' and ''The Girl with Something Extra.'' He wrote for CBC, BBC and three American networks.

Slade also developed a special talent—creating pilots for television. ''I kept signing four-year contracts to do three half-hour pilots a year, and gradually got to the point where I had lots of freedom and even a degree of control such as approval of casting . . . working for TV, you censor yourself at the typewriter. You become very wise about what will be acceptable. . . . TV does teach you a certain economy of technique and some . . . comedy. . . .''

Then came *Same Time, Next Year.* When the play was finished, Slade felt that since he had been on salary at Columbia's Screen Gems while writing it, he should offer it to them first. He sent it to the president of Columbia Pictures, who sent it back two weeks later saying that the company was not interested in it. He then gave the play to his agent, Jack Hutto, who sent copies to several Broadway producers with the stipulation that a decision be made within twenty-four hours. Almost all of the producers were unable to do this on such short notice with the exception of Morton Gottlieb, who phoned immediately to say he wanted an option. It became the biggest comedy hit in years and won Ellen Burstyn a Tony award for Best Actress. A subsequent film version starred Ellen Burstyn and Alan Alda and earned Slade an Academy Award nomination for Best Screen Adaptation.

Slade has also written: ''Everything Money Can't Buy'' (an ABC television series); ''Bridget Loves Bernie'' (a television comedy series); *Stand Up and Be Counted* (for film); *Romantic Comedy* and *Tribute* (for both theatre and film); and *Special Occasions* (a two-character play).

ACT ONE

SCENE ONE

The Time:
A day in February 1951.
The Place:
A bed-sitting room in the cottage of a country-style inn near Mendocino, north of San Francisco. The beamed ceilings, wood-burning fireplace, wallpaper, durable antique furniture, and burnished brass lamps and fittings give the setting a feeling of comfortable warmth and respectable tradition. The room is large enough to contain a sturdy double bed, chintz-covered sofa and armchairs, and a baby grand piano. There are two leaded-pane glass windows, a closet door, a door leading to a bathroom and another door that opens to an outside patio. The room's aura of permanence is not an illusion. The decor has been the same for the past twenty-five years and will not change for the next twenty-five.
At Rise:
GEORGE *and* DORIS *are asleep in bed. He is twenty-seven with a likable average face and an intense nervous energy that gives everything he does a slightly frenetic quality but doesn't always cover his deep-seated insecurity. Something wakes him and as he groggily turns over his eyes fall upon the sleeping form of* DORIS *beside him. He sits bolt upright in bed, instantly wide awake.*

_____

GEORGE.
(Fervently)
Oh Jesus.
(He slips out of bed and we see he is wearing only boxer shorts. He grabs his sports coat from the floor, puts it on and surveys the clothes strewn about the room. They include the rest of his clothes and her blouse, skirt, stockings, bra, girdle, and shoes)
Jesus H. Christ.
(He looks back at DORIS *and then quickly moves to the dresser where he grabs a bottle of Wildroot Cream Oil, massages it into his scalp and starts to comb his short, tousled hair.*
While he is doing this DORIS *wakes up, sits up in bed, watches him. At this point in time she is slightly overweight with ordinary pretty looks and a friendly, unself-conscious, ingenuous manner that makes her immediately appealing despite the fact that at twenty-four she*

hasn't had the time or the education to find out who or what she is yet. When she speaks there is a forced gaiety to her voice)*
DORIS.
Hey, that's a real sharp-looking outfit.
(At the sound of her voice he turns around to look at her)
GEORGE.
Uh—hi.
(They eye one another for a moment)
DORIS.
What time is it?
GEORGE.
Uh—my watch is on the bedside table.
(As she leans over to look at his watch, he makes a distracted attempt to clean up the room. This consists of picking up his trousers and his right shoe. He puts on his trousers during the following)
DORIS.
(Puzzled)
It says ten to eleven.
GEORGE.
No, it's twenty-five after seven. It's always three hours and twenty-five minutes fast.
DORIS.
Why?
GEORGE.
When I got it back from being fixed at the watchmaker's it was set three hours and twenty-five minutes fast. I decided to keep it that way.
DORIS.
(Bewildered)
Doesn't that mix you up?
GEORGE.
No, I'm very quick with figures.
DORIS.
But what about other people?
GEORGE.
(Agitated)
Look, it's *my* watch!
DORIS.
What are you so sore about?
(He takes a deep breath)
GEORGE.
(Grimly)
Because we're in a lot of trouble.
DORIS.
Yeah?
GEORGE.
God, why do you have to look so—so luminous!
DORIS.
Luminous?
GEORGE.
I mean it would make everything so much easier if you woke up with puffy eyes and blotchy

skin like most women.

DORIS.

I guess God figured chubby thighs was enough.

GEORGE.

Look, this thing is not just going to go away. We've got to talk about it.

DORIS.

Okay.

(She gets out of bed, pulls the sheet out, puts it around her over her slip and heads across the room)

GEORGE.

What are you doing?

DORIS.

I thought I'd clean my teeth first.

GEORGE.

Dorothy, sit down.

(She opens her mouth to speak)

Please—sit.

(She moves to a chair, sits with the sheet wrapped around her.

He paces for a moment, gathering his thoughts before he turns to face her. When he speaks it is with great sincerity)

Dorothy, first of all, I want you to know last night was the most beautiful, fantastic, wonderful, crazy thing that's ever happened to me and I'll never forget it—or you.

DORIS.

Doris.

GEORGE.

What?

DORIS.

My name's Doris.

GEORGE.

(Thrown)

Why didn't you say so earlier? All last night I called you Dorothy and you never said anything.

DORIS.

I didn't expect us to end up this—you know—

(She trails off)

Then when I did try to tell you—you weren't listening.

GEORGE.

When?

DORIS.

(Embarrassed)

It was—you know—in the middle of—things.

(He fixes her with a look of smoldering intensity)

GEORGE.

It was incredible, wasn't it?

DORIS.

It was—nice.

(Sensing he expects something more)

Especially the last time.

GEORGE.

(Anguished)

I know—I'm an animal!

(He throws the shoe he is holding into the sofa, moves away to look out of the window.

She takes this opportunity to kneel down to gather up some of her clothes)

I don't know what got into me. I just—what was the matter with the other two times?

DORIS.

What? Oh—well, the first time was so fast and the second—look, I feel funny talking about this.

GEORGE.

(Earnestly)

It was a very beautiful thing, Doris. There was nothing disgusting or dirty in what we did.

DORIS.

Then how come you're looking so down in the dumps?

GEORGE.

Because my wife is going to *kill* me!!

DORIS.

Why should she find out?

GEORGE.

She knows already.

DORIS.

You said she was in New Jersey!

GEORGE.

(Gloomily)

It doesn't matter. She *knows*.

DORIS.

How come?

GEORGE.

Look, I don't want to talk about it!

(He stares at her)

Doris, was it as incredible for you as it was for me?

DORIS.

(Curiously)

Do all men like to talk about it a lot afterwards?

GEORGE.

(Defensively)

Why? You think I'm some sort of—of eccentric or something?

DORIS.

No, I just wondered. See, I was a virgin when I got married. At least technically.

GEORGE.

Technically?

DORIS.

Well, I was pregnant. I don't count that.

GEORGE.

(Doubtfully)

Doris, that counts.

DORIS.

I mean it was by the man I married.

GEORGE.

Oh, I'm sorry.

(She sits, puts on stocking during following)

DORIS.

That's okay. Harry and me would've got married anyway. It just hurried things up a bit.

(Brightly)

Turns out I get pregnant if we drink from the same cup.

(He looks at her, pales a little, and gulps)

What's the matter?

GEORGE.

(Quickly)

It's okay. Trojans are very reliable.

DORIS.

Who are?

GEORGE.

Never mind.

(He stares at her)

We're in a lot of trouble, Doris.

DORIS.

Why?

GEORGE.

I think I love you.

DORIS.

Better not start up something we can't finish, George.

GEORGE.

Maybe it's too late for that.

(Suddenly)

It's crazy! It's really crazy! I mean I don't even know if you like *Catcher in the Rye*!

DORIS.

What?

GEORGE.

I have this test for people. If they don't like *Catcher in the Rye* or *Death of a Salesman* I won't even date them!

DORIS.

I never even finished high school.

GEORGE.

(Wildly)

You see? I don't even *care*! And I'm really a *snob* about education!

(He moves and bleakly stares out of window. DORIS *puts on her skirt and blouse during the following)*

Of course I should've known this would happen. You see, there's something I didn't tell you about me, Doris.

DORIS.

What?

GEORGE.

When it comes to life I have a brown thumb.

I mean nothing goes right. Ever.

DORIS.

How do you mean?

GEORGE.

Well, let me think of something that will give you the picture.

(He thinks)

Okay. I was eighteen when I first had sex. It was in the back seat of a parked 1938 Dodge sedan. Right in the middle of it—we were rear ended.

DORIS.

Gee, that's terrible. Did you have insurance?

GEORGE.

And take last night. You know what they were playing on the juke box when we met?

(She shakes her head)

"If I Knew You Were Coming I'd've Baked a Cake"!

DORIS.

(Puzzled)

So?

GEORGE.

So that's going to be "our song"!

(He moves to angrily throw a log on the smoldering fire)

Other people would get "Be My Love" or "Hello, Young Lovers." Me—I get "If I Knew You Were Coming I'd've Baked a Cake"!

DORIS.

(Sentimentally)

You're very romantic. I like that.

(He looks at her)

GEORGE.

And what about you? I think I've fallen in love with you, Doris. Now you want to know the luck I have? I'm happily married!

DORIS.

(Curiously)

Are you Jewish?

GEORGE.

(Thrown)

No, I'm not Jewish.

(He takes off coat, puts on shirt)

As a matter of fact, I'm the result of a very strict Methodist upbringing.

DORIS.

Is that why you feel so guilty?

GEORGE.

Don't *you* feel guilty?

DORIS.

Are you kidding? Half my high school graduating class became nuns.

GEORGE.

Yeah, I guess Catholics have rules about this sort of thing.

DORIS.

They have rules about everything. That's what's so great about being Catholic. You know where you stand and all.

(He looks at her for a moment, shakes his head, starts to pace)

GEORGE.

I tell you, Doris, I feel like slitting my wrists.

DORIS.

Are you Italian?

GEORGE.

What's with you and nationalities?

DORIS.

You're so emotional.

GEORGE.

I happen to be a C.P.A. I mean I can be as logical as the next person.

DORIS.

You don't strike me as an accountant type.

GEORGE.

It's very simple

(He shrugs)

My whole life has always been a mess. Figures always come out right. Black and white, nice and tidy. I like that. What are you?

DORIS.

Italian.

GEORGE.

(Thrown)

Then why aren't you more emotional?

(She moves to fire and warms her hands)

DORIS.

If you're brought up in a large Italian family it's enough to turn you off emotion for life, you know?

GEORGE.

I wondered why you weren't crying or yelling or anything.

DORIS.

I got up this morning and did all that in the john.

GEORGE.

Crying?

DORIS.

Yelling.

GEORGE.

I didn't hear you.

DORIS.

I put a towel in my mouth.

GEORGE.

Oh, I'm sorry.

DORIS.

That's okay. There's no use crying over spilt milk.

GEORGE.

You're right.

DORIS.

Then why are we feeling so lousy?

GEORGE.

(Soberly)

Because we're both decent, honest people and this thing is tearing us apart. I mean I know it wasn't our fault but I keep seeing the faces of my children and the look of betrayal in their eyes. I keep thinking of the trust my wife has placed in me. The times we've shared together. Our wedding vows. And you know the worst part of it all? Right at this moment, while I'm thinking all these things I have this fantastic hard on!

(She looks at him for a moment, not moving)

DORIS.

(Finally)

I wish you hadn't said that.

GEORGE.

I'm sorry. I just feel we should be totally honest with each other.

DORIS.

No, it's not that. I have to go to confession.

(He looks at her for a second, breaks into rather a forced, incredulous laugh, moves away, turns to her, chuckles)

GEORGE.

This is really very funny, you know that?

DORIS.

Tell me—I could use a good laugh.

GEORGE.

We're both crazy! I mean this sort of thing happens to millions of people every day. We're just normal, healthy human beings who did a perfectly healthy, normal thing. You don't use actual names in confession, do you?

DORIS.

No.

GEORGE.

Good. You want to know what I think about marriage and sex?

DORIS.

I don't want to miss confession, George.

GEORGE.

After you've heard what I have to say maybe you won't need to even go.

(He moves and sits cross-legged before her)

Look, suppose you compare a husband or a wife to a good book. So you got this great book and you read it—it's terrific; you love it. So you read the book again. Still good. So you read it again and again and again and even after maybe a hundred times you still enjoy it. Well, you know the book by heart now, so for a little variety you read it standing up, then lying down, then upside down, backwards,

sideways, every way you can think of. You still like it, but Jesus, how many ways are there to read a book? Just once in a while you want to hear a new story, right? It doesn't mean you *hate* the old book. You'll read it again—later. Who knows? Maybe you'll appreciate it more.
(A beat)
You understand what I'm saying?
DORIS.
There's no use crying over spilt milk?
GEORGE.
(Getting to his feet)
Doris, you've missed the whole point!
DORIS.
What is the point?
GEORGE.
(Intensely)
I've got to go to bed with you right now!
(He embraces her passionately and starts to smother her with kisses)
DORIS.
George, we can't!
GEORGE.
Why not?
DORIS.
You'll feel even worse afterwards!
GEORGE.
(Still kissing her)
I won't, I won't! I'm over that now!
DORIS.
How come?
GEORGE.
I just remembered something!
DORIS.
What?
GEORGE.
The Russians have the bomb! We could all die tomorrow!
DORIS.
(Somewhat out of breath)
George—you're clutching at straws!
(He grabs her by the shoulders, looks deep into her eyes)
GEORGE.
Don't you understand? We're both grown-up people who have absolutely nothing to be ashamed or afraid of!!!
(There is a knock at the door. Both freeze, their eyes reflecting total panic. Then they go into frantic action as they both dive for the clothes on the floor. He gets her girdle but is not aware of what is in his hand. She, clutching the sheet and her shoes, bumps into him as she first tries to get under the bed and then heads for the bathroom door)

GEORGE.
(Panic-stricken—in a desperate hiss)
Don't go into the bathroom!
(She freezes.)
DORIS.
Why not?
GEORGE.
It's the first place they'll look!
(She heads for the window and climbs out onto the balcony as he frantically tries to make the room presentable.
He looks around, sees she has disappeared but doesn't know where as he heads for the door)
I'm coming!
(He opens the door about six inches and squeezes outside, closing the door behind him.
We hear a muffled exchange offstage before the door reopens and he reenters pushing a cart containing breakfast)
Doris?
(She doesn't appear and, puzzled, he looks under the bed, then in the closet, then moves to the window, pushes it open and leans outside)
Doris?
(While he is doing this she comes back into the room through the other window, moves to behind him, claps a firm hand on his shoulder, speaks in a deep voice)
DORIS.
You have a woman in here?
(He leaps about a foot in the air with a yelp, turns to face her. She giggles and finally he gives a sheepish grin)
GEORGE.
It's okay, it was old Mr. Chalmers with my breakfast. I was very calm. He didn't suspect a thing.
DORIS.
He didn't ask about the girdle?
GEORGE.
What girdle?
(He looks in his hand, sees he is still clutching her girdle. Anguished)
Oh—great! Now he probably thinks I'm a—a homo!
DORIS.
What do you care?
GEORGE.
I stay here every year.
(She moves to peek under platters on breakfast cart)
DORIS.
How come?
GEORGE.
There's this guy I went to school with who

went into the wine business near here. I fly out the same weekend every year to do his books.

DORIS.

From New Jersey?

GEORGE.

He was my first client. It's kind of a sentimental thing.

DORIS.

Oh.

(She looks at him)

Uh—can I have my girdle back?

GEORGE.

Oh, sorry—sure.

(He extends girdle, she reaches for it but he keeps hold of the other end, so they are both holding an end)

Doris, there's something I want to tell you.

DORIS.

What?

GEORGE.

You probably think I do this sort of thing all the time. I mean I know I must appear smooth and glib—sexually. Well, I want you to know that since I've been married this is the very first time I've done this.

(A beat)

Do you believe me?

DORIS.

Sure, I could tell. Hey, you mind if I have some of your breakfast? I'm starved!

GEORGE.

Oh sure—help yourself, I'm not hungry.

(She takes her girdle, pulls a chair up to the cart and starts to eat as he starts to pace)

It's funny, even when I was single I was no good at quick, superficial affairs. I had to be able to really *like* the person before—

(Turning to her suddenly)

What do you mean, you could tell?

DORIS.

What? Oh—I don't know—the way you tried to get your pants off over your shoes and then tripped and hit your head on the bed post.

(Her eyes twinkling)

Little things like that.

(He smiles at her affectionately)

GEORGE.

It's great to be totally honest with another person, isn't it?

DORIS.

It sure is.

(His expression changes)

GEORGE.

Doris, I haven't been totally honest with you.

DORIS.

No?

GEORGE.

No.

(He takes a deep breath)

Okay—here it comes—the big one.

(She waits expectantly.)

I told you I was a married man with two children.

DORIS.

You're not?

GEORGE.

No. I'm a married man with *three* children.

DORIS.

I don't get it.

GEORGE.

I thought it would make me seem less married.

(Under her gaze he becomes agitated and starts to pace)

Look, I just didn't think it through. Anyway, it's been like a lead weight inside me all morning. I mean denying little Debbie like that. I'm sorry, I was under a certain stress or I wouldn't have done it. You understand?

DORIS.

Sure, we all do nutty things sometimes.

(He smiles in relief)

So how come your wife doesn't travel with you?

GEORGE.

Phyllis won't get on a plane.

DORIS.

She's afraid of flying?

GEORGE.

Crashing.

(He watches her eat for a moment. She looks up)

DORIS.

What's the matter?

GEORGE.

Nothing. I just love the way you eat.

(She grins at him, holds up coffee pot)

DORIS.

You wanta share a cup of coffee?

(He nods, pulls up a chair opposite her, gazes at her as she pours coffee)

GEORGE.

Doris, I've been thinking. Sometimes if you *know* why something happened it makes it easier to understand.

DORIS.

You mean like us?

GEORGE.

Right. Doris, do you believe that two total strangers can look across a room and both have this sudden, overwhelming, totally irrational desire to possess one another in every possible way?

(She considers for a moment)

DORIS.

No.

GEORGE.

(Puzzled)

Neither do I—so I guess that can't be it. Then how did this whole thing start?

DORIS.

It started when you sent me over that steak in the restaurant.

GEORGE.

They didn't serve drinks. Steak was all they had.

DORIS.

What made you do it?

GEORGE.

Impulse. Usually I never do that sort of thing. I have this—this friend who says that life is saying "yes."

(He shrugs)

The most I can generally manage is "maybe."

DORIS.

Your wife sounds like a nice person.

(He reacts)

So why'd you do it?

GEORGE.

I guess I was lonely and you looked so—so vulnerable and—well, you had a run in your stocking and your lipstick was smeared.

DORIS.

You thought I looked cheap?

GEORGE.

(Quickly)

No—beautiful. I'm attracted by flaws. I don't know—somehow they make people seem more human and—approachable.

(She gazes at him affectionately)

That's why I like Pete Reiser better than say— Joe DiMaggio.

DORIS.

Pete Reiser's a baseball player?

GEORGE.

He keeps running into walls. I like that.

DORIS.

(Gently)

You know something, George? You're a real nice guy.

(They smile tenderly at one another)

What made you think I was a medium rare?

GEORGE.

I'm very intuitive.

DORIS.

I'm well-done.

(This jolts George out of his romantic mood)

GEORGE.

Well-done? How can anyone like meat well-done?

DORIS.

Harry always has his that way.

GEORGE.

Oh. What were you doing in the restaurant anyway?

DORIS.

I was on my way to a retreat. I go this same weekend every year.

GEORGE.

(Thrown)

To—uh—meditate?

DORIS.

Yeah, you might call it that. But not about God or anything. More about—well—myself.

(He waits, awkwardly)

See, I got pregnant when I was just eighteen and so I never had a chance to—well—live it up. Oh, I don't know what I'm trying to say.

(She shakes her head, gives a little laugh)

Sometimes I think I'm crazy.

GEORGE.

Why?

DORIS.

(Awkwardly, thinking it out)

Well, look at my life. I got three little kids underfoot all the time, so I'm never alone. I live in a two-bedroom duplex in downtown Oakland, we got a 1948 Kaiser that's almost half paid for, a blond three-piece dinette set, a Motorola TV, and we go bowling at least once a week.

(A beat)

I mean, what else could anyone ask for? But sometimes things get me down, you know? It's dumb!

GEORGE.

I don't think it's dumb.

DORIS.

I don't know. Sometimes I—I don't know what I *think* about anything, you know? I mean I'm almost twenty-five and I still feel—well—half-formed.

(He doesn't say anything. A look of wonder comes to her face)

Will you listen to me? Honest, you make me say things out loud I haven't even *thought* to myself.

(She smiles at him)

I noticed that right after I met you last night.

GEORGE.

(Eagerly)

We had instant rapport! Did you notice that too?

DORIS.

No, but I know we really hit it off.

(A beat)

You want some more coffee?

(He shakes his head and watches her as she rises, moves to get sheet from where it was stuffed under the sofa, takes it to bed and starts to make bed)

GEORGE.

What happens to your kids when you go on your retreat?

DORIS.

Oh, Harry takes them to see his mother in Bakersfield. It's her birthday.

GEORGE.

She doesn't mind you not going?

DORIS.

No, she hates me.

GEORGE.

Why?

DORIS.

Because I got pregnant.

(He moves to help her make up bed)

GEORGE.

But her son had something to do with that too.

DORIS.

She's blocked that out of her mind. Oh, I don't blame her. You see, Harry was in first year of dental college.

GEORGE.

I don't get the connection.

DORIS.

He had to drop out of school and take a job selling waterless cooking.

GEORGE.

Oh.

(He moves away, watches her make up bed for a moment)

Look, Doris, naturally we're both curious about each other's husband and wife. But rather than dwelling on it and letting it spoil everything, why don't we do this? I'll tell you two stories—one showing the best side of my wife and the other showing the worst. Then you do the same about your husband. Okay?

DORIS.

Okay.

GEORGE.

I think I should go first.

DORIS.

Why?

GEORGE.

Because I already have my stories prepared.

(She nods, sits cross-legged on bed)

I'll start with the worst side of her.

DORIS.

Go ahead.

GEORGE.

(Grimly)

Phyllis knows about us.

DORIS.

You said that before. How could she possibly know?

GEORGE.

Because she has this—thing in her head.

DORIS.

You mean like a plate?

GEORGE.

(Thrown)

Plate?

DORIS.

I got this uncle who was wounded in the war so they put this steel plate in his head and he says he can tell when it's going to rain.

(He looks at her for a moment)

GEORGE.

Jesus, I'm in a lot of trouble.

DORIS.

Why?

GEORGE.

Because I find everything you say absolutely *fascinating*!

DORIS.

Tell me about your wife's steel plate.

GEORGE.

What?

(Brought back to earth, miserably)

No, it's not a plate—it's more like a bell.

(Becoming agitated)

I could be a million miles away but whenever I even *look* at another woman it goes off like a fire alarm! Last night at 1:22. I just know she sat bolt upright in bed with her head going, ding, ding, ding, ding!

(He nervously moves to breakfast cart and absently starts wiping off the lipstick marks on the coffee cup with his handkerchief)

DORIS.

How'd you know it was 1:22?

GEORGE.

I have peripheral vision and I noticed my watch said 4:47.

GEORGE.

Look, you owe me one rotten story.

DORIS.

Okay. This is not really rotten but—well—

(She gets off the bed, moves to fire, looks into it for a moment)

On our fourth anniversary we were having kind of a rough time. The kids were getting us down and—well, we'd gotten in over our heads financially but we decided to have some friends over anyway.

(She moves to look out of window)

Now Harry doesn't drink much, but that night he had a few beers and after the Gillette fights he and some of the guys started to talk and I overheard him say his time in the Army were the best years of his life.

GEORGE.

(Puzzled)

What's wrong with that? A lot of guys feel that way about the service.

(She turns to face him)

DORIS.

Harry was in the Army four years. Three of those years were spent in a Japanese prison camp!

(A beat)

And he said this on our anniversary! Oh, I know he didn't mean to hurt me—Harry would never hurt anyone—but, well, it—hurt, you know?

(A beat)

You're the only person I've ever told.

GEORGE.

You want some more coffee?

DORIS.

I'll get lipstick on the cup.

GEORGE.

I don't care.

(He moves to pour her coffee)

DORIS.

You wanta hear a story about the good side of him?

GEORGE.

Not really.

DORIS.

But you have to! I mean, I don't want you to get the wrong impression about Harry.

GEORGE.

Okay, if you insist.

(She moves to bed, plumps pillows)

DORIS.

Well, Harry's a real big, kind of heavyset sort of guy, you know?

GEORGE.

I wish you hadn't told me that.

DORIS.

Oh, you don't have to worry. He's gentle as—as a puppy.

(She sits on the downstage side of the bed, facing front and clasps a pillow to her chest)

Anyway, he tries to do different things with each of the kids, you know?

(He sits beside her on the bed, hands her coffee)

Thanks. So, he was having a hard time finding something special to do with Tony, our four-

year-old. Then he gets the idea to take him out to the park and fly this big kite. Well, he tells Tony about it—really builds it up—and Tony gets real excited. So this one Saturday last winter they go out together, but there's no wind and Harry has trouble getting the kite to take off. Well, it's kind of cold and Tony, who's pretty bored by now—he's only four years old—asks if he can sit in the car. Harry says, "Sure."

(She starts to smile)

About an hour later I happen to come by on my way home from the laundromat and I see Tony fast asleep in the car and Harry, all red in the face and out of breath, pounding up and down, all alone in the park, with this kite dragging along behind him on the ground.

(Her smile fades)

I don't know—somehow it really got to me.

(He looks at her, touched more by her reaction than by the story itself)

GEORGE.

Yeah, I know. Helen has some nice qualities too.

DORIS.

Who's Helen?

GEORGE.

(Puzzled)

My wife of course.

DORIS.

You said her name was Phyllis.

(Caught—a split moment of panic)

GEORGE.

I know—I lied.

(She stares at him bewildered. Agitated)

Helen—Phyllis—what's the difference? I'm married!

(He gets up, paces)

Look, I was nervous and I didn't want to leave any *clues*! I mean I was scared you'd try to look me up or something!

DORIS.

Is your real name George?

GEORGE.

Of course it is! You don't think I'd lie about my own name do you?

DORIS.

(Baffled)

You're crazy.

GEORGE.

Well, I never claimed to be consistent!

DORIS.

(Gently)

Crazy.

(She holds out the coffee cup to him, their hands touch and they become aware of the

contact. Their eyes meet. He sits beside her)
GEORGE.
(Tenderly)
It's funny, isn't it? Here we are having break-
fast in a hotel room, gazing into each other's
eyes, and we're both married with six kids
between us.
DORIS.
You got pictures?
GEORGE.
(Thrown)
What?
DORIS.
Pictures of your kids.
GEORGE.
(Uncomfortably)
Well, sure, but I don't think this is the time
or place to—
(She moves for her purse)
DORIS.
I'll show you mine if you show me yours.
(Getting snapshots from purse)
I keep them in a special folder we got free
from Kodak.
(She returns to bed, hands him snaps)
Where are yours?
GEORGE.
(Still off-balance)
Uh—you have to take the whole wallet.
*(He extracts wallet from his back pocket,
hands it to her.*
*They are now seated side by side on the bed,
looking at each other's snapshots)*
DORIS.
Oh, they're cute! Is the one in the glasses and
baggy tights the oldest?
GEORGE.
(Looking at snap)
Yes, that's Michael. Funny-looking kid isn't
he?
DORIS.
He wants to be Superman?
GEORGE.
Peter Pan. Sometimes it worries me.
(Looking at snaps in his hand)
Why is this one's face all screwed up?
DORIS.
Oh, that's Paul—it was taken on a roller coaster.
Isn't it natural? He threw up right after that.
GEORGE.
Yeah, he's really—something. I guess he looks
like Harry, huh?
DORIS.
Both of us really.
(Looking at snap)
What's your little girl's name?

GEORGE.
Debbie. That was taken on her second birth-
day. We were trying to get her to blow out the
candles.
DORIS.
She has her hand in the cake.
GEORGE.
Yeah, neat is not her strong suit.
(They look at one another)
DORIS.
You have great-looking kids, George.
GEORGE.
You too.
DORIS.
Thanks.
(There is a slight pause)
GEORGE.
Doris?
DORIS.
Yeah?
GEORGE.
Let's dump the lot of them and run away
together!
*(She looks at him astonished, and the lights
fade for the—)*

END OF ACT ONE, SCENE ONE

SCENE TWO

The Time:
A day in February 1956.
The Place:
The same.
At Rise:
GEORGE, *wearing a charcoal suit and pink shirt
of the period, has just hung a home-made sign
reading "HAPPY FIFTH ANNIVERSARY,
DARLING" on the front door. He has put on
a few pounds, his hair has just started to thin,
and at thirty-two he gives the impression of
more substance. It is just an impression. Although his manner is more subdued than five
years ago and his insecurities flash through
less frequently, it is only because he has learned
a degree of control of his mercurial moods.
He takes a small birthday cake from a box and
places it beside two plates and forks on the
coffee table.*

_____

DORIS.
(Offstage)
Damn!
GEORGE.
What's the matter?

DORIS.
(Offstage)
It's my merry widow.
GEORGE.
Your what?
DORIS.
(Offstage)
Merry widow. It mashes you in and pushes you out in all the right places. It also gives you this pale, wan look because it cuts off all circulation.
GEORGE.
Be sure and let me know when you're coming out.
DORIS.
(Offstage)
Right now.
GEORGE.
Wait a minute!
(He quickly moves to the piano, sits)
Okay—now!
(As she enters he sings and plays "If I Knew You Were Coming I'd Have Baked a Cake."
She is dressed in a strapless, black cocktail dress that was considered chic in the suburbs in the fifties; is slimmer than before and more carefully put together. The most striking physical change in her is her very blond hair, shaped in a Gina Lollobrigida cut. She has acquired some of the social graces of middle-class suburbia, is more articulate than before, and has developed a wry, deprecating wit that doesn't hide a certain terseness of manner.
He stops playing, moves to her and embraces her)
GEORGE.
Happy anniversary, darling.
(He hands her a glass of champagne, they toast, drink, and he indicates the cake)
Cut the cake and make a wish.
(They move to sit on the sofa and he watches her as she cuts the cake)
What did you wish?
DORIS.
I only have one wish.
GEORGE.
What?
DORIS.
That you keep showing up every year.
(They kiss)
GEORGE.
I'm always surprised that you do. I was really surprised the second year.
(He crosses to the piano and refills their glasses with champagne. He gives one to DORIS)
Of course I had less confidence in my personal magnetism then. You know that was one of the best ideas you ever had?
DORIS.
Meeting here every year?
GEORGE.
No, refusing to run off with me. Weren't you even tempted?
DORIS.
Sure I was. I still am. But I had the feeling that if we had run off together we'd end up with—well—with pretty much the same sort of nice, comfortable marriage we both already had at home.
(They sit and drink)
GEORGE.
How are things at home?
DORIS.
We moved to the suburbs. Right now everyone's very excited. Next week they're going to connect the sewers. Well it's not exactly the life of Scott and Zelda, but we'll survive.
GEORGE.
(Surprised)
You started reading!
DORIS.
Oh, you don't know the half of it. I joined the Book-of-the-Month Club.
GEORGE.
Good for you.
DORIS.
(Kidding herself)
Listen, sometimes I even take the *alternate* selections.
GEORGE.
(Sincerely)
I'm really proud of you, honey.
DORIS.
Well, it was either that or group mambo lessons. You still live in New Jersey?
GEORGE.
No, we moved to Connecticut. We bought an old barn and converted it.
DORIS.
What's it like?
GEORGE.
Drafty. Helen's got the decorating bug. At my funeral just as they're closing the lid on my coffin I have this mental picture of Helen throwing in two fabric swatches and yelling, "Which one do you like?" That's the bad story about her.
DORIS.
What else is new?
GEORGE.
We had a baby girl.

DORIS.

Oh, George, that's marvelous! You have pictures?

GEORGE.

(Grins)

I knew you'd ask that.

(He takes out pictures, hands them to her)

DORIS.

(Looking at snaps)

Oh, she's adorable. It's funny. I still like to look at new babies but I don't want to *own* one anymore. You think that's a sign of maturity?

GEORGE.

Could be.

(He takes out cigar)

Here, I even kept one of these for you to give to Harry. It's from Havana.

DORIS.

Harry still thinks I go on retreat. What should I tell him? It came from a Cuban nun?

(She takes cigar, moves to put it in her purse)

So how are the rest of the kids? How's Michael?

GEORGE.

Oh, crazy as ever. He had this homework assignment, to write what he did on his summer vacation. Trouble is, he chose to write what he actually did.

DORIS.

What was that?

GEORGE.

Tried to get laid. He wrote in great comic detail about his unfortunate tendency to get an erection on all forms of public transportation. The school almost suspended him.

DORIS.

You're crazy about him, aren't you?

GEORGE.

He's a very weird kid, Doris.

DORIS.

And he really gets to you. Come on—admit it.

GEORGE.

Okay. I admit it. He's a nice kid.

DORIS.

See? Was that so hard?

(He looks at her for a moment, crosses to her, impulsively kisses her)

DORIS.

What was that for?

GEORGE.

Everything. This. One beautiful weekend every year with no cares, no ties and no responsibilities. Thank you, Doris.

(He kisses her again. The embrace grows more passionate. They break)

DORIS.

(Breathlessly)

Gee, I just got all dressed up.

(They sink onto the bed. He is lying half on top of her when the phone rings)

DORIS.

Someone has a rotten sense of timing.

GEORGE.

Let it ring. It's probably only Pete wanting to know how much he owes the I.R.S.

DORIS. Chalmers probably told him we're in.

GEORGE.

Damn.

(Without changing his position he reaches out and takes the phone)

Hello.

(His expression changes—slowly but drastically)

Is there anything wrong? Yes, this is Daddy— Funny?

(He slowly rolls off DORIS to a tense position on the edge of the bed)

Well, that's probably because Daddy was just— uh—I had a frog in my throat, sweetheart. It came out huh? Which one was it?

(He sits with the phone in his hand, bent over, almost as if he has a stomachache)

Of course, the tooth-fairy will come, sweetheart—Why tonight, of course—It doesn't matter if you can't find it, darling, the tooth-fairy will know—Well, I wish I could be there to find it for you too, honey, but Daddy's working—Oh, in my room.

(At this point DORIS gets off the bed and unobtrusively starts to clean up the room)

Yes, it's a very nice room—Well, it has a fireplace and a sofa and a big comfortable b—

(He can't bring himself to say "bed")

—bathroom. Well I'd like you to come with me too, sweetheart. Maybe next year—I'm afraid not, sweetheart. You see Daddy has to finish up his—business—well, I'll try—Yes, I love you too, honey—Yes, very much.

(He hangs up and puts his head in his hands. DORIS crosses to him and wordlessly puts a comforting hand on his shoulder)

Oh, God, I feel so *guilty!*

(He rises and moves away)

DORIS.

Debbie?

GEORGE.

Her tooth came out. She can't find it and she's worried the tooth-fairy won't know! Oh, God, that thin, reedy little voice. Do you know what that *does* to me!

DORIS.

Sure, that calm exterior doesn't fool me for a minute.

GEORGE.

You think this is *funny*?

DORIS.

Honey, I understand how you feel but I really don't think it's going to help going on and on about it.

GEORGE.

Doris, my little girl said, "I love you, Daddy," and I answered her with a voice still *hoarse with passion*!

DORIS.

I think I've got the picture, George.

GEORGE.

Don't you ever feel guilty?

DORIS.

Sometimes.

GEORGE.

You've never said anything.

DORIS.

I just deal with it in a different way.

GEORGE.

How?

DORIS.

Privately.

(Agitated, GEORGE *starts pacing around the room)*

GEORGE.

I don't know, maybe men are more—sensitive than women.

DORIS.

Have a drink, George.

GEORGE.

Perhaps women are more pragmatic than men.

DORIS.

What's that mean?

GEORGE.

They adjust to rottenness quicker. I mean, they're more inclined to live for the moment.

(Offhandedly)

Anyway, you have the church.

DORIS.

The church?

GEORGE.

Well, you're Catholic, aren't you? You can get rid of all your guilt at one sitting. I have to live with mine.

DORIS.

I think I'll have a drink.

(She moves to pour herself a drink)

GEORGE.

Boy, something like that really brings you up short!

(Holding out his trembling hands)

I mean look at me! I tell you, Doris—when she started talking about the tooth-fairy—well, it affected me in a very profound manner.

(A beat)

On top of that I have indigestion you can't believe. It hit me that hard, you know?

DORIS.

George, I have three children too.

GEORGE.

Sure, sure—I know. I don't mean that you don't understand. It's just that we're different people and your guilt is less—acute.

DORIS.

Honey, what do you want to do? Have a guilt contest? Is that going to solve anything?

GEORGE.

What do you want me to do, Doris?

DORIS.

I think it might be a terrific idea if you stopped talking about it. It's only making you feel worse.

GEORGE.

I can't feel worse. That pure little voice saying—

(He stops, tries to shake it off with a jerk of his head)

No, you're right. Forget it.

(Shakes his head again)

Forget it. Talk about something else. Tell me about Harry. Tell me the good story about Harry.

(During the following, GEORGE *tries to concentrate but is obviously distracted and nervous)*

DORIS.

Okay. He went bankrupt.

(This momentarily jolts him out of his problem)

GEORGE.

How can anyone go bankrupt selling TV sets?

DORIS.

Harry has this one weakness as a salesman. It's a compulsion to talk people out of things they can't afford. He lacks the killer instinct.

(Reflectively)

It's one of the things I like best about him. Anyway, he went into real estate.

(GEORGE is staring out of the window)

Your turn.

GEORGE.

What?

DORIS.

Tell me your story about Helen.

GEORGE.

I already did.

DORIS.

You just told me the bad one. Why do you

always tell that one first?

GEORGE.

It's the one I look forward to telling the most.

DORIS.

Tell me the nice story about her.

GEORGE.

Oh.

(Moving about the room)

Well—Chris—that's our middle one—ran into a lawn sprinkler and gashed his knee really badly. Helen drove both of us to the hospital.

DORIS.

Both of you?

GEORGE.

I fainted.

DORIS.

Oh.

GEORGE.

The nice part was she never told anybody.

DORIS.

You faint often?

GEORGE.

Only in emergencies.

DORIS.

Is it the sight of blood that—

GEORGE.

Please, Doris! My stomach's squeamish enough already. Maybe I will have that drink.

(He moves to liquor, speaks overcasually)

Oh, listen, something just occurred to me. Instead of my leaving at the usual time tomorrow night would you mind if I left a little earlier?

DORIS.

(Puzzled)

When did you have in mind?

GEORGE.

Well, there's a plane in half an hour.

(She stares at him astounded)

DORIS.

You want to leave twenty-three hours early?

(He moves to suitcase, starts to pack and continues through the following as she watches with unbelieving eyes)

GEORGE.

Look, I know how you feel—I really do—and I wouldn't even suggest if if you weren't a mother yourself and didn't understand the situation. I mean I wouldn't even think of it if this crisis hadn't come up. Oh, it's not just the tooth-fairy—she could have swallowed the tooth. I mean it could be lodged God knows where! Now I know this leaves you a bit—uh—at loose ends but there's no reason for you to leave too. The room's all paid up. Anyway, I'm probably doing you a favor. If I did stay I wouldn't be very good company. Uh—

have you seen my hairbrush?

(He looks around, sees it is beside her)

Doris, would you hand me my hairbrush?

(Without a word, she picks it up and throws it at him with much more force than necessary. It sails past his head and crashes against the wall. There is a pause)

I think I can explain that. You feel somewhat rejected and, believe me, I can understand that but I want you to know my leaving has nothing to do with you and me!

(She just stares at him)

Doris, this is an emergency! I have a sick child at home!

DORIS.

(Exploding)

Oh, will you stop it! It's got nothing to do with the goddam tooth-fairy! You're consumed with guilt and the only way you can deal with it is by getting as far away from me as possible!

GEORGE.

Okay, I feel guilty. Is that so strange?

(Intensely)

Doris, don't you understand? We're *cheating*! Once a year we lie to our families and sneak off to a hotel in California and commit adultery!

(Holding up his hand)

Not that I want to stop doing it! But yes, I feel guilt. I admit it.

DORIS.

(Incredulous)

You admit it!? You take out ads! You probably stop strangers in the street! It's a wonder you haven't hired a *sky writer*! I'm amazed you haven't had your shorts monogrammed with a scarlet 'A' as a conversation starter! You think that by talking about it, by wringing your hands and beating your breast it will somehow excuse what you're doing? So you wander around like—like an open nerve saying, "I'm cheating but look how guilty I feel so I must really be a nice guy!" And to top it all, you have the incredible arrogance to think you're the only one in the world with a conscience! Well, that doesn't make you a nice guy. You know what it makes you? A horse's ass!

(There is a pause)

GEORGE.

(Finally)

You know something? I liked you better before you started reading.

DORIS.

That's not why you're leaving, George.

GEORGE.

Doris, it's not the end of the world. I'm not leaving you permanently.

(Turning to finish packing)

We'll see each other again next year.

(He shuts suitcase, snaps locks)

DORIS.

(Quietly—with finality)

There's not going to be a next year, George.

(He turns to face her)

GEORGE.

You don't mean that.

(He suspects by her face that she does)

I can't believe that! Just because I have to leave early one year you're willing to throw away a lifetime of weekends? How can you be so— so *casual*?

DORIS.

I don't see any point in going on.

(He starts to shake his head)

GEORGE.

Oh no. Don't do that to me, Doris.

(He takes suitcase, moves to deposit it by the door during following)

Don't try to manipulate me. I get enough of that at home.

(Getting raincoat, putting it on)

That's not what our relationship is about.

DORIS.

(Soberly)

What is it about, George?

GEORGE.

You don't know?

DORIS.

Yes. But it seems to be completely different from how you think about us. That's why I think we should stop seeing each other.

GEORGE.

(Finally)

My God, you really are serious.

DORIS.

George, what's the point of going on if we're going to come to each other burdened down with guilt and remorse? What joy is there in that?

GEORGE.

(Frustrated—indicating door)

Doris, I have a commitment there.

DORIS.

(Quietly)

And you don't have a commitment here?

GEORGE.

(Bewildered)

Here? I thought our only commitment was to show up every year.

DORIS.

Nice and tidy, huh? Just two friendly sexual partners who meet once a year, touch and let go.

GEORGE.

Okay—so maybe I was kidding myself. I'm human.

DORIS.

Well, so am I.

GEORGE.

(Sincerely)

But you're different. Stronger. You always seem able to—cope.

(She moves away, looks into the fire. She speaks slowly, deliberately unemotional)

DORIS.

George, during the past year I picked up the phone and started to call you five times. I couldn't seem to stop thinking about you. You kept slopping over into my real life and it scared hell out of me. More to the point, I felt *guilty*. So I decided to stop seeing you.

(He is shaken. She turns to face him)

At first I wasn't going to show up at all but then I thought I at least owed you an explanation. So I came.

(She turns away)

When you walked in the door I knew I couldn't do it. That despite the price it was all worth it.

(A pause)

GEORGE.

(Finally—anguished)

Oh God, I feel so guilty!!

DORIS.

(Quietly—flatly)

I think you'd better leave, George.

(There is a pause)

GEORGE.

I love you, Doris.

(A beat)

I'm an idiot. I suspect I'm deeply neurotic, and I'm no bargain—but I do love you.

(He moves to her, gently turns her to face him)

Will you let me stay?

(They embrace, break, and gaze at one another)

Doris, what are we going to do?

(She reaches out and takes his hand)

DORIS.

Touch and hold on very tight. Until tomorrow.

(They embrace. The lights slowly fade and the curtain falls)

END OF ACT ONE, SCENE TWO

SCENE THREE

The Time:
A day in February 1961.

The Place:
The same.
    At Rise:
GEORGE, *still wearing his raincoat and hat, is talking on the phone. His unpacked suitcase is in the middle of the floor and it is apparent that he has just arrived. As he talks he takes off his raincoat and throws it on the bed.*

———

GEORGE.
(Irritably—into phone)
No of course I haven't left Helen. I'm on a business trip. I come out here every year—I am not running away from the problem!
(Becoming more angry)
Of course I know it's serious. I still don't think it's any reason to phone me long distance and—Look, frankly, I don't think this is any of your business and to be totally honest I resent—
(He gives an exasperated sigh)
Yes, I saw a doctor—He said it's no big deal, that every man has this problem at one time or another and—Look, if we have to discuss this you may as well learn to pronounce it correctly. It's impotence, not im*p*otence—
(Incredulous)
What do you mean, did I catch it in time? It's a slight reflex problem not a terminal illness!
(Frustrated)
It's not something you have to "nip in the bud." Look, how did you find out about this anyway?—Dropped a few hints? What sort of hints?—You asked her and she looked funny. Terrific.
(Exasperated again)
Yes, of course I'm trying to do something about it—I don't have to tell you that—Look, will you let me deal with this in my own way? I'm going to be okay—Soon—I just *know,* that's all.
(Flaring)
I just feel it, okay?—I'm seeing someone out here who's an expert.
(His patience exhausted)
Look, I don't think we should be even *discussing* this!—I'm sorry,′ I'm going to hang up now.
(Firmly)
Goodbye, Mother!
(He slams the receiver down, picks up his raincoat, looks at bed, throws raincoat over chair, turns blankets and sheets down, tosses hat into chair revealing that his hairline has receded noticeably. He then crosses to his suitcase, puts it on rack, opens it, extracts paja-

mas and robe and exits to bathroom. There is a slight pause before the front door opens and DORIS *enters. She is obviously very, very pregnant. Her hair is back to her normal color and her face looks softer than before. Perspiring slightly, she puts her case down)*
DORIS.
(Calling)
George!
GEORGE.
(Offstage—from bathroom)
Be right out, darling!
*(*DORIS, *holding her back, moves to look out of the window. When* GEORGE, *now dressed in robe and pajamas, enters from the bathroom her back is towards him. He stops, smiles at her tenderly)*
How are you, lover?
(She turns to face him, revealing her eight months pregnant stomach. His smile fades and his expression becomes frozen. He just stares, unable to speak)
DORIS.
(Finally)
I know. I've heard of middle-aged spread but this is ridiculous.
GEORGE.
(In a strangled voice)
My God, what have you done to yourself?
DORIS.
Well, I can't take all the credit. It was a mutual effort.
(He continues to stare at her)
Honey, when you haven't seen an old friend for a year isn't it customary to kiss them hello?
GEORGE.
(Still stunned)
What? Oh, sure.
(He moves to her, gives her a rather perfunctory kiss)
DORIS.
Are you okay? You look funny.
GEORGE.
(Flaring—moving away)
Funny? I'm hysterical!
DORIS.
What's that mean?
(He tries to regain control)
GEORGE.
Well—naturally, I'm—surprised, okay?
DORIS.
You're surprised. I insisted on visiting the dead rabbit's grave!
(Puzzled)
Why are you wearing your pajamas and robe in the afternoon?

GEORGE.
(Irritably)
I'm rehearsing for a Noël Coward play! Why the hell do you think?

DORIS.
Oh, I'm sorry, darling. I'm afraid all that dirty stuff is out. That is, unless you have a ladder handy.

GEORGE.
Doris, do you mind? I'm in no mood for bad taste jokes!

DORIS.
Oh, come on, honey—where's your sense of humor? Look at it this way—maybe it's nature's way of telling us to slow down.
(He watches her as she moves to a chair and awkwardly negotiates herself into the seat. She kicks off her shoes, massages her feet, looks up to find him staring at her with a baleful expression)
George, is there something on your mind?
(He moves away to the window)

GEORGE.
Not anymore.

DORIS.
Then why are you so jumpy?
(He wheels to face her)

GEORGE.
You must be eight months pregnant!

DORIS.
Why are you so shocked? I am married.

GEORGE.
You think that excuses it?

DORIS.
What exactly are you trying to say?

GEORGE.
I just consider it damned—irresponsible!

DORIS.
(Amused)
Well, I have to admit, it wasn't planned!

GEORGE.
(Frustrated)
I mean coming here in—that condition!

DORIS.
Well, I'm sorry you're disappointed, darling, but we'll just have to find some other way to—communicate.

GEORGE.
Great! You have any ideas?

DORIS.
We could talk.

GEORGE.
Talk? Talk I can get at home!

DORIS.
(Grinning)
Well, sex I can get at home. And as you can

see, that's not just talk.

GEORGE.
What the hell is that supposed to mean?

DORIS.
(Shrugs)
Well, I've never had any cause to complain about Harry in that department.

GEORGE.
Oh really? And what does that make me? Chopped liver?
(She has been watching him with a curious expression)

DORIS.
George, what is the matter with you?

GEORGE.
Matter? I'm the only man in America who just kept an illicit assignation with a woman who—who looks like a—frigate in full sail! And you ask what's the matter?

DORIS.
(Calmly)
No, there's something else. You're not yourself.

GEORGE.
Let me be the judge of who I am, okay?

DORIS.
Why are you so *angry*?

GEORGE.
What was that crack about Harry? Is that supposed to reflect on me? You don't think I have normal desires and sex drives?

DORIS.
Of course not. You're very normal. I just meant I look forward to seeing you for a lot of reasons beside sex. Do you think we would have lasted this long if that's all we had in common?

GEORGE.
(Grudgingly)
No, I guess not.

DORIS.
We're friends as well as lovers, aren't we?

GEORGE.
Yes.
(He sighs)
I'm sorry, Doris. I've—I've had a lot on my mind lately and—well, seeing you look like that took the wind out of my sails. You want a drink?

DORIS.
No, you go ahead. Alcohol makes me go a funny shade of pink.
(She watches him as he moves to extract a bottle from his suitcase)
You want to tell me about it?

GEORGE.
No, it's not something I can really talk about.
(He moves to get glass, pours drink, shrugs)

It's just I was looking forward to an—intimate weekend.

DORIS.
You think we can only be intimate through sex?

GEORGE.
I think it sure helps.

DORIS.
Oh, maybe at the beginning.

GEORGE.
The beginning?

DORIS.
Well, every year we meet it's a bit strange and awkward at first but we usually solve that in between the sheets with a lot of heavy breathing.

GEORGE.
Doris, if we're not going to do it, would you mind not talking about it?

DORIS.
I just meant maybe we need something else to—break the ice.

GEORGE.
(Pouring himself another drink)
I'm willing to try anything.

DORIS.
How about this? Supposing I tell you something about myself I've never told anyone before in my life?

GEORGE.
I think I've had enough surprises for one day.

DORIS.
You'll like this one.
(She gets out of the chair with some difficulty and moves to look out of window. He watches and waits)
I've been having these sex dreams about you.

GEORGE.
When?

DORIS.
Just lately. Almost every night.

GEORGE.
What sort of dreams?
(She turns to face him)

DORIS.
That's what's so strange. They're always the same. We're making love under water. In caves, grottos, swimming pools—but always under water. Isn't that weird?
(She shrugs)
Probably something to do with me being pregnant.

GEORGE.
Under water, huh?
(She nods)

DORIS.
Now you tell me some deep, dark secret about

yourself.

GEORGE.
I can't swim.

DORIS.
(Puzzled)
Literally?

GEORGE.
(Irritably)
Of course literally! When I tell you I can't swim I simply mean I can't swim!

DORIS.
How come?

GEORGE.
I just never learned when I was a kid. But I never told anybody—well, Helen found out when she pushed me off a dock and I almost drowned—but my kids don't even know. When we go to the beach I pretend I'm having trouble with my trick knee.

DORIS.
You have a trick knee?

GEORGE.
No. They don't know that either.
(She moves to him, puts her hand on his cheek)

DORIS.
You see, it worked.
(He looks puzzled)
We're talking just like people who have been to bed and everything.
(She moves to another chair, carefully lowers herself into it. The effort tires her)
Boy, I'll tell you—that Ethel Kennedy must really like kids.

GEORGE.
Hey, I'm sorry about—earlier. I'm glad to see you anyway.

DORIS.
You want to tell me what it was all about?
(He looks at her for a moment)

GEORGE.
Okay, I may as well get it out in the open. I mean it's nothing to be ashamed about.
(He takes a turn around the room)
It's very simple really. It's my—sex life. Lately, Helen hasn't been able to satisfy me.

DORIS.
(Surprised)
She's lost her interest in sex?

GEORGE.
Oh, she tries—God knows. But I can tell she's just going through the motions.

DORIS.
Do you have any idea why this is?

GEORGE.
Well, Helen's always had a lot of hangups

about sex. For one thing she's always thought of it as just a healthy, normal, pleasant function. Don't you think that's a bit twisted?

DORIS.

Only if you're Catholic.

GEORGE.

(Earnestly)

You're joking but there's a lot to be said for guilt. I mean if you don't feel guilty or ashamed about it I think you're missing half the fun. To Helen—sex has always been good, clean—*entertainment*. No wonder she grew tired of it.

(He finds DORIS' *gaze somewhat disconcerting)*

Look, I don't know, for some reason my sex drive has increased while hers has decreased.

DORIS.

That's odd. Usually, it's the other way around.

GEORGE.

(Defensively)

Are you accusing me of lying?

DORIS.

Of course not. Why are you so edgy?

GEORGE.

Because—well, I don't think it's fair to talk about this behind her back when she's not here to defend herself.

(She watches him as he moves to pour another drink)

DORIS.

Would you like to get to the more formal part of your presentation?

GEORGE.

What? Oh—okay. I'll start with the nice story about her.

DORIS.

You've never done that before. You must be mellowing.

GEORGE.

Doris, do you mind? Where was I? Oh—yeah. We were checking into a hotel in London and there was a man in a morning coat and striped trousers standing at the front entrance. Helen handed him her suitcases and sailed on into the lobby. The man followed her in with her suitcases and very politely pointed out that not only didn't he work at the hotel but that he was the Danish Ambassador. Without batting an eye she said, "Well, that's marvelous. Maybe you can tell us the good places to eat in Copenhagen." And he did. The point is it doesn't bother her when she makes a total ass of herself. I really admire that.

DORIS.

And what don't you admire?

GEORGE.

It's that damned sense of humor of hers!

DORIS.

Oh, those are the stories I like the best.

(He looks at her for a moment, then launches headlong into the story)

GEORGE.

We'd come home from a party and we'd had a few drinks and we went to bed and we started to make love. Well, nothing happened—for me—I couldn't—well, you get the picture. It was no big deal—and we laughed about it. Then about half an hour later, just as I was dropping off to sleep she said, "It's funny, when I married a C.P.A. I always thought it would be his eyes that would go first."

DORIS.

(Finally)

She was just trying to make you feel better, George.

GEORGE.

Well, it didn't. Some things aren't funny.

*(*DORIS *doesn't say anything)*

I suppose what I'm trying to say is that the thing that bugs me most about Helen is that she broke my pecker!

DORIS.

(Gently)

You're impotent?

GEORGE.

Slightly.

(He gives a shrug)

Okay, now five people know. Me, you, Helen and her mother.

DORIS.

Who's the fifth?

GEORGE.

Chet Huntley. I'm sure her mother has given him the bulletin for the six o'clock news.

DORIS.

I thought that might be it.

GEORGE.

You mean you can tell just by looking at me?

DORIS.

(Sympathetically)

When did it happen, honey?

GEORGE.

Happen? Doris, we're not talking about a freeway accident! I mean you don't wake up one morning and say, "Oh shoot, the old family jewels have gone on the blink." It's a—gradual thing.

DORIS.

And you really blame Helen for this?

GEORGE.

Of course not. I—I wanted to tell you but I

just couldn't think of a graceful way of working it into the conversation.

(He gives a short, hard laugh)

To tell you the truth I was just waiting for you
to say "What's new?" And I was going to say
"Nothing, but I can tell you what's old."

DORIS.

How's Helen reacting?

GEORGE.

Oh, we haven't talked about it much but I get
the feeling she regards it as a lapse in one's
social responsibility. You know, rather like
letting your partner down in tennis by not holding your serve.

(He gives a little laugh)

Look, it's not great tragedy. As they say in
Brooklyn, "Just wait 'til next year."

(She is not smiling)

Seriously, I'll be okay. Send no flowers. The
patient's not dead yet—just resting.

(She extends her hand)

Doris, that statement hardly calls for
congratulations.

DORIS.

I need help to get out of this chair.

*(He pulls her out of the chair. Takes his face
between her hands. Simply)*

I'm really sorry.

*(They look tenderly at one another for a
moment before he suddenly jerks away)*

GEORGE.

What the hell was that?

DORIS.

The baby kicking.

GEORGE.

(Moving away)

Well, everyone else has taken a shot at me.
Why not him?

DORIS.

(Puzzled)

It's strange. He hasn't been kicking lately.
Maybe he resents the bumpy ride up here.

(She sees that GEORGE is not really listening)

Is there anything I can say that will help?

GEORGE.

What? Honey, you can say anything you want
except "It's all in your head." I mean I'm no
doctor but I have a great sense of direction.

(As she starts to talk)

Look, to tell you the truth, I'm not too crazy
about this whole discussion. Let's forget it,
huh?

DORIS.

Okay. What do you want to talk about?

GEORGE.

Anything but sex. How'd you feel about

pregnant?

DORIS.

Catatonic, incredulous, angry, pragmatic, and
finally maternal. Pretty much in that order.

GEORGE.

Your vocabulary's improving.

DORIS.

Ah, you didn't know. You're talking to a high
school graduate.

GEORGE.

(Puzzled)

How come?

DORIS.

Well, I was confined to bed for the first three
months of my pregnancy, so rather than it being
a total loss I took a correspondence course.

GEORGE.

(Admiringly)

You're really something, you know that?

DORIS.

There's kind of an ironic twist to all this.

GEORGE.

Oh?

DORIS.

Well, I didn't graduate the first time because
I got pregnant. And now I did graduate because—

(She grins, taps her stomach)

Appeals to my sense of order.

GEORGE.

(Teasing).

I didn't know you had a sense of order.

DORIS.

That's unfair. I'm much better at housework
lately. Now I'm only two years behind in my
ironing. Must be the nesting instinct. Anyway,
the day my diploma came in the mail Harry
bought me a corsage and took me out dancing.
Well, we didn't really dance—we lumbered.
Afterwards we went to a malt shop and had a
fudge sundae. That's the nice story about him.

GEORGE.

He still selling real estate?

DORIS.

Insurance. He likes it. Gives him an excuse to
look up all his old Army buddies.

*(He regards her as she stands with her stom-
ach thrust out and both hands pressed on either
side of her back)*

GEORGE.

Doris, are you comfortable in that position?

DORIS.

Honey, when you're in my condition you're
not comfortable in any position.

(He takes her arm, leads her to a chair)

GEORGE.
Come on, sit over here.

(He helps lower her into the chair. As he does a strange expression comes to his face)

DORIS.
Thanks. How are the kids?

GEORGE.
(Vaguely)
What? Oh, fine. Michael got a job with Associated Press.

DORIS.
Oh, darling, that's marvelous. I'm so proud of him.

(She notices that he is staring at her with an odd, fixed expression)

George, why are you looking at me like that?

GEORGE.
(Too quickly)
No reason. It—it's nothing.

DORIS.
Does my stomach offend you?

GEORGE.
No, it's not that. Tell me your other story about Harry.

DORIS.
I had trouble telling him I was pregnant. When I finally did he looked at me for a moment and then said "Is there a revolver in the house?" George, you're doing it again! What is it?

GEORGE.
(Exploding)
It's obscene!

DORIS.
(Bewildered)
What is?

GEORGE. When I touched you I started to get excited!!!!

(He paces around)

What kind of pervert am I?

(He turns to look at her)

I'm staring at a two hundred pound woman and I'm getting hot! Just the sight of you is making me excited.

(She looks at him for a moment)

DORIS.
(Finally)
Let me tell you something. That's the nicest thing anyone's said to me in months.

GEORGE.
(Very agitated)
It's not funny!

DORIS.
Aren't you pleased?

GEORGE.
Pleased? It reminds me of my seventh birthday!

DORIS.
What?

GEORGE.
My uncle gave me fifty cents. I ran two miles and when I got there the candy store was closed!

DORIS.
(Puzzled)
But doesn't this solve your—problem?

GEORGE.
(Frustrated)
The idea doesn't solve anything! It's the execution that counts!

DORIS.
(Pleased)
I really got to you, huh?

GEORGE.
(Tightly)
Excuse me.

(Without another word, he marches to the piano, sits and aggressively launches into a Rachmaninoff concerto. Surprisingly, he plays extremely well. Not quite concert hall material but close enough to fool a lot of people. DORIS *watches, absolutely astounded. She finally recovers enough to get out of her chair and move to the piano where she watches him with an incredulous expression)*

DORIS.
(Finally)
That's incredible! Are you as good as I think you are?

(He continues to play until indicated)

GEORGE.
How good do you think I am?

DORIS.
Sensational.

GEORGE.
I'm not as good as you think I am.

DORIS.
You sound marvelous to me.

GEORGE.
It's the story of my life, Doris. All the form and none of the ability.

DORIS.
(Puzzled)
But for years that piano has been sitting there and you haven't touched it. Why tonight?

GEORGE.
It beats a cold shower.

DORIS.
You play to release sexual tension?

GEORGE.
Any kind of tension. Any frustration in my life and I head right for the piano.

(A wry shrug)

You don't even get this good without a lot of

practice.

(DORIS *shakes her head in wonder*)

DORIS.

George, you're full of surprises.

GEORGE.

Yeah, I know—you live with a man for ten days but you never really know him.

DORIS.

Why didn't you tell me you played before?

GEORGE.

I had other ways of entertaining you.

DORIS.

Well, I always knew you had wonderful hands.

(*He stops playing, looks at her*)

GEORGE.

Look, lady, I only work here. I'm not allowed to date the customers.

(*She smiles, moves away. He starts playing again*)

DORIS.

George? You still feel—frustrated?

GEORGE.

I have the feeling it's going to take all six Brandenburg concertos.

DORIS.

You'll be exhausted.

GEORGE.

That's the idea.

DORIS.

But—

GEORGE.

(*Irritably*)

Doris, I've been waiting three months for—for the balloon to up! Well, it's up and it's not going to come down until something—

DORIS.

Honey, come here.

(*He stops playing, looks at her*)

Come on.

(*He gets up from the piano and moves to her. She starts to untie his robe*)

GEORGE.

Doris—

DORIS.

It's okay. It'll be okay.

GEORGE.

But you can't—

DORIS.

I know that.

GEORGE.

Then how—

DORIS.

Don't worry, darling. We'll work something out.

(*She kisses him very tenderly. Gradually he becomes more involved in the kiss until they are in a passionate embrace. Suddenly she backs away, clutching her stomach, her face in a mixture of surprise and alarm. Then she grimaces with pain*)

GEORGE.

(*Alarmed*)

What is it?

(*She is too busy fighting off the pain to answer*)

Doris?

(*The pain has knocked the breath out of her and she gasps to catch her breath*)

Doris, for God's sake, what is it?

(*She looks at him unbelievingly, not saying anything*)

Doris, what the hell is the matter?

DORIS.

(*Finally*)

If—if memory serves me correctly—I just had a labor pain.

(*He stands stock still, trying to absorb this*)

GEORGE.

You—you can't have!

(*Clutching at straws*)

Maybe it's indigestion.

DORIS.

No, there's a difference.

GEORGE.

How can you be sure?

DORIS.

I've had both.

GEORGE.

But you can't be in labor! When is the baby due?

DORIS.

Not for another month.

(*He stares at her for a moment and then puts his hands to his head*)

GEORGE.

My God, what have I *done*?!

DORIS.

What have *you* done?

GEORGE.

I brought it on. My—my selfishness.

DORIS.

George, don't be ridiculous. You had nothing to do with it.

GEORGE.

Don't treat me like a child, Doris!

DORIS.

Will you stop getting so excited?

GEORGE.

Excited? I thought I had troubles before. Can you imagine what this is going to do to my sex life?

DORIS.
George, will you—
(She stops)
I think I'd better—sit down.
(He quickly moves to her, leads her to a chair)
GEORGE.
(Anguished)
Jesus, what kind of a man am I? What kind of man would do a thing like that?
DORIS.
George, may I say something?
GEORGE.
(Very agitated—moving around)
Look, I appreciate what you're trying to do, honey, but nothing you can say will make me feel any better.
DORIS.
I'm not trying to make you feel any better.
(This stops him in his tracks)
GEORGE.
What are you trying to say?
DORIS.
We're in a lot of trouble. I'm going to have a baby.
GEORGE.
I know that.
DORIS.
I mean now. I have a history of short labor and—
(She stops as another labor pain starts)
GEORGE.
Oh, Jesus!
(He quickly moves to her, kneels in front of her and she grabs his hand in a viselike grip as she fights off the pain)
Oh, Jesus!
(The pain starts to subside)
How—how do you feel?
DORIS.
Like—like I'm going to have a baby.
GEORGE.
Maybe it's a false alarm. It has to be a false alarm!
DORIS.
Honey, try and get a hold of yourself. Get on the phone and find out where the nearest hospital is.
GEORGE.
Hospital? You want to go to a hospital?
DORIS.
George, like it or not, I'm going to have a baby.
GEORGE.
But we're not married!
(She stares at him)

I mean it's going to look—odd!
(She gets up)
DORIS.
Get on the phone, George.
(Moving towards the bathroom)
And make sure you get the directions.
GEORGE.
Where are you going?
DORIS.
The bathroom.
GEORGE.
Why?
DORIS.
I don't have time to answer questions!
(She exits to bathroom. He quickly moves to telephone, frantically jiggles receiver bar)
GEORGE.
(Into phone)
Hello, Mr. Chalmers? George. Can you tell me where the nearest hospital is?—Well, it's my—my wife. Something—unexpected came up. She got pregnant and now she's going to have the baby—How far is that?
(With alarm)
Oh, my God!—Get—get them on the phone for me, will you?
(He covers receiver with hand, calls out)
Are you okay, Doris?
(There is no answer. Panicking)
Doris! Doris, answer me!
DORIS.
(Offstage from bathroom—obviously in pain)
In—a minute. I'm—busy.
GEORGE.
Oh, Jesus.
(Into phone)
Hello—Hello, I'm staying at the Sea Shadows Inn just outside Mendocino and—I—I heard this—this groaning from—the next room. Well, I knocked on the door and found this—this lady—who I'd never met before, in labor and— Do you have to know that?—I still don't see why—Okay, George Peterson!—Well, I didn't time it exactly but—About three or four minutes I think—Hold on.
(Calling out)
Doris, who's your doctor?
DORIS.
(Offstage—with an effort)
Doctor Joseph—Harrington. Oakland. 555-7878.
GEORGE.
(Into phone)
Doctor Joseph Harrington in Oakland. His number is 555-7878—Yes, I have a car and I'm certainly willing to help out if—I'll get

her there—Right, right—Uh, could you answer one question?—Would—uh—erotic contact during pregnancy be the cause of premature—No reason, I just wondered and—Right, I'll do that!

(He hangs up, calls out)

They're phoning your doctor. He'll meet us there at the hospital.

(DORIS appears in the doorway of the bathroom, a strange look on her face. She doesn't say anything)

Doris, did you hear me?

DORIS.

I don't think we're going to make it to the hospital.

(The blood drains from his face)

GEORGE.

What?

DORIS.

My water just burst.

GEORGE.

Oh, dear God.

DORIS.

We're going to have to find a doctor in the area.

GEORGE.

But supposing we can't!

DORIS.

You look terrible. You're not going to faint, are you?

GEORGE.

(In total shock)

Doris, I'm not a cab driver! I don't know how to deliver babies!

DORIS.

George, this is no time to start acting like Butterfly McQueen.

(She heads toward the bed)

Get the nearest doctor on the phone.

(He races back to phone as she half sits and half lies on the bed)

GEORGE.

(Into phone)

Who's the nearest doctor?—Get him on the phone! Fast! This is an emergency!

(DORIS has gone into another labor spasm. GEORGE, phone in hand, moves to her, puts his arm around her, grabs her hand)

It's okay—hold on. Hold on, Doris. Hold on. There—there—hold on. You okay?

DORIS.

(Weakly)

This'll—teach you to fool around—with a married woman.

(Blurting)

George, I'm scared!

GEORGE.

You're going to be okay. Everything—

(Into phone)

Yes?

(Standing up—yelling)

His answering service! You don't understand. She's in the last stages of labor!—Well, get in your car and drive down to the goddam course! Just get him!

(He hangs up)

It's okay—he's on the golf course but it's just down the road. Chalmers is getting him.

(DORIS is staring at him with a look of total panic)

Doris, what is it?

DORIS.

I—I—can feel the baby!!

(He stares at her, absorbs the situation, and we see a definite transformation take place. He rolls up the sleeves of his robe)

GEORGE.

(Calmly)

All right, lean back and try to relax. I'll be right back.

(He exits quickly to the bathroom)

DORIS.

(Screaming)

George, don't leave me!

GEORGE.

(Offstage)

Hold on, baby.

DORIS.

George!

(He reappears with a pile of towels)

GEORGE.

It's okay. I'm here. It'll be all right.

DORIS.

What—are those—for?

GEORGE.

Honey, we're going to have a baby.

DORIS.

We?

GEORGE.

Right. But I'm going to need your help.

(She goes into a spasm of labor and he sits on the bed beside her)

Okay—bear down—bear down. Come on, baby.

(The lights start to fade)

You're going to be fine. Just fine. You think I play the piano well? Wait until you get a load of how I deliver babies.

(The lights have faded and the stage is dark)

END OF ACT ONE, SCENE THREE

ACT TWO

Scene One

The Time:
A day in February 1965.
The Place:
The same.
At Rise:
GEORGE *is unpacking his suitcase. Thinner than the last time we saw him, he is wearing an expensive conservative suit, his hair is gray and is worn unfashionably short. His manner is more subdued than before and he looks and acts older than his years. The door opens and* DORIS *bursts into the room. She is wearing a brightly colored granny gown, beads, sandals, and her hair is long and flowing. She is carrying a decal decorated duffel bag.*

DORIS.
Hey, baby! What do ya say?
(She throws her duffel bag into a chair and herself into the arms of a very surprised GEORGE. *She kisses him passionately, backs off and looks at him)*
So—you wanta fuck?
(He takes an astonished moment to absorb this)
GEORGE.
(Finally)
What?
DORIS.
(Grins)
You didn't understand the question?
GEORGE.
Of course I did. I just think it's a damned odd way to start a conversation.
DORIS.
Yeah? I've always found it to be a great little icebreaker. Besides, I thought you might be feeling horny after your flight.
*(*GEORGE *continues to eye* DORIS *with a mild consternation)*
GEORGE.
I didn't fly, I drove.
DORIS.
From Connecticut?
GEORGE.
From Los Angeles. We moved to Beverly Hills about ten months ago.
(He manages to yank his eyes away from (to him) DORIS'*s bizarre appearance and resumes hanging up his clothes)*

DORIS.
How come?
GEORGE.
Oh, a number of reasons.
(Shrugs)
I got fed up standing knee-deep in snow trying to scrape the ice off my windshield with a credit card. Besides, there are a lot of people out here with a lot of money who don't know what to do with it.
DORIS.
And you tell them?
GEORGE.
I'm what they call a Business Manager.
DORIS.
Things going okay?
GEORGE.
I can't complain. Why?
DORIS.
Because you look shitty.
(He turns to look at her)
Are you all right, honey?
GEORGE.
I'm fine.
DORIS.
You sure there's not something bothering you?
GEORGE.
Yes—you. Do you always go around dressed like a bad finger painting?
DORIS.
(Grinning)
No. I have to admit that today I am a little—well—visually overstated.
GEORGE.
Why?
DORIS.
I guess I wanted to make sure you knew you were dealing with the "new me." Sort of "show and tell."
GEORGE.
You look like a refugee from Sunset Strip.
DORIS.
Berkeley. I went back to school.
GEORGE.
(Bewildered)
What for?
DORIS.
(Grins)
You mean what do I want to be when I grow up?
GEORGE.
Well, you have to admit it's a bit strange becoming a schoolgirl at your age.
DORIS.
Are you kidding? Listen, it's not easy being the only one in the class with clear skin.

(She moves to get her duffel bag, unpacks it through the following)

GEORGE.

(Sitting)

What made you do it?

DORIS.

It was a dinner party that finally pushed me into it. Harry's boss invited us for dinner and I panicked.

GEORGE.

Why?

DORIS.

I'd spent so much time with kids I didn't know if I was capable of carrying on an intelligent conversation with anyone over five who wasn't a supermarket check-out clerk. Anyway, I went and was seated next to the boss. Well, I surprised myself. He talked—then I talked—you know, just like a real conversation. I was feeling real cool until I noticed him looking at me in a weird way. I looked down and realized that all the time we'd been talking I'd been cutting up the meat on his plate. At that moment I knew I had to get out of the house.

GEORGE.

But why school?

(She stretches out on the bed)

DORIS.

It's hard to explain. I felt restless and—undirected and I thought an education might give me some answers.

GEORGE.

What sort of answers?

DORIS.

(Shrugs)

To find out where it's really at.

GEORGE.

(Gets up)

Jesus.

DORIS.

What's the matter?

GEORGE.

That expression.

DORIS.

Okay. To find out who the hell I was.

GEORGE.

You don't get those sort of answers from a classroom.

DORIS.

I'm not in the classroom all the time. The demonstrations are a learning experience in themselves.

GEORGE.

Demonstrations against what?

DORIS.

The war of course. Didn't you hear about it?

It was in all the papers.

GEORGE.

(Curtly)

Demonstrations aren't going to stop the war.

DORIS.

You have a better idea?

GEORGE.

Look, I didn't come up here to discuss politics.

DORIS.

Well, so far you've turned down sex and politics. You want to try religion?

GEORGE.

I think I'll try a librium.

(She watches him as he takes pill out and moves to take it with a glass of water from the drink tray)

DORIS.

George, why are you so uptight?

GEORGE.

That's another expression I hate.

DORIS.

Uptight?

GEORGE.

There's no such word.

DORIS.

You remind me of when I was nine years old and I asked my mother what "fuck" meant. Know what she said? "There's no such word."

GEORGE.

And now you've found out there is you feel you have to use it in every other sentence?

DORIS.

George, what's bugging you?

GEORGE.

Bugging me? I'll tell you what's "bugging" me. The blacks are burning down the cities, there's a Harvard professor telling my children the only way to happiness is to become a doped up zombie, and I have a teen-age son with hair so long that from the back he looks exactly like Yvonne de Carlo.

DORIS.

(Grins)

That's right, baby—let it all hang out.

GEORGE.

I wish people would stop letting it "all hang out." Especially my daughter. It's a wonder she hasn't been arrested for indecent exposure.

DORIS.

That's a sign of age, honey.

GEORGE.

What is?

DORIS.

Being worried about the declining morality of the young. Besides, there's nothing you can do about it.

GEORGE.

We could start by setting some examples.

DORIS.

What are you going to do, George? Bring back public flogging?

GEORGE.

It might not be a bad idea. We could start with the movie producers. My God, have you seen the films they're making today? Half the time the audience achieves a climax before the movie does!

DORIS.

It's natural for people to be interested in sex. You can't kid the body, George.

GEORGE.

Maybe not but you can damn well be firm with it.

(She giggles, gets off the bed, moves toward him)

DORIS.

When you were younger I don't remember you as being exactly a monk about that sort of thing.

GEORGE.

That was different! Our relationship was not based upon a casual one night stand!

(She affectionately rumples his hair)

DORIS.

No, it's been *fifteen* one night stands.

GEORGE.

It's not the same. We've shared things. My God, I helped deliver your child, remember?

DORIS.

Remember? I think of it as our finest hour.

(She kisses him lightly, moves away to pour herself a drink)

GEORGE.

How is she?

DORIS.

Very healthy, very noisy and very spoiled.

GEORGE.

You don't feel guilty about leaving her alone while you're at school?

DORIS.

Harry's home a lot. The insurance business has been kind of slow lately.

GEORGE.

How does he feel about all this?

DORIS.

When I told him I wanted to go back to school because I wanted some identity he lost his temper and said, "You want identity? Go build a bridge! Invent penicillin but get off my back!"

GEORGE.

I always said Harry had a good head on his shoulders.

DORIS.

George, that was the bad story about him. How's Helen?

GEORGE.

Helen's fine. Just fine.

DORIS.

Tell me a story that shows how really lousy she can be.

GEORGE.

(Surprised)

That's not like you.

DORIS.

We seem to need something to bring us closer together.

GEORGE.

I don't understand.

DORIS.

I thought a really bad story about Helen might make you appreciate me more.

(This finally gets a small smile from GEORGE)

GEORGE.

Okay.

(She sits with her drink and listens)

As you know, she has this funny sense of humor.

DORIS.

By funny I take it you mean peculiar?

GEORGE.

Right. And it comes out at the most inappropriate times. I had signed this client—very proper, very old money. Helen and I were invited out to his house for cocktails to get acquainted with him and his wife. Well, it was all pretty awkward but we managed to get through the drinks all right. Then as we went to leave, instead of walking out the front door I walked into the hall closet. Now that wasn't so bad—I mean anybody can do that. The mistake I made was that I *stayed* in there.

DORIS.

You stayed in the closet?

GEORGE.

Yes. I don't know—I guess I figured they hadn't noticed and I'd stay there until they'd gone away—okay, I admit I didn't think things through. I was in there for about a minute before I realized I'd—well—misjudged the situation. When I came out the three of them were just staring at me. All right, it was an embarrassing situation but I probably could have carried it off. Except for Helen. You know what she did?

DORIS.

What?

GEORGE.

She peed on the carpet.

DORIS.
(Incredulous)
She did what?
GEORGE.
Oh, not right away. First of all, she started to laugh. Her face was all screwed up and the laughter was sort of—squeaky. Then she held her stomach and tears started to roll down her face. Then she peed on their Persian rug.
(DORIS is having trouble keeping a straight face)
DORIS.
What did you say?
GEORGE.
I said, "You'll have to excuse my wife. Ever since her last pregnancy she's had a problem." Then I offered to have the rug cleaned.
DORIS.
Did that help?
GEORGE.
They said it wasn't necessary. They had a maid.
(DORIS finally explodes into peals of laughter)
You think that's funny?
DORIS.
I've been meaning to tell you this for years but I think I'd like Helen.
GEORGE.
(Irritated)
Would she come off any worse if I told you I lost the account?
DORIS.
George, when did you get so *stuffy?*
GEORGE.
Stuffy? Just because I don't like my wife urinating on my clients' carpets does not mean I'm stuffy!
DORIS.
Okay, maybe not just that but—well—look at you.
(She gets up, gestures at him)
I mean—Jesus—you scream Establishment.
GEORGE.
I am not a faddist!
DORIS.
What's that mean?
GEORGE.
I have no desire to be like those middle-aged idiots with bell bottom trousers and Prince Valiant haircuts who go around saying "Ciao."
DORIS.
I wasn't talking about *fashion.* I was talking about your attitudes.
GEORGE.
My attitudes are the same as they always were. I haven't changed at all.

DORIS.
Yes, you have. You used to be crazy and— and insecure and dumb and a terrible liar and— *human.* Now you seem so *sure* of yourself.
GEORGE.
That's the last thing I am.
(She is surprised by his admission)
DORIS.
Oh?
(He looks at her for a moment, frowns, moves to look into the fire)
GEORGE.
I picked up one of Helen's magazines the other day and there was this article telling women what quality of *orgasms* they should have. It was called "The Big O."
(He turns to face her)
You know what really got to me? This was a magazine my mother used to buy for its *fruit cake* recipes.
DORIS.
The times they are a changing, darling.
GEORGE.
(Troubled)
Too fast. I don't know, twenty, thirty years ago we were brought up with standards—all right, they *were* blacks and whites but they were standards. Today—it's so confusing.
DORIS.
Well, that's at least a step in the right direction.
(She moves to him and kisses him)
GEORGE.
When did I suddenly become so appealing?
DORIS.
When you went from pompous to confused.
(They kiss again)
So what's your pleasure? A walk by the ocean, dinner, or me?
GEORGE.
You.
DORIS.
Gee, I thought you'd never ask.
(She steps back a pace and whips her dress off over her head revealing that she is just wearing a pair of bikini panties)
GEORGE.
My God.
DORIS.
What is it?
GEORGE.
Doris—you're not wearing a bra!
(She giggles, embraces him)
DORIS.
Oh, George, you're so forties.
(She starts to nibble on his ear)

GEORGE.
(Becoming passionate)
I happen to be an old-fashioned—man.
DORIS.
The next thing you'll be telling me you voted for Goldwater.
GEORGE.
I did.
(She takes a step back from him)
DORIS.
Are you putting me on?
GEORGE.
Of course not.
(Without another word, she picks up her dress and puts it on)
What—what are you doing?
DORIS.
(Furious)
If you think I'm going to bed with any son of a bitch who voted for Goldwater you've got another think coming!
GEORGE.
Doris, you can't do this to me! Now now!
DORIS.
Oh, can't I? I'll tell you something—not only will I not go to bed with you—I want fifteen years of fucks back!
GEORGE.
Doris, this is a very *delicate mechanism*!!
(She stares at him unbelievingly)
DORIS.
My God, how could you vote for a man like that?
GEORGE.
(Moving toward her)
Could we talk about this later?
DORIS.
(Pushing him away)
No, we'll talk about it *now*! Why?
GEORGE.
(Frustrated—yelling)
Because I have a son who wants to be a rock musician!!
DORIS.
What kind of reason is *that*?
GEORGE.
(Sitting)
The best reason I can come up with right now in my condition!
DORIS.
Well, you're going to have to do a lot better!
GEORGE.
Okay, he was going to end the war!
DORIS.
By bombing the hell out of innocent people!

GEORGE.
What innocent people? They're *Reds*!
DORIS.
They just wanted their country back!
GEORGE.
Oh, I'm sick of hearing all that liberal crap! We've got the H bomb. Why don't we use it!
DORIS.
Are you serious?
GEORGE.
Yes, I'm serious. Wipe the sons of bitches off the face of the earth!
(She stares at him for a moment)
DORIS.
(Quietly, incredulous)
My God, I don't know anything about you. What sort of a man are you?
GEORGE.
Right now—very frustrated.
DORIS.
All this time I thought you were a liberal Democrat. You told me you worked for Stevenson.
GEORGE.
(In a tired voice)
That was years ago.
DORIS.
What changed you? What happened to you?
GEORGE.
(Bitterly)
I grew up.
DORIS.
Yeah, well in my opinion you didn't turn out too well.
GEORGE.
Let's forget it, huh?
DORIS.
Forget it? How can I forget it? I mean being stuffy and—and old-fashioned is one thing but being a Fascist is another!
GEORGE.
(Flaring)
I am not a Fascist!
DORIS.
You're advocating mass murder!
GEORGE.
Doris—drop it, okay! Just—drop it!
DORIS.
How could you *do* this to me? Why, you stand for everything I'm against!
GEORGE.
Then maybe you're against the wrong things!
DORIS.
You used to think the same way I did.
GEORGE.
I changed!

DORIS.

Why?

GEORGE.

Because Michael was killed! How the hell else did you expect me to feel!!

(There is a long pause as she stands transfixed, trying to absorb this)

DORIS.

(Finally)

Oh—dear—God. How?

GEORGE.

He was trying to get a wounded man onto a Red Cross helicopter and a sniper killed him.

(Without a word, she moves to him, starts to put her arms around him. He brushes her away, rises and moves to window and stares out)

DORIS.

(Finally—almost in a whisper)

When?

(There is a pause)

GEORGE.

(Dispassionately)

We heard in the middle of a big July 4th party. Helen went completely to pieces—I'll never forget it. I didn't feel a thing. I thought I was in shock and it would hit me later.

(He turns to face her)

But you know something? It never did. The only emotion I can feel is blind anger. I didn't shed a tear.

(She doesn't say anything)

Isn't that the darnedest thing? I can't cry over my own son's death. I loved him but—for the life of me—I can't seem to cry over him.

(She doesn't move as he crosses to shakily pour himself a drink)

Doris, I'm sorry about—everything. Lately I've been a bit on edge and—

(The glass slips out of his hand, he tries to save it but it hits the dresser and smashes)

Oh, great! Will you look at that—I've gone and cut myself. If it isn't—one—damn thing—after—

(He starts to sob. DORIS moves to him and puts her arms around him. He sinks into a chair, and buries his head into her chest as the curtain falls)

END OF ACT TWO, SCENE ONE

SCENE TWO

The Time:

A day in February 1970.

The Place:

The same.

At Rise:

DORIS *and* GEORGE *are lying on top of the rumpled bed lazily enjoying the afterglow of lovemaking.* GEORGE *is wearing jeans with a butterfly on the seat and longish hair. His manner reflects a slightly self-conscious inner serenity.* DORIS *is wearing an attractive kimono but during the scene will don clothes and makeup that will project an image of chic, expensive, good taste.*

———

DORIS.

It's amazing how good it can be after all these years, isn't it?

GEORGE.

All these years? Honey, if you add up all the times we've actually made it together we're still on our honeymoon.

(A slight pause)

DORIS.

George, did you know I'm a grandmother?

GEORGE.

No, but I think you picked a weird time to announce it.

DORIS.

You think it's decadent having sex with a grandmother?

GEORGE.

Only if it's done well.

(He pats her hand)

Anyway, you're the youngest looking grandmother I've ever had a peak experience with.

DORIS.

(Getting off bed)

My mother thanks you, my father thanks you, my hairdresser thanks you and my plastic surgeon thanks you.

(He watches her as she lights a cigarette, sits at dresser, peers into mirror, starts to brush hair and apply makeup)

When Harry says, "You're not the girl I married," he doesn't know how right he is.

GEORGE.

Didn't Harry like your old nose?

DORIS.

He thinks this is my old nose.

GEORGE.

He never noticed?

DORIS.

(Flippantly)

Pathetic, isn't it? A new dress I could understand—but a whole nose?

GEORGE.
Well, to be totally honest I really can't see much of a difference either.

DORIS.
Who cares? It looks different from my side. Makes me act more attractive.

GEORGE.
Why do you feel you need a validation of your attractiveness?

DORIS.
(A slight shrug)
A woman starts feeling a little insecure when she gets to be forty-four.

GEORGE.
Forty-five.

DORIS.
See what I mean? Anyway, that's this year's rotten story about Harry. Got one about Helen?
(He grins, gets off bed, dons shirt, denim jacket and sandals during the following)

GEORGE.
There was a loud party next door. Helen couldn't sleep and she didn't want to take a sleeping pill because she had to get up at six the next morning. So she stuffed two pills in her ears. During the night they melted. The next morning as the doctor was digging the stuff out of her ears he said, "You know these can be taken orally." Helen just laughed.

DORIS.
If that's the worst story you can tell about her you must be a very happy man.
(He sits on the piano bench)

GEORGE.
Well, let's say I've discovered I have the potential for happiness.
(The phone rings. DORIS immediately moves to answer it)

DORIS.
(Into phone)
Hello.
(Just a hint of disappointment)
Oh, hi, Liz. No, it's sixty—not sixteen guests— That's right—a brunch—We've catered a couple of parties for her before—No problem. She sets up tables around the pool and there's room for the buffet on the patio—Right. Anyone else call?—Okay, I'll be at this number.
(She hangs up, turns to GEORGE, who has been watching her)
Sorry, busy weekend. I had to leave the number.

GEORGE.
Does Harry know you're here?

DORIS.
No, he still thinks I go on the retreat. Don't worry.

(She moves and proceeds to get dressed during the following)

GEORGE.
I'm not worried.

DORIS.
Then why are you frowning?

GEORGE.
I'm getting some bad vibes again.

DORIS.
Again?

GEORGE.
When you first walked into the room I picked up on your high tension level. Then after we made love I sensed a certain anxiety reduction but now I'm getting a definite negative feedback.

DORIS.
How long you been in analysis?

GEORGE.
How did you know I was in analysis?

DORIS.
(Drily)
Just a wild guess. What made you go into therapy?

GEORGE.
(With a shrug)
My value system changed.
(He casually plays some soft, pleasant chords at the piano as he talks)
One day I took a look at my $150,000 house, the three cars in the garage, the swimming pool, and the gardeners and I thought— "Why?" I mean did I really want the whole status trip? So—I decided to try and find out what I did want and who I was.

DORIS.
And you went from analysis to Esalen to Gestalt to Transactional to encounter groups to Nirvana.
(He stops playing, swivels to face her, speaks in a calm, reasonable voice)

GEORGE.
Doris, just because many people are trying to expand their emotional horizons doesn't make the experience any less valid. I've learned a lot.

DORIS.
I've noticed. For one thing you learned to talk as if you're reasoning with someone about to jump off a skyscraper ledge.

GEORGE.
(Grins)
Okay—okay. I know I tend to overcompensate for my emotionalism and sometimes there's a certain loss of spontaneity. I'm working on that.

DORIS.

I'm glad to hear it. What else did you find out?

GEORGE.

(Simply)

That behind the walls I've built around myself I'm a warm, caring, loving human being.

(She looks at him for a moment)

DORIS.

I could have told you that twenty years ago. How does Helen feel about this "voyage of self discovery"?

GEORGE.

At first she tended to overact.

DORIS.

In what way?

GEORGE.

She threw a grapefruit at me in the Thriftimart. It was natural that we'd have some interpersonal conflicts to work through but now it's cool. She's into pottery.

DORIS.

But how do you make a living?

GEORGE.

We live very simply, Doris—we don't need much. What bread we do need I can provide by simple, honest labor.

DORIS.

Like what?

GEORGE.

I play cocktail piano in a singles bar in the Valley.

(The phone rings again. DORIS quickly moves to answer it)

DORIS.

(Into phone)

Hello—Oh, hi, Liz—No way. Tell him that's our final offer—I don't care how good a location it is—That's bull, Liz, he needs us more than we need him. If he doesn't like it he can shove it but don't worry—he won't. Anything else?—Okay, you know the number.

(She hangs up)

I'm buying another store.

GEORGE.

Why?

DORIS.

Money.

(She continues to dress)

GEORGE.

Is that why you went into business? Just to make money?

DORIS.

Of course not. I wanted money *and* power. And it finally penetrated my thick little head that attending C.R. groups with ten other frustrated housewives wasn't going to change

anything.

GEORGE.

C.R. groups?

DORIS.

Consciousness raising.

(He nods)

I take it you *are* for Women's Liberation?

GEORGE.

Listen, I'm for any kind of liberation.

DORIS.

That's a cop out. Women have always been exploited by men and you know it.

GEORGE.

We've *all* been shafted, Doris, and by the same things.

(He gets up)

Look, let me lay this on you. I go to a woman doctor. The first time she gave me a rectal examination she said, "Am I hurting you or are you tense?" I said, "I'm tense." Then she said, "Are you tense because I'm a woman?" and I said, "No, I get tense when *anybody* does that to me."

(A beat)

You see what I mean?

DORIS.

I don't know but I *do* know that the only time a woman is taken seriously in this country is when she has the money to back up her mouth. The business has given me that.

GEORGE.

(Mildly)

Well, I guess it's nice to have a hobby.

DORIS.

Hobby? We grossed over half a million dollars the first year.

GEORGE.

Honey, if that's what you want I'm very happy for you.

(A slight shrug)

It's just that I'm not into the money thing anymore.

(She looks at him for a moment)

DORIS.

(Lightly)

George, you ever get the feeling we're drifting apart?

GEORGE.

No. In many ways I've never felt closer to you.

DORIS.

Really? I don't know, sometimes I think our lives are always—out of sync.

GEORGE.

We all realize our potential in different ways at different times. All I ask is that you don't

lay your trip on me, that's all.
(She moves to purse, extracts check)
DORIS.
Then let me lay this on you.
(She hands him check)
Here—it's the money you loaned me to start the store.
GEORGE.
(Looking at check)
It's three times the amount I gave you.
DORIS.
Return on your investment.
GEORGE.
I can't accept this, Doris.
DORIS.
(Firmly)
You can and you will. I'm not going to have any lover of mine playing piano in a singles bar. Sounds tacky.
(They smile at one another)
GEORGE.
You never used to order me around.
DORIS.
I've come a long way, baby.
GEORGE.
The important thing is does it give you a sense of fulfillment?
DORIS.
Fulfillment? Let me tell you about fulfillment.
(She moves to finish dressing)
I went into Gucci's the other day and I noticed a suede suit I liked and asked one of their snotty salesgirls the price. She said, "Seven hundred dollars," and started to walk away. I said, "I'll take five." She turned and said, "Five? Why on earth would you want five?" and I said, "I want them for my bowling team." *That's* fulfillment.
GEORGE.
So you have everything you want?
DORIS.
(Lighting cigarette—flippantly)
With one minor exception. Somewhere along the way I seem to have lost my husband.
GEORGE.
Lost him?
DORIS.
Well, I don't know if I've lost him or simply misplaced him. He walked out of the house four days ago and I haven't heard from him since.
GEORGE.
How do you feel about that?
DORIS.
George, do me a favor—stop acting as if you're leading a human potential group. It really pisses

me off.
GEORGE.
That's cool.
DORIS.
What's cool?
GEORGE.
For you to transfer your hostility and feelings of aggression from Harry to me. As long as you *know* that's what you're doing.
DORIS.
You mind if I tell you something, George? You're beginning to get on my nerves.
GEORGE.
That's cool too.
DORIS.
Jesus.
GEORGE.
I mean it. At least it's *honest*. That's the key to everything—total honesty.
DORIS.
Oh really? And are you totally honest with Helen?
GEORGE.
I'm trying.
DORIS.
Have you told her about us?
GEORGE.
No—but I could.
(She grimaces)
Really, I think that today she's mature enough to handle it.
DORIS.
George, you're full of shit.
GEORGE.
I can buy that—if you're really being *honest*.
DORIS.
Believe me, I'm being honest!
GEORGE.
Well, at least it's a start. But what about that other garbage?
(She starts to speak)
Oh come on, Doris!
(Imitating her)
"I don't know if I lost him or simply misplaced him." I mean, what sort of crap is that?
(She looks at him for a moment)
DORIS.
Okay, you have a point.
GEORGE.
Is there someone else?
DORIS.
I don't think so. I know there isn't with me.
(Getting agitated)
That's what really gets to me. Did you know I've been married for over twenty-five years and I've never cheated on him *once*!

(He doesn't say anything.)
Well, you know what I mean.
GEORGE.
What is it then? Boredom?
DORIS.
No. Oh, Harry's not exactly Cary Grant any-more but then neither is Cary Grant.
GEORGE.
So how do you feel about all this?
DORIS.
You're doing it again, George.
(He doesn't say anything)
Okay, I think—
GEORGE.
No, don't tell me what you think. Tell me what you *feel.*
DORIS.
Like I've been kicked in the stomach.
GEORGE.
That's good.
(She looks at him)
What else?
DORIS.
Angry, hurt, betrayed and—okay, a little guilty. But you know something? I *resent* the fact that he's made me feel guilty.
GEORGE.
Why do you feel resentment?
DORIS.
(Angrily)
Look, I didn't marry Harry because he had a head for business! Okay, it so happens that I discovered *I* did. Or maybe I was just lucky—I don't know. The point is, I don't love Harry any less because he's a failure as a provider. Why should he love me any less because I'm a success?
(He doesn't say anything, she sighs)
I don't know—one of these days I'm going to know exactly how I *do* feel.
GEORGE.
You don't know?
DORIS.
It varies between Joan of Arc, Rosalind Russell and Betty Crocker.
GEORGE.
Well, I suppose most women are going through a transitional period.
DORIS.
(With a wry grimace)
Yeah, but what am I going to do tonight?
GEORGE.
Have you told him you still love him?
DORIS.
Love him? Why does he think I've been hang-ing around with him for twenty-seven years?

GEORGE.
(In his calm, reasonable voice)
I just mean that right now his masculinity is being threatened and he probably needs some validation of his worth as a man.
DORIS.
And how the hell do I do all that? I mean that's some trick.
GEORGE.
Total honesty, Doris. Is it so hard for you to tell him that you understand how he feels?
DORIS.
Right now—it is, yes.
GEORGE.
Oh?
DORIS.
I mean why the hell should I apologize for doing something well? It's *his* ego that's screwed us up. I mean I really *resent* that!
GEORGE.
You want him back?
DORIS.
Right at this moment I'm not sure I do. Ask me tomorrow and I'll probably give you a dif-ferent answer.
GEORGE.
Why?
DORIS.
(Simply)
Tomorrow I won't have you.
GEORGE.
I'm always with you in spirit.
DORIS.
It's not easy to spiritually put your cold feet on someone's back.
GEORGE.
Is that a proposal, Doris?
DORIS.
You interested?
GEORGE.
Are you?
DORIS.
For two cents.
GEORGE.
Leave Helen and Harry?
DORIS.
Sure. Present a united back.
(He is looking at her, trying to determine whether she's serious)
Don't look so panicky, George. I'm only three quarters serious.
(There is a pause)
GEORGE.
Well, when you have your head together and are completely serious why don't you ask me again.

DORIS.

I bet you say that to all the girls.

GEORGE.

No.

(She cups his face in her hands and kisses him)

DORIS.

Thanks.

GEORGE.

And stop feeling so insecure.

DORIS.

About what?

GEORGE.

You're as feminine as you always were.

(She looks at him for a moment)

DORIS.

I know Gloria Steinem would hate me but I'm glad you said that.

(She gives a little shrug)

I guess I'm not as emancipated as I thought I was.

GEORGE.

None of us are.

(She grins at him)

DORIS.

You hungry?

GEORGE.

Yes.

DORIS.

Well, you're a lucky man because tonight our dinner is being catered by the chicest, most expensive French delicatessen in San Francisco.

GEORGE.

How'd we swing that?

DORIS.

The owner has a thing about you.

(As she moves toward the door)

It's all in the trunk of my car.

GEORGE.

You need any help?

DORIS.

Yes. Set the table, light the candles, and when I come back make me laugh.

GEORGE.

I'll try.

DORIS.

That's okay. If you can't make me laugh just hold my hand.

(She exits. He moves to prepare the table for the food. The phone rings. He hesitates for a moment before picking up the receiver)

GEORGE.

(Into the phone)

Hello—No, she's not here right now. Who is this?

(His face freezes)

Harry!—Uh, hold—hold on a moment.

(He places the phone on the floor, stares at it for a moment. Then he paces in a circle around it, his mind wrestling with the alternatives. He stops, stares at it, takes a deep breath, picks up the receiver)

Hello—Harry, we're two adult, mature human beings and I've decided to be totally honest with you—No, Doris is not here right now but *I'd* like to talk to you—Because I know you and Doris have been having a rough time lately and—We're very close friends. I've known Doris for twenty years and through her I feel as if I know you—Well, we've been meeting this same weekend for twenty years—The Retreat? Well, we can get into that later but first I want you to know something. She loves you, Harry—she really loves you—I just know, Harry—Look, maybe if I told you a story she just told me this morning it would help you understand. A few months ago Doris was supposed to act as a den mother for your ten-year-old daughter Georgina and her Indian guide group. Well, she got hung up at the store and was two hours late getting home. When she walked into the house she looked into the living room and do you know what she saw? A rather overweight, balding, middle-aged man with a feather on his head sitting cross-legged on the floor very gravely and gently telling a circle of totally absorbed little girls what it was like to be in a World War II Japanese prison camp. She turned around, walked out of the house, sat in her car and thanked God for being married to a man like you—Are you still there, Harry?—Well, sometimes married people get into an emotional straitjacket and find it difficult to communicate how they truly feel about each other. Honesty is the key to everything— Yes, we've had a very close, very intimate relationship for twenty years and I'm not ashamed to admit that it's been one of the most satisfying experiences of my life—My name? My name is Father Michael O'Herlihy.

(The lights start to dim as he keeps talking)

No, she's out saying a novena right now— Yes, my son, I'll tell her to call you.

(The curtain has fallen)

END OF ACT TWO, SCENE TWO

SCENE THREE

The Time:
A day in February 1975.

The Place:
The same.
At Rise:
DORIS *is alone on the stage silently mouthing "twenty-one, twenty-two, twenty-three" as she finishes transferring some red roses from a box into a silver vase. She is well dressed but her clothes are softer, more feminine and less fashionable than the last time we saw her. She turns as* GEORGE *enters. His hair has been trimmed to a "conservatively long" length and his raincoat covers his comfortably rumpled sports coat, pants, and turtle neck sweater. They drink one another in for a moment before they embrace affectionately.*

———

GEORGE.
You feel *good*.
DORIS.
So do you.
(She looks at him)
But you *look* tired.
GEORGE.
(Grins)
I've looked this way for years. You just haven't noticed.
(She doesn't say anything but we see the concern in her eyes. He turns away, takes off his raincoat and throws it over a chair during the following)
Anyway, I feel better now I'm here. This room's always had that effect on me.
DORIS.
I know what you mean. I guess it proves that maybe you can't buy happiness but you can certainly rent it.
(She gazes around the room affectionately)
It never changes, does it?
GEORGE.
About the only thing that doesn't.
DORIS.
I find that comforting.
GEORGE.
Even old Chalmers is the same. He must be seventy-five by now.
(He smiles at her)
Remember when we first met how even then we called him Old Chalmers?
(She nods)
He must have been about the same age we are now.
DORIS.
That I don't find comforting.
GEORGE.
We were very young.

(They gaze at one another for a moment)
DORIS.
Have we changed, George?
GEORGE.
Of course. I grew up with you. Remember the dumb lies I used to tell?
DORIS.
(Nods)
I miss them.
GEORGE.
I don't. It was no fun being that insecure.
DORIS.
And what about me? Have I grown up too?
GEORGE.
Oh, I have the feeling you were already grown up when I met you.
(They smile at one another)
Tell me something.
DORIS.
Anything.
GEORGE.
Why is it that every time I look at you I want to put my hands all over you?
(She moves to embrace him)
DORIS.
That's another thing that hasn't changed. You always were a sex maniac.
GEORGE.
(Nuzzling her)
Softest thing I've touched in months is Rusty, my cocker spaniel.
(She looks at him in surprise)
DORIS.
Oh?
(He avoids the unspoken query by moving away to the fireplace)
GEORGE.
Let's see if I can get this fire going.
(She watches him as he throws another log on)
You know I figured out with the cost of firewood today it's cheaper to buy Akron furniture, break it up, and burn *it*.
DORIS.
Things that tight?
GEORGE.
No, I'm okay. I've been doing some teaching at U.C.L.A.
DORIS.
Music?
GEORGE.
Accounting.
(He shrugs, gestures at the window)
It seems with everything that's happening out there figures are still the only things that don't lie.

(She moves to pour two cups of coffee from a coffee pot that has been set up on a tray)
Doris, why'd you sell your business?
DORIS.
(Surprised)
How did you know that?
GEORGE.
I'll tell you later. What made you do it?
DORIS.
I was bought out by a chain.
(A slight shrug)
It was the right offer at the right time.
GEORGE.
But I thought you loved working.
DORIS.
Well, there was another factor. Harry had a heart attack.
(She hands him a cup of coffee)
It turned out to be a mild one but he needed me to look after him—so—
(She shrugs)
GEORGE.
You don't miss the action?
DORIS.
Not yet. I guess I'm still enjoying being one of the idle rich.
(He sits with his coffee as she moves to get a cup for herself)
GEORGE.
But what do you do with yourself?
DORIS.
Oh—read, watch TV, play a little golf, visit our grandchildren—you know, all the jet set stuff.
GEORGE.
Harry's okay now?
(She sits opposite him)
DORIS.
Runs four miles a day and has a body like Mark Spitz.
(Grins)
Unfortunately, his face is still like Ernest Borgnine's. You want to hear a nice story about him?
GEORGE.
(Unenthusiastically)
Sure.
DORIS.
Right after the heart attack when he came out of intensive care he looked up at the doctor and said, "Doc, give it to me straight. After I get out of the hospital will I be able to play the piano?" The doctor said, "Of course" and Harry said, "Funny, I couldn't play it *before*."
(GEORGE gives a polite smile, gets up, moves to look out of the window)

You don't understand—it wasn't that it was that funny. It's just that Harry *never* makes jokes but he saw how panicky I was and wanted to make me feel better.
GEORGE.
Doris, how are you and Harry? You know— emotionally.
DORIS.
Comfortable.
GEORGE.
You're willing to settle for that?
(She moves to pick up his raincoat)
DORIS.
Oh, it's not such a bad state. The word's been given a bad reputation by the young.
(She looks around for his luggage)
Where's your luggage? Still in the car?
GEORGE.
I didn't bring any.
(She looks at him)
I—I can't stay, Doris.
DORIS.
(Puzzled)
Why?
GEORGE.
Look, I have a lot to say and a short time to say it so I'd better start now.
(She waits. He takes a breath)
First of all, Helen's known about us for over ten years.
DORIS.
(Finally)
When did you find out?
GEORGE.
Two months ago.
DORIS.
She never confronted you with it before?
GEORGE.
No.
(She slowly sits)
DORIS.
I always wondered how we managed to pull it off. I guess we didn't. What made her finally tell you?
GEORGE.
She didn't. She has this—this old friend— Connie—maybe I've mentioned her before. She told me.
(He shakes his head unbelievingly)
All those years and Helen never even hinted that she knew.
(A beat)
I guess that's the nicest story I've ever told about her.
DORIS.
Your wife's an amazing woman, George.

GEORGE.
She's dead.
(She just looks at him)
She died six months ago. Cancer. It was all—very fast.
(She slowly gets up, moves to look into the fire)
I'm sorry to blurt it out like that. I just couldn't think of a—graceful way to tell you.
(She nods, her back still to him)
You okay, honey?
DORIS.
It's so strange. I never met Helen. But—but I feel as if I've just lost my best friend. It's—crazy.
(He doesn't say anything. She turns to face him)
It must have been awful for you.
GEORGE.
You cope. You don't think you can but—you cope.
(She moves to him, touches his cheek with her hand)
DORIS.
The kids okay?
GEORGE.
They'll survive. I don't think I could have got through the whole thing without them.
(He moves away)
Then of course there was—Connie.
DORIS.
Connie?
GEORGE.
She'd lost her husband a few years ago so there was a certain—empathy.
DORIS.
Oh?
GEORGE.
She's a friend, Doris. A very good friend. We've always felt very—comfortable—together. I suppose it's because she's a lot like Helen.
(She reacts with a slight frown)
Is there something the matter?
DORIS.
I just wish you'd tried to reach me.
GEORGE.
I did. That's when I found out you'd sold the stores. I called and they gave me your home number. I let the phone ring four times, then I hung up. But it made me feel better knowing you were there if I needed you.
DORIS.
I wish you'd spoken to me.
GEORGE.
I didn't want to intrude. I didn't feel I had the

right.
DORIS.
My God, that's terrible. We should have been together.
GEORGE.
I've been thinking about us a lot lately. Everything we've been through together. The things we shared. The times we've helped each other. Did you know we've made love a hundred and thirteen times? I figured it out on my Bomar calculator.
(He is fixing fresh cups of coffee)
It's a wonderful thing to know someone that well. You know, there is nothing about you I don't know. It's two sugars, right?
DORIS.
No, one.
GEORGE.
Cream?
(She shakes her head)
So, I don't know everything about you. I don't know who your favorite movie stars are and I couldn't remember the name of your favorite perfume. I racked my brain but I couldn't remember.
DORIS.
(Smiles)
That's funny. It's My Sin.
GEORGE.
But I do know that in twenty-four years I've never been out of love with you. I find that incredible. So what do you say, Doris, you want to get married?
DORIS.
(Lightly)
Married? We shouldn't even be doing this.
GEORGE.
I'm serious.
DORIS.
(Looking at him)
You really are, aren't you?
GEORGE.
What did you think I was—just another summer romance? A simple "yes" will do.
DORIS.
There's no such thing, George.
GEORGE.
What is it?
DORIS.
I was just thinking of how many times I've dreamed of you asking me this. It's pulled me through a lot of bad times. I want to thank you for that.
GEORGE.
What did you say to me all those times?

DORIS.
I always said yes.
GEORGE.
Then why are you hesitating now?
(Pause)
Do you realize I'm giving you the opportunity to marry a man who has known you for twenty-four years and every time you walk by still wants to grab your ass?
DORIS.
You always were a sweet talker.
GEORGE.
That's because if I told you how I really felt about you it would probably sound like a medley of clichés from popular songs. Will you marry me?
DORIS.
(Pause)
I can't.
GEORGE.
Why not?
DORIS.
I'm already married.
GEORGE.
You feel you have to stay because he needs you?
DORIS.
No, it's more than that. George, try and understand.
(She moves away and turns to him)
When I look at Harry I don't only see the way he is now. I see all the other Harrys I've known. I'm sure he feels the same way about me. When we look at our children—our grandchildren—old movies on TV—anything—we share the same memories.
(A beat)
It's—comfortable. Maybe that's what marriage is all about in the end—I don't know.
(A slight pause)
Didn't you feel that way with Helen?
(There is a short pause)
GEORGE.
(Exploding)
Goddamit!
(He smashes his coffee cup into the fireplace)
I was the one who got you back together three years ago! Why did I do a stupid thing like that! I mean why the hell was I so goddam generous!?
DORIS.
Because you felt the same way about Helen then as I do about Harry now.
GEORGE.
What's that got to do with anything?!

DORIS.
If I hadn't gone back to Harry you might have been stuck with me permanently and you were terrified.
(He looks at her, manages a sheepish grin)
GEORGE.
You could always see through me, couldn't you?
DORIS.
That's okay. I always liked what I saw.
GEORGE.
Well, I want you now.
DORIS.
I'm still available once a year.
(He doesn't say anything)
Same time, same place?
(She catches a certain look in his eyes)
What is it?
(He looks at her for a moment, paces, turns to face her)
GEORGE.
(Awkwardly)
Doris—I—I need a wife. I'm just not the kind of man who can live alone. I want you to marry me but when I came here I—I knew there was an outside chance you'd say no. What I'm trying to say is—if you don't marry me I'll probably end up marrying Connie. No—that's a lie—I will marry her. She knows why I came here today. She knows—all about you. The point is, she's not the sort of woman who would go along with our—relationship.
(A beat)
You understand?
(DORIS manages a nod)
I suppose what I'm saying is that if you don't marry me we won't ever see each other again.
(DORIS is frozen, he moves to take her hand)
You're trembling.
DORIS.
The thought of never seeing you again terrifies me.
GEORGE.
Doris, for God's sake—marry me!
DORIS.
(Finally—torn)
I'm sorry—I can't.
(He looks at her for a long moment)
Don't hate me, George.
GEORGE.
I could never hate you. I was just trying to think of something that would break your heart, make you burst into tears and come with me.
DORIS.
You know us Italians. We never cry.
(He makes a gesture of helplessness, stands)

GEORGE.
What time is it?
(She holds out her wrist, he looks at her watch, reacts)
Five-fifty-five.
DORIS.
No, it's only two-thirty. I always keep my watch three hours and twenty-five minutes fast.
GEORGE.
(Puzzled)
How long you been doing that?
DORIS.
About twenty-odd years.
GEORGE.
Why would anyone want to do that?
DORIS.
Personal idiosyncrasy.
(There is an awkward pause)
GEORGE.
Well—I—have a plane to catch.
(She nods, stands. They look at one another)
You know, I can't believe this is happening to us.
(She doesn't say anything)
Yeah. Well—
(They embrace and kiss, clumsily and awkwardly, almost like two strangers. They break, he picks up his raincoat, moves to door, turns to look at her)
GEORGE.
Who were your favorite movie stars?
DORIS.
Lon McAllister, Howard Keel, Cary Grant, Marlon Brando, and Laurence Olivier.
GEORGE.
You've come a long way.
DORIS.
We both have.
(He opens door, looks at her)
GEORGE.
Always keep your watch three hours and twenty-five minutes fast, huh?
(He exits quickly, shutting the door behind him. DORIS stands for a moment trying to absorb the shock of his departure. Then, trancelike, she moves to the closet where she gets her suitcase, puts it on the sofa, and starts to pack but stops to look lovingly around the room, drinking in the memories before her eyes come to rest upon the vase of roses. She slowly moves to the roses, takes one out, closes her eyes and rests it gently against her cheek. She holds this pose for a long moment before her eyes jolt

open as the door crashes open and GEORGE, perspiring and very agitated, bursts into the room, holding his suitcases. He drops his cases with a thump, fixes her with an angry, frustrated look)
Okay, you win goddamit! You can't look a gift horse in the mouth!
DORIS.
(Astounded)
But—but what about Connie?
GEORGE.
(Yelling)
There is no Connie! I made her up!
(She just stares at him, dumbfounded)
No, that's a lie too. There is a Connie but she's sixty-nine years old!
(DORIS is still speechless)
Doris, I wanted you to marry me and I figured if you thought there was someone else you'd okay, maybe I didn't think it through. I was desperate, okay?
(Getting even more agitated)
Look, for once in my life I wanted a happy ending, can't you understand that?! Listen, I don't want to talk about it anymore!
(Still speechless she watches him march to the bed and start to furiously undress. He turns to look at her)
Okay! You're right about that too! If you had married me we might have just ended up with a "comfortable" ending!
(She opens her mouth to speak)
Look, I'm in no mood to figure it out right now. All I know is I'm back and I'm going to keep coming back every year until our bones are too brittle to risk contact.
(She starts to laugh, her laughter builds and then almost imperceptibly changes to something else and we realize that she is crying. She moves blindly into his arms, still sobbing. He gently tips her face up so that he can look at her and speaks very softly)
After twenty-four years? Why now?
DORIS.
(Through her tears)
Because I love—happy—endings!
(He picks her up, places her on the bed and as he lies beside her the lights slowly dim until there is just a pin spot on the vase of roses. Finally, this too fades, the stage is dark, and the play is over)

THE END

for colored girls
who have considered suicide/
when the rainbow is enuf

A *choreopoem by Ntozake Shange*

FOR THE SPIRITS OF MY GRANDMA VIOLA BENZENA MURRAY OWENS AND MY GREAT AUNT EFFIE OWENS JOSEY

First presented by Woodie King, Jr. at the Henry Street Settlement's New Federal Theatre, the New York Shakespeare Festival Public Theatre, and then at the Booth Theatre on Broadway where it opened on September 15, 1976, with the following cast:

(*in order of appearance*)

LADY IN BROWN	Janet League
LADY IN YELLOW	Aku Kadogo
LADY IN RED	Trazana Beverley
LADY IN GREEN	Paula Moss
LADY IN PURPLE	Risë Collins
LADY IN BLUE	Laurie Carlos
LADY IN ORANGE	Ntozake Shange

Directed by Oz Scott
Scenery by Ming Cho Lee
Costumes by Judy Dearing
Lighting by Jennifer Tipton
Choreography by Paula Moss
Music for "I Found God in Myself" by Diana Wharton

for colored girls who have considered suicide/when the rainbow is enuf is a choreopoem, not a play, according to its author, Ntozake Shange. "It was just my poems, any poems I happened to have." *for colored girls* . . . is a medley of music, dance and poetry in idiomatic free verse that incorporates elements of jazz, mime and song. "A poem should fill you up with something . . . make you swoon, stop in your tracks, change your mind or make it up. A poem should happen to you like cold water or a kiss."

On September 15, 1976, *for colored girls* . . . opened at the Booth Theatre on Broadway where it ran for nearly two years. Trazana Beverly won the Tony Award for the best featured actress and the play itself was nominated for a Tony Award for Best Play of 1976. *For colored girls* . . . won the Outer Critics Circle Award in 1977 and an award from the Coalition of One Hundred Black Women's Arts and Cultural Committee.

Ntzoke Shange was born Paulette Williams on October 18, 1948, in Trenton, New Jersey. "We were the American dream, four children, two cars, a mother who works, a father who works, family picnics, grandmothers, Christmas, all of that." Shange's family moved frequently, and eventually lived on Windermere Place in northern St. Louis, "one of the truly integrated streets in the city." Their neighbors were Haitians, Chinese, East Indians, Jamaicans and "regular whites and regular blacks."

"That street was like a buffer against everything that happened to me in the South. St. Louis has a hold on me . . . I lived there from age eight to age thirteen and it has great meaning—the jumping off place to the West, the place from which runaway slaves might reach freedom and Canada via the Underground Railroad, the place where Jesse James and his men hid out in the same caves used by the runaway slaves. . . . The Mississippi River. I am deeply affected by that mighty river. The St. Louis Municipal Opera would perform *Tom Sawyer* and I was there, entranced and can see it even today . . . Above all, I wanted to be a Mississippi gambler like Tyrone Power done up with his fancy frock coat and his ruffled sleeves and his big hat. . . ."

Her childhood was an extraordinarily privileged one. A child of the black upper middle class, she had violin and dance lessons, after-dinner poetry readings and Sunday afternoon family variety shows in which, "My mama would read from Dunbar, Shakespeare, Countee Cullen, T. S. Eliot. My dad would play congas and do magic tricks, my two brothers and my sisters would do soft shoe and then pick up the instruments for a quartet of some sort: a violin, cello, flute and saxophone. We all read constantly—anything, anywhere."

Yet Shange felt that she was "living a lie" for the first sixteen years of her life. "It was living in a world that defined reality as most black people or most white people understood it . . . feeling that there was something I could do, then realizing that nobody was expecting me to do anything because I was colored and I was also female. . . ."

She refers to her childhood as a "double life." There were debutante cotillions, memberships in the Jack and Jill Society (reserved only for children of black upper middle class professionals) and comfortable homes in pleasant surroundings, yet there was also racial prejudice encountered at an early age. Shange's most traumatic memory is the treatment she received when she was one of fifteen children chosen to integrate a previously all white school in St. Louis. Her happy, loving childhood had not prepared her for this. "I was being harassed and chased around by these white kids. My parents were busy being proud."

Music played a large part in Shange's education and this is very evident in *for colored girls* . . . "I am filled with rhythm and blues. . . . There was a time when rhythm and blues was my only reality. . . . My daddy plays some percussion, knows Miles Davis, Dizzy Gillespie, knew Charlie Parker . . . From the time I was eight until I was thirteen, I would sit by the radio and listen to George Logan's show . . . B. B. King, the Olympics, the Shirelles, Ike and Tina Turner. . . ."

Shange always wanted to write. "It was the only way to express my frustrations. . . . I lived in language, sound falls around me like rain on other people. . . ." The language of her poetry comes from the live-in maids who cared for her as a child.

At her father's insistence that she do something useful like teaching, Shange went to Barnard and received an honors degree in American Studies with a major in Afro-American music and poetry. While at Barnard her many experiences—marriage, divorce, suicide attempts, student protest activities, participation in civil rights and black liberation movements—helped to shape the ideas and feelings expressed in *for colored girls* . . . .

Shange received her bachelor's degree in 1970 and went on to the University of Southern California in Los Angeles where she worked part-time and held a teaching fellowship while earning her master's degree in American Studies. It was there, in 1971, that she decided to change her name. "I had a violent resentment of carrying a slave name; poems and music came from the pit of myself and the pit of myself isn't a slave." The name, Ntozake Shange, comes from the Xhosa tribe in South Africa and means "she who comes with her own things" and "who walks like a lion."

After obtaining her master's degree, she taught in the Women Studies program at Sonoma State College. Living in Oakland, "a sort of fairyland, where I loved the three-story wooden houses, the picket fences, the man who sold fish from a truck, the man who sold vegetables from a horse drawn wagon . . . ", Shange wrote most of the poems in *for colored girls* . . . at night during those three years and would read them in bars and bookstores in San Francisco. These poems were a release for her frustrations and an expression of the feminist and Third World attitudes developing in her. "All this stuff came pouring out of me. I started writing poetry as if I couldn't stop." Paula Moss recalls the genesis of *for colored girls* . . .: "She had this poetry and I had this dance and so we just started to put it out there and see if it would work."

They began in small bars, bookstores and schools, playing to standing-room-only audiences. Exhausting their "creative and emotional possibilities in San Francisco," they came to New York. They first performed at the Studio Rivbea, a jazz loft in Soho. Director Oz Scott saw a performance and offered to stage it, recruiting actresses to fill out the cast of seven women. It moved to the Old Reliable Bar and DeMonte's where it was seen by producer Woodie King, Jr., who subsequently produced it at the Henry Street Settlement's New Federal Theatre in November 1975. In June 1976, Joseph Papp produced the play at his New York Shakespeare Festival's Public Theatre. After its highly successful Off-Broadway run, *for colored girls* . . . opened to good reviews at the Booth Theatre on Broadway.

for colored girls . . . speaks to things that women experience, particularly black women. The word *colored* in the title was chosen because "it was a word that meant I belong somewhere" and because of Shange's deep affection for the grandmother who used to say to her, "You're such a good little colored girls . . ." Then, as she was driving home to Oakland after class one day, the sight of a rainbow inspired her with the thought that "women, especially black women, could survive on the realization that they have as much right and as much purpose for being here as air and mountains do . . ." The rainbow is ". . . the possibility to start all over again with the power and beauty of ourselves . . ."

for colored girls . . . explores the realities of different kinds of women and the terror, pain, anger, delight and cultural confusion of black women. A series of monologues written in colloquial, street-wise verse delivered by seven women, their story begins with childhood reminiscences (the eight-year-old who discovered the Haitian poet Toussaint L'Overture) and moves on through adolescence until it comes to the adult griefs of coping with men, which Shange feels is even more difficult for blacks.

Women are portrayed as victims in the play. They are ignored, raped, beaten, prostituted and never loved. Yet they endure with a miraculous kind of hope and anger. At their breaking point they collapse but then pick themselves up and find God within them. In this choreopoem, one can clearly see Shange's own struggle for independence, loving, losing and then discovering deep within herself a reason to live, a reason for life itself. "Poems come on their own time. I am offering these to you as what I've received from this world so far."

Ntozake Shange has also written *Closets; Cypress; A Photograph: A Study of Cruelty; In the Middle of a Flower, Sassafrass, Cypress and Indigo; Where the Mississippi Meets the Amazon; From Okra to Greens; Spell #7; Nappy Edges; Some Men; Mouths: A Daughter's Geography* and *Natural Disasters and Other Festive Occasions.*

Her work has appeared in *Black Scholar, Yardbird Reader, Invisible City, Third World Women, Times to Greez, Margins, Black Maria, West End Magazine, Broadway Boogie, APR, Shocks* and *Ms.* magazine.

_____

*The stage is in darkness. Harsh music is
heard as dim blue lights come up. One after
another, seven women run onto the stage
from each of the exits. They all freeze in
postures of distress. The follow spot picks up
the lady in brown. She comes to life and
looks around at the other ladies. All of the
others are still. She walks over to the lady in
red and calls to her. The lady in red makes
no response.*

   lady in brown
dark phrases of womanhood
of never havin been a girl
half-notes scattered
without rhythm/no tune
distraught laughter fallin
over a black girl's shoulder
it's funny/it's hysterical
the melody-less-ness of her dance

don't tell nobody don't tell a soul
she's dancin on beer cans & shingles

this must be the spook house
another song with no singers
lyrics/no voices
& interrupted solos
unseen performances

are we ghouls?
children of horror?
the joke?

don't tell nobody don't tell a soul
are we animals? have we gone crazy?

i can't hear anythin
but maddening screams
& the soft strains of death
& you promised me
you promised me . . .
somebody/anybody
sing a black girl's song
bring her out
to know herself
to know you
but sing her rhythms
carin/struggle/hard times
sing her song of life
she's been dead so long
closed in silence so long
she doesn't know the sound
of her own voice
her infinite beauty
she's half-notes scattered
without rhythm/no tune
sing her sighs
sing the song of her possibilities
sing a righteous gospel
the makin of a melody
let her be born
let her be born
& handled warmly.

   lady in brown
i'm outside chicago

lady in yellow
i'm outside detroit

lady in purple
i'm outside houston

lady in red
i'm outside baltimore

lady in green
i'm outside san francisco

lady in blue
i'm outside manhattan

lady in orange
i'm outside st. louis

lady in brown
& this is for colored girls who have considered
suicide
but moved to the ends of their own rainbows.

everyone
mama's little baby likes shortnin, shortnin,
mama's little baby likes shortnin bread
mama's little baby likes shortnin, shortnin,
mama's little baby likes shortnin bread

little sally walker, sittin in a saucer
rise, sally, rise, wipe your weepin eyes
an put your hands on your hips
an let your backbone slip
o, shake it to the east
o, shake it to the west
shake it to the one
that you like the best

lady in purple
you're it

*As the lady in brown tags each of the other
ladies they freeze. When each one has been
tagged the lady in brown freezes.
Immediately "Dancing in the Streets" by
Martha and the Vandellas is heard. All of
the ladies start to dance. The lady in green,
the lady in blue, and the lady in yellow do*

*the pony, the big boss line, the swim, and
the nose dive. The other ladies dance in
place.*
    lady in yellow
it was graduation nite & i waz the only
        virgin in the crowd
bobby mills martin jerome & sammy yates
        eddie jones & randi
all cousins
all the prettiest niggers in this factory town
carried me out wit em
in a deep black buick
smellin of thunderbird & ladies in heat
we rambled from camden to mount holly
laughin at the afternoon's speeches
& danglin our tassles from the rear view
        mirror
climbin different sorta project stairs
movin toward snappin beer cans &
GET IT GET IT THAT'S THE WAY TO
        DO IT MAMA
all mercer county graduated the same nite
        cosmetology secretarial pre-college
        autoshop & business
all us movin from mama to what ever waz
        out there

that nite we raced a big ol truck from the
        barbeque stand
trying to tell him bout the party at jacqui's
where folks graduated last year waz waitin
        to hit it wid us
i got drunk & cdnt figure out
whose hand waz on my thigh/but it didn't
        matter
cuz these cousins martin eddie sammy
        jerome & bobby
waz my sweethearts alternately since the
        seventh grade
& everybody knew i always started cryin if
        somebody actually
tried to take advantage of me
        at jacqui's
ulinda mason was stickin her mouth all out
while we tumbled out the buick
eddie jones waz her lickin stick
but i knew how to dance
        it got soo hot
vincent ramos puked all in the punch
& harly jumped all in tico's face
cuz he was leavin for the navy in the mornin
hadda kick ass so we'd all remember how
        bad he waz
seems like sheila & marguerite waz fraid
to get their hair turnin back

so they laid up against the wall
lookin almost sexy
didnt wanna sweat
but me & my fellas   we waz dancin

since 1963 i'd won all kinda contests
wid the cousins at the POLICE ATHLETIC
    LEAGUE DANCES
all mercer county knew
any kin to martin yates cd turn somersaults
fore smokey robinson cd get a woman
    excited

The Dells singing "Stay" is heard

we danced   doin nasty ol tricks

*The lady in yellow sings along with the Dells
for a moment. The lady in orange and the
lady in blue jump up and parody the lady in
yellow and the Dells. The lady in yellow
stares at them. They sit down.*

doin nasty ol tricks i'd been thinkin since
    may
cuz graduation nite had to be hot
& i waz the only virgin
so i hadda make like my hips waz inta some
    business
that way everybody thot whoever was gettin
    it
was a older man cdnt run the streets wit
    youngsters
martin slipped his leg round my thigh
the dells bumped "stay"
up & down—up & down the new carver
    homes
WE WAZ GROWN   WE WAZ
    FINALLY GROWN

ulinda alla sudden went crazy
went over to eddie cursin & carryin on
tearin his skin wid her nails
the cousins tried to talk sense to her
tried to hold her arms
lissin bitch sammy went on
bobby whispered i shd go wit him
fore they go ta cuttin
fore the police arrived
we teetered silently thru the parkin lot
no un uhuh
we didn't know nothin bout no party
bobby started lookin at me
yeah
he started looking at me real strange
like i waz a woman or somethin/

started talkin real soft
in the backseat of that ol buick
WOW
by daybreak
i just cdnt stop grinnin.

*The Dells singing "Stay" comes in and all
of the ladies except the lady in blue join in
and sing along*

> *lady in blue*
you gave it up in a buick?

> *lady in yellow*
yeh, and honey, it was wonderful.

> *lady in green*
we used to do it all up in the dark
in the corners . . .

> *lady in blue*
some niggah sweating all over you.

> *lady in red*
it was good!

> *lady in blue*
i never did like to grind.

> *lady in yellow*
what other kind of dances are there?

> *lady in blue*
mambo, bomba, merengue

when i waz sixteen i ran off to the south
    bronx
cuz i waz gonna meet up wit willie colon
& dance all the time
                    mamba bomba merengue

> *lady in yellow*
do you speak spanish?

> *lady in blue*
olà
my papa thot he was puerto rican & we wda
    been
cept we waz just reglar niggahs wit hints of
    spanish
so off i made it to this 36 hour marathon
    dance
con salsa con ricardo
'suggggggggggar' ray on southern blvd
next door to this fotografi place
jammed wit burial weddin & communion
    relics

next door to la real ideal genuine spanish
    barber
  up up up up up stairs & stairs & lotsa
    hallway
wit my colored new jersey self
didn't know what anybody waz saying
cept if dancin waz proof of origin
   i was jibarita herself that nite
& the next day
i kept smilin & right on steppin
if he cd lead i waz ready to dance
if he cdnt lead
i caught this attitude
      i'd seen rosa do
& wd not be bothered
i waz twirlin hippin givin much quik feet
& bein a mute cute colored puerto rican
til saturday afternoon when the disc-jockey
   say
'SORRY FOLKS WILLIE COLON AINT
   GONNA MAKE IT TODAY'
& alla my niggah temper came outta control
& i wdnt dance wit nobody
& i talked english loud
& i love you more than i waz mad
uh huh uh huh
more than more than
when i discovered archie shepp & subtle
   blues
doncha know i wore out the magic of juju
heroically resistin being possessed
ooooooooooooooh the sounds
sneakin in under age to slug's
to stare atà real 'artiste'
& every word outta imamu's mouth waz
   gospel
& if jesus cdnt play a horn like shepp
waznt no need for colored folks to bear no
   cross at all

& poem is my thank-you for music
& i love you more than poem
more than aureliano buendia loved macondo
more than hector lavoe loved himself
more than the lady loved gardenias
more than celia loves cuba or graciela loves
   el son
more than the flamingoes shoo-do-n-doo-wah
   love bein pretty

oyè négro
te amo mas que   te amo mas que
when you play
yr flute

everyone (very softly)
te amo mas que   te amo mas que

  lady in red
without any assistance or guidance from you
i have loved you assiduously for 8 months 2
   wks & a day
i have been stood up four times
i've left 7 packages on yr doorstep
forty poems 2 plants & 3 handmade
   notecards i left
town so i cd send to you have been no help
   to me
on my job
you call at 3:00 in the mornin on weekdays
so i cd drive 27½ miles cross the bay before i
   go to work
charmin charmin
but you are of no assistance
i want you to know
this waz an experiment
to see how selfish i cd be
if i wd really carry on to snare a possible
   lover
if i waz capable of debasin my self for the
   love of another
if i cd stand not being wanted
when i wanted to be wanted
& i cannot
so
with no further assistance & no guidance
   from you
i am endin this affair

this note is attached to a plant
i've been waterin since the day i met you
you may water it
yr damn self

  lady in orange
i dont wanna write
in english or spanish
i wanna sing   make you dance
like the bata   dance   scream
twitch hips wit me cuz
i done forgot all abt words
aint got no definitions
i wanna whirl
     with you

*Music starts, "Che Che Cole" by Willie
Colon. Everyone starts to dance.*

our whole body
wrapped like a ripe mango
ramblin whippin thru space

on the corner in the park
where the rug useta be
let willie colon take you out
swing your head
push your leg to the moon with me

i'm on the lower east side
in new york city
and i can't   i can't
talk witchu no more

   lady in yellow
we gotta dance to keep from cryin

   lady in brown
we gotta dance to keep from dyin

   lady in red
so come on

   lady in brown
come on

   lady in purple
come on

   lady in orange
hold yr head like it was ruby sapphire
i'm a poet
who writes in english
come to share the worlds witchu

   everyone
come to share our worlds witchu
we come here to be dancin
       to be dancin
       to be dancin
     baya

*There is a sudden light change, all of the
ladies react as if they had been struck in the
face. The lady in green and the lady in
yellow run out up left, the lady in orange
runs out the left volm, the lady in brown
runs out up right.*

   lady in blue
a friend is hard to press charges against

   lady in red
if you know him
you must have wanted it

   lady in purple
a misunderstanding

   lady in red
you know
these things happen

   lady in blue
are you sure
you didnt suggest

   lady in purple
had you been drinkin

   lady in red
a rapist is always to be a stranger
to be legitimate
someone you never saw
a man wit obvious problems

   lady in purple
pin-ups attached to the insides of his lapels

   lady in blue
ticket stubs from porno flicks in his pocket

   lady in purple
a lil dick

   lady in red
or a strong mother

   lady in blue
or just a brutal virgin

   lady in red
but if you've been seen in public wit him
danced one dance
kissed him good-bye lightly

   lady in purple
wit closed mouth

   lady in blue
pressin charges will be as hard
as keepin yr legs closed
while five fools try to run a train on you

   lady in red
these men friends of ours
who smile nice
stay employed
and take us out to dinner

   lady in purple
lock the door behind you

   lady in blue
wit fist in face
to fuck

lady in red
who make elaborate mediterranean dinners
& let the art ensemble carry all ethical
    burdens
while they invite a coupla friends over to
    have you
are sufferin from latent rapist bravado
& we are left wit the scars

lady in blue
bein betrayed by men who know us

lady in purple
& expect
like the stranger
we always thot waz comin

lady in blue
that we will submit

lady in purple
we must have known

lady in red
women relinquish all personal rights
in the presence of a man
who apparently cd be considered a rapist

lady in purple
especially if he has been considered a friend

lady in blue
& is no less worthy of bein beat witin an
    inch of his life
bein publicly ridiculed
havin two fists shoved up his ass

lady in red
than the stranger
we always thot it wd be

lady in blue
who never showed up

lady in red
cuz it turns out the nature of rape has
    changed

lady in blue
we can now meet them in circles we
    frequent for companionship

lady in purple
we see them at the coffeehouse

lady in blue
wit someone else we know

lady in red
we cd even have em over for dinner
& get raped in our own houses
by invitation
a friend

*The lights change, and the ladies are all hit
by an imaginary slap, the lady in red runs
off up left.*

lady in blue
eyes

lady in purple
mice

lady in blue
womb

lady in blue & lady in purple
nobody

The lady in purple exits up right.

lady in blue
tubes tables white washed windows
grime from age wiped over once
legs spread
anxious
eyes crawling up on me
eyes rollin in my thighs
metal horses gnawin my womb
dead mice fall from my mouth
i really didnt mean to
i really didnt think i cd
just one day off . . .
get offa me alla this blood
bonees shattered like soft ice-cream cones

i cdnt have people
lookin at me
pregnant
i cdnt have my friends see this
dyin danglin tween my legs
& i didnt say a thing
not a sigh
or a fast scream
to get
those eyes offa me
get them steel rods outta me
this hurts
this hurts me
& nobody came

cuz nobody knew
once i was pregnant & shamed of myself.

The lady in blue exits stage left volm.

*Soft deep music is heard, voices calling
"Sechita" come from the wings and volms.
The lady in purple enters from up right.*

   lady in purple
once there were quadroon balls/ elegance in
   st. louis/ laced
mulattoes/ gamblin down the mississippi/ to
   memphis/ new
orleans n okra crepes near the bayou/ where
   the poor white trash
wd sing/ moanin/ strange/ liquid tones/ thru
   the swamps/

*The lady in green enters from the right
volm; she is Sechita and for the rest of the
poem dances out Sechita's life.*

sechita had heard these things/ she moved
as if she'd known them/ the silver n high-
   toned laughin/
the violins n marble floors/ sechita pushed
   the clingin
delta dust wit painted toes/ the patch-work
   tent waz
poka-dotted/ stale lights snatched at the
   shadows/ creole
carnival waz playin natchez in ten minutes/
   her splendid
red garters/ gin-stained n itchy on her thigh/
   blk-diamond
stockings darned wit yellow threads/ an ol
   starched taffeta
can-can fell abundantly orange/ from her
   waist round the
splinterin chair/ sechita/ egyptian/ goddess of
   creativity/
2nd millennium/ threw her heavy hair in a
   coil over her neck/
sechita/ goddess/ the recordin of history/
   spread crimson oil
on her cheeks/ waxed her eyebrows/ n
   unconsciously slugged
the last hard whiskey in the glass/ the
   broken mirror she
used to decorate her face/ made her forehead
   tilt backwards/
her cheeks appear sunken/ her sassy chin
   only large enuf/
to keep her full lower lip/ from growin into
   her neck/ sechita/

had learned to make allowances for the
   distortions/
but the heavy dust of the delta/ left a tinge
   of grit n
darkness/ on every one of her dresses/ on
   her arms & her
shoulders/ sechita/ waz anxious to get back
   to st. louis/
the dirt there didnt crawl from the earth into
   yr soul/
at least/ in st. louis/ the grime waz store
   bought
second-hand/ here in natchez/ god seemed to
   be wipin his
feet in her face/

one of the wrestlers had finally won
tonite/ the mulatto/ raul/ was sposed to hold
   the boomin
half-caste/ searin eagle/ in a bear hug/ 8
   counts/ get
thrown unawares/ fall out the ring/ n then do
   searin eagle
in for good/ sechita/ cd hear redneck whoops
   n slappin on
the back/ she gathered her sparsely sequined
   skirts/ tugged
the waist cincher from under her greyin
   slips/ n made her face
immobile/ she made her face like nefertiti/
   approachin her
own tomb/ she suddenly threw/ her leg full-
   force/ thru the
canvas curtain/ a deceptive glass stone/
   sparkled/ malignant
on her ankle/ her calf waz tauntin in the
   brazen carnie
lights/ the full moon/ sechita/ goddess/ of
   love/ egypt/
2nd millennium/ performin the rites/ the
   conjurin of men/
conjurin the spirit/ in natchez/ the
   mississippi spewed
a heavy fume of barely movin waters/
   sechita's legs slashed
furiously thru the cracker nite/ & gold pieces
   hittin the
makeshift stage/ her thighs/ they were aimin
   coins tween her
thighs/ sechita/ egypt/ goddess/ harmony/
   kicked viciously
thru the nite/ catchin stars tween her toes.

*The lady in green exits into the stage left
volm, the lady in purple exits into up stage
left.*

*The lady in brown enters from up stage
right.*

   lady in brown
de library waz right down from de trolly
   tracks
cross from de laundry-mat
thru de big shinin floors & granite pillars
ol st. louis is famous for
i found toussaint
but not til after months uv
cajun katie/ pippi longstockin
christopher robin/ eddie heyward & a pooh
   bear
in the children's room
only pioneer girls & magic rabbits
& big city white boys
i knew i waznt sposedta
but i ran inta the ADULT READING
   ROOM
       & came across

        TOUSSAINT

       my first blk man
(i never counted george washington carver
cuz i didnt like peanuts)
        still
TOUSSAINT waz a blk man a negro like
   my mama say
who refused to be a slave
& he spoke french
& didnt low no white man to tell him nothin
       not napolean
       not maximillien
       not robespierre

TOUSSAINT L'OUVERTURE
waz the beginnin uv reality for me
in the summer contest for
who colored child can read
15 books in three weeks
i won & raved abt TOUSSAINT
   L'OUVERTURE
at the afternoon ceremony
waz disqualified
   cuz Toussaint
      belonged in the ADULT READING
        ROOM
      & i cried
& carried dead Toussaint home in the book
he waz dead & livin to me
cuz TOUSSAINT & them
they held the citadel gainst the french
wid the spirits of ol dead africans from outta
   the ground

TOUSSAINT led they army of zombies
walkin cannon ball shootin spirits to free
   Haiti
& they waznt slaves no more

      TOUSSAINT L'OUVERTURE
became my secret lover at the age of 8
i entertained him in my bedroom
widda flashlight under my covers
way inta the night/ we discussed strategies
how to remove white girls from my
   hopscotch games
& etc.
TOUSSAINT
was layin in bed wit me next to raggedy ann
the night i decided to run away from my
   integrated home
      integrated street
       integrated school
1955 waz not a good year for lil blk girls

Toussaint said 'lets go to haiti'
i said 'awright'
& packed some very important things in a
   brown paper bag
so i wdnt haveta come back
then Toussaint & i took the hodiamont
   streetcar
to the river
last stop
only 15¢
cuz there waznt nobody cd see Toussaint
   cept me
& we walked all down thru north st. louis
where the french settlers usedta live
in tiny brick houses all huddled together
wit barely missin windows & shingles
   uneven
wit colored kids playin & women on low
   porches sippin beer

i cd talk to Toussaint down by the river
like this waz where we waz gonna stow
   away
on a boat for new orleans
& catch a creole fishin-rig for port-au-prince
then we waz just gonna read & talk all the
   time
& eat fried bananas
   we waz just walkin & skippin past ol
   drunk men
when dis ol young boy jumped out at me
   sayin
'HEY GIRL YA BETTAH COME OVAH
   HEAH N TALK TO ME'
well

i turned to TOUSSAINT (who wuz furious)
& i shouted
'ya silly ol boy
ya bettah leave me alone
or TOUSSAINT'S gonna get yr ass'
de silly ol boy came round de corner laughin
    all in my face
'yellah gal
ya sure must be somebody to know my
    name so quick'
i waz disgusted
& wanted to get on to haiti
widout some tacky ol boy botherin me
still he kept standin there
kickin milk cartons & bits of brick
tryin to get all in my business
    i mumbled to L'OUVERTURE 'what shd
    I do'
finally
i asked this silly ol boy
'WELL WHO ARE YOU?'
he say
'MY NAME IS TOUSSAINT JONES'
well
i looked right at him
those skidded out cordoroy pants
a striped teashirt wid holes in both elbows
a new scab over his left eye
& i said
      'what's yr name again'
he say
'i'm toussaint jones'
'wow
i am on my way to see
TOUSSAINT L'OUVERTURE in HAITI
are ya any kin to him
he dont take no stuff from no white folks
& they gotta country all they own
& there aint no slaves'
that silly ol boy squinted his face all up
'looka heah girl
i am TOUSSAINT JONES
& i'm right heah lookin at ya
& i dont take no stuff from no white folks
ya dont see none round heah do ya?'
& he sorta pushed out his chest
then he say
'come on   lets go on down to the docks
& look at the boats'
i waz real puzzled goin down to the docks
wit my paper bag & my books
i felt TOUSSAINT L'OUVERTURE sorta
    leave me
& i waz sad
til i realized
TOUSSAINT JONES waznt too different

from TOUSSAINT L'OUVERTURE
cept the ol one waz in haiti
& this one wid me speakin english & eatin
    apples
yeah.
toussaint jones waz awright wit me
no tellin what all spirits we cd move
down by the river
st. louis 1955   hey wait.

The lady in brown exits into the stage right
volm.

The lady in red enters from the stage left
volm.

    lady in red
orange butterflies & aqua sequins
ensconsed tween slight bosoms
silk roses dartin from behind her ears
the passion flower of southwest los angeles
meandered down hoover street
past dark shuttered houses where
women from louisiana shelled peas
round 3:00 & sent their sons
whistlin to the store for fatback & black-
    eyed peas
she glittered in heat
& seemed to be lookin for rides
when she waznt & absolutely
eyed every man who waznt lame white or
    noddin out
she let her thigh slip from her skirt
crossin the street
she slowed to be examined
& she never looked back to smile
or acknowledge a sincere 'hey mama'
or to meet the eyes of someone
purposely findin sometin to do in
her direction
    she waz sullen
    & the rhinestones etchin the corners of her
    mouth
    suggested tears
    fresh kisses that had done no good
she always wore her stomach out
lined with small iridescent feathers
the hairs round her navel seemed to dance
& she didnt let on
she knew
from behind her waist waz aching to be held
the pastel ivy drawn on her shoulders
to be brushed with lips & fingers
smellin of honey & jack daniels
    she waz hot
    a deliberate coquette

who never did without
what she wanted
& she wanted to be unforgettable
she wanted to be a memory
a wound   to every man
arragant enough to want her
     she waz the wrath
        of women in windows
             fingerin shades/ ol lace curtains
                  camoflagin despair &
                       stretch marks
so she glittered honestly
delighted she waz desired
& allowed those especially
schemin/ tactful suitors
to experience her body & spirit
tearin/ so easily blendin with theirs/
& they were so happy
& lay on her lime sheets full & wet
from her tongue   she kissed
them reverently   even ankles
edges of beards . . .

The stage goes to darkness except for a
special on the lady in red, who lies
motionless on the floor; as the lights slowly
fade up the lady in red sits up.

at 4:30 AM
she rose
movin the arms & legs that trapped her
she sighed affirmin the sculptured man
& made herself a bath
of dark musk oil egyptian crystals
& florida water to remove his smell
to wash away the glitter
to watch the butterflies melt into
suds & the rhinestones fall beneath
her buttocks like smooth pebbles
in a missouri creek
layin in water
she became herself
ordinary
brown braided woman
with big legs & full lips
reglar
seriously intendin to finish her
night's work
she quickly walked to her guest
straddled on her pillows & began
          'you'll have to go now/ i've a lot of
          work to do/ & i cant with a man
          around/ here are yr pants/ there's
          coffee on the stove/ its been very
          nice/ but i cant see you again/ you
          got what you came for/ didnt you'

& she smiled
he wd either mumble curses bout crazy
     bitches
or sit dumbfounded
while she repeated
          'i cdnt possibly wake up/ with a
          strange man in my bed/ why dont
          you go home'
she cda been slapped upside the head
or verbally challenged
but she never waz
& the ones who fell prey to the
dazzle of hips painted with
orange blossoms & magnolia scented wrists
had wanted no more
than to lay between her sparklin thighs
& had planned on leavin before dawn
& she had been so divine
devastatingly bizarre the way
her mouth fit round
& now she stood a
reglar colored girl
fulla the same malice
livid indifference as a sistah
worn from supportin a wd be hornplayer
or waitin by the window
               & they knew
               & left in a hurry
she wd gather her tinsel &
jewels from the tub
& laugh gayly or vengeful
she stored her silk roses by her bed
& when she finished writin
the account of her exploit in a diary
embroidered with lilies & moonstones
she placed the rose behind her ear
& cried herself to sleep.

All the lights fade except for a special on the
lady in red; the lady in red exits into the
stage left volm.

The lady in blue enters from up right.

     lady in blue
i usedta live in the world
then i moved to HARLEM
& my universe is now six blocks

when i walked in the pacific
i imagined waters ancient from accra/ tunis
cleansin me/ feedin me
now my ankles are coated in grey filth
from the puddle neath the hydrant

my oceans were life

what waters i have here sit stagnant
circlin ol men's bodies
shit & broken lil whiskey bottles
left to make me bleed

i usedta live in the world
now i live in harlem & my universe is six
    blocks
a tunnel with a train
i can ride anywhere
remaining a stranger
      NO MAN YA CANT GO WIT ME/ I
      DONT EVEN KNOW YOU/ NO/ I
      DONT WANNA KISS YOU/ YOU
      AINT BUT 12 YRS OLD/ NO MAN/
      PLEASE PLEASE PLEASE LEAVE
      ME ALONE/ TOMORROW/ YEAH/
      NO/ PLEASE/ I CANT USE IT
    i cd stay alone
    a woman in the world
    then i moved to
HARLEM
i come in at dusk
stay close to the curb

The lady in yellow enters, she's waiting for
a bus.

round midnite
praying wont no young man
think i'm pretty in a dark mornin

The lady in purple enters, she's waiting for
a bus.

wdnt be good
not good at all
to meet a tall short black brown young man
    fulla his power
in the dark
in my universe of six blocks
straight up brick walls
women hangin outta windows
like ol silk stockings
cats cryin/ children gigglin/ a tavern wit red
    curtains
bad smells/ kissin ladies smilin & dirt
sidewalks spittin/ men cursing/ playin

The lady in orange enters, she is being
followed by a man, the lady in blue becomes
that man.

'I SPENT MORE MONEY YESTERDAY
THAN THE DAY BEFORE & ALL
   THAT'S MORE N YOU

NIGGAH EVER GOTTA HOLD TO
COME OVER HERE BITCH CANT YA
   SEE THIS IS $5'

never mind sister
dont pay him no mind
go go go go go go sister
do yr thing
never mind

i usedta live in the world
really be in the world
free & sweet talkin
good mornin & thank-you & nice day
uh huh
i cant now
i cant be nice to nobody
nice is such a rip-off
reglar beauty & a smile in the street
is just a set-up

i usedta be in the world
a woman in the world
i hadda right to the world
then i moved to harlem
for the set-up
a universe
six blocks of cruelty
piled up on itself
a tunnel
closin

The four ladies on stage freeze, count 4,
then the ladies in blue, purple, yellow and
orange move to their places for the next
poem.

    lady in purple
three of us like a pyramid
three friends
one laugh
one music
one flowered shawl
knotted on each neck
we all saw him at the same time
& he saw us
i felt a quick thump in each one of us
didnt know what to do
we all wanted what waz comin our way
so we split
but he found one
& she loved him

the other two were tickled
& spurned his advances
when the one who loved him waz

somewhere else
he wd come to her saying
yr friends love you very much
i have tried
& they keep askin where are you
she smiled
wonderin how long her friends
wd hold out
he waz what they were lookin for
he bided his time
he waited til romance waned
the three of us made up stories
bout usedta & cda been nice
the season waz dry
no men
no quickies
not one dance or eyes unrelentin
one day after another
cept for the one who loved him
he appeared irregularly
expectin graciousness no matter what
she cut fresh strawberries
her friends callt less frequently
went on hunts for passin fancies
she cdnt figure out what waz happenin
then the rose
she left by his pillow
she found on her friends desk
& there waz nothing to say
she said
i wanna tell you
he's been after me
all the time
says he's free & can explain
what's happenin wit you
is nothin to me
& i dont wanna hurt you
but you know i need someone now
& you know
how wonderful he is

her friend cdnt speak or cry
they hugged & went to where he waz
wit another woman
he said good-bye to one
tol the other he wd call
he smiled a lot

she held her head on her lap
the lap of her sisters soakin up tears
each understandin how much love stood
    between them
how much love between them
love between them
love like sisters

*Sharp music is heard, each lady dances as if
catching a disease from the lady next to her,
suddenly they all freeze.*

   lady in orange
ever since i realized there waz someone callt
a colored girl an evil woman a bitch or a
    nag
i been tryin not to be that & leave bitterness
in somebody else's cup/ come to somebody
    to love me
without deep & nasty smellin scald from lye
    or bein
left screamin in a street fulla lunatics/
    whisperin
slut bitch bitch niggah/ get outta here wit
    alla that/
i didnt have any of that for you/ i brought
    you what joy
i found & i found joy/ honest fingers round
    my face/ with
dead musicians on 78's from cuba/ or live
    musicians on five
dollar lp's from chicago/ where i have never
    been/ & i love
willie colon & arsenio rodriquez/ especially
    cuz i can make
the music loud enuf/ so there is no me but
    dance/ & when
i can dance like that/ there's nothin cd hurt
    me/ but
i get tired & i haveta come offa the floor &
    then there's
that woman who hurt you/ who you left/
    three or four times/
& just went back/ after you put my heart in
    the bottom of
yr shoe/ you just walked back to where you
    hurt/ & i didnt
have nothin/ so i went to where somebody
    had somethin for me/
but he waznt you/ & i waz on the way back
    from her house
in the bottom of yr shoe/ so this is not a
    love poem/ cuz there
are only memorial albums available/ & even
    charlie mingus
wanted desperately to be a pimp/ & i wont
    be able to see eddie
palmieri for months/ so this is a requium for
    myself/ cuz i
have died in a real way/ not wid aqua
    coffins & du-wop cadillacs/
i used to joke abt when i waz messin round/
    but a real dead
lovin is here for you now/ cuz i dont know

anymore/ how
to avoid my own face wet wit my tears/ cuz
     i had convinced
myself colored girls had no right to sorrow/
     & i lived
& loved that way & kept sorrow on the
     curb/ allegedly
for you/ but i know i did it for myself/
i cdnt stand it
i cdnt stand bein sorry & colored at the same
     time
it's so redundant in the modern world

lady in purple
i lived wit myths & music waz my ol man &
     i cd dance
a dance outta time/ a dance wit no partners/
     take my
pills & keep right on steppin/ linger in non-
     english
speakin arms so there waz no possibility of
     understandin
& you YOU
came sayin i am the niggah/ i am the
     baddest muthafuckah
out there/
i said yes/ this is who i am waitin for
& to come wit you/ i hadta bring everythin
the dance & the terror
the dead musicians & the hope
& those scars i had hidden wit smiles &
     good fuckin
lay open
& i dont know i dont know any more tricks
i am really colored & really sad sometimes
     & you hurt me
more than i ever danced outta/ into oblivion
     isnt far enuf
to get outta this/ i am ready to die like a lily
     in the
desert/ & i cdnt let you in on it cuz i didnt
     know/ here
is what i have/ poems/ big thighs/ lil tits/ &
so much love/ will you take it from me this
     one time/
please this is for you/ arsenio's tres cleared
     the way
& makes me pure again/ please please/ this
     is for you
i want you to love me/ let me love you/ i
     dont wanna
dance wit ghosts/ snuggle lovers i made up
     in my drunkenness/
lemme love you just like i am/ a colored
     girl/ i'm finally bein

real/ no longer symmetrical & impervious to
     pain

lady in blue
we deal wit emotion too much
so why dont we go on ahead & be white
     then/
& make everythin dry & abstract wit no
     rhythm & no
reelin for sheer sensual pleasure/ yes let's go
     on
& be white/ we're right in the middle of it/
     no use
holdin out/ holdin onto ourselves/ lets think
     our
way outta feelin/ lets abstract ourselves some
     families
& maybe maybe tonite/ i'll find a way to
     make myself
come witout you/ no fingers or other objects
     just thot
which isnt spiritual evolution cuz its empty
     & godliness
is plenty is ripe & fertile/ thinkin wont do
     me a bit of
good tonite/ i need to be loved/ & havent
     the audacity
to say
where are you/ & dont know who to say it
     to

lady in yellow
i've lost it
touch wit reality/ i dont know who's doin it
i thot i waz but i waz so stupid i waz able to
     be hurt
& that's not real/ not anymore/ i shd be
     immune/ if i'm
still alive & that's what i waz discussin/ how
     i am still
alive & my dependency on other livin beins
     for love
i survive on intimacy & tomorrow/ that's all
     i've got goin
& the music waz like smack & you knew
     abt that
& still refused my dance waz not enuf/ & it
     waz all i had
but bein alive & bein a woman & bein
     colored is a metaphysical
dilemma/ i havent conquered yet/ do you see
     the point
my spirit is too ancient to understand the
     separation of
soul & gender/ my love is too delicate to
     have thrown
back on my face

*The ladies in red, green, and brown enter
quietly; in the background all of the ladies
except the lady in yellow are frozen; the lady
in yellow looks at them, walks by them,
touches them; they do not move.*

   lady in yellow
my love is too delicate to have thrown back
     on my face

*The lady in yellow starts to exit into the
stage right volm. Just as she gets to the
volm, the lady in brown comes to life.*

   lady in brown
my love is too beautiful to have thrown back
     on my face

   lady in purple
my love is too sanctified to have thrown
     back on my face

   lady in blue
my love is too magic to have thrown back
     on my face

   lady in orange
my love is too saturday nite to have thrown
     back on my face

   lady in red
my love is too complicated to have thrown
     back on my face

   lady in green
my love is too music to have thrown back
     on my face

   everyone
music
music

*The lady in green then breaks into a dance,
the other ladies follow her lead and soon
they are all dancing and chanting together.*

   lady in green
yank dankka dank dank

   everyone
music

   lady in green
yank dankka dank dank

   everyone
music

   lady in green
yank dankka dank dank

   *everyone (but started by the lady in
     yellow)*
delicate
delicate
delicate

   *everyone (but started by the lady in
     brown)*
and beautiful
and beautiful
and beautiful

   *everyone (but started by the lady in
     purple)*
oh sanctified
oh sanctified
oh sanctified

   everyone (but started by the lady in blue)
magic
magic
magic

   *everyone (but started by the lady in
     orange)*
and saturday nite
and saturday nite
and saturday nite

   everyone (but started by the lady in red)
and complicated
and complicated
and complicated
and complicated
and complicated
and complicated
and complicated
and complicated

*The dance reaches a climax and all of the
ladies fall out tired, but full of life and
togetherness.*

   lady in green
somebody almost walked off wid alla my
     stuff
not my poems or a dance i gave up in the
     street
but somebody almost walked off wid alla my
     stuff
like a kleptomaniac workin hard & forgettin

while stealin
this is mine/ this aint yr stuff/
now why dont you put me back & let me
    hang out in my own self
somebody almost walked off wid alla my
    stuff
& didnt care enuf to send a note home sayin
i waz late for my solo conversation
or two sizes too small for my own tacky
    skirts
what can anybody do wit somethin of no
    value on
a open market/ did you getta dime for my
    things/
hey man/ where are you goin wid alla my
    stuff/
this is a woman's trip & i need my stuff/
to ohh & ahh abt/ daddy/ i gotta mainline
    number
from my own shit/ now wontchu put me
    back/ & let
me play this duet/ wit this silver ring in my
    nose/
honest to god/ somebody almost run off wit
    alla my stuff/
& i didnt bring anythin but the kick & sway
    of it
the perfect ass for my man & none of it is
    theirs
this is mine/ ntozake 'her own things'/ that's
    my name/
now give me my stuff/ i see ya hidin my
    laugh/ & how i
sit wif my legs open sometimes/ to give my
    crotch
some sunlight/ & there goes my love my
    toes my chewed
up finger nails/ niggah/ wif the curls in yr
    hair/
mr. louisiana hot link/ i want my stuff back/

my rhythms & my voice/ open my mouth/ &
    let me talk ya
outta/ throwin my shit in the sewar/ this is
    some delicate
leg & whimsical kiss/ i gotta have to give to
    my choice/
without you runnin off wit alla my shit/
now you cant have me less i give me away/
    & i waz
doin all that/ til ya run off on a good thing/
who is this you left me wit/ some simple
    bitch
widda bad attitude/ i wants my things/
i want my arm wit the hot iron scar/ & my
    leg wit the

flea bite/ i want my calloused feet & quik
    language back
in my mouth/ fried plantains/ pineapple pear
    juice/
sun-ra & joseph & jules/ i want my own
    things/ / how i lived them/
& give me my memories/ how i waz when i
    waz there/
you cant have them or do nothin wit them/
stealin my shit from me/ dont make it yrs/
    makes it stolen/
somebody almost run off wit alla my stuff/
    & i waz standin
there/ lookin at myself/ the whole time
& it waznt a spirit took my stuff/ waz a man
    whose
ego walked round like Rodan's shadow/ waz
    a man faster
n my innocence/ waz a lover/ i made too
    much
room for/ almost run off wit alla my stuff/
& i didnt know i'd give it up so quik/ & the
    one running wit it/
dont know he got it/ & i'm shoutin this is
    mine/ & he dont
know he got it/ my stuff is the anonymous
    ripped off treasure
of the year/ did you know somebody almost
    got away with me/
me in a plastic bag under their arm/ me
danglin on a string of personal carelessness/
    i'm spattered wit
mud & city rain/ & no i didnt get a chance
    to take a douche/
hey man/ this is not your perogative/ i gotta
    have me in my
pocket/ to get round like a good woman shd/
    & make the poem
in the pot or the chicken in the dance/ what i
    got to do/
i gotta have my stuff to do it to/
why dont ya find yr own things/ & leave this
    package
of me for my destiny/ what ya got to get
    from me/
i'll give it to ya/ yeh/ i'll give it to ya/
round 5:00 in the winter/ when the sky is
    blue-red/
& Dew City is gettin pressed/ if it's really
    my stuff/
ya gotta give it to me/ if ya really want it/
    i'm
the only one/ can handle it

lady in blue
that niggah will be back tomorrow, sayin

'i'm sorry'

lady in yellow
get this, last week my ol man came in sayin,
   'i don't know
how she got yr number baby, i'm sorry'

lady in brown
no this one is it, 'o baby, ya know i waz
   high, i'm sorry'

lady in purple
'i'm only human, and inadequacy is what
   makes us human, &
if we was perfect we wdnt have nothin to
   strive for, so you
might as well go on and forgive me pretty
   baby, cause i'm sorry'

lady in green
'shut up bitch, i told you i waz sorry'

lady in orange
no this one is it, 'i do ya like i do ya cause i
   thot
ya could take it, now i'm sorry'

lady in red
'now i know that ya know i love ya, but i
   aint ever gonna
love ya like ya want me to love ya, i'm
   sorry'

lady in blue
one thing i dont need
is any more apologies
i got sorry greetin me at my front door
you can keep yrs
i dont know what to do wit em
they dont open doors
or bring the sun back
they dont make me happy
or get a mornin paper
didnt nobody stop usin my tears to wash cars
cuz a sorry

i am simply tired
of collectin
   'i didnt know
     i was so important toyou'
i'm gonna haveta throw some away
i cant get to the clothes in my closet
for alla the sorries
i'm gonna tack a sign to my door
leave a message by the phone
   'if you called

to say yr sorry
call somebody
else
   i dont use em anymore'
i let sorry/ didnt meanta/ & how cd i know
   abt that
take a walk down a dark & musty street in
   brooklyn
i'm gonna do exactly what i want to
& i wont be sorry for none of it
letta sorry soothe yr soul/ i'm gonna soothe
   mine

you were always inconsistent
doin somethin & then bein sorry
beatin my heart to death
talkin bout you sorry
well
i will not call
i'm not goin to be nice
i will raise my voice
& scream & holler
& break things & race the engine
& tell all yr secrets bout yrself to yr face
& i will list in detail everyone of my
   wonderful lovers
& their ways
i will play oliver lake
loud
& i wont be sorry for none of it

i loved you on purpose
i was open on purpose
i still crave vulnerability & close talk
& i'm not even sorry bout you bein sorry
you can carry all the guilt & grime ya wanna
just dont give it to me
i cant use another sorry
next time
you should admit
you're mean/ low-down/ triflin/ & no count
   straight out
steada bein sorry alla the time
enjoy bein yrself

lady in red
there waz no air/ the sheets made ripples
   under his
body like crumpled paper napkins in a
   summer park/ & lil
specks of somethin from tween his toes or
   the biscuits
from the day before ran in the sweat that
   tucked the sheet
into his limbs like he waz an ol frozen
   bundle of chicken/

& he'd get up to make coffee, drink wine,
    drink water/ he
wished one of his friends who knew where
    he waz wd come by
with some blow or some sht/ anythin/ there
    waz no air/
he'd see the spotlights in the alleyways
    downstairs movin
in the air/ cross his wall over his face/ & get
    under the
covers & wait for an all clear or til he cd
    hear traffic
again/

there waznt nothin wrong with him/ there
    waznt nothin wrong
with him/ he kept tellin crystal/
any niggah wanna kill vietnamese children
    more n stay home
& raise his own is sicker than a rabid dog/
that's how their thing had been goin since he
    got back/
crystal just got inta sayin whatta fool niggah
    beau waz
& always had been/ didnt he go all over
    uptown sayin the
child waznt his/ waz some no counts
    bastard/ & any ol city
police cd come & get him if they wanted/
    cuz as soon as
the blood type & shit waz together/
    everybody wd know that
crystal waz a no good lyin whore/ and this
    after she'd been
his girl since she waz thirteen/ when he
    caught her
on the stairway/

he came home crazy as hell/ he tried to get
    veterans benefits
to go to school & they kept right on puttin
    him in
remedial classes/ he cdnt read wortha damn/
    so beau
cused the teachers of holdin him back & got
    himself
a gypsy cab to drive/ but his cab kept
    breakin
down/ & the cops was always messin wit
    him/ plus not
gettin much bread/

& crystal went & got pregnant again/ beau
    most beat
her to death when she tol him/ she still gotta
    scar

under her right tit where he cut her up/ still
    crystal
went right on & had the baby/ so now beau
    willie had
two children/ a little girl/ naomi kenya & a
    boy/ kwame beau
willie brown/ & there waz no air/

how in the hell did he get in this mess
    anyway/ somebody
went & tol crystal that beau waz spendin alla
    his money
on the bartendin bitch down at the merry-go-
    round cafe/
beau sat straight up in the bed/ wrapped up
    in the sheets
lookin like john the baptist or a huge baby
    wit stubble
& nuts/ now he hadta get alla that shit outta
    crystal's
mind/ so she wd let him come home/ crystal
    had gone &
got a court order saying beau willie brown
    had no access
to his children/ if he showed his face he waz
    subject
to arrest/ shit/ she'd been in his ass to marry
    her
since she waz 14 years old & here when she
    22/ she wanna
throw him out cuz he say he'll marry her/
    she burst
out laughin/ hollerin whatchu wanna marry
    me for now/
so i can support yr
ass/ or come sit wit ya when they lock yr
    behind
up/ cause they gonna come for ya/ ya
    goddamn lunatic/
they gonna come/ & i'm not gonna have a
    thing to do
wit it/ o no i wdnt marry yr pitiful black ass
    for
nothin & she went on to bed/

the next day beau willie came in blasted &
    got ta swingin
chairs at crystal/ who cdnt figure out what
    the hell
he waz doin/ til he got ta shoutin bout how
    she waz gonna
marry him/ & get some more veterans
    benefits/ & he cd
stop drivin them crazy spics round/ while
    they tryin
to kill him for $15/ beau waz sweatin

terrible/ beatin
on crystal/ & he cdnt do no more with the
   table n chairs/
so he went to get the high chair/ & lil
   kwame waz in it/
& beau waz beatin crystal with the high
   chair & her son/
& some notion got inta him to stop/ and he
   run out/

crystal most died/ that's why the police wdnt
   low
beau near where she lived/ & she'd been
   tellin the kids
their daddy tried to kill her & kwame/ & he
   just wanted
to marry her/ that's what/ he wanted to
   marry her/ &
have a family/ but the bitch waz crazy/ beau
   willie
waz sittin in this hotel in his drawers drinkin
coffee & wine in the heat of the day spillin
   shit all
over hisself/ laughin/ bout how he waz
   gonna get crystal
to take him back/ & let him be a man in the
   house/ & she
wdnt even have to go to work no more/ he
   got dressed
all up in his ivory shirt & checkered pants to
   go see
crystal & get this mess all cleared up/
he knocked on the door to crystal's rooms/
   & she
didnt answer/ he beat on the door & crystal
   & naomi
started cryin/ beau gotta shoutin again how
   he wanted
to marry her/ & waz she always gonna be a
   whore/ or
did she wanna husband/ & crystal just kept
   on
screamin for/ him to leave us alone/ just
   leave us
alone/ so beau broke the door down/ crystal
   held
the children in fronta her/ she picked kwame
   off the
floor/ in her arms/ & she held naomi by her
   shoulders/
& kept on sayin/ beau willie brown/ get
   outta here/
the police is gonna come for ya/ ya fool/ get
   outta here/
do you want the children to see you act the
   fool again/

you want kwame to brain damage from you
   throwin him
round/ niggah/ get outta here/ get out & dont
   show yr
ass again or i'll kill ya/ i swear i'll kill ya/
he reached for naomi/ crystal grabbed the lil
   girl &
stared at beau willie like he waz a leper or
   somethin/
dont you touch my children/ muthafucker/ or
   i'll kill
you/

beau willie jumped back all humble &
   apologetic/ i'm
sorry/ i dont wanna hurt em/ i just wanna
   hold em &
get on my way/ i dont wanna cuz you no
   more trouble/
i wanted to marry you & give ya things
what you gonna give/ a broken jaw/ niggah
   get outta here/
he ignored crystal's outburst & sat down
   motionin for
naomi to come to him/ she smiled back at
   her daddy/
crystal felt naomi givin in & held her
   tighter/
naomi/ pushed away & ran to her daddy/
   cryin/ daddy, daddy
come back daddy/ come back/ but be nice to
   mommy/
cause mommy loves you/ and ya gotta be
   nice/
he sat her on his knee/ & played with her
   ribbons &
they counted fingers & toes/ every so often
   he
looked over to crystal holdin kwame/ like a
   statue/
& he'd say/ see crystal/ i can be a good
   father/
now let me see my son/ & she didnt move/
   &
he coaxed her & he coaxed her/ tol her she
   waz
still a hot lil ol thing & pretty & strong/
   didnt
she get right up after that lil ol fight they
   had
& go back to work/ beau willie oozed
   kindness &
crystal who had known so lil/ let beau hold
   kwame/

as soon as crystal let the baby outta her

arms/ beau
jumped up a laughin & a gigglin/ a hootin &
    a hollerin/
awright bitch/ awright bitch/ you gonna
    marry me/
you gonna marry me . . .
i aint gonna marry ya/ i aint ever gonna
    marry ya/
for nothin/ you gonna be in the jail/ you
    gonna be
under the jail for this/ now gimme my kids/
    ya give
me back my kids/

he kicked the screen outta the window/ &
    held the kids
offa the sill/ you gonna marry me/ yeh, i'll
    marry ya/
anything/ but bring the children back in the
    house/
he looked from where the kids were hangin
    from the fifth
story/ at alla the people screamin at him/ &
he started sweatin again/ say to alla the
    neighbors/
you gonna marry me/

i stood by beau in the window/ with naomi
    reachin
for me/ & kwame screamin mommy mommy
    from the fifth
story/ but i cd only whisper/ & he dropped
    em

  lady in red
i waz missin somethin

  lady in purple
somethin so important

  lady in orange
somethin promised

  lady in blue
a layin on of hands

  lady in green
fingers near my forehead

  lady in yellow
strong

  lady in green
cool

  lady in orange
movin

  lady in purple
makin me whole

  lady in orange
sense

  lady in green
pure

  lady in blue
all the gods comin into me
layin me open to myself

  lady in red
i waz missin somethin

  lady in green
somethin promised

  lady in orange
somethin free

  lady in purple
a layin on of hands

  lady in blue
i know bout/ layin on bodies/ layin outta
    man
bringin him alla my fleshy self & some of
    my pleasure
bein taken full eager wet like i get
    sometimes
i waz missin somethin

  lady in purple
a layin on of hands

  lady in blue
not a man

  lady in yellow
layin on

  lady in purple
not my mama/ holdin me tight/ sayin
i'm always gonna be her girl
not a layin on of bosom & womb
a layin on of hands
the holiness of myself released

  lady in red
i sat up one nite walkin a boardin house
screamin/ cryin/ the ghost of another woman
who waz missin what i waz missin

i wanted to jump up outta my bones
& be done wit myself
leave me alone
& go on in the wind
it waz too much
i fell into a numbness
til the only tree i cd see
took me up in her branches
held me in the breeze
made me dawn dew
that chill at daybreak
the sun wrapped me up swingin rose light
    everywhere
the sky laid over me like a million men
i waz cold/ i waz burnin up/ a child
& endlessly weavin garments for the moon
wit my tears

i found god in myself
& i loved her/ i loved her fiercely

*All of the ladies repeat to themselves softly
the lines 'i found god in myself & i loved
her.' It soon becomes a song of joy, started
by the lady in blue. The ladies sing first to
each other, then gradually to the audience.
After the song peaks the ladies enter into a
closed tight circle.*

   lady in brown
& this is for colored girls who have
    considered
suicide/ but are movin to the ends of their
    own
rainbows

A Lovely Sunday for Creve Coeur

Tennessee Williams

First presented by Craig Anderson at the Hudson Guild Theatre in New York City on January 10, 1979, with the following cast:

(*in order of appearance*)

DOROTHEA	Shirley Knight
BODEY	Peg Murray
HELENA	Charlotte Moore
MISS GLUCK	Jan Lowry

Directed by Keith Hack
Scenery by John Conklin
Costumes by Linda Fisher
Lighting by Craig Miller

The career of Tennessee Williams is too well known in the theatre to require the extensive notice it is possible to give it. A brief recapitulation for the record would say that he was born in Columbus, Mississippi, in 1914, the son of mismatched parents, the mother a cultivated woman and daughter of an Episcopalian clergyman, the father a more or less typical American go-getter who would have preferred to get his son into business and into general conformity with Main Street. The family tension, also reflected in the disturbed character of a loved sister long ago institutionalized, has been variously translated and transmuted in the body of Mr. Williams' work.

After a rather desultory education in St. Louis, where he spent much of his youth, and graduation from the State University of Iowa, he clerked in a shoe factory, operated an elevator in an office, and worked in hotels, movie houses, and restaurants. His first professionally produced play, *Battle of Angels,* was completed in an advanced seminar for playwrights given in 1940 by Theresa Helburn and John Gassner, both the Theatre Guild. It was quickly optioned for production by the Guild and assigned to Margaret Webster to direct—no doubt as a tribute to her success in staging poetic drama ever since her superb *Richard II* production with Maurice Evans excelling in the title role. Although the play, owing to a series of difficulties during the tryout in Boston, was not brought to New York, Tennessee Williams, who had been writing fiction, verse, and drama assiduously since boyhood, proceeded to dramatize a D. H. Lawrence story with a friend, Donald Windham. The play, called *You Touched Me,* was staged by the late Guthrie McClintic with his customary skill and sensitivity, and had a moderate run on Broadway. But the author's fortunes first underwent a change for the better and his enormous talent first won general recognition in 1945 with the Eddie Dowling production of *The Glass Menagerie,* starring Laurette Taylor.

Thereafter, he moved from success to success, attaining worldwide repute with *A Streetcar Named Desire* (1947), *Summer and Smoke* (1948), *The Rose Tattoo* (1951), *Cat on a Hot Tin Roof* (1955), and *The Night of the Iguana* (1962), and receiving qualified appreciation for several other long plays (*Camino Real, Orpheus Descending, Sweet Bird of Youth, Period of Adjustment*) and a few remarkable one-acters. *The Milk Train Doesn't Stop Here Anymore,* too hastily thrust on Broadway after a tryout production at the Spoleto Festival in Italy in 1962, disappointed his friends and pleased the growing number of his detractors.

The Night of the Iguana is the expanded version of the shorter play tried out at the Spoleto Festival the summer before, but the author's essential concept remained unchanged. The defeated characters with whom the playwright symphathizes are entrapped by life like the iguana of the title—the lizard captured and tormented by the natives of Acapulco and kept overnight for eating the next day. "Eating" has preyed on the author's mind, as may be seen also in the cannibalism theme of *Suddenly Last Summer,* produced during the same period. Symbol-hunting critics and amateur psychoanalysts are welcome to make of this what they will, so far as I am concerned. The effectiveness of the play comes in any case not from the author's perfunctory treatment of the "eaters" but from the nature of those who are "eaten," and effectiveness stems as much from the life of these characters as from their author's dramatic skill and poetic imagination. The corrective for overpraise of the author's dramatic impact may well be Alan Downer's trenchant compaint that "Williams has become a kind of latter-day Belasco with his genius for making effective theatrical statements of the intellectual clichés of the day." (*Quarterly Journal of Speech,* October 1962, p. 265.) I take it that Mr. Downer had in mind chiefly the reliance on sexual motivations and relationships as exemplified in the current offering, *A Lovely Summer for Creve Coeur.* The corrective to undervaluing the author's atmospheric power and suggestiveness might be the reflection that in the American theatre very few playwrights have even approached Tennessee Williams' ability to make one feel that the theatre is a form of poetry no matter how much melodramatic motion it entails. His death in 1983 leaves an incalculable gap for all of us.

SCENE ONE

It is late on a Sunday morning, early June, in St. Louis.

The interior is what was called an efficiency apartment in the period of this play, the middle or late thirties. It is in the West End of St. Louis. Attempts to give the apartment brightness and cheer have gone brilliantly and disastrously wrong, and this wrongness is emphasized by the fiercely yellow glare of light through the oversize windows which look out upon vistas of surrounding apartment buildings, vistas that suggest the paintings of Ben Shahn: the dried-blood horror of lower middle-class American urban neighborhoods. The second thing which assails our senses is a combination of counting and panting from the bedroom, to the left, where a marginally youthful but attractive woman, Dorothea, is taking "setting-up exercises" with fearful effort.

SOUND. Ninety-one, *ha!*—ninety-two, *ha!*—ninety-three, *ha!*—ninety-four, *ha!*

This breathless counting continues till one hundred is achieved with a great gasp of deliverance. At some point during the counting, a rather short, plumpish woman, early middle-aged, has entered from the opposite doorway with a copy of the big Sunday St. Louis Post-Dispatch.

The phone rings just as Bodey, who is hard-of-hearing, sits down on a sofa in the middle of the room. Bodey, absorbed in the paper, ignores the ringing phone, but it has caused Dorothea to gasp with emotion so strong that she is physically frozen except for her voice. She catches hold of something for a moment, as if reeling in a storm, then plunges to the bedroom door and rushes out into the living room with a dramatic door-bang.

DOROTHEA. WHY DIDN'T YOU GET THAT PHONE?

BODEY *(rising and going to the kitchenette at the right)*. Where, where, what, what phone?

DOROTHEA. Is there more than one phone here? Are there several other phones I haven't discovered as yet?

BODEY. —Dotty, I think these setting-up exercises get you overexcited, emotional, I mean.

DOROTHEA *(continuing)*. That phone was ringing and I told you when I woke up that I was expecting a phone call from Ralph Ellis who told me he had something very important to tell me and would phone me today before noon.

BODEY. Sure, he had something to tell you but he didn't.

DOROTHEA. Bodey, you are not hearing, or comprehending, what I'm saying at all. Your face is a dead giveaway. I said Ralph Ellis—you've heard me speak of Ralph?

BODEY. Oh, yes, Ralph, you speak continuously of him, that name Ralph Ellis is one I got fixed in my head so I could never forget it.

DOROTHEA. Oh, you mean I'm not permitted to mention the name Ralph Ellis to you?

BODEY *(preparing fried chicken in the kitchenette)*. Dotty, when two girls are sharing a small apartment, naturally each of the girls should feel prefectly free to speak of whatever concerns her. I don't think it's possible for two girls sharing a small apartment *not* to speak of whatever concerns her whenever—whatever—*concerns* her, but, Dotty, I know that I'm not your older sister. However, if I was, I would have a suspicion that you have got a crush on this Ralph Ellis, and as an older sister, I'd feel obliged to advise you to, well, look before you leap in that direction. I mean just don't put all your eggs in one basket till you are one hundred percent convinced that the basket is the right one, that's all I mean. . . . Well, this is a lovely Sunday for a picnic at Creve Coeur. . . . Didn't you notice out at Creve Coeur last Sunday how Buddy's slimmed down round the middle?

DOROTHEA. No, I didn't.

BODEY. Huh?

DOROTHEA. Notice.

BODEY. Well, it was noticeable, Dotty.

DOROTHEA. Bodey, why should I be interested in whatever fractional—fluctuations—occur in your twin brother's waistline—as if it was the Wall Street market and I was a heavy investor?

BODEY. You mean you don't care if Buddy shapes up or not?

DOROTHEA. Shapes up for what?

BODEY. Nacherly for you, Dotty.

DOROTHEA. Does he regard me as an athletic event, the high jump or pole vault? Please, please, Bodey, convince him his shape does not concern me at all.

BODEY. Buddy don't discuss his work with me often, but lately he said his boss at Anheuser-Busch has got an eye on him.

DOROTHEA. How could his boss ignore such a sizeable object?—Bodey, what are you up to in that cute little kitchenette?

BODEY. Honey, I stopped by Piggly-Wiggly's yesterday noon when I got off the streetcar on the way home from the office, and I picked up three beautiful fryers, you know, nice and plump fryers.

DOROTHEA. I'd better remain out here till Ralph calls back, so I can catch it myself. *(She lies on the purple carpet and begins another series of formalized exercises.)*

BODEY. The fryers are sizzling so loud I didn't catch that, Dotty. You know, now that the office lets out at noon Saturday, it's easier to lay in supplies for Sunday. I think that Roosevelt did something for the country when he got us half Saturdays off because it used to be that by the time I got off the streetcar from International Shoe, Piggly-Wiggly's on the corner would be closed, but now it's still wide open. So I went in Piggly-Wiggly's, I went to the meat department and I said to the nice old man, Mr. Butts, the butcher, "Mr. Butts, have you got any real nice fryers?"—"You bet your life!" he said, "I must of been expectin' you to drop in. Feel these nice plump fryers." Mr. Butts always lets me feel his meat. The feel of a piece of meat is the way to test it, but there's very few modern butchers will allow you to feel it. It's the German in me. I got to feel the meat to know it's good. A piece of meat can look good over the counter but to know for sure I always want to feel it. Mr. Butts, being German, he understands that, always says to me, "Feel it, go on, feel it." So I felt the fryers. "Don't they feel good and fresh?" I said, "Yes, Mr. Butts, but will they keep till tomorrow?" "Haven't you got any ice in your icebox?" he asked me. I said to him, "I hope so, but ice goes fast in hot weather. I told the girl that shares my apartment with me to put up the card for a twenty-five pound lump of ice but sometimes she forgets to." Well, thank goodness, this time you didn't forget to. You always got so much on your mind in the morning, civics and—other things at the high school.—What are you laughin' at, Dotty? *(She turns around to glance at Dorothea who is covering her mouth to stifle breathless sounds of laughter.)*

DOROTHEA. Honestly, Bodey, I think you missed your calling. You should be in Congress to deliver a filibuster. I never knew it was possible to talk at such length about ice and a butcher.

BODEY. Well, Dotty, you know we agreed when you moved in here with me that I would take care of the shopping. We've kept good books on expenses. Haven't we kept good books? We've never had any argument over expense or disagreements between us over what I should shop for.—OW!

DOROTHEA. Now what?

BODEY. The skillet spit at me. Some hot grease flew in my face. I'll put bakin' soda on it.

DOROTHEA. So you are really and truly frying chickens in this terrible heat?

BODEY. And boiling eggs, I'm going to make deviled eggs, too. Dotty, what is it? You sound hysterical, Dotty!

DOROTHEA *(half strangled with laughter)*. Which came first, fried chicken or deviled eggs?—I swear to goodness, you do the funniest things. Honestly, Bodey, you are a source of continual astonishment and amusement to me. Now, Bodey, please suspend this culinary frenzy until the phone rings again so you can hear it this time before it stops ringing for me.

BODEY. Dotty, I was right here and that phone was not ringin'. I give you my word that phone was not makin' a sound. It was quiet as a mouse.

DOROTHEA. Why, it was ringing its head off!

BODEY. Dotty, about some things everyone is mistaken, and this is something you are mistaken about. I think your exercises give you a ringing noise in your head. I think they're too strenuous for you, 'specially on Sunday, a day of rest, recreation . . .

DOROTHEA. We are both entitled to separate opinions, Bodey, but I assure you I do not suffer from ringing in my head. That phone was RINGING. And why you did not hear it is simply because you don't have your hearing aid on!

(The shouting is congruent with the fiercely bright colors of the interior.)

BODEY. I honestly ain't that deaf. I swear I ain't that deaf, Dotty. The ear specialist says I just got this little calcification, this calcium in my—eardrums. But I do hear a telephone ring, a sharp, loud sound like that, I hear it, I hear it clearly.

DOROTHEA. Well, let's hope Ralph won't imagine I'm out and will call back in a while. But do put your hearing aid in. I don't share your confidence in your hearing a phone ring or a dynamite blast without it, and anyway, Bodey, you must adjust to it, you must get used to it, and after a while, when you're accustomed to it, you won't feel complete without it.

BODEY. —Yes, well—This is the best Sunday yet for a picnic at Creve Coeur . . .

DOROTHEA. That we'll talk about later. Just put your hearing aid in before I continue with my exercises. Put it in right now so I can see you.

BODEY. You still ain't finished with those exercises?

DOROTHEA. I've done one hundred bends and I did my floor exercises. I just have these bust development exercises and my swivels and—BODEY! PUT YOUR HEARING AID IN!

BODEY. I hear you, honey, I will. I'll put it on right now.

(She comes into the living room from the kitchenette and picks up the hearing aid and several large artificial flowers from a table. She hastily moves the newspaper from the sofa to a chair behind her, then inserts the device in an ear with an agonized look.)

DOROTHEA. It can't be that difficult to insert it. Why, from your expression, you could be performing major surgery on yourself! . . . without anesthesia . . .

BODEY. It'm just—not used to it yet. *(She covers the defective ear with an artificial chrysanthemum.)*

DOROTHEA *(in the doorway)*. You keep reminding yourself of it by covering it up with those enormous artificial flowers. Now if you feel you have to do that, why don't you pick out a flower that's suitable to the season? Chrysanthemums are for autumn and this is June.

BODEY. Yes. June. How about this poppy?

DOROTHEA. Well, frankly, dear, that big poppy is tacky.

BODEY. —The tiger lily?

DOROTHEA *(despairing)*. Yes, the tiger lily! Of course, Bodey, the truth of the matter is that your idea of concealing your hearing aid with a big artificial flower is ever so slightly fantastic.

BODEY. —Everybody is sensitive about something . . .

DOROTHEA. But complexes, obsessions must not be cultivated. Well. Back to my exercises. Be sure not to miss the phone. Ralph is going to call me any minute now. *(She starts to close the bedroom door.)*

BODEY. Dotty?

DOROTHEA. Yes?

BODEY. Dotty, I'm gonna ask Buddy to go to Creve Coeur with us again today for the picnic. That's okay with you, huh?

DOROTHEA *(pausing in the doorway)*. Bodey, Buddy is your brother and I fully understand your attachment to him. He's got many fine things about him. A really solid character and all that. But, Bodey, I think it's unfair to Buddy for you to go on attempting to bring us together because—well, everyone has a type she is attracted to and in the case of Buddy, no matter how much—I appreciate his sterling qualities and all, he simply isn't—*(She has gone into the bedroom and started swiveling her hips.)*

BODEY. Isn't what, Dotty?

DOROTHEA. A type that I can respond to. You know what I mean. In a romantic fashion, honey. And to me—romance is—essential.

BODEY. Oh—but—well, there's other things to consider besides—romance . . .

DOROTHEA *(swiveling her hips as she talks)*. Bodey, can you honestly feel that Buddy and I are exactly right for each other? Somehow I suspect that Buddy would be better looking about for a steady, German-type girl in South St. Louis—a girl to drink beer with and eat Wiener schnitzel and get fat along with him, not a girl—well, a girl already romantically—pour me a little more coffee? —Thanks. — Why do you keep forgetting the understanding between me and Mr. Ellis? Is that fair to Buddy? To build up his hopes for an inevitable letdown?

(Dorothea stops her swivels and returns to the living room to get the coffee Bodey has poured for her.)

BODEY. This Mr. T. Ralph Ellis, well . . .

DOROTHEA. Well, *what?*

BODEY. Nothing except . . .

DOROTHEA. *What?*

BODEY. He might not be as reliable as Buddy—in the long run.

DOROTHEA. What is "the long run," honey?

BODEY. The long run is—*life.*

DOROTHEA. Oh, so that is the long run, the long run is life! With Buddy? Well, then give the the short run, I'm sorry, but I'll take the short run, much less exhausting in the heat of the day and the night!

BODEY. Dotty, I tell you, Dotty, in the long run or the short run I'd place my bet on Buddy, not on a—fly-by-night sort of proposition like this, this—romantic idea you got about a man that mostly you see wrote up in—society pages . . .

DOROTHEA. *That is your misconception!* — Of something about which you are in total ignorance, because I rarely step out of the civics classroom at Blewett without seeing Ralph

Ellis a few steps down the corridor, pretending to take a drink at the water cooler on my floor which is two floors up from his office!

BODEY. Not really taking a drink but just pretending? Not a good sign, Dotty—pretending . . .

DOROTHEA. What I mean is—we have to arrange secret little encounters of this sort to avoid gossip at Blewett.

BODEY. —Well—

DOROTHEA. *WHAT?*

BODEY. I never trusted pretending.

DOROTHEA. Then why the paper flowers over the hearing aid, dear?

BODEY. That's—just—a little—sensitivity, there . . .

DOROTHEA. Look, you've got to live with it so take off the concealment, the paper tiger lily, and turn the hearing aid up or I will be obliged to finish my hip swivels out here to catch Ralph's telephone call.

BODEY *(as she is turning up the hearing aid, it makes a shrill sound).* See? See?

DOROTHEA. I think you mean hear, hear! —Turn it down just a bit, find the right level for it!

BODEY. Yes, yes, I—*(She fumbles with the hearing aid, dislodging the paper flower.)*

DOROTHEA. For heaven's sake, let me adjust it for you! *(She rushes over to Bodey and fiddles with the hearing aid.)* Now! —Not shrieking. —But can you hear me? I said can you hear me! At this level!?

BODEY. Yes. Where's my tiger lily?

DOROTHEA. Dropped on the fierce purple carpet. Here. *(She picks it up and hands it to Bodey.)* What's wrong with you?

BODEY. I'm—upset. Over this maybe—dangerous—trust you've got in Ralph Ellis's—intentions . . .

DOROTHEA *(dreamily, eyes going soft).* I don't like discussing an intimate thing like this but—the last time I went out in Ralph Ellis's Reo, that new sedan he's got called the Flying Cloud . . .

BODEY. Cloud? Flying?

DOROTHEA *(raising her voice to a shout).* The Reo is advertised as "The Flying Cloud."

BODEY. Oh. Yes. He'd be attracted to that.

DOROTHEA. It was pouring down rain and Art Hill was deserted, no other cars on it but Ralph and I in his Reo. The windows curtained with rain that glistened in the lamplight.

BODEY. Dotty, I hope you're not leading up to something that shouldn't of happened in this Flying Cloud on Art Hill. It really scares me, Dotty . . .

DOROTHEA. Frankly, I was a little frightened myself because—we've never had this kind of discussion before, it's rather—difficult for me but you must understand. I've always drawn a strict line with a man till this occasion.

BODEY. Dotty, do you mean—?

DOROTHEA. It was so magical to me, the windows curtained with rain, the soft look in his eyes, the warmth of this breath that's always scented with clove, his fingers touching so gently as he—

BODEY. Dotty, I don't think I want to know any more about this—experience on Art Hill because, because—I got a suspicion, Dotty, that you didn't hold the line with him.

DOROTHEA. The line just—didn't exist when he parked the car and turned and looked at me and I turned and looked at him. Our eyes, our eyes—

BODEY. Your eyes?

DOROTHEA. Burned the line out of existence, like it had never existed!

BODEY. —I'm not gonna tell this to Buddy!

DOROTHEA. You know, I wasn't aware until then that the Reo was equipped with adjustable seats.

BODEY. Seats that—?

DOROTHEA. Adjusted to pressure, yes, reclined beneath me when he pushed a lever.

BODEY *(distracted from the phonebook which she had begun to leaf through).* —How far did this seat recline beneath you, Dotty?

DOROTHEA. Horizontally, nearly. So gradually though that I didn't know till later, later. Later, not then—the earth was whirling beneath me and the sky was spinning above.

BODEY. Oh-ho, he got you drunk, did he, with a flask of liquor in that Flying Cloud on—

DOROTHEA. Drunk on a single Pink Lady?

BODEY. Pink?

DOROTHEA. Lady. —The mildest sort of cocktail! Made with sloe gin and grenadine.

BODEY. The gin was slow, maybe, but that man is a fast one, seducing a girl with adjustable seats and a flask of liquor in that Flying Cloud on—

DOROTHEA. Not a flask, a cocktail, and not in the Reo but in a small private club called The Onyx, a club so exclusive he had to present an engraved card at the entrance.

BODEY. Oh yes, I know such places!

DOROTHEA. How would you know such places?

BODEY. I seen one at the movies and so did you, at the West End Lyric, the last time you was all broke up from expectin' a call from this Ellis which never came in, so we seen Roy D'Arcy take poor Janet Gaynor to one of them—private clubs to—!

(Bodey has not found the Blewett number in the phonebook. She dials the operator.)

Blewett, Blewett, get me the high school named Blewett.

DOROTHEA. Bodey, what are you doing at the phone which I begged you not to use till Ralph called?

BODEY. Reporting him to Blewett!

DOROTHEA. Bodey, that takes the cake, reporting on the principal of Blewett to Blewett that's closed on Sundays. What a remarkable—

BODEY *(darting about)*. Paper, pen!

DOROTHEA. Now what?

BODEY. A written report to the Board of Education of St. Louis. I tell you, the Board will be interested in all details of how that principal of the school system got you lying down drunk and defenseless in his Flying Cloud in a storm on Art Hill, every advantage taken with Valentino sheik tricks on a innocent teacher of civics just up from Memphis.

DOROTHEA. YOU WILL NOT—

BODEY. DON'T TELL ME NOT!

DOROTHEA. LIBEL THE REPUTATION OF A MAN THAT I LOVE, GAVE MYSELF TO NOT JUST FREELY BUT WITH ABANDON, WITH JOY!

BODEY *(aloud as she writes)*. Board of Education of St. Louis, Missouri. I think you should know that your principal at Blewett used his position to take disgusting advantage of a young teacher employed there by him for that purpose. I know, I got the facts, including the date and—

(Dorothea snatches up and crumples the letter.)

My letter, you tore up my—!

DOROTHEA. Bodey, if you had written and mailed that letter, do you know what you'd have obliged me to do? I would be morally obliged to go personally down to the Board of Education and tell them an *opposite* story which happens to be the *true* one; that I *desired* Ralph Ellis, possibly even more than he did me!

(Bodey huffs and puffs wordlessly till she can speak.)

BODEY. —Well, God help you, Dotty. — But I give you my word I won't repeat this to Buddy.

DOROTHEA. How does it concern Buddy?

BODEY. It concerns Buddy and me because Buddy's got deep feelings and respect for you,

Dotty. He would respect you too much to cross the proper line before you had stood up together in the First Lutheran Church on South Grand.

DOROTHEA. Now you *admit* it!

BODEY. It's you that's makin' admissions of a terrible kind that might shock Buddy out of his serious intentions.

DOROTHEA. You are admitting that—

(As she had threatened, Dorothea has begun doing her hip swivels in the living room, but now she stops and stares indignantly at Bodey.)

—you've been deliberately planning and plotting to marry me off to your twin brother so that my life would be just one long Creve Coeur picnic, interspersed with knockwurst, sauerkraut—hot potato salad dinner.—Would I be asked to prepare them? Even in summer? I know what you Germans regard as the limits, the boundaries of a woman's life—*Kirche, Küche, und Kinder*—while being asphyxiated gradually by cheap cigars. I'm sorry but the life I design for myself is not along those lines or in those limits. My life must include romance. Without romance in my life, I could no more live than I could without breath. I've got to find a partner in life, or my life will having no meaning. But what I must have and finally do have is an affair of the heart, two hearts, a true consummated romance—yes consummated, I'm not ashamed! *(She gasps and sways.)*

BODEY. Dotty, Dotty, set down and catch your breath!

DOROTHEA. In this breathless efficiency apartment? —I've got to have space in my life.

BODEY. —Did I tell you that Buddy has made a down payment on a Buick?

DOROTHEA. No, you didn't and why should you, as it does not concern—Oh, my God, Blessed Savior!

BODEY. Dotty, what Dotty? D'you want your, your whatamacallit tablets?

DOROTHEA. Mebaral? No, I have not collapsed yet, but you've just about driven me to it.

BODEY. Take a breather, take a seventh inning stretch while I—

DOROTHEA. Bodey, this room is GLARING; it's not cheerful but GLARING!

BODEY. Stretch out on the sofa and look up, the ceiling is white!

DOROTHEA. I don't know why I'm so out of breath today.

BODEY. Don't do no more exercises. You drink too much coffee an' Cokes. That's stimulants for a girl high-strung like you. With a nervous heart condition.

DOROTHEA. It's functional—not nervous.

BODEY. Lie down a minute.

DOROTHEA. I will rest a little—but not because you say so. *(Between gasps she sinks into a chair.)* You're very bossy—and very inquisitive, too.

BODEY. I'm older'n you, and I got your interests at heart.

DOROTHEA. Whew!

BODEY. Think how cool it will be on the open-air streetcar to Creve Coeur.

DOROTHEA. You must have had your hearing off when I said I had other plans.

BODEY. Buddy, I been telling Buddy to cut down on his beer, and Buddy is listening to me. He's cut down to eight a day—from a dozen and will cut down more . . .

DOROTHEA. Bodey, could you stop talking about Buddy this hot Sunday morning? It's not a suitable subject for hot weather. I know brother-sister relationships are deep, but it's not just the beer, it's the almost total lack of interests in common, no topics of conversations, of—of mutual—interest.

BODEY. They could develop. I know Buddy just feels embarrassed. He hasn't opened up yet. Give him time and he will.

DOROTHEA. Bodey, this discussion is embarrassingly pointless in view of the fact that I'm already committed to Ralph Ellis. I still have to do my hip swivels . . .

(Sipping coffee as she goes, Dorothea returns to the bedroom and resumes her exercises.)

BODEY *(rushing to the phone)*. Olive 2697, Olive 2697! Buddy? Me! *Grosser Gott!* I can't talk now, but you absolutely got to go to Creve Coeur with us this Sunday. —Dress good! Don't smoke cigars! And laugh at her witty remarks. —Well, they *are,* they're witty! She teaches *civics.*

(The doorbell rings.)

Now be at the Creve Coeur station at 1:30, huh? —Please!—Somebody's at the door, I can't talk now. *(Leaving the phone off the hook, she rushes to the door and opens it.)* Oh. Hello.

HELENA. Good morning.

BODEY. Are you a friend of Dotty's?

(A stylishly dressed woman with the eyes of a predatory bird appears.)

HELENA. Of Dorothea's? —Yes

BODEY. Well, then come on in. Any friend of Dotty's is a friend of mine.

HELENA. Is that so?

BODEY *(discomfited)*. Yes, I—got grease on my hand. I was fryin' up some chickens for a picnic.

HELENA. —Well! This is a surprise! *(She makes several turns in a mechanical, rigid fashion, eyes staring.)*

BODEY. Excuse me, I should of—interduced myself.

HELENA. You are Miss Bodenheifer.

BODEY. Hafer, not heifer. *(She laughs nervously.)* Heifer meaning a cow.

HELENA. No conscious association whatsoever. *(She advances forward a step.)* So this is Schlogger Haven?

BODEY. Oh, Schlogger Haven, that's just a joke of Dotty's. The landlord's name is Schlogger, that's all—that's all . . .

HELENA. Dorothea was joking, was she?

BODEY. Yes, she jokes a lot, full of humor. We have lots of laughs. *(Bodey extends her hand.)*

HELENA. I can imagine you might, Miss Bodenheifer.

BODEY. You can forget the Miss. —Everyone at the office calls me Bodey.

HELENA. But we are not at the office—we are here in Schlogger Haven. *(She continues enigmatically.)* Hmmm . . . I've never ventured this side of Blewett before.

BODEY. Never gone downtown?

HELENA. I do nearly all my shopping in the West End, so naturally it amazed me to discover street after street without a shade tree on it, and the glare, the glare, and the heat refracted by all the brick, concrete, asphalt— was so overpowering that I nearly collapsed. I think I must be afflicted with a combination of photo- and heliophobia, both.

BODEY *(unconsciously retreating a step as if fearing contagion)*. I never heard of neither—but you got *both?*

HELENA. An exceptional sensitivity to both heat and strong light.

BODEY. Aw.

HELENA. Yes. Now would you please let Dorothea know I'm here to see her?

BODEY. Does Dotty expect you, Miss, uh—

HELENA. Helena Brookmire, no, she doesn't expect me, but a very urgent business matter has obliged me to drop by this early.

BODEY. She won't have no one in there with her. She's exercising.

HELENA. But Dorothea and I are well acquainted.

BODEY. Well acquainted or not acquainted at all, makes no difference. I think that modern girls emphasize too much these advertised treatments and keep their weight down too much for their health.

HELENA. The preservation of youth requires some sacrifices.

(She continues to stare about her, blinking her birdlike eyes as if dazzled.)

BODEY. —I guess you and Dotty teach together at Blewett High?

HELENA. —Separately.

BODEY. You mean you're not at Blewett where Dotty teaches civics?

HELENA *(as if addressing a backward child).* I teach there, too. When I said separately, I meant we teach separate classes.

BODEY. Oh, naturally, yes. *(She tries to laugh.)* I been to high school.

HELENA. Have you?

BODEY. Yes. I know that two teachers don't teach in the same class at the same time, on two different subjects.

HELENA *(opening her eyes very wide).* Wouldn't *that* be peculiar.

BODEY. Yes. That would be peculiar.

HELENA *(chuckling unpleasantly).* It might create some confusion among the students.

BODEY. Yes, I reckon it would.

HELENA. Especially if the subjects were as different as civics and the history of *art.*

(Bodey attempts to laugh again; Helena imitates the laugh almost exactly. Pause)

That *is,* it really *is!*

BODEY. Is *what?*

HELENA. The most remarkable room that I've ever stepped into! Especially the combination of colors! Such a *vivid* contrast! May I sit down?

BODEY. Yeh, yeh, excuse me, I'm not myself today. It's the heat and the—

HELENA. Colors? —The vivid contrast of colors? *(She removes a pair of round, white-rimmed dark glasses from her purse and puts them on.)* Did Dorothea assist you, Miss Bodenheifer, in decorating this room?

BODEY. No, when Dotty moved in, it was just like it is now.

HELENA. Then you are solely responsible for this inspired selection of colors?

(There is a loud sputter of hot fat from the kitchenette.)

BODEY. Excuse me a moment, I got to turn over the fryers in the skillet.

HELENA. Don't let me interrupt your preparations for a picnic.

BODEY. Didn't catch that. I don't hear good sometimes.

HELENA. Oh?

BODEY. You see, I got this calcium deposit in my ears . . . and they advised me to have an operation, but it's very expensive for me and sometimes it don't work.

PHONE VOICE. Booow-deee!

(Helena notices but doesn't comment on the unhooked phone.)

HELENA. I would advice you against it. I had an elderly acquaintance who had this calcification problem and she had a hole bored in her skull to correct it. The operation is called fenestration—it involves a good deal of danger and whether or not it was successful could not be determined since she never recovered consciousness.

BODEY. Never recovered?

HELENA. Consciousness.

BODEY. Yeh, well, I think maybe I'd better learn to live with it.

PHONE VOICE *(shouting again).* Bodeyyyyy—Bodeyyyy—

BODEY. What's that?

HELENA. I was wondering, too. Very strange barking sounds are coming out of the phone.

BODEY *(laughing).* Oh, God, I left it unhooked. *(She snatches it up.)* Buddy, sorry, somebody just dropped in, forgot you was still on the line. Buddy, call me back in a few minutes, huh, Buddy, it's, uh, very important. *(She hangs up the phone.)* That was my brother. Buddy. He says he drunk two beers and made him a liverwurst sandwich before I got back to the phone. Thank God he is so good-natured. . . . He and me are going out on a picnic at Creve Coeur with Dotty this afternoon. My brother is very interested in Dotty.

HELENA. Interested? Romantically?

BODEY. Oh, yes, Buddy's a very serious person.

HELENA *(rising).* —I am very impressed!

BODEY. By what, what by?

HELENA *(with disguised fury).* The ingenuity with which you've fitted yourself into this limited space. Every inch seems to be utilized by some appliance or—*decoration? (She picks up a large painted china frog.)* —A frahg?

BODEY. Yes, frawg.

HELENA. So realistically colored and designed you'd almost expect it to croak. —Oh, and you have a canary . . . stuffed!

BODEY. Little Hilda . . . she lived ten years. That's the limit for a canary.

HELENA. Limit of longevity for the species?

BODEY. She broke it by three months.

HELENA. Establishing a record. It's quite

heroic, enduring more than ten years in such confinement. What tenacity to existence some creature do have!

BODEY. I got so attached to it, I took it to a, a—

HELENA. Taxidermist.

BODEY. Excuse me a moment. *(She rushes to the stove in the alcove.)* OW!—Got burnt again.

HELENA *(following curiously).* You were burnt before?

(Bodey profusely powders her arms with baking soda. Helena backs away.)

Miss Bodenheifer, *please!* You've sprinkled my clothes with that powder!

BODEY. Sorry, I didn't mean to.

HELENA. Intentional or not, I'm afraid you have! May I have a clothes brush?

BODEY. Look at that, I spilt it on the carpet. *(She rushes to fetch a broom.)*

HELENA. Miss Bodenheifer, I WOULD LIKE A CLOTHES BRUSH, IF YOU HAVE A *CLOTHES* BRUSH! Not a broom. I am not a carpet.

BODEY. AW. SURE. Dotty's got a clothes brush. Oh. Help yourself to some coffee. *(She drops the broom and enters the bedroom.)*

(Through the open door, Dorothea can be heard counting as she swivels.)

DOROTHEA'S VOICE. Sixty, *ha!* Sixty-one, *ha! (She continues counting but stops when she notices Bodey.)* —The PHONE? Is it the PHONE?

BODEY. Clothes brush. *(Bodey closes the bedroom door and begins opening and shutting drawers as she looks for the clothes brush.)*

DOROTHEA. DON'T, DON'T, DON'T— slam a drawer shut like that! I feel like screaming!

(Helena opens a closet in the kitchenette; a box falls out.)

HELENA. The hazards of this place almost equal the horrors.

DOROTHEA *(in the bedroom).* I asked you if the phone rang.

BODEY. No, no, the doorbell.

HELENA *(who has moved to the icebox).* Ah. Ice, mostly melted, what squalor!

(This dual scene must be carefully timed.)

DOROTHEA. I presume it's Miss Gluck from upstairs in boudoir cap and wrapper. Bodey, get her out as quickly as possible. The sight of that woman destroys me for the whole day.

HELENA *(still in the kitchenette).* This remnant of ice will not survive in this steaming glass of coffee.

(A knock at the door is heard.)

What's that?

(Sophie Gluck opens the front door and sticks her head in. At the sight of Helena, she withdraws in alarm.)

Another tenant. *Demented!*

(Helena moves to the door and slams and bolts it with such force that Sophie, outside, utters a soft cry of confused panic.)

BODEY. Don't do no more calisthenics if it affects you this way.

DOROTHEA. Just, just—knock at the door when Miss Gluck has gone back upstairs, that's my—whew!—only—request . . .

BODEY. —Yes, well . . .

DOROTHEA. No coffee, no crullers or she— will stay—down here—forever—ha!

(The phone rings; Helena picks it up. Bodey emerges from the bedroom with a whisk broom, closing the door behind her. Helena is at the phone.)

HELENA. Oh, she seems engaged for the moment . . .

BODEY. Aw, the phone! Is it that principal, Ellis?

HELENA *(aside from the phone).* I'm afraid not. It seems to be Dorothea's other admirer— *quel embarras de richesses . . .*

BODEY *(rushing to the phone).* Must be Buddy. —Buddy? Well? —Yeh, good, what suit you got on? Well, take it off. It don't look good on you, Buddy. Put on the striped suit, Buddy an' the polka dot tie, and, Buddy, if you smoke a cigar at Creve Coeur, excuse yourself and smoke it in the bushes.

HELENA. This is—

BODEY. That's right, 'bye.

HELENA. —absolutely bizarre! You found a clothes brush? That's not a clothes brush. It's a whisk broom. Sorry. It doesn't look clean.

BODEY. Sorry. My nerves.

HELENA *(taking it and brushing herself delicately here and there).* What was that counting I heard? Is Dorothea counting something in there?

BODEY. She's counting her swivels in there.

HELENA. Swivels of what?

BODEY. Hip swivels, that's what. She's counting. Every morning she does one hundred bends and one hundred set-ups and one hundred hip swivels.

HELENA. Regardless of weather?

BODEY. That's right, regardless of weather.

HELENA. And regardless of—Hmmm . . .

(Bodey senses a touch of malice implicit in this unfinished sentence.)

BODEY. —What else, huh?

HELENA. Dorothea has always impressed me as an emotionally fragile type of person who might collapse, just suddenly collapse, when confronted with the disappointing facts of a situation about which she'd allowed herself to have—romantic illusions.

(It is now Bodey's turn to say, "Hmmm . . .")

—No matter how—well, I hate to say foolish but even intelligent girls can make mistakes of this nature . . . of course we all felt she was attaching too much importance to—

BODEY. "We all" is who?

HELENA. Our little group at Blewett.

BODEY. Yeh, there's always a gossipy little group, even down at International Shoe where I work there is a gossipy little group that feels superior to the rest of us. Well, personally, I don't want in with this gossipy little group because the gossip is malicious. Oh, they call it being concerned, but it's not the right kind of concern, naw, I'd hate for that gossipy little group to feel concerned about me, don't want that and don't need it.

HELENA. Understandably, yaiss. I will return this whisk broom to Dorothea.

BODEY. No, no, just return it to me.

HELENA. I have to speak to her and in order to do that I'll have to enter that room. So if you'll excuse me I'll—

(She starts toward the bedroom. Bodey snatches the whisk broom from her with a force that makes Helena gasp.)

BODEY. Miss Brooksit, you're a visitor here but the visit was not expected. Now you excuse me but I got to say you sort of act like this apartment was yours.

HELENA. —What a dismaying idea! I mean I—

BODEY. And excuse me or don't excuse me but I got a very strong feeling that you got something in mind. All right, your mind is your mind, what's in it is yours but keep it to yourself, huh?

HELENA *(cutting in)*. Miss Bodenheifer, you seem to be implying something that's a mystery to me.

BODEY. You know what I mean and I know what I mean so where's the mystery, huh?

DOROTHEA *(calling from the bedroom)*. Is somebody out there, Bodey?

BODEY. Just Sophie Gluck.

DOROTHEA. Oh, Lord!

HELENA. What was that you called me?

BODEY. I told Dotty that you was Miss Gluck from upstairs.

HELENA. —Gluck?

BODEY. Yeah, Miss Gluck is a lady upstairs that comes downstairs to visit.

HELENA. She comes down to see Dorothea?

BODEY. No, no, more to see me, and to drink coffee. She lost her mother, an' she's got a depression so bad she can't make coffee, so I save her a cup, keep her a cup in the pot. You know for a single girl to lose her mother is a terrible thing. What else can you do? She oughta be down. Weekdays she comes down at seven. Well, this is Sunday.

HELENA. Yes. This is Sunday.

BODEY. Sundays she comes down for coffee and a cruller at ten.

HELENA. Cruller? What is a cruller?

BODEY. Aw. You call it a doughnut, but me, bein' German, was raised to call it a cruller.

HELENA. Oh. A cruller is a doughnut but you call it a cruller. Now if you'll excuse me a moment, I will go in there and relieve Dorothea of the mistaken impression that I am Miss Gluck from upstairs who has come down for her coffee and—cruller.

BODEY. Oh, no, don't interrupt her calisthenics.

(Helena ignores this admonition and opens the bedroom door.)

DOROTHEA. Why, Helena Brookmire!— What a surprise. I—I—look a—*mess!*

HELENA. I heard this counting and gasping. Inquired what was going on. Your friend Miss—what?

DOROTHEA. You've met Miss Bodenhafer?

HELENA. Yes, she received me very cordially. We've dispensed with introductions. She says any friend of yours is a friend of hers and wants me to call her Bodey as they do at the office. Excuse me, Miss Bodenheifer, I must have a bit of private conversation—

(Helena closes the bedroom door, shutting out Bodey.)

DOROTHEA. Well, I wasn't expecting a visitor today, obviously not this early. You see, I—never receive a visitor here. . . . Is there something too urgent to hold off till Monday, Helena?

HELENA. Have our negotiations with the realty firm of Orthwein and Muller slipped your flighty mind?

DOROTHEA. Oh, the real estate people, but surely on Sunday—

HELENA. Mr. Orthwein called Cousin Dee-Dee last night and she called me this morning that now the news has leaked out and there's competitive bidding for the apartment on

Westmoreland Place and the deal must be settled at once.

DOROTHEA. You mean by—?

HELENA. Immediate payment, yes, to pin it down.

DOROTHEA. *Today? Sunday?*

HELENA. The sanctity of a Sunday must sometimes be profaned by business transactions.

(Bodey has now entered.)

DOROTHEA. Helena, if you'll just have some coffee and wait in the living room, I will come out as soon as I've showered and dressed.

BODEY. Yeh, yeh, do that. You're embarrassing Dotty, so come back out—

(Bodey almost drags Helena out of the bedroom, kicking the bedroom door shut.)

HELENA. Gracious!

BODEY. Yes, gracious, here! Set down, I'll get you some coffee.

HELENA *(with a sharp laugh)*. She said, ''I look a mess,'' and I couldn't contradict her.

BODEY. Here! Your coffee! Your cruller!

HELENA *(haughtily)*. I don't care for the cruller, as you call it. Pastries are not included in my diet. However—I'd like a clean napkin. You've splashed coffee everywhere.

BODEY. Sure, we got plenty of napkins. You name it, we got it. *(She thrusts a paper napkin at Helena like a challenge.)*

HELENA. This paper napkin is stained. Would you please give me—

BODEY. Take 'em all. You stained that napkin yourself. *(She thrusts the entire pile of napkins at Helena.)*

HELENA. You shoved the cup at me so roughly the coffee splashed.

(Helena fastidously wipes the tabletop. There is a rap at the door.)

BODEY. Aw, that's Sophie Gluck.

HELENA. I don't care to meet Miss Gluck.

BODEY. Will you set down so I can let in Sophie Gluck?

HELENA. So if you're going to admit her, I will take refuge again in Dorothea's bedroom. . . . There is another matter I've come here to . . .

BODEY *(seizing Helena's arm as she crosses toward the bedroom)*. I know what you're up to! —JUST A MINUTE, *BITTE,* SOPHIE! I can guess the other matter you just can't hold your tongue about, but you're gonna hold it. It's not gonna be mentioned to cloud over the day and spoil the Creve Coeur picnic for Dotty, Buddy, an' me! —COMIN', SOPHIE! *(Then, to Helena, fiercely.)* YOU SET BACK DOWN!

(During this altercation, Dorothea has been standing in the bedroom paralyzed with embarrassment and dismay. Now she calls sweetly through the door, opened a crack.)

DOROTHEA. Bodey, Bodey, what *is* going on out there? How could a phone be heard above that shouting? Oh, My Blessed Savior, I was bawn on a Sunday, and I am convinced that I shall die on a Sunday! Could you please tell me what is the cause of the nerve-shattering altercations going on out there?

HELENA. Dorothea, Miss Bodenheifer's about to receive Miss Gluck.

DOROTHEA. Oh, no, oh no, Bodey, entertain her upstairs! I'm not in shape for another visit today, especially not—Bodey!

BODEY. Sophie, Sophie, you had me worried about you.

HELENA. I'm afraid, Dorothea, your request has fallen upon a calcified eardrum.

BODEY. You come downstairs so late.

MISS GLUCK. *Sie hat die Tür in mein Kopf zugeschlagen!*

BODEY *(to Helena)*. You done that to Sophie!

HELENA. An unknown creature of demented appearance entering like a sneak thief!

BODEY. My best friend in the building!

HELENA. What a pitiful admission!

BODEY. You come here uninvited, not by Dotty or me, since I never heard of you, but got the nerve to call my best friend in the building . . .

MISS GLUCK. *Diese Frau ist ein Spion.*

BODEY. What did you call her?

HELENA. I called that woman demented. What I would call you is intolerably offensive.

MISS GLUCK. *Verstehen Sie?* Spy. *Vom Irrenhaus.*

BODEY. We live here, you don't. See the difference?

HELENA. Thank God for the difference. *Vive la différence.*

DOROTHEA *(coming just inside the living room)*. Helena, Bodey.

HELENA. Be calm Dorothea—don't get overexcited.

MISS GLUCK. *Zwei Jahre.* Two years.

DOROTHEA. Why is she coming at me like this?

MISS GLUCK. State asylum.

BODEY. You come here to scrounge money outta Dotty which she ain't got.

MISS GLUCK. *Sie ist heir—mich noch einmal—im Irrenhaus zu bringen.* To take back to hospital.

HELENA. Aside from the total inaccuracy of

your assumption and the insulting manner in which you express it—. As you very well know, Dorothea and I are both employed at Blewett. We are both on salary there! And I have not come here to involve myself in your social group but to rescue my colleague from it.

BODEY. Awright, you put it your way, it adds up to the same thing. You want money from Dotty which she ain't got to give you. Dotty is broke, flat broke, and she's been on a big buying spree, so big that just last night I had to loan her the price of a medium bottle of Golden Glow Shampoo, and not only that, I had to go purchase it for her because she come home exhausted. Dotty was too exhausted to walk to the drugstore. Well, me, I was tired, too, after my work at International Shoe and shopping, but out I hoofed it to Liggett's and forked out the forty-nine cents for the medium size Golden Glow from my own pockets, money I set aside for incidentals at the Creve Coeur picnic. There's always—

HELENA (cutting in). Miss Bodenheifer, you certainly have a gift for the felicitous phase such as "out you hoofed it to Liggett's," sorry, sorry, but it does evoke an image.

BODEY. I know what you mean by "hoof it" since you keep repeating "heifer" for "hafer." I'm not too dumb like which you regard me to know why you're struck so funny by "hoof it."

HELENA. You said you "hoofed it," not me.

BODEY. You keep saying "heifer" for "hafer." Me, I'm a sensitive person with feelings I feel, but sensitive to you I am not. Insults from you you bounce off me. I just want you to know that you come here shaking your tin cup at the wrong door.

(As a soft but vibrant counterpoint to this exchange, Sophie, sobbing and rolling her eyes like a religieuse in a state of sorrowful vision, continues her slow shuffle toward Dorothea as she repeats in German an account of her violent ejection by Helena.)

DOROTHEA (breathlessly). Bodey, what is she saying? Translate and explain to her I have no knowledge of German.

HELENA. Babbling, just lunatic babbling!

BODEY. One minute, one minute, Dotty. I got to explain to this woman she's wasting her time here and yours—and had the moxie to slam Sophie out of the door.

HELENA. Miss Bodenheifer, it's useless to attempt to intimidate me. . . . I would like the use of your phone for a moment. Then—

DOROTHEA. No calls on the phone!

BODEY. Dotty don't want this phone used; she's expecting a call to come in, but there is a pay phone at Liggett's three blocks east on West Pine and Pearl.

HELENA. Drugstores are shut on Sundays!

DOROTHEA. Quiet! Listen! All! This thing's getting out of hand!

HELENA. I want only to call a taxi for myself and for Dorothea. She's trapped here and should be removed at once. You may not know that just two weeks after she came to Blewett she collapsed on the staircase, and the staff doctor examined her and discovered that Dorothea's afflicted with neuro-circulatory asthenia.

(Dorothea has disappeared behind the sofa. Miss Gluck is looking down at her with lamentations.)

MISS GLUCK. BODEY.

BODEY. Moment, Sophie.

MISS GLUCK. Dotty, Dotty . . .

HELENA. What is she saying? Where's Dorothea?

BODEY. Dotty?

MISS GLUCK. Hier, auf dem Fussboden. Ist fallen.

HELENA. This Gluck creature has thrown Dorothea onto the floor.

BODEY. Gott im—! Wo ist—Dotty?

HELENA. The Gluck has flung her to the floor behind the sofa!

BODEY. Dotty!

HELENA. Dorothea, I'm calling us a cab. Is she conscious?

DOROTHEA. Mebaral—tablet—quick!

BODEY. Mebarals, where?

(Sophie wails loudly.)

DOROTHEA. My pocketbook!

BODEY. Hold on now, slowly, slowly—

DOROTHEA. Mebaral! Tablets!

HELENA. My physician told me those tablets are only prescribed for persons with—extreme nervous tension and asthenia.

BODEY. Will you goddam shut up? —Dotty, you just need to—

HELENA. What she needs is to stop these strenuous exercises and avoid all future confrontations with that lunatic from upstairs!

BODEY. Dotty, let me lift you.

DOROTHEA. Oh, oh, noooo, I—can't, I—I am paralyzed, Bodey!

BODEY. HEY, YOU BROOKS-IT, TAKE DOTTY'S OTHER ARM. HELP ME CARRY HER TO HER BED WILL YUH?

(Sophie is moaning through clenched fists.)

HELENA. All right, all right, but then I shall call my physician!

(Dorothea is carried into the bedroom and deposited on the bed. Sophie props pillows behind her.)

DOROTHEA. Meb—my meb . . .

BODEY. Tablets. Bathroom. In your pocketbook.

(Bodey rushes into the bathroom, then out with a small bottle. Dorothea raises a hand weakly and Bodey drops tablets in it.)

Dotty, don't swallow, that's three tablets!

DOROTHEA. My sherry to wash it down with—

BODEY. Dotty, take out the *two extra tablets,* Dotty!

HELENA. Sherry? Did she say sherry? Where is it?

DOROTHEA. There, there.

BODEY. Dotty, open your mouth, I got to take out those extras!

HELENA. No glass, you must drink from the bottle.

BODEY. NO! NOOOO!

HELENA. STOP CLUTCHING AT ME!

(Miss Gluck utters a terrified wail. Dorothea drinks from the bottle and falls back onto the pillows with a gasp.)

BODEY *(so angry she speaks half in German).* You *Schwein,* you bitch! *Alte böse Katze. (She then goes on in English.)* You washed three tablets down Dotty!

DOROTHEA. Now will you BOTH get out so I can breathe!

HELENA. The door's obstructed by Gluck.

BODEY. Sophie, go out, Sophie, go out of here with me for coffee and crullers!

(Sobbing, Sophie retreats. Bodey grabs a strong hold of Helena's wrist.)

HELENA. Let go of my wrist. Oh, my God, you have broken. . . . I heard a bone snap in my—!

BODEY. WALK! OUT! MOVE IT! . . .

HELENA *(turning quickly about and retreating behind the sofa).* Miss Bodenheifer, you are a one-woman demonstration of the aptness of the term "Huns" for Germans. . . And, incidentally, what you broke was not my wrist but my Cartier wristwatch, a birthday present from my Cousin Dee-Dee; you shattered the crystal, and you've broken the minute hand and bent the two others. I am afraid the repair bill will cost you considerably more than keeping Dorothea in Golden Glow Shampoo.

BODEY. It's all right, Sophie, set down right here and I'll . . . Coffee's still hot for you. Have a coupla crullers. Blow your nose on this napkin and—

(Helena laughs tonelessly.)

What's funny, is something funny? You never been depressed, no sorrows in your life ever, yeh, and you call yourself a human.

HELENA. Really, this is fantastic as the—color scheme of this room or the—view through the windows.

(In the bedroom, Dorothea has staggered from the bed and stumbled to the floor.)

DOROTHEA. Bodey.

HELENA. Dorothea.

BODEY *(calling through).* Dotty.

HELENA. You really must let me check on her condition.

DOROTHEA *(in the bedroom).* Don't forget . . . phone call.

BODEY. No, Dotty.

DOROTHEA *(faintly, clinging to something).* Tell Miss Brookmire I've retired for the day.

HELENA. *What?*

BODEY. She's not coming out. She's not coming out till you leave here—

(Bodey bolts the bedroom door.)

HELENA. I beg to differ. She *will* and I'll sit here till she does!

(Miss Gluck has taken a bite of a cruller, dunked in coffee, and begins to blubber, the coffee-soaked cruller dribbling down her chin.)

BODEY. Look, you upset Sophie!

MISS GLUCK. *Eine—Woche vor—Sonntag— meine Mutter—*

BODEY *(comfortingly). Ich weiss,* Sophie, *ich weiss.*

MISS GLUCK. *Gestorben!*

BODEY. But she went *sudden,* huh, Sophie? *(She crouches beside Miss Gluck, removing the dribblings of cruller and coffee from her mouth and chin.)*

HELENA. I don't understand the language, and the scene appears to be private.

BODEY. Yeh, keep out of it. *(She turns to Miss Gluck.)*—Your mother, she didn't hang on like the doctor thought she would, Sophie. Now, face it, it was better sudden, no big hospital bill, just went and is waiting for you in Heaven.

HELENA. With open arms, I presume, and with coffee and crullers.

BODEY. So, Sophie, just be grateful that she went quick with no pain.

MISS GLUCK *(grotesquely tragic). Nein, nein, sie hat geschrien!* I woke up runnin'!

BODEY. To her bed, you reached it and she was dead. Just one scream, it was over—wasn't that a mercy?

(Helena laughs.)

Sophie, honey, this woman here's not sympathetic. She laughs at sorrow, so maybe you better take the coffee, the cruller—here's another—upstairs, Sophie, and when we get back from the Creve Coeur picnic, I will bring you beautiful flowers, *schöne Blume*. Then I'll come up and sing to you in German—I will sing you to sleep.

(Miss Gluck slowly rises with coffee and crullers. Bodey conducts her gently to the door.)

MISS GLUCK *(crying out)*. *Ich bin allein, allein! In der Welt, freundlos!*

BODEY. No, no, Sophie, that is negative thinking.

MISS GLUCK. *Ich habe niemand in der Welt!*

BODEY. Sophie, God is with you, I'm with you. Your mother, all your relations are waiting for you in Heaven!

(Shepherding Miss Gluck into the hall, Bodey repeats this assurance in German.)

HELENA. Sometimes despair is just being realistic, the only logical thing for certain persons to *feel*. *(She addresses herself with a certain seriousness, now.)* Loss. Despair. I've faced them and actually they have—fortified and protected, not overcome me at all . . .

BODEY *(in the hall with Miss Gluck)*. Okay? *Verstehst du*, Sophie?

HELENA *(still ruminating privately)*. The weak. The strong. Only important division between living creatures. *(She nods birdlike affirmation.)*

(Miss Gluck remains visible in the hall, afraid to return upstairs.)

MISS GLUCK. *Allein, allein.*

(There is a change in the light. Helena moves a small chair downstage and delivers the following to herself.)

HELENA. *Allein, allein* means alone, alone. *(A frightened look appears in her eyes.)* Last week I dined alone, alone three nights in a row. There's nothing lonelier than a woman dining alone, and although I loathe preparing food for myself, I cannot bear the humiliation of occupying a restaurant table for one. Dining *au solitaire!* But I would rather starve than reduce my social standards by accepting dinner invitations from that middle-aged gaggle of preposterously vulgar old maids that wants to suck me into their group despite my total abhorrence of all they stand for. Loneliness in the company of five intellectually destitute spinsters is simply loneliness multipled by five . . .

(There is a crash in the hallway.)

DOROTHEA *(from the bedroom)*. Is it the phone?

HELENA. Another visit so soon? Miss Bodenheifer, your bereaved friend from upstairs is favoring you with another visit.

MISS GLUCK *(wildly)*. *Mein Zimmer is gespukt, gespukt!*

HELENA. "Spooked, spooked"?

BODEY. Sophie, your apartment isn't haunted.

HELENA. Perhaps if you went up with her, it would despook the apartment.

BODEY. Aw, no, I got to stay down and keep a sharp eye on *you*.

HELENA. Which means that she will remain here?

BODEY. Long as she pleases to. What's it to you? She got nothin' contagious. You can't catch heartbreak if you have got no heart.

HELENA. May I suggest that you put her in the back yard in the sun. I think that woman's complexion could stand a touch of color.

BODEY. I am puttin' her nowhere she don't want to be. How about you settin' in the back yard? Some natural color would do your face good for a change.

(Sensing the hostile "vibes," Miss Gluck moans, swaying a little.)

HELENA. Miss Bodenheifer, I will not dignify your insults with response or attention!

(Miss Gluck moans louder.)

Aren't you able to see that this Miss Gluck is mental? Distressing to hear and to look at! . . . Be that as it may, I shall wait.

BODEY. Sitting? Tight as a tombstone? Huh?

HELENA. I can assure you that for me to remain in this place is at least as unpleasant to me as to you. *(She cries out to Dorothea who is still in the bedroom.)* Dorothea? Dorothea? Can you hear me?

DOROTHEA *(clinging to something in the bedroom)*. See you—Blewett—t'morrow . . .

HELENA. No, no, at once, Dorothea, the situation out here is dreadful beyond endurance.

(Abruptly, Miss Gluck cries out, clutching her abdomen.)

BODEY. Sophie, what is it, Sophie?

MISS GLUCK. *Heisser Kaffee gibt mir immer Krampf und Durchfall.*

(This episode in the play must be handled carefully to avoid excessive scatology but keep the humor.)

BODEY. You got the runs? *Zum Badezimmer?* Sophie's got to go to the bathroom, Dotty.

DOROTHEA. Hasn't she got one upstairs?

BODEY. After hot coffee, it gives her diarrhea!

DOROTHEA. Must she have it down here?

MISS GLUCK *(in German)*. *KANN NICHT*

WARTEN!

BODEY. She can't wait, here, bathroom, Sophie! *Badezimmer!*

(Miss Gluck rushes through the bedroom into the bathroom.)

DOROTHEA. What a scene for Helena to report at Blewett. Miss Gluck, turn on both water faucets full force.

BODEY. Sophie, *beide Wasser rennen.*

DOROTHEA. Bodey, while I am here don't serve her hot coffee again since it results in these—crises!

BODEY. Dotty, you know that Sophie's got this problem.

DOROTHEA. Then send her coffee upstairs.

BODEY. Dotty, you know she needs companionship, Dotty.

DOROTHEA. That I cannot provide her with just now!

(Bodey returns to the living room.)

HELENA. How did Dorothea react to Miss Gluck's sudden indisposition?

BODEY. Dotty's a girl that understands human afflictions.

(There is a crash in the bathroom.)

DOROTHEA. Phone, Ralph's call—has he— did he?

BODEY. Phone, Dotty? No, no phone.

HELENA. I wouldn't expect—

BODEY *(to Helena).* Watch it!

HELENA. Watch what, Miss Bodenheifer? What is it you want me to watch?

BODEY. That mouth of yours, the tongue in it, with such a tongue in a mouth you could dig your grave with like a shovel!

HELENA *(her laugher tinkling like ice in a glass).* —The syntax of that sentence was rather confusing. You know, I suspect that English is not your native language but one that you've not quite adequately adopted.

BODEY. I was born on South Grand, a block from Tower Grove Park in this city of St. Louis!

HELENA. Ah, the German section. Your parents were German speaking?

BODEY. I learned plenty English at school, had eight grades of school and a year of business college.

HELENA. I see, I see, forgive me. *(She turns to a window, possibly in the "fourth wall.")* Is a visitor permitted to look out the window?

BODEY. A visitor like you's permitted to jump out it.

HELENA *(laughing indulgently).* With so many restrictions placed on one's speech and actions—

(Bodey turns up her hearing aid so high that

it screeches shrilly.)

DOROTHEA. Is it the phone?

HELENA. Please. Is it controllable, that electric hearing device?

BODEY. What did you say?

(The screeching continues.)

HELENA. Ow . . . ow . . .

(Bodey finally manages to turn down the hearing aid.)

DOROTHEA. Oh please bring a mop, Bodey. Water's streaming under—the bathroom door. Miss Gluck's flooded the bathroom.

BODEY. What? Bring?

HELENA. *Mop, mop!*

(Helena moves toward the bedroom door but Bodey shoves her back.)

BODEY. Stay! Put! Stay put!

(Bodey grabs a mop from the closet and then rushes into the bedroom.)

DOROTHEA. See? Water? Flooding?

BODEY. You told her to turn on both faucets. SOPHIE! *Halte das Wasser ab,* Sophie! *(Bodey opens the bathroom door and thrusts in the mop.)* Here, *das Wust, das Wust,* Sophie!

DOROTHEA *(to herself).* This is incredible to me, I simply do not believe it! *(She then speaks to Bodey who has started back toward the living room.)* May I detain you a moment? The truth has finally struck me. Ralph's calls have been intercepted. He has been repeatedly calling me on that phone, and you have been just as repeatedly lying to me that he hasn't.

BODEY. LYING TO—?

DOROTHEA. YES, LYING! *(She stumbles to the door of the bedroom.)* Helena, will *you* please watch that phone for me now?

HELENA *(crossing to the bedroom door).* I'm afraid, Dorothea, that a watched phone never rings!

(Bodey emerges from the bedroom. She and Helena return to the living room while Dorothea retreats to the bed, shutting the door behind her.)

What a view through this window, totally devoid of—why, no, a living creature, a pigeon! Capable of flight but perched for a moment in this absolute desolation . . .

INTERVAL

SCENE TWO

The scene is the same as before. The spotlight focuses on the lefthand, "bedroom" portion of the stage where Dorothea, seated at her vanity table and mellowed by her mebaral and sherry "cocktail," soliloquizes.

DOROTHEA *(taking a large swallow of sherry).* Best years of my youth thrown away, wasted on poor Hathaway James. *(She removes his picture from the vanity table and with closed eyes thrusts it out of sight.)* Shouldn't say wasted but so unwisely devoted. Not even sure it was love. Unconsummated love, is it really love? More likely just a reverence for his talent—precocious achievements . . . musical prodigy. Scholarship to Juilliard, performed a concerto with the Nashville Symphony at fifteen. *(She sips more sherry.)* But those dreadful embarrassing evenings on Aunt Belle's front porch in Memphis! He'd say: "Turn out the light, it's attracting insects." I'd switch it out. He'd grab me so tight it would take my breath away, and invariably I'd feel plunging, plunging against me that—that—frantic part of him . . . then he'd release me at once and collapse on the porch swing, breathing hoarsely. With the corner gas lamp shining through the wisteria vines, it was impossible not to notice the wet stain spreading on his light flannel trousers. . . . Miss Gluck, MOP IN!!

(Miss Gluck, who has timidly opened the bathroom door and begun to emerge, with the mop, into the bedroom, hastily retreats from sight.)

Such affliction—visited on the gifted. . . . Finally worked up the courage to discuss the—Hathaway's—problem with the family doctor, delicately but clearly as I could. "Honey, this Hathaway fellow's afflicted with something clinically known as—chronic case of—premature ejaculation—must have a large laundry bill. . . ." "Is it curable, Doctor?" —"Maybe with great patience, honey, but remember you're only young once, don't gamble on it, relinquish him to his interest in music, let him go."

(Miss Gluck's mop protrudes from the bathroom again.)

MISS GLUCK, I SAID MOP IN. REMAIN IN BATHROOM WITH WET MOP TILL MOP UP COMPLETED. MERCIFUL HEAVENS.

(Helena and Bodey are now seen in the living room.)

HELENA. Is Dorothea attempting a conversation with Miss Gluck in there?

BODEY. No, no just to herself—you gave her the sherry on top of mebaral tablets.

HELENA. She talks to herself? That isn't a practice that I would encourage her in.

BODEY. She don't need no encouragement in it, and as for you, I got an idea you'd encourage nobody in nothing.

DOROTHEA *(in the bedroom).* After Hathaway James, there was nothing left for me but—CIVICS.

HELENA *(who has moved to the bedroom door the better to hear Dorothea's "confessions").* This is not to B. B.!

BODEY. Stop listening at the door. Go back to your pigeon watching.

HELENA. How long is this apt to continue?

DOROTHEA. Oh God, thank you that Ralph has no such affliction—is healthily aggressive.

HELENA. I have a luncheon engagement in La Due at two!

BODEY. Well, go keep it! On time!

HELENA. My business with Dorothea must take precedence over anything else! *(Helena pauses to watch with amused suspicion as Bodey "attacks" the Sunday* Post-Dispatch *which she has picked up from the chair.)* What is that you're doing, Miss Bodenheifer?

BODEY. Tearing a certain item out of the paper.

HELENA. A ludicrous thing to do since the news will be all over Blewett High School tomorrow.

BODEY. Never mind tomorrow. There's ways and ways to break a piece of news like that to a girl with a heart like Dotty. You wouldn't know about that, no, you'd do it right now—malicious! —You got eyes like a bird and I don't mean a songbird.

HELENA. Oh, is that *so?*

BODEY. Yeh, yeh, that's so, I know!

(Pause. Bodey, who has torn out about half of the top page of one section, puts the rest of the paper on the sofa, and takes the section from which the piece has been torn with her as she crosses to the kitchenette, crumpling and throwing the torn piece into the wastebasket on her way.)

HELENA. Miss Bodenheifer.

BODEY *(from the kitchenette).* Hafer!

HELENA. I have no wish to offend you, but surely you're able to see that for Dorothea to stay in these circumstances must be extremely embarrassing to her at least.

BODEY. Aw, you think Dotty's embarrassed here, do you?

(Bodey has begun to line a shoebox with the section of newspaper she took with her. During the following exchange with Helena, Bodey

packs the fried chicken and other picnic fare in the shoebox.)

HELENA. She has hinted it's almost intolerable to her. The visitations of this Gluck person who has rushed to the bathroom, this nightmare of clashing colors, the purple carpet, orange drapes at the windows looking out at that view of brick and concrete and asphalt, lamp shades with violent yellow daisies on them, and wallpaper with roses exploding like bombshells, why it would give her a breakdown! It's giving me claustrophobia briefly as I have been here. Why, this is not a place for a civilized person to possibly exist in!

BODEY. What's so civilized about you, Miss Brooks-it? Stylish, yes, civilized, no, unless a hawk or a buzzard is a civilized creature. Now you see, you got a tongue in your mouth, but I got one in mine, too.

HELENA. You are being hysterical and offensive!

BODEY. You ain't heard nothing compared to what you'll hear if you continue to try to offer all this concern you feel about Dotty to Dotty in this apartment.

HELENA. Dorothea Gallaway and I keep nothing from each other and naturally I intend, as soon as she has recovered, to prepare her for what she can hardly avoid facing sooner or later and I—

BODEY *(cutting in)*. I don't want heartbreak for Dotty. For Dotty I want a—life.

HELENA. A life of—?

BODEY. A life, a *life*—

HELENA. You mean as opposed to death?

BODEY. Don't get smart with me. I got your number the moment you come in that door like a well-dressed snake.

HELENA. So far you have compared me to a snake and a bird. Please decide which—since the archaeopteryx, the only known combination of bird and snake, is long extinct!

BODEY. Yes, well, you talk with a kind of hiss. Awright, you just hiss away but not in this room which you think ain't a civilized room. Okay, it's too cheerful for you but for me and Dotty it's fine. And this afternoon, at the picnic at Creve Coeur Lake, I will tell Dotty, gentle, in my own way, if it's necessary to tell her, that this unprincipled man has just been using her. But Buddy, my brother Buddy, if in some ways he don't suit her like he is now, I will see he quits beer, I will see he cuts out his cigars, I will see he continues to take off five pounds a week. And by Dotty and Buddy there will be children—children! I will

never have none, myself, no! But Dotty and Buddy will have beautiful kiddies. Me? Nieces—nephews. . . . —Now you! I've wrapped up the picnic. It's nice and cool at Creve Coeur Lake and the ride on the open-air streetcar is lickety-split through green country and there's flowers you can pull off the bushes you pass. It's a fine excusion. Dotty will forget not gettin' that phone call. We'll stay out till it's close to dark and the fireflies—fly. I will slip away and Buddy will be alone with her on the lake shore. He will smoke no smelly cigar. He will just respectfully hold her hand and say—"I love you, Dotty. Please be mine," not meanin' a girl in a car parked up on Art Hill but—for the long run of life.

HELENA. —Can Dorothea be really attached to your brother? Is it a mutual attraction?

BODEY. Dotty will settle for Buddy. She's got a few reservations about him so far, but at Creve Coeur she'll suddenly recognize the—wonderful side of his nature.

HELENA. Miss Bodenheifer, Dorothea is not intending to remain in this tasteless apartment. Hasn't she informed you that she is planning to share a lovely apartment with me? The upstairs of a duplex on Westmoreland Place?

BODEY. Stylish? Civilized, huh? And too expensive for you to swing it alone, so you want to rope Dotty in, rope her into a place that far from Blewett? Share expenses? You prob'ly mean pay most.

HELENA. To move from such an unsuitable environment must naturally involve some expense.

(Miss Gluck falls out of the bathroom onto Dorothea's bed.)

DOROTHEA. MISS GLUCK! CAREFUL! Bodey, Bodey, Sophie Gluck's collapsed on my bed in a cloud of steam!

HELENA. Has Miss Gluck broken a steam pipe?

(Bodey rushes from the kitchenette into the bedroom.)

BODEY *(to Helena)*. You stay out.

(Dorothea emerges from the bedroom. She closes the door and leans against it briefly, closing her eyes as if dizzy or faint.)

HELENA. At last.

DOROTHEA. I'm so mortified.

HELENA. Are you feeling better?

DOROTHEA. Sundays are always different—

HELENA. This one exceptionally so.

DOROTHEA. I don't know why but—I don't quite understand why I am so—agitated. Something happened last week, just a few evenings ago that—

HELENA. Yes? What?

DOROTHEA. Nothing that I'm—something I can't discuss with you. I was and still am expecting a very important phone call—

HELENA. May I ask you from whom?

DOROTHEA. No, please.

HELENA. Then may I hazard a guess that the expected call not received was from a young gentleman who cuts a quite spectacular figure in the country club set but somehow became involved in the educational system?

DOROTHEA. If you don't mind, Helena, I'd much prefer not to discuss anything of a—private nature right now.

HELENA. Yes, I understand, dear. And since you've located that chair, why don't you seat yourself in it?

DOROTHEA. Oh, yes, excuse me. *(She sits down, weakly, her hand lifted to her throat.)* The happenings here today are still a bit confused in my head. I was doing my exercises before you dropped in.

HELENA. And for quite a while after.

DOROTHEA. I was about to—no, I'd taken my shower. I was about to get dressed.

HELENA. But the Gluck intervened. Such discipline! Well! I've had the privilege of an extended meeting with Miss Bodenheifer—*(She lowers her voice.)* She seemed completely surprised when I mentioned that you were moving to Westmoreland Place.

DOROTHEA. Oh, you told her.—I'm glad.—I'm such a coward, I couldn't.

HELENA. Well, I broke the news to her

DOROTHEA. I—just hadn't the heart to.

(Miss Gluck advances from the bedroom with a dripping wet mop and a dazed look.)

HELENA *(to Dorothea)*. Can't you see she's already found a replacement?

DOROTHEA. Oh, no, there's a limit even to Bodey's endurance! Miss Gluck, would you please return that wet mop to the kitchen and wring it out. *Küche*—mop—Sophie.

HELENA. Appears to be catatonic.

DOROTHEA *(as she goes into the bedroom to get Bodey)*. Excuse me.

(Bodey enters from the bedroom and takes Miss Gluck, with mop, into the kitchenette.)

BODEY *(singing nervously in the kitchenette)*. "I'm just breezing along with the breeze, pleasing to live, and living to please!"

(Dorothea returns to the living room.)

DOROTHEA. How did Bodey take the news I was moving?

HELENA. "That far from *Blewett!*" she said

as if it were transcontinental.

DOROTHEA. Well, it is a bit far, compared to this location.

HELENA. Surely you wouldn't compare it to *this* location.

DOROTHEA. Oh, no, Westmoreland Place is a—fashionable address, incomparable in that respect, but it is quite a distance. Of course, just a block from Delmar Boulevard and the Olive Street car-line, that would let me off at—what point closest to Blewett?

HELENA. Dorothea, forget transportation, that problem. We're going by automobile.

DOROTHEA. By—what automobile do you—?

HELENA. I have a lovely surprise for you, dear.

DOROTHEA. Someone is going to drive us?

HELENA. Yes, I will be the chauffeur and you the passenger, dear. You see, my wealthy cousin Dee-Dee, who lives in La Due, has replaced her foreign-made car, an Hispano-Suiza, no less, practically brand-new, with a Pierce Arrow limousine and has offered to sell us the Hispano for just a song! Immediately, as soon as she made me this offer, I applied for a driver's license.

(A moment of shocked silence is interrupted by a short squawk from Bodey's hearing aid.)

BODEY *(advancing quickly from the kitchenette)*. Limazine? What limazine? With a show-fer?

HELENA. Miss Bodenheifer, how does this concern you?

BODEY. Who's gonna foot the bill for it, that's how!

HELENA. My cousin Dee-Dee in La Due will accept payment on time.

BODEY. Whose time and how much?

HELENA. *Negligible! A rich cousin!* —Oh, my Lord, I've always heard that Germans—

BODEY. Lay off Germans!

HELENA. Have this excessive concern with money matters.

BODEY. *Whose* money?

HELENA. Practicality can be a stupefying—

MISS GLUCK. Bodey?

HELENA. —virtue, if it *is* one.

MISS GLUCK. *Ich kann nicht*—go up.

HELENA. Go up just one step to the kitchen! Please, Dorothea, can't we—have a private discussion, briefly?

MISS GLUCK. *Das Schlafzimmer is gespukt!*

HELENA. Because you see, Dorothea, as I told you, I do have to make a payment on the Westmoreland Place apartment early tomorrow, and so must collect your half of it today.

DOROTHEA. —My half would amount to—?

HELENA. Seventy.

DOROTHEA. Ohh! —Would the real estate people accept a—postdated check?

HELENA. Reluctantly—very.

DOROTHEA. You see, I had unusually heavy expenses this week—clothes, lingerie, a suitcase . . .

HELENA. Sounds as if you'd been purchasing a trousseau.—Miss Bodenhafer says that her brother, "Buddy," is seriously interested in you. How selfish of you to keep it such a secret!—even from me!

DOROTHEA. Oh, my heavens, has Miss Bodenhafer—how fantastic!

HELENA. Yes, she is a bit, to put it politely.

DOROTHEA. I meant has she given you the preposterous impression that I am interested in her brother? Oh, my Lord, what a fantastic visit you've had! Believe me, the circumstances aren't always so—chaotic. Well! *Il n'y a rien à faire.* When I tell you that she calls her brother Buddy and that he is her *twin! (She throws up her arms.)*

HELENA. Identical?

DOROTHEA. Except for gender, alike as two peas in a pod. You're not so gullible, Helena, that you can really imagine for a moment that I'd—you know me better than that!

HELENA. Sometimes when a girl is on the rebound from a disappointing infatuation, she will leap without looking into the most improbable sort of—liaison—

DOROTHEA. Maybe some girl, but certainly not I. And what makes you think that I'm the victim of a "disappointing infatuation," Helena?

HELENA. Sometimes a thing will seem like the end of the world, and yet the world continues.

DOROTHEA. I personally feel that my world is just beginning. . . . Excuse me for a moment. I'll get my checkbook. . . .

(Dorothea goes into the bedroom. Miss Gluck wanders back into the living room from the kitchenette, wringing her hands and sobbing.)

HELENA. MISS BODENHEIFER!

BODEY. Don't bother to tell me good-bye.

HELENA. I am not yet leaving.

BODEY. And it ain't necessary to shake the walls when you call me, I got my hearing aid on.

HELENA. Would you be so kind as to confine Miss Gluck to that charming little kitchen while I'm completing my business with Dorothea?

(Bodey crosses toward Miss Gluck.)

BODEY. Sophie, come in here with me. You like a deviled egg don't you? And a nice fried drumstick when your—digestion is better? Just stay in here with me.

(Bodey leads Miss Gluck back to the kitchenette, then turns to Helena.)

I can catch every word that you say to Dotty in there, and you better be careful the conversation don't take the wrong turn!

MISS GLUCK *(half in German). Ich kann nicht* liven opstairs no more, *nimmer, nimmer—kann nicht*—can't go!

BODEY. You know what, Sophie? You better change apartments. There's a brand-new vacancy. See . . . right over there, the fifth floor. It's bright and cheerful . . . I used to go up there sometimes . . . it's a sublet, furnished, everything in cheerful colors. I'll speak to Mr. Schlogger, no, no, to *Mrs.* Schlogger, she makes better terms. Him, bein' paralyzed, he's got to accept 'em, y'know.

MISS GLUCK. I think— *(She sobs.)* —Missus Schlogger don't like me.

BODEY. That's—*impossible,* Sophie. I think she just had a little misunderstanding with your—*(She stops herself.)*

MISS GLUCK. *Meine Mutter, ja—*

BODEY. Sophie, speak of the Schloggers, she's wheeling that old *Halunke* out on their fire escape.

(The Schloggers are heard from offstage.)

MR. SCHLOGGER'S VOICE. I didn't say *out* in the sun.

MRS. SCHLOGGER'S VOICE. You said out, so you're out.

BODEY *(shouting out the window).* Oh, my *Gott,* Missus Schlogger, a stranger that didn't know you would think you meant to push him offa the landin'. Haul him back in, you better. Watch his cane, he's about to hit you with it. Amazin' the strength he's still got in his good arm.

MRS. SCHLOGGER'S VOICE. Now you want back in?

(Helena rises to watch this episode on the fire escape.)

MR. SCHLOGGER'S VOICE. Not in the kitchen with you.

HELENA *(to herself but rather loudly).* Schloggers, so those are Schloggers.

BODEY *(to Miss Gluck).* She's got him back in, I'm gonna speak to her right now —HEY MISSUS SCHLOGGER, YOU KNOW MISS GLUCK? AW, SURE YOU REMEMBER SOPHIE UPSTAIRS IN 4–F? SHE LOST HER MOTHER LAST SUNDAY. Sophie, come here, stick your head out, Sophie. NOW YOU REMEMBER HER, DON'T YOU?

MRS. SCHLOGGER'S VOICE. *Ja, ja.*

BODEY. *JA, JA,* SURE YOU REMEMBER! MRS. SCHLOGGER, POOR SOPHIE CAN'T LIVE ALONE IN 4–F WHERE SHE LOST HER MOTHER. SHE NEEDS A NEW APARTMENT THAT'S BRIGHT AND CHEERFUL TO GET HER OUT OF DEPRESSION. HOW ABOUT THE VACANCY ON THE FIFTH FLOOR FOR SOPHIE. WE GOT TO LOOK OUT FOR EACH OTHER IN TIMES OF SORROW. *VERSTEHEN SIE?*

MRS. SCHLOGGER'S VOICE. I don't know.

BODEY. GIVE SOPHIE THAT VACANCY UP THERE. THEN TERMS I'LL DISCUSS WITH YOU. *(She draws Miss Gluck back from the window.)* Sophie, I think that done it, and that apartment on five is bright and cheerful like here. And you're not gonna be lonely. We got three chairs at this table, and we can work out an arrangement so you can eat here with us, more economical that way. It's no good cooking for one, cookin' and eatin' alone is— lonely after—

(Helena resumes her seat as Bodey and Miss Gluck return to the kitchenette.)

HELENA *(with obscure meaning).* Yes— *(She draws a long breath and calls out.)* Dorothea, can't you locate your checkbook in there?

(Dorothea returns from the bedroom wearing a girlish summer print dress and looking quite pretty.)

DOROTHEA. I was just slipping into a dress. Now, then, here it is, my checkbook.

HELENA. Good. Where did you buy that new dress?

DOROTHEA. Why, at Scruggs-Vandervoort.

HELENA. Let me remove the price tag. *(As she removes the tag, she looks at it and assumes an amused and slightly superior air.)* Oh, my dear. I must teach you where to find the best values in clothes. In La Due there is a little French boutique, not expensive but excellent taste. I think a woman looks best when she dresses without the illusion she's still a girl in her teens. Don't you?

DOROTHEA *(stung).* —My half will be—how much did you say?

HELENA. To be exact, $82.50.

DOROTHEA. My goodness, that will take a good bite out of my savings. Helena, I thought you mentioned a lower amount. Didn't you say it would be seventy?

HELENA. Yes, I'd forgotten—utilities, dear.

Now, we don't want to move into a place with the phone turned off, the lights off. Utilities must be *on,* wouldn't you say?

DOROTHEA. —Yes. —Of course, I don't think I'll be dependent on my savings much longer, and a duplex on Westmoreland Place— *(She writes out a check.)* —is a—quite a— worthwhile—investment . . .

HELENA. I should think it would strike you as one after confinement with Miss Bodenhafer in this nightmare of colors.

DOROTHEA. Oh. —Yes. —Excuse me . . . *(She extends the check slightly.)*

HELENA. —Are you holding it out for the ink to dry on it?

DOROTHEA. —Sorry. —Here. *(She crosses to Helena and hands the check to her.)*

(Helena puts on her glasses to examine the check carefully. She then folds it, puts it into her purse, and snaps the purse shut.)

HELENA. Well, that's that. I hate financial dealings but they do have to be dealt with. Don't they?

DOROTHEA. Yes, they seem to . . .

HELENA. Require it. —Oh, contract.

DOROTHEA. Contract? For the apartment?

HELENA. Oh, no, a book on contract bridge, the bidding system and so forth. You do play bridge a little? I asked you once before and you said you did sometimes.

DOROTHEA. Here?

HELENA. Naturally not here. But on Westmoreland Place I hope you'll join in the twice-weekly games. You remember Joan Goode?

DOROTHEA. Yes, vaguely. Why?

HELENA. We were partners in duplicate bridge, which we usually played, worked out our own set of bidding conventions. But now Joan's gone to Wellesley for her Master's degree in, of all things, the pre-Ptolemaic dynasties of Egypt.

DOROTHEA. Did she do that? I didn't know what she did.

HELENA. You were only very casually—

DOROTHEA. Acquainted.

HELENA. My cousin Dee-Dee from La Due takes part whenever her social calendar permits her to. She often sends over dainty little sandwiches, watercress, tomato, sherbets from Zeller's in the summer. And a nicely uniformed maid to serve. Well, now we're converting from auction to contract, which is more complicated but stimulates the mind. —Dorothea, you have an abstracted look. Are you troubled over something?

DOROTHEA. Are these parties mixed?

HELENA. "Mixed" in what manner?

DOROTHEA. I mean would I invite Ralph?

HELENA. I have a feeling that Mr. T. Ralph Ellis might not be able to spare the time this summer. And anyway, professional women do need social occasions without the—male intrusion . . .

DOROTHEA *(with spirit)*. I've never thought of the presence of men as being an intrusion.

HELENA. Dorothea, that's just a lingering symptom of your Southern belle complex.

DOROTHEA. In order to be completely honest with you, Helena, I think I ought to tell you— I probably won't be able to share expenses with you in Westmoreland Place for very long, Helena!

HELENA. Oh, is that so? Is that why you've given me the postdated check which you could cancel tomorrow?

DOROTHEA. You know I wouldn't do that, but—

HELENA. Yes, but—you could and possibly you would. . . . Look before you, there stands the specter that confronts you ˆ. . .

DOROTHEA. Miss??

HELENA. Gluck the perennial, the irremediable, Miss Gluck! You probably think me superficial to value as much as I do, cousin Dee-Dee of La Due, contract bridge, possession of an elegant foreign car. Dorothea, only such things can protect us from a future of descent into the Gluck abyss of surrender to the bottom level of squalor. Look at it and tell me honestly that you can afford not to provide yourself with the Westmoreland Place apartment . . . its elevation, its style, its kind of *éclat*.

(Miss Gluck, who has come out of the kitchenette and moved downstage during Helena's speech, throws a glass of water in Helena's face.)

DOROTHEA. Bodey, RESTRAIN HER, RESTRAIN MISS GLUCK, SHE'S TURNED VIOLENT.

BODEY. Sophie, no, no. I didn't say you done wrong. I think you done right. I don't think you did enough.

HELENA. Violence does exist in the vegetable kingdom, you see! It doesn't terrify me since I shall soon be safely out of its range. . . . Just let me draw two good deep breaths and I'll be myself again. *(She does so.)* That did it. . . . I'm back in my skin. Oh, Dorothea, we must, must advance in appearances. You don't seem to know how vastly important it is, the move to Westmoreland Place, partic-

ularly now at this time when you must escape from reminders of, specters of, that alternative there! Surrender without conditions . . .

DOROTHEA. Sorry. I am a little abstracted. Helena, you sound as if you haven't even suspected that Ralph and I have been dating . . .

HELENA. Seriously?

DOROTHEA. Well, now that I've mentioned it to you, yes, quite. You see, I don't intend to devote the rest of my life to teaching civics at Blewett. I dream, I've always dreamed, of a marriage someday, and I think you should know that it might become a reality this summer.

HELENA. With whom?

DOROTHEA. Why, naturally with the person whom I love. And obviously loves me.

HELENA. T? RALPH? ELLIS?

(Bodey, still in the kitchenette, nervously sings "Me and My Shadow.")

DOROTHEA. I thought I'd made that clear, thought I'd made everything clear.

HELENA. Oh, Dorothea, my dear. I hope and pray that you haven't allowed him to take advantage of your—generous nature.

DOROTHEA. Miss Bodenhafer has the same apprehension.

HELENA. That is the one and only respect in which your friend, Miss Bodenhafer, and I have something in common.

DOROTHEA. Poor Miss Bodenhafer is terribly naïve for a girl approaching forty.

HELENA. Miss Bodenhafer is not approaching forty. She has encountered forty and continued past it, undaunted.

DOROTHEA. I don't believe she's the sort of girl who would conceal her age.

HELENA *(laughing like a cawing crow)*. Dorothea, no girl could tell me she's under forty and still be singing a song of that vintage. Why, she knows every word of it, including— what do they call it? The introductory verse? Why is she cracking hard-boiled eggs in there?

DOROTHEA. She's making deviled eggs for a picnic lunch.

HELENA. Oh. In Forest Park.

DOROTHEA. No, at Creve Coeur.

HELENA. Oh, at Creve Coeur, that amusement park on a lake, of which Miss Bodenheifer gave such a lyrical account. Would you like a Lucky?

DOROTHEA. No. Thank you. My father smoked Chesterfields. Do you know Creve Coeur?

HELENA. Heard of it. Only. You go out, just the two of you?

DOROTHEA. No, her brother, Buddy, usually goes with us on these excursions. They say they've been going out there since they were children, Bodey and Buddy. They still ride the Ferris wheel, you know, and there's a sort of loop-the-loop that takes you down to the lake shore. Seats much too narrow sometimes. You see, it's become embarrassing to me lately, the brother you know . . .

HELENA. Who doesn't interest you?

DOROTHEA. Heavens, no, it's—pathetic. I don't want to hurt Bodey's feelings, but the infatuation is hardly a mutual thing and it never could be, of course, since I am—well, involved with—

HELENA. The dashing, the irresistible new principal at Blewett.

(Bodey sings.)

DOROTHEA. —I'd rather not talk about that—prematurely, you know. Ralph feels it's not quite proper for a principal to be involved with a teacher. He's—a very, very scrupulous young man.

HELENA. Oh? Is that the impression he gives you? I'm rather surprised he's given you that impression.

DOROTHEA. I don't see why. Is it just because he's young and attractive with breeding, background? Frequently mentioned in the social columns? Therefore beyond involvement with a person of my ignominious position.

HELENA. Personally, I'd avoid him like a—snakebite!

(Bodey, in the kitchenette, sings "I'm Just Breezing along with the Breeze" again.)
Another one of her oldies! The prospect of this picnic at Creve Coeur seems to make her absolutely euphoric.

DOROTHEA. I'm afraid that they're the high points in her life. Sad . . . Helena, I'm very puzzled by your attitude toward Ralph Ellis. Why on earth would a girl want to avoid a charming young man like Ralph?

HELENA. Perhaps you'll understand a little later.

(Dorothea glances at her watch and the silent phone.)

DOROTHEA *(raising her voice)*. Bodey, please not quite so loud in there! Miss Brookmire and I are holding a conversation in here, you know. *(She turns back to Helena and continues the conversation with an abrupt vehemence.)* — Helena, that woman wants to absorb my life like a blotter, and I'm not an ink splash! I'm sorry you had to meet her. I'm awfully—embarrassed, believe me.

HELENA. I don't regret it at all. I found her most amusing. Even the Gluck!

DOROTHEA *(resuming with the same intensity)*. Bodey wants me to follow the same, same old routine that she follows day in and day out and I—feel sympathy for the loneliness of the girl, but we have nothing, nothing, but *nothing* at all, in common. *(She interrupts herself.)* Shall we have some coffee?

HELENA. Yes, please. I do love iced coffee, but perhaps the ice is depleted.

BODEY *(from the kitchenette)*. She knows darn well she used the last piece.

HELENA. Is it still warm?

(Dorothea has risen and gone into the kitchenette where she pours two cups of coffee.)

DOROTHEA. It never cools off in this electric percolator, runs out, but never cools off. Do you take cream?

HELENA. No, thank you.

DOROTHEA *(bringing the coffee into the living room)*. Bodey does make very good coffee. I think she was born and raised in a kitchen and will probably die in a kitchen if ever she does break her routine that way.

(Bodey crosses to the kitchen table with Dorothea's purse and hat which she has collected from the living room while Helena and Dorothea sip their coffee.)

BODEY. Dotty, remember, Buddy is waiting for us at the Creve Coeur station, we mustn't let him think we've stood him up.

DOROTHEA *(sighing)*. Excuse me, Helena, there really has been a terrible problem with communication today. *(She crosses to Bodey and adjusts her hearing aid for her.)* Can you hear me clearly, now at last?

BODEY. You got something to tell me?

DOROTHEA. Something I've told you already, frequently, loudly, and clearly, but which you simply will not admit because of your hostility toward Ralph Ellis. I'm waiting here to receive an important call from him, and I am not going anywhere till it's come through.

BODEY. Dotty. It's past noon and he still hasn't called.

DOROTHEA. On Saturday evening he's out late at social affairs and consequently sleeps late on Sundays.

BODEY. This late?

HELENA. Miss Bodenhafer doesn't know how the privileged classes live.

BODEY. No, I guess not, we're ignorant of the history of art, but Buddy and me, we've got a life going on, you understand, we got a life . . .

DOROTHEA. Bodey, you know I'm sorry to disappoint your plans for the Creve Coeur picnic, but you must realize by now—after our conversation before Miss Brookmire dropped in—that I can't allow this well-meant design of yours to get me involved with your brother to go any further. So that even if I were *not* expecting this important phone call, I would not go to Creve Coeur with you and your brother this afternoon—or ever! It wouldn't be fair to your brother to, to—lead him on that way . . .

BODEY. Well, I did fry up three chickens and I boiled a dozen eggs, but, well, that's—

HELENA. Life for you, Miss Bodenhafer. We've got to face it.

BODEY. But I really was hoping—expecting—

(Tears appear in Bodey's large, childlike eyes.)

HELENA. Dorothea, I believe she's beginning to weep over this. Say something comforting to her.

DOROTHEA. Bodey? Bodey? This afternoon you must break the news to your brother that—much as I appreciate his attentions—I am seriously involved with someone else, and I think you can do this without hurting his feelings. Let him have some beer first and a—cigar. . . . And about this superabundance of chicken and deviled eggs, Bodey, why don't you call some girl who work in your office and get her to go to Creve Coeur and enjoy the picnic with you this afternoon?

BODEY. Buddy and I, we—don't have fun with—strangers . . .

DOROTHEA. Now, how can you call them strangers when you've been working in the same office with these girls at International Shoe for—how many years? Almost twenty? Strangers? Still?

BODEY. —Not all of 'em have been there long as me . . . *(She blows her nose.)*

DOROTHEA. Oh, some of them must have, surely, unless the death rate in the office is higher than—a cat's back.

(Dorothea smiles half-apologetically at Helena. Helena stifles a malicious chuckle.)

BODEY. —You see, Dotty, Buddy and me feel so at home with you now.

DOROTHEA. Bodey, we knew that I was here just for a while because it's so close to Blewett. Please don't make me feel *guilty.* I have no reason to, do I?

BODEY. —No, no, Dotty—but don't worry about it. Buddy and me, we are both—big eaters, and if there's somethin' left over, there's

always cute little children around Creve Coeur that we could share with, Dotty, so—

DOROTHEA. Yes, there must be. Do that. Let's not prolong this discussion. I see it's painful to you.

BODEY. —Do you? No. It's—you I'm thinking of, Dotty.—Now if for some reason you should change your mind, here is the schedule of the open-air streetcars to Creve Coeur.

HELENA. Yellowing with antiquity. Is it legible still?

BODEY. We'll still be hoping that you might decide to join us, you know that, Dotty.

DOROTHEA. Yes, of course—I know that. Now why don't you finish packing and start out to the station?

BODEY. —Yes. —But remember how welcome you would be if—shoes. *(She starts into the bedroom to put on her shoes.)* I still have my slippers on.

DOROTHEA *(to Helena after Bodey has gone into the bedroom).* So! You've got the post-dated check. I will move to Westmoreland Place with you July first, although I'll have to stretch quite a bit to make ends meet in such an expensive apartment.

HELENA. Think of the advantages. A fashionable address, two bedrooms, a baby grand in the front room and—

DOROTHEA. Yes, I know. It would be a very good place to entertain Ralph.

HELENA. I trust that entertaining Ralph is not your only motive in making this move to Westmoreland Place.

DOROTHEA. Not the only, but the principal one.

HELENA *(leaning forward slowly, eyes widening).* Oh, my dear Dorothea! I have the very odd feeling that I saw the name Ralph Ellis in the newspaper. In the society section.

DOROTHEA. In the society section?

HELENA. I think so, yes. I'm sure so.

(Rising tensely, Dorothea locates the Sunday paper which Bodey has left on the sofa, in some disarray, after removing the "certain item"—the society page. She hurriedly looks through the various sections trying to find the society news.)

DOROTHEA. Bodey?—BOOO-DEYY!

BODEY. What, Dotty?

DOROTHEA. Where is the society page of the *Post-Dispatch?*

BODEY. —Oh . . .

DOROTHEA. What does "oh" mean? It's disappeared from the paper and I'd like to know where.

BODEY. Dotty, I—

DOROTHEA. What's wrong with you? Why are you upset? I just want to know if you've seen the society page of the Sunday paper?

BODEY. —Why, I—used it to wrap fried chicken up with, honey.

DOROTHEA *(to Helena)*. The only part of the paper in which I have any interest. She takes it and wraps fried chicken in it before I get up in the morning! You see what I mean? Do you understand now? *(She turns back to Bodey)*. Please remove the fried chicken from the society page and *let me have it!*

BODEY. —Honey, the chicken makes the paper so greasy that—

DOROTHEA. *I will unwrap it myself! (She charges into the kitchenette, unwraps the chicken, and folds out the section of pages.)* —A section has been torn out of it? Why? What for?

BODEY. Is it? I—

DOROTHEA. Nobody possibly could have done it but you. What did you do with the torn out piece of the paper?

BODEY. —I—*(She shakes her head helplessly.)*

DOROTHEA. Here it is! —Crumpled and tossed in the wastebasket!—What for, I wonder? *(She snatches up the crumpled paper from the wastebasket and straightens it, using both palms to press it hard against the kitchen table so as to flatten it. She holds up the torn-out section of the paper so the audience can see a large photograph of a young women, good looking in a plain fashion, wearing a hard smile of triumph, then she reads aloud in a hoarse, stricken voice.)* Mr. and Mrs. James Finley announce the engagement of their daughter, Miss Constance Finley, to Mr.—T. Ralph Ellis, principal of—

(Pause. There is much stage business. Dorothea is stunned for some moments but then comes to violent life and action. She picks up the picnic shoebox, thrusts it fiercely into Bodey's hands, opens the door for her but rushes back to pick up Bodey's small black straw hat trimmed with paper daises, then opens the door for Bodey again with a violent gresture meaning, "Go quick!" Bodey goes. In the hall we hear various articles falling from Bodey's hold and a small, panting gasp. Then there is silence. Helena gets up with a mechanical air of sympathy.)

HELENA. That woman is sly all right but not as sly as she's stupid. She might have guessed you'd want the society page and notice Mr. Ellis's engagement had been torn out. Anyhow, the news would have reached you at the school tomorrow. Of course I can't understand how you could be taken in by whatever little attentions you may have received from Ralph Ellis.

DOROTHEA. —"Little—attentions?" I assure you they were not—"little attentions," they were—

HELENA. Little attentions which you magnified in your imagination. Well, now, let us dismiss the matter, which has dismissed itself! Dorothea, about the postdated check, I'm not sure the real estate agents would be satisfied with that. Now surely, Dorothea, surely you have relatives who could help you with a down payment in cash?

DOROTHEA. —Helena, I'm not interested in Westmorcland Place. —Now.

HELENA. What!

DOROTHEA. I've—abandoned that idea. I've decided not to move.

HELENA *(aghast)*. —Do you realize what a shockingly irresponsible thing you are doing? Don't you realize that you are placing me in a very unfair position? You led me to believe I could count on your sharing the expense of the place, and now, at the last moment, when I have no time to get hold of someone else, you suddenly—pull out. It's really irresponsible of you. It's a really very irresponsible thing to do.

DOROTHEA. —I'm afraid we wouldn't have really gotten along together. I'm not uncomfortable here. It's only two blocks from the school and—I won't be needing a place I can't afford to entertain—anyone now.—I think I would like to be alone.

HELENA. All I can say is, the only thing I can say is—

DOROTHEA. Don't say it, just, just—leave me alone, now, Helena.

HELENA. Well, that I shall do. You may be right, we wouldn't have gotten along. Perhaps Miss Bodenheifer and her twin brother are much more on your social and cultural level than I'd hoped. And of course there's always the charm of Miss Gluck from upstairs.

DOROTHEA. The prospect of that is not as dismaying to me, Helena, as the little card parties and teas you'd had in mind for us on Westmoreland Place . . .

HELENA. *Chacun à son goût.*

DOROTHEA. Yes, yes.

HELENA *(at the door)*. There is rarely a graceful way to say good-bye. *(She exits.)*

(Pause. Dorothea shuts her eyes very tight and raises a clenched hand in the air, nodding her head several times as it affirming an unhappy suspicion regarding the way of the world. This gesture suffices to discharge her sense of defeat. Now she springs up determinedly and goes to the phone. While waiting for a connection, she notices Miss Gluck seated disconsolately in a corner of the kitchenette.)

DOROTHEA. Now Miss Gluck, now Sophie, we must pull ourselves together and go on. Go on, we must just go on, that's all that life seems to offer and—demand. *(She turns her attention to the phone.)* Hello, operator, can you get me information, please?—Hello? Information? Can you get me the number of the little station at the end of the Delmar car-line where you catch the, the—open streetcar that goes out to Creve Coeur Lake?—Thank you.

MISS GLUCK *(speaking English with difficulty and a heavy German accent)*. Please don't leave me alone. I can't go up!

DOROTHEA *(her attention still occupied with the phone)*. Creve Coeur car-line station? Look. On the platform in a few minutes will be a plumpish little woman with a big artificial flower over one ear and a stoutish man with her, probably with a cigar. I have to get an important message to them. Tell them that Dotty called and has decided to go to Creve Coeur with them after all so will they please wait. You'll have to shout to the woman because she's—*deaf* . . .

(For some reason the word "deaf" chokes her and she begins to sob as she hangs up the phone. Miss Gluck rises, sobbing louder.)

No, no, Sophie, come here. *(Impulsively she draws Miss Gluck into her arms.)* I know, Sophie, I know, crying is a release, but it—inflames the eyes.

(She takes Miss Gluck to the armchair and seats her there. Then she goes to the kitchenette, gets a cup of coffee and a cruller, and brings them to Sophie.)

Make yourself comfortable, Sophie.

(She goes to the bedroom, gets a pair of gloves, then returns and crosses to the kitchen table to collect her hat and pocketbook. She goes to the door, opens it, and says . . .)

We'll be back before dark.

THE LIGHTS DIM OUT

That Championship Season

Jason Miller

First presented by Joseph Papp and the New York Shakespeare Festival at the Public Theater in New York City on May 2, 1972, with the following cast:

(*in order of appearance*)

TOM DALEY	Walter McGinn
GEORGE SIKOWSKI	Charles Durning
JAMES DALEY	Michael McGuire
PHIL ROMANO	Paul Sorvino
COACH	Richard A. Dysart

Directed by A. J. Antoon
Setting by Santo Loquasto
Costumes by Theori V. Aldredge
Lighting by Ian Calderon

PLACE: The coach's house, somewhere in the Lackawanna Valley.

Jason Miller wrote *That Championship Season* while appearing as one of the poker players in *The Odd Couple* at a dinner theatre in Fort Worth, Texas. The play was written during his free afternoons, three hours a day for ten weeks. "I read a lot of Odets, Williams and Albee to see how to put a play together." His work was almost lost through a catastrophic oversight. While driving to the Dallas airport Miller forgot that he had put his only copy of the manuscript on top of the car while loading his baggage. When he realized that it was gone, he drove back to Fort Worth and searched his room. In despair, he drove back to Dallas again and on the way he suddenly saw what appeared to be a blizzard of yellow pages; he hopped out of the car and started collecting them. "Miraculously, every one of one hundred fifty-three pages was in that lovely field. It was like picking flowers."

Miller then showed the manuscript to A. J. Antoon, who took it to Joseph Papp, and the three had "lots of late-night Scotch drinking over the script. It was very collaborative, very creative and we finally got it back to the way I wanted it originally." *That Championship Season* won a Tony award, a Pulitzer Prize for drama, the Outer Circle Critics Award and the New York Drama Critics Circle Award for the best play of the 1971–72 season.

That Championship Season is a play filled with keen observation and insight. It is a bitter commentary on the American way—the *deal*. Five men meet annually to celebrate the triumph of their past: the 1952 Pennsylvania High School Basketball Championship. This particular occasion is the twentieth anniversary of that event. Four of the five are present: George, the mayor of the town, worried about his reelection; Phil, the town's chief industrialist and a lover of fast cars and women; James, a junior high school principal and George's campaign manager; and George's brother Tom, a drunk. Their old coach watches over them like a stern father trying to relive and reinforce their success story—the American dream—a shattered dream that never existed. The coach's motto is success at any price, to win at any cost. "Never settle for less than success. . . . I carved you in silver," he says as the four turn on one another, their pride, loyalty and friendship vanishing in the confrontations that ensue. The play is also an indictment of small-town America. Miller has stated that he is writing about "men going into their middle age with a sense of terror and defeat. They are desperately holding on to their youth. The only thing that holds them together is the memory of when they *were* together."

Miller sees the play as somewhat autobiographical. "There are traces of autobiography in the play, only I did not know any politicians directly in Scranton. I played on the high school basketball team, but it came in second. I was never involved in a state championship, and I never had a coach like that. It is, however, the stuff of my life." He feels that with certain changes in language, interpretation and situation, the play could be taking place anywhere. "What wouldn't change is the inhibition, the fear and despair that motivates these people." Also, the setting is totally familiar to the author. "I love this room; it's distinctly the sixth character in my play. Even before I wrote the play, I visualized this dark and spacious room with its Tiffany lamp over the table, the lace curtains, the panes of colored glass, the sporting photographs, the staircase, the porch outside. . . ."

Jason Miller was born John Miller in Long Island City, New York, in 1939. He attended St. Patrick's High School and found the nuns there a very positive influence, especially one nun, Sister Celine, who taught him debating, rhetoric and public speaking. "They gave me encouragement at a time when I might have stolen cars." Miller's first exposure to theatre was "attending high mass and watching all the pomp and circumstance" as an altar boy. "I feel that the theatre should take the place of the church today—give us an image of ourselves, help us find where we're at. . . . All good theatre has something religious about it." From rhetoric and public speaking he went on to acting, acting in his first role as a private secretary in *Victoria Regina* at Marywood College, while still a senior at St. Patrick's.

Miller entered the University of Scranton (a Jesuit institution) on an athletic scholarship but soon afterward began to concentrate on acting and writing for the theatre. His first play, *The Winner,* a one-act drama about a prize fighter, won first prize in the Jesuit Eastern Play Contest. Upon graduation in 1961, he entered graduate school at Catholic University in Washington, D.C., to study drama. In 1963 he married Linda Gleason, another drama student, and they moved to New York. Here Miller found occasional work in television commercials and soap operas and small roles in Off Broadway and Off-Off-Broadway productions. Between acting jobs, he worked as a messenger, a truck loader and driver, a waiter and a welfare investigator.

In his spare time, he wrote three one-act plays. *The Perfect Son, The Curious Lady* and *Lou Gehrig Didn't Die of Cancer,* which were presented at the Triangle Theatre. *Lou Gehrig* also appeared at Lincoln Center in 1970 and at the Festival Theatre in 1981. In 1970, his full-length three-act play, *Nobody Hears a Broken Drum,* about the Molly McGuires, was also presented at the Triangle Theatre and then moved Off-Broadway to the Fortune Theatre.

Miller's first substantial acting roles were outside New York, at the Champlain Shakespeare Festival in Vermont, the Cincinnati Shakespeare Festival, the Baltimore Center Stage and the Hartke Theatre in Washington, D.C. His first involvement with Joseph Papp and the New York Public Theater was in the role of Rogozhin in *Subject to Fits* in 1971, under the direction of A. J. Antoon. He has also converted Studs Terkel's *Hard Times* into a musical, and he has written a ninety-minute ABC television movie, *Reward,* a mystery dealing with murder and drugs. Miller was nominated for an Academy Award for Best Supporting Actor for his portrayal of Father Karras in *The Exorcist.* He has also appeared in *The Nickel Ride,* directed by Robert Mulligan, in *Long Day's Journey Into Night* opposite Helen Hayes and in *Juno and the Paycock* with Geraldine Fitzgerald.

ACT ONE

Set: A large and expansive living room in a Gothic-Victorian tradition. The dominant mood of the room is nostalgia. Its furnishings are frayed, dusty; the cool and airless serenity of a museum fills the room. The furniture is a compilation of decades. Downstage left, a large mahogany table, over it, a Tiffany lamp. A Stromberg-Carlson console upstage center. Large leather sofa and matching chairs are scattered around the room. Gun-racks, with shotguns, on both walls. Doilies on the sofa and chairs. Glass bookcase upstage right, filled with leather bound books, on top of it a small collection of silver trophies. Upstage center a large spiralling staircase winds up into the second floor. Overlarge and faded pictures of Teddy Roosevelt, John Kennedy, Senator Joseph McCarthy hang from the walls. Floor lamps flank the staircase. The wall paper is faded and stained and the oriental rug covering the floor is worn and obviously in need of cleaning. An early make, 1950ish, fourteen-inch television set, with rabbit ears, sits neglected in the corner. Upstage center is the main entrance. Downstage left is the entrance to the kitchen. Soiled lace curtains cover the two narrow upstage windows. On the dining table sits a huge silver trophy.

At Rise: TOM DALEY *stands at the gun-racks. He suddenly takes a shotgun from the wall-rack.*

———

GEORGE *(Off-stage)*. Hey Tom, Scotch and water on the rocks?

TOM *(Holding gun)*. No ice.

GEORGE. Scotch and water comin' up.

TOM. Bring in the bottle, no one's going to steal it. Hey George, you know he keeps these guns loaded?

GEORGE. Yeah, I know. Hey, put it down, I'm out of season! Those guns have hair triggers.

TOM. I got the safety on.

GEORGE. Only my laundry man will know how scared I was. *(Pause.)* You've been missed around here, Tom.

TOM. It's only been, what, a couple of years?

GEORGE. Three years, Tom. You've missed three reunions. Remember the time you put the winter-green in my jock? I thought my balls were on fire. Those were the days, the good old days. I am sincerely more proud of winning that championship than I am of being mayor

of this town. Do you believe that?

TOM. No.

GEORGE. Dirty bastard. I'll never forget you; You were a great guard. Brilliant playmaker.

TOM *(Deadpan)*. You were a great guard too, George.

GEORGE. I mean it. Bottom of my heart. This is me talking, no politician. Tremendous ball-handler. . . . I wonder what's keeping them.

TOM. They'll be here.

GEORGE *(Pops a pill)*. Feena-mint. Pressure is murderous. Tense. Get a little constipated now and then. Mostly now.

TOM. When do you start your campaign?

GEORGE. I campaign every day of my life. The real grind begins . . . one week.

TOM. I never thought Sharmen would end up a politician.

GEORGE. Everybody ends up a politician. I'll beat his ass. He can't touch me in this town. Sharmawitz was his real name. That was his family's original name. The coach and me did some research on Mr. Sharmen. The only thing a Jew changes more than his politics is his name. *(Pause.)* He wants this town. Yeah. He wants to take it away from me.

TOM. Ready for another one, your honor?

GEORGE. James is going to be pissed at me if you're high when he gets here.

TOM. Brother James wouldn't dare get pissed at you.

GEORGE. After the election I'm going to endorse him for superintendent of schools. Too valuable a man to waste his time being a junior high school principal.

TOM. That's patronage, George.

GEORGE. I know. Is there any other way?

TOM. What did they find when they opened him up?

GEORGE. Who, the coach? Nothing. An ulcerated stomach. That's all. He'll live forever. I love that man, as we all do. I owe my whole life, success to that man. He convinced me that I could be mayor of this town. He ran me. Do you know how goddam close that first election was? Any idea?

TOM. I don't remember.

GEORGE. Thirty-two votes. I beat Hannrin by thirty-two votes. I looked it up. Closest election in the history of Pennsylvania politics.

TOM. The coach sent me a mass card when I was in the hospital. Mass card . . . I thought I was dead when I saw it.

GEORGE. How the hell long does it take to pick up fried chicken?

TOM. How's Marion?

GEORGE. She's my conscience, for God's sake. My severest critic. She knows the political scene . . . she's almost as sharp as I am *(Pause.)* You know, after the baby, she was . . . very depressed, not quite herself. She's coming around now, thank God.

TOM. That's good.

GEORGE. Hey, do you know what would make this reunion truly memorable?

TOM. Martin would come walking in that door.

GEORGE. Magic on the court, wasn't he?

TOM. Unbelievable.

GEORGE. Greatest high school basketball player I ever saw.

TOM. Unbelievable. *(Pouring.)* Bless me, Father, for I have sinned. *(Drinks.)*

GEORGE. Make that the last, huh.

TOM. It's only six o'clock, George.

GEORGE. Six. It's nine. Where the hell have you been?

TOM. I drink on Pacific Coast time. That way I'm three hours behind everybody else.

GEORGE *(Seriously).* Do you have a drinking problem, Tom?

TOM. No problem. I get all the booze I want.

GEORGE. Look at you, you're underweight, restless, your memory's going, you forget people's names.

TOM. Almost forty, George.

GEORGE. Forty, yeah, it's like half-time.

TOM. Hey, I remembered somebody. I saw her standing by the library yesterday. Mary . . . what's-her-name.

GEORGE. Who?

TOM. The epileptic. Mary . . . you know, the one we banged in your garage . . . we were freshmen or something.

GEORGE. I don't remember.

TOM. We humped her in your garage. She took fits or something.

GEORGE. Don't ever breathe a word . . . she wasn't an epileptic. She was only retarded. Not a word. It could ruin me. She was raped here about two years ago. Scandal. Remember Mike Pollard?

TOM. No.

GEORGE. The guy with the glass eye. Yeah. He raped her in the cemetery. The one and only serious crime I had in four years. Dumb bastard. Where the hell is everybody? The coach loves to drive Phil's caddie. That's why they're not here. Phil's got three cars now. Got a German car goes like a rocket. I cancel at least five speeding tickets for him a month. He's going out with this seventeen year old, believe that, up in Scranton. Had to take her to Philadelphia for an abortion.

TOM. He gave me a big hug and kiss.

GEORGE. Oh, hugs and kisses everybody. Italians are like that. Can't keep their hands off you. Hey, what's air pollution? Five hundred Italian paratroopers.

TOM. What has an I.Q. of 100?

GEORGE. Poland. See, I'm Polish, but I don't mind that, don't mind at all. But Phil gets pissed. Moody bastard. You can never tell what he's thinking. But right now I'm waiting for Phil to kick in thirty thousand for my campaign.

TOM. Thirty thousand . . .

GEORGE. But in return, Phil keeps all the strip land he's leased from the city. Sharmen wants to break that lease. Mr. Sharmen is an ecology nut. The fashionable issue, right? If he gets elected mayor, you won't be able to piss in your toilet. And I'm going to whip Sharmen's ass all over this town. Not this town. Not here. This town is not going to change hands. I love this town, Tom, love the people. Sure we have problems, but if we pull together I can make it the greatest little city in the country. That's one of my campaign slogans. ''Greatest Little City In The Country.''

TOM. Original.

GEORGE. Yeah. We have some information for Phil that's going to knock him on his ass. He's holding back. He knows we need him. See, Phil's not bright, really. James has often said that about Phil. Marion went up to see Phil last month about the contribution. He stalled. She doesn't trust him either *(The men enter.* JAMES *leads the way.* PHIL *follows.* JAMES *carries the beer.* PHIL *carries buckets of fried chicken.)* Where'd you guys go for the beer, New Jersey?

JAMES. Phil wanted *Schlitz.* We had to go to Old Forge.

PHIL. Cop stopped us on the way back. But he . . .

JAMES. Speeding. It's a wonder he saw us at the speed we're going.

PHIL. He recognized the coach and me and ripped up the ticket.

GEORGE. Where's the coach?

PHIL. He's parking the car.

GEORGE. I'm gonna put this in the oven.

PHIL *(Grabs* GEORGE*).* Who do you love, George? (GEORGE *goes into kitchen with chicken.* PHIL *follows with beer.)*

JAMES *(Entering, to* TOM*).* How're you doin'? Stay sober. I may need you tonight.

TOM. When the shit hits the fan I'll be right

behind you.

JAMES. You can handle this stuff in moderation. You can handle anything in moderation. *(To* GEORGE, *who is entering.)* He didn't say a word. Evaded the subject completely.

GEORGE. Didn't he even mention . . . ? (PHIL *enters with beer in hand*).

PHIL. Chicken's in the oven.

GEORGE. Hey, Phil, did you bring along your dirty movies? He's got pornographic movies, the dirty bastard. I love him. I should arrest him.

PHIL. Arrest me? I rent them from your brother-in-law, the Chief of Police. *(To* TOM.*)* The Police Department is a library for stag films.

GEORGE. He sells what he's confiscated. Isn't free enterprise something else?

PHIL. How do you think I raised the money for the Little League Fund? Rented the V.F.W., charged five bucks a head and showed *Olga's Massage Parlor* and selected shorts.

GEORGE. *Rin Tin Tin Gets In.*

JAMES. Incredible. I couldn't believe my eyes.

PHIL. Who are you kidding. You bought a German Shepherd the next day. *(Loud whistle on porch.* COACH *comes in dressed in a brown suit, 1940 cut. White shirt. Tie. Gold watch chain. Huge man. Old Testament temperament. A superb actor. A man of immense and powerful contradictions.)*

COACH. All right. Line it up. Shape it. Twenty laps around the room. Too much fat in the ass around here. I want my boys lean and mean. *(Great laughter.)* A voice from the past boys, the old gunner can still bray with the best. *(Pouring whiskey.)* Hit those boards hard, Romano . . . and you, Sikowski, don't just stand there with your finger up you know where, move! . . . And you, Daley, have a drink . . . *(Laughs.)* and you big Daley [James], hustle some of this whiskey into you, Imported. *Jamison.* Boil your brains, this stuff!

GEORGE. You haven't changed in twenty years.

COACH. I haven't changed in sixty years. I can take the four of you around the court 'til you drop, run you into the ground. *(Proudly.)* Even 185. Weighed that in 1940. *(Gets down and does ten quick push-ups.)* And that's after having my belly cut open, twenty stitches. *(Opens shirt.)* Look at that sonofabitch. Belly looks like a baseball.

JAMES. What's the secret?

COACH. "Walk softly and carry a big stick."

(Pause. Great joy, shy almost.) Oh, Christ, boys, Christ, it's so good . . . the joy in my heart to feel you around me again, *(He pats, feels, whacks them all.)* together again, can't find words to say it . . . magnificent! My boys standing around me again! A toast to the 1952 Pennsylvania State High School Basketball Champions! *(They drink.)* You were a legend in your time, boys, a legend. Never forget that, never.

GEORGE. We owe it all to you, coach. *(Men ad-lib agreement.)*

COACH. I used to tell people you boys were like a fine watch. My very expensive and fine watch that kept perfect time. You froze the ball against Tech for three minutes. Fantastic. Stay in shape. Lean and mean. You're in your thirties and that's the heart attack season, boys. Most important muscle in your body, boys . . . the heart . . . keep it in shape, work it out!

GEORGE. Bought one of those exercise bikes. Keeps the stomach flat.

PHIL. But your ass is still down around your knees.

GEORGE. That's it, start on me, the old scapegoat.

TOM. You love it.

GEORGE. Yeah.

COACH. Drink up, boys, put it away, night's young! Take off your jackets, relax.

GEORGE. Chicken is in the stove.

COACH. You're working on your third chin yourself, Phil.

PHIL. I'm an executive.

COACH. James, you're starting to sag a little too, you look tired.

JAMES. I haven't been sleeping well, coach.

COACH. Why?

JAMES. My teeth.

COACH. What's the matter?

JAMES. They're gone.

COACH. Gone.

JAMES *(Embarrassed).* They took them out last month.

COACH. You got plates?

JAMES. Yeah.

COACH. Let's see. Open your mouth. Uh, uh. Good job. They look almost real. *(Phil laughs.)* Never had enough Vitamin C in your diet!

JAMES *(Half-smile).* Try feeding five kids.

COACH. You didn't feed them your teeth did you? You need iron in your blood . . . *(Opens mouth.)* I got twenty-seven originals. *(Men laugh.)*

JAMES. Actually they've recently completed

studies proving that nerves can cause severe damage to teeth.

COACH. Really! Maybe you should have gotten your nerves out! *(Laugh.)* Have another shot and relax, James. Better put that chicken on low, George. Tom, *(Hugs him. They touch glasses and drink.)* I'm so goddam happy, so grateful you're back with us again. Doesn't he look wonderful, boys?

TOM *(Pouring)*. Nothing keeps the old gunner down, either.

COACH. You were a thing of rare . . . beauty, boys. Life is a game and I'm proud to say I played it with the best. We were one flesh twenty years ago; never forget that as long as you live! *(Pause.)* Ten seconds left on that clock . . . we were down by one point . . . remember . . .

GEORGE *(Quiet intensity)*. I passed inbounds to Tom.

TOM. I brought the ball up.

PHIL. Passed to me in the corner.

COACH *(Urgent)*. Six seconds left!

PHIL. I hit James coming . . .

JAMES. Across the court and I saw . . .

COACH. Three seconds left!

JAMES. Martin at the foul line . . .

GEORGE. Martin caught the ball in mid-air . . . he went up . . .

JAMES. Up . . .

COACH. One second . . .

GEORGE *(Jumping up)*. Yes!

COACH. State Champions! They said we couldn't do it, boys. We beat a school three times our size. We beat them in Philadelphia. We performed the impossible, boys, never forget that, never. Jesus, remember they had an eight foot nigger, jumped like a kangaroo. *(Proudly.)* There's the trophy, boys. Fast, Jesus, fast, you were a flash of legs . . . gone, like lightning!

GEORGE. Martin was a pressure ballplayer.

COACH. He thrived on it . . . loved it.

JAMES. He had a great eye.

COACH. Priceless.

GEORGE. The perfect ballplayer.

COACH. Not a flaw. he made it all go . . . magnificent talent! *(Pause. Quietly.)* Yeah. Not a word in twenty years. Let's say a little prayer for him boys, a prayer that he's safe and happy and still a champion. *(They lay their hands together, moment of silence.)* We never had a losing season, boys; there's not many that can say that . . .

GEORGE *(Testing)*. Sharmen won't be able to say that after next month, will he, coach?

COACH. He'll see politics played like he's never seen it played before. We'll run him off the court, that little mockie is going to think . . . he's trying to ruin Phil. Put Phil out of business.

PHIL. I strip-mine coal and the sonofabitch makes me out to look like a criminal.

COACH. Phil is one of the most respected businessmen in the state and this . . . Sharmawitz is trying to ruin his good name. Cop ripped up that speed ticket tonight when he recognized Phil.

PHIL. He knew you too, Coach.

GEORGE. He attacked me.

TOM. Who, the cop?

GEORGE. Sharmen. I'm not prejudiced. Live and let live. But that Jew attacked me, the mayor of the town, attacked me in print!

TOM. He's running against you, for Christ . . .

GEORGE. There's still such a thing as respect for the office! He said I wasn't smart enough to be corrupt . . . in the papers. Do you believe that?

TOM. Yes . . .

COACH. Fashion politics; he's running on all the headlines.

PHIL. The women love him. Looks like Robert Goulet.

GEORGE. You can't beat experience. He said under my term this town took five giant steps into the past. Believe that? I gave this town four memorable years!

COACH. And you'll give us four more! Like old T.R. said, Teddy was fond of sayin', "Never settle for less than success." And, boys, they carved that man's face into a mountain. They don't make Teddies any more, a man among men, a giant. Took Panama from the spics, boys, just walked in and took her.

TOM. I'll drink to that . . . feat.

COACH. And I'm proud to see all of you climbing to the top of your professions, politics, business . . . education . . . travel.

JAMES *(Sentimental)*. And there's only one man I know who's responsible for it and he's sitting right across from me.

COACH. No, not me. You did it yourselves. Best advice I gave you . . . get yourselves a name, remember? Listen up, Phil, your little league team lost its third in a row I hear.

PHIL *(Laughing)*. Lost my best pitcher and my center fielder.

COACH. Injured?

PHIL. They go to camp in June.

JAMES. Use my James. He can play center field.

PHIL. He can't hit a curve.

JAMES. He's only twelve years old, for God's sake.

PHIL. Work with him. He needs a lot of work.

JAMES. You're the coach, not me. He learns fast.

PHIL. I don't think he's interested if you want the truth . . .

JAMES. He's a gifted child.

COACH. Very smart.

JAMES. He has an I.Q. of one fifty-five.

PHIL. That's about two points higher than his batting average.

TOM. Maybe you could trade him, Phil . . .

JAMES. It's not funny. The boy is first team material. His self-esteem is being damaged, not playing, sitting on the bench.

COACH. George, get me a beer. *(He does.)*

JAMES. He's just not your ordinary kid.

PHIL. He doesn't like the game . . .

JAMES. Not sitting on the end of the bench.

TOM. James, he told me he didn't want to play ball.

JAMES. I want him to play.

TOM. He knows that but he doesn't share your enthusiasm.

JAMES. He's in that difficult age now. Avoids me. Keeps to himself. *(Pause.)* I think he's masturbating.

TOM. On the bench!

JAMES. You're ridiculous!

COACH. Did you say anything?

JAMES. What can I say? I certainly am not going to tell him those old horror stories. My father told us we'd go insane. Grow hair on the palm of your hands.

COACH. You kept it in your pants when you played for me.

JAMES. He'll do it, he will. I'll see to it. He's the cream of the crop, that boy . . .

COACH. You keep him playing. You quit on the field you'll quit in life. It's on the playing fields the wars are won.

JAMES. He's a good boy, a respectful boy.

COACH. He couldn't be anything else, being your son. You were the perfect son. You took care of your father.

JAMES *(Simply)*. Someone had to do it.

COACH. There's no respect, no personal sacrifice, not today. There's not many who'd have made the sacrifice you did, James.

GEORGE. There's a decline of respect, an absolute decline . . .

COACH. You see, there's no discipline, George.

GEORGE. The high school newspaper had a picture of a pig with Phil's name under it, believe that? Sharmen was behind that.

PHIL. Number one threat to the environment. They called me that. The stupid bastards don't realize you can't kill a mountain. Mountains grow back . . .

GEORGE *(Mollifying)*. I fixed it up, Phil. Don't forget that, don't worry about it.

PHIL. What, me worry? I could buy and sell those little bastards a hundred times. I got a shovel working for me now, looks like a dinosaur, right?

GEORGE. I can still get you an apology in print.

PHIL. I don't need it.

GEORGE. I called the principal and gave him hell, chewed his ass out.

TOM *(Going upstairs)*. That's it! I've got it! That's your campaign poster, George. A picture of you on your knees, salivating. Caption—"I'll chew the ass out of unemployment."

GEORGE *(Laughing)*. I want him. Hire that man.

TOM. Where's the john?

COACH. Where it always was. *(Laughs.)*

JAMES. He was very sick. I think it's affected his memory. He's getting back in shape.

COACH. Nothing's going to beat that boy. He's comin' along, comin' along . . . let's put him to work on your campaign. Write press releases, speeches . . .

GEORGE. My speechwriter.

JAMES. I'd love it but he's leaving. He bought his ticket today, he said.

COACH. Why?

JAMES. That's him, here today, gone tomorrow. Says he wants to leave by Sunday.

COACH. I'll talk to him. Give me an hour with him. Talk some sense into that boy's head.

GEORGE. We could use him.

PHIL. We need something . . . a miracle or something.

GEORGE. What does that mean, Phil?

PHIL. It means we've got problems.

GEORGE. Who?

PHIL. You. Us.

GEORGE. I've got a great record . . . wonderful. This town loves me. *(Laughs.)* Tell him how popular I am, coach.

COACH *(Pause)*. Let's hear Phil . . . don't overestimate your strength, George.

GEORGE. What?

COACH. What I mean to say is never underestimate your opponent.

GEORGE *(Pressing)*. I'm putting this town back on its feet again!

PHIL. Not with your taxes. A four per cent increase in property tax. You're lucky you weren't hung!

GEORGE. We were broke. The city was broke when I took over. We needed money, operating capital.

PHIL. No work around, no money, taxes raised every year. People . . . want . . . change. Look, it's a small town . . . forty, maybe. . . .

JAMES. Fifty-four thousand is our total population. There is unemployment but studies have shown that our unemployment is below the average.

GEORGE. You can't tell me that the working man's not behind me.

PHIL. Working man. The ammunition plant closes in September.

GEORGE. Phil, I didn't end the war.

PHIL. Look, I'm only reciting history. We had a garbage strike here lasted for five weeks. City smelled like a whorehouse.

JAMES. George has given this city the finest playground facilities in the state. I mean the program is considered a model by other cities.

COACH. That's a fact.

PHIL. And Sharmen has IBM ready to come in here tomorrow.

COACH. You bring those gigantic companies in here and in five years the briefcases will run this town.

GEORGE. I'm popular. Extremely popular. Wasn't there five thousand people cheering in the rain when I opened the zoo?

PHIL. They were waiting to see the new elephant . . .

GEORGE. But I bought the goddam thing.

PHIL. And it died in a month, George. It lived for one month only.

GEORGE. I'm the mayor, not a vet. How was I to know it was sick.

JAMES. I think what Phil is trying to say is that this . . .

PHIL. I know what I'm trying to say, James. It took you a month to bury the goddam thing.

GEORGE. Ten days, not a month, ten days.

PHIL. You could have burned the thing in a day.

GEORGE. You can't burn dead elephants. It's against the health laws. Don't you people know that?

COACH *(Pause)*. The goddam thing drew more people dead than alive.

JAMES. Well, we got rid of it.

PHIL. You advised him, James.

GEORGE. Yes, I finally had to throw the damn thing down a mine shaft. Goddam city council make me look foolish.

PHIL. Had to rent a crane. Another 500 bucks. The newspapers weren't kind, George.

GEORGE. They came around after I called them up and chewed some ass.

PHIL. They called you Sabu for a month. It hurt your image. *(TOM enters.)*

GEORGE. And I have a fantastic image in this town. If the city council was behind me, I'd get action and you know it. How can I work with a divided council, the bastards . . .

COACH. Trash it out, boys, trash it out. Have another drink, George.

GEORGE. No riots on my streets, no niggers burning down my town . . .

PHIL. The last nigger here was Joe Lewis and he was passing through.

GEORGE. No radicals, here, hippies. One rape in four years. One felony. My streets are safe any hour, day, night.

JAMES. We are not even certain she was raped.

COACH. Who?

GEORGE. The girl that Mike Pollard raped . . . he had a glass eye, you remember . . .

JAMES. She claimed he assaulted her . . . forced perverted acts. Said he performed cunnilingus on her.

COACH. Cunny-what?

JAMES. Oral sex. The male performing an oral act on the woman.

COACH. Oh yes, oh yeah. Jesus, that's a fancy name for it. *(Laughs.)*

PHIL. If that's a perversion I should be in a cage.

COACH *(Sudden change)*. Let's not get away from the subject, boys, we are on a very serious subject. I'm talking about dissension, boys, I can sense dissension in this room. Dissension is destroying this country, tearing it apart. *(To* TOM.*)* You're George's speechwriter. This country is hurting, boys, hurting, so let's pull together here . . . teamwork!

JAMES. Dangerous times all over.

COACH. We are killing off, murdering the best among us, gunning down the best we have! . . . Kennedy . . . killed by his own . . . such a waste.

JAMES. We don't take care of our own any more. Bobby Kennedy, too.

COACH. They killed McCarthy, boys, his own kind killed a great American. Looked under the rock and found the place infested with communists. Joe McCarthy. Turned his name into a dirty word. They kill the good ones, they kill them quick.

JAMES. It's been a tough decade.

COACH. It never changes. Father Coughlin . . . you're too young to remember . . . he told the truth about certain people, on the radio, international bankers, Jews, fellow travellers, and they muzzled him, a priest of God telling the truth and they put him away, exiled him. And that's a fact, boys. We are the country, boys, never forget that, never. Thousands of cities like ours; we fire the furnace, keep it all going round, indispensable! But no dissension, none, stick together. We stick together. *(Grabs* GEORGE, *dances.)* And "There'll be a hot time in the old town" come election night.

GEORGE *(Singing).* "A hot time in the old town tonight." Come on, you guys, sing . . . sing. This is a reunion, remember?

PHIL *(Clapping).* You sing, George.

GEORGE. Get the women, Phil, I think he's getting horny. *(Men ad-lib remarks.)*

COACH. I'll run them into the ground. *(The* COACH *stands frozen with pain.)*

GEORGE. What's the matter? Are you all right?

COACH. Bring me that chair.

JAMES. Can you move? Take a drink.

PHIL. What is it?

COACH *(Doesn't sit).* My stomach.

PHIL. Do you have pills?

COACH. It comes and goes. I overdid it. Adhesions, that's all it is. The incision is healing.

GEORGE. What can we do?

COACH *(Trying to joke).* Give me a hand upstairs.

GEORGE. I'll take him.

COACH. I'll put on that goddam girdle they gave me. It gives me a rash in this weather. *(On landing, as* GEORGE *helps him upstairs.)* It's nothing serious, it's only a healing pain, I'll be down in a few minutes. *(Pause.)*

PHIL. He didn't look good to me.

JAMES *(Uncertain).* All that dancing around. He gets like a boy. He overdid it.

PHIL. He looks yellow or something.

TOM. He's sick.

JAMES. He overdid it.

GEORGE *(On landing).* He's all right. He's mixing something. Kelp. Says it's an organic painkiller. I'll stay with him. *(Goes back to* COACH.)

JAMES. Go ahead.

PHIL. Kelp?

JAMES. Yeah. He doesn't believe in pain killers. No pills.

PHIL. He is going to get assholed by Sharmen.

JAMES. Shhh. Why are you so down on him?

PHIL. Because he's a loser. Four years ago he beat that old alcoholic we had by thirty-two votes, remember. Five recounts! You know it and I know it.

JAMES. Is that the only reason you're against him now?

PHIL. Isn't that enough?

JAMES *(Pause).* I thought it might be because you're having an affair with his wife.

TOM. Christ. Not now, James.

JAMES. I'll handle this.

PHIL. Who told you?

JAMES. It could easily become common knowledge.

PHIL *(Almost pleased).* It's a rumor.

JAMES. Don't deny it, Phil.

PHIL. She never got over me since high school.

TOM. Old Marion. I hope she improved with age.

JAMES. You keep quiet, understand!

TOM. Humping Marion was part of the curriculum.

PHIL. Not when she went with me.

JAMES. Don't get involved with her, Phil, she's sick, she's unstable.

PHIL. She was a great girl till she married that asshole.

JAMES. That asshole stands between you and a complete business disaster.

PHIL *(Shouting).* I know that, you think I don't know that!

JAMES. You need him as much as he needs you.

PHIL. Sharmen needs contributions, too.

JAMES *(Stunned).* Jesus, you'd do that to us? You'd jump to Sharmen?

PHIL. An investment. Politics is just another way of makin' money. Sharmen is no different than any other politician.

JAMES. I don't care what you do with your private life, but when it endangers—

PHIL. You're in it for what you can get, a piece of the action, don't shit me.

JAMES. He's all we have right now.

PHIL. And he's not enough. *(Pause.)*

JAMES. There is another alternative. My career is politics, Phil. I'm a political animal. I hoped to run, as you know, for school superintendent next year with George's endorsement. *(Pause.)* I want you to realize that this is ahead of my time-schedule, and I only offer my candidacy because we seem to be faced with an insoluble crisis.

PHIL *(Pause)*. You're not serious.

JAMES. Run me, Phil. I can carry this town.

PHIL *(Stunned)*. Why don't you have a drink, James?

JAMES. Someone has to challenge Sharmen's charisma.

PHIL. I'll have one with you.

JAMES. My reputation is spotless. I'm a respected public official. Known all over town. George could be convinced . . .

PHIL. I don't believe you're serious.

JAMES. I'm a seasoned politician.

PHIL. You . . . against Sharmen.

JAMES. I can be mayor of this town.

PHIL. Half the time, more than half, it was your advice that turned George into the village idiot.

JAMES. Phil, I kept his head above water. He suggested stuffing the elephant and putting it in the museum.

PHIL. James, take a look at yourself. Take an honest look. Sharmen attracts people, he's young . . . new . . . he's poised. You're a school principal, and you also work for the mayor, a patronage job . . . (GEORGE *enters with basketball*.)

GEORGE. He's putting on his girdle. Recognize this, huh? *(He passes the ball suddenly to* PHIL. PHIL *throws it to* TOM. TOM *to* JAMES. JAMES *back to* GEORGE.*)*

TOM. Can't get the rhythm going without Martin.

GEORGE. But it's still there. All we need is some practice. James, tell them my campaign slogan.

JAMES. Not now, George . . .

GEORGE. "Four more years of serenity and progress" . . . *(Pause.)* Don't you think it has a ring of security about it?

PHIL. If you have a choir of angels singing it.

GEORGE. It'll be expensive. We saturate the local stations with it, billboards, etc., etc.

JAMES. Later, George, this is not the time . . .

GEORGE. We have a whole new image for me. A grassroots guy. Show me moving among the people. No egghead. Dynamic shots.

JAMES. George, will you please . . .

GEORGE. I'm dynamite on television.

JAMES. George, shut up a minute, will you!

GEORGE. What's the matter . . . something gone wrong here?

JAMES. Phil has serious doubts about us.

GEORGE. What?

JAMES. He doesn't think we can beat Sharmen.

GEORGE. Not after he hears a piece of very hot news we picked up last week.

JAMES. What are you talking about?

GEORGE. My ace in the hole, James. Me and the coach kept it even from you. A little research goes a long way, my friends! Sharmen's uncle was a communist. *New York Times.* June fifth. 1952. A blacklisted writer. Hollywood.

PHIL. Old news. No one cares anymore. He's probably dead.

GEORGE. He is!

PHIL. Can't hurt Sharmen.

GEORGE. In this town he is dead with a resume like that!

JAMES. Are you sure, George? Are you absolutely positive, not a shadow . . . ?

GEORGE. Uncontestable. The coach can give you more details. Well, Phil, how do you stand now? There was a communist in his family!

PHIL. Times have changed. I can't depend on a hate vote. Nobody knows or cares about his dead communist uncle.

JAMES. It's a whole new ball game, Phil.

PHIL. Ancient history.

JAMES. It's gotta hurt him. There's no way it can't hurt him.

PHIL. Wake up. It's 1972 already.

JAMES *(Dangerous)*. George has taken good care of you, Phil . . .

PHIL. I paid for it. My money got him elected last time.

JAMES. There's more to it than that and you know it.

PHIL. Is there?

JAMES. Yes, there is. See this suit? One hundred dollars. Yours is silk, tailor made. Three hundred, huh? Five kids. One a genius, maybe. I support my alcoholic brother. Shut up! You're an alcoholic, a marathon drunk. I am working my ass off for George's victory because I want a share of the spoils. I am a talented man being swallowed up by anonymity! I want my share!

PHIL *(Trying not to shout)*. You two guys fucked up. Share that!

JAMES. What's the next step, Phil, lunch with Sharmen?

PHIL. You son of a bitch.

GEORGE. James, calm down

JAMES. Betrayal! It's nothing less than betrayal!

PHIL. Betrayal! Don't you mention betrayal to me.

JAMES. Listen to me, don't you understand what—

PHIL. Don't talk to me about betrayal, not after . . .

JAMES. Why are you so thick?

PHIL. Can I help it if you're nobody . . .

JAMES. Pig-headed—

PHIL. Go on welfare!

JAMES. He's fucking your wife, George, that's why he won't support you.

GEORGE *(Pause)*. Fucking who? What?

JAMES. Your wife, Marion.

GEORGE *(Shock)*. When? Why?

PHIL. That is not why I won't support him.

GEORGE. Wait a minute, you're doing what with Marion?

PHIL. Georgie, we had a thing . . . it just happened.

GEORGE. Marion. Unfaithful. I'm the mayor, for Chrissakes!

PHIL. This was the wrong thing to do.

GEORGE. I need some . . . drink. *(Suddenly.)* You should be dead! Wiped away like a dirty stain!

JAMES. George, my intention was not . . .

GEORGE. I know your intention. *(To PHIL.)* You prey on people, you fucking animal. *(Rips shotgun from wall.)* Dead. You dirty dumb dago fucking animal bastard. *(Points gun at PHIL.)*

COACH *(Enters)*. Boys, here's the record. I hope I have a good needle. Watch it, George, she's loaded.

GEORGE. I'm going to put Phil out of his misery!

COACH. What's the matter, what's happened, boys?

TOM. George, the safety is on. (GEORGE *flicks the safety off.*)

BLACKOUT

ACT TWO

Men are in exact positions that ended ACT ONE. *Long pause. Gun trembles in* GEORGE'S *hands.*

————

GEORGE. Fucking animal!

COACH. That's a hair-trigger, a . . . it's loaded. I keep them loaded.

GEORGE *(Whisper)*. Dumb, dangerous animal.

JAMES. Why don't you put the gun down, George.

TOM. Yeah, we give up.

JAMES. You've got your career to think about. Killing Phil is not worth it.

COACH *(Careful)*. Don't lose your poise, boy, be a man and give me the gun. (GEORGE *hands over the gun and begins to sob. Seating him.*) It's all right . . . sit here . . . okay. Easy boy. *(To* JAMES.*)* Get him some Scotch . . . whiskey. We'll work it out, George, put our heads together.

GEORGE. I couldn't even shoot the fucking pig.

COACH. You've had too much to drink, can't hold it. You've got a load of tension in you, boy. Tense. Take deep breaths, George, breathe deeply.

TOM *(With drink)*. Maybe he should do some push ups . . . run in place. *(Men stare at him.)*

COACH. Now, can you talk, George?

GEORGE *(Weakly)*. Yes.

COACH. Fine. Now let's get to the bottom of this. What happened between you and Phil?

GEORGE. It's a private thing . . .

COACH. Private? Nothing's private. There's been nothing private between the people in this room for twenty years.

JAMES. Phil is—   PHIL. Look, I—

GEORGE. It's my wife. I'll tell it. *(Gets up.)* It's my story, right Phil, old pal . . . friend, great guy . . . prick!

COACH. George!

GEORGE. I'm all right. Calm. Phil is having an affair with my Marion.

COACH *(Pause)*. Your Marion?

GEORGE. My Marion.

COACH. Continue, George.

GEORGE. I saved the man's business, put my political future on the line. I trusted my friend. You prick.

COACH. Get some air, George. Take him on the porch, James . . . is this true, Phil?

PHIL. It's over, coach, you know, it just happened.

COACH. No, I don't know because I've never laid my friend's wife. What in Christ's name are you playin', boy, huh?

GEORGE. He's nothing but a whore, an old diseased whore!

COACH. I said enough! *(To* PHIL.*)* You're pussy-whipped, boy, pussy-whipped! Get some discipline. You think with your cock and it's going to ruin you, boy, ruin you quicker than Sharmen, understand me? Somebody is going to scatter you someday . . . all over the ground and goddamit, there are people being hurt, people who have their whole lives invested in this game you're playin'. I'm stunned . . . shocked. I'm damn glad I have a good heart 'cause this . . . *(Sits.)*

GEORGE. Did she tell you you were the best, Phil, huh? Was she good, tell your friends, you dumb dago . . .

COACH. Get him in here. You'll announce it to the neighborhood.

GEORGE. Sex maniac! *(Bumps head on window. Crazy laugh.)* I want to know if my wife was a good lay.

COACH. What's wrong with you, it's none of your business!

GEORGE. What? . . .

COACH *(Pause)*. What happened from beginning to end?

PHIL. She was there one day in my office, and . . .

COACH. When?

PHIL. Last month. She came to see me about campaign money.

GEORGE. She went to all the businessmen in town.

TOM. Wonder how much she raised.

JAMES. I'm warning you.

PHIL. We talked, had some drinks, it just happened . . .

GEORGE. Right there in the office for Chrissakes!?

PHIL. It's a private office . . .

COACH *(Pause)*. On the floor?

PHIL. I have a couch in there. I asked her if she wanted to a . . . a . . .

TOM. Fuck. The word is fuck.

PHIL *(To JAMES)*. Shut that rummy up! And she said yes.

COACH. Just like that, like buying butter. Christ, Marion never struck me as a whore.

GEORGE. Now wait a minute . . .

COACH. Jesus, you're really something. You're some dago. Did you take her clothes off?

GEORGE. Now wait a minute . . .

COACH. I'm trying to establish who made the first advance.

PHIL. I don't remember, coach.

TOM. This is better than *Rin Tin Tin Gets In*.

PHIL. We had a few drinks.

COACH. I see what you did. You doubled her drinks, got her hot on booze and memories, and humped her on the floor.

GEORGE. The couch, goddamit.

COACH. Enough said. You turn on each other,

and you don't have a chance alone, not a solitary chance.

GEORGE. She's not a whore.

COACH. Nobody said she was. You need each other, boys, need . . .

GEORGE. I don't . . . need him.

COACH. I'm talking about survival. I'm talking about survival in the twentieth century.

GEORGE. I'm done with him.

COACH. You can't make it alone, George, not anymore. Gone forever, those days, gone.

GEORGE. You can't, after what's happened, expect me . . .

COACH. I didn't rot and die in the hospital . . .

GEORGE. . . . to even talk to . . .

COACH. . . . because I had you boys around me and . . .

GEORGE. Phil has betrayed everything and . . .

COACH *(Shouting)*. I wasn't alone! I had you boys around me! They didn't experiment with their needles on me, no sir, I had you around me.

JAMES. George, the point he's trying to make . . .

GEORGE. I know the point, I know it, but it doesn't apply to me, this situation.

COACH. I never could deal with ignorance, George, it disgusts me!

GEORGE. He took advantage . . . of my wife. She hasn't been the same since the baby, never got over it. She resents me for putting it away. I wanted to adopt a child, I told her, adopt right away.

COACH. You did the right thing. No man in this room faults you, right?

JAMES *(Trying to sit GEORGE down)*. Speaking for myself, I couldn't see any other way.

GEORGE *(Trying to come back)*. I had chances to be unfaithful. The widows when they cashed in the policy. I could have fucked fifty widows. It was there! They wanted somebody to keep them company.

COACH. Booze and women. I tried to protect you from it. I got the Jesuits, got you scholarships, got the Jesuits to teach you, boys. I graduated in three years from the Jesuits. They all wanted me to become a Jesuit. *(Pause.)* My father used to say the Jesuits were the scholars of the Church. *(Pause.)* But I liked my women . . . my booze . . . and after a while I had my mother . . . I was all she had. *(Pause.)* Someday, I said, someday, I'll marry. But time does strange things. It's high tide before you know it, as my father said, high tide. *(Pause.)* Miss Moriss, remember her, the music teacher.

(Slyly.) We knew each other for years. Biblically. Used to visit her on Saturday afternoon. She'd make me honey biscuits. A very cultured woman. Protestant. Would never think of becoming a Catholic, my mother was alive then, couldn't bring her here. *(Smiles.)* She read poetry in French and wore silk stockings and smoked cigarettes. Elegant. And she could hump like a hundred dollar whore and she loved me on those Saturday afternoons. Fell dead in the street seven years ago. *(Pause.)* I never had the time. Teaching the game was not just a profession, it was a vocation. Like a priest. Devoted my life to excellence . . . superiority. So don't fall apart before my eyes, boys. Not in front of me, because, you, boys, are my real trophies, never forget that, never.

JAMES. Every man in this room realizes that, coach.

COACH. "Never take less than success."

JAMES. I still hear that in my sleep.

COACH. That's a philosophy of life, boys. Not a slogan, a philosophy! We got a challenge comin' up. We beat them by the rules, boys. Pride. Loyalty. Teamwork. No other way.

TOM *(Mocking chant)*. Beat the Jew, Beat that Jew, beat that Jew—Gooo Gentile!

JAMES. You are ridiculous!

TOM. I'm absurd, are you kidding?

COACH *(Directly)*. Why don't you take a walk, Tom.

TOM. I took one, remember?

COACH. But you came back. (JAMES *sits* TOM *on stairs*.)

PHIL *(Flatly)*. I can't support George.

COACH. You will, Phil, after you hear some news . . .

GEORGE. I told him already about Sharmen.

COACH *(Driving on)*. Do you want to win this campaign, George?

GEORGE. I don't need him . . .

COACH. I didn't ask you that; I asked if you wanted to *win!*

GEORGE. Yes, I do but not . . .

COACH. Then you have to pay the price.

TOM. Who pays what? Huh? I mean, what price, what is it?

COACH. Pain. The price is pain. Endurance. You endure pain to win, a law of life, no other way, none. The pain in my gut. It's been there all my life. It's good to hurt. The mind overcomes pain. You keep your marriage, George. Hold onto it. *(Pause.)* We are waiting for your answer, Phil.

PHIL. I have to protect myself.

JAMES. You've already made a choice, haven't you?

COACH *(Unthinkable)*. Not Phil, not my Phil. *(Hug.)* Ya big moose, ya! I had to keep a bed check on you in high school, make sure you were in your own bed. *(Laughs.)*

PHIL *(Adamant)*. Look, I'm sorry, but Sharmen's uncle could today be the head of the red army and he'd still beat George.

COACH. He was a commie.

PHIL. I don't even know if that's true!

COACH *(Pause)*. When have I ever lied to you or you, anyone?

PHIL. No, I mean so what . . .

COACH. FBI came to the school in the 'fifties. McCarthy was in his heyday then on television. They asked about the uncle. Very casual. I knew what was up. I didn't know the man, never saw him. They said good-bye and that was that. I forgot all about it until I was flat on my back in that hospital. We researched it and discovered the whole truth!

PHIL. Why didn't you say something back in the 'fifties?

COACH. Why hurt a young boy? He wasn't a communist.

TOM. Why hurt him now?

COACH. He's on the other side now.

JAMES. He's opposition. *(Pause.)*

PHIL. I'm telling you, public opinion wants George back in the insurance business.

JAMES. Public opinion is changed every day.

TOM *(Half-serious)*. He's right, you know. *(Pause.)* An hour listening to this and I'm ready to campaign for Sharmen.

COACH. I don't like that talk here you . . .

JAMES. It's the liquor talking, Coach. Go to sleep, you're drunk.

TOM. I would but I think I pissed myself.

JAMES. Oh, Christ!

TOM. I think I should get up and go upstairs.

JAMES. Well, go up, for God's sake!

TOM *(Getting up)*. Is it still in the same place? *(Looks down.)* No. False alarm. I spilled my beer.

COACH. Don't let the booze beat you, boy. I'm behind you. Stand on your own two feet like the man you are.

GEORGE. Do you mind if I go up first? My stomach.

TOM. After you, your honor. *(Sits.)*

GEORGE *(On landing)*. I expect that nothing will be settled without consulting me.

JAMES. I want to say now, especially for Phil's benefit, that what I did tonight was done, not for personal reasons, but for the good of us all.

COACH. We all know that, James. Here, have a drink, Phil?

PHIL. Yeah.

JAMES. Let me explain myself. I felt only the truth would bring us together again. I wouldn't hurt you intentionally for the world, Phil.

PHIL. You don't have to convince me, James.

COACH *(Pause)*. He took the fifth amendment eleven times. *(Pause.)* A communist came through here, 1930 maybe. Bad times. Poverty like a plague. Joyce's across the street ate their horse, gave some of it to my mother. He came to organize. We broke his legs. Broke his legs with a two by four and sent him packing.

PHIL *(Pause)*. Things have changed today.

COACH. Nothing's different. Communists are at work today. Worse! Students burning down colleges. They're bringing a defeated army home. They kill you in the womb, today, in the womb. Worse than the 'thirties. Niggers shooting the police. Government gone bad. And there's no McCarthy to protect us.

JAMES. He's out to get you, Phil.

COACH. Wants to ruin you, boy.

TOM. He's a Jew—that's good enough to beat him in this town.

COACH. He's a smart Jewboy.

TOM. Why smear him with this communist thing?

COACH. Who's smearing? We are telling the truth. We win within the rules.

JAMES. He's not smearing Phil?

COACH *(To TOM directly)*. Exploiting a man's weakness is the name of the game. He can't move to the left you left him to death. Can't stop a hook, you hook away on him. Find his weak spot and go after it. Punish him with it. I drilled that into you a thousand times!

JAMES. My brother is accusing us of guilt by association!

TOM. Wrong. Guilt by accident. He can't choose his uncle.

COACH. You think that kike wouldn't use Marion against us? Wave her at us like a dirty flag.

TOM. Maybe he wouldn't. (GEORGE *comes down and stops at landing.*)

JAMES. Listen, he took the fifth amendment . . .

TOM *(Flaring)*. I've lived my life by taking the fifth. So have you, James. *(To himself.)* Everybody . . . along the line . . . sometime or another.

JAMES. There was a communist in his family and that is all we are interested in.

TOM *(Ruefully)*. The Jesuits would be pissed at you, James. *(On stairs, deadpan.)* I expect that nothing will be settled without consulting me. *(Goes.)*

COACH. Breaks my heart to see him come apart like that, a tragedy! *(Pause.)* It's up to you, Phil.

PHIL. I'm not convinced. I can't take a chance on him. Can't you understand if I lose that business I'm nothing? It's too late, there's nowhere to start over.

JAMES *(Holding phone)*. Call him, Phil, right now.

PHIL. Who?

JAMES. Sharmen. You're planning to do it anyway.

PHIL. You're full of shit.

JAMES. Do it in front of us. Offer him a contribution. Call 953-8220.

PHIL *(Smiling)*. How come you know his number?

JAMES *(Flustered)*. Don't try to insinuate against my loyalty. I called him about a picture of a pig in a high school newspaper! Oh forget it. He wouldn't take a contribution from you, anyway.

PHIL *(Taking phone, dialing)*. Hello, Norman? This is the number one threat to the environment. *(Pause.)* Right. Phil Romano. The friendly pollutionist. *(Laughs.)* It's all politics, right? Listen, I'll come right out with it and say I like your style. In fact, I'd like to talk over your campaign with you. What? Oh. Everybody needs some help. Money's tight, don't forget. I've been known to make a few political contributions now and then. What? No. No. You scratch my back and I scratch yours, it's that simple. *(Pause.)* Is that so? *(Pause.)* How's your uncle the communist, huh? You won't be laughing so hard when you read about it in the newspapers. You listen to me, you kike bastard, listen . . . *(Slams phone, enraged.)* It was his cousin, not his uncle. Christ Almighty! *(Mutters in Italian.)*

COACH. It's still in the family, it's all right, we can still use it!

PHIL *(Accusing)*. He laughed at me, fucking kike. *(To JAMES.)* You made me blow it, James, you pushed me into blowing it!

JAMES. Phil, listen, if I wasn't your friend . . .

PHIL. Don't shit me. My money's made my friends! Without my money, in school even, you wouldn't piss on me if I was on fire, my old man's money. Everybody got laid in the back seat of my car.

COACH *(Excited).* No goddam mockie is going to beat us on our home court! The crowd love us.

PHIL *(Angry).* Politics is not basketball.

COACH. Hell, yes. You get the crowd behind you and you can't lose! Everybody votes for a winner, boys, you know that.

PHIL. We can't sit around fingering the Past. Nobody but us remembers that game for . . .

COACH. Cop stopped us tonight, took one look at me and ripped up the ticket. Because he happened to *(Elated.)* remember that we gave this defeated town something to be proud of . . . a victory! We won the town that year.

PHIL. I'm no dummy and I know you can't fight progress . . .

COACH. Progress? Nothing changes but the date.

GEORGE. Put a Jew in my place and you'll have progress all right.

COACH. Jews ruin a country. Nobody says it out loud but many think it, people never forget, they know.

JAMES. I think we should go easy on Sharmen being Jewish. It could be labeled antisemitism.

COACH. Yea Israel. I'm all for Israel. Give that one-eyed sonofabitch the seventh day and he would have blown those greasy Arabs off the face of the earth. Arabs are communists. Wash their hair in camel piss. Let the Jews blow them the hell away. They're good and bad in every race. Nobody's anti-anything. Some of the greatest athletes in the world were Jews. Sid Luckman—magnificent! Nobody could punch like Barney Ross, pound for pound. Jesse Owens, alone, beat the goddam Germans, a splendid nigger, fast as the wind. But as a rule, watch them, can't trust them . . . Jews the same

TOM *(Top of stairs).* My friends, "In the kingdom of the blind . . ." *(He falls suddenly all the way down the steps. Men rush to him.)*

COACH. Don't move him. Broken bones.

JAMES. Tom, are you all right, Tom!

GEORGE. Maybe he's knocked out.

JAMES. Can you hear me, Tom?

COACH. Put him on the couch.

TOM. Somebody *(To* GEORGE.*)* just fell down the steps over there. *(Sits.)* James, this drinking in moderation is murder.

COACH. Get him a drink.

TOM. Get him a drink! *(*TOM *drinks.)* . . . "the one-eyed man is king." Before I was so rudely interrupted.

COACH *(Angry).* None of you can hold your liquor! Drink like women. You'll be squatting to piss next.

PHIL. I want to talk to you alone, Coach.

COACH *(Getting drunk).* Uh, oh. Are you sober?

PHIL. Yeah.

COACH. Come out on the porch. *(They exit.)*

GEORGE. I don't trust Phil. Something's up.

JAMES. Let's let the coach handle it.

TOM. Why not? He's handled everything else . . .

GEORGE *(To* TOM*).* We have nothing more to say to one another . . . ever.

TOM. Fuck you and the horse you rode in on, as my grandmother used to say. Love you, George. *(Pause.)* How's the little woman, huh?

JAMES. Shut up. Insensitive sonofabitch! *(*COACH *enters from porch, gets Fillmore H.S. sweater from coat rack, exits to porch, closing door behind him.)*

GEORGE *(Pause).* You think I don't feel things, you think the old clown doesn't have deep feelings, huh? Phony bullshit artist, huh? None of you know what goes on in my head, nobody knows. I can understand . . . understand what makes a man take a gun, go up a tower, and start blowing people apart. I know the feeling. All smiles, huh? I have rage in me . . . I hate, hate like everybody, hate . . . things. I could have taken his head off.

TOM. Why didn't you?

GEORGE. He wasn't worth it . . . I have a career to think about. *(Pause.)* In the hospital. Looked like something that floats . . . in formaldehyde. Freakish. Blue eyes.

JAMES. This is not the time, George.

GEORGE. We put it away. Boy. never even named it. Institutionalized it. Coach advised me . . . us, to give it up. I pay four hundred a month.

JAMES. What else could you do?

GEORGE. A child like that . . . mongoloid . . . doesn't help my career.

TOM. I need a beer.

GEORGE. It casts reflection . . . unfavorable to my image. People get suspicious . . . advised me to put it away immediately.

TOM. You lose the mongoloid vote, George, hands down and . . .

JAMES. George, don't get drunk. *(High.)* We have to make some important decisions tonight.

GEORGE. I can't get drunk enough. I don't need that bitch either! We were going to renew our vows on our fifteenth anniversary . . . on the altar . . .

TOM. Why don't we stone her?

JAMES. Shut up.

TOM. There's an old Jewish custom, George.

GEORGE. Why are you doing this to me?

TOM. Stop leaking all over everybody. Stop the tragic act and take the money. Stop this . . . dishonesty.

GEORGE. You always thought I was a phony, didn't you?

JAMES. Don't pay any attention . . .

TOM *(To himself)*. Unfuckingbelievable.

JAMES. George, *(Commanding.)* the coach is out there trying to convince Phil to back us. Now I know he can do it. Question is—will you accept the money from Phil? Now I think we should consider . . .

TOM. Would you accept the money if it was Helen.

JAMES. Sonofabitch, I'm . . .

GEORGE. Yes, wait a minute, how about that question.

JAMES. I'm not in any such situation . . . it wouldn't apply.

GEORGE. Be me, James, imagine yourself me and a friend, boy you grew up with, champions, was fucking your wife. Imagine that awhile.

JAMES. It wouldn't happen.

GEORGE *(Shouting)*. Pretend, just pretend you're me and answer me. Would you take the money?

JAMES *(Anger)*. Yes, I'd take it, yes yes, take it all!

TOM. The Jesuits would really be pissed at you . . .

JAMES. You're nothing but a . . . a complete and total disgrace. All cheap cynicism and booze.

TOM *(Warning)*. Don't let's do my biography tonight, James.

JAMES. I saved your life, boy!

TOM *(Flaring)*. You sound like him . . . "boy."

JAMES. Saved your life, and now I'm trying to save what's left of mine so stay out of it!

GEORGE *(Maudlin)*. Stop it. Don't fight. Brothers should love . . . take care of each other.

JAMES. I carried him all my life, carried everybody. I'm exhausted at thirty-eight.

TOM. James never did anything out of . . . love. James never loved anything. He's just obedient. An obedient man. Press a button . . .

JAMES. No one's listening.

TOM. . . . and he shoulders a responsibility. But he can't sleep at night and his teeth fell out.

GEORGE *(Very maudlin)*. I'm thirty-eight years old, used to have a thirty-two inch waist. Shit! Used to be the most popular boy in the school, used to have friends. Everything is in the past . . . tense. I'm in the past tense.

JAMES. Your future is politics, George.

GEORGE. I can't find . . . myself . . . I lose myself behind all the smiles, handshakes, speeches. I don't think I'm the man I wanted to be, I seem to myself to be somebody else. I'm always . . . can't stop watching myself . . .

JAMES. It's all in the way you look at things. Your angle of vision. Take Marion for example. She may have gone to Phil, did what she did, I'm not condoning it, but she may have . . . with Phil, did the whole thing for the money.

GEORGE. Why?

JAMES. Support you. Help you. It's entirely possible . . . it's in the realm of possibility.

GEORGE *(Wanting to believe)*. She was devoted to my career . . . I don't know, maybe I don't even care.

JAMES. It's been done before.

GEORGE. She always said he couldn't be trusted, used the stupid slob, you may be right, James.

JAMES. She probably recognized the problem before we did.

GEORGE. I wouldn't put it past her, you could be right, yes, you could.

TOM. I think she just humped him out of plain old lust, George.

GEORGE *(Bravado)*. I'll see you when I'm sober for that remark!

TOM. You're up for sale tonight, George, going cheap tonight.

JAMES. See what he does to me, me who went to another city to find him. He called and I went to another city to find him. How many times? How many cities? You were nothing but rags! Filth. I picked you up, carried you screaming into a hospital.

TOM. Nobody held a gun . . .

JAMES. I had no choice!

TOM. Only alkis like me have no alternatives, James.

JAMES. Do you know what the old man left me? He left me when he finally died six-thousand in medical bills and twelve-hundred for the funeral. And me, old faithful, ends up ten years behind everyone else and for what?

GEORGE. We all have great respect for you, James, you sacrificed, well, you know.

JAMES. Mediocrity. My son, Jimmy, the

bright one, asked me what it meant, definition of the word mediocrity. "It means of low excellence." You know why he asked? Because that's what he thinks of me, how he sees me, how I'm beginning to see myself.

GEORGE. The school super job is all yours after the elections.

JAMES. That's only the beginning. I found my talent late in life. I didn't get into politics until I was over thirty. There's always Congress, George, Congress in the distance. I'm going to make my stand in the political arena. (PHIL *comes in.*)

PHIL. He wants to talk to you, George.

GEORGE. Me?

PHIL. Yeah.

GEORGE. No.

PHIL. He's waiting. (*Pause.* GEORGE *fixes tie—exits to porch.*)

TOM (*Pause*). The suspense is killing.

PHIL. Like before a game. Drink?

TOM. Thank you.

JAMES. George will accept the money, Phil.

PHIL. Good. Ice?

TOM. No.

JAMES. How are you disposed?

PHIL. You mean how do I feel about it? Iffy. It's all iffy.

JAMES. What's the coach say?

PHIL. We got a town of dress factories, right, car lots, bars and empty mines and some Jew thinks he's going to turn it into Miami Beach.

JAMES. He's going to try. But if we can coordinate ourselves . . .

PHIL. Who cares? Do I really care? I'm so bored half the time it's killing me. Watching the same old faces get old, same bullshit, day in and day out. Bored. Sometimes I get on the turnpike and just drive until I feel like getting off. Alone. I ended up in Binghamton last week. One hundred miles on a Friday night by myself. Believe that! What's left? Hit a few bars, some music, drink, play old basketball games over in my head. Pick up some strange pussy now and then, here and there, you know. Always need something young and juicy sitting beside me. Mostly sit and replay the good games in my head, believe that?

JAMES. We were good.

PHIL. Could call each other's moves . . . everytime.

JAMES. We had some good times, great.

PHIL. Sometimes I think that's the only thing I can still feel, you know, still feel in my gut, still feel that championship season, feel the crowds . . . my best memory to date, yeah,

nothing matched it, nothing.

JAMES (*Warmly*). We were good then.

TOM. Martin.

PHIL. Think about him all the time, too. (*Pause.*) I loved that guy.

JAMES. The perfect ballplayer, wasn't he?

PHIL. Yeah. Know what I do for excitement now?

TOM. We all have a good idea!

PHIL. No, no. Everybody does that. I got a Porsche now. Fuel injector, water pump. James Dean, right? Upped it to 120 coming back from Binghamton. Smashed. Everything a blur. Can't see the road but I'm laughing my ass off, laughing so hard I have to wipe my eyes and now I'm hitting 135 and have only one hand on the wheel, pissed out of my mind, radio blaring and suddenly, it's crazy, but I think I'm just speed and I know nothing can catch me, nothing alive can touch me and I open her up to 140. Shit-scared. And everything becomes a blur but I'm laughing because I know nothing on earth can catch me. (*Pause.*) Some Friday night they'll be putting pieces of me in a rubber bag. (*Pause.*) Wonder what it's like to get it at 140 miles an hour.

TOM. Splat.

PHIL. Yeah. Like a bug hitting the windshield.

JAMES. Sounds more dangerous than married women.

PHIL (*Laughs*). James is offended by . . .

JAMES. No, no, it was a joke.

PHIL. Offended. Know why I like married women. Nobody gets involved. They don't yell, tell, swell, and they're grateful as hell. Marion took my cherry in school . . . nobody gets involved . . . I really cared for her. She's a bitch now, a bitch on wheels, he did a job on her, she's finished. I thought maybe we could go back to something, see if it was still there . . . it ain't like the movies, she's a bitch now.

JAMES. I don't understand women like her, never did, never wanted to.

PHIL. Better watch your Helen.

JAMES. My Helen. Never happen. Helen does everything by the book. No, Helen is a champion of chastity. Sex is children, children is sex. She'd be happy spending the rest of her life putting coco-butter on her tits . . . breasts. She's only happy when she's pregnant. Clears up her skin.

PHIL. She still paint?

JAMES. Not really.

PHIL. She won all the art prizes. She was the only that didn't laugh at me that time.

Remember? In art class, we had to identify paintings for the exam and I said mine was an El Gresso and you laughed out loud and somebody else laughed behind me and soon the whole class was laughing, even me, but I remember she didn't . . . laugh . . . *(Pause.)*

JAMES. You smell something?

PHIL. What? The chicken! (JAMES *into kitchen.)* Burned bad?

JAMES. No. Hot. I'll bring it out.

TOM. Did old Marion laugh?

PHIL. Don't worry about George. He'll get over it.

TOM. Think so, huh?

PHIL. You could rub the two of them together and you wouldn't get a sound. All this shit about her being ripped up about the baby.

TOM. She didn't want it?

PHIL. No. She had to convince him! He wanted to keep it. Wouldn't give it up until the coach damn near ordered him to. Hey, I'm not the first guy she laid, she's been running around the last few years.

TOM. Why doesn't she leave him?

PHIL. Where's she going at thirty-eight? *(Pause.)* You're an alcoholic.

TOM. What ever gave you that idea.

PHIL. Jesus Christ . . . what happened? *(Pause.)* Do you need money?

TOM. I'll let you know.

PHIL. Sharmen's got class, style. George is like Bugs Bunny on television. "This is the mayor. What's up, folks." We got Looney Tunes for a mayor. (JAMES *enters with chicken, then runs upstairs. To* TOM.) George isn't a modern man. It's that simple. I am; maybe you, too. You know, Claire and me, we have an arrangement. *(Pause.)* It's civilized. Nothing lasts forever. As long as she doesn't make it with anyone in the town, none of my friends, fine, you know, it's a mutual arrangement. You have to change with the times . . . be modern. *(Pause.)* Don't say anything to the rest, between me and you.

TOM *(To himself).* I think I'm medieval, yeah, probably somewhere in the Dark Ages.

PHIL. Yeah, she and her old lady fly all over. She's never home. On my money. The old lady knows she makes it with other men. Isn't that something, believe that, they talk about it . . . I wonder if it's a crime in this state to fuck your mother-in-law?

TOM. Ask Brother James. He's the keeper of perversions.

PHIL. I'm going to get a vasectomy.

TOM. Is that so? (JAMES *enters.)*

PHIL. They tie up your tubes. You come but you don't come sperm. Sterilized. *(Pause.)* I fuck a lot, you know, and I can't afford any more abortions. And two kids is enough. I told Claire, we discussed it and . . . she agrees . . . it's the intelligent thing to do. *(Pause.)* You're right, everybody around here lives in the Dark Ages, pitch black.

GEORGE. He wants to talk to you, James. (JAMES *exits front door.)*

TOM. George, have some chicken. *(Long pause.* COACH *and* JAMES *enter.)*

JAMES. You want me to step down as your campaign manager.

GEORGE. Phil has contacted these . . .

JAMES. You dump me now and my politics are over.

GEORGE. James, Phil has contacted these advertising people in Philadelphia.

JAMES. People will know I've been dumped. I wouldn't be able to buy a vote. You'd ruin me in this town.

GEORGE. After the election I can still endorse you for superintendent.

JAMES. After dumping me from running your campaign.

COACH. James, we need a very experienced man in that position. We are just bringing in some professional help. You'll still be involved in the campaign.

JAMES *(To* PHIL). Wait a minute. You did this, you've turned them against me.

PHIL. James, I can't put twenty-five thousand, thirty, in the hands of an amateur.

JAMES. I am not going to take this lying down. Spoiled ignorant lout is not going . . .

PHIL. It's not what you think.

JAMES. You're an ignoramus!

PHIL. You're a shabby man.

JAMES. And you're a goddamnn ignoramus! (PHIL *slaps* JAMES *across the face. A dental plate falls from* JAMES' *mouth.)* My teeth . . . *(On knees.)* You've broken my teeth. I'll kill you . . . ignorant . . . *(Near impotent rage.)*

TOM *(Picks it up).* It's not broken. Go on upstairs. *(Pause. To* PHIL.) If I had my wits, some anger, some guts, I'd take your head off, Phil.

PHIL. I'm just money to you guys! I'm money to everybody! I'm not giving it away, no more charity from the dumb dago!

JAMES *(Controlled).* If you people do this to me I will walk every street in this town, near me, and tell every single person about Phil and Marion.

PHIL. Shabby.

•

JAMES. I will not be abused like this. I will turn George into the village idiot.

GEORGE. You wouldn't do that, James.

JAMES. I swear it by Christ, and your brother-in-law, and the kickbacks on the city's jobs.

GEORGE. You'd ruin me . . . you'd ruin us . . .

JAMES. What did you just do to me?

PHIL. An hour ago he suggested that we back him for mayor.

COACH. I don't believe that.

PHIL. Ask him.

JAMES. I proposed an alternative!

GEORGE. I'm sick . . . help me . . . my stomach is upset.

COACH. Can you make it upstairs?

GEORGE. I think so. *(Suddenly he lunges toward trophy.)*

COACH. Not in the trophy.

BLACKOUT

ACT THREE

The men are in the same positions as the end of ACT TWO. _____

TOM. Nice shot, George.

COACH. I'll take him upstairs. Clean him up.

GEORGE. I can't get my breath . . .

COACH. Then stop talking. *(On stairs.)* Wash out the trophy, James. Under cold water (JAMES *exits.)*

TOM. Dull night. Maybe I should go and fall down the stairs again.

PHIL. It gets more desperate, people get more desperate. *(Yelling.)* Why is everyone so fucking desperate? Everyone wants a piece of me. Like Namath, right? I'm only my money . . . nothing else. *(Takes out paper.)* This is a dentist's bill. Four thousand dollars. My wife. For four thousand dollars you could cap a shark's mouth. I'm expected to finance everybody's life. *(Pause.)* Marion brought up the campaign money. About the third time I laid her, she brought it up, very casually, and then talked about it for three hours. *(Pause.)* I expected it . . . I knew it . . . she laid it in. Well, she worked for it! I made her earn it!

TOM. You wanted George to . . . find out.

PHIL. Yeah. Maybe. I don't know. She worked for it. I took her up to the Holiday one afternoon and fucked her on the bed, floor, chair, tub, toilet . . . everywhere but the ice machine. *(Pause.)* You know the only woman I ever loved . . . my mother, fuck the psychiatrists . . . my mother is the only . . . woman I ever knew. The rest are all cunts.

TOM. I don't care, you know. The truth is I don't care about the melodrama of your life. (JAMES *enters.)*

JAMES *(Pause).* I have been betrayed by my friends. *(No response.)* I carried that imbecile Polack four years, him and his nymphomaniac wife.

PHIL. Watch it.

JAMES. I know, I was his best man. The ushers were comparing notes on her. George got sick before the wedding too. Threw up with joy.

PHIL. We know her past history, James. No lectures . . .

JAMES. You don't know anything. You fornicated and read the newspapers. That's what you know. But nobody is going to abuse me, use me, nobody.

TOM. "Now we won't have James to kick around any more."

JAMES. Exactly. I'm a new man. And I come high. My success has been delayed by my responsibilities and now it is my turn, and now I am going to demand my right to success . . . demand. I had, Christ I'm ashamed, to borrow the money from Phil to bury him.

PHIL. You don't owe me anything.

JAMES. I owe. Everybody. I don't own a goddam thing.

PHIL. I won big on the Colts.

JAMES. And now you knife me in the back.

PHIL. James, I like being rich, okay. I need money. I want two of everything, Cars, boats, women, etc., etc. Around expensive things I get a hard on, turned on, I want them. My old man was like you, James, desperate. He built a business twenty-four hours a day, didn't have time to learn the language, two words he knew money and work; no, three, the business. The business killed him at forty-fucking-three and we buried a man nobody ever knew, I worked for my old man, slept with him, ate, and I have no memory of who he was, what he was. The fucking business is mine now. *(Pause.)* It's all mine. (COACH *enters.)*

COACH. He's cleaned up. Going to call his wife. I'm bewildered. *(Pause.)* Stunned. Never. Knocked on my ass! Never did I think I'd live to see you turn savagely , , , savagely turn on each other. You're not the same people who played for me.

TOM *(Drunkenly to himself).* We are a myth.

COACH. What?

TOM. Myths.

COACH. Is that trophy a myth! See the names engraved on it! Don't grow old on me, boys, don't lose faith, don't get old on me. I carved your names in silver, last forever, forever, never forget that, never. Nothing changes but the date, boys. You're all still immensely talented . . .

JAMES. I'm a junior high school principal who has to have the walls scrubbed every day because inevitably some little bastard scribbles all over them, "Mr. Daley eats it . . . Daley is a shit head."

COACH. Taking care of your father slowed you up.

JAMES (Pause). Slowed me up. I wiped the man's ass, like a baby, rubbed his body with oil, washed him, I had to feed him before he died and in all those years I never felt . . . love from him. He'd get drunk and abuse me.

COACH. In fever, bedridden, a man can say strange things.

JAMES. I just want . . .

COACH. What?

JAMES. I just want . . . wanted.

COACH. What!

JAMES. I WANTED HIM TO RESPECT ME . . . respect me, that's all I wanted.

COACH. Whine! You're a thirty-eight year old whine! Bitch and whine and blame your life on everybody. You got the eyes of a beggar . . . did they respect me? Thirty years a teacher . . . a coach, a teacher devoted to excellence. Did they respect me when they forced me into retirement? Gave me a farewell dinner, gold watch and a pension. A pension is a ticket to death, a goddam passport. Said I was old-fashioned, said I abused a student . . . the boy made an obscene gesture to my face and I hit him—what's old-fashioned about that?

JAMES. You broke his jaw . . .

COACH. And the next thing I know I'm walking the streets at eight o'clock in the morning with nowhere to go . . . start listening to the radio . . . (To himself.) I watch more t.v. than any man alive. You make them respect you. (GEORGE enters.)

GEORGE (Pause). I talked to Marion. (To JAMES.) You were right. Absolutely.

JAMES (Weary). Was I?

COACH. What did she say?

GEORGE. She did it for me, for the money.

COACH. You heard that, Phil.

PHIL. I know.

TOM. Next time, the ice machine, right, Phil?

GEORGE. It's late. I better leave now . . .

TOM. She convince you to take the money, George?

GEORGE. That's none of your goddam business.

TOM. After old James gets through, they're going to give you a pair of horns on the steps of city hall.

COACH. That is not going to happen.

JAMES. I meant what I said.

GEORGE. Marion said the whole . . .

COACH (Sharply). I don't care what the hot pantsed bitch said. Go home and kick her ass all over the kitchen. All that slutting around . . .

GEORGE. She's not a slut . . .

COACH. She was punished for slutting, wasn't she? She was punished and so were you!

GEORGE. That's a terrible thing to say.

COACH. Leave her the hell out of the campaign . . . lock her in her room . . . she's trouble, she is.

GEORGE. You know I have pride in . . .

COACH. You have no pride, none. You got a face for everybody. All slick smiles and empty eyes. You lost something, boy, lost something . . . (Pacing.) Phil playin' the lout screwing and ruining his life away. Lost something (To TOM.) You stumbling and reeling through the streets like some broken thing, hearing people laugh at you, breaks my . . . you were a gifted boy . . .

TOM. Past tense.

COACH. Gifted! Unbelievable talent. All of you. Not just basketball. I remember, James, remember sitting in that auditorium watching James win, what contest was it, what?

JAMES. I speak for democracy . . .

COACH. I speak for democracy. (Sincere pitch.) You held that audience spellbound. When you stood up to speak the whole crowd hushed, no movement, still. They were spellbound. You overwhelmed them. I'll never forget it.

JAMES. I won a hundred dollar bond . . . (Rueful.) The old man cashed it in and drank it up. (Pause.)

TOM. Yeah . . . gave you a little gold cup.

COACH. "Run to win." St. Paul said that, a saint, run always to win. I drilled that into you. "Healthy minds, healthy bodies," Greeks said that, boys, and they started it all, great athletes, the Greeks, magnificent!

TOM. Greeks were pederasts.

COACH. What the hell is he talking about?

JAMES. He means the Greeks were homosexuals.

COACH *(Shocked)*. The Greeks homos? Not the Greeks, the Romans maybe but not the Greeks! Don't come around me with the liberal bullshit. I won't listen. The Greeks made their men into gods. *(Pause. Recites with deep conviction.)*

"The credit belongs to the man who is
    actually in the arena,
Whose face is marred by dust and sweat
    and blood.
A man who knows the great enthusiasms
    and the great devotions.
Who spends himself in a worthy cause.
Who in the end knows the triumph of high
    achievement
And if he fails, at least fails while daring
    greatly
So that his place shall never be with those
    cold and timid souls
Who know neither victory nor defeat."

That's a great man's words. A man among men. Monday morning, boys, we start on Sharmawitz, we get into the arena and draw some blood.

JAMES *(Not taken in)*. Not James, not me, not till my participation is settled.

COACH. It's been settled!

JAMES. Not to my satisfaction.

COACH. Phil, as soon as possible, contact those people in Philadelphia.

PHIL. OK.

JAMES. You will not change your minds?

COACH. Get them up here by Monday?

JAMES. Goddammit. No one is going to walk over me. I'm done. My back's against the wall.

GEORGE. James I . . .

JAMES. Who are you? I don't know you. I will walk the streets of this town . . . I will . . . do you hear me . . . I'm going out there and open up . . . I will . . . *(Pause.)* low excellence.

TOM. Welcome to anonymity, James. No bench. No depth. Playing with too many injuries.

COACH. You've been sneering at us all night. Laughing in our faces.

TOM. Don't start on me. I'm not here. I'm in New Orleans.

COACH. You're finished. Useless. And you had talent. You quit on everyone who needed you . . .

TOM. Stop lying to us. Stop telling us how good we were.

COACH *(To TOM)*. We never had a losing season and we're not starting now . . .

TOM. That's not what Martin said.

COACH. What?

TOM. Martin? Remember him?

COACH. Yeah.

TOM. But he's not here. You know why he left, why he never came back to a reunion.

COACH *(Pause)*. Do I?

TOM. He told us the truth, twenty years ago.

COACH. Did he?

TOM. He wanted you to publicly refuse the trophy, remember. You told him in the third quarter to get that nigger center, the kangaroo, remember? He did. He went out and broke the guy's ribs.

COACH. I told him to stop him. That nigger was playing him off the court, and I told him to get tough under the boards and stop him.

TOM. He came to you a week after the game.

COACH. That's right, he did. He came to me . . . he walked in here. He came babbling something about the truth. What truth, I said, we won. That trophy is the truth, the only truth. I told him to get mean, punish some people, put some fear into them, you have to hate to win, it takes hate to win. I didn't tell him to break anybody's ribs. *(Pause.)* You don't believe me, boys? *(Appeal to majority.)*

GEORGE. I believe you, Coach.

TOM. We have gone through this phony ritual, champions? Shit! We stole it.

COACH. I told him there is no such thing as second place.

TOM. Never less than success. Pay the price. Get yourself a name. I did. I really did. I fell on my ass in ten cities, that's a record. *(Takes whiskey.)* Here's my trophy.

COACH. I read the fine print on you.

TOM. Find the other man's weaknesses— exploit him—hook him to death. *(Manic.)* Watch out—they're out to get you . . . *(Laughs.)* Get that sonofabitch before he gets you, win, win, only sin is losing, bless me Father for I . . . Christ, I'm sick.

COACH. Need to lose.

TOM. Look it in the eye, old man, we stole that trophy, championship season is a lie. Say that out loud . . .

COACH *(Putting trophy in TOM's hands)*. Deny that. You can feel it. It has weight. Deny it. Read the names in silver there.

TOM *(Anguish)*. I don't believe in trophies anymore! (COACH *slaps him across the face. Pause.)* . . . Empty.

COACH. Get out.

TOM. And Martin?

COACH. Out.

TOM. I got a ticket somewhere. *(Exits.)*

GEORGE. Coach, Martin tried to tell me the same story.

PHIL. Martin was a real sonofabitch when you think about it.

JAMES. Martin didn't have a brain in his head.

COACH. We don't need them, boys . . . it's history now. In the books. You were a rare and beautiful thing, boys . . . a miracle to see people play beautifully together . . . like when I was a boy . . . long time past . . . the whole town would come together. We'd have these huge picnics, great feasts of picnics. My father ran the only bank in town. An elegant man. Bach was played in this house. He quoted Shakespeare, "To be or not to be, that's the question." Shoulders like a king . . . he carried me on his back into the freezing, God, yes, waters of the lake. So clear you could see the white pebbles on the bottom. Gone now, all gone, vanished. Lake, picnic grounds, gone now. All concrete and wires and glass now. Used car lots now. Phil's trucks came and took it away.

GEORGE. We can bring it back, Coach, urban renewal, preserve the environment.

COACH. Jesus, I can still see buckets of ice cream . . . great red slabs of beef . . . kites, yes, the sky full of blue and red kites, men playing horseshoes, big silver pails of beer, in the late afternoon the men would dive from the high rocks, so high they made you dizzy to look down. I watched my father dive and turn and glisten in the sun, falling like a bird falls, and knife the water so clean as to leave only ripples. The depression killed him. The bank went under. His hair turned white. He threw his wedding ring away, threw his teeth across the room, stopped talking. He died a year later in his prime. Wouldn't let anybody in the room, not even my mother, died alone in the room. He lost faith in everything, the country. He told me, the man who listened to Bach, quoted Shakespeare, elegant man, he told me, "never forget Marx was a Jew, Jews will ruin the country." Twenty-nine killed him dead. *(Sudden rage.)* Not enough of them jumped out of windows in '29, the whole race should have splattered on the sidewalks in '29. The man didn't know how to fight back. He lost his character. Lost his character. *(Pause.)* I chose my country, God forgive me. I made the supreme sacrifice and went to work in the mines for my country. You got to fight back,

fight back, fight forever! They killed McCarthy too. Kennedy. Patton, even. *(Pause.)* There are no leaders, boys, all the great ones in stone. Somebody has to lead the country back again. I'm talking about survival. All we have is ourselves, boys, and the race is to the quickest and this country is fighting for her life, and we are the heart and we play always to win! *(Drunk but in control.)* You won't lose, boys— because I won't let you lose, I'll whip your ass to the bone, drive you into the ground. Your soul belongs to God but your ass belongs to me, remember that one, yes sir, we can do it, we are going to win because we can't lose, dare not lose, won't lose, lose is not in our vocabulary! I shaped you boys, never forget that. I ran you till the blisters busted, ran you right into perfection, bloody socks and all; you had no character, you couldn't put on your jocks, awkward, all legs, afraid, a mistake a second. I made you winners. I made you winners. (COACH *puts on the record. During the playing of the record, the men sit, transfixed by the memory. No movement.*)

RECORD *(Harsh, cracked tones).* Ten seconds left. Fillmore High School has fought their way back from a near disastrous first half. They are behind now by one point, 71–70. But they have the ball with ten seconds on the clock. George Sikowski will throw the ball to either Tom Daley or Martin Roads. Ten seconds. Pennsylvania State Basketball Championship game comes down to one shot, one play. Here we go, time in. Sikowski passes to Daley, Daley in the back court. A pass to James Daley in the corner, Daley across court to Romano. Five seconds! Romano to Daley, Daley to Roads at the foul line. Two seconds! Roads up and shoots! Yes, yes! Fillmore High School wins it! *(Loud crowd noise, then silence.* TOM *enters—goes to the* COACH. *Then sits.* GEORGE *drunkenly starts the school song. The others join in.)*

GEORGE AND OTHERS.

Another victory for Fillmore

as we swing into the fray

for the loyal sons of Fillmore are out to win today,

with hope and courage never failing

as we swing right down the field

our hearts will e'er be faithful

to the foe we'll never yield.

(Suddenly PHIL *starts to sob.)*

COACH *(Goes to* PHIL*).* Don't punish yourselves, boys, the world will do that, protect . . . survive. *(Pause.)* Phil, do you have something to say to George?

PHIL *(Goes to him)*. I'm sorry. Forgive me. Sorry. *(They hug and cry. Pause.)*

TOM. Whoop whoop. Us and the whooping cranes . . .

COACH. What's that?

TOM. On the way out. Cranes. Whoop.

COACH. Love one another, boys. No way a man can do it alone. Got to belong to something more than yourself.

JAMES. George, I'll do anything you want, I'm behind you.

GEORGE. You dirty bastard, I love you like a brother.

COACH *(With camera)*. All right, album time. *(The men gather around the trophy.)*

GEORGE. We better get together and start mapping it all out.

COACH. Monday at twelve. The mayor's office. You need a speech for the K of C next Thursday.

GEORGE. James?

JAMES. We'll have it to you by Monday.

(Men gather around trophy.)

COACH. Smile. Let's see them new teeth, James. *(Takes their picture. Pause.)*

JAMES. Let's have one of you, Coach.

COACH. No. Not me, not me, not me.

GEORGE. One for the album, Coach. (COACH *goes to the trophy. Holds it in his arms and poses for the picture.)*

PHIL. Why don't you come over tomorrow and watch the playoffs in color?

COACH. No. The game's changed. The good little man is extinct. They all shoot down at the basket now. I hardly watch it anymore. It's not my game. No longer the white man's game.

GEORGE. C'mon, smile, Coach

TOM. Say cunnilingus. *(The lights on stage fade out, leaving only a spot on the COACH. The flash of a camera.)*

JAMES. I got you, Coach.

COACH. Yeah.

FADEOUT

Talley's Folly

Lanford Wilson

FOR HAROLD CLURMAN

First presented by the Circle Repertory Company in New York City on May 3, 1979, with the following cast:

(*in order of apperance*)
MATT FRIEDMAN   Judd Hirsch
SALLY TALLEY   Trish Hawkins

Directed by Marshall W. Mason
Setting by John Lee Beatty
Costumes by Jennifer Von Mayhauser
Lighting by Dennis Parichy
Sound by Chuck London

PLACE: An old boathouse on the Talley place, a farm near Lebanon, Missouri

TIME: July 4, 1944
      Early evening

Talley's Folly is to be played without intermission

Lanford Wilson was one of the first playwrights to emerge into prominence from the Off-Off-Broadway scene, and he remains one of the most interesting. People are always asking where the new young American playwrights are, and the answer is almost always the same—everywhere and anywhere but Broadway, although Wilson is one of the exceptions in once having had a play produced on Broadway.

Wilson was born in Lebanon, Missouri, and was brought up in Ozark, Missouri, and he later attended the University of Chicago. It was here that he started writing plays. He arrived in New York in 1963, where he gravitated toward the Café Cino, a pioneering, Off-Off-Broadway café theatre run by Joseph Cino.

It was at the Café Cino in 1964 that he made his professional playwrighting debut with *Home Free!,* a play that subsequently transferred to the Cherry Lane Theatre. During the following ten years, Wilson had nine plays produced in New York, and many have been given across the country and abroad. He has also written the libretto for Lee Hoiby's opera, *Summer and Smoke,* based on Tennessee Williams's play.

Before he wrote *Lemon Sky,* Wilson had a number of successes to his credit. His one-acter, *The Madness of Lady Bright,* won many plaudits both in New York and London: *The Rimers of Eldritch* had a long New York run and also won the Drama Desk Vernon Rice Award, and both *The Gingham Dog* and *Lemon Sky* were extremely well reviewed. But neither was really successful with the public.

The Gingham Dog is a particularly interesting case in point because it appeared to have everything going for it. It had a most sensitive story about a man and a woman—he is white and she is black—and the closing down of their marriage. It was most sensitively written, and rather than exploring racial issues and tensions (although these certainly symbolized and concentrated the incompatibility between the couple) Wilson wrote about two loving people for whom love is not enough. It was beautifully directed by Alan Schneider, and the acting by Diana Sands (her last Broadway appearance) and George Grizzard was impeccable. It opened on April 23, 1969, and it ran a sad total of five performances. It was one of the first indications that Broadway, except in very special circumstances, might not be hospitable to serious drama.

It must have been with this in mind that *Lemon Sky* was produced Off Broadway rather than on Broadway. *Lemon Sky* had originally been produced by the Buffalo Studio Arena Theatre, and its New York premiere, at the Playhouse Theatre on May 17, 1970, was partly produced under the Arena Theatre's auspices. Staged by Warren Enters and starring Christopher Walken as Alan, a seventeen-year-old boy trying to establish a relationship with his father, played by Charles Durning, the play ran for only seventeen performances.

Once again there was muttering and despair, for, even more than *The Gingham Dog,* this seemed to many people to be one of the best of contemporary American plays. *Lemon Sky* later moved to Chicago where it had a much longer and more successful engagement. Wilson's story does have a happy ending, however, because in 1970 he became playwright-in-residence at the Off-Off-Broadway Circle Theatre. It was there on February 4, 1973, that his *The Hot l Baltimore* was staged, and this, transferred to Off Broadway, ran for more than a year. The critics' faith in Wilson was finally justified by public response.

Wilson is a naturalistic playwright, for the most part, with an abiding interest in American themes. His concern is with contemporary American society and morals, the way we live, the way we act, the way we think. He is not experimental in his techniques but clear-sighted in his honesty and sharp in his perceptions. *Talley's Folly* almost plays like a love poem. The tale is, as Matt Friedman tells us, ''a waltz . . . a no-holds-barred romantic story.'' But the play goes beyond even this, to explore the pain and pleasure involved in recognizing and mastering old fears and prejudices. In a way he is an old-fashioned playwright—it is not for nothing that his *The Hot l Baltimore* has been compared with William Saroyan—but there is nothing old-fashioned about his vision of America and his remarkable skill at capturing that vision on the stage.

A Victorian boathouse constructed of louvers, lattice in decorative panels, and a good deal of Gothic Revival gingerbread. The riverside is open to the audience. The interior and exterior walls have faded to a pale gray. The boathouse is covered by a heavy canopy of maple and surrounded by almost waist-high weeds and the slender, perfectly vertical limbs of a weeping willow. Lighting and sound should be very romantic: the sunset at the opening, later the moonlight, slant through gaps in the ceiling and walls reflecting the river in lambent ripples across the inside of the room.

The boathouse contains two boats, one turned upside down, buckets, boxes, no conventional seating. Overhead is a latticework attic in which is stored creels, bamboo poles, nets, seines, minnow buckets, traps, floats, etc., all long past use.

At opening: All this is seen in a blank white work light; the artificiality of the theatrical set quite apparent. The houselights are up.

___

MATT *(Enters in front of the stage. MATT FRIEDMAN is forty-two, dark, and rather large. Warm and unhurried, he has a definite talent for mimicry. In his voice there is still a trace of a German-Jewish accent, of which he is probably unaware. He speaks to the audience).* They tell me that we have ninety-seven minutes here tonight—without intermission. So if that means anything to anybody; if you think you'll need a drink of water or anything . . .

You know, a year ago I drove Sally home from a dance; and while we were standing on the porch up at the house, we looked down to the river and saw this silver flying thing rise straight up and zip off. We came running down to the river, we thought the Japanese had landed some amazing new flying machine, but all we found was the boathouse here, and—uh, that was enough.

I'll just point out some of the facilities till everybody gets settled in. If everything goes well for me tonight, this should be a waltz, one-two-three, one-two-three; a no-holds-barred romantic story, and since I'm not a romantic type, I'm going to need the whole valentine here to help me: the woods, the willows, the vines, the moonlight, the band—there's a band that plays tonight, over in the park. The trees, the berries, the breeze, the sounds, water and crickets, frogs, dogs, the light, the bees, working all night.

Did you know that? Bees work—worker bees—work around the clock. Never stop. Collecting nectar, or pollen, whatever a bee collects. Of course their life expectancy is twenty days. Or, in a bee's case, twenty days and twenty nights. Or possibly "expectancy" is wrong in the case of a bee. Who knows what a bee expects. But whatever time there is in a life is a lifetime, and I imagine after twenty days and twenty nights a bee is more or less ready to tuck it in.

(In a craggy, Western, "Old-Timer" voice) "I been flyin' now, young sprout, nigh-on to nineteen days an' nineteen nights."

(Imitating a young bee) "Really, Grandpa Worker Bee?"

(Old-Timer) "An' I'm 'bout ready to tuck it in."

(Slight pause. Reflectively) Work. Work is very much to the point. *(showing the set)* We have everything to help me here. There's a rotating gismo in the footlights (do you believe footlights) because we needed the moon out there on the water. The water runs right through here, so you're all out in the river—sorry about that. They promise me moonlight by the baleful, all through the shutters. We could do it on a couple of folding chairs, but it isn't bare, it isn't bombed out, it's rundown, and the difference is all the difference. And valentines need frou-frou.

We have a genuine Victorian folly here. A boathouse. Constructed of louvers, and lattice and geegaws. I feel like a real estate salesman. Of course there's something about the term "real estate" that strikes me as wrong. Estate maybe, but real is arguable. But to start you off on the right foot . . . Everybody ready? This is a waltz, remember, one-two-three, one-two-three.

There was a time—or, all right, I think that has to be: Once upon a time—there was a hope throughout the land. From the chaos of the Great Depression, people found strength in union, believing their time had come. But even as this hope was perceived, once again a dark power rose up from the chaos in another land. Once again this country pitched its resources and industry into battle. Now, after almost three years of war, it has become apparent that the battle is turning. Once again we are told that "peace and prosperity" are in the air. But in the midst of battle, that "hope" the people had known has been changed into the enemy. Peace and—more to the point—prosperity, is our ally now. Once again, we are told the country has been saved by war.

Now, you would think that in this remote wood, on this remote and unimportant, but sometimes capricious, river—that world events would not touch this hidden place. But such is not the case. There is a house on the hill up there, and there is a family that is not at peace but in grave danger of prosperity. And there is a girl in the house on the hill up there who is a terrible embarrassment to her family because she remembers that old hope, and questions this new fortune, and questioning eyes are hard to come by nowadays. It's hard to use your peripheral vision when you're being led by the nose.

Now I know what you're thinking. You're saying if I'd known it was going to be like this, I wouldn't have come. Or if I'd known it was going to be like this, I would have listened. But don't worry, we're going to do this first part all over again for the late-comers. I want to give you and me both every opportunity. So. Okeydokey. *(Checks pocket watch)* Oh, boy, this has gotta be fast. So: *(Deep breath, then all in a run)* They tell me that we have ninety-seven minutes here tonight without intermission so if that means anything to anybody if you think you'll need a drink of water or anything I'll just point out some of the facilities till everybody gets settled in if everything goes well for me tonight this should be a waltz one-two-three, one-two-three a no-holds-barred romantic story and since I'm not a romantic type I'm going to need the whole shmeer here to help me the woods the willows the vines the moonlight the band there's a band that plays tonight over in the park the trees the berries the breeze the sounds water and crickets frogs dogs the light the bees . . . *(Pauses. With a slight hill accent)* Frogs, dogs . . . *(to stage manager in sound booth)* Could we have a dog? I'd like a dog. *(He listens a second. Nothing. Then a furious, yapping, tiny terrier is heard)* Fellas! Fellas! A dog! *(Beat. Then a low, distant woof-woof-woof that continues until* SALLY's *entrance.* MATT *listens a beat, pleased)*

Oh, yeah. Old man Barnette kicked out Blackie and called in the kids, and about now the entire family is sitting down to supper. Even Blackie, out by the smokehouse. But a car pulled off the road about a mile downstream, and someone got out. And at this hour it begins to be difficult to see, the chickens have started to go to bed, and noises carry up the river as though there was someone there in the barnyard. And Blackie wants to let ev-

erybody know the Barnette farm is well guarded. *(Beat. Then back to run-on narration)*

Working all night did you know that bees work worker bees work around the clock never stop collecting nectar or pollen whatever a bee collects of course their life expectancy is twenty days or in a bee's case twenty days and twenty nights or possibly expectancy is wrong in the case of a bee who knows what a bee expects but whatever time there is in a life is a lifetime and I imagine after twenty days and . . .

SALLY *(Off, yelling)*. Matt? (MATT *is silent. He almost holds his breath)* Matt? *(The houselights begin to dim. The sunset and reflection from the river begin to appear; we hear the sound of the river and birds)* Matt?

MATT *(Softly, to the audience)*. This is a waltz, remember. One-two-three, one-two-three . . .

SALLY *(Off)*. Are you in that boathouse? I'm not going to come down there if you're not there 'cause that place gives me the creeps after dark. Are you down there?

MATT. No.

SALLY *(Coming closer)*. I swear, Matt Friedman, what in the devil do you think you're doing down here? *(Coming through the tall weeds and willow)* Oh, my—everything is soaking wet here. Buddy said he chased you off with a shotgun. I thought, good, we're maybe rid of you. I saw your car parked up there, I could not believe my eyes! *(She enters)* Not even you! And there you sit. Wiping your glasses. (SALLY TALLEY *is thirty-one. Light, thin, quite attractive, but in no way glamorous or glamorized. Straightforward, rather tired, and just now quite angry. In this state she has a pronounced Ozark accent, but when she concentrates on what she is saying, the accent becomes much less pronounced)*

MATT. The better to see you with, my dear.

SALLY. Don't even begin with me, Matt, I'm in no mood.

MATT. Were you hiding behind the window curtains when I was out in the yard talking to your brother? You like to hide from me so much.

SALLY. I got home five minutes ago. You know what time I get off work. Rachel and Ida dropped me out front, we could hear Buddy cussin' all the way out to the road.

MATT. You talk to your Aunt Charlotte? How did you know I'd be here?

SALLY. I was inside that house exactly thirty seconds. I walked in the door, Momma and Buddy lit in on me like I was ten years old, screaming about the Communist traitor infidel I'd let in the house. Buddy said he run you off with a shotgun.

MATT. He had a large two-barreled weapon, yes, with apertures about like so.

SALLY. If they knew you were still on the place, they'd have Cliffy on you.

MATT. You want the sheriff, all you have to do is keep yelling. Your sister-in-law called him. He's probably at your house right now.

SALLY (Near whisper). Whatever possessed you to come down here and get into a fight with my brother? You know I can't stand livin' there as it is.

MATT. Sally, one of us had better go for a walk and cool off. Both of us can't be angry.

SALLY. What better happen is you better march right back up there to your car and head back to St. Louis.

MATT. No, see, the way they build those things now they require gasoline to really get them running good. Especially Plymouths.

SALLY. Matt Friedman, you did not run out of gas.

MATT. You want to go try it? See if you can get it to catch?

SALLY. Oh, if that isn't just . . . typical.

MATT. That's what saves it, I think. I was just thinking that that was typical.

SALLY. That car is gonna kill me. I mean, I'm a strong person, but that car is gonna do it. Not one time has that car gone from one place to another place without breaking down.

MATT. Sally, you don't deprecate a man's car. A man's car reflects his pride in himself and his status in society. Castigate my car, you castigate me.

SALLY. Well, good. And you may be full of hot air on most things, but you are right about that. That—that—haybailer!—is a good reflection of you.

MATT. Boy, you get angry, you really are a mountain daughter, aren't you? Where's the still? I was looking for the still you said was down here.

SALLY. Matt, I'm exhausted. I've been up since five. I was at the hospital at six-thirty. I don't want to argue. The still was right there. They busted it up—broke it up.

MATT. Your dad get raided by Cliffy?

SALLY. Cliffy wasn't sheriff then, Mc-Conklin was sheriff. Him and Dad were half-partners in the still. They broke it up to sell for scrap after the repeal. Matt—

MATT. They were runnin' liquor, were they?

SALLY. Is the only thing keeping you here a gallon of gas for your car? 'Cause we have a can in the pump house.

MATT. Better wait till it gets a little darker if you're gonna start stealing Buddy's gas.

SALLY. You've alienated Buddy. You've almost paralyzed Olive.

MATT (Snapping his fingers). Olive! Olive! I could not think of your sister-in-law's darn name! I'm thinking pickled herring, I'm thinking caviar, I'm thinking boiled egg. I knew she was on a relish tray.

SALLY. Why are you always barging in places?

MATT. No, ma'am. I wrote you how many times I'd be down today.

SALLY. You barge into a person's home, you barge into where they work!

MATT. I telephoned your house here. I had a nice Missouri telephone chat with your Aunt Charlotte.

SALLY. Aunt Lottie would invite the devil into the parlor for hot cocoa.

MATT. Actually, I came here to talk to your father. That's the way I've been told these things are done in the South.

SALLY. You're not in the South. You're in the Midwest.

MATT. Sally, I've been all over the country, and there is New York City, isolated neighborhoods in Boston, and believe me, the rest is all the South.

SALLY. Would you please just tell me what happened up there so I'll know how to handle them?

MATT. Sally, I know I told you we'd have the whole weekend, and I've been looking forward to it just as much as you have, but there was—

SALLY. You are the most conceited, blind, deaf—

MATT. —just no way out of it. I have to go back tonight. We have a hearing on the iceman and his horse, there was no way—

SALLY. On what?

MATT. You know, I wrote you, the iceman, with a horse and wagon. We had him consecrated as a church and that worked for two years, till they caught on, but—

SALLY. I don't have any idea what you are talking about.

MATT (Going on). —churches don't pay taxes. We had him ordained. They didn't like it. So we set up a trust fund in the name of Daisy; now they want a hearing on that, because horses can't hold trusts. It was just sprung on us. I have to be back in St. Louis tomorrow.

SALLY. Would you just tell me what happened up there?

MATT. It was crazy to come down here, only I promised you, but we have to work fast here tonight.

SALLY. What was Buddy so mad about?

MATT. Did you hear me? I've only got tonight; I have to get back.

SALLY. Would you please just—

MATT. Sally, it is unimportant, but if it makes you happy! I came down here as I said I would; I parked my car, went to the front door, and knocked. Your sister-in-law—from the relish tray? You said?

SALLY. Olive.

MATT. Olive! I cannot remember that woman's—Olive! Olive! Olive came to the door, with very big eyes, shaking all over. I said, "Oh, hello, I'm Matt Friedman. I thought I'd come over this beautiful evening and have a chat with Mr. Talley." So she stood there doing her imitation of a fish, and—

SALLY. She did what?

MATT. She couldn't speak, I think. She was paralyzed. She goes—(Imitates a fish)

SALLY. It isn't necessary to characterize every—

MATT. Sally, I'm trying to tell this in a way that I don't get angry again.

SALLY. Okay!

MATT. Finally she swims off, after having said all of not one word, and Buddy came— Does your entire family have such absurd names?

SALLY. His real name is Kenny. We call him Buddy.

MATT. Kenny? Is his real name? This is better, for a grown man, Kenny? Kenny Talley, Lottie Talley, Timmy Talley, Sally Talley? Your brother also does not know how to converse. Your brother talks in rhetorical questions: "You're Sally's Jewish friend, ain't ya? What do you think you want here? Did you ever hear that trespassing was against the law?"

SALLY. Oh, they're all such hyprocrites and fools.

MATT. They was nothing hypocritical about, believe me.

SALLY. You deserve it, coming down here. I told you Dad said you weren't invited back.

MATT. So Buddy said, If you want to see your friend Sally, you can go to Springfield, where she works, and I said I'd wait there in the yard—and he went in and got a two-barreled hunting gun.

SALLY. And Olive called the sheriff.

MATT. I am omitting the yelling and the screaming and the deprecating.

SALLY. Who was yelling?

MATT. Well, there was your Aunt Charlotte yelling: "This man came to see me." And your mother yelling: "You are not to see my daughter." And Olive yelling, "Get back in the house" at everybody, at Charlotte, at Buddy, at the dog that was barking, at your brother's business friend—who was out in the yard to protect Buddy; he mostly said, "You tell 'em, Buddy, you tell 'em, Buddy." (Pause)

SALLY (Moves away, turns to him). I'm not even gonna apologize, you had it coming to you.

MATT. Of course, your mother and Olive stayed up there on the screened-in porch, protected from the mosquitoes and Communists and infidels.

SALLY (Turning away). I have absolutely got to get out of that place. Rachel and Ida and I have been looking for an apartment in town for months.

MATT (Watches her. Lightly). Actually you don't get mosquitoes here, do you? Rich people always know where to build their houses. With the house on the hill, in the breeze, the river always moving, mosquitoes don't nest around here. The breeze blows them off. Do they nest? Mosquitoes? Do mosquistoes nest? Does everything that lays eggs nest? Do fish nest? That's a funny idea.

SALLY. Don't try to make me feel good, Matt, it isn't going to work. Fish spawn.

MATT. What do mosquitoes do?

SALLY. I do not know what mosquitoes do. They breed.

MATT. You know, I'll bet you're right. (Beat) See, I thought you'd be glad to see me. That's my problem. I got no sounding board. I sit up there in St. Louis in this dusty office sneezing away, I get to daydreaming. I start thinking: (Ozark accent) Well, now, listen here, Matthew, what ort to happen is you ort to head on down into them hills an—

SALLY. Please don't do that. Don't make fun of the way we talk. Oh! Everything you do! You're enough to make a—

MATT (Beat). Preacher cuss. (beat) Sailor blush.

SALLY. I don't make fun of your accent, I don't see why—

MATT (With an unconscious but pronounced accent). I have no accent. I worked very hard and have completely lost any trace of accent.

SALLY. Very well.

MATT. And daydreaming away up there, I said to myself: *(Bogart)* This—uh—Sally dame. She—uh—looks to me like a good deal, Matt. She—uh—showed you a good time. The least you could do is reciprocate.

SALLY. That's supposed to be someone, I guess. That isn't you.

MATT. What do you mean, "someone"? You don't know Humphrey Bogart?

SALLY. We don't go to the pictures.

MATT. How did you know he was a movie actor? He might be the Secretary of the Interior; he—

SALLY. My grandmother knows Humphrey Bogart and she's never been to a—

MATT. You don't castigate a guy's imitations, Sal.

SALLY. The Secretary of the Interior has been Harold Ickes since Sitting Bull.

MATT. You don't go to the movies?

SALLY. Pictures are an excuse to sit alone in the dark.

MATT. To sit together in the dark.

SALLY. Not necessarily.

MATT. But you go alone.

SALLY. Not always.

MATT *(With sexual overtones).* Oh, ho . . . now, that's—interesting.

SALLY. Sometimes with some of the other nurse's aides from work.

MATT *(After a pause).* That's a big business, isn't it? Caring for the wounded. It's a nice place for the boys to forget about the hard realities of making a buck when they get out.

SALLY. The boys we take care of have seen their share of hard realities.

MATT. It's a very sunny building. The boys all have a very sunny attitude. The doctors are very sunny, the nurses are very sunny, the nurse's aides sunny. You expect the whole place to go up with spontaneous combustion.

SALLY. We try to be pleasant, yes. What would you have us do? Say, "Oh my gosh, you look terrible, I don't think you're going to make it through the night"? "Good Lord, you poor man, both hands missing and all you know is auto mechanics; you're never going to find a job you're happy with."

MATT. No, I wouldn't have you do—

SALLY *(Almost angry).* We don't have to fake anything. When you work with them every day you can see progress. Some of them will recover completely.

MATT. I'm not criticizing, I admire it.

SALLY. I was there last February when you barged in, I wasn't home!

MATT. Oh, yes, yes, that was funny. One girl said you had a cold that day, and another girl said you had gone to Kansas City to help requisition more beds. She was very imaginative, but under sympathetic questioning she was not a good fibber.

SALLY. So you drove all that way down to Springfield and all that way back for nothing.

MATT. It wasn't a wasted afternoon. I had the honor to be shown by a Negro private from California twenty-five different ways I can lose the game of checkers. Also, I had time to puzzle. Why would Sally tell every person with whom she works that if this hairy Jewish accountant comes down like a crazy man to see her . . . everybody tell him she's not here and Sally will hide in a closet.

SALLY. I was working in the kitchen that morning, where visitors are not allowed. It was not necessary to hide.

MATT. With little nurses coming into the kitchen every ten minutes to say: "Well, I don't know, Sally, he's still up there. Looks like he intends to stay all day." Puzzles don't waste my time, Sally. I'm very good at puzzles. I have great powers of ratiocination. I'm a regular Sherlock. He was a terrible anti-Semite. He was a rather shallow, ignorant man. Did you know that?

SALLY. I'm sorry, I wasn't listening. I was trying to figure out what "ratiocination" means.

MATT. Oh, forgive me. I don't have a speaking vocabulary. I have a reading vocabulary. I don't talk that much.

SALLY. I haven't noticed the problem.

MATT. Last year, weren't you always saying how quiet I was? Matt, why don't you say something—weren't you always asking me questions?

SALLY *(Moving toward the door).* I retract everything I said last summer.

MATT *(Moving to cut her off with rather surprising agility).* But unlike Sherlock Holmes, I'm not quick. I'm steady and I stay at something, but I'm thick. *First,* it took a long time for me to know something as thick as me. And *then,* going back over the mystery of Sally in the closet, I decided what was called for was an on-the-spot investigation.

SALLY. Matt, I'm—

MATT *(Taking a notepad from his pocket).* So I have a few questions I'd like to put to you.

SALLY. There is no mystery.

MATT. Mystery isn't bad, Sally. Mystery is the spice of life.

SALLY. Variety is the spice of life.

MATT. Well, variety has always been a mystery to me. Give me one choice and I can take it or leave it. Give me two and I can't decide. Give me three, I don't want any of it. Now—

SALLY. I cannot understand why you can't get the message. You sound like a functioning human being; but you've got a wire crossed or something.

MATT. A screw loose.

SALLY. You are one total, living loose screw. That much is certain. You've been away a solid year. The one time you come to the hospital to hunt me down I refuse to see you—

MATT. No, no, you didn't refuse, you hid in the kitchen.

SALLY. And you sat up there in that dayroom the entire blessed afternoon.

MATT. I was not made to feel unwelcome.

SALLY. *Not made to feel unwelcome?* You do not have the perception God gave lettuce. I did not answer but one letter and in that one short note I tried to say in no uncertain terms that I didn't want you to write to me. You have sent me an almost *daily* chronicle of your life in your office. The most mundane details of your accounting life. Why did you come back here?

MATT. It was a very pleasant way to begin the morning: writing, Dear Sal. Cleared out my head, like reading the newspaper, only not so depressing. I could tell you about the intrigue in the office; mull over the problems I anticipated. And knowing you—you sort of spoke along with me. Your carefully balanced and rational judgment was a great boon to my disposition. Improved the weather. And the weather in St. Louis needs all the improvement it can get. I'll bet I made you laugh.

SALLY. No, you did not.

MATT. No?

SALLY. Not once.

MATT. That's a blow.

SALLY. I knew you were trying to, but I didn't find anything particularly funny.

MATT. Not trying. I just thought you might. You didn't get lonely. It wasn't like being away from me this whole year, was it?

SALLY. Not at all.

MATT. Didn't you come to look forward to the mail in the morning?

SALLY. I dreaded each new day.

MATT. Now see, if I believed that, I'd leave.

SALLY. I did gain a fondness for the calm respectability of Sunday.

MATT. Holidays must have been nice.

SALLY. Holidays were a benediction.

MATT. Did you make the recipe I sent you? I couldn't make it because I don't have a timer. Baking in an oven, I forget what I'm doing and I go off and leave. I come back, the apartment is terrible. I cook well—

SALLY. —I don't cook. Why don't you just go on up the road to the Barnettes'? It isn't that far. They'll give you enough gas to get into town.

MATT. You have no sense of nostalgia, Sal. You have no romance.

SALLY. No, I do not. Not right now. I can't remember feeling less romantic.

MATT. Alone. Together again in the sunset—well, sundown—twilight. *(Pause, looks around and out over the river)* This country. I mean, this countryside. Is so beautiful. Do you think about that when you live in it all the time? Surrounded by all this lovely scenery? Or do you take it for granted?

SALLY. We know it's beautiful. Why wouldn't we appreciate it? There has to be some compensation in the place. It isn't particularly fertile; it's rocky; it's got poor drainage; it's all hills.

MATT. How can it have poor drainage if it's all hills?

SALLY. Hills have nothing to do with drainage. Water has to soak into the ground, not run off. The weather is too dry in the summer, the crops just curl up in the field. The spring is nothing but a cycle of floods. The winters are too cold, and damp, and . . .

MATT. But it's beautiful. *(He has been rubbing his hands on a side of the upturned boat. His finger has just jabbed a hole in the side)* Gottenyu! Look at that. That goes right through. Not what I'd call seaworthy. Riverworthy. When was the last time anybody was down here? Aside from you, coming down here to get away from the house? Aside from you and me coming down here last summer?

SALLY. I wouldn't know.

MATT. Ought maybe to fix the place up.

SALLY. Nobody has any use of it any more. You couldn't get materials now if you wanted to.

MATT. Fancy place to let rot away. Nobody even knows who spent all that much time building some crazy place like this. It isn't really grand, it's just silly. Is it not silly? Must have broke a lot of jigsaw blades.

SALLY. Uncle Whistler.

MATT. What?

SALLY. Everett Talley. Built the boathouse

in 1870. Built follies all over town. He wanted to build a gazebo up by the house, but Grandpa said it was a frivolity, so he built a boathouse.

MATT. And made it look like a gazebo.

SALLY. Well, that's what he wanted to do in the first place. He did the bandstand in the park across the river. The town didn't want it, but he'd seen it in a picture somewhere so he went over and built it. They tried to stop him, he went right on; said they could tear it down after he had finished. Painted it maroon and pink and gold. Said, "Now, tear it down." Eventually they used it for high school band concerts.

MATT. Sounds like a frustrated guy.

SALLY. Not at all! Why does everything have to be cynical? He was not in the least frustrated. He was a happily married man with seven kids. He made toys. Tap-dancing babies and whirligigs. He got pleasure out of making things for people. He did exactly what he wanted to do. He was the healthiest member of the family. Everybody in town knew him. They all called him Whistler.

MATT. Because he was the artist in the family?

SALLY. Because he sang and whistled. He used to go stomping through the woods singing *"Una furtiva lagrima"* at the top of his lungs; nobody outside the Talleys knew what he was singing, so they all said he was crazy, but he certainly wasn't frustrated.

MATT *(He has found an ice skate)*. What is that? An ice skate? Somebody had big feet. Do you skate?

SALLY. No.

MATT. Me too. Did you use to roller skate on the sidewalk?

SALLY. There isn't a sidewalk closer than a mile and a half, in town.

MATT. Me too. All the other kids had skates. Fly past me, knock me down, I was only five. Some memories linger.

SALLY. In St. Louis?

MATT *(Beat. He does not answer her)*. In the winter they skated on the lake. Frozen solid. I tried another boy's skates on once. Nearly broke my neck. Well, that's what I should have expected. I am not what you would call a beautifully coordinated individual.

SALLY. Oh, don't put those on!

MATT. That roller rink in Lebanon where the soldiers all hang out. That's the principal recreation here, it ooomo.

SALLY. People come up from Springfield.

MATT. Fellas and their dates?

SALLY. Girls looking for soldiers.

MATT. Looks like everybody is having a good time. All that drinking and all that skating, I'd get sick.

SALLY. They do.

MATT. You go?

SALLY. I went once, Matt, I didn't like it. *(He has put the skates on his feet)* Don't stand up in those, you'll go right through the floor.

MATT. No, no, it's all a matter of balance. *(stands, nearly falls over, grabs the wall)*

SALLY. Don't do that—Oh, for crying out loud.

MATT. Unfortunately, I have almost no sense of balance at all. *(He is holding on)* What do you do? You have to push off to start. Then you glide.

SALLY. You don't have to push off, but I suppose you could.

MATT. Eventually you come to a standstill. How do you keep going?

SALLY. You take steps. Step, push. And you glide on that foot. Your weight on that one foot.

MATT. How do you get your weight off one foot and onto another?

SALLY. The other foot has to come up.

MATT. How can the other foot come up?

SALLY. Lift it! *(She goes to him, pulls at one foot)* Oh, for godsake, lift it!

MATT *(Unsteady, still holding on to the wall)*. Oh . . . One foot.

SALLY. Now, you're gliding on that one foot. Before you start to slow down, you lean your weight over onto the other.

MATT. Oh, sure. What's to catch me if I shift my weight off of this foot?

SALLY. The other foot. You've got two, stupid.

MATT. Sally, I'm awkward, I'm not stupid.

SALLY. Put the *other foot* down! *(He does)*

MATT *(On both feet again)*. That's much easier.

SALLY. Now, lift the other foot.

MATT. I know, I know. And glide on that. *(He has taken hold of her and let go of the wall)* Why don't the skaters get tangled up?

SALLY. Because they're synchronized.

MATT. I'm not going to worry about what you do, okay? You'll confuse me *(Singing "Over the Waves," waltz-tempo, low at first, gaining in confidence)* La-la-la-la-la-bop-bop-bop—

SALLY *(For one moment they appear to be skating)*. Come on, not so loud.

MATT. La-la-la-la-la-la-la-la-bop-bop-boom-bop-bop—

SALLY. Come on, Matt, stop. They'll hear you across the river.

MATT. I'm having an old-fashioned skate with my girl.

SALLY. I'm not your girl, Matt. Come on. Let go, you're ridiculous.

MATT. Don't let go. Don't let go! We're coming to the end of the pond.

SALLY *(Has disentangled herself. He is flailing his arms with nothing to hold on to)*. I'm going to go get gasoline for your car.

MATT *(As if heading for the edge of the pond)*. I'm going too fast! I don't know how to turn. Sally! I'm gonna crash! Help! The trees are looming up in front of me. They're coming right at me. Fir trees and big old maple trees. Oak trees! They're black against the snow. Firelight flickering on them from the campfire. They're frozen hard as stone and deadly. It's the end of a brilliant career! Here they come. I can't slow down! Here they come! AAAAAAAAaaaaaaaaa! *(Falls down)* Oh, oh . . . I'm in serious—Where are you going? Sally?

SALLY *(She has stood with her arms crossed, watching him. Now she turns to leave)*. I'm going for your gas.

MATT. Sally? Hey, I can't run after you in these.

SALLY. Good. I'm good and sick of you running after me, Matt. *(She is gone)*

MATT. Come on. *(He tries to run after her)* Where do you think you are going— *(As his leg crashes through the floor, he grabs at the overhead lattice. It gives way and falls on him, dumping the reels, creels, baskets, nets, etc., over him)* Oh, my God! Sally? Help. Sally? *(He fights his way clear of the mess to see her standing in the doorway again)* I fell through the floor.

SALLY *(Somewhat concerned)*. Where are you hurt. What did you hurt?

MATT. Sally. Come on—uh . . . *(Fends her off a moment)* I appreciate your concern, but— just let me think a second. *(Pause)* Uh, no, in all honesty, I think I'm not injured at all. Except maybe my head. That stuff came down on me. *(Laughs)* Look at you standing there with your arms crossed. *(Tries to rise)* Uh. There's one problem. I don't know how I'm supposed to get out of this. My leg's through the floor. Give me a lift.

SALLY. Oh, good Lord. *(Tries to help)* They must have heard you up to the house; across the river.

MATT. I was having fun. It's very good exercise, skating.

SALLY *(Giving up)*. I can't. You're too big. And you're not helping.

MATT. I'm helping, I'm helping.

SALLY. You'll have to get out by yourself. What a baby.

MATT. It's not so bad here. *(Looking around)* It's not an uncomfortable position. My vanity is a little confused, but outside of that.

SALLY. You're not going to be so comfortable when you get your foot snake-bit.

MATT. Oh, my God. *(He manages to scramble out of the hole)* You know all the right things to say. *(Looking his leg over)* I think I'm not injured. No, I'm not even skinned. The wood is too rotten to scrape me even.

SALLY. You could have scratched yourself on a rusty nail and gotten blood poisoning.

MATT. No, I had a tetanus shot before I came down. That's what you have to get when you go fishing. I read about it. In case you prick your finger with a fish hook. Most painful thing I ever paid to have done to myself. *(Sits, takes off the skates)* Were you serious about the snakes?

SALLY. Copperheads, water moccasins, cottonmouths. I mean, they won't prey on you. But I imagine if you stuck your foot right in their nest, they wouldn't like it.

MATT. Snake's nest? *(He gets up, pushes something over the hole)* Had you told me about the snakes last year when we came down here, there would never have been an affair between Sally and Matt. *(Sits again to put his shoes on)*

SALLY. There was no affair.

MATT. Of course there was an affair. How many times in seven days did I see you?

SALLY. I don't know.

MATT. Seven.

SALLY. Seven.

MATT. Seven. I got hoarse screaming over the music of that dance band. I could hardly speak all week long.

SALLY. The kids nowadays like it so loud they don't have to think.

MATT. I don't blame them.

SALLY. Neither do I.

MATT. You didn't mind me talking to you. Out on the porch of the Shriners' mosque.

SALLY. I didn't mind talking to you; I didn't mind you driving me home; I didn't even mind changing the tire.

MATT. I thought we made a very good team. Most girls would have stayed in the car. You at least held the flashlight.

SALLY. *Held the flashlight?*

MATT. Well, and told me how to change the tire.

SALLY. And lit matches so you could see, when the flashlight batteries burned out. I could have done it much faster myself. What I minded was the very next evening walking two miles when the carburetor failed.

MATT. I told you to wait in the car. I told you not to come.

SALLY. What is someone going to say, with me sitting alone in the car on a road where lovers park, where I have never been before in my life. Even during school.

MATT. I tried to hitchhike us a ride; you hid in the bushes every time a car came by. I'm looking around for you, the drivers all think I'm drunk and pull over into the other lane. You almost caused three head-on collisions that night.

SALLY. Aside from that night, the other times I saw you were a lot of fun. Except maybe the night you came to dinner.

MATT. I am not responsible for your family. That evening was your idea.

SALLY. Everyone is always saying what a crazy old-maid Emma Goldman I'm becoming, I wanted to show them how conservative and ignorant I really am.

MATT. You are not conservative, you are not ignorant, and Emma Goldman, believe me, was no old maid.

SALLY. You know what I mean. Between being what they consider out-and-out anti-American and being over forty years old, and having a beard, you made a grand hit with Mom and Dad, let me tell you.

MATT. I could tell.

SALLY. You left the house, Dad said, That man is more dangerous than Roosevelt himself.

MATT. What they were hoping was that I would be a proper Christian suitor and take crazy Sally off their hands.

SALLY (She gets up to go). No, at least they've stopped hoping that. That's something.

MATT. Where are you going? When we're getting on so well.

SALLY. We are not getting on so well.

MATT (Manages to get between SALLY and the door, blocking her way). Sally, listen. You're scared and I'm scared, but we both have to realize that we're going to deal with this before either of us leaves.

SALLY. There's nothing to deal with, Matt.

MATT. No, there's quite a lot. We can't have it both ways. You can chase me away or you can put on a pretty dress. But you can't put

on a pretty dress to come down here and chase me away. (Beat) You remember I've seen you come home from work in your uniform.

SALLY. I changed out of my uniform at work tonight.

MATT. Because you thought I'd meet you in Springfield, outside the hospital.

SALLY. I didn't know you'd be down here; I thought I'd come down here to listen to the band.

MATT. You were coming to the boathouse because this is where we came last year.

SALLY. This is my place. I come down here every day.

MATT. Okay, fine, I'll believe that. You go to the boathouse to forget your family. Maybe you have a cigarette to unwind, knowing you can't smoke up at the house; maybe you take a nip from a whiskey bottle you keep here somewhere.

SALLY. I won't stay up there forever. I'm as eager to leave as they are eager to get rid of me.

MATT. Maybe get an apartment in Springfield. Share with Rachel and Ida, so the three of you don't have to drive to work every morning.

SALLY. They're nice girls.

MATT. They're very nice. Maybe get a pet dog. A dachshund, maybe, name him Matt. Smoke all you want to in your own apartment. Go out to the movies on Saturday night. Maybe go sometimes to the USO dances? Not get too involved with any of the boys, not Sally.

SALLY. Is that bad?

MATT. No, ma'am, it is not. You do real work at the hospital. All the boys said they like you best. All those other nurses, though, with their eyes they were saying: "Don't you go away, Matt, Sally is gonna come around."

SALLY. They enjoyed the game.

MATT. Yes, me too. But they weren't telling me to go away.

SALLY. Well, then I'm telling you to go away; nothing will come from it, Matt—

MATT. See, they could tell that I was in love with you, and they were telling me you might be in love with me, and wouldn't that be a catastrophe.

SALLY (Beat). I don't think I even know what that means; I don't know if you know what that—

MATT. Aside from that, though, you're afraid you might love me.

SALLY. I don't think that is even a desirable state to be in—

MATT. Agreed, a hundred percent; all you have to say is, No, I am not.

SALLY. Why don't you just leave and make us all happier.

MATT. I don't know that leaving would make you happy. It wouldn't make me happier. It would be easier. See, I can take no for an answer; I can't take evasion, I can't take I'm scared, I can't take hiding in the kitchen.

SALLY. Just put it out of your mind, Matt. It's impossible.

MATT. So the future is pug dogs and apartments and USO get-togethers and drinking with the girls.

SALLY. It sounds wonderful.

MATT. Sally has decided she is an eccentric old maid, and she is going to be one.

SALLY. I'm looking forward to it.

MATT *(He sighs. Pause. Gets out a notebook)*. Well, see, I'll show you how far Sherlock got. My first solution to the Sally-in-the-closet puzzle—

SALLY. Kitchen.

MATT. Sally hiding in the kitchen—was, she don't want nothing to do with this Jew-type. *(Mild Jewish accent)* It no matter that she never saw one before, she has heard great much about dem. Days alvays beink shased from place to place, must be somethink wrong. Anyvay, *shiksas* are gullible breeds an belief everythink they hear.

SALLY. Oh, you don't think that at all. I'm a liberal Midwestern college graduate. You were very exotic to me. I reread the Old Testament.

MATT. Well, I hate to disillusion you, but I didn't reread the New Testament. *(Tearing off the page of the notebook; throwing it away)* So it is not that. Everything must be in a list for me or I get confused. Then I said maybe the reason Sally is so scared is it's this *(German accent)* Yerman she can't abide. All the boys are off fighting these Yerman types, there's one right in the middle of us.

SALLY. There are old families of German descent here.

MATT. Ha-ha. You know nothing about dis Friedman. Might be anybody. Dis enemy maybe infiltrate de home front, ja?

SALLY. Don't. That's creepy.

MATT. You should only know. So! She does not think of Matt as a German *(Tears off another page, looks at the next)* Then Matt says: *(Carefully)* This Sally puzzle, She's how old? *(*SALLY *freezes)* Stop looking at yourself, Matt. It is not just Matt she is not liking. She is *well*

over how old? All her friends and all her relatives were married by what age? And with all the prospering young men down here, some—

SALLY. All the prospering young men are off to war, Matt.

MATT. I think we are getting somewhere. Well, then all the handsome and pathetic and brave soldiers at the hospital she sees every day.

SALLY. They're kids. They're ten years younger than me; more, most of them.

MATT. This has got to be the most particular girl that ever was. Whoever heard of such a situation? Where is her bright-red hair net? Where're the rolled garters on her legs to drive men out of their mind. Why isn't she exposing half her bosom with a plunging neckline like every other female? Where is the come-hither? The invitation? *(Moves to* SALLY*)* Here is an unmarried, attractive, not fanatically religious young lady who actually thinks of herself as a human being rather than a featherbed. And you say there is no mystery? Also, I talked to the patients at the hospital, remember? Some are not so young. And they all say, "Are you Sally's beau? Every time we say something sweet to Sally, try to get fresh, she says, 'Come on, now, I got a beau.'"

SALLY *(A long pause. She is trying to speak and can't. After two attempts she says shakily)*. There's time . . . enough . . . for . . .

MATT *(Pause. Quietly)*. It's just a friendly conversation, Sally. No reason to be upset.

SALLY. Oh, come . . . on. My life is no concern to you. If we get through the war, there's time to think about the future.

MATT. Nobody thinks like that any more. Live for today.

SALLY. Everything is upside down.

MATT *(Turns her to face him)*. No, no. We're not waiting for when Johnny comes marching home this time.

SALLY. I can't hear a word you're saying. You have a thing of blood on your face.

MATT *(Alarmed. A spot of blood from a scratch has appeared over one eye)*. Blood? Where? How did I get?

SALLY. You said that junk fell on you. Don't touch it. Don't—just put both your hands down. *(She takes a handkerchief from her purse, and a bottle from a hiding place. Lights a lantern, and hands it to him)* Hold this.

MATT *(Looking at bottle, as she dabs handkerchief)*. What is that?

SALLY. Never you mind.

MATT. What is that? *(She dabs at his fore-*

head) Ai! That stings. What are you putting on . . . ?

SALLY. Gin. You're not hurt; don't faint. Sit down.

MATT. I'm inoculated; it won't give me lockjaw.

SALLY. I'm sorry to hear it.

MATT. I had a tetanus shot. Ouch.

SALLY. I know. Because you read in a book how to be a fisherman.

MATT *(As she chases him)*. Some skills have to be acquired, you know. Man is not born with a knowledge of the river or nobody would ever drown. Ouch! This is a professional nurse's aide's bedside manner? Also, I read. In my business I had to learn to read very fast because they change the tax laws every week.

SALLY *(A last dab at him)*. One more.

MATT. So now I read like a madman, and I retain nothing at all. But I read like lightning.

SALLY. I read very slowly and practically memorize every word.

MATT. Jack Sprat. Am I okay?

SALLY. You'll live. *(She takes a nip from the bottle and passes it to him. He takes a drink, reacts, hands the bottle back.)*

MATT. You have Sen-Sen for your breath? *(She opens her purse)* No, no. *(He takes a cigarette, offers her one. She sighs, takes it. He gets a lighter from his pocket. It doesn't work. She opens her purse, produces a lighter, and lights his and hers. Looking around)* Poor Whistler. He should see what is happening to his boathouse. He'd sing *"Una furtiva Lagrima."*

SALLY. I used to think that he made the place for me. I was little when he died, but I thought he knew I'd come along, so he built it just the way it is—falling down—the way people used to build Roman ruins for their gardens. That way nobody else would come here and discover the magic of the place except me.

MATT. It was falling down? Even then?

SALLY. Well, it wasn't that long ago. I played in it when I was eight or ten, I'm twenty-seven now, so—

MATT. No, you're counting wrong.

SALLY. I'm what?

MATT. You're thirty-one.

SALLY. I am certainly not thirty-one. Who do—

MATT. Oh, my goodness. She does have a vanity as well as a temper. You are thirty-one because you were fired from teaching Sunday school on your twenty-eighth birthday and that's three years ago.

SALLY. What?

MATT. I've become great friends with your Aunt Charlotte. There's a counterspy in your very home. You're infiltrated. I didn't tell you. You're ambushed. I've come up on you from behind.

SALLY. When did you talk to Aunt Charlotte?

MATT. Last year. For a second today. And every few weeks during the winter. On the telephone. *(He laughs)* I had never heard of anyone being fired from Sunday school before.

SALLY. I quit, we didn't get along.

MATT. I like it better the way she told me. The preacher told you you were supposed to be teaching from the Methodist reader, not from Thorstein Veblen.

SALLY. They were having problems with union organizers at the garment factory.

MATT. Some of the kids' mothers work there.

SALLY. They asked me what was happening.

MATT. I like that. So you read to them from . . . ?

SALLY. *The Theory of the Leisure Class.*

MATT. How much of the garment factory does your family own?

SALLY. Almost twenty-five percent. Dad and the minister and the newspaper editor suggested we all concentrate on the text: "And he who does not work, neither shall he eat."

MATT. And scare the pants off the sluggards.

SALLY. Make the unreligious infidels buckle down.

MATT. Be good Christian workers.

SALLY. I also read from St. Augustine.

MATT. "Profit is a sin."

SALLY. "Businessmen will never enter the Kingdom."

MATT. He was also a terrible anti-Semite.

SALLY. Worse, he was Catholic.

MATT. Sally, you know that unmarried daughters are supposed to help the menfolk keep the social status quo.

SALLY. Organize food baskets for the poor.

MATT. Keep their mouths shut.

SALLY. There was a time when Dad had great hopes for me.

MATT. No wonder they are so eager to get you out of their house.

SALLY. You're older than I am.

MATT. Oh, more than you know. I'm forty-two.

SALLY. That's about what I imagined.

MATT. Sally, you don't say that. Whatever you think.

SALLY. Under the draft by the skin of your teeth.

MATT. Yes.

SALLY. You could have volunteered.

MATT. Yes.

SALLY. You've been married?

MATT. No, ma'am.

SALLY. Why?

MATT. Never asked anybody. Nobody ever asked me.

SALLY. You should have heard the other nurse's aides, after you left. They thought you were the bee's knees.

MATT. They still say that down here?

SALLY. They still say cat's pajamas. Only something is wrong. Something is goofy, isn't it? A single man, forty-two years old. It doesn't make sense that a good man hasn't made a fool of himself at least once by your age.

MATT. Well, puzzles. Why does the chicken cross the road? A man I know says some riddle to me every day. I say, Don't tell me, don't tell me. Later in the day I say, Okay, I give up. Puzzles and jokes.

SALLY. They couldn't quite put you together so they decided you weren't quite right. Maybe you had a wife and six kids in Germany.

MATT. You like jokes? Old Ben Franklin was standing at the kitchen window one morning flying his kite out the window. And his missus, Mrs. Franklin, comes in, looks out at the kite, and says to Ben, "You need more tail." (SALLY reacts) And Ben says to her: "That's what I told you this morning. And you told me to go fly a kite."

SALLY. I heard that before I was twelve.

MATT. I hadn't heard it before. Mrs. Blumenfeld in the office told us that yesterday morning.

SALLY. English wasn't your first language. What was?

MATT. Questions and answers. What is the shortest month? May is the shortest month, there are only three letters in May.

SALLY. German? Yiddish?

MATT. What was Matthew's first language? It doesn't come out funny. What does it matter; he can't talk to the old man at the cafeteria in Lithuanian any more. Not the way he would like to. Some. Pieces: "The weather is hot today." "Yes, the weather is hot. I read the Germans marched into Russia." "Yes, what happened to the German-Russian friendship, ho, ho, ho?" I yell to him like he was deaf.

SALLY. Where were you born?

MATT. I don't know.

SALLY. Where was the sidewalk they skated on?

MATT. (Almost abrupt). I lived in many cities. (Sighs, maybe sits, or walks around) Oh, dear. We are a lot alike, you know? To be different. We are two such private people. A guy the other day—I eat at this cafeteria, I talk to a lot of nutty guys—

SALLY. I don't want to hear another story, I—

MATT. No, no, no, this is not like that. I came down here to tell you this. This guy told me we were eggs.

SALLY. Who? You and me?

MATT. All people. He said people are eggs. Said we had to be careful not to bang up against each other too hard. Crack our shells, never be any use again. Said we were eggs. Individuals. We had to keep separate, private. He was very protective of his shell. He said nobody ever knows what the other guy is thinking. We all got about ten tracks going at once, nobody ever knows what's going down any given track at any given moment. So we never can really communicate. As I'm talking to you on track number three, over on track five I might be thinking about . . . (Puts his hand on her back) Oh, any number of things. (Really asking) And when I think you're listening to me, what are you really thinking?

SALLY. (Removes his hand). And you think he's right or you think he's wrong?

MATT. Well, that's two ways of looking at it. I told him he was paranoid. Ought not to worry too much about being understood. Ought to work at it. We . . . (Puts his hand on her knee) Got our work cut out for us, don't we? I told him . . .

SALLY. (Gently pushes his hand away, and crosses her legs). What?

MATT. (Up and pacing). Well, it's all right there in his analogy, ain't it? What good is an egg? Gotta be hatched or boiled or beat up into something like a lot of other eggs. Then you're cookin'. I told him he ought not to be too afraid of gettin' his yolk broke.

SALLY. Where were you born?

MATT. He didn't appreciate it either.

SALLY. Why are you being such a private person? Such an egg?

MATT. (His back to us, staring out). Where was Matt born? Uh, Rostock maybe or Dansk or Kaunas, but probably Kaunas, which became the capital of . . .

SALLY. Lithuania.

MATT. What was Lithuania. (Turning) So! there! Omelette!

SALLY. When did you come to America?

MATT. This is one you haven't heard; this is a city joke. The Kaiser's architect had a little outhouse he wanted plastered and painted, so he asked for bids from three contractors: a Polish man, an Italian, and a Jew.

SALLY. Matt—

MATT. So first the Pole says, Well, that job will cost you three thousand marks. Kaiser's architect says, How do you figure that? The Pole says, One thousand for the plasterer, one thousand for the painter, and one thousand for me. So the Italian says, That will be six thousand marks. Kaiser's architect says, How is that six thousand marks? The Italian says, Two thousand for the plasterer, two thousand for the painter, two thousand for me. So he goes to the Jewish contractor and he says, That job will be nine thousand marks. Nine thousand marks! How can you figure that? So the Jew says, Three thousand for you, three thousand for me, and three thousand for the Pole.

SALLY. You said you were German, why were you born in Lithuania?

MATT. Probably Lithuania.

SALLY. Did you come here with your family? *(Pause)* To this country? *(Pause)* Or don't you know that either.

MATT. I know, I know. *(Pause. Finally decides)* Very well, Miss Sally Talley. There was a Prussian and a Uke (Ukrainian, yes?). A Prussian and a Uke and a Lat and a Probable Lit, who all traveled over Europe.

SALLY. Matt, you're maddening—I don't know if this is a story or a—

MATT. I will tell this, Sally, in the only way I can tell it. The Prussian had been a soldier, but then he realized that, being Jewish, he could not advance in the Kaiser's army, so then he became an engineer.

SALLY. There's no such thing as a Prussian Jew.

MATT *(Rather Prussian)*. Prussian is the way the Prussian thought of himself, and Prussian he was. *(She sighs, perhaps says, "Very well")* So he became a Wandering . . . Engineer. The Kaiser sent the Prussian and the Uke and the Lat and the Probable Lit to study engineering wonders: many months in the Swiss mountains to watch the building of a funicular, yes?

SALLY. Yes.

MATT. And in the evening the Prussian liked to sit stiffly and talk with other stiff Prussian Jews sitting around the cafés of the capitals of Europe. But unfortunately, one of the people with whom the Prussian spoke was—

SALLY. Matt, you're confusing me and I don't know if this is a joke or this is—

MATT. This is the joke about how the Probable Lit came to America that you said you wanted to hear. So one of the people with whom he spoke was an inventor named—who remembers—such is fame—who had discovered how to get nitrogen out of air. Like magic. So one day the Prussian and the Uke and the Lat and the Probable Lit lit out for Naples but were detained in Nice, where there is a large police force, because people try to board boats there to cross borders, Europe being mostly made up of borders that people get upset when you try to cross. Europe is the child's game of May I. You know May I? "Captain, may I cross into Yugoslavia?" "Yes, you may take three scissor steps." "Okay, I take three scissor steps." "Oh, oh, go back to Czechoslovakia. You forgot to say, 'May I.' ".

SALLY. Who is the Uke and who is the Lat? You're the Lit and the Prussian is your father? Who is the Uke?

MATT. This is all on the up-and-up, Sally, the Prussian was married to the Uke. She said she was Sephardic, but that wasn't true.

SALLY *(Knows somehow that he is talking about something important)*. Okay. I want to understand this, Matt. Who was the Lat?

MATT. The Lat was their daughter, who had been born in Latvia two years before the Probable Lit had been born probably in Lithuania.

SALLY. I didn't know you have a sister.

MATT *(Looking across the river. Low)*. It turned out to be of little consequence, people in Europe being very wasteful of people.

SALLY *(Beat)*. And your family was detained in Nice?

MATT. Yes, by the Nice police. Which was very unlucky, as the French are very much the natural enemy of the Prussians, and the French very much wanted to know from the Prussian engineer . . . What? *(Beat)* Something he had overheard in a café.

SALLY *(Long pause. Troubled answer)*. How to get nitrogen from the air.

MATT. Like magic!

SALLY. Why?

MATT. Everyone was happily looking forward to the Great War.

SALLY. This was when?

MATT. This was 1911, the Lit was nine. And this nitrogen is not used in the fields as fertilizer. This nitrogen is used in the manufacture of gunpowder. So one should be very careful what your friends tell you in cafés. *(This is difficult to say, and there is a bitterness un-*

derlying it which he does not show) So the French torture the Prussian—

SALLY. Oh, no—

MATT. Who, being Prussian and Jewish, says nothing, and the French decide to torture the Lat daughter to make the Prussian speak.

SALLY. Matt, you don't have to say anything, I know—

MATT. The consequences being that the Lat fell into a coma from which she did not recover and the French were convinced that they had the wrong Prussian, Uke, Lat, and Lit, and let the whole lot of them go. So they went to the authorities in Germany, leaving the little Lit with his uncle in Lübeck. The irony turned out to be that the German government reasoned that this gregarious Prussian engineer knew something vital to the interest of the Kaiser—

SALLY. Oh, no—

MATT. Well, as he did. So the Prussian and the Uke tried to slip across the border into Denmark. But, we understand, they forgot to say, "May I?"

SALLY. They wouldn't kill their own people just because they knew something they might or might not tell—

MATT. —Well, they didn't consider them their own, of course. And people were not killed in Germany. They were indefinitely detained.

SALLY. I never heard that there were persecutions in the First World War.

MATT. I thought you said you reread the Old Testament.

SALLY. How did he get to America? The Lit?

MATT. Who said the little Lit came to America?

SALLY. How did he get to America?

MATT. Norway to Caracas to America on a banana boat.

SALLY. By himself? Or with refugees?

MATT. Refugees, smefugees. With the uncle from Lübeck and his wife and four kids.

SALLY. Little kids?

MATT. What does it matter what size kids? No. Grown people. Not little kids. There is always something thrilling about the broad canvas of a European story, isn't there? *(Pause)* But I am afraid that the Probable Lit had seen too much. No allegiances would claim him any more, no causes.

SALLY. So the lit didn't volunteer for the army.

MATT. Oh, war. What did he know except war; life was war, war was life. Against the French he would almost have gone this time. No. *(Looking at her)* The resolve was never to be responsible for bringing into such a world another living soul. He would not bring into this world another child to be killed for a political purpose. This boy knew blank about sitting alone without a woman to talk to. *(Pause)* So the little Lit was a little crazy, and I'm afraid as he grew older he got a little crazier, but he has witnessed nothing to cause him to alter his conviction. *(Watching her closely)* And what woman would be interested in such a grown Probable Lit with such a resolve? *(Pause. She doesn't answer)* Anyway, he doesn't think about it. The day is over in a second. I spend my life adding figures. It breaks my head.

SALLY *(Very level). He* does. The Lit.

MATT. Does what?

SALLY. You said "I." You mean the Lit. The Lit spends his life adding figures.

MATT. Yes, well, I do too. We are much alike. We work together.

SALLY. You've both gone to a lot of work for nothing.

MATT. What work? What do you mean?

SALLY. Or do you naturally invent stories about your sister and father and mother being killed by Germans?

MATT. One by the French; two by the Germans.

SALLY. You've been talking to Aunt Lottie? Who else have you talked to? People in town? Have you looked in the Lebanon newspaper? The old files? I don't know how detectives work.

MATT. This is bad. Why are you speaking like this?

SALLY. Why did you tell me that story?

MATT. To make you see why I had not spoken last year.

SALLY. That's what you came down here to tell me?

MATT. Yes.

SALLY. Well, now you've told me. Now I know. Now you can leave.

MATT *(Worried)*. I have said something I don't know that I have said.

SALLY *(She hurries to leave)*. It was a calculated risk; you just miscalculated. *(Hides the gin, grabs her jacket and purse)* You're not good at manipulation. I've been worked over by experts. *(Blows out the lantern)* They're good down here. *(The boathouse is flooded in moonlight)*

MATT. Sally, you have mistaken something—

SALLY. —Get gone now. Leave before I hit

you with something. You can walk to the Barnettes', they'll give you some gas for a couple of coupons.

MATT. Now who is making the disturbance?

SALLY *(Angry; quite loud)*. Get off this property or get out of my way so I can go back to the house, or I'll disturb you for real.

MATT. We are going to settle this before anyone goes anywhere.

SALLY. I won't be made a fool just because I fell in love again, Matt, and I won't be pushed around again.

MATT. You're not getting away from me.

SALLY. Get out of here!

MATT. Do you realize what you said? Did you hear yourself?

SALLY *(Yelling toward the door)*. Buddy! Cliffy! Here he is. Matt Friedman is down here! *(Her last words are muffled by MATT's hand as he grabs her and holds her fast. She tries to speak over his lines)*

MATT *(Grabbing her)*. *Vilde Chaya!* You are a crazy woman! We could both be shot with that gun. People do not scream and yell and kick. *(She stops struggling)* People are blessed with the beautiful gift of reason and communication. *(He starts to release her)*

SALLY. Cliffy!

MATT *(Grabbing her again)*. How can such a thing happen? When they passed out logic everybody in the Ozarks went on a marshmallow roast. You are rational now? *(He releases her. She moves away, MATT stands where he can block her exit)* Life is going to be interesting with you. You're hurt?

SALLY. No.

MATT. My hand is bleeding. Where did you hide the alcohol? *(He goes to the gin bottle, keeping an eye on her)* I called my uncle and my aunt. Seventy years old. They say, Matt, don't get mixed up with the *goyim*. They have my cousins call me; old neighbors I haven't heard from in years. I say I must live my own life. I come down here protected from tetanus; I am getting rabies from an *alte moid*.

SALLY *(Level)*. Why did you tell me about your family, and about you?

MATT *(Pouring the gin on his hand)*. Because you asked me. Why have you not married? Where were you born? How did you get to this stupid country? Because I am a crazy person. Your nurse friends all say something is wacky with Matt that he has never made a fool of himself over some woman; I said, Matt, go down, tell Sally who you are. Once in your life *risk* something. At least you will know that

you did what you could. What do you think she is going to do, bite you?

SALLY *(Pause)*. Charlotte told you nothing. She may be silly. She may like you.

MATT. One does not necessarily follow the other.

SALLY. But she doesn't gossip about me. She didn't tell you anything.

MATT. So you tell me. No, Charlotte told me nothing except that there was something to tell. I said, Charlotte, Sherlock thinks that there is some dark mystery down here and Charlotte said, Mr. Holmes, Sally will have to tell you that herself.

SALLY. There is nothing to tell.

MATT. You were screaming up to the house for the sheriff because there is—Oh, my— *(Listens)* They could all be coming down here now.

SALLY. They're all listening to the radio.

MATT. Saved by Miss Fanny Brice. We stick together. Oh, my gosh! I do not know how to begin! I am walking into an unfriendly church in my underdrawers, here.

SALLY. What are you talking about?

MATT. You don't have that dream? I congratulate you. That is a terrible dream. I mean, I am at such a disadvantage here. *(With an energy born from frustration)* None of my skills is appropriate to the situation I find myself in. And I have amazing skills. I could be an attraction in a sideshow. Give me a list of three, six, up to fifteen numbers, five digits each, I'll tell you the sum immediately. In my head, Mr. Adding Machine. Everybody gapes. How does he do that? He's got it all written down. I know the multiplication table up to seventy-five times seventy-five. Truly. It's something I know. What is sixty-seven times sixty-eight? Four thousand five hundred fifty-six. I have amazing skills. Only I feel like Houdini in the iron box under the ice at the bottom of the river. I forgot where I put the key to the handcuffs. Such a frustrating dream.

SALLY. One of the boys at the hospital is an artist. He's developed a facility for when a dream starts to go bad. It starts to get scary. He, in the dream, changes it all into a drawing, wads it up, and throws it away.

MATT. Freud wouldn't like it.

SALLY. Oh, drive him crazy.

MATT. I am foolish to insinuate myself down here and try to feel like one of the hillbillies. Who ever heard of this Friedman? I don't blame you. I won't be Matt Friedman any more. I'll join the throng. Call myself . . . August

Hedgepeth. Sip moonshine over the back of my elbow. Wheat straw in the gap in my teeth. I'm not cleaning my glasses, I'm fishing for crappie. Bass.

SALLY. Sun perch.

MATT. Oh, heck yes. Only I'm not. I can't even take off my shoes without feeling absurd.

SALLY. People don't walk around with their shoes off here, sipping moonshine. It isn't really the Hatfields and the McCoys. The ones who go barefoot only do it because they can't afford shoes, Matt . . . I . . .

MATT. Matt? Who's that? I don't even hear you. My name is August. Call me August.

SALLY. I couldn't possibly.

MATT. That's my name as of this minute.

SALLY. Matt, you—

MATT. Who? Huh? Wha?

SALLY *(A pause. Finally)*. August . . .

MATT. I don't like it. What is that fragrance? What are you wearing?

SALLY. It isn't me.

MATT. Smell.

SALLY. Honeysuckle.

MATT. That's honeysuckle? No wonder they make songs about it. It blooms at night?

SALLY. No, that's something else. It blooms during the day, the night, whenever.

MATT. It's wonderful.

SALLY. You've never had to grub it out of a garden.

MATT. You know that folk song? *(Sings)* "Lindy, did you smell that honeysuckle vine last night? Honey, it was smellin' so sweet in de moonlight.''

SALLY. No. I mean sure, but I don't know it.

MATT. We heard the Lebanon band play it last summer. Isn't that a Missouri folk song?

SALLY. No. I don't know. I don't know Missouri folk songs.

MATT *(Sings)*. "Oh, God, I'd lay me down and die, If I could be as sweet as that to you.'' *(Directly to her, low and trying to sing well)* "Oooooo-oooooo. My little Lindy Lou . . .''

SALLY. Don't sing to me, it's ridiculous. And my name is not Lindy Lou. It's Sally Talley. *(They both smile)*

MATT. I know, I came down to talk to you about that.

SALLY. Well, I'm not going to change— *(Dead stop. Count fifteen)*

MATT. Why is your chin trembling? You okay? Sally?

SALLY. You didn't say that. Don't say that.

MATT. It's what I want to say.

SALLY. Well, don't. Talk about your socialism, talk about your work or something, like you did in your letters.

MATT. I don't talk Socialism, I don't talk Communism, I talk common sense. I don't think much of isms. In no time at all you start defending isms like they were something tangible. What are you afraid of? Why—

SALLY *(Cutting him off)*. And that's what made Buddy so angry? And Olive? Talking common sense?

MATT. No, your brother is a baiter. You want to change the subject? Fine.

SALLY. A what?

MATT *(Almost angry)*. A baiter! A baiter. He baits people. Buddy thinks that if all the factory workers went on strike for better wages, as they were trying to do in his factory, it would bring the country to its knees. He is a very poetic speaker.

SALLY. Well, it would bring Buddy to his knees, and that's a position with which he is very unfamiliar, believe me.

MATT. What are you afraid of?

SALLY. People are working now at least.

MATT. Economics, you want to talk? I say to you: This is my life. This is what I want. Say no or say yes, and you say: Talk about economics?

SALLY. Will there really be strikes after the war is over?

MATT *(Glares at her)*. You are playing games, yes?

SALLY. I don't know what—

MATT. You are a peach. After the war they'll strike, yes. People say. Shaking in their boots. Sure. They'll strike. Everybody from soda jerks to grease monkeys. It gives them the illusion that the system is working.

SALLY *(Also worried. Trying one more diversion)*. People are afraid to admit it, but I think they're worried about what's going to happen when the boys come back.

MATT *(Increasingly angry)*. Down here they're afraid to admit it? I'm glad to hear it. It shows humility. Humility is good for the soul. In St. Louis they tremble in their beds at night. Headlines in the papers. One businessman said the war had to last another two years or the nation would never recover.

SALLY. They're afraid that there will be another Depression.

MATT. They who?

SALLY. They. They. Who do we ever mean when we say they?

MATT. Man I know says, "They-sayers are all liars."

SALLY. They see it happening all over again: the Depression, unemployment, with the factories shut down, higher taxes.

MATT. No.

SALLY. What do you mean, no?

MATT. No. It won't happen.

SALLY. You can't know that.

MATT. There is a lot I do not know. On people I am utterly ignorant. On girls I am more than ignorant. On money I am an expert only. On taxes I am an authority. Businesses ask *me* about taxes. People who cry depression are blind and frightened.

SALLY. Why should it be different this time?

MATT. You are worried? About what is going to be?

SALLY. Yes. It was no fun. Hobos coming up to the back door four and five at a time. Every day. Asking for work and having to accept handouts.

MATT. It's different. It won't be like that again. Roosevelt himself will be the one passing out lollipops.

SALLY. I don't know why you're acting like this. All I—

MATT. How much money do you have?

SALLY. What?

MATT *(Furious)*. You're an average person in a less-than-average job. You've been working only two and a half, three years. How much money do you have saved? You have nothing to spend it on, you put it in a savings account, you buy bonds to save capitalism, excuse me, democracy—er—a—freedom of speech, were you not terrified to express yourself—how much have you saved?

SALLY. What's wrong? I'm not going to let you talk to—

MATT. Forget it. How much?

SALLY *(Beat)*. I do know how much money I've saved. That's what bothers me. Money makes me greedy and guilty at the same time.

MATT. So how much?

SALLY. Half my check every week for three years. I make thirty dollars a week.

MATT. Twenty-three hundred forty dollars!

SALLY. A little less. Twenty-two hundred.

MATT. Multiply that times one hundred twenty million people.

SALLY. You're the mathematician, what does it come to?

MATT. A lot of money. That nobody had before the war. Burning a hole in everybody's pockets. How many people have bought war bonds? Eighty-five million people! How much money is in savings banks? One hundred thirty billion dollars! Everybody is going to be spending and building and working. The sideshow is over! End of financial exhibition. I'll go. Why did I come? You aren't going to be honest with me.

SALLY. Honest about what?

MATT. About you, about me, about Sally and Matt. You think I intend to sit here and talk finance? What will happen after the war.' Why should there be an after-the-war?

SALLY. I was being perfectly honest with you.

MATT. Perfectly honest and perfectly evasive. Perfectly mysterious and perfectly frightened out of your wits. *(Bogart)* "You know somethin', baby? You dames are all alike. Ya yella. Ya all got a yella streak a mile wide right down the middle of ya back."

SALLY. Is that supposed to be Cagney?

MATT *(Crushed)*. No; oh, my goodness! Cagney! That's still Bogart. You have no sense of flattery.

SALLY. And we're all yella. You know that many women, you can make a generalization like that?

MATT. Oh, good grief. Now what are you going to be? Jealous and possessive about something you don't even want? No. I know no women. What I told you I have never before spoken for the same reason that you speak nothing to anybody, because we are terrified that if once we allow ourselves to be cracked— I think people really do think that they're eggs. They're afraid they are the—who is the egg-man, all the king's horses and—

SALLY. Humpty Dumpty.

MATT. We all have a Humpty Dumpty complex. So now I take a big chance. I come down here to tell you I am in love for the only time in my life with a girl who sees the world exactly as I see it. I say to you, I am sorry, Sally, I will not have children, but if there is a life for the two of us, will you have me or not? You scream and yell bloody murder, you kick, you—ah, breathe fast, what do you call it, breathing fast in and out, in and out—?

SALLY. Hyperventilate.

MATT. You hyperventilate and say, Matthew, talk about finance. *(Sighs)* Oh, boy, oh, boy.

SALLY *(A long pause)*. You can come with me to the road. I'll get you some gas. I'll go into the yard by myself.

MATT. The car isn't out of gas.

SALLY *(Beat)*. What is it out of?

MATT. Hope! The car is out of hope. The car is in fine running condition. I turn the key, it goes; I turn it off, it stops. I turned it off. I didn't say it was out of gas, I said it needs gas to run. You assumed it was out of gas. *(Pause)* I wasn't talking to Buddy about isms up at the house, I was telling him about you and me down here in the boathouse last summer.

SALLY. Oh, my God! Oh!

MATT. Hey, come on, you'll drown out Fibber McGee.

SALLY. You didn't!

MATT. They'll arrest us both. Shhhh! They'll hear you swear right across the river at the park. You want to hear the band play in Whistler's band shell? So the night shouldn't be a waste?

SALLY. You didn't.

MATT. They ought to start any time. We can watch the fireworks.

SALLY. They won't have fireworks; you can hear the band from here. Matt, you have no idea how prejudiced Buddy and Olive are! Really!

MATT. You kidding me? I don't imagine your father will let you sleep under his roof after Buddy tells them. Your aunt thought it was very likely you'd be kicked out of the house. We think maybe they'll shave your head.

SALLY. Aunt Lottie put you up to this?

MATT. She said you were anxious to get out of the house, but you didn't have much courage. She is a very bold strategist.

SALLY. You told her about last summer?

MATT. No, she told me. You told Rachel, Rachel told her cousin Rose, Rose told your Aunt Charlotte.

SALLY. I'll brain them, every one.

MATT. You been listening to anything I've said?

SALLY. What? Oh, Matt, I told you, put it out of your head.

MATT. You're hard. You're tough.

SALLY. Well, I can't think about it now.

MATT. Maybe you better.

SALLY. There is no place to go or I'd be out of there, Matt.

MATT. There's a hospital in St. Louis. St. Ann's. St. Louis's St. Ann's. Where you could work. They're crying for help.

SALLY. Too long a drive.

MATT. Well, it happens my apartment is conveniently located four blocks away.

SALLY. You have room for three nurse's aides?

MATT. I rescind the offer. You like St. Louis?

The Browns, you never know. The Cardinals are okay. We can go to the game, watch the Cooper brothers.

SALLY. Matt, you can see I don't want you to talk like that.

MATT. I hear you say that. I think I see something different. You aren't afraid of me. This minute, are you afraid of me right now?

SALLY. I've never been afraid of you.

MATT. Put everything I've said behind. I didn't sing "Lindy Lou" and ask Sally to marry me. Sally didn't say, Don't sing. We are friends talking together, looking at the river and the upside-down black trees with the shaky moon in the water. *(Suddenly noticing)* Hey! There's no color. In moonlight. What a gyp. Very little color. Look at you.

SALLY *(Looks at him)*. Some.

MATT. You might as well have blue eyes. Amazing the things you get so used to that you don't know them any more. Okay. So I ask you. Why did your aunt say, "There is something you don't know, Matt, and something only Sally can tell you"?

SALLY. It was a long time ago.

MATT. You're thirty-one years old. How long—

SALLY. It was another life, really—

MATT. So what happened in this other life?

SALLY. Say I was disappointed in love. It was a long time ago. I was another person.

MATT. No, I don't believe in disappointed in love.

SALLY. It was more of a financial arrangement than anything.

MATT. Oh, well. Disappointed in a financial arrangement, I understand.

SALLY. I was engaged to Harley Campbell, his dad owned—

MATT. I don't believe it.

SALLY. You don't even know who he is.

MATT. I met him up at the house. He was the one that was saying, "You tell 'em, Buddy. You tell 'em, Buddy."

SALLY. Well, he used to be very good-looking.

MATT. I don't believe that either.

SALLY *(Not rhapsodic; detached, but this is an unpleasant memory)*. He was a guard on the basketball team; I was a cheerleader. We grew up together. We were the two richest families in town. We were golden children. Dad owned a quarter of the garment factory; Harley's dad owned a third. These two great families were to be united in one happy factory. We used to walk through the plant holding hands, waving at all the girls; they loved us. When the workers asked for a showdown to discuss their demands, Dad brought us right into the meeting, onto the platform. Everybody applauded.

MATT. The youth, the beauty . . .

SALLY. The money. Here they are, folks. The future of the country. Do you love them or do you love them? Now back to work. They still don't have a union.

MATT. So how did it happen that Sally was disappointed in love?

SALLY. It all became academic. The Depression happened. Maybe we didn't look so golden. The factory almost closed.

MATT. I know the Depression came. So how did it happen that Sally was disappointed in love?

SALLY *(With some difficulty)*. I was sick for a long time. I got TB and missed school. I didn't graduate until a year after Harley did. It was a good excuse to drift apart. *(Easier)* Then he went to Princeton, became engaged to a girl from New Jersey, his father killed himself.

MATT. Because he was engaged to a girl from New Jersey?

SALLY. Because by then it was 1931. He was in debt. He thought he would lose the factory. He didn't know how to live poor.

MATT. So?

SALLY. Harley quit school, Buddy and Harley and Dad worked at the factory, trying to save it. They're doing fine now.

MATT. I know. A government contract for army uniforms. So?

SALLY. Harley's wife left him eight years ago; he remarried a girl from Rogersville.

MATT *(Looks at her a moment)*. So that's the truth, the whole truth, and nothing but the truth, so help you, Hannah.

SALLY. Yes.

MATT. You're real cute. *(Pause)* Might as well get the gas, don't you think?

SALLY. You're not out of gas.

MATT. Yes, maybe I am. Maybe I lied.

SALLY. Well, if that's what it takes.

MATT. You know what I'm thinking? Over on track number nine? That Sally may not be who I thought she was, after all.

SALLY. Maybe not.

MATT. May not be. Maybe not. What kind of an answer to a mystery is that? What happened to change this Golden Girl into an embarrassment to the family? Into a radical old maid who is fired from teaching Sunday school?

Why would this nice Harley leave you after all this time while you were sick with such a romantic disease? See, I'm a logical person. I have to have it all laid out like in a list, and that isn't logical.

SALLY. His family didn't want him to marry me, obviously.

MATT. They thought you weren't good enough for him?

SALLY. Come on. *(As she starts to move past him to the door, he reaches out and takes her wrist. The band, rather distant, plays a fanfare)*

MATT. What?

SALLY. Yes. Don't do that.

MATT. Mr. Campbell was in debt and worried about being overextended, but the rich partner's daughter gets TB and the wedding is off?

SALLY. I don't know.

MATT. There's your music. Wasn't Harley the richest boy in town, you said?

SALLY. Yes.

MATT. And Sally was the richest girl in the countryside. This was the match of the decade. Bells were going to ring for such a match.

SALLY. Well, they didn't.

MATT. When the Depression comes, rich families must pool their resources.

SALLY. They didn't see it that way.

MATT. The Campbells are a large Missouri family, are they? Fifteen little Campbells?

SALLY. No.

MATT. No. Only Harley, two brothers, and one sister?

SALLY. No.

MATT. Only Harley and his brother?

SALLY. Harley and his sister.

MATT. Harley was the only son of a very prominent Laclede County family.

SALLY. Yes.

MATT. So why didn't they want their only son to marry the beautiful, popular, cheerleader Talley girl whom he had been going steady with for three years?

SALLY. They didn't like me.

MATT. All those years he dated you over their protest?

SALLY. Not on your life.

MATT. No, because Harley did not do things against his parents' wishes.

SALLY. No.

MATT. But in fact you didn't graduate with Harley. You were delayed a full year.

SALLY. That's beginning to hurt, Matt.

MATT. You're pulling, I'm not pulling. *(Releases her, but stands in her path)* Why weren't you good enough for Harley?

SALLY. I got sick.

MATT. You got TB and went to Arizona, where you lived for the rest of your life.

SALLY. No.

MATT. You gave this contagious disease to their only son and he went away to Arizona and was never heard from again.

SALLY. The TB was not serious. There were complicating circumstances that caused me to be out of school.

MATT. There were complications. Sally was pockmarked and ugly and nobody wanted anything to do with her.

SALLY. You might say that.

MATT. This only son was repulsed by the sight of you.

SALLY. No, Matt. I was in the hospital for a month. I had a fever.

MATT. This Harley has a morbid fear of hospitals. I'm getting a fever is who's getting a fever.

SALLY. They didn't want it.

MATT. But your dad insisted.

SALLY. He didn't want it either.

MATT. You were pale and white and would not look good in a wedding dress.

SALLY. Matt.

MATT. You were a tramp and a vamp and would have ruined the reputation of this prominent family. Is that what the story is?

SALLY. He was the heir. He had to carry on the family name!

MATT. And you were irresponsible; you had uncontrollable kleptomania and could not be trusted around the family money.

SALLY. I was sick! I had a fever.

MATT. You were delirious and drunken and no family would allow such a woman to marry their only son.

SALLY (She tries to run past him). I was sick for a year.

MATT (Holds her again). You were not sick. You went away. Why did you go away?

SALLY. I was at the house.

MATT (Driving). Why were you in the house for a year?

SALLY. I had a fever.

MATT. No. Because you had disgraced yourself.

SALLY. I had a pelvic infection.

MATT. Is that what you told people?

SALLY. They didn't know what was wrong with me.

MATT. Why were you hiding in the house?

SALLY. They couldn't get the fever down!

MATT. Why were you hiding?

SALLY (Hitting him). They couldn't break the fever! By the time they did, it didn't matter.

MATT. What were you hiding—

SALLY. Because it had eaten out my insides! I couldn't bear children. I can't have children! Let go of me. (She breaks away, crying, falls against something, and sits)

MATT. What do you mean?

SALLY. I couldn't have children.

MATT. Sally, I'm here, you're okay. It's okay.

SALLY. Go away. Go away.

MATT (Sitting beside her). I didn't know. I thought you had had a child.

SALLY. I have had no child. There was no scandal. I was no longer of value to the merger.

MATT. It's okay. It's okay.

SALLY. Oh, stop. That's what I tell the boys. It's okay. Only they're dying of blood poisoning. Don't comfort me. I'm fine. Blast you. Let go.

MATT. I thought you had had a child by someone else. You're so crazy.

SALLY. I only wish I had.

MATT. This was a result of the TB?

SALLY (She looks at him for a long moment. Then finally, no longer crying). The infection descended into the fallopian tubes; it's not uncommon with women at all. And so there couldn't be an heir to the garment empire. (Almost laughing) It was all such a great dance. Everyone came to the hospital. Everyone said it made no difference. By the time Harley graduated, the Campbells weren't speaking to the Talleys. By then Dad was looking at me like I was a broken swing. It was a very interesting perspective.

MATT. Did you think that your aunt had told me you couldn't have children and I was making up the story of my life just to tease you?

SALLY. Possibly.

MATT (To the sky). Eggs! Eggs! Eggs! Eggs! We're so terrified. But we still hope. You take a beautiful dress to work—Did you tell the nurses I was coming to see you?

SALLY. No!

MATT. And look at me. For five years I have been wearing the same tie to work. It is a matter of principle with me not to wear a different tie. I buy a new tie to come and see Sally. You see how corruption of principle begins.

SALLY. I had nothing to do with that.

MATT. Is that a new dress, by the way? I didn't know that dress.

SALLY. Yes. It's no big deal.

MATT. It is an enormous deal! It is the New Deal! It is a Big Deal!

SALLY. You didn't even say you liked it.

MATT. I like it, I love the dress. *(Pause)* I was sitting up in St. Louis all this winter in a terrible quandary. It is not that I have been happy or not happy, but that I have not thought that I *could* be happy. *(Beat)* But this winter I was terribly unhappy and I *knew* I was unhappy. I had fallen for a girl and could not give her the life she would surely expect, with a family, many children. *(Pause. Taking her hand)* You know what has happened? Some mischievous angel has looked down and saw us living two hundred miles apart and said, You know what would be a kick in the head? Let's send Matt on a vacation to Lebanon.

SALLY. You believe in angels?

MATT. I do now, most definitely. Her name might be Lottie Talley, maybe. *(Pause)* We missed your marching band.

SALLY. They'll play all evening.

MATT *(Pause)*. So. We'll go up to the city tonight. Leave the car here—

SALLY. Oh, Matt, it's absurd to be talking like that; we're practically middle-aged.

MATT. So. We'll go up to the city tonight. Leave the car in town, take the midnight bus.

SALLY *(Pause)*. I'll be up in a week or so.

MATT *(Pause)*. I'll stay here at the hotel in Lebanon and wait.

SALLY. You have to work tomorrow.

MATT. So what?

SALLY *(Pause)*. We'll go tonight. *(They kiss. The distant band strikes up a soft but lightly swinging rendition of "Lindy Lou." They laugh)*

MATT. "Lindy Lou." *(Pause. They are sitting holding hands, perfectly relaxed.* MATT *looks around)* You live in such a beautiful country. Such a beautiful countryside. Will you miss it?

SALLY. Yes.

MATT. Me too. Once a year we'll come back down, so we don't forget.

SALLY. All right.

MATT *(Looks at her for a long while, then his gaze drifts to the audience)*. And so, all's well that ends . . . *(Takes out his watch, shows time to* SALLY, *then to audience)* . . . right on the button. Good night. *(They embrace.)*

The song continues as the light fades

A Little Night Music

Hugh Wheeler and *Stephen Sondheim*

First presented by Harold Prince in association with Ruth Mitchell at the Shubert Theatre in New York City on February 25, 1973, with the following cast:

(*in order of appearance*)

MR. LINDQUIST	Benjamin Rayson
MRS. NORDSTROM	Teri Ralston
MRS. ANDERSSEN	Barbara Lang
MR. ERLANSON	Gene Varrone
MRS. SEGSTROM	Beth Fowler
FREDRIKA ARMFELDT	Judy Kahan
MADAME ARMFELDT	Hermione Gingold
FRID, HER BUTLER	George Lee Andrews
HENRIK EGERMAN	Mark Lambert
ANNE EGERMAN	Victoria Mallory
FREDRIK EGERMAN	Len Cariou
PETRA	D. Jamin-Bartlett
DESIREE ARMFELDT	Glynis Johns
MALLA, HER MAID	Despo
BERTRAND, A PAGE	Will Sharpe Marshall
COUNT CARL-MAGNUS MALCOLM	Laurence Guittard
COUNTESS CHARLOTTE MALCOLM	Patricia Elliott
OSA	Sherry Mathis

Directed by Harold Prince
Scenery by Boris Aronson
Costumes by Florence Clotz
Lighting by Tharon Musser

A Little Night Music is the result of a collaboration of three gifted minds: Harold Prince, the producer and director; Steven Sondheim, the composer and lyricist; and Hugh Wheeler, the playwright. The play won seven Tony Awards: Best Musical of the Season, Best Book of a Musical, Best Music, Best Lyrics, Best Leading Actress's Performance in a Musical, Best Supporting Actress's Performance in a Musical and Best Costumes in a Musical. It was also chosen as one of the Ten Best Plays in the Annual Burns Mantle Yearbook. The title of the play was taken from Mozart's *Eine Kleine Nachtmusik* and its plot and characters from *Smiles of a Summer Night,* a film which was released in 1956 by Ingmar Bergman, one of his few attempts at comedy.

The story is set in Sweden at the turn of the century and concerns a middle-aged lawyer, Fredrik Egerman, who is enchanted by Anne, the eighteen-year-old daughter of a friend. He marries her under the delusion that he is regaining part of his lost youth. But the bride is still a child and a virgin after eleven months of marriage. She is attracted instead to Egerman's son, Henrik, and he to her. At the center of this story is an actress, Desiree. Disillusioned with her touring life, she decides to recapture Egerman, a former lover and the father of her illegitimate teen-age daughter Fredrika.

Madame Armfeldt, Desiree's mother, tells Fredrika to watch for the summer night to smile. "It smiles three times, first for the young, who know nothing; second for the fools, who know too little and third for the old, who know too much." At the end of the play she tells her granddaughter that the night has already smiled twice, once for the young and once for the fools. "The smile for the fools was particularly broad tonight."

A Little Night Music is structured in the form of a waltz musical. Prince and Sondheim had been contemplating such a production since their collaboration on *West Side Story.* The entire score is in 3/4 time or variations of it (9/8, 12/16, etc.), and is filled with ballads, waltzes and straight Broadway tunes. These provide the production with mood, tempo and style.

Harold Prince has worked in dual capacities as producer and director for *Follies, Company, Zorba, Cabaret, It's a Bird . . . It's a Plane . . . It's Superman!,* and *She Loves Me.* He has produced *Pajama Game; Damn Yankees; New Girl in Town; West Side Story; Fiorello; Take Her, She's Mine; A Funny Thing Happened on the Way to the Forum; Poor Bitos; Fiddler on the Roof;* and *The Great God Brown.* Prince has also directed two films: *Cabaret* and *Something for Everyone.*

Stephen Sondheim was born in 1930, in New York, the son of a dress manufacturer. At age ten, already a gifted pianist, his childhood ambition was to write songs for Broadway musicals. As a teenager, he met and was influenced by Oscar Hammerstein. Sondheim attended Williams College, where he won the Hutchinson Prize for Musical Composition. After graduation, he did further musical study on a scholarship at Princeton. In 1957 he wrote the lyrics for *West Side Story,* and in 1959, for *Gypsy.* This was followed by his composition of both lyrics and music for *Invitation to a March, A Funny Thing Happened on the Way to the Forum, Company, Follies* and *A Little Night Music.* He has also written scripts for the television series "Topper" and created the complex puzzles that appeared in *New York Magazine's* first issues, 1966–1968. In addition to his awards for music, Sondheim has received the Edgar Award from the Mystery Writers of America for the screenplay he wrote in collaboration with Anthony Perkins for the film *The Last of Sheila.*

Hugh Callingham Wheeler was born on March 19, 1912, in London, England, the son of Harold Wheeler and Florence Scammell Wheeler. His father was a British civil servant. "My father was the official reviewer of bankruptcy—he worked wearing a wig and, because of his job, harassed many poor souls." He began to write at an early age. "Of course I wrote from the cradle . . . when I was fifteen, I was writing three-act plays about ladies with long cigarette holders who would elope to the south of France."

He became a professional writer at the age of nineteen, after receiving his bachelor of arts degree from the University of London in 1932. "I'd just been graduated from the University . . . when a friend of my father came to visit us. He told us that a woman [Patsy Kelly] with whom he'd written four mysteries had flown off to get married. So I came to America and became his collaborator. We were rather prolific and for a while, we turned out mystery novels under the name of Patrick Quentin as well as Q. Patrick. Then I began doing the Patrick Quentins myself. . . ."

During World War II, Wheeler served in the United States Army Corps. He became a naturalized citizen while he was in the army. "I never left Fort Dix. They just asked me if I wanted to be in the Medical Corps and handed me a white coat."

After the war, Wheeler wrote mystery novels, short stories, novelettes and one novel, *The Crippled Muse,* until 1961, when he began to write for the legitimate theatre. His first play, *Big Fish, Little Fish,* starred Jason Robards, Jr., and was staged by Sir John Gielgud. It ran for 101 performances. This was followed by *Look: We've Come Through,* staged by José Quintero and featuring Burt Reynolds in a supporting role. Wheeler's third play, *We Have Always Lived in the Castle,* was an adaptation of a novel by Shirley Jackson and was produced in 1966 with Shirley Knight and Tom Stern in the starring roles, directed by Garson Kanin. His first hit came in 1973, with *A Little Night Music.* He was asked by Harold Prince to write the play after their previous collaboration on the film *Something for Everyone.*

The genesis of *A Little Night Music* occurred in 1957. Prince recalls, "We wanted to do something based on the kind of material that's called a 'masque.' Something that deals with encounters in a country house, love and lovers and mismatched partners . . ." The idea lay dormant for fifteen years for want of suitable material. Then, in 1971, Sondheim saw Ingmar Bergman's film *Smiles of a Summer Night.* "We knew we had it. The next step was to obtain the stage rights for the movie. . . ." Wheeler states, "We looked at a lot of properties like Renoir films and then decided that the one we could jump off from was Bergman's thing. . . ." Bergman sold the rights when he was assured that the producer did not intend a "rigid adaptation" of his film but rather a musical freely suggested by it. Bergman's lawyer refused to haggle over terms and just told them to draw up their own contract.

The show opened on February 25, 1973, in New York after several drafts and with some changes in plot and characterization. The actress's child, a four-year-old boy, had been turned into a thirteen-year-old girl and the role of the actress's mother, a retired courtesan, had been expanded to provide a "basic spine" for the production. It was rechristened *A Little Night Music* and its setting was changed from Vienna to Sweden.

Before the houselights are down, MR. LIND-QUIST *appears and sits at the piano. He removes his gloves, plunks a key, and begins to vocalize.* MRS. NORDSTROM *enters, hits a key on the piano, and vocalizes with him.* MRS. ANDERSSEN, MR. ERLANSEN *and* MRS. SEGSTROM *come out and join the vocalizing.*

MEN.
La, La La La
La La La La

GIRLS.
La, La La La
La, La La La

MRS. NORDSTROM.
    The old deserted beach that we
      walked—
    Remember?

MR. ANDERSSEN.
    Remember?
    The tenor on the boat that we chartered,
    Belching ''The Bartered Bride''

MR. ERLANSEN.
    Remember?
    The cafe in the park where we talked—
    Remember?

ALL.
    Ah, how we laughed,
    Ah, how we cried,

MR. LINDQUIST.
    Ah, how you promised

GIRLS AND MEN.
La, La La La

    And
    Ah, how
    I lied.

Ah . . .
Lie . . . lie . . . lie . . .

MRS. SEGSTROM.
    That dilapidated inn—
    Remember, darling?

MR. LINDQUIST.
    And the canopy in red,
    Needing repair.

MR. ERLANSEN.
    The proprietress' grin,
    Also her glare.

ALL.
    Soon, I promise.
    Soon I won't shy away,
    Dear old—

MRS. NORDSTROM.
    Yellow gingham on the bed—
    Remember, darling?

    Soon. I want to.
    Soon, whatever you say.
    Even

GIRLS.
Now
When we're close and
We
Touch
And you're kissing my
Brow,
I don't mind it
Too much.
And you'll have to

MEN.
Now, when we touch,

Touching my brow,

Ahhhh . . .

ALL.
    Admit I'm endearing,
    I help keep things humming,
    I'm not domineering,
    What's one small shortcoming?
    And
    Unpack the luggage, La La La

Pack up the luggage, La La La
Unpack the luggage, La La La
Hi-ho, the glamorous life!
Unpack the luggage, La La La
Pack up the luggage, La La La
Unpack the luggage, La La La
Hi-ho, the glamorous life!

MR. LINDQUIST.
    Ahhhhh . . .

OTHER MEMBERS OF QUINTET.
Unpack the luggage, La La La
Pack up the luggage, La La La

MRS. NORDSTROM.
    Ahhhh . . .

OTHER MEMBERS OF THE QUINTET.
Unpack the luggage, La La La
Hi-ho, the glamorous life!

ALL.
    Bring up the curtain, La La La
    Bring down the curtain, La La La
    Bring up the curtain, La La La

Hi-ho, hi-ho
For the glamorous life!

(After the applause, the QUINTET *starts to waltz. The show curtain flies out, revealing the* MAIN CHARACTERS *doing a strangely surreal waltz of their own, in which partners change partners and recouple with others. The* QUINTET *drifts up into the waltzing* COUPLES, *and reappears to hum accompaniment for the last section of the dance.* FREDRIKA *wanders through the waltz, too, watching)*

ACT ONE

PROLOGUE

At the end of the Opening Waltz, MADAME ARMFELDT *is brought on in her wheelchair by her butler,* FRID. *In her lap is a tray containing a silver cigarette box, a small vase with four yellow bud-roses, and the cards with which she is playing solitaire. She is watched by* FREDRIKA ARMFELDT, *13—a grave, very self-contained and formal girl with the precise diction of the convent-trained.*

———

FREDRIKA. If you cheated a little, it would come out.

MADAME ARMFELDT *(Continuing to play)*. Solitaire is the only thing in life that demands absolute honesty. As a woman who has numbered kings among her lovers, I think my word can be taken on that point.

(She motions to FRID, *who crosses down and lights her cigarette)*

What was I talking about?

FREDRIKA. You said I should watch.

MADAME ARMFELDT. Watch—what?

FREDRIKA. It sounds very unlikely to me, but you said I should watch for the night to smile.

MARAME ARMFELDT. Everything is unlikely, dear, so don't let that deter you. Of course the summer night smiles. Three times.

FREDRIKA. But how does it smile?

MADAME ARMFELDT. Good heavens, what sort of a nanny did you have?

FREDRIKA. None, really. Except Mother, and the other actresses in the company—and the stage manager.

MADAME ARMFELDT. Stage managers are not nannies. They don't have the talent.

FREDRIKA. But if it happens—how does it happen?

MADAME ARMFELDT. You get a feeling. Suddenly the jasmine starts to smell stronger, then

a frog croaks—then all the stars in Orion wink. Don't squeeze your bosoms against the chair, dear. It'll stunt their growth. And then where would you be?

FREDRIKA. But why does it smile, Grandmother?

MADAME ARMFELDT. At the follies of human beings, of course. The first smile smiles at the young, who know nothing.

(She looks pointedly at FREDRIKA)

The second, at the fools who know too little, like Desiree.

FREDRIKA. Mother isn't a fool.

MADAME ARMFELDT *(Going right on)*. Um hum. And the third at the old who know too much—like me.

(The game is over without coming out. Annoyed at the cards, MADAME ARMFELDT *scatters them at random, and barks at* FRID)

Frid, time for my nap.

FREDRIKA *(Intrigued in spite of herself, gazes out at the summer night)*. Grandmother, might it really smile tonight?

MADAME ARMFELDT. Why not? Now, practice your piano, dear, preferably with the soft pedal down. And as a treat tonight at dinner, I shall tell you amusing stories about my liaison with the Baron de Signac, who was, to put it mildly, peculiar.

(FRID wheels her off and FREDRIKA *goes to sit at the piano)*

ACT ONE

SCENE ONE

THE EGERMAN ROOMS

Two rooms—the parlor and the master bedroom, indicated on different levels. ANNE EGERMAN, *a ravishingly pretty girl of 18, is on the bed. She goes to the vanity table, toys with her hair, and then enters the parlor.* HENRIK EGERMAN, *her stepson, a brooding young man of 19, is seated on the sofa, playing his cello. Beside him on the sofa is a book with a ribbon marker.* ANNE *looks at* HENRIK, *then leans over the sofa to get his attention.*

———

ANNE. Oh Henrik, dear, don't you have anything less gloomy to practice?

HENRIK. It isn't gloomy, it's profound.

ANNE *(Reaches down, takes* HENRIK'S *book, and begins reading from it)*. " . . . in discussing temptation, Martin Luther says: 'You cannot prevent the birds from flying over your head, but you can prevent them from nesting in your hair.' '' Oh dear, that's gloomy too! Don't they teach you anything at the seminary a little more cheerful?

HENRIK *(Grand)*. A man who's going to serve in God's Army must learn all the ruses and stratagems of the Enemy.

ANNE *(Giggling)*. And which of your professors made that historic statement?

HENRIK *(Caught out)*. Pastor Ericson, as a matter of fact. He says we're like generals learning to win battles against the devil.

(Her ball of silk falls off her lap)

ANNE. Oh dear, my ball!

*(*HENRIK *bends down to pick up the ball. He stands beside her, obviously overwhelmed by her nearness.* ANNE *pats her lap)*
You can put it there, you know. My lap isn't one of the Devil's snares.

(Flushing, HENRIK *drops the ball into her lap and moves away from her)*

HENRIK. Anne, I was wondering—could we go for a walk?

ANNE. Now?

HENRIK. I've so much to tell you. What I've been thinking, and everything.

ANNE. Silly Henrik, don't you realize it's almost tea-time? And I think I hear your father.

(She rises, puts down the ball of silk)
I'm sure you've made the most wonderful discoveries about life, and I long to talk, but— later.

*(*FREDRIK *enters, followed by* PETRA*)*
Fredrik dear!

HENRIK *(Mutters to himself)*. Later.

ANNE. Look who's come home to us—holier than ever.

FREDRIK. Hello, son. How was the examination?

HENRIK. Well, as a matter of fact . . .

FREDRIK *(Breaking in)*. You passed with flying colors, of course.

ANNE. First on the list.

HENRIK *(Trying again)*. And Pastor Ericson said . . .

FREDRIK *(Breaking in)*. Splendid—you must give us a full report. Later.

ANNE. He'd better be careful or he'll go straight to heaven before he has a chance to save any sinners.

FREDRIK. Don't tease him, dear.

ANNE. Oh, Henrik likes to be teased, don't you, Henrik? Fredrik, do you want your tea now?

FREDRIK. Not now, I think. It's been rather

an exhausting day in Court and as we have a long evening ahead of us, I feel a little nap is indicated.

(He produces theater tickets from his pocket)

ANNE *(Grabbing at them, delighted as a child)*. Tickets for the theater!

FREDRIK. It's a French comedy. I thought it might entertain you.

ANNE. It's ''Woman Of The World,'' isn't it? With Desiree Armfeldt! She's on all the posters! Oh, Fredrik, how delicious!

(To HENRIK, *teasing)*
What shall I wear? My blue with the feathers—

*(*FREDRIK *pours water)*
genuine angel's feathers—? Or the yellow? Ah, I know. My pink, with the bosom. And Henrik, you can do me up in the back.

(She goes into the bedroom)

FREDRIK. I'm sorry, son. I should have remembered you were coming home and got a third ticket. But then perhaps a French comedy is hardly suitable.

*(*FREDRIK *takes a pill)*

HENRIK *(Outburst)*. Why does everyone laugh at me? Is it so ridiculous to want to do some good in this world?

FREDRIK. I'm afraid being young in itself can be a trifle ridiculous. Good has to be so good, bad so bad. Such superlatives!

HENRIK. But to be old, I suppose, is not ridiculous.

FREDRIK *(Sigh)*. Ah, let's not get into that. I love you very much, you know. So does Anne—in her way. But you can't expect her to take your mother's place. She's young too; she has not yet learned . . .

HENRIK. . . . to suffer fools gladly?

FREDRIK *(Gentle)*. You said that, son. Not I.

ANNE. Fredrik!

(As FREDRIK *moves into the bedroom,* HENRIK *picks up his book and reads.* ANNE *is buffing her nails)*
You were sweet to think of the theater for me.

FREDRIK. I'll enjoy it too.

ANNE. Who wouldn't—when all the posters call her The One And Only Desiree Armfeldt?

*(*FREDRIK *begins to try to kiss her. She rattles on)*
I wonder what it would feel like to be a One and Only! The One and Only—Anne Egerman!

(She leaves FREDRIK *on the bed and moves to the vanity table. As aware as he is of her rejection)*
Poor Fredrik! Do I still make you happy? After eleven months? I know I'm foolish to be so

afraid—and you've been so patient, but, soon—
I promise. Oh, I know you think I'm too silly
to worry, but I do . . .

(As FREDRIK *looks up to answer, she gives
a little cry)*

Oh no! For heaven's sakes, can that be a pim-
ple coming?

*(*FREDRIK, *deflated, begins to sing)*

FREDRIK *(Singing).*

> Now, as the sweet imbecilities
> Tumble so lavishly
> Onto her lap . . .

ANNE. Oh Fredrik, what a day it's been!
Unending drama! While Petra was brushing
my hair, the doorbell . . .

FREDRIK.

> Now, there are two possibilities:
> A, I could ravish her,
> B, I could nap.

ANNE. . . . that grumpy old Mrs. Nordstrom
from next door. Her sister's coming for a visit.

FREDRIK.

> Say it's the ravishment, then we see
> The option
> That follows, of course:

ANNE. . . . do hope I'm imperious enough
with the servants. I try to be. But half the time
I think they're laughing at me.

FREDRIK.

> A, the deployment of charm, or B,
> The adoption
> Of physical force.
> *(Music)*
> Now B might arouse her,
> But if I assume
> I trip on my trouser
> Leg crossing the room . . .
> *(Music)*
> Her hair getting tangled,
> Her stays getting snapped,
> My nerves will be jangled,
> My energy sapped . . .
> *(Music)*
> Removing her clothing
> Would take me all day
> And her subsequent loathing
> Would turn me away—
> Which eliminates B
> And which leaves us with A.

ANNE. Could you ever be jealous of me?

FREDRIK.

> Now, insofar as approaching it,
> What would be festive
> But have its effect?

ANNE. Shall I learn Italian? I think it would
be amusing, If the verbs aren't too irregular.

FREDRIK.

> Now, there are two ways of broaching
> it:
> A, the suggestive
> And B, the direct.

ANNE. . . . but then French is a much chic-
er language. Everyone says so. Parlez-vous
Français?

FREDRIK.

> Say that I settle on B, to wit,
> A charmingly
> Lecherous mood . . .
> *(Music)*
> A, I could put on my nightshirt or sit
> Disarmingly,
> B, in the nude . . .
> *(Music)*
> That might be effective,
> My body's all right—
> But not in perspective
> And not in the light . . .
> *(Music)*
> I'm bound to be chilly
> And feel a buffoon,
> But nightshirts are silly
> In midafternoon . . .
> *(Music)*
> Which leaves the suggestive,
> But how to proceed?
> Although she gets restive,
> Perhaps I could read . . .
> *(Music)*
> In view of her penchant
> For something romantic,
> De Sade is too trenchant
> And Dickens too frantic,
> And Stendhal would ruin
> The plan of attack,
> As there isn't much blue in
> "The Red and the Black."
> *(Music)*
> De Maupassant's candor
> Would cause her dismay.
> The Brontës are grander
> But not very gay.
> Her taste is much blander,
> I'm sorry to say,
> But is Hans Christian Ander-
> Sen ever risque?
> Which eliminates A.
> *(Exits upstage)*

ANNE. And he said, "You're such a pretty
lady!" Wasn't that silly?

FREDRIK *(As he walks back on).*

> Now, with my mental facilities
> Partially muddied

And ready to snap . . .

ANNE *(At the jewel box now)*. . . . I'm sure about the bracelet. But earrings, earrings! *Which* earrings?

FREDRIK.

> Now, though there are possibilities
> Still to be studied,
> I might as well nap . . .

ANNE. Mother's rubies? . . . Oh, the diamonds are—Agony! I know . . .

FREDRIK.

> Bow though I must
> To adjust
> My original plan . . .

ANNE. Desiree Armfeldt—I just know she'll wear the most glamorous gowns!

FREDRIK.

> How shall I sleep
> Half as deep
> As I usually can? . . .

ANNE. Dear, distinguished old Fredrik!

FREDRIK.

> When now I still want and/or love you,
> Now, as always,
> Now,
> Anne?

(FREDRIK turns over and goes to sleep. They remain frozen. PETRA, 21, the charming, easygoing maid, enters the parlor)

PETRA. Nobody rang. Doesn't he want his tea?

HENRIK *(Still deep in book)*. They're taking a nap.

PETRA *(Coming up behind him, teasingly ruffling his hair)*. You smell of soap.

HENRIK *(Pulling his head away)*. I'm reading.

PETRA *(Caressing his head)*. Do those old teachers take a scrubbing brush to you every morning and scrub you down like a dray horse? *(Strokes his ear)*

HENRIK *(Fierce)*. Get away from me!

PETRA *(Jumping up in mock alarm)*. Oh what a wicked woman I am! I'll go straight to hell! *(Starting away, she goes toward the door, deliberately wiggling her hips)*

HENRIK *(Looking up, even fiercer)*. And don't walk like that!

PETRA *(Innocent)*. Like—what? *(Wiggles even more)* Like this?

HENRIK *(Pleadingly)*. Stop it. Stop it? *(He rises, goes after her, clutches her, and starts savagely, clumsily, to kiss her and fumble at her breasts. She slaps his hand)*

PETRA. Careful! *(Breaks away)*

That's a new blouse! A whole week's wages and the lace extra! *(Looks at him)* Poor little Henrik! *(Then affectionately pats his cheek)* Later! You'll soon get the knack of it! *(She exits. HENRIK puts down the book, gets his cello and begins to sing, accompanying himself on the cello)*

HENRIK.

> Later . . .
> When is later? . . .
> All you ever hear is "Later, Henrik!
>   Henrik, later . . ."
> "Yes, we know, Henrik.
> Oh, Henrik—
> Everyone agrees, Henrik—
> Please, Henrik!"
> You have a thought you're fairly bursting with,
> A personal discovery or problem, and it's
> "What's your rush, Henrik?
> Shush, Henrik—
> Goodness, how you gush, Henrik—
> Hush, Henrik!"
> You murmur,
> "I only . . .
> It's just that . . .
> For God's sake!"
> "Later, Henrik . . ."
>
> "Henrik" . . .
> Who is "Henrik?" . . .
> Oh, that lawyer's son, the one who
>   mumbles—
> Short and boring,
> Yes, he's hardly worth ignoring
> And who cares if he's all dammed—
> *(Looks up)*
> —I beg your pardon—
> Up inside?
> As I've
> Often stated,
> It's intolerable
> Being tolerated.
> "Reassure Henrik,
> Poor Henrik."
> "Henrik, you'll endure
> Being pure, Henrik."
>
> Though I've been born, I've never been!
> How can I wait around for later?
> I'll be ninety on my deathbed
> And the late, or rather later,
> Henrik Egerman!

Doesn't anything begin?
(ANNE, in the bedroom, gets up from the vanity table and stands near the bed, singing to FREDRIK)
ANNE.

    Soon, I promise.
    Soon I won't shy away,
    Dear old—
       (She bites her lip)
    Soon. I want to.
    Soon, whatever you say.
    Even now,
    When you're close and we touch,
    And you're kissing my brow,
    I don't mind it too much.
    And you'll have to admit
    I'm endearing,
    I help keep things humming,
    I'm not domineering,

What's one small shortcoming?
And think of how I adore you,
Think of how much you love me.
If I were perfect for you,
Wouldn't you tire of me
Soon,
All too soon?
Dear old—
(The sound of HENRIK's cello. FREDRIK stirs noisily in the bed. ANNE goes into the parlor)
Henrik! That racket! Your father's sleeping!
(She remains, half-innocent, half-coquettish, in her negligee. For a second, ANNE watches him. She closes her nightgown at the neck and goes back into the bedroom)
ANNE *(Back at the bed)*. Soon—
HENRIK. "Later" . . .
ANNE. I promise.
HENRIK. When is "later?"
(Simultaneously)

ANNE.	HENRIK.
Soon	"Later, Henrik, later,"
I won't shy	All you ever hear is,
Away,	"Yes, we know, Henrik, oh, Henrik,
Dear old—	Everyone agrees, Henrik, please, Henrik!"

(FREDRIK stirs. Simultaneously)

ANNE	HENRIK	FREDRIK
Soon.	"Later" . . .	Now,
I want to.	When is "later?"	As the sweet
Soon,	All you ever	imbecilities
	Hear is	Trip on my trouser leg,
Whatever you	"Later, Henrik,	
Say.		
		Stendhal
		eliminates
	Later."	A,
	As I've often	
	Stated:	But
	When?	When?
Even	Maybe	Maybe
Now,		
When you're close	Soon, soon	Later,
And we touch	I'll be ninety	
	And	
And you're kissing	Dead.	When I'm kissing
My brow,		
I don't mind it		Your brow
Too much,		And I'm stroking
	I don't mind it	your head,
	Too much,	You'll come into
		my bed.

ANNE	HENRIK	FREDRIK
And you'll have	Since I have to	And you have to
To admit	Admit	Admit
I'm endearing,	I find peering	I've been hearing
I help	Through life's	All those
Keep things	Gray windows	tremulous cries
Humming, I'm	Impatiently	Patiently,
Not domineering,	Not very cheering.	Not interfering
What's one small	Do I fear death?	With those
		tremulous thighs.
Shortcoming?	Let it	
And	Come to me	Come to me
Think of how	Now,	Soon,
I adore you,		
Think of how	Now,	Soon,
Much you love me.		
If I were perfect	Now,	Soon,
For you,		
Wouldn't you tire	Now.	Soon.
Of me		
Later?	Come to me	Come to me
	Soon. If I'm	Soon,
	Dead,	
We will,	I can	
Later.	Wait.	Straight to me,
		never mind
	How can I	How.
We will . . .	Live until	Darling,
Soon.	Later?	Now—
		I still want and/or
	Later . . .	Love
		You,
Soon.		
		Now, as
	Later . . .	Always,
Soon.		Now,
		(He does a kiss)
		Desiree.

(ANNE *stares out, astonished, as the lights go down.* FREDRIKA, *still at the piano, is playing scales)*

FREDRIKA *(Singing)*.

    Ordinary mothers lead ordinary lives:
    Keep the house and sweep the parlor,
    Cook the meals and look exhausted.
    Ordinary mothers, like ordinary wives,
    Fry the eggs and dry the sheets and
    Try to deal with facts.
    Mine acts.

(DESIREE *sweeps on with* MALLA *in tow.* MALLA *carries a wig box, suitcase, and parasol)*

DESIREE *(Singing)*.

    Darling, I miss you a lot
    But, darling, this has to be short
    As mother is getting a plaque

From the Halsingborg Arts Council
Amateur Theatre Group.
Whether it's funny or not, . . .
I'll give you a fuller report
The minute they carry me back
From the Halsingborg Arts Council
Amateur Theatre Group . . .
Love you . . .

    (THE QUINTET *appears)*

QUINTET.

    Unpack the luggage, La La La
    Pack up the luggage, La La La
    Unpack the luggage, La La La
    Hi-ho, the glamorous life!

MRS. SEGSTROM.

    Ice in the basin, La La La

MR. ERLANSEN.

Cracks in the plaster, La La La

MRS. ANDERSSEN.
　　Mice in the hallway, La La La
THE QUINTET.
　　Hi-ho, the glamorous life!
MEN.
　　Run for the carriage, La La La
WOMEN.
　　Wolf down the sandwich, La La La
THE QUINTET.
　　Which town is this one? La, La, La
　　Hi-ho, the glamorous life!
(FRID *wheels* MADAME ARMFELDT *onstage*)
MADAME ARMFELDT *(Singing).*
　　Ordinary daughters ameliorate their lot,
　　Use their charms and choose their
　　　futures,
　　Breed their children, heed their mothers.
　　Ordinary daughters, which mine, I fear,
　　　is not,
　　Tend each asset, spend it wisely
　　While it still endures . . .
　　Mine tours.
DESIREE *(Singing).*
　　Mother, forgive the delay,
　　My schedule is driving me wild.
　　But, mother, I really must run,
　　I'm performing in Rottvik
　　And don't ask where is it, please.
　　How are you feeling today
　　And are you corrupting the child?
　　Don't. Mother, the minute I'm done
　　With performing in Rottvik,
　　I'll come for a visit
　　And argue.
MEN.
　　Mayors with speeches, La La La
WOMEN.
　　Children with posies, La La La
MEN.
　　Half-empty houses, La La La
ALL THE QUINTET.
　　Hi-ho, the glamorous life!
MRS. NORDSTROM.
　　Cultural lunches,
ALL THE QUINTET.
　　La La La
MRS. ANDERSSEN.
　　Dead floral tributes,
ALL THE QUINTET.
　　La La La
MR. LINDQUIST.
　　Ancient admirers,
ALL THE QUINTET.
　　La La La
　　Hi-ho, the glamorous life!

DESIREE.
　　Pack up the luggage, La La La!
　　Unpack the luggage, La La La
　　Mother's surviving, La La La
　　Leading the glamorous life!
　　　(Holds up a mirror)
　　Cracks in the plaster, La La La
　　Youngish admirers, La La La
　　Which one was that one? La La La
　　Hi-ho, the glamorous life!
DESIREE and THE QUINTET.
　　Bring up the curtain, La La La
　　Bring down the curtain, La La La
　　Bring up the curtain, La La La
　　Hi-ho, the glamorous . . .
　　Life.

ACT ONE

SCENE TWO

STAGE OF LOCAL THEATER
　　*The show curtain is down. Two stage boxes
　　are visible. Sitting in one are* MR. LINDQUIST,
　　MRS. NORDSTROM, *and* MR. ERLANSEN. ANNE
　　and FREDRIK *enter, and speak as they walk to
　　their box.*

———

ANNE. Does she look like her pictures?
FREDRIK. Who, dear?
ANNE. Desiree Armfeldt, of course.
FREDRIK. How would I know, dear?
ANNE *(Pause).* I only thought . . .
FREDRIK. You only thought—what?
ANNE. Desiree is not a common name. I
mean, none of your typists and things are called
Desiree, are they?
FREDRIK. My typists and things in descend-
ing order of importance are Miss Osa Svensen,
Miss Ona Nilsson, Miss Gerda Bjornson, *and*
Mrs. Amalia Lindquist.
(A PAGE *enters, and knocks three times with
the staff he is carrying. The show curtain rises
revealing the stage behind it, a tatty Louis XIV
"salon." For a moment it is empty. Then* TWO
LADIES, *in rather shabby court costumes, enter)*
FIRST LADY (MRS. SEGSTROM). Tell me some-
thing about this remarkable Countess, Madame.
SECOND LADY (MRS. ANDERSSEN). I shall try
as best I can to depict the personality of the
Countess, Madame, although it is too rich in
mysterious contradictions to be described in a
few short moments.
FIRST LADY. It is said that her power over

men is most extraordinary.

SECOND LADY. There is a great deal of truth in that, Madame, and her lovers are as many as the pearls in the necklace which she always wears.

FIRST LADY. Your own husband, Madame, is supposed to be one of the handsomest pearls, is he not?

SECOND LADY. He fell in love with the Countess on sight. She took him as a lover for three months and after that I had him back.

FIRST LADY. And your marriage was crushed?

SECOND LADY. On the contrary, Madame! My husband had become a tender, devoted, admirable lover, a faithful husband and an exemplary father. The Countess' lack of decency is most moral.

(THE PAGE re-enters)

PAGE. The Countess Celimène de Francen de la Tour de Casa.

(The Countess—DESIREE—*makes her sensational entrance. A storm of applause greets her.* FREDRIK *claps.* ANNE *does not as she glares at the stage.*

During the applause, DESIREE *makes a deep curtsey, during which, old pro that she is, she cases the house. Her eye falls on* FREDRIK. *She does a take and instantly all action freezes)*

MR. LINDQUIST *(sings).*
Remember?

MRS. NORDSTROM *(sings).*
Remember?

(MR. LINDQUIST and MRS. NORDSTROM leave the stage box)

MRS. NORDSTROM.
The old deserted beach that we walked—
Remember?

MR. LINDQUIST.
Remember?
The cafe in the park where we talked—
Remember?

MRS. NORDSTROM.
Remember?

MR. LINDQUIST.
The tenor on the boat that we chartered, Belching "The Bartered Bride"—

BOTH.
Ah, how we laughed,
Ah, how we cried.

MR. LINDQUIST.
Ah, how you promised and
Ah, how I lied.

MRS. NORDSTROM.
That dilapidated inn—
Remember, darling?

MR. LINDQUIST.
The proprietress' grin,
Also her glare . . .

MRS. NORDSTROM.
Yellow gingham on the bed—
Remember, darling?

MR. LINDQUIST.
And the canopy in red,
Needing repair?

BOTH.
I *think* you were there.

(They return to the stage box and the action continues)

ANNE *(Fierce, to* FREDRIK*).* She looked at us. Why did she look at us?

DESIREE *(To* SECOND LADY*).* Dear Madame Merville, what a charming mischance to find you here this evening.

FREDRIK. I don't think she looked especially at us.

ANNE.	SECOND LADY.
She did! She peered, then she smiled.	Charming, indeed, dear Celimène.

SECOND LADY. May I be permitted to present my school friend from the provinces? Madame Vilmorac—whose husband, I'm sure, is in dire need of a little expert polishing.

FIRST LADY. Oh, dear Countess, you are all but a legend to me. I implore you to reveal to me the secret of your success with the hardier sex!

ANNE. She smiled at us!

(Grabs FREDRIK*'s opera glasses and studies the stage)*

DESIREE. Dear Madame, that can be summed up in a single word—

ANNE. She's ravishingly beautiful.

FREDRIK. Make-up.

DESIREE. —dignity.

TWO LADIES. Dignity?

ANNE *(Turning on* FREDRIK*).* How can you be sure—if you've never seen her?

FREDRIK. Hush!

DESIREE *(Playing her first-act set speech).* Dignity. We women have a right to commit any crime toward our husbands, our lovers, our sons, as long as we do not hurt their dignity. We should make men's dignity our best ally and caress it, cradle it, speak tenderly to it, and handle it as our most delightful toy. Then a man is in our hands, at our feet, or anywhere else we momentarily wish him to be.

ANNE.	FREDRIK
(Sobbing). I	Anne!

want to go
home!
ANNE. I want to go home!
FREDRIK. Anne!
(They run off)

ACT ONE

SCENE THREE

THE EGERMAN ROOMS
In the parlor, PETRA, *lying on the couch, is calmly rearranging her blouse.* HENRIK, *in a storm of tension, is pulling on his trousers. On the floor beside them is a bottle of champagne and two glasses.*
———

HENRIK. We have sinned, and it was a complete failure!
(Struggling with his fly buttons)
These buttons, these insufferable buttons!
PETRA. Here dear, let me.
(She crosses, kneels in front of him, and starts to do up the fly buttons)
Don't you worry, little Henrik. Just let it rest a while.
(She pats his fly)
There. Now you put on your sweater and do a nice little quiet bit of reading.
(She gets his sweater from the back of a chair and helps him into it.
ANNE *enters, still crying. She sees* HENRIK *and* PETRA, *lets out a sob, and runs into the bedroom.* FREDRIK *enters.*
Perfectly calm, to FREDRIK*)*
My, that was a short play.
FREDRIK. My wife became ill; I had to bring her home.
(He gives HENRIK *a look, sizing up the situation approvingly, before following* ANNE *into the bedroom)*
Anne!
*(*HENRIK *starts again toward* PETRA, *who avoids him)*
PETRA. No, lamb. I told you. Give it a nice rest and you'll be surprised how perky it'll be by morning.
(She wriggles her way out.
FREDRIK *has now entered the bedroom,* ANNE *is no longer visible—as if she had moved into an inner room. In the parlor,* HENRIK *picks up the champagne bottle and glasses and puts them on the table)*
ANNE *(Off, calling).* Fredrik!

FREDRIK. Yes, dear.
ANNE *(Off).* Did you have many women between your first wife and me? Sometimes when I think of what memories you have, I vanish inside.
FREDRIK. Before I met you I was quite a different man. Many things were different. Better?
*(*ANNE *comes back into the bedroom)*
Worse? Different, anyway.
ANNE. Do you remember when I was a little girl and you came to my father's house for dinner and told me fairy tales? Do you remember?
FREDRIK. Yes, I remember.
ANNE *(Sitting on* FREDRIK'*s lap).* Then you were "Uncle Fredrik" and now you're my husband. Isn't that amusing? You were so lonely and sad that summer. I felt terribly sorry for you, so I said: Poor thing, I'll marry him. Are you coming to bed yet?
FREDRIK. Not just yet. I think I'll go out for a breath of fresh air.
ANNE. That wasn't an amusing play, was it?
FREDRIK. We didn't see that much of it.
ANNE. I wonder how old that Armfeldt woman can be. At least fifty—don't you think?
FREDRIK. I wouldn't say that old.
ANNE. Well, goodnight.
FREDRIK. Goodnight.
(As FREDRIK *moves into the parlor,* MR. LINDQUIST *and* MRS. NORDSTROM *appear. There is a musical sting and* FREDRIK *[and* HENRIK*] freeze)*
MRS. NORDSTROM *(Sings).*
Remember?
MR. LINQUIST *(Sings).*
Remember?
BOTH.
Remember?
Remember
*(*FREDRIK *unfreezes, clasps his hands together and goes into the parlor.* HENRIK *looks anxiously at his* FATHER*)*
HENRIK. Is she all right now?
FREDRIK. Oh yes, she's all right.
HENRIK. It wasn't anything serious?
FREDRIK. No, nothing serious.
HENRIK. You don't think—a doctor? I mean, it would be terrible if it was something— serious.
FREDRIK. Pray for her, son. Correction— pray for me. Goodnight.
HENRIK. Goodnight, father.
*(*FREDRIK *exits, and* MRS. NORDSTROM *and*

MR. LINDQUIST *sweep downstage)*
  MRS. NORDSTROM *(Sings).*
      The local village dance on the green—
      Remember?
  MR. LINDQUIST *(Sings).*
      Remember?
      The lady with the large tambourine—
      Remember?
  MRS. NORDSTROM.
      Remember?
      The one who played the harp in her boa
      Thought she was so a-
      Dept.
  BOTH.
      Ah, how we laughed,
      Ah, how we wept.
      Ah, how we polka'd
  MRS. NORDSTROM.
      And ah, how we slept.
      How we kissed and how we clung—
      Remember, darling?
  MR. LINDQUIST.
      We were foolish, we were young—
  BOTH.
      More than we knew.
  MRS. NORDSTROM.
      Yellow gingham on the bed,
      Remember, darling?
      And the canopy in red,
  MR. LINDQUIST.
      Or was it blue?

(MRS. NORDSTROM *and* MR. LINDQUIST *are joined by* MRS. SEGSTROM, MRS. ANDERSSEN *and* MR. ERLANSEN, *who appear downstage)*
  MRS. SEGSTROM.
      The funny little games that we played—
        Remember?
  MR. ERLANSEN.
      Remember?
      The unexpected knock of the maid—
      Remember?
  MRS. ANDERSSEN.
      Remember?
      The wine that made us both rather merry
      And, oh, so very
      Frank.
  ALL.
      Ah, how we laughed.
      Ah, how we drank.
  MR. ERLANSEN.
      You acquiesced
  MRS. ANDERSSEN.
      And the rest is a blank.
  MR. LINDQUIST.
      What we did with your perfume—

MR. ERLANSEN.
    Remember, darling?
MRS. SEGSTROM.
    The condition of the room
    When we were through . . .
MRS. NORDSTROM.
    Our inventions were unique—
    Remember, darling?
MR. LINDQUIST.
    I was limping for a week,
    You caught the flu . . .
ALL.
    I'm *sure* it was—
    You.
(They drift off as DESIREE's *digs come on)*

ACT ONE

SCENE FOUR

DESIREE'S DIGS
    FREDRIK *walks on, as* DESIREE, *in a robe, enters, munching a sandwich and carrying a glass of beer.*

_____

FREDRIK. They told me where to find you at the theater.
DESIREE. Fredrik!
FREDRIK. Hello, Desiree.
(For a moment they gaze at each other)
DESIREE. So it *was* you! I peered and peered and said: "Is it . . . ? Can it be . . . ? Is it possible?" And then, of course, when you walked out after five minutes, I was sure.
FREDRIK. Was my record that bad?
DESIREE. Terrible. You walked out on my Hedda in Helsingborg. And on my sensational Phaedra in Ekilstuna.
FREDRIK *(Standing, looking at her).* Fourteen years!
DESIREE. Fourteen years!
FREDRIK. No rancor?
DESIREE. Rancor? For a while, a little. But now—no rancor, not a trace.
(Indicating a plate of sandwiches)
Sandwich?
FREDRIK *(Declining).* Hungry as ever after a performance, I see.
DESIREE. Worse. I'm a wolf. Sit down.
(Pouring him a glass of schnapps)
Here. You never said no to schnapps.
(FREDRIK *sits down on the love seat. She stands, looking at him)*
FREDRIK. About *this* walking out! I'd like to

explain.

DESIREE. The girl in the pink dress, I imagine.

FREDRIK. You still don't miss a thing, do you?

DESIREE. Your wife.

FREDRIK. For the past eleven months. She was so looking forward to the play, she got a little overexcited. She's only eighteen, still almost a child.

(A pause)

I'm waiting.

DESIREE. For what?

FREDRIK. For you to tell me what an old fool I've become to have fallen under the spell of youth, beginnings, the blank page.

(Very coolly, DESIREE *opens the robe, revealing her naked body to him)*

DESIREE. The page that has been written on— *and* rewritten.

FREDRIK *(Looking, admiring)*. With great style. Some things—schnapps, for example— improve with age.

DESIREE. Let us hope that proves true of your little bride.

(She closes the wrapper and stands, still very cool, looking at him)

So you took her home and tucked her up in her cot with her rattle and her woolly penguin.

FREDRIK. Figuratively speaking.

DESIREE. And then you came to me.

FREDRIK. I wish you'd ask me why.

DESIREE *(Deadpan)*. Why did you come to me?

FREDRIK. For old times' sake? For curiosity? To boast about my wife? To complain about her? Perhaps—Hell, why am I being such a lawyer about it?

(Pause)

This afternoon when I was taking my nap . . .

DESIREE. So you take afternoon naps now!

FREDRIK. Hush! . . . I had the most delightful dream.

DESIREE. About . . . ?

FREDRIK. . . . you.

DESIREE. Ah! What did we do?

FREDRIK. Well, as a matter of fact, we were in that little hotel in Malmo. We'd been basking in the sun all day.

DESIREE *(Suddenly picking it up)*. When my back got so burned it was an agony to lie down so you . . . ?

FREDRIK. As vivid as . . . Well, *very* vivid! So you see. My motives for coming here are what might be called—mixed.

*(*DESIREE *suddenly bursts into laughter)*

FREDRIK *(Tentative)*. Funny?

DESIREE *(Suddenly controlling the laughter, very mock solemn)*. No. Not at all.

(There is a pause, distinctly charged with unadmitted sex)

FREDRIK *(Looking around, slightly uncomfortable)*. How familiar all this is.

DESIREE. Oh yes, nothing's changed. Uppsala one week. Orebroe the next. The same old inevitable routine.

FREDRIK. But it still has its compensations?

DESIREE. Yes—no—no—yes.

FREDRIK. That's a rather ambiguous answer. *(Pause)*

You must, at least at times, be lonely.

DESIREE *(Smiling)*. Dear Fredrik, if you're inquiring about my love life, rest assured. It's quite satisfactory.

FREDRIK. I see. And—if I may ask—at the moment?

DESIREE. A dragoon. A very handsome, very married dragoon with, I'm afraid, the vanity of a peacock, the brain of a pea, but the physical proportions . . .

FREDRIK. Don't specify the vegetable, please. I am easily deflated.

(They both burst into spontaneous laughter)

Oh, Desiree!

DESIREE. Fredrik!

(Another charged pause. FREDRIK *tries again)*

FREDRIK. Desiree, I . . .

DESIREE. Yes, dear?

FREDRIK. I—er . . . That is . . .

(Loses his nerve again)

Perhaps a little more schnapps?

DESIREE. Help yourself.

*(*FREDRIK *crosses to the writing desk, where, next to the schnapps, is a framed photograph of* FREDRIKA. *He notices it)*

FREDRIK. Who's this?

DESIREE *(Suddenly rather awkward)*. That? Oh—my daughter.

FREDRIK. Your daughter? I had no idea . . .

DESIREE. She happened.

FREDRIK. She's charming. Where is she now?

DESIREE. She's with my mother in the country. She used to tour with me, and then one day Mother swept up like the Wrath of God and saved her from me—You never knew my mother! She always wins *our* battles.

(Wanting to get off the subject)

I think perhaps a little schnapps for me too.

FREDRIK. Oh yes, of course.

*(*FREDRIK *pours a second schnapps. The charged pause again)*

DESIREE *(Indicating the room)*. I apologize for all this squalor!

FREDRIK. On the contrary, I have always associated you—very happily—with chaos.
(Pause)
So.

DESIREE. So.

FREDRIK *(Artificially bright)*. Well, I think it's time to talk about my wife, don't you?

DESIREE. Boast or complain?

FREDRIK. Both, I expect.
(Singing)
She lightens my sadness,
She livens my days,
She bursts with a kind of madness
My well-ordered ways.
My happiest mistake,
The ache of my life:
You must meet my wife.
She bubbles with pleasure,
She glows with surprise,
Disrupts my accustomed leisure
And ruffles my ties.
I don't know even now
Quite how it began.
You must meet my wife, my Anne.
One thousand whims to which I give in,
Since her smallest tear turns me ashen.
I never dreamed that I could live in
So completely demented,
Contented
A fashion.
So sunlike, so winning,
So unlike a wife.
I do think that I'm beginning
To show signs of life.
Don't ask me how at my age
One still can grow—
If you met my wife,
You'd know.

DESIREE. Dear Fredrik, I'm just longing to meet her. Sometime.

FREDRIK *(Singing)*.
She sparkles.

DESIREE *(Singing)*.
How pleasant.

FREDRIK.
She twinkles.

DESIREE.
How nice.

FREDRIK.
Her youth is a sort of present—

DESIREE.
Whatever the price.

FREDRIK.
The incandescent—what?—the—

DESIREE *(Proffering a cigarette)*.
Light?

FREDRIK.
—of my life!
You must meet my wife.

DESIREE.
Yes, I must, I really must. Now—

FREDRIK.
She flutters.

DESIREE.
How charming.

FREDRIK.
She twitters.

DESIREE.
My word!

FREDRIK.
She floats.

DESIREE.
Isn't that alarming?
What is she, a bird?

FREDRIK.
She makes me feel I'm—what?—

DESIREE.
A very old man?

FREDRIK.
Yes—no!

DESIREE.
No.

FREDRIK.
But—

DESIREE.
I must meet your Gertrude.

FREDRIK.
My Anne.

DESIREE.
Sorry—Anne.

FREDRIK.
She loves my voice, my walk, my mustache,
The cigar, in fact, that I'm smoking.
She'll watch me puff until it's just ash,
Then she'll save the cigar butt.

DESIREE.
Bizarre, but
You're joking.

FREDRIK.
She dotes on—

DESIREE.
Your dimple.

FREDRIK.
My snoring.

DESIREE.
How dear.

FREDRIK.
The point is, she's really simple.

DESIREE *(Smiling)*.
　　Yes, that much seems clear.
FREDRIK.
　　She gives me funny names.
DESIREE.
　　Like—?
FREDRIK.
　　"Old dry-as-dust."
DESIREE.
　　Wouldn't she just?
FREDRIK.
　　You must meet my wife.
DESIREE.
　　If I must—
(Looks over her shoulder at him and smiles)
　　Yes, I must.
FREDRIK.
　　A sea of whims that I submerge in,
　　Yet so lovable in repentance.
　　Unfortunately, still a virgin,
　　But you can't force a flower—
DESIREE *(Rises)*.
　　Don't finish that sentence!
　　She's monstrous!
FREDRIK.
　　She's frightened.
DESIREE.
　　Unfeeling!
FREDRIK.
　　Unversed.
　　She'd strike you as unenlightened.
DESIREE.
　　No, I'd strike her first.
FREDRIK.
　　Her reticence, her apprehension—
DESIREE.
　　Her crust!
FREDRIK.
　　No!
DESIREE.
　　Yes!
FREDRIK.
　　No!
DESIREE.
　　Fredrik . . .
FREDRIK.
　　You must meet my wife.
DESIREE.
　　Let me get my hat and my knife.
FREDRIK.
　　What was that?
DESIREE.
　　I must meet your wife.

FREDRIK.	DESIREE.
Yes, you must.	Yes, I must.

DESIREE *(Speaks)*. A virgin.

FREDRIK. A virgin.
DESIREE. Eleven months?
FREDRIK. Eleven months.
DESIREE. No wonder you dreamed of me!
FREDRIK. At least it was you I dreamed of, which indicates a kind of retroactive fidelity, doesn't it?
DESIREE. At least.
FREDRIK *(Suddenly very shy)*. Desiree, I—
DESIREE. Yes?
FREDRIK. Would it seem insensitive if I were to ask you—I can't say it!
DESIREE. Say it, darling.
FREDRIK. Would you . . .
(He can't)
DESIREE. Of course. What are old friends for?
(She rises, holds out her hand to him. He takes her hand, rises, too)
Wait till you see the bedroom! Stockings all over the place, a rather rusty hip-bath—and the Virgin Mary over the headboard.
(They exit, laughing, into the bedroom.
MADAME ARMFELDT *appears and sings with one eye on the room)*
MADAME ARMFELDT.
　　At the villa of the Baron de Signac,
　　Where I spent a somewhat infamous
　　　year,
　　At the villa of the Baron de Signac
　　I had ladies in attendance,
　　Fire-opal pendants . . .

　　Liaisons! What's happened to them?
　　Liaisons today.
　　Disgraceful! What's become of them?
　　Some of them
　　Hardly pay their shoddy way.

　　What once was a rare champagne
　　Is now just am amiable hock,
　　What once was a villa at least
　　Is "digs."

　　What was once a gown with train
　　Is now just a simple little frock,
　　What once was a sumptuous feast
　　Is figs.
　　No, not even figs—raisins.
　　Ah, liaisons!

　　Now let me see . . . Where was I? Oh
　　　yes . . .

　　At the palace of the Duke of Ferrara,
　　Who was prematurely deaf but a dear,

At the palace of the Duke of Ferrara
I acquired some position
Plus a tiny Titian . . .

Liaisons! What's happened to them?
Liaisons today.
To see them—indiscriminate
Women, it
Pains me more than I can say,
The lack of taste that they display.

Where is style?
Where is skill?
Where is forethought?
Where's discretion of the heart,
Where's passion in the art,
Where's craft?
With a smile
And a will,
But with more thought,
I acquired a chateau
Extravagantly o-
Verstaffed.

Too many people muddle sex with mere
desire,
And when emotion intervenes,
The nets descend.
It should on no account perplex, or
worse, inspire.
It's but a pleasurable means
To a measurable end.
Why does no one comprehend?
Let us hope this lunacy is just a trend.

Now let me see . . . Where was I? Oh,
yes . . .

In the castle of the King of the Belgians,
We would visit through a false
chiffonier.
In the castle of the King of the Belgians
Who, when things got rather touchy,
Deeded me a duchy . . .

Liaisons! What's happened to them?
Liaisons today.
Untidy—take my daughter, I
Taught her, I
Tried my best to point the way.
I even named her Desiree.

In a world where the kings are
employers,
Where the amateur prevails and deli-
cacy fails to pay,

In a world where the princes are
lawyers,
What can anyone expect except to
recollect
Liai . . .

(She falls asleep. FRID *appears and carries
her off. A beat)*

CARL-MAGNUS *(Offstage)*. All right, all right.
It's broken down. So *do* something! Crank it
up—or whatever it is!

*(*FREDRIK *and* DESIREE *appear at the bedroom door,* FREDRIK *in a bathrobe,* DESIREE *in
a negligee)*

FREDRIK. What can it be?

DESIREE. It can't!

FREDRIK. The dragoon?

DESIREE. Impossible. He's on maneuvers.
Eighty miles away. He couldn't . . .

CARL-MAGNUS *(Offstage, bellowing)*. A garage, idiot! That's what they're called.

DESIREE. He could.

FREDRIK. Is he jealous?

DESIREE. Tremendously.
(Suppresses a giggle)
This shouldn't be funny, should it?

FREDRIK. Let him in.

DESIREE. Fredrik . . .

FREDRIK. I am not a lawyer—nor are you
an actress—for nothing. Let him in.

*(*DESIREE *goes to open the door.* CARL-MAG-
NUS *enters, immaculate but brushing imaginary dust from his uniform. He is carrying a
bunch of daisies)*

DESIREE *(With tremendous poise)*. Carl-
Magnus! What a delightful surprise!

(Totally ignoring FREDRIK, CARL-MAGNUS
bows stiffly and kisses her hand)

CARL-MAGNUS. Excuse my appearance. My
new motorcar broke down.

(Hand kiss. Presents the daisies)
From a neighboring garden.

DESIREE *(Taking them)*. How lovely! Will
you be staying—long?

CARL-MAGNUS. I have twenty hours leave.
Three hours coming here, nine hours with you,
five hours with my wife and three hours back.

(Still ignoring FREDRIK*)*
Do you mind if I take off my uniform and put
on my robe?

DESIREE. Well—at the moment it's occupied.

CARL-MAGNUS *(Not looking at* FREDRIK*)*. So
I see.

DESIREE. Mr. Egerman—Count Malcolm.

FREDRIK. Sir.

CARL-MAGNUS *(Still ignoring* FREDRIK*)*. Sir.

FREDRIK. I feel I should give you an explanation for what may seem to be a rather unusual situation.

(With tremulous aplomb)

For many years, I have been Miss Armfeldt's mother's lawyer and devoted friend. A small lawsuit of hers—nothing major, I'm happy to say—comes up in Court tomorrow morning and at the last minute I realized that some legal papers required her daughter's signature. Although it was late and she had already retired . . .

DESIREE. I let him in, of course.

CARL-MAGNUS *(Turning the icy gaze on her)*. And then?

DESIREE. Ah, yes, the—the robe. Well, you see . . .

FREDRIK. Unfortunately, sir, on my way to the water-closet—through Miss Armfeldt's darkened bedroom—I inadvertently tripped over her hip-bath and fell in. Miss Armfeldt generously loaned me this garment while waiting for my clothes to dry in the bedroom.

CARL-MAGNUS. In that case, Miss Armfeldt, I suggest you return to the bedroom and see whether this gentleman's clothes are dry by now.

DESIREE. Yes. Of course.

(She crosses between FREDRIK *and* CARL-MAGNUS *and exits.*

Pacing, CARL-MAGNUS *begins to whistle a military march.* FREDRIK *counters by whistling a bit of Mozart)*

CARL-MAGNUS. Are you fond of duels, sir?

FREDRIK. I don't really know. I haven't ever tried.

CARL-MAGNUS. I have duelled seven times. Pistol, rapier, foil. I've been wounded five times. Otherwise fortune has been kind to me.

FREDRIK. I must say I'm impressed.

CARL-MAGNUS *(Picking up fruit knife)*. You see this fruit knife? The target will be that picture. The old lady. Her face. Her eye.

(Throws knife, which hits target)

FREDRIK *(Clapping)*. Bravo.

CARL-MAGNUS. Are you being insolent, sir?

FREDRIK. Of course—sir.

*(*DESIREE *returns from the bedroom. She is carrying* FREDRIK'*s clothes in a soaking wet bundle. She has dipped them in the hip-bath)*

DESIREE. They're not *very* dry.

FREDRIK. Oh dear me, they're certainly not, are they?

CARL-MAGNUS. A predicament.

FREDRIK. Indeed.

CARL-MAGNUS. I imagine, Miss Armfeldt, you could find this gentleman one of my nightshirts.

FREDRIK. Thank you, thank you. But I think I'd prefer to put on my own—er—garments.

*(*FREDRIK *takes the wet bundle from* DESIREE*)*

CARL-MAGNUS. Unfortunately, sir, you will not have the time for that.

(To DESIREE*)*

Perhaps you could tell him where to look.

DESIREE. Oh yes, yes. The left hand—no, the right hand bottom draw of the—er—

(Indicating a chest of drawers)

. . . thing.

*(*FREDRIK *gives her the wet clothes)*

FREDRIK *(Hesitating, then:)*. Thank you.

(He goes into the bedroom

While he is away, DESIREE *and* CARL-MAGNUS *confront each other in near-silence:* CARL-MAGNUS *only whistles a bit of the march that he whistled at* FREDRIK *earlier)*

FREDRIK *(Returns in a nightshirt, carrying the robe, which he holds out to* CARL-MAGNUS*)*. Your robe, sir.

*(*CARL-MAGNUS *receives it in silence.*

FREDRIK *puts on the nightcap that goes with the nightshirt)*

Well—er—goodnight. Miss Armfeldt, thank you for your cooperation.

*(*FREDRIK *takes the wet bundle from* DESIREE *and exits)*

CARL-MAGNUS *(Singing, to himself)*.
>She wouldn't . . .
>Therefore they didn't . . .
>So then it wasn't . . .
>Not unless it . . .
>Would she?
>She doesn't . . .
>God knows she needn't . . .
>Therefore it's not.

>He'd never . . .
>Therefore they haven't . . .
>Which makes the question
> absolutely . . .
>Could she?
>She daren't . . .
>Therefore I mustn't . . .
>What utter rot!

>Fidelity is more than mere display,
>It's what a man expects from life.

(The unit that DESIREE *is sitting on starts to ride off as* CHARLOTTE, *seated at her breakfast table, rides on)*

>Fidelity like mine to Desiree
>And Charlotte, my devoted wife.

ACT ONE

Scene Five

BREAKFAST ROOM IN MALCOLM COUNTRY HOUSE
Breakfast for one (CHARLOTTE's)—and an extra coffee cup—stands on an elegant little table. Music under.

———

CHARLOTTE. How was Miss Desiree Armfeldt? In good health, I trust?

CARL-MAGNUS. Charlotte, my dear. I have exactly five hours.

CHARLOTTE *(Deadpan)*. Five hours this time? Last time it was four. I'm gaining ground.

CARL-MAGNUS *(Preoccupied)*. She had a visitor. A lawyer in a nightshirt.

CHARLOTTE. Now, *that* I find interesting. What did you do?

CARL-MAGNUS. Threw him out.

CHARLOTTE. In a nightshirt?

CARL-MAGNUS. In *my* nightshirt.

CHARLOTTE. What sort of lawyer? Corporation, Maritime, Criminal—Testamentary?

CARL-MAGNUS. Didn't your sister's little school friend Anne Sorensen marry a Fredrik Egerman?

CHARLOTTE. Yes, she did.

CARL-MAGNUS. Fredrik Egerman.

(He sings)
> The papers,
> He mentioned papers,
> Some legal papers
> Which I didn't see there . . .
> Where were they,
> The goddamn papers
> She had to sign?
>
> What nonsense . . .
> He brought her papers,
> They were important
> So he had to be there . . .
> I'll kill him . . .
> Why should I bother?
> The woman's mine!
>
> Besides, no matter what one might infer,
> One must have faith to some degree.
> The least that I can do is trust in her
> The way that Charlotte trusts in me.

(Speaks)
What are you planning to do today?

CHARLOTTE. *After* the five hours?

CARL-MAGNUS. Right now. I need a little sleep.

CHARLOTTE. Ah! I see. In that case, my plans will have to be changed. What will I do?
(Sudden mock radiance)
I know! Nothing!

CARL-MAGNUS. Why don't you pay to visit to Marta's little school friend?

CHARLOTTE. Ah ha!

CARL-MAGNUS. She probably has no idea what *her* husband's up to.

CHARLOTTE. And I could enlighten her. Poor Carl-Magnus, are you *that* jealous?

CARL-MAGNUS. A civilized man can tolerate his wife's infidelity, but when it comes to his mistress, a man becomes a tiger.

CHARLOTTE. As opposed, of course, to a goat in a rut. Ah, well, if I'm back in two hours, that still leaves us three hours. Right?

CARL-MAGNUS *(Unexpectedly smiling)*. You're a good wife, Charlotte. The best.

CHARLOTTE. That's a comforting thought to take with me to town, dear. It just may keep me from cutting my throat on the tram.

(CHARLOTTE exits)

CARL-MAGNUS *(Sings)*.
> Capable, pliable . . .
> Women, women . . .
> Undemanding and reliable,
> Knowing their place.
> Insufferable, yes, but gentle,
> Their weaknesses are incidental,
> A functional but ornamental
> *(Sips coffee)*
> Race.
> Durable, sensible . . .
> Women, women . . .
> Very nearly indispensable
> Creatures of grace.
> God knows the foolishness about them,
> But if one had to live without them,
> The world would surely be a poorer,
> If purer, place.
>
> The hip-bath . . .
> About that hip-bath . . .
> How can you slip and trip into a hip-bath?
> The papers . . .
> Where were the papers?
> Of course, he might have taken back the papers . . .
> She wouldn't . . .
> Therefore they didn't . . .
> The woman's mine!
> *(He strides off)*

ACT ONE

SCENE SIX

THE EGERMAN ROOMS
In the bedroom, ANNE, *in a negligee, sits on the bed while* PETRA *combs her hair.*

___

ANNE. Oh, that's delicious. I could purr. Having your hair brushed is gloriously sensual, isn't it?

PETRA. I can think of more sensual things.

ANNE *(Giggles, then suddenly serious).* Are you a virgin, Petra?

PETRA. God forbid.

ANNE *(Sudden impulse).* I am.

PETRA. I know.

ANNE *(Astonished and flustered).* How on earth can you tell?

PETRA. Your skin, something in your eyes.

ANNE. Can everyone see it?

PETRA. I wouldn't think so.

ANNE. Well, that's a relief.

(Giggles)

How old were you when—

PETRA. Sixteen.

ANNE. It must have been terrifying, wasn't it? *And* disgusting.

PETRA. Disgusting? It was more fun than the rolly-coaster at the fair.

ANNE. Henrik says that almost everything that's fun is automatically vicious. It's so depressing.

PETRA. Oh him! Poor little puppy dog!

ANNE *(Suddenly imperious).* Don't you dare talk about your employer's son that way.

PETRA. Sorry, Ma'am.

ANNE. I forbid anyone in this house to tease Henrik.

(Giggles again)

Except me.

*(*ANNE *goes to the vanity, sits, opens the top of her robe, studies her reflection in the table-mirror)*

It's quite a good body, isn't it?

PETRA. Nothing wrong there.

ANNE. Is it as good as yours?

(Laughing, she turns and pulls PETRA *onto the bed, trying to undo* PETRA'*s uniform)*

Let me see!

(For a moment, PETRA *is shocked. Laughing,* ANNE *continues,* PETRA *starts laughing too. They begin struggling playfully together)*

If I was a boy, would I prefer you or me? Tell me, tell me!

(Still laughing and struggling they stumble across the room and collapse in a heap on the bed)

You're a boy! You're a boy!

PETRA *(Laughing).* God forbid!

(As they struggle, the front doorbell rings)

ANNE *(Sits up).* Run, Petra, run. Answer it.

*(*PETRA *climbs over* ANNE *to get off of the bed.*

As PETRA *hurries into the parlor and exits to answer the door,* ANNE *peers at herself in the mirror)*

Oh dear, oh dear, my hair! My—everything!

*(*PETRA *returns to the parlor with* CHARLOTTE*)*

PETRA. Please have a seat, Countess. Madame will be with you in a minute.

*(*CHARLOTTE *looks around the room—particularly at* FREDRIK'*s picture—*

PETRA *hurries in the bedroom. Hissing)*

It's a Countess!

ANNE. A Countess?

PETRA. Very grand.

ANNE. How thrilling! Who on earth can she be?

(After a final touch at the mirror, she draws herself up with great dignity and, with PETRA *behind her, sweeps into the living room. At the door, she stops and stares. Then delighted, runs to* CHARLOTTE*)*

Charlotte Olafsson! It is, isn't it? Marta's big sister who married that magnificent Count Something or other—and I was a flower girl at the wedding.

CHARLOTTE. Unhappily without a time-bomb in your lily of the valley bouquet.

ANNE *(Laughing).* Oh, Charlotte, you always did say the most amusing things.

CHARLOTTE. I still do. I frequently laugh myself to sleep contemplating my own future.

ANNE. Petra, ice, lemonade, cookies.

*(*PETRA *leaves. Pause)*

CHARLOTTE. Well, dear, how are you? And how is your marriage working out?

ANNE. I'm in bliss. I have all the dresses in the world and a maid to take care of me and this charming house and a husband who spoils me shamelessly.

CHARLOTTE. That list, I trust, is in diminishing order of priority.

ANNE. How dreadful you are! Of course it isn't. And how's dear Marta?

CHARLOTTE. Ecstatic. Dear Marta has renounced men and is teaching gymnastics in a school for retarded girls in Beetleheim. Which brings me or . . .

(Glancing at a little watch on her bosom)
. . . rather should bring me, as my time is strictly limited—to the subject of men. How do you rate your husband as a man?

ANNE. I—don't quite know what you mean.

CHARLOTTE. I will give you an example. As a man, my husband could be rated as a louse, a bastard, a conceited, puffed-up, adulterous egomaniac. He constantly makes me do the most degrading, the most humiliating things like . . . like . . .

(Her composure starts to crumble. She opens a little pocketbook and fumbles)

ANNE. Like?

CHARLOTTE. Like . . .

(Finding tiny handkerchief from purse, dabbing at her nose and bursting into tears)
Oh, why do I put up with it? Why do I let him treat me like—like an intimidated corporal in his regiment? Why? Why? Why? I'll tell you why. I despise him! I hate him! I *love* him! Oh damn that woman! May she rot forever in some infernal dressing room with lipstick of fire and scalding mascara! Let every billboard in hell eternally announce: Desiree Armfeldt in—in—in *The Wild Duck*!

(Abandons herself to tears)

ANNE. Desiree Armfeldt? But what has she done to you?

CHARLOTTE. What has she *not* done? Enslaved my husband—enslaved yours . . .

ANNE. Fredrik!

CHARLOTTE. He was there last night in her bedroom—in a nightshirt. My husband threw him out into the street and he's insanely jealous. He told me to come here and tell you . . . and I'm actually *telling* you! Oh what a monster I've become!

CHARLOTTE.
I'm before him
On my knees
And he kisses me.

CHARLOTTE.
He assumes I'll lose my reason,
And I do.
Men are stupid, men are vain,
Love's disgusting, love's insane,
A humiliating business!

ANNE. Oh, how true!

CHARLOTTE. Ah, well . . .

CHARLOTTE.
In the curtains,
In the silver,
In the buttons,
In the bread.

ANNE. Charlotte, is that the truth? Fredrik was there—in a nightshirt?

(CHARLOTTE sobs)

CHARLOTTE. My husband's nightshirt!

ANNE. Oh I knew it! I was sure he'd met her before. And when she *smiled* at us in the theater . . .

(She begins to weep)

CHARLOTTE. Poor Anne!

(PETRA enters with the tray of lemonade and cookies and stands gazing at the two women in astonishment)

PETRA. The lemonade, Ma'am.

ANNE *(Looking up, controlling herself with a great effort, to the weeping CHARLOTTE)*. Lemonade, Charlotte?

CHARLOTTE *(Looking up too, seeing the lemonade)*. Lemonade! It would choke me!

(Sings)
Every day a little death
In the parlor, in the bed,
In the curtains, in the silver,
In the buttons, in the bread.
Every day a little sting
In the heart and in the head.
Every move and every breath,
And you hardly feel a thing,
Brings a perfect little death.

He smiles sweetly, strokes my hair,
Says he misses me.
I would murder him right there
But first I die.
He talks softly of his wars,
And his horses
And his whores,
I think love's a dirty business!

ANNE. So do I!

ANNE.
So do I . . .

ANNE.
Every day a little death,
CHARLOTTE.
Every day a little death,
ANNE.
On the lips and in the eyes,
CHARLOTTE.
In the parlor, in the bed,
ANNE.
In the murmurs,
In the pauses,
In the gestures,
In the sighs.
Every day a little dies,

CHARLOTTE.
Every day a little sting

In the heart
And in the head.
Every move and
Every breath,
And you hardly feel a
Thing,
Brings a perfect little
Death.

ANNE.
In the looks and in
The lies.

And you hardly feel a
Thing,
Brings a perfect little
Death.

(After the number, HENRIK *enters, taking off his hat and scarf)*

HENRIK. Oh, excuse me.

ANNE *(Trying to rise to the occasion)*. Charlotte, this is Henrik Egerman.

HENRIK *(Bows and offers his hand)*. I am happy to make your acquaintance, Madam.

CHARLOTTE. Happy! Who could ever be happy to meet *me*?

(Holding HENRIK*'s hand, she rises and then drifts out.* ANNE *falls back sobbing on the couch.* HENRIK *stands, gazing at her)*

HENRIK. Anne, what is it?

ANNE. Nothing.

HENRIK. But what did that woman say to you?

ANNE. Nothing, nothing at all.

HENRIK. That can't be true.

ANNE. It is! It is! She—she merely told me that Marta Olafsson, my dearest friend from school is—teaching gymnastics . . .

(Bursts into tears again, falls into HENRIK*'s arms.* HENRIK *puts his arms around her slowly, cautiously)*

HENRIK. Anne! Poor Anne! If you knew how it destroys me to see you unhappy.

ANNE. I am not unhappy!

HENRIK. You know. You must know. Ever since you married Father, you've been more precious to me than . . .

ANNE *(Pulls back, suddenly giggling through her tears)*. . . . Martin Luther?

*(*HENRIK, *cut to the quick, jumps up)*

HENRIK. Can you laugh at me even now?

ANNE *(Rises)*. Oh dear, I'm sorry. Perhaps, after all, I am a totally frivolous woman with ice for a heart. Am I, Henrik? *Am* I?

*(*PETRA *enters)*

MADAME ARMFELDT'S VOICE. *(Off. Pushed in chair by* FRID*)*. Seven of hearts on the eight of spades.

ANNE *(Laughing again)*. Silly Henrik, get your book, quick, and denounce the wickedness of the world to me for at least a half an hour.

*(*ANNE *runs off as the bedroom and parlor go.* HENRIK *follows her, as does* PETRA, *carrying the lemonade tray)*

MADAME ARMFELDT'S VOICE. The Ten of Hearts! Who needs the Ten of Hearts!!

ACT ONE

SCENE SEVEN

ARMFELDT TERRACE

MADAME ARMFELDT *is playing solitaire with* FRID *standing behind her.* FREDRIKA *sits at the piano, playing scales.*

————

MADAME ARMFELDT. Child, I am about to give you your advice for the day.

FREDRIKA. Yes, Grandmother.

MADAME ARMFELDT. Never marry—or even dally with—a Scandinavian.

FREDRIKA. Why not, Grandmother?

MADAME ARMFELDT. They are all insane.

FREDRIKA. All of them?

MADAME ARMFELDT. Uh-hum. It's the latitude. A winter when the sun never rises, a summer when the sun never sets, are more than enough to addle the brain of any man. Further off, further off. You practically inhaled the Queen of Diamonds.

DESIREE *(Off)*. Who's home?

FREDRIKA *(Jumps up, thrilled)*. Mother!

*(*DESIREE *enters and* FREDRIKA *rushes to her, throwing herself into* DESIREE*'s arms)*

DESIREE. Darling, you've grown a mile; you're much prettier, you're irresistible! Hello, Mother.

MADAME ARMFELDT *(Continuing to play, unfriendly)*. And to what do I owe the honor of this visit?

DESIREE. I just thought I'd pop out and see you both. Is that so surprising?

MADAME ARMFELDT. Yes.

DESIREE. You're in one of your bitchy moods, I see.

MADAME ARMFELDT. If you've come to take Fredrika back, the answer is no. I do not object to the immorality of your life, merely to its sloppiness. Since I have been tidy enough to have acquired a sizeable mansion with a fleet of servants, it is only common sense that my granddaughter should reap the advantages of it.

(To FREDRIKA*)*

Isn't that so, child?

FREDRIKA. I really don't know, Grandmother.

MADAME ARMFELDT. Oh yes you do, dear. Well, Desiree, there must be something you want or you wouldn't have "popped out." What is it?

DESIREE. All right. The tour's over for a while, and I was wondering if you'd invite some people here next weekend.

MADAME ARMFELDT. If they're actors, they'll have to sleep in the stables.

DESIREE. Not actors, Mother. Just a lawyer from town and his family—Fredrik Egerman.

MADAME ARMFELDT. In my day, one went to lawyers' offices but never consorted with their *families*.

DESIREE. Then it'll make a nice change dear, won't it?

MADAME ARMFELDT. I am deeply suspicious, but very well. ·

DESIREE *(Producing a piece of paper)*. Here's the address.

MADAME ARMFELDT *(Taking it)*. I shall send 'round a formal invitation by hand.

(She snaps her fingers for FRID. *As he wheels her off:)*

Needless to say, I shall be polite to your guests. However, they will not be served my best champagne. I am saving that for my funeral.

*(*FREDRIKA *runs to* DESIREE; *they embrace, and freeze in that pose. The screens divide the stage so that we see, in another area,* PETRA *bringing* ANNE *an invitation on a small tray)*

PETRA *(Sings)*.

    Look, ma'am,
    An invitation.
    Here, ma'am,
    Delivered by hand.
    And, ma'am,
    I notice the station-
    Ery's engraved and very grand.

ANNE.

    Petra, how too exciting!
    Just when I need it!

    Petra, such elegant writing,
    So chic you hardly can read it.
    What do you think?
    Who can it be?
    Even the ink—
    No, here, let me . . .
    "Your presence . . ."
    Just think of it, Petra . . .
    "Is kindly . . ."
    It's at a chateau!
    "Requested . . ."
    Et cet'ra, et cet'ra,
    " . . . Madame Leonora Armf—"
    Oh no!
    A weekend in the country!

PETRA.

    We're invited?

ANNE.

    What a horrible plot!
    A weekend in the country!

PETRA.

    I'm excited.

ANNE.

    No, you're not!

PETRA.

    A weekend in the country!
    Just imagine!

ANNE.

    It's completely depraved.

PETRA.

    A weekend in the country!

ANNE.

    It's insulting!

PETRA.

    It's engraved.

ANNE.

    It's that woman,
    It's that Armfeldt . . .

PETRA.

    Oh, the actress . . .

ANNE.

    No, the ghoul,
    She may hope to
    Make her charm felt,
    But she's mad if she thinks
    I would be such a fool
    As to weekend in the country!

PETRA.

    How insulting!

ANNE.

    And I've nothing to wear!

ANNE and PETRA.

    A weekend in the country!

ANNE.

    Here!

*(*ANNE *gives the invitation back to* PETRA*)*

The last place I'm going is there!

(ANNE and PETRA exit behind a screen. DE-SIREE and FREDRIKA unfreeze and begin to move downstage)

DESIREE (Speaks). Well, dear, are you happy here?

FREDRIKA. Yes. I think so. But I miss us.

DESIREE. Oh, so do I!

(Pause)

Darling, how would you feel if we had a home of our very own with me only acting when I felt like it—and a man who would make you a spectacular father?

FREDRIKA. Oh I see. The lawyer! Mr. Egerman!

DESIREE. Dear child, you're uncanny.

(DESIREE and FREDRIKA freeze once again, and the screens close in to provide a stagette for the appearance of FREDRIK, ANNE, and

ANNE.
                                    Oh, no!

ANNE.
    A weekend
    With that woman . . .
FREDRIK.
    In the country . . .
ANNE.
    In the flesh!
FREDRIK.
    I've some business
    With her mother.
PETRA.
    See, it's business!
ANNE.
    . . . Oh, no doubt!
    But the business
    With her mother
    Would be hardly the business I'd worry
        about.
FREDRIK and PETRA.
    Just a weekend in the country,
FREDRIK.
    Smelling jasmine . . .
ANNE.
    Watching little things grow
FREDRIK and PETRA.
    A weekend in the country . . .
ANNE
    Go!
FREDRIK.
    My darling,
    We'll simply say no.

PETRA)
PETRA (Sings).
    Guess what, an invitation!
ANNE.
    Guess who, begins with an "A" . . .
    Armfeldt—
    Is that a relation
    To the decrepit Desiree?
PETRA.
    Guess when we're asked to go, sir—
    See, sir, the date there?
    Guess where—a fancy chateau, sir!
ANNE.
    Guess, too, who's lying in wait there,
    Setting her traps,
    Fixing her face—
FREDRIK.
    Darling,
    Perhaps a change of pace . . .
FREDRIK.
A
Weekend in the country
Would be charming,
And the air would be fresh.
    ANNE.
        Oh!
(They exit.
FREDRIKA and DESIREE unfreeze)
    FREDRIKA (Speaks). Oh Mother, I know it's none of my business, but . . . that dragoon you wrote me about—with the mustache?
    DESIREE. Oh, him! What I ever saw in him astounds me. He's a tin soldier—arms, legs, brain—tin, tin, tin!
(They freeze on the downstage bench.
The screens close in, providing a new play-ing area for ANNE and CHARLOTTE)
ANNE (Sings).
    A weekend!
CHARLOTTE.
    How very amusing.
ANNE.
    A weekend!
CHARLOTTE.
    But also inept.
ANNE.
    A weekend!
    Of course, we're refusing.
CHARLOTTE.
    Au contraire,
    You must accept.
ANNE.
    Oh, no!
CHARLOTTE.
    A weekend in the country . . .

ANNE.
But it's frightful!
CHARLOTTE.
No, you don't understand.
A weekend in the country
Is delightful
If it's planned.
Wear your hair down
And a flower,
Don't use make-up,
Dress in white.
She'll grow older
By the hour
And be hopelessly shattered by
Saturday night.
Spend a weekend in the country.
ANNE.
We'll accept it!
CHARLOTTE.
I'd a feeling
You would.
BOTH.
A weekend in the country!
ANNE.
Yes, it's only polite that we should.
CHARLOTTE.
Good.

(ANNE *and* CHARLOTTE *both disappear behind the screens.* DESIREE *and* FREDRIKA *unfreeze*)

FREDRIKA. Count Malcolm's insanely jealous, isn't he? You don't suppose he'll come galloping up on a black stallion, brandishing a sword?

DESIREE. Oh dear, I hadn't thought of that. But no, no, thank heavens. It's his wife's birthday this weekend—sacred to domesticity. At least we're safe from him.

(*They freeze.* CARL-MAGNUS *enters from behind a screen;* CHARLOTTE *follows opposite to meet him*)

CARL-MAGNUS (*Sings*).
Well?
CHARLOTTE.
I've an intriguing little social item.
CARL-MAGNUS.
What?
CHARLOTTE.
Out at the Armfeldt family manse.
CARL-MAGNUS.
Well, what?
CHARLOTTE.
Merely a weekend,
Still I thought it might am-
Use you to know who's invited to go,
This time with his pants.

CARL-MAGNUS.
You don't mean—?
CHARLOTTE.
I'll give you three guesses.
CARL-MAGNUS.
She wouldn't!
CHARLOTTE.
Reduce it to two.
CARL-MAGNUS.
It can't be . . .
CHARLOTTE.
It nevertheless is . . .
CARL-MAGNUS.
Egerman!
CHARLOTTE.
Right! Score one for you.
CARL-MAGNUS (*Triumphantly*).
Aha!
CHARLOTTE (*Triumphantly*).
Aha!
CARL-MAGNUS (*Thoughtfully*).
Aha!
CHARLOTTE (*Worriedly*).
Aha?
CARL-MAGNUS.
A weekend in the country . . .
We should try it—
CHARLOTTE.
How I wish we'd been asked.
CARL-MAGNUS.
A weekend in the country . . .
Peace and quiet—
CHARLOTTE.
We'll go masked.
CARL-MAGNUS.
A weekend in the country . . .
CHARLOTTE.
Uninvited—
They'll consider it odd.
CARL-MAGNUS.
A weekend in the country—
I'm delighted!
CHARLOTTE.
Oh, my God.
CARL-MAGNUS.
And the shooting should be pleasant
If the weather's not too rough.
Happy Birthday,
It's your present.
CHARLOTTE.
But . . .
CARL-MAGNUS.
You haven't been getting out nearly
enough,
And a weekend in the country . . .

CHARLOTTE.
It's perverted!
CARL-MAGNUS.
Pack my quiver and bow.
CHARLOTTE and CARL-MAGNUS.
A weekend in the country—
CARL-MAGNUS.
At exactly 2:30, we go.
CHARLOTTE.
We can't.

CARL-MAGNUS.
Go and pack my suits!
CHARLOTTE.
I won't!
CARL-MAGNUS.
My boots!
Pack everything I own
That shoots.
CHARLOTTE.
No!

CARL-MAGNUS.
Charlotte!
CHARLOTTE.
I'm thinking it out.
CARL-MAGNUS.
Charlotte!
CHARLOTTE.
There's no need to shout.
CARL-MAGNUS.
Charlotte!
CHARLOTTE.
All right, then,

BOTH
We're off on our way,
What a beautiful day
For

ALL.
A weekend in the country,
How amusing,
How delightfully droll,
A weekend in the country
While we're losing our control.
A weekend in the country,
How enchanting
On the manicured lawns.
A weekend in the country,
With the panting and the yawns.
With the crickets and the pheasants
And the orchards and the hay,
With the servants and the peasants,
We'll be laying our plans
While we're playing croquet

CARL-MAGNUS.
We shall.
CHARLOTTE.
We shan't.
CARL-MAGNUS.
I'm getting the car
And we're motoring down.
CHARLOTTE.
Yes, I'm certain you are
And I'm staying in town.

(The screens open to reveal ANNE, FREDRIK, and PETRA)

ANNE.
We'll go.
PETRA.
Oh good!
FREDRIK.
We will?

ANNE.
We should.
Pack everything white.
PETRA.
Ma'am, it's wonderful news!
FREDRIK.
Are you sure it's all right?
ANNE.
We'd be rude to refuse.
FREDRIK.
Then we're off!
PETRA.
We are?
FREDRIK.
We'll take the car.
ALL THREE.
We'll bring champagne
And caviar!
We're off on our way,
What a beautiful day
For

For a weekend in the country,
So inactive that one has to lie down.
A weekend in the country
Where . . .

(HENRIK enters)

HENRIK.
A weekend in the country,
The bees in their hives,
The shallow worldly figures,
The frivolous lives.
The devil's companions
Know not whom they serve.
It might be instructive
To observe.

(DESIREE and FREDRIKA unfreeze)

DESIREE. However, there is one tiny snag.

FREDRIKA. A snag?

DESIREE. Lawyer Egerman is married.

FREDRIKA. That could be considered a snag.

DESIREE. Don't worry, my darling. I was not raised by your Grandmother for nothing.

(DESIREE holds out her arm, and FREDRIKA runs to her. Together, they walk upstage as the screens open, revealing, for the first time, the facade of the Armfeldt Mansion. FRID stands at the door, and once DESIREE and FREDRIKA have entered, he closes it behind them)

CARL-MAGNUS
Charlotte!

FREDRIK
We're off!

HENRIK
A weekend in the
Country,
The bees in their
Hives . . .

CHARLOTTE
I'm thinking it out.

PETRA
We are?

CARL-MAGNUS
Charlotte!

FREDRIK and ANNE
We'll take the car.

FREDRIK, ANNE, and
PETRA
We'll bring
Champagne and
Caviar!

MRS SEGSTROM and
MRS. ANDERSSEN
We're off! We are?
We'll take the car.

CHARLOTTE
There's no need
To shout.

MRS. NORDSTROM
and MR. ERLANSEN
A weekend of
        playing
Croquet,

MR. LINDQUIST
Confiding our
        motives
And hiding our
        yawns,

We'll
Bring
Champagne

MRS. NORDSTROM
and MR. ERLANSEN
A weekend of
        strolling
The lawns,

MRS. SEGSTROM and
MRS. ANDERSSEN
And caviar!

CARL-MAGNUS, CHARLOTTE
FREDRIK, ANNE, and PETRA.
We're off and away,
What a beautiful day!

ALL THE QUINTET.

The weather is spectacular!

ALL.
        With riotous laughter
        We quietly suffer
        The season in town,
        Which is reason enough for
        A weekend in the country,
        How amusing,
        How delightfully droll!
        A weekend in the country,
        While we're losing our control.
        A weekend in the country,
        How enchanting
        On the manicured lawns.
        A weekend in the country,
        With the panting and the yawns.

With the crickets and the pheasants
And the orchards and the hay,
With the servants and the peasants
We'll be laying our plans
While we're playing croquet
For a weekend in the country,
So inactive
That one has to lie down.
A weekend in the country
Where
We're twice as upset as in,
Twice as upset as in,
Twice as upset as in,
Twice as upset as in . . .

(ALL, simultaneously)

CARL-MAGNUS.
        Charlotte, we're going!
        Charlotte, we're going!
        Charlotte, we're going!
        Charlotte, we're going!

CHARLOTTE.
We're uninvited!
We're uninvited!
We're uninvited!
We should stay in . . .

ANNE	FREDRIK	PETRA
A weekend!	Are you sure you want to go?	A weekend!
A weekend!	Are you sure you want to go?	A weekend!
A weekend!	Are you sure you want to go	A weekend!
A weekend!	Away and leave,	A weekend!
A weekend!	Go and leave	A weekend!
A weekend!		A weekend!
A weekend!		A weekend!
A weekend		A weekend
In		In

HENRIK.
    World's shallow people going,
    Shallow world's people going
    To

THE QUINTET.
Twice as upset as in
Twice as upset as in
Twice as upset as in
Twice as upset as in
Twice as upset as in
Twice as upset as in
Twice as upset as in
Twicc as upset as in

GIRLS.
    Crickets calling,
ALL.
    The vespers ring,
    The nightingale's waiting to sing.
    The rest of us wait on a string.
    Perpetual sunset
    Is rather an unset-
    Tling thing.
(The show curtain rises on Scene One)

ALL.
    Town!
CURTAIN

ENTR'ACTE

After a musical Entr'Acte, THE QUINTET *enters.*

_____

MRS. ANDERSSEN.
    The sun sits low,
    Diffusing its usual glow.
    Five o'clock . . .
    Twilight . . .
    Vespers sound,
    And it's six o'clock . . .
    Twilight
    All around,
ALL.
    But the sun sits low,
    As low as it's going to go.
MR. ERLANSEN.
    Eight o'clock . . .
MR. LINDQUIST.
    Twilight . . .
GIRLS.
    How enthralling!
MR. ERLANSEN.
    It's nine o'clock . . .
MR. LINDQUIST.
    Twilight . . .
GIRLS.
    Slowly crawling towards
MR. ERLANSEN.
    Ten o'clock . . .
MR. LINDQUIST.
    Twilight . . .

ACT TWO

SCENE ONE

THE ARMFELDT LAWN
    FRID *is serving champagne to* DESIREE *and* MALLA. FREDRIKA, *upstage, is playing croquet with the help of* BERTRAND, MADAME ARM-FELDT'*s page.* FRID *returns to* MADAME ARM-FELDT. OSA *passes with a tray of cookies, and* FREDRIKA *takes one.* DESIREE *gets a mallet and begins to play croquet.*

_____

MADAME ARMFELDT. To lose a lover or even a husband or two during the course of one's life can be vexing. But to lose one's teeth is a catastrophe. Bear that in mind, child, as you chomp so recklessly into that ginger snap.
    FREDRIKA. Very well, Grandmother.
    MADAME ARMFELDT (*Holding up her glass to* FRID). More champagne, Frid.
    (FRID *gets a fresh bottle*)
One bottle the less of the Mumms '87 will not, I hope, diminish the hilarity at my wake.
    (DESIREE *sits on the rise.* FRID *opens the bottle with a loud* POP!)

THE QUINTET.
> The sun won't set.
> It's fruitless to hope or to fret.
> It's dark as it's going to get.
> The hands on the clock turn,
> But don't sing a nocturne
> Just yet.

(Off, we hear a car-horn)

DESIREE. They're coming!

MADAME ARMFELDT. Nonsense!

DESIREE. But they are!

MADAME ARMFELDT. Impossible. No guest with the slightest grasp of what is seemly would arrive before five-fifteen on a Friday afternoon.

(We hear the car-horn again, and this time it's louder)

Good God, you're right!

DESIREE. Malla!

(DESIREE runs up into the house, followed closely by MALLA, and OSA. BERTRAND exits with the croquet set)

MADAME ARMFELDT. Frid! We cannot be caught squatting on the ground like Bohemians!

(FRID scoops her up and carries her into the house. FREDRIKA follows.

THE QUINTET *runs on to collect the furniture and props left on stage:* MR. ERLANSEN *gets the champagne buckets,* MRS. NORDSTROM *the fur rug,* MRS. ANDERSSEN *the cookie stand,* MR. LINDQUIST *the wickets and croquet pole,* MRS. SEGSTROM MADAME's *wicker stool. They freeze for a moment at the sound of the car-horn, and then all run off.*

A beat later, CARL-MAGNUS' *sports car drives on.* CARL-MAGNUS *is driving;* CHARLOTTE *sits beside him.* CARL-MAGNUS *stops the car and gets out)*

> ANNE *(Hissing).*
> So you did come?
> *(Pause)*
> Talk later.

(HENRIK, tremendously solicitous, holds out the handkerchief to ANNE)

HENRIK. Your handkerchief, Anne.

ANNE *(Taking it, moving away).* Thank you.

HENRIK. You must have dropped it.

(PETRA taps HENRIK on the shoulder)

PETRA. Your book, Master Henrik.

HENRIK *(Taking it).* Thank you.

PETRA *(With soupy mock-solicitousness).* You must have dropped it.

(PETRA moves to get the luggage.

FRID, *seeing and immediately appreciating* PETRA, *goes to her)*

FRID. Here. Let me.

CHARLOTTE *(Looking around).* Happy birthday to me!

CARL-MAGNUS *(Inspecting a wheel).* What was that?

CHARLOTTE. I merely said . . . oh, never mind.

CARL-MAGNUS. If that damn lawyer thinks he's going to get away with something—Haha!

CHARLOTTE. Haha! indeed, dear.

(CARL-MAGNUS helps CHARLOTTE out of the car)

CARL-MAGNUS. Watch him, Charlotte. Watch them both like a . . .

CHARLOTTE. Hawk, I know, dear. You're a tiger, I'm a hawk. We're our own zoo.

(As she speaks, a touring car sweeps on from the opposite side. It is driven rather erratically by FREDRIK *with* ANNE *beside him.* HENRIK *and* PETRA *are in the back seat with a pile of luggage. The car only just misses* CARL-MAGNUS' *car as it comes to a stop. Recognition comes.* FREDRIK *gets out of his car)*

FREDRIK. Good day, sir. I was not aware that you were to be a fellow guest.

(FREDRIK opens the car and helps ANNE out. HENRIK *helps* PETRA *out of the back seat)*

CARL-MAGNUS. Neither is Miss Armfeldt. I hope our arrival will in no way inconvenience you.

FREDRIK. Not at all, not at all. I am happy to see that you have gotten through yet another week without any serious wounds.

CARL-MAGNUS. What's that? Wounds, sir?

FREDRIK. Rapier? Bow and arrow? Blow dart?

(At this point, ANNE *and* CHARLOTTE *see each other. They run together.*

On the way, ANNE *drops her handkerchief)*

CHARLOTTE *(Hissing).*
So you did come?
(Pause)
Talk later.

PETRA *(Handing him two suitcases).* Let you—what?

(PETRA, with one suitcase, enters the house, followed by FRID, *who is carrying two.* HENRIK *is moodily drifting away as* DESIREE *emerges from the house. She is followed by* FREDRIKA, *and smiling dazzlingly for the* EGERMANS)*

DESIREE. Ah, here you all are . . .

(CARL-MAGNUS clears his throat noisily. The smile dies)

Count Malcolm!

CARL-MAGNUS *(Bowing frigidly over her hand).* My wife and I were in the neighborhood to visit her cousin. Unhappily, on arrival, we discovered the chateau was quarantined for . . .

(Flicks his fingers at CHARLOTTE*)*

CHARLOTTE. Plague.

CARL-MAGNUS. Since I am due back to maneuvers by dawn, we venture to propose ourselves for the night.

DESIREE *(Concealing no little fluster)*. Well, yes. Indeed. Why not? Mother will be honored!—surprised, but honored.

*(*DESIREE *crosses to* CHARLOTTE, *and sweeps past her, barely touching her hand)*
Countess Malcolm, I presume?

CHARLOTTE *(As* DESIREE *sweeps past her)*. You do indeed, Miss Armfeldt.

DESIREE. And Mr. Egerman! How kind of you all to come. Mother will be overjoyed.

FREDRIK *(Bending over her hand)*. It is your mother who is kind in inviting us. Allow me to present my rather anti-social son, Henrik.

(Points to the drifting away HENRIK, *who turns to acknowledge her)*
And this is my wife.

(He presents ANNE*)*

DESIREE. How do you do?

ANNE *(Icy)*. How do you do?

DESIREE *(Indicating* FREDRIKA*)*. And this is *my* daughter.

(Pause)
You must all be exhausted after your journeys; my daughter will show you to your rooms. Mother likes dinner at nine.

*(*FREDRIKA *leads them into the house:* CHARLOTTE, *then* ANNE, *then* HENRIK, *then* OSA. FREDRIKA *then stays on the terrace.*

Simultaneously, both FREDRIK *and* CARL-MAGNUS *turn, both with the same idea: to get* DESIREE *alone)*

CARL-MAGNUS *and* FREDRIK. Where shall I put the car?

(They exchange a hostile glare)

DESIREE *(Even more flustered)*. Ah, the cars, the cars! Now let me see.

CARL-MAGNUS *(Hissing)*. I must speak to you at once!

DESIREE *(Hissing)*. Later.

(Out loud)
How about the stables? They're straight ahead.

FREDRIK *(Hissing)*. I must speak to you at once!

DESIREE *(Hissing)*. Later.

(Reassured, CARL-MAGNUS *and* FREDRIK *return to their cars. Calling after him)*
You can't miss them, Mr. Egerman. Just look for the weather vane. A huge tin cockerel.

(Spinning to FREDRIKA, *pulling her downstage)*
Disaster, darling!

FREDRIKA. But what are you going to do? The way he glared at Mr. Egerman! He'll kill him!

DESIREE. Let us keep calm.

*(*FREDRIK *and* CARL-MAGNUS, *both with autocranks in hand, start back toward* DESIREE*)*

FREDRIKA *(Noticing)*. They're coming back!

DESIREE *(Totally losing her calm)*. Oh no! Oh God!

*(*DESIREE *starts to run up to the house)*

FREDRIKA *(Calling after her)*. But what should I say?

DESIREE. Anything!

(She runs into the house, as FREDRIK *and* CARL-MAGNUS, *gazing after* DESIREE *in astonishment, come up to* FREDRIKA*)*

FREDRIKA *(On the spot but gracious, seemingly composed)*. Mr. Egerman—Count Malcolm . . . Mother told me to tell you that she suddenly . . .

(She breaks)
. . . oh dear, oh dear.

(She scurries up into the house. The two men react, then, ignoring each other, return to their cars. They each crank their cars and get into them. The screens close in as the cars back out offstage. MR. ERLANSEN *and* MRS. NORDSTROM *enter)*

MRS. NORDSTROM *(Sings)*.
The sun sits low
And the vespers ring,

MR. ERLANSEN.
And the shadows grow
And the crickets sing,
And it's . . .

MRS. NORDSTROM.
Look! Is that the moon?

MR. ERLANSEN.
Yes.
What a lovely afternoon!

MRS. NORDSTROM.
Yes.

MR. ERLANSEN.
The evening air
Doesn't feel quite right

MRS. NORDSTROM.
In the not-quite glare
Of the not-quite night,
And it's . . .
Wait! Is that a star?

MR. ERLANSEN.
No.
Just the glow of a cigar.

MRS. NORDSTROM.
Oh.
(They exit)

ACT TWO

SCENE TWO

THE OTHER PART OF THE GARDEN
ANNE *leads* CHARLOTTE *on. Both women carry parasols.*

_____

ANNE. . . . After I spoke to you, I thought: I will go! I won't! Then I thought: Why not? We'll go to that awful woman's house and I'll say to her: "How dare you try to steal my husband? At your age you should have acquired at least some moral sense." And then— then in the motorcar coming here, I thought: "Oh dear, I'll never have the courage and maybe it's all my fault." And oh, I want to go home.
(Bursts into sobs)
CHARLOTTE. Have no fears. Miss Armfeldt has met her match.
ANNE *(Astonished, even through her tears).* She has? Who?
CHARLOTTE. Me. When I told my husband, he instantly became a tiger—his word, of course—and then, as if from heaven, a plan flashed into my mind.
(Pause)
Do you feel up to hearing my plan, dear?
(ANNE gives a little nod)
I shall make love to your husband.
ANNE *(Aghast).* You too?
CHARLOTTE. Confident of my own charms, I shall throw myself into your husband's arms. He will succumb. Why not? Carl-Magnus, in a storm of jealousy, will beg my forgiveness and swear eternal fidelity. And as for Miss Desiree Armfeldt, she will be back peddling her dubious commodities elsewhere. At least, that is the plan.
ANNE *(Suddenly forgetful of her tears).* Oh how amusing. How extremely amusing. Poor old Fredrik. And it serves him right, too.
CHARLOTTE. I am not sure I appreciate that remark, dear.
(FREDRIK appears, walking toward them)
FREDRIK. Ah, here you are, ladies.
CHARLOTTE *(Sudden devastating smile at FREDRIK).* Oh, Mr. Egerman! If you'll pardon my saying so, that's a simply ravishing cravat.

FREDRIK *(slightly bewildered).* It is?
CHARLOTTE *(Taking FREDRIK's left arm; ANNE takes his right arm).* I can't remember when I have seen so seductive a cravat.
(As ANNE suppresses giggles, they all walk off together. As ANNE, CHARLOTTE, and FREDRIK exit, MR. LINDQUIST and MRS. SEGSTROM appear)
MR. LINDQUIST *(Sings).*
The atmosphere's becoming heady,
The ambiance thrilling,
MRS. SEGSTROM.
The spirit unsteady,
The flesh far too willing.
MR. LINDQUIST.
To be perpetually ready
Is far from fulfilling . . .
MRS. SEGSTROM.
But wait—
The sun
Is dipping.
MR. LINDQUIST.
Where?
You're right.
It's dropping.
Look—!
At last!
It's slipping.
MRS. SEGSTROM.
Sorry,
My mistake,
It's stopping.
(They exit)

ACT TWO

SCENE TWO-A

THE OTHER PART OF THE GARDEN
FREDRIKA *enters.*

_____

FREDRIKA. Oh, I do agree that life at times can seem complicated.
(HENRIK enters behind her)
HENRIK. Complicated! If only you knew! Oh, Miss . . . Miss . . .
FREDRIKA. Armfeldt. I am not legitimate.
HENRIK. I see. Oh, Miss Armfeldt, all my life, I've made a fiasco of everything. If you knew how poor an opinion I have of myself! If you knew how many times I wish I had been one of the spermatazoa that never reached the womb.

(He breaks from her)
There, there! You see? I've done it again!

FREDRIKA. Mr. Egerman, I have toured with mother, you know. I'm broadminded.

HENRIK. You are? Then in that case, might I make a confession to you?

FREDRIKA. Of course.

HENRIK. I hate to burden you on so slight an acquaintance, but bottling it up inside of me is driving me insane.

(Pause. With great effort)
Oh, Miss Armfeldt, for the past eleven months, although I am preparing to enter the Ministry, I—

(He can't get it out)
FREDRIKA. What, Mr. Egerman?

HENRIK. I have been madly, hopelessly in love with my stepmother. Do you realize how many mortal sins that involves? Oh, damn everything to hell! I beg your pardon.

(They link arms and walk off. MR. LINDQUIST, MRS. SEGSTROM, MR. ERLANSEN, MRS. ANDERSSEN *and* MRS. NORDSTROM *enter and sing)*

ALL.
    The light is pink
    And the air is still
    And the sun is slinking
    Behind the hill.
    And when finally it sets,
    As finally it must,
    When finally it lets
    The moon and stars adjust,
    When finally we greet the dark
    And we're breathing amen,

MRS. ANDERSSEN.
    Surprise of surprises,
    It instantly rises
    Again.

(THE QUINTET exits)

ACT TWO

SCENE THREE

ARMFELDT TERRACE
Both dressed for dinner, FREDRIK *and* CARL-MAGNUS *are discovered;* FREDRIK *downstage,* CARL-MAGNUS *pacing on the porch.* FREDRIK *has a cigar and a small liqueur glass;* CARL-MAGNUS *carries a champagne glass.*

———

FREDRIK *(Sings).*
    I should never have
    Gone to the theater.
    Then I'd never have come
    To the country.
    If I never had come
    To the country,
    Matters might have stayed
    As they were.

CARL-MAGNUS *(Nods).* Sir . . .

FREDRIK *(Nods).* Sir . . .
    If she'd only been faded,
    If she'd only been fat,
    If she'd only been jaded
    And bursting with chat,
    If she'd only been perfectly awful,
    It would have been wonderful.

    If . . . if . . .
    If she'd been all a-twitter
    Or elusively cold,
    If she'd only been bitter,
    Or better,
    Looked passably old,
    If she'd been covered with glitter
    Or even been covered with mold,
    It would have been wonderful.

    But the woman was perfection,
    To my deepest dismay.
    Well, not quite perfection,
    I'm sorry to say.
    If the woman were perfection,
    She would go away,
    And that would be wonderful.
    Sir . . .

CARL-MAGNUS. Sir . . .
    If she'd only look flustered
    Or admitted the worst,
    If she only had blustered
    Or simpered or cursed,
    If she weren't so awfully perfect,
    It would have been wonderful.

    If . . .
    If . . .
    If she'd tried to be clever,
    If she'd started to flinch,
    If she'd cried or whatever
    A woman would do in a pinch,
    If I'd been certain she never
    Again could be trusted an inch,
    It would have been wonderful.

    But the woman was perfection,
    Not an action denied,

The kind of perfection
I cannot abide.
If the woman were perfection,
She'd have simply lied,
Which would have been wonderful.
FREDRIK.
If she'd only been vicious . . .
CARL-MAGNUS.
If she'd acted abused . . .
FREDRIK.
Or a bit too delicious . . .
CARL-MAGNUS.
Or been even slightly confused . . .
FREDRIK.
If she had only been sulky . . .
CARL-MAGNUS.
Or bristling . . .
FREDRIK.
Or bulky . . .
CARL-MAGNUS.
Or bruised . . .
BOTH.
It would have been wonderful.
CARL-MAGNUS.
If . . .
BOTH.
If . . .
FREDRIK.
If she'd only been willful . . .
CARL-MAGNUS.
If she only had fled . . .
FREDRIK.
Or a little less skillful . . .
CARL-MAGNUS.
Insulted, insisting . . .
FREDRIK.
In bed . . .
CARL-MAGNUS.
If she had only been fearful . . .
FREDRIK.
Or married . . .
CARL-MAGNUS.
Or tearful . . .
FREDRIK.
Or dead . . .
BOTH.
It would have been wonderful.
But the woman was perfection,
And the prospects are grim.
That lovely perfection
That nothing can dim.
Yes, the woman was perfection,
So I'm here with him . . .
CARL-MAGNUS. Sir . . .
FREDRIK. Sir . . .

BOTH.
It would have been wonderful.
(FREDRIKA *enters from the house*)
FREDRIKA. Excuse me, Count Malcolm, but Mother says she would like a word with you in the green salon.
(CARL-MAGNUS, *glaring triumphantly at* FREDRIK, *jumps up and strides into the house.* FREDRIKA *stands and grins shyly at* FREDRIK, *then follows* CARL-MAGNUS *into the house.* DESIREE *enters*)
DESIREE. Fredrik, you wanted a moment alone with me, I believe. Here it is.
FREDRIK (*Puzzled*). But that child said . . .
DESIREE. Oh, that was just Fredrika's little strategem.
FREDRIK. Fredrika? Your child is called Fredrika?
DESIREE. Yes.
FREDRIK. Ah!
DESIREE. Really Fredrik, what vanity. As if you were the only Fredrik in the world.
(*Brisk*)
Now, what is it you want to tell me?
FREDRIK. As a matter of fact, I thought you should know that my wife has no inkling of that nightshirt episode. So we should be discreet.
DESIREE. Dear Fredrik, of course. I wouldn't dream of giving that enchanting child a moment's anxiety.
FREDRIK. Then you do see her charm?
DESIREE. How could anyone miss it? How lovely to see you, Fredrik.
FREDRIK. In spite of Count Malcolm's invasion? You're sure we're not complicating . . .
CARL-MAGNUS (*Off*). Desiree!
FREDRIK. Oh God! Something tells me I should make myself scarce.
CARL-MAGNUS (*Off*). Desiree!
FREDRIK. Later, perhaps?
DESIREE. Any time.
FREDRIK. In your room?
DESIREE. In my room.
(FREDRIK *looks around for a place to hide. He finds the statue, puts his glass on it, and hides behind it. He douses his cigar in another glass resting on the statue*)
CARL-MAGNUS (*Comes out of the house*). Desiree!
DESIREE (*Calling, excessively sweet*). Here, dear!
CARL-MAGNUS. That child said the green salon.
DESIREE. She did? How extraordinary.

CARL-MAGNUS. Where's that goddamn lawyer?

DESIREE *(Airy)*. Mr. Egerman? Oh, somewhere about, no doubt.

CARL-MAGNUS. What's he doing here anyway?

DESIREE. He's visiting my mother, of course. He told you. They're the most devoted old friends.

CARL-MAGNUS. That had better be the truth. If I catch him so much as touching you, I'll call him out—with rapiers!

(Glares)

Where is your bedroom? Readily accessible, I trust.

DESIREE *(Aghast)*. But, Carl-Magnus!

(FRID enters from the house, crosses downstage)

With your *wife* here . . . !

CARL-MAGNUS. Charlotte is irrelevant. I shall visit your bedroom at the earliest opportunity tonight.

FRID. Madame, Count Malcolm! Dinner is served.

(As he moves past them to pick up FREDRIK's glass, he sees FREDRIK behind the statue. Totally unaware of complications)

Dinner is served, Mr. Egerman.

(FRID exits up into the house)

DESIREE *(Rising to it)*. Ah, there you are, Mr. Egerman!

(FREDRIK comes out from behind the statue, laughing)

Gentlemen, shall we proceed?

(Gives one arm to each as they start up into the house and freeze in place)

ACT TWO

SCENE FOUR

THE DINING ROOM

As the dining room table and GUESTS come on, MRS. NORDSTROM, MRS. SEGSTROM and MRS. ANDERSSEN sing.

———

MRS. NORDSTROM
Perpetual
anticipation is
Good for the soul
But it's bad for the
heart.
It's very good for
practicing

Self-control.
It's very good for
Morals,
But bad for morale.
It's very bad.
It can lead to

Going quite mad.

It's very good for

Reserve and

Learning to do

What one should.
It's very good.

Perpetual
Anticipation's
A delicate art,

MRS. SEGSTROM
Perpetual antici-
Pation is good for

The
Soul, but it's bad
For the
Heart.
It's very good for
Practicing self-
Control. It's
Very good for
Morals but bad

For morale. It's

Too unnerving.

It's very good,

Though, to have
Things to contem-

Plate.

Perpetual

MRS. ANDERSSEN
Per-
Petual antici-

Pation is good
For
The soul, but
It's
Bad for the
Heart.
It's
Very good,
Though,
To learn to
Wait.

MRS. NORDSTROM	MRS. SEGSTROM	MRS. ANDERSSEN
	Anticipation's A	Perpetual Anticipation's
Playing a role,	Delicate art,	A Delicate art,
Aching to start,		
	Aching to start,	
Keeping control	Keeping control	Keeping control
While falling	While falling	While falling
Apart.	Apart.	Apart.
Perpetual		
Anticipation is	Perpetual	
Good for the soul	Anticipation is	Perpetual
But it's bad for the	Good	Anticipation is
	But it's bad for the	Bad for the
Heart.	Heart.	Heart.

(The dining room table has moved onstage with MADAME ARMFELDT *already seated in place, facing the audience in solitary splendor. The table is elaborately dressed with fruit and floral pieces and expensive dinnerware. There are also two large candelabra, one at each end of the table. Parallel to the table and upstage of it, the line of* SERVANTS *has come on:* BERTRAND, OSA, PETRA, *and* FRID. OSA *and* PETRA *stand with trays as* FRID *and* BERTRAND *light the candelabra.*

Once the table is in place, FREDRIK *and* CARL-MAGNUS *move up to it with* DESIREE. FREDRIK *pulls out a chair for* DESIREE *and she sits.* FREDRIK *gets* ANNE *and seats her.* CHARLOTTE *enters,* CARL-MAGNUS *seats her on the extreme right end of the table. He then moves to the extreme left, and sits down next to* DESIREE. HENRIK *sits between* DESIREE *and* ANNE, FREDRIK *between* ANNE *and* CHARLOTTE. *The* GUESTS *all sit facing upstage.* FRID *and* BERTRAND *pour, and* MADAME ARMFELDT *raises her glass. The* OTHERS *follow her. When the glasses come down, there is a burst of laughter and noise from the* GUESTS.

FREDRIKA, *seated at the piano, "accompanies" the scene)*

DESIREE. . . . So you won the case after all, Mr. Egerman! How splendid!

FREDRIK. I was rather proud of myself.

DESIREE. And I'm sure you were tremendously proud of him too, Mrs. Egerman.

ANNE. I beg your pardon? Oh, I expect so, although I don't seem to remember much about it.

(CHARLOTTE *extends her glass;* BERTRAND *fills it)*

FREDRIK. I try not to bore my wife with my dubious victories in the courtroom.

DESIREE. How wise you are. I remember when I was her age, anything less than a new dress, or a ball, or a thrilling piece of gossip bored me to tears.

FREDRIK. That is the charm of youth.

CHARLOTTE. Dearest Miss Armfeldt, do regale us with more fascinating reminiscences from your remote youth.

CARL-MAGNUS. Charlotte, that is an idiotic remark.

FREDRIK. A man's youth may be as remote as a dinosaur, Countess, but with a beautiful woman, youth merely accompanies her through the years.

CHARLOTTE. Oh, Mr. Egerman, that is too enchanting!

(Leaning over her chair)

Anne, dear, where on earth did you find this simply adorable husband?

ANNE *(Leans. In on the "plan," of course, giggling).* I'm glad you approve of him.

CHARLOTTE *(To* HENRIK*).* Your father

(HENRIK *leans)*

is irresistible.

(CARL-MAGNUS *leans)*

I shall monopolize him for the entire weekend.

(DESIREE leans. Then, to ANNE*)*

Will you lease him to me, dear?

ANNE *(Giggling).* Freely. He's all yours.

(FREDRIK *looks at* ANNE, *then at* CHARLOTTE, *then leans)*

. . . unless, of course, our hostess has other plans for him.

DESIREE *(Smooth, getting out of her seat).* I

had thought of seducing him into rolling the croquet lawn tomorrow, but I'm sure he'd find the Countess less exhausting.

CHARLOTTE *(Rising)*. I wouldn't guarantee that!

(Clapping her hand over her mouth)

Oh, how could those wicked words have passed these lips!

CARL-MAGNUS *(Astonished. Rising)*. Charlotte!

CHARLOTTE. Oh, Carl-Magnus, dear, don't say you're bristling!

(To FREDRIK who has also risen. From here the two of them move to the music in a stylized fashion.)

My husband, Mr. Egerman, is a veritable porcupine. At the least provocation he is all spines—or is it quills? Beware. I am leading you down dangerous paths!

CARL-MAGNUS *(Frigid)*. I apologize for my wife, sir. She is not herself tonight.

FREDRIK *(Both amused and gracious)*. If she is this charming when she is *not* herself, sir, I would be fascinated to meet her when she *is*.

CHARLOTTE. Bravo, bravo! My champion!

(HENRIK and ANNE get up from the table and join the stylized dance)

May tomorrow find us thigh to thigh pushing the garden roller in tandem.

FREDRIK *(Turning it into a joke)*. That would depend on the width of the rollers.

(To DESIREE)

Miss Armfeldt, as a stranger in this house, may I ask if your roller . . .

CARL-MAGNUS *(Instantly picking this up)*. Stranger, sir? How can you call yourself a stranger in *this* house?

FREDRIK *(Momentarily bewildered)*. I beg your pardon?

CARL-MAGNUS *(Triumphantly sure he has found FREDRIK and DESIREE out, to MADAME ARMFELDT)*. I understand from your daughter, Madame, that Mr. Egerman is an old friend of yours and consequently a frequent visitor to this house.

MADAME ARMFELDT *(Vaguely aware of him, peering through a lorgnette)*. Are you addressing me, sir? Whoever you may be.

CARL-MAGNUS. I am, Madame.

MADAME ARMFELDT. Then be so kind as to repeat yourself.

DESIREE *(Breaking in)*. Mother, Count Malcolm—

MADAME ARMFELDT *(Overriding this, ignoring her, to CARL-MAGNUS)*. Judging from the level of the conversation so far, young

man, you can hardly expect me to have been paying attention.

(CARL-MAGNUS is taken aback)

CHARLOTTE. Splendid! The thrust direct! I shall commandeer that remark and wreak havoc with it at all my husband's regimental dinner parties!

(DANCE SECTION. Finally MADAME ARMFELDT tings on a glass with her fork for silence)

MADAME ARMFELDT *(As FRID and BERTRAND serve)*. Ladies and gentlemen, tonight I am serving you a very special dessert wine. It is from the cellars of the King of the Belgians who—during a period of intense intimacy—presented me with all the bottles then in existence. The secret of its unique quality is unknown, but it is said to possess the power to open the eyes—even of the blindest among us . . .

(Raising her glass)

To Life!

(The GUESTS all raise their glasses)

THE OTHERS. To Life!

MADAME ARMFELDT. And to the only other reality—Death!

(Only MADAME ARMFELDT and CHARLOTTE drink. A sudden chilly silence descends on the party as if a huge shadow had passed over it. The GUESTS slowly drift back to the table in silence.

At length the silence is broken by a little tipsy giggle from CHARLOTTE)

CHARLOTTE. Oh I *am* enjoying myself! What an unusual sensation!

(Raises her glass to DESIREE)

Dearest Miss Armfeldt, at this awe-inspiring moment—let me drink to *you* who have made this evening possible. The One and Only Desiree Armfeldt, beloved of hundreds—regardless of course of their matrimonial obligations!

(Hiccups)

CARL-MAGNUS. Charlotte, you will go to your room immediately.

(There is general consternation)

FREDRIK. Miss Armfeldt, I'm sure the Countess—

ANNE. Oh, dear, oh, dear, I am beside myself.

HENRIK *(Suddenly jumping up, shouting, smashing his glass on the table)*. Stop it! All of you! Stop it!

(There is instantly silence)

FREDRIK. Henrik!

HENRIK *(Swinging to glare at him)*. Are *you* reproving me?

FREDRIK. I think, if I were you, I would sit

down.

HENRIK. Sit, Henrik. Stand, Henrik. Am I to spend the rest of my life at your command, like a lapdog? Am I to respect a man who can permit such filthy pigs' talk in front of the purest, the most innocent, the most wonderful . . . ? I despise you all!

ANNE *(Giggling nervously)*. Oh Henrik! How comical you look!

DESIREE *(Smiling, holding out her glass to him)*. Smash this too. Smash every glass in the house if you feel like it.

HENRIK *(Bewildered and indignant)*. And you! You're an artist! You play Ibsen and—and Racine! Don't any of the great truths of the artists, come through to you at all? Are you no better than the others?

DESIREE. Why don't you just laugh at us all, my dear? Wouldn't that be a solution?

HENRIK. How can I laugh, when life makes me want to vomit?

(He runs out of the room)

ANNE. Poor silly Henrik. Someone should go after him.

(She gets up from the table, starts away)

FREDRIK *(Very authoritative)*. Anne. Come back.

(Meekly, ANNE *obeys, sitting down again at the table. Total silence.* FREDRIK *sits. Then, after a beat: A hiccup from* CHARLOTTE*)*

DESIREE. Dear Countess, may I suggest that you try holding your breath—for a very long time?

(The screens close in on the scene, and the table moves off)

ACT TWO

SCENE FIVE

ARMFELDT GARDEN

HENRIK, *who has run from the dining room, runs and stands near the bench in despair.* FREDRIKA, *at the piano sees him.*

————

FREDRIKA *(Stops playing)*. Mr. Egerman!

*(*HENRIK *ignores her)*

Mr. Egerman?

*(*HENRIK *looks up)*

HENRIK. I have disgraced myself—acting like a madman, breaking an expensive glass, humiliating myself in front of them all.

FREDRIKA. Poor, Mr. Egerman!

HENRIK *(Defending himself in spite of himself)*. They laughed at me. Even Anne. She said, "Silly Henrik, how comical you look!" Laughter! How I detest it! Your mother—everyone—says, "Laugh at it all." If all you can do is laugh at the cynicism, the frivolity, the lack of heart—then I'd rather be dead.

ANNE *(Off)*. Henrik!

HENRIK. Oh God! There she is!

(He runs off)

ANNE *(Off)*. Henrik dear!

FREDRIKA *(Calls after him)*. Mr. Egerman! Please don't do anything rash!

*(*ANNE *runs on)*

Oh Mrs. Egerman, I'm so terribly worried.

ANNE. You poor dear. What about?

FREDRIKA. About Mr. Egerman—Junior, that is.

ANNE. Silly Henrik! I was just coming out to scold him.

FREDRIKA. I am so afraid he may do himself an injury.

ANNE. How delightful to be talking to someone younger than myself. No doubt he has been denouncing the wickedness of the world—and quoting Martin Luther? Dearest Fredrika, all you were witnessing was the latest crisis in his love affair with God.

FREDRIKA. Not with God, Mrs. Egerman—with you!

ANNE *(Totally surprised)*. Me!

FREDRIKA. You may not have noticed, but he is madly, hopelessly in love with you.

ANNE. Is that really the truth?

FREDRIKA. Yes, he told me so himself.

ANNE *(Thrilled, flattered, perhaps more)*. The poor dear boy! How ridiculous of him—and yet how charming. Dear friend, if you knew how insecure I constantly feel, how complicated the marriage state seems to be. I adore old Fredrik, of course, but . . .

FREDRIKA *(Interrupting)*. But Mrs. Egerman, he ran down towards the lake!

ANNE *(Laughing)*. To gaze over the ornamental waters! How touching! Let us go and find him.

*(*ANNE *takes* FREDRIKA*'s arm and starts walking off with her)*

Such a good looking boy, isn't he? Such long, long lashes . . .

(They exit giggling, arm-in-arm)

ACT TWO

SCENE FIVE-A

ANOTHER PART OF THE GARDEN

FRID *runs on from behind a screen, followed*

by a more leisurely PETRA. *They have a bottle of wine and a small bundle of food with them.*

———

PETRA. Who needs a haystack? Anything you've got to show, you can show me right here—that is, if you're in the mood.

FRID *(Taking her into his arms)*. When am I not in the mood?

PETRA *(Laughing)*. I wouldn't know, would I? I'm just passing through.

FRID. I'm in the mood.

(Kiss)

I'm in it twenty-four hours a day.

(Kiss. FREDRIKA *runs across stage)*

FREDRIKA. Mr. Egerman!

PETRA. Private here, isn't it?

(ANNE runs across stage)

ANNE. Henrik! Henrik!

PETRA. What *are* they up to?

FRID. Oh, them! What are they ever up to?

(ANNE runs back across)

ANNE. Henrik!

(FREDRIKA runs back across)

FREDRIKA. Mr. Egerman!

FRID. You saw them all at dinner, dressed up like waxworks, jabbering away to prove how clever they are. And never knowing what they miss.

(Kiss)

ANNE's VOICE. Henrik!

FRID. Catch one of them having the sense to grab the first pretty girl that comes along—and do her on the soft grass, with the summer night just smiling down.

(Kiss)

Any complaints yet?

PETRA. Give me time.

FRID. You've a sweet mouth—sweet as honey.

(The screen moves, wiping out FRID *and* PETRA. *It reveals* HENRIK, *who has been watching them make love. After an anguished moment, he runs straight up into the house, slamming the doors behind him)*

ACT TWO

SCENE SIX

DESIREE'S BEDROOM

DESIREE *sits on the bed, her long skirt drawn up over her knees, expertly sewing up a hem.*

FREDRIK *enters and clears his throat.*

———

FREDRIK. Your dragoon and his wife are glowering at each other in the green salon, and all the children appear to have vanished, so when I saw you sneaking up the stairs . . .

DESIREE. I ripped my hem on the dining room table in all that furore.

FREDRIK *(Hovering)*. Is this all right?

DESIREE. Of course. Sit down.

(Patting the bed beside her, on which tumbled stockings are strewn)

FREDRIK. *On* the stockings?

DESIREE. I don't see why not.

(There is a long pause)

Well, we're back at the point where we were so rudely interrupted last week, aren't we?

FREDRIK. Not quite. If you'll remember, we'd progressed a step further.

DESIREE. How true.

FREDRIK. I imagine neither of us is contemplating a repeat performance.

DESIREE. Good heavens, with your wife in the house, and my lover and his wife and my daughter . . .

FREDRIK. . . . and my devoted old friend, your mother.

(They both laugh)

DESIREE *(During it, like a naughty girl)*. Isn't my dragoon awful?

FREDRIK *(Laughs)*. When you told me he had the brain of a pea, I think you were being generous.

(They laugh more uproariously)

DESIREE. What in God's name are we laughing about? Your son was right at dinner. We don't fool that boy, not for a moment. The One and Only Desiree Armfeldt, dragging around the country in shoddy tours, carrying on with someone else's dim-witted husband. And the Great Lawyer Egerman, busy renewing his unrenewable youth.

FREDRIK. Bravo! Probably that's an accurate description of us both.

DESIREE. Shall I tell you why I really invited you here? When we met again and we made love, I thought: Maybe here it is at last—a change to turn back, to find some sort of coherent existence after so many years of muddle.

(Pause)

Of course, there's your wife. But I thought: perhaps—just perhaps—you might be in need of rescue too.

FREDRIK. From renewing my unrenewable youth?

DESIREE *(Suddenly tentative)*. It was only a thought.

FREDRIK. When my eyes are open and I look at you, I see a woman that I have loved for a long time, who entranced me all over again when I came to her rooms . . . who gives me such genuine pleasure that, in spite of myself, I came here for the sheer delight of being with her again. The woman who could rescue me? Of course.

(Pause)

But when my eyes are not open—which is most of the time—all I see is a girl in a pink dress teasing a canary, running through a sunlit garden to hug me at the gate, as if I'd come home from Timbuctu instead of the Municipal Courthouse three blocks away . . .

DESIREE *(Sings)*.
　　Isn't it rich?
　　Are we a pair?
　　Me here at last on the ground,
　　You in mid-air.
　　Send in the clowns.

　　Isn't it bliss?
　　Don't you approve?
　　One who keeps tearing around,
　　One who can't move.
　　Where are the clowns?
　　Send in the clowns.

　　Just when I'd stopped
　　Opening doors,
　　Finally knowing
　　The one that I wanted was yours,
　　Making my entrance again
　　With my usual flair,
　　Sure of my lines,
　　No one is there.

　　(FREDRIK rises)

　　Don't you love farce?
　　My fault, I fear.
　　I thought that you'd want what I want—
　　Sorry, my dear.
　　But where are the clowns?
　　Quick, send in the clowns.
　　Don't bother, they're here.

FREDRIK. Desiree, I'm sorry. I should never have come. To flirt with rescue when one has no intention of being saved . . . Do try to forgive me.

(He exits)

DESIREE.
　　Isn't it rich?
　　Isn't it queer?
　　Losing my timing this late

　　In my career?
　　And where are the clowns?
　　There ought to be clowns.
　　Well, maybe next year . . .

(The lights iris out on DESIREE)

ACT TWO

SCENE SEVEN

THE TREES

As DESIREE'*s bedroom goes off,* HENRIK *emerges from the house, carrying a rope. He runs downstage with it.*

ANNE *and* FREDRIKA *run on; when* HENRIK *hears them, he runs behind the screens to hide.*

———

ANNE *(As she runs on)*. Henrik!
(To FREDRIKA*)*
Oh, I'm quite puffed! Where can he be?
(Noticing FREDRIKA'*s solemn face)*
Poor child, that face! Don't look so solemn. Where would you go if you were he?

FREDRIKA. Well, the summer pavilion? And then, of course, there's the stables.

ANNE. Then you go to the stables and I'll take the summer pavilion.
(Laughing)
Run!
(She starts off)
Isn't this exciting after that stodgy old dinner!
(They run off, and HENRIK *runs back on. He stops at the tree, stands on the marble bench, and, after circling his noose around his neck, throws the other end of the rope up to the tree limb)*

ANNE'*s* VOICE. Henrik!
*(*HENRIK *falls with a loud thud, as* ANNE *enters)*

ANNE. What an extraordinary . . . ! Oh, Henrik—how comical you look!
(Pulling him up by the noose still around his neck)
Oh, no! You didn't!
(Pause)
For me?
(She gently removes the noose from his neck)
Oh, my poor darling Henrik.
(She throws herself into his arms)
Oh, my poor boy! Oh, those eyes, gazing at me like a lost Saint Bernard . . .
(They start to kiss passionately)

HENRIK. I love you! I've actually *said* it!

ANNE *(Returning his kisses passionately)*.

Oh how scatterbrained I was never to have realized. Not Fredrik . . . not poor old Fredrik . . . not Fredrik at all!

(They drop down onto the ground and start to make passionate love. The trees wipe them out, revealing PETRA *and* FRID. FRID *is still asleep)*

PETRA *(Sings).*

> I shall marry the miller's son,
> Pin my hat on a nice piece of property.
> Friday nights, for a bit of fun,
> We'll go dancing.
> Meanwhile . . .
> It's a wink and a wiggle
> And a giggle in the grass
> And I'll trip the light fanadango,
> A pinch and a diddle
> In the middle of what passes by.
> It's a very short road
> From the pinch and the punch
> To the paunch and the pouch and the pension.
> It's a very short road
> To the ten thousandth lunch
> And the belch and the grouch and the sigh.
> In the meanwhile,
> There are mouths to be kissed
> Before mouths to be fed,
> And a lot in between
> In the meanwhile.
> And a girl ought to celebrate what passes by.

> Or I shall marry the businessman,
> Five fat babies and lots of security.
> Friday nights, if we think we can,
> We'll go dancing.
> Meanwhile . . .
> It's a push and a fumble
> And a tumble in the sheets
> And I'll foot the highland fancy,
> A dip in the butter
> And a flutter with what meets my eye.
> It's a very short fetch
> From the push and the whoop
> To the squint and the stoop and the mumble.
> It's not much of a stretch
> To the cribs and the croup
> And the bosoms that droop and go dry.
> In the meanwhile,
> There are mouths to be kissed
> Before mouths to be fed,
> And there's many a tryst
> And there's many a bed

> To be sampled and seen
> In the meanwhile.
> And a girl has to celebrate what passes by.

> Or I shall marry the Prince of Wales—
> Pearls and servants and dressing for festivals.
> Friday nights, with him all in tails,
> We'll have dancing.
> Meanwhile . . .
> It's a rip in the bustle
> And a rustle in the hay
> And I'll pitch the quick fantastic,
> With flings of confetti
> And my petticoats away up high.
> It's a very short way
> From the fling that's for fun
> To the thigh pressing under the table.
> It's a very short day
> Till you're stuck with just one
> Or it has to be done on the sly.
> In the meanwhile,
> There are mouths to be kissed
> Before mouths to be fed,
> And there's many a tryst
> And there's many a bed.
> There's a lot I'll have missed
> But I'll not have been dead when I die!
> And a person should celebrate everything
> Passing by.

> And I shall marry the miller's son.

(She smiles, as the lights fade on her)

ACT TWO

SCENE EIGHT

ARMFELDT HOUSE AND GARDEN

FREDRIKA *is lying on the grass reading.* MADAME ARMFELDT, *seated in a huge wing-chair upstage.* DESIREE, *on the bed, is writing in her diary.* CARL-MAGNUS *paces on the terrace and then goes into the house.* MRS. SEGSTROM *and* MR. LINDQUIST *are behind trees,* MR. ERLANSEN *and* MRS. ANDERSSEN *are behind opposite trees. Charlotte sits downstage on a bench.*

After a beat, FREDRIK *enters, sees the* FIGURE *on the bench. Is it* ANNE? *He hurries toward her.*

———

FREDRIK. Anne?—Oh, forgive me, Countess. I was looking for my wife.

CHARLOTTE (*Looking up, through sobs*). Oh Mr. Egerman, how can I face you after that exhibition at dinner? Throwing myself at your head!

FREDRIK. On the contrary, I found it most morale-building.

(*Sits down next to her*)

It's not often these days that a beautiful woman does me that honor.

CHARLOTTE. I didn't.

FREDRIK. I beg your pardon?

CHARLOTTE. I didn't do you that honor. It was just a charade. A *failed* charade! In my madness I thought I could make my husband jealous.

FREDRIK. I'm afraid marriage isn't one of the easier relationships, is it?

CHARLOTTE. Mr. Egerman, for a woman it's impossible!

FREDRIK. It's not all that possible for men.

CHARLOTTE. Men! Look at you—a man of an age when a woman is lucky if a drunken alderman pinches her derierre at a village fete! And yet, you have managed to acquire the youngest, prettiest . . . I hate you being happy. I hate *anyone* being happy!

(HENRIK *and* ANNE *emerge from the house, carrying suitcases. They start stealthily downstage*)

HENRIK. The gig should be ready at the stables.

ANNE (*Giggling*). Oh Henrik darling, I do hope the horses will be smart. I do detest riding in a gig when the horses are not smart.

(HENRIK *stops, pulls her to him. They kiss*)

MRS. SEGSTROM (*Turns, looking onstage, sings*).

> Think of how I adore you,
> Think of how much you love me,
> If I were perfect for you,
> Wouldn't you tire of me
> Soon . . . ?

HENRIK. Let all the birds nest in my hair!

ANNE. Silly Henrik! Quick, or we'll miss the train! (THEY *are now downstage. Unaware of* FREDRIK *and* CHARLOTTE, *they move past them. For a long moment,* FREDRIK *and* CHARLOTTE *sit, while* FREDRIK'*s world tumbles around his ears*)

CHARLOTTE. It was, wasn't it?

FREDRIK. It was.

CHARLOTTE. Run after them. Quick. You can catch them at the stables.

FREDRIK (*Even more quiet*). After the horse has gone?

(*Pause*)

How strange that one's life should end sitting on a bench in a garden.

MR. ERLANSEN (*Leans, looking onstage, sings*).

> She lightens my sadness,
> She livens my days,
> She bursts with a kind of madness
> My well-ordered ways.
> My happiest mistake,
> The ache of my life . . .

(*As they sit, the lights come up on* DESIREE'*s* BEDROOM, *as* CARL-MAGNUS *enters*)

DESIREE. Carl-Magnus, go away!

CARL-MAGNUS (*Ignoring her, beginning to unbutton his tunic*). I'd have been here half an hour ago if I hadn't had to knock a little sense into my wife.

DESIREE. Carl-Magnus, do not take off your tunic.

CARL-MAGNUS (*Still ignoring her*). Poor girl. She was somewhat the worse for wine, of course. Trying to make me believe that she was attracted to that asinine lawyer fellow.

DESIREE. Carl-Magnus, listen to me! It's over. It was never anything in the first place, but now it's OVER!

CARL-MAGNUS (*Ignoring this, totally self-absorbed*). Of all people—that lawyer! Scrawny as a scarecrow and without a hair on his body, probably.

(*He starts removing his braces*)

DESIREE (*Shouting*). Don't take off your trousers!

CARL-MAGNUS (*Getting out of his trousers*). Poor girl, she'd slash her wrists before she'd let any other man touch her. And even if, under the influence of wine, she did stray a bit, how ridiculous to imagine I would so much as turn a hair!

(*As he starts to get out of his trouser leg, he stumbles so that he happens to be facing the "window." He stops dead, peering out*) Good God!

DESIREE. What is it?

CARL-MAGNUS (*Peering*). It's her! And him! Sitting on a bench! She's touching him! The scoundrel! The conniving swine! Any man who thinks he can lay a finger on *my* wife!

(*Pulling up his pants and grabbing his tunic as he hobbles out*)

DESIREE. Carl-Magnus, what are you doing?

CARL-MAGNUS. My duelling pistols!

(And he rushes out. DESIREE *runs after him)*
DESIREE. Carl-Magnus!
(The bed rolls off)
MADAME ARMFELDT. A great deal seems to be going on in this house tonight.
(Pause)
Child, will you do me a favor?
FREDRIKA. Of course, Grandmother.
MADAME ARMFELDT. Will you tell me what it's all for? Having outlived my own illusions by centuries, it would be soothing at least to pretend to share some of yours.
FREDRIKA *(After thought)*. Well, I think it must be worth it.
MADAME ARMFELDT. Why?
FREDRIKA. It's all there is, isn't it? Oh, I know it's often discouraging, and to hope for something too much is childish, because what you want so rarely happens.
MADAME ARMFELDT. Astounding! When I was your age I wanted everything—the moon—jewels, yachts, villas on the Riviera. And I got 'em, too,—for all the good they did me.
(Music. Her mind starts to wander)
There was a Croatian Count. He was my first lover. I can see his face now—such eyes, and a mustache like a brigand. He gave me a wooden ring.
FREDRIKA. A wooden ring?
MADAME ARMFELDT. It had been in his family for centuries, it seemed, but I said to myself: a wooden ring? What sort of man would give you a wooden ring, so I tossed him out right there and then. And now—who knows? He might have been the love of my life.
(In the GARDEN, FREDRIK *and* CHARLOTTE *pause)*
CHARLOTTE. To think I was actually saying: How I hate you being happy! It's—as if I carry around some terrible curse.
(CARL-MAGNUS enters from house, runs down steps)
Oh, Mr. Egerman . . . I'm sorry.
(CHARLOTTE breaks from FREDRIK with a little cry. FREDRIK, still dazed, merely turns, gazing vaguely at CARL-MAGNUS)
CARL-MAGNUS *(Glaring, clicks his heels)*. Sir, you will accompany me to the pavilion.
(CHARLOTTE looks at the pistol. Slowly the wonderful truth begins to dawn on her. He really cares! Her face breaks into a radiant smile)
CHARLOTTE. Carl-Magnus!
CARL-MAGNUS *(Ignoring her)*. I think the situation speaks for itself.
CHARLOTTE *(Her ecstatic smile broaden-*

ing). Carl-Magnus, dear, you won't be *too* impulsive, will you?
CARL-MAGNUS. Whatever the provocation, I remain a civilized man.
(Flourishing the pistol)
The lawyer and I are merely going to play a little Russian Roulette.
CHARLOTTE. Russian Roulette?
CARL-MAGNUS *(To* FREDRIK*)*. Well, sir? Are you ready, sir??
FREDRIK *(Still only half aware)*. I beg your pardon. Ready for what??
CHARLOTTE *(Thrilled)*. Russian Roulette!
FREDRIK. Oh, Russian Roulette. That's with a pistol, isn't it? And you spin the . . .
(Indicating)
Well, why not?
(Very polite, to CHARLOTTE*)*
Excuse me, Madame.
(CARL-MAGNUS clicks his heels and struts off. FREDRIK *follows him off slowly)*
MR. LINDQUIST *(Sings)*.
A weekend in the country . . .
MR. LINDQUIST and MRS. ANDERSSEN.
So inactive
MR. LINDQUIST, MRS. ANDERSSEN and MR. ERLANSEN.
That one has to lie down.
MR. LINDQUIST, MRS. ANDERSSEN, MR. ERLANSEN, MRS. SEGSTROM, MRS. NORDSTROM.
A weekend in the country
Where . . .
(FRID and PETRA *enter, unobserved, and lean against a tree.* GUNSHOT*)*
We're twice as upset as is in town!
(THE QUINTET scatters and runs off, except for MRS. ANDERSSEN *who stands behind a tree.* DESIREE *runs out of the house and down to* CHARLOTTE*)*
DESIREE. What is it? What's happened?
CHARLOTTE. Oh, dear Miss Armfeldt, my husband and Mr. Egerman are duelling in the pavilion!
DESIREE. Are you insane? You let them do it?
(She starts to run to the PAVILION. CARL-MAGNUS *enters, carrying* FREDRIK *over one shoulder. Quite roughly, he tosses him down on the grass, where* FREDRIK *remains motionless)*
DESIREE. You lunatic! You've killed him! Fredrik!
CHARLOTTE. Carl-Magnus!
CARL-MAGNUS. My dear Miss Armfeldt, he merely grazed his ear. I trust his performance in the Law Courts is a trifle more professional.

(He clears his throat. To CHARLOTTE*)*
I am prepared to forgive you, dear. But I feel this house is no longer a suitable place for us.

CHARLOTTE. Oh yes, my darling, I agree!

CARL-MAGNUS. You will pack my things and meet me in the stables. I will have the car ready.

CHARLOTTE. Yes, dear. Oh, Carl-Magnus! You became a tiger for me!

(They kiss)

MRS. ANDERSSEN *(Sings).*
    Men are stupid, men are vain,
    Love's disgusting, love's insane,
    A humiliating business . . .

MRS. SEGSTROM.
    Oh, how true!

*(*CARL-MAGNUS *and* CHARLOTTE *break the kiss.* CARL-MAGNUS *exits.* CHARLOTTE *runs up to the house)*

MRS. ANDERSSEN.
    Aaaah,

(When CHARLOTTE *closes the house doors)*
    Well . . .

DESIREE. Fredrik? Fredrik!

FREDRIK *(Stirs, opens his eyes, looks dazedly around).* I don't suppose this is my heavenly reward, is it?

DESIREE. Hardly, dear, with *me* here.

FREDRIK *(Trying to sit up, failing, remembering).* Extraordinary, isn't it? To hold a muzzle to one's temple—and yet to miss! A shaky hand, perhaps, is an asset after all.

DESIREE. Does it hurt?

FREDRIK. It hurts—spiritually. You've heard, I imagine, about the evening's other event?

DESIREE. No, what?

FREDRIK. Henrik and Anne—ran off together.

DESIREE. Fredrik!

FREDRIK. Well, I think I should get up and confront the world, don't you?

DESIREE *(Sings).*
    Isn't it rich?

FREDRIK *(Sings).*
    Are we a pair?
    You here at last on the ground.

DESIREE.
    You in mid-air.
        (Speaks)
    Knees wobbly?

FREDRIK. No, no, it seems not. In fact, it's hardly possible, but . . .

DESIREE *(Sings).*
    Was that a farce?

FREDRIK *(Sings).*
    My fault, I fear.

DESIREE.
    Me as a merry-go-round

FREDRIK.
    Me as King Lear.
        (Speaks)
How unlikely life is! To lose one's son, one's wife, and practically one's life within an hour and yet to feel—relieved. Relieved, and, what's more, considerably less ancient.

(He jumps up on the bench)
Aha! Desiree!

DESIREE. Poor Fredrik!

FREDRIK. No, no, no. We will banish "poor" from our vocabulary and replace it with "coherent."

DESIREE *(Blank).* Coherent?

FREDRIK. Don't you remember your manifesto in the bedroom? A coherent existence after so many years of muddle? You and me, and of course, Fredrika?

(They kiss. The music swells)

FREDRIK *(Sings).*
    Make way for the clowns.

DESIREE *(Sings).*
    Applause for the clowns.

BOTH.
    They're finally here.

(The music continues)

FREDRIK *(Speaks).* How does Malmo appeal to you? It'll be high sunburn season.

DESIREE. Why not?

FREDRIK. Why not?

DESIREE. Oh God!

FREDRIK. What is it?

DESIREE. I've got to do Hedda for a week in Halsingborg.

FREDRIK. Well, what's wrong with Purgatory before Paradise? I shall sit through all eight performances.

(They go slowly upstage.

FREDRIKA *wakes up)*

FREDRIKA. Don't you think you should go to bed, Grandmother?

MADAME ARMFELDT. No, I shall stay awake all night for fear of missing the first cock-crow of morning. It has come to be my only dependable friend.

FREDRIKA. Grandmother—

MADAME ARMFELDT. What, dear?

FREDRIKA. I've watched and watched, but I haven't noticed the night smiling.

MADAME ARMFELDT. Young eyes are not ideal for watching. They stray too much. It has already smiled. Twice.

FREDRIKA. It has? Twice? For the young— and the fools?

MADAME ARMFELDT. The smile for the fools was particularly broad tonight.

FREDRIKA. So there's only the last to come.

MADAME ARMFELDT. Only the last.

(MADAME ARMFELDT dies.

We become more aware of the underscoring, the same used under the opening waltz.

HENRIK *and* ANNE *suddenly waltz on, and then all of the* OTHER COUPLES, *at last with their proper partners, waltz through the scene.*

The screens close, and MR. LINDQUIST *appears at the piano. He hits one key of the piano, just as he did at the opening.*

And the play is over)

The River Niger

Joseph A. Walker

THIS PLAY IS DEDICATED TO MY MOTHER AND FATHER AND TO HIGHLY UNDERRATED BLACK DADDIES EVERYWHERE.

First presented by the Negro Ensemble Company, Inc., New York City, December 5, 1972. It opened at the Brooks Atkinson Theatre in New York City on April 3, 1973, with the following cast:

(in order of appearance)

JOHN WILLIAMS	Douglas Turner Ward
MATTIE WILLIAMS	Roxie Roker
GRANDMA WILHEMINA BROWN	Frances Foster
DR. DUDLEY STANTON	Graham Brown
JEFF WILLIAMS	Les Roberts
ANN VANDERGUILD	Grenna Whitaker
MO	Neville Richen
GAIL	Saundra McClain
CHIPS	Lennal Wainwright
AL	Dean Irby
SKEETER	Charles Weldon

Directed by Douglas Turner Ward
Scenery by Gary James Wheeler
Costumes by Edna Watson
Lighting by Shirley Prendergast

The River Niger is a powerful play about love, sacrifice, family bonds, race hatred, physical death and the death of innocence. It centers around the inner life of the Williams family and the struggle of Jeff Williams, a young black air force dropout, to become a man. Although the story focuses on Jeff Williams, the real hero of the play is his father, Johnny, whose goal is to find poetry and meaning in his life and who, at a moment's notice, is willing to sacrifice himself for this ideal and to protect his son. Joseph Walker, the play's talented author, writes in a realistic and naturalistic style, which he feels best suits his situation and characters. Walker's family was very much like the Williams family, and most of the material in the play is derived from autobiographical sources.

Walker grew up in a Washington D.C. ghetto in a close-knit family. His father, like Johnny Williams, was a philosopher and a scholar who painted houses for a living, as well as an alcoholic who died at the age of fifty-eight. Walker feels that his father was the single most important influence in his life. Mr. Walker wanted to be a physicist and knew a great deal about mathematics. He introduced his son to philosophy at an age when most of his friends were still reading comic books. He also taught his son a sense of pride, both in himself and as a black man. His parents, according to the author, had an unusual love relationship, supportive yet at times antagonistic, which is touched on in the play through the relationship between Johnny and Mattie.

Walker's mother was a schoolteacher and also worked as a statistical clerk for the government. She was cultivated and soft-spoken. She would read Homer and Shakespeare to him as bedtime stories and stressed the power of knowledge much as Jeff Williams does when he tries to explain to his friends why he prefers to fight injustice in his own way.

Joseph Walker was born on February 24, 1935, in Washington, D.C., and, like Jeff Williams, was an only son. He attended Howard University, where he received his bachelor of arts degree in philosophy. He enlisted in the air force and rose to the rank of second lieutenant. He quit navigator's school two weeks before graduation at Harlenton Air Force Base, as did Jeff Williams. Jeff's monologue to his father in Act Three, an attempt to explain why he left the air force, is taken directly from Walker's own experience. Like Jeff, Walker wrote a poem instead of taking his final exam in navigation, and this gave him the realization that he wanted to write. Writing poetry led to writing plays, which led to a career in acting, directing, stage design and choreography.

He has written many plays in both a naturalistic and an abstract style (an example of the latter is *Yin-Yang*). He writes in many genres and his other dramatic efforts include *The Hiss, Old Judge Moses Is Dead, Themes of Black Experience* and *The Harranges*. Walker's musicals include *Ododo, The Lion Is a Soul Brother* and *The Believers,* which he wrote in collaboration with Josephine Jackson. *Out of the Ashes* and *Yin-Yang* are his two ensemble pieces.

Walker received a master of fine arts in drama from Catholic University and a doctorate in film from New York University. In 1970, he was a playwright in residence at the Yale University School of Drama and has taught speech and drama at City College of New York. He narrated *In Black America* for CBS and acted in an Emmy-nominated episode of ''NYPD,'' ''Deadly Circle of Violence.'' He also appeared in the movie *April Fools* and in Woody Allen's *Bananas.* He replaced Moses Gunn in *Cities of Besiques* at the Public Theatre. While at Howard University, he played Luke in the first production of James Baldwin's *The Amen Corner,* and at Catholic University he played the lead roles in *Prometheus Bound, Requiem for a Heavyweight* and *No Exit.* Walker has also appeared at the Olney Theatre and the Arena Stage in Washington, D.C., and in the television movie *A Man Called Adam.*

Joseph Walker is the cofounder of Demi-Gods, a black dance/music/theatre repertory company that was an outgrowth of his theatre classes at City College of New York. He and his wife, Dorothy Dinrue Walker, train the company. In 1972–1973, he received the Drama Desk Award, the Elizabeth Hull/Kate Warriner Award from the Dramatists Guild, the Village Voice Off Broadway Award, the 1973 Audelco Award, the 1973 Tony Award for Best Play and a Guggenheim fellowship for creative writing. *The River Niger* was first produced by the Negro Ensemble Company Off Broadway, where it received the 1972–1973 Obie Award. The play moved to Broadway on April 3, 1973, to the Brooks Atkinson Theatre.

Time: February 1, the Present: 4:30 p.m.
Place: New York City—Harlem.

Setting: *Brownstone on 133rd between Lenox and Seventh. Living room and kitchen cross section. Living room a subdued green. Modest living-room suite consisting of coffee table, two easy chairs, and a sofa. The chairs and sofa are covered with transparent plastic slip-covers. There is a television set with its back to the audience.*

The kitchen is almost as large as the living room. There are a large kitchen table and four chairs. Stage right is an entrance from the back porch to the kitchen. Stage left is an entrance that leads from a small vestibule to a hallway—to the living room. In the hallway is a stairway that leads upstairs.

The house is not luxuriously decorated, of course, but it is not garish either. The "attempt" is to be cozy. Even though the place is very clean, there are many magazines and old newspapers around—giving the general appearance of casual "clutter."

(At rise, a bass counterpoint creeps in, and GRANDMA WILHEMINA BROWN, *a stately, fair-skinned black woman in her middle eighties is in the kitchen. She is humming "Rock of Ages" and pouring herself an oversized cup of coffee. She drops in two teaspoons of sugar and a fraction of cream, which she returns to the refrigerator. For a moment she stops humming and looks around stealthily. She goes to the kitchen window and peeps out into the back-yard. Satisfied that she is alone, she opens the cabinet under the sink. With one final furtive glance around, she reaches under the cabinet and feels about till she finds what she's been looking for—a bottle of Old Grand-dad. Apparently, she unhooks it from under the top of the cabinet, glances around once more, then pours an extremely generous portion into her coffee. There is a sound from the backyard— as if someone or something has brushed by a trash can. She freezes for a second. With un-believable speed she "hooks" the bottle back into her secret hiding place, snatches her cof-fee, and hurries out of the kitchen.* GRANDMA *pauses on the stairs. In the next moment we hear a key in the back door.* GRANDMA *hurries out of view. The back door opens cautiously. It is* JOHN WILLIAMS, *a thin, medium-sized brown man in his middle fifties. His hair is gray at the temples and slicked down. He has a salt-and-pepper mustache. He wears a brown topcoat, combat boots, corduroy pants—on his head a heavily crusted painter's cap. He is obviously intoxicated but very much in control.*

From his topcoat pocket he removes a bottle of Johnnie Walker Red Label, which he opens, and takes a long swallow, grimacing as he does so. He then stuffs the bottle into his "hiding place," behind the refrigerator. He pushes the refrigerator back in place and removes his topcoat. Pulling out his wallet, he begins counting its contents. Extremely dissatisfied with the count, he sits heavily and ponders his plight. A second later he takes out a piece of paper.

———

JOHN

(Reading aloud to himself as bass line comes back in).

I am the River Niger—hear my waters.
I wriggle and stream and run.
I am totally flexible—
Damn!

(He crumples the paper and stuffs it into his pants pocket. In the very next instant, he re-members something—goes out the back door and returns with a small cedar jewelry box which he places on the table with great pride. There is a rapping at the back door. Bass fades out. JOHN *is startled. He begins sneaking out of the room when he hears . . .)*

VOICE

(Softly but intensely).

Johnny Williams! Open the damn door.

(Raps again.)

It's me, Dudley. Open up!

*(*JOHN *goes to the door.)*

It's Dudley Stanton, fool.

*(*JOHN *opens the door.* DUDLEY STANTON, *a thin, wiry, very dark black man—in his late fifties—graying. He is impeccably but conser-vatively dressed. The two men stare at each other. Much love flows between them.)*

JOHN.

Well, I'll be a son-of-a-bitch.

DUDLEY

(In a thick and beautiful Jamaican accent).

Yeah, man, that's what you are, a son-of-a-bitch. Now, will a son-of-a-bitch let a son-of-a-whore in? It's very cold out here, man! Did I ever tell you my ma was a whore?

JOHN.

Only a thousand times. Come on in, ya mon-key chaser.

DUDLEY

(Coming in).

Now, you know I can't stand that expression. Why do you want to burden our friendship with that expression?

JOHN.

Where in the hell you been?

DUDLEY.

Can I take off my coat first?

JOHN.

Take off your jockstrap for all I care. Where in the hell you been?

DUDLEY.

To Mexico on vacation—fishing, man. And oh, what fishing. Man, I tell you.

JOHN.

Did it ever occur to you that your old buddy might like go fishing too? Did that ever cross your mind?

DUDLEY.

You ain't never got no vacation time coming. You use it up faster than you earn it.

JOHN.

Well, at least you could have let a buddy know you were going.

(Sees the bottle under DUDLEY'*s arm.)*

Give me a drink?

DUDLEY. Sure thing.

(Hands JOHN *the bottle.)*

JOHN.

Vodka! I be damned! You know I can't stand vodka.

DUDLEY.

You don't want my vodka, go on behind the refrig and get your Scotch. I saw you hide it there.

JOHN.

You been spying on me with that damn telescope again.

DUDLEY.

Yeah. I saw you coming in. Closed my office.

JOHN.

You old monkey chaser.

DUDLEY.

One day, I'm going to brain you for that expression.

JOHN.

Goddamn black Jew doctor. You make all the money in the world and you can't even buy your poor buddy a bottle of Scotch.

DUDLEY.

Hell, I shouldn't even drink with you.

(Pause.)

If you don't stop boozing the way you do, you'll be dead in five years. You're killing yourself bit by bit, Johnny.

JOHN.

Well, that's a helluva sight better than doing it all at once. Besides, I can stop any time I want to.

DUDLEY.

Then why don't you?

JOHN.

I don't want to.

(Changing the subject purposely.)

Dudley, my son's due home tomorrow.

DUDLEY.

Jeff coming home? No lie! That's wonderful! Old Jeff. Let's take a run up to the Big Apple and celebrate!

JOHN.

That's where I'm coming from. I left work early today—I got so damned worked up, you know. I mean, all I could see was my boy—big-time first lieutenant in the United States of America Air Force—Strategic Air Command—navigator—walking through the front door with them bars—them shining silver bars on his goddamn shoulders.

(He begins saluting an imaginary Jeff.)

Yes, sir. Whatever you say, sir. Right away, Lieutenant Williams. Lieutenant Jeff Williams.

DUDLEY.

Johnny Williams, you are the biggest fool in God's creation. How in the name of your grandma's twat could you get so worked up over the white man's air force? I've always said, "That's what's wrong with these American niggers. They believe anything that has a little tinsel sprinkled on it." "Shining silver bars." Fantasy, man!

JOHN.

He's my son, Dudley, and I'm proud of him.

DUDLEY.

You're supposed to be, but because he managed to survive this syphilitic asshole called Harlem, not because he's a powerless nub in a silly military grist mill. What you use for brains, man?

JOHN.

I'm a fighter, Dudley. I don't like white folks either, but I sure do love their war machines. I'm a fighter who ain't got no battlefield. I woke up one day, looked around, and said to myself, "There's a war going on, but where's the battlefield?" I'm gonna find it one day—you watch.

DUDLEY.

In other words, you'd gladly give your life for your poor downtrodden black brothers and sisters if you only knew where to give it?

JOHN.

Right! For my people!

DUDLEY.

I wonder how many niggers have said those words: "For my people!"

JOHN.

Give me the right time and I'd throw this rubbish on the rubbish heap in a minute.

DUDLEY.

Cop-out! That's all that is!

JOHN.

Ya goddamn monkey chaser—you're the cop-out!

DUDLEY.

Cop-out! The battlefield's everywhere. That's what's wrong with niggers in America—everybody's waiting for *the* time. I don't delude myself, nigger. I know that there's no heroism in death—just death, dirty nasty death.

(Pours another drink.)

The rest is jive, man! Black people are jive. The most unrealistic, unphilosophical people in the world.

JOHN.

Philosophy be damned. Give me a program—a program!

DUDLEY.

A program!?! We're just fools, Johnny, white and black retarded children, playing with matches. We don't have the slightest idea what we're doing. Do you know, I no longer believe in medicine. Of all man's presumptions medicine is the most arrogantly presumptuous. People are supposed to die! It's natural to die. If I find that a patient has a serious disease, I send him to one of my idealistic colleagues. I ain't saving no lives, man. I treat the hypochondriacs. I treat colds, hemorrhoids, sore throats. I distribute sugar pills and run my fingers up the itching vaginas of sex-starved old bitches. Women who're all dried up, past menopause—but groping for life. They pretend to be unmoved, but I feel their wrigglings on my fingers. I see 'em swoon with ecstasy the deeper I probe. Liars—every one of them who would never admit their lives are up—what they really want is a good dose of M and M.

JOHN.

M and M?

DUDLEY.

Male meat! Old biddies clinging to life like tenants in condemned houses, and medicine keeps on finding cures. Ridiculous! Nature has a course. Let her take it!

JOHN.

But what I do is part of nature's course, ya idiot!

DUDLEY.

Go on, Johnny, be a hero and a black leader, and die with a Molotov cocktail in your hand, screaming, "Power to the People." The only value your death will have is to dent the population explosion. You can't change your shitting habits, let alone the world.

JOHN.

You know what your trouble is, Dudley? You're just floating, man, floating downwind like a silly daisy.

DUDLEY.

Come on! What the hell are you rooted to?

JOHN.

To the battlefield. To my people, man!

DUDLEY.

You ain't got no people, nigger. Just a bunch of black crabs in a barrel, lying to each other, always lying and pulling each other back down.

JOHN.

Who do you suppose made us that way?

DUDLEY.

You want me to say *whitey,* don't you?

JOHN.

Who else?

DUDLEY.

You goddamn idealists kill me. You really do, you know. No matter what the *cause* is, the fact remains that we *are* crabs in a barrel. Now deal with that, nigger!

JOHN.

Aw, go screw yourself.

DUDLEY.

There you go. Hate the truth, don't you? The truth is, you're a dying wino nigger who's trying to find some reason for living. And now you're going to put that burden on your son. Poor Jeff! Doesn't know what he's in for.

JOHN

(Pause).

The fact remains, monkey-chasing son-of-a-bitch, the fact remains that I got a son coming home from the air force tomorrow and you ain't got nobody—

(A loving afterthought.)

but me—

DUDLEY.

You are a big fool! Jessie wanted children. Every time she missed her period, I'd give her something to start it over again. Poor lovable bitch, till the day she died she never knew. But I knew—I knew it was a heinous crime to bring any more children into this pile of horse shit.

JOHN.

You're sick, you know that, monkey chaser—sick. To satisfy your own perverted outlook, you'd destroy your wife's right to motherhood. Sick!

DUDLEY.

. . . The day Jessie died she made me promise I'd marry again and have children, and I lied to her—told her I would—Didn't make her dying any easier, though. She still died twitching and convulsing, saliva running from the corners of her mouth—death phlegm rattling in her throat. She still died gruesomely. That's the way it is. That's life! I'm the last of my line—thank God. No more suffering for the Stantons. Thank God—that cruel son-of-a-bitch.

JOHN.

You depress the shit out of me, you know that, monkey chaser—but you can still be my friend, even if you're just a chickenhearted rabbit, afraid to make a motion.

DUDLEY

(Genuinely angry).

Look, nigger—any motion you make is on a treadmill.

JOHN.

Aw, drink ya drink. What's the matter with you? It don't take no genius to figure out that none of this shit's gonna matter a hundred years from now—that the whole thing's a game of musical chairs—so what? What's your favorite word—presumptuous? Well, man, it is presumptuous as hell of you to even think you can figure this shit out.

DUDLEY.

Ain't that what we're here for, stupid? What we've got brains for? To figure it out?

JOHN.

Hell no! To play a better game, fool. Just play the motherfucker, that's all. And right now the game is Free My People. Ya get that! And if you don't play it, nigger, you know what you're gonna become—what you *are*—you know what you are, Dr. Dudley Stanton? You're a goddamn spiritual vegetable. Thinking's for idiots—wise men act; thinking is all dribble anyhow, and idiots can do a helluva damn better job at it than you can. My advice to you, Mr. Monkey Chaser, is fart, piss, screw, eat, fight, run, beat your meat, sympathize, and criticize, but for God's sake, stop thinking. It's the white folks' sickness.

DUDLEY.

I'm talking to a bloody amoeba.

JOHN.

Amoebas are the foundation, man, and they ain't got no blood. Now loan me one hundred and ninety dollars.

DUDLEY.

What?

JOHN.

A hundred and ninety dollars—shit. Don't I speak clearly? I had two years of college, you know.

DUDLEY.

You drank all your money away?

JOHN.

Hell yes.

DUDLEY.

At the Apple?

JOHN.

Right!

DUDLEY.

Setting up everybody and his ma?

JOHN.

Uh huh!

DUDLEY.

Bragging like a nigger about how your first lieutenant, Air Force, Strategic Air Command son is due home tomorrow?

JOHN.

Right!

DUDLEY.

And they all smiled, patted you on your back, and ordered two more rounds of three-for-one bar slop?

JOHN.

Right, nigger. Now, do I get the bread or not—Shit, I ain't required to give you my life story for a measly handout—

DUDLEY.

Of a hundred and ninety dollars—

JOHN.

Shit! Right!

DUDLEY.

You already owe me three hundred and forty.

JOHN.

That much?

DUDLEY

(Takes out a small notebook)

See for yourself—

JOHN.

Well, a hundred and ninety more won't break you. Do I get it or not?

(There is a knock on the front door.)

Come on, man, that's Mattie.

DUDLEY.

Well, well, well, look at the great warrior now—about to get his ass kicked!

JOHN.

Come on! Yes or no?

DUDLEY.

But here's your battlefield, man. Start fighting! I tell you one thing though, I'm putting my money on Mattie, man.

(Again there is a knock on the front door.)

JOHN.

See ya later.

(Starts for the back door.)

DUDLEY.

Wait a minute! If it were Mattie, she'd use her key, right?

JOHN
(Comes back).
Hey, yeah, that's right. Didn't think of that!

DUDLEY.
You don't believe in thinking.

(JOHN goes to door and sneaks a look through the pane.)

JOHN
(Comes back).
Hey, it's a young chick. Good legs—like she might have a halfway decent turd cutter on her.

DUDLEY.
Let her in, man, let her in!

JOHN.
Look—am I going to get the money?

DUDLEY
(Interrupting him).
We'll talk about it. I ain't saying yes and I ain't saying no.

JOHN.
Sadistic bastard!

(A more insistent knock.)

DUDLEY.
Open the goddamn door, nigger!

(JOHN opens the door. ANN VANDER-GUILD—a very attractive black woman in her early twenties—enters. She sparkles on top of a deep brooding inner core. A bass line of beautiful melancholy comes in.)

JOHN.
Yes, ma'am.

ANN.
I'm Ann—

JOHN.
Uh huh.

ANN.
I'm a friend of Jeff Williams's. This, uh, is his, where he lives, isn't it?

JOHN.
When he's home, yes. He won't be here until noon tomorrow.

ANN.
Yes, I know—may I come in?

JOHN.
Oh, I'm sorry. Come in.

ANN.
Would you help me with my suitcases? They're in the cab.

JOHN.
Suitcases!

ANN.
Yes, I'd like to spend the night—if I may.

JOHN.
Spend the night—

DUDLEY
(Coming in from the kitchen).
Go get the young lady's suitcases, man. And close the damn door. It's colder than a virgin's—

(Catches himself.)

JOHN.
Suitcases!

(JOHN exits. DUDLEY and ANN size each other up.)

DUDLEY.
Come on in. Let me have your coat.

ANN.
Thank you.

DUDLEY.
So you're Jeff's intended?

ANN.
Well, not exactly, sir. We're very good friends, though.

DUDLEY.
But you intend to make yourself Jeff's intended. Am I right?

(ANN smiles.)

What a nice smile! Then I am right. Have a seat—

(JOHN staggers into the room with an armful of suitcases, plops them down, stares at ANN for a second. Bass fades.)

JOHN.
There's more.

(Exits.)

DUDLEY.
Planning a long stay?

ANN.
I'll go to a hotel tomorrow.

DUDLEY.
I wasn't saying that for that. I'm merely intrigued with your determination. Young women—strong-willed young women—always fascinate me.

(JOHN enters with a small trunk on his back which he unloads heavily.)

JOHN.
That'll be three dollars and fifty cents, young lady.

DUDLEY.
I've got it, Miss— What's your last name?

ANN.
Vanderguild.

DUDLEY.
Miss Vanderguild.

ANN.
I wouldn't think of it.

DUDLEY
(Hurriedly pays JOHN, who is somewhat bewildered).
I told you about my weakness for strong women. My mother was strong. Lord, how strong. Could work all day and half the night.

JOHN.

Flat on her back! Anybody can do that.

DUDLEY.

Only a strong woman, man. Besides, who says she was always on her back. I'm certain she was versatile. Sorry, dear. We're two very dirty old men. Stick out your tongue!

ANN.

What is this—

DUDLEY

(Grabs her wrist, examining her pulse).

Stick out your tongue, young lady!

(She obeys like a child.)

Had a rather severe cold recently, girl?

ANN.

Why yes, but . . .

DUDLEY.

You're all right now. Can tell a lot from tongues.

JOHN.

There you go, getting vulgar again. You can take a man out, of his mother, but you can't take the mother out of the man.

DUDLEY.

That's just his way of getting back at me. Actually, I loved my mother very much. She worked my way through college and medical school, though I didn't find out how until the day I graduated.

JOHN.

Stop putting your business in the street!

DUDLEY.

I'm not. It's all in the family. Miss Ann Vanderguild here's a part of the family, or almost. Ann, here, is your prospective daughter-in-law, and she'll make a good one too, Johnny. I stamp her certified.

JOHN

(To ANN).

Jeff never wrote us about you.

ANN.

Well, he doesn't exactly know I'm here, sir. I mean we never discussed it or anything.

JOHN.

Where you from, little lady?

ANN.

Canada, sir—I mean, originally I'm from South Africa, sir.

JOHN.

This gentleman here is Dudley Stanton. Dr. Dudley Stanton.

ANN

(To DUDLEY).

My EKG is excellent too, sir.

DUDLEY.

Excellent?

ANN.

I mean it's within normal limits, sir. I guess my pulse is very slow, because I used to run track—the fifty-yard dash. I'm a nurse. Perhaps you can help me find a job, sir?

DUDLEY.

Oh, these strong black women!

ANN.

I'm only strong if my man needs me to be, sir.

JOHN

(Genuinely elated).

You hear that, Dudley, a warrior's woman! A fighter—

DUDLEY.

Women always were the real fighters, man, don't you know that? Men are the artists, philosophers—creating systems, worlds. Silly dreams and fictions!

JOHN.

Fiction is more real, stupid.

DUDLEY.

You see, young lady, your prospective father-in-law here is a philosopher-poet!

JOHN.

A poet!

DUDLEY.

Philosopher-poet!

JOHN.

I'm a poet! A house painter and a poet!

DUDLEY.

Then read us one of your masterpieces.

JOHN.

Do I have to, Dudley?

DUDLEY.

A hundred and ninety bucks' worth—hell yes! You don't think I come over here to hear your bull, do you? Your poems, man, by far the better part of you—now read us one—then give it to me.

(To ANN)

You see, I'm collecting them for him, since he doesn't have enough sense to do it for himself—One day I'm gonna publish them—

JOHN.

Probably under your own name, you goddamn Jew.

DUDLEY.

Read us your poem!

JOHN

(Fumbles through his pants pockets and comes up with several scraps of paper, which he examines for selection. He smooths out one piece of paper and begins reading).

I am the River Niger—hear my waters—

No, that one ain't right yet.

ANN.

Please go on!

JOHN.

No, it ain't complete yet. Let's see, yeah, this one's finished.

(Begins reading from another scrap of paper as lights fade to a soft amber. A bass jazz theme creeps in. JOHN is spotlighted.)
"Lord, I don't feel noways tired."
And my soul seeks not to be flabby.
Peace is a muscleless word,
A vacuum, a hole in space,
An assless anesthesia,
A shadowy phantom,
Never settling anyway—Even in sleep.
In my dreams I struggle; slash and crash and cry,
"Damn you, you wilderness! I will cut my way through!"
And the wilderness shouts back!
"Go around me!"
And I answer,
"Hell, no! The joke's on both of us
And I will have the last laugh."
The wilderness sighs and grows stronger
As I too round out my biceps in this ageless, endless duel.
Hallelujah! Hallelujah! Hallelujah!
I want a muscle-bound spirit,
I say, I want a muscle-bound soul—'cause,
Lord, I don't feel noways tired.
I feel like dancing through the valley of the shadow of death!
Lord, I don't feel noways tired.

ANN.

Beautiful!

(Bass fades.)

DUDLEY

(Takes sheet of paper).

This is a blank sheet of paper!

JOHN.

I made it up as I went along. Hell, I'll write it down for you.

(Holds out his hand insistently for the money. DUDLEY counts it out. The doorbell rings suddenly and MATTIE's voice is heard—"Mama— John." JOHN takes the money eagerly, stuffs it in his pocket, then starts for the door. En route he stops suddenly, looks at ANN as if in a dilemma, thinks quickly, then crosses to ANN and whispers urgently.)

Look, Ann, if my wife thinks for one minute that you're trying to get Jeff hooked, she and her crazy mama'll reduce the whole thing to ashes. Tell 'em you're just passing through— you and Jeff were friends up there in Canada— just friends, see—

DUDLEY.

Gradually—you've got to ease in gradually. They think Jeff fell off a Christmas tree or something. No one's good enough for Jeff— Not even Jeff.

JOHN.

Act like a good-natured sleep-in—

ANN.

Sleep-in?

DUDLEY.

A maid!

MATTIE.

Will someone please open the door! I can't get to my key.

GRANDMA

(At the top of the stairs; she is slightly intoxicated).

I'm coming, daughter. I'm coming—

(Starts humming "Rock of Ages" as she descends the stairs.)

JOHN

(To ANN).

Now remember.

(Opens door.)

Hello, Mattie!

MATTIE.

The groceries—help me with the groceries.

ANN.

Let me give you a hand, Mrs. Williams.

(DUDLEY gestures to ANN approvingly. MATTIE takes off her coat, kicks off her shoes, and settles in an easy chair while ANN and JOHN take the groceries to the kitchen.)

MATTIE.

Who's that young lady?

DUDLEY.

A friend of the family.

GRANDMA.

How you feeling, daughter? Look a bit peaked to me.

MATTIE.

Not too well, Mama; almost fainted on the subway. Was all I could do to get the groceries.

JOHN

(Coming back).

Just need a little soda and water, that's all.

MATTIE.

That's what you always say. Something is wrong with me, John. I don't know what, but something's wrong.

DUDLEY.

Tomorrow's Saturday. Why don't you come into my office around eleven, let me take a look at you?

MATTIE.

No thanks, Dudley. You always manage to scare a person half to death. Have you ever heard of a doctor who ain't got no bedside manner at all, Mama?

(Laughs.)

DUDLEY.

Well, what do you want—the truth or somebody to hold your hand?

GRANDMA.

Both, fool.

MATTIE.

Mama!

GRANDMA.

Well, he is a fool.

DUDLEY.

Well, I guess that's my cue to go home!

JOHN.

I'll be damned! Mrs. Wilhemina Brown is going to apologize—

GRANDMA.

Over my dead husband's grave—

MATTIE.

Mama. You must not feel well yourself.

GRANDMA.

I don't, child, I don't. Planned to have your dinner ready, but I been feeling kinda poorly here lately.

JOHN.

That's what she always says.

MATTIE.

Come to think of it, Mama, your eyes—

GRANDMA

(Defensively).

What about my eyes?

MATTIE.

Well, they look kinda glassy—

JOHN

(Knowingly).

I wonder why?

GRANDMA

(On her feet).

And what in the Lord's name is that supposed to mean?

MATTIE

(Raising her voice).

Will you stop it—all of you.

GRANDMA.

(To MATTIE).

Are you talking to me? You screaming at your mama?

MATTIE.

At everybody, Mama.

GRANDMA.

My own daughter, my own flesh and blood, taking a no-good drunk's part against her own mother.

MATTIE.

I'm not taking anybody's part. I just want some peace and quiet when I come home. Now I

think you owe Dr. Stanton an apology.

GRANDMA.

I'll do no such thing.

(Starts humming "Rock of Ages.")

MATTIE.

I apologize for my mother, Dudley.

DUDLEY.

That's okay, Mattie, I wasn't going anywhere anyway.

GRANDMA.

I got two more daughters and two manly sons. They'd just love to have me. Maybe I should go live with Flora.

JOHN.

Good idea! Plenty of opportunity to get glassy-eyed over at Flora's. Yes, indeed.

MATTIE.

John, what are you agitating her for?

DUDLEY.

. . . Are you afraid, Mattie? To have a checkup, I mean?

MATTIE

(Pause).

Stay for dinner, Dudley.

DUDLEY.

Thanks, I will.

ANN

(At the door).

Would you like for me to fix dinner, Mrs. Williams?

(Pause.)

MATTIE.

Who is this child?

JOHN.

Ann Vanderguild. She's from South Africa. She's a friend of Jeff's—just passing through. I asked her to spend the night.

GRANDMA.

Where's she going to spend it—the bathroom?

MATTIE.

Mama, what's wrong with you tonight?

JOHN.

She had a little too much, that's all.

MATTIE

(To ANN).

You're welcome, dear. You can stay in Jeff's room tonight. I got it all cleaned up for him. He'll be here tomorrow, you know? Thank the Lord.

ANN.

Yes, ma'am! It certainly will be pleasant to see him again.

(MATTIE *looks at* ANN *curiously.*)

I make a very good meat loaf, ma'am. I noticed you've got all the ingredients as I was putting the food away.

MATTIE.

You put the food away?

ANN.

You seem so bushed.

MATTIE.

What a nice thing for you to do. And you read my mind too. Meat loaf is exactly what I was planning to fix. Yes, indeed. Such a pretty girl too.

JOHN

(To DUDLEY*).*

Why don't we make a little run and leave these black beauties to themselves. To get acquainted—

GRANDMA.

Don't be calling me no black nothing. I ain't black! I'm half-full-blooded Cherokee Indian myself. Black folks is "hewers of wood and drawers of water" for their masters. Says so in the Scriptures. I ain't no hewer of no wood myself. I'm a Cherokee aristocrat myself.

JOHN.

Go on, Grandma, show us your true Cherokee colors, yes, indeed.

GRANDMA

(She is obviously inebriated—sings at the top of her voice).

Onward, Christian soldiers,

Marching on to war,

With the cross of Jesus

Going on before!

(Begins shouting as if in church.)

I'm a soldier myself. I ain't no nigger. A soldier of the Lord. I ain't no common nigger. So don't you be calling me no black nothing. Bless my Jesus. Don't know what these young folks is coming to, calling everybody black! *I'm going home to see my Jesus.*

This little light of mine,

Let it shine, let it shine, oh, let it shine. Do Jesus!

(Shouting gestures.)

DUDLEY.

What I tell you,, Johnny. Crabs in a barrel, waiting for a hand from Canaan land to lift 'em out. Each one shoving and pushing, trying to be first to go. And if Jesus was to put his hand down there, they'd probably think it belonged to just another nigger crab and pinch it off.

JOHN.

Ain't that poetic. I can just read the headlines: "Jesus extends his hand to bless his chosen"— 'cause we are the chosen, Dudley—"and a hustling dope addict takes out his blade and cuts it off at the wrist."

DUDLEY.

For the ring on his little finger. Rub-a-dub-dub, niggers in a tub. Christ extends a helping hand and (JOHN *joins in and they deliver the end of the line in unison*) draws back a nub.

MATTIE.

Will you two please stop it!

(GRANDMA's *still singing.*)

Mama, why don't you go upstairs and take a rest. Ya'll 'bout to drive me crazy.

GRANDMA.

My own daughter treats me like a child. Sending me upstairs. Punishing me 'cause I got the spirit.

(Starting for the stair. Starts singing once again, but in a more subdued and soulful manner.)

I know his blood will make me whole.

I know his blood will make me whole.

If I just touch the hem of his garment

I know his blood will make me whole.

(JOHNNY *tries to help her up the stairs.*)

Don't need no help from nobody but Jesus.

(Starts up steps.)

I got Minerva and Flora, and Jacob and Jordan—fine children. Any one of 'em be tickled pink to have me—tickled pink! I don't have to stay here.

MATTIE.

Mama, go lie down for a while.

GRANDMA.

And ain't none of 'em black either. Christian soldiers every last one of 'em. Mattie's the only black child I ever spawned—my first and last, thank Jesus.

(GRANDMA *starts up the steps—on the verge of tears.*)

I don't have to stay here—

(Sings.)

I ain't got long,

I ain't got long

To stay here.

Ben Brown was black though. Looked like an eclipse—sho' nuff. Lord, my God, hallelujah and do Jesus—he was the ace of spades. And a man, afore God, he was a man—you hear me, Johnny Williams? My man was a man.

(Exits, humming "Steal Away.")

MATTIE

(To ANN*).*

She gets like that every now and then.

JOHN.

More like every other night.

MATTIE.

We have a guest, John.

JOHN.

Come on, Dudley, let's make that run!

MATTIE.

Hold on, Johnny Williams. Where is it?

JOHN.

Where's what?

MATTIE.

Don't play games, John. This is rent week—remember. Now give it to me.

DUDLEY.

All right, great African warrior, do your stuff.

JOHN.

Mind your business—

MATTIE.

John, I don't feel well. Now, do we have to play your games tonight—Now give it to me.

(JOHN *counts out the money and gives it to her. She counts it rapidly.*)

It's ten dollars short, John.

JOHN.

Come on, Mattie. I got to have train fare and cigarettes for the next two weeks.

MATTIE.

Stop playing, Johnny. You know if I don't keep it for you, you'll drink it up all at once. Come on, now.

(He gives her the ten.)

JOHN.

Look, let me have five at least. There's more than enough for the rent.

(Pause.)

Good God, woman, Jeff'll be here tomorrow. Dudley and I just want to do a little celebrating. Five, woman, hell.

MATTIE.

Promise you won't be out late. We got a lot of gettin' ready to do tomorrow morning.

JOHN.

I got this chick, see, sixteen years old, and she is as warm as gingerbread in the winter time, and we gon' lay up all night—

MATTIE.

We have a young lady here, Johnny.

JOHN.

Jeff'll be here by noon. Now, let's see! My little mama just might let me out of the saddle by noon. Yes, indeed—she just might!

MATTIE.

John!

JOHN.

But if I'm not back in time, Jeff'll understand—ain't too often a man my age gets himself into some young and tender, oven-ready, sixteen-year-old stuff what can shake her some tail feathers like the leaves in March.

(She hands him the five.)

MATTIE.

Get out of here, Johnny Williams.

DUDLEY.

Whew! What a warrior—have mercy! You sure do win your battles, man!

JOHN.

Oh, shut up! Why fight when you know you're wrong. Let's go!

MATTIE.

Dudley—don't let him overdo it. Tomorrow's gonna be a long day.

(JOHN *gets their coats from the hallway.*)

DUDLEY.

I'll do my best, Mattie . . .

JOHN

(Coming back).

Don't worry—this black-ass Jew ain't gon' spend enough to even get a buzz—he'll watch over me—just like an old mongrel hound dog I used to own. Damn dog stayed sober all the time—wouldn't even drink beer. He was the squarest, most unhip dog in the world! Come on, monkey chaser, let me tell you 'bout that dog. Named him Shylock!

DUDLEY.

Niggers invented name-calling. Mouth, that's all they are, mouth. Good night, ladies. Ann, see you tomorrow.

JOHN.

Come on, sickle head. See ya, Ann!

DUDLEY.

I'm coming, O great African warrior!

(They exit.)

MATTIE.

Well, Ann, now you've met the whole family. I hope Johnny's cussing don't bother you too much.

ANN.

No, ma'am! I think he's delightful—he and Dr. Stanton. My father had a friend like him—always attacking each other something terrible.

MATTIE.

Sometimes they get to going at each other so hard you think they're gonna come to blows.

ANN.

But when they put my father in prison—

MATTIE.

In prison—for what?

ANN.

They accused him of printing these pamphlets which criticized the government—

MATTIE.

Lord, you can't criticize the government over there?

ANN.

No, ma'am. Anyway, just after my father was jailed, his friend just pined away. God—those two men loved each other.

MATTIE.

Men can really love each other, and the funny thing about it is, don't nobody really know it but them.

ANN.

Women don't seem to be able to get along with each other that way—I mean that deep-loving way. You know what I mean, Mrs. Williams?

MATTIE.

Of course I do. It's all 'cause women don't trust one another. Your father? Is he still in prison?

ANN.

Yes, ma'am. This is going on his ninth year.

MATTIE.

Nine years in prison, my God! How does your mother take it?

ANN

(Bass melancholy enters).

Quietly. Ma takes everything quietly. Dad turned himself in to protect my two brothers. They were the ones operating the press. Dad was just as surprised as the rest of us when the police found the setup in an old chest of drawers in the attic. Before anyone could say a word, Dad was confessing to everything. This dirty old sergeant got mad and hit him in the stomach with his billy club. Dad had a violent temper, but when he got back on his feet, I could see it in his eyes, the decision, I mean. He turned and said, ''Boss, if I said something offensive, please forgive an old black fool.'' And you know what that sergeant did? He hit him again. He hit him again, Mrs. Williams!

(Overcome with rekindled grief.)

MATTIE.

Oh, I'm sorry, Ann. I must write your mother.

ANN.

She'd like that.

(Pause. She collects herself.)

My brothers escaped though—stole their way across the border. At first they didn't want to go, they wanted to turn themselves in for Dad, but Ma made 'em go. They live in England now and have families of their own. It wasn't long before the authorities found out that Dad was really innocent, but just because my brothers got away and are free, and just to be plain mean, they kept him in prison anyway. Nine years—nine long years. Those bastards! I despise white people, Mrs. Williams.

MATTIE.

Let's talk about something nicer. Tell me about Jeff—

(Bass fades.)

ANN.

Yes, ma'am.

MATTIE.

And you—

ANN.

Ma'am?

MATTIE.

About Jeff and you . . . or you and Jeff.

ANN.

I was nursing in Quebec when they brought him into the hospital. He had fractured his ankle skiing. Every time it started paining him, he'd laugh—

MATTIE.

He's such a fool.

ANN.

Said his dad had taught him to do that. The second night there were some minor complications and he was in so much pain until the doctor ordered me to give him a shot of morphine. Then he got to talking. Very dreamily at first, like he was drifting in a beautiful haze. He told me all about you and Mr. Williams and Grandma Wilhemina Brown and Dr. Stanton. I almost lost my job—I kept hanging around his room so much, listening to one episode after another.

MATTIE.

And that's when you started loving him half to death.

ANN

(Pause).

Yes, ma'am.

MATTIE.

That boy sure can talk up a storm. He'll make a fine lawyer. Don't you think so?

ANN

(Pause).

I won't get in his way, Mrs. Williams.

MATTIE

(After a long pause).

No, I don't think you will.

(Pause.)

Well, let's see if we can trust each other good enough to make that meat loaf. Why don't you chop the onions while I do the celery?

(Starts to rise.)

ANN

(Stopping her).

Oh, no, ma'am, this one's on me.

MATTIE

(Laughing).

I'm very particular, you know.

ANN.

I know you are. Jeff's told me a lot about how good your cooking is.

MATTIE

(Happy to hear it).

That boy sure can eat—Lord today. Well, all

right, Ann. Let me go on up and get myself comfortable. I'll be right back.

(She sees the jewelry box on the table—opens it up—takes out a card.)

What's this?

(Reads card.)

"Big-legged woman, keep your dress tail down. Big-legged woman, keep your dress tail down, 'cause you got something under—"

ANN.

Go on, Mrs. Williams.

MATTIE.

Lord, child, that man of mine.

ANN.

Read it, please, ma'am.

MATTIE.

"Big-legged woman, keep your dress tail down, 'cause you got something under there to make a bulldog hug a hound."

(They laugh.)

Tomorrow's our anniversary, you know.

ANN.

Congratulations!

MATTIE.

He made this. Can do anything with his hands, or with his head for that matter, when he ain't all filled up on rotgut.

(Pause.)

He's killing himself drinking. I guess I'm to blame though.

ANN.

Oh, you don't mean that, Mrs. Williams.

MATTIE.

It's true.

ANN.

But he seems so full of life.

MATTIE.

Is it "life" he's full of—or something else?

(MATTIE exits up the steps. ANN busies herself about the kitchen. There is a knock on the front door.)

MATTIE'S VOICE.

Will you get that, please, Ann.

ANN.

Yes, ma'am.

(She crosses and opens the door. A tall, rangy young man in his early twenties rudely pushes his way in. He looks around boldly. He has an air of "I'm a bad nigger" about him.)

CHIPS.

Jeff here?

ANN

(Sarcastically).

Come in!

CHIPS.

I'm already in. Is Jeff home yet?

ANN.

Are you a friend of Jeff's?

CHIPS.

Could be. You a friend of Jeff's?

ANN.

Yes.

CHIPS

(Looking her over lewdly).

Not bad! As a matter of fact, you look pretty stacked up there.

ANN.

Jeff's not home.

CHIPS.

Hey, what kinda accent is that? You puttin' on airs or something—

(She opens the door.)

Yeah, yeah, I'm going. Tell him Chips came by. Big Mo wants to see him at headquarters as soon as possible. Like it's urgent, ya dig it?

ANN.

He won't be here until noon tomorrow.

CHIPS.

That's what he wrote the family. He wrote Mo—

ANN.

Who's Mo?

CHIPS

(Laughs).

Who's Mo? Mo's the leader.

ANN.

The leader of what?

CHIPS.

The leader! Wrote Mo he'd be here tonight. Tell him we'll be back around midnight.

(Leers at ANN)

Yes, sir—just like a brick shithouse.

(Slaps her on the rear. ANN instinctively picks up a heavy ashtray.)

Now, don't get rambunctious! If there's anything I can't stand it's a rambunctious black bitch.

ANN.

You get the hell out of here!

CHIPS

(Takes out a switchblade).

Now, what's that ashtray gonna do? If I wanted to, I could cut your drawers off without touching your petticoat and take what I want. Now, dig on that?

ANN.

Over my dead body.

CHIPS.

I made it with a corpse once. Knew a guy that worked in a funeral home. Pretty chick too—looked something like you. Wasn't half bad either—once I got into it.

ANN.
You damn dog—get out of here!

CHIPS
(Laughing).
Yeah, little fox. I'm going, but I'll be back tonight with Big Mo.
(Exits.)

(ANN *slams the door. She is obviously shaken.* MATTIE *comes down the steps wearing a robe and house slippers.*)

MATTIE.
Who was that, honey?
(Sees ANN'*s fear.)*
What happened?

ANN.
Some fellow to see Jeff. Called himself Chips.

MATTIE.
Chips! That bum! If he or any of them other bums show up around here again, you call somebody. They're vicious! Come on, sit down. Catch your breath.

ANN.
I'm fine.

MATTIE.
Do as I say now!
(ANN *sits.*)
. . . I wonder what they want with Jeff. Jeff used to be the gang leader around here when he was a teenager. By the time he got to college, Jeff and his friend Mo had made the gang decent—you know, doing good things to help the neighborhood. But I heard lately, the bums gone back to their old ways. I wonder what they want with Jeff now . . . Well, let's get this thing ready, and into the oven so we can eat and you can get a good night's rest. You must be exhausted. Bought a new bed for Jeff. You'll sleep like a log.

ANN.
Doesn't the couch in the living room let out into a bed, ma'am?

MATTIE.
Why, yes.

ANN.
Then I'll sleep on the couch. If it's all right with you.

MATTIE.
Jeff wouldn't mind a bit you sleeping in his new bed, child! He'll probably say something vulgar about it. Chip off the old block, you know.

ANN.
Let it be fresh for him, ma'am, let him christen it with that pretty long frame of his.

MATTIE
(Laughs).
Is he skinny, Ann?

ANN.
As a rail.

MATTIE.
You're welcome to stay as long as you want. But no tomfoolery between you two, ya understand?

ANN.
Oh, no, ma'am.

MATTIE.
And another thing. Between you and me and the lamppost, don't let on to my mother how you feel about Jeff. She don't think nobody's good enough for Jeff. Says he's the spittin' image of my father. Lord, child, she sure loved my father. I'm very lucky in a way, Ann. I come from very loving parents—in their fashion.

ANN.
Yes, ma'am, I can see that!

MATTIE.
I've often wondered why my sisters turned out to be such hogs.
(They start on food preparations as lights fade out.)

(When the lights come up once more, the house is in darkness. ANN *is asleep on the living-room couch. It is 2 a.m. There is a low rapping at the front door.* ANN *bolts upright. The knocking becomes insistent. Sleepily she answers the door.)*

ANN.
Is that you, Mr. Williams?
(No response.)
Mr. Williams?
(No answer. She opens the door. MO, *an athletic-looking young man in his mid-twenties; his girl friend,* GAIL, *sincere and very much in love with* MO; SKEETER, *who seems constantly out of it and desperate;* AL, *who appears to be intensely observant; and* CHIPS— *all force their way in.)*

CHIPS.
Ann—Big Mo. Big Mo—Ann.

MO.
Hello, Ann.

CHIPS.
Ain't she fine, Mo?

GAIL.
Why don't you hush your lips! Simpleton!

MO
(To GAIL*).*
Cool it!
(To CHIPS*)*
Get yourself together, Chips!

AL.
Yeah! Get yourself together, nigger. It's past

the witching hour.

MO

(Ferociously to everybody).

Ease off! Ease off me!

(Silent respect.)

Is Jeff home?

ANN.

No!

MO.

No! How ya mean—no?

ANN.

Just what I said—no!

CHIPS.

She's a smarty, Mo.

MO.

. . . Okay. You sound like you're for real!

CHIPS.

She is, Mo, baby—she is! Let me squeeze up on her a bit.

MO

(Intensely).

Shut the fuck up! Excuse me, Ann.

(To CHIPS*)*

And sit down somewhere.

(To SKEETER, *falling asleep in the chair)*

You fall asleep—I'm gonna crack your skull, nigger!

SKEETER.

Just meditating, chief—just meditating.

MO

(To ANN*).*

Pardon that dumb shit, baby, but, er, we gonna wait right here till your man shows—all right?

ANN.

Look! It is 2 a.m. in the morning. Jeff won't be here until noon. Now what is it that can't wait till noon?

MO.

I can't wait.

(Pause.)

Besides—said he'd be here tonight!

ANN.

You know what I think? I think you're being very rude—a bunch of very rude bastards! That's what I think.

CHIPS.

Let me squeeze up on her a bit, Big Mo!

(The conversation is interrupted by the somewhat noisy entrance of JOHN *and* DUDLEY *through the back door.)*

DUDLEY.

That's all you ever do! Blow off at the mouth! Blow off! Blow off! Pardon me, but kiss my brown eye!

JOHN.

Looks too much like your face.

DUDLEY.

You gimme a royal pain. Give me one for the road, and let me go home.

JOHN.

One for the road! Why didn't you buy one for the road before we hit the road. Shylock stingy bastard.

ANN.

Mr. Williams! Mr. Williams!

JOHN

(Coming into the living room—closely followed by DUDLEY*).*

Yes, Ann—sweet Ann?

(Sees the crowd.)

Company, I see.

ANN.

Unwanted company, sir.

MO.

We're gonna wait for Jeff, Mr. Williams—that's all.

JOHN.

Is that Mo—Mo Hayes?

MO.

Yes, it is.

JOHN.

Well, well, well—I ain't seen you since Skippy was a punk.

MO.

I've been around, Mr. Williams.

JOHN.

Nice to see you again, son. Who're your friends?

MO

(Introducing them).

Well, sir, this is Gail—my girl. Chips and Skeeter, remember? And Al.

JOHN.

Nice to meet you.

(They exchange greetings.)

Now go home, gentlemen. It's the wee hours of the morning.

MO.

We're gonna wait for Jeff.

GAIL.

Let's go, Mo, we can come back later.

JOHN.

What'd you say, Li'l Mo? Ain't that your nickname? Li'l Mo? Ain't that what we used to call you?

MO.

I said, "We're gonna wait for Jeff."

JOHN.

We're planning a celebration for Jeff noon tomorrow, and you're welcome to come—all of you. But that's noon tomorrow.

MO.

Can't leave until I see Jeff. Sorry.

JOHN.

You're "sorry." You wait until you see how
sorry I am when I get back—okay.

(Exits.)

GAIL.

Mo, baby, let's go. Jeff ain't goin' run nowhere. I mean, what's the hurry?

CHIPS

(Eyeing ANN).

Yeah, what's the hurry?

GAIL

(Turning on him).

You should be in the biggest hurry, nigger,
'cause when Jeff finds out how you been insulting his woman, you're gonna be in a world
of trouble.

DUDLEY

Gentlemen, I'd advise you all to leave. Before
something presumptuous happens. Can never
tell about these black African warrior niggers.

AL

(Pushing DUDLEY into a chair).

Shut up.

DUDLEY

(Blessing himself).

Father, forgive them, for they know not what
they do.

(JOHN *comes back with an M-1 and a World
War II hand grenade.)*

JOHN

*(Highly intoxicated but even more deadly
serious because of it).*

Yeah—well, Father may forgive 'em, but I
don't, not worth a damn.

CHIPS.

You ain't the only one in here with a smoking
machine, man.

*(Opens his coat to reveal a shoulder holster
and a revolver.)*

MO.

Close your jacket, stupid.

JOHN.

Come over here, Ann. Dudley, get your drunk
self outta that chair and make it on over here.

(They follow his instructions. To them)

I don't know if this old grenade'll work or not,
but when I pull the pin and throw it at them
niggers, we duck into the kitchen—all right.

AL.

This old stud's crazy as shit.

MO.

Shut up.

CHIPS.

I bet he's faking.

(Reaching for his revolver. JOHN instantly

*throws the bolt on the M-1. They all freeze for
a long moment; finally . . .)*

MO

(Laughing).

You win. You win, Mr. Williams. Dig it?
We'll see ya 'round noon. Let's go.

*(They file out. MO stops at the door, still
laughing.)*

Ya got some real stuff going for you, Mr.
Williams.

DUDLEY.

Impressive. Presumptuous as hell, but
impressive.

*(At this moment GRANDMA comes down the
steps. She pretends to be sleepwalking. She
hums "Rock of Ages" under her breath.)*

JOHN.

Shh. The old bag's dreaming.

DUDLEY.

What?

JOHN.

I've been waiting for this a solid week, Dudley.

DUDLEY.

What?

JOHN.

Shh. You said you wanted one for the road,
didn't you? Then be patient, nigger, be patient.

*(GRANDMA makes her way into the kitchen—
seeing nobody. Bass line enters.)*

GRANDMA.

Possum ain't nothing but a big rat. I used to
say so to Big Ben Brown. "Call it what you
want, wife." Always called me wife, you
know. "Possum sure got a powerful wild taste
to it."

*(She finds her hiding place, pours herself a
huge glass of whiskey—talking all the time.)*

That big old black man of mine. Sure could
hunt him some possum. Always knew exactly
where to find 'em. I sure hated picking out the
buckshot though. Sometimes I'd miss one or
two, and I'd jes' be eating and all a sudden I
chomp down on one. Lordy, that was a hurting
thing. Felt like my tooth was gonna split wide
open. Sassafras root—and burning pine cones.
Do Jesus! Possum's got a wild taste.

*(Bass line fades out. JOHN throws his keys
into the hall. Startled, GRANDMA caps the bottle, hides it, and mumbles her way back up the
steps, intermittently humming "Rock of Ages."
When she's out of sight, JOHN lets out a yelp,
gets GRANDMA's bottle, and pours each of them
a drink.)*

JOHN.

Here's to Grandmammy.

*(They drink as JEFF enters silently, loaded
down with duffel bags and luggage. He sees*

*them, sneaks into hallway without being seen,
and hides.)*
Here's to us.
(Again.)
Here's to Jeff.
(Again.)
Here's to his daddy.
(Again.)
Here's to his sweet old mama. Here's to Jesus
Christ—one of the baddest cats to ever drop.
(They exchange "good nights." DUDLEY *exists front door.* JOHN *goes upstairs.* ANN *goes
back to sofa—switches off light. Lights fade to
night. Music covers.* JEFF *enters, sees* ANN *on
sofa, and is very pleased. He is a lanky young
man in his middle twenties. There is a heavy
seriousness about him, frosted over with the
wildness he has inherited from his father. His
presence is strong and commanding. He is
dressed casually in a turtleneck, bell-bottom
slacks, boots, and long-styled topcoat. Magazines protrude from his overcoat pocket. His
hair is a modified or shortened afro. His face
is clean. He takes off his coat, sits directly
opposite* ANN, *fumbles in his pockets, comes
up with a plastic bag of marijuana, rolls a
joint, and lights up. After a couple of puffs,
he leans over and kisses* ANN *on the lips. She
groans; he then takes a heavy drag on the joint
and blows it full in her face. She awakens with
a soft sputter. She is overwhelmed at seeing
him. Without saying a word, he extends the
joint to her. She sits upright and drags on it.
He grabs her foot and gently kisses the arch.)*
JEFF.
Three whole days—um, um—and I sho' have
missed them big old feet of yours.
ANN
(Hands him the joint).
Are my feet big?
JEFF.
Why do you think I always walk behind you
in the snow? You got natural snowshoes, baby.
*(He grabs her roughly but lovingly and kisses
her.)*
ANN.
I had to come, Jeff.
JEFF.
I know. Now, let's get down to the nitty-gritty.
How 'bout some loving, mama?
ANN.
Oh, Jeff—I promised your mother.
JEFF.
She won't know. And whatcha don't know—
*(Starts taking off his clothes, talking as he
does.)*
My dad taught me that where there's a will,

there's a way.
ANN.
Your dad taught you a lot of things.
JEFF.
Yeah. Now we're banging away, right. Oo,
ahh, oo, ahh. And it's sweet—like summer
time in December, right? And just when it
really gets good, right? And we're about to
reach the top of the mountain, down the steps
comes Grandma—on one of her frequent
sleepwalking things. And what do I do? I roll
over to the wall and drop down to the other
side. Like this—
(Demonstrates.)
And nobody knows but us.
(She kisses him.)
Daddy Johnny says before a man settles down—
which shouldn't oughta be until he's damn near
thirty or more—
(She kisses him.)
A young man's mission is the world.
ANN.
Well, isn't that what you've been trying to do?
(She kisses him.)
JEFF.
You keep taking up my time.
ANN.
Uh huh.
*(Kisses him as the lights begin to dim. Bass
line plays under.)*
You like my feet?
JEFF.
Is the Pope Catholic? Can a fish swim? Do
black folks have rhythm? Do hound dogs chase
rabbits? Your feet got more beauty than sunshine, mama.
*(They kiss as the lights fade to black. Bass
line fades.)*

It is 10:45 the next morning. JOHN, *wearing
coveralls made rough with dry paint and a
painter's cap, is sweating heavily as he sits
pondering his poem. It is obvious that he has
suspended the activity of mopping the kitchen
floor.*

_____

JOHN
(Bass enters).
I am the River Niger—here my waters!
I wriggle and stream and run.
I am totally flexible.
I am the River Niger—hear my waters!
My waters are the first sperm of the world—
*When the earth was but a faceless whistling
     embryo*
Life burst from my liquid kernels like popcorn.

Hear my waters—rushing and popping in muf-
fled finger-drum staccato.
It is life you hear stretching its limbs in my
waters—
(To himself)
Yeah.

(Quietly he gathers his multiple scraps of
paper, folds them neatly, stuffs them into his
pocket. Bass fades. He rises to continue mop-
ping the still-half-wet floor. Abruptly he de-
cides to quit and starts for the closet to get his
overcoat. He stops as a knock is heard at the
kitchen door. He answers it. It is DUDLEY.*)*

JOHN.

Man, you just in time.

DUDLEY.

For what?

JOHN.

To make it with me to the Big Apple. The
labor's too deep around here for me. Mattie's
gon' off her head. Do you know that, I—me—
Lightnin' John Williams—more powerful than
a speeding locomotive—do you realize that I
have mopped this entire house by myself? And
now I am making it.

DUDLEY.

Without telling the captain?

JOHN.

What's that suppose to mean?

DUDLEY.

It means that the African warrior is always
sneaking around like Brer Rabbit instead of
walking up to the captain and saying, "Captain
Mattie, I's worked hard 'nuff—I's taking a rest
and a mint julep at the Apple!" I mean, I want
to see some evidence of your spear-throwing,
baby—not just words. Words are outta style.

JOHN

(Goes to closet in living room. Gets over-
coat, comes back, stepping lightly on wet floor).
Look, my West Indian corn roaster, I accept
the fact that you're a gutless black aristocrat,
going thumbs up or thumbs down while your
brothers and sisters are being fed to the Lion's
Club—So beat your meat while Rome burns—
I don't give a piss. Just allow me to paint my
own self-portraits—okay, ugly?

DUDLEY.

It's pretty chilly out there, man, you better put
on a sweater or something, you know.

JOHN.

You mean it's pretty chilly for you—that's
what I'm trying to tell you. That's you, man,
not me!

DUDLEY.

Johnny—

JOHN.

And don't step on my floor—

DUDLEY.

Mattie came over this morning—early. I examined her—and, well, I felt a lot of—irreg-
ularities—Anyway—

JOHN

(Sardonically).

Well, what're you quacks gonna do now—
remove her other tit?

DUDLEY.

Johnny.

(Pause.)

Maybe even worse. I don't want to alarm her
until I'm sure. I made an appointment for her
at Harlem—they'll do a biopsy—anyway, I'll
know as soon as the lab gets done with it.

(Pause.)

JOHN

(Stricken but defensive).

Why you telling me all this if you don't know
for sure?

(Pause.)

DUDLEY.

She came over while you were still asleep—
she doesn't want you to know. I promised I
wouldn't tell you.

JOHN.

Does she suspect?

DUDLEY.

I was very honest with her.

JOHN.

That figures! Honesty sticks to some people's
mouths like peanut butter.

DUDLEY.

Like you just said, man, I have to deal with
things the way I think best.

MATTIE'S VOICE

(From upstairs).

Johnny—Johnny—have you finished the
kitchen?

JOHN.

She just keeps going, Dudley. I don't know
how in hell, but she keeps on keeping on.

(Pause.)

When'll you know for sure?

DUDLEY.

By Friday evening.

MATTIE'S VOICE.

If you've finished the kitchen, John, how about
taking out those bags of trash.

JOHN.

Just keeps on keeping on!

(Pause.)

MATTIE'S VOICE.

John! Johnny!

JOHN

(Quietly).

Johnny's gone to the Apple, you amazing bitch, to celebrate an amazing bitch.

(He and DUDLEY *exit just as* MATTIE *and* ANN *come down the steps.)*

MATTIE

(On the landing, followed by ANN*).*

Ann, I do believe that man's gone! Sneaked out!

ANN.

I'll finish, Mrs. Williams.

MATTIE.

Ann, thank you so much for your help. I don't think we coulda finished without you, and that's a fact.

(Pause.)

Mama, will you please hurry!

(To ANN*)*

The store will be jam-packed when we get there.

GRANDMA'S VOICE

(From upstairs).

If you can't wait for your mother, then go on without me!

MATTIE.

Please, Mama!

GRANDMA.

Just go on without me, just go on!

MATTIE

(To ANN*).*

There's too much drinking in this house. That's the problem. She's probably hungover.

ANN.

Pardon me, Mrs. Williams, but you know about your mother's drinking?

MATTIE.

Of course! It's all in her eyes.

ANN.

But last night I thought—well—

MATTIE.

Child, you got to swallow a lot of truth 'round here to give folks dignity. If Mama knew I knew—I mean really knew I knew—she'd be so embarrassed. Don't you know, I even pretend that John ain't the alcoholic he really is?

ANN.

But you're not helping them that way.

MATTIE.

Helping them! Who says I ain't? Johnny soon be pushing sixty. he ain't got but a few more years left. If he wants to spend 'em swimming in a fifth a day, who am I to tell him he can't? And Mama, she'll be eighty-three this September. I'm supposed—as the youngsters on my job say—"to blow their cool"? Honey, all we're doing in this life is playing what we

ain't. And well, I play anything my folks need me to play.

ANN.

I guess that makes sense.

MATTIE

(Bass enters).

That man had two years of college, Ann. Wanted to be a lawyer like Jeff wants to be, you know. He had to stop school because my mother and my two sisters—Flora and Minerva—came up from the South to live with us—for a short time, so they said. Ignorant country girls—they weren't trained to do nothing. I got a job, and together Johnny and I fed 'em, clothed 'em. In a couple of years, John was ready to go back to school, raring to go, don't you know. Then Flora's boy friend came up from good old South Carolina and didn't have a pot to piss in or a window to throw it out of. He and Flora got married, and where do you think they stayed?

(Yells upstairs.)

Mama!

(Back to ANN*.)*

On top of it all, Minerva got herself pregnant by some silly, buck-toothed nineteen-year-old who just vanished. So here comes another mouth to feed—Child, Johnny was painting houses all morning, working the graveyard shift at the Post Office, and driving a cab on his days off.

(Again yells.)

Mama please!

(Back to ANN*.)*

He kept on reading though. And I mean heavy reading. Smart, Lord know that man is smart. Student friends of his were always coming 'round here getting his help in stuff like trigonometry, organic chemistry, philosophy—heavy stuff, you know. They used to call him Solomon. Some of his bummified wino friends still call him that at the Apple. Solomon!

ANN.

Every other word out of Jeff's mouth is "Daddy Johnny says—"

MATTIE.

That's what he did. He poured himself into Jeff. Lord, had that boy reading Plato and Shakespeare when he was thirteen years old.

(Yelling upstairs.)

I gonna leave without you, Mama.

GRANDMA'S VOICE.

I'm a child to be told when to come and go!

MATTIE.

You can be too good, Ann. I was actually proud of the way John worked himself. I read somewhere—in one of John's psychology magazines—where it's called a Christ fixation, or something like that.

ANN.

But that's kinda nice, isn't it?

MATTIE.

Honey, the meek ain't never inherited nothing. No, Ann, if I had to do all over again, I'd do it a whole lot different, believe me. What did we get for it? A chest full of bitterness, that's all. These past few years I've had nothing but bile in my mouth. No, Ann, we got nothing, honey. I mean you'd think they'd call every once in a while.

ANN.

My mother used to say, "The giver receives all."

MATTIE.

Not in this world, child.

ANN.

Somewhere! It must be somewhere—some place—

MATTIE

(Growing heated).

In heaven, honey?

ANN.

In a manner of speaking. Treasures—

MATTIE

(Brooding with anger).

In heaven! Treasures in heaven! My man is an alcoholic, the city's trying to condemn this firetrap we ain't even finished paying for yet, and Flora's got a fancy house and a fancy lawnmower upstate. There were times, Ann, times when I wanted John to get mad—really mad—get a bull whip and whip 'em out—just whip 'em right on out. Johnny woulda done it, ya know. Started to several times, but I'd always manage to cool him down. I got nobody to blame but myself.

(Pause.)

Treasures in heaven—shit. A good man is a treasure. White folks proclaim that our men are no good and we go 'round like fools trying to prove them wrong. And I fell right into the same old dumb trap myself. That's why I can't get angry with that man no more. Oh, I pretend to be, but I'm not. Johnny ran a powerful race with a jockey on his back who weighed a ton. So now he's tired. Do you hear me? Tired— and he's put himself out to pasture—with his fifth a day; and I say good for Johnny. I knew he was a smart man. Good for Johnny.

(On the verge of tears.)

If our men are no good, then why are all these little white girls trying to gobble 'em up faster than they can pee straight? I rejoice in you young people, Ann. You're the spring rains we need, 'cause we as a people got a lot of growing to do. Bless our young folk.

GRANDMA

(Down the steps).

Well, I ain't young like them people you blessing. Them steps is mighty steep.

(Bass line fades.)

ANN.

Morning, Mrs. Brown.

GRANDMA.

You still here?

MATTIE.

Mama, she's here on my invitation. Let's go.

GRANDMA.

The gall of a young girl, planting herself right on the boy's doorstep.

(Crosses to the kitchen.)

ANN.

I'm leaving as soon as Jeff's party's over—

MATTIE.

You'll do no such thing. Mama, hush!

(Embarrassed.)

Ann, would you kinda give Jeff's room a onceover? I started to do it myself, but for some strange reason the door was locked. Been searching for the key half the morning.

(Hands ANN the key from her apron pocket.)

ANN

(Exiting up the stairs).

Yes, ma'am.

MATTIE

(Going to the hall closet, which gives GRANDMA a chance to check her bottle in the kitchen. MATTIE gets their coats, plus an old creaky shopping cart).

Mama, will you stop insulting that child!

GRANDMA

(Astonished to see empty bottle).

That boy needs some time to grow up.

MATTIE.

Who's stopping him?

GRANDMA.

That audacious girl! That's who.

MATTIE.

Mama, she's a nice girl. Besides, Jeff has a mind of his own.

GRANDMA.

Ain't no such thing. Not when it comes to a pretty face. And I got a feeling she's animal-natured.

MATTIE.

Then you admit she's pretty?

GRANDMA.

Well, she's halfway light skin—got good hair. You know what that does to a colored man's mind!

MATTIE.
Not today, Mama.
(Yelling upstairs.)
Ann, Ann, would you come here a minute.
GRANDMA.
Young niggers—old niggers—they all the same! High yellows is still what they want! Young girls these days just like vipers! Anyhow, why you rushing the boy?
MATTIE.
I'm not doing a thing, Mama. It's all in your mind.
(ANN appears at the top of the stairs. She looks like a cyclone has hit her.)
My God, child, what on earth—is the room that dirty?
ANN.
It's a very strong room, ma'am, I can tell you that.
MATTIE.
Listen, honey, I got a roast in the oven. Take it out in twenty-five minutes exactly.
ANN.
Yes, ma'am.
MATTIE.
Come on, Mama.
GRANDMA
(Ice wind hits her full in the face as MATTIE opens the door).
Do Jesus!
(MATTIE and GRANDMA exit. JEFF appears at the top of the stairs.)
JEFF.
How your feets feeling this morning, mama?
ANN.
You're insane, you know that—trying to pull my clothes off with your mother right downstairs.
JEFF.
Hey, ain't I got a groovy mama?
ANN.
She's wonderful.
JEFF.
You ever look at her feet? She's got some boss dogs—
ANN.
Jeff, I'm moving into a hotel this evening—your grandma's a little too much—even for me.
JEFF.
Look, today's my homecoming and tomorrow's Sunday—a day of rest. Monday we'll find you a place—okay? Now, why don't you cool your heels and let's get a quickie before the inmates return—
(Pause.)
Don't worry! Dad won't be back for at least

an hour and Mama always gets carried away shopping—
(Knock on the front door.)
And you will not be saved by the bell. See who it is.
(She goes to peephole in door.)
ANN.
It's Mo's friend—Skeeter, and I believe the other one's called Al.
JEFF.
Skeeter! Send them away! No! That wouldn't be cool. That means Mo's not far behind. Let them in! Tell them to make themselves comfortable, that you've got some last-minute cleaning to do upstairs, and come on up. For all they know, I'm not here yet.
ANN.
As simple as that, huh?
JEFF.
Right!
(Another knock.)
ANN.
You're crazy.
JEFF
(Starts upstairs).
Can I help it if I'm in heat for your feet?
(Exits. ANN answers the door.)
SKEETER.
Hey, we come for the party. Mo wanted us to break in early so's we could rap a taste before Jeff's folks gits into him, ya dig.
ANN.
Come on in. Skeeter, isn't it?
SKEETER.
Ain't it.
ANN.
And Al?
(AL nods. They enter. SKEETER is jittery. It is obvious he is in heavy need of a fix, but he's clever enough to hide the chilling cold running through him.)
Can I take your coat?
(AL gives her his coat.)
What about you?
SKEETER.
That's okay—I mean, I'm cool.
ANN.
Can I get you a beer or something?
AL.
Not right now, thanks.
ANN.
Skeeter?
SKEETER.
I'm cool, sister, I'm cool. Is Jeff here?
ANN.
Not yet.
(There is a pounding from upstairs.)

SKEETER.
What's that?

ANN.
Please make yourselves comfortable. Jeff's due shortly, I've got to get his room cleaned up a bit.

(Starts up the stairs.)

There's beer and stuff in the refrig. Just call if you need me.

SKEETER.
Yeah. Everything's everything.

(ANN exits.)

I hate smart-ass black bitches.

(Lights a cigarette.)

AL.
So do I, sweet baby.

SKEETER.
Stop being so obvious. If Mo ever finds out about your sweet shit—

AL.
He won't, sweet baby.

SKEETER.
Don't give me that sweet-baby jive. Have you got it?

AL.
Well, fuck you. I hate smart-ass dope fiends.

SKEETER.
Aw, come on, Al, don't catch an attitude.

AL.
I'll catch a 'tude if I so desire. I got the shit and you want it, so walk soft or go to Phoenix House, nigger man.

SKEETER
(Shivering).

Come on, man. I'm sorry.

AL.
You sure is. You the sorriest motherfucker I ever run across.

SKEETER.
Come on, man. Mo'll be here in a minute.

AL.
Finish telling me 'bout Buckley.

SKEETER.
Gimme the stuff first.

AL.
I want to know 'bout Buckley.

SKEETER
(Shivering).

I'm cold, man—cold.

AL.
Then talk to me, sugar baby.

SKEETER.
What you want to know?

AL.
Who ripped him off?

SKEETER.
Why you so anxious to know?

AL.
Those motherfuckers in Queens claim they did it. They always claiming credit for what we do.

SKEETER.
We? You weren't even heard of when it happened.

AL.
Well, it's we now, ain't it? Had to be you, Chips, or Mo!

SKEETER.
Why's that?

AL.
Well, I know you cats wouldn't trust none of the young bloods in the organization to do an important job like that.

SKEETER.
Why you want to know 'bout Buckley? You sure you from the home office, nigger? Ever since they sent you here, you been bugging me 'bout Buckley!

AL.
Look, I fight for niggers, 'cause I hate the devil pig—but I don't trust niggers as far as I can spit. If there's a finger man on the team, I want to know who it is. Somebody might make a mistake and put him on my ass. You sure get heated up 'bout simple party gossip. So heated up, sugar baby, you clean forget all 'bout that deep-freeze chill slipping and sliding through your bones. You even bite the hand that lights your fire, don't you, sugar baby?

(In furious desperation, SKEETER suddenly reaches inside his coat, but AL is too quick. At about the same time they both produce their revolvers.)

Don't make the mistake of thinking a sissy can't play that Gary Cooper shit if he want to, nigger man.

(They face each other.)

SKEETER
(Seething).

I hate your guts.

AL.
All that's cool. But I got what it takes to get your guts together, and don't you forget it. I can draw a gun like Sammy Davis, and I was a Golden Gloves champion two years in a row. I got all the hole cards, baby. I could even pull the trigger faster than you right now, 'cause I stays in shape, baby, and you is a dope fiend.

(SKEETER puts his gun away. AL follows suit. SKEETER paces about the room, clutching his stomach as AL watches, underneath enjoying SKEETER's pain. Finally, SKEETER turns to AL, pleading in anguish.)

SKEETER.

Give me the shit, Al.

AL.

I had it for you all the time. You just been
running backward and now you're facing the
right way, that's all, sugar baby. Just answer
me one teeny-tiny little question. Was it you?

SKEETER.

No.

AL.

Chips?

SKEETER

(Almost screaming).

It was an outside dude.

AL.

Who?

SKEETER

(He clutches his stomach).

He wouldn't give his name. He just did it and
split. Last I heard he was in Frisco.

*(Satisfied, AL searches his pockets. Un-
known to AL, SKEETER suppresses a chuckle.)*

AL

(Handing him a package of wrapped tin foil).

Here, snort on this. It oughta hold you till after
the meeting. It's strong as a horse's ass.

*(Using the tip of his little finger, SKEETER
snorts greedily—first one nostril, then the next.)*

Later on we can really take care of business.

(Watches SKEETER awhile.)

Why'd ya'll hate Buckley so?

SKEETER

(Calming down rapidly).

He was on the narco squad. Useta raid and
steal scag and push it to the school kids. Always little girls. He'd get 'em hooked, strung
out, then make 'em do freakish shit for a fix.
Any one of us woulda blown him away.

(Pause.)

Hey, I seen you trying to feel up on Chips's
little brother.

AL

(Excitedly).

You lie, nigger.

SKEETER.

If you'd make it with Chips, you'd make it
with anybody. Don't give me that funny look,
nigger.

AL.

You lie!

SKEETER.

If I tell Mo 'bout it, he'll bust both of you
mothers. Ain't that some shit. And you mean
to tell me you don't know 'bout Chips? He
stuck his joint in an embalmed cunt. And he
brags about it! You know what Mo calls him
when he really gets mad at him? Femaldehyde

Dick. *(Laughs.)*

AL.

That shit you just snorted ain't gon' last forever, you know.

SKEETER.

Oughta call you Femaldehyde Brown Eye.

AL.

Ya never miss the water till the well runs dry.

SKEETER.

Don't give me that shit. We got a working
relationship—the three of us.

AL.

What three?

SKEETER.

You, me, and Chips. You give me scag 'cause
you know I know where you at—I don't tell
Mo where you at 'cause I need the scag. Chips
don't tell him 'cause he digs fags. That's where
he's at! Now, you keep your eye—your brown
eye—on that relationship 'cause all three of us
is walking on the same razor blade, sugar baby,
and don't you forget it, 'cause our asses could
get cut in half!

*(Laughs uproariously. There is a knock on
the door.)*

AL.

Answer the door, dope fiend!

(SKEETER goes to the door, peeks through.)

SKEETER.

It's Femaldehyde himself.

AL.

Flake off, nigger—I'm warning you!

SKEETER.

You want to know something else, Alfreida?
That shit about an outside man ripping off
Buckley—I made that up.

AL.

Your ass is gon' be mine. Wait and see!

SKEETER

(Laughing).

You wanta know something else? I'm supposed to pick up some good stuff as soon as
we finish rapping with Jeff. I don't really need
your shit.

(Laughs and opens the door.)

CHIPS

(To AL).

What's this clown laughing about?

SKEETER

(Holding his sides).

Gary Cooper here just got some lemon in his
sucker—

(Laughs. The front door is left slightly ajar.)

CHIPS.

Dig these happenings. A young dude who said
he was from the *Times* was hanging around
headquarters all morning, asking questions

about you know who.

SKEETER.

Buckley!

CHIPS.

Dig it!

SKEETER

(Eyeing AL).

Ain't that interesting!

(Laughs.)

CHIPS.

The pigs is restless. So you cats be careful.

(ANN *appears at top of stairs.*)

Well, bless my soul—if it ain't foxy mama.
How 'bout a hug and a squeeze, foxy mama?

(To SKEETER)

Who else is here?

SKEETER.

Just us chickens.

CHIPS.

You mean foxy mama is by her little old self—
in this big house?

ANN

(Trying to ignore him).

Jeff'll be here in a minute, everybody.

CHIPS.

Then we got to git it before he gets here, right,
mama? All I want you to do is show me the
upstairs.

(CHIPS *starts up the steps after her.*)

ANN.

What are you trying to prove?

AL.

Chips—

SKEETER.

Man, can't you act civilized?

CHIPS.

Mind ya business.

SKEETER.

Chips—come on, man.

ANN.

It's all right—he wants to see upstairs—I'll
show him.

CHIPS

(Swats her on her rear).

Now you talking, foxy mama. All I wants is
a hug and a squeeze. You dudes take it easy
now. And call me when you see Mo coming.

(ANN *hesitates, and he shoves her ahead of
him.*)

He who hesitates is lost, mama.

(They exit upstairs.)

AL.

Some niggers ain't got no couth—

SKEETER.

There goes Femaldehyde!

*(In the next moment we hear a loud yell from
JEFF and much commotion. A second later JEFF*

comes down the stairs with CHIPS's *revolver
pressed against* CHIPS's *head.* ANN *brings up
the rear.)*

Here comes Femaldehyde!

CHIPS.

Come on, Jeff, man, I was only fooling, man.
I mean, you know me, Jeff. I didn't know she
was your woman, man. Honest!

(JEFF *smacks him brutally across the face.*)

SKEETER.

Lighten up, Jeff.

AL.

Yeah, like you made your point, man.

(JEFF *turns and looks at them, saying nothing. The ferocity of his stare silences them.*)

ANN.

Jeff—it's okay.

(JEFF *wallops* CHIPS *in the pit of his stomach.*
CHIPS's *knees buckle to the floor.*)

CHIPS.

It's your world, baby! It's your world!

ANN.

He's not worth it, Jeff. Please, baby, for me—
okay?

(MO *and* GAIL *enter, almost unseen.*)

CHIPS.

I was only fooling, Jeff. Honest.

JEFF.

Fooling with a gun at my woman's head?

CHIPS.

I wouldn't hurt ya woman, man. It ain't even
loaded.

JEFF

(Places gun against CHIPS's *temple).*

So if I pull the trigger, it won't matter.

(Cocks hammer.)

CHIPS

(Hysterical).

Oh shit—oh shit—Don't do that, Jeff. Please
don't do that.

JEFF.

The next time I catch you looking cross-eyed
at my woman, I'm gonna rid the world of one
more jive-ass nigger. Now, get out of here.

MO.

Let him stay, Jeff. As a favor to me.

JEFF

(Turns to see MO).

I despise irresponsible niggers, Mo.

MO.

I'll be responsible for him.

JEFF.

Then he'd better become shy, quiet, and unassuming. 'Cause that's the only kind of nigger
I tolerate in my house.

MO.

Well, you sound like the Jeff I used to know back when.

GAIL

(To CHIPS*).*

You act more like a pig than the pigs.

MO.

Old Femaldehyde!

SKEETER

(Laughing).

Rides again.

MO

(Referring to the revolver).

Is that your steel, man?

SKEETER.

It's Chips's.

(Laughs.)

MO

(Collaring CHIPS *angrily).*

What! Not only do you insult a personal friend of mine—but you let him take your steel! That's unforgivable, cluck. You better get it back or another one just like it—posthaste—you dig me. Loss of a weapon is a crime against the organization. Do you dig them apples, Femaldehyde?

(SKEETER *holds his sides laughing.)*

(To SKEETER*)*

Shut up!

GAIL

(Extends her hand to a still angry JEFF*).*

I'm Gail.

JEFF.

Hi!

MO.

This is my woman, Jeff. And of course you know Skeeter—

JEFF.

Hey, Skeets.

SKEETER

(Shaking JEFF*'s hand).*

What's happening, big Jeff?

MO.

And Al here I wrote you 'bout.

(They shake hands.)

Now, can we all settle down awhile and rap?

(Everybody finds a comfortable spot, and there is an uneasy silence.)

ANN.

Who wants a beer?

(Everybody nods.)

MO.

Why don't you help her, Gail?

GAIL.

Sure.

(ANN *and* GAIL *cross the room to the kitchen.)*

MO.

Now, dig this, Brother Jeff. What I'm about to run down to you is only to make a point, and stop being so pissed. Everybody's edgy.

JEFF.

I'm not edgy, baby, I'm about to draw blood.

CHIPS.

Look, man, I'm sorry—okay.

JEFF.

Negative, baby—not okay, not okay worth a damn.

MO.

Jeff—Jeff—why do you think Chips had the nerve to shoot on your woman like he did? I think it's because of your letters, man!

JEFF.

You showed *them* my personal letters to you!

MO.

Yeah! And you know why? 'Cause they sounded like you were turning, man, dig it— turning into a weak, halfway-in-between, nei- ther here nor there Oreo cookie. I mean, the last thing we expected was Big Brother, bad- ass Jeff, our main man who we been waiting to welcome back to the trenches suddenly de- ciding to go trip off to law school, rapping 'bout the Constitution and a whole lot of the upside of the wall shit . . . Jeff, remember the time I had to fight Billy Richardson? Remem- ber how his brothers kept clipping me and pushing on me every time it looked like I was winning? Remember that shit?

JEFF.

What's the point?

MO.

It was suppose to be a fair fight to see who was to gain control over St. Nicholas Avenue, right? I mean we parlayed and parlayed, and it was agreed upon—we had a verbal contract. And what they do? Billy's older brothers held you against the fence while he and the younger punks in his gang went to work on me. I was ready to give up, man, I mean all the wind was outta my sail, baby. And I looked up, and there you were, crying, baby, crying—trying to break loose from cats twice your size, can you dig it? Trying to break loose to help your main man, your brother, and crying, and some- how your shit got into me, and I beat Billy until he was screaming for mercy—his own boys let up when they dug what was happen- ing! Well, a dumb-ass nigger and a pig are one and the same! They don't understand agree ments and contracts; they're beasts—the only thing a beast understands is guts and deter- mination. We ran the whole goddamn neigh- borhood after that, and we had one motto,

"Keep on keeping on!" And anybody who gave up in a fight got his ass kicked when he got back to the club. All that shit about legal pressure, the democratic process bullshit. I tell you, man, the law ain't never helped the black man do nothing. The law is the will of the prevailing force, which is the pig in this country—and you want to be a lawyer? That Constitution ain't nothing but bullshit, don't you know that yet, man?

JEFF.

Make it work and you've got a formidable weapon.

MO.

I say, burn the motherfucker! Look, man, we've gone all those routes. We've petitioned, we've sat in, shitted in, demonstrated until we got fallen arches, etc., etc., etc., and where did it get us, huh? Things are worse! Contracts!? I'm talking 'bout revolution, man.

JEFF.

That word's been talked to death. The revolution ain't nothing but talk, talk, talk, and I ain't gonna waste my life on talk. Niggers are jiving, man, can't you see it? That's all I heard from the black troops in the air force—revolution. Where's the gun factory, the bomb-assembly plant? We're shucking and jiving, man—that's all. Law is something concrete, something I can do, not talk about.

MO.

To a certain extent, you're right, Brother Jeff. Black people have been shucking and jivin', passing the buck. Well, we are the buck-ending committee. We ain't just talking, baby. We proving it. And in a few days we gonna serve notice on whitey that the shit has only begun to hit the fan. We want you with us, man.

JEFF.

You've got it all figured out, Mo. You don't need me.

MO.

We don't need nothing, baby, we just want you with us.

JEFF.

Maybe I'm out of it, Mo. Maybe I don't know what's really happening any more. Yes, I'm still for whatever advances the cause of black folks, but I reserve the right to choose my own weapons. I don't have to fight with yours, Mo, and I respect your right not to have to fight with mine . . . All I know is that right now my convictions rest elsewhere . . . Now, gentlemen, my folks will be making it back pretty soon and I'd like the atmosphere to change into something a little bit more groovy, ya dig?

MO.

Yes, sir, Lieutenant Williams, sir.

JEFF.

Or leave.

MO.

Is that an order, sir?

JEFF.

You're in my house, nigger.

MO.

I don't play that word, man. You throw it 'round a little too much.

JEFF.

Oh yeah, well, you pat your foot while I play it, nigger.

MO.

You either gon' be with us or against us, Brother Jeff. Nobody stays uncommitted in this neighborhood. Besides, we can make you do anything we want you to do.

JEFF.

How you gonna do that, brother?

MO.

Every time you poke your head out your door, you can be greeted with rocks, broken glass, garbage bags, or doo-do. And if that don't work . . .

(ANN and GAIL return from kitchen.)

And if that don't work . . .

JEFF

(Furious).

If that don't work, what?

MO.

We can work on your moms and pops. They might come home and find the whole house empty, no furniture or nothing, motherfucker.

JEFF.

Oh no, baby, you're the motherfucker. You really are the motherfucker!

(Controlling his fury at MO.)

You jive-ass nigger. Mr. Zero trying to be Malcolm X. List' old world, list' to the revolutionary. See him standing there with his Captain America uniform on. Look at his generals. Skeeter the dope head and Chips the sex pervert. Mo the magnificent, playing cops and robbers in his middle twenties, trying to be somebody and don't know how. The one advantage I have over you, Mo, is my daddy taught me to see through my own bullshit, to believe that I don't need bullshit to be somebody. Go back to school, Mo, you're smart enough.

GAIL.

Don't talk to him like that!

MO.

You been thinking this shit for a long time, ain't you nigger?

JEFF.

Affirmative. And if you try any shit on my folks, your ass is mine, nigger. Or have you forgotten what a mean, evil, black bastard I can be, how you could whip everybody in the neighborhood and how I could whip the piss out of you, how I got more determination in my little toenail than you got in your whole soul, nigger!

MO.

At least you still talk bad.

JEFF.

I ain't bad. I'm crazy, motherfucker. Now you, your dope fiend, and Marquis de Sade, get the fuck outta here, and don't call me—I'll call you.

MO

(Not too frightened but impressed).

Let's go. This ain't the end, Jeff. I suggest you think about what I said and think hard.

JEFF.

Just make it, man. And remember

(Places gun to CHIPS's *temple.)*

I'm fully armed, thanks to General Chips here.

MO.

Don't make fun of me, Jeff.

JEFF.

Why should I do that, you're a self-made comedian.

CHIPS.

I think we should—

MO.

You ain't had a thought in your life, cluck.

(They all exit.)

JEFF

(Walking around the room).

Goddamn, goddamn! . . . Where's the hootch? I know Pop got some somewhere.

(Looks around frantically.)

I know the refrig used to be one of his favorite places.

(Finds it)

Damn! Almost half full! Lawd hep me! 'Cause these niggers don' gon' crazy.

(Takes a drink.)

Hep me, Lawd. Hep me, hep me, Lawd.

(Takes another drink and sings the words . . .)

" 'Cause the niggers don' gon' crazy!''

ANN.

That's enough.

JEFF.

Ann, my love, the most glorious bitch I ever don' run across—let's get married. Let's get married and screw right at the ceremony. Monday we'll get the license. There's a three-day wait—Tuesday, Wednesday, and Thursday—Friday we'll get high off this bad-ass smoke I been saving and fly on to the preacher.

ANN.

Are you serious?

JEFF.

Indubitably.

ANN.

Oh, Jeff, why so sudden?

JEFF.

Honey, with the way these niggers is acting up 'round here, I figure I better get me some hep.

ANN.

Jeff, I—

JEFF.

I know you love me to pieces, and I don't blame you one bit.

ANN.

You conceited—

JEFF.

The problem is, I don't really love you.

(Pause.)

I glory for you, baby. Besides, you got the bossest dogs I ever seen.

(They kiss and embrace. There's a knock at the door. It's GAIL.*)*

GAIL.

Can I come in?

ANN.

Of course.

(ANN *brings her into the kitchen.*)

GAIL.

Mo thinks I stopped at the store to get cigarettes.

ANN.

Would you like a drink?

GAIL.

No, I don't drink.

ANN.

Relax, Gail.

GAIL.

Jeff, when I was a little girl, all I used to do was watch you and Mo running everything, the whole neighborhood together, always cool—no strain, ya know what I mean? You two cats were so beautiful together . . . Maybe it was wrong for Mo to come down on you so hard tonight, Jeff, after three years—but you the only person he trusts, Jeff. Writing to you the years you were away was his way of forgetting you had ever left. Now he needs you more than ever, Jeff. The organization has gotten to be a real hassle.

JEFF.

How could it be anything else with those nothings he's got at his back? I mean, it's hard to be out front when you got shit at your back.

GAIL.

That's why he needs you bad, Jeff. Mo only looks at the good in people. Skeeter and Chips been with you cats ever since you started gang-bopping. Mo's not dumb, he knows their hang-ups. But they swore to him they'd stay clean. Anyway, when you trying to build an army outta people who been buried in garbage all their lives, you can't expect they gon' all of a sudden start smelling like roses. In time, Mo believes, the movement will straighten 'em out for good.

JEFF.

Mo's a saint. I'm a realist.

GAIL.

Then help him, Jeff, help him.

JEFF.

It's not just those okeydoke creeps 'round him, Gail. We don't see eye to eye. Mo thinks he's still back in the old days, leading a gang. Times have changed.

GAIL.

You could influence him, Jeff.

JEFF.

He doesn't need me, Gail. He's sure about where he's going and confident about how to get there—

GAIL.

That's not true, Jeff.

JEFF.

And all that bull about threatening me and my folks—I'd jump in an elephant's chest behind that jive.

GAIL.

He was only saying that for them—

JEFF.

Why crucify me for a bunch of nothings, baby?

GAIL.

Do you know Mo, Jeff?

JEFF.

I thought I did.

GAIL.

If you really know him, Jeff, then you know he didn't mean what he said. He's desperate, Jeff. Things are all mixed up. A few years ago, everything was straight up and down—simple—*right on for the people*. Now every-thing's falling apart, splitting up, people going every which way. And Mo's gotten into some heavy, scary things, Jeff. Right now the heat's on 'cause a pig cop was wasted a few months ago. And this Friday Mo plans to destroy a new state office building going up, or else mess with one of the police stations. You think he's so cocksure? Well, he ain't. He don't even

know if what he's doing is right any more. I know—'cause I see him get up in the middle of the night and stare out the window and talk to himself—talk to his demons. Don't let his tough act fool you, Jeff. Behind his real to-gether front, he's about to snap. You hear me, Jeff, he's gonna snap. I know it. Lord God, help him, Jeff Williams. Even if you don't see eye to eye with him, find a way to help him. The hell with the movement, help HIM! Help him, please, before he breaks apart. Help him, Jeff.

(She sobs uncontrollably. ANN *comforts her.)*

ANN.

He will, Gail, he will—I know he will.

(To JEFF*)*

I like him, Jeff. His approach may be all wrong, but he's fighting. He's honest and he's fight-ing. He's a determined black man, just like you, Jeff.

JEFF.

All right. I'll try, Gail, I'll try. I promise you.

(The front door swings open. It's MATTIE *and* GRANDMA, GRANDMA *pushing a shopping cart,* MATTIE *loaded down with grocery bags. Bass line enters.)*

MATTIE.

Lawdamercy. The door's wide open!

GANDMA.

That hussy girl's doings!

*(*MATTIE *sees* JEFF.*)*

MATTIE.

Lawdamercy! Lawdamercy! Jeff!

(She rushes to embrace him.)

You big old good-for-nothing thing.

*(*GRANDMA *starts for him.)*

GRANDMA.

Ben Brown! The spitting image of Ben Brown. Ben Brown all over again.

(She embraces him.)

Ain't black like Ben Brown, but he sho' do carve himself out a fine figure, don't he, Mattie?

JEFF

(Eyeing her lewdly).

You don't do so bad yourself, sweet meat!

GRANDMA.

You ought to be ashamed of yourself.

(Hugs him once more.)

MATTIE.

You weren't supposed to be here till noon.

JEFF.

I'll go back and come at noon.

MATTIE.

Go on, boy, stop acting so simple.

JEFF.

Can't help it, Mama. I got my two foxes back again—Cleopatra—

(Referring to GRANDMA.*)*
and her sidekick.

(Referring to his mother.)

MATTIE.

I'll sidekick you.

JEFF

(Hugging them both at the same time).

Got my two womens back again.

MATTIE.

Stop being so rough with your simple self. What they been feeding you—bread and water? You too thin to say grace over.

JEFF.

Know what I wants for dinner? Some corn bread, yeah. And some of Grandma's mustard greens, Mama.

GRANDMA

(Salutes him).

Yes, sir.

JEFF.

And black-eyed peas. And some of your candied sweets, Grandma, with lemon and raisins all over 'em, yeah!

GRANDMA.

And roast beef!

JEFF.

Do Jesus, and bless my soul, Grandma Brown! And don't forget the lemonade.

GRANDMA.

A gallon of it. Made it myself.

JEFF.

And some sassafras tea.

GRANDMA.

Got it fresh from that new health-food store.

(Pause.)

JEFF.

Ma, do you realize that I'm home for good—

MATTIE.

Thank God!

JEFF.

No more okeydoke. No more time outta my race against time. No more stuff, messing with my mind. I'm me—Jeff Williams, because Daddy Johnny named me—before ya'll claimed me on your income tax! And ya'll sho' is looking gooooooooood—good God, good!

MATTIE.

Go on, boy!

JEFF.

Mama, this is Gail. Mo Hayes's girl friend.

MATTIE.

Nice to know you, Gail.

GAIL

(Extending her hand).

Heard a lot about you, Mrs. Williams.

JEFF.

And this is my grandma. Gail. Grandma Wil-

hemina Geneva Brown.

GRANDMA.

There you go, acting the fool, Jeff Williams. You know I can't stand "Geneva."

GAIL.

My pleasure, Mrs. Brown.

GRANDMA.

What? Oh, yes. How do, child.

JEFF.

And this is Ann!

GRANDMA

(Disapprovingly).

We've met.

MATTIE.

The best—of—friends!

*(*GRANDMA *grunts.)*

JEFF

(Ignoring GRANDMA*).*

Well, I'm glad 'cause this foxy mama here and your son—me—the baddest dude to catch an attitude—God's gift to the female race—"for God so loved the world that he gave—"

MATTIE.

I'll take off my shoe and knock holes in your head, boy!

JEFF.

Mama, what I'm trying to tell you—

GRANDMA.

You gon' marry this here brazen gal?

(Bass fades.)

MATTIE.

Mama!

JEFF.

Indubitably!

GAIL.

That's beautiful! Just beautiful!

GRANDMA.

Do Jesus, Uncle Sam don' took my child—

MATTIE.

Your child—

GRANDMA.

And turned him into a cockeyed ignoramus.

MATTIE.

Don't pay any attention to her, Ann.

ANN.

Jeff, I think I'll walk to the corner with Gail.

JEFF.

You will not!

GRANDMA.

You too young to fart good—talking 'bout getting married.

JEFF.

I'm twenty-five!

GRANDMA.

Stop lying! You ain't outta your teens.

JEFF.

I was twenty-two when I left, Grandma.

GRANDMA
(To MATTIE*).*

Lawd, Mattie, is my child don' got that old on me?

MATTIE.

Your *grandson* is that old, Mama.

GRANDMA.

Do Jesus! Time sho' do fly, don't it? 'Tweren't yesterday I was getting myself all sprayed up changing your diapers.

JEFF
(Slowly, deliberately).

That was twenty-five years ago, Grandma.

GRANDMA
(Coming out of her reveries).

Don't make no difference. You're too young to get yourself saddled with a wife. Next thing you know, here comes one crumbsnatcher—then two—

JEFF.

Then three—then four. It's pretty lonely not having any brothers and sisters, I can tell you.

GRANDMA.

A lodestone! A lodestone 'round your neck, a-dragging you down.

MATTIE.

What about law school, Jeff?

JEFF.

Oh, we gon' do that too. I mean them crumb-snatchers ain't coming until we are ready for 'em. Ann's gonna use the loop, birth-control pills, the rhythm methods, and the diaphragm, and Emko!

GRANDMA.

There sure is a whole lot Emko babies walking 'round here.

MATTIE
(To JEFF*).*

Well, you certainly seem to know an awful lot 'bout it.

JEFF.

Like I said before, I'm *twenty-five*. Be twenty-six the twenty-fourth of this month, Mama.

MATTIE.

You still don't have to know so much in front of your mother.

JEFF.

I apologize.

GRANDMA
(Blurting out a long-pent-up reality).

Look at your father. He wanted to be a lawyer, didn't he? Then I jumped on his back, then them two no good daughters of mine, then their two empty-headed husbands—then you. The load was so heavy till he couldn't move no more. He just had to stand there, holding it up.

MATTIE
(Very serious).

Then you know about it?

GRANDMA.

What do you think I am? A sickle-headed, lopsided, cockeyed ignoramus like your son here?

MATTIE.

Oh, so you admit he's my son?

GRANDMA.

He's your son, but he's my child.

MATTIE
(Turning to ANN*).*

Have ya'll given it serious thought, Ann?

ANN.

He just asked me, Mrs. Williams.

GRANDMA.

Is that all you gon' do? Talk? You gon' let this brazen hussy just take my child away?

MATTIE.

Mama, why don't you go to your room and cool off a bit.

GRANDMA.

She is brazen. Camping right on his doorstep. I call that bold, brash, and brazen! And con-niving too! A pretty face'll sho' kill a man—even a good man.

(To ANN*)*

And not even mean to! You gon' take that on your shoulders, child, you gon' kill your man before he can stand up good yet? Is that what you gon' do? I did it. Mattie did it. She let me help her do it.

MATTIE.

Mama!

GRANDMA.

Don't mama me. Where's my medicine? I don't want to be here and watch my child leap into deep water. Lawdamercy, no! Where is my medicine? Where's my pocket book?

JEFF
(To MATTIE*).*

Is Grandma sick, Ma?

MATTIE.

In a manner of speaking.

(GRANDMA *finds her purse. There is a large bulge in it. She seems satisfied. She starts up the stairs, singing "Rock of Ages.")*

GRANDMA.

Hep him, Lawd! Hep my child!

(She exists, singing.)

JEFF
(To ANN*).*

Is this what you've been putting up with?

MATTIE.

Ann's a fine girl, Jeff. You know I believe that, don't you, Ann?

ANN.

Thank you, Mrs. Williams.

MATTIE.

And you know women get silly over their sons and, well, grandsons.

ANN.

Yes, ma'am.

MATTIE.

My personal opinion—if ya'll are interested—is that you should wait awhile—at least until Jeff's finished law school.

JEFF.

Ever since I got home, people been telling me what to do and what not to do. You talking about a lodestone—that's the heaviest lodestone in the world . . . I want to marry Ann 'cause she is a fine girl, Mama. Something rare—came home and found my sweet baby here—it was like God was saying, "This is your woman, son. I can't let you do nothing that dumb. I can't let you leave her. I made her for you!" And goddamn it—

MATTIE.

Jeff!

JEFF.

I'm following what I hear inside my soul!

MATTIE

(Pauses for a long moment, finally embracing him strongly, on the verge of tears).

Then you do that, baby. You follow the Lord. As mad as He makes me sometimes, I don't think He's ever really told me wrong.

(Hugs ANN *lovingly.)*

Come on in here and help me fix this food, girl. You're one of the family now. I guess I knew you were the moment I laid eyes on you.

(To JEFF*)*

Why do you like to shock people so? You know how your grandmother dotes on you.

(She exits into the kitchen.)

GAIL.

A beautiful black brother and sister, doing a beautiful thing.

(She embraces ANN*.)*

JEFF.

Gail, I'll try to talk to Mo. I'm not certain it will do any good, but I'll try to talk to him—when he's alone—Just him and me. Okay?

GAIL.

I appreciate it, Jeff.

(She exits as JOHN, *very intoxicated, and* DUDLEY, *still in control of himself, enter. They are arguing some philosophical point.* JOHN *sees* JEFF.*)*

JOHN.

Jeff! Well, I'll be goddamned. Jeff!

(He ruffles JEFF's *hair.)*

JEFF.

How you been, Pop?

JOHN.

Where's your uniform?

JEFF.

Dr. Stanton.

DUDLEY.

You're looking fine, boy! Just fine. Skinny, but fine.

JOHN.

Where's your uniform?

MATTIE

(Coming back in, followed by ANN, *with a cake)*

John, you're drunk.

JOHN.

Yes, my love.

*(*GRANDMA *comes down the stairs. She too is loaded. She's singing "Onward, Christian Soldiers.")*

JEFF.

Why don't you take the load off your feet, Pop.

JOHN.

Where's your uniform, Jeff? Go put it on.

JEFF.

If it's all the same to you, Pop—

JOHN.

I've got a theory, Dudley—Dr. Dudley Stanton—

MATTIE.

Why don't you go sleep it off—

JOHN.

My theory is that if you as a doctor don't try to keep the living from dying, then you're dead yourself. You're a dead doctor.

*(*GRANDMA *crosses to* JOHN *and sings directly into his ear.)*

Mrs. Brown, I have never hit an old lady in my life—

GRANDMA.

Ya hit this old lady—

JOHN.

And what?

GRANDMA.

She's gon' jump down your throat—

JOHN.

And what?

GRANDMA.

Straddle your gizzard—

JOHN.

And what?

GRANDMA.

And gallop your brains out!

(He picks her up and whirls her around the room, laughing.)

JOHN.

Grandma, you are the biggest fool in the world, but I sure do love me some Grandma Wilhemina Geneva Brown.

GRANDMA.

Stinking old wino.

JOHN.

I love you too, Dudley—Dr. Dudley Stanton—even if you do walk through life with a broomstick up your ass.

(To ANN*)*

And even though we just met, I loves me some Ann—sweet fighting lady that you are. Jeff, ya got yourself a mama—a mama who's gonna protect your flanks—a sweet fighting lady.

JEFF.

I know, Pop.

(GRANDMA *grunts disapprovingly.)*

JOHN.

And my son I loves better than I love myself. My big old big-time United States Air Force lieutenant son. He's coming home today—

JEFF.

I'm here, Pop.

JOHN

(Really annoyed).

No you ain't—you ain't here. 'Cause if you were, you'd have on your uniform—

JEFF.

I don't like to wear it, Daddy Johnny.

JOHN.

Why not?

JEFF.

Well, I guess—

JOHN.

Spit it out.

JEFF.

I feel ashamed of it. I feel that it's a kinda cop-out, Pop—it makes me feel like a buffoon every time I put it on. I should have burned my commission, not shown up, made it to Canada or something. I really don't believe in this country any more.

DUDLEY.

Boy, you don't believe in the United States of America—land of the free, home of the brave, this democratic, constitutional, industrial giant?

JEFF.

I don't believe in lies any more, Dr. Stanton.

DUDLEY

(Jokingly but meaning it).

Welcome home, Jeff. Welcome home, Brother Jeff.

(Pats him on the back.)

JOHN.

Have I been waiting around here, waiting to see you in that goddamn uniform—for you to—Go put it on!

JEFF.

I made a vow with myself, Daddy Johnny.

JOHN

(Getting angry).

It's an accomplishment, fool. How many of us ever get there—to be an officer? God knows, this country needs to be torn down, but don't we want it torn down for the right to be an officer if you're able? It's an accomplishment. And I'm proud of your accomplishment.

DUDLEY.

A dubious accomplishment.

JOHN.

Laugh and ridicule the damn thing all you want, goddamn it, but recognize that it's another fist jammed through the wall.

DUDLEY.

Man, he became the protector of a system he believes should be destroyed.

JOHN.

So we're contradictions—so what else is new? That could apply to every black man, woman, and child who ever lived in this country. Especially the taxpayers. They been financing the system for a long time. Besides, who ever said we wanted total destruction anyway? If you get right on down to the real nitty-gritty, I don't want to totally destroy what, by rights, belongs to me anyway. I just want to weed out the bullshit. Change the value system so that the Waldorf has as many welfare tenants as Rockafellows.

JEFF.

The Rockafellows will never allow it.

JOHN.

They will if you put *them* on welfare.

DUDLEY.

How in hell you gonna do that, fool?

JOHN.

By finding the battlefield—like I told you—like I been telling you—each and every motherfucker—

MATTIE.

John!

JOHN.

Whoever dropped from a pretty black poontang has got to find his own battlefield and go to war. In his own way—his own private war.

DUDLEY.

All hail to the philosopher-poet.

JOHN

(Grabbing DUDLEY *roughly in the collar and screaming as bass line enters).*

I'm a poet, ya hear me, a poet! When this country—when this world, learns the meaning of poetry—Don't you see, Jeff, poetry is what the revolution's all about—never lose sight of the true purpose of the revolution, all revolutions—to restore poetry to the godhead! Poetry is religion, the alpha and the omega, the cement of the universe. The supereye under which every other eye is scrutinized, and it stretches from one to infinity, from bullshit to the beatific, the rocking horse of the human spirit—God himself. God himself is pure distilled poetry.

DUDLEY.
Bravissimo!

JOHN.
Preserve the Empire State Building—if you can. It was built from over three hundred years of black poetry, 'cause sweat is poetry too, son. Kick out the money changers and reclaim it. Ain't none of us gonna be free until poetry rides a mercury-smooth silver stallion.

(Pause.)

Seeing you in your uniform with bars on your shoulders and them navigator wings on your chest is a kinda—

(Bass fades.)

DUDLEY
(Undaunted).

Heresy!

JOHN.
Poetry, Jeff. Black poetry.

JEFF.
Pop, I didn't make it through navigator school—I washed out—flunked out—whatever.

JOHN
(Furious).

My son flunked out—You lie—Go get that uniform!

JEFF.
No, Daddy Johnny, no!

MATTIE.
Leave him alone, Johnny.

JOHN.
I'm the head of this house.

MATTIE.
Ain't nobody disputing that.

JOHN.
And when I ask my son—who I ain't seen but three or four times in three years—to do me one simple favor—

ANN.
But if it's against his principles, Mr. Williams—

JOHN.
There goes the little fighting lady, protecting your flanks.

JEFF.
I don't need nobody to protect my flanks.

ANN.
I know you don't, baby.

GRANDMA
(Half high).

"I know you don't, baby!" Brazen hussy.

JEFF.
Don't call her that again, Grandma!

GRANDMA.
I calls 'em as I sees 'em. My Ben Brown told me—

MATTIE.
Hush, Ma!

JEFF.
I'll leave, Pop. I'll leave now—tonight—ya dig that? 'Cause I've had me enough homecoming for a lifetime.

JOHN.
Ain't nobody asking you to leave—

JEFF.
Ya telling me what to do like I was sweet sixteen or something. Everybody 'round here wants to tell me what to do.

MATTIE.
You didn't write to us about flunking out, Jeff.

JEFF.
Ya want to know why I didn't write home about it, Mama? 'Cause every single letter I got from you or Pop was telling me how proud you were of your navigator son.

JOHN.
We thought you were doing all right.

JEFF.
You thought that because that's what you wanted to think!

JOHN.
What else could we think?

JEFF.
About me, Daddy Johnny, about Jeff—damn your pride! You coulda thought about me.

(Strained pause.)

I hated navigation! You know how I hate figures, Pop.

JOHN.
You never worked hard enough!

JEFF.
So you say, Daddy Johnny—'cause that's what you want to believe. "Jeff Williams is my son, everybody! Just like me. Anything I can do he can do."

JOHN.
You can! It's all in how you think of yourself—

JEFF.
Right, Pop, right. As a matter of fact, I may be able to do a few things you can't do. But not math, Pop. That's you, not me. Don't you dig that?

JOHN.

Say what you got to say.

JEFF.

Haven't I said it already? You said it yourself! We got to find our own battlefields. Don't you dig how that statement relates to what I'm saying?

JOHN.

No! Hell, no, I don't. You flunked out. My boy, my boy failed. That's all I can see.

JEFF.

Ya'll had a piece of my big toe, Pop. *Everybody* had a piece of my toe. Not just those white-pig instructors who kept checking and rechecking my work, 'cause I was what they called a belligerent nigger. There were only eight black officers out of three hundred in that school, and they kept telling me, "Man, you got to make it. You got to be a credit to your race."

JOHN.

What's wrong with that?

JEFF.

Then there was this girl I was shacking up with.

MATTIE.

Shacking up!

JEFF.

Shacking up, Mama!

GRANDMA.

Another brazen hussy!

JEFF.

She was the fox to end all foxes, Pop. An afro so soft and spongy, until my hands felt like they were moving through water. And she kept telling me, "Honey, we needs that extra hundred and thirty a month flight pay to keep me in the style to which you have made me accustomed."

JOHN.

Come to the point!

JEFF.

Don't you see the point, Pop? Everybody had a piece of my nigger toe—my fine fox, my fellow black brother officers, the pig instructors, you and Mama, Pop—everybody had a piece—but me—Jeff Williams!

JOHN.

Jeff Williams is Johnny Williams's son, god-damn it!

JEFF.

You mean none of me belongs to me, Pop?

JOHN.

I want to see you in your uniform! Now, what is all this talk talk about?

JEFF.

It's about you and me and the battlefields. About who is Jeff Williams, Pop.

JOHN.

Then tell me who in the hell is he!

JEFF.

A dude who hated navigation to the point where he got migraines. Who wanted to throw up on every flight—motion-sickness pills notwith-standing. Whose ears pained him from takeoff to landing. Do you know what it feels like when your ears don't clear?

MATTIE.

My baby!

JEFF

(Bass enters).

Don't baby me, Mama. I still think I'm the baddest, but I ain't—nor do I want to be a supernigger, 'cause that's all a supernigger is, a *super*nigger. Someone who spends his life trying to prove he's as good as the Man. On my last flight exam—a night celestial—I wound up eighty miles into Mexico, according to my computations, while everybody else's figures put us at Harlingen Air Force Base, Texas. We were circling the field. The sun was coming up, soft and pastel like someone had sprinkled red pepper all over the clouds. I tore off a piece of my flight log and began writing a poem. You see, Pop, I do believe in poetry. It was a simple poem—all about the awe of creation. Anyway—along came this Lieutenant Forth-right—a Texas cracker whose one joke, re-peated over and over again, was "Hee, haw, students, never worry about being lost. At least you knows ya'll is in the airplane. Yuk, yuk." This creep caught sight of my poem, and this big Howdy Doody grin spread all over his face, and he started laughing. This Howdy Doody pig started laughing. This subhuman, cave-man, orangutan was laughing at something he couldn't even understand. Then he showed the poem to the other instructor orangutans, and they started laughing. And that did it, Pop. I said to myself, "This ain't my stick. What am I doing this for? What am I doing this shit for? This navigator jive ain't for me." They sent me before a board of senior officers. You see, this was the second time I'd failed my night celestial flying exam, and they gave me a flat-ass white all-American lieutenant for counsel, and you know what he told me? He told me to cop a plea, to cop a plea, Pop, to express my love of country and dedication to the air force! To lick ass! That way, he said, they'd only wash me back a few months and I could still come through. But I told that board, "Let go my toe!" And they replied, "What?" You know, the way white people do when they don't believe their ears. So I screamed at the top of my voice, "Let go my nigger toe so I can stand up and be a man.'' . . . I guess they thought I was insane. They hemmed and hawed and cleared their thoughts, but they let go my toe, Mama. I had cut loose the man. Then I went right home and I cut loose my fine fox, and I cut loose my so-called black brother officers, and I felt like there was no more glue holding my shoes to the track; I felt I could almost fly, Pop, 'cause I was a supernigger no more . . . So I ain't proving nothing to nobody—white, black, blue, or polka dot—to nobody! Not even to you, Daddy Johnny . . . Mama, you give that thing—that uniform thing to the Salvation Army or to the Goodwill or whatever, 'cause it will never have the good fortune to get on my back again.

DUDLEY.

Bravo! Bravissimo!

(Bass fades. GRANDMA *sings "Onward, Christian Soldiers," and for some time no one says anything.)*

JEFF

(Quietly).

It's all about battlefields—just like you said, Pop.

(JOHN *pauses for an infinite time, looking at* JEFF, *then at* MATTIE *and the others. With great deliberation he then collects his coat and starts walking out slowly.)*

MATTIE

(Trying to stop him).

John! It's Jeff's coming-home party!

(He doesn't stop, exiting through the front door—leaving everyone suspended in a state of sad frustration. Lights fade as they all avoid looking at each other.)

It is Friday evening. DUDLEY, MATTIE, GRANDMA, *and* JEFF *are seated in the living room.* ANN *is in the kitchen busily putting away dishes. The air is very heavy. After a long pause,* JEFF *rises, moves toward the window.*

JEFF.

I noticed the kids tore down the baskets on the basketball court, Ma.

MATTIE.

Yeah, well, they weren't made to be swung on, that's for sure.

JEFF.

Why are we so damn destructive, Ma?

MATTIE.

I guess 'cause we're so mad . . . Lord, where could he be?

GRANDMA

(Intoxicated).

Ain't nothing strange about a man staying away from home. Does 'em good.

MATTIE.

Mama, it's Friday. He's been gone since Saturday.

DUDLEY.

Oh, he'll be all right, Mattie.

MATTIE.

It's like he just disappeared—

JEFF.

Mama, have you checked the police station today?

MATTIE.

Five times!

DUDLEY.

Well, won't do any good to worry. He's a strong, capable man with a whole lot of sense. He's probably in some hotel writing.

GRANDMA.

You mean *drinking!*

DUDLEY.

Well—both then.

MATTIE

(On the verge of tears).

Anything could happen to him. All these dope fiends running 'round Harlem, banging people in the head for a quarter. He could be laying in some vacant lot—hurt—or, or—

JEFF.

No, Mama—he's all right!

MATTIE.

Six days!

DUDLEY.

I'm gonna have to give you a sedative if you don't calm down, Mattie.

GRANDMA.

I like sedatives myself.

DUDLEY.

You starting on your medicine a little early, aren't you, Grandma?

GRANDMA.

I takes my medicine whenever I need it. It opens up my chest and cuts the phlegm.

MATTIE.

Poor thing—he could be seriously injured—

GRANDMA

(Bass enters).

Now, that's exactly what happened to my Ben Brown. He was wild as a pine cone and as savage as a grizzly, and black! Black as a night what ain't got no moon. He'd stay out in the woods for days at a time—always come back with a mess of fish or a sack of rabbits, and possums—that man could tree a possum like he was a hound dog. I guess he was so black till they musta thought he was a shadow, creeping up on 'em.

(Pause.)

One day he just didn't come back.

MATTIE.

Mama, do we have to hear *it* again?

GRANDMA.

A load of buckshot ripped his guts right out—right out on the ground!

MATTIE.

Mama!

GRANDMA.

It was an old redneck cracker named Isaiah what been poaching on our land. Ben said he'd kill any white man he caught hunting on our land. So there they were—both dead—Ben musta been strangling him. I guess Isaiah figured a load of buckshot would put a stop to him. But there was Ben, still holding on to that cracker's throat when we found 'em. Couldn't nothing stop my husband from doing what he had a mind to do. They had to pry his hands loose. Folks come from miles around to attend his funeral. White folks too. Yes, they did. He was a king in his own right, and they knew it. Gawdamercy, my man was a king. And I know he's in *Glory!* Just awaiting for his Wilhemina. I knows it.

(Starts humming "Rock of Ages." Bass fades.)

DUDLEY.

The reason I asked to see you all tonight—well—well—because Mattie and I have something very serious to discuss with you.

MATTIE.

Do they have to know, Dudley?

DUDLEY.

It's only fair that they should know, Mattie. Mattie is going to have to be hospitalized. I guess that's why Johnny hasn't been home—I guess he's off somewhere—brooding.

MATTIE.

Dudley! You promised me you wouldn't tell him—

DUDLEY.

I made a decision, Mattie. It was either keep my promise to you or prepare Johnny ahead of time for what might kill him—if he heard it too sudden-like . . .

MATTIE.

Then you're responsible—If anything's happened to him—you're responsible.

DUDLEY.

I made a judgment—

JEFF.

Will somebody please tell me what's going on?

DUDLEY.

Jeff, we got the report today. Mattie's got, well, several growths—malignant growths. Mattie's got cancer.

MATTIE.

There you go again—about as gentle as a sledgehammer.

JEFF.

How serious?

DUDLEY.

Very serious, but not hopeless—the location prevents removal, but radium treatments might arrest the—

MATTIE.

Jeff, you don't see me upset, do you, son?

JEFF

(Cupping her face in his hands lovingly).

Mama!

MATTIE.

I'm gonna die—that's all there is to it.

GRANDMA.

No such thing! You know Dudley here's a cockeyed quack—

MATTIE.

Mama, the only thing I'm worried about is the whereabouts of my man.

JEFF.

But you can't think negative like that—

(GRANDMA *sings loudly, "For His eye is on the sparrow, and I know He watches me."*)

MATTIE.

Hush, Mama.

(ANN *comes to the door. Bass enters.*)

Now, what old negative? Look at me! I've had a full life with an extraordinary man who fell upon me and fed my soul like manna from heaven—bless him, God bless him wherever he is—And you—where could I get a finer-looking, stronger-looking, more loving son than my Jeff? And I'll be around to see you marry Ann—a gift to you, Jeff, and don't you abuse her. I got my mother beside me, still alive and kicking. And Dudley Stanton—a mainstay—your father's and my spiritual brother—

DUDLEY.

Thank you, sweetheart—

MATTIE.

No, Dudley! Thank you. Now, what old negative thinking? If Johnny were to come through that door right now, I'd be the happiest woman in God's creation—and like my Johnny says, "Lord, I don't feel noways tired—I could go on for another century."

JEFF

(Very upset).

You will, Mama. You will.

MATTIE.

But it's my time, baby. I guess maybe I've done whatever He put me here to do.

(There is a knock on the front door. ANN *answers it. It is* MO *and* GAIL. ANN *shows them into the living room.)*

MO.

Dr. Stanton! Mrs. Williams—Grandma—

MATTIE.

How've you been, Li'l Mo? Lord, you sure have grown.

GAIL.

Mrs. Williams—everybody—

(GRANDMA *grunts.)*

MO.

I got to see you, Jeff.

JEFF.

Is it important?

MO.

I need your help, Jeff.

JEFF.

Let's go into the kitchen. I'll be right back, Mama.

(JEFF, MO, GAIL, *and* ANN *move toward kitchen. Living-room conversation continues.)*

MATTIE.

Looks like rain.

GRANDMA.

I sure hate this dirty city when it rains—looks like a cesspool.

DUDLEY.

One thing good about rain in February—it means an early spring.

JEFF

(From the kitchen).

Look, man, I know I promised Gail—but that's gonna have to wait. My folks are in heavy trouble.

MO.

Yeah, I heard about your father.

ANN.

We just found out Mrs. Williams has cancer.

GAIL.

Oh, Jeff, I'm so sorry.

MO.

Wow, me too, man—I see what you mean. Wow!

MATTIE

(From the living room).

Don't you think—well—we could go on without Jeff, Dudley? He's just a child.

DUDLEY.

He's a man now, Mattie, and with Grandma getting up there and Johnny—taking it so hard—

GRANDMA.

Who's getting up where? A body ain't no older than their toes, and mine twinkle a damn sight

better than yours—

DUDLEY.

When you've had your medicine.

GAIL

(From the kitchen).

How serious is it, Jeff?

ANN.

It's inoperable. The only hope is radium treatment.

MO.

I'm sorry, man. I really am.

JEFF.

Thanks.

MATTIE

(From living room).

Mama, sing that song for me.

GRANDMA.

Which song, daughter?

MATTIE.

"Rock of Ages."

(GRANDMA *begins singing soothingly.* MATTIE *joins her from time to time.)*

MO

(From kitchen).

All them years we was running together, Mrs. Williams was like a mother to me too, remember, Jeff?

JEFF.

Yeah.

MO.

I guess that changes things 'round. I wouldn't want to put more weight on you now, especially behind news like that.

ANN.

What is the problem, Gail?

GAIL.

There's a stool pigeon in the organization. It's gotta be either Chips, Skeeter, or Al.

ANN.

Oh no.

GAIL.

If we don't find him out quick, everything's liable to blow up in our faces. Remember what I told y'all 'bout that cop Buckley?

ANN.

What can Jeff do?

GAIL.

Mo's laying a trap tonight where the stoolie's gonna hafta phone his boss. He'll hafta do it from either the pool-hall phone next to headquarters, or the bar phone down the street. Mo's got both phones bugged, ready to be monitored. I'll be listening in the pool-hall basement, and we wanted Jeff to cover the phone in the bar. Jeff's the only person we can trust.

MO.

What about it, Jeff?

JEFF

(Angrily).

I got no time for this cloak-and-dagger shit—my folks are hurting, man, didn't you hear?

MO.

Okay, man. Okay, I dig.

ANN.

What about me?

JEFF

(Adamantly).

Hell, no. I won't let you or my family get implicated in this shit—

ANN.

Jeff, I don't intend to get implicated—but what Gail and Mo are asking doesn't seem unreasonable. Remember?—my brothers were betrayed once, Jeff. My father is still in prison as a result. Nine years with still no release in sight. No matter what you and I might think about Mo's activities, he certainly does not deserve betrayal. I could not live with myself knowing that I had an opportunity to help and didn't.

MO.

Thanks for the offer, baby. But I'm afraid it's no good. What has to be done and where it's gotta happen, a woman would only draw suspicion.

JEFF.

How long would it take, Mo?

MO.

No more than an hour's time, Jeff. All together, you should be back here three hours from right now. I promise you, Jeff, it'll be no sweat. I just need to know, you dig?

JEFF.

Why you sure he'll make contact?

MO.

He's gotta. Tonight is the night of our big thing, Jeff. I'm ordering a change of plan at the last minute that's gonna make the rat hafta contact the pigs. Meanwhile, nobody but me knows that I'm crossing everybody up by following through with my original plan. Nobody's gonna get hurt, Jeff, just some property damaged. While everybody is on their way to the police station, I'll be headed—

JEFF.

I don't want to know, Mo. I'll monitor the phone for you, but I don't want to know nothing. Don't crowd me, Mo, you understand?

MO.

That's cool, Jeff.

JEFF.

This is as far as I go, Mo.

MO.

I gotcha, Brother Jeff. I dig.

ANN.

And I will sit with Gail at the pool hall.

JEFF.

No!

ANN.

She shouldn't be alone, Jeff.

JEFF.

I *said no!*

MO.

It's safe, Jeff. I swear. You know I wouldn't have my woman doing anything that would put her in a trick. No jeopardy, man, I promise.

MATTIE

(From living room).

What time you got, Dudley?

DUDLEY.

Five after seven.

MATTIE.

You think he's had his dinner?

DUDLEY.

Sure, sweetheart. Keep singing, Grandma.

JEFF

(From the kitchen).

All right, Ann.

MO.

Groovy. Make it to the bar about 8:45, Jeff. Take a cab so you'll be seen as little as possible. The bartender, a buddy of mine, will take you to the setup. About the same time Jeff leaves here, Gail will pick you up outside, Ann. Okay, we'll split now—by the back door. So we won't disturb—Like I said, Jeff, I really am sorry about Mrs. Williams. I really mean it.

JEFF.

Yeah, later, Mo.

MO.

Okay.

(MO *and* GAIL *exit out the kitchen door.* JEFF *and* ANN *return to the living room.*)

MATTIE.

What happened to Mo and his girl?

JEFF.

They went out the back, Mama.

(There is an awkward silence.)

DUDLEY.

Jeff, Mattie will be admitted to the hospital on Monday.

MATTIE.

Couldn't I be treated at home, Dudley? Ann's a nurse. She could—

ANN.

You need special equipment, Mrs. Williams, but of course I'll be your nurse.

MATTIE.

Would you, Ann? I hate those nurses at Harlem. They're so indifferent and snooty.

JEFF.

Goddamn!

GRANDMA.

Watch your mouth! Can't even pee straight and using that kind of language.

(There's a second sound at the back door. JOHN: *"I'm all right! I can make it!"* JEFF *and* ANN *rush to open the door, exiting. We hear voices outside—*MO *and* GAIL *explaining.* JOHN *enters, assisted by* JEFF *and* ANN. *He has a week's growth of beard. His eyes have the deep-socket look of an alcoholic who's been on a substantial bender. His overall appearance is gaunt and shoddy. His clothes are filthy and wrinkled. He obviously smells. His hands have a slight tremor. Thee is a deep gash above his left eye. Bass enters.* JOHN *is helped into a chair,* MATTIE *embracing him.)*

MATTIE.

Johnny, sweet Johnny! We've been so worried about you.

JOHN.

Don't, Mattie! I smell something awful.

DUDLEY.

Move, Mattie. Let me take a look at that cut.

(Moves MATTIE *aside.)*

Jeff, bring my bag. It's in the hallway there.

(JEFF exits to hallway.)

Hand me a towel, Grandma.

GRANDMA.

Old wino, nigger.

DUDLEY.

Wet it with cold water. Maybe we can stop the bleeding.

ANN.

I'll hold it, Dr. Stanton.

DUDLEY.

Good girl.

(She presses the folded paper towel to JOHNNY's *cut.)*

JOHN.

Fighting lady Ann. I sure needed me a fighting lady out there. You shoulda seen me, Mattie, when them young hoods jumped me.

MATTIE.

I saw you, baby. Every second.

JOHN.

I was like a cornered wildcat. I was battlin' 'em to a draw. Then Li'l Mo and his fighting lady came up.

DUDLEY.

It's a bird, it's a plane, it's a Supercullud Guy!

JOHN.

Super Black Man, sicklehead. I ain't been

hanging out with them militant winos for nothing.

DUDLEY.

Folks, take a look at an aging African warrior, trying to make a comeback.

JOHN

(Singing to a made-up tune).

When I get home to Africa

I'll buy myself a mango.

Grab myself a monkey gal

And do the monkey tango.

DUDLEY.

When'd you eat last?

JOHN.

Niggers used to sing that to make fun of Marcus Garvey. Can you imagine. The great Marcus Garvey.

DUDLEY.

Answer my question! When was the last time you had a decent meal?

JOHN.

Wednesday. Or was it Tuesday?

DUDLEY.

What are you trying to do, Johnny?

(JEFF returns with the bag.)

ANN.

I'll do it.

(She swabs the wound and bandages it.)

MATTIE.

Where've you been, baby?

JOHN.

In the desert, Mattie. Out in the desert, like Christ, talking to myself.

GRANDMA.

Christ was talking to the devil, ya old wino.

JOHN.

Same difference. But I took care of the old bastard. I said, Get thee behind me, Prince of Darkness! Then I got thirsty and came home. I wanted to see me some angels.

JEFF.

Pop, you okay now? I mean, for real?

JOHN.

Yeah, Jeff. Welcome home, son. My son is really home. And I'm happy he's found his battlefield.

MATTIE.

You won't do it again, will you, Johnny? If something's troubling you, let's talk about it. Okay? Now promise!

JOHN.

I was all right, Mattie—really. Dulcey gave me a room over her store. I told her I wanted to think—to write some poetry. I wanted to write a love poem—to you, Mattie. Words are like precious jewels, did you know that? But I couldn't find any jewels precious enough to match you, Mattie. So I took to drinking, and before I knew it, I was drunk all the time. I couldn't stop. Then yesterday these little men came to visit me—about one foot tall. They both had a T-shirt on with a zero on the chest. And they crried two little satchels. I asked 'em what they were carrying in 'em, and they opened up the satchels, and they were empty. I asked them their names, and they said, "The Nothing Brothers." That's when I figured it was time to go home.

DUDLEY.

Delirium tremens—D.T.'s from not eating.

JOHN.

Whatever. I knew it was time to come home. I knew it was Friday too. Dudley told me he'd have some information for me on Friday.

(Tense silence.)

DUDLEY

(Avoiding it).

What kind of information?

JEFF.

We all know, Pop.

JOHN.

You all know? Then—

DUDLEY.

Mattie will be admitted Monday morning.

(At this point, JOHN *goes berserk. Screams at the top of his voice. Racing around the room, whipping with an imaginary whip, and screaming, "Get out, get out, you motherfuckers. Get out of my father's house!" He falls to the floor—somewhat exhausted, looks up as if to heaven. Bass counterpoint increases.)*

JOHN.

You son-of-a-bitch, why do you keep fucking with me? What do you want from me, you bastard?

MATTIE.

Johnny, don't talk like that. That's blasphemy.

JOHN.

He keeps fucking with me, Mattie. When I was a kid, the bigger kids used to always pick on me. I had to fight every day. They said it was because I was a smart aleck.

(To the heavens)

Is that why, you bastard, 'cause I'm a smart aleck?

MATTIE.

You can't talk to Him like that. He'll turn His back on you.

JOHN.

You know what I'm gonna do on Judgment Day? I'm gonna grab that motherfucker by the throat and squeeze and squeeze and squeeze until I get an answer.

MATTIE.

He doesn't have to give you an answer. I thought you said, "Get thee behind me—" I thought you took care a Satan!

JOHN

(Breaks into tears).

I tried, Mattie. I tried—you don't know how fucking hard I tried.

MATTIE

(Embraces him).

I know, baby. I see you every second.

JOHN.

You shoulda let me whip 'em out, Mattie. You shoulda let me whip out the bullshit.

MATTIE.

We weren't made that way, baby.

JOHN.

You shoulda let me whip out the money changers. You deserve so much more than this nothing. I wanted to do so much for you, Mattie.

MATTIE.

I got *you,* baby. I got the kindest, sweetest man in the world. I got the Rolls-Royce, baby.

JOHN.

I coulda done it, Mattie. God knows, I coulda done it!

MATTIE.

I know, baby. I put it on you. I stopped you and I'm sorry. I'm sorry. Will you forgive me, sweet baby? Please forgive me! I was selfish, Johnny. I've been so goddam happy! All I ever cared about was seeing you walk, stumble, or stagger through that door. I only complained because I felt I should say something—but I never meant it, Johnny, I never meant a word. You couldn't have given me nothing more, baby. I'da just keeled over and died from too much happiness. Just keeled over and died.

(Lights begin to dim as bass rises. Music remains as long as it takes actors to exit and get into place for next scene. When lights finally rise again, MATTIE *and* DUDLEY *are sitting in living room,* MATTIE *under heavy sedation, intermittently knitting, nodding from time to time.* DUDLEY *is watching TV, smoking a cigar. Silence ensues for a long time. Finally* MATTIE *addresses* DUDLEY.*)*

MATTIE.

What'd you give me, Dudley? Sure is strong. Can hardly keep my head up.

DUDLEY.

Do you feel any pain?

MATTIE.

Not now.

DUDLEY.

Then it's doing its job. You'll rest good when you go to bed.

MATTIE.

Which can't be too long from now. The way I'm feeling.

(JOHN *appears at the top of the stairs; descends slowly, as he is absorbed in reading some pages. He enters the living room and announces quietly . . .*)

JOHN.

I finished it.

MATTIE.

What?

JOHN.

A poem I been working on, Mattie. It's your poem, Mattie. "The River Niger." It ain't a love poem, but it's for you, sugar, dedicated to my superbitch, Mattie Jean Williams.

DUDLEY.

Read it to us, nigger.

(ANN *and* GAIL *are seen entering the back door.* JEFF *too.* JOHN *begins to read, and bass begins low with African motif and gradually rises.* JEFF *and girls begin to engage in conversation, but desist when they hear* JOHN. *They drift to living room.*)

JOHN.

I am the River Niger—hear my waters!
I am totally flexible.
I am the River Niger—hear my waters!
My waters are the first sperm of the world.
When the earth was but a faceless whistling embryo,
Life burst from my liquid kernels like popcorn.
Hear my waters—rushing and popping in muffled finger-drum staccato.
It is life you hear, stretching its limbs in my waters—

I am the River Niger! Hear my waters!
When the Earth Mother cracked into continents,
I was vomited from the cold belly of the Atlantic
To slip slyly into Africa
From the underside of her brow.
I see no—
Hear no—
Speak no evil,
But I know.
I gossip with the crocodile
And rub elbows with the river horse.
I have swapped morbid jokes with the hyena
And heard his dry cackle at twilight.
I see no—
Hear no—
Speak no evil,
But I know.

I am the River Niger—hear my waters!
Hear, I say, hear my waters, man!

They is Mammy-tammys, baby.
I have lapped at the pugnacious hips of brown mamas.
Have tapped on the doors of their honeydews, yeah!
I have shimmered like sequins
As they sucked me over their blueberry tongues,
As they sung me to sleep in the glittering afternoon, yeah!
I have washed the red wounds of clay-decorated warriors—
Bad, bad dudes who smirked at the leopard.
I have cast witches from gabbling babies, yeah!
Have known the warm piss from newly circumcized boys.
Have purified the saliva from sun-drenched lions—
Do you hear me talking?

I am the River Niger!
I came to the cloudy Mississippi
Over keels of incomprehensible woe.
I ran 'way to the Henry Hudson
Under the sails of ragged hope.
I am the River Niger,
Transplanted to Harlem
From the Harlem River Drive.
Hear me, my children—hear my waters!
I sleep in your veins.
I see no—
Hear no—
Speak no evil,
But I know, and I know that you know.
I flow to the ends of your spirit.
Hold hands, my children, and I will flow to the ends of the earth,
And the whole world will her my waters.
I am the River Niger! Don't deny me!
Do you hear me? Don't deny me!
(Pause. Bass fades.)

MATTIE.

That's very beautiful, Johnny.

JEFF.

Yeah, Pop, that's pretty nice.

DUDLEY

(Sarcastically).

Interesting!

JOHN.

Ya monkey chaser.

JEFF.

How you feeling, Mama?

MATTIE.

Okay, I guess. A little woozy, but I'm going to bed now, and I couldn't think of a better time than after Johnny's poem. Thank you, dear.

JOHN.
Be up soon, Mattie.

MATTIE.
Take your time.

DUDLEY.
Yeah, I'd better get home, too.

JEFF.
Good night, Mama.

ANN and GAIL.
Good night, Mrs. Williams.

MATTIE.
Good night.

(She exits.)

(GRANDMA enters, humming "Rock of Ages." They pass each other on the stairs.)
Good night, Mama.

GRANDMA.
Sleep tight! Don't let the bedbugs bite.

(MATTIE exits, shaking her head. GRANDMA hums throughout this scene. She comes into the living room.)

JEFF.
How ya feel, Pop?

JOHN.
Fine! Fine, still a little shaky, but all right.

JEFF.
Ya got any booze, Pop?

JOHN.
No, I'm drying out. Doctor's orders.

GRANDMA.
Where the *TV Guide?*
(She searches for it.)

DUDLEY
(Finding it underneath him).
Oh, here it is, Mrs. Brown. I was sitting on it.

GRANDMA.
It was under you all this time?

DUDLEY.
I guess so.

GRANDMA.
Then let it cool off a little bit before you give it to me.

JEFF
(To ANN and GAIL).
Let's make it into the kitchen.

ANN.
I'm still cold from outside.

DUDLEY
(To JEFF).
Has it started raining yet?

JEFF.
It's raining and snowing at the same time.
(They move to kitchen.)

JOHN.
See, Dudley, life's full of contradictions.

DUDLEY.
Ain't nothing contradictory about nature, man. Nature is everything. It's human beings who are contradictions.

JOHN.
Well, ain't human beings a part of nature?

DUDLEY
(Seriously).
Guess so, now that you mention it.

JOHN.
That's why we're so messed up. We forget that we're just a part of nature.
(Pause.)
Put on the TV, Dudley.

DUDLEY.
I should be going home.

JOHN.
Relax, man.
(DUDLEY switches on the TV.)

JEFF
(From the kitchen).
What'd *you* hear, Gail?

GAIL.
Nothing but Skeeter, making a horse connection.

ANN.
We thought it might be a code, but it sounded innocent enough.

GAIL.
What about you?

JEFF.
I heard something all right. But I couldn't identify the voice. The bartender was no help; he was somewhere else when the call was made.

GAIL.
What did the caller say?

JEFF.
Plan B.

GAIL.
That's all—"Plan B"?

JEFF.
Right. And the voice on the other end said, "You sure?" The caller said, "Yes—Plan B."

GAIL.
You couldn't recognize the voice?

JEFF.
No, but I might if I heard it again.

GAIL.
I shouldn't have let you talk me into coming here. Mo might need me.

JEFF.
Calm down, baby. We'll hear soon.

GAIL.
But something might have happened.

ANN.
He wanted you to come with us.

JEFF.

Stop worrying, Mo's all right.

GAIL.

I can't help . . .

(She attempts to calm herself, crossing to the back door and looking out.)

It sure is beginning to come down. Beginning to stick.

ANN.

I've been away from South Africa for a long time, but I still can't get used to snow.

GAIL.

Snow makes everything so quiet. It's spooky.

GRANDMA

(Entering the kitchen).

Ya wants some spirits?

JEFF.

We sure do, Grandma.

GRANDMA.

Turn your backs.

(She produces a bottle of Old Grand-dad from her new hiding place on top of the cabinet—pours each of them a drink.)

The way things been happening 'round here today, a body needs some spirits. Here! Besides, this child's so fidgety—

(Referring to GAIL.)

—done got my phlegm acting up again.

(GRANDMA *downs hers. For a second they watch in amazement—then down theirs. There is a noise at the back door.* JEFF *goes to the door.)*

JEFF.

It's Mo and Skeets.

(Opens door. MO *drags* SKEETER *in. It's obvious he's been hurt.)*

MO.

Pigs are swarming all over headquarters!

(DUDLEY *enters, followed closely by* JOHN. DUDLEY *examines* SKEETER.)

DUDLEY.

Gunshot wound. What's going on 'round here? Bring me my bag, Ann. You're very lucky, young man—no bones broken. Put a tourniquet on that arm, Ann, while I clean it out.

(ANN *and* DUDLEY *work on* SKEETER. JEFF *pulls* MO *into the living room.)*

JEFF.

Why in the hell did you bring him here?

MO.

I figured Dr. Stanton would be here—

JEFF.

I told you I don't want my family implicated in this shit—Why didn't you take him to your place?

MO

JOHN *comes to the door).*

I live over headquarters! The pigs—

JEFF.

Oh, shit—shit—what happened?

MO.

It's stupid—stupid. I mean, we had just crossed the street. I mean, we were just walking 'round the fence when this pig started blowing his whistle and yelling at us.

JEFF.

They musta been alerted.

MO.

Fucking Skeeter panicked—started running— what the hell am I supposed to do? I'm carrying a tote bag with four sticks of dynamite. So I start running too. Next thing I know, there're four pigs chasing us. One fires and spins Skeets clean 'round. Skeets is screaming and shit, and they're gaining, so I blast off a couple and knock trigger-happy on his ass.

JEFF.

What—you crazy motherfucker, coming here after that?

JOHN.

You mean, they just started shooting? You didn't shoot first?

MO.

Why would we do that?

JOHN.

You sure?

MO.

I don't want to hurt nobody if I can help it, Mr. Williams.

JOHN.

You think he's dead?

MO.

I don't know. He hit the ground so hard I could almost feel it.

JOHN.

I sure hope you killed the bastard. But if you call yourself a revolutionary, then you supposed to know where you gonna take your wounded. Takes more'n wearing a goddamn beret.

DUDLEY

(From the kitchen).

Yeah! Why don't I set up another office over here?

(There is a wild banging on the front door. JEFF *answers the door.* AL *enters, followed closely by* CHIPS.)

JEFF

(Angrily).

What's going on?

AL.

There are wall-to-wall pigs at headquarters. And Mo said—

JEFF

(To MO*).*

And you told them to come here if that happened—

(Silence.)

Didn't you? Didn't you? Didn't I tell you not to crowd me, ya stupid bastard?

MO.

I was wrong, Jeff. I'm sorry.

JEFF.

You're sorry.

*(*JEFF *leaps on* MO *and is separated by* JOHN*.)*

I'll kill him, Pop, so help me. I'll kill him!

JOHN.

You'll wake up your mother.

(In the next second, a confusion of sirens and police whistles—lights shining through the front windows and the back door, and a policeman on a bullhorn.)

LIEUTENANT STAPLES'S VOICE

(From outside).

This is Lieutenant Staples from the Thirty-second Police Precinct. We know you are in there and who's in there. We gotcha front and back, plus men on the roof. You got five minute to throw out your weapons and come out of there. And let me remind whoever else is in there not to harbor criminals from the law. You got five minutes. If there're innocent people in there, their blood will be on your hands.

JOHN.

Give me those goddamn guns.

(Pause.)

Come on, come on! They can't prove a thing—except those guns. Dudley, get Skeeter's. Come on, Mo, give it to me.

*(*MO *hesitates, but gives it to him.)*

CHIPS.

Al's the one, Mo. A fucking Judas faggot.

AL.

You lie!

CHIPS.

There were cops everywhere. You said not to do nothing when we got to the police station until you and Skeeter showed, right? Well, when you didn't show, he ran across the street and deliberately bumped into one of 'em—

AL.

He's lying.

CHIPS.

And whispered something in his ear. Next thing I know, every pig and his mother is jumping into a car—that's when it hit me you was pulling a trick, and the state office building plan was still on.

AL.

I didn't have a damn thing to do with that.

CHIPS.

You shoulda heard the squawk boxes, "State office building—emergency—emergency." The block was vacant inside of a minute.

AL.

You're not believing this shit?

CHIPS.

Then he tried to shake me, Mo. Caught a cab, and you know what he told him? Told him to go to the state office building.

AL.

I gave him the address of headquarters.

CHIPS.

You lie, nigger. I overheard you.

SKEETER

(Coming out of the kitchen).

And the way you keep questioning me about Buckley—

MO.

Why didn't you tell me about that?

AL.

He's your informer, Mo. He'd do anything for horse.

(Pause.)

He told them pigs to go to the state office building. He's the one.

MO.

He was with me.

JEFF

(To AL*).*

It was you. I heard you.

AL.

Heard me what?

JEFF.

The phone—you phoned. It was your voice. You said, "B." The voice at the other end said, "Are you sure?" and you repeated, "B!"

AL.

That don't prove nothing—Skeeter left too—we both went to the phone.

JEFF.

Okay, if it wasn't you then, suppose I were to tell you I killed Buckley?

AL.

What do you know about Buckley?

JEFF.

I did it. I killed him.

AL.

How'd he die?

JEFF,

Two slugs in the chest.

AL.

What caliber?

JEFF.

Forty-five. I stole it from the air force.

AL.

Don't shit me. Buckley was killed almost a month ago. Ya only been here a week.

JEFF.

What makes you so sure?

MO.

What are you doing, Jeff?

JEFF.

I was released from active duty exactly one month from last Friday.

AL.

Bullshit!

JEFF.

Wanta see my release papers?

ANN.

Jeff!

JEFF.

Stay out of it, Ann!

(Fumbles through wallet and gives AL *his release papers.* AL *reads them.)*

AL

(Pulling out his revolver).

All right, stand still, all of you! I took this assignment for one reason and one reason only, to find out who killed Buckley. And now I know.

(To JEFF*)*

You killed Buckley. He was worth ten of you Brillo heads. Now his friends out there are gonna take this place apart, and all of you are in trouble, you hear. You motherfuckers, fucking up the country with your slogans and your jive-ass threats. Militants, ain't that a bitch. Black cripples, trying to scale a mountain. I hate the smell of you assholes.

MO.

Jeff's lying, can't you see that? I killed Buckley.

SKEETER.

I did it.

CHIPS.

I did it.

AL.

No, no, it fits. It fits. I know where each of you mothers were when Buckley was killed. None of you coulda done it. He did it. Why didn't I think of good old Jeff? All I heard about was good old Jeff. Jeff this—Jeff that— till you bastards staged your phony scene to throw me off the track when he got here.

MO.

Don't be stupid. It was an outside job.

AL

(To JEFF*).*

Yeah . . . him.

ANN.

What are you doing, Jeff? You know you were with me that whole month in Canada!

(This causes AL *to pause for a moment in frozen doubt.* JOHN *seizes the opportunity to raise the gun still in his hand, point it at* AL.*)*

JOHN.

Drop it son.

*(*AL *whirls and shoots. There is an exchange of gun play between the two men.* AL *goes down, killed instantly.* JOHN *also goes down, mortally wounded.)*

JEFF

(Rushing to his father's side, followed closely by DUDLEY*).*

Pop!

JOHN.

The guns, Jeff . . . put 'em in the drain in the basement. Al's still holding his? Good.

JEFF.

Pop!

JOHN.

Hurry, you don't want Daddy Johnny to die for nothing, do you?

*(*JEFF *grabs* SKEETER's *and* CHIPS's, *tries to take* MO's.*)*

No! We need Mo's—this is yours, ain't it, Mo?

MO.

Yes, sir.

JOHN.

Go on, son.

*(*JEFF *exits.)*

(To DUDLEY, *who's been trying to get at* JOHN's *wound)*

Don't worry about that, ya monkey chaser. They'll be in here in a second.

DUDLEY.

You're hurt, man. Ann—my bag—

*(*ANN *starts off.)*

JOHN.

Fuck your bag, Dudley. Go to the door—tell that Lieutenant Staples—tell him—to give us five more minutes—just five more—then he can make his arrests—

DUDLEY.

You'll die if I don't—

JOHN.

I'll die anyway. Do as I say! Before they shoot up Mattie's house.

*(*ANN *comes back with bag, starts preparing dressings.* JEFF *returns.* MATTIE *appears at the top of the stairs.)*

MATTIE.

(Extremely drowsy. JEFF *and* GAIL *run to her, the rest are stupefied.)*

I had a dream, and I heard this noise in the middle of it.

DUDLEY

(Waving a handkerchief out the front door

and shouting).
Lieutenant Staples—Lieutenant Staples.
STAPLES'S VOICE.
This is Lieutenant Staples—what's going on in there?
DUDLEY.
I'm Dr. Dudley Stanton—next-door neighbor. A man's been seriously wounded in here. Call an ambulance.
STAPLES'S VOICE.
Throw out your guns.
DUDLEY.
I think it would be best for you to see the situation for yourself.
JOHN.
Good boy, Dudley. They don't care nothing 'bout niggers killing themselves nohow.
DUDLEY
(To STAPLES*).*
Both weapons are secured. I have them. Give us five minutes, then come in.
STAPLES'S VOICE.
If anyone tries to escape, my men have orders to shoot—
MATTIE.
What on earth's going on?
DUDLEY.
No one will. I give my word. Five minutes.
(Closes the door.)
CHIPS.
We *got* to get outta here!
MO.
Shut up, and stay tight!
JEFF
(To MO*).*
Do you see what you brought in here tonight?
(Leaps for MO *once again.)*
JOHN.
Jeff, stop it. Don't make a mockery out of my death. Sit down, all of you, and listen to me.
MATTIE
(For the first time realizing JOHN'*s hurt).*
Johnny! Johnny!
JOHN.
Keep Mattie away, Dudley—keep her away—
DUDLEY
(Restraining her).
Try and be calm, Mattie.
JOHN.
Wipe off the handle on Mo's gun, Jeff.
*(*JEFF *does it.)*
Okay, now give it to me.
(He grips the gun firmly several times.)
I don't want nobody's fingerprints on it but mine.
MATTIE.
Johnny, you're bleeding—

JOHN
(With savage power).
Mattie, I love ya, Mattie. I ain't got much life left.
MATTIE.
Johnny, no!
JOHN.
I got to get our children straight before I go—now be my superbitch and shut the fuck up.
*(*MATTIE *understands and obeys.)*
Now you youngbloods listen to me. Here's the story: I am the real leader of the organization—ya got me. I was with Skeeter when he got shot. I fired the shot which hit the cop at the office building. I made it back here—found out that Al here is a Judas, and we had a shoot-out. The rest of you have never owned a gun—only your leader—me! Ya got that?
GRANDMA
(Drunk, and in a state of shock, comes strangely alive. She thinks JOHN *is her Ben; she rushes up and falls at* JOHN'*s knees).*
Ben—Ben Brown!
(Reaches for JOHN'*s gun.)*
Gimme that shotgun.
*(*MATTIE *blocks her.)*
MATTIE
(Very calm and solemn, almost eerie).
No, Mama.
GRANDMA.
I'll just shoot right into the crowd, daughter. See 'em, look at their faces! They's glad to see my Ben dead. Lawdamercy! He's dead!
(Crying from an ancient wound.)
Gimme that shotgun, child. Ten for one, ten for one—my man is a king—you crackers—ya dirty old redneck crackers.
(Breaks into ''Rock of Ages.'' Bass counterpoint seeps in.)
JOHN.
Hear that, Mattie. The old battle-ax finally gave me a compliment. Where's my Mattie? Let me see my Mattie.
*(*MATTIE'*s let through. They embrace.)*
MATTIE.
I'm with you every second, baby.
JOHN.
I knew she'd slip one day. I'm sorry, Mattie.
MATTIE.
What for, baby?
JOHN.
I'm cheating ya, honey—going first this way.
MATTIE.
Hush now!
JOHN.
Don't suffer long, honey. Just give up and take my hand. The children—the children will be

all right now.

(Pause.)

Look at Dr. Dudley Stanton down there. Trying to save my life. Ain't that a bitch! See what a big old fake you've been all along. Don't worry, Dudley—fighting lady Ann—Jeff—ya got a fighting lady to protect your flanks, son—don't worry, I don't feel nothing now. Just sweetness—a sweet sweetness.

DUDLEY.

Your poems—I'll get 'em published.

JOHN.

Fuck them poems—this is poetry, man—what I feel right here and now. This sweetness. Sing on, Grandma.

(Pause. He shivers)

I found it, Dudley—I found it.

DUDLEY.

What, Johnny?

JOHN.

My battlefield—my battlefield, man! I was a bitch too, ya monkey chaser. See my shit! I got two for the price of one.

DUDLEY.

Yeah, chief.

(JOHN *dies. Pause.*)

CHIPS

(Whimpering).

Oh God, oh my God!

MATTIE.

Shut up! And tell it like Johnny told ya. He ain't gonna die for nothing, 'cause you ain't gonna let him! Jeff—open the door, son! Tell 'em to come on in here!

(JEFF *crosses to the door.*)

And you better not fuck up!

Buried Child

Sam Shepard

FOR JOE CHAIKIN

First presented at the Magic Theatre in San Francisco on June 27, 1978, with the following cast:

(*in order of appearance*)

DODGE	Joseph Gistirak
HALIE	Catherine Willis
TILDEN	Dennis Ludlow
BRADLEY	William M. Carr
SHELLY	Betsy Scott
VINCE	Barry Lane
FATHER DEWIS	Rj Frank

Directed by Robert Woodruff
Scenery by David Gropman
Costumes by Ms. Brookes and Joan E. Weiss
Lighting by John P. Dodd

Buried Child by Sam Shepard premiered on June 27, 1978, at the Magic Theatre in San Francisco's Fort Mason Center, where Sam Shepard is the Playwright-in-Residence. It was directed by Robert Woodruff. In October 1978, the play moved to the Theatre for the New City in New York. In January 1979, *Buried Child* began playing simultaneously in two separate productions, one at the Yale Repertory Theatre in Connecticut and the other at the Theatre De Lys in New York. After 152 performances at the Theatre De Lys, the production moved to the Circle Repertory Theatre where it played through September 1979. The Yale Repertory production moved to Trinity Square Repertory Theatre in Rhode Island and played until April 1980.

Second only to Tennessee Williams, Sam Shepard is one of America's most produced playwrights, with forty productions to his credit. He has won seven Obie awards for distinguished playwriting and was awarded the Pulitzer Prize for *Buried Child* in 1979. He was also the recipient of a Rockefeller grant, a Guggenheim Foundation grant, a CBS Fellowship at the Yale School of Drama and a National Institute for Arts and Letters Award. Ironically, though Shepard is considered the most outstanding spokesman for contemporary American drama, he has never had a commercial Broadway production. He has written and collaborated with Patti Smith, Bob Dylan, Michelangelo Antonioni, Mick Jagger and Joseph Chaikin. *Buried Child* became Shepard's first real commercial success.

Buried Child is the second in a trilogy of plays on the disintegration of the family and of the American Dream. It was preceded by *The Curse of the Starving Class*, in 1977, and followed by *True West*, in 1980. *Buried Child* is the story of an Illinois farm family, a mother, father, two grown sons, and a grandson, Vince, who visits them with his girlfriend Shelley. After a six-year absence, his family pretends not to know or to recognize him. Three generations come together in this play in a bitter, chilling view of the American family: Dodge, a grandfather who slumbers in front of a television with a bottle of whiskey; Halie, a mother whose cheery voice belies the terrible secret within her; and Bradley and Tilden, middle-aged former sportsmen who have deteriorated both physically and spiritually. Vince and Shelley seem normal, but as the play progresses we see that Vince has inherited the family's bad blood. He goes berserk, deserts his girlfriend and decides to live in the house and inherit it by force. The plot revolves around a crime committed by the father twenty years before the opening of the play. For the rest of their lives, each family member is committed by loyalty or fear to keep this crime hidden from the outside world, only hinting at it among themselves. It is this secret that ultimately destroys them.

Shepard makes a searing indictment of the American family, seeing it as a destructive unit rather than a supportive one. Vince's girlfriend, Shelley, is the audience's point of identity, a measure of normality in an alien, hostile environment. The play deals with many themes: homecoming, recognition, belonging, identity, fertility, aggression, pain, pride and rebirth. *Buried Child* is also about heritage: the inheritance of a house, land and goods and also the inheritance of family secrets, guilts and transgressions. It is an eerie tale with bewildering and frightening images that haunt long after the play has been seen or read.

The American setting, the bleak atmosphere and surreal quality are all hallmarks of Shepard's writing. His characters are distinctly American: Old West cowboys, fading rock-and-roll stars, sci-fi monsters, Hollywood agents and screenwriters. Elements of American popular culture are found as well: B movies, melodramas, the occult, detective novels, criminology and revolution. Shepard blends satire and suspense to form a theatre of comedy and menace; his plays exude an aura of mystery and enigma.

Sam Shepard, America's most controversial playwright, whose works are described by critics as "epic fables about the nation's ruthlessness," was born November 5, 1943, in an army basic training camp at Fort Sheridan, Illinois, to Sam Shepard and Jane Schook Rogers. The family moved to South Dakota, Guam, the Philippines and finally to Duarte, a rural suburb east of Los Angeles. They lived on a farm and grew avocados and raised sheep. Shepard developed a knack for animal husbandry; one year, his ram won grand prize at the Los Angeles County Fair. Duarte made a great impact on Shepard as he watched "the dissolution of an agricultural society that had a powerful effect on me—seeing the move toward the suburban octopus." After graduating from high school in 1961, Shepard studied agricultural science at San Antonio Junior College. Like many of his friends, he read the Beat writers: Ferlinghetti, Corso and Kerouac. One day while sitting in a friend's house, he was tossed a book. It was *Waiting for*

Godot. Although at the time he could not make much sense of Beckett, he was fascinated by the language. Soon afterward he wrote his first play, an "imitation of Tennessee Williams."

After three semesters in college, Shepard was faced with two career choices: to take a job managing a sheep ranch or to tour churches with a repertory company as an actor. He needed to leave Duarte for personal reasons, so he chose the latter; after a few months this led him to New York. He decided to seek his fortune as an actor in "the urban badlands of Manhattan's Avenue C with Charles Mingus, Jr., an old high school friend." This was 1963 and Shepard was twenty. The son of the legendary jazz artist helped Shepard to find a job busing tables at the Village Gate, adding to his varied job experiences as sheep shearer, car wrecker, rancher, farmer and actor.

At the Village Gate, Shepard met Ralph Cook, the headwaiter and founder of Theatre Genesis. Shepard had been writing poetry in the Beat style, and Cook encouraged him to write for Off-Off-Broadway theatre. He began writing one-act plays which were really impressionistic mood pieces. In early 1964 a new theatre, St. Marks-in-the-Bouwerie, was looking for new playwrights and Shepard offered them *Cowboys*. Then *Cowboys* and *Rock Garden* opened Theatre Genesis's first season in the fall of 1964. Shepard recalls feeling "at home for the first time" at Theatre Genesis. "Whenever I was feeling lost on the streets, I never went back to my apartment. I always ended up going back to the theatre. . . . It was literally home—I slept there, ate there . . . I spent a lot of time there." However, the critics' reviews were disastrous, and Shepard was planning to go back to California when the *Village Voice* gave him a rave review. This encouraged him to continue to write, and he did so at a furious pace. "The early plays, many written in one night, poured out in a kind of fever. There was so much to write, I felt I couldn't spend time rewriting. I had to move on to the next thing. It was a furious kind of writing. Obsessive . . ." His plays, *Dog, Up to Thursday* and *Rocking Chair,* were produced at the Cafe La Mama Experimental Theatre Club.

An important milestone in Shepard's career occurred when he was included in a New Playwrights Series at the Cherry Lane Theatre in February 1965. Three plays, *Chicago, Icarus' Mother,* and *Red Cross,* won Obie awards for Off and Off-Off-Broadway excellence in 1966. Also in 1966, one of his plays was produced at the University of Minnesota, to be followed by productions in later years at Princeton and Yale. In 1967, he won a Rockefeller Foundation grant and formed a rock group, the Holy Modal Rounders, for which he became the drummer. Drugs and jazz greatly influenced his writing at this point. "I identified a lot with jazz at the time—there was no reason why writing shouldn't be exactly like a jazz improvisation . . ." He went to Mexico and wrote *La Turista,* which was presented at the American Place Theatre. *Forensic and the Navigator* and *Melodrama Play* earned him another Obie for the 1967–68 season. *Operation Sidewinder* was presented at Lincoln Center in 1970, and afterward, due to many internal and external pressures, Shepard left for London with his wife, O-Lan, and his son, Jesse Mojo.

Shepard believes that he learned two very important things in England: how much work it takes to make good theatre, and that it means something to be an American. In London, he produced and directed *The Tooth of Crime* at the Royal Court's Theatre Upstairs. It was there that he began to work with actors for the first time and came under Peter Brooks' influence. Brooks "told me I should start thinking about characters more. . . ."; I used to be a lot more interested in situations or just the sound of words and what that did to characters. Characters seemed like a corny idea, a narrow relevance. Now, I'm interested in character on a big scale." Regarding his experience working with actors, Shepard states: ". . . a playwright has to understand what an actor goes through. . . . I don't see how any playwright can grow if he doesn't get involved with the production of his work. . . . It's the difference between training a horse and getting on his back. Until you get up on stage and put yourself inside the character you'll never realize the dilemmas an actor faces."

Shepard and his family returned to California in 1974, "to find our roots." He now lives on a ranch in Northern California where he writes his plays in longhand on yellow pads, before typing them. He has been greatly influenced by music, both rock and jazz, and by film. He uses Kerouac's technique of "jazz sketching," or jamming with words. Like a musician jumping from key to key, improvising as he goes, Shepard treats dialogue as jazz riffs. "I see actors as musicians, playing to each other, using their voices instead of instruments. I am always surprised by the similarities between music and writing: the inner structure, tonality, rhythm, harmony. . . . Listening is essential in writing and it takes a lot of practice . . . it's that inner sort of listening. It's like listening to yourself when you're driving long distances . . . or listening to yourself play an instrument. . . .''

Writing for film, as well as viewing it, has had an important effect on Shepard's work. He is strongly influenced by the rapid cutting between scenes and characters. This gives an improvisational quality to his plays and has helped to discipline his writing. ''I used to be dead set against rewriting. My attitude was that if a play had faults . . . any attempt to correct them was cheating.'' Now, he states, ''I burn a whole lot in the sink.''

Sam Shepard has also written *Cowboys No. 2;* the screenplay for Antonioni's *Zabriski Point; The Unseen Hand; Mad Dog Blues; Cowboy Mouth,* written with Patti Smith; *The Rolling Thunder Log* Book; *Tooth of Crime; Killer's Head; Angel City; Suicide in Bb; Seduced; Inacoma; Action; The Holy Ghostly; Geography of a Horse Dreamer; Tongues; Savage/Love,* written with Joseph Chaikin; and *Hawk Moon,* a book of fiction and poetry.

CHARACTERS:

DODGE—In his seventies
HALIE—His wife. Mid-sixties
TILDEN—Their oldest son
BRADLEY—Their next oldest son, an amputee
VINCE—Tilden's son
SHELLY—Vince's girl friend
FATHER DEWIS—A Protestant minister

While the rain of your fingertips falls,
while the rain of your bones falls,
and your laughter and marrow fall down,
you come flying.

Pablo Neruda

ACT ONE

Scene: Day. Old wooden staircase down left with pale, frayed carpet laid down on the steps. The stairs lead off stage left up into the wings with no landing. Up right is an old, dark green sofa with the stuffing coming out in spots. Stage right of the sofa is an upright lamp with a faded yellow shade and a small night table with several small bottles of pills on it. Down right of the sofa, with the screen facing the sofa, is a large, old-fashioned brown T.V. A flickering blue light comes from the screen, but no image, no sound. In the dark, the light of the lamp and the T.V. slowly brighten in the black space. The space behind the sofa, upstage, is a large screened-in porch with a board floor. A solid interior door to stage right of the sofa, leading into the room on stage; and another screen door up left, leading from the porch to the outside. Beyond that are the shapes of dark elm trees.

Gradually the form of DODGE is made out, sitting on the couch, facing the T.V., the blue light flickering on his face. He wears a well-worn T-shirt, suspenders, khaki work pants and brown slippers. He's covered himself in an old brown blanket. He's very thin and sickly looking, in his late seventies. He just stares at the T.V. More light fills the stage softly. The sound of light rain. DODGE slowly tilts his head back and stares at the ceiling for a while, listening to the rain. He lowers his head again and stares at the T.V. He turns his head slowly to the left and stares at the cushion of the sofa next to the one he's sitting on. He pulls his left arm out from under the blanket, slides his hand

under the cushion, and pulls out a bottle of whiskey. He looks down left toward the staircase, listens, then uncaps the bottle, takes a long swig and caps it again. He puts the bottle back under the cushion and stares at the T.V. He starts to cough slowly and softly. The coughing gradually builds. He holds one hand to his mouth and tries to stifle it. The coughing gets louder, then suddenly stops when he hears the sound of his wife's voice coming from the top of the staircase.

———

HALIE'S VOICE. Dodge?

(DODGE just stares at the T.V. Long pause. He stifles two short coughs.)

HALIE'S VOICE. Dodge! You want a pill, Dodge?

(He doesn't answer. Takes the bottle out again and takes another long swig. Puts the bottle back stares at T.V., pulls blanket up around his neck.)

HALIE'S VOICE. You know what it is, don't you? It's the rain! Weather. That's it. Every time. Every time you get like this, it's the rain. No sooner does the rain start then you start. *(pause)* Dodge?

(He makes no reply. Pulls a pack of cigarettes out from his sweater and lights one. Stares at T.V., pause.)

HALIE'S VOICE. You should see it coming down up here. Just coming down in sheets. Blue sheets. The bridge is pretty near flooded. What's it like down there? Dodge?

(DODGE turns his head back over his left shoulder and takes a look out through the porch. He turns back to the T.V.)

DODGE *(to himself).* Catastrophic.

HALIE'S VOICE. What? What'd you say, Dodge?

DODGE *(louder).* It looks like rain to me! Plain old rain!

HALIE'S VOICE. Rain? Of course it's rain! Are you having a seizure or something! Dodge? *(pause)* I'm coming down there in about five minutes if you don't answer me!

DODGE. Don't come down.

HALIE'S VOICE. What!

DODGE *(louder).* Don't come down!

(He has another coughing attack. Stops.)

HALIE'S VOICE. You should take a pill for that! I don't see why you just don't take a pill. Be done with it once and for all. Put a stop to it.

(He takes bottle out again. Another swig. Returns bottle.)

HALIE'S VOICE. It's not Christian, but it works. It's not necessarily Christian, that is. We don't know. There's some things the ministers can't even answer. I, personally, can't see anything wrong with it. Pain is pain. Pure and simple. Suffering is a different matter. That's entirely different. A pill seems as good an answer as any. Dodge? *(pause)* Dodge, are you watching baseball?

DODGE. No.

HALIE'S VOICE. What?

DODGE *(louder)*. No!

HALIE'S VOICE. What're you watching? You shouldn't be watching anything that'll get you excited! No horse racing!

DODGE. They don't race on Sundays.

HALIE'S VOICE. What?

DODGE *(louder)*. They don't race on Sundays!

HALIE'S VOICE. Well they shouldn't race on Sundays.

DODGE. Well they don't!

HALIE'S VOICE. Good. I'm amazed they still have that kind of legislation. That's amazing.

DODGE. Yeah, it's amazing.

HALIE'S VOICE. What?

DODGE *(louder)*. It is amazing!

HALIE'S VOICE. It is. It truly is. I would've thought these days they'd be racing on Christmas even. A big flashing Christmas tree right down at the finish line.

DODGE *(shakes his head)*. No.

HALIE'S VOICE. They used to race on New Year's! I remember that.

DODGE. They never raced on New Year's!

HALIE'S VOICE. Sometimes they did.

DODGE. They never did!

HALIE'S VOICE. Before we were married they did!

*(*DODGE *waves his hand in disgust at the staircase. Leans back in sofa. Stares at T.V.)*

HALIE'S VOICE. I went once. With a man.

DODGE *(mimicking her)*. Oh, a "man."

HALIE'S VOICE. What?

DODGE. Nothing!

HALIE'S VOICE. A wonderful man. A breeder.

DODGE. A what?

HALIE'S VOICE. A breeder! A horse breeder! Thoroughbreds.

DODGE. Oh, Thoroughbreds. Wonderful.

HALIE'S VOICE. That's right. He knew everything there was to know.

DODGE. I bet he taught you a thing or two huh? Gave you a good turn around the old stable!

HALIE'S VOICE. Knew everything there was to know about horses. We won bookoos of money that day.

DODGE. What?

HALIE'S VOICE. Money! We won every race I think.

DODGE. Bookoos?

HALIE'S VOICE. Every single race.

DODGE. Bookoos of money?

HALIE'S VOICE. It was one of those kind of days.

DODGE. New Year's!

HALIE'S VOICE. Yes! It might've been Florida. Or California! One of those two.

DODGE. Can I take my pick?

HALIE'S VOICE. It was Florida!

DODGE. Aha!

HALIE'S VOICE. Wonderful! Absolutely wonderful! The sun was just gleaming. Flamingos. Bougainvilleas. Palm trees.

DODGE *(to himself, mimicking her)*. Bougainvilleas. Palm trees.

HALIE'S VOICE. Everything was dancing with life! There were all kinds of people from everywhere. Everyone was dressed to the nines. Not like today. Not like they dress today.

DODGE. When was this anyway?

HALIE'S VOICE. This was long before I knew you.

DODGE. Must've been.

HALIE'S VOICE. Long before. I was escorted.

DODGE. To Florida?

HALIE'S VOICE. Yes. Or it might've been California. I'm not sure which.

DODGE. All that way you were escorted?

HALIE'S VOICE. Yes.

DODGE. And he never laid a finger on you I suppose? *(long silence)* Halie?

(No answer. Long pause.)

HALIE'S VOICE. Are you going out today?

DODGE *(gesturing toward rain)*. In this?

HALIE'S VOICE. I'm just asking a simple question.

DODGE. I rarely go out in the bright sunshine, why would I go out in this?

HALIE'S VOICE. I'm just asking because I'm not doing any shopping today. And if you need anything you should ask Tilden.

DODGE. Tilden's not here!

HALIE'S VOICE. He's in the kitchen.

*(*DODGE *looks toward stage left, then back toward T.V.)*

DODGE. All right.

HALIE'S VOICE. What?

DODGE *(louder)*. All right!

HALIE'S VOICE. Don't scream. It'll only get your coughing started.

DODGE. All right.

HALIE'S VOICE. Just tell Tilden what you want and he'll get it. *(pause)* Bradley should be over later.

DODGE. Bradley?

HALIE'S VOICE. Yes. To cut your hair.

DODGE. My hair? I don't need my hair cut!

HALIE'S VOICE. It won't hurt!

DODGE. I don't need it!

HALIE'S VOICE. It's been more than two weeks Dodge.

DODGE. I don't need it!

HALIE'S VOICE. I have to meet Father Dewis for lunch.

DODGE. You tell Bradley that if he shows up here with those clippers, I'll kill him!

HALIE'S VOICE. I won't be very late. No later than four at the very latest.

DODGE. You tell him! Last time he left me almost bald! And I wasn't even awake! I was sleeping! I woke up and he'd already left!

HALIE'S VOICE. That's not my fault!

DODGE. You put him up to it!

HALIE'S VOICE. I never did!

DODGE. You did too! You had some fancy, stupid meeting planned! Time to dress up the corpse for company! Lower the ears a little! Put up a little front! Surprised you didn't tape a pipe to my mouth while you were at it! That woulda' looked nice! Huh? A pipe? Maybe a bowler hat! Maybe a copy of the Wall Street Journal casually placed on my lap!

HALIE'S VOICE. You always imagine the worst things of people!

DODGE. That's not the worst! That's the least of the worst!

HALIE'S VOICE. I don't need to hear it! All day long I hear things like that and I don't need to hear more.

DODGE. You better tell him!

HALIE'S VOICE. You tell him yourself! He's your own son. You should be able to talk to your own son.

DODGE. Not while I'm sleeping! He cut my hair while I was sleeping!

HALIE'S VOICE. Well he won't do it again.

DODGE. There's no guarantee.

HALIE'S VOICE. I promise he won't do it without your consent.

DODGE *(after pause)*. There's no reason for him to even come over here.

HALIE'S VOICE. He feels responsible.

DODGE. For my hair?

HALIE'S VOICE. For your appearance.

DODGE. My appearance is out of his domain! It's even out of mine! In fact, it's disappeared! I'm an invisible man!

HALIE'S VOICE. Don't be ridiculous.

DODGE. He better not try it. That's all I've got to say.

HALIE'S VOICE. Tilden will watch out for you.

DODGE. Tilden won't protect me from Bradley!

HALIE'S VOICE. Tilden's the oldest. He'll protect you.

DODGE. Tilden can't even protect himself!

HALIE'S VOICE. Not so loud! He'll hear you. He's right in the kitchen.

DODGE *(yelling off left)*. Tilden!

HALIE'S VOICE. Dodge, what are you trying to do?

DODGE *(yelling off left)*. Tilden, get in here!

HALIE'S VOICE. Why do you enjoy stirring things up?

DODGE. I don't enjoy anything!

HALIE'S VOICE. That's a terrible thing to say.

DODGE. Tilden!

HALIE'S VOICE. That's the kind of statement that leads people right to the end of their rope.

DODGE. Tilden!

HALIE'S VOICE. It's no wonder people turn to Christ!

DODGE. TILDEN!!

HALIE'S VOICE. It's no wonder the messengers of God's word are shouted down in public places!

DODGE. TILDEN!!!!

*(*DODGE *goes into a violent, spasmodic coughing attack as* TILDEN *enters from stage left, his arms loaded with fresh ears of corn.* TILDEN *is* DODGE's *oldest son, late forties, wears heavy construction boots, covered with mud, dark green work pants, a plaid shirt and a faded brown windbreaker. He has a butch haircut, wet from the rain. Something about him is profoundly burned out and displaced. He stops center stage with the ears of corn in his arms and just stares at Dodge until he slowly finishes his coughing attack.* DODGE *looks up at him slowly. He stares at the corn. Long pause as they watch each other.)*

HALIE'S VOICE. Dodge, if you don't take that pill nobody's going to force you.

(The two men ignore the voice.)

DODGE *(to* TILDEN*)*. Where'd you get that?

TILDEN. Picked it.

DODGE. You picked all that?

*(*TILDEN *nods.)*

DODGE. You expecting company?

TILDEN. No.

DODGE. Where'd you pick it from?

TILDEN. Right out back.

DODGE. Out back where!

TILDEN. Right out in back.

DODGE. There's nothing out there!

TILDEN. There's corn.

DODGE. There hasn't been corn out there since about nineteen thirty five! That's the last time I planted corn out there!

TILDEN. It's out there now.

DODGE (yelling at stairs). Halie!

HALIE'S VOICE. Yes dear!

DODGE. Tilden's brought a whole bunch of corn in here! There's no corn out in back is there?

TILDEN (to himself). There's tons of corn.

HALIE'S VOICE. Not that I know of!

DODGE. That's what I thought.

HALIE'S VOICE. Not since about nineteen thirty five!

DODGE (to TILDEN). That's right. Nineteen thirty five.

TILDEN. It's out there now.

DODGE. You go and take that corn back to wherever you got it from!

TILDEN (After pause, staring at DODGE). It's picked. I picked it all in the rain. Once it's picked you can't put it back.

DODGE. I haven't had trouble with neighbors here for fifty-seven years. I don't even know who the neighbors are! And I don't wanna know! Now go put that corn back where it came from!

(TILDEN stares at DODGE then walks slowly over to him and dumps all the corn on DODGE's lap and steps back. DODGE stares at the corn then back to TILDEN. Long pause.)

DODGE. Are you having trouble here, Tilden? Are you in some kind of trouble?

TILDEN. I'm not in any trouble.

DODGE. You can tell me if you are. I'm still your father.

TILDEN. I know you're still my father.

DODGE. I know you had a little trouble back in New Mexico. That's why you came out here.

TILDEN. I never had any trouble.

DODGE. Tilden, your mother told me all about it.

TILDEN. What'd she tell you?

(TILDEN pulls some chewing tobacco out of his jacket and bites off a plug.)

DODGE. I don't have to repeat what she told me! She told me all about it!

TILDEN. Can I bring my chair in from the kitchen?

DODGE. What?

TILDEN. Can I bring in my chair from the kitchen?

DODGE. Sure. Bring your chair in.

(TILDEN exits left. DODGE pushes all the corn off his lap onto the floor. He pulls the blanket off angrily and tosses it at one end of the sofa, pulls out the bottle and takes another swig. TILDEN enters again from left with a milking stool and a pail. DODGE hides the bottle quickly under the cushion before Tilden sees it. TILDEN sets the stool down by the sofa, sits on it, puts the pail in front of him on the floor. TILDEN starts picking up the ears of corn one at a time and husking them. He throws the husks and silk in the center of the stage and drops the ears into the pail each time he cleans one. He repeats this process as they talk.)

DODGE (after pause). Sure is nice looking corn.

TILDEN. It's the best.

DODGE. Hybrid?

TILDEN. What?

DODGE. Some kinda fancy hybrid?

TILDEN. You planted it. I don't know what it is.

DODGE (pause). Tilden, look, you can't stay here forever. You know that, don't you?

TILDEN (spits in spittoon). I'm not.

DODGE. I know you're not. I'm not worried about that. That's not the reason I brought it up.

TILDEN. What's the reason?

DODGE. The reason is I'm wondering what you're gonna do.

TILDEN. You're not worried about me, are you?

DODGE. I'm not worried about you.

TILDEN. You weren't worried about me when I wasn't here. When I was in New Mexico.

DODGE. No, I wasn't worried about you then either.

TILDEN. You shoulda worried about me then.

DODGE. Why's that? You didn't do anything down there, did you?

TILDEN. I didn't do anything.

DODGE. Then why should I have worried about you?

TILDEN. Because I was lonely.

DODGE. Because you were lonely?

TILDEN. Yeah. I was more lonely than I've ever been before.

DODGE. Why was that?

TILDEN (pause). Could I have some of that whiskey you've got?

DODGE. What whiskey? I haven't got any whiskey.

TILDEN. You've got some under the sofa.

DODGE. I haven't got anything under the sofa! Now mind your own damn business! Jesus God, you come into the house outa the middle of nowhere, haven't heard or seen you in twenty years and suddenly you're making accusations.

TILDEN. I'm not making accusations.

DODGE. You're accusing me of hoarding whiskey under the sofa!

TILDEN. I'm not accusing you.

DODGE. You just got through telling me I had whiskey under the sofa!

HALIE'S VOICE. Dodge?

DODGE *(to* TILDEN*)*. Now she knows about it!

TILDEN. She doesn't know about it.

HALIE'S VOICE. Dodge, are you talking to yourself down there?

DODGE. I'm talking to Tilden!

HALIE'S VOICE. Tilden's down there?

DODGE. He's right here!

HALIE'S VOICE. What?

DODGE *(louder)*. He's right here!

HALIE'S VOICE. What's he doing?

DODGE *(to* TILDEN*)*. Don't answer her.

TILDEN *(to* DODGE*)*. I'm not doing anything wrong.

DODGE. I know you're not.

HALIE'S VOICE. What's he doing down there!

DODGE *(to* TILDEN*)*. Don't answer.

TILDEN. I'm not.

HALIE'S VOICE. Dodge!

(The men sit in silence. DODGE *lights a cigarette.* TILDEN *keeps husking corn, spits tobacco now and then in spittoon.)*

HALIE'S VOICE. Dodge! He's not drinking anything, is he? You see to it that he doesn't drink anything! You've gotta watch out for him. It's our responsibility. He can't look after himself anymore, so we have to do it. Nobody else will do it. We can't just send him away somewhere. If we had lots of money we could send him away. But we don't. We never will. That's why we have to stay healthy. You and me. Nobody's going to look after us. Bradley can't look after us. Bradley can hardly look after himself. I was always hoping that Tilden would look out for Bradley when they got older. After Bradley lost his leg. Tilden's the oldest. I always thought he'd be the one to take responsibility. I had no idea in the world that Tilden would be so much trouble. Who would've dreamed. Tilden was an All-American, don't forget. Don't forget that. Fullback. Or quarterback. I forget which.

TILDEN *(to himself)*. Fullback. *(still husking)*

HALIE'S VOICE. Then when Tilden turned out to be so much trouble, I put all my hopes on Ansel. Of course Ansel wasn't as handsome, but he was smart. He was the smartest probably. I think he probably was. Smarter than Bradley, that's for sure. Didn't go and chop his leg off with a chain saw. Smart enough not to go and do that. I think he was smarter than Tilden too. Especially after Tilden got in all that trouble. Doesn't take brains to go to jail. Anybody knows that. Course then when Ansel died that left us all alone. Same as being alone. No different. Same as if they'd all died. He was the smartest. He could've earned lots of money. Lots and lots of money.

*(*HALIE *enters slowly from the top of the staircase as she continues talking. Just her feet are seen at first as she makes her way down the stairs, a step at a time. She appears dressed completely in black, as though in mourning. Black handbag, hat with a veil, and pulling on elbow length black gloves. She is about sixty-five with pure white hair. She remains absorbed in what she's saying as she descends the stairs and doesn't really notice the two men who continue sitting there as they were before she came down, smoking and husking.)*

HALIE. He would've took care of us, too. He would've seen to it that we were repaid. He was like that. He was a hero. Don't forget that. A genuine hero. Brave. Strong. And very intelligent. Ansel could've been a great man. One of the greatest. I only regret that he didn't die in action. It's not fitting for a man like that to die in a motel room. A soldier. He could've won a medal. He could've been decorated for valor. I've talked to Father Dewis about putting up a plaque for Ansel. He thinks it's a good idea. He agrees. He knew Ansel when he used to play basketball. Went to every game. Ansel was his favorite player. He even recommended to the City Council that they put up a statue of Ansel. A big, tall statue with a basketball in one hand and a rifle in the other. That's how much he thinks of Ansel.

*(*HALIE *reaches the stage and begins to wander around, still absorbed in pulling on her gloves, brushing lint off her dress and continuously talking to herself as the men just sit.)*

HALIE. Of course, he'd still be alive today if he hadn't married into the Catholics. The Mob. How in the world he never opened his eyes to that is beyond me. Just beyond me. Everyone around him could see the truth. Even Tilden. Tilden told him time and again. Catholic women are the Devil incarnate. He wouldn't listen. He was blind with love. Blind. I knew. Everyone knew. The wedding was more like a funeral. You remember? All those Italians. All that horrible black, greasy hair. The smell of cheap cologne. I think even the priest was wearing a pistol. When he gave her the ring I knew he was a dead man. I knew it. As soon as he gave her the ring. But then it was the honeymoon that killed him. The honeymoon. I knew he'd never come back from the honeymoon. I kissed him and he felt like a corpse. All white. Cold. Icy blue lips. He never used to kiss like that. Never before. I knew then that she'd cursed him. Taken his soul. I saw it in her eyes. She smiled at me with that Catholic sneer of hers. She told me with her eyes that she'd murder him in his bed. Murder my son. She told me. And there was nothing I could do. Absolutely nothing. He was going with her, thinking he was free. Thinking it was love. What could I do? I couldn't tell him she was a witch. I couldn't tell him that. He'd have turned on me. Hated me. I couldn't stand him hating me and then dying before he ever saw me again. Hating me in his death bed. Hating me and loving her! How could I do that? I had to let him go. I had to. I watched him leave. I watched him throw gardenias as he helped her into the limousine. I watched his face disappear behind the glass.

(She stops abruptly and stares at the corn husks. She looks around the space as though just waking up. She turns and looks hard at TILDEN *and* DODGE *who continue sitting calmly. She looks again at the corn husks.)*

HALIE *(pointing to the husks).* What's this in my house! *(kicks husks)* What's all this!

*(*TILDEN *stops husking and stares at her.)*

HALIE *(to* DODGE*).* And you encourage him!

*(*DODGE *pulls blanket over him again.)*

DODGE. You're going out in the rain?

HALIE. It's not raining.

*(*TILDEN *starts husking again.)*

DODGE. Not in Florida it's not.

HALIE. We're not in Florida!

DODGE. It's not raining at the race track.

HALIE. Have you been taking those pills? Those pills always make you talk crazy. Tilden, has he been taking those pills?

TILDEN. He hasn't took anything.

HALIE *(to* DODGE*).* What've you been taking?

DODGE. It's not raining in California or Florida or the race track. Only in Illinois. This is the only place it's raining. All over the rest of the world it's bright golden sunshine.

*(*HALIE *goes to the night table next to the sofa and checks the bottle of pills.)*

HALIE. Which ones did you take? Tilden, you must've seen him take something.

TILDEN. He never took a thing.

HALIE. Then why's he talking crazy?

TILDEN. I've been here the whole time.

HALIE. Then you've both been taking something!

TILDEN. I've just been husking the corn.

HALIE. Where'd you get that corn anyway? Why is this house suddenly full of corn?

DODGE. Bumper crop!

HALIE *(moving center).* We haven't had corn here for over thirty years.

TILDEN. The whole back lot's full of corn. Far as the eye can see.

DODGE *(to* HALIE*).* Things keep happening while you're upstairs, ya know. The world doesn't stop just because you're upstairs. Corn keeps growing. Rain keeps raining.

HALIE. I'm not unaware of the world around me! Thank you very much. It so happens that I have an over-all view from the upstairs. The back yard's in plain view of my window. And there's no corn to speak of. Absolutely none!

DODGE. Tilden wouldn't lie. If he says there's corn, there's corn.

HALIE. What's the meaning of this corn Tilden!

TILDEN. It's a mystery to me. I was out in back there. And the rain was coming down. And I didn't feel like coming back inside. I didn't feel the cold so much. I didn't mind the wet. So I was just walking. I was muddy but I didn't mind the mud so much. And I looked up. And I saw this stand of corn. In fact I was standing in it. So, I was standing in it.

HALIE. There isn't any corn outside Tilden! There's no corn! Now, you must've either stolen this corn or you bought it.

DODGE. He doesn't have any money.

HALIE *(to* TILDEN*).* So you stole it!

TILDEN. I didn't steal it. I don't want to get kicked out of Illinois. I was kicked out of New Mexico and I don't want to get kicked out of Illinois.

HALIE. You're going to get kicked out of this house, Tilden, if you don't tell me where you got that corn!

*(*TILDEN *starts crying softly to himself but keeps husking corn. Pause.)*

DODGE *(to* HALIE*).* Why'd you have to tell him that? Who cares where he got the corn? Why'd you have to go and tell him that?

HALIE *(to* DODGE*).* It's your fault you know!

You're the one that's behind all this! I suppose you thought it'd be funny! Some joke! Cover the house with corn husks. You better get this cleaned up before Bradley sees it.

DODGE. Bradley's not getting in the front door!

HALIE *(kicking husks, striding back and forth)*. Bradley's going to be very upset when he sees this. He doesn't like to see the house in disarray. He can't stand it when one thing is out of place. The slightest thing. You know how he gets.

DODGE. Bradley doesn't even live here!

HALIE. It's his home as much as ours. He was born in this house!

DODGE. He was born in a hog wallow.

HALIE. Don't you say that! Don't you ever say that!

DODGE. He was born in a goddamn hog wallow! That's where he was born and that's where he belongs! He doesn't belong in this house!

HALIE *(she stops)*. I don't know what's come over you, Dodge. I don't know what in the world's come over you. You've become an evil man. You used to be a good man.

DODGE. Six of one, a half dozen of another.

HALIE. You sit here day and night, festering away! Decomposing! Smelling up the house with your putrid body! Hacking your head off til all hours of the morning! Thinking up mean, evil, stupid things to say about your own flesh and blood!

DODGE. He's not my flesh and blood! My flesh and blood's buried in the back yard!

(They freeze. Long pause. The men stare at her.)

HALIE *(quietly)*. That's enough, Dodge. That's quite enough. I'm going out now. I'm going to have lunch with Father Dewis. I'm going to ask him about a monument. A statue. At least a plaque.

(She crosses to the door up right. She stops.)

HALIE. If you need anything, ask Tilden. He's the oldest. I've left some money on the kitchen table.

DODGE. I don't need anything.

HALIE. No, I suppose not. *(she opens the door and looks out through porch)* Still raining. I love the smell just after it stops. The ground. I won't be too late.

(She goes out door and closes it. She's still visible on the porch as she crosses toward stage left screen door. She stops in the middle of the porch, speaks to DODGE but doesn't turn to him.)

HALIE. Dodge, tell Tilden not to go out in the back lot anymore. I don't want him back there in the rain.

DODGE. You tell him. He's sitting right here.

HALIE. He never listens to me Dodge. He's never listened to me in the past.

DODGE. I'll tell him.

HALIE. We have to watch him just like we used to now. Just like we always have. He's still a child.

DODGE. I'll watch him.

HALIE. Good.

(She crosses to screen door, left, takes an umbrella off a hook and goes out the door. The door slams behind her. Long pause. TILDEN husks corn, stares at pail. DODGE lights a cigarette, stares at T.V.)

TILDEN *(still husking)*. You shouldn't a told her that.

DODGE *(staring at T.V.)*. What?

TILDEN. What you told her. You know.

DODGE. What do you know about it?

TILDEN. I know. I know all about it. We all know.

DODGE. So what difference does it make? Everybody knows, everybody's forgot.

TILDEN. She hasn't forgot.

DODGE. She should've forgot.

TILDEN. It's different for a woman. She couldn't forget that. How could she forget that?

DODGE. I don't want to talk about it!

TILDEN. What do you want to talk about?

DODGE. I don't want to talk about anything! I don't want to talk about troubles or what happened fifty years ago or thirty years ago or the race track or Florida or the last time I seeded corn! I don't want to talk!

TILDEN. You don't wanna die do you?

DODGE. No, I don't wanna die either.

TILDEN. Well, you gotta talk or you'll die.

DODGE. Who told you that?

TILDEN. That's what I know. I found that out in New Mexico. I thought I was dying but I just lost my voice.

DODGE. Were you with somebody?

TILDEN. I was alone. I thought I was dead.

DODGE. Might as well have been. What'd you come back here for?

TILDEN. I didn't know where to go.

DODGE. You're a grown man. You shouldn't be needing your parents at your age. It's unnatural. There's nothing we can do for you now anyway. Couldn't you make a living down there? Couldn't you find some way to make a living? Support yourself? What'd ya come back here for? You expect us to feed you forever?

TILDEN. I didn't know where else to go.

DODGE. I never went back to my parents. Never. Never even had the urge. I was independent. Always independent. Always found a way.

TILDEN. I didn't know what to do. I couldn't figure anything out.

DODGE. There's nothing to figure out. You just forge ahead. What's there to figure out?

(TILDEN *stands*.)

TILDEN. I don't know.

DODGE. Where are you going?

TILDEN. Out back.

DODGE. You're not supposed to go out there. You heard what she said. Don't play deaf with me!

TILDEN. I like it out there.

DODGE. In the rain?

TILDEN. Especially in the rain. I like the feeling of it. Feels like it always did.

DODGE. You're supposed to watch out for me. Get me things when I need them.

TILDEN. What do you need?

DODGE. I don't need anything! But I might. I might need something any second. Any second now. I can't be left alone for a minute!

(DODGE *starts to cough*.)

TILDEN. I'll be right outside. You can just yell.

DODGE (*between coughs*). No! It's too far! You can't go out there! It's too far! You might not ever hear me!

TILDEN (*moving to pills*). Why don't you take a pill? You want a pill?

(DODGE *coughs more violently, throws himself back against sofa, clutches his throat.* TILDEN *stands by helplessly*.)

DODGE. Water! Get me some water!

(TILDEN *rushes off left.* DODGE *reaches out for the pills, knocking some bottles to the floor, coughing in spasms. He grabs a small bottle, takes out pills and swallows them.* TILDEN *rushes back on with a glass of water.* DODGE *takes it and drinks, his coughing subsides*.)

TILDEN. You all right now?

(DODGE *nods. Drinks more water.* TILDEN *moves in closer to him.* DODGE *sets glass of water on the night table. His coughing is almost gone*.)

TILDEN. Why don't you lay down for a while? Just rest a little.

(TILDEN *helps* DODGE *lay down on the sofa. Covers him with blanket*.)

DODGE. You're not going outside are you?

TILDEN. No.

DODGE. I don't want to wake up and find you not here.

TILDEN. I'll be here.

(TILDEN *tucks blanket around* DODGE.)

DODGE. You'll stay right here?

TILDEN. I'll stay in my chair.

DODGE. That's not a chair. That's my old milking stool.

TILDEN. I know.

DODGE. Don't call it a chair.

TILDEN. I won't.

(TILDEN *tries to take* DODGE's *baseball cap off*.)

DODGE. What're you doing! Leave that on me! Don't take that offa me! That's my cap!

(TILDEN *leaves the cap on* DODGE.)

TILDEN. I know.

DODGE. Bradley'll shave my head if I don't have that on. That's my cap.

TILDEN. I know it is.

DODGE. Don't take my cap off.

TILDEN. I won't.

DODGE. You stay right here now.

TILDEN (*sits on stool*). I will.

DODGE. Don't go outside. There's nothing out there.

TILDEN. I won't.

DODGE. Everything's in here. Everything you need. Money's on the table. T.V. Is the T.V. on?

TILDEN. Yeah.

DODGE. Turn it off! Turn the damn thing off! What's it doing on?

TILDEN (*shuts off T.V., light goes out*). You left it on.

DODGE. Well turn it off.

TILDEN (*sits on stool again*). It's off.

DODGE. Leave it off.

TILDEN. I will.

DODGE. When I fall asleep you can turn it on.

TILDEN. Okay.

DODGE. You can watch the ball game. Red Sox. You like the Red Sox don't you?

TILDEN. Yeah.

DODGE. You can watch the Red Sox. Pee Wee Reese. Pee Wee Reese. You remember Pee Wee Reese?

TILDEN. No.

DODGE. Was he with the Red Sox?

TILDEN. I don't know.

DODGE. Pee Wee Reese. (*falling asleep*) You can watch the Cardinals. You remember Stan Musial.

TILDEN. No.

DODGE. Stan Musial. (*falling into sleep*) Bases loaded. Top a' the sixth. Bases loaded. Runner on first and third. Big fat knuckle ball.

Floater. Big as a blimp. Cracko! Ball just took off like a rocket. Just pulverized. I marked it. Marked it with my eyes. Straight between the clock and the Burma Shave ad. I was the first kid out there. First kid. I had to fight hard for that ball. I wouldn't give it up. They almost tore the ears right off me. But I wouldn't give it up.

(DODGE *falls into deep sleep.* TILDEN *just sits staring at him for a while. Slowly he leans toward the sofa, checking to see if* DODGE *is well asleep. He reaches slowly under the cushion and pulls out the bottle of booze.* DODGE *sleeps soundly.* TILDEN *stands quietly, staring at* DODGE *as he uncaps the bottle and takes a long drink. He caps the bottle and sticks it in his hip pocket. He looks around at the husks on the floor and then back to* DODGE. *He moves center stage and gathers an armload of corn husks then crosses back to the sofa. He stands holding the husks over* DODGE *and looking down at him he gently spreads the corn husks over the whole length of* DODGE's *body. He stands back and looks at* DODGE. *Pulls out bottle, takes another drink, returns bottle to his hip pocket. He gathers more husks and repeats the procedure until the floor is clean of corn husks and* DODGE *is completely covered in them except for his head.* TILDEN *takes another long drink, stares at* DODGE *sleeping then quietly exits stage left. Long pause as the sound of rain continues.* DODGE *sleeps on. The figure of* BRADLEY *appears up left, outside the screen porch door. He holds a wet newspaper over his head as a protection from the rain. He seems to be struggling with the door then slips and almost falls to the ground.* DODGE *sleeps on, undisturbed.)*

BRADLEY. Sonuvabitch! Sonuvagoddamnbitch!

(BRADLEY *recovers his footing and makes it through the screen door onto the porch. He throws the newspaper down, shakes the water out of his hair, and brushes the rain off of his shoulders. He is a big man dressed in a grey sweat shirt, black suspenders, baggy dark blue pants and black janitor's shoes. His left leg is wooden, having been amputated above the knee. He moves with an exaggerated, almost mechanical limp. The squeaking sounds of leather and metal accompany his walk coming from the harness and hinges of the false leg. His arms and shoulders are extremely powerful and muscular due to a lifetime dependency on the upper torso doing all the work for the legs. He is about five years younger than* TILDEN.

He moves laboriously to the stage right door and enters, closing the door behind him. He doesn't notice DODGE *at first. He moves toward the staircase.)*

BRADLEY *(calling to upstairs).* Mom!

(He stops and listens. Turns upstage and sees DODGE *sleeping. Notices corn husks. He moves slowly toward sofa. Stops next to pail and looks into it. Looks at husks.* DODGE *stays asleep. Talks to himself.)*

BRADLEY. What in the hell is this?

(He looks at DODGE's *sleeping face and shakes his head in disgust. He pulls out a pair of black electric hair clippers from his pocket. Unwinds the cord and crosses to the lamp. He jabs his wooden leg behind the knee, causing it to bend at the joint and awkwardly kneels to plug the cord into a floor outlet. He pulls himself to his feet again by using the sofa as leverage. He moves to* DODGE's *head and again jabs his false leg. Goes down on one knee. He violently knocks away some of the corn husks then jerks off* DODGE's *baseball cap and throws it down center stage.* DODGE *stays asleep.* BRADLEY *switches on the clippers. Lights start dimming.* BRADLEY *cuts* DODGE's *hair while he sleeps. Lights dim slowly to black with the sound of clippers and rain.)*

ACT TWO

Scene: Same set as Act One. Night. Sound of rain. DODGE *still asleep on sofa. His hair is cut extremely short and in places the scalp is cut and bleeding. His cap is still center stage. All the corn and husks, pail and milking stool have been cleared away. The lights come up to the sound of a young girl laughing off stage left.* DODGE *remains asleep.* SHELLY *and* VINCE *appear up left outside the screen porch door sharing the shelter of* VINCE's *overcoat above their heads.* SHELLY *is about nineteen, black hair, very beautiful. She wears tight jeans, high heels, purple T-shirt and a short rabbit fur coat. Her makeup is exaggerated and her hair has been curled.* VINCE *is* TILDEN's *son, about twenty-two, wears a plaid shirt, jeans, dark glasses, cowboy boots and carries a black saxophone case. They shake the rain off themselves as they enter the porch through the screen door.*

———

SHELLY *(laughing, gesturing to house).* This is it? I don't believe this is it!

VINCE. This is it.

SHELLY. This is the house?

VINCE. This is the house.

SHELLY. I don't believe it!

VINCE. How come?

SHELLY. It's like a Norman Rockwell cover or something.

VINCE. What's a' matter with it? It's American.

SHELLY. Where's the milkman and the little dog? What's the little dog's name? Spot. Spot and Jane. Dick and Jane and Spot.

VINCE. Knock it off.

SHELLY. Dick and Jane and Spot and Mom and Dad and Junior and Sissy!

(She laughs. Slaps her knee.)

VINCE. Come on! It's my heritage. What dya' expect?

(She laughs more hysterically, out of control.)

SHELLY. "And Tuffy and Toto and Dooda and Bonzo all went down one day to the corner grocery store to buy a big bag of licorice for Mr. Marshall's pussy cat!"

(She laughs so hard she falls to her knees holding her stomach. VINCE stands there looking at her.)

VINCE. Shelly will you get up!

(She keeps laughing. Staggers to her feet. Turning in circles holding her stomach.)

SHELLY *(continuing her story in kid's voice)*. "Mr. Marshall was on vacation. He had no idea that the four little boys had taken such a liking to his little kitty cat."

VINCE. Have some respect would ya'!

SHELLY *(trying to control herself)*. I'm sorry.

VINCE. Pull yourself together.

SHELLY *(salutes him)*. Yes sir.

(She giggles.)

VINCE. Jesus Christ, Shelly.

SHELLY *(pause, smiling)*. And Mr. Marshall—

VINCE. Cut it out.

(She stops. Stands there staring at him. Stifles a giggle.)

VINCE *(after pause)*. Are you finished?

SHELLY. Oh brother!

VINCE. I don't wanna go in there with you acting like an idiot.

SHELLY. Thanks.

VINCE. Well, I don't.

SHELLY. I won't embarrass you. Don't worry.

VINCE. I'm not worried.

SHELLY. You are too.

VINCE. Shelly look, I just don't wanna go in there with you giggling your head off. They might think something's wrong with you.

SHELLY. There is.

VINCE. There is not!

SHELLY. Something's definitely wrong with me.

VINCE. There is not!

SHELLY. There's something wrong with you too.

VINCE. There's nothing wrong with me either!

SHELLY. You wanna know what's wrong with you?

VINCE. What?

(SHELLY laughs.)

VINCE *(crosses back left toward screen door)*. I'm leaving!

SHELLY *(stops laughing)*. Wait! Stop. Stop! *(VINCE stops)* What's wrong with you is that you take the situation too seriously.

VINCE. I just don't want to have them think that I've suddenly arrived out of the middle of nowhere completely deranged.

SHELLY. What do you want them to think then?

VINCE *(pause)*. Nothing. Let's go in.

(He crosses porch toward stage right interior door. SHELLY follows him. The stage right door opens slowly. VINCE sticks his head in, doesn't notice DODGE sleeping. Calls out toward staircase.)

VINCE. Grandma!

(SHELLY breaks into laughter, unseen behind VINCE. VINCE pulls his head back outside and pulls door shut. We hear their voices again without seeing them.)

SHELLY'S VOICE *(stops laughing)*. I'm sorry. I'm sorry Vince. I really am. I really am sorry. I won't do it again. I couldn't help it.

VINCE'S VOICE. It's not all that funny.

SHELLY'S VOICE. I know it's not. I'm sorry.

VINCE'S VOICE. I mean this is a tense situation for me! I haven't seen them for over six years. I don't know what to expect.

SHELLY'S VOICE. I know. I won't do it again.

VINCE'S VOICE. Can't you bite your tongue or something?

SHELLY'S VOICE. Just don't say "Grandma," okay? *(she giggles, stops)* I mean if you say "Grandma" I don't know if I can stop myself.

VINCE'S VOICE. Well try!

SHELLY'S VOICE. Okay. Sorry.

(Door opens again. VINCE sticks his head in then enters. SHELLY follows behind him. VINCE crosses to staircase, sets down saxophone case and overcoat, looks up staircase. SHELLY notices DODGE's baseball cap. Crosses

to it. Picks it up and puts it on her head. VINCE *goes up the stairs and disappears at the top.* SHELLY *watches him then turns and sees* DODGE *on the sofa. She takes off the baseball cap.)*

VINCE'S VOICE *(from above stairs).* Grandma!

*(*SHELLY *crosses over to* DODGE *slowly and stands next to him. She stands at his head, reaches out slowly and touches one of the cuts. The second she touches his head,* DODGE *jerks up to a sitting position on the sofa, eyes open.* SHELLY *gasps.* DODGE *looks at her, sees his cap in her hands, quickly puts his hand to his bare head. He glares at* SHELLY *then whips the cap out of her hands and puts it on.* SHELLY *backs away from him.* DODGE *stares at her.)*

SHELLY. I'm uh—with Vince.

*(*DODGE *just glares at her.)*

SHELLY. He's upstairs.

*(*DODGE *looks at the staircase then back to* SHELLY.*)*

SHELLY *(calling upstairs).* Vince!

VINCE'S VOICE. Just a second!

SHELLY. You better get down here!

VINCE'S VOICE. Just a minute! I'm looking at the pictures.

*(*DODGE *keeps staring at her.)*

SHELLY *(to* DODGE*).* We just got here. Pouring rain on the freeway so we thought we'd stop by. I mean Vince was planning on stopping anyway. He wanted to see you. He said he hadn't seen you in a long time.

(Pause. DODGE *just keeps staring at her.)*

SHELLY. We were going all the way through to New Mexico. To see his father. I guess his father lives out there. We thought we'd stop by and see you on the way. Kill two birds with one stone, you know? *(she laughs,* DODGE *stares, she stops laughing)* I mean Vince has this thing about his family now. I guess it's a new thing with him. I kind of find it hard to relate to. But he feels it's important. You know. I mean he feels he wants to get to know you all again. After all this time.

(Pause. DODGE *just stares at her. She moves nervously to staircase and yells up to* VINCE.*)*

SHELLY. Vince will you come down here please!

*(*VINCE *comes half way down the stairs.)*

VINCE. I guess they went out for a while.

*(*SHELLY *points to sofa and* DODGE. VINCE *turns and sees* DODGE. *He comes all the way down staircase and crosses to* DODGE. SHELLY *stays behind near staircase, keeping her distance.)*

VINCE. Grandpa?

*(*DODGE *looks up at him, not recognizing him.)*

DODGE. Did you bring the whiskey?

*(*VINCE *looks back at* SHELLY *then back to* DODGE.*)*

VINCE. Grandpa, it's Vince. I'm Vince. Tilden's son. You remember?

*(*DODGE *stares at him.)*

DODGE. You didn't do what you told me. You didn't stay here with me.

VINCE. Grandpa, I haven't been here until just now. I just got here.

DODGE. You left. You went outside like we told you not to do. You went out there in back. In the rain.

*(*VINCE *looks back at* SHELLY. *She moves slowly toward sofa.)*

SHELLY. Is he okay?

VINCE. I don't know. *(takes off his shades)* Look, Grandpa, don't you remember me? Vince. Your Grandson.

*(*DODGE *stares at him then takes off his baseball cap.)*

DODGE *(points to his head).* See what happens when you leave me alone? See that? That's what happens.

*(*VINCE *looks at his head.* VINCE *reaches out to touch his head.* DODGE *slaps his hand away with the cap and puts it back on his head.)*

VINCE. What's going on Grandpa? Where's Halie?

DODGE. Don't worry about her. She won't be back for days. She says she'll be back but she won't be. *(he starts laughing)* There's life in the old girl yet! *(stops laughing)*

VINCE. How did you do that to your head?

DODGE. I didn't do it! Don't be ridiculous!

VINCE. Well who did then?

(Pause. DODGE *stares at* VINCE.*)*

DODGE. Who do you think did it? Who do you think?

*(*SHELLY *moves toward* VINCE.*)*

SHELLY. Vince, maybe we oughta' go. I don't like this. I mean this isn't my idea of a good time.

VINCE *(to* SHELLY*).* Just a second. *(to* DODGE*)* Grandpa, look, I just got here. I just now got here. I haven't been here for six years. I don't know anything that's happened.

(Pause. DODGE *stares at him.)*

DODGE. You don't know anything?

VINCE. No.

DODGE. Well that's good. That's good. It's much better not to know anything. Much, much better.

VINCE. Isn't there anybody here with you?

*(*DODGE *turns slowly and looks off to stage*

left.)

DODGE. Tilden's here.

VINCE. No, Grandpa, Tilden's in New Mexico. That's where I was going. I'm going out there to see him.

(DODGE turns slowly back to VINCE.)

DODGE. Tilden's here.

(VINCE backs away and joins SHELLY. DODGE stares at them.)

SHELLY. Vince, why don't we spend the night in a motel and come back in the morning? We could have breakfast. Maybe everything would be different.

VINCE. Don't be scared. There's nothing to be scared of. He's just old.

SHELLY. I'm not scared!

DODGE. You two are not my idea of the perfect couple!

SHELLY *(after pause)*. Oh really? Why's that?

VINCE. Shh! Don't aggravate him.

DODGE. There's something wrong between the two of you. Something not compatible.

VINCE. Grandpa, where did Halie go? Maybe we should call her.

DODGE. What are you talking about? Do you know what you're talking about? Are you just talking for the sake of talking? Lubricating the gums?

VINCE. I'm trying to figure out what's going on here!

DODGE. Is that it?

VINCE. Yes. I mean I expected everything to be different.

DODGE. Who are you to expect anything? Who are you supposed to be?

VINCE. I'm Vince! Your Grandson!

DODGE. Vince. My Grandson.

VINCE. Tilden's son.

DODGE. Tilden's son, Vince.

VINCE. You haven't seen me for a long time.

DODGE. When was the last time?

VINCE. I don't remember.

DODGE. You don't remember?

VINCE. No.

DODGE. You don't remember. How am I supposed to remember if you don't remember?

SHELLY. Vince, come on. This isn't going to work out.

VINCE *(to SHELLY)*. Just take it easy.

SHELLY. I'm taking it easy! He doesn't even know who you are!

VINCE *(crossing toward DODGE)*. Grandpa, Look—

DODGE. Stay where you are! Keep your distance!

(VINCE stops. Looks back at SHELLY then to DODGE.)

SHELLY. Vince, this is really making me nervous. I mean he doesn't even want us here. He doesn't even like us.

DODGE. She's a beautiful girl.

VINCE. Thanks.

DODGE. Very Beautiful Girl.

SHELLY. Oh my God.

DODGE *(to SHELLY)*. What's your name?

SHELLY. Shelly.

DODGE. Shelly. That's a man's name isn't it?

SHELLY. Not in this case.

DODGE *(to VINCE)*. She's a smart-ass too.

SHELLY. Vince! Can we go?

DODGE. She wants to go. She just got here and she wants to go.

VINCE. This is kind of strange for her.

DODGE. She'll get used to it. *(to SHELLY)* What part of the country do you come from?

SHELLY. Originally?

DODGE. That's right. Originally. At the very start.

SHELLY. L.A.

DODGE. L.A. Stupid country.

SHELLY. I can't stand this Vince! This is really unbelievable!

DODGE. It's stupid! L.A. is stupid! So is Florida! All those Sunshine States. They're all stupid! Do you know why they're stupid?

SHELLY. Illuminate me.

DODGE. I'll tell you why. Because they're full of smart-asses! That's why.

(SHELLY turns her back to DODGE, crosses to staircase and sits on bottom step.)

DODGE *(to VINCE)*. Not she's insulted.

VINCE. Well you weren't very polite.

DODGE. She's insulted! Look at her! In my house she's insulted! She's over there sulking because I insulted her!

SHELLY *(to VINCE)*. This is really terrific. This is wonderful. And you were worried about me making the right first impression!

DODGE *(to VINCE)*. She's a fireball isn't she? Regular fireball. I had some a' them in my day. Temporary stuff. Never lasted more than a week.

VINCE. Grandpa—

DODGE. Stop calling me Grandpa will ya'! It's sickening. "Grandpa." I'm nobody's Grandpa!

(DODGE starts feeling around under the cushion for the bottle of whiskey. SHELLY gets up from the staircase.)

SHELLY *(to VINCE)*. Maybe you've got the wrong house. Did you ever think of that? Maybe this is the wrong address!

VINCE. It's not the wrong address! I recognize the yard.

SHELLY. Yeah but do you recognize the people? He says he's not your Grandfather.

DODGE *(digging for bottle)*. Where's that bottle!

VINCE. He's just sick or something. I don't know what's happened to him.

DODGE. Where's my goddamn bottle!

(DODGE gets up from sofa and starts tearing the cushions off it and throwing them downstage, looking for the whiskey.)

SHELLY. Can't we just drive on to New Mexico? This is terrible, Vince! I don't want to stay here. In this house. I thought it was going to be turkey dinners and apple pie and all that kinda stuff.

VINCE. Well I hate to disappoint you!

SHELLY. I'm not disappointed! I'm fuckin' terrified! I wanna' go!

(DODGE yells toward stage left.)

DODGE. Tilden! Tilden!

(DODGE keeps ripping away at the sofa looking for his bottle, he knocks over the night stand with the bottles. VINCE and SHELLY watch as he starts ripping the stuffing out of the sofa.)

VINCE *(to SHELLY)*. He's lost his mind or something. I've got to try to help him.

SHELLY. You help him! I'm leaving!

(SHELLY starts to leave. VINCE grabs her. They struggle as DODGE keeps ripping away at the sofa and yelling.)

DODGE. Tilden! Tilden get your ass in here! Tilden!

SHELLY. Let go of me!

VINCE. You're not going anywhere! You're going to stay right here!

SHELLY. Let go of me you sonuvabitch! I'm not your property!

(Suddenly TILDEN walks on from stage left just as he did before. This time his arms are full of carrots. DODGE, VINCE and SHELLY stop suddenly when they see him. They all stare at TILDEN as he crosses slowly center stage with the carrots and stops. DODGE sits on sofa, exhausted.)

DODGE *(panting, to TILDEN)*. Where in the hell have you been?

TILDEN. Out back.

DODGE. Where's my bottle?

TILDEN. Gone.

(TILDEN and VINCE stare at each other. SHELLY backs away.)

DODGE *(to TILDEN)*. You stole my bottle!

VINCE *(to TILDEN)*. Dad?

(TILDEN just stares at VINCE.)

DODGE. You have no right to steal my bottle! No right at all!

VINCE *(to TILDEN)*. It's Vince. I'm Vince.

(TILDEN stares at VINCE then looks at DODGE then turns to SHELLY.)

TILDEN *(after pause)*. I picked these carrots. If anybody wants any carrots, I picked 'em.

SHELLY *(to VINCE)*. This is your father?

VINCE *(to TILDEN)*. Dad, what're you doing here?

(TILDEN just stares at VINCE, holding carrots, DODGE pulls the blanket back over himself.)

DODGE *(to TILDEN)*. You're going to have to get me another bottle! You gotta get me a bottle before Halie comes back! There's money on the table. *(points to stage left kitchen)*

TILDEN *(shaking his head)*. I'm not going down there. Into town.

(SHELLY crosses to TILDEN. TILDEN stares at her.)

SHELLY *(to TILDEN)*. Are you Vince's father?

TILDEN *(to SHELLY)*. Vince?

SHELLY *(pointing to VINCE)*. This is supposed to be your son! Is he your son? Do you recognize him? I'm just along for the ride here. I thought everybody knew each other!

(TILDEN stares at VINCE. DODGE wraps himself up in the blanket and sits on sofa staring at the floor.)

TILDEN. I had a son once but we buried him.

(DODGE quickly looks at TILDEN. SHELLY looks to VINCE.)

DODGE. You shut up about that! You don't know anything about that!

VINCE. Dad, I thought you were in New Mexico. We were going to drive down there and see you.

TILDEN. Long way to drive.

DODGE *(to TILDEN)*. You don't know anything about that! That happened before you were born! Long before!

VINCE. What's happened, Dad? What's going on here? I thought everything was all right. What's happened to Halie?

TILDEN. She left.

SHELLY *(to TILDEN)*. Do you want me to take those carrots for you?

(TILDEN stares at her. She moves in close to him. Holds out her arms. TILDEN stares at her arms then slowly dumps the carrots into her arms. SHELLY stands there holding the carrots.)

TILDEN *(to SHELLY)*. You like carrots?

SHELLY. Sure. I like all kinds of vegetables.

DODGE *(to* TILDEN*).* You gotta get me a bottle before Halie comes back!

*(*DODGE *hits sofa with his fist.* VINCE *crosses up to* DODGE *and tries to console him.* SHELLY *and* TILDEN *stay facing each other.)*

TILDEN *(to* SHELLY*).* Back yard's full of carrots. Corn. Potatoes.

SHELLY. You're Vince's father, right?

TILDEN. All kinds of vegetables. You like vegetables?

SHELLY *(laughs).* Yeah. I love vegetables.

TILDEN. We could cook these carrots ya' know. You could cut 'em up and we could cook 'em.

SHELLY. All right.

TILDEN. I'll get you a pail and a knife.

SHELLY. Okay.

TILDEN. I'll be right back. Don't go.

*(*TILDEN *exits off stage left.* SHELLY *stands center, arms full of carrots.* VINCE *stands next to* DODGE. SHELLY *looks toward* VINCE *then down at the carrots.)*

DODGE *(to* VINCE*).* You could get me a bottle. *(pointing off left)* There's money on the table.

VINCE. Grandpa why don't you lay down for a while?

DODGE. I don't wanna lay down for a while! Every time I lay down something happens! *(whips off his cap, points at his head)* Look what happens! That's what happens! *(pulls his cap back on)* You go lie down and see what happens to you! See how you like it! They'll steal your bottle! They'll cut your hair! They'll murder your children! That's what'll happen.

VINCE. Just relax for a while.

DODGE *(pause).* You could get me a bottle ya' know. There's nothing stopping you from getting me a bottle.

SHELLY. Why don't you get him a bottle Vince? Maybe it would help everybody identify each other.

DODGE *(pointing to* SHELLY*).* There, see? She thinks you should get me a bottle.

*(*VINCE *crosses to* SHELLY*.)*

VINCE. What're you doing with those carrots.

SHELLY. I'm waiting for your father.

DODGE. She thinks you should get me a bottle!

VINCE. Shelly put the carrots down will ya'! We gotta deal with the situation here! I'm gonna need your help.

SHELLY. I'm helping.

VINCE. You're only adding to the problem! You're making things worse! Put the carrots down!

*(*VINCE *tries to knock the carrots out of her arms. She turns away from him, protecting the carrots.)*

SHELLY. Get away from me! Stop it!

*(*VINCE *stands back from her. She turns to him still holding the carrots.)*

VINCE *(to* SHELLY*).* Why are you doing this! Are you trying to make fun of me? This is my family you know!

SHELLY. You coulda' fooled me! I'd just as soon not be here myself. I'd just as soon be a thousand miles from here. I'd rather be any-' where but here. You're the one who wants to stay. So I'll stay. I'll stay and I'll cut the carrots. And I'll cook the carrots. And I'll do whatever I have to do to survive. Just to make it through this.

VINCE. Put the carrots down Shelly.

*(*TILDEN *enters from left with pail, milking stool and a knife. He sets the stool and pail center stage for* SHELLY. SHELLY *looks at* VINCE *then sits down on stool, sets the carrots on the floor and takes the knife from* TILDEN. *She looks at* VINCE *again then picks up a carrot, cuts the ends off, scrapes it and drops it in the pail. She repeats this,* VINCE *glares at her. She smiles.)*

DODGE. She could get me a bottle. She's the type a' girl that could get me a bottle. Easy. She'd go down there. Slink up to the counter. They'd probably give her two bottles for the price of one. She could do that.

*(*SHELLY *laughs. Keeps cutting carrots.* VINCE *crosses up to* DODGE, *looks at him.* TILDEN *watches* SHELLY*'s hands. Long pause.)*

VINCE *(to* DODGE*).* I haven't changed that much. I mean physically. Physically I'm just about the same. Same size. Same weight. Everything's the same.

*(*DODGE *keeps staring at* SHELLY *while* VINCE *talks to him.)*

DODGE. She's a beautiful girl. Exceptional.

*(*VINCE *moves in front of* DODGE *to block his view of* SHELLY. DODGE *keeps craning his head around to see her as* VINCE *demonstrates tricks from his past.)*

VINCE. Look. Look at this. Do you remember this? I used to bend my thumb behind my knuckles. You remember? I used to do it at the dinner table.

*(*VINCE *bends a thumb behind his knuckles for* DODGE *and holds it out to him.* DODGE *takes a short glance then looks back at* SHELLY. VINCE *shifts position and shows him something else.)*

VINCE. What about this?

*(*VINCE *curls his lips back and starts drum-*

ming on his teeth with his fingernails making little tapping sounds. DODGE *watches a while.* TILDEN *turns toward the sound.* VINCE *keeps it up. He sees* TILDEN *taking notice and crosses to* TILDEN *as he drums on his teeth.* DODGE *turns T.V. on. Watches it.)*

VINCE. You remember this Dad?

(VINCE keeps on drumming for TILDEN. TIL-DEN *watches a while, fascinated, then turns back to* SHELLY. VINCE *keeps up the drumming on his teeth, crosses back to* DODGE *doing it.* SHELLY *keeps working on carrots, talking to* TILDEN.)*

SHELLY *(to* TILDEN*).* He drives me crazy with that sometimes.

VINCE *(to* DODGE*).* I Know! Here's one you'll remember. You used to kick me out of the house for this one.

(VINCE pulls his shirt out of his belt and holds it tucked under his chin with his stomach exposed. He grabs the flesh on either side of his belly button and pushes it in and out to make it look like a mouth talking. He watches his belly button and makes a deep sounding cartoon voice to synchronize with the movement. He demonstrates it to DODGE *then crosses down to* TILDEN *doing it. Both* DODGE *and* TILDEN *take short, uninterested glances then ignore him.)*

VINCE *(deep cartoon voice).* "Hello. How are you? I'm fine. Thank you very much. It's so good to see you looking well this fine Sunday morning. I was going down to the hardware store to fetch a pail of water."

SHELLY. Vince, don't be pathetic will ya'!

(VINCE stops. Tucks his shirt back in.)

SHELLY. Jesus Christ. They're not gonna play. Can't you see that?

(SHELLY keeps cutting carrots. VINCE slowly moves toward TILDEN. TILDEN *keeps watching* SHELLY. DODGE *watches T.V.)*

VINCE *(to* SHELLY*).* I don't get it. I really don't get it. Maybe it's me. Maybe I forgot something.

DODGE *(from sofa).* You forgot to get me a bottle! That's what you forgot. Anybody in this house could get me a bottle. Anybody! But nobody will. Nobody understands the urgency! Peelin carrots is more important. Playin piano on your teeth! Well I hope you all remember this when you get up in years. When you find yourself immobilized. Dependent on the whims of others.

(VINCE moves up toward DODGE. *Pause as he looks at him.)*

VINCE. I'll get you a bottle.

DODGE. You will?

VINCE. Sure.

(SHELLY stands holding knife and carrot.)

SHELLY. You're not going to leave me here are you?

VINCE *(moving to her).* You suggested it! You said, "why don't I go get him a bottle." So I'll go get him a bottle!

SHELLY. But I can't stay here.

VINCE. What is going on! A minute ago you were ready to cut carrots all night!

SHELLY. That was only if you stayed. Something to keep me busy, so I wouldn't be so nervous. I don't want to stay here alone.

DODGE. Don't let her talk you out of it! She's a bad influence. I could see it the minute she stepped in here.

SHELLY *(to* DODGE*).* You were asleep!

TILDEN *(to* SHELLY*).* Don't you want to cut carrots anymore?

SHELLY. Sure. Sure I do.

(SHELLY sits back down on stool and continues cutting carrots. Pause. VINCE *moves around, stroking his hair, staring at* DODGE *and* TILDEN. VINCE *and* SHELLY *exchange glances.* DODGE *watches T.V.)*

VINCE. Boy! This is amazing. This is truly amazing. *(keeps moving around)* What is this anyway? Am I in a time warp or something? Have I committed an unpardonable offence? It's true, I'm not married. *(SHELLY looks at him, then back to carrots)* But I'm also not divorced. I have been known to plunge into sinful infatuation with the Alto Saxophone. Sucking on number 5 reeds deep into the wee wee hours.

SHELLY. Vince, what are you doing that for? They don't care about any of that. They just don't recognize you, that's all.

VINCE. How could they not recognize me! How in the hell could they not recognize me! I'm their son!

DODGE *(watching T.V.).* You're no son of mine. I've had sons in my time and you're not one of 'em.

(Long pause. VINCE *stares at* DODGE *then looks at* TILDEN. *He turns to* SHELLY.)*

VINCE. Shelly, I gotta go out for a while. I just gotta go out. I'll get a bottle and I'll come right back. You'll be o.k. here. Really.

SHELLY. I don't know if I can handle this Vince.

VINCE. I just gotta think or something. I don't know. I gotta put this all together.

VINCE. Can't we just go?

VINCE. No! I gotta find out what's going on.

SHELLY. Look, you think you're bad off, what about me? Not only don't they recognize me but I've never seen them before in my life. I don't know who these guys are. They could be anybody!

VINCE. They're not anybody!

SHELLY. That's what you say.

VINCE. They're my family for Christ's sake! I should know who my own family is! Now give me a break. It won't take that long. I'll just go out and I'll come right back. Nothing'll happen. I promise.

(SHELLY stares at him. Pause.)

SHELLY. All right.

VINCE. Thanks. *(he crosses up to DODGE)* I'm gonna go out now, Grandpa and I'll pick you up a bottle. Okay?

DODGE. Change of heart huh? *(pointing off left)* Money's on the table. In the kitchen.

(VINCE moves toward SHELLY.)

VINCE *(to SHELLY)*. You be all right?

SHELLY *(cutting carrots)*. Sure. I'm fine. I'll just keep real busy while you're gone.

(VINCE looks at TILDEN who keeps staring down at SHELLY's hands.)

DODGE. Persistence see? That's what it takes. Persistence. Persistence, fortitude and determination. Those are the three virtues. You stick with those three and you can't go wrong.

VINCE *(to TILDEN)*. You want anything, Dad?

TILDEN *(looks up at VINCE)*. Me?

VINCE. From the store? I'm gonna get grandpa a bottle.

TILDEN. He's not supposed to drink. Halie wouldn't like it.

VINCE. He wants a bottle.

TILDEN. He's not supposed to drink.

DODGE *(to VINCE)*. Don't negotiate with him! Don't make any transactions until you've spoken to me first! He'll steal you blind!

VINCE *(to DODGE)*. Tilden says you're not supposed to drink.

DODGE. Tilden's lost his marbles! Look at him! He's around the bend. Take a look at him.

(VINCE stares at TILDEN. TILDEN watches SHELLY's hands as she keeps cutting carrots.)

DODGE. Now look at me. Look here at me!

(VINCE looks back to DODGE.)

DODGE. Now, between the two of us, who do you think is more trustworthy? Him or me? Can you trust a man who keeps bringing in vegetables from out of nowhere? Take a look at him.

(VINCE looks back at TILDEN.)

SHELLY. Go get the bottle Vince.

VINCE *(to SHELLY)*. You sure you'll be all right?

SHELLY. I'll be fine. I feel right at home now.

VINCE. You do?

SHELLY. I'm fine. Now that I've got the carrots everything is all right.

VINCE. I'll be right back.

(VINCE crosses stage left.)

DODGE. Where are you going?

VINCE. I'm going to get the money.

DODGE. Then where are you going?

VINCE. Liquor store.

DODGE. Don't go anyplace else. Don't go off some place and drink. Come right back here.

VINCE. I will.

(VINCE exits stage left.)

DODGE *(calling after VINCE)*. You've got responsibility now! And don't go out the back way either! Come out through this way! I wanna' see you when you leave! Don't go out the back!

VINCE'S VOICE *(off left)*. I won't!

(DODGE turns and looks at TILDEN and SHELLY.)

DODGE. Untrustworthy. Probably drown himself if he went out the back. Fall right in a hole. I'd never get my bottle.

SHELLY. I wouldn't worry about Vince. He can take care of himself.

DODGE. Oh he can, huh? Independent.

(VINCE comes on again from stage left with two dollars in his hand. He crosses stage right past DODGE.)

DODGE *(to VINCE)*. You got the money?

VINCE. Yeah. Two bucks.

DODGE. Two bucks. Two bucks is two bucks. Don't sneer.

VINCE. What kind do you want?

DODGE. Whiskey! Gold Star Sour Mash. Use your own discretion.

VINCE. Okay.

(VINCE crosses to stage right door. Opens it. Stops when he hears TILDEN.)

TILDEN *(to VINCE)*. You drove all the way from New Mexico?

(VINCE turns and looks at TILDEN. They stare at each other. VINCE shakes his head, goes out the door, crosses porch and exits out screen door. TILDEN watches him go. Pause.)

SHELLY. You really don't recognize him? Either one of you?

TILDEN *turns again and stares at SHELLY's hands at she cuts carrots.*

DODGE *(watching T.V.)*. Recognize who?

SHELLY. Vince.

DODGE. What's to recognize?

(DODGE *lights a cigarette, coughs slightly and stares at T.V.*)

SHELLY. It'd be cruel if you recognized him and didn't tell him. Wouldn't be fair.

(DODGE *just stares at T.V., smoking.*)

TILDEN. I thought I recognized him. I thought I recognized something about him.

SHELLY. You did?

TILDEN. I thought I saw a face inside his face.

SHELLY. Well it was probably that you saw what he used to look like. You haven't seen him for six years.

HALIE. I haven't?

SHELLY. That's what he says.

(TILDEN *moves around in front of her as she continues with carrots.*)

TILDEN. Where was it I saw him last?

SHELLY. I don't know. I've only known him for a few months. He doesn't tell me everything.

TILDEN. He doesn't?

SHELLY. Not stuff like that.

TILDEN. What does he tell you?

SHELLY. You mean in general?

TILDEN. Yeah.

(TILDEN *moves around behind her.*)

SHELLY. Well he tells me all kinds of things.

TILDEN. Like what?

SHELLY. I don't know! I mean I can't just come right out and tell you how he feels.

TILDEN. How come?

(TILDEN *keeps moving around her slowly in a circle.*)

SHELLY. Because it's stuff he told me privately!

TILDEN. And you can't tell me?

SHELLY. I don't even know you!

DODGE. Tilden, go out in the kitchen and make me some coffee! Leave the girl alone.

SHELLY (*to* DODGE). He's all right.

(TILDEN *ignores* DODGE, *keeps moving around* SHELLY. *He stares at her hair and coat.* DODGE *stares at T.V.*)

TILDEN. You mean you can't tell me anything?

SHELLY. I can tell you some things. I mean we can have a conversation.

TILDEN. We can?

SHELLY. Sure. We're having a conversation right now.

TILDEN. We are?

SHELLY. Yes. That's what we're doing.

TILDEN. But there's certain things you can't tell me, right?

SHELLY. Right.

TILDEN. There's certain things I can't tell you either.

SHELLY. How come?

TILDEN. I don't know. Nobody's supposed to hear it.

SHELLY. Well, you can tell me anything you want to.

TILDEN. I can?

SHELLY. Sure.

TILDEN. It might not be very nice.

SHELLY. That's all right. I've been around.

TILDEN. It might be awful.

SHELLY. Well, can't you tell me anything nice?

(TILDEN *stops in front of her and stares at her coat.* SHELLY *looks back at him. Long pause.*)

TILDEN (*after pause*). Can I touch your coat?

SHELLY. My coat? (*she looks at her coat then back to* TILDEN) Sure.

TILDEN. You don't mind?

SHELLY. No. Go ahead.

(SHELLY *holds her arm out for* TILDEN *to touch.* DODGE *stays fixed on T.V.* TILDEN *moves in slowly toward* SHELLY, *staring at her arm. He reaches out very slowly and touches her arm, feels the fur gently then draws his hand back.* SHELLY *keeps her arm out.*)

SHELLY. It's rabbit.

TILDEN. Rabbit.

(He *reaches out again very slowly and touches the fur on her arm then pulls back his hand again.* SHELLY *drops her arm.*)

SHELLY. My arm was getting tired.

TILDEN. Can I hold it?

SHELLY (*pause*). The coat? Sure.

(SHELLY *takes off her coat and hands it to* TILDEN. TILDEN *takes it slowly, feels the fur then puts it on.* SHELLY *watches as* TILDEN *strokes the fur slowly. He smiles at her. She goes back to cutting carrots.*)

SHELLY. You can have it if you want.

TILDEN. I can?

SHELLY. Yeah. I've got a raincoat in the car. That's all I need.

TILDEN. You've got a car?

SHELLY. Vince does.

(TILDEN *walks around stroking the fur and smiling at the coat.* SHELLY *watches him when he's not looking.* DODGE *sticks with T.V., stretches out on sofa wrapped in blanket.*)

TILDEN (*as he walks around*). I had a car once! I had a white car! I drove. I went everywhere. I went to the mountains. I drove in the snow.

SHELLY. That must've been fun.

TILDEN (*still moving, feeling coat*). I drove all day long sometimes. Across the desert. Way out across the desert. I drove past towns. Anywhere. Past palm trees. Lightning. Anything. I would drive through it. I would drive through it and I would stop and I would look around and I would drive on. I would get back in and drive! I loved to drive. There was nothing I loved more. Nothing I dreamed of was better than driving.

DODGE (*eyes on T.V.*). Pipe down would ya'!

(TILDEN *stops. Stares at* SHELLY.)

SHELLY. Do you do much driving now?

TILDEN. Now? Now? I don't drive now.

SHELLY. How come?

TILDEN. I'm grown up now.

SHELLY. Grown up?

TILDEN. I'm not a kid.

SHELLY. You don't have to be a kid to drive.

TILDEN. It wasn't driving then.

SHELLY. What was it?

TILDEN. Adventure. I went everywhere.

SHELLY. Well you can still do that.

TILDEN. Not now.

SHELLY. Why not?

TILDEN. I just told you. You don't understand anything. If I told you something you wouldn't understand it.

SHELLY. Told me what?

TILDEN. Told you something that's true.

SHELLY. Like what?

TILDEN. Like a baby. Like a little tiny baby.

SHELLY. Like when you were little?

TILDEN. If I told you you'd make me give your coat back.

SHELLY. I won't. I promise. Tell me.

TILDEN. I can't. Dodge won't let me.

SHELLY. He won't hear you. It's okay.

(*Pause.* TILDEN *stares at her. Moves slightly toward her.*)

TILDEN. We had a baby. (*motioning to* DODGE) He did. Dodge did. Could pick it up with one hand. Put it in the other. Little baby. Dodge killed it.

(SHELLY *stands.*)

TILDEN. Don't stand up. Don't stand up!

(SHELLY *sits again.* DODGE *sits up on sofa and looks at them.*)

TILDEN. Dodge drowned it.

SHELLY. Don't tell me anymore! Okay?

(TILDEN *moves closer to her.* DODGE *takes more interest.*)

DODGE. Tilden? You leave that girl alone!

TILDEN (*pays no attention*). Never told Halie.

Never told anybody. Just drowned it.

DODGE (*shuts off T.V.*). Tilden!

TILDEN. Nobody could find it. Just disappeared. Cops looked for it. Neighbors. Nobody could find it.

(DODGE *struggles to get up from sofa.*)

DODGE. Tilden, what're you telling her! Tilden!

(DODGE *keeps struggling until he's standing.*)

TILDEN. Finally everybody just gave up. Just stopped looking. Everybody had a different answer. Kidnap. Murder. Accident. Some kind of accident.

(DODGE *struggles to walk toward* TILDEN *and falls.* TILDEN *ignores him.*)

DODGE. Tilden you shut up! You shut up about it!

(DODGE *starts coughing on the floor.* SHELLY *watches him from the stool.*)

TILDEN. Little tiny baby just disappeared. It's not hard. It's so small. Almost invisible.

(SHELLY *makes a move to help* DODGE. TILDEN *firmly pushes her back down on the stool.* DODGE *keeps coughing.*)

TILDEN. He said he had his reasons. Said it went a long way back. But he wouldn't tell anybody.

DODGE. Tilden! Don't tell her anything! Don't tell her!

TILDEN. He's the only one who knows where it's buried. The only one. Like a secret buried treasure. Won't tell any of us. Won't tell me or mother or even Bradley. Especially Bradley. Bradley tried to force it out of him but he wouldn't tell. Wouldn't even tell why he did it. One night he just did it.

(DODGE's *coughing subsides.* SHELLY *stays on stool staring at* DODGE. TILDEN *slowly takes* SHELLY's *coat off and holds it out to her. Long pause.* SHELLY *sits there trembling.*)

TILDEN. You probably want your coat back now.

(SHELLY *stares at coat but doesn't move to take it. The sound of* BRADLEY's *leg squeaking is heard off left. The others on stage remain still.* BRADLEY *appears up left outside the screen door wearing a yellow rain slicker. He enters through screen door, crosses porch to stage right door and enters stage. Closes door. Takes off rain slicker and shakes it out. He sees all the others and stops.* TILDEN *turns to him.* BRADLEY *stares at* SHELLY. DODGE *remains on floor.*)

BRADLEY. What's going on here? (*motioning to* SHELLY) Who's that?

(SHELLY *stands, moves back away from*

BRADLEY *as he crosses toward her. He stops next to* TILDEN. *He sees coat in* TILDEN'*s hand and grabs it away from him.)*

BRADLEY. Who's she supposed to be?

TILDEN. She's driving to New Mexico.

*(*BRADLEY *stares at her.* SHELLY *is frozen.* BRADLEY *limps over to her with the coat in his fist. He stops in front of her.)*

BRADLEY *(to* SHELLY, *after pause)*. Vacation?

*(*SHELLY *shakes her head "no", trembling.)*

BRADLEY *(to* SHELLY, *motioning to* TILDEN). You taking him with you?

*(*SHELLY *shakes her head "no".* BRADLEY *crosses back to* TILDEN.*)*

BRADLEY. You oughta'. No use leaving him here. Doesn't do a lick a' work. Doesn't raise a finger. *(stopping, to* TILDEN*)* Do ya'? *(to* SHELLY*)* 'Course he used to be an All American. Quarterback or Fullback or somethin'. He tell you that?

*(*SHELLY *shakes her head "no".)*

BRADLEY. Yeah, he used to be a big deal. Wore lettermen's sweaters. Had medals hanging all around his neck. Real purty. Big deal. *(he laughs to himself, notices* DODGE *on floor, crosses to him, stops)* This one too. *(to* SHELLY*)* You'd never think it to look at him would ya'? All bony and wasted away.

*(*SHELLY *shakes her head again.* BRADLEY *stares at her, crosses back to her, clenching the coat in his fist. He stops in front of* SHELLY.*)*

BRADLEY. Women like that kinda' thing don't they?

SHELLY. What?

BRADLEY. Importance. Importance in a man?

SHELLY. I don't know.

BRADLEY. Yeah. You know, you know. Don't give me that. *(moves closer to* SHELLY*)* You're with Tilden?

SHELLY. No.

BRADLEY *(turning to* TILDEN*)*. Tilden! She with you?

*(*TILDEN *doesn't answer. Stares at floor.)*

BRADLEY. Tilden!

*(*TILDEN *suddenly bolts and runs off up stage left.* BRADLEY *laughs. Talks to* SHELLY. DODGE *starts moving his lips silently as though talking to someone invisible on the floor.)*

BRADLEY *(laughing)*. Scared to death! He was always scared!

*(*BRADLEY *stops laughing. Stares at* SHELLY.*)*

BRADLEY. You're scared too, right? *(laughs again)* You're scared and you don't even know me. *(stops laughing)* You don't gotta be scared.

*(*SHELLY *looks at* DODGE *on the floor.)*

SHELLY. Can't we do something for him?

BRADLEY *(looking at* DODGE*)*. We could shoot him. *(laughs)* We could drown him! What about drowning him?

SHELLY. Shut up!

*(*BRADLEY *stops laughing. Moves in closer to* SHELLY. *She freezes.* BRADLEY *speaks slowly and deliberately.)*

BRADLEY. Hey! Missus. Don't talk to me like that. Don't talk to me in that tone a' voice. There was a time when I had to take that tone a' voice from pretty near everyone. *(motioning to* DODGE*)* Him, for one! Him and that half brain that just ran outa' here. They don't talk to me like that now. Not any more. Everything's turned around now. Full circle. Isn't that funny?

SHELLY. I'm sorry.

BRADLEY. Open your mouth.

SHELLY. What?

BRADLEY *(motioning for her to open her mouth)*. Open up.

(She opens her mouth slightly.)

BRADLEY. Wider.

(She opens her mouth wider.)

BRADLEY. Keep it like that.

(She does. Stares at BRADLEY. *With his free hand he puts his fingers into her mouth. She tries to pull away.)*

BRADLEY. Just stay put!

(She freezes. He keeps his fingers in her mouth. Stares at her. Pause. He pulls his hand out. She closes her mouth, keeps her eyes on him. BRADLEY *smiles. He looks at* DODGE *on the floor and crosses over to him.* SHELLY *watches him closely.* BRADLEY *stands over* DODGE *and smiles at* SHELLY. *He holds her coat up in both hands over* DODGE, *keeps smiling at* SHELLY. *He looks down at* DODGE *then drops the coat so that it lands on* DODGE *and covers his head.* BRADLEY *keeps his hands up in the position of holding the coat, looks over at* SHELLY *and smiles. The lights black out.)*

ACT THREE

Scene: Same set. Morning. Bright sun. No sound of rain. Everything has been cleared up again. No sign of carrots. No pail. No stool. VINCE'*s saxophone case and overcoat are still at the foot of the staircase.* BRADLEY *is asleep on the sofa under* DODGE'*s blanket. His head toward stage left.* BRADLEY'*s wooden leg is leaning against the sofa right by his head. The shoe is left on it. The harness hangs down.*

DODGE *is sitting on the floor, propped up against the T.V. set facing stage left wearing his baseball cap.* SHELLY's *rabbit fur coat covers his chest and shoulders. He stares off toward stage left. He seems weaker and more disoriented. The lights rise slowly to the sound of birds and remain for a while in silence on the two men.* BRADLEY *sleeps very soundly.* DODGE *hardly moves.* SHELLY *appears from stage left with a big smile, slowly crossing toward* DODGE *balancing a steaming cup of broth in a saucer.* DODGE *just stares at her as she gets close to him.*

———

SHELLY *(as she crosses).* This is going to make all the difference in the world, Grandpa. You don't mind me calling you Grandpa do you? I mean I know you minded when Vince called you that but you don't even know him.

DODGE. He skipped town with my money ya' know. I'm gonna hold you as collateral.

SHELLY. He'll be back. Don't you worry.

(She kneels down next to DODGE *and puts the cup and saucer in his lap.)*

DODGE. It's morning already! Not only didn't I get my bottle but he's got my two bucks!

SHELLY. Try to drink this, okay? Don't spill it.

DODGE. What is it?

SHELLY. Beef bouillon. It'll warm you up.

DODGE. Bouillon! I don't want any goddamn bouillon! Get that stuff away from me!

SHELLY. I just got through making it.

DODGE. I don't care if you just spent all week making it! I ain't drinking it!

SHELLY. Well, what am I supposed to do with it then? I'm trying to help you out. Besides, it's good for you.

DODGE. Get it away from me!

(SHELLY stands up with cup and saucer.)

DODGE. What do you know what's good for me anyway?

(She looks at DODGE *then turns away from him, crossing to staircase, sits on bottom step and drinks the bouillon.* DODGE *stares at her.)*

DODGE. You know what'd be good for me?

SHELLY. What?

DODGE. A little massage. A little contact.

SHELLY. Oh no. I've had enough contact for a while. Thanks anyway.

(She keeps sipping bouillon, stays sitting. Pause as DODGE *stares at her.)*

DODGE. Why not? You got nothing better to do. That fella's not gonna be back here. You're not expecting him to show up again are you?

SHELLY. Sure. He'll show up. He left his horn here.

DODGE. His horn? *(laughs)* You're his horn?

SHELLY. Very funny.

DODGE. He's run off with my money! He's not coming back here.

SHELLY. He'll be back.

DODGE. You're a funny chicken, you know that?

SHELLY. Thanks.

DODGE. Full of faith. Hope. Faith and hope. You're all alike you hopers. If it's not God then it's a man. If it's not a man then it's a woman. If it's not a woman then it's the land or the future of some kind. Some kind of future.

(Pause.)

SHELLY *(looking toward porch).* I'm glad it stopped raining.

DODGE *(looks toward porch then back to her).* That's what I mean. See, you're glad it stopped raining. Now you think everything's gonna be different. Just 'cause the sun comes out.

SHELLY. It's already different. Last night I was scared.

DODGE. Scared a' what?

SHELLY. Just scared.

DODGE. Bradley? *(looks at* BRADLEY*)* He's a push-over. 'Specially now. All ya' gotta' do is take his leg and throw it out the back door. Helpless. Totally helpless.

(SHELLY turns and stares at BRADLEY's *wooden leg then looks at* DODGE. *She sips bouillon.)*

SHELLY. You'd do that?

DODGE. Me? I've hardly got the strength to breathe.

SHELLY. But you'd actually do it if you could?

DODGE. Don't be so easily shocked, girlie. There's nothing a man can't do. You dream it up and he can do it. Anything.

SHELLY. You've tried I guess.

DODGE. Don't sit there sippin' your bouillon and judging me! This is my house!

SHELLY. I forgot.

DODGE. You forgot? Whose house did you think it was?

SHELLY. Mine.

(DODGE just stares at her. Long pause. She sips from cup.)

SHELLY. I know it's not mine but I had that feeling.

DODGE. What feeling?

SHELLY. The feeling that nobody lives here but me. I mean everybody's gone. You're here, but it doesn't seem like you're supposed to be.

(pointing to BRADLEY*)* Doesn't seem like he's supposed to be here either. I don't know what it is. It's the house or something. Something familiar. Like I know my way around here. Did you ever get that feeling?

*(*DODGE *stares at her in silence. Pause.)*

DODGE. No. No, I never did.

*(*SHELLY *gets up. Moves around space holding cup.)*

SHELLY. Last night I went to sleep up there in that room.

DODGE. What room?

SHELLY. That room up there with all the pictures. All the crosses on the wall.

DODGE. Halie's room?

SHELLY. Yeah. Whoever "Halie" is.

DODGE. She's my wife.

SHELLY. So you remember her?

DODGE. Whad'ya mean! 'Course I remember her! She's only been gone for a day—half a day. However long it's been.

SHELLY. Do you remember her when her hair was bright red? Standing in front of an apple tree?

DODGE. What is this, the third degree or something! Who're you to be askin' me personal questions about my wife!

SHELLY. You never look at those pictures up there?

DODGE. What pictures!

SHELLY. Your whole life's up there hanging on the wall. Somebody who looks just like you. Somebody who looks just like you used to look.

DODGE. That isn't me! That never was me! This is me. Right here. This is it. The whole shootin' match, sittin' right in front of you.

SHELLY. So the past never happened as far as you're concerned?

DODGE. The past? Jesus Christ. The past. What do you know about the past?

SHELLY. Not much. I know there was a farm.

(Pause.)

DODGE. A farm?

SHELLY. There's a picture of a farm. A big farm. A bull. Wheat. Corn.

DODGE. Corn?

SHELLY. All the kids are standing out in the corn. They're all waving these big straw hats. One of them doesn't have a hat.

DODGE. Which one was that?

SHELLY. There's a baby. A baby in a woman's arms. The same woman with the red hair. She looks lost standing out there. Like she doesn't know how she got there.

DODGE. She knows! I told her a hundred times it wasn't gonna' be the city! I gave her plenty a' warning.

SHELLY. She's looking down at the baby like it was somebody else's. Like it didn't even belong to her.

DODGE. That's about enough outa' you! You got some funny ideas. Some damn funny ideas. You think just because people propagate they have to love their offspring? You never seen a bitch eat her puppies? Where are you from anyway?

SHELLY. L.A. We already went through that.

DODGE. That's right, L.A. I remember.

SHELLY. Stupid country.

DODGE. That's right! No wonder.

(Pause.)

SHELLY. What's happened to this family anyway?

DODGE. You're in no position to ask! What do you care? You some kinda' Social Worker?

SHELLY. I'm Vince's friend.

DODGE. Vince's friend! That's rich. That's really rich. "Vince!" "Mr. Vince!" "Mr. Thief" is more like it! His name doesn't mean a hoot in hell to me. Not a tinkle in the well. You know how many kids I've spawned? Not to mention Grand kids and Great Grand kids and Great Great Grand kids after them?

SHELLY. And you don't remember any of them?

DODGE. What's to remember? Halie's the one with the family album. She's the one you should talk to. She'll set you straight on the heritage if that's what you're interested in. She's traced it all the way back to the grave.

SHELLY. What do you mean?

DODGE. What do you think I mean? How far back can you go? A long line of corpses! There's not a living soul behind me. Not a one. Who's holding me in their memory? Who gives a damn about bones in the ground?

SHELLY. Was Tilden telling the truth?

*(*DODGE *stops short. Stares at* SHELLY. *Shakes his head. He looks offstage left.)*

SHELLY. Was he?

*(*DODGE*'s tone changes drastically.)*

DODGE. Tilden? *(turns to* SHELLY, *calmly)* Where is Tilden?

SHELLY. Last night. Was he telling the truth about the baby?

(Pause.)

DODGE *(turns toward stage left)*. What's happened to Tilden? Why isn't Tilden here?

SHELLY. Bradley chased him out.

DODGE *(looking at* BRADLEY *asleep)*. Bradley? Why is he on my sofa? *(turns back to*

SHELLY) Have I been here all night? On the floor?

SHELLY. He wouldn't leave. I hid outside until he fell asleep.

DODGE. Outside? Is Tilden outside? He shouldn't be out there in the rain. He'll get himself into trouble. He doesn't know his way around here anymore. Not like he used to. He went out West and got himself into trouble. Got himself into bad trouble. We don't want any of that around here.

SHELLY. What did he do?

(Pause.)

DODGE *(quietly stares at* SHELLY*).* Tilden? He got mixed up. That's what he did. We can't afford to leave him alone. Not now.

(Sound of HALIE *laughing comes from off left.* SHELLY *stands, looking in direction of voice, holding cup and saucer, doesn't know whether to stay or run.)*

DODGE *(motioning to* SHELLY*).* Sit down! Sit back down!

*(*SHELLY *sits. Sound of* HALIE*'s laughter again.)*

DODGE *(to* SHELLY *in a heavy whisper, pulling coat up around him).* Don't leave me alone now! Promise me? Don't go off and leave me alone. I need somebody here with me. Tilden's gone now and I need someone. Don't leave me! Promise!

SHELLY *(sitting).* I won't.

*(*HALIE *appears outside the screen porch door, up left with* FATHER DEWIS*. She is wearing a bright yellow dress, no hat, white gloves and her arms are full of yellow roses.* FATHER DEWIS *is dressed in traditional black suit, white clerical collar and shirt. He is a very distinguished grey haired man in his sixties. They are both slightly drunk and feeling giddy. As they enter the porch through the screen door,* DODGE *pulls the rabbit fur coat over his head and hides.* SHELLY *stands again.* DODGE *drops the coat and whispers intensely to* SHELLY*. Neither* HALIE *nor* FATHER DEWIS *are aware of the people inside the house.)*

DODGE *(to* SHELLY *in a strong whisper).* You promised!

*(*SHELLY *sits on stairs again.* DODGE *pulls coat back over his head.* HALIE *and* FATHER DEWIS *talk on the porch as they cross toward stage right interior door.)*

HALIE. Oh Father! That's terrible! That's absolutely terrible. Aren't you afraid of being punished?

(She giggles.)

DEWIS. Not by the Italians. They're too busy punishing each other.

(They both break out in giggles.)

HALIE. What about God?

DEWIS. Well, prayerfully, God only hears what he wants to. That's just between you and me of course. In our heart of hearts we know we're every bit as wicked as the Catholics.

(They giggle again and reach the stage right door.)

HALIE. Father, I never heard you talk like this in Sunday sermon.

DEWIS. Well, I save all my best jokes for private company. Pearls before swine you know.

(They enter the room laughing and stop when they see SHELLY. SHELLY *stands.* HALIE *closes the door behind* FATHER DEWIS. DODGE*'s voice is heard under the coat, talking to* SHELLY.*)*

DODGE *(under coat, to* SHELLY*).* Sit down, sit down! Don't let 'em buffalo you!

*(*SHELLY *sits on stair again.* HALIE *looks at* DODGE *on the floor then looks at* BRADLEY *asleep on sofa and sees his wooden leg. She lets out a shriek of embarrassment for* FATHER DEWIS.*)*

HALIE. Oh my gracious! What in the name of Judas Priest is going on in this house!

(She hands over the roses to FATHER DEWIS.*)*

HALIE. Excuse me Father.

*(*HALIE *crosses to* DODGE*, whips the coat off him and covers the wooden leg with it.* BRADLEY *stays asleep.)*

HALIE. You can't leave this house for a second without the Devil blowing in through the front door!

DODGE. Gimme back that coat! Gimme back that goddamn coat before I freeze to death!

HALIE. You're not going to freeze! The sun's out in case you hadn't noticed!

DODGE. Gimme back that coat! That coat's for live flesh not dead wood!

*(*HALIE *whips the blanket off* BRADLEY *and throws it on* DODGE. DODGE *covers his head again with blanket.* BRADLEY*'s amputated leg can be faked by having half of it under a cushion of the sofa. He's fully clothed.* BRADLEY *sits up with a jerk when the blanket comes off him.)*

HALIE *(as she tosses blanket).* Here! Use this! It's yours anyway! Can't you take care of yourself for once!

BRADLEY *(yelling at* HALIE*).* Gimme that blanket! Gimme back that blanket! That's my blanket!

*(*HALIE *crosses back toward* FATHER DEWIS *who just stands there with the roses.* BRADLEY

thrashes helplessly on the sofa trying to reach blanket. DODGE *hides himself deeper in blanket.* SHELLY *looks on from staircase, still holding cup and saucer.)*

HALIE. Believe me, Father, this is not what I had in mind when I invited you in.

DEWIS. Oh, no apologies please. I wouldn't be in the ministry if I couldn't face real life.

(He laughs self-consciously. HALIE *notices* SHELLY *again and crosses over to her.* SHELLY *stays sitting.* HALIE *stops and stares at her.)*

BRADLEY. I want my blanket back! Gimme my blanket!

(HALIE turns toward BRADLEY and silences him.)

HALIE. Shut up Bradley! Right this minute! I've had enough!

(BRADLEY slowly recoils, lies back down on sofa, turns his back toward HALIE and whimpers softly. HALIE *directs her attention to* SHELLY *again. Pause.)*

HALIE *(to* SHELLY*).* What're you doing with my cup and saucer?

SHELLY *(looking at cup, back to* HALIE*).* I made some bouillon for Dodge.

HALIE. For Dodge?

SHELLY. Yeah.

HALIE. Well, did he drink it?

SHELLY. No.

HALIE. Did you drink it?

SHELLY. Yes.

(HALIE stares at her. Long pause. She turns abruptly away from SHELLY and crosses back to FATHER DEWIS.)

HALIE. Father, there's a stranger in my house. What would you advise? What would be the Christian thing?

DEWIS *(squirming).* Oh, well. . . . I. . . . I really—

HALIE. We still have some whiskey, don't we?

(DODGE slowly pulls the blanket down off his head and looks toward FATHER DEWIS. SHELLY stands.)

SHELLY. Listen, I don't drink or anything. I just—

(HALIE turns toward SHELLY viciously.)

HALIE. You sit back down!

(SHELLY sits again on stair. HALIE *turns again to* DEWIS*.)*

HALIE. I think we have plenty of whiskey left! Don't we Father?

DEWIS. Well, yes. I think so. You'll have to get it. My hands are full.

(HALIE giggles. Reaches into DEWIS'*s pockets, searching for bottle. She smells the roses*

as she searches. DEWIS *stands stiffly.* DODGE *watches* HALIE *closely as she looks for bottle.)*

HALIE. The most incredible things, roses! Aren't they incredible, Father?

DEWIS. Yes. Yes they are.

HALIE. They almost cover the stench of sin in this house. Just magnificent! The smell. We'll have to put some at the foot of Ansel's statue. On the day of the unveiling.

(HALIE finds a silver flask of whiskey in DEWIS'*s vest pocket. She pulls it out.* DODGE *looks on eagerly.* HALIE *crosses to* DODGE*, opens the flask and takes a sip.)*

HALIE *(to* DODGE*).* Ansel's getting a statue, Dodge. Did you know that? Not a plaque but a real live statue. A full bronze. Tip to toe. A basketball in one hand and a rifle in the other.

BRADLEY *(his back to* HALIE*).* He never played basketball!

HALIE. You shut up, Bradley! You shut up about Ansel! Ansel played basketball better than anyone! And you know it! He was an All American! There's no reason to take the glory away from others.

(HALIE turns away from BRADLEY, crosses back toward DEWIS sipping on the flask and smiling.)

HALIE *(to* DEWIS*).* Ansel was a great basketball player. One of the greatest.

DEWIS. I remember Ansel.

HALIE. Of course! You remember. You remember how he could play. *(she turns toward* SHELLY*)* Of course, nowadays they play a different brand of basketball. More vicious. Isn't that right, dear?

SHELLY. I don't know.

(HALIE crosses to SHELLY*, sipping on flask. She stops in front of* SHELLY*.)*

HALIE. Much, much more vicious. They smash into each other. They knock each other's teeth out. There's blood all over the court. Savages.

(HALIE takes the cup from SHELLY and pours whiskey into it.)

HALIE. They don't train like they used to. Not at all. They allow themselves to run amuck. Drugs and women. Women mostly.

(HALIE hands the cup of whiskey back to SHELLY *slowly.* SHELLY *takes it.)*

HALIE. Mostly women. Girls. Sad, pathetic little girls. *(she crosses back to* FATHER DEWIS*)* It's just a reflection of the times, don't you think Father? An indication of where we stand?

DEWIS. I suppose so, yes.

HALIE. Yes. A sort of a bad omen. Our youth becoming monsters.

DEWIS. Well, I uh—

HALIE. Oh you can disagree with me if you want to, Father. I'm open to debate. I think argument only enriches both sides of the question don't you? *(she moves toward* DODGE*)* I suppose, in the long run, it doesn't matter. When you see the way things deteriorate before your very eyes. Everything running down hill. It's kind of silly to even think about youth.

DEWIS. No, I don't think so. I think it's important to believe in certain things.

HALIE. Yes. Yes, I know what you mean. I think that's right. I think that's true. *(she looks at* DODGE*)* Certain basic things. We can't shake certain basic things. We might end up crazy. Like my husband. You can see it in his eyes. You can see how mad he is.

*(*DODGE *covers his head with the blanket again.* HALIE *takes a single rose from* DEWIS *and moves slowly over to* DODGE*.)*

HALIE. We can't not believe in something. We can't stop believing. We just end up dying if we stop. Just end up dead.

HALIE *throws the rose gently onto* DODGE*'s blanket. It lands between his knees and stays there. Long pause as* HALIE *stares at the rose.* SHELLY *stands suddenly.* HALIE *doesn't turn to her but keeps staring at rose.*

SHELLY *(to* HALIE*).* Don't you wanna' know who I am! Don't you wanna know what I'm doing here! I'm not dead!

*(*SHELLY *crosses toward* HALIE.HALIE *turns slowly toward her.)*

HALIE. Did you drink your whiskey?

SHELLY. No! And I'm not going to either!

HALIE. Well that's a firm stand. It's good to have a firm stand.

SHELLY. I don't have any stand at all. I'm just trying to put all this together.

*(*HALIE *laughs and crosses back to* DEWIS*.)*

HALIE *(to* DEWIS*).* Surprises, surprises! Did you have any idea we'd be returning to this?

SHELLY. I came here with your Grandson for a little visit! A little innocent friendly visit.

HALIE. My Grandson?

SHELLY. Yes! That's right. The one no one remembers.

HALIE *(to* DEWIS*).* This is getting a little far fetched.

SHELLY. I told him it was stupid to come back here. To try to pick up from where he left off.

HALIE. Where was that?

SHELLY. Wherever he was when he left here! Six years ago! Ten years ago! Whenever it was. I told him nobody cares.

HALIE. Didn't he listen?

SHELLY. No! No he didn't. We had to stop off at every tiny little meatball town that he remembered from his boyhood! Every stupid little donut shop he ever kissed a girl in. Every Drive-In. Every Drag Strip. Every football field he ever broke a bone on.

HALIE *(suddenly alarmed, to* DODGE*).* Where's Tilden?

SHELLY. Don't ignore me!

HALIE. Dodge! Where's Tilden gone?

*(*SHELLY *moves violently toward* HALIE*.)*

SHELLY *(to* HALIE*).* I'm talking to you!

*(*BRADLEY *sits up fast on the sofa,* SHELLY *backs away.)*

BRADLEY *(to* SHELLY*).* Don't you yell at my mother!

HALIE. Dodge! *(she kicks* DODGE*)* I told you not to let Tilden out of your sight! Where's he gone to?

DODGE. Gimme a drink and I'll tell ya'.

DEWIS. Halie, maybe this isn't the right time for a visit.

*(*HALIE *crosses back to* DEWIS*.)*

HALIE *(to* DEWIS*).* I never should've left. I never, never should've left! Tilden could be anywhere by now! Anywhere! He's not in control of his faculties. Dodge knew that. I told him when I left here. I told him specifically to watch out for Tilden.

BRADLEY *reaches down, grabs* DODGE*'s blanket and yanks it off him. He lays down on sofa and pulls the blanket over his head.*

DODGE. He's got my blanket again! He's got my blanket!

HALIE *(turning to* BRADLEY*).* Bradley! Bradley, put that blanket back!

*(*HALIE *moves toward* BRADLEY. SHELLY *suddenly throws the cup and saucer against the stage right door.* DEWIS *ducks. The cup and saucer smash into pieces.* HALIE *stops, turns toward* SHELLY. *Everyone freezes.* BRADLEY *slowly pulls his head out from under blanket, looks toward stage right door, then to* SHELLY. SHELLY *stares at* HALIE. DEWIS *cowers with roses.* SHELLY *moves slowly toward* HALIE. *Long pause.* SHELLY *speaks softly.)*

SHELLY *(to* HALIE*).* I don't like being ignored. I don't like being treated like I'm not here. I didn't like it when I was a kid and I still don't like it.

BRADLEY *(sitting up on sofa).* We don't have to tell you anything, girl. Not a thing. You're not the police are you? You're not the government. You're just some prostitute that Tilden brought in here.

HALIE. Language! I won't have that language in my house!

SHELLY (to BRADLEY). You stuck your hand in my mouth and you call me a prostitute!

HALIE. Bradley! Did you put your hand in her mouth? I'm ashamed of you. I can't leave you alone for a minute.

BRADLEY. I never did. She's lying!

DEWIS. Halie, I think I'll be running along now. I'll just put the roses in the kitchen.

(DEWIS moves toward stage left. HALIE stops him.)

HALIE. Don't go now, Father! Not now.

BRADLEY. I never did anything, mom! I never touched her! She propositioned me! And I turned her down. I turned her down flat!

(SHELLY suddenly grabs her coat off the wooden leg and takes both the leg and coat down stage, away from BRADLEY.)

BRADLEY. Mom! Mom! She's got my leg! She's taken my leg! I never did anything to her! She's stolen my leg!

BRADLEY reaches pathetically in the air for his leg. SHELLY sets it down for a second, puts on her coat fast and picks the leg up again. DODGE starts coughing softly.

HALIE (to SHELLY). I think we've had about enough of you young lady. Just about enough. I don't know where you came from or what you're doing here but you're no longer welcome in this house.

SHELLY (laughs, holds leg). No longer welcome!

BRADLEY. Mom! That's my leg! Get my leg back! I can't do anything without my leg.

(BRADLEY keeps making whimpering sounds and reaching for his leg.)

HALIE. Give my son back his leg. Right this very minute!

(DODGE starts laughing softly to himself in between coughs.)

HALIE (to DEWIS). Father, do something about this would you! I'm not about to be terrorized in my own house!

BRADLEY. Gimme back my leg!

HALIE. Oh, shut up Bradley! Just shut up! You don't need your leg now! Just lay down and shut up!

(BRADLEY whimpers. Lays down and pulls blanket around him. He keeps one arm outside blanket, reaching out toward his wooden leg. DEWIS cautiously approaches SHELLY with the roses in his arms. SHELLY clutches the wooden leg to her chest as though she's kidnapped it.)

DEWIS (to SHELLY). Now, honestly dear, wouldn't it be better to try to talk things out? To try to use some reason?

SHELLY. There isn't any reason here! I can't find a reason for anything.

DEWIS. There's nothing to be afraid of. These are all good people. All righteous people.

SHELLY. I'm not afraid!

DEWIS. But this isn't your house. You have to have some respect.

SHELLY. You're the strangers here, not me.

HALIE. This has gone far enough!

DEWIS. Halie, please. Let me handle this.

SHELLY. Don't come near me! Don't anyone come near me. I don't need any words from you. I'm not threatening anybody. I don't even know what I'm doing here. You all say you don't remember Vince, okay, maybe you don't. Maybe it's Vince that's crazy. Maybe he's made this whole family thing up. I don't even care any more. I was just coming along for the ride. I thought it'd be a nice gesture. Besides, I was curious. He made all of you sound familiar to me. Every one of you. For every name, I had an image. Every time he'd tell me a name, I'd see the person. In fact, each of you was so clear in my mind that I actually believed it was you. I really believed when I walked through that door that the people who lived here would turn out to be the same people in my imagination. But I don't recognize any of you. Not one. Not even the slightest resemblance.

DEWIS. Well you can hardly blame others for not fulfilling your hallucination.

SHELLY. It was no hallucination! It was more like a prophecy. You believe in prophecy, don't you?

HALIE. Father, there's no point in talking to her any further. We're just going to have to call the police.

BRADLEY. No! Don't get the police in here. We don't want the police in here. This is our home.

SHELLY. That's right. Bradley's right. Don't you usually settle your affairs in private? Don't you usually take them out in the dark? Out in the back?

BRADLEY. You stay out of our lives! You have no business interfering!

SHELLY. I don't have any business period. I got nothing to lose.

(She moves around, staring at each of them.)

BRADLEY. You don't know what we've been through. You don't know anything!

SHELLY. I know you've got a secret. You've all got a secret. It's so secret in fact, you're all convinced it never happened.

(HALIE moves to DEWIS.)

HALIE. Oh, my God, Father!

DODGE *(laughing to himself)*. She thinks she's going to get it out of us. She thinks she's going to uncover the truth of the matter. Like a detective or something.

BRADLEY. I'm not telling her anything! Nothing's wrong here! Nothing's ever been wrong! Everything's the way it's supposed to be! Nothing ever happened that's bad! Everything is all right here! We're all good people!

DODGE. She thinks she's gonna suddenly bring everything out into the open after all these years.

DEWIS *(to* SHELLY*)*. Can't you see that these people want to be left in peace? Don't you have any mercy? They haven't done anything to you.

DODGE. She wants to get to the bottom of it. *(to* SHELLY*)* That's it, isn't it? You'd like to get right down to bedrock? You want me to tell ya'? You want me to tell ya' what happened? I'll tell ya'. I might as well.

BRADLEY. No! Don't listen to him. He doesn't remember anything!

DODGE. I remember the whole thing from start to finish. I remember the day he was born. *(Pause.)*

HALIE. Dodge, if you tell this thing—if you tell this, you'll be dead to me. You'll be just as good as dead.

DODGE. That won't be such a big change, Halie. See this girl, this girl here, she wants to know. She wants to know something more. And I got this feeling that it doesn't make a bit a' difference. I'd sooner tell it to a stranger than anybody else.

BRADLEY *(to* DODGE*)*. We made a pact! We made a pact between us! You can't break that now!

DODGE. I don't remember any pact.

BRADLEY *(to* SHELLY*)*. See, he doesn't remember anything. I'm the only one in the family who remembers. The only one. And I'll never tell you!

SHELLY. I'm not so sure I want to find out now.

DODGE *(laughing to himself)*. Listen to her! Now she's runnin' scared!

SHELLY. I'm not scared!

*(*DODGE *stops laughing, long pause.* DODGE *stares at her.)*

DODGE. You're not huh? Well, that's good. Because I'm not either. See, we were a well established family once. Well established. All the boys were grown. The farm was producing enough milk to fill Lake Michigan twice over.

Me and Halie here were pointed toward what looked like the middle part of our life. Everything was settled with us. All we had to do was ride it out. Then Halie got pregnant again. Outa' the middle a' nowhere, she got pregnant. We weren't planning on havin' any more boys. We had enough boys already. In fact, we hadn't been sleepin' in the same bed for about six years.

HALIE *(moving toward stairs)*. I'm not listening to this! I don't have to listen to this!

DODGE *(stops* HALIE*)*. Where are you going! Upstairs! You'll just be listenin' to it upstairs! You go outside, you'll be listenin' to it outside. Might as well stay here and listen to it.

*(*HALIE *stays by stairs.)*

BRADLEY. If I had my leg you wouldn't be saying this. You'd never get away with it if I had my leg.

DODGE *(pointing to* SHELLY*)*. She's got your leg. *(laughs)* She's gonna keep your leg too. *(to* SHELLY*)* She wants to hear this. Don't you?

SHELLY. I don't know.

DODGE. Well even if ya' don't I'm gonna' tell ya'. *(pause)* Halie had this kid. This baby boy. She had it. I let her have it on her own. All the other boys I had had the best doctors, best nurses, everything. This one I let her have by herself. This one hurt real bad. Almost killed her, but she had it anyway. It lived, see. It lived. It wanted to grow up in this family. It wanted to be just like us. It wanted to be a part of us. It wanted to pretend that I was its father. She wanted me to believe in it. Even when everyone around us knew. Everyone. All our boys knew. Tilden knew.

HALIE. You shut up! Bradley, make him shut up!

BRADLEY. I can't.

DODGE. Tilden was the one who knew. Better than any of us. He'd walk for miles with that kid in his arms. Halie let him take it. All night sometimes. He'd walk all night out there in the pasture with it. Talkin' to it. Singin' to it. Used to hear him singing to it. He'd make up stories. He'd tell that kid all kinds a' stories. Even when he knew it couldn't understand him. Couldn't understand a word he was sayin'. Never would understand him. We couldn't let a thing like that continue. We couldn't allow that to grow up right in the middle of our lives. It made everything we'd accomplished look like it was nothin'. Everything was cancelled out by this one mistake. This one weakness.

SHELLY. So you killed him?

DODGE. I killed it. I drowned it. Just like

the runt of a litter. Just drowned it.

(HALIE *moves toward* BRADLEY.)

HALIE *(to* BRADLEY). Ansel would've stopped him! Ansel would've stopped him from telling these lies! He was a hero! A man! A whole man! What's happened to the men in this family! Where are the men!

(Suddenly VINCE *comes crashing through the screen porch door up left, tearing it off its hinges. Everyone but* DODGE *and* BRADLEY *back away from the porch and stare at* VINCE *who has landed on his stomach on the porch in a drunken stupor. He is singing loudly to himself and hauls himself slowly to his feet. He has a paper shopping bag full of empty booze bottles. He takes them out one at a time as he sings and smashes them at the opposite end of the porch, behind the solid interior door, stage right.* SHELLY *moves slowly toward stage right, holding wooden leg and watching* VINCE.)

VINCE *(singing loudly as he hurls bottles).* "From the Halls of Montezuma to the Shores of Tripoli. We will fight our country's battles on the land and on the sea."

(He punctuates the words "Montezuma", "Tripoli", "battles" and "sea" with a smashed bottle each. He stops throwing for a second, stares toward stage right of the porch, shades his eyes with his hand as though looking across to a battle field, then cups his hands around his mouth and yells across the space of the porch to an imaginary army. The others watch in terror and expectation.)

VINCE *(to imagined Army).* Have you had enough over there! 'Cause there's a lot more here where that came from! *(pointing to paper bag full of bottles)* A helluva lot more! We got enough over here to blow ya' from here to Kingdomcome!

(He takes another bottle, makes high whistling sound of a bomb and throws it toward stage right porch. Sound of bottle smashing against wall. This should be the actual smashing of bottles and not tape sound. He keeps yelling and heaving bottles one after another. VINCE *stops for a while, breathing heavily from exhaustion. Long silence as the others watch him.* SHELLY *approaches tentatively in* VINCE's *direction, still holding* BRADLEY's *wooden leg.)*

SHELLY *(after silence).* Vince?

*(*VINCE *turns toward her. Peers through screen.)*

VINCE. Who? What? Vince who? Who's that in there?

*(*VINCE *pushes his face against the screen from the porch and stares in at everyone.)*

DODGE. Where's my goddamn bottle!

VINCE *(looking in at* DODGE). What? Who is that?

DODGE. It's me! Your Grandfather! Don't play stupid with me! Where's my two bucks!

VINCE. Your two bucks?

*(*HALIE *moves away from* DEWIS, *upstage, peers out at* VINCE, *trying to recognize him.)*

HALIE. Vincent? Is that you, Vincent?

*(*SHELLY *stares at* HALIE *then looks out at* VINCE.)*

VINCE *(from porch).* Vincent who? What is this! Who are you people?

SHELLY *(to* HALIE). Hey, wait a minute. Wait a minute! What's going on?

HALIE *(moving closer to porch screen).* We thought you were a murderer or something. Barging in through the door like that.

VINCE. I am a murderer! Don't underestimate me for a minute! I'm the Midnight Strangler! I devour whole families in a single gulp!

*(*VINCE *grabs another bottle and smashes it on the porch.* HALIE *backs away.)*

SHELLY *(approaching* HALIE). You mean you know who he is?

HALIE. Of course I know who he is! That's more than I can say for you.

BRADLEY *(sitting up on sofa).* You get off our front porch you creep! What're you doing out there breaking bottles? Who are these foreigners anyway! Where did they come from?

VINCE. Maybe I should come in there and break them!

HALIE *(moving toward porch).* Don't you dare! Vincent, what's got into you! Why are you acting like this?

VINCE. Maybe I should come in there and usurp your territory!

*(*HALIE *turns back toward* DEWIS *and crosses to him.)*

HALIE *(to* DEWIS). Father, why are you just standing around here when everything's falling apart? Can't you rectify this situation?

*(*DODGE *laughs, coughs.)*

DEWIS. I'm just a guest here, Halie. I don't know what my position is exactly. This is outside my parish anyway.

*(*VINCE *starts throwing more bottles as things continue.)*

BRADLEY. If I had my leg I'd rectify it! I'd rectify him all over the goddamn highway! I'd pull his ears out if I could reach him!

*(*BRADLEY *sticks his fist through the screening of the porch and reaches out for* VINCE, *grabbing at him and missing.* VINCE *jumps away from* BRADLEY's *hand.)*

VINCE. Aaaah! Our lines have been penetrated! Tentacles animals! Beasts from the deep!

(VINCE strikes out at BRADLEY's hand with a bottle. BRADLEY pulls his hand back inside.)

SHELLY. Vince! Knock it off will ya'! I want to get out of here!

(VINCE pushes his face against screen, looks in at SHELLY.)

VINCE *(to SHELLY)*. Have they got you prisoner in there, dear? Such a sweet young thing too. All her life in front of her. Nipped in the bud.

SHELLY. I'm coming out there, Vince! I'm coming out there and I want us to get in the car and drive away from here. Anywhere. Just away from here.

SHELLY *moves toward VINCE's saxophone case and overcoat. She sets down the wooden leg, downstage left and picks up the saxophone case and overcoat. VINCE watches her through the screen.*

VINCE *(to SHELLY)*. We'll have to negotiate. Make some kind of a deal. Prisoner exchange or something. A few of theirs for one of ours. Small price to pay if you ask me.

(SHELLY crosses toward stage right door with overcoat and case.)

SHELLY. Just go and get the car! I'm coming out there now. We're going to leave.

VINCE. Don't come out here! Don't you dare come out here!

(SHELLY stops short of the door, stage right.)

SHELLY. How come?

VINCE. Off limits! Verboten! This is taboo territory. No man or woman has ever crossed the line and lived to tell the tale!

SHELLY. I'll take my chances.

(SHELLY moves to stage right door and opens it. VINCE pulls out a big folding hunting knife and pulls open the blade. He jabs the blade into the screen and starts cutting a hole big enough to climb through. BRADLEY cowers in a corner of the sofa as VINCE rips at the screen.)

VINCE *(as he cuts screen)*. Don't come out here! I'm warning you! You'll disintegrate!

(DEWIS takes HALIE by the arm and pulls her toward staircase.)

DEWIS. Halie, maybe we should go upstairs until this blows over.

HALIE. I don't understand it. I just don't understand it. He was the sweetest little boy!

DEWIS *drops the roses beside the wooden leg at the foot of the staircase then escorts HALIE quickly up the stairs. HALIE keeps looking back at VINCE as they climb the stairs.*

HALIE. There wasn't a mean bone in his body. Everyone loved Vincent. Everyone. He was the perfect baby.

DEWIS. He'll be all right after a while. He's just had a few too many that's all.

HALIE. He used to sing in his sleep. He'd sing. In the middle of the night. The sweetest voice. Like an angel. *(she stops for a moment)* I used to lie awake listening to it. I used to lie awake thinking it was all right if I died. Because Vincent was an angel. A guardian angel. He'd watch over us. He'd watch over all of us.

(DEWIS takes her all the way up the stairs. They disappear above. VINCE is now climbing through the porch screen onto the sofa. BRADLEY crashes off the sofa, holding tight to his blanket, keeping it wrapped around him. SHELLY is outside on the porch. VINCE holds the knife in his teeth once he gets the hole wide enough to climb through. BRADLEY starts crawling slowly toward his wooden leg, reaching out for it.)

DODGE *(to VINCE)*. Go ahead! Take over the house! Take over the whole goddamn house! You can have it! It's yours. It's been a pain in the neck ever since the very first mortgage. I'm gonna die any second now. Any second. You won't even notice. So I'll settle my affairs once and for all.

(As DODGE proclaims his last will and testament, VINCE climbs into the room, knife in mouth and strides slowly around the space, inspecting his inheritance. He casually notices BRADLEY as he crawls toward his leg. VINCE moves to the leg and keeps pushing it with his foot so that it's out of BRADLEY's reach then goes on with his inspection. He picks up the roses and carries them around smelling them. SHELLY can be seen outside on the porch, moving slowly center and staring in at VINCE. VINCE ignores her.)

DODGE. The house goes to my Grandson, Vincent. All the furnishings, accoutrements and parapernalia therein. Everything tacked to the walls or otherwise resting under this roof. My tools—namely my band saw, my skill saw, my drill press, my chain saw, my lathe, my electric sander, all go to my eldest son, Tilden. That is, if he ever shows up again. My shed and gasoline powered equipment, namely my tractor, my dozer, my hand tiller plus all the attachments and riggings for the above mentioned machinery, namely my spring tooth harrow, my deep plows, my disk plows, my automatic fertilizing equipment, my reaper, my swathe, my seeder, my John Deere Harvester, my post hole digger, my jackhammer, my lathe—*(to himself)* Did I mention my lathe? I already mentioned my lathe—my Bennie Goodman records, my harnesses, my bits, my halters, my brace, my rough rasp, my force, my welding equipment, my shoeing nails, my levels and bevels, my milking stool—no, not my milking stool—my hammers and chisels, my hinges, my cattle gates, my barbed wire, self-tapping augers, my horse hair ropes and all related materials are to be pushed into a gigantic heap and set ablaze in the very center of my fields. When the blaze is at its highest, preferably on a cold, windless night, my body is to be pitched into the middle of it and burned til nothing remains but ash.

(Pause. VINCE takes the knife out of his mouth and smells the roses. He's facing toward audience and doesn't turn around to SHELLY. He folds up knife and pockets it.)

SHELLY *(from porch)*. I'm leaving, Vince. Whether you come or not, I'm leaving.

VINCE *(smelling roses)*. Just put my horn on the couch there before you take off.

SHELLY *(moving toward hole in screen)*. You're not coming?

(VINCE stays downstage, turns and looks at her.)

VINCE. I just inherited a house.

SHELLY *(through hole, from porch)*. You want to stay here?

VINCE *(as he pushes BRADLEY's leg out of reach)*. I've gotta carry on the line. I've gotta see to it that things keep rolling.

(BRADLEY looks up at him from floor, keeps pulling himself toward his leg. VINCE keeps moving it.)

SHELLY. What happened to you Vince? You just disappeared.

VINCE *(pause, delivers speech front)*. I was gonna run last night. I was gonna run and keep right on running. I drove all night. Clear to the Iowa border. The old man's two bucks sitting right on the seat beside me. It never stopped raining the whole time. Never stopped once. I could see myself in the windshield. My face. My eyes. I studied my face. Studied everything about it. As though I was looking at another man. As though I could see his whole race behind him. Like a mummy's face. I saw him dead and alive at the same time. In the same breath. In the windshield, I watched him breathe as though he was frozen in time. And every breath marked him. Marked him forever without him knowing. And then his face changed. His face became his father's face.

Same bones. Same eyes. Same nose. Same breath. And his father's face changed to his Grandfather's face. And it went on like that. Changing. Clear on back to faces I'd never seen before but still recognized. Still recognized the bones underneath. The eyes. The breath. The mouth. I followed my family clear into Iowa. Every last one. Straight into the Corn Belt and further. Straight back as far as they'd take me. Then it all dissolved. Everything dissolved.

(SHELLY stares at him for a while then reaches through the hole in the screen and sets the saxophone case and VINCE's overcoat on the sofa. She looks at VINCE again.)

SHELLY. Bye Vince.

She exits left off the porch. VINCE watches her go. BRADLEY tries to make a lunge for his wooden leg. VINCE quickly picks it up and dangles it over BRADLEY's head like a carrot. BRADLEY keeps making desperate grabs at the leg. DEWIS comes down the staircase and stops half way, staring at VINCE and BRADLEY. VINCE looks up at DEWIS and smiles. He keeps moving backwards with the leg toward upstage left as BRADLEY crawls after him.

VINCE *(to DEWIS as he continues torturing BRADLEY)*. Oh, excuse me Father. Just getting rid of some of the vermin in the house. This is my house now, ya' know? All mine. Everything. Except for the power tools and stuff. I'm gonna get all new equipment anyway. New plows, new tractor, everything. All brand new. *(VINCE teases BRADLEY closer to the up left corner of the stage.)* Start right off on the ground floor.

(VINCE throws BRADLEY's wooden leg far off stage left. BRADLEY follows his leg off stage, pulling himself along on the ground, whimpering. As BRADLEY exits VINCE pulls the blanket off him and throws it over his own shoulder. He crosses toward DEWIS with the blanket and smells the roses. DEWIS comes to the bottom of the stairs.)

DEWIS. You'd better go up and see your Grandmother.

VINCE *(looking up stairs, back to DEWIS)*. My Grandmother? There's nobody else in this house. Except for you. And you're leaving aren't you?

(DEWIS crosses toward stage right door. He turns back to VINCE.)

DEWIS. She's going to need someone. I can't help her. I don't know what to do. I don't know what my position is. I just came in for some tea. I had no idea there was any trouble.

No idea at all.

(VINCE *just stares at him.* DEWIS *goes out the door, crosses porch and exits left.* VINCE *listens to him leaving. He smells roses, looks up the staircase then smells roses again. He turns and looks upstage at* DODGE. *He crosses up to him and bends over looking at* DODGE'*s open eyes.* DODGE *is dead. His death should have come completely unnoticed by the audience.* VINCE *covers* DODGE'*s body with the blanket, then covers his head. He sits on the sofa, smelling roses and staring at* DODGE'*s body. Long pause.* VINCE *places the roses on* DODGE'*s chest then lays down on the sofa, arms folded behind his head, staring at the ceiling. His body is in the same relationship to* DODGE'*s. After a while* HALIE'*s voice is heard coming from above the staircase. The lights start to dim almost imperceptibely as* HALIE *speaks.* VINCE *keeps staring at the ceiling.*)

HALIE'S VOICE. Dodge? Is that you Dodge? Tilden was right about the corn you know. I've never seen such corn. Have you taken a look at it lately? Tall as a man already. This early in the year. Carrots too. Potatoes. Peas. It's like a paradise out there, Dodge. You oughta' take a look. A miracle. I've never seen it like this. Maybe the rain did something. Maybe it was the rain.

(*As* HALIE *keeps talking off stage,* TILDEN *appears from stage left, dripping with mud from the knees down. His arms and hands are covered with mud. In his hands he carries the corpse of a small child at chest level, staring down at it. The corpse mainly consists of bones wrapped in muddy, rotten cloth. He moves slowly downstage toward the staircase, ignoring* VINCE *on the sofa.* VINCE *keeps staring at the ceiling as though* TILDEN *wasn't there. As* HALIE'*s VOICE continues,* TILDEN *slowly makes his way up the stairs. His eyes never leave the corpse of the child. The lights keep fading.*)

HALIE'S VOICE. Good hard rain. Takes everything straight down deep to the roots. The rest takes care of itself. You can't force a thing to grow. You can't interfere with it. It's all hidden. It's all unseen. You just gotta wait til it pops up out of the ground. Tiny little shoot. Tiny little white shoot. All hairy and fragile. Strong though. Strong enough to break the earth even. It's a miracle, Dodge. I've never seen a crop like this in my whole life. Maybe it's the sun. Maybe that's it. Maybe it's the sun.

(TILDEN *disappears above. Silence. Lights go to black.*)

A Prayer For My Daughter

Thomas Babe

FOR CHARISSA

First presented by Joseph Papp at the Public Theater in New York City on January 17, 1978, with the following cast:
(*in order of appearance*)

KELLY	George Dzundza
JACK	Jeffrey De Munn
JIMMY	Alan Rosenberg
SEAN	Lawrence Luckinbill

Directed by Robert Allan Ackerman
Scenery by Bil Mikulewicz
Costumes by Bob Wojiwodski
Lighting by Arden Fingerhut

A Prayer for My Daughter by Thomas Babe is a play set in a New York police station on Independence Day. Two homosexuals are picked up for the brutal slaying of an elderly shop-keeper. In the following investigation, both suspects and one of the policemen shoot themselves up with narcotics, the elder policeman's daughter commits suicide and the older suspect, the actual killer, goes free. The play deals with a cross section of ethnic types and ethical values. Its four main characters are Kelly, an alcoholic Irish policeman; Jack, an Italian policeman who is also an addict; Simon, a homosexual criminal and killer; and Jimmy, a young Hispanic junkie. The idea that emerges from their interaction is that those who keep the peace and those who disturb it differ only in the clothes that they wear; they are really indistinguishable from each other.

The themes of the play as espoused by Babe are: we are all enmeshed in corruption; every man has a bit of woman in him and to survive the evils of existence one must betray one's friends and oneself. To underscore these themes, Babe employs the daughter as a metaphor. All four characters in the play have daughters. The two police officers each have two, Jimmy has one, and Simon refers to Jimmy as his daughter. Daughters in the play represent the feminine virtues: affection, vulnerability, compassion, poetry—attributes which, according to Babe, every man has inside himself, but longs to kill because they threaten his ability to function amid the evil that surrounds him.

Kelly, a sergeant, weary of his work, allows his favorite daughter to kill herself with a gun. Jack, married three times, has a murderous hatred for women yet cannot be without one. Simon, a malicious "spiritualist" of the Charles Manson type, is a homicidal killer who wants to destroy the woman inside himself, the woman who aches for the men she has known. Jimmy, a young junkie, somewhat schizophrenic, becomes the vessel through which all the other characters pour their feelings and seek absolution. Through him, they realize their fantasies of incest and paternal love.

A Prayer for My Daughter was first presented at the Eugene O'Neill National Playwright's Conference in 1977. Shortly afterward Babe sent a copy of his manuscript to Joseph Papp at the New York Public Theater. His was one of the fifteen hundred unsolicited manuscripts received every year by the Theater. On January 17, 1978, it was produced by Papp at the New York Public's Anspacher Theatre. In the same year, on July 24, the play also opened at the Royal Court's "Theatre Upstairs" in London, and in November the play moved to the Royal Court Theatre itself to accommodate a larger audience. The play was also produced at the Actors Workshop of the New York Chapter of the National Academy of Television Arts and Sciences in an Actor's Equity Showcase on October 26, 1980.

Thomas Babe was born in 1941, in Buffalo, and was raised in both Buffalo and Rochester. He speaks of his childhood with reluctance and remembers it as dreary, oppressive and deadening. "There was something mean about that stretch of country—nothing to encourage or reward you if you had any imagination or ambition, especially if you were not self-conscious enough to know or demand what you wanted. The life of the imagination seemed something wicked to them downstate. At times, writing was a desperate act. Even the manual activity of writing was liberating, with more life going on on paper than in the outside world."

During his first year as a Harvard freshman, Babe set a record for a concert reading of Voltaire's *Candide* and won a $100 prize for writing the best play. He wrote another play during his sophomore year that won the Phyllis Anderson Award. He graduated in 1963 and went to Cambridge as a Marshall Scholar. While studying in England, he realized the experience and intensity of being an American. " . . . It made me feel that if I could ever do anything worthwhile, it would be out of the gut of America."

Babe returned to Harvard in 1965 as an English graduate student. With another classmate, he managed the Summer Players at Radcliffe College, staging Shakespeare, Brecht and Greek plays. He also directed his own play, *A Winter's Tale in Georgia*. He left Harvard before finishing his doctoral thesis and gave up drama to attend Yale Law School. In the turmoil of the late sixties, Babe believed that politics was the way to affect change in society; he became an assistant speech writer for John Lindsay and, finding himself surrounded by lawyers, con-cluded that it was more legitimate to be a lawyer than a playwright, "I was looking for legitimacy, and that seemed a good place to find it."

Babe graduated law school in 1972, but instead of studying for the bar, he wrote a play called

A Hero for Our Times. In the next two years he wrote seven more plays. "What it was, was a progressive deterioration in happiness. I was evading what I had to do. . . . Everyone looked at me strangely. A law degree but no lawyering? I began writing. Fortunately I could. Susan [his wife] is the beneficiary of a trust fund. We both wanted to work. . . . Once I wrote the first play, things began happening very quickly in my mind."

The three plays that have influenced Thomas Babe most are *Spring Awakening, In the Jungle of Cities* and *Measure for Measure.* Each of these plays, according to Babe, "is daring and tries to make a difficult point." Babe has a definite system for preparing himself to write. "I spend two months reading, boosting myself up. Then I write very fast. It's like being a prize fighter in training and then knocking it out. A scene a day. I have to work quickly to keep all the connections I've been working out in my head. I know when it's true. It's like the truth is chasing me to write. It's like a mania. My hands start to sweat. I feel it in my nervous system. . . . The period when I'm writing is really rough. Writing is a psychic process. It's not quite possession. More like ecstasy. I get so wound up I have to consume immoderate quantities of rum just to get to sleep at night. . . . You let one voice inside you come to the front of your consciousness and you push the others back. It's like listening to something inside your head. I only get to hear it once."

In 1980 Babe collaborated for the first time with another artist, Twyla Tharp. The two produced a dance-play, *When We Were Very Young,* a fantasy about children, a look at adults through the eyes of children. Babe thoroughly enjoyed this partnership. ". . . If I could choose a way of working, this would be it. It's in process and continues to be in process, and nobody seems to be terrified that it's in process. . . . This has been a lot harder than writing a play by myself because of all of the elements involved, but it is also one of the most exciting things I've worked on in my life. It's like trying to discover penicillin. You don't know what the result will be but you know you're getting close."

Babe's other works include *Kid Champion,* a multi-media play with music; *Fathers and Sons,* a play about Wild Bill Hickock's last days with his bastard son; *Rebel Women,* about Sherman's march to the sea; *Anna; The Leaf People; Great Solo Town,* a play concerned with the loss of teenage innocence; *Taken in Marriage; Justice; Salt Lake City Skyline,* a play about Joe Hill and the judge who presided over his trial; and *Billy Irish,* a play about heroes and villains and how they change into each other.

ACT ONE

*The squad room of a downtown precinct.
The place has all its affinities to a toilet bowl—
vilely littered, postered; papers, coffee cups,
butts, busted typewriters and some that work,
phones, injured furniture, radiators exposed,
high, dirty windows, strange perspectives, a
ceiling too vaulted, demented angles to the
walls. The room is empty. A moment. It is one
a.m. The door opens and four men come in.
Of the cops,* KELLY *is heading for a fat forties,
beer-gut and all;* JACK *is lean, more than a
little cruel looking, more than a little dangerous. Of the crooks,* JIMMY *is a kid, that's all,
pure punk but with the aspect of a choir boy;*
SEAN, *bearded and lean, has a little of the
professor about him, the air that he is the
cleanest thing that's been in this room in a
decade or two. The crooks are manacled.*

*At the very opening moment, as the four men
enter, the squad room has been decorated;
streamers in red, white and blue from the lamp
in the center. Leavings of a party. A balloon
tied to the telephone, other balloons elsewhere. The four stand dumbfounded; then*
KELLY *wades in.*

———

KELLY. What is this, for Christ's sake?
JACK. Looks like the glorious Fourth.
KELLY. In here?
JACK. What do I know, Kelly? *(*KELLY
shrugs, as if to say he doesn't care, and begins
to methodically remove all the decorations
while:* JACK *to the two felons.)* Sit. *(pause;
angry.)* I said sit, garbage, so you sit. *(pushes*
JIMMY *down in a chair with a balloon on it,
which pops.)*
JIMMY *(happy).* Car-a-zeee!
JACK. Yeah?
JIMMY. May I?
JACK. Shut it.
JIMMY. May I please—
JACK *(as a threat).* Hey, all right?
KELLY. Knee him in the nuts, he gives you
trouble.
JIMMY. They gonna hurt us?
JACK. Might just be, sonny.
KELLY *(about the decorations he is taking
down).* I mean, who done this?
JACK. Who didn't, Frannie? The moon is
full, it's a national holiday today, right now,
as we speak. Inde-fucking-pendence Day. I
gotta tell you, Frannie, people drink beer, they
get in car wrecks, they drown by the hundreds,
hunh?

KELLY. Yeah, and Fourth of July last year,
they booked that transvestite whore for stab-
bing somebody with a flag, Lorelie, right?
JACK. In other words, Leonard. Leonard,
and no last name.
KELLY. She was dancing in here when I
came in, in a red white and blue dress with a
sash that says, you remember, ''Auntie Sam?''
I mean . . .
JACK. And silver shoes, I'll never forget em!
KELLY. And which of you proposed mar-
riage to her—I mean, him, before I got here?
JACK. Not me, I didn't do it. Mrs. Delasan-
te's little boy Jackie here has one glass of the
old vino and fell asleep in the cardboard box
the desk came in.
KELLY. Yeah, did you? I guess I recall. Well,
I don't know.
JIMMY *(to* JACK*).* How bout some *agua,*
sheriff?
JACK. What?
JIMMY. Water. Please, I'm thirsty.
JACK. Yeah?
JIMMY. I'm thirsty.
SEAN. He's thirsty. He's a drug addict—
JIMMY. But I'm clean now.
SEAN. His mouth gets dry.
JACK. No shit, no fuckin shit. *(*JACK *goes
over to the water cooler and fills a cup.* KELLY
is reading a note on his telephone.)
KELLY. Why don't I get these notes when
they're fresh? Hey, Jack, how the fuck long
has this note been around? There's no date on
it, there's no time.
JACK. I don't know about it. That's Kra-
marsky's birdlike hand.
KELLY. *Pollock. (starts dialing)*
JACK *(holding the water out to* JIMMY*).* Here.
JIMMY. I can't drink that when I'm sittin on
my goddamn hands.
JACK. Hey, hey, you're right.
JIMMY. Shit.
JACK. Here. *(Teases him with the water;
then throws it in his face.* JIMMY *looks at him,
water running off.* SEAN *leans over and whispers in his ear . . .* JACK *sits at a typewriter
and starts to type out a report. Throughout,*
KELLY *on the phone.)*
KELLY. Hiyah, sweetie? No, me. Yeah. No,
I knew I'd wake you, see, I had the message
you called and I didn't know when, I didn't
know nothin it was important, it wasn't important, so I called. So, did you call your
mother, too? Don't say that, no, I mean, don't

say that again, you know she's okay, she's been . . . the mind business. I said, the mind business. No, no, not like that, like a little thing, you know . . . ?

JACK *(with many papers and files, reading).* What's the woman's name again?

SEAN. The who?

JACK. You killed, the one of you.

JIMMY. Got no idea of the drift of *this* conversation.

JACK. Yeah? Maybe. *(pause, looking at papers; sings:)*

>YOU ARE MY SUNSHINE,
>MY ONLY SUNSHINE,
>YOU MAKE ME HAPPY—

KELLY *(hand over receiver, to JACK).* Hey, could you?

JACK *(continuing softly).*

>WHEN SKIES ARE GRAY,
>YOU'LL NEVER KNOW, DEAR,
>HOW MUCH I MISS YOU—

SEAN *(correcting).* Love you!

JACK. Yeah, *love* you . . . *(sings)*

>PLEASE DON'T TAKE MY SUN-
>SHINE AWAY.

(spoken) Yep.

KELLY *(to phone).* I told you I didn't think you ought to, sweetie, I mean, I don't like him, you don't like him. No, I don't think you did. *(pause)* You did. *(long pause)* Goddamnit! *(pause)* I said, goddamnit. You whooor. *(pause)* No, I didn't say that. I didn't mean that. I meant you should've—*(pause)* Aw, for the Christ's sake, don't cry. *(pause)* No, look, I'll bring you some ice cream later, you can't sleep. Tell him to walk. *(pause)* You got the .38, lock the door. We got a little garbage to clean up here. *(pause)* No, I do, I do understand. *(pause)* Butter pecan. Yeah, I love you, too, light of my life, yeah, I can. *(hangs up; to no one)* Son of a faithless bitch.

JACK. Margie?

KELLY. She married that number one asshole in secret. Last week.

JACK. You didn't straighten her out so cool.

KELLY. She was straightened. I think she gets her mother's mental lapses. Shit.

JACK. Why don't you go visit her, kick the shit's head in. You know, she sees you kick his head in, she knows what a man is.

KELLY. He's a faggot, anyway, bad for her.

JACK. No shit.

KELLY. Stick this garbage someplace, I wanna talk.

JACK. Yeah? *(rising)* Okay, walk, in there. Walk is walk, it's flashing in green. Walk.

*(*JIMMY *and* SEAN *are put in separate rooms.)*

KELLY. So?

JACK. So?

KELLY. I think we drop the smart stuff, the I'm-a-good-cop and you're-a-bad-cop routines, and hurt em a little, physically.

JACK. Why?

KELLY. The other psychological crap don't work.

JACK. We can knock em around later; we should take them apart a little mentally first, and you can do that you're the kid's father while I do that I'm the beard's best friend.

KELLY. Don't work.

JACK. Why?

KELLY. Because.

JACK. You want a conviction?

KELLY. I'm fuckin fucked out, Delasante. If it weren't so late, I'd say, sure, let's do a little dance with them. But you don't do that well so late at night, and I wanna take care of my kid.

JACK. What's late at night?

KELLY. Don't ask me.

JACK. I'm asking, you know?

KELLY. Just we had that floater last year and he talked you up and you wanted to make such a big impression on him that you let him go out to take a piss and he walked right out of the fuckin building.

JACK. Yeah, so?

KELLY. So? Don't engage in conversation. I say they're nothin, hit them a lot. I don't trust your instinct to impress the bright ones.

JACK. That's what you're afraid of?

KELLY. I told you.

JACK. You really think that, don't you?

KELLY. I told you. I'm tired. I wanna straighten my kid. Okay?

JACK. Maybe you're right. Maybe you'd get a little close to the vest with that kid, anyway. He's pretty.

KELLY. Don't bait me. You're wasting a z-hour here.

JACK. Maybe you're right, yeah, you son of a bitch. *(pause)* You don't trust me?

KELLY. Aw, come on.

JACK. You don't really fuckin trust me?

KELLY. Jackie, I'm shit out flat and my brain feels like it's fading and I just wanna operate when I still have that last little edge. I wanna straighten Margie. You're a good cop.

JACK. You bet your fuckin fat ass.

KELLY. I said it.

JACK. You don't trust me? Shit, that burns

me. How come I didn't hear this last year?

KELLY. I trust you. I was a little out of line there, okay. I just think this beard is wily . . . and . . . you tend to get entranced with the wilies whereas I kick em, that's all, it's a character trait.

JACK. Yeah?

KELLY. Yeah. A trait.

JACK. Yeah? *(The phone rings.* JACK *picks it up.)* Who? *(pause, sings)*

    FOR IT WAS MA-RY, MA-RY,
    LONG BEFORE—

(hands the phone to KELLY*)* The wife, Kelly.

KELLY *(to phone).* Yeah? No, I talked to her, no, she's all right. No, she is, I'm sure. You shouldn't get worried about what she threatens to do, that's an act. No, I'm tired, that's all. I'll take her a little ice cream, she can't sleep. They're shootin off fireworks in the street outside her window. No, I haven't been, I haven't in a month. No. Don't let the bedbugs bite. *(hangs up)* I think she's . . . *(long pause)* Insane, my wife. *(pause)* I don't know . . . what I don't know is what I don't know. Bring the weird in here and you be a nice big brother to the kid. I wanna have it all written in 30 minutes.

JACK. Which one you figure?

KELLY. I figure the bearded homo pulled the trigger.

JACK. Betcha. I got the kid.

KELLY. Even money.

JACK. Fuck it, the beard's a long shot. He's too delicate, you know what I mean, to let blood.

KELLY. Dead wrong, He's *(pause)* Insane.

JACK. Okay, even money.

KELLY. Fifty.

JACK. Twenty-five.

KELLY. Forty. *(pause)* . . . I wanna make sure when you say you're sure of something, you're sure; that's so I know I can trust you, when you put your money where you mouth is.

JACK. Forty, you son of a bitch. *(He laughs, they both do, then:* KELLY *takes a drink;* JACK *exits and gets* SEAN, *who is shoved in.* JACK *re-exits into the room where* JIMMY *is. Silence.)*

KELLY. Yeah, Sean.

SEAN. Simon.

KELLY. Sean de Kahn.

SEAN. Simon Cohn.

KELLY. You really let some nice hardworking Hebraic parents down when you embarked on this life of crime, didn't you?

SEAN. If you please . . .

KELLY. I don't care, see, we all let somebody down somewheres. Your folks still living?

SEAN. I want to call my attorney.

KELLY. What do you want to call him, your attorney, courageous?

SEAN. I don't have to—

KELLY. You don't have to do anything, right? *(picks up phone book)* It's Brooklyn, if memory serves.

SEAN. What?

KELLY. Your folks. *(looking)* A lotta you in Brooklyn, Cohns. But I remember, Flatbush Avenue, right? Didn't I have to bust you there once. Yeah, used goods, here.

SEAN. I want to call my attorney.

KELLY. He's in bed.

SEAN. So are my parents.

KELLY. I know . . . the same bed, fifty years now. Where the fuck do you sleep?

SEAN. Really . . .

KELLY. All over town, I know. Well, Sean . . .

SEAN. You're a bum, officer. Of all the low-grade moron operatives in the various departments of your department, you have the odor, officer, of a bum.

KELLY *(unruffled).* And you're just a ponce. So it's 682–7738, is that right?

SEAN. I want to see my attorney.

KELLY. I'm gonna have your father call one. He probably knows a good one, family friend, who'll work cheap.

SEAN. I—want to see my attorney, now!

KELLY. Yeah, well your father, Abraham, I see by the entry in the book here, Abraham Cohn, he must know somebody. *(pause;* KELLY *dials the phone)*

SEAN. Hang up. I'll talk to you.

KELLY. Yeah?

SEAN. I'LL TALK.

KELLY *(hanging up; a pause).* So, I'm waiting, Sean, I'm all ears for the talk.

SEAN. Obviously.

KELLY. Obviously you are not quite making music yet.

SEAN. Obviously. *(*KELLY *picks up the phone again.)* What I wanted to tell you, at the outset . . . *(*KELLY *puts down the phone.)*

KELLY. Was?

SEAN. That boy I was arrested with in there . . .

KELLY. Jimmy?

SEAN. Is a very disturbed, very disturbing young man, do you know what I mean, very deeply disturbing?

KELLY. He don't bother me none.

SEAN. I mean, he's very difficult young man to get a line on, if you see what I mean, that's what's disturbing.

KELLY. Is this by way of saying you're gonna let him take the fall for this, the little druggie?

SEAN *(contemptuous)*. You're silly. That wasn't my point at all.

KELLY. No, Sean?

SEAN. Simon. Mr. Cohn.

KELLY. I figure either of you two could've actually blown Mrs. Linowitz away. Old cons like you got icewater for blood, but young guys like Jimmy, they can be very impetuous.

SEAN. I know.

KELLY. I know you know.

SEAN. You're silly. We'll beat it.

KELLY. I know. That's why we do this.

SEAN. What's "this?"

KELLY. We try and sneak in a little punishment before the court has a chance to decide you don't deserve it on a technicality, like you were born incurable homo, or I didn't read you your rights Shakespeare-perfect.

SEAN. No one's read me my rights.

KELLY. I don't read 'em to homos.

SEAN. Then what you're doing here is a dreadful farce.

KELLY. You wanna talk Miranda and Escobedo with me, Sean, okay. You're entitled to a lawyer, except you're not really entitled to a lawyer, because you got blood on your hands and it stinks. Now this is my house, Sean, I make the rules. That's your warning, you have the right to be very careful around me, okay?

SEAN. You're worse than silly. You're . . . insane.

KELLY. I'm tired, Sean. Got this daughter who's got her head wedged up in trouble, you know, family stuff, I stake a dry cleaning establishment all day, my ass is sore, you and your friend treat me to an old woman, her head half off—I'm just not as used to shit like that, like you imagine I am: I get tired, edgy. *(pause)* You got any kids? No, you wouldn't, otherwise you'd be home, in bed fifty years, I'd have to call you, say, Mr. Cohn, your son, your daughter just stiffed somebody just like you, got bail money? Hear the tears on the phone, yours, Simon. How old are you?

SEAN. I am entitled to one phone call.

KELLY. You know, we ain't gonna squeeze a fly turd out of this if you don't tell me what I can readily discern from your rap sheet. Forty . . . uh . . . one. Gettin on.

SEAN. I don't know why you do this, if you don't mind my saying so. You're silly. Everything you're doing is silly. That other detective in there will have Jimmy crying and signing anything he wants in ten minutes, and you and I can sit here until you drop dead, officer, which frankly doesn't seem to me too far in the distance.

KELLY. Forty-one, you got no job at all, no profession, nothin, you got to turn little old lady dry cleaners into hamburger. Hunh? What are you? I mean, talk.

SEAN. Everything.

KELLY. Name it.

SEAN. I'm a teacher, in fact. I'm Jimmy's teacher.

KELLY. What do you teach him?

SEAN. A way of life.

KELLY. What way of life?

SEAN. Eclectic spiritualism.

KELLY. Don't say. And you *do* like him, right, the kid?

SEAN. Jimmy.

KELLY. Too much to come right out here and pin the rap on him?

SEAN. He's my son.

KELLY. No kidding.

SEAN. And my daughter.

KELLY. That sounds more like it.

SEAN. They're all my children, who need me.

KELLY. You been in his pants, then, is that the teaching part?

SEAN. You're silly, I'm a celibate.

KELLY. Or a masturbate.

SEAN. No, officer, the things that detain you don't bother me, don't concern me at all. Hard for you to believe, I can understand that.

KELLY. Me, naw, I'm easy, I'll believe anything. I can appreciate your predatory streak, Sean, stalk and catch and like that, and move on. I've never been longtime attached to any of the garbage I've put away, but for the moment, you're everything, baby, you're all I want.

SEAN. I can see that.

KELLY. A drink?

SEAN. You drink on the job.

KELLY. Sometimes, when I wanna mellow out, when I understand everything perfectly and feel entitled to swallow one or two for a guiltless reward.

SEAN. It's against regulations for you to drink on duty. You're armed.

KELLY. Tell you what we're gonna do. In a few minutes, I'm gonna be slightly drunk and I'm gonna get up and beat the holy shit out of you. I mean, there's gonna be very little you can do to influence that decision, I mean, if you confessed now, you don't confess, you tell me to fuck off, you kiss my ass—so before it gets unpleasant, which won't be wholly your fault, if you'd like to tell me was it you or was it Jimmy Rosehips who blasted Mrs. Linowitz, then I'll be able to think while I'm tap-dancing on your forehead—hey, this is a killer, or hey, this is just an accomplice. *(pause)* I may be. *(pause)* Insane. *(pause)*

SEAN. I don't want anything to happen to Jimmy, I don't want anything to happen to me.

KELLY. Sure.

SEAN. Protect him, protect myself.

KELLY. I follow.

SEAN. That's all I wanted to say.

KELLY. You wanted to say more, didn't you, one motherfuckall of a lot more.

SEAN. Maybe I did, or didn't.

KELLY. Okay, I'm gonna beat you up a little bit now because that's gonna make me feel better there and then we can get back to this nice talk.

SEAN. Don't hit my face.

KELLY. I never hit faces. I'm not sadistic.

JACK *(enters suddenly)*. He wants some junk.

KELLY. Fuck him.

JACK. Look, sorry to interrupt and like that, but he wants some junk.

SEAN. Don't give him any.

KELLY. Shut up.

JACK. I wanna give him some junk. He's gonna cop but I can't deal with no guy who's melting in front of my eyes.

KELLY. No junk. *(The phone rings. The three look at each other.* JIMMY *comes to the door of the other room. It rings and rings. Finally* KELLY.*)* Kelly. Yeah, hi honey. Listen, I'll be there with the—what? No, you don't think you want to . . . *(Pause;* KELLY *holds the phone away from his head; a woe on his face.)* Jack, would you, on another phone? She's got the .38 in her mouth. I can't understand a word she's saying. She's left her apartment, she's checked into some bide-a-wee in the Bronx. Get a trace on it. *(back to the phone)* Yeah, say, sweetie, listen, I can't hear you when you talk like that. I know what you're saying is important—*(hand over phone, to* JACK, *on other phone.)* She took something, too. Sweet Jesus on the Cross. *(to* JIMMY*)* Get your ass back in that room, or I'll break it. *(to the phone;* JIMMY *doesn't really move)* Look, I wanna ask you something, sweetie. No, goddamnit, listen to me: I wanna ask you something. I can't fuckin

understand you, would you put that thing down, there's all that fuckin banging on the receiver. You know, this is very inconsiderate of you . . . *(pause)* No, I hear you, yeah. *(pause,* KELLY *touched by what he hears)* I know, sweetie, I know. I love you too. No, it'll be all right, no, what? The morning? What morning? The glorious morning after what? *(pause)* Hello? *(to* JACK*)* She hung up, I think.

JACK. We got it.

KELLY. Take care of it.

JACK. What?

KELLY. What's the extension of the loonie squad? Morris works midnight to eight, see if he's there. He's always talking jumpers down and shit like that.

JACK. You don't wanna go yourself?

KELLY. Suicides are a disgrace. They don't even get buried in church ground.

JACK. She ain't dead.

KELLY. Yeah, jerkoff, yeah!

JACK. Hey?

KELLY. I don't know. She gets a radiance about her, Margie, and then she gets blue, shit-eating blue and I don't know nothing what to do . . .

JACK. Go see her.

KELLY. What, dead?

JACK. You ain't sure what's happening.

KELLY. I got a feelin. *(walks up to* JIMMY*)* If you don't go back in there and sit down, I'm gonna break you over my knee like a pencil. Now park your fuckin toosh.

JACK *(on the phone)*. That was the trace, Morris, baby. She says she has a gun, Kelly says he thinks she took somethin as well . . . Naw, he don't want to . . . I don't know why . . . Kelly?

KELLY. I got nothin to say. Morris knows his job.

JACK *(to phone)*. He's got nothin to say. He says you know your job. Yeah. *(hangs up)* He says he'll try, but fuck you.

KELLY *(sudden energy)*. Okay, I'm taking Sean de Kahn in the other room, you drag Narcissus out here. I want somethin quick from him, from you, all of you. The kid's his daughter, if you follow that.

JACK *(one last try)*. Kelly, if you wanna go see about Margie . . . ?

KELLY *(ignoring)*. And no junk!

JACK. Yeah, no junk, so . . . till the cows come home we'll be.

KELLY *(to* SEAN*)*. Walk.

SEAN. What they do to me, mine enemies, I thrive upon. A German philosopher said,

Jimmy.

JIMMY *(intimately)*. What's that, baby?

SEAN. *Lebt wohl, liebes Kind. (The two are forcefully separated.)*

JIMMY *(to the departing* SEAN*)*. No, what, Simon, really? *(*KELLY *and* SEAN *are gone. Pause.)*

JACK. I don't believe you. *(pause)* Daughter, hunh?

JIMMY. That's lingo. That's talk. Talk-talk. You don't get talk-talk.

JACK. Sounds weird to me, Jimmy.

JIMMY. Yeah, it would.

JACK. Prison talk. I thought I heard all the prison talk.

JIMMY. It's lingo-language.

JACK. How come I don't know lingo-language if I been collecting the garbage for so long.

JIMMY. Cause.

JACK. Yeah?

JIMMY. You don't know me.

JACK. This is the first time we busted you.

JIMMY. It's been a real pleasure.

JACK. I'll know you now and next time I'll know you're Sean's little girl so I'll know which pocket you're in.

JIMMY. You don't know shit.

JACK. Enlighten me.

JIMMY. Come on.

JACK. I don't like to think there's something you know, the garbage rats, that I don't know about what certain things are—heads, queens, squats, daughters, you know?

JIMMY. You know all you want.

JACK. Yeah? *(Pause. He removes junk from the desk drawer. Also, a needle and equipment for a hit. He begins cooking a fix.)*

JIMMY. What's that?

JACK. Stuff. Benny DeMartino's stuff. Evidence.

JIMMY. It's sugar. I don't want none.

JACK. Don't worry, you ain't gettin.

JIMMY. He said you shouldn't gimme none.

JACK. You're not getting.

JIMMY. I mean it.

JACK. Yeah?

JIMMY. It's sugar.

JACK. You're sugar. You're the beard's sugar. This is Dilaudid.

JIMMY. You ain't shittin me?

JACK. Benny handles Dilaudid because he's not too bright, he thinks Dilaudid is like Methadone and he feels good pushin it. But Dilaudid is pure poison, like horse. Stupid Benny. You know him?

JIMMY. He's okay.

JACK. He's in the can.

JIMMY. He ain't. His old lady made bail before you got him printed. I know. Man, I know what I know.

JACK. Ever hit on Dilaudid?

JIMMY. How come he didn't go?

JACK. Who?

JIMMY. The other officer.

JACK. Go where, Jimmy.

JIMMY. Ain't he got a suicide working there?

JACK. He didn't want to go. He's seen one dead person today. The old lady you did.

JIMMY. He must be a fun man, he must be a real fun sugar daddy he can't move his ass for . . . whoever it was.

JACK. Who was it?

JIMMY. His daughter, man, I heard that. I wasn't supposed to, but I heard.

JACK. I mean who was it, which one of you, killed Mrs. Linowitz.

JIMMY. From nothin I know nothin from. *(pause)* You wanna know about my daughter?

JACK. Nope.

JIMMY. I wanna tell you.

JACK. I don't want to hear. I want to know how it was Mrs. Linowitz had to get killed for twenty-six dollars and fifteen cents.

JIMMY. You don't give a shit. My daughter—

JACK. I'm bored. When I get bored, I get shitty. *(holds up the loaded fix)* There she is.

JIMMY. You're a bastard. How do I know what that is? How do I know that ain't sodium pentothal. That's sodium pentothal or it's milk sugar.

JACK. You're milk sugar. This is for me. *(rolls up his sleeve; fixes during the following)* How I got it figured is that Sean says, Jimmy, just this once, Jimmy honey, a little money and you and me, we'll settle out a bit, and Jimmy says, Look, man, I don't do nothing with an armory in it, I'm clean, I take teevees, class-C felonies only, and Sean de Kahn says, Jimmy, this Mrs. Linowitz keeps a pile in a tin box under the presser, she don't trust banks, and we take this, we make ten thousand minimum and no old lady is gonna offer any resistance, she reads the papers, she'll think we're garbage, she'll remember the grandchildren and get scared like all ladies of any type, she'll cave right in, and Jimmy says, I don't know, and Sean de Kahn gets Jimmy a little hit and next thing you know, there's Jimmy and Sean, and Sean has a gun in his hand and Jimmy is scraping up the money and suddenly Jimmy hears this terrible roaring explosion and fire by his ear and sees this poor dumb old woman get blasted backwards and he says, Shit, Sean, why'd you do that, man?, and old Sean just smiles and smiles and says it was necessary, philosophically necessary. Right? *(pause; JACK relaxes into a sort of euphoria, but alert)* Hey, Jimmy, it's pins and needles for about eight seconds, then it's whoosh. This Dilaudid, what can I say about it, hunh? Nectar for the gods.

JIMMY. I gotta have some.

JACK. Yeah?

JIMMY. I GOTTA HAVE SOME.

JACK *(offering)*. Be my guest. If your lips move and your mouth is filled with truth afterwards.

JIMMY. Shit, you know I'll sing.

JACK. In key.

JIMMY. Gimme. It's a holiday, man. I want some fireworks, too. *(JIMMY fixes; talks during; his euphoria takes over. He does it like a pro, pumping, regulating for the maximum.)* This is the philosophy, right here, this is religion.

JACK. Don't blaspheme, Jimmy. Take your junk, okay, but keep some respect.

JIMMY. It's light. You know, officer, there's light in the world and there's dark and this is light and sometimes, some nights, just a kiss, on the cheek, too, not even on the lips or anywhere, that's luminous and when your devils knock out for maybe half an hour and you're blending and shaking, the darkness is banished, it is gone. The darkness is the evil, the black everywhere, all the time; it's permanent, the dark, unloseable, and you and me and everybody are the only real source of illumination we got . . . people. Well, now, you give off, officer, well, it's not much more than the warm glow from a cigar butt, a little orange, I'd find you in the dark, but your light ain't as the light of ten suns, and mine is only sporadically, but it's the thing to shoot for.

JACK. You're shooting.

JIMMY. You're gonna break the mood.

JACK. You're gonna break the needle. *(JACK removes the needle from JIMMY's arm.)*

JIMMY. I know what I'm doing. I'm practicing my religion.

JACK. Yeah? You learn your religion from the beard.

JIMMY. He's my teacher. I'm his student. I'm a shit student. He's here now, he'd say there's no light in that dropper, Jimmy, that's the dark, that's the thru-way round the light, that junk you're pumpin into your veins.

JACK. I had some good teachers once. Jesuits.

JIMMY. Higher formal education?

JACK. Yep.

JIMMY. And you couldn't get no job better than a police officer?

JACK. Naw, you got that wrong. I wanted to. My father was a cop.

JIMMY. Figures. Mine was a crook.

JACK. My teachers at the university told me we didn't need the darkness, that the light was inevitable. You're a good Catholic, I presume, I'd just like to find out if your thinking isn't a little out of line here, in other words, are you a heretic?

JIMMY. You're makin fun.

JACK. No, look, I wanna understand.

JIMMY. Woooweee, I feel righteous! Ask any goddamn thing you want, I am bathed, I am positively immersed in a mega-killowat radiance!

JACK. Okay, that's what I was gonna ask.

JIMMY. What?

JACK. Okay, then, here I go.

JIMMY *(giggling)*. He's gonna ask me something to see if I'm a fairytic.

JACK. Heretic. I mean, I wanna know, do you believe the dark has to be there?

JIMMY. Sure. How the fuck else are you gonna know when it's light if you ain't emerging from something, getting out from under?

JACK. In other words, the dark *has* to be there.

JIMMY. Yeah.

JACK. In other words, in order to have light you have to have dark.

JIMMY. Does that make me a hermaphratic?

JACK. There, you see, that's what I mean. You think there has to be you, darkness, legally speaking, for there to be me, high noon, on the same scale. And that's a heresy, Jimmy, they used to burn people for that. The fathers always used to say, the dark wasn't necessary, it was just there, because none of us knew enough about the light.

JIMMY. Listen, I wanna tell you about my daughter.

JACK. Yeah, sure, in a minute. I was gettin into this theology business here not just, you know, out of idle batting-the-breeze—I was trying to teach you something, in other words, be a teacher to you, like Sean de Kahn is a teacher. I was trying to resurrect the old one-to-one, you and me—like *he's* your teacher, say, sort of your father, would you say, you're his daughter . . . ?

JIMMY. Like that.

JACK. See, that's the part I don't get. You're a daughter? You pardon my persistence here, since we're swimming right along?

JIMMY. You can have anything you want, officer.

JACK. Okay, I was curious, since you say you have a daughter of your own, how you could be sort of his daughter. I mean, you got obligations.

JIMMY. I take good care of my family.

JACK. No doubt.

JIMMY. Pay the bills. I'm there a lot. Just sometimes . . .

JACK. You and old Sean gotta . . .

JIMMY. He provides a different kind of light.

JACK. You were sayin. How did you get to be his daughter, say, in other words, rather than his son?

JIMMY. You really want to know, I mean, this isn't a send-up?

JACK. What do you think?

JIMMY. I think I'm feelin good *(pause)*

JACK. Yeah?

JIMMY. There are guys flattered if they think somebody looks at them the way somebody—that person—might look at a really pretty chick.

JACK. Why's that?

JIMMY. I don't know.

JACK. You get off on it, in other words?

JIMMY. Yeah, sometimes.

JACK. Why?

JIMMY. Cause things work better that way, sometimes.

JACK. You mean you make it, then?

JIMMY. It's like affection more, if you can follow. I mean, no guy but an upfront deviate is gonna make it with his own daughter, but there's affection there, a lot of just affection. The kind most guys don't hand out to sons. Who's gonna kiss his own son a lot or pat him on the ass, like that, without the bullshit, hunh?

JACK. And you don't get ashamed?

JIMMY. Sometimes, ashamed. That's when I stop and go home, when I'm ashamed. I go back and forth.

JACK. You'll just pardon me, of course, but it sounds strange, that's all, in other words, not strictly normal.

JIMMY. It's not, man, but it should be: it's part of the spectrum. *(pause)*

JACK. Look, we're gettin along pretty good here . . .

JIMMY. Seems so.

JACK. In other words, we're practically bein innocent and friendly, that's how good.

JIMMY. That's the light from the junk.

JACK. Yeah, but . . .

JIMMY. Okay, man, I hear you, we're cooking, we're rolling right along . . .

JACK. Okay, see, that's what I mean. Now I want you to tell me something else.

JIMMY. Okay.

JACK. Look, I mean, I want you to tell me about *your* daughter.

JIMMY. Why?

JACK. Cause we're rolling along so nice here, in other words, cooking with the light.

JIMMY. Why do you want me to tell you?

JACK *(His tone changes)*. Cause I don't think you have one.

JIMMY. I thought we was approaching a little sunshine here. Ain't it light enough for you?

JACK. In other words, I don't think you have a daughter because I think it's your second instinct to lie about everything, habitually; you'd lie about your own dork if it was stiff in your pants. See, you're just a punk, garbage—

JIMMY. Man, it is getting very dark in here.

JACK. A punk, somebody's punk all the time, and there isn't a woman in the world who'd get down with you, let alone anything in you that'd make a child, let alone a daughter. Just another lie, Jim-bo, just one more piece of heretical, mendacious shit from your punko mouth, so don't talk theology with me cause I know. You're damned. You're midnight on the desert under a heavy cloud cover. You're shit.

JIMMY. Hey, I thought we were cooking, there, simmering. Man, you are confusing.

JACK. I want the story, Jimmy, the whole thing. Who pulled the trigger? We're gonna be friends again, you know, or look at it this way, when this little thing is cleaned up here, you might find I'm gonna be your friend. I mean, we're all in the same bed, we gotta get along. So'd you pop her, or what, or did he? *(pause)* Well?

JIMMY. Man, I'm feeling so good here, we were coasting. I was getting to like you, getting to trust you. I was gonna tell you stuff not even about that robbery, but about myself because I think we're getting cool and I always wanted to get cool with a cop. I always wanted one for a buddy, a friend, some cop, and you're surprising because you seem to know a little shit about religion even, but now, I don't know, man, I'm confused, you really confused me, you just came on there and I don't think there's any light left between us, you know?

JACK. Yeah?

JIMMY. I mean, there's no light. I'm feeling pretty good, but there's no light. *(He cries.)*

JACK. Yeah? In other words, you lost your trust in me?

JIMMY. Fuck, I don't want you watch me cry. I don't want you to see me like this.

JACK. Yeah?

JIMMY. I don't want you to think anything.

JACK. Yeah? *(JACK walks away, he is angry, he bangs a filing case.)* Goddamnit!

JIMMY. I'm confused, man, that's all, don't look.

JACK. Yeah, well, goddamnit, don't crack on me. One shit of a punk you are, you're supposed to come back, you're supposed to fight back.

JIMMY. You confused me.

JACK. Goddamnit it. *(pause)* How old's your daughter?

JIMMY. Five.

JACK. You're kidding!

JIMMY. Five. I got married when I was sixteen.

JACK *(pause)*. Five, hunh?

JIMMY. Five and a third.

JACK. Is she pretty?

JIMMY. She's got hair like the top of a candle.

JACK. Smart, precocious-like, dull, what?

JIMMY. Pretty smart.

JACK. You ever think about her?

JIMMY. What do you mean?

JACK. Think about what she's gonna think about you.

JIMMY. She'll be all right.

JACK. Her daddy's scum?

JIMMY. Not to her I ain't, officer.

JACK. Yeah?

JIMMY. Want me to tell you?

JACK. In other words, you're a psychopath *(pause: they look at each other)* Well, you had me going, Jim-bo *(laughs)* A daughter. Goddamnit, you guys are all alike. *(suddenly serious)* You pop her or what, or did your friend pop her, the proprietress?

JIMMY. I don't know. I'm confused.

JACK. I want to know!

JIMMY. I don't know, it's this junk, it's a black hole in the universe.

JACK. I want to fuckin know!

JIMMY. I think he did. He did. He did it. I hate guns. He did it. I don't know.

JACK *(throwing him in the chair)*. He did it, yeah, punk, he did it, while you were thinking about your daughter. *(Pause; the door opens; KELLY comes in with SEAN. SEAN is in pain. So is KELLY, though a little less, rubbing his knuckles.)*

KELLY. Jesus, what garbage, soft as pig shit. One belt and Sean de Kahn becomes Sean de total collapse.

SEAN. I think my spleen is ruptured.

KELLY. Yeah?

SEAN. I was a medical technician in Asia. I know the symptoms, I think it's a ruptured spleen.

JACK. Couldn't take a little one-two, hunh, Sean?

SEAN. It'll go badly for you if I die. If my condition gets worse it'll be very hard for you to deny that I was beaten. A man doesn't rupture a spleen falling over a chair or any of the other excuses you would be tempted to report. An autopsy will show that I was beaten.

KELLY. You ain't dead yet, so shut up. Sit.

SEAN. I think—

KELLY. Sit! *(no one looks at anyone else; pause.)*

JACK. What *I* think . . . is . . .

KELLY. We were havin a nice interval here, Delasante, we were being wholly wiped out and not halfway through the night yet, so I wonder, not what the fuck do you think, but truthfully, why you're botherin to think at all.

SEAN. It occurs to me . . .

KELLY. Sweet Jeeesus!

SEAN. We don't need to do this.

KELLY. What?

SEAN. This.

KELLY. What this?

SEAN. The both of you . . . officers, have doubtless someplace to go to. *(pause)* That's true, isn't it?

KELLY. Someplace?

JACK. He means, like home.

KELLY. O, yeah, I see. Home is someplace. Sean, you shoulda stood there, at home, or had one yourself.

SEAN. What I meant, detective—

KELLY. Shut up!

JACK *(laughing a little too wildly)*. Sean de Kahn thinks *we* wanna go home?! That's too much!

KELLY *(joining)*. He really thinks so, don't he?

JACK. Stupid sonofabitch.

KELLY. Lemme ask you, Sean—

SEAN. Simon—

KELLY. Yeah, you really believe we wanna go home?

SEAN *(grim)*. I said so.

KELLY. Jackie, you wanna go home, or to a bar, or get laid . . . or someplace?

JACK (sobers). Eventually . . . someplace.

KELLY (an edge). Yeah, but not now.

JACK. Naw, not now, of course.

KELLY. Me neither.

JIMMY (after a brief pause). Neither would I if I had your shit.

KELLY. You don't talk. (pause) What shit?

JIMMY. Fuck you guys. This is like wadin through mud.

SEAN. I think you ought to swear out a formal complaint against us and then you two can go home, or wherever. And when I'm booked properly, I can have the services of a physician. I mean, do we have to be here?

KELLY. That's a very pointed interrogatory, Sean. Wanna go, Jackie? You, Jimmy, wanna get some sleep, too? Sean, you really wanna see el medico so bad?

SEAN. I gave my opinion.

JIMMY. Do what you want with me: I'm hummin like a filament.

KELLY. Jackie, what? You got anything waitin for you again?

JACK. Me? Nothin. Forget me. But I think you wanna find Margie and stop her killing herself.

KELLY. Yeah?

JACK. Or you're gonna regret it a long time.

KELLY. Wrong again. I wanna sit right here, that's all I want.

SEAN. You behave as though you were . . . (pause) Insane.

JIMMY. He hates his daughter, that's the shit.

JACK. Frannie, hunh? Why don't you take the car to the Bronx, call Margie's sister, something . . . take the pressure off. Right?

KELLY. Margie?

JIMMY. She wants you.

KELLY. Are you talking?

JIMMY. O, man, don't it hurt you someplace that you got a daughter who's gonna kill herself cause you're her total-darkness daddy on the phone? No pain, nothin?

KELLY (to JIMMY). Who told you anything, garbage?

JIMMY. I eavesdropped.

KELLY. Don't, not any more.

JIMMY. Sure. I just wondered if it don't hurt.

KELLY (grim anger). If I was you, I'd shut my face. (pause) Yeah, sure, it hurts a lot, sonny-Jim. (pause) And not very much at all. (pause) I pride myself on my ability to absorb the blows. After while, these things don't hurt much. (pause, takes a drink) Boys, boys, I don't know. (pause) What it was, was that my father was a good man, see? That's the trouble

right there, he was a hero.

JACK. Yeah, well, sure.

KELLY. He was. He cared, but he didn't hurt much.

JACK. Yeah, and I wish I could lie to you, Frannie, but my old man was a bum.

KELLY. Your old man was a good cop, Jack, don't forget it.

JACK. But a bum. A bum to me, to my mother, to his daughter, a bum to his own mother.

JIMMY. I didn't have no old man.

JACK. You said he was a crook, your old man, you just told me.

JIMMY. I didn't have no old man.

JACK. In other words, another of your crummy, punko lies.

JIMMY. Yeah, yeah, another of my lies.

SEAN. My father was Thomas Aquinas. My father was a saint.

KELLY. Your father was a commie, Sean. Lost his job in the 50s. He was a commie traitor, Sean.

SEAN. I rely on Aquinas.

KELLY. Sure thing. How's the spleen there?

SEAN. I'm not so sure it's the spleen now because it's not getting worse and it should've.

KELLY. Good, I'm glad. I mean, I just wanted to punish you, not kill you. (takes a drink) Shit, you don't have to tell me, Delasante, the kid blamed the beard.

JACK. You got it.

SEAN. I would've thought it was disturbing . . .

KELLY. What?

SEAN. To have a daughter. That would be a very deeply disturbing thing.

KELLY. Who can say? (Pause; KELLY takes a drink. JIMMY starts to giggle; he can't help himself.) And you give him a pop, Delasante?

JACK. Yeah, I gave him a pop.

KELLY. Jesus, what a bunch of hyperventilated creeps. I don't know. (KELLY drinks again; JIMMY stifles his giggles.) What it is there is that Margie's the only person in the world I'm on a sure foot with. I don't want anything from her, except I'm her father and she's my daughter and that will never get removed. It goes back to the times she was little and all the stuff along the way, and the smiles, and she'd shout at me and get pissed off sometimes . . . but that there is perrmanent; even when she sticks it to me, it's permanent. It's more like a thing I read about Alfred Einstein, who invented the big bomb, who said when he was a kid he read a lot of dead scientists and authors and said he didn't feel alone, he didn't think he ever would feel alone, because those dead guys were his unloseable friends. That's how I think of her, my daughter, my unloseable friend. And I don't want a goddamn thing from her but she knows it, she's unloseable, and she prospers. That's the limit of it. *(pause;* JIMMY *giggles again)*

SEAN. "Feeling does not influence even in the smallest degree the subject's thought processes," the Army concluded after they gave me a psychological test. "Very highly unusual," they concluded. *(*JIMMY *starts to laugh.* KELLY *pins him with a glance.)*

KELLY. You and me, sonny, we talk next, make book on it.

JACK *(sings).*

YOU ARE MY SUNSHINE

MY ONLY SUNSHINE

(The phone rings.)

YOU MAKE ME HAPPY

WHEN SKIES ARE GRAY—

KELLY. Jesus Christ, with the music . . . !

JACK.

YOU'LL NEVER KNOW, DEAR—

*(*JACK *picks up the phone.)* What? *(pause)*

KELLY. So? Who is it?

JACK. Disconnect. *(He hangs up the phone.)*

BLACKOUT.

ACT TWO

It's somewhat later, JIMMY *is asleep on a desk.* SEAN *is sitting.* JACK *is reading a book.* KELLY *is on the phone. At the end of this act, outside and through the windows, dawn comes, and with it, light and noise.*

KELLY *(to the phone).* Yeah, I hear you, but I don't know how the phone number can be unlisted for the police department. No, I'll hold. I'd like to talk to your supervisor. *(to the others)* Jesus, I don't know. *(to the phone)* But, see, that's where I'm having my problem—operator—yes, that's where, because you can't de-list the police department. Yes. Sergeant Francis Kelly, New York City Police Department, shield number 28469. Yeah, but there's also a problem there since that office don't open till 9 a.m. I know this is a holiday and all but this is an emergency. So gimme the state police. *(to the others)* Fuckin rinky-dink fifth rate state, Vermont.

JACK. We're lucky, I gotta tell you, luck of the duck. Kelly, we're a fluke.

SEAN. Is there coffee, or something?

JACK. I think there's coffee.

SEAN. Can I have some?

JACK. What's it worth to you?

SEAN. Nothing, nothing at all. I'm starting to fall asleep and I don't want to.

JACK. I'll get you coffee.

SEAN. Are you going to throw it in my face?

JACK. Naw, shit, I'm in a good, benevolent mood. I always mellow out at 4 a.m.

KELLY. Fuckin-A.

SEAN. When I get very tired, I find I tend to get careless. Do you find that?

JACK. You get the coffee without opinions, homocide, okay? *(handing him coffee)*

SEAN. Thank you.

JACK. Don't mention it, I'm sure. *(pause)* We're lucky, you and me and him and him, Sean de Kahn.

KELLY. Yeah? Stockmeister, listen, I'm with the New York Police Department, if that means anything, and I'm trying to get to a daughter of mine, except, for crying out loud, the police in Chelsey is unlisted. *(hand over the receiver)* Would you ever . . . ? I mean, Jesus. *(to the phone)* Yeah, it's Kelly on the Old Fork Road up there in the southwest quandrant and you tell her to get on the horn to her old man, there's a neighbor has the phone, like double-quick pronto because her nutty sister is going to kill herself if she hasn't, yeah, and call me at area code 212-780-2122. Yeah, listen, I appreciate this, Stockmeister, I'll return it sometime. Yeah, you, too; no, no, I won't let nobody sell me the Brooklyn bridge. Yeah, you, too. *(hangs up the phone)* Dumb pansy copy. How do you de-list the police?

JACK. You wanna hear something, Kelly?

KELLY. My mind is one long brush-burn here, Delasante, you got something to say that has a little freight of kindness on it. De-list the fuckin local police, I mean.

JACK. Yeah, this writer. You shoot a wad and you lay out a 100 million, you ready for this, seeds, which all resemble tadpoles, and, you ready for this, they're swimming like mad where you done it—

KELLY *(grabbing the book).* What the hell are you reading? *Prisoner of Sex?*

JACK. That old broad whoor dropped it last week. *The Prisoner of Sex.*

KELLY. Yeah, I don't care. Let's try it your way.

JACK. I wanna go home, let 'em both fall,

even-steven.

KELLY. No, I gotta do something.

JACK. I don't.

KELLY. You'll get a lotta money sitting up half the night with this garbage. Come on.

JACK. What am I gonna do with money?

KELLY. What is it?

JACK. The "it" is nothing. I'm crapped out.

KELLY. Yeah?

JACK. I don't know how you manage. Don't you never get bushed?

KELLY. I have reserves of energy. It comes from bein even with everybody. I still live with my woman, Delasante, I have a sense of obligation.

JACK. I'm payin child support times two, alimony times three. Don't talk to me about bein serene with my conscience. Talk to me about Margie, hunh? I know you want to be there with her; I ain't fooled.

KELLY. You don't know shit. If you care so much, why don't you go out and tell her all that intolerable grief she says she has is really tolerable. You always liked her.

JACK. I don't believe you, Frannie.

KELLY. Leave Margie alone, leave me alone.

JACK. Anything you say, but don't play the obligation symphony to me, hunh? That's all.

KELLY. I'm takin the kid and I want the beard to sing like Renata Tavori.

SEAN. Tibaldi.

KELLY. Okay, Tibaldi.

SEAN. The coffee is acid. It's been boiled.

KELLY. You ever seen Renata Tavori?

SEAN. Boiled coffee is spoiled coffee.

KELLY. Yeah? *(to JACK)* You're gonna have fun. *(waking JIMMY)* Okay, Rosehips, up and at 'em.

JIMMY *(waking)*. Hey, what?

KELLY. You get the absolution when I get the confession. Up.

JIMMY. I don't know about you people. You people are crazy.

KELLY. We're crazy. Move it. *(JIMMY gets up wearily and makes for the room; KELLY follows.)* If the phone disturbs your deliberations with some news, get me out here, okay?

JACK. You'd be happier someplace else, Kelly, like wherever Margie is.

KELLY. I don't know where she is, asshole. She's wherever: the ice cream could melt by now, if I had it. Fuck it, just listen for the phone.

JACK. Yeah, well, you, too: write if you get work.

KELLY. Hang by your thumbs. *(Pushes JIMMY*

into the other room; closes the door. JACK *and* SEAN *look at each other. Pause.)*

JACK *(singing)*.
YOU ARE MY SUNSHINE,
MY ONLY SUNSHINE,
YOU MAKE ME HAPPY,
WHEN SKIES ARE GRAY . . .

SEAN *(snapping)*. Don't. *(softening it)* Please.

JACK *(referring to KELLY)*. Kelly, he won't listen, he don't listen to shit, well, maybe that's his problem, who can say, hunh? You work with a man a long time and like tonight he said to me he didn't trust me and you think you work with a man and suddenly it appears on the horizon he doesn't trust you, on the horizon where the sun rises, the light you know, you being into the light and all, he doesn't trust you, and that's the futile black, right, Sean, I mean, in other words, Simon? Right? *(pause, sings)*
YOU MAKE ME HAPPY WHEN SKIES ARE GRAY
I mean, you ever been with a woman, Sean, Simon . . . ?

SEAN. Of course.

JACK. No, I mean, not with, like let's-have-a-drink, but with-with, intimate.

SEAN. Is this relevant to anything?

JACK. So, when you said, "of course," you meant you been intimate to the degree of penetration and ejaculation?

SEAN. You're very quick.

JACK. Are you a little condescending to me? You killed an old Jewish merchant lady and I'm not good enough to talk to?

SEAN. I didn't kill anybody.

JACK. That's not what I heard.

SEAN. You heard nothing.

JACK *(sings)*.
AND I HUNG MY HEAD
AND I CRIED.
YOU ARE MY—
So who was she?

SEAN. Who?

JACK. The woman. *(pause)*

SEAN. Oh, the one-I-was-with woman?

JACK. I don't necessarily think I'm speaking in a foreign tongue.

SEAN. There wasn't *one*. As in, you were married, officer, but you didn't exclusively cover the same loins all the time.

JACK. That's funny. You know what, I think you're condescending to me, that's what I think though I don't want to think that, and it pisses me off, a little, Sean.

SEAN. Simon.

JACK. De Kahn.

SEAN. There was more than one.

JACK. What?

SEAN. Woman.

JACK. A lot?

SEAN. A number.

JACK. Pretty virile.

SEAN. They were happy.

JACK. So? I got it. Mrs. Linowitz shot herself. How about that? *(pause)* Nothin. *(pause; sings:)*

> YOU ARE MY SUNSHINE,
> MY ONLY SUNSHINE—

SEAN. Okay, I'll bite.

JACK. On what?

SEAN. What is it, precisely, you want?

JACK. O, shit, junior, I want a confession. This is the basketball court. I wanna dunk, win by one, and go sweet-Jesus home. You got that?

SEAN. Tell me what to say.

JACK. You know, whichever way, in your own words, twist the idiom a little, so it don't sound like we wrote it and some bullshit lawyer makes some bullshit judge laugh at Kelly and me for being a little old fashioned and going to the source of the felony. Like that. Whatever. The truth.

SEAN. I don't want to condescend to you, officer.

JACK. Delasante, Jack.

SEAN. I'd rather we were square.

JACK. Me, too. I want the kid for this one. I get no pleasure from burning you.

SEAN. You can have him.

JACK. All the way. I want him stapled in a shroud.

SEAN. Take him. What should I say?

JACK. Hey, let's resist a little. I thought you had some love for him, he was your daughter.

SEAN. You can have him.

JACK. What's the problem, there?

SEAN. Nothing *(pause)*

JACK. Is he Sunshine?

SEAN. He's Jimmy Rosehips.

JACK. I know what the rap sheet says, pussy.

SEAN. I don't care if you use narcotics, but you shouldn't've given him any.

JACK. Who gives a shit? You just said I could have him. Maybe he'll OD, you get him good and hooked, and then you're rid of him. *(pause)* Nice lookin kid. Is he sunshine?

SEAN *(angry)*. How the fuck do you know so much?

JACK *(pointing)*. Your package, Sean, it's all in there. (SEAN *makes for the file, angrier*

still) Hey, come on, sit down. Let's be civil a little.

SEAN. What do you have in there, just what, what exactly?

JACK. A little this, a little that.

SEAN. You cheap son-of-a-bitch.

JACK. Yeah, well. When you got the shit kicked out of you in '68 after you were arrested for extortion, you remember, Kitty Langelia, another woman you hurt, you talked a blue-streak through delirium at Bellevue emergency and we sat there by your bed and wrote and wrote, cause we knew, we just knew, we were gonna see you again.

SEAN. I beat that rap, you bastard. That stuff should've been removed from my file. You know, I can sue to have that stuff removed from my file.

JACK. Yeah, well, sue. *(sings)*

> YOU ARE MY SUNSHINE,
> MY ONLY SUNSHINE
> YOU MAKE ME HAPPY
> WHEN SKIES ARE GRAY
> YOU'LL NEVER KNOW, DEAR
> HOW MUCH I MISS YOU—

SEAN *(On the edge)*. How much I *love* you.

JACK. Yeah, love you.

> PLEASE DON'T TAKE MY SUN-
> SHINE AWAY.

SEAN. I wanna say something.

JACK. I know, that's the point. And you know what? I'm gonna listen.

SEAN. Why?

JACK. Just talk. *(pause)*

SEAN. A while ago, in Vietnam, in actual fact, I saw something, a man, and he was a soldier, well, everybody was a soldier but me, and I ignored them, I figured it was better not to know a single one of them personally because I might have to save his life and the pressure would've been wrong on me to save the life of a man I knew or maybe loved so I didn't. But there was this one man I didn't know, had never even ever seen before, sitting under a tree; he had his shirt off, he was all bloody and dirty from a fire fight, and he was doing nothing, just smoking a joint, and I was watching him the way I sometimes watched the men, thinking the dumbest crap, like how much I wanted to touch his shoulder, and he was nobody special at all and suddenly he turned toward me and waved and I thought, he must be waving at somebody behind me, so I turned around and saw there was nobody else but the two of us, and he waved again, and I started to be sort of pleased because I could see his eyes were intelligent and kind, and then he pointed right at me, and I thought, what is this, does he like me, this stranger, and then he said something that I couldn't hear, and I think I smiled and made the I can't hear you gesture, so he stood up and started to shout and I still couldn't hear, but I wanted to, so then he stood all the way up and that's when I heard the shot and he was nailed in the neck by a sniper and dropped like a ton of bricks, and of course, the shooting started again and me, by instinct, crawled on my belly to him, to where I stuck a wad in his neck and turned him over and cradled his head in my lap and wiped the shit off his forehead, because I always comforted the men I knew I couldn't help who were going to die and then I realized, Christ on the bloody cross, you shitbucket, you know you're going to weep, and so it was, for the first time ever, I opened my kit and gave myself a shot of morphine, and I sat there I'm told, for twelve hours, with his head in my lap, and he seemed to me to be an angel and every time I came out of it I fixed again. The sergeant said to me afterwards: shit, son, you were holdin onto that stiff so dear, goddamn if we didn't think we were gonna have to stuff the *both* of you in the body bag. *(pause)* Give me a hit, officer, Just a little hit, please. *(SEAN gets his hit.)* What's wrong is, I should've taken that beating he gave me better, it shouldn't've hurt so much, I should've ignored it, or been able to, but that's what's wrong, this thing is getting through to me again. *(pause)* You know how many times I didn't say a thing and didn't do a thing, not one goddamn thing, and I know you'll find that hard to believe, considering my package, but I was good a long time a very long time until I was overwhelmed with it. *(pause; a different tone: sad)* There's a woman inside me, officer, and she aches for the men she has known. She flirts with them and cries for them when they have to go in the morning; she likes to please them but she likes to have her cigarette lit, at least when I used to smoke . . . and I hate her so much that most often I want to kill her, because she loves her men so completely that if terrifies me . . . and she says to me, whenever I think there is no woman in me, that I am a liar and a fool, and she is the one who makes me cry and she's the one who makes me sing goddamn songs to men . . . live men, dead men, it doesn't matter. *(pause)* And he was her first, my woman, her first man. Nothing came of it but that I ran my fingers through his hair for, they tell me, twelve hours,

and I sang:
> YOU ARE MY SO FORTH
> MY ONLY SO FORTH
> YOU MAKE ME SO FORTH

(Pause, SEAN's tone changes slightly back to its old crispness.) Does a word of this makes the least little sense to you?

JACK. Oh, I'm gettin it all, but it's a little vague. You have a woman . . .

SEAN. Inside.

JACK. How'd that happen?

SEAN. I don't know.

JACK. Would I like her? I mean, is she a real piece of ass?

SEAN. You bet your life she is. That's why I want to kill her.

JACK. You ever think about a good shrink? *(SEAN laughs.)* No. really, I'm bein quite serious.

SEAN. I've thought about it.

JACK. Have you considered the alternative?

SEAN. What alternative?

JACK. Just one way? Hetero?

SEAN. Didn't you hear me just talking to you?

JACK. I heard. Sounded just like a woman. But I let you talk. I was entranced. All my life I been curious about guys like you because I only ever known guys like me. So I let you talk.

SEAN. What an incredibly stupid thing to say!

JACK. Hey, don't play dumb with me! I been married three times, I got two daughters: I know things about women it would pay you not to be dumb about around me. A man needs them. I mean, I *need* them . . .

SEAN. Hey, so do I.

JACK. It ain't been proved.

SEAN. The fuck not.

JACK. Let's say, "maybe", considering your needs. But somebody like me, without the bends, I go crazy without that sort of female contact yeah, look how crazy I am, four times a day dipping into the hard shit—I go certifiable. But what it is if you need them, you can't live *with* them, you think about murder all the time. Which is why I let you talk, guys like you—I wonder and I'm pained at your type. You got it easy. And to me, you're just another woman, or the one inside you is, and I wanna hit you.

SEAN. Relax, King Kong. Don't take things so literally.

JACK. Don't tell me how to take things. My first wife was the only one of the long number

I was crazy in love with—crazy Debby—and it was okay there for a long time, several years even, till I caught her one night lookin at me. Every fuckin time I woke up, with nothin to hide me in a very hot July, she'd be there on one elbow, lookin at me, which I pretended not to see. I didn't know what to think—she's after something, she's not, she's thinking I want to sneak off, and I'm thinking, she wants to slip it to me . . .

SEAN. She was just watching.

JACK. Yep, for where to stick it.

SEAN. Maybe she loved you.

JACK. Such crap. If she loved me, we'd still be married, to this day.

SEAN. If I loved you, Jack—

JACK. I don't know I gave you the liberty to nickname me.

SEAN. That didn't happen?

JACK. I don't know it did, is what I meant.

SEAN. I'm sorry.

JACK. No, I mean, what were you going to say there.

SEAN. Nothing. If I loved you, Jack, I'd spend a night watching you sleep. I've done that.

JACK. I don't want to know much more, I'm sure.

SEAN. Try.

JACK. What?

SEAN. To listen to me, Jack.

JACK. Save your breath. In that sex book there, you'll find yourself a most vivid description. A man lays down his little present to his woman, and the spermazoos are swimming, and it turns out that the spermazoos that make a little girl can live forever in the Phillips tube, whereas the spermazoos that make a man die fast in the Phillips tube, minutes, seconds, something in the solution kills them, and even when you've given her your delight, and hers, something in the uterine contractions of the moment gets up another flush of these acids that are squeezed out that kill the male spermazoos, which are very active in the manic sense, but have no staying power. There's a moral there, get it? *(pause)* Women always kill the men, given half a chance. And I don't give 'em half a chance.

SEAN. You're a funny man, you know?

JACK. Yeah? Whenever I hear that, I check for my wallet.

SEAN. I mean, you're not as dumb as you'd like me to believe, are you? In fact, you're. . . ?

JACK. Tell me I'm sweetness and light, that the woman inside you has a thing for me. That would make my night . . . complete. *(pause, they look at each other; phone rings)* Ja-wohl. Hi. How are you? Long time not to talk with. Yeah, he's in concert with a suspect in a particularly horrid and abhorrent homicide, but what's that, okay? Hold it. *(calls out)* Kelly, the other daughter from Vermont, and what's her name again?

KELLY *(voice through the door)*. What?

JACK. Your other daughter!

KELLY. Sasha!

JACK. Sasha?

KELLY. A minute!

JACK. Sasha's Russian, ain't it. *(picks up the phone)* Hi, Sasha-love, you know, your name just came back to me, Sasha, your old daddy's on the hundred yard dash to el-telefono. Sorry about the crap about your sister— No, I don't know, I don't anything, honey, but, hey, you sound great, vigorous, healthy, natural, hunh? Yeah, I'm gonna put you on hold, listen: you grow marijuana up there? Yeah, that's funny, yeah. *(puts the phone on hold)* She said "You grow smart down there?" I don't know her for shit. *(putting away the drug materials)* We could just cool it with Kelly I gave you a pop . . . ?

SEAN. Sure thing, boss.

JACK. And we agree, Jimmy pulled the chain on the old lady?

SEAN. Right on.

JACK. And he *did*, right?

SEAN. What do you think?

JACK. I think he did.

SEAN. Then he did.

JACK. And you really think so, I mean . . . ?

SEAN. I'm pretty committed to thinking he did, yeah.

JACK. Yeah.

SEAN. As, in another words, you just heard me explain.

JACK. I heard you.

SEAN *(sings as he reaches out and takes JACK's hand)*

YOU ARE MY SUNSHINE
MY ONLY SUNSHINE . . .
YOU MAKE ME HAPPY
WHEN SKIES ARE GRAY

So?

JACK *(pulling his hand away)*. Nothin. There's no woman in me *(SEAN laughs.)*, and I wouldn't talk about the one in you too much outside this room, or you're worth nothing to us. When you've given us your statement as to how Jimmy killed the woman he killed—

SEAN. I haven't yet.

JACK. Fuck it, you will—I don't want Jimmy's attorney to rip you up and down in front of a jury and make you out to be, frankly, a vicious and insane fruitloop . . . which, frankly, is what I think you are. Okay? *(They look at each other.* JACK *picks up the phone and presses the button.)* Sasha-pots, Delasante again. Daddy's rounding third and heading for home, and hold on, eat some yogurt. *(puts the phone back on hold; calls)* KELLY! *(to* SEAN*)* She's the sweetest piece of Christmas candy, that Sasha, last time I saw her, all hellos and you're-my-funny-uncle-Jack. Nothin like screwy Margie. *(pause)* So, I ain't it, sorry, but we dispose of Jimmy and I'm happy and you're happy, and it doesn't matter a lot whether he pulled the trigger or not, *he's* the one I want tonight.

SEAN. Why?

JACK. What?

SEAN. I can see why *I'd* like to see Jimmy removed from circulation for a very long time. I just don't know why you want him.

JACK. I want him because he's young and I like to nip these things in the bud. The kid is a deviate, up front.

SEAN. Yeah?

JACK. And we're agreed on that, at least? *(*KELLY *enters, pushing* JIMMY *into the room before. A moment of eye-contact between* SEAN *and* JIMMY. KELLY *makes for the phone.)*

SEAN. Agreed!

KELLY *(to* JIMMY*)*. Sit! *(to phone)* Hello, hey, hi, yeah, hi, I'm sorry but your sister married somebody last week and today she wants to kill herself and she's moving here and moving there, all over the Bronx and we can't find her to stop her from doing that, but I wanna know if she calls again, which she's been doing time to time, can I call you and put you on and you talk to her because frankly I don't know what to say to stop her till we can get help—Yeah, I had a drink or two, the tension mounts, that's not the problem I'm having—no, no, headaches anymore. No, I can't do that, I can't run, I'm a fatass—What do you mean? No, I'd've come, but it's a long drive, I think—How let you down, let down what, I work for a living—No, that doesn't make sense. No, it doesn't. No. No. I mean, no. What are you two, a conspiracy? Hunh? I love her, I mean, I'll love her later when this thing straightens. There'll be time there. Can I depend on you? No, look, I don't know why you'd say, like, what, what did you say—What's made out of stone? What?—O, Jesus,

fuck off! *(slams the phone down)* Jesus. *(pause)*

JACK. I'm gonna go get the News. I don't care. I wanna see if Catfish Hunter's elbow got better yet.

SEAN. The game was over already when you busted us at the dry cleaners. Indians four, Yankees two.

JACK. No shit. I'm gonna go get the News, anyway.

KELLY. Would you haul Sean de Kahn into the other room and get the last least little part of some shit that will hold up in court, now.

JACK. I dunno. Sean, you ready to write it finally?

SEAN. Anyway you'd like.

KELLY. That's nice. That's cooperation.

JACK. Okay, Sean, I mean, there, Simon, one last turn.

SEAN *(weary, obedient)*. Can I have a soft drink?

JACK. Anything you like, Simon. Pepsi, Orange Crush, Fresca.

SEAN *(a pause)*. One of each, actually.

JACK *(happy)*. Okay, okay, confessionville lies just down the road. One of each. *(Pushes* SEAN *out of the room.* KELLY *and* JIMMY *alone. Silence.)*

KELLY. Dumb junkies I work with and chase, and winos and homos and psychos and dumbos, the worst, and edge-of-the-ledge jumpos and sapphos and pimpos, and uh-ohs . . . like my daughter there. *(pause)* Ask again.

JIMMY *(catching his meaning)*. No.

KELLY. Okay, I'll tell you. I'm here because I don't want to be there in the Bronx with Margie, and I couldn't stand to be anywhere else. And since I wanna be here, you gotta be here and Sergeant Delasante, and Sean de Kahn gotta be here. And since I never figured out how to ask for anything I really wanted, I don't ask, I tell. And if I want, or wanted, anything from you, you wouldn't know unless I told you, which I don't intend to. *(pause)* I wanted all that clear. *(pause)*

JIMMY. Who said to be a man was easy?

KELLY. What?

JIMMY. Look, I didn't kill anybody.

KELLY. Oh, I didn't think, oh no, unh-unh, you'd killed nobody. Just why?

JIMMY. What?

KELLY. The stuff.

JIMMY. What stuff? *(*JIMMY *starts giggling.)*

KELLY. You know what?

JIMMY *(in his giggles)*. What?

KELLY. I guess you're high?

JIMMY. High? On what, man?

KELLY. Dilaudid.

JIMMY. Me? Where?

KELLY. Don't gimme where. I know where, and I know why.

JIMMY (*still giggling*). Oh, shit, no, not me, I'm clean.

KELLY. I don't think so.

JIMMY (*sings*)

> WHITER THAN THE WHITEWASH
> ON THE WALL,
> WHITER THAN THE WHITEWASH
> ON THE WALL,
> WASH ME IN THE WATER
> THAT YOU WASH YOUR DIRTY
> DAUGHTER IN
> AND I SHALL BE WHITER THAN
> THE
> WHITEWASH ON THE WALL.

KELLY. My brain, you know, is a plate glass window, and you just hit it, sonny, and the fragments are stardust.

JIMMY. That's nice.

KELLY. Yeah. (*pause*) So, strip.

JIMMY. Hey!

KELLY. You just leapfrog from felony to felony, you know that? I mean, we had you here for robbery, murder, now we got you for using narcotics and I gotta see you aren't concealing. Hippity hop, Jimmy, through the whole criminal code.

JIMMY. Shit.

KELLY. Now. Strip search.

JIMMY. Boy, I know this routine.

KELLY. Better know it by heart.

JIMMY. I do. Are you serious?

KELLY. Do I look the leastways bereft of seriousness, outside that I'm fat?

JIMMY. Oh, boy.

KELLY. Yeah, oh boy. Strip.

JIMMY (*as he strips down to nothing, facing* KELLY, *upstage*). I never had this roust before in a stationhouse. I had it in jail, officer—

KELLY. Sergeant.

JIMMY. Sergeant. I got that there because that's what they do, the old turnkeys, get all the men out and stick them in the tile room and line them up, you know . . . they say, okay, boys, put your front to the back of the man in front of you and your backside to the man behind, pecker and ass, and then they wait a couple minutes and then the headman says to us, Well, any of you boys, you get sexually excited, you can get dressed and walk, you're okay; any of you don't get excited, you stay, we know what to do with you.

KELLY. I don't know about that. I wanna see if you have narcotics about your person, in a legal sense.

JIMMY (*indicating* JACK *offstage*). HE GAVE ME THE POP!

KELLY. A police officer gave you junk?

JIMMY. You know that.

KELLY. Boy, if you went into court and said, My God, I was in this precinct station and one officer was a junky and the other was an alky and I was arrested with a beard, boy, what would the judge say, what, Jimmy? You're in this court because you *killed* somebody. A fix from a cop? Hey, you're in trouble here, do you understand?

JIMMY. I know, I know, I'm sorry.

KELLY. Yeah, about what?

JIMMY. I don't know.

KELLY. Thought you were gonna say something, there.

JIMMY (JIMMY *is naked now*). I don't know.

KELLY. Well, I can see you ain't holdin, so get dressed.

JIMMY. No.

KELLY. Aw, come on.

JIMMY. I don't know. (*pause*)

KELLY. Shit-Jesus, I'm ashamed, you know. (*pause*) Put the clothes on.

JIMMY. I don't want to.

KELLY. I said, put your clothes on.

JIMMY. I don't know.

KELLY. What don't you know? Who done it?

JIMMY. That's not it, that's not what I don't know.

KELLY. I get so pissed off at people saying they don't know, I do.

JIMMY. Does she say "I don't know" a whole lot?

KELLY. Who?

JIMMY. Your daughter.

KELLY. Don't touch my daughter, Jimmy.

JIMMY. Okay, yeah, I'm sorry, I thought you might wanna say.

KELLY. Get dressed, would you?

JIMMY (*after a pause*). It's okay.

KELLY. I know that, I know it's okay.

JIMMY. You want me to fight you still, is that it?

KELLY. Just a little.

JIMMY. I'm way out of my depth here.

KELLY. Are you? I wonder.

JIMMY. It's just not easy, man.

KELLY. Sergeant.

JIMMY. No, man, it's "man", sergeant.

KELLY. Who said easy? I can't figure the taking of a human life, your own, somebody else's, and that's the only last fuckin thing on God's green earth I can't figure. Every other sin is bullshit. *(pause)*

JIMMY. I know, and it's okay, it really is.

KELLY. Christ I'm tired.

JIMMY. If you're tired, I'm just dead. *(JIMMY puts his head on KELLY's lap.)*

KELLY. Yeah, I know. *(as he takes JIMMY in his arms; a moment)* There was a time for months, years even, after she was born, I couldn't say her name. I had to say something else but her real name—I'd call her Margarine, she liked that, Magpie, Mag-poos, from the mess she used to leave in her diapers, Mugs, Mike, even Mikey, and then some day there, she dawned on me like Margaret, which is her real name, and Margie, which is her real nickname, and I had possession of the belief that my daughter was the most extraordinary human being who ever moved shoes over the earth. I couldn't for the life of me tell you what happened there later, how she got moody, how she smart-assed me around and sneaked around with those pin-dicks she was always callin "My man,"—maybe all that started when she started to get her monthlies, but nobody's ever got from me what she got with her sayin crap, her sayin "Hi daddy . . . " her sayin "I love you daddy . . ." *(kisses JIMMY on the head)* You know what's funny, to me, and I'm tired, maybe I'm dead, since I never had my arms around a man like this, is I feel your beard, like a woman would've felt your beard, if I was one, or if I was ever . . . you know. *(pause)* You know what else is funny, I mean, to me? I can tell you're not excited, I mean, that's there, but what's funny is that I am. That's very funny.

JIMMY. Okay. *(pause)* I want to put my clothes on now.

KELLY. I can understand.

JIMMY. May I?

KELLY. Yeah, sure.

JIMMY. It's still okay, you know, still really okay.

KELLY. I know. *(They embrace again.)* I gotta ask, are you trying to be affectionate or steal my gun there?

JIMMY. I don't know

KELLY. You tryin to steal my gun? You haven't got any clothes on.

JIMMY. I don't know.

KELLY. You stole my gun. *(pause)*

JIMMY. I know.

KELLY. You got it.

JIMMY. Yep.

KELLY. Where?

JIMMY. In my hand.

KELLY. Which hand.

JIMMY. You got two guesses.

KELLY. Okay, okay, you gonna shoot me? I'm tired.

JIMMY. I'm not gonna shoot you.

KELLY. I'd like the gun back.

JIMMY. I know.

KELLY. Tel you, let's make a deal.

JIMMY. What deal?

KELLY. Let's just stand like we were, before, just relaxed, close our eyes, feel nothin . . . nothin at all. *(KELLY makes to be affectionate.)*

JIMMY. Stop doin that, it's not that hand.

KELLY. I figured that. Let's just relax.

JIMMY. It's— *(The gun goes off.)* Aw, shit, you're such bad luck.

KELLY. I know. Get me a chair.

JIMMY. How bad is it, hunh?

KELLY. I don't know, but it hurts like a son-of-a-bitch. Get dressed, hunh, get dressed fast, I mean, this is a constabulary.

JIMMY *(doing so)*. Okay, I'm gettin dressed. I know this doctor, man, he can fix you. I even got money Sean don't know about, she don't know about, my wife, nobody knows about . . .

KELLY. I'm very tired here, and I think I'm feelin, for the first time in a long time, a feelin of . . . I don't know.

JIMMY. Don't be afraid, sergeant.

KELLY. I didn't say nothin of it was being afraid or not. I feel sort of . . . well, Jesus, Jimmy, pretty comfortable here. Does that make you laugh?

JIMMY. What? *(JACK opens the door and comes in.)*

JACK. What's the commotion?

JIMMY *(pointing the gun at JACK)*. Just be careful, man, okay? Okay, I don't want to hurt you.

JACK. No shit, Jimmy, and what did you go and do but shoot a police officer, hunh? Now would you like to drop it easy and plant your hands on the desk?

JIMMY. I don't know, but maybe not.

JACK *(helpless)*. Kelly, what the fuck?

KELLY. No, Jackie, don't get big about this.

JACK. Do you mind If I take a look at his backside?

JIMMY. Yeah, sure, okay.

KELLY. I know it's back there someplace, I can feel it, but it feels kind've nice; I mean, it ain't yet.

JACK *(looking)*. Yeah?

KELLY. My time's coming five, ten years from now . . . myocardial infarction.

JACK. I hope to tell you. You took it in the wallet, Kelly: the stupid bullet's stickin out the back of your pants. *(With a nod to* JIMMY, *stuffs a towel or something in back of* KELLY, *to stop the bleeding.)*

KELLY. No shit, the wallet? I'll drink to that. *(does)*

JACK. The gun, Jimmy, Now! *(a tense moment, then the phone rings)* Okay, so, in other words, if I answer the phone, that'd be okay, Jimmy . . . or, let me put it like this, you won't shoot me?

JIMMY. Fuck, no, what do you think?

JACK. Nice. *(picks up the phone)* Who? Yep. Yep. Yeah. O, Jesus. (puts the phone down, shaken)

SEAN *(entering; seeing the scene)*. What happened?

JIMMY. I don't know, but don't do nothing, okay?

JACK. If you remember how, anyone, a short prayer.

KELLY. What're you talking about?

JACK. A short prayer, anyone.

KELLY. Aw, fuck. *(pause)* All over?

JACK. Morris was late.

KELLY. I'll bet.

JACK. He was so late, Frannie, he was so late.

JIMMY *(to* SEAN*)*. We can go, man.

SEAN. Don't say hippy stuff to me, Jimmy. Don't say "man."

JIMMY. Let's go.

SEAN. You want to go?

JIMMY. I don't know.

JACK *(recollecting)*. In other words, it took her half an hour to kick the bucket, because, Kelly, I gotta inform you, if you do to yourself what she done to herself, you don't die just like that. But oh, she had such determination, that's the way it seems, such a will to get it done—Morris says, her voice was clear, he says, her voice was proud; it was something, Morris said, that she sounded like she was lookin forward to, like makin love, in other words . . . I don't know. *(pause)* You shits didn't know her . . . a crystal radiance . . . Bingo!

KELLY. Bingo.

JACK. Yeah, bingo. It ain't nice what she done to her head, Morris says.

KELLY. Did you get something from Sean de Kahn?

JACK. Your daughter's dead, for Christ's sake!

KELLY. From Sean, anything?

JACK. Yeah, a very moving piece of prose.

KELLY. Okay, you won your forty bucks. So, would you, disarm the felon so we can go someplace . . . home, to sleep, whatever?

JACK *(eyeing* JIMMY*)*. Yeah, of course.

JIMMY. Don't.

JACK. Gimme the gun, Jimmy, or I'll take you apart with these couple hands.

JIMMY *(enraged)*. I wanna say something and if you don't go over there and sit down, I mean, like now, I'm gonna blow your fuckin brains out. I mean it. All right, I said to myself, Jimmy, sweetheart, you may haul dog-do for the rest of your life, and uphill, but you and this woman of yours, blown up like a balloon, you've both come to the sacred place and you are about to have a son. Well, I was, you can laugh, but I was going to, and she thought so, too, she said, I'm that good—what is that kind of good?—she said, I'll deliver you a son, and we were ready, and he says, Here, excuse me, I am in transit between births and smoke cigars to get the fetal fluid off my hands, and I said, Great, Doc, just awful great, but be good and at your level best, and we ended up in a room that was just about as bad a room as you would ever want to be in, yeah, it was like a men's room, and everybody was all smiles, even Lisa, because it had crowned—my first look was peachfuzz on the cranium, damp as September rain, peeking through her mommie's opening, and at first I said, No thank you, but the nurses are making me ashamed, they say the father is so important, and Lisa's saying, We got up for this together so don't chicken on me, Jimmy, and I'm crying, thinking, whatever it is, it's alive, it's got wet hair on it. So I donned the blue suit and the blue booties and the blue mask and the blue hat and I waited, and I was saying, James, you are a progenitor, and Lisa, you are the other thing—I'm thinking, what's it, what's it, the progenetrix, and we neither of us know, we don't fuckin know, but we hope it works, and it was coming, man, was it ever coming, and then it got stuck: and there was panic everywhere except for Lisa, I mean, she didn't know, and the doctors looked at each other, back and forth, and they heated up the vacuum cleaners and the scalpels and they said, everybody, put your hands on her, all together, and push, let's gather together and push, and this male doctor said push, and this male intern said push, and this male father said push, and this male whatever-the-hell-he-was said push, and we helped her, we pushed while she pushed, and the only other woman in the room, who was the nurse, didn't push but listened with a stethoscope to see if it was alive, what we were pushing at and just like suddenly, one last push, and Bingo! a baby appeared, all covered completely in some shitstorm of coldcream and tied by a cord to her mommy, and I said, thanks, yeah, I said that, and it's likely more than thanks . . . and I noticed, well, I mean what can I say, yes, it was a little girl, right there, dressed in cream and a little poopy, stuck in the tubes like she was when I didn't even know the lady was a lady, and I thought only, Not fuck off little person, you are not the man I wanted to come from there, I didn't think at all how bad my disappointment was. I didn't think anything, okay? Okay, I thought, just, you are my daughter and those people will wash the cream off you and in a while, I'm afraid, daughter, you'll be mine—and this is on a two-minute acquaintance in a delivery room—I thought, daughter, fuck it, from now till I die, I'll have to answer to you. When she popped out, whole and perfect, I mean, a little pooped, too long in the birth canal, all the light I ever had ran to her, all what I hoped, and in the bar around the corner from the hospital I told the keeper there, I'm glad I didn't have a son, but what else could I say? *(pause)* What could I say? Somebody's got to tell *me*. *(pause)* I mean, did you ever think, Sergeant, when you saw your daughter the first time, that some part of you—was in her? Did you ever feel that, looking at Margie? Do you know what I mean? I mean, do you feel nothin at all, anyway at all, now she's dead? Say something!

KELLY. I'll tell you, since you wanna know all that crap. When Jack just told me Bingo and brains on the wall, I'll tell you how I felt. I felt okay. I felt like the stone is off my chest. She's safe now. Now I'm gonna love her a lot and think about her, I'm gonna be closer to her than I ever been in my life, because all that stuff is past now and it was so complicated. Now she's set kind of perfect, bein dead, and bingo! . . . I find myself relieved.

JIMMY *(points gun at* KELLY'*s temple for a long moment then tosses the gun on the desk in defeat).* All right, Sergeant, man, you win.

KELLY. Okay, Jackie, he ain't got the gun anymore. So you beat him up a little now, right?

JACK. Yeah, I can, but I'm not going to, Kelly, you know, in other words, not now.

Jimmy, he ain't got a prayer of surviving his next birthday, look at him.

KELLY. You're all bullshit, Jackie.

JACK. Yeah?

KELLY. Yeah.

JACK. Yeah, maybe, Frannie, and I'm not gonna tell you what I finally conclude about you, not now. This is Margie's wake. I'm gonna write my reports up, and yours, like a very good police officer, which is what I happen to be. And here's how it comes out, just so everybody knows, including the sergeant there—that Sean has given me a statement that makes Jimmy take the whole big total fall, which Jimmy knows, and Jimmy's got nothin to say in his own defense, really, because he knows, after all, he's the rabbit here, everybody's darlin little girl, which Sean knows likewise, and I know, and the sergeant there knows. Just like we all know, in reality, that Sean, in reality, killed the old lady and Jimmy was so hopped up at the time he's practically innocent. I don't know why things turn out like this, but they do, they always do. And I'm gonna wait five seconds for anybody here to tell me I'm out of line, in other words, wrong *(pause)* Okay, Jimmy.

JIMMY. Say what you want, but I know why you all gotta be rid of me and I don't kiss off so easy.

JACK. Yeah? Whatever gets you through the night, but just so you know, honey, just so the record's straight, that's all. In other words, happy Fourth of July, friends. *(pause)*

KELLY. There's a nice breeze comin in through the window there, you notice?

JACK. Gonna be a hot one, though.

JIMMY. Looks like the dawn.

SEAN. Or what passes for dawn.

KELLY. You bitter, Sean? You sound bitter. I'm not, even though I'm entitled to be, so I can ask.

SEAN. You stupid, sentimental, Irish drunk. You've lost her, your daughter: But you didn't stop her when you could've because you didn't want to, and what more can I say about that? *(pause)*

KELLY. Boys, boys, let's look lively here, it's time for the morning watch. Jimmy, put your shirt on there. Jesus, Sean, you look like shit: pinch your cheeks or something to get the color up. Put the cuffs on em, Jackie, we'll finish the paperwork tomorrow. *(*JACK *does so,* KELLY *rises, with difficulty.)* Shall we, some part of this new morning, say a prayer for my daughter?

JACK. Why, for Christ's sake?

KELLY. Because you pray, or you pretend to pray, because that's what people do to balm the griefs all, and you know that. And Jimmy there knows, and even Sean. You do something people ordinarily do. *(pause; a little build in the noise outside)*

SEAN *(sings; KELLY prays).*
> THE OTHER NIGHT, DEAR,
> AS I LAY SLEEPING
> I DREAMED I HELD YOU
> IN MY ARMS
> WHEN I AWOKE, DEAR
> I WAS MISTAKEN
> AND I HUNG MY HEAD
> AND I CRIED.

(KELLY finishes prayer. JIMMY joins in sing-ing, then JACK, and finally, KELLY.)
> YOU ARE MY SUNSHINE,
> MY ONLY SUNSHINE,
> YOU MAKE ME HAPPY
> WHEN SKIES ARE GRAY
> YOU'LL NEVER KNOW, DEAR,
> HOW MUCH I LOVE YOU,
> PLEASE DON'T TAKE MY SUN-
> SHINE AWAY.

(SEAN laughs. A moment when they are frozen after the song. Noise outside intrudes: KELLY busts it by moving; he and JACK are then suddenly businesslike.)

KELLY. Move, garbage. The bus for the Tombs leaves in five minutes. You boys'll just make it.

(They go, perfectly cop and crook. Blackout.)

Loose Ends

Michael Weller

First presented by Circle in the Square Theater in New York City on June 7, 1979, with the following cast:

(*in order of appearance*)

PAUL	Kevin Kline
SUSAN	Roxanne Hart
JANICE	Patricia Richardson
BALINESE FISHERMAN	Earnest Abuba
DOUG	Jay O. Sanders
MARAYA	Celia Weston
BEN	Steve Vinovich
SELINA	Jodi Long
RUSSELL	Michael Kell
LAWRENCE	Michael Lipton
PHIL	Jeff Brooks

Directed by Alan Schneider
Scenery by Zac Brown
Costumes by Kristina Watson
Lighting by David F. Segal

Loose Ends is a play about its own generation. Weller's play reflects the lifestyle of certain couples in the seventies: their aspirations, their expectations and their yearnings. *Loose Ends* focuses on one couple, Paul and Susan, and their search over a span of nine years for sincerity, love, meaning and self worth in their marriage while growing up in a decade of transitory relationships and "open" morality. It is a story about two people who discover as they develop and mature that their goals and needs become incompatible even as they continue to love each other. *Loose Ends* is not only a play about the difficulties of keeping a marriage together in the seventies; it also touches upon Zen Buddhism, women's liberation, the sexual revolution, divorce, abortion and the choice between career and marriage. Another idea, which is expressed in the play, is that in order to gain material success you have to surrender your ideals.

Michael Weller states, "The children of the seventies are sad, happy, lonely, hemmed in and groping for an answer to all of the paradoxes freedom of choice has brought us." *Loose Ends* reflects the shifting values and patterns of our current existence. It typifies the era of Spock children who have become adults in the me generation.

Loose Ends had its genesis in a one act play that Schneider commissioned from Weller. "One of the things I did when I became director of the Julliard Theatre Center was to ask Michael to write a short play for the Lincoln Center touring program. . . . He wrote a play called *Split* about couples splitting up. But the Lincoln Center people decided divorce was too mature a subject for high school audiences, so we never put it on. Michael then sat down and wrote a full-length version, and that became *Loose Ends.*" Before this, *Split* was produced in a showcase production at the Ensemble Studio Theatre. Once it was rewritten it was sent to David Chambers. The play was accepted and premiered in 1971 at the Arena Theatre in Washington. Prior to its premiere there, it was shown at the Royal Court Theatre in London.

Michael Weller was born in 1943 in New York City. His father is a New York photographer who had been an artist with the Works Progress Administration (WPA), as had his mother, "a beautiful woman named Rosa Rush who died young and in tragic circumstances. . . ."

"My background was artistic rather than commercial. . . . I had it pretty easy, there was never any pressure on me to do anything. My rebellion would have been to be a banker." Weller attended Brandeis University where he studied musical composition and began to write plays. "My college education ended in 1965. During my last year I shared a house with several people. I managed to learn very little about them. Most of the things they did baffled me."

At Brandeis, Weller thought of becoming a composer. He wrote several scores for student musicals, including one for the adaptation of Nathaniel West's *A Cool Million.* But he decided after his senior year that he'd rather write words than notes. He became a playwright almost by accident when he was disappointed with the book that someone had written for his musical adaptation. He bought a manual on playwriting and copied the rules he learned from it on cocktail napkins, studying them while he worked as a bartender. From this he developed "a very cool attitude" toward his writing. "I was never very romantic about it."

Another accident that led him to playwriting was when he was asked to help write a college show. One of his instructors encouraged his developing interest in drama and urged him to go to England to study. He chose Manchester University because ". . . it was possible in just one year to get a degree in drama." At Manchester, the theatre course ". . . consisted largely of a teacher bringing the aspiring writers, directors and actors into a small theatre and telling them that he never wanted to see it empty. That gave me a dream of theatre I've never lost."

Weller feels that studying in Manchester was invaluable because it gave him the English habit of close observation of character. "The British use language as a series of very interesting clues, which you have to watch very carefully." Then Weller moved to London where he wrote at night and supported himself by day at various jobs: running a pub, janitorial work and teaching. ". . . Oh, it was lovely, I was the only janitor with a graduate degree. I used to go around listening to the teachers say all this wrong stuff about drama, and after classes I'd call these kids back and tell 'em what they really ought to be reading."

Weller's career began at the *Sunday Times* Student Drama Festivals. After studying drama at Manchester in 1964, he appeared as an actor in the Festival in 1965. In 1968 his play *How Ho Ho Rose and Fell in Seven Short Scenes,* an expressionistic study of dictatorship, was shown at the Festival. Then *Moonchildren* began to attract interest and was performed at the Royal Court Theatre in London under the title of *Cancer* in 1970. It came to America and catapulted him to fame. Before *Moonchildren* he had written more than fourteen plays, six of which had been produced in London in "lunchtime theatres," an opportunity he does not think he would have had here in the States. He also believes that the *Sunday Times* Festivals were responsible for his development and for his career's inception. In 1973 he became the first Playwright in Residence at the Mark Taper Forum of the Los Angeles Music Center and the recipient of a $10,000 grant.

Weller's inspiration for *Loose Ends* came from the lives of many of his female friends. "I've seen a lot of professional women stumbling on to their talent by accident. Suddenly it becomes very important to them and to their sense of themselves. I also accidentally happened on to a certain talent that I had. My dedication to it has caused a lot of problems. I'm drawn to the contradictions that come up in a woman who wants a job and also wants love. . . . It's often difficult for the person you're with to understand the kind of private passion that draws you to your work, that's as strong in motivating you as the love you have for that person. . . ."

Weller does not like autobiographical interpretations of his work. "There is a temptation to get mixed up between what the author's life is and what his plays are about. . . . I'd rather have my works presented with no explanation, let them be taken for what they are. . . . I just want to feel free to present each work as if it was the first one, so there's no explanation of my style or my development. I like to work in different styles and I like to be completely free to change when and where I will."

For Weller, writing plays is his compulsion. "I like pushing . . . to get theatre forms expanded. Theatre is a fantastic medium. Every single night an audience is a different animal and you see things that will never take place again. . . . I want to . . . expand theatre . . . to bring it back to what it came out of . . . great acrobatics and vocal skills in the actors . . . make it more . . . exuberant, more baccanalian."

Other works by Michael Weller are *Fred; Happy Valley; The Body Builders; The Making of Theodore Thomas, Citizen; Tira Tells Everything There Is to Know About Herself; Grant's Movie; Three Sketches* (for *Oh, Calcutta*); *The Greatest Show on Earth; More Than You Deserve; Fishing;* the screenplays for *Hair, Ragtime* and *Loose Ends; Now There's Just the Three of Us; 23 Years Later; At Home* and *The Dwarfman, Master of a Million Shapes.*

AUTHOR'S PRODUCTION NOTE

In its original production the scene changes of *Loose Ends* were accompanied by photographs. These showed scenes from Paul and/or Susan's life in the spans of time between the dates of each scene. Two things were accomplished by this. The audience's attention was taken off the stage where, in-the-round, there was nothing to hide from view the frantic scurrying of cast and crew while pieces of scenery were changed. And, more important, the pictures supplied information about the world of Paul and Susan and their friends. They were not intended to represent photographs taken by Susan. Their point of view, so to speak, was neutral.

Each scene ended with the actors freezing in position on stage as the lights dimmed and a slide of those actors in that position was projected on a screen. The photograph had been taken in a "real life" equivalent of the stage set. During the scene change there followed a number of slides taken in various settings never seen in the play, then as a scene change was ending, we concluded with a slide of the next scene with actors in position. When the stage lights came up we saw the theatrical equivalent of the last slide. There were no slides at the beginning and end of each act.

SCENE ONE

Slide: 1970 A beach. Night. Full Moon.
Waves. On bare stage, PAUL *and* SUSAN, *early*
mid-20s, naked, clothes around. He sits facing
ocean (us) and she lies curled up.

PAUL. It was great at the beginning. I could
speak the language almost fluently after a month
and the people were fantastic. They'd come
out and help us. Teach us songs. Man, we
thought it was all going so well. But we got
all the outhouses dug in six months and we
had to stay there two years, that was the deal.
And that's when we began to realize that none
of the Nglele was using these outhouses. We'd
ask them why and they'd just shrug. So we
started watching them carefully and what we
found out was the Nglele use their feces for
fertilizer. It's like gold to them. They thought
we were all fucking crazy expecting them to
waste their precious turds in our spiffy new
outhouses. Turns out they'd been helping us
because they misunderstood why we were there.
They thought it was some kind of punishment
and we'd be allowed to go home after we finished digging the latrines, that's why they were
helping us and then when we stayed on they
figured we must be permanent outcasts or
something and they just stopped talking to us
altogether. Anyway, me and Jeff, the guy I
told you about, we figured maybe we could
salvage something from the fuckup so we got
a doctor to make a list of all the medicines
we'd need to start a kind of skeleton health
program in Ngleleland and we ordered the
medicine, pooled both our salaries for the two
years to pay for it. Paid for it. Waited. Never
came. So we went to the capitol to trace it and
found out this very funny thing. The Minister
of Health had confiscated it at the dock, same
man who got our team assigned to the Nglele
Tribal Territories in the first place. We were
furious, man, we stormed into his office and
started yelling at him. Turned out to be a real
nice guy. Educated in England, British accent
and everything. Had this office lined with sets
of Dickens and Thackeray all in leather bind-
ings. Unbelievable. Anyway, he said he
couldn't help us about the medicine, he'd been
acting on orders from higher up, which we
knew was bullshit, then he said he really admired our enthusiasm and our desire to help
his people but he wanted to know just out of
curiosity, if we'd managed to start the

medical program and save a thousand lives,
let's say, he wanted to know if we were prepared to feed and clothe those thousand people
for the next ten years, twenty years, however
long they lived. He made us feel so goddamned
naive, so totally helpless and unprepared powerless. We went out of there, got drunk, paid
the first women we could find and spent the
rest of the week fucking our brains out. And
then for the next year and two months we just
sat around in Ngleleland stoned out of our minds
counting off the days we had left before we
could go home. Anyway, since you asked,
that's what the Peace Corps was like.

SUSAN. Sounds pretty shitty.

PAUL. Well. At least now I speak fluent
Nglele. You never know when that'll come in
handy in Philadelphia.

SUSAN. You got another cigarette? (PAUL
finds his shirt, gets out cigarettes, lights two
of them.) I got this American newspaper yesterday, they sell 'em at that hotel by the market
place, they're about a week old but I just wanted
to read a newspaper. . . . It was so weird. I
took it back to the shack . . . Oh, we rented
this shack just down the beach . . . me and
Janice, she's the girl you saw me with . . .
(PAUL *hands cigarette to* SUSAN.) . . . thanks
. . . I should stop . . . anyway, I made a cup
of coffee and sat on the beach and read this
paper. And, you know, all the stories were out
of date and I didn't know what most of 'em
were about anyway because we've been traveling for over a month and I just started thinking,
you know, all this news could be from another
planet, you know what I mean, like is this stuff
they're writing about happening on the planet
earth because I live on earth, I'm sitting right
here, right on the earth and none of this stuff
is happening to me. I just thought of that while
you were talking. I don't know why. Do you
ever think about things like that? (PAUL *starts*
chuckling.) What? What are you laughing at?

PAUL. Nothing.

SUSAN. You do that a lot, you know.

PAUL. Do what?

SUSAN. You start laughing when something
isn't funny and when I ask you what you're
laughing at you say "nothing."

PAUL. It's just. I don't know. I was just
thinking I spent two years going through a lot
of very weird stuff but when I try to talk about
it it's just a story, just some stuff that happened
and now it's over. It doesn't mean anything
more.

SUSAN. That's not funny.

PAUL. No. No, it isn't.

SUSAN. You want me to tell you about something weird that happened to me? You know, that way we'll each have weird stories about each other.

PAUL. Sure. Go ahead.

SUSAN. O.K. When I was ten. No, eleven, I had my tonsils out and my dad was on a business trip, but I really wanted him to see my tonsils, so I made the doctor promise to put them in formaldehyde and I took them home. But they were real ugly and I decided I didn't want him to see them after all so I made a little fire in the backyard and said a few prayers and had a tonsil cremation and then I put the ashes in this vase on the mantelpiece. That was my big secret. It was really great because wherever I went I knew something that no one else knew and that seemed like something very important. I don't know why exactly. Then the maid cleaned the vase one day and that was that. Except that a year later the maid choked to death and they found two grapes lodged in her trachea, so I knew my tonsils had their revenge. I'm kidding. How long are you staying here?

PAUL. In Bali?

SUSAN. Yeah.

PAUL. I have a job that starts in two weeks.

SUSAN. Where?

PAUL. Philadelphia.

SUSAN. What kind of a job?

PAUL. Teaching English at this private school.

SUSAN. Is that what you're going to do? Teach English? I mean, you know, sort of forever?

PAUL. It's all I could get for now.

SUSAN. Do you know what you're going to do?

PAUL. When I grow up, you mean?

SUSAN. Yeah, you know.

PAUL. We'll see. What about you?

SUSAN. Oh, I don't know. I guess I'll travel with Janice for a while. Then I'll probably go home and do something or other that'll make me incredibly rich and respected and happy and fulfilled in every possible way and then, let's see, I'll move to the country and buy a little house with lots of stained glass and two cats, oh, and a solar heating panel and . . . and a servant called Lothar or something like that . . . I don't know.

PAUL. Sounds nice.

SUSAN. Want to go in again?

PAUL. Do you?

SUSAN. I asked first.

PAUL. Sure.

SUSAN. O.K.

(They stand, remove clothes.)

PAUL. Ready? One . . . two . . . three . . . *Go!* (PAUL *runs forward.* SUSAN *doesn't.* PAUL *stops, turns.* SUSAN *laughs.* PAUL *chases her down the beach, offstage. Shrieks, happy yelling.* SUSAN *runs back on.* PAUL *catches her. Tickle, kiss, passion. They roll on sand, kissing. Stop. Roll apart. They are full.)* This is incredible. Fucking incredible.

SUSAN. Listen, what do you think if . . . me and Janice made a pact that if anything happened while we were on this trip it was O.K. to split up and go on alone. And I like her, you know, she's a good friend, but she's into this whole thing about a guru she heard about in India, that's kind of how this trip started in the first place, but I like it right here and I was thinking maybe . . . I mean, if I told her to go on alone would you like to stay here for a while, see how things worked out and if it feels good maybe we could travel together, you know. Does that sound good? Paul?

PAUL. I have this job.

SUSAN. You didn't sound too enthusiastic about it.

PAUL. I'm not. That's not the point. I'm broke.

SUSAN. It doesn't cost anything to travel, you know. You can live for nothing if you do it right.

PAUL. Yeah, I guess so.

SUSAN. And I got a little saved up.

PAUL. I couldn't do that . . .

SUSAN. Why not? I mean, well, O.K. It's up to you.

PAUL. Is it? Yeah, I guess it is. I could just do it, couldn't I. I could just say fuck it. And I'd love to, jesus god would I ever love to. *(Pause.)* I don't believe this is happening. I really don't. *(They giggle.* PAUL *suddenly alert.)*

SUSAN. What's that?

PAUL. I heard something. *(They peer into darkness.)* Over there, look, someone's coming. There's a flashlight. *(They start dressing quickly.)* Hello! Hello! Who's there? *(Flashlight beam on them.)* Americans. We're Americans. Tourists. Who is it?

JANICE *(offstage).* Susan, is that you?

SUSAN. Shit.

PAUL. What's the matter?

SUSAN. It's Janice. My friend.

JANICE. Are you all right?

(Enter JANICE with flashlight.)

SUSAN. What are you doing?

JANICE. I just wondered what happened to you.

SUSAN. I went for a walk.

JANICE. I just got worried, that's all. You said you'd be back by five.

SUSAN. Things happened.

JANICE. Yeah, 'cause it's almost ten. I got worried.

SUSAN. This is Paul.

PAUL. Hi.

JANICE. Hi. So, are you coming back?

SUSAN. Janice, what's the matter with you?

JANICE. Someone was walking around outside the shack. I heard footsteps. I didn't want to stay back there. I mean a tourist did get killed here, you know.

PAUL. Wasn't that last year?

JANICE. The point is, it *can* happen.

PAUL. I thought I heard his wife killed him.

JANICE. Susan, I don't want to go back there alone. Those blue spiders are all over the place tonight. I tried to spray with a bug bomb, but it just makes the legs come off and they keep moving around. Please, Susan, I know it's a drag, I know we decided to be loose about the traveling, but I don't want to go back to that place by myself.

SUSAN. Can we talk about this later?

JANICE. Yes, I think we should do that, Susan.

SUSAN. Good night, Janice.

(JANICE *turns to go. Screams. Drops flashlight.*)

JANICE. Oh my God.

(They look. Nearby stands a BALINESE *holding a large fish.)*

SUSAN. Who's that?

(BALINESE *advances with a smile, holds the fish out.*)

BALINESE. *(Something in Balinese)*

JANICE. Oh, Jesus, it's him again.

SUSAN. Who?

JANICE. He's been following me around all day. He was in the marketplace. What do you want?

BALINESE. *(Something in Balinese)*

JANICE. I don't understand you. I don't speak your language. Please go away.

PAUL. Is that fish for us?

BALINESE. *(Something in Balinese)*

PAUL. Are you trying to sell the fish? You want money? Dollars. Dollars?

(PAUL *goes toward* BALINESE *reaching into pocket for money.* BALINESE *backs away and holds fish from him.*)

BALINESE. *(Something in Balinese)*

PAUL. O.K., O.K., take it easy.

(BALINESE *kneels before* JANICE *and proffers fish.*)

BALINESE. *(Something in Balinese)*

JANICE *(pause)*. Let's just buy the fish, O.K.?

SUSAN. What are we gonna do with a fish. We don't even have a place to cook it.

JANICE. We'll make a fire on the beach, I don't care. Let's just get rid of him.

PAUL. I think I read somewhere the Balinese offer a fish when they're in love. Seriously, I think he's proposing marriage.

JANICE. O.K., mister, look, I've had enough of this. Get up. I'll buy your fish, O.K. Buy. Money. Then you go away and leave me alone. Do you understand me. Comprenez? Shit.

BALINESE. *(Something in Balinese)*

JANICE. You go away. Away. You go away.

BALINESE. Ooo gow weh.

JANICE. Here. (JANICE *hands money to* BALINESE *and takes fish.*) . . . Now you go. Go. (BALINESE *backs away, then stands watching.*) No. Go all the way. Go completely away. All the way. (BALINESE *backs away into the night.*)

PAUL. He's gone.

JANICE. No he's not. He's just waiting out there. As soon as we start back he'll follow us.

SUSAN. Janice, I wish you'd cool it.

JANICE. I'm telling you, he's been after me all day.

SUSAN. All right, all right. He's gone now.

JANICE. Are you coming back?

SUSAN. Yes, I'm coming back. In a few minutes.

JANICE. It's really great to find out who your friends are. *(exits)*

PAUL. Good night . . .

SUSAN. Oh, man she is crazy. I mean I knew she could get a little weird sometimes, but this is ridiculous. This is a mistake. This trip is definitely a mistake.

PAUL. She seems O.K.

SUSAN. You don't have to travel with her. Do you have another cigarette? (PAUL *lights one for her.*) I was feeling so good. Was that really true about the fish?

PAUL. No.

SUSAN *(laughs)*. I like you.

PAUL. You have a pen?

SUSAN. What for?

PAUL. Get your address. Maybe I'll see you back in the States.

SUSAN. But I thought . . . ?

PAUL. I can't. I mean, yeah, sure, I could.

I could. But I can't. It's ridiculous. I mean, look at what I have after two years. A bunch of stories and a ticket home. I have to do something now. You know, where I end up with something I can . . . something that doesn't just go away, you know what I mean?

SUSAN. Hey, that's O.K. You don't have to explain it. I had a good time.

PAUL. Yeah.

SUSAN. You want to come back to the shack? I got a pen there. You can stay tonight if you want, there's room.

PAUL. I have to confirm a flight back at the hotel.

SUSAN. You're staying at the hotel?

PAUL. After two years in Ngleleland, are you kidding?

SUSAN. Does it have a shower? I got sand everywhere.

PAUL. Want to come back?

SUSAN. If it's O.K.

PAUL. Sure.

(They start out. SUSAN *stops.)*

SUSAN. Shit.

PAUL. What's the matter?

SUSAN. I can't leave her alone. Janice, jesus. Look, I'll tell you what. Why don't I meet you at the hotel tomorrow. We could rent a couple of bikes and go out to the mountains . . .

PAUL. I'm leaving in the morning.

SUSAN. Oh. You didn't say. O.K. Well, I'm in the Denver phone book. Steen. That's two ees. We're the only Steens. That's my family.

PAUL. O.K., Susan Steen. Two ees.

SUSAN. What's your last name?

PAUL. Baumer.

SUSAN. Paul Baumer.

PAUL. Right.

SUSAN. So. Maybe I'll see you.

PAUL. O.K. Take it easy.

*(*PAUL *and* SUSAN *stand for a moment. They exit in opposite directions. Fade.)*

SCENE TWO

Slide: 1971 DOUG *and* MARAYA's *yard. Noon. On one side of stage rear end of a shingle covered trailer home on cinderblocks. Some shingles have fallen off and you can see painted metal beneath. There is a window in rear end. At other side of stage is nearly completed 2 x 4 frame for part of house. Tools, etc.* DOUG *and* PAUL, *stripped to waist, working on frame.*

DOUG. Listen, man, I've been there, you

don't have to tell me about horny. Shit, when I found out ole Maraya was pregnant with baby-Jake I got a hard on—wouldn't go down for six months. Everything got me off and I mean everything. Even ole Doofus the dog. Even looking at flowers.

PAUL. Well, what I was . . .

DOUG. Man, there was this one time it was raining and I was walking home from the swimming hole and I just started thinking wow, this rain reminds me of Maraya's big ole tummy. Don't ask me why. And before I knew what I was doing there I was standing in the rain, standing, man, holding my pecker in my hand, pumping away just like I was in the shower or something, I don't know. This dude came driving right by, I didn't give a shit, nothing was gonna stop me. He gets about fifty yards down the road and hits the brakes, tires screeching all over the place when he realizes he's just seen a sex maniac whacking off in the rain. I'm telling you, man, when the feeling hits you like that, fuck holding back, right.

PAUL. Yeah, but the thing is . . .

DOUG. I don't know. Maybe I'm just getting weird living up here. I'm not saying I'd ever go back to the city, ungh-uh, you can have that shit, but still . . . (PAUL *hands him piece of 2 x 4.*) What's this one for? Oh, yeah, Damn, I interrupted you again. I *am* getting weird, I'm telling you. Cisco came up here a couple weeks ago, stayed for two days, I couldn't stop talking. Nobody up here talks. How do I seem?

PAUL. What do you mean?

DOUG. Since the last time you saw me. Do I seem any weirder?

PAUL. No.

DOUG. You do.

PAUL. What do you mean?

DOUG. I don't know. So you're walking on this beach in Bali and you see this chick, right?

PAUL. Well, you know, we started talking and it felt really good. I mean after two years in Africa it felt really good to be talking to someone again . . .

DOUG. So you whipped out the big boy and shagged her on the beach.

PAUL. Douglas, you have a mind like a sewer, you know that.

DOUG. You didn't fuck her? You mean I been listening to all this shit for nothing?

PAUL. You haven't been listening, you've been talking the whole time.

DOUG. O.K., you got five minutes to get to the fuck or I'm quitting for lunch.

PAUL. You want to hear this or not?

DOUG. Shit, man, she really got to you, huh?

PAUL. I guess you could say that.

DOUG. And I did. So it's real serious, huh?

PAUL. Well, you know, for now. What do you want me to say?

DOUG. You don't know if it's serious?

PAUL. We'll see.

DOUG. O.K., you go to bed at night sometimes and you lie there together but you don't feel like you *have* to fuck before you go to sleep, right.

PAUL. What are you talking about?

DOUG. Just answer me, does that ever happen?

PAUL. Sure, sometimes.

DOUG. Then it's serious. So you fucked her on the beach. Hey, O.K., I'm sorry, what happened?

PAUL. I've been trying to tell you.

DOUG. Well, I been waiting for it to get interesting. I can't help it if you don't know how to tell a story.

PAUL. O.K., look, the school closed . . .

DOUG. What school . . .

PAUL. Doug!

DOUG. What school? You didn't say anything about a school.

PAUL. Philadelphia. Where you wrote me that time?

DOUG. Oh, yeah. How come it closed?

PAUL. Oh, you know, it was one of those experimental places, develop the inner person, that kind of shit. Anyway, the parents must've got wise or something 'cause the school ran out of money halfway through the year and they had to close down. So there's me out of a job, nothing to do, so I got a bus up to Boston to check out a few possibilities and she was on the bus.

DOUG. You're shitting?

PAUL. I swear. I couldn't believe it.

DOUG. You didn't even know she was back in America? That's really far out. I mean that's definitely in the land of spooky events.

PAUL. Well, actually, I left out the part where I called her family in Denver and found out she was living in Boston.

DOUG. Why you little devil.

PAUL. I mean I wasn't sure I was going to try to look her up or anything. In fact I had a little thing going in Philadelphia and I wasn't even sure I wanted to leave.

DOUG. Listen.

PAUL. What?

DOUG. She's real cute. I like her. Really. And I want to get back to the part where you fucked on the beach. And I want a sandwich. You want a sandwich?

PAUL. You're never gonna get this house built.

DOUG. Fuck the house, man, I'm hungry. *(calls) Maraya!*

(MARAYA *appears in rear window of trailer.*)

MARAYA. What do you want?

DOUG. What's for food? We're getting hungry.

MARAYA. It's not ready yet.

DOUG. How 'bout a couple of beers?

MARAYA. Get 'em yourself, I'm not your waitress.

DOUG. I won't build your house. (MARAYA *withdraws her head.*) Want a beer?

PAUL. Sure

(DOUG *goes toward the trailer, passes* SUSAN *who is coming out. She has a camera over shoulder. She is eating an apple.*)

DOUG. Beer my dear?

SUSAN. Lunch is coming in a minute.

DOUG. There goes that darn Doug, ruining his appetite again.

(DOUG *goes into trailer.* SUSAN *comes to* PAUL.)

SUSAN. How's it coming?

PAUL. Pretty slow.

SUSAN. Maraya told me about this waterfall where you can go swimming. It's only about a mile. You want to go after lunch?

PAUL. Come here.

SUSAN. What?

PAUL. I want to go right now.

SUSAN. You want to go after lunch.

PAUL. Sure.

SUSAN. It's nice here.

PAUL. Do you like them?

SUSAN. Yeah. Maraya's a little weird with that baby, but I like them.

PAUL. Are you O.K.?

SUSAN. Sure.

PAUL. You seem a little, I don't know . . . something or other.

SUSAN. I always am a little something or other.

PAUL. Am I supposed to leave it alone? Am I supposed to not push it?

SUSAN. Babe, I'm fine, really.

PAUL. O.K. It's just, sometimes I'm not sure how you're feeling, that's all.

SUSAN. Don't worry about it.

PAUL. In other words, something's on your mind but you don't feel like talking about it right now?

SUSAN. It's nothing, really. I'm fine. Let's

change the subject.

PAUL. O.K.

SUSAN. We'll talk about it later.

PAUL. O.K.

(DOUG *comes from trailer with three beers.*)

DOUG. Maraya wants to know, lunch out here or in the west wing?

PAUL. Out here's fine.

DOUG. Did I interrupt something?

PAUL. No, no.

DOUG *(yells). Out here, and hurry up, I gotta go get that battery for the truck.*

MARAYA *(offstage, yells). It'll be there when it's ready.*

DOUG. I'm gonna haveta start whuppin' that woman if she don't behave herself better. (DOUG *sits by* PAUL.) How come you didn't finish the house? (*Apple in mouth,* SUSAN *backs away and takes pictures of* PAUL *and* DOUG *together.* DOUG *clowns.*)

SUSAN. Hey, come on, just relax, I want to get you two together. Just act natural.

DOUG *(in a weird pose).* I'm stuck, I can't move.

SUSAN. Doug. (DOUG *relaxes.*) O.K., now move a little closer.

DOUG *(moves closer).* Don't get fresh.

(Enter MARAYA *from trailer carrying baby-*JAKE *in one arm and balancing a plate of sandwiches with her free hand. She sees what's going on and stops, talks to baby-*JAKE.*)*

MARAYA. Look, honey, they're taking pictures, see? That little thing she's holding goes click and that makes a picture and then you have something to look at so you can remember how it used to be. Done?

SUSAN. Yeah.

(SUSAN *shoulders camera.* MARAYA *sets plate down.*)

MARAYA. O.K., troops, dig in.

baby-JAKE *(cries).* (MARAYA *takes out breast and feeds baby-*JAKE.*)

SUSAN. How much did you pay for this place?

DOUG. Fifteen. It's eleven acres. Goes right down to the bluestone quarry in back and then over the woods that way. Be worth about sixty–seventy when the house is finished and you figure inflation. You guys looking for something.

SUSAN. I was just wondering. It's nice up here.

DOUG. Listen, there's a place coming on the market soon, no one knows about it yet, state land on three sides so no one can build. I'll check it out for you if you're interested. It'd be great if you guys moved up here. Want me

to check it out?

MARAYA *(to baby-*JAKE*).* Ouch, honey, you're biting really hard, you know. You shouldn't do that 'cause it just makes my nipples sore and I get all tense and that stops the milk from flowing and you'll just get angrier. It's a vicious circle.

DOUG. You want me to check out that land?

PAUL *(to* SUSAN*).* What do you think?

SUSAN. I don't know. You want to?

PAUL. Do you?

SUSAN. I asked first.

PAUL *(to* DOUG*).* Sure. Why not?

DOUG. Hot damn, all right, you got it. This afternoon. Shit, I gotta get that batter. *(stands)* Who's coming to town? *(no one moves)* Gee, I don't know if I'll have room for all of you.

PAUL. We're going to the waterfall.

DOUG. The waterfall, eh. We all know what happens at the waterfall, ho-ho. How 'bout you, Marsie, want to come to town?

MARAYA. I gotta do some stuff. Can you get me some smokes? Two packs. I'm trying to cut down, that's for all week. They say you can taste it in the milk, but I think that's bullshit. You can't taste it, can you honey? No, of course not.

DOUG *(to* PAUL*).* Give me a push down the hill, wouldya. (PAUL *and* DOUG *exit*)

SUSAN. Do you mind if I take a few pictures?

MARAYA. No, that'd be great.

SUSAN. Just stay like that. Don't worry about anything. (SUSAN *takes pictures*)

MARAYA. Hey, I really like that thing you gave us with the guy dancing.

SUSAN. Oh, right. I got 'em in Tibet. It's a woodcut on silk.

MARAYA. Did you buy a lot of 'em? I bet you could sell 'em.

SUSAN. That's what I did. Sold about a hundred of them. They only cost like a dollar each in Tibet.

MARAYA. How much you get for 'em, if you don't mind my asking?

SUSAN. Twenty-five.

MARAYA. Far out.

SUSAN. Yeah, that's how I got all this camera stuff. I went on a real splurge. Hold that, yeah, like that, that's nice.

MARAYA. Oww, shit Jake, you're getting obnoxious, come on. Hold still. She's taking our picture.

SUSAN. Why don't you try the other one?

MARAYA. What other one? Oh. (MARAYA *gives baby-*JAKE *the other teat*) Is that kind of a serious trip, the photography?

SUSAN. Oh, I don't know. I enjoy it.

MARAYA. You're taking a lot of pictures, is why I asked. Hey, this is a lot better, you know. He's not biting. I can't wait'll he can talk. It's weird 'cause you know he's got a lotta stuff on his mind, you can tell he's thinking about things all the time, but you can't ask him about it. It's really frustrating. Are you gonna have kids?

SUSAN. Probably. Someday. I don't know.

MARAYA. You should have 'em pretty soon though. They come out healthier when you have 'em young and if you wait too long you might get a mutation. You'd probably be a good mother.

SUSAN. Why do you say that?

MARAYA. I don't know, just a feeling. Like how you knew about changing the breast. *(pause)* You guys living together?

SUSAN. We're getting a place back in Boston this fall. Supposedly.

MARAYA. You sound sort of like you're not too sure.

SUSAN. Oh, you know. If we do, we do, if we don't we don't.

MARAYA. I know what you mean. (SUSAN *is looking at* MARAYA) What are you looking at?

SUSAN. Did you know a lot of guys before Doug?

MARAYA. Oh yeah, a lot. Well, a medium lot. I mean compared to some of my friends it wasn't hardly any, but compared to some of my other friends it was more than them.

SUSAN. Was it strange at first? Being with just one guy?

MARAYA. Well, I like Doug, you know. I mean he's not the easiest guy in the world, but then again he says I'm not all that great either. I guess it's how you look at it.

SUSAN. But did you? . . . Like we decided we'd get this place together, right, but then when I thought about it . . . I don't know, you go through this whole number in your head, like are you really ready for this? Is this what you really want? . . .

MARAYA. Try it out. What can you lose. You know, if it doesn't work, you split.

SUSAN. No, what I mean is . . . I thought this was supposed to happen a lot later . . . living with someone. You know how there's things you're gonna do now and thing you're gonna do later and living with someone was definitely supposed to be a later. But now I feel like really O.K. about it. I want to try it.

MARAYA. So tell him.

SUSAN. I already have. After five times. He

always says "yeah, great" and then he never does anything about it. I remember this one week I even left newspapers around his apartment, you know, open to the classified . . . apartments for rent. Really. You see yourself doing this stuff and you don't believe it's you. And like now, we're travelling around meeting all of his friends, right? And everyone wants to know where it's at with us and it's weird because I just don't know. I don't know. And I don't want to keep pushing him, either. I always hate it when people do that to me. I mean that's one of the thing I really like about Paul. He always knows when to back off, but sometimes he's like so blasé you just want to strangle him. Shit. Listen to me. I'm making it sound like some kind of big deal. I don't even know why I brought it up.

MARAYA. That's O.K. Look, I'll tell you how I think about it. If you want something, you ask for it. The worst thing that can happen is the guy says no and I'm used to that so it's O.K. and then sometimes he says yes and then you feel really good.

SUSAN. Don't say anything to Paul, O.K.?

MARAYA. My lips are sealed. Hey, Jakeypoo, you like that, don't you? That's nice, yes, nice. You can always tell when he's enjoying it from how he sucks. It's funny, it even turns me on sometimes. Really. I love sex. Sometimes when I really depressed I think "how bad can it be if there's still sex?" *(Truck motor coughing to life offstage)* Yea truck! They got the truck started, honey. Go "Yea truck!" He could care less. Are you O.K.?

SUSAN. Sure. *(goes back to loading camera)*

PAUL *(returns sweaty)*. O.K., who's for the waterfall? I gotta cool off.

MARAYA. Do you have a cigarette?

(PAUL *gets them out. Lights one for* MARAYA.)

MARAYA. . . . Phew, Jake, you really stink. I swear, sometimes I think this kid borrows shit from somewhere. We don't feed him half of what comes out of him.

SUSAN. You want to come to the waterfall?

MARAYA. Can you just wait while I change the baby . . . maybe I better just put him to bed. Maybe I'll catch up with you later. (MARAYA *starts off*)

PAUL. Hey, your cigarette.

MARAYA. Oh, thanks. I gotta stop, I really do.

(MARAYA *exits into trailer, puffing.*)

PAUL. You ready?

SUSAN. Sure.

PAUL. O.K., let's go (SUSAN *gets up, points*

camera somewhere.) Susan . . .

SUSAN. What?

PAUL. I want to talk.

SUSAN. Stay like that for a second. C'mon, don't look so serious. We'll talk at the waterfall. (SUSAN *takes a few shots.*) O.K., let's go. *(exits, off)* You coming?

(PAUL *looks after her, follows. Fade.*)

SCENE THREE

Slide: 1973 Backyard of PAUL *and* SUSAN's *apartment house. Children's swing and wrought-iron filigree table and chairs painted white but rusting. Low picket fence and gate.* SUSAN *organizes masses of small photos into rows on 4 x 8 panel, which lies flat on the wrought-iron table. One complete board leans against frame of swing. Transistor cassette on ground plays Shubert's Trout Quintet, Third Movement, Scherzo. Hold on* SUSAN *at work for a moment. Then, through gate, enter* BEN BAUMER *36, in seersucker suit, jacket over shoulder, tie undone, paper bag in one hand. He stops and watches for a moment.*

BEN. Susan?

SUSAN. Hi. You found us.

BEN. Oh yeah. You give a mean set of directions. Didn't get lost once. I'm parked right in front, is that O.K.?

SUSAN. Sure. Hang on a second. (SUSAN *turns off the cassette.*) So. You're Ben.

BEN. Always was, always will be.

SUSAN. Well, it's nice to meet you at last.

BEN. Same to you. And everything you've heard about me is true.

SUSAN. I was expecting a mustache.

BEN. Oh, that. Shaved it off years ago. Paul told you about the mustache, eh?

SUSAN. No, in the picture.

BEN. No kidding. Funny, I don't remember any pictures with a mustache. I only had it a few months.

SUSAN. It's three couples on a beach.

BEN. Oh, God, no. Not the naked one.

SUSAN. It's a great picture. We put it on the bureau.

BEN. Well, god darn! That little so and so! Wouldn't you know it. I have a hundred great pictures of myself and wouldn't you know he'd pick that one. What can you do? The whole family's crazy. Say, where is the little stinker anyway?

SUSAN. Who? Oh, you mean Paul. He's still

at the editing room.

BEN. Editing room? What's that all about?

SUSAN. He's editing film. Well, he's learning.

BEN. I thought he was teaching.

SUSAN. He was. Now he's editing film.

BEN. You're trying to tell me he's editing film, right?

SUSAN. Right.

BEN. Well, you live and learn. He never said anything about it.

SUSAN. Can I get you anything . . . beer, Coke . . .

BEN. Leave the liquid refreshments to me.

(BEN *takes champagne and paper cups from bag.*)

SUSAN. What's that for?

BEN. *Celebrazzione.*

SUSAN. Shouldn't we wait for Paul?

BEN. No, I got some cheap stuff for him. This is for us. The real thing, a little Dom Pergweenon. Chilled. Just got it in Cambridge.

SUSAN. What's the occasion?

BEN. Hahahaha. Just you wait, Mrs. Higgins, just you wait. *(twist cork)* Hold your nose and wiggle your toes. *(cork pops)* Ahhh, thank you. I needed that. O.K., one for you, one for me, quick, quick . . . waste not want not . . . a little more for you . . . a lot more for me . . . perfecto. O.K., here's glue in your shoe. *(They drink.)* I'll tell you something. My little brother is a real so and so. He doesn't deserve a beautiful girl like you, and that's my humble opinion. I'll tell you what. Why don't you and me catch the next flight to London before he gets home?

SUSAN. Why London?

BEN. I thought you'd never ask. I got the job.

SUSAN. Oh.

BEN. The job. The London job. He told you about the job, didn't he?

SUSAN. I don't think so.

BEN. He didn't mention anything about . . .

SUSAN. He probably just forgot to tell me. We've had a lot of stuff going on.

BEN. Yeah. Well, I guess it's just not that important. Can't imagine how I got excited about it in the first place.

SUSAN. What is it? Tell me.

BEN. It's only a little matter of opening a multi-million dollar European opeation which I'm in charge of. In fact, I created the idea. He did tell you I was in securities?

SUSAN. He said you were a salesman.

BEN. Near enough. Refill?

SUSAN. I'm fine.

(BEN *pours for himself.*)

BEN. No, you see Randle & Lane, that's my company, they've been kind of conservative on overseas markets so I doped out a whole campaign, did a little presentation and they liked it. They liked it a lot. So now I'm in charge of setting the whole thing up. Europe.

SUSAN. That sounds fantastic.

BEN. Listen to this. Sixty thousand a year basic plus commission. Free car. Six-week vacation a year. Five-room apartment overlooking jolly old Hyde Park. And the girls in London! I mean talk about yummy! All you want to do is tear the wrappers off and lick 'em to death, I swear.

SUSAN. Aren't you married?

BEN. Yep. Ten years. Great lady, the best. *(drains cup)* Little more?

SUSAN. I'm O.K.

(BEN *pours for himself. Looks at* SUSAN's *work.*)

BEN. What's all this?

SUSAN. You like it?

BEN. Very nice. Very nice.

SUSAN. I'm serious. Do you really like it?

BEN. Absolutely. It's . . . different. You work for a photographer?

SUSAN. I *am* a photographer.

BEN. Oh, I'll be darned. So this is your stuff, huh? What do you sell it or is it a sort of a hobby or what?

SUSAN. I've sold a few. I might be having an exhibit next month. There's a guy that's interested. Just local but . . . gotta start somewhere.

PAUL *(voice, off, as from second floor window).* What's going on out there?

BEN. Hey, guy . . .

SUSAN. Hi, sweetie.

BEN. Get your rusty butt down here.

PAUL *(off).* Be right down.

SUSAN *(pause).* Listen, congratulations on the job.

BEN. Oh, thank you. Thank you very much. And, ah, fingers crossed for your exhibit. And you never know the way things catch on. There was that movie a couple years ago about surfing. A guy just went out and took a lot of film, just people surfing. Darn movie made him a fortune. You never know.

(PAUL *enters through gate.*)

PAUL. Hi Ben.

BEN. Hey, guy, look at you. *(They stand awkwardly.)* You're just in time for a little warm champagne. (PAUL *kisses* SUSAN *hello.*)

PAUL. Hi, babe, how's it going?

SUSAN. O.K. The panel . . .

PAUL. Looks good.

SUSAN. It's coming. You're back early.

(Enter through gate SELINA, *very beautiful Chinese-American. Totally American manner and accent.)*

PAUL. Yeah, the lab fucked up the film again so there's nothing to edit. They gave us the afternoon off.

(BEN *is watching* SELINA.)

BEN. Can I help you?

SUSAN. Hi Soolie . . .

PAUL. Oh, Selina, this is my brother Ben. This is Selina. She works in the editing room.

BEN. Ah, so that's why he stopped teaching.

SELINA. Excuse me?

PAUL. Soolie wanted to see some of the panels.

SELINA. I didn't know you had company. I'll stop by tomorrow.

SUSAN. Why don't you stay for dinner? Please. I want to show you one of the panels It still doesn't feel right.

SELINA. How many panels are you going to have?

SUSAN. Twenty, I think.

SELINA. Twenty, wow.

SUSAN. Well, I have like over a thousand pictures, right? I set the timer for once every fiften seconds and the wedding was about nine hours. Figure it out.

BEN *(at panel).* This is a wedding? I thought it was one of those you know, what do you call it . . . a happening . . .

SELINA. It was beautiful. That farm is perfect. If they ever want to sell it, let me know. I really love New Hampshire. Listen, I was thinking, you know, you could maybe try a series with the camera going around in a circle. You know. Time the shutter to the motor and you'd see the background changing a little in each picutre.

SUSAN. I've thought about that, but I really like it to be one background—just one space and everything that happens in it so you have a reference point. You know, Space portrait. That's what it is. A portrait of one space.

SELINA. You could call it Circular Space Portrait. I don't know. I was just thinking.

PAUL. Can I say something?

SUSAN. What?

PAUL. You're going up? With Soolie? To look at a panel?

SUSAN. Yeah.

PAUL. If you find yourself anywhere near

the fridge . . .

SUSAN. Two beers?

BEN. What? Oh, sure.

(SUSAN *and* SELINA *start to go.*)

SELINA *(to* BEN*).* Nice to meet you.

BEN. Well, I hope there's more to come.

SELINA. Excuse me?

PAUL. Never mind.

(SUSAN *and* SELINA *exit, talking.*)

SELINA. Avra's really sorry she missed the wedding. She has this great present for you guys. She wants to know when she can come over with it . . .

SUSAN. What is it?

SELINA. She made me promise not to tell.

(They are gone.)

PAUL. So, d'you drive up?

BEN. Wait a minute. Wait just a minute. I probably heard this wrong. Did that Oriental sweetie say something about a present for you? A wedding present?

PAUL. Oh, yeah, Avra. She wanted to watch Watergate so she missed the wedding. Avra's really strange.

BEN. Whose wedding?

PAUL. I was coming to that.

BEN. You're married?

PAUL. Yeah.

BEN. Well, surprise, surprise. When did this happen?

PAUL. Last weekend.

BEN. Gee, guy, excuse me for being a little surprised, here. I mean I talked to Mom on the phone yesterday and she didn't say anything about it. I suppose you didn't tell her, either.

PAUL. Not yet.

BEN. Jesus Christ, Paul, what is it with you?

PAUL. Is this going to be a lecture?

BEN. But your own mother.

PAUL. Did you tell Mom about you and Marlene splitting up? Did you tell her Marlene had enough of your drinking and fucking around and doesn't want to come to London with you if you get that job?

BEN. I got it.

PAUL. Congratulations. Did you tell Mom?

BEN. Of course I told her. I told her the moment I knew.

PAUL. But you didn't tell her about Marlene. Gee, Ben, are you trying to keep things from Mom?

BEN. Don't be a wise-ass.

PAUL. All right, then, don't start in about our duties to Mom. I'm not interested in this game you're trying to play about the two won-derboys living a great life, making their little fortunes, raising happy little families. What's the point? She's sitting there in Seattle bleeding Dad for all the alimony she can and dumping it into that ridiculous Ecole de Beauté she runs. I mean, come on, Ben. What's that got to do with my life?

BEN. I don't get it. Same family, same house, but I swear to God there's Chinamen I understand better than I understand you.

PAUL. I noticed. Look. Me and Susan . . . we've been together for like two years . . . more. It's working out real good, so . . . and if we pay joint taxes it'll be better for both of us and . . . well, she needed to get a lot of people together for this Space Portrait she had in mind and we thought a wedding was a great idea. And we happen to love each other. So. And we didn't really dig the idea of a lot of relatives crying their ass off at the beauty of it all and shoving Waring blenders and matched dinnerware down our throat, that's all. O.K.

BEN. No, it's not O.K. because that's not what I'm talking about and you know it.

PAUL *(exploding).* How the fuck am I supposed to know what you're talking about? I haven't seen you for three years and I never understood you back then anyway. I just told you why I got married and why I didn't tell Mother. Now if that isn't what we're talking about, suppose you tell me just what the fuck we are talking about.

BEN. O.K., let's calm down.

PAUL. I'm calm. I'm calm. What? Tell me. What are we talking about?

BEN. Look. I know what you're going to say, but just listen to me and let me finish, O.K. I'm going to have a lot of contacts with this job, very important contacts . . .

PAUL. Forget it . . .

BEN. Just shut up a second. You've got fantastic qualifications . . . your background in the Peace Corps, your honors in college. They look at that résumé and it looks good. It looks good and then they get to these years and what do they see? A little teaching here, a little what is it? Film editing . . . a little of that . . . And they want to know what was going on. Believe me, Paul, you can go anywhere you want from here, but you can't keep faffing around forever.

PAUL. Well, then I'd just better get my act together lickety-split or I'll miss my golden opportunity to sell securities, whatever they are.

BEN. I'm not talking about selling securities. I'm talking about diplomatic work, travel, foreign relations, all the stuff you were interested in in college.

PAUL. That was a long time ago.

BEN. O.K., look, Paul, I understand, you're going through something.

PAUL. Oh. What am I going through?

BEN. Well, don't ask me for Christ sake, that's what I'd like to know. That's what we'd all like to know.

PAUL. All? Suddenly I'm so important. But what am I going through? You said you understood that I was going through something and I was just real curious to know what that was because I keep thinking of it as my life, but you seem to be anxious for me to get over it or through it or whatever.

BEN. I'm talking about . . .

PAUL. I know what you're talking about, but your arrogance just, I don't know, I just can't believe it sometimes. You come to me with your life in a shambles . . . Oh, oh yeah, I know you got a great new job, but I'm not talking about your job. I'm talking about your life, Big Ben, your life. I have a little job. I like it. I know it doesn't take full advantage of my fluency in Nglele, I know it might raise questions about whatever happened to somebody or other everybody seems to have thought I was, but that's . . . never mind. The point is, I'm happy. I have food in the ice box. When I'm hungry I go there and eat. I have a little money in the bank. Not too much, but enough; and it's more than many. There's someone in bed next to me. I'm not lonely. That's my life, Ben, that's all I want, just a home, Susan, some kids, just what I can see and touch. Do you understand what I'm saying? All the other stuff was and is and will be bullshit forever and evermore, amen. I'm happy. And this seems to worry you.

BEN. I'm not worried. I didn't say I was worried.

PAUL. Good for you.

BEN. Look, what are we fighting for? I haven't seen you for four years. Truce, huh? What do you say? Let me buy you guys dinner. We'll go out to the snazziest goddamn restaur . . .

PAUL. Susan's cooking.

BEN. Come on, give the little lady a break, huh? What do you say? My treat . . .

PAUL. We got food in. Some friends are coming over. We planned a big dinner for you. You don't have to impress us, Ben.

(BEN *takes a swig of champagne.*)

BEN. It's not final you know. Me and Marlene. We're taking a year to think it over.

There's the kids.

(BEN *pours himself more champagne.*)

PAUL. Why don't you hold off on that stuff 'til dinner. We got some nice wine.

BEN. What this? This is nothing. Carbonated French piss. So you're married.

PAUL. Yep.

BEN. Damn. *(long pause)* Hey, how come there aren't ice cubes in Poland?

PAUL. Oh, jesus, Ben not now.

BEN. No, this is a good one. You know why?

PAUL. Why?

BEN. I thought you'd never ask. The lady with the recipe died. (BEN *laughs.* PAUL *laughs sadly at* BEN. BEN *thinks he's got* PAUL *with him.*) The lady died . . . dumb, huh? O.K., there's this convention of astronauts . . . this is a quickie . . . they're from all over the world . . . (SUSAN *enters with two beers. Gives* BEN *one.*) Thank you little milkmaid.

SUSAN *(walking away).* It's beer.

BEN. What? Oh, oh, so it is, so it is. Well then, thank you little beermaid . . .

(SUSAN *hands* PAUL *beer and starts out.*)

PAUL. Hey.

SUSAN. What?

PAUL. Come here. (SUSAN *does.*) What's going on up there?

SUSAN. Soolie's making a call. I'm just starting dinner.

PAUL. Want a hand?

SUSAN. It's all under control. She's just calling the gallery.

PAUL. O.K. (SUSAN *starts out.*) Wait a minute. What do you mean she's calling the gallery?

SUSAN. She knows the guy. I mean, like real well. She's gonna get him to come over later. She thinks he'll give me my own show when he sees the new stuff.

PAUL. Serious?

SUSAN. Yeah.

PAUL. Well, I mean, how come you're so calm? Isn't this sort of woopie-hooray-fucking incredible?

SUSAN. Yeah. I'm a genius. I gotta start the potatoes.

PAUL. Babe!

(They embrace, kiss. BEN *stands awkwardly, wanders. Blackout.)*

SCENE FOUR

Slide: 1974 PAUL *and* SUSAN's *living room. Easy chair. Couch. Worn Indian rug. Bricks 'n' boards bookcase. On couch sit* JANICE *and*

RUSSELL. *They wear loose fitting Indian mystic style garments.* PAUL *sits in easy chair, a pile of papers by his feet.*

————

JANICE. Remember, this is a dream I'm talking about. Russell dreamed this. Anyway, then what was it? The girl climbed on the back of this huge white bird . . .

RUSSELL. Swan.

JANICE. Oh yeah right. The bird was a swan and he described this girl and it was a perfect description of Susan who he's never seen a picture of, O.K.? But every detail. And that was on Sunday night which was the same night you said Susan flew to New York. Now, I think that's more than a coincidence.

PAUL. She didn't fly. She took a Greyhound bus.

JANICE. Oh, I thought you said she flew.

RUSSELL. Swan. Greyhound. Animals. Travel. Animals carrying people to new places.

JANICE. And here's the amazing part. The swan put her down and she took out all these pictures out of a case she was carrying and started putting them up on these tall tall buildings and you say Susan's in New York putting up an exhibition of her photography. Russell dreamed this.

PAUL. You sure you don't want a beer or something?

RUSSELL. No alcohol.

PAUL. Oh yeah, I forgot.

RUSSELL. We'll take food later. Thank you.

JANICE. No, but you see what I mean?

PAUL. Well, I'm sorry she's not here.

RUSSELL. No problem.

(They sit for a moment.)

PAUL. If you say you might pass through New York I could give you her number there. You did say you might pass through New York, right?

RUSSELL. Yes.

PAUL. O.K. Well, I'll give you her number. I'll write it down. *(starts writing)* So, you two met in India, huh?

RUSSELL. Yes.

PAUL. That must've been interesting.

RUSSELL. It was.

PAUL. Was it?

RUSSELL. Yes.

PAUL. How? In what way was it interesting?

RUSSELL *(thinks)*. Have you been to India?

PAUL. No.

RUSSELL. You should go.

PAUL. Why?

RUSSELL. Different trip. Very different.

JANICE. We used to have these meetings in the ashram where Master would answer questions and . . . he's read a lot of Western literature and he can explain things in a very clear way. He's very modern in a lot of ways . . .

RUSSELL. He's trained in a very ancient tradition.

JANICE. Yeah, the tradition is ancient. I'm not saying about the tradition. I mean as far as that goes I'm not even sure they know how far back—I mean it's one of the oldest schools, right? But when he explains things you just feel he's talking to you, right now, today. Don't you think so, Russ?

RUSSELL. Yes.

JANICE. Yeah, you see, that's really what I mean, like even outside the meetings there was this incredible energy everywhere in the ashram—all kinds of different energy at different levels, spiritual, psychic, sexual, oh but let me give you an example of the kind of stuff Master could get into. Like remember I told you that . . . oh, I didn't tell you this, O.K., they had this war India and Pakistan, about something and Master made the whole ashram, all the buildings and everything, he made it invisible from the air so the bombers couldn't see where . . .

RUSSELL. Jan. (JANICE *stop immediately.*) Certain times, certain ideas.

JANICE. I was only. I just meant . . .

(RUSSELL smiles. JANICE *smiles back weakly.* RUSSELL *takes her hand. She is reassured.)*

PAUL. Here's the number.

(Enter SELINA from the kitchen.)

SELINA. I can't find that pole thing for the middle of the coffee pot.

PAUL. I'll get it.

(PAUL exits into kitchen. SELINA sits. Pause.)

JANICE. So what's the film about? Paul said you and him were working on a script while Susan's in New York.

SELINA. We work on it while she's here too. Where do you know Susan from?

JANICE. We grew up together. We traveled around the world. We're like best friends.

SELINA. Oh, right, you're the one that bought the fish in Bali.

JANICE *(to RUSSELL)*. We can stop in New York, can't we? All we need to do is change the tickets to New York–Tokyo.

RUSSELL. It could happen.

SELINA. You're going to Tokyo?

RUSSELL. Tokyo, Singapore, Agadir, Cologne, Paris, Leeds, New York again. Circles.

SELINA. You travel a lot, huh?

RUSSELL. Master can't be everywhere. The physical things. Someone has to check them.

SELINA. That's what you do? You check things for this guy Master?

RUSSELL. Master checks. I'm just there.

SELINA. What does he check?

RUSSELL. Everything. Anything.

SELINA. Covers a lot, huh?

RUSSELL. Really.

JANICE. What's the film about?

SELINA. The American Revolution.

RUSSELL. Heavy topic. Historical.

SELINA. It's mainly about this whorehouse in Concord where the British army used to get laid. The producers want to make kind of a porno-musical. We can't figure out if they're crazy or incredibly smart. They used to sell dope and write children's books. They keep their money in this old ice box. Big piles of it. Very weird. Anyway, I guess with the Bicentennial coming up they figure they can cash in if they get the film out in time.

(Enter PAUL from kitchen carrying tray of cookies.)

PAUL. Who's that, Ira and Nick?

SELINA. Yeah. D'you find it?

PAUL. It's perking away.

RUSSELL *(stands abruptly)*. Thank you.

PAUL. What?

JANICE. We're going? O.K. Well, I guess we'll see Susan in New York. Anything you want us to take her?

PAUL. No, that's O.K.

JANICE. Is everything all right?

PAUL. Fine. Fine.

JANICE. O.K.

(JANICE and RUSSELL exit. PAUL picks up pages from floor.)

PAUL. So. Where were we?

SELINA. Do you feel like working?

PAUL. Sure. Why not?

SELINA. You seem distracted.

PAUL. I'm fine. I wasn't expecting company.

SELINA. You were out of it even before they came.

PAUL. No, it was just Janice. I knew what she was thinking . . . Susan in New York . . . you and me here. I mean, you can't say anything.

SELINA. O.K., let's work.

PAUL. You're right, I am out of it. She's only been in New York for five days and already I feel like a fucking basket case. You know, we haven't been apart for even a whole

day since we started living together. Three years almost.

SELINA. Call her.

PAUL. She's probably still at the gallery.

SELINA. So call her there.

PAUL. She didn't leave the number.

SELINA. You know the name of the place. Call New York information.

PAUL. Soolie, she doesn't want me to call her there or she'd've given me the number. That's code for "this is my space, do not invade."

SELINA. You guys are so weird sometimes.

PAUL. Let's just work on the script.

SELINA. We'll get a lot done, I can tell.

PAUL *(opens binder, stops)*. She was out last night when I called. We usually talk at eleven. She wasn't there. She wasn't there all night. She never called.

SELINA. Look, if she was hurt or she got into some kind of trouble somebody'd've called you, don't worry.

PAUL. That's not what I was thinking exactly.

SELINA. You think she's fucking around?

PAUL. I don't know.

SELINA. What would you do if she was?

PAUL. How should I know?

SELINA. If I was in love with a guy and I found out he was doing something like that to me I know what I'd do.

PAUL. What would you do?

SELINA. I'd kill him.

PAUL. We've always had this kind of understanding, not like a formal thing. Just we picked it up talking to each other, that it'd be all right if we . . . in theory, that is, in theory it was O.K. If we . . . we weren't like exclusively tied down to each other, you know. If we were attracted to someone . . . and we didn't have to necessarily tell each other if we ever . . . unless we were afraid it was getting out of hand . . . like it was getting too serious and we couldn't handle it. But the thing is, we've never been unfaithful. Unfaithful. Funny how it comes back to words like that. We haven't slept with other people. At least I haven't. And I don't think she has except of course there's no way to know for sure since we said we didn't necessarily have to tell each other. But I really don't think she has. She's probably wanted to. I mean I've wanted to so it stands to reason that she's probably wanted to and the fact that she hasn't, or probably hasn't, uncool though it is to admit it, the fact that there's probably this thing she's wanted to do but didn't do it because she knew how it'd make me feel . . . that always made me feel, like admire her. Not admire exactly. Maybe trust. Respect. Trust. Something like that. Some combination of those things.

SELINA. I know what you mean.

PAUL. Yeah, but now that I don't know where she was last night I've been feeling pretty ridiculous, you know. Kind of foolish. Stupid, I don't know what. I was awake all last night thinking about it. I mean, here I am all this time . . . I've known you for what, two years and all that time I've found you like very very attractive, but so what? That's how it goes and now if she's just gone and slept with someone what was all this about? All this holding back for the sake of someone else's feelings . . . and the most ridiculous thing of all is maybe she was in New York thinking you and me were getting it on behind her back and that's what made her . . . if in fact she did do anything, maybe she did it to get even. Or maybe she hasn't done anything. In which case where was she? And why didn't she call?

SELINA. Do you want to sleep with me? Is that what you're saying?

PAUL. No, no that's not what I'm saying. I mean, I have wanted to but that's not the point. Primarily. Although I did say it, didn't I? But I always assumed you sort of . . . it was just one of those things. Have you ever thought about it?

SELINA. Yes, of course.

PAUL. Well. How do you feel about that?

SELINA. About the fact that people are attracted to each other?

PAUL. Have you wanted to sleep with me?

SELINA. I've wanted to do a lot of things I wouldn't do.

PAUL. So you have wanted to. But you wouldn't.

SELINA. If Susan had been in last night, would you?

PAUL. I wish I hadn't brought this up.

SELINA. I think it was a good idea. Bringing it up, I mean. I smell coffee.

(SELINA *exits to kitchen*)

PAUL *(calling)*. Selina?

SELINA *(off)*. What?

PAUL. Thank you.

SELINA *(off)*. You're welcome.

(PAUL *takes script, lies on couch, glances at a few pages. Pause. He lays script aside, can't concentrate. Enter* SUSAN *slowly. Carries small bag. She watches* PAUL *for a moment.*)

SUSAN. Paul.

PAUL *(sits up)*. What happened? Why are you back?

SUSAN. Nothing happened. I took the day off. Are you working?

PAUL. Where were you last night?

SUSAN. I stayed with a friend. Are you glad to see me?

PAUL. Susan. (PAUL *and* SUSAN *embrace.* SELINA *appears with two cups of coffee. Stands for a moment.*) You didn't call. I was worried.

SUSAN. I was going to. I'm sorry.

PAUL. Why didn't you?

(SELINA *withdraws into kitchen*)

SUSAN. I was here.

PAUL. Where? In Boston?

SUSAN. Yeah.

PAUL. Last night?

SUSAN. Paul, I have to tell you something.

PAUL. Oh shit. What is it?

SUSAN. I stayed with Katie last night.

PAUL. Katie. Katie Moffatt? That's downstairs. You stayed downstairs? You came up from New York and you stayed downstairs?

SUSAN. Let me tell you what happened.

PAUL. Yeah, why don't you do that.

SUSAN. I came up. I flew up. I wanted to surprise you. And then at the airport I just . . . I don't know. I just got angry that I'd come all this way because I missed you. I was gonna call. I was going to pretend I was still in New York, but then, I don't know . . . I didn't.

PAUL. I noticed.

SUSAN. Paul, I'm sorry, I'm trying to explain. I mean I don't feel wonderful about this, In fact, I feel pretty damn stupid. I know it was a dumb thing to do and I felt even worse when I realized why I'd . . . I wanted you to worry. I wanted that. I know it's shitty, but I wanted to get back at you for making me come all the way up to Boston when I should be working on the show . . . Yeah, I know. I just have to tell you that. What I'm trying to say is . . . I seem to have this little problem accepting the fact that I . . . I'm just so fucking in love with you, Paul. That's all it is, and I can't stand being away from you.

(SUSAN *controlling herself.* PAUL *comes to her. They embrace.* SUSAN *weepy.*)

PAUL. Hey. Hey.

(*They kiss. Passionately.* SELINA *comes back. Stands. Fade.*)

SCENE FIVE

Slide: 1975 Central Park. Afternoon. Benches and garbage can. PAUL, SUSAN *and*

MARAYA *eat from "family-size" bucket of Kentucky Fried Chicken.* PAUL *holds baby-*MATTY *while* MARAYA *prepares a bottle.* MARAYA *is pregnant.*

———

MARAYA. I don't know. I guess he was just pissed off about somehting. I don't even remember what it was any more, but he picked up this big ole kitchen knife and slammed it into the table. Went in about an inch and that table's solid oak. I mean he was really mad. (*to baby-*MATTY) I'm just telling about daddy, honey. Don't worry, everything's O.K.

(MARAYA *gives bottle to* PAUL *who feeds baby-*MATTY.)

SUSAN. But how'd he hurt his hand?

MARAYA. Oh, he wasn't holding the handle tight enough. It slipped down over the blade.

SUSAN. Yech!

MARAYA. Really. Poor Doug. Twenty-three stitches. He's O.K. now, but he has to take these pain killers and that could be a drag in the interview 'cause these pills are like super zappo strong and they make you really high. And they don't kill the pain, either.

(PAUL *looks at* SUSAN'*s watch.*)

PAUL. It's ten past one.

MARAYA (*yelling*). Doug!! (*to Baby-*MATTY) Sorry, honey, I was just calling daddy.

(*Enter* DOUG *looking back over his shoulder. He has a huge bandage-wrap and position brace on right hand. Dog barks, offstage.*)

DOUG. You heard what I said, Jake. Stay away from that doggie. Hey, man I'm serious. I'll punch your fucking head in.

MARAYA. Doug, don't talk to him like that. He can play with the dog. It's not gonna hurt him.

DOUG. Yeah and when it bites him and he gets rabies who's gonna pay the hospital bills?

PAUL. It's ten past, Doug. It'll take you a good half hour to get down to Wall Street from here.

SUSAN. It takes fifteen minutes.

DOUG. I gotta have a joint. Where's your purse, Marsie?

MARAYA. You can't get stoned now, honey. You're going to see the president of a bank.

DOUG. Fuck him. Man, my hand hurts. If he doesn't want to lend me the bread, I'll get it someplace else.

MARAYA. Doug, you're talking about five hundred thousand dollars. Another bank wouldn't let you in the door. (*to* SUSAN) The president is Cisco's uncle.

DOUG. What do you know about it anyway? Man, if I can't get a few bucks from some sucker unless he's my buddy's uncle I don't even want it.

MARAYA. He's not just your buddy—he's your partner.

DOUG. Some fucking partner. If I didn't do all the work myself we'd finish about one house a century. Come on, where's the dope?

MARAYA. No, Doug, you can't have it.

DOUG. My hand's killing me. I can't think straight.

(*Dog barks, offstage*)

MARAYA. No.

DOUG (*yelling*). Jake, what'd I tell you about that doggie? Leave him alone or I'm gonna hurt you. If you want to stay over there . . . (*Barking stops*) O.K., that's better.

SUSAN. He's cute.

DOUG. I'll tell you one thing. If I get this bread I'm gonna buy Cisco out and run the business myself, unless you want to come in with me.

PAUL. Me?

DOUG. You never think I'm being serious. Man, I mean it. You don't know some of the shit I'm getting into. I'm gonna be a rich man. That guy I built the house for, you remember him. Mr. Conklin, the guy with the big lump on his neck? Well, he was real pleased with my work—real pleased. And he bought this big ole chunk of prime lakefront property and when he found out I was with the twenty-third tactical in Nam . . . that was his outfit in the second world war . . . that did it, man. Got the contract just like that. Fourteen houses. You know what that'll be worth?

MARAYA. Doug, you haven't even got the money yet.

DOUG. Listen, man, with this deal going any bank that ain't standing in line to lend me the bread is a bank with its head up its ass. One joint, Marsie, huh?

MARAYA. No.

DOUG. One toke. One fucking toke is all.

MARAYA. No, Doug, you can't.

(PAUL *looks at* SUSAN'*s watch.*)

PAUL. It's twenty past.

MARAYA. We better get moving.

DOUG. Yeah, O.K. (*yells*) Hey, Jake, come on, kid, it's bank time. Man, I'll tell ya, I'm no good at this shit. I'm just not. I don't know why the fuck Cisco can't take care of it. It's his uncle.

SUSAN. Why doesn't he?

DOUG. He doesn't have a suit. Naa, I don't

know. *Jake!* He hates his uncle. In fact, I think it's mutual, but I'm supposed to promise this dude Cisco'll straighten out if he lends us the bread. The family's impressed that Cisco's a partner in a company. Shitkicker Construction Unlimited. I'll tell you what I can't figure out is how anyone'd think it's worth half a million to get Cisco right. I like the dude. He's my partner and I'll carry him through a lot of shit for sure, but Cisco, man, you could get him straight as a ruler and I still wouldn't pay you more'n a dollar for him.

MARAYA. Are we going or not?

DOUG. Yeah, yeah, we're going. This is weird. This is definitely nonnormal. I gotta go talk bullshit to a bank president. Doug Superfreak meets Mr. Straightmoney. You guys'll come up, right?

SUSAN. We'll see you soon. Good luck.

DOUG. I don't know how you guys can live in this city. Look at that squirrel. He's got hepatitis, no shit. Look at him. Pathetic. Shooting up with a dirty needle. Give him an hour in the country and he'd forget there ever was a Central Park. You should move up. I'm serious. I dump Cisco, we go 50-50 on the business, you bring your camera, take pictures of trees and shit like that. It's so pretty up there.

MARAYA. Doug.

DOUG. O.K., O.K., take it easy. See you guys. Hey, Jakie-poo. *(exits)*

SUSAN. When are you expecting?

PAUL. Susan, they have to go.

MARAYA. November, and that's absolutely the last one. It was a mistake believe me. *(to baby-*MATTY*)* Not you, honey, the next one. All I can tell you is don't listen to doctors. They said I was safe for a couple months after Matty here . . . four weeks later, bang. Four weeks. Oh well, gotta go. You guys take care, huh. *(for baby-*MATTY*)* "Bye-bye." Go "bye-bye." Bye. *(exits)*

(Pause. SUSAN *offers some chicken.)*

SUSAN. Want some more?

PAUL. No.

(Pause.)

SUSAN. How've you been?

PAUL. Great. You?

SUSAN. O.K.

PAUL. So much for the good news.

SUSAN. Did you sell the script yet?

PAUL. No.

SUSAN. It'll happen, don't worry.

PAUL. No it won't. It's a piece of shit.

SUSAN. I read it. I thought it was good.

PAUL. Yet another point of agreement.

SUSAN. Paul, what's the matter?

PAUL. Why'd you have to go invite Doug and Maraya?

SUSAN. I thought you'd want to see them. They're your friends.

PAUL. But now?

SUSAN. They're only in town for the day. They have to go back this afternoon.

PAUL. Susan, for christ sakes, we haven't seen each other for three months. We do have things to talk about.

SUSAN. I'm sorry. I thought you'd want to see them. We have all afternoon to talk.

PAUL. I thought you had to work.

SUSAN. I can take the afternoon off.

PAUL. Nice job.

SUSAN. Yes, as a matter of fact, it's a very nice job.

PAUL. Taking pictures of rich people's houses.

SUSAN. I knew that's how you'd see it.

PAUL. Sorry.

SUSAN. Paul, it does happen to be the best architectural journal in the country. In fact, it's one of the best in the world. And I like working there. I like the people. I like their ideas. I like what they're trying to do with the magazine and I like the fact that I'm beginning to feel like I can take my work seriously for the first time.

PAUL. I said I'm sorry.

SUSAN. I heard you.

PAUL. Moving right along.

SUSAN. And another thing, Paul. I need to make my own living. I never realized it before, how much I hated taking money from you, from my family. Now I don't feel like I have to apologize for anything any more and that's important, Paul. You're not the only one around here that's proud, you know.

PAUL. You're right. And I'm sorry. Really. That was stupid. I didn't mean to put you down.

SUSAN. I know you didn't. I just had to tell you. Oh, babe, it's so nice to see you.

PAUL. I miss you.

SUSAN. Well, I miss you too.

PAUL. A lot?

SUSAN. Yeah, pretty much a whole lot.

PAUL. Were you . . . have you been with anyone else?

SUSAN. As in guys? A few. How about you?

PAUL. Guys? Not many.

SUSAN. 'Cause I was with a woman. Once. Life's infinite variety.

PAUL. How interesting. Was it nice?

SUSAN. No. I mean yes, in a way, but no, not really. I miss making love to you.

PAUL. Yeah, that part was always pretty good.

SUSAN. Was? Why do you talk about it like it's over? *(pause)* Is it?

PAUL. I don't know, is it?

SUSAN. Isn't that what we're supposed to be talking about? This wasn't supposed to be permanent. I thought we were just trying out a little time on our own. You want to end it?

PAUL. No.

SUSAN. So let's talk about it.

PAUL. That's what we're doing.

SUSAN. O.K. Things are going pretty well for me, you know.

PAUL. So I gathered.

SUSAN. What I mean is, I can't move back to Boston.

PAUL. Can't? You're being physically restrained?

SUSAN. I don't want to.

PAUL. Ah. So I'd have to move to New York, is that it?

SUSAN. You don't have to make it sound like the end of the world. You always talked about moving to New York.

PAUL. I'm just trying to clarify the situation.

SUSAN. You could do so well here, Paul.

PAUL. I'm doing just fine in Boston. All our friends are there. I've been made a full editor. I like it there.

SUSAN. But you said you wanted your own business one day. You can do it here. There's a lot more film happening here than there is in Boston. And I'm meeting a lot of people who might be able to help.

PAUL. You sound like my brother.

SUSAN. Well, what's wrong with getting a little help, for God sake? Soolie helped me. I've helped some people here. It's not just a favor, you know. You do it because you think someone's good. And you are, babe. You should be doing . . . just, something more like what I know you're capable of doing. Why do you keep fighting it?

PAUL. We should have a sex change before we think about getting back together.

SUSAN. Well, you're the one that always said it. "If you're white, middle class and American you have to work twenty-four hours a day to not make it." So stop working so hard.

PAUL. O.K., let's say I move to New York. That's condition number one, right? So let's say I accept that . . .

SUSAN. Don't do me any favors.

PAUL. Well, for christ sake, that's what you're saying, isn't it? If I want you, I have to have New York.

SUSAN. It isn't a condition.

PAUL. Everything is a condition, Susan. Everything.

SUSAN. What are you saying?

PAUL. I just want to know what I get in exchange.

SUSAN. What do you want?

PAUL. You know what I want.

SUSAN. Oh.

PAUL. Have you thought about it?

SUSAN. I don't think either of us is ready for that.

PAUL. That's bullshit . . .

SUSAN. I'm not.

PAUL. Well when? We can't start when we're sixty.

SUSAN. I'm thirty-one.

PAUL. Great. Only twenty-nine years to go.

SUSAN. Would you want to be our child, Paul? I mean honestly, at this point in time do you really think you'd want to have the two of us for parents?

PAUL. We're no worse than a few I grew up with.

SUSAN. That's what I mean. I want to have kids someday. I do. Just not now.

PAUL. So what's the score so far? Paul moves to New York. Susan remains childless. That's two to nothing. I need some points here.

SUSAN. We'll talk about it, O.K.?

PAUL. We'll talk about it? That sounds familiar.

SUSAN. Well, you can't just expect me to say yeah, great. "You want kids, we'll have kids." It is something we have to talk about.

PAUL. O.K. That's half a point, right?

SUSAN. Can you stay for the weekend? I think we should spend some time together. I'd like you to meet some of my friends. I've bored them to death talking about you. I don't think they believe you exist. There's a party tomorrow night. I have room at my place.

PAUL. Is that an offer?

SUSAN. Can you stay?

PAUL. Yeah.

SUSAN. Good. *(They kiss)* Let's clear up here.

PAUL. Are we going somewhere?

SUSAN. We can talk at my place.

PAUL. As opposed to here where we can't talk?

SUSAN. You want to stay here?

PAUL. No, I want to go back to your place. And talk.

SUSAN. I'm expecting a call, that's all.

PAUL. Oh.

SUSAN. Come on.

(They rise.)

PAUL. Susan.

SUSAN. What?

PAUL. What is it? I feel like . . . I don't know.

SUSAN. It's been three months. We need time. Let's go. *(exits, off)* You coming, babe?

(PAUL *follows. Fried chicken on bench. Fade.)*

SCENE SIX

Slide: 1977 PAUL *and* SUSAN's *living room, Central Park West. Evening. Painter's drop cloth on floor. Ladder, buckets of paint, paint tray, brushes. Pile of boxes covered with sheet. Armchair.* SUSAN *and* SELINA *sit on floor finishing take-out Chinese meal. They are in work clothes. As light go up, they are convulsed with laughter.*

———

SUSAN. I don't believe it. What's yours say?

(SELINA *breaks her fortune cookie and reads*)

SELINA. "He who knows not, but knows not that he knows not is a fool. Shun him." That's a fortune?

SUSAN. Whew. Heavy.

SELINA. Someone at the cookie factory's been working overtime.

SUSAN *(looks into food container)*. Want some more?

SELINA. I'm stuffed.

SUSAN. All in all I'd call that a pretty shitty meal.

SELINA. It's better than I could do.

PAUL *(off)*. What time is it?

SUSAN. Ten past.

SELINA. Is he really serious about the job?

SUSAN. Why would he joke about something like that?

SELINA. He's already got two editors working for him. I don't see why he needs me.

SUSAN. 'Cause Bert's a jerk. Paul ought to fire him but he won't so he's gonna need someone else around who really knows what they're doing. Look, it's a big deal. First feature film. He doesn't want to fuck up.

SELINA. I thought he didn't have it yet. Isn't that why he's going to California?

SUSAN. That's just a formality. He already knows definitely they want him, but there's this whole ritual you have to do . . . meet the director . . . meet the producer . . . sit around for a few days snorting coke. That's how they do business.

SELINA. I've never worked on a feature.

PAUL *(off)*. What time is it?

SUSAN. Quarter past. I wish he'd get a watch. Listen, I know you're worried. It's a big move. I mean I was terrified when I came to New York the first time. Remember my show . . . ?

SELINA. The Space Portraits?

SUSAN. Right. Jesus, the things I didn't know about photography. It feels like about a million years ago.

SELINA. I liked the Space portraits.

SUSAN. Oh, sure, they were O.K., I mean for what I knew then, they were great, but until I met people who really knew what they were doing . . . 'cause if they see you've got something, they'll open right up . . . let you pick their brains, ask questions, tell you what you're doing wrong, show you all the stuff you have to know to get really good and, I mean, that's what it's all about finally. Just, when you can see yourself making real choices in the work and you know they're right, even though you don't know how you know any more. Like now my eye just sees when it's perfect, when it's clear, you know, when it's simple. You know what it is. It's when you finally see a whole pattern under everything and you know exactly how much of it you have to show to suggest the whole thing. Anyway. I'm rambling, aren't I? I keep doing that lately. What were we talking about? Oh yeah, New York.

SELINA. I'll think about it.

SUSAN. Promise?

SELINA. Cross my heart and hope to die.

PAUL *(off)*. What time is it?

SUSAN *(ignores him)*. 'Cause Paul's really convinced you're one of the best editors he's ever worked with. You taught him for god sake. But who'sever gonna know how good you are when you're stuck up in Boston?

(PAUL *rushes in with small suitcase. He wears a three-piece suit, has mustache, looks trendy.)*

PAUL. Susie, what the hell did I do with my . . . oh, here they are. *(pats his jacket)*

SUSAN. What?

PAUL. My joints. I forgot I had 'em. Man, do I hate flying. Let me have a little vino. What time is it?

SUSAN. Calm down, babe.

PAUL. I'm calm, I'm calm. *(takes swig from bottle)* That's better. Well, I guess I'd better get moving.

SUSAN. Can't you wait a few more minutes? He's on his way.

PAUL. Who?

SUSAN. Lawrence.

PAUL. Oh yeah, right. What time is it?

SUSAN. Twenty-two past.

PAUL. I don't want to get caught in traffic. The plane's leaving in forty-five minutes.

SUSAN. There won't be any traffic.

PAUL. That's what you said the last time and it took an hour.

SUSAN. Last time wasn't the Fourth of July weekend. Everyone's out of town. Calm down.

PAUL. Look, I saw Lawrence a few days ago. Just tell him I had to go. Tell him I'm sorry I missed him. I'm not trying to avoid him. I think he's a wonderful human being. I love the new beds. He has marvelous taste and we'll all have dinner when I get back, O.K.?

SUSAN. You know he's going to be hurt. He thinks you don't like him.

PAUL. He thinks everybody doesn't like him. Now come on. Wish me luck. I have to go.

SUSAN (hugs him). Good luck. I'll miss you.

PAUL. I'll call as soon as I get to the hotel. You gonna watch the fireworks from the terrace?

SUSAN. I guess so.

PAUL. I'll tell the pilot to buzz Central Park West and waggle his wings.

SUSAN. O.K., we'll wave.

PAUL. Bye, Soolie. (They hug) You still be here Friday night?

SELINA. I don't know yet.

PAUL. If you're not, I'll call you.

SELINA. Good luck.

PAUL. It's in the bag. Shit, I hate flying. (starts out)

SUSAN. Hey.

PAUL. What?

SUSAN. What about Bert?

PAUL. What about him?

SUSAN. You're not going to let him do that final cut on the Slumbermax commercial by himself? Come on, babe.

PAUL. I left instructions on the wall. He'll know what to do.

SUSAN. Like he did the last time?

PAUL. What can I do? Everyone else is tied up.

SUSAN. Everyone?

PAUL. Lindzee's busy, Stan's busy, Al's busy, Mike's busy, everyone's busy.

(Pause. SUSAN is looking at SELINA.)

SELINA. Hey, come on, I can't . . .

PAUL. It's a piece of cake, Soolie . . .

SELINA. This is my vacation.

PAUL. You could do it in your sleep. It'll take a day. I've got it all laid out, even the frame counts.

SELINA. You guys are real subtle.

PAUL. Yes?

SELINA. O.K. One day.

PAUL (to SUSAN). The log book's on top of the film rack. My work sheet's taped to the back of my office door. Warn Bert, by the way. Do you have his number in the country?' Can you remember all that?

SUSAN. Logbook, filmrack, work sheet, back of door, warn Bert, country number, twenty-five past.

PAUL. What?

SUSAN. It's twenty-five past.

PAUL. Oh, O.K. Shit. Bye. (exits)

SUSAN. Thanks.

SELINA. Yeah, good old Soolie. (SUSAN sits, leans back.) . . . You feeling O.K.?

SUSAN. Huh? Oh, yeah, I'm fine. I guess I had too much wine or something. Maybe it's the monosodium.

SELINA. Maybe you ought to lie down.

SUSAN. No, I'm O.K. Lawrence'll be here in a minute. I'll be all right.

SELINA. You don't look all right.

SUSAN. Excuse me. (rises, starts out, stops, breathes deep, returns, sits) False alarm.

SELINA. Are you pregnant or something?

SUSAN. Yeah.

SELINA. Really?

SUSAN. Really.

SELINA. Paul didn't say anything.

SUSAN. I just found out, and don't say anything until I get a chance to tell him, O.K.?

SELINA. Man, I'd really like to be pregnant right now. I was thinking of just doing it, you know. Since it doesn't look like I'm having too much luck finding a guy I can put up with for more than a day or two. Just get someone to, you know, just contribute. Are you happy?

SUSAN. I don't know. That's the whole problem. I just don't know how I feel. We had all these heavy talks when we got back together. You know—well, we didn't really decide anything. Just we'd, we wouldn't exactly try, but then again we wouldn't exactly not try and then if something happened we'd deal with it.

SELINA. So something happened.

SUSAN. Yeah, and here I am, dealing with it. You know, I had such an incredible feeling when I got the results of the test. Just . . . there you are, it finally happened. I was like

totally serene, just sort of floated home and I
had this whole fantasy, you know, all those
pregnant women you see walking around with
that funny little smile on their face, the big
secret . . .

SELINA. . . . and huge tits . . .

SUSAN. God, Paul would love that. Oh, and
I got this idea for a series of self portraits all
through the pregnancy, the different stages.
You could do it with a permanent camera in
the bedroom so everything would be the same
in the picture except I'd be getting bigger and
bigger. But the thing is, when I started thinking
about it I realized I was really into the idea of
the photographs, but I wasn't really all that
into the idea of being pregnant.

SELINA. You don't really want to tell him,
do you?

SUSAN. Of course I want to tell him. I mean,
O.K. I guess maybe I just want to get comfortable with the idea first so I know how I
feel about it. We're the ones who have to do
all the work, right?

SELINA. Yeah, I guess.

SUSAN. I don't know. It's just so nice the
way things are now and the thing is he hasn't
said anything about a baby for like . . . well,
ever since the business started doing well. Not
one word. So I guess it really was some kind
of competitive thing. You know, I get pregnant
so I can't work as much and that makes me
less of a threat. The old story. Does that make
sense?

SELINA. Oh, yeah. It makes sense. Sure.

SUSAN. So what do you think?

SELINA. I don't see why you don't want to
tell him. He's doing well, you're doing well.
Everything seems to be working out. So what's
the problem?

SUSAN. There's no problem.

SELINA. Oh. Then what are we talking about?

SUSAN (pause). Why do you always take his
side?

SELINA. Whose side?

SUSAN. Whenever I try to talk to you about
something you always . . . like, I really thought
you'd understand about something like this . . .
sisterhood and all that. I mean I have a right
to my own thoughts, don't I? It's not so terrible
that I don't want to say anything to him until
I know for sure how I feel about what my body
is going to have to be doing for the next how
ever many months and then when I know for
sure I'll tell him about it and that way it won't
get all messy with me getting my feelings all
tangled up in the way he feels about it until we

don't know who feels what about anything
anymore, which is what always seems to happen with us. But whenever I try to talk to you
I feel like you think I'm being . . . I don't
know . . . like you automatically think I'm
doing the wrong thing. Well?

SELINA. What are you asking me?

SUSAN. Yeah, you see? Like that kind of
remark. What's that supposed to mean? Oh,
shit, Soolie, listen to me. I sound like a witch.
I'm sorry. I really am sorry. I just, I don't
know what to do about this. (Phone by SUSAN
rings. She picks up.) Hello? Yeah, he can come
up. (hangs up) I'm thirty-three. If I don't have
it now . . . God, why is everything so fucking
complicated? They ought to have a course in
making up your mind. I'm sorry, but you see
what I mean, don't you?

SELINA. Oh. Sure. You have a problem, that's
all. It's O.K. You just have a problem.

SUSAN. I'm glad you think so.

SELINA. I don't really think anything you
know. All I think is I'm always in the middle
with you two. Paul talks to me. You talk to
me. Don't you ever talk to each other? I don't
know what you should do. It's not my life. I
mean I have enough of my own stuff to figure
out and I don't go around asking people what
I should do because they're my problems and
they're not very interesting unless you're me.
In which case, they're mostly just a pain in
the ass. I'd like to move to New York, for
instance. I'd like to work for Paul. I think I'm
probably ready for it although I think there
must be a lot of editors around as good as me
and that makes me wonder why you want me
to move here. Is it because I'm good at my
job or because you like me or because you and
Paul don't know how to deal with each other
and you need me as a middle man?

SUSAN. I didn't know you felt that way.

SELINA. You never asked. And I don't always feel that way either.

SUSAN. I think we better straighten this out.

SELINA. O.K.

(Doorbell rings)

SUSAN. Shit. I'll be right back. (exits)

(SELINA pours more wine. Talking offstage,
then enter SUSAN followed by LAWRENCE,
talking.)

LAWRENCE. . . . and then in the middle they
had this incredible column of balloons right up
to the ceiling and out like branches, god, I love
balloons. I decided that's what's been missing
from my life. I'm going to have balloons in
my life. I'm going to just walk around my

apartment and kick balloons in front of me. Doesn't that sound fabulous? Just kicking balloons around in your own apartment. Except I'm going to only have one color—just white ones. Too many different colors would just get confusing and who needs more confusion? Hello. I'm Lawrence.

SUSAN. This is Selina.

LAWRENCE. Hi, Selina.

SELINA. Hello.

LAWRENCE. I love your turquoise. Where'd you get it, Arizona?

SELINA. Boston.

LAWRENCE. God, the Navahoes are everywhere. I always wanted a pendant like that. Isn't it funny how everyone's wearing turquoise nowadays? I never used to like it, but now everyone's wearing it and I'm beginning to see what they mean. There's nothing like a trend to change the way you feel about things.

SUSAN. If you want to see how the beds look, they're here.

LAWRENCE. The beds. What beds? Oh, the beds. Did they arrive already?

SUSAN. In the two end rooms. Why don't you have a look.

LAWRENCE. Was this a heavy conversation or something?

SUSAN. Yeah.

LAWRENCE. God, what a Fourth of July. I've spent the whole day being rejected by everyone. Sylvia thinks I hate her because I was staring again. I swear I don't know what to do about it. I just can't help it. She's so glamorous for her age all she has to do is start talking to me and all I can do is stare at her and for some reason that makes her think I don't like her. Maybe I stare wrong. Maybe I should learn a new way to stare. Do you have a mirror? I'll practice. Do you like the beds?

SUSAN. Oh, yeah. They're great.

LAWRENCE. Aren't they sensational? I was going to get one for myself, but then I'd have to redo the bedroom and I'm not in the mood. How long is this going to take?

SUSAN. We'll just be a few minutes.

LAWRENCE. All right. Call me when you're done. May I have some wine? (SUSAN *pours him a glass.*) Maybe I'll watch some TV after I look at the beds. Do you have a *TV Guide?*

SUSAN. In the bedroom.

LAWRENCE. Where's Paul?

SUSAN. He had to catch a flight.

LAWRENCE. They all say that, don't they? Story of my life. (*the wine.*) That's some champagne for later. (*the bag.*) I stole it from Syl-

via's party and whatever you do, don't tell her I came here. I said I was sick. God, I hope she doesn't call my place. I forgot to take the phone off the hook. It's just her parties are always the pits. She has fabulous decorations and terrible company. It's always the same thing. She just doesn't know who to invite. I mean D minus for people. This time it was all these *On the Waterfront* types. You know the kind—leather jackets and keys hanging off their jeans. God, I can't wait till that style goes out. It reminds me of the janitor at my high school. And the silliest thing is I know she's doing it for me, but I don't know where she got the idea I was into leather. I hate it to death. Oh, and then she stopped me on the way out, Sylvia, did you ever notice how she does that? Waits till you're on the way out the door and then she hits you with some heavy dilemma? Some earth shattering problem? Like this time it was, "Shoud she have a face lift?" I mean, really. I just had to stand there and pretend to think about it when I knew she'd already made up her mind and all she wanted is for me to agree. That's all anybody ever wants. And then there I was staring at her again. Yes, I know, you're talking. I'm sorry. If you'd had the day I just had you'd understand. Don't be too long. (*exits toward bedroom*)

SELINA. Who is he?

SUSAN. My boss. You know, on the magazine. He's helping us decorate. He found us the beds. Do you feel like talking?

SELINA. I don't have anything to say, really.

SUSAN. You think I should tell Paul?

SELINA. It's up to you.

SUSAN. I don't really feel like talking anymore. Maybe tomorrow. Are you angry?

SELINA. Why should I be angry?

SUSAN. Should I tell Lawrence to come back? Jesus, what do I keep asking you for?

PAUL (*rushes in*). I forgot my fucking ticket. I got all the way to the Midtown Tunnel and I realized I didn't have my ticket. I could've sworn I put it in my travel wallet. I put my wallet in my bag . . . Wait a minute. Oh no. I think I might've just done a very dumb thing.

SUSAN. What?

PAUL (*opens jacket, looks, closes it quickly*). I just did a very dumb thing. I have my ticket. My ticket is in my pocket.

SUSAN. Are you stoned?

PAUL. I was on my way to the airport. Of course I'm stoned.

SUSAN. You can still make it. It only takes half an hour.

PAUL. Yeah . . . but I think I don't want to. There seems to be something bigger than all of us telling me to stay.

SUSAN. You have a meeting, babe.

PAUL. Not 'til late tomorrow. I can make it if I catch an early flight and I remember my ticket. Remember that I have my ticket, that is.

LAWRENCE *(re-enter)*. Oh, good. I thought I heard something. How was California?

PAUL. Not bad. How was the party?

LAWRENCE. It was just on the verge of complete catastrophe when I left. Thank god you're here. They banished me to the bedroom with nothing good on TV.

SUSAN. So do you want to try to make the flight or stay and watch the fireworks?

PAUL. Is that champagne?

LAWRENCE. Chateau Sylvia.

PAUL. I'll stay and watch the fireworks.

LAWRENCE. Can I open it? *(takes out the bottles, opening one)* Oh, dear, good old America. Two hundred and one years old and looking every minute of it. Actually, I think we should have stopped the whole show last year. I mean two hundred years is enough for any country, don't you think? There's just no way we can go anywhere, but downhill after this. Hold your breath. *(Uncorks bottle. No pop. No fizz. Looks into bottle.)* God, and I thought Sylvia was flat. (PAUL *laughs.* LAWRENCE *laughs. Others join. They stop abruptly.)* What are we laughting at?

PAUL. I don't know.

(They laugh again. Fade.)

SCENE SEVEN

Slide: 1978 Terrace of PAUL *and* SUSAN's *apartment. Deck Chairs. Doors to apartment. Portable barbeque.* SUSAN *and* JANICE *on deck chairs taking the sun.* JANICE *smokes constantly and drinks a beer.*

JANICE. I think it's just a question of respect. Mutual respect.

SUSAN. Yeah.

JANICE. Phil repsects me. I respect him. I mean, that's it.

SUSAN. Yeah.

JANICE. Like with Russell, well, you never met him, but believe me . . . O.K. . . . a typical example of Russell. This time we were in Boston, but you'd gone to New York and I wanted to stop and see you. It was no big deal,

real easy to change the tickets, but he wouldn't do it. You know why? Get this. I was too attached to the things of this world. That's what he said. O.K. So one time we were back in San Francisco and he saw this sports car and he bought it. I couldn't believe it. He wasn't even into cars or if he was I never knew about it. I never knew a lot of things about him, but when I said what about the things of this world, I mean, you can go buy a car, but I can't see a friend. You know what he says? He can buy the car because he isn't attached to it. He doesn't need it. Great. And the dumb thing is, I believed him. Like completely. No, not completely. No, that's right, that's what I was starting to say. *(offers cigarette)* Want one?

SUSAN. No, I quit.

JANICE. Oh, yeah? When.

SUSAN. Six months ago.

JANICE. Wow. But, you know . . . I really do believe there's this part of you that knows better and all it takes is for one thing to happen. Like with Russell we were meditating one day. Well, he was. I couldn't get into it, so I was just sort of pretending. I did that a lot. That's another thing. I used to wonder if he knew I was pretending, 'cause if he's supposed to be so spiritual he should be able to tell, right? But he never said anything. Anyway, this one time I was telling you about, I just started watching him, sort of squinting, and all of a sudden he like started changing shape in front of me and I could see the pores in his skin and all these little hairs all over his body. It's like he just turned evil right in front of me. I was even thinking later that maybe it was this really ironic thing happening. You know. Like the first time I finally had a mystical insight while I was meditating and what I saw was the guy that had got me into it in the first place, was this really evil creep. Anyway, I just got up and walked out. He was still meditating. I never saw him again. It's weird how these things work out. Oh, by the way, my mother says hi. That's another great thing about being with Phil. I can go home again. I never wanted my folks to meet Russell. Phil and Paul really seem to be hitting it off. Phil usually takes a long time to like people. It's mostly he's just shy, I guess. I remember on our honeymoon we went to the Grand Canyon and he hardly talked to anyone at the hotel. I thought maybe he was angry. He's just shy. Do you like him. Sue. Susie? Susan.

SUSAN *(waking)*. Huh? Sorry. What?

JANICE. Do you like Phil?

SUSAN. Who's Phil? Oh, Phil. Yeah. He seems like a nice guy.

JANICE. You guys seem real happy. Paul's in a great mood.

SUSAN. The film went well. They finished editing last month.

JANICE. I never realized he was so like, well, I never really knew him or anything, but he's really lively. Sometimes I'm not sure how to take him.

(Airplane flies over. They watch.)

SUSAN. Where is everybody?

JANICE. They're inside.

BEN *(enters)*. How are the bathing beauties doing out here?

SUSAN. What's going on in there?

(Singing from inside. Enter PAUL and PHIL with birthday cake.)

PAUL and PHIL.
  Happy birthday to you
  Happy birthday to you . . .

SUSAN. Oh no!!!

ALL.
  Happy birthday dear Susan
  Happy birthday to youuuuu!!!!!!

SUSAN. I thought there was something fishy going on.

BEN. Admit it. Admit it. We got you. You weren't expecting it.

PAUL. Happy Birthday . . . *(sets down cake)*

BEN. O.K. Make a wish and blow out the candles.

SUSAN *(thinks)*. Got it. *(blows out candles)*

BEN. *Geronimo!!!!*

SUSAN. Shhh, Ben the neighbors.

BEN. Well invite 'em over goddamn it. *(yells down) We're having a party!!!*

SUSAN. I'll get the plates. Everybody want? *(Yes. Goes in.)*

BEN. And the champagne. Leave us never forget la champagne. *(Goes in.)*

PHIL. Your brother's a real character.

PAUL. Oh yeah. He's a real character all right. Actually, what he really is, is he's a helluva guy.

PHIL. He told me this great joke. I don't know if you know it. Why aren't there any ice cubes in Poland? Do you know that one?

PAUL. There aren't any ice cubes in Poland? I'm sure that's not true.

PHIL. No. No, it's a joke.

PAUL. I was in Warsaw last year and we had cocktails at this hotel and I'm sure they had ice cubes. Yes, yes, they definitely did. I remember . . . ice cubes.

PHIL. No, you're supposed to . . .

JANICE. He's putting you on, honey.

(PAUL acknowledges this with good humor.)

PHIL *(laughs quietly)*. You already heard it.

PAUL. He's my brother. We talk about everything. I'll tell you the problem I have with that joke, though. I'm supposed to say "why" and you're supposed to say "the lady with the recipe died." O.K., but the thing is, Poland's been trading a lot with the West, so even if this lady had forgotten to write the recipe down, let's say, and then let's say she died. Well, there's all these other people in Poland who would've come into contact with Europeans who had the recipe. So the whole premise of the joke is too far fetched to be genuinely amusing.

PHIL. You guys are both crazy.

PAUL. Why are we both crazy?

PHIL. What?

PAUL. Oh, I thought that was the beginning of another joke. Hey, I'm just feeling good.

PHIL *(laughs)*. Have you thought about that story idea at all?

PAUL. I have. I have thought about it.

PHIL. Do you think it could work? Tell me the truth.

PAUL. I think it could be very commercial.

PHIL. Seriously?

PAUL. Why not?

JANICE. Honey, what have you been bothering Paul about?

PHIL. I haven't been bothering him. I just asked him.

JANICE. Phil, nobody's going to want to make a movie about city planners. You think it's interesting because that's what you do. I told you not to bring it up . . .

PAUL. Now wait a minute. Wait a minute. I don't agree. I think if you handled it right there could be a big market for something like that. I'm telling you, people are sick and tired of violence and sex and glamour and fantasy. They want to see real life up on the screen.

PHIL. If I could write I'd do it myself, but I'm not really an artistic kind of person. I have it all up here. Like before I was just thinking about this one time when the computer broke down over at dispatch and all the busses got routed downtown to the city center. It was crazy. They were all lined up there bumper to bumper. People were yelling at each other. You shouldn't've seen it.

PAUL. Now that's what I'm saying. That's exactly the kind of thing that's missing from movies nowdays, scenes like that. Busses all tangled up in the middle of town.

(PAUL *hugs* PHIL. *Enter* SUSAN *with plates, followed by* BEN *with champagne.)*

BEN. . . . but I already made reservations. It's all set.

SUSAN. Well, you'll have to ask them about it. They're the ones that have to catch a flight.

BEN. Janice and Phil, may I have your undivided attention for just one moment? A suggestion has been made by yours truly that we celebrate Susan's birthday with a disgustingly lavish dinner tonight at the Four Seasons compliments of. Now, Susan has very reasonably pointed out that you two have to leave tonight, but I say nuts to that and furthermore, a certain company I work for happens to maintain a lovely suite of rooms at a very lovely hotel where you can stay after dinner and . . . and said company will provide you with a limousine to the airport tomorrow to meet any flight of your choosing. Now what do you say to that?

JANICE. Great!

BEN. Phil? Now think carefully before you say yes.

PHIL. Well, I'd really like to but . . .

JANICE. Honey, you don't have to be back at work on Monday . . .

PHIL. I was just thinking we shouldn't leave Jesse with my folks for another day. We've already taken advantage of them.

JANICE. Sweetie, they love taking care of her. They'll spoil her rotten.

PHIL. Well, I guess we could call.

JANICE. We'll stay.

PHIL. Never argue with a lady.

BEN. I'll drink to that. O.K. Now I suggest we open the champagne, cut the cake and embarrass the hell out of Susan by watching her open all her presents. All in favor say nothing. Motion passed.

PAUL. Ben, you're really great, you know that.

BEN. Aw shucks, guy . . .

PAUL. No, really. I mean how many people would come all the way from England for a birthday? And this is the man who's broken every sales record in the history of Randle & Lane Securities. And, not only that, he's also managed to set up permanent offices in Spain, Greece, Italy, in East Germany. Where else, Ben? Have I missed any? Haven't you managed to break into a few other countries?

BEN. Let's get the presents.

JANICE. Phil, come on.

(BEN *exists into apartment.* PHIL *and* JANICE

follow. PAUL *starts out.)*

SUSAN. Paul . . .

PAUL. Huh?

SUSAN. Don't do that to Ben. He means well.

PAUL. I have to get the present.

SUSAN. Paul.

PAUL. What?

SUSAN. What's going on?

PAUL. Nothing. *(Exits, Jet passes over.* SUSAN *watches.)*

BEN *(Enters with two presents, Gives one to* SUSAN*).* For you, my dear. Happy birthday.

SUSAN. What's that one?

BEN. Oh, just a little even-Steven, old family custom. Didn't Paul ever tell you about this? We always used to get a little even-Steven when the other one had a birthday. Dad had a theory that it would prevent sibling rivalry. So much for *that* theory.

SUSAN. I'm sorry about the way he's behaving. I don't know what's going on. I really don't.

BEN. I'm used to it. *(pause)* It's a watch.

SUSAN. Good thinking.

(Re-enter PAUL *with* PHIL *and* JANICE, *bearing gifts.)*

BEN. Ah, here it comes. O.K., guy, hand it over and face the music.

PAUL. Me?

BEN. You know what they say about presents—lovers first. Theirs are always the worst. Friends later. Theirs are always greater.

PAUL. Do they say that? I didn't know. Happy birthday. *(gives* SUSAN *present)*

SUSAN *(surprised by coolness).* Thank you. *(starts to open it)*

PAUL. I should explain this, by the way. I thought I'd get something really special this year and . . . there's these places midtown you never hear about. At least, I never did. They're shops, right, stores, like they sell things, but. Like where I found this thing. All they sell there is ancient Chinese treasures and you have to make an appointment to even get in the place. So . . . you're like the only customer. It's incredible. You get inside and you're in a different world. It's completely quiet. You can't hear any sounds from the street and all the stuff is under glass cases like a museum and the lady that shows you around says things like "Now here's an unusual little figurine . . . very rare T'ang Dynasty, perhaps you'd like me to take it out for you." I mean, that's what I call shopping. Do you like it?

(SUSAN *holds up figurine of a horse. it has*

an opening in its back.)

SUSAN. It's beautiful.

PAUL. Isn't it nice? Genuine Ming Dynasty. There's only about twenty of them in the world. That's what the lady said. They were only for the royal family. That's why I thought it was a nice idea. What they'd do is if the Emperor had a son that died before he was old enough to rule they'd cremate the body and put the ashes in that hole in the back and then they'd bury the whole works. I guess that's why they're so rare. But listen to this. This is the great part. It's shaped like a horse because they had this belief that the horse would take the child's spirit on a ride where it'd see its whole life passing by . . . the life it would have had if it hadn't died. And that way it could go to its final resting place in peace. At least that's what the lady explained.

BEN. Jesus, guy, this must've set you back a few pennies.

PAUL. Oh, yeah. But like I said, I wanted to get something really special and I think I got a pretty good deal. They were asking ninety-seven thousand, but I got 'em down to ninety-three. Not bad.

BEN. A steal at twice the price.

(They're getting uneasy.)

PAUL. Still, I had to sell the business, all the editing machines, the office equipment, the lease on the building and I had to cash in my stocks and take out all my savings, but I finally scraped it all together.

SUSAN. Paul . . . ?

PAUL. I just thought it was worth it. We need something in this apartment for all the ashes. The unborn embryos. Isn't that what they do after they take 'em out. Don't they burn 'em, or did you have one of those guys that just pops it in a baggie and into the trash can . . . ?

SUSAN. Would you leave us alone, please.

BEN. Hey, guy, what is this . . .

SUSAN. Just leave us alone. All of you. Please.

(BEN, PHIL and JANICE exit inside.)

PAUL. You mean you don't like it after all that?

SUSAN. Paul, is this for real?

PAUL. Is what for real?

SUSAN. This. *(the horse)*

PAUL. Oh, yes. *That's* for real. . . . I thought you meant the embryo and I was going to ask you about that because it seems to have slipped your mind.

SUSAN. Is that what this is all about?

PAUL. I just thought it might be worth bringing up.

SUSAN. Who told you? Selina?

PAUL. Oh, is that what's important? Who told me? It wasn't you, that's for sure. And it's a pretty god damn weird thing to find out about from someone else. That your wife had an abortion six months ago and didn't bother to tell you about it. I guess I must just be one of those naturally curious people because when I found out it made me want to know all kinds of things, Susan. Like just what the fuck has been going on in our life? All these wonderful little human dramas going on under my nose and I didn't know a thing about it. Was it mine?

SUSAN. Yes.

PAUL. Why didn't you tell me?

SUSAN. Paul, I don't know. I really don't know. I meant to. I wanted to.

PAUL. I see. Anything else, or is that sort of the full explanation?

SUSAN. I don't know anything else. I didn't mean not to tell you.

PAUL. That's very illuminating. That really makes me feel like this is something we can work out. I mean what are we, Susan? Remind me because it's getting kind of vague in my mind. Are we married? Something like that? Is there some kind of unique relationship here? Something that might be worth looking into? Are you saying you didn't tell me because it isn't an interesting fact, or it's just not a very important thing for me to know about? Or it's an unpleasant topic of conversation or it's none of my business? I mean, what is this shit???

SUSAN. Stop it . . .

PAUL. *Susan!!!!*

BEN *(appears on terrace)*. Hey, is everything . . .

PAUL. *Get out!!!*

BEN. I'm just inside if . . .

PAUL. *Get the fuck out of here!!!!* (BEN *retreats*) *(Quiet.)* It hurts, Susan. It just hurts. All this silence between us. All this unknown stuff. You know how much I want a kid. You know that. I mean what've I been doing for the past three years? Running my ass off building up a business—working twelve hours a day? Am I supposed to have been doing that for the deep satisfaction it gave me? Do you think I'm a mental defective or something? I mean at very worst, I thought this was all some kind of weird test I was going through—some bizarre nest-building ritual to prove I was worthy of fertilizing your eggs. That was the only way I could look at it and still feel marginally sane . . .

SUSAN. I don't believe this. Are you saying you did everything you did so I'd let you make a baby? Is that what you're saying? Because if it is . . . well, nice to know what you're keeping me around for. Thank you.

PAUL. Susan, you know that's not what I meant.

SUSAN. All I know is it's a pretty shitty thing to lay on me. Nobody forced you to do anything you didn't want to do. So what's this thing like it's all been some kind of terrible ordeal? Jesus, Paul, what's the matter with you? You are allowed to enjoy it, you know. There's no law that says you have to feel terrible about it. You earned it, for god sake. You deserve it. And I'm proud of you, babe. I really am. I just want to see you be happy with it.

PAUL. Ah, so that's why you had the abortion. That's why you didn't tell me—because you wanted me to be happy. You were doing it all for me. Gee, why didn't I see it that way? We really are wonderful people, aren't we Susan? We just do everything for each other.

SUSAN. All right. I didn't tell you. I was wrong—mea culpa. What can I say, Paul? I'm sorry? Because I am. But that doesn't have very much to do with anything right now, does it?

PAUL. But why? Why?

SUSAN. Babe, you don't get a whole lot of time to think about what you should do when there's this thing growing inside you. And it's not getting smaller. And the more you think things over the less small it's getting. It's not like I just popped down to the friendly neighborhood abortionist. I did think it over just a little bit before I went through with it.

PAUL. But why didn't you say anything?

SUSAN (quiet). Paul. I like what we have. I guess I just don't want anything to change it all.

PAUL. And telling me would have changed it all.

SUSAN. I don't know. Wouldn't it?

PAUL. Well, if it would then what the hell is it we have that's so great?

SUSAN. Oh, so now we have nothing . . .

PAUL. Well tell me, Susan, what do we have? Tell me what we have . . .

SUSAN. Everything you've done. Everything I've done. Everything we've got. It's all nothing? None of it means anything to you? My god, Paul, how you must be suffering.

PAUL. We really hate each other, don't we?

SUSAN. Babe, I don't hate you. I just don't

understand why we always make everything so complicated for each other. Hasn't this been a good time? I mean, I was under the impression we were more or less happy. In fact, I was even thinking if Greg and Francine get divorced we'll be the longest couple of all our friends.

PAUL. Except for Doug and Maraya.

SUSAN. That doesn't count. They're not married. Shit!

PAUL. What?

SUSAN. I'm smoking.

(They smile.)

PAUL. I don't know what it is, Susan. I mean, yes, I want all this. Sometimes. Sometimes I'm really amazed it's me that's doing all this. There's been whole weeks when I went around thinking, "hey, this is a pretty good deal. I'm happy." I mean, this is it, right? This must be it. I must be happy. But then one day I'll come home, I'll go in there and try to get comfortable, read or something and for some reason I just can't concentrate. Try to watch TV, can't even manage that. So I start walking around the apartment and I see all the stuff we have. All this stuff. And I start thinking about what we do to get it. You pick up a little box and go click. I tape together pieces of film. Presto. We have everything we want. We're so good at doing these little things that make us able to have all this stuff, but we can't get it together to have one stupid little baby. Us. The two of us. Together. Doesn't that ever seem strange to you? You know, sort of intuitively wrong? Absurd. Something like that?

SUSAN. No, Paul. I'm sorry, it doesn't. The only thing I find strange is the way I keep feeling like I have to have a baby to be enough for you. I mean, what if I decide a baby isn't as important to me as a lot of other things? What happens if I decide that all I want is you? And our life together? And our work? I mean, couldn't that be enough? Paul. (pause) Paul. Paul, answer me. Am I enough for you without a baby? (Pause) I see. And you wanted to know why I couldn't tell you.

PAUL. I don't know. I don't know. Why didn't you say something before this?

SUSAN. Maybe I didn't want to know what I just found out. Well, Paul, I'm sorry. I'm sorry you feel so badly about your accomplishments because I'm feeling pretty good about mine and I can't see any reason why I shouldn't. Doug starts doing well, you laugh about it. You think it's funny. You do well and suddenly it's wrong. I don't get it. You can't have it all ways, babe. We're not children any more. You have what you have. If you want it, keep it and stop making excuses for it. And if you want to be a saint, go back and dig outhouses for the Nglele.

PAUL. Oh boy.

SUSAN. What?

PAUL. We're in a lot of trouble, aren't we?

SUSAN. I guess we are.

PAUL. So now what?

SUSAN. I don't know. Should we be talking about this now?

PAUL. No. I want to go out and have a great time with Ben and Janice and Phil.

SUSAN. All right. We'll talk about it now. What are we going to do?

PAUL. I don't know.

SUSAN. Well, we're going to have to do something, aren't we?

PAUL. Like a divorce, you mean?

SUSAN. Is that what you want?

PAUL. Do you?

SUSAN. Well, I hadn't exactly been thinking about it a whole lot. Not today. Are you serious?

PAUL. Isn't that what's going on here? Can you think of anything else we could do?

SUSAN. Well, well, happy birthday.

PAUL. I meant it to hurt, Susan.

SUSAN. Yes. We'll call a lawyer in the morning.

PAUL. Lawyer? *(pause)* O.K.

SUSAN. Fine.

PAUL. Jesus.

(Plane flies over. They look at each other. Blackout.)

SCENE EIGHT

Slide: 1979   The cabin, winter, snow outside. Early evening. Open potbelly stove with fire. Old couch with crochet-square afghan covering it. PAUL and SUSAN wrapped in blankets, naked beneath. PAUL sits on couch. SUSAN showing slides on wall from projector with a carousel. Slide' of DOUG and MARAYA and three children standing proudly in front of construction firm's office building. Then the carousel is at an end leaving white square on wall.

PAUL. Wait a minute. Go back. Let me see the last one again.

(SUSAN backs up to DOUG and MARAYA and family.) Doug and Maraya. He shaved off his beard.

SUSAN. Yeah, a couple of months ago. That's

his office. I used it for background on a job. *(turns the lights on)* I think he's a little upset you haven't been in touch.

PAUL. It's the first time I've been back east.

SUSAN. You could've called. Written a letter.

PAUL. Hey.

SUSAN. What?

PAUL. This is real nice. I'd sort of forgotten. Well, I hadn't forgotten, but I hadn't remembered with total accuracy if you know what I mean.

SUSAN. I think I know what you mean.

PAUL. So you actually went and bought this place.

SUSAN. Yeah, nostalgia. I got a good deal. The Pearsons let me have it cheap because we'd been married here. They're sentimental.

PAUL. Opportunist.

SUSAN. How come you haven't been in touch with anyone? Selina was asking about you. Gary and Linda. Even Lawrence. You hiding in San Francisco?

PAUL. No, I just . . . it didn't feel real until the divorce came through. I don't know. I just didn't want to think about all that.

SUSAN. Who's Edie?

PAUL. Edie?

(SUSAN exits into bedroom, keeps talking.)

SUSAN *(off)*. Yeah. I called you in San Francisco a couple months ago and someone called Edie answered the phone.

PAUL. Oh. She never said anything.

SUSAN *(off)*. What?

PAUL. I said she never said anything.

SUSAN *(off)*. I didn't tell her who I was.

PAUL. More secrets, huh.

SUSAN *(off)*. Who is she?

PAUL. Just a woman I'm seeing.

SUSAN *(off)*. Ah-hah. Seeing a woman called Edie, eh?

PAUL. She's nice. She has a kid.

SUSAN *(off)*. Is it serious?

PAUL. I don't know. She's a photographer, speaking of making the same mistake twice.

(SUSAN enters, dressing. PAUL puts wood in the stove.)

SUSAN. You're kidding.

PAUL. Not only that. She picked the same yellow tiles for her bathroom as you picked for ours.

SUSAN. She has good taste.

PAUL. Well, she picked me.

SUSAN. Are you happy?

PAUL. Happy? Why? I mean, yeah. I guess so. What about you?

SUSAN. Oh, I'm O.K. It's just . . . like this.

Today, being with you again, I just started remembering how nice it was. Sometimes. When it was nice. We should've married other people and had a long affair.

PAUL. It's a nice school where I'm teaching. Nice kids. Very bright. Rich, of couse. I like it, though. I really do. I guess I'm happy.

SUSAN. Good.

PAUL. Hey.

SUSAN. Do you do that with Edie? Say "hey"?

PAUL. Come here.

SUSAN *(watching him)*. I knew it'd happen like this. You'd just show up all of a sudden. Wouldn't phone. I'd've been able to say no if you phoned. It's funny how we can't seem to keep our hands off each other, even now.

PAUL. Come here.

SUSAN. Hang on a second. *(Exits again. Off)* How's Ben doing?

PAUL. Better. They did a cardiogram and discovered he'd had another heart attack three years before this one. Hadn't even known about it. Just cured himself.

SUSAN *(off)*. Still drinking?

PAUL. Not for now. What are you doing in there?

SUSAN *(off)*. Looking for my boots.

PAUL. What are you getting dressed for? Let's raid the ice-box. It's almost time for— *(Watch)* . . . jesus, it's only five. I forgot how early it gets dark up here in the winter.

SUSAN *(off)*. Go ahead. Help yourself. I think there's some chicken.

PAUL. Aren't you hungry? You always used to get hungry afterwards.

SUSAN *(enters, dressed)*. How do I look?

PAUL. Terrible. Come here.

SUSAN. Why don't you get some food?

PAUL. Are you going somewhere?

SUSAN. Paul, I have a life. I can't just stop everything just because you show up unannounced. I'd made plans for dinner.

PAUL. Oh, you didn't say.

SUSAN. I wasn't really expecting anything like this to happen. It didn't leave much time for talking, did it.

PAUL. No, I guess not. Who's the lucky man?

SUSAN. You don't know him.

PAUL. What's his name?

SUSAN. Jerry.

PAUL. He's coming here?

SUSAN. Don't worry. I'll go out to the car.

PAUL. Can I come? Sorry. Can I wait for you?

SUSAN. I don't think that'd be a very good idea.

PAUL. You're coming back with him?

SUSAN. We usually do.

PAUL. You see him a lot, huh?

SUSAN. He has a place near here. It's convenient. He lives in New York. He's an illustrator. He's 5'11", 165 pounds, vegetarian, blue eyes. Anything else you'd like to know?

PAUL. He sounds fabulous.

SUSAN. He's all right. Actually, he's very nice.

PAUL. Nice. Funny, that's what I said about Edie. Maybe we should introduce them. When'll I see you again?

SUSAN. When'll you be back east?

PAUL. Depends. I might come back real soon if you made me a good offer. Another dirty weekend in New Hampshire.

SUSAN. I don't think we should do this again.

PAUL. Why not?

SUSAN. Well . . . we're being unfaithful. I don't know, Paul. I guess you just don't get over nine years so easily. I don't.

PAUL. No.

(Car noise outside)

SUSAN. Jesus, he's early. What time is it?

(PAUL has a watch.)

PAUL. Ten past.

SUSAN. Damn. Do I look O.K.? Sorry. Listen, when you go just throw a few logs on the fire and make sure the damper's turned down. Bye, Paul. (SUSAN *takes winter coat and starts out door. Stops. Yells outside . . .*) Hang on, Jerry, I'll be right out. I . . . I forgot my bag. (SUSAN *comes back into room. She and* PAUL *embrace, kiss, hold each other. Then it's over.*) Bye, babe.

PAUL. Bye.

(SUSAN *goes.* PAUL *watches car from window. When it's gone he sits, turns on projector, watches slides. Fade.*)

The Ritz

Terrence McNally

First presented at the Longacre Theatre in New York City on January 20, 1975, by Adela Holzer, with the following cast:

(*in order of appearance*)

ABE	George Dzundza
CLAUDE PERKINS	Paul B. Price
GAETANO PROCLO	Jack Weston
CHRIS	F. Murray Abraham
GOOGIE GOMEZ	Rita Moreno
MAURINE	Hortensia Colorado
MICHAEL BRICK	Stephen Collins
TIGER	John Everson
DUFF	Christopher J. Brown
CARMINE VESPUCCI	Jerry Stiller
VIVIAN PROCLO	Ruth Jaroslow
PIANIST	Ron Abel
POLICEMAN	Bruce Bauer
CRISCO	Richard Boccelli
SHELDON FARENTHOLD	Tony DeSantis
PATRON IN CHAPS	John Remme
PATRON FROM SHERIDAN SQUARE	Steve Scott

Directed by Robert Drivas
Scenery and Costumes by Michael H. Yeargan and Lawrence King
Lighting by Martin Aronstein

The Ritz, Terrence McNally's tenth play, is a comedy in three acts. It was originally presented as *The Tubs* at the Yale Repertory Theatre in 1974 and ran for thirty-five performances. It was then presented at the National Theatre in Washington for two weeks in December of the same year. It opened on Broadway at the Longacre Theatre in January 1975. *The Ritz* won a Tony award for both its author and for Rito Moreno, who played the character of Googie Gomez.

McNally describes *The Ritz* as "a comedy of mayhem, mishaps and mistaken identities that occur when a garbage man from Cleveland goes to a Turkish bath in Manhattan." A small time businessman, Gaetano Proclo, played by Jack Weston, is on the run from his mobster brother-in-law and hides out in an obscure bath house, The Ritz. What he does not immediately know is that it is patronized exclusively by males. At no point is his life or his manhood entirely safe, and in his battle to preserve both he meets some unforgetable characters: Googie Gomez, a night club singer disguised as a man; Claude Perkins, a "Chubby Chaser" and Carmine Vespucci, Procolo's homicidal brother-in-law, played by Jerry Stiller.

Puppets provided McNally's first interest in the theatre. There was no theatre in Corpus Christi, Texas, where he was born and grew up, but "Kukla, Fran and Ollie," a puppet show, was presented on television. While a young man, McNally dreamed of being a writer, a journalist. He recalls his youth as a combination of *American Graffiti* and Bach's Mass in B Minor— *American Graffiti* because he rode around Mac's Drive-In in cars with his friends, going to the beach, drinking beer, playing poker on Sundays after having skipped church and Bach's Mass in B Minor because he read poetry and plays and listened to Bach without being considered a misfit. He had a high-school English teacher who encouraged him to read by including him in a salon at her home where she discussed Shelley and Shakespeare on Sunday afternoons.

McNally's parents had migrated from New York to Texas. His father, a beer distributor, "made Schlitz the best-selling beer in Corpus Christi." At the age of five he went to see *Annie Get Your Gun* starring Ethel Merman, and it made a lasting impression. At twelve, a nun in a parochial school introduced him to opera, turning him into an "opera freak." As a youngster he used to write stories and start small newspapers. His first effort was created from the background notes on a George Gershwin album. "My first play had George marrying a pretty girl named Ira, and it ended with George dying and the cast, including Ginger Rogers and Ethel Merman, saying 'he'd want us to go on with the show.' "

McNally received a bachelor of arts in English literature from Columbia University. A creative-writing prize awarded during his senior year led him to Mexico for a year to write a novel. Instead he wrote an autobiographical play called *This Side of the Door,* which won the Stanley award from the New York City Writers Conference in 1962. It was produced at a New York drama workshop run by Richard Barr and Edward Albee. McNally turned down a proposed Off-Broadway production because he felt that the personal nature of the play would embarrass his parents. Still, the play led to a stage manager's job at the Actor's Studio, after he sent a copy of it to Mollie Kazan, who thought that he had talent but not much experience.

While at the Actor's Studio, he joined the author's workshop, where in 1965, he wrote *And Things That Go Bump in the Night.* Alan Schneider, a director at the Studio, urged him to send it to the Tyrone Guthrie Theatre in Minneapolis where it was staged in a very successful production. It then came to Broadway where it flopped, McNally believes, because of a changed cast and revisions made in the script under pressure from the producers. He was so crushed that he almost quit writing entirely. After a few years, encouraged by his friends Robert Drivas and Elaine May, he wrote *Next,* directed by May and performed first at the Berkshire Theatre Festival and then Off Broadway; *Sweet Eros,* produced Off Broadway in 1968; and *Where Has Tommy Flowers Gone,* performed at the Yale Rep in 1969.

Bad Habits was his next commercial success, composed of two short plays, *Dunelawn* and *Ravenswood.* Originally *Dunelawn* was performed at East Hampton and was then paired with *Ravenswood* at the Manhattan Theatre Club in 1973 and then at the Astor Place Theatre in 1974. It eventually made its way to Broadway, where it was performed at the Longacre Theatre in 1975.

McNally has also written *Witness; Noon* from *Morning, Noon and Night* in collaboration with Israel Horovitz and Leonard Melfi; *Apple Pie,* three short plays for WNET; *Tour,* part of *Collision Course* with Horovitz and Melfi; *Cuba-si; Whiskey* from *Wine, Whiskey and Wild, Wild Women,* also with Horovitz and Melfi; *Bye Bye Broadway;* and *Adaptation,* produced by

Lyn Austin and Oliver Smith. He was also the librettist of the musical *Here's Where I Belong* based on John Steinbeck's *East of Eden*, produced by Mitch Miller and United Artists at the Billy Rose Theatre in 1968.

McNally has been awarded the Harry Evans Traveling Fellowship in Creative Writing, a Guggenheim Fellowship in 1967 for *And Things That Go Bump in the Night*, an Obie award and the Elizabeth Hull-Kate Warriner award for *Bad Habits* in 1974.

The time of the play is now.

The place of the play is a men's bathhouse in New York City.

The people of the play are:

GAETANO PROCLO: *He is in his early 40s, balding and stout.*

CHRIS: *He is in his early 30s with a big, open face and features.*

MICHAEL BRICK: *He is in his mid-20s, very rugged and very handsome.*

CARMINE VESPUCCI: *He is in his 40s, balding and stout.*

CLAUDE PERKINS: *He is in his 40s and quite lean.*

TIGER: *He is in his early 20s, wiry and has lots of curly hair.*

DUFF: *He too is in his early 20s, wiry and has lots of curly hair. In fact, he looks a lot like Tiger.*

ABE: *He is in his 50s and stocky.*

THE PATRONS: *They come in all sizes, shapes and ages.*

GOOGIE GOMEZ: *She is in her 30s and has a sensational figure.*

VIVIAN PROCLO: *She is in her early 40s and stout.*

MAURINE: *She's in her mid-40s and very thin.*

ACT ONE

The house curtain is in, the house lights are on and the overture from "Tancredi" is playing as the audience comes in. The house goes to black. In the darkness we hear the sounds of the Rosary being recited. Occasionally a stifled sob overrides the steady incantation of the prayers.

———

PRIESTS AND RELATIVES. Hail Mary, full of grace, the Lord is with thee. Blessed art thou amongst women and blessed is the fruit of thy womb, Jesus. Holy Mary, Mother of God, pray for us sinners now and at the hour of our death. Amen. *(Underneath all this, the funeral march from "Nabucco" is heard. The lights have revealed* OLD MAN VESPUCCI'S *death bed. Relatives and family are grouped around him, all in silhouette. Kneeling to his right is* CARMINE. *Kneeling to his left is* VIVIAN. *They are weeping profusely.)*

CARMINE. Poppa . . .

VIVIAN. Poppa . . . *(The death rattles are beginning.* OLD MAN VESPUCCI *feebly summons*

the others to draw close for his final words.)

AUNT VERA. *Aspetta! Aspetta!*

COUSIN HORTENSIA. Sshh! Speak to us, Poppa!

AUNT VERA. Give us your blessing, Poppa!

COUSIN HORTENSIA. One final word, Poppa!

AUNT VERA. *Un poccita parole,* Poppa!

VIVIAN. Give us your blessing, Poppa!

OLD MAN VESPUCCI. Vivian.

VIVIAN. Yes, Poppa?

OLD MAN VESPUCCI. *Vieni qua.*

VIVIAN. Yes, Poppa.

OLD MAN VESPUCCI. Get Proclo.

VIVIAN. Get Proclo, Poppa? Yes, Poppa. He's coming. The plane was late from Cleveland. He'll be here for your blessing. *(*OLD MAN VESPUCCI *dismisses his daughter with a hand gesture.)*

OLD MAN VESPUCCI. Carmine, my son.

CARMINE. Yes, Poppa. I'm here, Poppa.

OLD MAN VESPUCCI. Get Proclo.

CARMINE. Get Proclo, Poppa?

OLD MAN VESPUCCI. Get Proclo. *Qui brute. Qui boce. Tha botania!* Kill him! Kill him! Kill him! Kill the son of a bitch!

VIVIAN. Proclo is my husband, Poppa!

OLD MAN VESPUCCI *(Finally mustering all the strength he can, he raises himself up).* GET PROCLO!!! *(He falls back dead.)*

RELATIVES *(simultaneously).* Aaaaaiiiieeeee!

AUNT VERA. *Poppa è morto!*

PRIEST. *In nomine partis et filii et spiritu sancti requiescat in . . . (The lights fade on the death bed. At the same time, the sound of a pounding drum is heard. It is the opening of "One of a Kind." The lights come up, revealing activity inside The Ritz behind scrims. The main things we see are doors. Doors and doors and doors. Each door has a number. Outside all these are corridors. Lots and lots of corridors. Filling these corridors are men. Lots and lots of men. They are prowling the corridors. One of the most important aspects of the production in this sense of men endlessly prowling the corridors outside the numbered doors. The same people will pass up and down the same corridors and stairways over and over again. After a while, you'll start to think some of them are on a treadmill. Most of them are dressed exactly alike; i.e., they are wearing bathrobes. A few men wear towels around their waists. Every so often we see someone in bikini underwear or an additional accoutrement, such as boots or a vest. The nubmer of men, referred to from now on as the patrons, can vary, but each actor must be*

encouraged to develop a specific characteri-
zation. Even though they seldom speak, these
various patrons must become specific, integral
members of the cast. We also see TIGER *and*
DUFF, *two attendants. They are sweeping up*
and making beds. Over the music, we hear
announcements.)

ABE *(over the loudspeaker).* 217 coming up,
Duff! . . . Tiger, they're out of soap in the
showers! On the double! And check the linens
and robes on the third floor . . . Just a reminder
that every Monday and Thursday is Buddy
Night at the Ritz. So bring a friend. Two entrances for the price of one. *(The lights dim,*
and the entrance area is flown in. The inner
door and Abe's booth are moved on from left
to right. The center scrim flies as the lights
come up bright, and we are in the admissions
area of The Ritz. The various patrons will pay,
check their valuables, receive a room key and
then be buzzed through the inner door adjacent
to the booth. One patron has just finished
checking in. As he is buzzed through the door,
we see ABE *announce his room number over*
a loudspeaker.) 274! That's 274 coming up,
Duff! *(The patron disappears. The phone on*
ABE's *desk rings, and he answers.)* Hello. The
Ritz. No, we don't take reservations! *(He hangs*
up, as another PATRON *enters.)*

PATRON. Good evening.

ABE. Yeah?

PATRON. Nasty night.

ABE. Is it?

PATRON. I'm one big puddle.

ABE. Well watch where you're dripping. I
just had that floor mopped.

PATRON. I'd like a room, please.

ABE. That's ten bucks. Sign the registration
book and check in your valuables. *(The* PA-
TRON *begins the check-in procedure.* CLAUDE
PERKINS *has entered from the outside. He is*
wearing a rincoat over rather ordinary clothes.
He carries a bag from Zabar's Delicatessen
and has a Valet Pack slung over one shoulder.
He gets in line behind the PATRON.)

PATRON. You're dripping.

CLAUDE. What?

PATRON. I said, you're dripping.

CLAUDE. Of course I'm dripping. It's pouring out there.

PATRON. Well try not to. They don't like
you dripping here. *(He starts for the door.)*
See you. *(He is buzzed through.)*

CLAUDE. I hope not.

ABE *(over the loudspeaker).* 376! That's room
376! Coming up, Duff!

CLAUDE. That's a good floor for that one.
Nobody goes up there.

ABE. Well look who's back. Hello, stranger.

CLAUDE. Hello, Abe.

ABE. I thought you'd sworn off this place.

CLAUDE. I thought I had, too.

ABE. You got homesick for us, right?

CLAUDE. I didn't have much choice. I don't
speak Spanish, so the Continental is out. The
Club Baths are just too far downtown, I'm
boycotting the Beacon, Man's Country's had
it and I've been barred from the Everard.

ABE. You've been barred from the Everard?

CLAUDE. They'll regret it.

ABE. Nobody gets barred from the Everard.
How'd you manage that?

CLAUDE. There was this man there.

ABE. A fat man, right?

CLAUDE. Fat? He was the magic mountain.
He drove me into one of my frenzies. I went
berserk and I kicked his door in. So they threw
me out and told me never to come back. I was
willing to pay for it. I just wanted to talk to
him.

ABE. Pick on somebody your own size, why
don't you, Claude?

CLAUDE. I wouldn't like that. How much do
you weight?

ABE. Forget it.

CLAUDE. Are you up to 200 yet?

ABE. Forget it!

CLAUDE. Couldn't we just install a weigh-
in station here?

ABE. I said forget it! You want to check that?

CLAUDE. It's my costume for the talent show.
(He is heading for the door, still carrying the
Valet Pack and Zabar's shopping bag.) It's
good to be back, Abe. I'm feeling strangely
optimistic this evening.

ABE. Just don't kick any doors in.

CLAUDE. I hope I don't have to. *(Claude is*
buzzed through the door.)

ABE. 205! Coming up! That's 205! (GAE-
TANO PROCLO *comes dashing in. He is carrying*
a suitcase and a big box of Panettone, the
Italian bakery specialty. He is wearing a wet
raincoat, a cheap wig, a big bushy moustache
and dark glasses. He goes directly to ABE.)

PROCLO. Can you cash a check for me? It's
on Ohio State National.

ABE. What do I look like? A teller in a bank?

PROCLO. You don't understand. I've got a
cab waiting. I'll be right back. That's why I
got into the cab in the first place, to go somewhere, and it's to here I've come. *(sounds of*
a horn blowing) You hear that? That's him!

ABE. You got a traveler's check?

PROCLO. No.

ABE. Travelers are supposed to have traveler's checks.

PROCLO. Well this traveler doesn't. We left Cleveland in a hurry. Traveler's checks are for people who plan! *(more honking)* There he goes again!

ABE. I'm sorry.

PROCLO. Look, I've got all the identification in the world. Driver's license, Social Security, Blue Cross, voter registration, Rotary Club. . . . What about my business card? "Proclo Sanitation Services, Gaetano Proclo, President." That's me.

ABE. You got a credit card?

PROCLO. I don't want credit, I want cash!

ABE. N-o, buddy.

PROCLO. Oh come on! Do I look like someone who would try to pass a bad check? *(a realization)* Why of course I do! *(He takes off his dark glasses.)* There! Now can you see me? *(more honking)* Oh all right! *(He removes his moustache.)* Now are you satisfied?

ABE. I don't make the rules here.

PROCLO. Wait! Wait! *(He takes off his wig.)* Everything else is real.

ABE. I'd like to help you out, mac, but—

PROCLO. The only thing that's gonna calm me down is *you* cashing my check. My brother-in-law is a maniac and he's going to kill me tonight. If you don't let me in there I'm going to be a dead person. Please, mister, you are making a grown man cry. I'm begging you. It's a matter of life and death! *(more honking)*

ABE. I shouldn't really be doing this but . . .

PROCLO. You are a good man . . .

ABE. Abe.

PROCLO. Abe. I'm gonna have a novena said for you when I get back to Cleveland. What's your last name? Abe what?

ABE. Lefkowitz.

PROCLO. I'm *still* gonna have that novena said for you! *(More honking.* CHRIS *has entered from the outside. He wears jeans, a blue nylon windbreaker, and a bright purple shirt. He carries an overnight bag. Also, he is wearing a policeman's whistle and a "popper" holder around his neck.)*

CHRIS. Does anybody have a cab waiting?

PROCLO. What?

CHRIS. Is that your cab out there?

PROCLO. Oh yes, yes, it is!

CHRIS. Well you've also got one very pissed off driver.

PROCLO *(To* ABE*).* Can you cash this for me

now? *(to* CHRIS*)* How pissed off is he?

CHRIS. On a ten scale? Ten. *(more honking)*

PROCLO. Christ! *(*PROCLO *is fumbling with the money and heading for the door.)* Keep an eye on those for me, will you?

CHRIS. Sure thing. *(*PROCLO *hurries out.* CHRIS *looks at the suitcase and the Panettone.)* Planning a big night of it, honey? *(to* ABE*)* I had a friend who tried moving into the baths.

ABE. What happened?

CHRIS. He died from a lack of sunshine. He died happy and blind, but he still died.

ABE. We missed you last week.

CHRIS. How do you think your customers felt? I'm a legend in my own lifetime. *(yelling into* ABE'*s microphone)* Try to hold out, men! Help is on the way!

ABE. Hold your horses, Chris.

CHRIS. That's all I've been holding all week.

ABE. You wanna sign in?

CHRIS *(while he writes).* How's that gorgeous son of yours?

ABE. You're too late. He's getting married.

CHRIS. That's terrific. Give him my love, will you?

ABE. Sure thing, Chris.

CHRIS. Does he need anyone to practice with?

ABE. He's been practicing too much. That's why he's getting married.

CHRIS. Compared to me, Abe, she'd have to be an amateur. *(He returns the registration book.)*

ABE. Ronald Reagen! Aw, c'mon, Chris!

CHRIS. You know, he used to be lovers with John Wayne.

ABE. Sure he was.

CHRIS. Right after he broke up with Xavier Cugat.

ABE. People like you think the whole world's queer.

CHRIS. It's lucky for people like you it is. *(*PROCLO *comes rushing back in.)*

PROCLO. He can't change a ten! Do you believe it? New York City, one of the great cities of the world, and this driver I have can't change a ten!

CHRIS. They still don't take anything over a five.

PROCLO. In Cleveland even a paper boy can change a ten!

CHRIS. Did I ever have you?

PROCLO. What?

CHRIS. I've got a rotten memory that way. You never used to live in Rego Park?

PROCLO. No!

CHRIS. 'Cause you look like someone I knew

once who was from Rego Park.

PROCLO. I'm afraid not.

CHRIS. He was a large man like you and he was in ladies' shoes, I remember.

PROCLO. Well I'm from Cleveland and I'm in refuse.

CHRIS. I guess not then. Sorry.

PROCLO. That's perfectly all right. *(He hurries back out.)*

CHRIS. A gay garbageman!

ABE. You never can tell.

CHRIS. That's true. I mean, look at me. If you just saw me walking down the street, you'd think I was a queen. *(CHRIS blows his whistle as he is buzzed through the door.)* All right, men! Up against the wall. This is a raid!

ABE. 240! Two-four-oh. She's here, boys! *(A young man has entered from outside. His name is MICHAEL BRICK. He steps up to the admissions booth.)*

MICHAEL. I'd like a room, please. *(The first time we hear MICHAEL's voice we are in for a shock. It is a high, boy soprano-ish treble. A timbre totally incongruous with his rugged physique.)* One of your private rooms. How much is that?

ABE. You want what?

MICHAEL. A room, please. I was told you have private rooms.

ABE. Yeah, we got rooms.

MICHAEL. Then I'd like one, sir. How much is that?

ABE. How long?

MICHAEL. Is what, sir?

ABE. How long do you want it for?

MICHAEL. Three or four hours should be sufficient for my purposes.

ABE. I don't care what your purposes are: twelve's our minimum.

MICHAEL. All right, twelve then, sir.

ABE. That's ten bucks. Sign in and I'll take your valuables.

MICHAEL. Tell me something. Has a balding, middle-aged fat man come in here recently?

ABE. I don't believe what just came in here recently.

MICHAEL. Think hard. I'll repeat his description. A balding, middle-aged fat man.

ABE. We got all kinds inside. Fat, thin, short, tall, young, old. I can't keep track.

MICHAEL. Well I guess I'll just have to go in and see for myself, sir.

ABE. I guess you will. You're not a cop, are you?

MICHAEL. I'm a detective, sir. Michael Brick. The Greybar Agency. Our client wants the goods on him and I'm just the man to get them. I've never failed a client yet. What do I do now?

ABE. Through there and up the stairs. Someone'll show you your room.

MICHAEL. Thank you, sir.

ABE. Let me give you a little tip, Brick. Stay out of the steam room.

MICHAEL. Why, sir?

ABE. It gets pretty wild in there.

MICHAEL. Oh, I can take it, sir. In my line of work I get to do a lot of wild things. This is my first seduction job. Wish me luck.

ABE. With that voice, you'll need it. *(MICHAEL is buzzed through the door and is gone.)* 101 coming up! That's one-oh-one! Oh boy, oh boy, oh boy! *(GOOGIE GOMEZ comes into the admissions area, protecting herself from the rain with a wet copy of Variety. She is carrying a wig box and wardrobe bag.)*

GOOGIE. No rain, he tells me! No rain, he says! No rain! That fucking Tex Antoine! That little *Maricon*! I'd like to pull his little beard off! One spot on this dress and I'm finished! The biggest night of my life and it's pissing dogs and cats.

PROCLO *(who has entered behind GOOGIE).* That's cats and dogs. *(GOOGIE has been so busy worrying about rain spots on her dress she really hasn't noticed PROCLO yet. When she does, there is a marked change in her behavior and vocabulary.)*

GOOGIE. Joe Papp. Hello, Mr. Papp. It's a real pleasure to meet you. I seen all your shows. Uptown, downtown, in the park. They're all fabulous. *Fabulosa!* And I just know, in my heart of hearts, that after you see my show tonight you're going to want to give me a chance at one of your wonderful theatres. Uptown, downtown, in the park. I'll even work the mobile theatre. Thank you for coming, Mr. Papp. Excuse me, I got a little laryngitis. But the show must go on, *si?*

PROCLO. My name isn't Papp.

GOOGIE. You're not Joe Papp?

PROCLO. I'm sorry.

GOOGIE. But you are a producer?

PROCLO. No.

GOOGIE. Are you sure?

PROCLO. Yes.

GOOGIE. That's okay. I heard there was gonna be a big producer around tonight and I wasn't taking any chances. You never know. It's hard for me to speak English good like that. *(A new outburst.)* Aaaaiiieee! My God, not the hairs! *Coño! (Her hands are hovering in the vicinity of her head.)* Okay. Go ahead and say it. It's okay. I can take it. Tell me I look like shit.

PROCLO. Why would I want to say a thing like that to such an attractive young lady?

GOOGIE. You boys really know how to cheer a girl up when she's dumps in the down. *(She gives* PROCLO *a kiss on the cheek.)* My boyfriend Hector see me do that: *ay! cuidado!* He hates you *maricones,* that Hector! He's a ballbreaker with me, too, mister. You know why you're not a producer? You're too nice to be a producer. But I'm gonna show them all, mister, and tonight's the night I'm gonna do it. *(*GOOGIE *is moving toward the door.)* One day you gonna see the name Googie Gomez in lights and you gonna say to yourself ''Was that *her?''* And you gonna answer yourself ''That was her!'' But you know something, mister? I was *always* her. Just nobody knows it. *Yo soy Googie Gomez, estrellita del future!* (GOOGIE *is buzzed through the door and is gone.)*

PROCLO. Who the hell was that?

ABE. Googie.

PROCLO. I thought this was a bathhouse.

ABE. It is.

PROCLO. A *male* bathhouse!

ABE. It is.

PROCLO. Then what's she doing in there?

ABE. Googie sings in The Pits.

PROCLO. The pits? What pits?

ABE. The nightclub.

PROCLO. You've got a nightclub in there?

ABE. We've got a nighclub, movies, TV, swimming pool, steam room, sauna, massage table, discotheque, bridge, amateur night and free blood tests every Wednesday. . . . *(*PROCLO *turns at the sound of* MAURINE *entering behind him from outside. She is wearing a duffel coat with the hood up, pants and tall rubber rain boots. No chic dresser,* MAURINE. *She seems deep in concentration and takes no notice of* PROCLO *as she moves toward the door.)* How'd it go today, Mo? *(*MAURINE *just shrugs. She is buzzed through the door and is gone.)*

PROCLO. I don't even want to *think* what she does.

ABE. Mo's just our accountant.

PROCLO. I asked that cab driver to bring me to the last place in the world anybody would think of looking for me.

ABE. You found it.

PROCLO. Except everybody in the world is already in there. I need calm, privacy, safety tonight.

ABE. So stay in your room and keep your door locked.

PROCLO. Don't worry. I will. How much is that?

ABE. Ten dollars. *(*PROCLO *looks at the registration book.)*

PROCLO. Ronald Reagan!

ABE. You can write John Doe for all I care. Just so long as we get some kind of a name down there.

PROCLO. Any name at all? Oh, Abe, I'm gonna speak to the Pope about getting you canonized! *(reads what he's written)* ''Carmine Vespucci, Bensonhurst, Brooklyn.''

ABE. Who's that?

PROCLO. My maniac brother-in-law who was going to kill me tonight!

ABE. What did you do to him?

PROCLO. I got born and I married his sister.

ABE. That's all?

PROCLO. Just my whole life. *(*PROCLO *gathers his suitcase and Panettone, ready to enter now.)*

ABE. Do you mind if I ask you a personal question?

PROCLO. The man who just saved my life can ask me anything.

ABE. You ever been in a place like this?

PROCLO. Oh sure. We got a Jack LaLanne's in Cleveland. *(The door is buzzed and* PROCLO *goes through.)*

ABE. 196! That's one-nine-six coming up, Duff. Oh boy, oh boy, oh boy! *(While* ABE *is speaking, the lights will fade on the admissions area and ''Just Can't Get You Out of My Mind'' comes up. The admissions area and the scrims are flown. Other lights are coming up and we are in the interior of The Ritz. On the lower level we see* TIGER *sweeping up. Chris enters behind him.)*

TIGER. Hey, Chris.

GHRIS. Hi, Tiger.

TIGER. What took you so long? They called your number ten minutes ago.

CHRIS. I was in the boutique.

TIGER. What'd you buy?

CHRIS. A red light bulb for my room and this month's *Viva.*

TIGER. You don't need a red light bulb.

CHRIS. And I hope I don't need this month's *Viva.* Much action tonight?

TIGER. With you here I'm sure there will be.

CHRIS. Slow, hunh?

TIGER. Real dead, so far.

CHRIS. Don't worry, honey, I'll shake this place up good.

TIGER. If anybody can it's you.

CHRIS. The thing that no one understands about me is that sex is just my way of saying hello.

TIGER. Yeah, but you want to say hello to everybody you meet.

CHRIS. Don't you?

TIGER. I work here!

CHRIS. I wish I did. *(They go.* CLAUDE PERKINS *has come up to the wandering and lost* PROCLO. *The love theme from "Now, Voyager" plays.)*

CLAUDE. Hello, there.

PROCLO. Hello.

CLAUDE. What seems to be the problem?

PROCLO. I can't seem to find my room.

CLAUDE. Well you just come with me.

PROCLO. Why thank you. That's very kind of you. *(They leave together. On the upper level we see* DUFF. CHRIS *comes up the stairs and pokes his head into the steam room.)*

CHRIS. Guess who!

DUFF. Hey, Chris.

CHRIS. Hi, Duffie.

DUFF. 240 again?

CHRIS. And it better be clean! Last time they were having a crab race on the sheets.

DUFF. I did it myself, first thing when I came on. *(He opens the door with* CHRIS's *key.)*

CHRIS. Home sweet home! If these walls could talk . . . !

DUFF. They don't have to.

CHRIS. I've spent some of the happiest hours of my life in this room.

DUFF. I know. We've all heard you.

CHRIS. When are we gonna get together, you cute little hump?

DUFF. I don't know. Ask Tiger.

CHRIS. That means "forget it." Out! Out! I've got a busy night ahead of me. I hope. *(calling out loudly)* There will be an orgy beginning in room 240 in exactly four minutes! That's an orgy in room 240 in exactly four minutes! *(He goes into his room and closes the door. We have been watching* CLAUDE *lead* PROCLO *to his—that is,* CLAUDE's*—room.* CLAUDE *has followed* PROCLO *in and has closed the door.)*

PROCLO. Are you sure this is 196? I think this is someone else's room. Look, see the clothes?

CLAUDE. You'll never guess what I made for dinner tonight, so I'm just going to have to tell you.

PROCLO. I beg your pardon?

CLAUDE. A nice rich ground pork meat loaf with a mozzarella cheese center, gobs of mashed potatoes swimming in gravy, carrots floating in butter and for a salad, avocado chunks smothered in Roquefort dressing. Could you just die?

PROCLO. I could just . . . ! I don't know what I could just!

CLAUDE. And then: Dutch Chocolate layer cake with two big scoops of Baskin-Robbins mocha walnut ice cream and a fudge malted.

PROCLO. It sounds delicious.

CLAUDE. You could've been there.

PROCLO. I was in Brooklyn. Now if you'll excuse me, I'll—

CLAUDE. Wait! *(He is rummaging in his shopping bag.)* You want a bagel with lox and cream cheese?

PROCLO. No, thank you. I've eaten.

CLAUDE. An eclair? Some homemade brownies? I know! A corned beef on rye with a dill pickle!

PROCLO. Really, I'm not hungry. *(CLAUDE is blocking his way.)*

CLAUDE. How much do you weigh?

PROCLO. What?

CLAUDE. Your weight! 210? 220?

PROCLO. 226. *(CLAUDE has started to undulate, dance almost, and move towards* PROCLO.)*

CLAUDE *(singing in a low, sexy growl).* "Jelly Roll Baby/You're my Jelly Roll Man . . ."

PROCLO. I think there is some confusion here.

CLAUDE. "Jelly Roll Cupcake/I'm your Jelly Roll fan . . ."

PROCLO. In fact, I *know* there is some confusion going on in here.

CLAUDE. "You got the roll/and I got the soul/that strictly adores/paying Jelly Roll toll . . ." *(CLAUDE is still singing as he pulls* PROCLO *toward him and they collapse heavily on the bed.)*

PROCLO. Stop it! Please! You're hurting me!

CLAUDE. I'm hurting *you?*

PROCLO. Help! Help! *(TIGER has been seen running along the corridor and uses his passkey now to come into the room. A small crowd of patrons starts forming in the corridor outside the room.)*

TIGER *(Pulling* PROCLO *off* CLAUDE*).* Okay, fat man! Leave the little guy alone! What are you trying to do? Pull his head off? *(He takes* PROCLO's *key.)* Let me see your key. 196! Now get down there and don't cause any more trouble. What do you think this is? The YMCA? *(He puts* PROCLO's *suitcase in the corridor and turns back to* CLAUDE.)* I'm sorry, sir. It won't happen again. *(CLAUDE is moaning happily.)*

CLAUDE. I certainly hope not.

TIGER. Get down there, man! *(He goes.)*

PROCLO. He ought to be locked up! *(The crowd of patrons are all looking at* PROCLO.*)* Hello. Whew! I just had quite a little experience in there. I think that guy's got a problem. People like that really shouldn't be allowed in a place like this. *(stony silence from the PA-TRONS)* What unusual pants. They look like cowboy chaps.

PATRON IN CHAPS. They are cowboy chaps.

PROCLO. I was thinking I thought they looked like cowboy chaps. Well gentlemen, if you'll excuse me, and let me get out of these clothes. Bye. Nice talking to you. *(PROCLO beats an embarrassed retreat down the stairs. The group of PATRONS will slowly disband.* CHRIS *opens the door to his room, sticks his head out and yells.)*

CHRIS. Okay, boys, room 240! Soup's on, come and get it! *(He goes back into his room.* PROCLO *hurries to his room.* MICHAEL BRICK *has appeared in the area of a pay telephone. He dials a number and waits.)*

MICHAEL. Hello, Bimbi's? Is this the bar across the street from The Ritz? There's a Mr. Carmine Vespucci there. I've got to speak to him. It's urgent.

ABE *(over the loudspeaker).* Tiger! Duff! The linen people are here. On the double!

MICHAEL. Mr. Vespucci? My name is Michael Brick. I'm with the Grebar Detective Agency. You hired my partner to get something on a Mr. Gaetano Proclo, only my partner's sick so I'm taking over the case for him. I'm calling you from the Ritz. I just got here. Now let me see if I've got his description right. A balding middle-aged fat men? That's not much to go on, but I'll do my best. *(GOOGIE enters and signals to him.)* One of those tranvestites is standing right next to me. Now you just stay by the phone in that bar across the street and I'll get back to you.

GOOGIE. *Ay, que cosa linda!*

MICHAEL. I can't talk now. I think he's surrounding me for unnatural things. *(MICHAEL hangs up, gives GOOGIE a horrified look and hurries off.)*

GOOGIE. Hey *chico,* I was just gonna talk to you! *(TIGER enters.)* Tiger, is he here yet?

TIGER. Who?

GOOGIE. Who? What do you mean who? There is only one *who* I am interested in you telling me about! Listen, you told me there was gonna be a big producer here tonight. I dress special. I do the hairs special. If you're

lying to me, Tiger. . . .

TIGER. Can't you take a little joke?

GOOGIE. My career is no joke. Nobody's career is never no joke.

TIGER. I was just trying to build you up.

GOOGIE. I tell you something and I mean this: You ever hear of instant laryngitis? No producer be out there tonight and that's what I got—instant laryngitis—and you and Duff are gonna do the show alone. Those are my words, they are from the heart and I am now officially sick!

TIGER. Googie! *(GOOGIE rasps an answer and leaves,* TIGER *following her.* PROCLO *comes wandering into view, still carrying his suitcase and still shaken from his experience with* CLAUDE.*)*

PROCLO. This place is like a Chinese maze. *(PROCLO is standing there when* DUFF *comes out of one of the rooms.)*

DUFF. Are you 196?

PROCLO. Something like that.

DUFF. I meant your room.

PROCLO. So did I.

DUFF. Follow me. *(He leads* PROCLO *to the room.)* 196. Here it is. *(DUFF has opened the door for him.* PROCLO *goes into the room. It is a shambles from the previous occupant.* DUFF *calls out into the corridors.)* Hey, Tiger! Room 196! On the double!

PROCLO. You're kidding. Tell me you're kidding.

DUFF. What did you expect?

PROCLO. I don't know. A room maybe. A normal size room.

DUFF. You should see some of the rooms they could've put you in.

PROCLO. You're telling me they come even smaller?

DUFF. Half this size.

PROCLO. Does Mickey Rooney know about this place?

DUFF. You got far out taste, mister.

PROCLO. Vespucci. Carmine Vespucci. What's your name?

DUFF. Duff.

PROCLO. It's good to see you, Duff.

DUFF. How do you mean?

PROCLO. I was beginning to think this place was a little to esoteric for my tastes, if you know what I mean. Like that guy up there with all the food.

DUFF. I think it's something to do with the weather. Rainy nights always bring out the weirdos.

PROCLO. They shouldn't let people like that

in here. It'll give this place a bad name.

DUFF. This place already has a bad name. *(TIGER has arrived with a mop and a change of linen. The room will be very crowded with the three of them and PROCLO's luggage.)*

TIGER. We're both up shit creek again.

DUFF. Who with this time?

TIGER. I told Googie there'd be a producer out front tonight.

DUFF. Maybe there will be.

TIGER. I promised her. No producer, she's not going on. She's locked in her dressing room with laryngitis.

PROCLO. She told me she was feeling better.

TIGER. You know Googie?

PROCLO. I met her downstairs. She thought I was a producer. She's very colorful.

TIGER. Right now she's also very pissed off.

DUFF. Let me talk to her.

PROCLO. Not so fast, Duff. What about slippers?

DUFF. Slippers?

PROCLO. Slippers.

DUFF. Where do you think you are? Slippers! *(DUFF leaves as TIGER continues to clean PROCLO's room and make up his bed.)*

PROCLO. I always thought they gave you slippers in a bathhouse. I mean, you could catch athlete's foot in a place like this.

TIGER. You're lucky if that's all you catch. *(trying to make up the bed)* Excuse me.

PROCLO. I'm sorry. *(He stands.)* Looking at you two, I think I'm seeing double.

TIGER. He's Duff. I'm Tiger.

PROCLO. How are people supposed to tell you apart?

TIGER. They don't usually. Just try to stay out of 205 this time.

PROCLO. What's in 205?

TIGER. That room I had to pull you out of. You could hurt someone doing that.

PROCLO. Now just a minute! I thought that guy was taking me to *my* room! You don't think I went in there because I wanted to?

TIGER *(dawning on him)*. You trying to tell me he's a chubby chaser?

PROCLO. A chubby what?

TIGER. Someone who likes . . . *(He gestures, indicating great bulk.)*

PROCLO. You mean like me?

TIGER. You're right up his alley.

PROCLO. I knew someone like that once. I just never knew what to call him. "Get away from me, Claude!" is all I could come up with. A chubby chaser! That's kind of funny. Unless, of course, you happen to be the chubby

they're chasing. Room 205. Thanks for the tip. I'll avoid it like the plague. *(DUFF has returned and is knocking loudly on the door.)*

DUFF. Fifteen minutes!

PROCLO. Oh my God!

TIGER. Relax! *(He opens the door.)*

DUFF. Come on, Tiger. Show time!

TIGER. What happened?

DUFF. Googie's Mr. Big is here. He's going to be sitting ringside for the first show tonight.

TIGER. How'd you manage that?

DUFF. I didn't. But with a little help from our friend here . . . !

PROCLO. Hey, now just a minute!

DUFF. Aw, now come on, Mr. Vespucci! Give two down and out go-go boys with aspirations for higher things a break.

PROCLO. I don't want to get involved in anything.

DUFF. All you have to do is listen to her act.

PROCLO. I don't want to listen to her act.

DUFF. I don't blame you, but that's not the point.

PROCLO. I'm not a producer.

DUFF. Googie's not really a singer.

TIGER. Come on, what do you say?

PROCLO. What if she finds out?

DUFF. That's our problem.

TIGER. Leave everything to us.

PROCLO. I came here to lay low.

TIGER. Man, you can't lay any lower than Googie's nightclub act.

DUFF. Come on, we gotta change.

TIGER. You're a prince, Mr. . . .

DUFF. Vespucci.

TIGER. An honest-to-God prince.

PROCLO. Thank you, Duff.

TIGER. He's Duff. I'm Tiger. *(They run off. PROCLO closes the door and shakes his head.)*

PROCLO. Seclusion! Is that asking so very much, God? Simple seclusion? I must be crazy! Allowing them to tell her I'm a producer! *(MICHAEL BRICK is seen outside CLAUDE's door, which is ajar. He sticks his head into the room.)*

MICHAEL. Excuse me.

CLAUDE. I'm resting.

MICHAEL. May I come in?

CLAUDE. I said I'm resting.

MICHAEL. I'm looking for someone.

CLAUDE. I told you I'm resting.

MICHAEL. That's okay. I just want to ask you—

CLAUDE. What do you need? A brick wall to fall on your head? "Resting!" It's a euphemism for "not interested"! Skinny! *(CLAUDE slams the door in MICHAEL's face.*

MICHAEL *knocks on another door.)*

MICHAEL. Excuse me. May I come in? *(Michael starts into the room, then comes rushing out.)* Oh, I beg your pardon. Excuse me, may I come in? Thank you very much. *(He goes into another room. This time he comes rushing out almost at once.)* Oh, my goodness! *(*MICHAEL'*s mother never told him there would be nights like this. He steels himself and enters the steam room. On the swing of the door, he is back out and gone.* PROCLO *has nearly finished changing when there is a knock on his door. He quickly puts his wig back on.)*

PROCLO. Yes?

CLAUDE. Are you there?

PROCLO. Who is it?

CLAUDE. Room service.

PROCLO. Who? *(He opens the door a crack, sees* CLAUDE *and slams it.)* Go away!

CLAUDE. I've got a box of Hershey bars. *(He begins throwing bars of candy through the transom.)*

PROCLO. I said go away!

CLAUDE. Peter Paul Mounds, Milky Ways . . .

PROCLO. I know what you are now!

CLAUDE. I can make you very happy!

PROCLO. You're a chubby chaser!

CLAUDE. I know.

PROCLO. Well stop it!

CLAUDE. How?

PROCLO. I don't know! *(*PROCLO *waits, listens)* Are you still there?

CLAUDE. I'm never leaving.

PROCLO. You can't stand out there all night. This is my room and that's my door to it. Now go away or I'll call Tiger and Duff.

CLAUDE. I'm not doing anything.

PROCLO. You're making me nervous.

CLAUDE *(he thinks, then sings).* "Love your magic spell is everywhere . . ." *(He thinks.)* "Then along came . . ." *(He stops singing.)* Who? Then along came who?

PROCLO. Vespucci.

CLAUDE *(An inspiration).* Vespucci!/I just met a boy named Vespucci!/And suddenly that name . . . *(*PROCLO *stops moaning and comes up with a plan.)*

PROCLO. Okay, you win. What room are you in?

CLAUDE. 205.

PROCLO. All right, you go back to 205. I'll be right up.

CLAUDE. Promise?

PROCLO. On my mother's grave! *(He is crossing his fingers.)* Just get away from that

door! 'Cause if you're still standing out there when I come out of this room, the deal is off.

CLAUDE. And if you're not up in my room in five minutes . . .

PROCLO. What?

CLAUDE. I'll find you.

PROCLO. And?

CLAUDE. You don't want to make me do anything rash, do you, Mr. Vespucci?

PROCLO. Oh no, oh no!

CLAUDE. Five minutes then. Room 205. If you're not up there, I'm gonna come down here and break your knees. Don't push your luck with Claude Perkins. *(He goes. His name seems to have struck a distant bell for* PROCLO.*)*

PROCLO. Claude Perkins. It can't be the same one. Claude Perkins. That's all I need. He's dead. He has to be dead. Claude Perkins. *(*PROCLO *opens the door and looks out. No sign of* CLAUDE. *Without realizing it, he shuts the door behind him and locks himself out.)* Oh no! Come on, will you? Open up. Damn! *(calling off)* Boys! Boys! You with the keys! Yoo hoo! Yoo hoo! *(*PROCLO *is suddenly aware of a patron who is just looking at him and smiling.)* Hello. Just clearing my throat. Ahoo! Ahoo! Too many cigarettes. Ahoo! Hello there. I hear the Knicks tied it up in the last quarter.

PATRON. Crisco.

PROCLO. What?

PATRON. Crisco oil party.

PROCLO. Crisco oil party?

PATRON. Room 419. Pass it on.

PROCLO. Pass what on?

PATRON. And bring Joey.

PROCLO. Who's Joey?

PATRON. You know Joey. But not Chuck. Got that?

PROCLO. Crisco oil party Room 419. I can bring Joey but not Chuck.

PATRON. Check.

PROCLO. What's wrong with Chuck? *(*PATRON *whispers something in* PROCLO'*s ear.* PROCLO'*s eyes grow wide. He can't wait to get out of there.)* Chuck's definitely out! If you'll excuse me now . . . ! *(He starts moving away. The* PATRON *leaves.* PROCLO *starts pacing in rapid circles.)* Now wait a minute. Wait a minute. Stay calm. Be rational. Don't get hysterical. All he did was invite you to a Crisco oil party, whatever the hell that is, and told you to bring Joey. Of course, I don't know Joey, and I don't think I want to, and not to bring Chuck because Chuck—. It can't be one of those places. I mean, one or two weird people do not a you-know-what make. People are just more normal in Cleveland.

CHRIS *(leaning out of his room)*. Telephone call for Joe Namath in room 240. Long distance for Mr. Joe Namath in room 240!

PROCLO. Well *there!* You see? I knew I wasn't a crazy person! *(*PROCLO *is heading toward* CHRIS'*s room.)* There's just no way. . . . *(On his way, he composes a speech to himself.)* Mr. Namath? Excuse me. I wonder if I might trouble you for an autograph. It's not for me. It's for my 12-year-old, Gilda. Say, did you hear the Knicks tied it up in the last quarter? Mr. Namath?

CHRIS *(from inside his room)*. No, don't! . . . I can't . . . Oooo! . . . Aaaa! . . . Oh my God! . . . Do it, do it! . . . Yes! Yes! *(He puts down the magazine he was thumbing through.)* If that doesn't get those queens up here nothing will.

PROCLO *(knocking on* CHRIS'*s door)*. Mr. Namath? *(*CHRIS *comes out of his room and sees* PROCLO.*)* You're not Joe Namath.

CHRIS. Neither are you.

PROCLO. I thought you were Joe Namath.

CHRIS. It's the lighting.

PROCLO. I was praying you were Joe Namath.

CHRIS. I don't blame you.

PROCLO. I mean, you just had to be him!

CHRIS. Eating your heart out, honey?

PROCLO. I don't know what I'm doing.

CHRIS. Join the club. It's like some strange heterosexual gypsy curse has been put on this place tonight. How's the orgy room doing?

PROCLO. I haven't—

CHRIS. The steam room?

PROCLO. No.

CHRIS. The pool? The sauna? The dormitory?

PROCLO. Sorry.

CHRIS. Well no wonder you haven't made out.

PROCLO. I don't want to make out.

CHRIS. Who are you trying to kid? This is me, sweetheart, your Aunt Chris. *(He starts pounding on closed doors.)* Fire drill! Everybody out for fire drill! *(A door opens. A* PATRON *looks out.)* I'm sorry. I thought this was the powder room.

PATRON. We're busy.

CHRIS *(To* PROCLO*)*. You like this one?

PROCLO. No!

CHRIS. Neither do I!

PATRON. I said we're busy! *(He slams the door.)*

CHRIS. You've got my son in there. Tell him his mother wants to see him.

PATRON *(from behind the door)*. Buzz off!

CHRIS. One mark on that boy's body, Wanda, and I'm calling the police! *(to* PROCLO*)* Well I tried.

PROCLO. Really. I don't want you to do anything for me.

CHRIS. You're not going to believe this line, but "You're new around here, aren't you?"

PROCLO. I'm afraid so.

CHRIS. I never forget a face and I've seen a lot of faces in this place. Some people think I'm a sex maniac. They're right. If I don't get laid at least twice a day I go home and beat my dog. Here's hoping for you, Jeanette! *(He offers a "popper" to* PROCLO, *who shakes his head no.)* It's fantastic stuff. I got it from this queen I know who just got back from a hairdresser's convention in Tokyo. He does Barbra Streisand's hair, so they gave him the Gene Hersholt Humanitarian Award. *(He laughs and backslaps* PROCLO.*)* Come on, I'll show you around.

PROCLO. That's all right. I was just going back to my room.

CHRIS. Come *on!* I don't do this for everyone. I'm an expert guide. A lesser person would charge for this sort of tour.

PROCLO. There's something I better tell you.

CHRIS. Sweetheart, relax, you're not my type. I just want to help you find yours. *(To a* SNOOTY PATRON *who is walking by.)* Hi. *(*SNOOTY PATRON *turns his back.)* We said hello. *(*SNOOTY PATRON *turns his back some more.* CHRIS *turns to* PROCLO, *gives him an eye signal and starts talking to him in a very loud voice.)* Do I know her? Darling, she is what is known as a Famous Face. She's out cruising 24 hours a day. She must live in a pup tent on Sheridan Square. If I had a nickel for every pair of shoes she's gone through . . . ! *(*SNOOTY PATRON *finally turns around and glares at him.)* Margaret Dumont! I thought you were dead!

SNOOTY PATRON. There's a reason some of us don't ride the subways and I'm looking right at him. *(He huffs off.)*

CHRIS. Is that supposed to mean me? *(after him)* Screw you, honey! *(To* PROCLO*)* One thing I can't stand is a queen without a sense of humor. *(After him.)* You can die with your secret! *(to* PROCLO*)* Miserable piss-elegant fairy.

PROCLO. I have to tell your something. I'm afraid I'm not a . . . *(He will try to convey something with his hands.)*

CHRIS. You're not gay?

PROCLO. No.

CHRIS. Then what are you doing here?

PROCLO. That's what I'd like to know.

CHRIS. Baby, you're very much in the minority around here.

PROCLO. That's what I'm afraid of.

CHRIS. Or maybe you're not and that's why I'm having such rotten luck tonight. What are you? A social worker or something?

PROCLO. You mean *everybody* here is . . . ?

CHRIS. Gay. It's not such a tough word. You might try using it some time.

PROCLO. Nobody is . . . the opposite?

CHRIS. I sure as hell hope not. I didn't pay ten bucks to walk around in a towel with a bunch of Shriners.

PROCLO. What about Tiger and Duff?

CHRIS. What about them?

PROCLO. I thought they were normal.

CHRIS. They are normal. They've also been lovers for three years.

PROCLO. I'm sorry. I didn't mean it like that.

CHRIS. Yes, you did.

PROCLO. Yes, I did.

CHRIS. I'll tell you something about straight people, and sometimes I think it's the only thing worth knowing about them. They don't like gays. They never have. They never will. Anything else they say is just talk.

PROCLO. That's not true.

CHRIS. Think about it.

PROCLO. I'm sorry. I didn't know what I was getting into when I came in here tonight. I'm in trouble, I'm scared and I'm confused. I'm sorry.

CHRIS. That's okay.

PROCLO. You're gonna think I'm crazy but somebody is planning to kill me tonight. My own brother-in-law.

CHRIS. Are you putting me on?

PROCLO. I wish I were. And if Carmine caught me in a place like this he'd have *double* grounds for murder.

CHRIS. What do you mean?

PROCLO. My brother-in-law. For twelve years I was the butt of every sissy joke played at Our Lady of Perpetual Sorrow. It was a good name for that place. And then, when I married his only sister . . . ! They're very close, even for Italian brothers and sisters, and you know what they're like. *(He clasps his hands together.)* Cement! Except for Vivian, Vivian's my wife, that whole family's always hated me. At our wedding, her own mother had a heart attack while we were exchanging vows. Vivian said "I do" to me and Mamma Vespucci keeled right over in the front pew.

CHRIS. It's kind of funny.

PROCLO. Not when it happens to you. Yesterday, at their own father's funeral even, Carmine had all the relatives giving me that look.

CHRIS. What look?

PROCLO. That look. *(He gives a look.)*

CHRIS. I would've laid him out.

PROCLO. That's you.

CHRIS. Why didn't you?

PROCLO. The truth? I'm scared to death of him. I guess I always have been.

CHRIS. Maybe that's why he always hated you.

PROCLO. "Get Proclo." Those were their father's dying words. Do you believe it? This far from his Maker and all he can say is "Get Proclo."

CHRIS. Get Proclo?

PROCLO. That's me. With their father dead now, there's a lot of money involved that Carmine would love to screw me out of. And I'm not so sure it's particularly clean money. Carmine can chase me all over town but this is one night he's not gonna "Get Proclo."

CHRIS. And you picked a gay baths to hide out in?

PROCLO. I didn't pick it exactly. I asked my cab driver to take me to the last place in the world anybody would think of looking for me.

CHRIS. Don't worry, you found it.

PROCLO. Only now I've got a chubby chaser and someone who thinks I'm a producer after me.

CHRIS. Listen, it beats someone like your brother-in-law trying to kill you. Why don't you just stay in your room and try to get some sleep?

PROCLO. Sleep!

CHRIS. Strange as it may seem, no one's gonna attack you.

PROCLO. Someone already has.

CHRIS. Beginner's luck! Standing around out here like this, you're just asking for it. Go to your room.

PROCLO. I can't! I locked myself out!

CHRIS. Well try and find Tiger and Duff. They'll let you in. Now if you'll excuse me, darling, I want to try my luck in there. Us B-girls work better solo.

PROCLO. See you.

CHRIS. See you. *(He throws open the door to the steam room and blows the whistle.)* Hello, everybody, my name is June! What's yours? *(He is gone.* PROCLO *is alone. He stands undecided for a moment but we can see that his curiosity is getting the better of him. He opens the door to the steam room and peers in. He goes in. The door closes. There is a long pause.)*

The stage is empty. And at once, PROCLO *comes bursting out of the steam room. You have never seen anyone move as fast. He comes tearing down the stairs and runs into* DUFF.)

PROCLO. The key to 196, quick!

DUFF. You're supposed to wear it.

PROCLO. I know!

DUFF. What's the matter?

PROCLO. Just let me in, please.

DUFF. Try to hang onto your key from here on out, okay?

PROCLO. Believe me, I'll make every effort. *(He is admitted.)* Thank you.

DUFF. The show's about to get started.

PROCLO *(puffing for breath).* Fine, fine!

DUFF. You won't be late?

PROCLO. Of course not!

DUFF. Googie's all keyed up.

PROCLO. So am I, so am I!

DUFF. Thanks a million for helping us out like this, Mr. Vespucci.

PROCLO. Tell me something, you and Tiger are . . . lovers?

DUFF. Three years. I think that's pretty good, don't you?

PROCLO. It's terrific.

DUFF. I better get ready. See you downstairs! *(He goes, closing the door.)*

PROCLO. I wouldn't go down there and see her act for a—! *Her* act? Of course! I knew there was something funny about that Gomez woman. She's not a woman! Female impersonators . . . chubby chasers . . . B-girls . . . Baby Junes! When I grow another head is when I'm gonna leave this room! *(He sits on the bed, exhausted. Where to go now? What to do? His eyes go to the Panettone. He looks a little more cheerful. Meanwhile,* MICHAEL *has raced back to the area of the telephones and dialed a number.)*

MICHAEL. Bimbi's? Oh! Mr. Vespucci. Michael Brick. No one fits your description. It's pretty hard getting the goods on someone you've never seen. And you didn't tell me about that steam room. *(We see* GOOGIE *entering. She sees* MICHAEL. *She stops. She eavesdrops.)* If you need me I'm at 929-9929. And I'm in room 101. 101!

GOOGIE. Room 101!

MICHAEL. He's here again. *(MICHAEL hangs up and hurries off.)*

GOOGIE. I'll be there, *chico*. Googie's gonna straighten you out between shows. *(She turns to* PROCLO'*s room.* PROCLO *is eating his Panettone when she knocks on the door. He jumps.)* Guess who, Mr. Vespucci? *(More*

knocking. PROCLO *tries to ignore it but it is very urgent. Finally he goes to the door and opens it a crack. A fatal mistake.)*

PROCLO. Now wait a minute! *(GOOGIE barges in and closes the door.)*

GOOGIE. I know what you're going to say.

PROCLO. You couldn't possibly!

GOOGIE. I don't believe in bugging producers just before they catch your act, so I just want to tell you one thing. In my second number, "Shine On Harvest Moon," the orchestra and me sometimes get into different keys, but if you know that it won't matter. Other than that, the act is fabulous and I just know you're gonna love it.

PROCLO. I'm sure of it!

GOOGIE. You know what *guapo* means? Handsome.

PROCLO. Oh no, I'm ugly. I'm very, very ugly.

GOOGIE. With a face like that, you could've been an actor. You still could. It's never too late. Look at Caterina Valente or Charo or Vicki Carr.

PROCLO. Of course they're *real* women.

GOOGIE. Oh no!

PROCLO. They're not?

GOOGIE. Plastic Puerto Ricans. I am the real thing. You are the real thing and I knew you were in show business.

PROCLO. Me?

GOOGIE. I knew I'd seen you someplace.

PROCLO. I was in the Cleveland Little Theatre Masque and Mummerr's spring production of "The Sound of Music," but I'd hardly call that show business.

GOOGIE. Oh yeah? What part?

PROCLO. It was really more of a walk-on.

GOOGIE. I was in that show.

PROCLO. You were in "The Sound of Music"?

GOOGIE. Oh sure.

PROCLO. Where was this?

GOOGIE. Broadway, the Main Stem, where else?

PROCLO. The original cast?

GOOGIE. I was more original than anyone else in it. They fired me the first day of rehearsal, those bastards. They said I wasn't right for the part.

PROCLO. What part was that?

GOOGIE. One of those fucking Trapp kids. But you know what the real reason was, mister?

PROCLO. They found out what you really were?

GOOGIE. Seymour Pippin!

PROCLO. Who?

GOOGIE. Seymour Pippin! If there's one man in this whole world I was born to kill with my own two hands it is Seymour Pippin. You want to hear something funny? If you didn't have all that hair you would look a lot like him and I would probably fly into a rage and tear all your eyes out! I never forget that face and I never forgive. He was the company manager and if there is one thing worse than a producer or a press agent, it is a company manager.

PROCLO. It *is* a family show.

GOOGIE. But I fix them. I picket that show till they was crazy. I picket, I picket, I picket. Every night! They couldn't stop me. I picket that show every night until I got a part in "Camelot."

PROCLO. You were in "Camelot," too?

GOOGIE. Oh sure.

PROCLO. That's a wonderful show.

GOOGIE. It's a piece of shit.

PROCLO. Oh, they fired you from that one, too?

GOOGIE. Sure they fired me! What do you expect? Thanks to Seymour Pippin I get fired from everything.

PROCLO. I can't imagine why.

GOOGIE. You see this face? It's a curse! *(She is moving in for the kill.* PROCLO *is backing off, horrified.)*

PROCLO. Keep away!

GOOGIE. Don't fight it, *chico!*

PROCLO. Believe me, you won't be happy! I won't be happy! You're making a terrible mistake.

GOOGIE. I am suddenly all woman.

PROCLO. No you're not. You're someone with a lot of problems.

GOOGIE. Make me feel like a real woman, *chico.*

PROCLO. I can't help you out in that department! It's out of my hands.

GOOGIE. Kiss me! *(Sounds of an orchestra striking up.)* Oh shit! That's my music! *(She is dragging* PROCLO *by the hand. She throws open the door.)* Come on, my Mr. Big Producer. You're gonna love my show. I got you the best seats. I see you ringside. We save the hanky-panky for later. *(GOOGIE hurries off.)*

PROCLO. Ringside! Hanky-panky! What am I doing here? *(CLAUDE appears on the third level.)*

CLAUDE. Vespucci!

PROCLO. It *is* the same Claude Perkins. We were in the Army together. Compared to those two, Carmine wanting to kill me is sanity! *(He*

rushes off, followed by CLAUDE.)*

CLAUDE. I warned you, Vespucci! You promised, I waited, and you didn't come! Hey, where are you? *(The music is building as the lights dim and the nightclub, complete with twinkle lights and mylar, flies in.)*

ABE *(Over the loudspeaker.).* And now, on the great Ritz stage, direct from her record-breaking bus and truck tour with "Fiddler on the Roof," the sensational Googie Gomez! With Duff and Tiger, those amazing now you see it, now you don't golden go-go boys! *(There is a roll of drums.)* Here's Duff. *(DUFF runs on. Another roll of drums.)* Here's Tiger. *(TIGER makes a great entrance. Another roll of drums.)* And here's Googie! *(GOOGIE bursts on and launches into her first number. She is very bad but very funny. It's the kind of number you watch in disbelief. Sincerity is what saves her. Such a lack of talent is appalling, yes, but it does come straight from the heart.* TIGER *and* DUFF *are doing their best, too. They dance well enough and they look pretty good up there. When the number ends, during the applause, we see* PROCLO *run across pursued by* CLAUDE. GOOGIE, *followed by* TIGER *and* DUFF, *goes after them.)* Hey, wait a minute! Where are you going? I was just gonna introduce you! *(They are gone. Suddenly the figure of a very wet, very angry balding middle-aged fat man comes storming through the mylar into* GOOGIE'*s spotlight.)*

CARMINE. I'm Carmine Vespucci of the Bensonhurst Vespuccis. I want a room in this here whorehouse and I don't want any shit. *(There is a mighty roll of drums as Scarpia's Theme from "Tosca" is heard. A crack of cymbals. Curtain.)*

ACT TWO

CARMINE *is seen coming along the corridor. He is still in street clothes. He looks all around and then knocks softly on the door of* MICHAEL BRICK'*s room.*

———

CARMINE. Brick? Are you in there, Brick? It's Vespucci. Don't open. I don't want anyone to see us. If you can hear me, knock once. If you can't, knock twice. Are you there, Brick? *(MICHAEL knocks once.)* Good. Our signals are working. Now listen to me, have you seen that balding fat brother-in-law of mine yet? *(MICHAEL knocks twice.)* What does that mean?

No? *(MICHAEL knocks once.)* Okay, I think I read you. Now I know he's in here somewhere. What I don't know is how you could miss him. He's a house. Listen, Brick, none of these fruits tried to pull anything with you, did they? *(MICHAEL knocks twice.)* You can thank Our Blessed Lady for that. Meet me in 102 in fifteen minutes. Knock three times. Got that? *(MICHAEL knocks three times.)* Not now, stupid, *then*. And you don't have to worry about him leaving this place. Leaving it in one piece I should say. I got all my men outside. Ain't that great, Brick? Hunh? *(MICHAEL knocks once.)* I knew you'd like that. Keep looking. *(CARMINE goes into his room, starts to undress. We will see him take out a revolver, a stiletto, a pair of brass knuckles. From offstage, CLAUDE calls.)*

CLAUDE. Vespucci! *(PROCLO appears on the third level and races into a room. CLAUDE runs past the room and sees a patron.)* Say, have you seen a Vespucci go by? *(PROCLO leaves his hiding place and heads down the stairs and they disappear.)* Vespucci! Vespucci! *(GOOGIE appears and pokes her head into Proclo's room.)*

GOOGIE. Where are you hiding, Mr. Vespucci? *(She disappears. PROCLO appears and starts down the stairs to his own room on the first level. Midway he crosses paths with TIGER and DUFF.)*

TIGER. There you are!

DUFF. Why did you run away? *(PROCLO escapes and continues down to his room. TIGER and DUFF disappear, looking for GOOGIE. Meanwhile GOOGIE appears in a corridor, now looking for CLAUDE.)*

GOOGIE. Where is this person who ruin my act? Where is this skinny little man? I kill him! *(She disappears. TIGER and DUFF appear and criss-cross again.)*

TIGER. Googie! Googie!

DUFF. Googie! Googie! *(They are gone. As soon as PROCLO reaches his room, CLAUDE comes down the corridor looking for him. He opens the door, but PROCLO has hidden behind it.)*

CLAUDE. Vespucci! *(As he leaves, he shuts the door, revealing PROCLO, who quickly makes the sign of the cross and starts gathering his things. Meanwhile GOOGIE has appeared down a corridor. She sneaks up on CLAUDE and tears his robe off.)*

GOOGIE. Ah hah! *Cabron! (CLAUDE races off, pursued by GOOGIE, who is in turn pursued by TIGER and DUFF.)*

TIGER. Googie!

DUFF. Googie! *(They are all gone. PROCLO is in a terrific hurry. We can hear him muttering to himself as he frantically packs his bag.)*

PROCLO. I'd rather spend the night in Central Park in the rain than spend another minute in this place! They're all mad! I thought *I* had problems! If I ever get my hands on that cab driver, he's finished! So long, room, I won't miss you. *(He comes out of the room carrying his clothes, his suitcase and the box of Panettone. He slams the door.)* Hello, Cleveland! *(He sees a PATRON walking by.)* Which is the way out of here?

PATRON. That way. *(PROCLO goes up the stairs to the second level, looking for an exit. CLAUDE appears on a side balcony.)*

CLAUDE. Vespucci! Vespucci! *(PROCLO has made his decision: it's the steam room or else. He goes rushing in with his clothes, his suitcase and the Panettone. CLAUDE leaps over the balcony in hot pursuit.)*

CLAUDE. I hope you know what a cul-de-sac is, because you're in one. *(He goes into the steam room. Now GOOGIE enters on the rampage. We see her tearing up and down the corridors, TIGER and DUFF following, trying to calm her down.)*

GOOGIE. Where is this skinny little man who chase a producer out of my number? No one chases no producer out of Googie Gomez' number! *(She is pounding on doors. One of them is opened by the PATRON IN CHAPS.)*

PATRON IN CHAPS. Howdy, pardner.

GOOGIE. Don't howdy me, you big leather sissy! *(She pushes him back into the room.)* You think I don't know what goes on around this place? All you men going hee-hee-hee, poo-poo-poo, hah-hah-hah! I get my boyfriend Hector in here with his hombres and he kill you all! *(She is heading for the steam room.)*

DUFF. You can't go in there!

TIGER. Googie, no! *(GOOGIE storms into the steam room, TIGER and DUFF following. The door closes behind them. A moment later, GOOGIE lets out a muffled yell.)*

GOOGIE. *Pendego! (PATRONS start streaming out. GOOGIE comes right after them. She has CLAUDE firmly in tow.)* There will be no more hee-hee-hee, poo-poo-poo, hah-hah-hah around this place tonight! *(She slings CLAUDE across the hall.)*

CLAUDE. You're hurting me!

GOOGIE. I'm just getting started! *(TIGER and DUFF attempt to subdue her.)*

CLAUDE. You could use a good psychiatrist, mister!

GOOGIE. What you call me?

TIGER. He didn't mean it!

GOOGIE. What you call me?

TIGER. Tell her you're sorry!

CLAUDE. I haven't seen such tacky drag since the Princeton Varsity Show!

GOOGIE. Tacky drag?

CLAUDE. Thirty years ago, sonny! *(GOOGIE has gotten herself into good street-fighting position by now. With a bloodcurdling yell she leaps for CLAUDE and chases him off, TIGER and DUFF close behind. The stage is bare for a moment. We hear CLAUDE.)*

CLAUDE. Help! *(From the yell, it sounds as if GOOGIE's got him. The steam room door opens and CHRIS comes out.)*

CHRIS. I'm going straight. *(Suddenly the steam room door slams open and PROCLO, or what's left of him, staggers out. He is fully dressed, wearing the wig, dark glasses and moustache from his first entrance, and carrying his suitcase. He has visibly wilted. He doesn't seem to know where he is.)*

PROCLO. I don't believe this whole night.

CHRIS. Were you in there for all that? *(PROCLO just nods.)* Where? *(PROCLO just shrugs.)* You don't want to talk about it? *(PROCLO just shakes his head.)* Why are you wearing your clothes?

PROCLO. I'm going to Central Park.

CHRIS. I thought you were going to stay in your room.

PROCLO *(blindly walking downstairs)*. I can't. I told Googie I was Carmine Vespucci. Claude thinks I'm Carmine Vespucci. Everybody thinks I'm Carmine Vespucci.

CHRIS. Well who are you?

PROCLO. Tonight I'm Carmine Vespucci.

CHRIS. I give up! *(CHRIS sees MICHAEL BRICK coming along a corridor.)* What have we here? Now this is a little more like it. Play it cool, Chris. *(He arranges himself attractively.)* If you don't mind, Mr. Vespucci, I'd like to try my luck with this one. Hey, Vespucci, I'm talking to you. Snap out of it!

MICHAEL. Are you Mr. Carmine Vespucci, sir?

CHRIS. You live around here, kid?

MICHAEL. No, I came in from Astoria. Are you Mr. Vespucci?

CHRIS. Say yes, say yes!

PROCLO. Yes!

MICHAEL. I'm Michael Brick. My room's right over here. *(He will start leading PROCLO to his room.)*

CHRIS. Hi, I'm Chris. My room's right up there.

MICHAEL. Hi, Chris. *(MICHAEL and PROCLO have gone into MICHAEL's room and closed the door.)* Am I glad to see you, Mr. Vespucci. *(CHRIS has been watching their encounter in envy and disbelief.)*

CHRIS. I don't date out-of-towners. *(He starts to exit, but is stopped by the ring of the pay phone. He answers it with an enormous scream of frustration. He hangs up and disappears. A somewhat still dazed PROCLO is sitting in MICHAEL's room.)*

MICHAEL. Now this is what I thought we'd do. Get under the bed.

PROCLO *(beginning to cry)*. Another one!

MICHAEL. All right, stay there. We'll pretend you're him and I'm me and the real you is under the bed.

PROCLO *(tears are really flowing)*. Only this one's the worst.

MICHAEL. Now get the picture. The lights are low, he's moving down the hallway and he sees me leaning against the door. I flex for him. Pecks and biceps are supposed to be a turn on. Don't ask me why. I catch his eye. I've got a cigarette dangling from my lips, I put one knee up. I wink, I kind of beckon with my head and finally I speak. "See something you like, buddy?" That's the tough guy approach.

PROCLO. Is that your own voice?

MICHAEL. Yes.

PROCLO. I mean, your real voice?

MICHAEL. Yes.

PROCLO. Your natural speaking one?

MICHAEL. Yes.

PROCLO. Thank you.

MICHAEL. Why? Does it bother you?

PROCLO. Oh no, no, no!

MICHAEL. Some people find it very irritating.

PROCLO. I can't see why.

MICHAEL. Me either. But of course I'm used to it. I've had it ever since I was a kid. I mean, I grew up and matured, only my voice didn't. Where was I?

PROCLO. The tough guy approach.

MICHAEL. Oh! And *then* . . . and this is where you're going to have to jump out—

PROCLO. I am having a nightmare.

MICHAEL. Very, very, very casually . . .

PROCLO. I can hardly wait.

MICHAEL. I thought I'd let my hand just kind of graze against my . . . *(He hesitates, then whispers in PROCLO's ear.)*

PROCLO. I'm getting out of here!

MICHAEL *(pulling him down).* But you're going to have to help me catch your brother-in-law, Mr. Vespucci.

PROCLO. My brother-in-law?

MICHAEL. I haven't seen anyone who fits Mr. Proclo's description.

PROCLO. Proclo? My brother-in-law?

MICHAEL. The balding middle-aged fat man you hired me to catch.

PROCLO. Where do you know my brother-in-law from?

MICHAEL. I don't yet. That's why I called you at that bar across the street.

PROCLO. What bar?

MICHAEL. Where you and your men have this place surrounded so Mr. Proclo can't leave in one piece.

PROCLO. Who are you?

MICHAEL. Michael Brick, sir.

PROCLO. What are you?

MICHAEL. A detective. *(MICHAEL is suddenly alerted by the alarm on his wristwatch.)* It's time!

PROCLO. For what?

MICHAEL. Get under the bed. He'll see you.

PROCLO. Who will?

MICHAEL. Your brother-in-law. He'll be here any second. Since I couldn't find Mr. Proclo I'm making him find me. I left a note by the coke machines saying "Any middle-aged balding fat man whose initials are G.P. interested in a good time should meet me in Room 101 at midnight sharp." When he gets here you're gonna have to help me. You see, I'm not queer.

PROCLO *(already climbing under the bed).* You could've fooled me.

MICHAEL. I'm right on top of you.

PROCLO. I can't tell you how comforting that is. *(CHRIS is seen moving along the corridors, playing "The Lady or the Tiger." He knocks softly at different doors, and finally on CARMINE's.)*

CARMINE. I said knock three times!

CHRIS. He's being masterful with me already, the brute. *(He knocks three times.)*

CARMINE. That's more like it.

CHRIS. I think I'm in love. *(CARMINE opens the door and pulls CHRIS violently into the room, slamming the door behind them.)*

CARMINE. Quick. Don't let anyone see you. Now let me get a look at you. *(He circles CHRIS appraisingly.)* I'm not a judge of fruit bait, but I guess you'll do.

CHRIS. Just cool it, sweetheart. This isn't the meat rack.

CARMINE. You can can the fag act with me, Brick. Now listen, I think I've come up with something. I know this sounds like the oldest stunt in the book, but I'm going to hide under your bed.

CHRIS. On the contrary, it's a first.

CARMINE. You never tried the old under-the-bed technique?

CHRIS. Not recently.

CARMINE. What kind of a detective are you?

CHRIS. That's a good question, honey.

CARMINE. Can it, Brick, just can it. One thing I don't like is a wise guy. The only thing I don't like more is a queer wise guy. I'm calling the shots now and I'm getting under your bed.

CHRIS. Where am I supposed to be?

CARMINE. On top of it, stupid!

CHRIS. It sounds fabulous. Then what?

CARMINE. You know, do what you have to do.

CHRIS. What's that?

CARMINE. How should I know? Wiggle your fanny, shake your towel in his face.

CHRIS. Whose face?

CARMINE. My brother-in-law's, you dummy! The guy I hired you to catch. And then I pop out, catching you both in the act of fragrant delicto and whammo! I got him.

CHRIS. Your brother-in-law?

CARMINE. Who else? Jesus, you're like talking to a yo-yo.

CHRIS. Dumb and dizzy, that's me, darling! *(In a very "butch" voice.)* Just a little more of that gay humor. Ho ho ho!

CARMINE. All right, now you go back to 101. *(CHRIS desperately starts to leave.)* Not yet! If the coast is clear, whistle like this. . . . *(He whistles with two fingers.)* . . . and I'll high tail it to your room and slide right under and we're in business. Got that?

CHRIS. Check.

CARMINE. It's about time.

CHRIS. Only I can't whistle.

CARMINE. Goddamnit, you can't whistle either?

CHRIS. Tell you what, Mr. . . .

CARMINE. Vespucci, Carmine Vespucci. Only don't call me that! He might hear us. I need a code name.

CHRIS. Evelyn.

CARMINE. Naw, I don't like Evelyn. Sounds effeminate.

CHRIS. How about Bunny?

CARMINE. Okay, Bunny.

CHRIS. All right then, Bunny, you get under

this bed. That way I won't have to whistle and you won't have to high tail it to 101.

CARMINE. Maybe you're not so dumb after all, Brick.

CHRIS. Just to refresh my memory, give me his name again.

CARMINE. It's Proclo, Gaetano Proclo.

CHRIS. What did he do?

CARMINE. He married my sister. I told her. I pleaded with her. I was on my knees to her. "Viv, honey, marry this Proclo character and you're marrying to stick a knife in me." She loves him, she tells me. Well I hate him, I tell her. I've always hated him. He's not of the family. He's not like us. He don't belong in Poppa's business. But she wouldn't listen to me. And so what happens? Twenty years she thinks she's happily married, my sister, but the truth is it's twenty years she's been a martyr, that woman. My sister is a saint and she don't even know it. I'll tell you one thing: with Poppa gone now . . . *(He breaks into uncontrollable sobs.)* . . . Poppa, God bless him . . . I ain't sharing Vespucci Sanitation Services and Enterprises, Inc., with no fairy!

CHRIS. Your brother-in-law is a fairy?

CARMINE. He's gonna be when I get through with him.

CHRIS. What are you going to do to him?

CARMINE. I'm gonna kill him!

CHRIS. Good!

CARMINE. You know what a *delitto di passione* is, Brick? 'Cause you're gonna see one tonight. A crime of passion. An enraged brother catching his dear sweet sister's balding fat slob husband in an unnatural act with one of these these fuitcakes around here! There's no court in the country that would convict me. Twenty years I waited for this night. You're looking at a man of great and terrible Italian passions, Brick.

CHRIS. I can see that, Bunny. *(He turns off the room lights.)*

CARMINE. What happened?

CHRIS. That's how they do it here. Now get under the bed. I'm leaving the door open so he can come in. Once he gets here, you take it from there. I'm right on top of you. Now don't say another word. *(CHRIS has tiptoed out of the room, leaving the door ajar and CARMINE under the bed. He knocks on MICHAEL's door.)*

MICHAEL. That must be your brother-in-law, Mr. Vespucci!

PROCLO *(ready to meet his Maker)*. I'm sure it is.

MICHAEL *(unlocking the closed door)*. Hold your horses, stud! *(He stretches out on the bed. We see PROCLO's face looking out from the foot of the bed.)* It's open! *(CHRIS enters.)* See something you like, buddy?

CHRIS. You've got to be kidding.

MICHAEL. False alarm, Mr. Vespucci.

CHRIS. Where's your friend?

MICHAEL. He's under the bed.

CHRIS. Why not? Everybody else is. I always wondered what you straight guys did together. Now that I know, I'm glad I'm gay. If you didn't have all that hair, I'd ask you if your name was Guy something.

PROCLO *(crawling out from under the bed)*. It is.

CHRIS. And you really do have a garbageman brother-in-law who's out looking for you, don't you?

PROCLO. Unh-hunh!

CHRIS. Well, the maniac is right across the hall and he's got a gun. I just thought I'd mention it.

MICHAEL. Now he's after you, Mr. Vespucci! And you didn't mention anything about a gun. *(GOOGIE appears in the corridor and knocks on the door.)* I'm scared! *(CHRIS dives under the bed.)*

PROCLO. You're scared? Move over!

CHRIS. There's not enough room.

PROCLO. I can fit.

CHRIS. I was here first.

PROCLO. It's my brother-in-law!

CHRIS. It's my ass! *(MICHAEL has opened the door a crack and peeked out. Now he slams it shut and dives under the bed from the other side. PROCLO still hasn't managed to get under.)*

PROCLO. Where do you think you're going?

MICHAEL. It's not him, Mr. Vespucci!

PROCLO. Well who is it then?

MICHAEL. It's that tranvestite again!

PROCLO. What are you talking about? *(The knocking is getting louder.)* Who's there?

GOOGIE. I know you in there, *chico!*

PROCLO. Oh, no! *(He goes to the door and opens it. GOOGIE comes flying in, closing the door behind her and clapping one hand over PROCLO's mouth.)* Now, look—!

GOOGIE. Don't speak. Don't say nothing. Say one word and Googie's out on her ass. She's breaking every book in the rule doing this. *(She has pushed PROCLO onto the bed and is lying on top of him.)* You know why you don't like women? Because you never tried it, that's all. Or maybe you did and that's why. She was a bad woman. Forget her. Believe me, *chico,* it don't hurt. It's nice. It's very nice. Just lie back and Googie's gonna show you how nice.

PROCLO. Look, I'd like to help you out—!

GOOGIE. Think of a tropical night! A beach.

PROCLO. What beach?

GOOGIE. The moon is shining on the sea and in the distance, over the waves, you hear music. . . . *(She sings.)* "Besame, besame mucho!" *(PROCLO is terrified. Almost involuntary, under the bed,* MICHAEL *and* CHRIS *join in singing. For several moments, there is almost a trio going between them, as* GOOGIE *tries to take off* PROCLO's *clothes.)*

GOOGIE, MICHAEL and CHRIS. Como si fuera esta noche/ La ultima vez/ Besame, besame mucho/ Piensa que tal vez mañana/ Estare lejos muy lejos/ De ti. *(Suddenly,* PROCLO *comes back to his senses.)*

PROCLO. This isn't going to work out, Mr. Googie!

GOOGIE. Mister?

PROCLO. There's just no way!

GOOGIE. Mister? You thought I was a drag queen? No such luck, *chico!*

PROCLO. You really are a miss?

GOOGIE. This is all real. *(She has clasped his hands to her breasts.* PROCLO *can't believe what he is feeling. His voice goes up at least an octave.)*

PROCLO. It feels real, it feels real!

GOOGIE. I just hope I'm gonna find me some *huevitos.*

PROCLO. What are *huevitos?*

GOOGIE *(Finding them under his raincoat.).* Ay ay ay!

PROCLO. They're real, too!

GOOGIE. We're gonna make such a whoo-pee, *chico!*

PROCLO. Thank you.

GOOGIE. Thank you? You're gonna thank me.

PROCLO. The trouble is my brother-in-law is trying to kill me and there's someone under this bed.

GOOGIE. Oh no you don't! I'm not falling for that old hat and dance routine. You're not pulling no wool over my ears so easy.

PROCLO. I swear to God there is!

GOOGIE. Never try to shit an old pro, *chico.*

MICHAEL. He's not! There is someone under this bed.

CHRIS. Us! And if you two want to bounce around like that I'll gladly go back to my own room.

GOOGIE *(leaping off the bed).* That's a rotten

stunt, mister. I could lose my job for this. I told you: I threw wind in caution coming down here!

PROCLO. It's really very simple.

GOOGIE. I don't need no explaining. you rather make hee-hee-hee, poo-poo-poo, hah-hah-hah with that *maricon* you got hiding under the bed!

CHRIS. Two *maricons,* Googie!

GOOGIE. Who's that down there?

CHRIS. It's me, Chris.

GOOGIE. Hi, Chris. What are you doing down there?

CHRIS. I wish I knew.

MICHAEL *(poking his head out now).* The reason we're under this bed—

GOOGIE. You!

MICHAEL. Now wait!

GOOGIE. Not only you got a fat boyfriend, you *maricon* hump—you got a mean one! *(She is hitting* MICHAEL *with the pillow.)*

MICHAEL. I'm not his boyfriend!

PROCLO. He's not!

MICHAEL. And I'm not gay!

GOOGIE. With a voice like that you're no straight arrow either.

MICHAEL. I was born with this voice.

GOOGIE. So was Yma Sumac. I saw you talking on the telephone and I said, "Googie, that boy could make your blood go boil."

PROCLO. I thought you said that about me.

GOOGIE. I say that about everyone. *(PROCLO is making an escape.)* Where are you going?

PROCLO. Look, I'm just someone who's in a lot of trouble, lady.

GOOGIE. You're not staying for my second show?

PROCLO. I'm not a producer. It was all your two friends' idea. Now if you'd just let me get out of here—

GOOGIE. Hey, now wait a minute!

PROCLO. Now what?

GOOGIE. Wait just one big fat minute! *(She grabs for* PROCLO's *wig. It comes off.)*

PROCLO. Hey!

GOOGIE. I thought maybe it was you!

PROCLO. Who are you talking about?

GOOGIE. Seymour Pippin! You don't fire Googie Gomez from no show and get away with it. *(She is trying to kill* PROCLO.) You think I forget a face like yours, you bastard? I'm gonna tear your eyes out! *(CHRIS and* MICHAEL *will eventually subdue her.)*

CHRIS. It's not him, Googie.

MICHAEL. That's Mr. Vespucci.

GOOGIE. You promise?

PROCLO. I promise.

GOOGIE. I thought you was Seymour Pippin.

PROCLO. I wish I were.

GOOGIE. What do you know? I thought he was Seymour Pippin!

MICHAEL. Seymour Pippin! (CARMINE *has come out of his room and knocks on the door.*)

PROCLO. Oh my God! (*They all start scrambling for a place under the bed.*)

GOOGIE. What about me?

CHRIS. That's my place!

MICHAEL. Hurry up!

GOOGIE. Suck your gut in!

PROCLO. I am!

GOOGIE. More!

PROCLO. Who is that?

CHRIS. Relax, mister. I told you: you're not my type.

PROCLO. Well just get your hand off my—.

GOOGIE. It's okay! It's my hand.

MICHAEL. If it's him, Mr. Vespucci, just give me the word. (PROCLO, CHRIS *and* GOOGIE *have somehow all managed to squeeze under the bed.* MICHAEL *opens the door.* CARMINE *storms in.*)

CARMINE. What the hell happened to you? You said you'd be on top! I've been under that damn bed so long I can hardly walk! (*As he turns he sees* MICHAEL, *who has gone into his flexing routine.*)

MICHAEL. See something you like, buddy?

CARMINE. What the—?

MICHAEL. You new around here, mac?

CARMINE. You're not Brick! Where's Brick? What have you done to him?

MICHAEL. Lie down.

CARMINE. Get your hands off me! (MICHAEL *shoves* CARMINE *onto the bed.* GOOGIE *cries out.*)

GOOGIE. Ow! Ay, coño!

PROCLO. Sshh!

CARMINE. What the—?

MICHAEL. Relax.

CARMINE. Somebody's under there!

MICHAEL. Just stretch out on the bed, now.

CARMINE. What are you doing in here?

MICHAEL. Just relax: I'm trying to seduce you.

CARMINE. Get your hands off me, you goddamn Greek, or I'll lay your head open.

MICHAEL (*Pinning* CARMINE *down*). Is it him, Mr. Vespucci?

PROCLO. Yes!

CARMINE. Vespucci? I'm Vespucci.

MICHAEL. Is it?

PROCLO. Yes, yes! It's him! It's him!

CARMINE. I know that voice! (*He leans over the bed just as* GOOGIE *rolls out.*) What the hell is this? One of them goddamn transvestites, sure you are!

GOOGIE. Seymour Pippin! (*She is attacking* CARMINE, *swatting him with a pillow.*)

CARMINE. Fight fair, you faggot! (MICHAEL *knocks* CARMINE *out with a karate blow.*)

MICHAEL. Hi-ya! (CARMINE *falls onto the bed.* PROCLO *groans.*)

GOOGIE. Aw, shit! Why you do that? I was gonna fix his wagon for him good!

MICHAEL. He's out cold, Mr. Vespucci!

PROCLO. Just get me out of here.

CHRIS. And we were just starting to have so much fun!

GOOGIE. You know something? This man is not Seymour Pippin either. He sure got a mean face though! I wonder who he is. (PROCLO *and* CHRIS *are up from under the bed now.*)

PROCLO. It's my brother-in-law.

GOOGIE. Is he in show business?

PROCLO. He's in garbage.

GOOGIE. A gay garbageman?

MICHAEL. You're sure it's him?

PROCLO. I'm afraid so.

GOOGIE. What are you two talking about?

MICHAEL. I'm a detective. Mr. Vespucci here hired me to get something on his brother-in-law Mr. Proclo there so Mr. Proclo doesn't inherit one-half the family business.

PROCLO. So that's it. (*He tries to strangle* CARMINE. *The others hold him back.*)

MICHAEL. Mr. Vespucci wanted to catch us together so he could commit a *delitto di passione*. What's a *delitto di passione*, Mr. Vespucci? (*Again* PROCLO *goes for* CARMINE's *throat.*)

PROCLO. You're about to see one!

CHRIS. Hey, now take it easy! You can't do that!

PROCLO. *He* was going to! (MICHAEL *has been getting ready to photograph* CARMINE *on the bed.*)

MICHAEL. Look out now. You'll be in the picture.

CHRIS (*primping his hair*). Picture? What picture? (*Suddenly* GOOGIE *grabs the camera.*)

GOOGIE. Oh no! I see what you do! If that man want to be here, let him be here. What you care? I don't stand still for no blackmail! I tell Tiger and Duff what you do and you're out on your ass, big boy! Come on, Chris! (*She goes with the camera.*)

CHRIS. Excuse me, but I promised Mark Spitz

we'd do a quick ten laps around the pool. *(He goes.)*

MICHAEL. Mark Spitz comes here, Mr. Vespucci?

PROCLO. I don't care!

MICHAEL. What should I do with him?

PROCLO. Kill him.

MICHAEL. I'm a private detective, Mr. Vespucci. I'm not a hit man.

PROCLO. You got something to tie him down with?

MICHAEL. Cuffs.

PROCLO. Hurry.

MICHAEL. Give me a hand with him, will you?

PROCLO. Can't you hit him again?

MICHAEL. That wouldn't be ethical, Mr. Vespucci.

PROCLO. Ethical? Your line of work and you're telling me what's ethical? Come on, let's get out of here.

MICHAEL. If you don't need me anymore, I want to find that Googie and get my camera back.

PROCLO. Fine, fine. *(MICHAEL goes. PROCLO stands looking after him, then down at CAR-MINE on the bed.)* You blew it, Carmine. By the time you get out of this place I'll be back in Cleveland with Vivian and the kids. *(He goes, leaving the door open. He passes into CARMINE's room. We will see him gather up CARMINE's clothes as he yells out.)* Fat man in 101! Come and get it. Fat man in 101! He's all yours. Fat man in 101! *(As PROCLO comes out of Carmine's room, he sees TIGER in the corridor.)*

PROCLO. Duff.

TIGER. I'm Tiger.

PROCLO. Whatever! Burn these for me, will you?

TIGER. Burn 'em?

PROCLO. You heard me.

TIGER *(Scooping up CARMINE's clothes).* You're sounding happy.

PROCLO. I'm close to feeling terrific!

TIGER. What happened?

PROCLO. I'm catching the next plane to Cleveland.

TIGER. Good luck.

PROCLO. You're too late. I've already got it! *(TIGER is gone. PROCLO grabs his suitcase and starts to head off. The pay phone rings and MICHAEL answers it.)*

MICHAEL. Hello? This is The Ritz. Michael Brick speaking. It's for you, Mr. Vespucci.

PROCLO. Who is it?

MICHAEL. Who is this? It's Mrs. Proclo, calling from that bar across the street.

PROCLO. Mrs. Proclo? My God, it's Vivian. Tell her I've left.

MICHAEL. I'm sorry but he just left, Mrs. Proclo. She doesn't believe me.

PROCLO. Tell her she has to believe you.

MICHAEL. He says you have to believe me. She says she's not staying there another minute. She's taking a man's hat and raincoat and coming right over here and nothing's going to stop her. Hello . . . hello? *(He hangs up.)* I didn't even get to tell her the good news.

PROCLO. What good news?

MICHAEL. That we got our man! *(GOOGIE is coming along on her way to the nightclub.)* Miss Gomez?

GOOGIE. Don't Miss Gomez me now, *chico.* I got a show to do.

MICHAEL. I can explain about downstairs.

GOOGIE. I don't talk to no detectives.

MICHAEL. Then about my cameras! *(They are gone.)*

PROCLO. He'll kill me. She'll divorce me. My children will grow up hating my memory. Oh my God! *(TIGER is passing.)*

TIGER. What happened?

PROCLO. I just ran out of luck! There's a woman trying to get in here. Keep her out.

TIGER. They don't let ladies in here.

PROCLO. It's my wife.

TIGER. Relax. She'll never get past Abe. *(He is gone.)*

PROCLO. I did! *(He runs into his room. We see CLAUDE come in behind him. PROCLO doesn't. Yet. He sits on the bed and pants.)*

CLAUDE. Your door was open.

PROCLO. What?

CLAUDE. I'm giving you one more chance. *(He starts to sing his song.)* "Jelly Roll Baby/ You're my Jelly Roll Man . . ."

PROCLO. Please, I'm too weak.

CLAUDE. "Jelly Roll cupcake/ I'm your Jelly Roll fan . . ."

PROCLO. Look, this is a lot of fun, I can't tell you! I don't know about you, Claude, but I'm in terrible trouble.

CLAUDE. Claude!

PROCLO. I didn't say that.

CLAUDE. Wait a minute! Wait a minute! Guy! It's you, Guy!

PROCLO. Absolutely no!

CLAUDE. Gaetano Proclo, the fifth division, Special Services, the Philippines.

PROCLO. I was 4-F. I never served.

CLAUDE. It's me, Claude! Claude Perkins.

PROCLO. Get away from me, Claude!

CLAUDE. That's right! "Get away from me" Claude! We had an act together. A trio with Nelson Carpenter. We pantomimed Andrews Sisters records. "Rum and Coca Cola." Remember?

PROCLO. I don't know what you're talking about. I hate the Andrews Sisters.

CLAUDE. You hate the Andrews Sisters?

PROCLO. Look, I'm in desperate, desperate trouble, mister, and I wish you'd just go away.

CLAUDE. Just wait until I write Nelson Carpenter about this!

ABE *(over the loudspeaker)*. 253 coming up! That's two-five-three. You're not going to believe what's coming up, boys!

PROCLO. O my God, it is Vivian!

CLAUDE. There are other fat fish in the ocean, Gaetano Proclo, and 253 just may be one of them.

PROCLO. Just don't touch 253, Claude!

CLAUDE. We'll see about that. *(He sweeps out.* PROCLO *returns to his room, kneels beside his bed, and quietly begins to pray. The patron in chaps walks in on the awakening* CARMINE *in* BRICK'*s room.)*

PATRON IN CHAPS. Howdy, pardner. Handcuffs? Outta sight! *(He sinks to his haunches and just stares.* TIGER, DUFF, GOOGIE *and* MICHAEL *are running by. The three entertainers are dressed to go on.)*

GOOGIE. If I don't hit that note, cover for me.

DUFF. How?

GOOGIE. Take your clothes off! Anything!

MICHAEL. Miss Gomez! *(They are gone.* CARMINE *is starting to come around. The* PATRON IN CHAPS *is still staring.)*

PATRON IN CHAPS. Far out! Far out! *(CHRIS pokes his head into the room.)*

CHRIS. Hi, girls!

CARMINE. Brick!

CHRIS. Don't believe a word she says. She thinks she's a detective or something.

CARMINE. Who she? What she?

CHRIS. You she. And who do you think you are? Dale Evans? *(He starts to go.)*

CARMINE. Let me out of here! I'll kill you!

CHRIS. I've got a date with 253. *(He is gone.)*

CARMINE. Gaetano! Gaetano! *(The* PATRON IN CHAPS *runs off. On the second level we see* VIVIAN. *She is wearing a man's hat and raincoat over her black pants suit. She carries a shopping bag.* CHRIS *approaches her.)*

CHRIS. I had a hunch it would be bad, but nothing like this. *(To* VIVIAN.*)* Welcome to the city morgue. *(VIVIAN recoils and lets out one of her giant sobs: an unearthly sound.)*

VIVIAN. Aaaaaaaeeeeee!

CHRIS. Forget it, mister, that's not my scene! *(Opening the door to the steam room.)* Avon calling! *(He goes in,* CLAUDE *has approached* VIVIAN *in the corridor, and again the strains of the "Now, Voyager" theme are heard.)*

CLAUDE. Looking for 253? *(VIVIAN nods, stifling her sobs.)* Right this way. *(He leads her to his own room, of course, carefully concealing the number as they enter. He slams the door and starts to sing.)* "Jelly Roll Baby/ You're my Jelly Roll Man . . ." *(VIVIAN really lets out a big sob as he starts moving towards her.)*

VIVIAN. Aaaaiiiieeeee! *(No sooner does she scream than* VIVIAN *faints dead away on* CLAUDE'*s bed. At that moment,* CARMINE *manages to free himself from his handcuffs by banging the bed noisily on the ground.* PROCLO, *in his room,* CARMINE'*s threats and* VIVIAN'*s screams ringing in his ears, is literally quivering, as he softly calls out.)*

PROCLO. Help. Help. Help. *(CARMINE is on the rampage. He shoots the lock off his own door. The door gives and he runs in.)*

CARMINE. My clothes! Somebody took my clothes! *(He runs out of the room, brandishing the revolver.)* Okay, Gaetano! I know you're in here! I'm gonna find you if it's the last thing I do! *(He disappears. Meanwhile,* CLAUDE *is trying to revive* VIVIAN.*)*

CLAUDE. All right, lie there like a beached whale. *(No response from* VIVIAN.*)* Look, I'd love to stay here and play Sleeping Beauty with you but I've got to get ready for the Talent Contest. *(He starts getting his things together for his record pantomime act.)* What's in the bag? You bring your own lunch? *(He is looking in* VIVIAN'*s shopping bag.)*

ABE *(over the loudspeaker)*. Just a reminder, boys and girls. It's amateur night at The Ritz.

CHRIS *(coming out of the steam room)*. You can say that again!

CLAUDE. You've got to be kidding. *(He takes a long mink coat out of* VIVIAN'*s shopping bag. He can't resist putting it on.)* What becomes a legend most? *(CARMINE comes storming up to* CHRIS.*)*

CHRIS. Hi, Bunny. How's tricks?

CARMINE. You! *(He points his gun.)*

CHRIS. Is that thing loaded?

CARMINE. And you're lucky I'm not using it on you. Now where is he?

CHRIS. Who?

CARMINE. My brother-in-law, you dumb dick!

CHRIS. He was just here.

CARMINE. And?

CHRIS. He went in there. *(He motions towards* CLAUDE'*s room.)*

CARMINE. Well why didn't you say so?

CHRIS. I just did. You're really planning to shoot him?

CARMINE. *You* if he's not in there! *(*CARMINE *starts for* CLAUDE'*s room.* CHRIS *hurries off in another direction.* CARMINE *starts banging on* CLAUDE'*s door.)*

CLAUDE. Who's that?

CARMINE. You know goddamn well who it is. *(*CLAUDE *opens the door, takes one look at* CARMINE, *and starts his song.)*

CLAUDE. "Jelly Roll Baby/ You're my Jelly Roll . . ."

CARMINE. What the—? *(He pulls his gun.)* Get out of here! *(*CLAUDE *escapes, taking his clothes and* VIVIAN'*s mink with him.* CARMINE *turns at a moan from* VIVIAN *on the bed.)* Okay, Gaetano, the jig is up! *(Then, realizing who it is.)* Viv! Vivian, baby. What have they done to you? *(He tries to revive her.)* Speak to me, Viv! Viv! *(*CHRIS *has come up to* PROCLO'*s door.* PROCLO *is slumped. He is too tired, too defeated, to call for help anymore.)*

CHRIS. It's me, Chris! Open the door! *(*PROCLO *does.)* That brother-in-law of yours means business.

PROCLO. Why can't he just find me and get it over with?

CHRIS. You're just going to sit there?

PROCLO. What's the use?

CHRIS. Hide somewhere.

PROCLO. I came here. He found me.

CHRIS. Wear a disguise.

PROCLO. I am! *(He tears off his wig and moustache.)* I thought you were mad at me.

CHRIS. I am but I prefer you alive to dead. I'm funny that way. *(*CLAUDE, *wearing the mink, comes along the corridor.)*

PROCLO. Claude!

CLAUDE. Oh, sure. Now you know me.

PROCLO. You've got to help me.

CLAUDE. I've got to get ready for the talent contest tonight.

PROCLO. My brother-in-law's here with a gun.

CLAUDE. So that's who that maniac is! *(*PROCLO, CLAUDE, *and* CHRIS *go.)*

CARMINE. Viv! Viv! Sis!

VIVIAN *(reviving).* Where am I? Carmine!

CARMINE. What are you doing here?

VIVIAN. I couldn't stand being in that bar anymore.

CARMINE. Do you know what kind of place this is?

VIVIAN. It was horrible, Carmine. He wanted me to roll on him.

CARMINE. Who?

VIVIAN. I don't know. Some little thin man.

CARMINE. I'll kill him. I'll kill 'em all.

VIVIAN. I was afraid something terrible had happened. I asked myself what Gilda would do.

CARMINE. Gilda? Gilda's twelve years old.

VIVIAN. Not my Gilda. The one in *Rigoletto.*

CARMINE. This isn't an opera, Viv.

VIVIAN. She disguised herself as a man for the man she loved and came to a place very similar to this one.

CARMINE. And then what happened?

VIVIAN *(new sobs).* She was stabbed to death!

CARMINE. You weren't stabbed. You were only rolled on.

VIVIAN. Take me home, Carmine, please.

CARMINE. Home? But he's here. I can prove it to you.

VIVIAN. I don't want proof. I just want to go back to Cleveland.

CARMINE. With a man like that?

VIVIAN. I don't care. He's my husband.

CARMINE. I'm gonna kill the son of a bitch when I find him.

VIVIAN. No killing, Carmine. I don't want killing.

CARMINE. All he's done to you.

VIVIAN. He hasn't done anything to me.

CARMINE. That's what you think. Now I want you to get out of here and take a cab back to Brooklyn. Leave that husband of yours to me.

VIVIAN. I'm not going!

CARMINE. Then stay in here and don't let anyone in.

VIVIAN. No!

CARMINE. This is between him and me, Viv!

VIVIAN. If you hurt him, I'll never speak to you again!

CARMINE. It's Poppa's honor that's at stake!

VIVIAN. Poppa's dead! *(This statement causes them both to collapse into sobs.)*

CARMINE. Poppa! He's stained the Vespucci honor!

VIVIAN. Carmine, please!

CARMINE. It's like he peed on Poppa's grave!

VIVIAN. Aaaaalllllleee!

CARMINE. I'm thinking about Poppa, Viv. Believe me, it's not for me.

VIVIAN. What about me?

CARMINE. You, too. He peed on you, too. You've been dishonored, too, sister.

VIVIAN. Give me the gun.

CARMINE. What?

VIVIAN. Give me the gun. I'm going to kill myself.

CARMINE. Are you crazy?

VIVIAN. I want to die, Carmine. You've made me so crazy I want to kill myself.

CARMINE. It's him I'm going to kill. *(By this time,* VIVIAN *will have the gun. Suddenly, she becomes aware that her mink is missing.)*

VIVIAN. Carmine! No, no!

CARMINE. What is it!

VIVIAN. No! . . . No! . . . No! . . .

CARMINE. What is it?

VIVIAN. My mink!

CARMINE. Your mink?

VIVIAN. It's gone. They've taken it. It was in here.

CARMINE. Why weren't you wearing it?

VIVIAN. I didn't want to get it wet. It cost 900 dollars.

CARMINE. I'll get your mink back, too.

VIVIAN. He gave it to me for our anniversary. Now I really want to kill myself.

CARMINE. I'll get your goddamn mink. Now let go of me.

VIVIAN. I'm coming with you.

CARMINE. You're staying here.

VIVIAN. I don't want him dead, Carmine.

CARMINE. It's not up to you. This is for Poppa! *(He starts off.)* Gaetano! Gaetano!

VIVIAN. Carmine! *(But he is gone.* VIVIAN *runs out of the room and sees the snooty patron.)* Stop him.

SNOOTY PATRON. Who?

VIVIAN. My brother. He'll kill him. You heard him. He's a violent man.

SNOOTY PATRON. Kill who?

VIVIAN. My husband. And my mink! They took my mink! *(*VIVIAN *and the* SNOOTY PATRON *disappear up a corridor.* PROCLO, CLAUDE *and* CHRIS *go running by on their way to the nightclub.)*

CHRIS. I don't know any Andrews Sisters numbers!

CLAUDE. We'll fake it!

PROCLO. This will never work!

CLAUDE. He never really knew any either. Nelson and I carried you for years. *(*CARMINE *enters and comes face to face with* CHRIS *and the others.* PROCLO *hides behind the mink coat as* CHRIS *blows his whistle.)*

CHRIS. He went up to the steam room, boss.

CARMINE. Thanks. *(He heads upstairs.*

CLAUDE, PROCLO *and* CHRIS *turn on their heels and run in the opposite direction.* VIVIAN *appears on the first level.)*

VIVIAN. Carmine, wait!

CARMINE. I said stay in there! *(He continues toward the steam room.* VIVIAN *sees* PROCLO *and his group just exiting.)*

VIVIAN. My mink! Stop, thief! *(They are gone,* VIVIAN *in pursuit.* CARMINE *runs into the steam room. This time all the patrons come flying out.* CARMINE *follows, brandishing his gun. They all run off. Music is heard. It is a bad baritone singing the end of an operatic aria.)*

BAD BARITONE *(singing over the loudspeaker).* Il concetto vidisi/ Or ascoltate/ Com-eglie svolto,/ Andiam./ Incominciate! *(This is the transition to the nightclub. The talent show is in progress. There is applause as* GOOGIE *steps onto the stage.)*

GOOGIE. That was Tiny Naylor singing "The Prologue" from *Pagliacci.* Bravo, Tiny, bravo. It's gonna be a close race tonight. *(She consults a card.)* Our next contestant is Sheldon Farenthold, song stylist. Take it away, Sheldon! *(Sheldon enters, encased in red balloons. He plays directly out front, thus making the audience in the theatre the audience in The Pits. During the number he will pop his balloons and do bumps and grinds.)*

SHELDON *(singing).*

Why are we here? What are we doing?
It's time we all found out.
We're not here to stay,
We're on a short holiday,
'Cause . . .
Life is just a bowl of cherries,
Don't take it serious,
Life's too mysterious.
You work, you slave, you worry so,
But you can't take your dough when
    you go, go, go,
So keep repeating it's the berries,
The strongest oak must fall . . .
        (Suddenly, two groups of patrons, one chased by CARMINE, *the other by* VIVIAN, *crisscross and disappear into the "backstage" area of the nightclub.* SHELDON *shoots them a blinder but goes on performing like a good little trouper that he is. Spoken.)*
Thanks a lot! *(sung)*
The sweet things in life,
To you were just loaned,
How can you lose what you've never

owned.
Life is just a bowl of cherries,
So live and laugh at it all.
C'mon . . .
Live
And laugh at it all!

(When the number ends, SHELDON *takes his bows and goes.* GOOGIE *steps forward.)*

GOOGIE. Thank you. You know, it gives me a real pleasure to emcee these amateur shows because I began as an amateur. *(Sounds of disbelief from the offstage band members.)* It's true! I didn't get where I am over night. Oh no, *chicos!* It took a long, long time. A star is born, that's true, I mean, you have "it" in the cradle or you don't, but she doesn't twinkle over no one night. *(She laughs at her own joke, then regains herself.)* Okay. *(Suddenly a group of patrons, led by* SHELDON *and his balloons, races across, chased by* CARMINE. GOOGIE *chooses to continue unflustered.)* Our last contestant is Mr. Claude Perkins and partners recreating their famous Army act. Hit it, boys! *(Music is heard. It is a '40s sounding swing orchestra. A spotlight picks up* CLAUDE *in his WAC uniform,* PROCLO *in his wife's mink coat and a long blonde wig, and* CHRIS *in an elaborate makeshift gown made from sheets. The Andrews Sisters are heard singing one of their big hits, "The Three Caballeros."* CLAUDE, CHRIS *and* PROCLO *begin to pantomime to the record and jitterbug. At first,* PROCLO *is all nerves and* CLAUDE *does a Herculean job of covering for him. But as the number progresses, we see* PROCLO *getting better and better as the act comes back to him. After a while, he's close to enjoying himself.)*

THE ANDREWS SISTERS *(prerecorded).*
We're three caballeros, three gay
    caballeros,
They say we are birds of a feather,
We're happy amigos,
No matter where he goes,
The one, two and three goes,
We're always together.

(Suddenly all of the patrons, including poor SHELDON, *balloons and all, with* TIGER *and* DUFF, *are chased across the stage and into the house by* CARMINE *and* VIVIAN.)

We're three happy chappies, with
    snappy serapes,
You'll find us beneath our sombreros;
We're brave and we'll stay so,
We're bright as a peso,

Who sez so, we say so,
The three caballeros.

*(CHRIS *accidentally steps on* PROCLO'*s foot, but the number continues.)*

Oh, we have ths stars to guide us,
Guitars here beside us,
To play as we go;
We sing and we samba;
We shout "Ay, *Caramba.*"
What means *Ay, Caramba?*
Oh yes, I don't know . . .

(The number is really building now. PROCLO *is boogying away like crazy. Suddenly* CARMINE *fires a shot in the air. There is total pandemonium as the group of patrons returns to the stage from the back of the house. They run into a big huddle.* PROCLO *and* CLAUDE *manage to lose themselves somewhere in the middle of the crowd.)*

CARMINE. Now everybody slow down! Nobody's going nowhere. And get some lights on. I want to see who I'm talking to. *(The follow-spot hits* CARMINE.*)* Not on me! I want the room lights, you dumb fruit! *(All the lights come on.)* Okay, I want all the fairies in a line.

CHRIS. What about us butch types, boss?

CARMINE. Shut up, you.

CHRIS. It's me, Bunny, Brick.

CARMINE. You're fired. Get over there! *(He motions with his gun for* CHRIS *to form a line. He turns and sees* MICHAEL.*)* I can't believe it. A good-looking, rugged boy like you.

MICHAEL. Believe what, sir?

CARMINE. I believe it. Get going.

GOOGIE. Wait a minute. All of this because some fat woman who lost her mink?

CARMINE. One more word out of you, you goddamn tranvestite and—

GOOGIE. What you call me?

SHELDON. Careful, Googie.

GOOGIE. You make me see red, mister, and when I see red I tear you apart. Shit! You think I'm scared of a little gun? *(CARMINE *fires in the air again.)* That's okay, mister. You don't bother me, I don't bother you. *(She backs into the main group of patrons.)*

CARMINE. Okay, Cowboy. Your turn.

PATRON IN CHAPS. I don't know what your name is but you belong in Bellevue.

CARMINE. Who says?

PATRON IN CHAPS. A trained psychiatrist.

CARMINE. Get outta here! *(DUFF *and* TIGER *try to sneak up on* CARMINE.*)* What are you two? The Cherry Sisters?

DUFF. Up yours, mister.

CARMINE. Get over there. All right. The rest

of you! *(The group crosses the stage, revealing* CLAUDE *and* PROCLO, *whose face is turned.* CLAUDE *approaches* CARMINE.*)*

CLAUDE. You really know how to mess up an act, you know that, mister?

CARMINE. Christ, another one!

CLAUDE. I'm an entertainer. Pantomime acts are coming back, you'll see.

CARMINE. In the meantime, you're still a tranvestite. Move! *(Only* PROCLO *remains now.* CARMINE *is savoring every moment of his humiliation.)* I guess that makes it you. Look at you. I could vomit. Jesus, Mary and Joseph! Is that her mink? *(*PROCLO *turns around. Not only is he wearing the mink and the Patty Andrews wig, he has added the dark glasses and the moustache. He nods.)* Give it back to her. *(*PROCLO *shakes his head.)*

VIVIAN. I don't want it now. That's not Gaetano. I just want to go home.

CARMINE. Okay, Gaetano, the jig's up. Take that crap off. The wig, the glasses, the moustache, the mink. Everything. I'm giving you three. *(to the others)* I want you all to meet my splendid brother-in-law, Gaetano Proclo.

MICHAEL. That's not Mr. Proclo! He is!

CARMINE. Who is?

MICHAEL. You are! *(*CARMINE *spins around.* PROCLO *bites his wrist and grabs the gun. The others subdue* CARMINE. *For a few moments he is buried as they swirl about him.* VIVIAN *just sobs hysterically.)*

CARMINE. Get your hands off me! This time you've really done it, Gaetano!

PROCLO. Shut up, Carmine.

CARMINE. Sure, you got some balls now, you're holding a gun.

PROCLO. Don't worry about my balls, Carmine.

CARMINE. I'm gonna kill you!

PROCLO. Keep him quiet. Sit on him. I don't want to hear that voice. *(*TIGER, DUFF, *and* CHRIS *hold* CARMINE *down and muffle his mouth, though* CARMINE *will try to get his two cents in during the conversation that follows.* PRO-CLO *has approached* VIVIAN.*)*

PROCLO. Don't cry, Viv.

VIVIAN. Don't cry, he says. Look at him like that, telling me not to cry!

PROCLO. You want your coat back?

VIVIAN. I want to know what you're doing in it!

PROCLO. It was the only thing that fit.

VIVIAN. Aaaaiiiieeee!

PROCLO. Carmine was going to kill me!

VIVIAN. AAAAIIIIEEEE!

PROCLO. Vivian, please!

VIVIAN. My husband, the man in the mink coat! I can't wait to go to Bingo with you like that next week but I won't be there if God is merciful because I'm going to have a heart attack right here.

CARMINE. This is grounds for annulment, sis. I asked Father Catini.

VIVIAN. I don't want an annulment. I want to die. *Mi fa morire, Dio, mi fa morire!*

PROCLO. Is this what you wanted, Carmine?

CARMINE. You're finished, Gaetano.

PROCLO. I can understand you hating me as a brother-in-law but killing someone over a garbage company?

VIVIAN. *Un delitto di passione,* Carmine?

CARMINE. *Si! Un delitto di passione!*

VIVIAN. *Ma perchè?*

CARMINE. *Perchè* you're married to a flaming homo, that's *perchè!*

VIVIAN. Aaaaiiiieeee!

CARMINE. He came here tonight, didn't he?

PROCLO. A cab driver brought me here.

CARMINE. Because you told him to.

PROCLO. I never heard of this place.

CARMINE. You see that Vivian? Even a cab driver knows what a *fata* he is!

VIVIAN. I just hope you're not going to insist on mentioning this in confession.

PROCLO. Mention what?

VIVIAN. He knows your voice, Guy.

PROCLO. Who knows my voice?

VIVIAN. Father Bonnelli. He knows everyone's *voce.* For my sake, Guy, for the children's, don't tell him about this.

PROCLO. I wasn't planning to!

VIVIAN. You're going through a stage. Last year it was miniature golf.

CARMINE. This ain't like no miniature golf, Viv.

VIVIAN. I'll get over this. I get over everything. It's my greatest strength.

PROCLO. There's nothing to get over, then or now!

VIVIAN. Aaaiiiieee!

PROCLO. Vivian, what do I have to do to convince you?

CARMINE. She is convinced! Cry your heart out, sis, it's all right. Carmine's here.

PROCLO. How the hell do you prove something like that to your wife? I give up. You win, Carmine. Let him go. *(*TIGER, DUFF *and* CHRIS *reluctantly release* CARMINE, *look at* PROCLO, *and then leave.)*

CARMINE. Come on, sis, let's get out of here.

PROCLO. Vivian, wait!

CARMINE. Don't you even speak to my sister! *(PROCLO stands there helpless. MAURINE has appeared. She goes directly to CARMINE and hands him a long sheet of figures.)*

MAURINE. Thirty seven thousand five hundred on the week. The rain killed us tonight. And next week we got the Jewish holidays coming up. Good night, boss. *(She goes.)*

VIVIAN. Who was that?

CARMINE. Just a person.

VIVIAN. She called you boss.

CARMINE. A lot of people call me boss. *(He starts to eat the sheet of figures.)*

VIVIAN. Give me that.

CARMINE. It's not what you're going to think, Vivian.

VIVIAN. "Vespucci Enterprises, Inc. Carmine Vespucci, President." This is a statement!

CARMINE. I was going to tell you about it.

VIVIAN. We own this place?

CARMINE. Poppa'd done a lot of expanding while you were in Cleveland.

VIVIAN. We own this place, Guy!

CARMINE. He doesn't have to know the family business, Viv! Now come on, this isn't the place to talk about it.

VIVIAN. So you knew what kind of place this was.

CARMINE. So did he obviously. That's why he came here. I can't help it if we own it. It's just a coincidence.

VIVIAN. What kind of cab was it, Guy?

PROCLO. What?

VIVIAN. The one that brought you here.

PROCLO. I don't remember.

CARMINE. A fairy cab!

VIVIAN. Do you remember the name of the company?

CARMINE. The Fairy Cab Company! Fairy cabs for fairy passengers! Now come on, Vivian, let's get out of here. What do you care what kind of cab it was?

VIVIAN. Think hard, Guy. It's important.

PROCLO. It was an opera . . . Aida Cab!

VIVIAN. Aida Cab! We own that company!

PROCLO. We do?

VIVIAN. Carmine, did you tell that driver to bring Guy here?

CARMINE. Of course I didn't!

VIVIAN. What did the driver look like, Guy?

PROCLO. All I remember about him is his stutter.

VIVIAN. His stutter?

PROCLO. He stuttered and smoked pot.

VIVIAN. Cousin Tito! I should've guessed. It's going to be very hard to forgive you for this, Carmine.

CARMINE. What's to forgive! I don't want no forgiving!

VIVIAN. Now take the hit off him, Carmine.

CARMINE. Vivian!

VIVIAN. Take it off!

CARMINE. No!

VIVIAN. If you don't take it off, Carmine, I am gonna tell Frankie di Lucca about you muscling into the Bingo concessions at the Feast of St. Anthony and then Frankie di Lucca is gonna put a hit out on you and you are gonna end up wearing cement shoes at the bottom of the East River and then there will be even more grief and less peace in our fucking family than there already is!

PROCLO. I am married to an extraordinary woman!

CARMINE. You wouldn't do this to me, sis!

VIVIAN. You know me, Carmine.

CARMINE. Vivian!

VIVIAN. I swear it, Carmine. *Lo giuro.*

CARMINE. *Non giura,* sis!

VIVIAN. *Lo giuro,* Carmine. *Lo giuro,* the Bingo and the cement shoes.

CARMINE. "Get Proclo." You heard Poppa.

VIVIAN. I've got Proclo, Carmine. Now take the hit off!

CARMINE. I'll lose face.

VIVIAN. Not under the East River!

CARMINE *(writhing in defeat)*. Aaaaiiieee!

VIVIAN. Now take the hit off him, Carmine! Is it off? *(He nods.)* On Poppa's grave? *(He shakes his head.)* I want it on Poppa's grave and I want it forever! *(He shakes his head.)* I'm calling Frankie di Lucca.

CARMINE. It's off on Poppa's grave!

VIVIAN *(finally breaking down)*. Poppa! All right, now I forgive you.

CARMINE. I told you: I don't want no forgiving.

VIVIAN. You already have it. And now I want to see you two forgive each other. *Il bacio del pace,* Carmine.

CARMINE. You gotta be kidding!

PROCLO. Over my dead body!

VIVIAN. I want you to kiss each other as brothers.

PROCLO. I wouldn't kiss him for a million dollars.

VIVIAN. That's exactly what it's worth, Guy.

PROCLO. I wouldn't kiss him, period.

VIVIAN. I want you to make your peace with Carmine.

PROCLO. Vivian!

VIVIAN. For me, Guy, for me.

PROCLO. I forgive you, Carmine. With a little luck nobody's gonna die in your family for a long, long time and we won't have to see each other for another twenty years. Just be sure to send the checks. *Andiamo! (By this time, all the patrons will have gathered as an audience to the proceedings.* PROCLO *opens his arms and moves towards* CARMINE *for the kiss of peace.)* Hey!

CARMINE. Hey! *(They make a slow, ritual-like circle. Of course, both men do look rather ludicrous as they circle one another.* PROCLO *in his wife's mink coat;* CARMINE *in his bathrobe.* CARMINE *hesitates.)*

VIVIAN. Frankie di Lucca! *(The circling resumes. Just as they are about to kiss.* CARMINE *gives* PROCLO *a good punch in the stomach. But as* PROCLO *bends over in pain, he knees* CARMINE *in the groin.* CARMINE *goes down. The others give a mighty cheer and congratulate* PROCLO.)

PROCLO *(amazed)*. I did it. I did it. *(now jubilant)* I won. I didn't fight fair but I won! *(to* CARMINE*)* You can go *va fangool* yourself, Carmine. People like you really do belong in garbage. People like me just marry into it. Get him out of here, men!

CHRIS. Bring her up to the steam room, girls! *(The others pounce on* CARMINE, *who is protesting mightily, and drag him off.)*

CARMINE. I'm coming back here and I'm gonna kill every last one of you fairies!

CHRIS. Sure you are, Nancy! *(It is a gleeful, noisy massed exit. All the patrons sing "La Marseillaise." For several moments we can still hear* CARMINE *yelling and the others cheering.* VIVIAN *has been following them in concern.* PROCLO *stops her.)*

PROCLO. Vivian!

VIVIAN. Where are your clothes? I want to go home.

PROCLO. I'm not leaving.

VIVIAN. Don't make any more waves in the family now, Guy.

PROCLO. It's the perfect time. If I don't do it now I never will. Your family's run herd on me since the day I met you. I'm sick of it. I'm sick of Carmine and Connie and Tony and Tommy and Sonny and Pipo and Silva and Beppe and Gina and your Aunt Rosa and Cousin Tito! I'm sick of all of them. The living and the dead. What am I? Some curse on a family? "Get Proclo." Those were your father's dying words!

VIVIAN. He was my father. I was his only girl. You expected him to like you?

PROCLO. Yes! Yes, I expect people to like me. I want people to like me. It's called self-esteem, Vivian.

VIVIAN. I think we have a wonderful marriage.

PROCLO. I do, too. It's nothing personal, Viv.

VIVIAN. A beautiful home, all paid for.

PROCLO. I'm not talking about that. I'm talking about me. I'm talking about wanting things. And I do want things. I've always wanted things. I wanted so many things I didn't get I can't even remember them. I wanted to send Momma back to Italy before she died. I didn't have the money in those days.

VIVIAN. Not many eight-year-old boys do, Guy.

PROCLO. I want us to be terrific forever. I want to go on a diet. No, I want to *stay* on one. I want a boat. I want a brand new fleet of trucks. I want Proclo Sanitation services to be number *one* in Cleveland. I want people to stop calling me a garbageman. I want to be known as a sanitary engineer. I want to be honored as an ecologist! I want changes! I want changes! I want changes! *(He has exhausted himself.)*

VIVIAN. I want to go back to Cleveland.

PROCLO. You know something? So do I. *(She goes to him and kisses his cheek.* CLAUDE *enters with three trophies.)*

CLAUDE. We won! We won! *(He hands one of the trophies to* PROCLO *and heads upstairs.)* We won the talent contest! We won! God bless the Andrews Sisters! Chris! Chris, where are you?

CHRIS. In the steam room!

CLAUDE. We won!

CHRIS. We won? *(CLAUDE meets* CHRIS *in the steam room with screams of joy.)*

PROCLO. You see that, Viv? I never won anything in my whole life. That was Claude Perkins. We were in Special Services together.

VIVIAN. He seems like a nice person.

PROCLO. I wouldn't go that far, Vivian. To him I look like Tyrone Power.

VIVIAN. So did I. Now where are your things? *(They return to* PROCLO's *room, where he will dress and pack.* GOOGIE *comes storming on, followed by* TIGER *and* DUFF. *She is dressed in street clothes and carrying all her belongings.)*

TIGER. We're sorry, Googie.

GOOGIE. You build someone up like that and it's all a lie. Ay, that's a low-down dirty trick to play.

TIGER. Look at it this way: one night there

will be a Mr. Big out there and you'll be all keyed up for it.

GOOGIE. There ain't never gonna be no Mr. Big in this place. There ain't never gonna be me no more in this place neither. I quit.

DUFF. Come on, Googie, we adore you.

GOOGIE. You adore yourself. (MICHAEL *appears.*) Would you believe it? They told me that Mr. Big was gonna be here tonight.

MICHAEL. Who's Mr. Big?

GOOGIE. Only the man you wait for all your life. Only the man who opens miracles. Only the man who can make you a star over one night. A producer, who else?

MICHAEL. My uncle is a producer, Miss Gomez.

GOOGIE. Oh yeah? What's he produce?

MICHAEL. Shows.

GOOGIE. Legitimate shows? I don't do no dirty stuff.

MICHAEL. Right now I think he's casting "Oklahoma" for a dinner theatre.

GOOGIE. "Oklahoma"? It's a stretch but I could do that part. You could get me an audition with him?

MICHAEL. Sure thing.

GOOGIE. You see? I had this hunch the whole evening. I got another show to do. I meet you in Bimbi's across the street. We run into my boy friend Hector and we tell him you're my agent. (*to* TIGER *and* DUFF) I see you two skunks later.

DUFF. I thought you quit.

GOOGIE. That's show business. (*She is gone.*)

TIGER. You got an uncle who's in show business?

MICHAEL. Seymour Pippin. He's a producer.

DUFF. Forget it, mister.

TIGER. Come on, Duff. (MICHAEL, TIGER *and* DUFF *leave.* CHRIS *has entered.*)

PROCLO (*to* VIVIAN). Are you ready?

CHRIS. I suppose you're wondering what happened to Bunny. We entered her in the Zinka Milanov look-alike contest. First prize is a gay guide to Bloomingdale's. We're still awaiting the judge's decision.

VIVIAN. Who's he talking about?

PROCLO. Carmine.

VIVIAN. He said she.

CHRIS. We've called the 16th Precinct. They'll be right over for him.

VIVIAN. Oh, Guy, you've got to do something for him.

PROCLO. I will, Vivian. Thanks for the help back there.

CHRIS. Just let me know the next time you three are coming in. I want to be sure not to be here. I haven't had so much fun since the day they raided Riis Park.

PROCLO. If you're ever in Cleveland Vivian makes a great lasagna.

CHRIS. Well, that's the best offer I've had all night.

PROCLO. Goodnight, Chris.

CHRIS. So long, boss. (*He heads back up to his room. We hear* GOOGIE *offstage, singing a song from her third show, "Shine On Harvest Moon.")*

ABE (*on the loudspeaker*). 316 coming up! That's three-one-six, Duff!

PROCLO. Let's go!

VIVIAN. Guy, promise me you'll take good care of Carmine.

PROCLO. Oh Poppa's grave.

VIVIAN (*a new outburst of grief*). Poppa! (*She exits.* PROCLO *calls off to her.*)

PROCLO. Not your Poppa's. Mine! (*As* PROCLO *starts off, a policeman races on.* PROCLO *stops to watch with a contented smile.* CHRIS *blows his whistle, and the policeman runs up to the steam room, where he finds* CARMINE, *bound and gagged and dressed in a green brocade ball gown.* CLAUDE *sees* CARMINE, *too, and sings his "Jelly Roll" song as he plays tug-o'-war with the policeman over* CARMINE. *Patrons are filling the halls.* DUFF *and* TIGER *start making fresh beds. And* PROCLO *just smiles.*)

CHRIS. Orgy! Orgy! Orgy in 240! (*The lights are fading. The play is over.*)

Streamers

David Rabe

FOR MIKE NICHOLS AND WYLIE WALKER

First presented by the Long Wharf Theater in New Haven on January 30, 1976, with the following cast:

(in order of appearance)

MARTIN	Michael-Raymond O'Keefe
RICHIE	Peter Evans
CARLYLE	Joe Fields
BILLY	John Heard
ROGER	Herbert Jefferson, Jr.
COKES	Dolph Sweet
ROONEY	Kenneth McMillan
M.P. LIEUTENANT	Stephen Mendillo
PFC HINSON (M.P.)	Ron Siebert
PFC CLARK (M.P.)	Michael Kell

Directed by Mike Nichols
Set by Tony Walton
Costumes by Bill Walker
Lighting by Ronald Wallace

David Rabe was a sensation and everyone knew it. Only the wise knew that it was going to be a difficult reputation to live down. In 1971, he became the flagship of Joseph Papp's American Shakespeare Festival. The boy most likely—the savior of American drama. Mr. Papp, an impresario extraordinary, and an entrepreneur with taste, love, and, significantly, aspiration, suggested that he was the best American playwright since Eugene O'Neill.

Rabe was born in 1940 in Dubuque, Iowa. He was the son of a schoolteacher and was educated in Dubuque, at Loras Academy and at Loras College, but the more significant part of his education came with his army service. He was drafted into the army in January 1965, and he served for two years, the final year being in Vietnam. This experience had a very large influence on his life.

On his release in 1967, he studied at a writing program at Villanova, and here he produced the first drafts of his first two plays, *The Basic Training of Pavlo Hummel* and *Sticks and bones.* For a time he worked on the New Haven *Register,* before the opportunity presented itself to him to become a full-time playwright and writer.

He met Joe Papp and his entire future changed. Mr. Papp first produced *Pavlo Hummel* on May 20, 1971, at the Newman Theater of the Shakespeare Festival's Public Theater complex on Lafayette Street. It was well received and ran for a total of 363 performances, which remains a record for the Lafayette Street complex.

His second play, *Sticks and Bones,* had originally been produced in a workshop production in Villanova. In 1971, in a revised version, it was staged at the Anspacher Theater, of the Public Theater Complex, while *Pavlo Hummel* was still running. It played 121 performances downtown and then on March 1, 1972, it was moved uptown to Broadway. After 245 performances at the Golden Theatre it closed on October 1, 1972.

During this time the play was operating at a consistent loss. However, Mr. Papp and his great nonprofit-making theatre subsidized it with money coming from his Broadway musical *Two Gentlemen of Verona.* There was also a television deal for *Sticks and Bones.* It was part of the package Mr. Papp had arranged with CBS Television. The television version was made, but then CBS, fearful of public opinion and aware of governmental orthodoxy, reneged on the arrangement and canceled the showing.

More controversy was lying in wait for Mr. Rabe and, of course, Mr. Papp. His final play in his Vietnam Trilogy was *The Orphan,* suggested by the Oresteia. This was very unsuccessful with the press and, it seems, the public. It opened at the Anspacher Theater on April 18, 1973, and closed on May 13.

On November 8, 1973, *The Boom-Boom Room* opened Joseph Papp's first season at the Vivian Beaumont Theater at Lincoln Center—it had been chosen as the first play to demonstrate Papp's and Lincoln Center's new stand as a platform for the new, young American playwright. Its reception was exceptionally mixed. Damned in some quarters, praised in others, it became a talking point of the season. Nevertheless, this analytical story of a go-go girl in Philadelphia won a Tony nomination in 1974. And, speaking of Tonys, *Sticks and Bones* actually won a Tony in 1972.

In *Sticks and Bones* Mr. Rabe takes that all-American family institution, the soap opera— even the characters are called Ozzie, Harriet, and Rick—and teases out of it a recognition of national malaise. It is a play about Vietnam, and why America had its involvement there.

Streamers, first presented on January 30, 1976, is again set in the early years of Vietnam. Its concerns, however, are universal: homosexuality, race relations, and the need to conform. The play's entire action is set in a claustrophobic army barracks—we watch as tensions and passions rise higher and higher. *Streamers* finally erupts in a burst of understanding but, like the parachute its title recalls, this grace comes too late. We land on the ground in a crumpled heap.

ACT ONE

*The set is a large cadre room thrusting an-
gularly toward the audience. The floor is
wooden and brown. Brightly waxed in places,
it is worn and dull in other sections. The back
wall is brown and angled. There are two lights
at the center of the ceiling. They hang covered
by green metal shades. Against the back wall
and to the stage right are three wall lockers,
side by side. Stage center in the back wall is
the door, the only entrance to the room. It
opens onto a hallway that runs off to the latrines, showers, other cadre rooms and larger
barracks rooms. There are three bunks.*
BILLY's *bunk is parallel to* ROGER's *bunk. They
are upstage and on either side of the room,
and face downstage.* RICHIE's *bunk is downstage and at a right angle to* BILLY's *bunk. At
the foot of each bunk is a green wooden footlocker. There is a floor outlet near* ROGER's
*bunk. He uses it for his radio. A reading lamp
is clamped on to the metal piping at the head
of* RICHIE's *bunk. A wooden chair stands beside the wall lockers. Two mops hang in the
stage left corner near a trash can.*

It is dusk as the lights rise on the room.
RICHIE *is seated and bowed forward wearily
on his bunk. He wears his long-sleeved khaki
summer dress uniform. Upstage behind him is*
MARTIN, *a thin, dark young man, pacing, worried. A white towel stained red with blood is
wrapped around his wrist. He paces several
steps and falters, stops. He stands there.*

———

RICHIE. Honest to God, Martin, I don't know
what to say anymore. I don't know what to
tell you.

MARTIN *(beginning to pace again).* I mean
it. I just can't stand it. Look at me.

RICHIE. I know.

MARTIN. I hate it.

RICHIE. We've got to make up a story. They'll
ask you a hundred questions.

MARTIN. Do you know how I hate it?

RICHIE. Everybody does. Don't you think I
hate it, too?

MARTIN. I enlisted, though. I enlisted and I
hate it.

RICHIE. I enlisted, too.

MARTIN. I vomit every morning. I get the
dry heaves. In the middle of every night.

(He flops down on the corner of BILLY's *bed
and sits there, slumped forward, shaking his
head.)*

RICHIE. You can stop that. You can.

MARTIN. No.

RICHIE. You're just scared. It's just fear.

MARTIN. They're all so mean; they're all so
awful. I've got two years to go. Just thinking
about it is going to make me sick. I thought it
would be different from the way it is.

RICHIE. But you could have died, for God's
sake.

*(*RICHIE *has turned now; he is facing*
MARTIN.*)*

MARTIN. I just wanted out.

RICHIE. I might not have found you, though.
I might not have come up here.

MARTIN. I don't care. I'd be out.

*(The door opens and a black man in filthy
fatigues—they are grease-stained and dark with
sweat—stands there. He is* CARLYLE, *looking
about.* RICHIE, *seeing him, rises and moves
toward him.)*

RICHIE. No. Roger isn't here right now.

CARLYLE. Who isn't?

RICHIE. He isn't here.

CARLYLE. They tole me a black boy livin'
in here. I don't see him.

(He looks suspiciously about the room.)

RICHIE. That's what I'm saying. He isn't
here. He'll be back later. You can come back
later. His name is Roger.

MARTIN. I slit my wrist.

*(Thrusting out the bloody, towel-wrapped
wrist toward* CARLYLE.*)*

RICHIE. Martin! Jesus!

MARTIN. I did.

RICHIE. He's kidding. He's kidding.

CARLYLE. What was his name? Martin?

*(*CARLYLE *is confused and the confusion has
made him angry. He moves toward* MARTIN.*)*
You Martin?

MARTIN. Yes.

*(*BILLY, *a white in his mid-twenties, blond
and trim, appears in the door, whistling, carrying a slice of pie on a paper napkin. Sensing
something, he falters, looks at* CARLYLE, *then*
RICHIE.*)*

BILLY. Hey, what's goin' on?

CARLYLE *(turning, leaving).* Nothin', man.
Not a thing.

*(*BILLY *looks questioningly at* RICHIE. *Then,
after placing the piece of pie on the chair beside the door, he crosses to his footlocker.)*

RICHIE. He came in looking for Roger, but
he didn't even know his name.

BILLY *(Sitting on his footlocker, he starts
taking off his shoes).* How come you weren't
at dinner, Rich? I brought you a piece of pie.

Hey, Martin.

(MARTIN thrusts out his towel-wrapped wrist.)

MARTIN. I cut my wrist, Billy

RICHIE. Oh, for God's sake, Martin!

(He whirls away.)

BILLY. Huh?

MARTIN. I did.

RICHIE. You are disgusting, Martin.

MARTIN. No. It's the truth. I did. I am not disgusting.

RICHIE. Well, maybe it isn't disgusting, but it certainly is disappointing.

BILLY. What are you guys talking about?

(Sitting there, he really doesn't know what is going on.)

MARTIN. I cut my wrists, I slashed them, and Richie is pretending I didn't.

RICHIE. I am not. And you only cut one wrist and you didn't slash it.

MARTIN. I can't stand the army anymore, Billy.

(He is moving now to petition BILLY, and RICHIE steps between them.)

RICHIE. Billy, listen to me. This is between Martin and me.

MARTIN. It's between me and the army, Richie.

RICHIE *(taking MARTIN by the shoulders as BILLY is now trying to get near MARTIN)*. Let's just go outside and talk, Martin. You don't know what you're saying.

BILLY. Can I see? I mean, did he really do it?

RICHIE. No!

MARTIN. I did.

BILLY. That's awful. Jesus. Maybe you should go to the infirmary.

RICHIE. I washed it with peroxide. It's not deep. Just let us be. Please. He just needs to straighten out his thinking a little, that's all.

BILLY. Well, maybe I could help him?

MARTIN. Maybe he could.

RICHIE *(Suddenly pushing at MARTIN. RICHIE is angry and exasperated. He wants MARTIN out of the room)*. Get out of here, Martin. Billy, you do some push-ups or something.

(Having been pushed toward the door, MARTIN wanders out.)

BILLY. No.

RICHIE. I know what Martin needs.

(RICHIE whirls and rushes into the hall after MARTIN, leaving BILLY scrambling to get his shoes on.)

BILLY. You're no doctor, are you? I just want to make sure he doesn't have to go to the infirmary, then I'll leave you alone.

(One shoe on, he grabs up the second and runs out the door into the hall after them.)

Martin! Martin, wait up!

(Silence. The door has been left open. Fifteen or twenty seconds pass. Then someone is heard coming down the hall. He is singing "Get a Job" and trying to do the voices and harmonies of a vocal group. ROGER, a tall, well-built black in long-sleeved khakis, comes in the door. He has a laundry bag over his shoulder, a pair of clean civilian trousers and a shirt on a hanger in his other hand. After dropping the bag on his bed, he goes to his wall locker, where he carefully hangs up the civilian clothes. Returning to the bed, he picks up the laundry and then, as if struck, he throws the bag down on the bed, tears off his tie and sits down angrily on the bed. For a moment, with his head in his hands, he sits there. Then, resolutely, he rises, takes up the position of attention, and simply topples forward, his hands leaping out to break his fall at the last instant and put him into the push-up position. Counting in a hissing, whispering voice, he does ten push-ups before giving up and flopping onto his belly. He simply doesn't have the will to do any more. Lying there, he counts rapidly on.)

ROGER. Fourteen, fifteen. Twenty. Twenty-five.

(BILLY, shuffling dejectedly back in, sees ROGER lying there. ROGER springs to his feet, heads toward his footlocker, out of which he takes an ashtray and a pack of cigarettes.)

You come in this area, you come in here marchin', boy: standin' tall.

(BILLY, having gone to his wall locker, is tossing a Playboy *magazine onto his bunk. He will also remove a towel, a Dopp kit and a can of foot powder.)*

BILLY. I was marchin'.

ROGER. You call that marchin'?

BILLY. I was as tall as I am; I was marchin'—what do you want?

ROGER. Outa here, man; outa this goddamn typin'-terrors outfit and into some kinda real army. Or else out and free.

BILLY. So go; who's stoppin' you; get out. Go on.

ROGER. Ain't you a bitch.

BILLY. You and me more regular army than the goddamn sergeants around this place, you know that?

ROGER. I was you, Billy boy, I wouldn't be talkin' so sacrilegious so loud, or they be doin' you like they did the ole sarge.

BILLY. He'll get off.

ROGER. Sheee-it, he'll get off.

(Sitting down on the side of his bed and facing BILLY, ROGER *lights up a cigarette.* BILLY *has arranged the towel, Dopp kit and foot powder on his own bed.)*

Don't you think L.B.J. want to have some sergeants in that Vietnam, man? In Disneyland, baby? Lord have mercy on the ole sarge. He goin' over there to be Mickey Mouse.

BILLY. Do him a lot of good. Make a man outa him.

ROGER. That's right, that's right. He said the same damn thing about himself and you, too, I do believe. You know what'd the old boy's MOS? His Military Occupation Speciality? Demolitions, baby. Expert is his name.

BILLY *(Taking off his shoes and beginning to work on a sore toe,* BILLY *hardly looks up).* You're kiddin' me.

ROGER. Do I jive?

BILLY. You mean that poor ole bastard who cannot light his own cigar for shakin' is supposed to go over there blowin' up bridges and shit? Do they wanna win this war or not, man?

ROGER. Ole sarge was over in Europe in the big one, Billy. Did all kinds a bad things.

BILLY *(Swinging his feet up onto the bed,* BILLY *sits, cutting the cuticles on his toes, powdering his feet).* Was he drinkin' since he got the word?

ROGER. Was he breathin', Billy? Was he breathin'?

BILLY. Well, at least he ain't cuttin' his fuckin' wrists.

(Silence. ROGER *looks at* BILLY, *who keeps on working.)*

Man, that's the real damn army over there, ain't it? That ain't shinin' your belt buckle and standin' tall. And we might end up in it, man.

(Silence. ROGER, *rising, begins to sort his laundry.)*

Roger . . . you ever ask yourself if you'd rather fight in a war where it was freezin' cold or one where there was awful snakes? You ever ask that question?

ROGER. Can't say I ever did.

BILLY. We used to ask it all the time. All the time. I mean, us kids sittin' out on the back porch tellin' ghost stories at night. 'Cause it was Korea time and the newspapers were fulla pictures of soldiers in snow with white frozen beards; they got these rags tied around their feet. And snakes. We hated snakes. Hated 'em. I mean, it's bad enough to be in the jungle duckin' bullets, but then you crawl right into a goddamn snake. That's awful. That's awful.

ROGER. It don't sound none too good.

BILLY. I got my draft notice, goddamn Vietnam didn't even exist. I mean, it existed, but not as in a war we might be in. I started crawlin' around the floor a this house where I was stayin' cause I'd dropped outa school, and I was goin' "Bang, bang," pretendin'. Jesus.

ROGER *(continuing with his laundry, he tries to joke).* My first goddamn formation in basic, Billy, this NCO's up there jammin' away about how some a us are goin' to be dyin' in the war. I'm sayin', "What war? What the crazy man talkin' about?"

BILLY. Us, too. I couldn't believe it. I couldn't believe it. And now we got three people goin' from here.

ROGER. Five.

(They look at each other, and then turn away, each returning to his task.)

BILLY. It don't seem possible. I mean, people shootin' at you. Shootin' at you to kill you.

(Slight pause)

It's somethin'.

ROGER. What did you decide you preferred?

BILLY. Huh?

ROGER. Did you decide you would prefer the snakes or would you prefer the snow? 'Cause it look like it is going to be the snakes.

BILLY. I think I had pretty much made my mind up on the snow.

ROGER. Well, you just let 'em know that, Billy. Maybe they get one goin' special just for you up in Alaska. You can go to the Klondike. Fightin' some snowmen.

*(*RICHIE *bounds into the room and shuts the door as if to keep out something dreadful. He looks at* ROGER *and* BILLY *and crosses to his wall locker, pulling off his tie as he moves. Tossing the tie into the locker, he begins unbuttoning the cuffs of his shirt.)*

RICHIE. Hi, hi, hi, everybody. Billy, hello.

BILLY. Hey.

ROGER. What's happenin', Rich?

(Moving to the chair beside the door, RICHIE *picks up the pie* BILLY *left there. He will place the pie atop the locker, and then, sitting, he will remove his shoes and socks.)*

RICHIE. I simply did this rather wonderful thing for a friend of mine, helped him see himself in a clearer, more hopeful light—little room in his life for hope? And I feel very good. Didn't Billy tell you?

ROGER. About what?

RICHIE. About Martin.

ROGER. No.

BILLY (*looking up and speaking pointedly*). No.

(RICHIE *looks at* BILLY *and then at* ROGER. RICHIE *is truly confused.*)

RICHIE. No? No?

BILLY. What do I wanna gossip about Martin for?

RICHIE (*He really can't figure out what is going on with* BILLY. *Shoes and socks in hand, he heads for his wall locker*). Who was planning to gossip? I mean, it did happen. We could talk about it. I mean, I wasn't hearing his goddamn confession. Oh, my sister told me Catholics were boring.

BILLY. Good thing I ain't one anymore.

RICHIE (*Taking off his shirt, he moves toward* ROGER). It really wasn't anything, Roger, except Martin made this rather desperate, pathetic gesture for attention that seems to have brought to the surface Billy's more humane and protective side.

(*Reaching out, he tousles* BILLY'*s hair.*)

BILLY. Man, I am gonna have to obliterate you.

RICHIE (*tossing his shirt into his locker*). I don't know what you're so embarrassed about.

BILLY. I just think Martin's got enough trouble without me yappin' to everybody.

(RICHIE *has moved nearer* BILLY, *his manner playful and teasing.*)

RICHIE. "Obliterate"? "Obliterate," did you say? Oh, Billy, you better say "shit," "ain't" and "motherfucker" real quick now or we'll all know just how far beyond the fourth grade you went.

ROGER (*having moved to his locker, into which he is placing hid folded clothes*). You hear about the ole sarge, Richard?

BILLY (*grinning*). You ain't . . . shit . . . motherfucker.

ROGER (*laughing*). All right.

RICHIE (*moving center and beginning to remove his trousers*). Billy, no, no. Wit is my domain. You're in charge of sweat and running around the block.

ROGER. You hear about the ole sarge?

RICHIE. What about the ole sarge? Oh, who cares? Let'e go to a movie. Billy, wanna? Let's go. C'mon.

(*Trousers off, he hurries to his locker.*)

BILLY. Sure. What's playin'?

RICHIE. I don't know. Can't remember. Something good, though.

(*With a Playboy magazine he has taken from his locker,* ROGER *is settling down on his bunk,*

his back toward both BILLY and RICHIE.)

BILLY. You wanna go, Rog?

RICHIE (*in mock irritation*). Don't ask Roger! How are we going to kiss and hug and stuff if he's there?

BILLY. That ain't funny, man.

(*He is stretched out on his bunk, and* RICHIE *comes bounding over to flop down and lie beside him.*)

RICHIE. And what time will you pick me up?

BILLY (*He pushes at* RICHIE, *knocking him off the bed and onto the floor*). Well, you just fall down and wait, all right?

RICHIE. Can I help it if I love you?

(*Leaping to his feet, he will head to his locker, remove his shorts, put on a robe.*)

ROGER. You gonna take a shower, Richard?

RICHIE. Cleanliness is nakedness, Roger.

ROGER. Is that right? I didn't know that. Not too many people know that. You may be the only person in the world who know that.

RICHIE. And godliness is in there somewhere, of course.

(*Putting a towel around his neck, he is gathering toiletries to carry to the shower.*)

ROGER. You got your own way a lookin' at things, man. You cute.

RICHIE. That's right.

ROGER. You g'wan, have a good time in that shower.

RICHIE. Oh, I will.

BILLY (*without looking up from his feet, which he is powdering*). And don't drop your soap.

RICHIE. I will if I want to.

(*Already out the door, he slams it shut with a flourish.*)

BILLY. Can you imagine bein' in combat with Richie—people blastin' away at you— he'd probably want to hold your hand.

ROGER. Ain't he somethin'?

BILLY. Who's zat?

ROGER. He's all right.

BILLY (*Rising, he heads toward his wall locker, where he will put the powder and Dopp kit*). Sure he is, except he's livin' under water.

(*Looking at* BILLY, ROGER *senses something unnerving; it makes* ROGER *rise, and return his magazine to his footlocker.*)

ROGER. I think we oughta do this area, man. I think we oughta do our area. Mop and buff this floor.

BILLY. You really don't think he means that shit he talks, do you?

ROGER. Huh? Awwww, man . . . Billy, No.

BILLY. I'd put money on it, Roger, and I

ain't got much money.

(BILLY *is trying to face* ROGER *with this, but* ROGER, *seated on his bed, has turned away. He is unbuttoning his shirt.*)

ROGER. Man, no, no. I'm tellin' you, lad, you listen to the ole Rog. You seen that picture a that little dolly he's got in his locker? He ain't swish, man, believe me—he's cool.

BILLY. It's just that ever since we been in this room, he's been different somehow. Somethin'.

ROGER. No, he ain't.

(BILLY *turns to his bed, where he carefully starts folding the towel. Then he looks at* ROGER.)

BILLY. You ever talk to any a these guys— queers, I mean? You ever sit down, just rap with one of 'em?

ROGER. Hell, no; what I wanna do that for? Shit, no.

BILLY (*crossing to the trash can in the corner, where he will shake the towel empty*). I mean, some of 'em are okay guys, just way up this bad alley, and you say to 'em, "I'm straight, be cool," they go their own way. But then there's these other ones, these bitches, man, and they're so crazy they think anybody can be had. Because they been had themselves. So you tell 'em you're straight and they just nod and smile. You ain't real to 'em. They can't see nothin' but themselves and these goddamn games they're always playin'.

(*Having returned to his bunk, he is putting on his shoes.*)

I mean, you can be decent about anything, Roger, you see what I'm sayin'? We're all just people, man, and some of us are hardly that. That's all I'm sayin'.

(*There is a slight pause as he sits there thinking. Then he gets to his feet.*)

I'll go get some buckets and stuff so we can clean up, okay? This area's a mess. This area ain't standin' tall.

ROGER. That's good talk, lad; this area a midget you put it next to an area standin' tall.

BILLY. Got to be good fuckin' troopers.

ROGER. That's right, that's right. I know the meanin' of the words.

BILLY. I mean, I just think we all got to be honest with each other—you understand me?

ROGER. No, I don't understand you; one stupid fuckin' nigger like me—how's that gonna be?

BILLY. That's right; mock me, man. That's what I need. I'll go get the wax.

(*Out he goes, talking to himself and leaving*

the door open. For a moment ROGER *sits, thinking, and then he looks at* RICHIE'*s locker and gets to his feet and walks to the locker which he opens and looks at the pinup hanging on the inside of the door. He takes a step backward, looking.*)

ROGER. Shee-it.

(*Through the open door comes* CARLYLE. ROGER *doesn't see him. And* CARLYLE *stands there looking at* ROGER *and the picture in the locker.*)

CARLYLE. Boy . . . whose locker you lookin' into?

ROGER (*He is startled, but recovers*). Hey, baby, what's happenin'?

CARLYLE. That ain't your locker, is what I'm askin', nigger. I mean, you ain't got no white goddamn woman hangin' on your wall.

ROGER. Oh, no—no, no.

CARLYLE. You don't wanna be lyin' to me, 'cause I got to turn you in you lyin' and you do got the body a some white goddamn woman hangin' there for you to peek at nobody around but you—you can be thinkin' about that sweet wet pussy an' maybe it hot an' maybe it cool.

ROGER. I could be thinkin' all that, except I know the penalty for lyin'.

CARLYLE. Thank God for that.

(*Extending his hand, palm up*)

ROGER. That's right. This here the locker of a faggot.

(*And* ROGER *slaps* CARLYLE'*s hand, palm to palm.*)

CARLYLE. Course it is; I see that; any damn body know that.

(ROGER *crosses toward his bunk and* CARLYLE *swaggers about, pulling a pint of whiskey from his hip pocket.*)

You want a shot? Have you a little taste, my man.

ROGER. Naw.

CARLYLE. C'mon. C'mon. I think you a Tom you don't drink outa my bottle.

(*He thrusts the bottle toward* ROGER *and wipes a sweat- and grease-stained sleeve across his mouth.*)

ROGER (*taking the bottle*). Shit.

CARLYLE. That right. How do I know? I just got in. New boy in town. Somewhere over there; I dunno. They dump me in amongst a whole bunch a pale, boring motherfuckers.

(CARLYLE *is exploring the room. Finding* BILLY'*s Playboy, he edges onto* BILLY'*s bed and leafs nervously through the pages.*)

I just come in from P Company, man, and I been all over this place, don't see too damn many of us. This outfit look like it a little short on soul. I been walkin' all around, I tell you, and the number is small. Like one hand you can tabulate the lot of 'em. We got few brothers I been able to see, is what I'm sayin'. You and me and two cats down in the small bay. That's all I found.

(As ROGER *is about to hand the bottle back,* CARLYLE, *almost angrily, waves him off.)*
No, no, you take another; take a real taste.

ROGER. It ain't so bad here. We do all right.

CARLYLE *(He moves, shutting the door. Suspiciously, he approaches* ROGER*).* How about the white guys? They give you any sweat? What's the situation? No jive. I like to know what is goin' on within the situation before that situation get a chance to be closin' in on me.

ROGER *(Putting the bottle on the footlocker, he sits down).* Man, I'm tellin' you, it ain't bad. They're just pale, most of 'em, you know. They can't help it; how they gonna help it? Some of 'em got little bit a soul, couple real good boys around this way. Get 'em little bit of Coppertone, they be straight, man.

CARLYLE. How about the NCOs? We got any brother NCO watchin' out for us or they all white, like I goddamn well *know* all the officers are? Fuckin' officers always white, man; fuckin' snow cones and bars everywhere you look.

*(*CARLYLE *cannot stay still. He moves to his right, his left; he sits, he stands.)*

ROGER. First sergeant's a black man.

CARLYLE. All right; good news. Hey, hey, you wanna go over the club with me, or maybe downtown? I got wheels. Let's be free.

(Now he rushes at ROGER.*)*
Let's be free.

ROGER. Naw . . .

CARLYLE. Ohhh, baby . . . !

(He is wildly pulling at ROGER *to get him to the door.)*

ROGER. Some other time. I gotta get the area straight. Me and the guy sleeps in here too are gonna shape the place up a little.

ROGER *has pulled free, and* CARLYLE *cannot understand. It hurts him, depresses him.)*

CARLYLE. You got a sweet deal here an' you wanna keep it, that right?

(He paces about the room, opens a footlocker, looks inside.)
How you rate you get a room like this for yourself—you and a couple guys?

ROGER. Spec 4. The three of us in here Spec 4.

CARLYLE. You get a room then, huh?

(And suddenly, without warning or transition, he is angry.)
Oh, man, I hate this goddamn army. I hate this bastard army. I mean, I just got outa basic—off leave—you know? Back on the block for two weeks—and now here. They don't pull any a that petty shit, now, do they—that goddamn petty basic training bullshit? They do and I'm gonna be bustin' some head—my hand is gonna be upside all kinds a heads, 'cause I ain't gonna be able to endure it, man, not that kinda crap—understand?

(And again, he is rushing at ROGER.*)*
Hey, hey, oh, c'mon, let's get my wheels and make it, man, do me the favor.

ROGER. How'm I gonna? I got my obligations.

(And CARLYLE *spins away in anger.)*

CARLYLE. Jesus, baby, can't you remember the outside? How long it been since you been on leave? It is so sweet out there, nigger; you got it all forgot. I had such a sweet, sweet time. They doin' dances, baby, make you wanna cry. I hate this damn army.

(The anger overwhelms him.)
All these mother-actin' jacks givin' you jive about what you gotta do and what you can't do. I had a bad scene in basic—up the hill and down the hill; it ain't somethin' I enjoyed even a little. So they do me wrong here, Jim, they gonna be sorry. Some-damn-body! And this whole Vietnam *thing*—I do not dig it.

(He falls on his knees before ROGER. *It is a gesture that begins as a joke, a mockery. And then a real fear pulses through him to nearly fill the pose he has taken.)*
Lord, Lord, don't let 'em touch me. Christ, what will I do, they *do*! Whoooooooooooooo! And they pullin' guys outa here, too, ain't they? Pullin' 'em like weeds, man; throwin' 'em into the fire. It's shit, man.

ROGER. They got this ole sarge sleeps down the hall—just today they got him.

CARLYLE. Which ole sarge?

ROGER. He sleeps just down the hall. Little guy.

CARLYLE. Wino, right?

ROGER. Booze hound.

CARLYLE. Yeh; I seen him. They got him, huh?

ROGER. He's goin'; gotta be packin' his bags. And three other guys two days ago. And two guys last week.

CARLYLE *(leaping up from* BILLY'S *bed).* Ohhh, them bastards. And everybody just takes it. It ain't our war, brother. I'm tellin' you. That's what gets me, nigger. It ain't our war nohow because it ain't our country, and that's what burns my ass—that and everybody just sittin' and takin' it. They gonna be bustin' balls, man—kickin' and stompin'. Everybody here maybe one week from shippin' out to get blown clean away and, man, whata they doin'? They doin' what they told. That what they doin'. Like you? Shit! You gonna straighten up your goddamn area! Well, that ain't for me; I'm gettin' hat, and makin' it out where it's sweet and the people's livin'. I can't cut this jive here, man. I'm tellin' you. I can't cut it.

(He has moved toward ROGER, *and behind him now* RICHIE *enters, runnin, his hair wet, traces of shaving cream on his face. Toweling his hair, he falters, seein* CARLYLE. *Then he crosses to his locker.* CARLYLE *grins at* ROGER, *looks at* RICHIE, *steps toward him and gives a little bow.)*

My name is Carlyle; what is yours?

RICHIE. Richie.

CARLYLE *(He turns toward* ROGER *to share his joke).* Hello. Where is Martin? That cute little Martin.

(And RICHIE *has just taken off his robe as* CARLYLE *turns back.)*

You cute, too, Richie.

RICHIE. Martin doesn't live here.

(Hurriedly putting on underpants to cover his nakedness)

CARLYLE *(Watching* RICHIE, *he slowly turns toward* ROGER). You ain't gonna make it with me, man?

ROGER. Naw . . . like I tole you. I'll catch you later.

CARLYLE. That's sad, man; make me cry in my heart.

ROGER. You g'wan get your head smokin'. Stop on back.

CARLYLE. Okay, okay. Got to be one man one more time.

(On the move for the door, his hand extended palm up behind him, demanding the appropriate response)

Baby! Gimme! Gimme!

(Lunging, ROGER *slaps the hand.)*

ROGER. G'wan home! G'wan home.

CARLYLE. You gonna hear from me.

(And he is gone out the door and down the hallway.)

ROGER. I can . . . and do . . . believe . . . that.

*(*RICHIE, *putting on his T-shirt, watches* ROGER, *who stubs out his cigarette, then crosses*

to the trash can to empty the ashtray.)

RICHIE. Who was that?

ROGER. Man's new, Rich. Dunno his name more than that "Carlyle" he said. He's new—just outa basic.

RICHIE *(powdering his thighs and under his arms).* Oh, my God . . .

(As BILLY *enters, pushing a mop bucket with a wringer attached and carrying a container of wax)*

ROGER. Me and Billy's gonna straighten up the area. You wanna help?

RICHIE. Sure, sure; help, help.

BILLY *(talking to* ROGER, *but turning to look at* RICHIE, *who is still putting powder under his arms).* I hadda steal the wax from Third Platoon.

ROGER. Good man.

BILLY *(moving to* RICHIE, *joking, yet really irritated in some strange way).* What? Whata you doin', singin'? Look at that, Rog. He's got enough jazz there for an entire beauty parlor. *(grabbing the can from* RICHIE'*s hand)* What is this? Baby Powder! *Baby Powder!*

RICHIE. I get rashes.

BILLY. Okay, okay, you get rashes, so what? They got powder for rashes that isn't baby powder.

RICHIE. It doesn't work as good; I've tried it. Have you tried it?

(Grabbing BILLY'*s waist,* RICHIE *pulls him close.* BILLY *knocks* RICHIE'*s hands away.)*

BILLY. Man, I wish you could get yourself straight. I'll mop, too, Roger—okay? Then I'll put down the wax and you can spread it?

(He has walked away from RICHIE.)

RICHIE. What about buffing?

ROGER. In the morning.

(He is already busy mopping up near the door.)

RICHIE. What do you want me to do?

BILLY *(Grabbing up a mop, he heads downstage to work).* Get inside your locker and shut the door and don't holler for help. Nobody'll know you there; you'll stay there.

RICHIE. But I'm so pretty.

BILLY. *Now!*

(Pointing to ROGER. *He wants to get this clear.)* Tell that man you mean what you're sayin', Richie.

RICHIE. Mean what?

BILLY. That you really think you're pretty.

RICHIE. Of course I do; I am. Don't you think I am? Don't you think I am, Roger?

ROGER. I tole you—you fulla shit and you cute, man. Carlyle just tole you you cute, too.

RICHIE. Don't you think it's true, Billy?

BILLY. It's like I tole you, Rog.

RICHIE. What did you tell him?

BILLY. That you go down; that you go up and down like a Yo-Yo and you go blowin' all the trees like the wind.

(RICHIE *is stunned. He looks at* ROGER, *and then he turns and stares into his own locker. The others keep mopping.* RICHIE *takes out a towel, and putting it around his neck, he walks to where* BILLY *is working. He stands there, hurt, looking at* BILLY.)

RICHIE. What the hell made you tell him I been down, Billy?

BILLY *(still mopping)*. It's in your eyes; I seen it.

RICHIE. What?

BILLY. You.

RICHIE. What is it, Billy, you think you're trying to say? You and all your wit and intelligence—your *humanity.*

BILLY. I said it, Rich; I said what I was tryin' to say.

RICHIE. Did you?

BILLY. I think I did.

RICHIE. Do you?

BILLY. Loud and clear, baby.

(Still mopping)

ROGER. They got to put me in with the wierdos. Why is that, huh? How come the army hate me, do this shit to me—know what to do.

(Whimsical and then suddenly loud, angered, violent)

Now you guys put socks in your mouths, right now—get shut up—or I am gonna beat you to death with each other. Roger got work to do. To be doin' it!

RICHIE *(turning to his bed, he kneels upon it).* Roger, I think you're so innocent sometimes. Honestly, it's not such a terrible thing. Is it, Billy?

BILLY. How would I know?

(He slams his mop into the bucket.)

Oh, go fuck yourself.

RICHIE. Well, I can give it a try, if that's what you want. Can I think of you as I do?

BILLY *(throwing down his mop)*. GODDAMMIT! That's it! IT!

(He exits, rushing into the hall and slamming the door behind him. ROGER *looks at* RICHIE. *Neither quite knows what is going on. Suddenly the door bursts open and* BILLY *storms straight over to* RICHIE, *who still kneels on the bed.)*

Now I am gonna level with you. Are you gonna listen? You gonna hear what I say, Rich, and not what you think I'm sayin'?

*(RICHIE *turns away as if to rise, his manner flippant, disdainful.)*

No! Don't get cute; don't turn away cute. I wanna say somethin' straight out to you and I want you to hear it!

RICHIE. I'm all ears, goddammit! For what, however, I do not know, except some boring evasion.

BILLY. At least wait the hell till you hear me!

RICHIE *(in irritation).* Okay, okay! What?

BILLY. Now this is level, Rich; this is straight talk.

(He is quiet, intense. This is difficult for him. He seeks the exactly appropriate words of explanation.)

No b.s. No tricks. What you do on the side, that's your business and I don't care about it. But if you don't cut the cute shit with me, I'm gonna turn you off. Completely. You ain't gonna get a good mornin' outa me, you understand, because it's gettin' bad around here. I mean, I know how you think—how you keep lookin' out and seein' yourself, and that's what I'm tryin' to tell you because that's all that's happenin', Rich. That's all there is to it when you look out at me and think there's some kind of approval or whatever you see in my eyes—you're just seein yourself. And I'm talkin' the simple quiet truth to you, Rich. I swear I am.

*(BILLY *looks away from* RICHIE *now and tries to go back to the mopping. It is embarrassing for them all.* ROGER *has watched, has tried to keep working.* RICHIE *has flopped back on his bunk. There is a silence.)*

RICHIE. How . . . do . . . you want me to be? I don't know how else to be.

BILLY. Ohhh, man, that ain't any part of it.

(The mop is clenched in his hands.)

RICHIE. Well, I don't come from the same kind of world as you do.

BILLY. Damn, Richie, you think Roger and I come off the same street?

ROGER. Shit . . .

RICHIE. All right. Okay. But I've just done what I wanted all of my life. If I wanted to do something, I just did it. Honestly. I've never had to work or anything like that and I've always had nice clothing and money for cab fare. Money for whatever I wanted. Always. I'm not like you are.

ROGER. You ain't sayin' you really done that stuff, though, Rich.

RICHIE. What?

ROGER. That fag stuff.

RICHIE *(He continues looking at* ROGER *and then he looks away).* Yes.

ROGER. Do you even know what you're sayin', Richie? Do you even know what it means to be a fag?

RICHIE. Roger, of course I know what it is. I just told you I've done it. I thought you black people were supposed to understand all about suffering and human strangeness. I thought you had depth and vision from all your suffering. Has someone been misleading me? I just told you I did it. I know all about it. Everything. All the various positions.

ROGER. Yeh, so maybe you think you've tried, but that don't make you it. I mean, we used to . . . in the old neighborhood, man, we had a couple dudes swung that way. But they was weird, man. There was this one little fella, he was a screamin' goddamn faggot . . . uh . . .

(He considers RICHIE, *wondering if perhaps he has offended him.)*

Ohhh, ohhh, you ain't no screamin' goddamn faggot, Richie, no matter what you say. And the baddest man on the block was my boy Jerry Lemon. So one day Jerry's got the faggot in one a them ole deserted stairways and he's bouncin' him off the walls. I'm just a little fella, see, and I'm watchin' the baddest man on the block do his thing. So he come bouncin' back into me instead of Jerry, and just when he hit, he gave his ass this little twitch, man, like he thought he was gonna turn me on. I'd never a thought that was possible, man, for a man to be twitchin' his ass on me, just like he thought he was a broad. Scared me to death. I took off runnin'. Oh, oh, that ole neighborhood put me into all kinds a crap. I did some sufferin', just like Richie says. Like this once, I'm swingin' on up the street after school, and outa this phone booth comes this man with a goddamned knife stickin' outa his gut. So he sees me and starts tryin' to pull his mother-fuckin' coat out over the handle, like he's worried about how he looks, man. "I didn't know this was gonna happen," he says. And then he falls over. He was just all of a sudden dead, man; just all of a sudden dead. You ever seen anything like that, Billy? Any crap like that?

*(*BILLY, *sitting on* ROGER'*s bunk, is staring at* ROGER.*)*

BILLY. You really seen that?

ROGER. Richie's a big-city boy.

RICHIE. Oh, no; never anything like that.

ROGER. "Momma, help me," I am screamin'. "Jesus, Momma, help me." Little fella, he don't know how to act, he sees somethin' like that.

(For a moment they are still, each thinking.)

BILLY. How long you think we got?

ROGER. What do you mean?

*(*ROGER *is hanging up the mops;* BILLY *is now kneeling on* ROGER'*s bunk.)*

BILLY. Till they pack us up, ship us out.

ROGER. To the war, you mean? To Disneyland? Man, I dunno; that up to them IBM's. Them machines is figurin' that. Maybe tomorrow, maybe next week, maybe never.

(The war—the threat of it—is the one thing they share.)

RICHIE. I was reading they're planning to build it all up to more than five hundred thousand men over there. Americans. And they're going to keep it that way until they win.

BILLY. Be a great place to come back from, man, you know? I keep thinkin' about that. To have gone there, to have been there, to have seen it and lived.

ROGER *(Settling onto* BILLY'*s bunk, he lights a cigarette).* Well, what we got right here is a fool, gonna probably be one a them five hundred thousand, too. Do you know I cry at the goddamn anthem yet sometimes? The flag is flyin' at a ball game, the ole Roger gets all wet in the eye. After all the shit been done to his black ass. But I don't know what I think about this war. I do not know.

BILLY. I'm tellin' you, Rog—I've been doin' a lot a readin' and I think it's right we go. I mean, it's just like when North Korea invaded South Korea or when Hitler invaded Poland and all those other countries. He just kept testin' everybody and when nobody said no to him, he got so committed he couldn't back out even if he wanted. And that's what this Ho Chi Minh is doin'. And all these other Communists. If we let 'em know somebody is gonna stand up against 'em, they'll back off, just like Hitler would have.

ROGER. There is folks, you know, who are sayin' L.B.J. is the Hitler, and not ole Ho Chi Minh at all.

RICHIE *(talking as if this is the best news he's heard in years).* Well, I don't know anything at all about all that, but I am certain I don't want to go—whatever is going on. I mean, those Vietcong don't just shoot you and blow you up, you know. My God, they've got these other awful things they do: putting elephant shit on these stakes in the ground and then you step on 'em and you got elephant shit in a wound in your foot. The infection is horrendous. And then there's these caves they hide in and when you go in after 'em, they've got these snakes that they've tied by their tails to the ceiling. So it's dark and the snake is furious from having been hung by its tail and you crawl right into them—your face. My God.

BILLY. They do not.

(BILLY *knows he has been caught; they all know it.*)

RICHIE. I read it, Billy. They do.

BILLY (*completely facetious, yet the fear is real*). That's bullshit, Richie.

ROGER. That's right, Richie. They maybe do that stuff with the elephant shit, but nobody's gonna tie a snake by its tail, let ole Billy walk into it.

BILLY. That's disgusting, man.

ROGER. Guess you better get ready for the Klondike, my man.

BILLY. That is probably the most disgusting thing I ever heard of. I DO NOT WANT TO GO! NOT TO NOWHERE WHERE THAT KINDA SHIT IS GOIN' ON! L.B.J. is Hitler; suddenly I see it all very clearly.

ROGER. Billy got him a hatred for snakes.

RICHIE. I hate them, too. They're hideous.

BILLY (*And now, as a kind of apology to* RICHIE, BILLY *continues his self-ridicule far into extreme*). I mean, that is one of the most awful things I ever heard of any person doing. I mean, any person who would hang a snake by its tail in the dark of a cave in the hope that some other person might crawl into it and get bitten to death, that first person is somebody who oughta be shot. And I hope the five hundred thousand other guys that get sent over there kill 'em all—all them gooks—get 'em all driven back into Germany, where they belong. And in the meantime, I'll be holding the northern border against the snowmen.

ROGER (*rising from* BILLY'*s bed*). And in the meantime before that, we better be gettin' at the ole area here. Got to be strike troopers.

BILLY. Right.

RICHIE. Can I help?

ROGER. Sure. Be good.

(*And* ROGER *crosses to his footlocker and takes out a radio.*)

Think maybe I put on a little music, though it's gettin' late. We got time. Billy, you think?

BILLY. Sure.

(*getting nervously to his feet*)

ROGER. Sure. All right. We can be doin' it to the music.

(*He plugs the radio into the floor outlet as* BILLY *bolts for the door.*)

BILLY. I gotta go pee.

ROGER. You watch out for the snakes.

BILLY. It's the snowmen, man; the snowmen.

(BILLY *is gone and "Ruby," sung by Ray Charles, comes from the radio. For a moment, as the music plays,* ROGER *watches* RICHIE *wander about the room, pouring little splashes of wax onto the floor. Then* RICHIE *moves to his bed and lies down, and* ROGER, *shaking his head, starts leisurely to spread the wax, with* RICHIE *watching.*)

RICHIE. How come you and Billy take all this so seriously—you know.

ROGER. What?

RICHIE. This army nonsense. You're always shining your brass and keeping your footlocker neat and your locker so neat. There's no point to any of it.

ROGER. We here, ain't we, Richie? We in the army.

(*Still working the wax*)

RICHIE. There's no point to any of it. And doing those push-ups, the two of you.

ROGER. We just see a lot a things the same way is all. Army ought to be a serious business, even if sometimes it ain't.

RICHIE. You're lucky, you know, the two of you. Having each other for friends the way you do. I never had that kind of friend ever. Not even when I was little.

ROGER (*after a pause during which* ROGER, *working, sort of peeks at* RICHIE *every now and then*). You ain't really inta that stuff, are you, Richie?

(*It is a question that is a statement.*)

RICHIE (*coyly he looks at* ROGER). What stuff is that, Roger?

ROGER. That fag stuff, man. You know. You ain't really into it, are you? You maybe messed in it a little is all—am I right?

RICHIE. I'm very weak, Roger. And by that I simply mean that if I have an impulse to do something, I don't know how to deny myself. If I feel like doing something, I just do it. I . . . will . . . admit to sometimes wishin' I . . . was a little more like you . . . and Billy, even, but not to any severe extent.

ROGER. But that's such a bad scene, Rich. You don't want that. Nobody wants that. Nobody wants to be a punk. Not nobody. You wanna know what I think it is? You just got in with the wrong bunch. Am I right? You just got in with a bad bunch. That can happen. And that's what I think happened to you. I bet you never had a chance to really run with the boys before. I mean, regular normal guys like Billy and me. How'd you come in the army, huh, Richie? You get drafted?

RICHIE. No.

ROGER. That's my point, see.

(He has stopped working. He stands, leaning on the mop, looking at RICHIE.*)*

RICHIE. About four years ago, I went to this party. I was very young, and I went to this party with a friend who was older and . . . this "fag stuff," as you call it, was going on . . . so I did it.

ROGER. And then you come in the army to get away from it, right? Huh?

RICHIE. I don't know.

ROGER. Sure.

RICHIE. I don't know, Roger.

ROGER. Sure, sure. And now you're gettin' a chance to run with the boys for a little, you'll get yourself straightened around. I know it for a fact; I know that thing.

(From off there is the sudden loud bellowing sound of Sergeant ROONEY.*)*

ROONEY. THERE AIN'T BEEN NO SOLDIERS IN THIS CAMP BUT ME. I BEEN THE ONLY ONE— I BEEN THE ONLY ME!

(And BILLY *comes dashing into the room.)*

BILLY. Oh, boy.

ROGER. Guess who?

ROONEY. FOR SO LONG I BEEN THE ONLY GODDAMN ONE!

BILLY *(leaping onto his bed and covering his face with a Playboy magazine as* RICHIE *is trying to disappear under his sheet and blankets and* ROGER *is trying to get the wax put away so he can get into his own bunk).* Hut who hee whor—he's got some Yo-Yo with him, Rog!

ROGER. Huh?

(As COKES *and* ROONEY *enter. Both are in fatigues and drunk and big-bellied. They are in their fifties, their hair whitish and cut short. Both men carry whiskey bottles, beer bottles.* COKES *is a little neater than* ROONEY, *his fatigue jacket tucked in and not so rumpled, and he wears canvas-sided jungle boots.* ROONEY, *very disheveled, chomps on the stub of a big cigar. They swagger in, looking for fun, and stand there side by side.)*

ROONEY. What kinda platoon I got here? You buncha shit sacks. Everybody look sharp.

(The three boys lie there, unmoving.)

Off and on!

COKES. *Off and on!*

(He seems barely conscious, wavering as he stands.)

ROGER. What's happenin', Sergeant?

ROONEY *(shoving his bottle of whiskey at* ROGER, *who is sitting up).* Shut up, Moore! You want a belt?

(Splashing whiskey on ROGER'*s chest)*

ROGER. How can I say no?

COKES. My name is Cokes!

BILLY *(rising to sit on the side of his bed).* How about me, too?

COKES. You wait your turn.

ROONEY *(He looks at the three of them as if they are fools. Indicates* COKES *with a gesture).* Don't you see what I got here?

BILLY. Who do I follow for my turn?

ROONEY *(suddenly, crazily petulant).* Don't you see what I got here? Everybody on their feet and at attention!

*(BILLY *and* ROGER *climb from their bunks and stand at attention. They don't know what* ROONEY *is mad at.)*

I mean it!

*(RICHIE *bounds to the position of attention.)*

This here is my friend, who in addition just come back from the war! The goddamn war! He been to it and he come back.

*(ROONEY *is patting* COKES *gently, proudly.)*

The man's a fuckin' hero!

*(ROONEY *hugs* COKES, *almost kissing him on the cheek.)*

He's always been a fuckin' hero.

*(COKES, *embarrassed in his stupor, kind of wobbles a little from side to side.)*

COKES. No-o-o-o-o-o . . .

(And ROONEY *grabs him, starts pushing him toward* BILLY'*s footlocker.)*

ROONEY. Show 'em your boots, Cokes. Show 'em your jungle boots.

(With a long, clumsy step, COKES *climbs onto the footlocker,* ROONEY *supporting him from behind and then bending to lift one of* COKES' *booted feet and display it for the boys.)* Lookee that boot. That ain't no everyday goddamn army boot. That is a goddamn jungle boot! That green canvas is a jungle boot 'cause a the heat, and them little holes in the bottom are so the water can run out when you been walkin' in a lotta water like in a jungle swamp.

(He is extremely proud of all this; he looks at them.)

The army ain't no goddamn fool. You see a man wearin' boots like that, you might as well see he's got a chestful a medals, 'cause he been to the war. He don't have no boots like that unless he been to the war! Which is where I'm goin' and all you slaphappy motherfuckers, too. Got to go kill some gooks.

(He is nodding at them, smiling.)

That's right.

COKES (*bursting loudly from his stupor*). Gonna piss on 'em. Old booze. 'At's what I did. Piss in the rivers. Goddamn GI's secret weapon is old booze and he's pissin' it in all their runnin' water. Makes 'em yellow. Ahhhha ha, ha, ha!

(*He laughs and laughs, and* ROONEY *laughs, too, hugging* COKES.)

ROONEY. Me and Cokesy been in so much shit together we oughta be brown.

(*And then he catches himself, looks at* ROGER.)

Don't take no offense at that, Moore. We been swimmin' in it. One Hundred and First Airborne, together. One-oh-one. Screamin' goddamn Eagles!

(*Looking at each other, face to face, eyes glinting, they make sudden loud screaming-eagle sounds.*)

This ain't the army; you punks ain't in the army. You ain't ever seen the army. The army is Airborne! Airborne!

COKES (*beginning to stomp his feet*). Airborne, Airborne! *All the way!*

(*As* RICHIE, *amused and hoping for a drink, too, reaches out toward* ROONEY)

RICHIE. Sergeant, Sergeant, I can have a little drink, too.

(ROONEY *looks at him and clutches the bottle.*)

ROONEY. Are you kiddin' me? You gotta be kiddin' me.

(*He looks to* ROGER.)

He's kiddin' me, ain't he, Moore?

(*And then to* BILLY *and then to* COKES)

Ain't he, Cokesy?

(COKES *steps forward and down with a thump, taking charge for his bewildered friend.*)

COKES. Don't you know you are tryin' to take the booze from the hand a the future goddamn Congressional Honor winner . . . Medal . . . ?

(*And he looks lovingly at* ROONEY. *He beams.*)

Ole Rooney, Ole Rooney.

(*He hugs* ROONEY's *head.*)

He almost done it already.

(*And* ROONEY, *overwhelmed, starts screaming "Aggggghhhhhhhhhh," a screaming-eagle sound, and making clawing eagle gestures at the air. He jumps up and down, stomping his feet.* COKES *instantly joins in, stomping and jumping and yelling.*)

ROONEY. Let's show these shit sacks how men are men jumpin' outa planes.

Aggggghhhhhhhhhh,

(*Stomping and yelling, they move in a circle,* ROONEY *followed by* COKES.)

A plane fulla yellin' stompin' men!

COKES. All yellin' stompin' men!

(*They yell and stomp, making eagle sounds, and then* ROONEY *leaps up on* BILLY's *bed and runs the length of it until he is on the footlocker,* COKES *still on the floor, stomping.* ROONEY *makes a gesture of hooking his rip cord to the line inside the plane. They yell louder and louder and* ROONEY *leaps high into the air, yelling, "*GERONIMO-O-O-O!*" as* COKES *leaps onto the locker and then high into the air, bellowing, "*GERONIMO-O-O-O!*" They stand side by side, their arms held up in the air as if grasping the shroud lines of open chutes. They seem to float there in silence.*)

What a feelin' . . .

ROONEY. Beautiful feelin' . . .

(*For a moment more they float there, adrift in the room, the sky, their memory.* COKES *smiles at* ROONEY.)

COKES. Remember that one guy, O'Flannigan . . . ?

ROONEY (*nodding, smiling remembering*). O'Flannigan . . .

COKES. He was this one guy . . . O'Flannigan . . .

(*He moves now toward the boys,* BILLY, ROGER *and* RICHIE, *who have gathered on* ROGER's *bed and footlocker.* ROONEY *follows several steps, then drifts backward onto* BILLY's *bed, where he sits and then lies back, listening to* COKES.)

We was testing chutes where you could just pull a lever by your ribs here when you hit the ground—see—and the chute would come off you, because it was just after a whole bunch a guys had been dragged to death in an unexpected and terrible wind at Fort Bragg. So they wanted you to be able to release the chute when you hit if there was a bad wind when you hit. So O'Flannigan was this kinda joker who had the goddamn sense a humor of a clown and nerves, I tell you, of steel, and he says he's gonna release the lever midair, then reach up, grab the lines and float on down, hanging.

(*His hand paws at the air, seeking a rope that isn't there.*)

So I seen him pull the lever at five hundred feet and he reaches up to two fistfuls a air, the chute's twenty feet above him, and he went into the ground like a knife.

(*The bottle, held high over his head, falls through the air to the bed, all watching it.*)

BILLY. Geezus.

ROONEY (nodding gently). Didn't get to sing the song, I bet.

COKES (standing, staring at the fallen bottle). No way.

RICHIE. What song?

ROONEY (He rises up, mysteriously angry). Shit sack! Shit sack!

RICHIE. What song, Sergeant Rooney?

ROONEY. "Beautiful Streamer," shit sack.

(COKES, gone into another reverie, is staring skyward.)

COKES. I saw this one guy—never forget it. Never.

BILLY. That's Richie, Sergeant Rooney. He's a beautiful screamer.

RICHIE. He said "streamer," not "screamer," asshole.

(COKES is still in his reverie.)

COKES. This guy with his chute goin' straight up above him in a streamer, like a tulip, only white, you know. All twisted and never gonna open. Like a big icicle sticking straight up above him. He went right by me. We met eyes, sort of. He was lookin' real puzzled. He looks right at me. Then he looks up in the air at the chute, then down at the ground.

ROONEY. Did he sing it?

COKES. He didn't sing it. He started going like this.

(COKES reaches desperately upward with both hands and begins to claw at the sky while his legs pump up and down.)

Like he was gonna climb right up the air.

RICHIE. Ohhhhh, Geezus.

BILLY. God.

(ROONEY has collapsed backward on BILLY's bed and he lies there and then he rises.)

ROONEY. Cokes got the Silver Star for rollin' a barrel a oil down a hill in Korea into forty-seven chinky Chinese gooks who were climbin' up the hill and when he shot into it with his machine gun, it blew them all to grape jelly.

(COKES, rocking a little on his feet, begins to hum and then sing "Beautiful Streamer," to the tune of Stephen Foster's "Beautiful Dreamer.")

COKES. "Beautiful streamer, open for me . . . The sky is above me . . ."

(And then the singing stops.)

But the one I remember is this little guy in his spider hole, which is a hole in the ground with a lid over it.

(And he is using RICHIE's footlocker before him as the spider hole. He has fixed on it, is moving toward it.)

And he shot me in the ass as I was runnin' by, but the bullet hit me so hard—

(His body kind of jerks and he runs several steps.)

—it knocked me into this ditch where he couldn't see me. I got behind him.

(Now at the head of RICHIE's bed, he begins to creep along the side of the bed as if sneaking up on the footlocker.)

Crawlin'. And I dropped a grenade into his hole.

(He jams a whiskey bottle into the footlocker, then slams down the lid.)

Then sat on the lid, him bouncin' and yellin' under me. Bouncin' and yellin' under the lid. I could hear him. Feel him. I just sat there.

(Silence. ROONEY waits, thinking, then leans forward.)

ROONEY. He was probably singin' it.

COKES (sitting there). I think so.

ROONEY. You think we should let 'em hear it?

BILLY. We're good boys. We're good ole boys.

COKES (Jerking himself to his feet, he staggers sideways to join ROONEY on BILLY's bed). I don't care who hears it, I just wanna be singin' it.

(ROONEY rises; he goes to the boys on ROGER's bed and speaks to them carefully, as if lecturing people on something of great importance.)

ROONEY. You listen up; you just be listenin' up, 'cause if you hear it right you can maybe stop bein' shit sacks. This is what a man sings, he's goin' down through the air, his chute don't open.

(Flopping back down on the bunk beside COKES, rooney looks at COKES and then at the boys. The two older men put their arms around each other and they begin to sing.)

ROONEY AND COKES (singing).

> Beautiful streamer,
> Open for me,
> The sky is above me,
> But no canopy.

BILLY (murmuring). I don't believe it.

ROONEY AND COKES.

> Counted ten thousand,
> Pulled on the cord.
> My chute didn't open,
> I shouted, "Dear Lord."
> Beautiful streamer,
> This looks like the end,
> The earth is below me,
> My body won't end.

Just like a mother
Watching o'er me,
Beautiful streamer,
Ohhhhh, open for me.
ROGER. Un-fuckin'-believable.
ROONEY *(beaming with pride)*. Ain't that a beauty.
(And then COKES *topples forward onto his face and flops limply to his side. The three boys leap to their feet.* ROONEY *lunges toward* COKES.*)*
RICHIE. Sergeant!
ROONEY. Cokie! Cokie!
BILLY. Jesus.
ROGER. Hey!
COKES. Huh? Huh?
*(*COKES *sits up.* ROONEY *is kneeling beside him.)*
ROONEY. Jesus, Cokie.
COKES. I been doin' that; I been doin' that. It don't mean nothin'.
ROONEY. No, no.
COKES *(Pushing at* ROONEY, *who is trying to help him get back to the bed.* ROONEY *agrees with everything* COKES *is now saying and the noises he makes are little animal noises)*. I told 'em when they wanted to send me back I ain't got no leukemia; they wanna check it. They think I got it. I don't think I got it. Rooney? Whata you think?
ROONEY. No.
COKES. My mother had it. She had it. Just 'cause she did and I been fallin' down.
ROONEY. It don't mean nothin'.
COKES *(He lunges back and up onto the bed)*. I tole 'em I fall down 'cause I'm drunk. I'm drunk all the time.
ROONEY. You'll be goin' back over there with me, is what I know, Cokie.
(He is patting COKES, *nodding, dusting him off.)*
That's what I know.
(As BILLY *comes up to them, almost seeming to want to be a part of the intimacy they are sharing)*
BILLY. That was somethin', Sergeant Cokes. Jesus.
*(*ROONEY *whirls on him, ferocious, pushing him.)*
ROONEY. Get the fuck away, Wilson! Whata you know? Get the fuck away. You don't know shit. Get away! You don't know shit.
(And he turns to COKES, *who is standing up from the bed.)*
Me and Cokes are goin' to the war zone like we oughta. Gonna blow it to shit.

(He is grabbing at COKES, *who is laughing. They are both laughing.* ROONEY *whirls on the boys.)*
Ohh, I'm gonna be so happy to be away from you assholes; you pussies. Not one regular army people among you possible. I swear it to my mother who is holy. You just be watchin' the papers for doin' darin' brave deeds. 'Cause we're old hands at it. Makin' shit disappear. Goddamn whooosh!
COKES. Whooosh!
ROONEY. Demnalitions. Me and . . .
(And then he knows he hasn't said it right.)
Me and Cokie . . . Demnal . . . Demnali . . .
RICHIE *(still sitting on* ROGER's *bed)*. You can do it, Sergeant.
BILLY. Get it.
(He stands by the lockers and ROONEY *glares at him.)*
ROGER. 'Cause you're cool with dynamite, is what you're trying' to say.
ROONEY *(charging at* ROGER, *bellowing)*. Shut the fuck up, that's what you can do; and go to goddamn sleep. You buncha shit . . . sacks. Buncha mothers—know-it-all motherin' shit sacks—that's what you are.
COKES *(shoulders back, he is taking charge)*. Just goin' to sleep is what you can do, 'cause Rooney and me fought it through two wars already and we can make it through this one more and leukemia that comes or doesn't come—who gives a shit? Not guys like us. We're goin' just pretty as pie. And it's lights-out time, ain't it, Rooney?
ROONEY. Past it, goddammit. So the lights are goin' out.
(There is fear in the room, and the three boys rush to their wall lockers, where they start to strip to their underwear, preparing for bed. ROONEY *paces the room, watching them, glaring.)*
Somebody's gotta teach you soldierin'. You hear me? Or you wanna go outside and march around awhile, huh? We can do that if you wanna. Huh? You tell me? Marchin' or sleepin'? What's it gonna be?
RICHIE *(rushing to get into bed)*. Flick out the ole lights, Sergeant; that's what we say.
BILLY *(climbing into bed)*. Put out the ole lights.
ROGER *(in bed and pulling up the covers)*. Do it.
COKES. Shut up.
(He rocks forward and back, trying to stand at attention. He is saying good night.)
And that's an order. Just shut up. I got gre-

nades down the hall. I got a pistol. I know where to get nitro. You don't shut up, I'll blow . . . you . . . to . . . fuck.

(Making a military left face, he stalks to the wall switch and turns the lights out. ROONEY *is watching proudly, as* COKES *faces the boys again. He looks at them.)*

That's right.

(In the dark, there is only a spill of light from the hall coming in the open door. COKES *and* ROONEY *put their arms around each other and go out the door, leaving it partly open.* RICHIE, ROGER *and* BILLY *lie in their bunks staring. They do not move. They lie there. The sergeants seem to have vanished soundlessly once they went out the door. Light touches each of the boys as they lie there.)*

ROGER *(He does not move).* Lord have mercy, if that ain't a pair. If that ain't one pair a beauties.

BILLY. Oh, yeh.

(He does not move.)

ROGER. Too much, man—too, too much.

RICHIE. They made me sad; but I loved them, sort of. Better than movies.

ROGER. Too much. Too, too much.

(Silence)

BILLY. What time is it?

ROGER. Sleep time, men. Sleep time.

(Silence)

BILLY. Right.

ROGER. They were somethin'. Too much.

BILLY. Too much.

RICHIE. Night.

ROGER. Night.

(Silence)

Night, Billy.

BILLY. Night.

*(*RICHIE *stirs in his bed.* ROGER *turns onto his side.* BILLY *is motionless.)*

BILLY. I . . . had a buddy, Rog—and this is the whole thing, this is the whole point—a kid I grew up with, played ball with in high school, and he was a tough little cat, a real bad man sometimes. Used to have gangster pictures up in his room. Anyway, we got into this deal where we'd drive on down to the big city, man, you know, hit the bad spots, let some queer pick us up . . . sort of . . . long enough to buy us some good stuff. It was kinda the thing to do for a while, and we all did it, the whole gang of us. So we'd let these cats pick us up, most of 'em old guys, and they were hurtin' and happy as hell to have us, and we'd get a lot of free booze, maybe a meal, and we'd turn 'em on. Then pretty soon they'd

ask us did we want to go over to their place. Sure, we'd say, and order one more drink, and then when we hit the street, we'd tell 'em to kiss off. We'd call 'em fag and queer and jazz like that and tell 'em to kiss off. And Frankie, the kid I'm tellin' you about, he had a mean streak in him and if they gave us a bad time at all, he'd put 'em down. That's the way he was. So that kinda jazz went on and on for sort of a long time and it was a good deal if we were low on cash or needed a laugh and it went on for a while. And then Frankie—one day he come up to me—and he says he was goin' home with the guy he was with. He said, what the hell, what did it matter? And he's sayin'—Frankie's sayin'—why don't I tag along? What the hell he's sayin', what does it matter who does it to you, some broad or some old guy, you close your eyes, a mouth's a mouth, it don't matter—that's what he's sayin'. I tried to talk him out of it, but he wasn't hearin' anything I was sayin'. So the next day, see, he calls me up to tell me about it. Okay, okay, he says, it was a cool scene, he says; they played poker, a buck minimum, and made a fortune. Frankie was eatin' it up, man. It was a pretty way to live, he says. So he stayed at it, and he had this nice little girl he was goin' with at the time. You know the way a real bad cat can sometimes do that—have a good little girl who's crazy about him and he is for her, too, and he's a different cat when he's with her?

ROGER. Uh-huh.

(The hall light slants across BILLY'*s face.)*

BILLY. Well, that was him and Linda, and then one day he dropped her, he cut her loose. He was hooked, man. He was into it, with no way he knew out—you understand what I'm sayin'? He had got his ass hooked. He had never thought he would and then one day he woke up and he was on it. He just hadn't been told, that's the way I figure it; somebody didn't tell him somethin' he shoulda been told and he come to me wailin' one day, man, all broke up and wailin', my boy Frankie, my main man, and he was a fag. He was a faggot, black Roger, and I'm not lyin'. I am not lyin' to you.

ROGER. Damn.

BILLY. So that's the whole thing, man; that's the whole thing.

(Silence. They lie there.)

ROGER. Holy . . . Christ. Richie . . . you hear him? You hear what he said?

RICHIE. He's a storyteller.

ROGER. What you mean?

RICHIE. I mean, he's a storyteller, all right; he tells stories, all right.

ROGER. What are we into now? You wanna end up like that friend a his, or you don't believe what he said? Which are you sayin'?

(The door bursts open. The sounds of machine guns and cannon are being made by someone, and CARLYLE, *drunk and playing, comes crawling in.* ROGER, RICHIE *and* BILLY *all pop up, startled, to look at him.)*

Hey, hey, what's happenin'?

BILLY. Who's happenin'?

ROGER. You attackin' or you retreatin', man?

CARLYLE *(looking up; big grin)*. Hey, baby . . . ?

(Continues shooting, crawling. The three boys look at each other.)

ROGER. What's happenin', man? Whatcha doin'?

CARLYLE. I dunno, soul; I dunno. Practicin' my duties, my new abilities.

(Half sitting, he flops onto his side, starts to crawl.)

The low crawl, man; like I was taught in basic, that's what I'm doin'. You gotta know your shit, man, else you get your ass blown so far away you don't ever see it again. Oh, sure, you guys don't care. I know it. You got it made. You got it made. I don't got it made. You got a little home here, got friends, people to talk to. I got nothin'. You got jobs they probably ain't ever gonna ship you out, you got so important jobs. I got no job. They don't even wanna give me a job. I know it. They are gonna kill me. They are gonna send me over there to get me killed, goddammit. WHAT'S A MATTER WITH ALL YOU PEOPLE?

(The anger explodes out of the grieving and ROGER *rushes to kneel beside* CARLYLE. *He speaks gently, firmly.)*

Hey, man, get cool, get some cool; purchase some cool, man.

CARLYLE. Awwwww . . .

(Clumsily, he turns away.)

ROGER. Just hang in there.

CARLYLE. I don't wanna be no DEAD man. I don't wanna be the one they all thinkin' is so stupid he's the only one'll go, they tell him; they don't even have to give him a job. I got thoughts, man, in my head; alla time, burnin', burnin' thoughts a understandin'.

ROGER. Don't you think we know that, man? It ain't the way you're sayin' it.

CARLYLE. It is.

ROGER. No. I mean, we all probably gonna go. We all probably gonna have to go.

CARLYLE. No-o-o-o-o.

ROGER. I mean it.

CARLYLE *(Suddenly he nearly topples over)*. I am very drunk.

(And he looks up at ROGER.)

You think so?

ROGER. I'm sayin' so. And I am sayin', "No sweat." No point.

*(CARLYLE *angrily pushes at* ROGER, *knocking him backward.)*

CARLYLE. Awwwww, dammit, dammit, mother . . . shit . . . it . . . ohhhhhhh.

(Sliding to the floor, the rage and anguish softening into only breathing)

I mean it. I mean it.

(Silence. He lies there.)

ROGER. What . . . a you doin' . . . ?

CARLYLE. Huh?

ROGER. I don't know what you're up to on our freshly mopped floor.

CARLYLE. Gonna go sleep—okay? No sweat . . .

(Suddenly very polite, he is looking up.)

Can I, soul? Izzit all right?

ROGER. Sure, man, sure, if you wanna, but why don't you go where you got a bed? Don't you like beds?

CARLYLE. Dunno where's zat. My bed. I can' fin' it. I can' fin' my own bed. I looked all over, but I can' fin' it anywhere. GONE!

(Slipping back down now, he squirms to make a nest. He hugs his bottle.)

ROGER *(moving to his bunk, where he grabs a blanket)*. Okay, okay, man. But get on top a this, man.

(He is spreading the blanket on the floor, trying to help CARLYLE *get on it.)*

Make it softer. C'mon, c'mon . . . get on this.

*(BILLY *has risen with his own blanket, and is moving now to hand it to* ROGER.)*

BILLY. Cat's hurtin', Rog.

ROGER. Ohhhhh, yeh.

CARLYLE. Ohhhhh . . . it was so sweet at home . . . it was so sweet, baby; so-o-o good. They doin' dances make you wanna cry. . . .

(Hugging the blankets now, he drifts in a kind of dream.)

ROGER. I know, man.

CARLYLE. So sweet . . . !

*(BILLY *is moving back to his own bed, where, quietly, he sits.)*

ROGER. I know, man.

CARLYLE. So sweet . . . !

ROGER. Yeh.

CARLYLE. How come I gotta be here?

(On his way to the door to close it, ROGER *falters, looks at* CARLYLE *then moves on toward the door.)*

ROGER. I dunno, Jim.

*(*BILLY *is sitting and watching, as* ROGER *goes on to the door, gently closes it and returns to his bed.)*

BILLY. I know why he's gotta be here, Roger. You wanna know? Why don't you ask me?

ROGER. Okay. How come he gotta be here?

BILLY *(smiling)*. Freedom's frontier, man. That's why.

ROGER *(settled on the edge of his bed and about to lie back)*. Oh . . . yeh . . .

(As a distant bugle begins to play taps and RICHIE, *carrying a blanket, is approaching* CARLYLE. ROGER *settles back;* BILLY *is staring at* RICHIE; CARLYLE *does not stir; the bugle plays.)*

Bet that ole sarge don't live a year, Billy. Fuckin' blow his own ass sky high.

*(*RICHIE *has covered* CARLYLE. *He pats* CARLYLE'*s arm, and then straightens in order to return to his bed.)*

BILLY. Richie . . . !

*(*BILLY'*s hissing voice freezes* RICHIE. *He stands, and then he starts again to move, and* BILLY'*s voice comes again and* RICHIE *cannot move.)*

Richie . . . how come you gotta keep doin' that stuff?

*(*ROGER *looks at* BILLY, *staring at* RICHIE, *who stands still as a stone over the sleeping* CARLYLE.)*

How come?

ROGER. He dunno, man. Do you? You dunno, do you, Rich?

RICHIE. No.

CARLYLE *(from deep in his sleep and grieving)*. It . . . was . . . so . . .pretty . . . !

RICHIE. No.

(The lights are fading with the last soft notes of taps.)

ACT TWO

Scene One

Lights come up on the cadre room. It is late afternoon and BILLY *is lying on his stomach, his head at the foot of the bed, his chin resting on his hands. He wears gym shorts and sweat socks; his T-shirt lies on the bed and his sneakers are on the floor.* ROGER *is at his footlocker,*

taking out a pair of sweat socks. His sneakers and his basketball are on his bed. He is wearing his khakis.

A silence passes, and then ROGER *closes his footlocker and sits on his bed, where he starts lacing his sneakers, holding them on his lap.*

———

BILLY. Rog . . . you think I'm a busybody? In any way?

(Silence. ROGER *laces his sneakers.)*

Roger?

ROGER. Huh? Uh-uh.

BILLY. Some people do. I mean, back home.

(He rolls slightly to look at ROGER.*)*

Or that I didn't know how to behave. Sort of.

ROGER. It's time we maybe get changed, don't you think?

*(*ROGER *rises and goes to his locker. He takes off his trousers, shoes and socks.)*

BILLY. Yeh. I guess. I don't feel like it, though. I don't feel good, don't know why.

ROGER. Be good for you, man; be good for you.

(Pulling on his gym shorts, ROGER *returns to his bed, carrying his shoes and socks.)*

BILLY. Yeh.

*(*BILLY *sits up on the edge of his bed.* ROGER, *sitting, is bowed over, putting on his socks.)*

I mean, a lot of people thought like I didn't know how to behave in a simple way. You know? That I overcomplicated everything. I didn't think so. Don't think so. I just thought I was seein' complications that were there but nobody else saw.

(He is struggling now to put on his T-shirt. He seems weary, almost weak.)

I mean, Wisconsin's a funny place. All those clear-eyed people sayin' "Hello" and lookin' you straight in the eye. Everybody's good, you think, and happy and honest. And then there's all of a sudden a neighbor who goes mad as a hatter. I had a neighbor who came out of his house one morning with axes in both hands. He started then attackin' the cars that were driving up and down in front of his house. An' we all knew why he did it, sorta.

(He pauses; he thinks.)

It made me wanna be a priest. I wanted to be a priest then. I was sixteen. Priests could help people. Could take away what hurt 'em. I wanted that, I thought. Somethin', huh?

ROGER *(He has the basketball in his hands)*. Yeh. But everybody's got feelin's like that sometimes.

BILLY. I don't know.

ROGER. You know, you oughta work on a little jump shot, my man. Get you some kinda fall-away jumper to go with that beauty of a hook. Make you tough out there.

BILLY. Can't fuckin' do it. Not my game. I mean, like that bar we go to. You think I could get a job there bartendin', maybe? I could learn the ropes.

(He is watching ROGER, *who has risen to walk to his locker.)*

You think I could get a job there off-duty hours?

ROGER *(pulling his locker open to display the pinup on the inside of the door).* You don't want no job. It's that little black-haired waitress you wantin' to know.

BILLY. No, man. Not really.

ROGER. It's okay. She tough, man.

(He begins to remove his uniform shirt. He will put on an O.D. T-shirt to go to the gym.)

BILLY. I mean, not the way you're sayin' it, is all. Sure, there's somethin' about her. I don't know what. I ain't even spoke to her yet. But somethin'. I mean, what's she doin' there? When she's dancin', it's like she knows somethin'. She's degradin' herself, I sometimes feel. You think she is?

ROGER. Man, you don't even know the girl. She's workin'.

BILLY. I'd like to talk to her. Tell her stuff. Find out about her. Sometimes I'm thinkin' about her and it and I got a job there, I get to know her and she and I get to be real tight, man—close, you know. Maybe we screw, maybe we don't. It's nice . . . whatever.

ROGER. Sure. She a real fine-lookin' chippy, Billy. Got nice cakes. Nice little titties.

BILLY. I think she's smart, too.

(ROGER starts laughing so hard he almost falls into his locker.)

Oh, all I do is talk. "Yabba-yabba." I mean, my mom and dad are really terrific people. How'd they ever end up with somebody so weird as me?

(ROGER moves to him, jostles him.)

ROGER. I'm tellin' you, the gym and a little ball is what you need. Little exercise. Little bumpin' into people. The soul is tellin' you.

(BILLY rises and goes to his locker, where he starts putting on his sweat clothes.)

BILLY. I mean, Roger, you remember how we met in P Company? Both of us brand-new. You started talkin' to me. You just started talkin' to me and you didn't stop.

ROGER *(hardly looking up).* Yeh.

BILLY. Did you see somethin' in me made you pick me?

ROGER. I was talkin' to everybody, man. For that whole day. Two whole days. You was just the first one to talk back friendly. Though you didn't say much, as I recall.

BILLY. The first white person, you mean.

(Wearing his sweat pants, BILLY is now at his bed, putting on his sneakers.)

ROGER. Yeh. I was tryin' to come outa myself a little. Do like the fuckin' head shrinker been tellin' me to stop them fuckin' headaches I was havin', you know. Now let us do fifteen or twenty push-ups and get over to that gymnasium, like I been sayin'. Then we can take our civvies with us—we can shower and change at the gym.

(ROGER crosses to BILLY, who flops down on his belly on the bed.)

BILLY. I don't know . . . I don't know what it is I'm feelin'. Sick like.

(ROGER forces BILLY up onto his feet and shoves him playfully downstage, where they both fall forward into the push-up position, side by side.)

ROGER. Do 'em, trooper. Do 'em. Get it.

(ROGER starts. BILLY joins in. After five, ROGER realizes that BILLY has his knees on the floor. They start again. This time, BILLY counts in double time. They start again. At about "seven," RICHIE enters. Neither BILLY nor ROGER sees him. They keep going.)

ROGER AND BILLY. . . . seven, eight, nine, ten . . .

RICHIE. No, no; no, no; no, no, no. That's not it; that's not it.

(They keep going, yelling the numbers louder and louder.)

ROGER AND BILLY. . . . eleven, twelve, thirteen . . .

(RICHIE crosses to his locker and gets his bottle of cologne, and then returning to the center of the room to stare at them, he stands there dabbing cologne on his face.)

ROGER AND BILLY. . . . fourteen, fifteen.

RICHIE. You'll never get it like that. You're so far apart and you're both humping at the same time. And all that counting. It's so unromantic.

ROGER *(rising and moving to his bed to pick up the basketball).* We was exercisin', Richard. You heard a that?

RICHIE. Call it what you will, Roger.

(With a flick of his wrist, ROGER tosses the basketball to RICHIE.)

Everybody has their own cute little pet names for it.

BILLY. Hey!

(And he tosses the ball at RICHIE, *hitting him in the chest, sending the cologne bottle flying.* RICHIE *yelps, as* BILLY *retrieves the ball and, grabbing up his sweat jacket from the bed, heads for the door.* ROGER, *at his own locker, has taken out his suit bag of civilian clothes.)* You missed.

RICHIE. Billy, Billy, Billy, please, please, the ruffian approach will not work with me. It impresses me not even one tiny little bit. All you've done is spill my cologne.

(He bends to pick up the cologne from the floor.)

BILLY. That was my aim.

ROGER. See you.

*(*BILLY *is passing* RICHIE. *Suddenly* RICHIE *sprays* BILLY *with cologne, some of it getting on* ROGER, *as* ROGER *and* BILLY, *groaning and cursing at* RICHIE, *rush out the door.)*

RICHIE. Try the more delicate approach next time, Bill.

(Having crossed to the door, he stands a moment, leaning against the frame. Then he bounces to BILLY's *bed, sings "He's just my Bill," and squirts cologne on the pillow. At his locker, he deposits the cologne, takes off his shirt, shoes and socks. Removing a hardcover copy of Pauline Kael's* I Lost It at the Movies *from the top shelf of the locker, he bounds to the center of the room and tosses the book the rest of the way to the bed. Quite pleased with himself, he fidgets, pats his stomach, then lowers himself into the push-up position, goes to his knees and stands up.)* Am I out of my fucking mind? Those two are crazy. I'm not crazy.

*(*RICHIE *pivots and strides to his locker. With an ashtray, a pack of matches and a pack of cigarettes, he hurries to his bed and makes himself comfortable to read, his head propped up on a pillow. Settling himself, he opens the book, finds his place, thinks a little, starts to read. For a moment he lies there. And then* CARLYLE *steps into the room. He comes through the doorway looking to his left and right. He comes several steps into the room and looks at* RICHIE. RICHIE *sees him. They look at each other.)*

CARLYLE. Ain't nobody here, man?

RICHIE. Hello, Carlyle. How are you today?

CARLYLE. Ain't nobody here?

(He is nervous and angrily disappointed.)

RICHIE. Who do you want?

CARLYLE. Where's the black boy?

RICHIE. Roger? My God, why do you keep calling him that? Don't you know his name

yet? Roger. Roger.

(He thickens his voice at this, imitating someone very stupid. CARLYLE *stares at him.)*

CARLYLE. Yeh. Where is he?

RICHIE. I am not his keeper, you know. I am not his private secretary, you know.

CARLYLE. I do not know. I do not know. That is why I am asking. I come to see him. You are here. I ask you. I don't know. I mean, Carlyle made a fool outa himself comin' in here the other night, talkin' on and on like how he did. Lay on the floor. He remember. You remember? It all one hype, man; that all one hype. You know what I mean. That ain't the real Carlyle was in here. This one here and now the real Carlyle. Who the real Richie?

RICHIE. Well . . . the real Richie . . . has gone home. To Manhattan. I, however, am about to read this book.

(Which he again starts to try to do)

CARLYLE. Oh. Shit. Jus' you the only one here, then, huh?

RICHIE. So it would seem.

(He looks at the air and then under the bed as if to find someone.)
So it would seem. Did you hear about Martin?

CARLYLE. What happened to Martin? I ain't seen him.

RICHIE. They are shipping him home. Someone told about what he did to himself. I don't know who.

CARLYLE. Wasn't me. Not me. I keep that secret.

RICHIE. I'm sure you did.

(Rising, walking toward CARLYLE *and the door, cigarette pack in hand)*
You want a cigarette? Or don't you smoke? Or do you have to go right away?

(Closing the door)
There's a chill sometimes coming down the hall, I don't know from where.

(Crossing back to his bed and climbing in)
And I think I've got the start of a little cold. Did you want the cigarette?

*(*CARLYLE *is staring at him. Then he examines the door and looks again at* RICHIE. *He stares at* RICHIE, *thinking, and then he walks toward him.)*

CARLYLE. You know what I bet? I been lookin' at you real close. It just a way I got about me. And I bet if I was to hang my boy out in front of you, my big boy, man, you'd start wantin' to touch him. Be beggin' and talkin' sweet to ole Carlyle. Am I right or wrong?

(He leans over RICHIE.)

What do you say?

RICHIE. Pardon?

CARLYLE. You heard me. Ohhh. I am so restless, I don't even understand it. My big black boy is what I was talkin' about. My thing, man; my rope, Jim. HEY, RICHIE!

(And he lunges, then moves his fingers through RICHIE'*s hair.)*

How long you been a punk? Can you hear me? Am I clear? Do I talk funny?

(He is leaning close.)

Can you smell the gin on my mouth?

RICHIE. I mean, if you really came looking for Roger, he and Billy are gone to the gymnasium. They were—

CARLYLE. No.

(He slides down on the bed, his arm placed over RICHIE'*s legs.)*

I got no athletic abilities. I got none. No moves. I don't know. *Hey, Richie!*

(Leaning close again)

I just got this question I asked. I got no answer.

RICHIE. I don't know . . . what . . . you mean.

CARLYLE. I heard me. I understood me. "How long you been a punk?" is the question I asked. Have you got a reply?

RICHIE *(confused, irritated, but fascinated).* Not to that question.

CARLYLE. Who do if you don't? I don't. How'm I gonna?

(Suddenly there is whistling in the hall, as if someone might enter, footsteps approaching, and RICHIE *leaps to his feet and scurries away toward the door, tucking in his undershirt as he goes.)*

Man, don't you wanna talk to me? Don't you wanna talk to ole Carlyle?

RICHIE. Not at the moment.

CARLYLE *(He is rising, starting after* RICHIE, *who stands nervously near* ROGER'*s bed).* I want to talk to you, man; why don't you want to talk to me? We can be friends. Talkin' back and forth, sharin' thoughts and bein' happy.

RICHIE. I don't think that's what you want.

CARLYLE *(He is very near to* RICHIE*).* What do I want?

RICHIE. I mean, to talk to me.

*(*RICHIE, *as if repulsed, crosses away. But it is hard to tell if the move is genuine or coy.*

CARLYLE. What am I doin'? I am talkin'. DON'T YOU TELL ME I AIN'T TALKIN' WHEN I AM TALKIN'! COURSE I AM. Bendin' over backwards.

(And pressing his hands against himself in his anger, he has touched the grease on his

shirt, the filth of his clothing, and this ignites the anger.)

Do you know they still got me in that goddamn P Company? That goddamn transient company. It like they think I ain't got no notion what a home is. No nose for no home—like I ain't never had no home. I had a home. IT LIKE THEY THINK THERE AIN'T NO PLACE FOR ME IN THIS MOTHER ARMY BUT K.P. ALL SUDSY AND WRINKLED AND SWEATIN'. EVERY DAY SINCE I GOT TO THIS SHIT HOUSE, MISTER! HOW MANY TIMES YOU BEEN ON K.P.? WHEN'S THE LAST TIME YOU PULLED K.P.?

(He has roared down to where RICHIE *had moved, the rage possessing him.)*

RICHIE. I'm E.D.

CARLYLE. You E.D.? You E.D.? You Edie, are you? I didn't ask you what you friends call you, I asked you when's the last time you had K.P.?

RICHIE *(Edging toward his bed. He will go there, get and light a cigarette).* E.D. is "Exempt from Duty."

CARLYLE *(moving after* RICHIE*).* You ain't got no duties? What shit you talkin' about? Everybody in this fuckin' army got duties. That what the fuckin' army all about. You ain't got no duties, who got 'em?

RICHIE. Because of my job, Carlyle. I have a very special job. And my friends don't call me Edie.

(Big smile)

They call me Irene.

CARLYLE. That mean what you sayin' is you kiss ass for somebody, don't it? Good for you.

(Seemingly relaxed and gentle, he settles down on RICHIE'*s bed. He seems playful and charming.)*

You know the other night I was sleepin' there. You know.

RICHIE. Yes.

CARLYLE *(gleefully, enormously pleased).* You remember that? How come you remember that? You sweet.

RICHIE. We don't have people sleeping on our floor that often, Carlyle.

CARLYLE. But the way you crawl over in the night, gimme a big kiss on my joint. That nice.

RICHIE *(Shocked, he blinks).* What?

CARLYLE. Or did I dream that?

RICHIE *(laughing in spite of himself).* My God, you're outrageous!

CARLYLE. Maybe you dreamed it.

RICHIE. What . . . ? No. I don't know.

CARLYLE. Maybe you did it, then; you didn't dream it.

RICHIE. How come you talk so much?

CARLYLE. I don't talk, man, who's gonna talk? YOU?

(He is laughing and amused, but there is an anger near the surface now, an ugliness.)

That bore me to death. I don't like nobody's voice but my own. I am so pretty. Don't like nobody else face.

(And then viciously, he spits out at RICHIE.)

You goddamn face ugly fuckin' queer punk!

(And RICHIE jumps in confusion.)

RICHIE. What's the matter with you?

CARLYLE. You goddamn ugly punk face. YOU UGLY!

RICHIE. Nice mouth.

CARLYLE. That's right. That's right. And you got a weird mouth. Like to suck joints.

(As RICHIE storms to his locker, throwing the book inside. He pivots, grabbing a towel, marching toward the door.)

Hey, you gonna jus' walk out on me? Where you goin'? You c'mon back. Hear?

RICHIE. That's my bed, for chrissake.

(He lunges into the hall.)

CARLYLE. You'd best.

(Lying there, he makes himself comfortable. He takes a pint bottle from his back pocket.)

You come back, Richie, I tell you a good joke. Make you laugh, make you cry.

(He takes a big drink.)

That's right. Ole Frank and Jesse, they got the stagecoach stopped, all the peoples lined up— Frank say, "All right, peoples, we gonna rape all the men and rob all the women." Jesse say, "Frank, no, no—that ain't it—we gonna—" And this one little man yell real loud, "You shut up, Jesse; Frank knows what he's doin'."

(Loudly, he laughs and laughs. BILLY enters. Startled at the sight of CARLYLE there in RICHIE's bed, BILLY falters, as CARLYLE gestures toward him.)

Hey, man . . . ! Hey, you know, they send me over to that Vietnam, I be cool, 'cause I been dodgin' bullets and shit since I been old enough to get on pussy make it happy to know me. I can get on, I can do my job.

(BILLY looks weary and depressed. Languidly he crosses to his bed. He still wears his sweat clothes. CARLYLE studies him, then stares at the ceiling.)

Yeh. I was just layin' here thinkin' that and you come in and out it come, words to say my feelin'. That my problem. That the black man's problem altogether. You ever considered that? Too much feelin'. He too close to everything. He is, man; too close to his blood, to his body.

It ain't that he don't have no good mind, but he *Believe* in his body. Is . . . that Richie the only punk in this room, or is there more?

BILLY. What?

CARLYLE. The punk; is he the only punk?

(Carefully he takes one of RICHIE's cigarettes and lights it.)

BILLY. He's all right.

CARLYLE. I ain't askin' about the quality of his talent, but is he the only one, is my question?

BILLY *(He does not want to deal with this. He sits there).* You get your orders yet?

CARLYLE. Orders for what?

BILLY. To tell you where you work.

CARLYLE. I'm P Company, man. I work in P Company. I do K.P. That all. Don't deserve no more. Do you know I been in this army three months and ten days and everybody still doin' the same shit and sayin' the same shit and wearin' the same green shitty clothes? I ain't been happy one day, and that a lotta goddamn misery back to back in this ole boy. Is that Richie a good punk? Huh? Is he? He takes care of you and Roger—that how come you in this room, the three of you?

BILLY. What?

CARLYLE *(emphatically).* You and Roger are hittin' on Richie, right?

BILLY. He's not queer, if that's what you're sayin'. A little effeminate, but that's all, no more; if that's what you're sayin'.

CARLYLE. I'd like to get some of him myself if he a good punk, is what I'm sayin'. That's what I'm sayin'! You don't got no understandin' how a man can maybe be a little diplomatic about what he's sayin' sorta sideways, do you? Jesus.

BILLY. He don't do that stuff.

CARLYLE *(lying there).* What stuff?

BILLY. Listen, man. I don't feel too good, you don't mind.

CARLYLE. What stuff?

BILLY. What you're thinkin'.

CARLYLE. What . . . am I thinkin'?

BILLY. You . . . know.

CARLYLE. Yes, I do. It in my head, that how come I know. But how do you know? I can see your heart, Billy boy, but you cannot see mine. I am unknown. You . . . are known.

BILLY *(as if he is about to vomit, and fighting it).* You just . . . talk fast and keep movin', don't you? Don't ever stay still.

CARLYLE. Words to say my feelin', Billy boy.

(RICHIE steps into the room. He sees BILLY and CARLYLE, and freezes.)

There he is. There he be.

(RICHIE *moves to his locker to put away the towel.*)

RICHIE. He's one of them who hasn't come down far out of the trees yet, Billy; believe me.

CARLYLE. You got rudeness in your voice, Richie—you got meanness I can hear about ole Carlyle. You tellin' me I oughta leave— is that what you think you're doin'? You don't want me here?

RICHIE. You come to see Roger, who isn't here, right? Man like you must have important matters to take care of all over the quad; I can't imagine a man like you not having extremely important things to do all over the world, as a matter of fact, Carlyle.

CARLYLE (*He rises. He begins to smooth the sheets and straighten the pillow. He will put the pint bottle in his back pocket and cross near to* RICHIE.). Ohhhh, listen—don't mind all the shit I say. I just talk bad, is all I do; I don't do bad. I got to have friends just like anybody else. I'm just bored and restless, that all; takin' it out on you two. I mean, I know Richie here ain't really no punk, not really. I was just talkin', just jivin' and entertainin' my own self. Don't take me serious, not ever. I get on out and see you all later.

(*He moves for the door,* RICHIE *right behind him, almost ushering him.*)

You be cool, hear? Man don't do the jivin', he the one gettin' jived. That what my little brother Henry tell me and tell me.

(*Moving leisurely, he backs out the door and is gone.* RICHIE *shuts the door. There is a silence as* RICHIE *stands by the door.* BILLY *looks at him and then looks away.*)

BILLY. I am gonna have to move myself outa here, Roger I decides to adopt that sonofabitch.

RICHIE. He's an animal.

BILLY. Yeh, and on top a that, he's a rotten person.

RICHIE (*He laughs nervously, crossing nearer to* BILLY). I think you're probably right.

(*Still laughing a little, he pats* BILLY's *shoulder and* BILLY *freezes at the touch. Awkwardly* RICHIE *removes his hand and crosses to his bed. When he has lain down,* BILLY *bends to take off his sneakers, then lies back on his pillow staring, thinking, and there is a silence.* RICHIE *does not move. He lies there, struggling to prepare himself for something.*)

Hey . . . Billy?

(*Very slight pause*)

Billy?

BILLY. Yeh.

RICHIE. You know that story you told the other night?

BILLY. Yeh . . . ?

RICHIE. You know . . .

BILLY. What . . . about it?

RICHIE. Well, was it . . . about you?

(*Pause*)

I mean, was it . . . ABOUT you? Were you Frankie?

(*This is difficult for him.*)

Are . . . you Frankie? Billy?

(BILLY *is slowly sitting up.*)

BILLY. You sonofabitch . . . !

RICHIE. Or was it really about somebody you knew . . . ?

BILLY (*sitting, outraged and glaring*). You didn't hear me at all!

RICHIE. I'm just asking a simple question, Billy, That's all I'm doing.

BILLY. You are really sick. You know that? Your brain is really, truly rancid! Do you know there's a theory now it's genetic? That it's all a matter of genes and shit like that?

RICHIE. Everything is not so ungodly cryptic, Billy.

BILLY. You. You, man, and the rot it's makin' outa your feeble fuckin' brain.

(ROGER, *dressed in civilian clothes, bursts in and* BILLY *leaps to his feet.*)

ROGER. Hey, hey, anyone got a couple bucks he can loan me?

BILLY. Rog, where you been?

ROGER (*throwing the basketball and his sweat clothes into his locker*). I need five. C'mon.

BILLY. Where you been? That asshole friend a yours was here.

ROGER. I know, I know. Can you gimme five?

RICHIE (*He jumps to the floor and heads for his locker*). You want five. I got it. You want ten or more, even?

(BILLY, *watching* RICHIE, *turns, and nervously paces down right, where he moves about, worried.*)

BILLY. I mean, we gotta talk about him, man; we gotta talk about him.

ROGER (*as* RICHIE *is handing him two fives*). 'Cause we goin' to town together. I jus' run into him out on the quad, man, and he was feelin' real bad 'bout the way he acted, how you guys done him, he was fallin' down apologizin' all over the place.

BILLY (*as* RICHIE *marches back to his bed and sits down*). I mean, he's got a lotta weird ideas about us; I'm tellin' you.

ROGER. He's just a little fucked up in his head is all, but he ain't trouble.

(He takes a pair of sunglasses from the locker and puts them on.)

BILLY. Who needs him? I mean, we don't need him.

ROGER. You gettin' too nervous, man. Nobody said anything about anybody needin' anybody. I been on the street all my life; he brings back home. I played me a little ball, Billy; took me a shower. I'm feelin' good!

(He has moved down to BILLY.)

BILLY. I'm tellin' you there's somethin wrong with him, though.

ROGER *(Face to face with BILLY, ROGER is a little irritated).* Every black man in the world ain't like me, man; you get used to that idea. You get to know him, and you gonna like him. I'm tellin' you. You get to be laughin' just like me to hear him talk his shit. But you gotta relax.

RICHIE. I agree with Billy, Roger.

ROGER. Well, you guys got it all worked out and that's good, but I am goin' to town with him. Man's got wheels. Got a good head. You got any sense, you'll come with us.

BILLY. What are you talkin' about—come with you? I just tole you he's crazy.

ROGER. And I tole you you're wrong.

RICHIE. We weren't invited.

ROGER. I'm invitin' you.

RICHIE. No, I don't wanna.

ROGER *(He moves to RICHIE; it seems he really wants RICHIE to go).* You sure, Richie? C'mon.

RICHIE. No.

ROGER. Billy? He got wheels, we goin' in drinkin', see if gettin' our heads real bad don't just make us feel real good. You know what I mean. I got him right; you got him wrong.

BILLY. But what if I'm right?

ROGER. Billy, Billy, the man is waitin' on me. You know you wanna. Jesus. Bad cat like that gotta know the way. He been to D.C. before. Got cousins here. Got wheels for the weekend. You always talkin' how you don't do nothin'—you just talk it. Let's do it tonight—stop talkin'. Be cruisin' up and down the strip, leanin' out the window, bad as we wanna be. True cool is a car. We can flip a cigarette out the window—we can watch it bounce. Get us some chippies. You know we can. And if we don't, he knows a cathouse, it fulla cats.

BILLY. You serious?

RICHIE. You mean you're going to a whore-house? That's disgusting.

BILLY. Listen who's talkin'. What do you want me to do? Stay here with you?

RICHIE. We could go to a movie or something.

ROGER. I am done with this talkin'. You goin', you stayin'?

(He crosses to his locker, pulls into view a wide-brimmed black and shiny hat, and puts it on, cocking it at a sharp angle.)

BILLY. I don't know.

ROGER *(stepping for the door).* I am goin'.

BILLY *(Turning, BILLY sees the hat).* I'm going. Okay! I'm going! Going, going, going!

(And he runs to his locker.)

RICHIE. Oh, Billy, you'll be scared to death in a cathouse and you know it.

BILLY. BULLSHIT!

(He is removing his sweat pants and putting on a pair of gray corduroy trousers.)

ROGER. Billy got him a lion-tamer 'tween his legs!

(The door bangs open and CARLYLE is there, still clad in his filthy fatigues, but wearing a going-to-town black knit cap on his head and carrying a bottle.)

CARLYLE. Man, what's goin' on? I been waitin' like throughout my fuckin' life.

ROGER. Billy's goin', too. He's gotta change.

CARLYLE. He goin', too! Hey! Beautiful! That beautiful!

(His grin is large, his laugh is loud.)

ROGER. Didn't I tell you, Billy?

CARLYLE. That beautiful, man; we all goin' to be friends!

RICHIE *(sitting on his bed).* What about me, Carlyle?

(CARLYLE looks at RICHIE, and then at ROGER and then he and ROGER begin to laugh. CARLYLE pokes ROGER and they laugh as they are leaving. BILLY, grabbing up his sneakers to follow, stops at the door, looking only briefly at RICHIE. Then BILLY goes and shuts the door. The lights are fading to black.)

SCENE TWO

In the dark, taps begins to play. And then slowly the lights rise, but the room remains dim. Only the lamp attached to RICHIE's bed burns and there is the glow and spill of the hallway coming through the transom. BILLY, CARLYLE, ROGER and RICHIE are sprawled about the room. BILLY, lying on his stomach, has his head at the foot of his bed, a half-empty bottle of beer dangling in his hand. He wears a blue oxford-cloth shirt and his sneakers lie beside his bed. ROGER, *collapsed in his own bed, lies upon his back, his head also at the foot, a* Playboy *magazine covering his face and a half-empty bottle of beer in his hands, folded on his belly. Having removed his civilian shirt, he wears a white T-shirt.* CARLYLE *is lying on his belly on* RICHIE's *bed, his head at the foot, and he is facing out.* RICHIE *is sitting on the floor, resting against* ROGER's *footlocker. He is wrapped in a blanket. Beside him is an unopened bottle of beer and a bottle opener.*

They are all dreamy in the dimness as taps plays sadly on and then fades into silence. No one moves.

_____

RICHIE. I don't know where it was, but it wasn't here. And we were all in it—it felt like—but we all had different faces. After you guys left, I only dozed for a few minutes, so it couldn't have been long. Roger laughed a lot and Billy was taller. I don't remember all the details exactly, and even though we were the ones in it, I know it was about my father. He was a big man. I was six. He was a very big man when I was six and he went away, but I remember him. He started drinking and staying home making model airplanes and boats and paintings by the numbers. We had money from mom's family, so he was just home all the time. And then one day I was coming home from kindergarten, and as I was starting up the front walk he came out the door and he had these suitcases in his hands. He was leaving, see, sneaking out, and I'd caught him. We looked at each other and I just knew and I started crying. He yelled at me, "Don't you cry; don't you start crying." I tried to grab him and he pushed me down in the grass. And then he was gone. G-O-N-E.

BILLY. And that was it? That was it?

RICHIE. I remember hiding my eyes. I lay in the grass and his my eyes and waited.

BILLY. He never came back?

RICHIE. No.

CARLYLE. Ain't that some shit. Now, I'm a jive-time street nigger. I knew where my daddy was all the while. He workin' in this butcher shop two blocks up the street. Ole Mom used to point him out. "There he go. That him—that your daddy." We'd see him on the street, "There he go."

ROGER. Man couldn't see his way to livin' with you—that what you're sayin'?

CARLYLE. Never saw the day.

ROGER. And still couldn't get his ass outa the neighborhood?

*(*RICHIE *begins trying to open his bottle of beer.)*

CARLYLE. Ain't that a bitch. Poor ole bastard just duck his head—Mom pointin' at him—he git this real goddamn hangdog look like he don't know who we talkin' about and he walk a little faster. Why the hell he never move away I don't know, unless he was crazy. But I don't think so. He come up to me once—I was playin'. "Boy," he says, "I ain't your daddy. I ain't. Your momma's crazy." "Don't you be callin' my momma crazy, Daddy," I tole him. Poor ole thing didn't know what to do.

RICHIE *(Giving up; he can't get the beer open)*. Somebody open this for me? I can't get this open.

*(*BILLY *seems about to move to help, but* CARLYLE *is quicker, rising a little on the bunk and reaching.)*

CARLYLE. Ole Carlyle get it.

*(*RICHIE *slides along the floor until he can place the bottle in* CARLYLE's *outstretched hand.)*

RICHIE. Then there was this once—there was this TV documentary about these bums in San Francisco, this TV guy interviewing all these bums, and just for maybe ten seconds while he was talkin' . . .

(Smiling, CARLYLE *hands* RICHIE *the opened bottle.)*

. . . to this one bum, there was this other one in the background jumpin' around like he thought he was dancin' and wavin' his hat, and even though there wasn't anything about him like my father and I didn't really ever see his face at all, I just kept thinkin': That's him. My dad. He thinks he's dancin'.

(They lie there in silence and suddenly, softly, BILLY *giggles, and then he giggles a little more and louder.)*

BILLY. Jesus!

RICHIE. What?

BILLY. That's ridiculous, Richie; sayin' that, thinkin' that. If it didn't look like him, it wasn't him, but you gotta be makin' up a story.

CARLYLE *(Shifting now for a more comfortable position, he moves his head to the pillow at the top of the bed)*. Richie first saw me, he didn't like me much nohow, but he thought it over now, he changed his way a thinkin'. I can see that clear. We gonna be one big happy family.

RICHIE. Carlyle likes me, Billy; he thinks

I'm pretty.

CARLYLE (*sitting up a little to make his point clear*). No, I don't think you pretty. A broad is pretty. Punks ain't pretty. Punk—if he good-lookin'—is cute. You cute.

RICHIE. He's gonna steal me right away, little Billy. You're so slow, Bill. I prefer a man who's decisive.

(*He is lying down now on the floor at the foot of his bed.*)

BILLY. You just keep at it, you're gonna have us all believin' you are just what you say you are.

RICHIE. Which is more than we can say for you.

(*Now* ROGER *rises on his elbow to light a cigarette.*)

BILLY. Jive, jive.

RICHIE. You're arrogant, Billy. So arrogant.

BILLY. What are you—on the rag?

RICHIE. Wouldn't it just bang your little balls if I were!

ROGER (*to* RICHIE). Hey, man. What's with you?

RICHIE. Stupidity offends me; lies and ignorance offend me.

BILLY. You know where we was? The three of us? All three of us, earlier on? To the wrong side of the tracks. Richard. One good black upside-down whorehouse where you get what you buy, no jive along with it—so if it's a lay you want and need, you go! Or don't they have faggot whorehouses?

ROGER. IF YOU GUYS DON'T CUT THIS SHIT OUT I'M GONNA BUST SOMEBODY'S HEAD!

(*Angrily he flops back on his bed. There is silence as they all lie there.*)

RICHIE. "Where we was," he says. Listen to him. "Where we was." And he's got more school, Carlyle, than you have fingers and . . .

(*He has lifted his foot onto the bed; it touches, presses,* CARLYLE'*s foot.*)

. . . toes. It's this pseudo-earthly quality he feigns—but inside he's all cashmere.

BILLY. That's a lie.

(*Giggling, he is staring at the floor.*)

I'm polyester, worsted and mohair.

RICHIE. You have a lot of school, Billy; don't say you don't.

BILLY. You said "fingers and toes"; you didn't say "a lot."

CARLYLE. I think people get dumber the more they put their butts into some schoolhouse door.

BILLY. It depends on what the hell you're talkin' about.

(*Now he looks at* CARLYLE, *and sees the feet touching.*)

CARLYLE. I seen cats back on the block, they knew what was shakin'—then they got into all this school jive and, man, every year they went, they come back they didn't know nothin'.

(BILLY *is staring at* RICHIE'*s foot pressed and rubbing* CARLYLE'*s foot.* RICHIE *sees* BILLY *looking.* BILLY *cannot believe what he is seeing. It fills him with fear. The silence goes on and on.*)

RICHIE. Billy, why don't you and Roger go for a walk?

BILLY. What?

(*He bolts to his knees. He is frozen on his knees on the bed.*)

RICHIE. Roger asked you to go downtown, you went, you had fun.

ROGER (*Having turned, he knows almost instantly what is going on*). I asked you, too.

RICHIE. You asked me; you begged Billy. I said no. Billy said no. You took my ten dollars. You begged Billy. I'm asking you a favor now—go for a walk. Let Carlyle and me have some time.

(*Silence*)

CARLYLE (*He sits up, uneasy and wary*). That how you work it?

ROGER. Work what?

CARLYLE. Whosever turn it be.

BILLY. No, no, that ain't the way we work it, because we don't work it.

CARLYLE. See? See? There it is—that goddamn education showin' through. All them years in school. Man, didn't we have a good time tonight? You rode in my car. I showed you a good cathouse, all that sweet black pussy. Ain't we friends? Richie likes me. How come you don't like me?

BILLY. 'Cause if you really are doin' what I think you're doin', you're a fuckin' animal!

(CARLYLE *leaps to his feet, hand sneaking to his pocket to draw a weapon.*)

ROGER. Billy, no.

BILLY. No, WHAT?!

ROGER. Relax, man; no need.

(*He turns to* CARLYLE; *patiently, wearily, he speaks.*)

Man, I tole you it ain't goin' on here. We both tole you it ain't goin' on here.

CARLYLE. Don't you jive me, nigger. You goin' for a walk like I'm askin', or not? I wanna get this clear.

ROGER. Man, we live here.

RICHIE. It's my house, too, Roger; I live here, too.

(RICHIE *bounds to his feet, flinging the blan-*

*ket that has been covering him so it flies and
lands on the floor near* ROGER's *footlocker.)*

ROGER. Don't I know that? Did I say somethin' to make you think I didn't know that?

(Standing, RICHIE *is removing his trousers
and throwing them down on his footlocker.)*

RICHIE. Carlyle is my guest.

*(Sitting down on the side of his bed and
facing out, he puts his arms around* CARLYLE's
thigh. ROGER *jumps to his feet and grabs the
blanket from the foot of his bed. Shaking it
open, he drops onto the bed, his head at the
foot of the bed and facing off as he covers
himself.)*

ROGER. Fine. He your friend. This your
home. So that mean he can stay. It don't mean
I gotta leave. I'll catch you all in the mornin'.

BILLY. Roger, what the hell are you doin'?

ROGER. What you better do, Billy. It's gettin' late. I'm goin' to sleep.

BILLY. What?

ROGER. Go to fucking bed, Billy. Get up in
the rack, turn your back and look at the wall.

BILLY. You gotta be kiddin'.

ROGER. DO IT!

BILLY. Man . . . !

ROGER. Yeah . . . !

BILLY. You mean just . . .

ROGER. It been goin' on a long damn time,
man. You ain't gonna put no stop to it.

CARLYLE. You . . .ain't . . .serious.

RICHIE *(Both he and* CARLYLE *are staring at*
ROGER *and then* BILLY, *who is staring at*
ROGER). Well, I don't believe it. Of all the
childish . . .infantile . . .

CARLYLE. Hey!

(silence)

HEY! Even I got to say this is a little weird,
but if this the way you do it . . .

(And he turns toward RICHIE *below him.)*
. . . it the way I do it. I don't know.

RICHIE. With them right there? Are you kidding? My God, Carlyle, that'd be obscene.

(Pulling slightly away from CARLYLE)
CARLYLE. Ohhh, man . . . they backs turned.

RICHIE. No.

CARLYLE. What I'm gonna do?

(Silence. He looks at them, all three of them.)
Don't you got no feelin' for how a man feel?
I don't understand you two boys. Unless'n you
a pair of motherfuckers. That what you are,
you a pair of motherfuckers? You slits, man.
DON'T YOU HEAR ME!? I DON'T UNDERSTAND
THIS SITUATION HERE. I THOUGHT WE MADE
A DEAL!

(RICHIE rises, starts to pull on his trousers.

CARLYLE *grabs him.)*

YOU GET ON YOUR KNEES, YOU PUNK, I MEAN
NOW, AND YOU GONNA BE ON MY JOINT FAST
OR YOU GONNA BE ONE BUSTED PUNK. AM I
UNDERSTOOD?

(He hurls RICHIE *down to the floor.)*

BILLY. I ain't gonna have this going on here;
Roger, I can't.

ROGER. I been turnin' my back on one thing
or another all my life.

RICHIE. Jealous, Billy?

BILLY *(getting to his feet).* Just go out that
door, the two of you. Go. Go on out in the
bushes or out in some field. See if I follow
you. See if I care. I'll be right here and I'll be
sleepin', but it ain't gonna be done in my house.
I don't have much in this goddamn army, but
here is mine.

(He stands beside his bed.)

CARLYLE. I WANT MY FUCKIN' NUT! HOW
COME YOU SO UPTIGHT? HE WANTS ME! THIS
BOY HERE WANTS ME! WHO YOU TO STOP IT?

ROGER *(spinning to face* CARLYLE *and*
RICHIE). That's right, Billy. Richie one those
people want to get fucked by niggers, man. It
what he know was gonna happen all his life—
can be his dream come true. Ain't that right,
Richie!

(Jumping to his feet, RICHIE *starts putting
on his trousers.)*

Want to make it real in the world, how a nigger
is an animal. Give 'em an inch, gonna take a
mile. Ain't you some kinda fool, Richie? Hear
me, Carlyle.

CARLYLE. Man, don't make me no nevermind what he think he's provin' an' shit, long
as I get my nut. I KNOW I ain't no animal,
don't have to prove it.

RICHIE *(pulling at* CARLYLE's *arm, wanting
to move him toward the door).* Let's go. Let's
go outside. The hell with it.

(But CARLYLE *tears himself free; he squats
furiously down on the bunk, his hands seizing
it, his back to all of them.)*

CARLYLE. Bull shit. Bullshit! I ain't goin'
no-fuckin'-where—this jive ass ain't runnin'
me. Is this you house or not?

*(He doesn't know what is going on; he can
hardly look at any of them.)*

ROGER *(bounding out of bed, hurling his
pillow across the room).* I'm goin' to the fuckin'
john, Billy. Hang it up, man; let 'em be.

BILLY. No.

ROGER. I'm smarter than you—do like I'm
sayin'.

BILLY. It ain't right.

ROGER. Who gives a big rat's ass!

CARLYLE. Right on, bro! That boy know; he do.

(He circles the bed toward them.)

Hear him. Look into his eyes.

BILLY. This fuckin' army takin' everything else away from me, they ain't takin' more than they got. I see what I see—I don't run, don't hide.

ROGER *(Turning away from BILLY, he stomps out the door, slamming it)*. You fuckin' well better learn.

CARLYLE. That right. Time for more schoolin'. Lesson number one.

(Stealthily he steps and snaps out the only light, the lamp clamped to RICHIE's bed.)

You don't see what you see so well in the dark. It dark in the night. Black man got a black body—he disappear.

(The darkness is so total they are all no more than shadows.)

RICHIE. Not to the hands; not to the fingers.

(Moving from across the room toward CARLYLE)

CARLYLE. You do like you talk, boy, you gonna make me happy.

(As BILLY, nervously clutching his sneaker, is moving backward.)

BILLY. Who says the lights go out? Nobody goddamn asked me if the lights go out.

(BILLY, lunging to the wall switch, throws it. The overhead lights flash on, flooding the room with light. CARLYLE is seated on the edge of RICHIE's bed, RICHIE kneeling before him.)

CARLYLE. I DO, MOTHERFUCKER, I SAY!

(And the switchblade seems to leap from his pocket to his hand.)

I SAY! CAN'T YOU LET PEOPLE BE?

(BILLY hurls his sneaker at the floor at CARLYLE's feet. Instantly CARLYLE is across the room, blocking BILLY's escape out the door.)

Goddamn you, boy! I'm gonna cut your ass, just to show you how it feel—and cuttin' can happen. This knife true.

RICHIE. Carlyle, now c'mon.

CARLYLE. Shut up, pussy.

RICHIE. Don't hurt him, for chrissake.

CARLYLE. Goddamn man throw a shoe at me, he don't walk around clean in the world thinkin' he can throw another. He get some shit come back at him.

(BILLY doesn't know which way to go, and then CARLYLE jabbing the knife at the air before BILLY's chest, has BILLY running backward, his eyes fixed on the moving blade. He stumbles, having run into RICHIE's bed. He

sprawls backward and CARLYLE is over him.)

No, no; no, no. Put you hand out there. Put it out.

(Slight pause; BILLY is terrified.)

DO THE THING I'M TELLIN'!

(BILLY lets his hand rise in the air and CARLYLE grabs it, holds it.)

That's it. That's good. See? See?

(The knife flashes across BILLY's palm; the blood flows. BILLY winces, recoils, but CARLYLE's hand still clenches and holds.)

BILLY. Motherfucker.

(Again the knife darts, cutting, and BILLY yelps. RICHIE, on his knees beside them, turns away.)

RICHIE. Oh, my God what are you—

CARLYLE *(In his own sudden distress, CARLYLE flings the hand away)*. That you blood. The blood inside you, you don't ever see it there. Take a look how easy it come out—and enough of it come out, you in the middle of the worst goddamn trouble you ever gonna see. And know I'm the man can deal that kinda trouble, easy as I smile. And I smile . . . easy. Yeah.

(BILLY is curled in upon himself, holding the hand to his stomach as RICHIE now reaches tentatively and shyly out as if to console BILLY, who repulses the gesture. CARLYLE is angry and strangely depressed. Forlornly he slumps onto BILLY's footlocker as BILLY staggers up to his wall locker and takes out a towel.)

Bastard ruin my mood, Richie. He ruin my mood. Fightin' and lovin' real different in the feelin's I got. I see blood come outa somebody like that, it don't make me feel good—hurt me—hurt on somebody I thought was my friend. But I ain't supposed to see. One dumb nigger. No mind, he thinks, no heart, no feelings a gentleness. You see how that ain't true, Richie. Goddamn man threw a shoe at me. A lotta people woulda cut his heart out. I gotta make him know he throw shit, he get shit. But I don't hurt him bad, you see what I mean?

(BILLY's back is to them, as he stands hunched at his locker, and suddenly his voice, hissing, erupts.)

BILLY. Jesus . . . H. . . . Christ . . . ! Do you know what I'm doin'? Do you know what I'm standin' here doin?

(He whirls now; he holds a straight razor in his hand. A bloody towel is wrapped around the hurt hand. CARLYLE tenses, rises, seeing the razor.)

I'm a twenty-four-year-old goddamn college graduate—intellectual goddamn scholar type—

and I got a razor in my hand. I'm thinkin' about comin' up behind one black human being and I'm thinkin' nigger this and nigger that— I wanna cut his throat. THAT IS RIDICULOUS. I NEVER FACED ANYBODY IN MY LIFE WITH ANYTHING TO KILL THEM. YOU UNDERSTAND ME? I DON'T HAVE A GODDAMN THING ON THE LINE HERE!

(The door opens and ROGER *rushes in, having heard the yelling.* BILLY *flings the razor into his locker.)*

Look at me, Roger, look at me. I got a cut palm—I don't know what happened. Jesus Christ, I got sweat all over me when I think a what I was near to doin'. I swear it. I mean, do I think I need a reputation as a killer, a bad man with a knife?

(He is wild with the energy of feeling free and with the anger at what these others almost made him do. CARLYLE *slumps down on the footlocker; he sits there.)*

Bullshit! I need shit! I got sweat all over me. I got the mile record in my hometown. I did four forty-two in high school and that's the goddamn record in Windsor County. I don't need approval from either one of the pair of you.

(And he rushes at RICHIE.*)*

You wanna be a goddamn swish—a goddamn faggot-queer—GO! Suckin' cocks and takin' it in the ass, the thing of which you dream—GO! AND YOU—

(Whirling on CARLYLE*)*

You wanna be a bad-assed animal, man, get it on—go—but I wash my hands. I am not human as you are. I put you down, I put you down—

(He almost hurls himself at RICHIE.*)*

—you gay little piece a shit cake—SHIT CAKE. AND YOU—

(Hurt, confused, RICHIE *turns away, nearly pressing his face into the bed beside which he kneels, as* BILLY *has spun back to tower over the pulsing, weary* CARLYLE.*)*

—you are your own goddamn fault, SAMBO! SAMBO!

(And the knife flashes up in CARLYLE'*s hand into* BILLY'*s stomach, and* BILLY *yelps.)*

Ahhhhhhhhh.

(And pushes at the hand. RICHIE *is still turned away.)*

RICHIE. Well, fuck you, Billy.

BILLY *(He backs off the knife).* Get away, get away.

RICHIE *(As* ROGER, *who could not see because* BILLY'*s back is to him, is approaching*

CARLYLE *and* BILLY *goes walking up toward the lockers as if he knows where he is going, as if he is going to go out the door and to a movie, his hands holding his belly).* You're so-o messed up.

ROGER *(to* CARLYLE*).* Man, what's the matter with you?

CARLYLE. Don't nobody talk that weird shit to me, you understand?

ROGER. You jive, man. That's all you do— jive!

*(BILLY, *striding swiftly, walks flat into the wall lockers; he bounces, turns. They are all looking at him.)*

RICHIE. Billy! Oh, Billy!

*(ROGER *looks at* RICHIE.*)*

BILLY. Ahhhhhhh. Ahhhhhhh.

*(ROGER *looks at* CARLYLE *as if he is about to scream, and beyond him,* BILLY *turns from the lockers, starts to walk again, now staggering and moving toward them.)*

RICHIE. I think . . . he stabbed him. I think Carlyle stabbed Billy. Roger!

*(ROGER *whirls to go to* BILLY, *who is staggering downstage and angled away, hands clenched over his belly.)*

BILLY. Shut up! It's just a cut, it's just a cut. He cut my hand, he cut gut.

(He collapses onto his knees just beyond ROGER'*s footlocker.)*

It took the wind out of me, scared me, that's all.

(Fiercely he tries to hide the wound and remain calm.)

ROGER. Man, are you all right?

(He moves to BILLY, *who turns to hide the wound. Till now no one is sure what happened.* RICHIE *only "thinks"* BILLY *has been stabbed.* BILLY *is pretending he isn't hurt. As* BILLY *turns from* ROGER, *he turns toward* RICHIE *and* RICHIE *sees the blood.* RICHIE *yelps and they all begin talking and yelling simultaneously.)*

CARLYLE You	ROGER You all right?
know what I was	Or what? He slit you?
learnin', he was	
learnin' to talk all that	BILLY Just took the
weird shit, cuttin',	wind outa me, scared
baby, cuttin', the	me.
ways and means a	
shit, man, razors.	
RICHIE Carlyle, you	
stabbed him; you	
stabbed him.	

CARLYLE. Ohhhh, pussy, pussy, pussy, Carlyle know what he do.

ROGER *(trying to lift* BILLY*).* Get up, okay?

Get up on the bed.

BILLY *(irritated, pulling free)*. I am on the bed.

ROGER. What?

RICHIE. No, Billy, no, you're not.

BILLY. Shut up!

RICHIE. You're on the floor.

BILLY. I'm on the bed. I'm on the bed.

(Emphatically. And then he looks at the floor.)

What?

ROGER. Let me see what he did.

*(*BILLY*'s hands are clenched on the wound.)*

Billy, let me see where he got you.

BILLY *(recoiling)*. NO-O-O-O-O-O, you nigger!

ROGER *(He leaps at* CARLYLE*)*. What did you do?

CARLYLE *(hunching his shoulders, ducking his head)*. Shut up.

ROGER. What did you do, nigger—you slit him or stick him?

(And then he tries to get back to BILLY*.)*

Billy, let me see.

BILLY *(doubling over till his head hits the floor)*. NO-O-O-O-O-O! Shit, shit, shit.

RICHIE *(suddenly sobbing and yelling)*. Oh, my God, my God, ohhhh, ohhhh, ohhhh.

(Bouncing on his knees on the bed)

CARLYLE. FUCK IT, FUCK IT, I STUCK HIM. I TURNED IT. This mother army break my heart. I can't be out there where it pretty, don't wanna live! Wash me clean, shit face!

RICHIE. Ohhhh, ohhhhh, ohhhhhhhhhhh. Carlyle stabbed Billy, oh, ohhhh, I never saw such a thing in my life. Ohhhhhhh.

(As ROGER *is trying gently, fearfully, to straighten* BILLY *up)*

Don't die, Billy; don't die.

ROGER. Shut up and go find somebody to help. Richie, go!

RICHIE. Who? I'll go, I'll go.

(Scrambling off the bed)

ROGER. I don't know. JESUS CHRIST! DO IT!

RICHIE. Okay. Okay. Billy, don't die. Don't die.

(Backing for the door, he turns and runs.)

ROGER. The sarge, or C.Q.

BILLY *(Suddenly doubling over, vomiting blood.* RICHIE *is gone)*. Ohhhhhhhhhh. Blood. Blood

ROGER. Be still, be still.

BILLY *(pulling at a blanket on the floor beside him)*. I want to stand up. I'm—vomiting—

(Making no move to stand, only to cover himself)

—blood. What does that mean?

ROGER *(slowly standing)*. I don't know.

BILLY. Yes, yes, I want to stand up. Give me blanket, blanket.

(He rolls back and forth, fighting to get the blanket over him.)

ROGER. RIICCHHHIIIEEEE!

(As BILLY *is furiously grappling with the blanket)*

No, no.

(He looks at CARLYLE, *who is slumped over, muttering to himself.* ROGER *runs for the door.)*

Wait on, be tight, be cool.

BILLY. Cover me. Cover me.

(At last he gets the blanket over his face. The dark makes him grow still. He lies there beneath his blanket. Silence. No one moves. And then CARLYLE *senses the quiet; he turns, looks. Slowly, wearily, he rises and walks to where* BILLY *lies. He stands over him, the knife hanging loosely from his left hand as he reaches with his right to gently take the blanket and lift it slowly from* BILLY*'s face. They look at each other.* BILLY *reaches up and pats* CAR-LYLE*'s hand holding the blanket.)*

I don't want to talk to you right now, Carlyle. All right? Where's Roger? Do you know where he is?

(Slight pause)

Don't stab me anymore, Carlyle, okay? I was dead wrong doin' what I did. I know that now. Carlyle, promise me you won't stab me anymore. I couldn't take it. Okay? I'm cold . . . my blood . . . is . . .

(From off comes a voice.)

ROONEY. Cokesy? Cokesy wokesy?

(And ROONEY *staggers into the doorway, very drunk, a beer bottle in his hand.)*

Ollie-ollie oxen-freeee.

(He looks at them. CARLYLE *quickly, secretly, slips the knife into his pocket.)*

How you all doin'? Everybody drunk, huh? I los' my friend.

(He is staggering sideways toward BILLY*'s bunk, where he finally drops down, sitting.)*

Who are you, soldier?

(And RICHIE, *running, comes roaring into the room. He looks at* ROONEY *and cannot understand what is going on.* CARLYLE *is standing.* ROONEY *is just sitting there. What is going on?* RICHIE *moves along the lockers, trying to get behind* ROONEY, *his eyes never off* CARLYLE*.)*

RICHIE. Ohhhhhh, Sergeant Rooney, I've been looking for you everywhere—where have you been? Carlyle stabbed Billy, he stabbed him.

ROONEY (sitting there). What?

RICHIE. Carlyle stabbed Billy.

ROONEY. Who's Carlyle?

RICHIE. He's Carlyle.

(As CARLYLE seems about to advance, the knife again showing in his hand)

Carlyle, don't hurt anybody more!

ROONEY (On his feet, he is staggering toward the door). You got a knife there? What's with the knife? What's goin' on here?

(CARLYLE steps as if to bolt for the door, but ROONEY is in the way, having inserted himself between CARLYLE and RICHIE, who has backed into the doorway.)

Wait! Now wait!

RICHIE (as CARLYLE raises the knife). Carlyle, don't!

(RICHIE runs from the room.)

ROONEY. You watch your step, you understand. You see what I got here?

(He lifts the beer bottle, waves it threateningly.)

You watch your step, motherfucker. Relax. I mean, we can straighten all this out. We—

(CARLYLE lunges at ROONEY, who tenses.)

I'm just askin' what's goin' on, that's all I'm doin'. No need to get all—

(And CARLYLE swipes at the air again; ROONEY recoils.)

Motherfucker. Motherfucker.

(He seems to be tensing, his body gathering itself for some mighty effort. And he throws his head back and gives the eagle yell.)

Eeeeeeeeeeeaaaaaaaaaaaaaaaaaahhhhhh!
Eeeeaaaaaaaaaaaaaahhhhhhhhhhhhhh!

(CARLYLE jumps; he looks left and right.)

Goddammit, I'll cut you good.

(He lunges to break the bottle on the edge of the wall lockers. The bottle shatters and he yelps, dropping everything.)

Ohhhhhhhh! Ohhhhhhhhhhhhhh!

(CARLYLE bolts, running from the room.)

I hurt myself, I cut myself. I hurt my hand.

(Holding the wounded hand, he scurries to BILLY's bed, where he sits on the edge, trying to wipe the blood away so he can see the wound.)

I cut—

(Hearing a noise, he whirls, looks; CARLYLE is plummeting in the door and toward him. ROONEY stands.)

I hurt my hand, goddammit!

(The knife goes into ROONEY's belly. He flails at CARLYLE.)

I HURT MY HAND! WHAT ARE YOU DOING? WHAT ARE YOU DOING? WAIT! WAIT!

(He turns away, falling to his knees, and the knife goes into him again and again.)

No fair. No fair!

(ROGER, running, skids into the room, headed for BILLY, and then he sees CARLYLE on ROONEY, the leaping knife. ROGER lunges, grabbing CARLYLE, pulling him to get him off ROONEY. CARLYLE leaps free of ROGER, sending ROGER flying backward. And then CARLYLE begins to circle ROGER's bed. He is whimpering, wiping at the blood on his shirt as if to wipe it away. ROGER backs away as CARLYLE keeps waving the knife at him. ROONEY is crawling along the floor under BILLY's bed and then he stops crawling, lies there.)

CARLYLE. You don't tell nobody on me you saw me do this, I let you go, okay? Ohhhhhhhh.

(Rubbing, rubbing at the shirt)

Ohhhhhh, how'm I gonna get back to the world now, I got all this mess to—

ROGER. What happened? That you—I don't understand that you did this! That you did—

CARLYLE. YOU SHUT UP! Don't be talkin' all that weird shit to me—don't you go talkin' all that weird shit!

ROGER. Nooooooooooooo!

CARLYLE. I'm Carlyle, man. You know me. You know me.

(He turns, he flees out the door. ROGER, alone, looks about the room. BILLY is there. ROGER moves toward BILLY, who is shifting, undulating on his back.)

BILLY. Carlyle, no; oh, Christ, don't stab me anymore. I'll die. I will—I'll die. Don't make me die. I'll get my dog after you. I'LL GET MY DOG AFTER YOU!

(ROGER is saying, "Oh, Billy, man, Billy." He is trying to hold BILLY. Now he lifts BILLY into his arms.)

ROGER. Oh, Billy; oh, man. GODDAMMIT, BILLY!

(As a MILITARY POLICE LIEUTENANT comes running in the door, his .45 automatic drawn, and he levels it at ROGER)

LIEUTENANT. Freeze, soldier! Not a quick move out of you. Just real slow, straighten your ass up.

(ROGER has gone rigid; the LIEUTENANT is advancing on him. Tentatively ROGER turns, looks.)

ROGER. Huh? No.

LIEUTENANT. Get your ass against the lockers.

ROGER. Sir, no. I—

LIEUTENANT *(hurling* ROGER *away toward the wall lockers).* MOVE!

(As another M.P., Pfc HINSON, *comes in, followed by* RICHIE, *flushed and breathless)* Hinson, cover this bastard.

HINSON *(Drawing his .45 automatic, moving on* ROGER*).* Yes, sir.

(The LIEUTENANT *frisks* ROGER, *who is spread-eagled at the lockers.)*

RICHIE. What? Oh, sir, no, no. Roger, what's going on?

LIEUTENANT. I'll straighten this shit out.

ROGER. Tell 'em to get the gun off me, Richie.

LIEUTENANT. SHUT UP!

RICHIE. But, sir, sir, he didn't do it. Not him.

LIEUTENANT *(Fiercely he shoves* RICHIE *out of the way).* I told you, all of you, to shut up.

(He moves to ROONEY's *body.)* Jesus, God, this Sfc is cut to shit. He's cut to shit.

(He hurries to BILLY's *body.)* This man is cut to shit.

(As CARLYLE *appears in the doorway, his hands cuffed behind him, a third M.P., Pfc* CLARK, *shoving him forward.* CARLYLE *seems shocked and cunning, his mind whirring.)*

CLARK. Sir, I got this guy on the street, runnin' like a streak a shit.

(He hurls the struggling CARLYLE *forward and* CARLYLE *stumbles toward the head of* RICHIE's *bed as* RICHIE, *seeing him coming, hurries away along* BILLY's *bed and toward the wall lockers.)*

RICHIE. He did it! Him, him!

CARLYLE. What is going on here? I don't know what is going on here!

CLARK *(Club at the ready, he stations himself beside* CARLYLE*.).* He's got blood all over him, sir. All over him.

LIEUTENANT. What about the knife?

CLARK. No, sir. he must have thrown it away.

(As a fourth M.P. has entered to stand in the doorway, and HINSON, *leaving* ROGER, *bends to examine* ROONEY. *He will also kneel and look for life in* BILLY.)*

LIEUTENANT. You throw it away, soldier?

CARLYLE. Oh, you thinkin' about how my sister got happened, too. Oh, you ain't so smart as you think you are! No way!

ROGER. Jesus God almighty.

LIEUTENANT. What happened here? I want to know what happened here.

HINSON *(rising from* BILLY's *body).* They're both dead, sir. Both of them.

LIEUTENANT *(confidential, almost whispering).* I know they're both dead. That's what I'm talkin' about.

CARLYLE. Chicken blood, sir. Chicken blood and chicken hearts is what all over me. I was goin' on my way, these people jump out the bushes be pourin' it all over. Chicken blood and chicken hearts.

(Thrusting his hands out at CLARK*)* You goin' take these cuffs off me, boy?

LIEUTENANT. Sit him down, Clark. Sit him down and shut him up.

CARLYLE. This my house, sir. This my goddamn house.

*(CLARK *grabs him, begins to move him.)*

LIEUTENANT. I said to shut him up.

CLARK. Move it; move!

(Struggling to get CARLYLE *over to* ROGER's *footlocker as* HINSON *and the other M.P. exit)*

CARLYLE. I want these cuffs taken off my hands.

CLARK. You better do like you been told. You better sit and shut up!

CARLYLE. I'm gonna be thinkin' over here. I'm gonna be thinkin' it all over. I got plannin' to do. I'm gonna be thinkin' in my quietness; don't you be makin' no mistake.

(He slumps over, muttering to himself. HINSON *and the other M.P. return, carrying a stretcher. They cross to* BILLY, *chatting with each other about how to go about the lift. They will lift him; they will carry him out.)*

LIEUTENANT *(to* RICHIE*).* You're Wilson?

RICHIE. No, sir.

(Indicating BILLY*)* That's Wilson. I'm Douglas.

LIEUTENANT *(to* ROGER*).* And you're Moore. And you sleep here.

ROGER. Yes, sir.

RICHIE. Yes, sir. And Billy slept here and Sergeant Rooney was our platoon sergeant and Carlyle was a transient, sir. He was a transient from P Company.

LIEUTENANT *(scrutinizing* ROGER*).* And you had nothing to do with this?

(To RICHIE*)* He had nothing to do with this?

ROGER. No, sir, I didn't.

RICHIE. No, sir, he didn't. I didn't either. Carlyle went crazy and he got into a fight and it was awful. I didn't even know what it was about exactly.

LIEUTENANT. How'd the Sfc get involved?

RICHIE. Well, he came in, sir.

ROGER. I had to run off to call you, sir. I wasn't here.

RICHIE. Sergeant Rooney just came in—I don't know why—he heard all the yelling, I guess—and Carlyle went after him. Billy was already stabbed.

CARLYLE (*rising, his manner that of a man who is taking charge*). All right now, you gotta be gettin' the fuck outa here. All of you. I have decided enough of the shit has been goin' on around here and I am tellin' you to be gettin' these motherfuckin' cuffs off me and you be gettin' me a bus ticket home. I am quittin' this jive-time army.

LIEUTENANT. You are doin' what?

CARLYLE. No, I ain't gonna be quiet. No way. I am quittin' this goddamn—

LIEUTENANT. You shut the hell up, soldier. I am ordering you.

CARLYLE. I don't understand you people! Don't you people understand when a man be talkin' English at you to say his mind? I have quit the army!

(*As* HINSON *returns*)

LIEUTENANT. Get him outa here!

RICHIE. What's the matter with him?

LIEUTENANT. Hinson! Clark!

(*They move, grabbing* CARLYLE, *and they drag him, struggling, toward the door.*)

CARLYLE. Oh, no. Oh, no. You ain't gonna be doin' me no more. I been tellin' you. To get away from me. I am stayin' here. This my place, not your place. You take these cuffs off me like I been tellin' you! My poor little sister Lin Sue understood what was goin' on here! She tole me! She knew!

(*He is howling in the hallway now.*)
You better be gettin' these cuffs off me!

(*Silence.* ROGER, RICHIE *and the* LIEUTENANT *are all staring at the door. The* LIEUTENANT *turns, crosses to the foot of* ROGER's *bed.*)

LIEUTENANT. All right now. I will be getting to the bottom of this. You know I will be getting to the bottom of this.

(*He is taking two forms from his clipboard.*)

RICHIE. Yes, sir.

(HINSON *and the fourth M.P. return with another stretcher. They walk to* ROONEY, *talking to one another about how to lift him. They drag him from under the bed. They will roll him onto the stretcher, lift him and walk out.* ROGER *moves, watching them, down along the edge of* BILLY's *bed.*)

LIEUTENANT. Fill out these forms. I want your serial number, rank, your MOS, and NCOIC of your work. Any leave coming up will be canceled. Tomorrow at 0800 you will report to my office at the provost marshal's headquarters. You know where that is?

ROGER (*as the two M.P.'s are leaving with the stretcher and* ROONEY's *body*). Yes, sir.

RICHIE. Yes, sir.

LIEUTENANT (*Crossing to* ROGER, *he hands him two cards*). Be prepared to do some talking. Two perfectly trained and primed strong pieces of U.S. Army property got cut to shit up here. We are going to find out how and why. Is that clear?

RICHIE. Yes, sir.

ROGER. Yes, sir.

(*The* LIEUTENANT *looks at each of them. He surveys the room. He marches out.*)

RICHIE. Oh, my God. Oh. Oh.

(*He runs to his bed and collapses, sitting hunched down at the foot. He holds himself and rocks as if very cold.* ROGER, *quietly is weeping. He stands and then walks to his bed. He puts down the two cards. He moves purposefully up to the mops hanging on the wall in the corner. He takes one down. He moves with the mop and the bucket to* BILLY's *bed, where* ROONEY's *blood stains the floor. He mops.* RICHIE, *in horror, is watching.*)

RICHIE. What . . . are you doing?

ROGER. This area a mess, man.

(*Dragging the bucket, carrying the mop, he moves to the spot where* BILLY *had lain. He begins to mop.*)

RICHIE. That's Billy's blood, Roger. His blood.

ROGER. Is it?

RICHIE. I feel awful.

ROGER (*He keeps mopping*). How come you made me waste all that time talkin' shit to you, Richie? All my time talkin' shit, and all the time you was a faggot, man; you really was. You shoulda jus' told ole Roger. He don't care. All you gotta do is tell me.

RICHIE. I've been telling you. I did.

ROGER. Jive, man, jive!

RICHIE. No!

ROGER. You did bullshit all over us! ALL OVER US!

RICHIE. I just wanted to hold his hand, Billy's hand, to talk to him, go to the movies hand in hand like he would with a girl or I would with someone back home.

ROGER. But he didn't wanna; he didn't wanna.

(*Finished now,* ROGER *drags the mop and bucket back toward the corner.* RICHIE *is sobbing; he is at the edge of hysteria.*)

RICHIE. He did.

ROGER. No, man.

RICHIE. He did. He did. It's not my fault.

(ROGER *slams the bucket into the corner and rams the mop into the bucket. Furious, he marches down to* RICHIE. *Behind him* SERGEANT COKES, *grinning and lifting a wine bottle, appears in the doorway.*)

COKES. Hey!

(RICHIE, *in despair, rolls onto his belly.* COKES *is very, very happy.*)

Hey! What a day, gen'l'men. How you all doin'?

ROGER (*crossing up near the head of his own bed*). Hello, Sergeant Cokes.

COKES (*Affectionate and casual, he moves near to* ROGER). How you all doin'? Where's ole Rooney? I lost him.

ROGER. What?

COKES. We had a hell of a day, ole Rooney and me, lemme tell you. We been playin' hide-and-go-seek, and I was hidin', and now I think maybe he started hidin' without tellin' me he was gonna and I can't find him and I thought maybe he was hidin' up here.

RICHIE. Sergeant, he—

ROGER. No. No, we ain't seen him.

COKES. I gotta find him. He knows how to react in a tough situation. He didn't come up here looking for me?

(ROGER *moves around to the far side of his bed, turning his back to* COKES. *Sitting,* ROGER *takes out a cigarette, but he does not light it.*)

ROGER. We was goin' to sleep. Sarge. Got to get up early. You know the way this mother army is.

COKES (*Nodding, drifting backward, he sits down on* BILLY'S *bed*). You don't mind I sit here a little. Wait on him. Got a little wine. You can have some.

(*Tilting his head way back, he takes a big drink and then, looking straight ahead, corks the bottle with a whack of his hand.*)

We got back into the area—we had been downtown—he wanted to play hide-and-go-seek. I tole him okay, I was ready for that. He hid his eyes. So I run and hid in the bushes and then under this Jeep. 'Cause I thought it was better. I hid and I hid and I hid. He never did come. So finally, I got tired—I figured I'd give up, come lookin' for him. I was way over by the movie theater. I don't know how I got there. Anyway, I got back here and I figured maybe he come up here lookin' for me, figurin' I was hidin' up with you guys. You ain't seen him, huh?

ROGER. No, we ain't seen him. I tole you that, Sarge.

COKES. Oh.

RICHIE. Roger!

ROGER. He's drunk, Richie! He's blasted drunk. Got a brain turned to mush!

COKES (*in deep agreement*). That ain't no lie.

ROGER. Let it be for the night, Richie. Let him be for the night.

COKES. I still know what's goin' on, though. Never no worry about that. I always know what's goin' on. I always know. Don't matter what I drink or how much I drink. I always still know what's goin' on. But . . . I'll be goin' maybe and look for Rooney.

(*But rising, he wanders down center.*)

But . . . I mean, we could be doin' that forever. Him and me. Me under the Jeep. He wants to find me, he goes to the Jeep. I'm over here. He comes here. I'm gone. You know, maybe I'll just wait a little while more I'm here. He'll find me then if he comes here. You guys want another drink.

(*Turning, he goes to* BILLY'S *footlocker, where he sits and takes another enormous guzzle of wine.*)

Jesus, what a goddamn day we had. Me and Rooney started drivin' and we was comin' to this intersection and out comes this goddamn Chevy. I try to get around her, but no dice. BINGO! I hit her in the left rear. She was furious. I didn't care. I gave her my name and number. My car had a headlight out, the fender bashed in. Rooney wouldn't stop laughin'. I didn't know what to do. So we went to D.C. to this private club I know. Had ten or more snorts and decided to get back here after playin' some snooker. That was fun. On the way, we picked up this kid from the engineering unit, hitchhiking. I'm starting to feel real clear-headed now. So I'm comin' around this corner and all of a sudden there's this car stopped dead in front of me. He's not blinkin' to turn or anything. I slam on the brakes, but it's like puddin' the way I slide into him. There's a big noise and we yell. Rooney starts laughin' like crazy and the kid jumps outa the back and says he's gonna take a fuckin' bus. The guy from the other car is swearin' at me. My car's still workin' fine, so I move it off to the side and tell him to do the same, while we wait for the cops. He says he wants his car right where it is and he had the right of way 'cause he was makin' a legal turn. So we're waitin' for the cops. Some cars go by. The guy's car is this big fuckin' Buick. Around the corner comes this little red Triumph. The driver's this blond kid got this blond girl next to him. You can see what's gonna happen. There's this fuckin' car sittin' there, nobody in it. So the Triumph goes crashin' into the back of the Buick with nobody in it. BIFF- BANG-BOOM. And everything stops. We're staring. It's all still. And then that fuckin' Buick kinda shudders and starts to move. With nobody in it. It starts to roll from the impact. And it rolls just far enough to get where the road starts a downgrade. It's driftin' to the right. It's driftin' to the shoulder and over it and onto this hill, where it's pickin' up speed 'cause the hill is steep and then it disappears over the side, and into the dark, just rollin' real quiet. Rooney falls over, he's laughin' so hard. I don't know what to do. In a minute the cops come and in another minute some guy comes runnin' up over the hill to tell us some other guy had got run over by this car with nobody in it. We didn't know what to think. This was fuckin' unbelievable to us. But we found out later from the cops that this wasn't true and some guy had got hit over the head with a bottle in a bar and when he staggered out the door it was just at the instant that this fuckin' Buick with nobody in it went by. Seein' this, the guy stops cold and turns around and just goes back into the bar. Rooney is screamin' at me how we been in four goddamn accidents and fights and how we have got out clean. So then we got everything all straightened out and we come back here to play hide-and-seek 'cause that's what ole Rooney wanted.

(He is taking another drink, but finding the bottle empty.)

Only now I can't find him.

(Near RICHIE's *footlocker stands a beer bottle and* COKES *begins to move toward it. Slowly he bends and grasps the bottle; he straightens, looking at it. He drinks. And settles down on* RICHIE's *footlocker.)*

I'll just sit a little.

*(*RICHIE, *lying on his belly, shudders. The sobs burst out of him. He is shaking.* COKES, *blinking, turns to study* RICHIE.*)*

What's up? Hey, what're you cryin' about, soldier? Hey?

*(*RICHIE *cannot help himself.)*

What's he cryin' about?

ROGER *(Disgustedly, he sits there).* He's cryin' 'cause he's a queer.

COKES. Oh. You a queer, boy?

RICHIE. Yes, Sergeant.

COKES. Oh.

(pause)

How long you been a queer?

ROGER. All his fuckin' life.

RICHIE. I don't know.

COKES *(turning to scold* ROGER*).* Don't be yellin' mean at him. Boy, I tell you it's a real strange thing the way havin' leukemia gives you a lotta funny thoughts about things. Two months ago—or maybe even yesterday—I'da called a boy who was a queer a lotta awful names. But now I just wanna be figurin' things out. I mean, you ain't kiddin' me out about ole Rooney, are you, boys, 'cause of how I'm a sergeant and you're enlisted men, so you got some idea a vengeance on me? You ain't doin' that, are you, boys?

ROGER. No.

RICHIE. Ohhhh. Jesus. Ohhhh. I don't know what's hurtin' in me.

COKES. No, no, boy. You listen to me. You gonna be okay. There's a lotta worse things in this world than bein' a queer. I seen a lot of 'em, too. I mean, you could have leukemia. That's worse. That can kill you. I mean, it's okay. You listen to the ole sarge. I mean, maybe I was a queer, I wouldn't have leukemia. Who's to say? Lived a whole different life. Who's to say? I keep thinkin' there was maybe somethin' I coulda done different. Maybe not drunk so much. Or if I'd killed more gooks, or more Krauts or more dinks. I was kind-hearted sometimes. Or if I'd had a wife and I had some kids. Never had any. But my mother did and she died of it anyway. Gives you a whole funny different way a lookin' at things, I'll tell you. Ohhhh, Rooney, Rooney.

(slight pause)

Or if I'd let that little gook outa that spider hole he was in, I was sittin' on it. I'd let him out now, he was in there.

(He rattles the footlocker lid under him.)

Oh, how'm I ever gonna forget it? That funny little guy. I'm runnin' along, he pops up outa that hole. I'm never gonna forget him—how'm I ever gonna forget him? I see him and dive, goddamn bullet hits me in the side, I'm midair, everything's turnin' around. I go over the edge of this ditch and I'm crawlin' real fast. I lost my rifle. Can't find it. Then I come up behind him. He's half out of the hole. I bang him on top of his head, stuff him back into the hole with a grenade for company. Then I'm sittin' on the lid and it's made outa steel. I can feel him in there, though, bangin' and yellin' under me, and his yelling I can hear is begging for me to let him out. It was like a goddamn Charlie Chaplin movie, everybody fallin' down and clumsy, and him in there yellin' and bangin' away, and I'm just sittin' there lookin' around. And he was Charlie Chaplin. I don't know who I was. And then he blew up.

(pause)

Maybe I'll just get a little shut-eye right sittin' here while I'm waitin' for ole Rooney. We figure it out. All of it. You don't mind I just doze a little here, you boys?

ROGER. No.

RICHIE. No.

(ROGER rises and walks to the door. He switches off the light and gently closes the door. The transom glows. COKES sits in a flower of light. ROGER crosses back to his bunk and settles in, sitting.)

COKES. Night, boys.

RICHIE. Night, Sergeant.

(COKES sits there, fingers entwined, trying to sleep.)

COKES. I mean, he was like Charlie Chaplin. And then he blew up.

ROGER *(suddenly feeling very sad for this ole man)*. Sergeant . . . maybe you was Charlie Chaplin, too.

COKES. No. No.

(pause)

No. I don't know who I was. Night.

ROGER. You think he was singin' it?

COKES. What?

ROGER. You think he was singin' it?

COKES. Oh, yeah. Oh, yeah; he was singin' it.

(Slight pause, COKES, sitting on the foot-locker, begins to sing a makeshift language imitating Korean, to the tune of "Beautiful Streamer." He begins with an angry, mocking energy that slowly becomes a dream, a lullaby, a farewell, a lament.)

> Yo no som lo no
> Ung toe lo knee
> Ra so me la lo
> La see see oh doe.
> Doe no tee ta ta
> Too low see see
> Ra mae me lo lo
> Ah boo boo boo eee.
> Boo boo eee booo eeee
> La so lee lem
> Lem lo lee da ung
> Uhhh so ba booooo ohhhh.
> Boo booo eee ung ba
> Eee eee la looo
> Lem lo lala la
> Eeee oohhh ohhh ohhh ohhhhh.

(In the silence, he makes the soft, whispering sound of a child imitating an explosion, and his entwined fingers come apart. The dark figures of RICHIE and ROGER are near. The lingering light fades.)

American Buffalo

David Mamet

First presented at the Goodman Theatre Stage Two in Chicago on November 23, 1975, with the following cast:

(*in order of appearance*)
BOBBY   William H. Macy
TEACH   Bernard Erhard
DONNY   J. J. Johnston

Directed by Gregory Mosher
Scenery by Michael Merritt
Lighting by Robert Christen

THE SCENE: Don's Resale Shop. A junkshop.

THE TIME: One Friday. Act One takes place in the morning; Act Two starts around 11:00 that night.

American Buffalo is a three-character play written in two acts. According to its author, David Mamet, "People will look back at the play in five years and say the language is garbage or they will say it's poetry."

American Buffalo is concerned with three men who spend most of their time on stage planning to burglarize the apartment of a coin collector who has recently bought a buffalo nickel from their junk shop. They assume that he has a valuable coin collection and plan to steal it. The burglary never comes off because the men are gradually undone, consumed by their own mistrust, ineptitude and connivance.

Donny Dubrow is the middle-aged owner of the junk shop. His disorganized store and his way of handling customers reveal that he is not a skilled businessman, but he manages to stay in business because he is a survivor. Donny's protégé and assistant is Bobby, a street kid and ex-addict who is confused and very vulnerable. Donny assumes the role of father, teaching Bobby about life and how to take care of himself. Teach is a friend of Donny's. He is explosive, vulnerable, vicious and immature. Assuming a cold and callous demeanor, he betrays himself as an anguished child who is jealous of Bobby and the attention he gets from Donny. Teach also assumes the role of guide at the end of the play; he becomes the catalyst between Donny and Bobby, helping them to realize their importance to each other. In trying to destroy their relationship, he brings them closer together and shows them the necessity of trust and loyalty.

American Buffalo zeroes in on the language of petty hoods and unleashes a relentless storm of raunchy expletives. It is an exercise in absurdity in which nothing of consequence happens. The play ends with betrayal and failure to execute the heist. The play expounds on a conflict of values—friendship, loyalty and business, business being defined as taking care of oneself. The play also tells of the price that is paid for lack of trust in human relationships. It speaks about the love, envy and distrust that fester among men who battle for each other's affections.

David Mamet has said, "*American Buffalo* is about what Thorstein Veblen calls the delinquent classes, '. . . To the middle classes they may look like petty crooks, but the crooks think of themselves as entrepreneurs . . . not that there's any significant difference between the stealing that goes on in a Madison Avenue advertising agency and in an Eighth Avenue stickup.' "

Mamet also states that "a lot of people thought the play was about criminals and low-lifes and losers. . . . The play is about an essential part of American consciousness, which is the ability to suspend an ethical sense and adopt in its stead a popular accepted mythology and use that to assuage your conscience like everyone else is doing. . . . America is a very . . . propaganda-prone nation. This willingness to be sold constitutes some of the basis for the actions in *American Buffalo*. . . . Americans have always been very susceptible to exhortations to do what is right but never to think what is right. . . ."

David Mamet was born on November 30, 1947, in Chicago and went to grade school and high school on the South Side, attending Rick Central and Frances Parker high schools. His roots are Russian and Polish Jewish and his parents are first-generation Americans. His father is a labor lawyer and his mother teaches retarded children. They were divorced after Mamet was eleven; each remarried and raised a second family. "I don't see how anyone can escape a stormy adolescence. I think some of my anger, perhaps unconscious anger comes out in my plays, in the gut language. I . . . used to read a lot and played the piano and I used to love going to the movies."

While living in Chicago, he worked as a gopher at the Hull House Theatre and as a busboy at Second City, Chicago's famed improvisational company. "It was a superb, superb training ground, and their rhythm—the rhythm of action, the rhythm of speech—influences the way I write." When there was spare time, ". . . we put on plays in garages and basements, everything used in the show was borrowed, stolen . . ." Summer jobs included work in the steel mills and in factories.

Upon graduation from high school, Mamet went to Goddard College in Vermont, majoring in drama, dance and acting. It was at Goddard that he began to write because "the actors I was working with needed some material to do." The piece he wrote was *Sexual Perversity in Chicago*. A dance teacher and choreographer at the college, Marl Ryder, read his plays and encouraged him to continue. Mamet also did some directing at Goddard and graduated as an actor with a job in Montreal, but he confesses "I was terrible and it bothered me a lot. . . . I have so much reverence for actors. What they do is incredibly beautiful and difficult and so stunning on stage."

In Montreal, in 1967, he worked as an acrobatic dancer in the Maurice Chevalier Show. He then worked for a year as a contributing editor to Hugh Hefner's magazine, *Oui,* and studied acting at the Neighborhood Playhouse School of Theatre in New York. He also served for a year in the merchant marine and says this helped to train his ear for language.

In 1971 he founded the St. Nicholas Theatre Company. He and his co-founders transferred the project from Vermont to Chicago three years later, where they performed *Sexual Perversity in Chicago* at the Organic Theatre Company very successfully. Then in October 23, 1975, *American Buffalo* opened at the Goodman Theatre's Center Stage Two. The play then came to New York and was presented at St. Clement's Church on January 23, 1976. It finally opened at the Ethel Barrymore Theatre on Broadway, February 16, 1977.

In Chicago when not busy at the St. Nicholas Theatre, which produced twenty of his plays, Mamet shot pool and worked odd jobs as a window washer, cab driver, short order cook and in a "boiler room" which he describes as ". . . a room with a lot of phones and a lot of people who work these phones, trying to sell people worthless land in Arizona and Florida. You don't make much money . . . but you do meet some colorful people."

He returned to Goddard to teach acting and writing, as an artist-in-residence. He has also taught at the University of Chicago, Marlboro College, Pontiac (Illinois) Penitentiary and Yale University. "I don't think you can teach people how to write plays. The most you can do is to tell them to read Aristotle's *Poetics* and to study acting."

It was *American Buffalo* that led Mamet away from the St. Nicholas Theatre to sleep on a friend's floor and spend his days trying to sell his plays to various producers. "Everybody in New York read it and nobody understood it. . . ." Finally, producer Joseph Beruh and Edgar Lansbury optioned the play in 1976.

Mamet has been acclaimed for his keen ear, which captures the language, idioms and speech rhythms of different social strata with remarkable accuracy and skill. One of Mamet's favorite methods is basic eavesdropping, which he translates into pages of dialogue and keeps in a filing cabinet. "I write all my plays in bound notebooks." He "squirrels" away his handwritten manuscripts and in fact has written an autobiographical play entitled *Squirrels.*

Concerning the language he uses in his plays, Mamet states, "The first thing I learned is that the exigent speak poetry. They don't speak the language of newspapers. I heard rhythms and verbal expressions that dealt with an experience not covered in anything I'd ever read. . . . I became fascinated by the notion of a native American language . . . words create behavior which is obviously crucial if you want to become a playwright . . . actually my main emphasis is on the rhythm of the language. . . ." Mamet's original interest in language came from his father, "an amateur semanticist" who played children's records and read nursery verses to him.

Conveying a thought in a single line or even a single word is something that Mamet is striving for. "My plays are getting more spare as I go along. Success has made it possible for me to . . . produce as much or as little as I want . . . What I write about is what I think is missing from our society and that's communication on a basic level. I understand my characters completely. I make no judgments about them . . . they're just people I have known."

David Mamet has won the Joseph Jefferson Award, the Obie award for the most promising playwright of 1976 and the New York Drama Critics' Circle Award. His other works include: *Duck Variations, Lone Canoe or the Explorer, Reunion, Dark Pony, The Water Engine, A Life in the Theatre, The Revenge of the Space Pandas, The Woods, Lakeboat, Sermon, The Poet and the Rent, The Sanctity of Marriage, Mr. Happiness, Prairie du Chien* and the screenplay for the second version of *The Postman Always Rings Twice.*

ACT ONE

Don's Resale Shop. Morning, DON *and* BOB
are sitting.
_____

DON. So?
(Pause.)
So what, Bob?
(Pause.)
BOB. I'm sorry, Donny.
(Pause.)
DON. All right.
BOB. I'm sorry, Donny.
(Pause.)
DON. Yeah.
BOB. Maybe he's still in there.
DON. If you think that, Bob, how come you're
here?
BOB. I came in.
(Pause.)
DON. You don't come in, Bob. You don't
come in until you do a thing.
BOB. He didn't come out.
DON. What do I care, Bob, if he came out
or not? You're s'posed to watch the guy, you
watch him. Am I wrong?
BOB. I just went to the back.
DON. Why?
(Pause.)
Why did you do that?
BOB. 'Cause he wasn't coming out the front.
DON. Well, Bob, I'm sorry, but this isn't
good enough. If you want to do business . . .
if we got a business deal, it isn't good enough.
I want you to remember this.
BOB. I do.
DON. Yeah, *now* . . . but later, what?
(Pause.)
Just one thing, Bob. Action counts.
(Pause.)
Action talks and bullshit walks.
BOB. I only went around to see he's coming
out the back.
DON. No, don't go fuck yourself around with
these excuses.
(Pause.)
BOB. I'm sorry.
DON. Don't tell me that you're sorry. I'm
not mad at you.
BOB. You're not?
DON *(pause).* Let's clean up here.
*(*BOB *starts to clean up the debris around
the poker table.)*
The only thing I'm trying to teach you some-
thing here.

BOB. Okay.
DON. Now lookit Fletcher.
BOB. Fletch?
DON. Now, Fletcher is a standup guy.
BOB. Yeah.
DON. I don't *give* a shit. He is a fellow stands
for something—
BOB. Yeah.
DON. You take him and you put him down
in some strange town with just a nickel in his
pocket, and by nightfall he'll have that town
by the balls. This is not talk, Bob, this is action.
(Pause.)
BOB. He's a real good card player.
DON. You're fucking A he is, Bob, and this
is what I'm getting at. Skill. Skill and talent
and the balls to arrive at your own conclusions.
The fucker won four hundred bucks last night.
BOB. Yeah?
DON. Oh yeah.
BOB. And who was playing?
DON. *Me* . . .
BOB. Uh-huh . . .
DON. And *Teach* . . .
BOB. (How'd Teach do?)*
DON. (Not too good.)
BOB. (No, huh?)
DON. (No.) . . . and Earl was here . . .
BOB. Uh-huh . . .
DON. And Fletcher.
BOB. How'd he do?
DON. He won four hundred bucks.
BOB. And who else won?
DON. Ruthie, she won.
BOB. She won, huh?
DON. Yeah.
BOB. She does okay.
DON. Oh yeah . . .
BOB. She's an okay card player.
DON. Yes, she is.
BOB. I like her.
DON. Fuck, I like her too. (There's nothing
wrong in that.)
BOB. (No.)
DON. I mean, she treats you right.
BOB. Uh-huh. How'd she do?
DON. She did okay.
(Pause.)
BOB. You win?
DON. I did all right.

_____

* Some portions of the dialogue appear in parentheses,
which serve to mark a slight change of outlook on the part
of the speaker—perhaps a momentary change to a more
introspective regard.—D.M.

BOB. Yeah?

DON. Yeah. I did okay. Not like Fletch . . .

BOB. No, huh?

DON. I mean, Fletcher, he plays *cards*.

BOB. He's real sharp.

DON. You're goddamn right he is.

BOB. I know it.

DON. Was he born that way?

BOB. Huh?

DON. I'm saying was he born that way or do you think he had to learn it?

BOB. Learn it.

DON. Goddamn right he did, and don't forget it. Everything, Bobby: it's going to happen to you, it's *not* going to happen to you, the important thing is can you deal with it, and can you *learn* from it.

(Pause.)

And this is why I'm telling you to stand up. It's no different with you than with anyone else. Everything that I or Fletcher know we picked up on the street. That's all business is . . . common sense, experience, and talent.

BOB. Like when he jewed Ruthie out that pig iron.

DON. What pig iron?

BOB. That he got off her that time.

DON. When was this?

BOB. On the back of her truck.

DON. That wasn't, I don't think, her pig iron.

BOB. No?

DON. That was *his* pig iron, Bob.

BOB. Yeah?

DON. Yeah. He bought it off her.

(Pause.)

BOB. Well, she was real mad at him.

DON. She was.

BOB. Yup.

DON. She was mad at him?

BOB. Yeah. That he stole her pig iron.

DON. He didn't steal it, Bob.

BOB. No?

DON. No.

BOB. She was *mad* at him . . .

DON. Well, that very well may be, Bob, but the fact remains that it was *business*. That's what business is.

BOB. What?

DON. People taking *care* of themselves. Huh?

BOB. No.

DON. 'Cause there's business and there's friendship. Bobby . . . there are many things, and when you walk around you *hear* a lot of things, and what you got to do is keep clear who your friends are, and who treated you like

what. Or else the rest is garbage, Bob, because I want to tell you something.

BOB. Okay.

DON. Things are not always what they seem to be.

BOB. I know.

(Pause.)

DON. There's lotsa people on this street, Bob, they want this and they want that. Do anything to get it. You don't have *friends* this life. . . . You want some breakfast?

BOB. I'm not hungry.

(Pause.)

DON. *Never* skip breakfast, Bob.

BOB. Why?

DON. Breakfast . . . is the most important meal of the day.

BOB. I'm not hungry.

DON. It makes no earthly difference in the world. You know how much nutritive benefits they got in coffee? Zero. Not one thing. The stuff eats *you* up. You can't live on coffee, Bobby. (And I've told you this before.) You cannot live on cigarettes. You may feel good, you may feel *fine,* but something's getting overworked, and you are going to pay for it. Now: What do you see me eat when I come in here every day?

BOB. Coffee.

DON. Come on, Bob, don't fuck with me. I *drink* a little coffee . . . but what do I *eat*?

BOB. Yogurt.

DON. Why?

BOB. Because it's good for you.

DON. You're goddamn right. And it wouldn't kill you to take a vitamin.

BOB. They're too expensive.

DON. Don't worry about it. You should just take 'em.

BOB. I can't afford 'em.

DON. Don't worry about it.

BOB. You'll buy some for me?

DON. Do you need 'em?

BOB. Yeah.

DON. Well, then, I'll get you some. What do you *think*?

BOB. Thanks, Donny.

DON. It's for your own good. Don't thank me . . .

BOB. Okay.

DON. I just can't use you in here like a zombie.

BOB. I just went around the back.

DON. I don't care. Do you see? Do you see what I'm getting at?

(Pause.)

BOB. Yeah.

(Pause.)

DON. Well, we'll see.

BOB. I'm sorry, Donny.

DON. Well, we'll see.

TEACH *(appears in the doorway and enters the store)*. Good morning.

BOB. Morning, Teach.

TEACH *(walks around the store a bit in silence)*. Fuckin' Ruthie, fuckin' Ruthie, fuckin' Ruthie, fuckin' Ruthie, fuckin' Ruthie.

DON. What?

TEACH. Fuckin' *Ruthie* . . .

DON. . . . yeah?

TEACH. I come into the Riverside to get a cup of *coffee,* right? I sit down at the table Grace and Ruthie.

DON. Yeah.

TEACH. I'm gonna order just a cup of coffee.

DON. Right.

TEACH. So Grace and Ruthie's having breakfast, and they're done. *Plates . . . crusts* of stuff all over . . . So we'll shoot the shit.

DON. Yeah.

TEACH. Talk about the *game* . . .

DON. . . . yeah.

TEACH. . . . *so* on. Down I sit. "Hi, hi." I take a piece of toast off Grace's plate . . .

DON. . . . uh-huh . . .

TEACH. . . . and she goes "Help yourself." Help myself. I should help myself to half a piece of toast it's four slices for a quarter. I should have a nickel every time we're over at the game, I pop for coffee . . . cigarettes . . . a *sweet roll,* never say word. "Bobby, see who wants what." Huh? A fucking *roast-beef* sandwich. *(to* BOB*) Am I right? (to* DON*)* Ahh, shit. We're sitting down, how many times do I pick up the check? But (No!) because I never go and make a big *thing* out of it—it's no big thing—and flaunt like "This one's on me" like some bust-out asshole, but I naturally assume that I'm with friends, and don't forget who's who when someone gets behind a half a yard or needs some help with (huh?) some fucking rent, or drops enormous piles of money at the track, or someone's *sick* or something . . .

DON *(to* BOB*)*. This is what I'm talking about.

TEACH. Only (and I tell you this, Don). Only, and I'm not, I don't think, casting anything on anyone; from the mouth of a Southern bulldyke asshole ingrate of a vicious nowhere cunt can this trash come. *(To* BOB*)* And I take nothing back, and I know you're close with them.

BOB. With Grace and Ruthie?

TEACH. Yes.

BOB. (I like 'em.)

TEACH. I have always treated everybody more than fair, and never gone around complaining. Is this true, Don?

DON. Yup.

TEACH. Someone is *against* me, that's their problem . . . I can look out for myself, and I don't got to fuck around behind somebody's back, I don't like the way they're treating me. (Or pray some brick *safe* falls and hits them on the head, they're walking down the street.) But to have that shithead turn, in one breath, every fucking sweet roll that I ever ate with them into *ground glass* (I'm wondering were they eating it and thinking "This guy's an idiot to blow a fucking *quarter* on his friends" . . .) . . . this hurts me, Don. This hurts me in a way I don't know what the fuck to do.

(Pause.)

DON. You're probably just upset.

TEACH. You're fuckin' A I'm upset. I am *very* upset, Don.

DON. They got their problems, too, Teach.

TEACH. *I* would like to have their problems.

DON. All I'm saying, nothing *personal* . . . they were probably, uh, *talking* about something.

TEACH. Then let them talk about it, then. No, I am sorry, Don, I cannot brush this off. They treat me like an asshole, they are an asshole.

(Pause.)

The only way to teach these people is to kill them.

(Pause.)

DON. You want some coffee?

TEACH. I'm not hungry.

DON. Come on, I'm sending Bobby to the Riverside.

TEACH. (Fuckin' joint . . .)

DON. Yeah.

TEACH. (They harbor *assholes* in there . . .)

DON. Yeah. Come on, Teach, what do you want? Bob?

BOB. Yeah?

DON *(to* TEACH*)*. Come on, he's going anyway. *(To* BOB, *handing him a bill)* Get me a Boston, and go for the yogurt.

BOB. What kind?

DON. You know, plain, and, if they don't got it, uh, something else. And get something for yourself.

BOB. What?

DON. Whatever you want. But get something to eat, and whatever you want to drink, and get Teacher a coffee.

BOB. Boston, Teach?

TEACH. No.

BOB. What?

TEACH. Black.

BOB. Right.

DON. And something for yourself to eat. *(to* TEACH*)* He doesn't want to eat.

TEACH *(to* BOB*).* You got to eat (And this is what I'm saying at The Riverside.)

(Pause.)

BOB. (Black coffee.)

DON. And get something for yourself to eat. *(to* TEACH*)* What do you want to eat? An English muffin? *(to* BOB*)* Get Teach an English muffin.

TEACH. I don't want an English muffin.

DON. Get him an English muffin, and make sure they give you jelly.

TEACH. I don't want an English muffin.

DON. What do you want?

TEACH. I don't want anything.

BOB. Come on, Teach, eat something.

(Pause.)

DON. You'll feel better you eat something, Teach.

(Pause.)

TEACH *(to* BOB*).* Tell 'em to give you an order of bacon, real dry, real crisp.

BOB. Okay.

TEACH. And tell the broad if it's for me she'll give you more.

BOB. Okay.

DON. Anything else you want?

TEACH. No.

DON. A cantaloupe?

TEACH. I never eat cantaloupe.

DON. No?

TEACH. It gives me the runs.

DON. Yeah?

TEACH. And tell him he shouldn't say anything to Ruthie.

DON. He wouldn't.

TEACH. No? No, you're right. I'm sorry, Bob.

BOB. It's okay.

TEACH. I'm upset.

BOB. It's okay, Teach.

(Pause.)

TEACH. Thank you.

BOB. You're welcome.

*(*BOB *starts to exit.)*

DON. And the plain if they got it.

BOB. I will. *(exits)*

DON. He wouldn't say anything.

TEACH. What the fuck do *I* care . . .

(Pause.)

Cunt.

(Pause.)

There is not one loyal bone in that bitch's body.

DON. How'd you finally do last night?

TEACH. This has nothing to do with that.

DON. No, I know. I'm just saying . . . for *talk* . . .

TEACH. Last night? You were here, Don.

(Pause.)

How'd *you* do?

DON. Not well.

TEACH. Mmm.

DON. The only one won any money, Fletch and Ruthie.

TEACH *(pause).* Cunt had to win two hundred dollars.

DON. She's a good card player.

TEACH. She is *not* a good card player, Don. She is a mooch and she is a locksmith and she plays like a woman.

(Pause.)

Fletcher's a card player. I'll give him that. But *Ruthie* . . . I mean, *you* see how she fucking plays . . .

DON. Yeah.

TEACH. And always with that cunt on her shoulder.

DON. Grace?

TEACH. Yes.

DON. Grace is her partner.

TEACH. Then let her *be* her partner, then. (You see what I'm talking about?) Everyone, they're sitting at the table and then Grace is going to walk around . . . fetch an *ashtray* . . . go for *coffee* . . . *this* . . . and everybody's all they aren't going to hide their cards, and they're going to make a show how they don't hunch *over,* and like that. I don't give a shit. I say the broad's her fucking partner, and she walks in back of me I'm going to hide my hand.

DON. Yeah.

TEACH. And I say anybody doesn't's out of their mind.

(Pause.)

We're talking about money for chrissake, huh? We're talking about cards. Friendship is friendship, and a wonderful thing, and I am all for it. I have never said different, and you know me on this point. Okay. But let's just keep it *separate* huh, let's just keep the two apart, and maybe we can deal with each other like some human beings.

(Pause.)

This is all I'm saying, Don. I know you got a soft spot in your heart for Ruthie . . .

DON. . . . yeah?

TEACH. I know you like the broad and Grace and, Bob, I know he likes 'em too.

DON. (He likes 'em.)

TEACH. And I like 'em too. (I know, I know.) I'm not averse to this. I'm not averse to sitting down. (I know we *will* sit down.) These things happen, I'm not saying that they don't . . . and yeah, yeah, yeah, I know I lost a bundle at the game and blah blah blah.

(Pause.)

But all I ever ask (and I would say this to her face) is only she remembers who is who and not to go around with *her* or Gracie either with this attitude. "The Past is Past, and this is Now, and so Fuck You." You see?

DON. Yes.

(Long pause.)

TEACH. So what's new?

DON. Nothing.

TEACH. Same old shit, huh?

DON. Yup.

TEACH. You seen my hat?

DON. No. Did you leave it here?

TEACH. Yeah.

(Pause.)

DON. You ask them over at The Riv?

TEACH. I left it here.

(Pause.)

DON. Well, you left it here, it's here.

TEACH. You seen it?

DON. No.

(Pause.)

TEACH. Fletch been in?

DON. No.

TEACH. Prolly drop in one or so, huh?

DON. Yeah, You know. You never know with Fletcher.

TEACH. No.

DON. He might drop in the *morning* . . .

TEACH. Yeah.

DON. And then he might, he's gone for ten or fifteen days you never know he's gone.

TEACH. Yeah.

DON. Why?

TEACH. I want to talk to him.

DON *(pause)*. Ruth would know.

TEACH. You sure you didn't seen my hat?

DON. I didn't see it. No.

(Pause.)

Ruthie might know.

TEACH. (Vicious dyke.)

DON. Look in the john.

TEACH. It isn't in the john. I wouldn't leave it there.

DON. Do you got something up with Fletch?

TEACH. No. Just I have to talk to him.

DON. He'll probably show up.

TEACH. Oh yeah . . . *(pause, indicating objects on the counter)* What're *these*?

DON. Those?

TEACH. Yeah.

DON. They're from 1933.

TEACH. From the thing?

DON. Yeah.

(Pause.)

TEACH. Nice.

DON. They had a whole market in 'em. Just like anything. They license out the shit and everybody makes it.

TEACH. Yeah? (I knew that.)

DON. Just like now. They had *combs,* and *brushes* . . . you know, brushes with the thing on 'em . . .

TEACH. Yeah. I know. They had . . . uh . . . what? Clothing too, huh?

DON. I think. Sure. Everything. And there're guys they just collect the stuff.

TEACH. They got that much of it around?

DON. *Shit* yes. (It's not that long ago.) The thing, it ran two years, and they had (*I* don't know) all kinds of people every year they're buying everything that they can lay their hands on that they're going to take it back to Buffalo to give it, you know, to their aunt, and it mounts up.

TEACH. What does it go for?

DON. The compact?

TEACH. Yeah.

DON. Aah . . . (*You* want it?)

TEACH. No.

DON. Oh. I'm just asking. I mean, *you* want it . . .

TEACH. No. I mean somebody walks *in* here . . .

DON. Oh. Somebody walks *in* here . . . (This shit's fashionable . . .)

TEACH. (I don't doubt it.)

DON. . . . and they're gonna have to go like fifteen bucks.

TEACH. You're fulla shit.

DON. My word of honor.

TEACH. No shit.

DON. Everything like that.

TEACH. (A bunch of fucking thieves.)

DON. Yeah. Everything.

TEACH *(snorts)*. What a bunch of crap, huh?

DON. *Oh* yeah.

TEACH. Every goddamn thing.

DON. Yes.

TEACH. If I kept the stuff that I threw *out* . . .

DON. . . . . yes.

TEACH. I would be a wealthy man today. I would be cruising on some European yacht.

DON. Uh-huh.

TEACH. (Shit my father used to keep in his *desk* drawer.)

DON. (My father, too.)

TEACH. (The *basement* . . .)

DON. (Uh-huh.)

TEACH. (Fuckin' toys in the back*yard*, for chrissake . . .)

DON. (Don't even talk about it.)

TEACH. It's . . . I don't know.

(Pause.)

You want to play some gin?

DON. Maybe later.

TEACH. Okay.

(Pause.)

I dunno.

(Pause.)

Fucking *day* . . .

(Pause.)

Fucking *weather* . . .

(Pause.)

DON. You think it's going to rain?

TEACH. Yeah. I do. Later.

DON. Yeah?

TEACH. Well, *look* at it.

(BOB *appears, carrying a paper bag with coffee and foodstuffs in it.)*

Bobby, Bobby, Bobby, Bobby, Bobby.

BOB. Ruthie isn't mad at you.

TEACH. She isn't?

BOB. No.

TEACH. How do you know?

BOB. I found out.

TEACH. How?

BOB. I talked to her.

TEACH. You talked to her.

BOB. Yes.

TEACH. I asked you you weren't going to.

BOB. Well, she asked me.

TEACH. What?

BOB. That were you over here.

TEACH. What did you tell her?

BOB. You were here.

TEACH. Oh. *(He looks at* DON.*)*

DON. What did you say to her, Bob?

BOB. Just Teach was here.

DON. And is she coming over here?

BOB. I don't think so. (They had the plain.)

DON *(to* TEACH*).* So? (This is all right.) *(to* BOB*)* All right, Bob.

(He looks at TEACH*)*

TEACH. That's all right, Bob. *(to self)* (Everything's all right to someone . . .)

(DON *takes bag and distributes contents to appropriate recipients.)*

(To DON*)* You shouldn't eat that shit.

DON. Why?

TEACH. It's just I have a feeling about health foods.

DON. It's not health foods, Teach. It's only yogurt.

TEACH. That's not health foods?

DON. No. They've had it forever.

TEACH. Yogurt?

DON. Yeah. They used to joke about it on "My Little Margie." *(to* BOB*)* (Way before your time.)

TEACH. Yeah?

DON. Yeah.

TEACH. What the fuck. A little bit can't hurt you.

DON. It's *good* for you.

TEACH. Okay, okay. Each one his own opinion. *(pause, to* BOB*)* Was Fletcher over there?

BOB. No.

DON. Where's my coffee?

BOB. It's not there?

DON. No.

(Pause.)

BOB. I told 'em specially to put it in.

DON. Where is it?

BOB. They forgot it.

(Pause.)

I'll go back and get it.

DON. Would you mind?

BOB. No.

(Pause.)

DON. You gonna get it?

BOB. Yeah.

(Pause.)

DON. What, Bob?

BOB. Can I talk to you?

(Pause. DON *goes to* BOB*.)*

DON. What is it?

BOB. I saw him.

DON. Who?

BOB. The guy.

DON. You saw the guy?

BOB. Yes.

DON. That I'm talking about?

BOB. Yes.

DON. Just now?

BOB. Yeah. He's going somewhere.

DON. He is.

BOB. Yeah. He's puttin' a suitcase in the car.

DON. The guy, or both of 'em?

BOB. Just him.

DON. He got in the car he drove off??

BOB. He's coming down the stairs . . .

DON. Yeah.

BOB. And he's got the suitcase . . .

DON *nods.*

He gets in the car . . .

DON. Uh-huh . . .

BOB. He drives away.

DON. So where is she?

BOB. He's goin' to pick her up.

DON. What was he wearing?

BOB. Stuff. Traveling clothes.

DON. Okay.

(Pause.)

Now you're talking. You see what I mean?

BOB. Yeah.

DON. All right.

BOB. And he had a coat, too.

DON. Now you're talking.

BOB. Like a raincoat.

DON. Yeah.

(Pause.)

Good.

(Pause.)

BOB. Yeah, he's gone.

DON. Bob, go get me that coffee, do you mind?

BOB. No.

DON. What did you get yourself to eat?

BOB. I didn't get anything.

DON. Well, get me my coffee, and get yourself something to eat, okay?

BOB. Okay. (Good.) *(Exits.)*

(Pause.)

DON. How's your bacon?

TEACH. Aaaahh, they always fuck it up.

DON. Yeah.

TEACH. This time they fucked it up too burnt.

DON. Mmmm.

TEACH. You got to be breathing on their neck.

DON. Mmmm.

TEACH. Like a lot of things.

DON. Uh-huh.

TEACH. *Any* business . . .

DON. Yeah.

TEACH. You want it run right, *be* there.

DON. Yeah.

TEACH. Just like you.

DON. What?

TEACH. Like the shop.

DON. Well, no one's going to run it, I'm not here

(Pause.)

TEACH. No.

(Pause.)

You have to be here.

DON. Yeah.

TEACH. It's a one-man show.

DON. Uh-huh.

(Pause.)

TEACH. So what is this thing with the kid?

(Pause.)

I mean, is it anything, uh . . .

DON. It's nothing . . . *you* know . . .

TEACH. Yeah.

(Pause.)

It's *what* . . . ?

DON. You know, it's just some *guy* we spotted.

TEACH. Yeah. Some *guy.*

DON. Yeah.

TEACH. (Some guy . . .)

DON. Yeah.

(Pause.)

What time is it?

TEACH. Noon.

DON. (Noon.) (Fuck.)

TEACH. What?

(Pause.)

DON. You parked outside?

TEACH. Yeah.

DON. Are you okay on the meter?

TEACH. Yeah. The broad came by already.

(Pause.)

DON. Good.

(Pause.)

TEACH. Oh, yeah, she came by.

DON. Good.

TEACH. You want to tell me what this thing is?

DON *(pause).* The thing?

TEACH. Yeah.

(Pause.)

What is it?

DON. Nothing.

TEACH. No? What is it, jewelry?

DON. No. It's nothing.

TEACH. Oh.

DON. You know?

TEACH. Yeah.

(Pause.)

Yeah. No. I don't know

(Pause.)

Who am I, a *police*man . . . I'm making conversation, huh?

DON. Yeah.

TEACH. Huh?

(Pause.)

'Cause you know I'm just asking for talk.

DON. Yeah. I know. Yeah, okay.

TEACH. And I can live without this.

DON *(reaches for phone).* Yeah. I know.

Hold on. I'll tell you.

TEACH. Tell me if you *want* to. Don.

DON. I want to, Teach.

TEACH. Yeah?

DON. Yeah.

(Pause.)

TEACH. Well, I'd fucking *hope* so. Am I wrong?

DON. No. No. You're right.

TEACH. I *hope* so.

DON. No, hold on; I gotta make this call.

TEACH. Well, all right. So what is it, jewelry?

DON. No.

TEACH. What?

DON. Coins.

TEACH. (Coins.)

DON. Yeah. Hold on, I gotta make this call.

(DON hunts for a card, dials telephone.)

(Into phone) Hello? This is Donny Dubrow. We were talking the other day. Lookit, sir, if I could get ahold of some of that stuff you were interested in, would you be interested in some of it?

(Pause.)

Those *things* . . . *Old,* yeah.

(Pause.)

Various pieces of various types.

(Pause.)

Tonight. Sometime late. Are they *what* . . . !!?? Yes, but I don't see what kind of a question is that (at the prices we're talking about . . .)

(Pause.)

No, hey, no, I understand *you* . . .

(Pause.)

Sometime late.

(Pause.)

One hundred percent.

(Pause.)

I feel the same. All right. Good-bye. *(hangs up)* Fucking asshole.

TEACH. Guys like that, I like to fuck their wives.

DON. I don't blame you.

TEACH. Fucking *jerk* . . .

DON. (I swear to God . . .)

TEACH. That guy's a collector?

DON. Who?

TEACH. The phone guy.

DON. Yeah.

TEACH. And the other guy?

DON. We spotted?

TEACH. Yeah.

DON. Him, too.

TEACH. So you hit him for his coins.

DON. Yeah.

TEACH. —And you got a buyer in the phone guy.

DON. (Asshole.)

TEACH. The thing is you're not sitting with the shit.

DON. No.

TEACH. The guy's an asshole or he's not, what do you care? It's business.

(Pause.)

DON. You're right.

TEACH. The guy with the suitcase, he's the mark.

DON. Yeah.

TEACH. How'd you find him?

DON. In here.

TEACH. Came in here, huh?

DON. Yeah.

TEACH. (No shit.)

(Pause.)

DON. He comes in here one day, like a week ago.

TEACH. For what?

DON. Just browsing. So he's looking in the case, he comes up and with this *buffalo-head* nickel . . .

TEACH. Yeah . . .

DON. From nineteen-something. (I don't know. I didn't even know it's there . . .)

TEACH. Uh-huh . . .

DON. . . . and he goes, "How much would that be?"

TEACH. Uh-huh . . .

DON. So I'm about to go, "Two bits," jerk that I am, but something tells me to shut up, so I go, "You tell me."

TEACH. Always good business.

DON. *Oh* yeah.

TEACH. How wrong can you go?

DON. That's what I mean, so then he thinks a minute, and he tells me he'll just shop a bit.

TEACH. Uh-huh . . . *(stares out of window)*

DON. And so he's *shopping* . . . What?

TEACH. Some cops.

DON. Where?

TEACH. At the corner.

DON. What are they doing?

TEACH. Cruising.

(Pause.)

DON. They turn the corner?

TEACH *(waits).* Yeah.

(Pause.)

DON. . . . And so he's shopping. And he's picking up a beat-up *mirror* . . . an old *kid's* toy . . . a *shaving* mug . . .

TEACH. . . . right . . .

DON. Maybe five, six things, comes to eight bucks. I get 'em and I put 'em in a box and then he tells me he'll go fifty dollars for the nickel.

TEACH. No.

DON. Yeah. So I tell him (get this), "Not a chance."

TEACH. (Took balls.)

DON. (Well, what-the-fuck . . .)

TEACH. (No, I mean it.)

DON. (I took a chance.)

TEACH. (You're goddamn right.)

(Pause.)

DON *(shrugs).* So I say, "Not a chance," he tells me eighty is his highest offer.

TEACH. (I knew it.)

DON. Wait. So I go, "Ninety-five."

TEACH. Uh-huh.

DON. We settle down on ninety, *takes* the nickel, leaves the box of shit.

TEACH. He pay for it?

DON. The box of shit?

TEACH. Yeah.

DON. No.

(Pause.)

TEACH. And so what was the nickel?

DON. *I* don't know . . . some rarity.

TEACH. Ninety dollars for a nickel.

DON. Are you kidding, Teach? I bet it's worth five *times* that.

TEACH. Yeah, huh?

DON. Are you kidding me, the guy is going to come in here, he plunks down ninety bucks like nothing. *Shit* yeah.

(Pause.)

TEACH. Well, what the fuck, it didn't cost you anything.

DON. That's not the point. The next day back he comes and he goes through the whole bit again. He looks at *this,* he looks at *that,* it's a nice *day* . . .

TEACH. Yeah . . .

DON. And he tells me he's the guy was in here yesterday and bought the buffalo off me and do I maybe have some other articles of interest.

TEACH. Yeah.

DON. And so I tell him, "Not offhand." He says that could I get in touch with him, I get some in, so I say "sure," he leaves his card. I'm s'posed to call him anything crops up.

TEACH. Uh-huh.

DON. He comes in here like I'm his fucking doorman.

TEACH. Mmmm.

DON. He takes me off my coin and will I call him if I find another one.

TEACH. Yeah.

DON. Doing me this favor by just coming in my shop.

TEACH. Yeah.

(Pause.)

Some people never change.

DON. Like he has done me this big favor by just coming in my shop.

TEACH. Uh-huh. (You're going to get him now.)

DON. (You know I am.) So Bob, we kept a lookout on his place, and that's the shot.

TEACH. And who's the chick?

DON. What chick?

TEACH. You're asking Bob about.

DON. Oh yeah. The guy, he's married. I mean (*I* don't know.) We *think* he's married. They got two names on the bell. . . . Anyway, he's living with this chick, *you* know . . .

TEACH. What the hell.

DON. . . . and you should see this chick.

TEACH. Yeah, huh?

DON. She is a knockout. I mean, she is *real* nice-lookin', Teach.

TEACH. (Fuck *him* . . .)

DON. The other day, last Friday like a week ago, Bob runs in, lugs me out to look at 'em, they're going out on bicycles. The ass on this broad, un-be-fucking-lievable in these bicycling shorts sticking up in the air with these short handlebars.

TEACH. (Fuckin' *fruits* . . .)

(Pause.)

DON. So that's it. We keep an eye on 'em. They both work. . . . (Yesterday he rode his bicycle to work.)

TEACH. He didn't.

DON. Yeah.

TEACH *(snorts).* (With the three-piece suit, huh?)

DON. I didn't see 'em. Bobby saw 'em.

(Pause.)

And that's the shot. Earl gets me in touch the phone guy, he's this coin collector, and that's it.

TEACH. It fell in your lap.

DON. Yeah.

TEACH. You're going in tonight.

DON. It looks that way.

TEACH. And who's going in?

(Pause.)

DON. Bobby.

(Pause.)

He's a good kid, Teach.

TEACH. He's a great kid, Don. You know how I feel about the kid.

(Pause.)

I *like* him.

DON. He's doing good.

TEACH. I can see that.

(Pause.)

But I gotta say something here.

DON. What?

TEACH. Only this—and I don't think I'm *getting* at anything—

DON. What?

TEACH *(pause)*. Don't send the kid in.

DON. I shouldn't send Bobby in?

TEACH. No. (Now, just wait a second.) Let's siddown on this. What are we saying here? Loyalty.

(Pause.)

You know how I am on this. This is great. This is admirable.

DON. What?

TEACH. This loyalty. This is swell. It turns my heart the things that you do for the kid.

DON. What do I do for him, Walt?

TEACH. Things. Things, you know what I mean.

DON. No. I don't do anything for him.

TEACH. In your mind you don't, but the things, I'm saying, that you actually go *do* for him. This is fantastic. All I mean, a guy can be too loyal, Don. Don't be dense on this. What are we saying here? Business. I mean, the guy's got you're taking his high-speed blender and a Magnavox, you send the kid in. You're talking about a real *job* . . . they don't come in right away and know they been *had* . . . You're talking maybe a safe, certainly a good lock or two, and you need a guy's looking for valuable shit, he's not going to mess with the stainless steel silverware, huh, or some digital clock.

(Pause.)

We both know what we're saying here. We both know we're talking about some job needs more than the kid's gonna skin-pop go in there with a *crowbar* . . .

DON. I don't want you mentioning that.

TEACH. It slipped out.

DON. You know how I feel on that.

TEACH. Yes. And I'm sorry, Don. I admire that. All that I'm saying, don't confuse business with pleasure.

DON. But I don't want that talk, only, Teach.

(Pause.)

You understand?

TEACH. I more than understand, and I apologize.

(Pause.)

I'm sorry.

DON. That's the only thing.

TEACH. All right. But I tell you. I'm glad I said it.

DON. Why?

TEACH. 'Cause it's best for these things to be out in the open.

DON. But I don't want it in the open.

TEACH. Which is why I apologized.

(Pause.)

DON. You know the fucking kid's clean. He's trying hard, he's working hard, and you leave him alone.

TEACH. Oh yeah, he's trying *real* hard.

DON. And he's no dummy, Teach.

TEACH. Far from it. All I'm saying, the job is beyond him. Where's the shame in this? This is not jacks, we get up to go home we give everything back. Huh? You want this fucked up?

(Pause.)

All that I'm saying, there's the least *chance* something might fuck up, you'd get the law down, you would take the shot, and couldn't find the coins *whatever:* if you see the least chance, you cannot afford to take that chance! Don? *I* want to go in there and gut this motherfucker. Don? Where is the shame in this? You take care of him, *fine.* (Now this is loyalty.) But Bobby's got his own best interests, too. And you cannot afford (and simply as a *business* proposition) you cannot afford to take the chance.

(Pause. TEACH picks up a strange object.) What is this?

DON. That?

TEACH. Yes.

DON. It's a thing that they stick in dead pigs keep their legs apart all the blood runs out.

(TEACH nods. Pause.)

TEACH. Mmmm.

(Pause.)

DON. I set it up with him.

TEACH. "You set it up with him." . . . You set it up and then you told him.

(Long pause.)

DON. I gave Earl ten percent.

TEACH. Yeah? for what?

DON. The connection.

TEACH. So ten off the top: forty-five, forty-five.

(Pause.)

DON. And Bobby?

TEACH. A hundred. A hundred fifty . . . we hit big . . .*whatever*.

DON. And *you* what?

TEACH. The *shot.* I go, I go *in* . . . I bring

the stuff *back* (or wherever . . .)
(Pause.)
DON. And what do I do?
TEACH. You mind the fort.
(Pause.)
DON. Here?
TEACH. Well, yeah . . . this is the fort.
(Pause.)
DON. (You know, this is real classical money we're talking about.)
TEACH. I know it. You think I'm going to fuck with Chump Change?
(Pause.)
So tell me.
DON. Well, hold on a second. I mean, we're still talking.
TEACH. I'm sorry. I thought we were done talking.
DON. No.
TEACH. Well, then, let's talk some more. You want to bargain? You want to mess with the points?
DON. No. I just want to think for a second.
TEACH. Well, you think, but here's a helpful hint. Fifty percent of some money is better than ninety percent of some broken *toaster* that you're gonna have, you send the kid in. (Which is providing he don't trip the alarm in the *first* place . . .) Don? You don't even know what the *thing* is on this. Where he lives. They got alarms? What *kind* of alarms? What kind of *this* . . . ? And what if (God forbid) the *guy* walks in? Somebody's nervous, whacks him with a table lamp—you wanna get touchy—and you can take your ninety dollars from the nickel shove it up your ass—the good it did you—and you wanna know *why*? (And I'm not *saying* anything . . .) because you didn't take the time to go first-class.
(BOB re-enters with a bag.)
Hi, Bob.
BOB. Hi, Teach.
(Pause.)
DON. You get yourself something to eat?
BOB. I got a piece of pie and a Pepsi.
(BOB and DON extract foodstuffs and eat.)
DON. Did they charge you again for the coffee?
BOB. For your coffee?
DON. Yes.
BOB. They charged me this time. I don't know if they charged me last time, Donny.
DON. It's okay.
(Pause.)
TEACH *(to BOB)*. How is it out there?
BOB. It's okay.

TEACH. Is it going to rain?
BOB. Today?
TEACH. Yeah.
BOB. I don't know.
(Pause.)
TEACH. Well, what do you think?
BOB. It might.
TEACH. You think so, huh?
DON. Teach . . .
TEACH. What? I'm not saying anything.
BOB. What?
TEACH. I don't think I'm saying anything here.
(Pause.)
BOB. It *might* rain.
(Pause.)
I think *later*.
TEACH. How's your pie?
BOB. Real good.
TEACH *(holds up the dead-pig leg-spreader)*. You know what this is?
(Pause.)
BOB. Yeah.
TEACH. What is it?
BOB. I know what it is.
TEACH. What?
BOB. I know.
(Pause.)
TEACH. Huh?
BOB. What?
TEACH. Things are what they are.
DON. Teach . . .
TEACH. What?
DON. We'll do this later.
BOB. I got to ask you something.
TEACH. Sure, that makes a difference.
DON. We'll just do it later.
TEACH. Sure.
BOB. Uh, Don?
DON. What?
(Pause.)
BOB. I got to talk to you.
DON. Yeah? What?
BOB. I'm wondering on the thing that maybe I could have a little bit up front.
(Pause.)
DON. Do you *need* it?
BOB. I don't *need* it . . .
DON. How much?
BOB. I was thinking that maybe you might let me have like fifty or something.
(Pause.)
To sort of *have* . . .
TEACH. You got any cuff links?
DON. Look in the case. *(to BOB)* What do you need it for?

BOB. Nothing.

DON. Bob . . .

BOB. You can trust me.

DON. It's not a question of that. It's not a question I go around trusting you, Bob . . .

BOB. What's the question?

TEACH. Procedure.

DON. Hold on, Teach.

BOB. I got him all spotted.

(Pause.)

TEACH. Who?

BOB. Some guy.

TEACH. Yeah?

BOB. Yeah.

TEACH. Where's he live?

BOB. Around.

TEACH. Where? Near here?

BOB. No.

TEACH. No?

BOB. He lives like on Lake Shore Drive.

TEACH. He does.

BOB. Yeah.

TEACH *(pause)*. What have you got, a job cased?

BOB. I just went for coffee.

TEACH. But you didn't get the coffee.

(Pause.)

Now, did you?

BOB. No.

TEACH. Why?

DON. Hold on, Teach. Bob . . .

BOB. What?

DON. You know what?

BOB. No.

DON. I was thinking, you know, we might hold off on this thing.

(Pause.)

BOB. You wanna hold *off* on it?

DON. I was thinking that we might.

BOB. Oh.

DON. And, on the money, I'll give you . . . forty, you owe me twenty, and, for now, keep twenty for spotting the guy.

(Pause.)

Okay?

BOB. Yeah.

(Pause.)

You don't want me to do the job?

DON. That's what I *told* you. What am I telling you?

BOB. I'm not going to do it.

DON. Now *now*. We aren't going to do it now.

BOB. We'll do it later on?

DON *(shrugs)*. But I'm giving you twenty just for spotting the guy.

BOB. I need fifty, Donny.

DON. Well, I'm giving you forty.

BOB. You said you were giving me twenty.

DON. No, Bob, I did not. I said I was giving you forty, of *which* you were going to owe me twenty.

(Pause.)

And you go *keep* twenty.

BOB. I got to give back twenty.

DON. That's the deal.

BOB. When?

DON. Soon. When you got it.

(Pause.)

BOB. If I don't *get* it soon?

DON. Well, what do you call "soon"?

BOB. I don't know.

DON. Could you get it in a . . . day, or a couple of days or so?

BOB. Maybe. I don't *think* so. Could you let me have fifty?

DON. And you'll give me back thirty?

BOB. I could just give back the twenty.

DON. That's not the deal.

BOB. We could *make* it the deal.

(Pause.)

Donny? We could *make* it the deal. Huh?

DON. Bob, lookit. Here it is: I give you fifty, next week you pay me back twenty-five.

(Pause.)

You get to keep twenty-five, you pay me back twenty-five.

BOB. And what about the thing?

DON. Forget about it.

BOB. You tell me when you want me to do it.

DON. I don't know *that* I want you to do it. At this point.

(Pause.)

You know what I mean?

(Pause.)

BOB. No.

DON. I mean, I'm *giving* you twenty-five, and I'm saying forget the thing.

BOB. Forget it for me.

DON. Yes.

BOB. Oh.

(Pause.)

Okay. Okay.

DON. You see what I'm talking about?

BOB. Yes.

DON. Like it never happened.

BOB. I know.

DON. So you see what I'm saying.

BOB. Yes.

(Pause.)

I'm gonna go.

(Pause.)

I'll see you later. *(Pause. He looks at* DON.*)*

DON. Oh. *(Reaches in pocket and hands bills to* BOB. *To* TEACH*)* You got two fives?

TEACH. No.

DON *(to* BOB*)*. I got to give you . . . thirty, you owe me back thirty.

BOB. You said you were giving me fifty.

DON. I'm sorry, I'm sorry, Bob, you're absolutely right. *(He gives* BOB *remainder of money.)*

(Pause.)

BOB. Thank you.

(Pause.)

I'll see you later, huh, Teach?

TEACH. I'll see you later, Bobby.

BOB. I'll see you, Donny.

DON. I'll see you later, Bob.

BOB. I'll come back later.

DON. Okay.

*(*BOB *starts to exit.)*

TEACH. *See* you.

(Pause. BOB *is gone.)*

You're only doing the right thing by him, Don.

(Pause.)

Believe me.

(Pause.)

It's best for everybody.

(Pause.)

What's done is done.

(Pause.)

So let's get started. On the thing. Tell me everything.

DON. Like what?

TEACH. ˙. . . the *guy* . . . where does he live . . .

DON. Around the corner.

TEACH. Okay, and he's gone for the weekend.

DON. We don't know.

TEACH. Of course we know. Bob saw him coming out the door. The kid's not going to lie to you.

DON. Well,, Bob just saw him coming *out* . . .

TEACH. He had a suitcase, Don, he wasn't going to the A&P . . . He's going for the weekend . . .

(Pause.)

Don, (Can you cooperate?) Can we get started? Do you want to tell me something about coins?

(Pause.)

DON. What about 'em?

TEACH. A crash course. What to look for. What to take. What to *not* take (. . . this they can trace) (that isn't *worth* nothing . . .)

(Pause.)

What looks like what but it's more *valuable* . . . *so* on . . .

DON. First off, I want that nickel back.

TEACH. Donny . . .

DON. No, I know, it's only a fuckin' nickel . . . I mean big deal, huh? But what I'm saying is I only want it back.

TEACH. You're going to get it back. I'm going in there for his coins, what am I going to take 'em all except your nickel? Wake up. Don, let's plan this out. The *spirit* of the thing?

(Pause.)

Let's not be loose on this. People are *loose,* people pay the price . . .

DON. You're right.

TEACH. (And I like you like a brother, Don.) So let's wake up on this.

(Pause.)

All right? A man, he walks in here, well-dressed . . . (With a briefcase?)

DON. (No.)

TEACH. All right . . . comes into a junkshop looking for coins.

(Pause.)

He spots a valuable nickel hidden in a pile of shit. He farts around, he picks up this, he farts around, he picks up that.

DON. (He wants the nickel.)

TEACH. No shit. He goes to check out, he goes ninety on the nick.

DON. (He would of gone five times that.)

TEACH. (Look, don't kick yourself.) All right, we got a guy knows coins. Where does he keep his coin collection?

DON. Hidden.

TEACH. The man hides his coin collection, we're probably looking the guy has a *study* . . . I mean, he's not the kind of guy to keep it in the *basement* . . .

DON. No.

TEACH. So we're looking for a study.

DON. (A den.)

TEACH. And we're looking, for, he hasn't got a *safe* . . .

DON. Yeah . . . ?

TEACH. . . . he's probably going to keep 'em . . . where?

(Pause.)

DON. I don't know. His desk drawer.

TEACH. (You open the middle, the rest of 'em pop out?)

DON. (Yeah.)

TEACH. (Maybe.) Which brings up a point.

DON. What?

TEACH. As we're moving the stuff tonight,

we can go in like Gangbusters, huh? We don't care we wreck the joint up. So what else? We *take* it, or leave it?

DON. . . . well . . .

TEACH. I'm not talking *cash,* all I mean, what other stuff do we take . . . for our *trouble* . . .

(Pause.)

DON. I don't know.

TEACH. It's hard to make up rules about this stuff.

DON. (You'll be in there under lots of pressure.)

TEACH. (Not so much.)

DON. (Come on, a little, anyway.)

TEACH. (That's only natural.)

DON. (Yeah.)

TEACH. (It would be unnatural I wasn't tense. A guy who isn't tense. I don't want him on my side.)

DON. (No.)

TEACH. (You know *why*?)

DON. (Yeah.)

TEACH. (Okay, then.) It's good to talk this stuff out.

DON. Yeah.

TEACH. You *have* to talk it out. Bad feelings, misunderstandings happen on a job. You can't get away from 'em, you have to deal with 'em. You want to quiz me on some coins? You want to show some coins to me? *List* prices . . . the blue book . . . ?

DON. You want to see the book?

TEACH. Sure.

DON *(hands large coin-book to* TEACH*).* I just picked it up last week.

TEACH. Uh-hum.

DON. All the values aren't *current* . . .

TEACH. Uh-huh . . .

DON. *Silver* . . .

TEACH *(looking at book).* Uh-huh . . .

DON. What's *rarity* . . .

TEACH. Well, that's got to be fairly steady, huh?

DON. I'm saying against what *isn't.*

TEACH. Oh.

DON. But the book gives you a general idea.

TEACH. You've been looking at it?

DON. Yeah.

TEACH. You got to have a feeling for your subject.

DON. The book can give you that.

TEACH. This is what I'm *saying* to you. One thing. Makes all the difference in the world.

DON. What?

TEACH. Knowing what the fuck you're talking about. And it's so rare, Don. So rare. What do you think a 1929 S Lincoln-head penny with the wheat on the back is worth?

(DON starts to speak.)

Ah! Ah! Ah! Ah! Ah! We got to know what *condition* we're talking about.

DON *(pause).* Okay. What condition?

TEACH. *Any* of 'em. You tell me.

DON. Well, pick one.

TEACH. Okay, I'm going to pick an easy one. Excellent condition 1929 S.

DON. It's worth . . . *about* thirty-six dollars.

TEACH. No.

DON. (More?)

TEACH. Well, guess.

DON. Just tell me is it more or less.

TEACH. What do you think?

DON. More.

TEACH. No.

DON. Okay, it's worth, I gotta say . . . eighteen-sixty.

TEACH. No.

DON. Then I give up.

TEACH. Twenty fucking cents.

DON. You're fulla shit.

TEACH. My mother's grave.

DON. Give me that fucking book. *(business)* Go beat that.

TEACH. This is what I'm saying, Don, you got to know what you're talking about.

DON. You wanna take the book?

TEACH. Naaa, *fuck* the book. What am I going to do, leaf through the book for hours on end? The important thing is to have the *idea* . . .

DON. Yeah.

TEACH. What was the other one?

DON. What other one?

TEACH. He stole off you.

DON. What do you mean what was it?

TEACH. The *date,* so on.

DON. How the fuck do *I* know?

TEACH *(pause).* When you looked it up.

DON. How are you getting in the house?

TEACH. The house?

DON. Yeah.

TEACH. Aah, you go in through a *window* they left open, something.

DON. Yeah.

TEACH. There's always something.

DON. Yeah. What else, if not the window.

TEACH. How the fuck do *I* know?

(Pause.)

If not the window, something else.

DON. What?

TEACH. We'll see when we get there.

DON. Okay, all I'm asking, what it *might* be.

TEACH. Hey, you didn't warn us we were going to have a quiz . . .

DON. It's just a question.

TEACH. I know it.

(Pause.)

DON. What is the answer?

TEACH. We're seeing when we get there.

DON. Oh. You can't answer me, Teach?

TEACH. You have your job. I have my job, Don. I am not here to smother you in theory. Think about it.

DON. I am thinking about it. I'd like you to answer my question.

TEACH. Don't push me, Don. Don't front off with me here. I am not other people.

DON. And just what does that mean?

TEACH. Just that nobody's perfect.

DON. They aren't.

TEACH. No.

(Pause.)

DON. I'm going to have Fletch come with us.

TEACH. Fletch.

DON. Yes.

TEACH. You're having him *come* with us.

DON. Yes.

TEACH. Now you're kidding me.

DON. No.

TEACH. No? Then why do you say this?

DON. With Fletch.

TEACH. Yes.

DON. I want some depth.

TEACH. You want depth on the team.

DON. Yes, I do.

TEACH. So you bring in Fletch.

DON. Yes.

TEACH. 'Cause I don't play your games with you.

DON. We just might need him.

TEACH. We won't.

DON. We might, Teach.

TEACH. We don't need him, Don. We do not need this guy.

(DON picks up phone.)

What? Are you *calling* him?

(DON nods.)

DON. It's busy. *(Hangs up.)*

TEACH. He's probably talking on the phone.

DON. Yeah. He probably is.

TEACH. We don't need this guy, Don. We don't need him. I see your point here, I do. So you're thinking I'm out there alone, and you're worried I'll rattle, so you ask me how I go in. I understand. I see this, I do. I could

go in the second floor, climb up a drainpipe. I could *this* . . .

(DON dials phone again.)

He's talking, he's talking, for chrissake, give him a minute, huh?

(DON hangs up phone.)

I am hurt, Don.

DON. I'm sorry, Teach.

TEACH. I'm not hurt for me.

DON. Who are you hurt for?

TEACH. Think about it.

DON. We can use somebody watch our rear.

TEACH. You keep your numbers down, you don't *have* a rear. You know what has rears? Armies.

DON. I'm just saying, something goes *wrong* . . .

TEACH. Wrong, wrong, you make your own right and wrong. Hey Biiig fucking deal. The shot is yours, no one's disputing that. We're talking business, let's *talk* business: you think it's good business call Fletch in? To help us.

DON. Yes.

TEACH. Well then okay.

(Pause.)

Are you sure?

DON. Yeah.

TEACH. All right, if you're *sure* . . .

DON. I'm sure, Teach.

TEACH. Then, all right, then. That's all I worry about.

(Pause.)

And you're probably right, we could use three of us on the job.

DON. Yeah.

TEACH. Somebody watch for the cops . . . work out a *signal* . . .

DON. Yeah.

TEACH. Safety in numbers.

DON. Yeah.

TEACH. Three-men jobs.

DON. Yeah.

TEACH. You, me, Fletcher.

DON. Yeah.

TEACH. A division of labor.

(Pause.)

(Security. Muscle. Intelligence.) Huh?

DON. Yeah.

TEACH. This means, what, a traditional split. Am I right? We get ten off the top goes to Earl, and the rest, three-way split. Huh? That's what we got? Huh?

DON. Yeah.

TEACH. Well, that's what's right.

(Pause.)

All right. Lay the shot out for me.

DON. For tonight?

TEACH. Yes.

DON. Okay.

(Pause.)

I stay here on the phone . . .

TEACH. . . . yeah . . .

DON. . . . for Fletcher . . .

TEACH. Yeah.

DON. We meet, ten-thirty, 'leven, back here.

TEACH. (Back here, the three . . .)

DON. Yeah. And go in.

(Pause.)

DON. Huh?

TEACH. Yeah. Where?

DON. Around the corner.

TEACH. Yeah.

(Pause.)

Are you mad at me?

DON. No.

TEACH. Do you want to play gin?

DON. Naaa.

TEACH. Then I guess I'll go home, take a nap, and rest up. Come back here tonight and we'll take off this fucking fruit's coins.

DON. Right.

TEACH. I feel like I'm trying to stay *up* to death . . .

DON. You ain't been to sleep since the game?

TEACH. *Shit* no (then that dyke cocksucker . . .)

DON. So go take a nap. You trying to kill yourself?

TEACH. You're right, and you do what you think is right, Don.

DON. I got to, Teach.

TEACH. You got to trust your instincts, right or wrong.

DON. I got to.

TEACH. I know it. I know you do.

(Pause.)

Anybody wants to get in touch with me, I'm over the hotel.

DON. Okay.

TEACH. I'm not the *hotel,* I stepped out for coffee, I'll be back one minute.

DON. Okay.

TEACH. And I'll see you around eleven.

DON. O'*clock.*

TEACH. *Here.*

DON. Right.

TEACH. And don't worry about anything.

DON. I won't.

TEACH. I don't want to hear you're worrying about a goddamned thing.

DON. You won't, Teach.

TEACH. You're sure you want Fletch coming with us?

DON. Yes.

TEACH. All right, then, so long as you're sure.

DON. I'm sure, Teach.

TEACH. Then I'm going to see you tonight.

DON. Goddamn right you are.

TEACH. I am seeing you later.

DON. I know.

TEACH. Good-bye.

DON. Good-bye.

TEACH. I want to make one thing plain before I go, Don. I am not mad at you.

DON. I know.

TEACH. All right, then.

DON. You have a good nap.

TEACH. I will.

(TEACH exits.)

DON. Fuckin' *business* . . .

(Lights dim to black.)

ACT TWO

Don's Resale Shop. 11:15 that evening. The shop is darkened. DON is alone. He is holding the telephone to his ear.

———

DON. Great. Great great great great great.

(Pause.)

(Cocksucking fuckhead . . .)

(Pause.)

This is greatness.

(DON hangs up phone. BOB appears in the door to the shop.)

What are you doing here?

BOB. I *came* here.

DON. For what?

BOB. I got to talk to you.

DON. Why?

BOB. Business.

DON. Yeah?

BOB. I need some money.

DON. What for?

BOB. Nothing. I can pay for it.

DON. For what?

BOB. This guy. I found a coin.

DON. A coin?

BOB. A buffalo-head.

DON. Nickel?

BOB. Yeah. You want it?

(Pause.)

DON. What are you doing here, Bob?

BOB. I need money.

(DON picks up phone and dials. He lets it

ring as he talks to BOB.)
You want it?
DON. What?
BOB. My buffalo.
DON. Lemme look at it.
(Pause.)
I got to look at it to know do I want it.
BOB. You don't know if you want it?
DON. I probably *want* it . . . what I'm saying, if it's *worth* anything.
BOB. It's a buffalo, it's worth something.
DON. The question is but what. It's just like everything else, Bob. Like every other fucking thing. *(Pause. He hands up phone.)* Were you at The Riv?
BOB. Before.
DON. Is Fletch over there?
BOB. No.
DON. Teach?
BOB. No. Ruth and Gracie was there for a minute.
DON. What the fuck does that mean?
(Pause.)
BOB. Nothing.
(Pause.)
Only they were there.
(Pause.)
I didn't *mean* anything . . . my nickel . . . I can tell you what it is.
(Pause.)
I can tell you what it is.
DON. What? What *date* it is? That don't mean shit.
BOB. No?
DON. Come on, Bobby? What's important in a coin . . .
BOB. . . . . yeah?
DON. What *condition* it's in . . .
BOB. (Great.)
DON. . . . . if you can (I don't know . . .) count the hair on the Indian, something. You got to look it up.
BOB. In the book?
DON. Yes.
BOB. Okay. And then you know.
DON. Well, no. What I'm saying, the book is like you use it like an *indicator* (I mean, right off with *silver* prices . . . so on . . .) *(He hangs up phone.)* Shit.
BOB. What?
DON. What do you want for the coin?
BOB. What it's worth only.
DON. Okay, we'll look it up.
BOB. But you still don't know.
DON. But you got an idea, Bob. You got an idea you can *deviate* from.

(Pause.)
BOB. The other guy went ninety bucks.
DON. He was a fuckin' sucker, Bob.
(Pause.)
Am I a sucker? (Bob, I'm busy here. You see?)
BOB. Some coins are worth that.
DON. Oddities, Bob. Freak oddities of nature. What are we talking about here? The silver? The silver's maybe three times face. You want fifteen cents for it?
BOB. No.
DON. So, okay. So what do you want for it?
BOB. What it's worth.
DON. Let me see it.
BOB. Why?
DON. To look in the goddamn . . . Forget it. Forget it. *Don't* let me see it.
BOB. But the book don't *mean* shit.
DON. The book gives us *ideas,* Bob. The book gives us a basis for *comparison.* Look, we're human beings. We can *talk,* we can negotiate, we can *this* . . . you need money? What do you need?
(Pause.)
BOB. I *came* here . . .
(Pause.)
DON. What do you need, Bob?
(Pause.)
BOB. How come you're in here so late?
DON. We're gonna play cards.
BOB. Who?
DON. Teach and me and Fletcher.
(TEACH enters the store.)
What time is it?
TEACH. Fuck is *he* doing here?
DON. What fucking time is it?
TEACH. Where's Fletcher?
(Pause.)
Where's Fletcher?
BOB. Hi, Teach.
TEACH *(to DON).* What is he doing here?
BOB. I came in.
DON. Do you know what time it is?
TEACH. What? I'm late?
DON. Damn right you're late.
TEACH. I'm fucked up since my watch broke.
DON. Your watch broke?
TEACH. I just told you that.
DON. When did your watch break?
TEACH. The fuck do *I* know?
DON. Well, you look at it. You want to know your watch broke, all you got to do is look at it.
(Pause.)
TEACH. I don't have it.
DON. Why not?

TEACH. I took it off when it broke. (What do you *want* here?)

DON. You're going around without a watch.

TEACH. Yes, I am, Donny. What am I, you're my *keeper* all a sudden?

DON. I'm paying you to do a thing, Teach, I expect to know where you are when.

TEACH. Donny. You aren't paying me to do a thing. We are doing something together. I know we are. My watch broke, that is my concern. The *thing* is your and my concern. And the concern of Fletcher. You want to find a reason we should jump all over each other all of a sudden like we work in a *bloodbank,* fine. But it's not good business.

(Pause.)

And so who knows what time it is offhand? Jerks on the radio? The phone broad?

(Pause.)

Now, I understand nerves.

DON. There's no fuckin' nerves involved in this. Teach.

TEACH. No, huh?

DON. No.

TEACH. Well, great. That's great, then. So what are we talking about? A little lateness? Some excusable fucking lateness? And a couple of guys they're understandably a bit excited?

(Pause.)

DON. I don't like it.

TEACH. Then *don't* like it, then. Let's do this. Let's everybody get a writ. I got a case. You got a case. Bobby—I don't know what the fuck *he's* doing here . . .

DON. Leave him alone.

TEACH. Now I'm picking on him.

DON. Leave him alone.

TEACH. What's he doing here?

DON. He came in.

BOB. I found a nickel.

TEACH. Hey, that's fantastic.

BOB. You want to see it?

TEACH. Yes, please let me see it.

BOB *(hands nickel, wrapped in cloth, to* TEACH*).* I like 'em because of the art on it.

TEACH. Uh-huh.

BOB. Because it *looks* like something.

TEACH *(to* DON*).* Is this worth anything?

BOB. We don't know yet.

TEACH. Oh.

BOB. We're going to look it up.

TEACH. Oh, what? Tonight?

BOB. I think so.

DON *(hangs up phone).* Fuck.

TEACH. So where is he?

DON. How the fuck do I know?

TEACH. He said he'd be here?

DON. Yes, he did, Teach.

BOB. Fletcher?

TEACH. So where is he, then? And what's *he* doing here?

DON. Leave him alone. He'll leave.

TEACH. He's going to leave, huh?

DON. Yes.

TEACH. You're sure it isn't like the bowling league. Fletch doesn't show up, we just suit up Bobby, give him a shot, and *he* goes in?

(Pause.)

Aaah, fuck. I'm sorry. I spoke in anger. I'm sorry, I'm sorry. (Everybody can make mistakes around here but me.) I'm sorry, Bob, I'm very sorry.

BOB. That's okay, Teach.

TEACH. All I meant to say, we'd give you a fuckin' suit, like in football . . .

(Pause.)

and you'd (You know, like, whatever . . .) and *you'd* go in. *(Pause. To* DON*)* So what do you want me to do? Dress up and lick him all over? I said I was sorry, what's going on here. Huh? In the *first* place. I come in, I'm *late* . . . *he's* here . . .

(Pause.)

DON. Bobby, I'll see you tomorrow, okay? *(He picks phone up and dials.)*

BOB. I need some money.

TEACH *(digging in pockets).* What do you need?

BOB. I want to sell the *buffalo* nickel.

TEACH. I'll buy it myself.

BOB. We don't know what it's worth.

TEACH. What do you want for it?

BOB. Fifty dollars.

TEACH. You're outta your fuckin' mind.

(Pause.)

Look. Here's a fin. Get lost. Okay?

(Pause.)

BOB. It's worth more than that.

TEACH. How the fuck do you know that?

BOB. I think it is.

(Pause.)

TEACH. Okay. You keep the fin like a loan. You *keep* the fuckin' nickel, and we'll call it a loan. Now go on. *(He hands nickel back to* BOB*.)*

DON *(hangs up phone).* Fuck.

BOB. I need more.

TEACH *(to* DON*).* Give the kid a couple of bucks.

DON. What?

TEACH. Give him some money.

DON. What for?

TEACH. The nickel.

(Pause.)

BOB. We can look in the book tomorrow.

DON *(to TEACH)*. You bought the nickel?

TEACH. Don't worry about it. Give him some money. Get him out of here.

DON. How much?

TEACH. What? I don't care . . .

DON *(to BOB)*. How much . . . *(to TEACH)* What the fuck am I giving him money for?

TEACH. Just give it to him.

DON. What? Ten? *(Pause. Digs in pocket, hands bill to BOB)* How is that, Bob? *(Pause. Hands additional bill to BOB)* Okay?

BOB. We'll look it up.

DON. Okay. Huh? We'll see you tomorrow.

BOB. And we'll look it up.

DON. Yes.

BOB *(to TEACH)*. You should talk to Ruthie.

TEACH. Oh, I should, huh?

BOB. Yes.

TEACH. Why?

BOB. Because.

(Pause.)

TEACH. I'll see you tomorrow, Bobby.

BOB. Good-bye, Teach.

TEACH. Good-bye.

DON. Good-bye, Bob.

BOB. Good-bye.

(Pause. BOB exits.)

DON. Fuckin' *kid* . . .

TEACH. So where is Fletcher?

DON. Don't worry. He'll be here.

TEACH. The question is but when. Maybe his watch broke.

DON. Maybe it just did, Teach. Maybe his actual watch broke.

TEACH. And maybe mine didn't, you're saying? You wanna bet? You wanna place a little fucking wager on it? How much money you got in your pockets? I bet you all the money in your pockets against all the money in my pockets, I walk out that door right now, I come back with a broken watch.

(Pause.)

DON. Calm down.

TEACH. I am calm. I'm just upset.

DON. I know.

TEACH. So where is he when I'm here?

DON. Don't worry about it.

TEACH. So who's going to worry about it then?

DON. (Shit.)

TEACH. This should go to prove you something.

DON. It doesn't prove anything. The guy's just late.

TEACH. Oh. And I wasn't?

DON. You were late, too.

TEACH. You're fuckin' A I was, and I got bawled out for it.

DON. He's late for a reason.

TEACH. I don't accept it.

DON. That's your privilege.

TEACH. And what was Bob doing here?

DON. He told you. He wanted to sell me the nickel.

TEACH. That's why he came here?

DON. Yes.

TEACH. To sell you the buffalo?

DON. Yes.

TEACH. Where did he get it?

DON. I think from some guy.

TEACH. Who?

(Pause.)

DON. I don't know.

(Pause.)

TEACH. Where's Fletcher?

DON. I don't know. He'll show up. *(picks up phone and dials)*

TEACH. He'll show up.

DON. Yes.

TEACH. He's not here now.

DON. No.

TEACH. You scout the guy's house?

DON. The guy? No.

TEACH. Well, let's do that, then. (He's not home. Hang up.)

DON *(hangs up phone)*. You wanna scout his house.

TEACH. Yeah.

DON. Why? Bob already saw him when he went off with the suitcase.

TEACH. Just to be sure, huh?

DON. Yeah. Okay.

TEACH. You bet. Now we call him up.

DON. We call the guy up.

TEACH. Yeah.

(Pause.)

DON. Good idea. *(He picks up phone. Hunts guy's number. Dials. To himself)* We can do this.

TEACH. This is planning. . . . This is preparation. If he answers . . .

(DON shhhhs TEACH.)

I'm telling you what to do if he answers.

DON. What?

TEACH. Hang up. *(DON starts to hang up phone.)* No. Don't hang up. Hang up now. Hang up *now*!

(DON hangs up phone.)

Now look: If he *answers* . . .

DON. . . . yeah?

TEACH. *Don't* arouse his fucking suspicions.

DON. All right.

TEACH. And the odds are he's not there, so when he answers just say you're calling for a wrong fucking *number*, something. Be simple.

(Pause.)

Give me the phone.

(DON hands TEACH the phone.)

Gimme the card.

(DON hands TEACH card.)

This is his number? 221-7834?

DON. Yeah.

TEACH *(snorts)*. All right. I dial. I'm calling for somebody named June, and we go interchange on number.

(Pause.)

We're gonna say like, "Is this 221-7834?"

DON. . . . yeah?

TEACH. And they go, "No." (I mean " -7843." It is -7834.)

So we go, very simply, "Is this 221-7843?" and they go "No." and right away the guy is home, we still haven't blown the shot.

DON. Okay.

(TEACH picks up the phone and dials.)

TEACH *(into phone)*. Hi. Yeah. I'm calling . . . uh . . . is June there?

(Pause.)

Well, is this 221-7843?

(Pause.)

It is? Well, look I must of got the number wrong. I'm sorry.

(He hangs up phone.)

(This is bizarre.) Read me that number.

DON. 221-7834.

TEACH. Right. *(Dials phone. Listens.)* Nobody home. See, this is careful operation . . . *(Pause. Hangs up.)* You wanna try it?

DON. No.

TEACH. I don't mind that you're careful, Don. This doesn't piss me off. What gets me mad, when you get loose.

DON. What do you mean?

TEACH. You know what I mean.

DON. No. I don't.

TEACH. Yes you do. I come in here. The kid's here.

DON. He doesn't know anything.

TEACH. He doesn't.

DON. No.

TEACH. What was he here for, then?

DON. Sell me the buffalo.

TEACH. Sell it tonight.

DON. Yeah.

TEACH. A valuable nickel.

DON. We don't know.

(Pause.)

TEACH. Where is Fletch?

DON. I don't know. *(Picks up phone and dials.)*

TEACH. He's not home. He's not home. Don. He's out.

DON *(into phone)*. Hello?

TEACH. He's in?

DON. This is Donny Dubrow.

TEACH. The Riv?

DON. I'm looking for Fletcher.

(Pause.)

Okay. Thank you. *(He hangs up.)*

TEACH. Cocksucker should be horsewhipped with a horsewhip.

DON. He'll show up.

TEACH. Fucking Riverside, too. (Thirty-seven cents for take-out coffee . . .)

DON. Yeah. *(picks up phone)*

TEACH. A lot of nerve you come in there for sixteen years. This is not free enterprise.

DON. No.

TEACH. You know what is free enterprise?

DON. No. What?

TEACH. The freedom . . .

DON. . . . yeah?

TEACH. Of the *Individual* . . .

DON. . . . yeah?

TEACH. To Embark on Any Fucking Course that he sees fit.

DON. Uh-huh . . .

TEACH. In order to secure his honest chance to make a profit. Am I so out of line on this?

DON. No.

TEACH. Does this make me a Commie?

DON. No.

TEACH. The country's *founded* on this, Don. You know this.

DON. Did you get a chance to take a nap?

TEACH. Nap nap nap nap nap. Big deal.

DON *(pause)*. Yeah.

TEACH. Without this we're just savage shitheads in the wilderness.

DON. Yeah.

TEACH. Sitting around some vicious campfire. That's why *Ruthie* burns me up.

DON. Yeah.

TEACH. (Nowhere dyke . . .) And take those fuckers in the concentration camps. You think they went in there by *choice*?

DON. No.

TEACH. They were *dragged* in there, Don . . .

DON. . . . yeah.

TEACH. Kicking and screaming. *Gimme* that

fucking phone.

(TEACH *grabs phone. Listens. Hangs up.*)
He's not home. I say *fuck* the cocksucker.

DON. He'll show up.

TEACH. You believe that?

DON. Yes.

TEACH. Then you are full of shit.

DON. Don't tell me that, Teach. Don't tell me I'm full of shit.

TEACH. I'm sorry. You want me to hold your hand? This is how you keep score. I mean, *we're* all here . . .

DON. Just, I don't want that talk.

TEACH. Don . . . I talk straight to you 'cause I respect you. It's kickass or kissass, Don, and I'd be lying if I told you any different.

DON. And what makes you such an authority on life all of a sudden?

TEACH. My life, Jim. And the way I've lived it.

(*Pause.*)

DON. Now what does that mean, Teach?

TEACH. What does that mean?

DON. Yes.

TEACH. What does that *mean*?

DON. Yes.

TEACH. Nothing. Not a thing. All that I'm telling you, the shot is yours. It's one night only. Too many guys know. All I'm saying. Take your shot.

DON. Who knows?

TEACH. You and me.

DON. Yeah.

TEACH. Bob and Fletcher. Earl, the phone guy, Grace and Ruthie, maybe.

DON. Grace and Ruth don't know.

TEACH. Who *knows* they know or not, all that I'm telling you, it's not always so clear what's going on. Like Fletcher and the pig iron, that time.

DON. What was the shot on that?

TEACH. He stole some pig iron off Ruth.

DON. (I *heard* that . . .)

TEACH. That's a fact. A fact stands by itself. And we must face the facts and act on them. You better wake up, Don, right now, or things are going to fall around your *head,* and you are going to turn around to find he's took the joint off by himself.

DON. He would not do that.

TEACH. He would. He is an animal.

DON. He don't have the address.

TEACH. He doesn't know it.

DON. No.

TEACH. Now, that is wise. Then let us go and take what's ours.

DON. We have a deal with the man.

TEACH. With Fletcher.

DON. Yes.

TEACH. We had a deal with Bobby.

DON. What does that mean?

TEACH. Nothing.

DON. It don't.

TEACH. No.

DON. What did you mean by that?

TEACH. I didn't mean a thing.

DON. You didn't.

TEACH. No.

DON. You're full of shit, Teach.

TEACH. I am.

DON. Yes.

TEACH. Because I got the balls to face some facts?

(*Pause.*)

You scare me sometimes, Don.

DON. Oh, yeah?

TEACH. Yes. I don't want to go around with you here, things go down, we'll settle when we're done. We have a job to do here. Huh? Forget it. Let's go, come on.

DON. We're waiting for him.

TEACH. Fletcher.

DON. Yes.

TEACH. Why?

DON. Many reasons.

TEACH. Tell me one. You give me one good reason, why we're sitting here, and I'll sit down and never say a word. One reason. One. Go on. I'm listening.

DON. He knows how to get in.

(*Pause.*)

TEACH. Good night, Don. (*He starts to go for door.*)

DON. Where are you going?

TEACH. Home.

DON. You're going home.

TEACH. Yes.

DON. Why?

TEACH. You're fucking with me. It's all right.

DON. Hold on. You tell me how I'm fucking with you.

TEACH. Come on, Don.

DON. You asked me the one reason.

TEACH. You make yourself ridiculous.

DON. Yeah?

TEACH. Yeah.

DON. Then answer it.

TEACH. What is the question?

DON. Fletch knows how to get in.

TEACH. "Get in." That's your reason?

DON. Yes.

(*Pause.*)

TEACH. What the fuck they live in Fort Knox? ("Get in.") *(snorts)* You break in a *window,* worse comes to worse you kick the fucking back door in. (What do you think this is, the Middle Ages?)

DON. What about he's got a safe?

TEACH. Biiiig fucking deal.

DON. How is that?

TEACH. You want to know about a safe?

DON. Yes.

TEACH. What you do, a *safe* . . . you find the combination.

DON. Where he wrote it down.

TEACH. Yes.

DON. What if he didn't write it down?

TEACH. He wrote it down. He's *gotta* write it down. What happens he forgets it?

DON. What happens he doesn't forget it?

TEACH. He's gotta forget it, Don. Human nature. The point being, even he doesn't forget it, *why* does he not forget it?

DON. Why?

TEACH. 'Cause he's got it *wrote down.*

(Pause.)

That's why he *writes* it down.

(Pause.)

Huh? Not because he's some fucking turkey can't even remember the combination to his own *safe* . . . but only in the event that (God forbid) he somehow *forgets* it . . . he's got it wrote down.

(Pause.) This is common sense.

(Pause.)

What's the good keep the stuff in the safe, every time he wants to get at it he's got to write away to the manufacturer?

DON. Where does he write it?

TEACH. What difference? *Here* . . . We go in, I find the combination fifteen minutes, tops.

(Pause.)

There are only just so many places it could be. Man is a creature of habits. Man does not change his habits overnight. This is not like him. (And if he does, he has a very good reason.) Look, Don: You want to remember something (you write it down). Where do you put it?

(Pause.)

DON. In my wallet.

(Pause.)

TEACH. *Exactly!*

(Pause.)

Okay?

DON. What if he didn't write it down?

TEACH. He wrote it down.

DON. I know he did. But just, I'm saying,

from *another* instance. Some made-up guy from my imagination.

TEACH. You're saying in the instance of some guy . . .

DON. (Some *other* guy . . .)

TEACH. . . . he didn't write it down?

(Pause.)

DON. Yes.

TEACH. Well, this is another thing.

(Pause.)

You see what I'm saying?

DON. Yeah.

TEACH. It's another matter. The guy, he's got the shit in the safe, he didn't write it *down* . . .

(Pause.)

Don . . . ?

DON. Yes?

TEACH. How do you know he didn't write it down?

DON. (I'm, you know, making it up.)

(Pause.)

TEACH. Well, then, this is not based on *fact.*

(Pause.)

You see what I'm saying? I can sit here and tell you *this,* I can tell you *that,* I can tell you any fucking thing you care to mention, but what is the point? You aren't telling me he didn't write it down. All that you're saying, you can't *find* it. Which is only natural, as you don't know where to look. All I'm asking for a little trust here.

DON. I don't know.

TEACH. Then you know what? Fuck you. (All day long. Grace and Ruthie Christ) What am I standing here convincing you? What am I doing demeaning myself standing here pleading with you to protect your best interests? I can't believe this, Don. Somebody told me I'd do this for you . . . (For *anybody*) I'd call him a liar. (I'm coming in here to efface myself.) I am not Fletch, Don, no, and you should thank God and fall *down* I'm not. (You're coming in here all the time that "He's so good at cards . . . ") The man is a cheat. Don. He *cheats* at cards—Fletcher, the guy that you're waiting for.

DON. He cheats.

TEACH. Fucking A right, he does.

DON. Where do you get this?

(Pause.)

You're full of shit, Walt. You're saying Fletch cheats at cards.

(Pause.)

You've seen him. You've *seen* him he cheats.

(Pause.)

You're *telling* me this?

TEACH. (The whatchamacallit is always the last to know.)

DON. Come on, Walt, I mean, forget with the job and all.

TEACH. You live in a world of your own, Don.

DON. Fletch cheats at cards.

TEACH. Yes.

DON. I don't believe you.

TEACH. Ah. You can't take the truth.

DON. No. I am sorry. I play in this fucking game.

TEACH. And you don't know what goes on.

DON. I leave Fletcher alone in my *store*. . . . He could take me off any time, day and night. What are you telling me, Walt? This is nothing but poison, I don't want to hear it. *(pause)*

TEACH. And that is what you say.

DON. Yes. It is.

(Pause.)

TEACH. Think back, Donny. Last night. On one hand. You lost two hundred bucks.

(Pause.)

You got the straight, you stand pat. I go down before the draw.

DON. Yeah.

TEACH. He's got what?

DON. A flush.

TEACH. That is correct. How many did he take?

DON. What?

TEACH. How many did he take?

(Pause.)

DON. One?

TEACH. No. Two, Don. He took two.

(Pause.)

DON. Yeah. He took two on that hand.

TEACH. He takes two on your standing pat, you kicked him thirty bucks? He draws two, comes out with a *flush*?

DON *(pause)*. Yeah?

TEACH. And spills his fucking Fresca?

DON. Yeah?

TEACH. Oh. You remember that?

DON *(pause)*. Yeah.

TEACH. And we look down.

DON. Yeah.

TEACH. When we look back, he has come up with a king-high flush.

(Pause.)

After he has drawed two.

(Pause.)

You're better than that, Don. You *knew* you had him beat, and you were right.

(Pause.)

DON. It could happen.

TEACH. Donny . . .

DON. Yeah?

TEACH. He laid down five red cards. A heart flush to the king.

(Pause.)

DON. Yeah?

TEACH. I swear to God as I am standing here that when I threw my hand in when you raised me out, that I folded the king of hearts.

(Pause.)

DON. You never called him out.

TEACH. No.

DON. How come?

TEACH. (He don't got the address the guy?)

DON. I told you he didn't.

(Pause.)

He's cheating, you couldn't say anything?

TEACH. It's not my responsibility, to cause bloodshed. I am not your keeper. You want to face facts, okay.

DON. I can't believe this, Teach.

TEACH. (Friendship is marvelous.)

DON. You couldn't say a word?

TEACH. I tell you now.

DON. He was cheating, you couldn't say anything?

TEACH. Don. Don, I see you're put out, you find out this guy is a cheat. . . .

DON. According to you.

TEACH. According to me, yes. I am the person it's usually according *to* when I'm talking. Have you noticed this? And I'm not crazed about it you're coming out I would lie to you on this. *Fuck* this. On anything. Wake up, Jim. I'm not the cheat. I know you're not mad at me, who are you mad at? Who fucked you up here, Don? Who's not here? Who?

DON. Ruth knows he cheats?

TEACH. Who is the bitch in league with?

DON. Him?

TEACH *(pause)*. You know how much money they took from this game?

DON. Yeah?

TEACH. Well, I could be wrong.

DON. Don't fuck with me here, Teach.

TEACH. I don't fuck with my friends, Don. I don't fuck with my business associates. I am a businessman, I am here to do business, I am here to face facts. (Will you open your eyes . . . ?) The kid comes in here, he has got a certain coin, it's like the one *you* used to have . . . the guy you brought in doesn't show, we don't know where *he* is.

(Pause.)

Something comes down, some guy gets his

house took off.

(Pause.)

Fletcher, he's not showing up. All right. Let's say I don't know why. Let's say *you* don't know why. But I know that we're both better off. We are better off, Don.

(Pause.)

What time is it?

DON. It's midnight.

(Pause.)

TEACH. I'm going out there now. I'll need the address.

(TEACH takes out revolver and begins to load it.)

DON. What's that?

TEACH. What?

DON. That.

TEACH. This "gun"?

DON. Yes.

TEACH. What does it look like?

DON. A gun.

TEACH. It *is* a gun.

DON *(rises and crosses to center)*. I don't like it.

TEACH. Don't look at it.

DON. I'm serious.

TEACH. So am I.

DON. We don't need a gun, Teach.

TEACH. I pray that we don't, Don.

DON. We don't, tell me why we need a gun.

TEACH. It's not a question do we *need* it . . . *Need* . . . Only that it makes me comfortable, okay? It helps me to relax. So, God forbid, something inevitable occurs and the choice is (And I'm saying "God forbid") it's either him or us.

DON. Who?

TEACH. The guy. I'm saying God forbid the *guy* (or somebody) comes in, he's got a knife . . . a cleaver from one of those magnetic boards . . . ?

DON. Yeah?

TEACH. . . . with the two *strips* . . . ?

DON. Yeah?

TEACH. And *whack,* and somebody is bleeding to death. This is all. Merely as a deterrent.

(Pause.)

All the preparation in the world does not mean *shit,* the path of some crazed lunatic sees you as an invasion of his personal domain. Guys go nuts, Don, *you* know this. Public *officials* . . . *Ax* murderers . . . all I'm saying, look out for your own.

DON. I don't like the gun.

TEACH. It's a personal thing, Don. A personal thing of mine. A silly personal thing. I just like to have it along. Is this so unreasonable?

DON. I don't want it.

TEACH. I'm not going without it.

DON. Why do you want it?

TEACH. Protection of me and my partner. Protection, deterrence. (We're only going around the fucking *corner* for chrissake . . .)

DON. I don't want it with.

TEACH. I can't step down on this, Don. I got to have it with. The light of things as they are.

DON. Why?

TEACH. Because of the way *things* are. *(He looks out window.)* Hold on a second.

DON. Fletcher?

TEACH. Cops.

DON. What are they doing?

TEACH. Cruising.

(Pause.)

DON. They turn the corner?

TEACH. Hold on.

(Pause.)

Yes. They have the right idea. Armed to the hilt. Sticks, Mace, knives . . . who knows *what* the fuck they got. They have the right idea. Social customs break down, next thing *everybody's* lying in the gutter.

(A knocking is heard at the door.)

(Get down.) (Douse the light.)

DON. (Lemme see who it is . . .)

TEACH. Don't answer it.

BOB *(from behind door)*. Donny?

TEACH. (Great.)

DON. (It's Bobby.)

TEACH. (I know.)

BOB. Donny?

(Pause.)

TEACH. (Don't let him in.)

DON. (He knows we're in here.)

TEACH. (So let him go away, then.)

BOB. I got to talk to you.

(DON looks at TEACH.)

DON *(to BOB)*. What is it?

BOB. I can't come in?

TEACH. (Get him outta here.)

(Pause.)

DON. Bob . . .

BOB. Yeah?

DON. We're busy here.

BOB. I got to talk to you.

(DON looks at TEACH.)

TEACH. (Is he alone?)

DON. (I think.)

TEACH *(pause)*. (Hold on.)

(TEACH opens door and pulls BOB in.)

What, Bob? What do you want? You know we

got work to do here, we don't need you to do it, so what are you doing here and what do you want?

BOB. To talk to Don.

TEACH. Well, Don does not want to talk to you.

BOB. I *got* to talk to him.

TEACH. You do not have to do anything, Bob. You do not have to do anything that we tell you that you have to do.

BOB. I got to talk to Donny. *(to* DON*)* Can I talk to you? *(Pause. To* DON*.)* I came here . . .

DON. . . . yeah?

BOB. . . . The Riverside?

DON. Yeah?

BOB. Grace and Ruthie . . . he's in the hospital. Fletch.

(Pause.)

I only wanted to, like, *come* here. I know you guys are only playing *cards* this . . . now. I didn't want to disturb you like up, but they just I found out he was in the hospital and I came over here to . . . tell you.

(Pause.)

TEACH. With what?

BOB. He got mugged.

TEACH. You're so full of shit.

BOB. I think some Mexicans.

*(*TEACH *snorts.)*

He did. He's in the hospital.

TEACH. You see this, Don?

DON. He's mugged?

BOB. Yeah, Grace, they just got back. They broke his jaw.

TEACH. They broke his jaw.

BOB. Yeah. Broke.

TEACH. And now he's in the hospital. Grace and Ruthie just got back. You thought that you'd come over.

BOB. Yeah.

TEACH. Well, how about this, Don? Here Fletch is in Masonic Hospital a needle in his arm, huh. How about this?

DON. How bad is he?

BOB. They broke his jaw.

DON. What else?

BOB. I don't know.

TEACH. Would you believe this if I told you this this afternoon?

DON. When did it happen, Bob?

BOB. Like before.

DON. Before, huh?

BOB. Yeah.

TEACH. How about this, Don?

BOB. We're going to see him tomorrow.

DON. When?

BOB. I don't know. In the morning.

DON. They got hours in the morning?

BOB. I guess so.

TEACH. Hey, thanks for coming here. You did real good in coming here.

BOB. Yeah?

TEACH *(to* DON*).* He did real good in coming here, huh, Donny? *(to* BOB*)* We really owe you something.

BOB. What for?

TEACH. Coming here.

BOB. What?

TEACH. Something.

BOB. Like what?

DON. He don't know. He's saying that he thinks we owe you something, but right now he can't think what it is.

BOB. Thanks, Teach.

TEACH. It's okay, Bob.

(Pause. BOB *starts to exit.)*

Stick around.

BOB. Okay. For a minute.

TEACH. What? You're busy?

BOB. I got, like, some things to do.

TEACH. Whaddaya got, a "date"?

BOB. No.

TEACH. What, then?

BOB. Business.

(Pause.)

DON. Where did they take him, Bob?

(Pause.)

BOB. Uh, Masonic.

DON. I don't think that they got hours start til after lunch.

BOB. Then we'll go then. I'm gonna go now.

TEACH. Hold on a second, Bob. I feel we should take care of you for coming here.

BOB. That's okay. I'll see you guys.

DON. Come here a minute, Bobby.

BOB. What, Donny?

DON. What's going on here?

BOB. Here?

DON. Yes.

(Pause.)

BOB. Nothing.

DON. I'm saying what's happening, Bob?

BOB. I don't know.

DON. Where did you get that nickel from?

BOB. What nickel?

DON. You know what nickel, Bob, the nickel I'm talking about.

BOB. I got it off a guy

DON. What guy?

BOB. I met downtown.

TEACH. What was he wearing?

BOB. Things.

(Pause.)

DON. How'd you get it off him, Bob?

BOB. We kinda talked.

(Pause.)

DON. You know what, you look funny, Bob.

BOB. I'm late.

DON. It's after midnight, Bob. What are you late for?

BOB. Nothing.

DON *(very sadly)*. Jesus. Are you fucking with me here?

BOB. No.

DON. (Bobby.)

BOB. I'm not fucking with you, Donny.

(Pause.)

DON. Where's Fletcher?

(Pause.)

BOB. Masonic.

(DON goes to telephone and dials information.)

DON *(into phone)*. For Masonic Hospital, please.

BOB. . . . I *think* . . .

DON *(to BOB)*. What?

BOB. He might not be Masonic.

DON *(to phone)*. Thank you. *(Hangs up phone. To BOB)* Now, *what?*

BOB. He might not *be* there . . .

DON. You said he was there.

BOB. Yeah, I just, like, I *said* it. I really don't remember what they said, Ruthie.

TEACH. (Ruthie.)

BOB. . . . so I just . . . *said* Masonic.

DON. Why?

BOB. I thought of it.

(Pause.)

DON. Uh-huh. *(to phone)* Yes. I'm looking for a guy was just admitted. Fletcher Post.

(Pause.)

Just a short time ago.

(Pause.)

Thank you. *(Pause. To BOB and TEACH)* She's lookins for it. *(to phone)* No?

BOB. (I told you . . .)

DON. You're sure?

(Pause.)

Thank you. *(Hangs up phone. To BOB)* He's not there.

BOB. I told you.

TEACH. (What did I tell you, Don?)

DON. Where is he?

BOB. Somewhere else.

DON. (This makes me nuts . . .) Bobby . . .

BOB. Yeah?

(Pause.)

They broke his jaw.

DON. Who?

BOB. Some spics. I don't know.

(TEACH snorts.)

They did.

DON. Who?

TEACH. Yeah.

DON. Who is this "they," Bob, that you're talking about?

TEACH. Bob. . . .

BOB. . . . yeah?

TEACH. Who are these people you're talking about?

BOB. They broke his jaw.

TEACH. They took it in them all of a sudden they broke his jaw.

BOB. They didn't care it was him.

TEACH. No?

BOB. No, Teach.

TEACH. So who is it takes him out by accident. Huh? Grace and Ruthie?

BOB. They wouldn't do that.

TEACH. I'm not saying they would.

BOB *(to DON)*. What is he saying, Donny?

TEACH. Bob, Bob, Bob . . . what am I saying . . .

(Pause.)

DON. Where's Fletch, Bobby?

BOB. Hospital.

TEACH. Aside from that.

BOB. All I know, that's the only place he is, Teach.

TEACH. Now, don't get smart with me, Bob, don't get smart with me, you young fuck, we've been sweating blood all day on this and I don't want your smart mouth on it (fuck around with Grace and Ruthie, and you come in here . . .), so all we want some answers. Do you understand?

(Pause.)

I told you: Do you understand this?

DON. You better answer him.

BOB. I understand.

TEACH. Then let's make *this* clear: Loyalty does not mean *shit* a situation like this; I don't know what you and them are up to, and I do not *care,* but only you come clean with us.

BOB. He might of been a different hospital.

TEACH. Which one?

BOB. *Any of* 'em.

DON. So why'd you say "Masonic"?

BOB. I just thought of it.

TEACH. Okay. Okay. . . . Bob?

BOB. . . . yes?

TEACH. I want for you to tell us here and now (and for your own protection) what is going *on,* what is set *up* . . . where *Fletcher* is . . . and everything you know.

DON *(sotto voce).* (I can't believe this.)

BOB. I don't know anything.

TEACH. You don't, huh?

BOB. No.

DON. Tell him what you know, Bob.

BOB. I don't know it, Donny. Grace and Ruthie . . .

(TEACH grabs a nearby object and hits BOB *viciously on the side of the head.)*

TEACH. Grace and Ruthie up your ass, you shithead; you don't fuck with us, *I'll* kick your fucking head in. (I don't give a shit . . .)

(Pause.)

You *twerp* . . .

(A pause near the end of which BOB *starts whimpering.)*

I don't give a shit. (Come in here with your fucking stories . . .)

(Pause.)

Imaginary people in the hospital . . .

*(*BOB *starts to cry.)*

That don't mean shit to me, you fruit.

BOB. Donny . . .

DON. You brought it on yourself.

TEACH. Sending us out there . . . who the fuck knows what . . .

BOB. He's in the hospital.

DON. Which hospital?

BOB. I don't know.

TEACH. Well, then, you better make one up, and quick.

DON. Bob . . .

TEACH. (Don't back down on this Don. Don't back down on me, here.)

DON. Bob . . .

BOB. . . . yeah?

DON. You got to see our point here.

BOB *(whimpering).* Yeah, I do.

DON. Now, we don't want to hit you.

TEACH. (No.)

BOB. I know you don't.

TEACH. No.

DON. But you come in here.

BOB. . . . yeah . . .

DON. . . . the only one who knows the score . . .

BOB. Yeah . . . (My ear is bleeding. It's coming out my ear.) Oh, fuck, I'm real scared.

DON. (Shit.)

BOB. I don't feel good.

TEACH. (Fuckin' kid poops out on us . . .)

BOB. Don . . .

TEACH. Now what are we going to do with this?

DON. You know, we didn't want to do this to you, Bob.

BOB. I know . . .

DON. We didn't want to do this.

(Phone rings.)

TEACH. (Great.)

DON *(to phone).* What? What the fuck do *you* want?

TEACH. (It's the guy?)

DON. (It's Ruthie.) *(To phone)* Oh yeah, we heard about that, Ruth.

TEACH. *(She's* got a lot of nerve . . .)

DON *(to phone).* From Bobby. Yeah. We'll *all* go.

(Pause.)

I thought he was at Masonic? Bobby. Well, okay, that's where we'll go then, Ruthie, we aren't going to go and see him at some hospital he isn't even *at* . . .

(Pause.)

Bobby's not here. I will. Okay. I will. Around eleven. Okay. *(He hangs up.)*

TEACH *(to* BOB). And you owe me twenty bucks.

DON *(dialing).* For Columbus Hospital, please.

TEACH. (Fuckin' medical costs . . .)

DON. Thank you.

TEACH *(singing softly to himself).* " . . . and I'm never ever sick at sea."

DON. Yes. For Fletcher Post, please, he was just admitted?

(Pause.)

No. I only want to know is he all right, and when we go to see him.

(Pause.)

Thank you.

TEACH. What?

DON. She's looking. *(to phone)* Yes? Yeah. Thank you very much. Yes. You've been very kind. *(He hangs up phone.)*

TEACH. What is he, *in* there?

DON. Yeah.

TEACH. And they won't let us talk to him?

DON. His jaw is broke.

BOB. I feel funny.

TEACH. Your *ear* hurts.

DON. Bob, it hurts. Bob?

TEACH. I never felt quite right on this.

DON. Go tilt your head the other way.

TEACH. I mean, we're fucked up here. We have not blown the shot, but we're fucked up.

DON. We are going to take you to the hospital.

TEACH. Yeah, yeah, we'll take you to the hospital, you'll get some *care,* this isn't a big deal.

DON. Bob, you fell downstairs, you hurt your ear.

TEACH. He understands?

DON. You understand? We're going to take you to the hospital, you fell downstairs.

TEACH *(at door)*. This fucking rain.

DON. You give 'em your right name, Bob, and you know what you can tell 'em. *(reaches in pocket, thrusts money at BOB)* You hold on to this, Bob. Anything you want inside the hospital.

BOB. I don't want to go to the hospital.

TEACH. You're going to the hospital, and that's the end of it.

BOB. I don't want to.

DON. You got to, Bob.

BOB. Why?

TEACH. You're fucked up, that's why.

BOB. I'm gonna do the job.

DON. We aren't going to do the job tonight, Bob.

TEACH. You got a hat or something keep my head dry?

DON. No.

BOB. I get to do the job.

TEACH. You shut up. You are going in the hospital.

DON. We aren't going to do the job tonight.

BOB. We do it sometime else.

DON. Yeah.

TEACH. He ain't going to do no job.

DON. Shut up.

TEACH. Just say he isn't going to do no job.

DON. It's done now.

TEACH. What?

DON. I'm saying, this is over.

TEACH. No, it's not, Don. It is not. He does no job.

DON. You leave the fucking kid alone.

TEACH. You want kids, you go have them. *I* am not your wife. *This* doesn't mean a thing to me. *I'm* in this. And it *isn't* over. This is for me, and this is my question:

(Pause.)

Where did you get that coin?

BOB. What?

TEACH. Where'd you get that fucking nickel, if it all comes out now.

(Pause.)

He comes in here, a fifty dollars for a nickel, where'd you get it?

BOB. Take me to the hospital.

(Pause.)

TEACH. Where did you get that nickel? (I want you to watch this.)

(Pause.)

BOB. I bought it.

TEACH. (Mother Fucking Junkies.)

DON. Shut up.

TEACH. What are you saying that you bought that coin?

BOB. Yeah.

TEACH. Where?

BOB. A coin store.

(Pause.)

TEACH. You bought it in a coin store.

BOB. Yeah.

(Pause.)

TEACH. Why?

DON. Go get your car.

TEACH. What did you pay for it?

(Pause.)

What did you pay for it?

BOB. Fifty dollars.

TEACH. You buy a coin for fifty dollars, you come back here.

(Pause.)

Why?

DON. Go get your fucking car.

TEACH. Why would you do a thing like that?

BOB. I don't know.

TEACH. Why would you go do a thing like that?

BOB. For Donny.

(Pause.)

TEACH. You people make my flesh crawl.

DON. Bob, we're going to take you out of here.

TEACH. I can not take this anymore.

DON. Can you walk?

BOB. No.

DON. Go and get your car.

TEACH. I am not your nigger. I am not your wife.

DON. I'm through with you today.

TEACH. You are.

DON. Yes.

TEACH. Why?

(Pause.)

DON. You have lamed this up real good.

TEACH. I did.

DON. Real good.

TEACH. I lamed it up.

BOB. He hit me.

DON. I know, Bob.

TEACH. Yes, I hit him. For his own good. For the good of all.

DON. Get out of here.

TEACH. "Get out of here"? And now you throw me out like *trash*? I'm doing this for *you*. What do I have to wreck this joint *apart*? He told you that he bought it in a *coin store*.

DON. I don't care.

TEACH. You don't care? (I cannot believe this.) You *believe* him?

DON. I don't *care.* I don't *care* anymore.

TEACH. You *fake.* You fucking *fake.* You fuck your friends. You *have* no friends. No *wonder* that you fuck this kid around.

DON. You shut your mouth.

TEACH. You seek your friends with *junkies.* You're a joke on this street, you and him.

DON. Get out.

TEACH. I do not go out, no.

BOB. (I eat shit.)

DON. You get out of here.

TEACH. I am not going anywhere. I have a piece of this.

DON. You have a piece of *shit,* you fucking lame. *(advancing on him)*

TEACH. (This from a man who has to buy his friends.)

DON. *I'll* tell you friends, *I'll* give you friends . . . *(still advancing)*

BOB. (Oh, fuck . . .)

DON. The stinking deals you come in here . . .

TEACH. You stay away from me . . .

DON. You stiff this one, you stiff that one . . . you come in here, you stick this poison in me . . . *(hitting him).*

TEACH. (Oh, Christ . . .)

BOB. (I eat shit.)

TEACH. (Oh, my God, I live with madmen.)

DON. All these years . . .

BOB. (A cause I missed him.)

DON *(advancing again).* All these fucking years . . .

TEACH. (You're going to hit me.)

BOB. Donny . . .

DON. You make life of garbage.

BOB. Donny!

TEACH. (Oh, my God.)

BOB. I missed him.

DON *(stopping).,* What?

BOB. I got to tell you what a fuck I am.

DON. What?

BOB. I missed him.

DON. Who?

BOB. The guy.

DON. What guy?

BOB. The guy this morning.

DON. What guy?

BOB. With the suitcase.

DON *(pause).* You missed him?

BOB. I eat shit.

DON. What are you saying that you lied to me?

BOB. I eat shit.

TEACH. What is he saying?

(Pause.)

DON. You're saying that you lied?

TEACH. What is he saying?

DON. You're saying you didn't see him with the suitcase?

TEACH. This kid is hysterical.

DON. You didn't see him?

TEACH. He's saying that he didn't see him?

DON. When he left this morning.

TEACH. He's saying that he lied?

BOB. I'm going to throw up.

TEACH. He's saying he didn't see the guy?

(Pause.)

When he came out. I was in here. *Then* you saw him. When he had the suitcase. *(pause)* Then.

(Pause.)

You saw him *then.*

(Pause. BOB *shakes his head.)*

My Whole Cocksucking Life.

(TEACH *picks up the dead-pig sticker and starts trashing the junkshop.)*

The Whole Entire World.

There Is No Law.

There Is No Right And Wrong.

The World Is Lies.

There Is No Friendship.

Every Fucking Thing.

(Pause.)

Every God-forsaken Thing.

DON. Calm down. Walt.

TEACH. We all live like the cavemen.

(During the speech, DON *tries to subdue* TEACH, *and finally does.)*

DON. (Siddown.)

(Pause.)

(TEACH *sits still.)*

TEACH. I went on a limb for you.

(Pause.)

You don't know what I go through. I put my dick on the chopping block.

(Pause.)

I hock my fucking watch . . .

(Pause.)

I go out there. I'm out there every day.

(Pause.)

There is nothing out there.

(Pause.)

I fuck myself.

(Pause.)

DON. Are you all right?

TEACH. What?

DON. Are you all right.

TEACH. How the fuck do I know?

DON. You tire me out, Walt.

TEACH. What?

DON. I need a rest.

TEACH. This fucking day.

DON *(pause)*. My shop's fucked up.

TEACH. I know.

DON. It's all fucked up.

(Pause.)

You fucked my shop up.

TEACH. Are you mad at me?

DON. What?

TEACH. Are you mad at me?

(Pause.)

DON. Come on.

TEACH. Are you?

DON. Go and get your car. Bob?

TEACH *(pause)*. Tell me are you mad at me.

DON. No.

TEACH. You aren't?

DON. No.

(Pause.)

TEACH. Good.

DON. You go and get your car.

TEACH. You got a hat?

DON. No.

TEACH. Do you have a piece of paper?

DON. Bob . . . ?

(TEACH walks to counter, takes a piece of newspaper, and starts making himself a paper hat.)

TEACH. He's all right?

DON. Bob . . . ?

TEACH. Is he all right?

DON. Bob . . . ?

BOB *(waking up)*. What?

DON. Come on. We're taking you the hospital.

(TEACH puts on paper hat and looks at self in window.)

TEACH. I look like a sissy.

DON. Go and get your car.

(Pause.)

TEACH. Can you get him to the door?

DON. Yeah.

(Pause.)

TEACH. I'm going to get my car.

DON. You gonna honk?

TEACH. Yeah.

DON. Good.

TEACH. I'll honk the horn.

(Pause.)

DON. Good.

(Pause.)

TEACH. This fucking day, huh?

DON. Yeah.

TEACH. I know it. You should clean this place up.

DON. Yeah.

(Pause.)

TEACH. Good. *(exits)*

DON. Bob.

BOB. What?

DON. Get up.

(Pause.)

Bob. I'm sorry.

BOB. What?

DON. I'm sorry.

BOB. I fucked up.

DON. No. You did real good.

BOB. No.

DON. Yeah. You did real good.

(Pause.)

BOB. Thank you.

DON. That's all right.

(Pause.)

BOB. I'm sorry, Donny.

DON. That's all right.

(Lights dim.)

Wings

Arthur Kopit

TO GEORGE KOPIT, MY FATHER 1913–1977

First presented at the Yale Repertory Theatre in New Haven, Connecticut, on March 3, 1978, with the following cast:

(in order of appearance)

EMILY STILSON	Constance Cummings
AMY	Marianne Owen
DOCTORS	Geoffrey Pierson
	Roy Steinberg
NURSES	Caris Corfman
	Carol Ostrow
BILLY	Richard Grusin
MR. BROWNSTEIN	Ira Bernstein
MRS. TIMMINS	Betty Pelzer

Directed by John Madden
Designed by Andrew Jackness
Costumes by Jeanne Button
Lighting by Tom Schraeder
Sound by Tom Voegeli
Music by Herb Pilhofer

"In the spring of 1976 . . . my father suffered a major stroke which rendered him incapable of speech. Furthermore, because of certain other complications all related to his aphasia, and all typical of stroke, it was impossible to know how much he comprehended . . . [He had] something which I felt possessed a kind of glow or flicker, rather like a lamp way off in the dark, something only barely perceptible. I took these faint flashes to be him signaling. . . . This thought was both heartening and frightful. To what extent was he still intact? To what extent was he aware of what had befallen him? *What was it like inside?*"

What it is like inside is the subject of the remarkable and poetic play *Wings*. Kopit takes us on a journey through the inner consciousness of the mind—an exhilarating, poignant, and at times, frightening experience. *Wings* is in the form of a loosely woven monologue that is structured into three sections: the stroke itself, the ensuing shock, the slow recovery back to the world of consciousness and the growing ability to deal with this consciousness. *Wings* investigates the nature of consciousness through its primary character, Emily Stilson, an elderly ex-aviatrix who struggles to regain her use of language after suffering a stroke. Kopit perceives this voyage as "Aeneas' descent into the netherworld with the hope of reemergence. . . ."

As a young woman, Emily Stilson was an aviatrix and a wing-walker. *Wings* is her odyssey back from paralysis to life as we view this experience through her own eyes. At first she is disoriented; later she is confounded by the process of speech, and finally she is led back into the world with a new awareness of life.

The portrayal of Emily Stilson, a virtual one-woman show, consists of disconnected fragments of memory, dislocated images and thoughts that whirl out of nowhere and disappear. Nothing is constant—time, space or objects. We hear the stroke through the character's own stream of consciousness. We hear an injured mind intact. We see a sequence of experiences inside out. We see, hear, feel and think as Emily does; it is an expressionistic ride through an impaired mind in which we, the audience, are endowed with a kind of double vision allowing us to see both what actually happens and what Emily perceives to be happening. Kopit describes his play as "a magnificent adventure into the mind and a revelation of the strength and mystery of the human spirit."

Seven months after Kopit's father's stroke, a Wisconsin-based radio drama series, *Earplay,* sponsored by the National Public Radio, commissioned Kopit to do a radio play. The structure of the play grew out of a seventy-year-old patient in Mr. Kopit's therapy group who had been an aviatrix and who had done stunt flying, and also out of Jacqueline Doolittle, a speech pathologist at the Burke Rehabilitation Center where Kopit's father was a patient. Doolittle had suffered a head injury in a car accident with resultant aphasia. "When Arthur began to work on the play, he used what I knew about both sides of the experience."

In the play, when Emily concludes in the hospital that she is really in a disguised farmhouse, "that was me," states Doolittle, "a nurse brought flowers into my room one day, and I resented those flowers dreadfully. I felt I had been captured and that my captors were . . . bringing me flowers to show we were in the country."

At the Burke Rehabilitation Center, Kopit researched his ideas for *Wings* for eight months, observing therapy sessions, talking with neurologists and psychologists, reading everything he could find on the subject. The problem was fitting all he learned into a format consistent with his heroine's personality. "I wrote on file cards in sections. Eliminating all the excess material was brutal. The most difficult part was selectivity. . . ." Kopit listened to tapes of stroke victims trying to regain the ability to talk, and he transcribed these to get a sense of their speech patterns. He also studied the days of stunt-walkers and "seat of the pants flying." He states: "The woman at Burke had been an adventurer, she had walked on the wings of her plane and had to keep her balance in the wind. The metaphor was almost too perfect and I would never have had the nerve to use it, but since it was given to me, almost as a gift, I couldn't reject it."

The *Earplay* presentation of *Wings* was produced and directed by John Madden who later directed the first staged production at the Yale Repertory Theatre on March 3, 1978. *Wings* then played at the New York Shakespeare Festival's Public Theatre and finally at Broadway's Lyceum Theatre for the 1978–79 season.

Arthur Lee Kopit was born on May 10, 1937, in New York City. Growing up in Lawrence, Long Island, a prosperous New York suburb, Kopit spent what he calls an "uneventful" childhood as the "victim of a healthy family life." He demonstrated an early interest in the theatre when he entertained his friends with improvised puppet shows. Radio was an important influence on his literary development. "It's a much more exciting medium than TV because it involves your creative faculties. When I was a wee lad, I used to look forward every day to those radio serials of Superman. I've always been involved with myths and heroism and I think it came from radio because there you had to imagine what the fabulous person would be like."

Upon graduation in 1965 from Lawrence High School where he was the sportswriter for the student newspaper, Kopit entered Harvard University on a scholarship to study electrical engineering. He soon lost interest in engineering (after taking some creative writing courses) and decided to become a playwright. In his sophomore year at Harvard, Kopit wrote *The Questioning of Nick*, which won a playwriting contest the following year. He then took a playwriting course with Robert Chapman and wrote *On the Runway of Life You Never Know What's Coming Off Next*, which was produced at Harvard. He next wrote *Don Juan in Texas* and *Tyndaradi*. During his senior year, he wrote and produced *Across the River and Into the Jungle, Sing to Me Through Open Windows* and *Aubade*.

Kopit graduated in 1959 and traveled to Europe on a Shaw Traveling Fellowship. It was during this time that he wrote *Oh Dad, Poor Dad, Mamma's Hung You in the Closet and I'm Feeling So Sad*. He sent it to Harvard and won the Adams House Playwriting Contest. In 1960, while Kopit was still traveling, Harvard's student production of *Oh Dad* was presented at the Agassiz Theatre in Cambridge. The play was published by Hill and Wang that same year. *Oh Dad . . .* won the Vernon Rice Award and the Outer Circle Award in 1962 and was produced again at the Phoenix Theatre in 1963. In 1965 *The Day the Whores Came Out to Play Tennis* was presented at the Players Theatre along with *Sing to Me Through Open Windows*. In 1969 *Indians* was produced in London at the Royal Shakespeare Company's Aldwych Theatre.

Arthur Kopit has also received grants from the Rockefeller and Guggenheim Foundations, the Center for the Humanities at Wesleyan University and CBS honors from the National Institute of Arts and Letters. He was the Playwright-in-Residence at Wesleyan University and has been an adjunct professor at the Yale School of Drama.

Arthur Kopit has also written *Chamber Music; Secrets of the Rich; Christmas with the Cannibals; How Sweet the Wine But How Dark the Color; To Dwell in a Palace of Strangers; Conquest of Everest; The Hero; Asylum, or What the Gentlemen Are up to Not to Mention the Ladies; Mhil'daiim; Gemini; Through a Labyrinth; Scientific Process* and the screenplay for *Indians*.

PRODUCTION NOTES

The play takes place over a period of two years; it should be performed without intermission. The stage as a void.

System of black scrim panels that can move silently and easily, creating the impression of featureless, labyrinthine corridors.

Some panels mirrored so they can fracture light, create the impression of endlessness, even airiness, multiply and confuse images, confound one's sense of space.

Sound both live and pre-recorded, amplified; speakers all around the theater.

No attempt should be made to create a literal representation of Mrs. Stilson's world, especially since Mrs. Stilson's world is no longer in any way literal.

The scenes should blend. No clear boundaries or domains in time or space for Mrs. Stilson any more.

It is posited by this play that the woman we see in the center of the void is the intact inner self of Mrs. Stilson. This inner self does not need to move physically when her external body (which we cannot see) moves. Thus, we infer movement from the context; from whatever clues we can obtain. It is the same for her, of course. She learns as best she can.

And yet, sometimes, the conditions change; then the woman we observe is Mrs. Stilson as others see her. We thus infer who it is we are seeing from the context, too. Sometimes we see both the inner and outer self at once.

Nothing about her world is predictable or consistent. This fact is its essence.

The progression of the play is from fragmentation to integration. By the end, boundaries have become somewhat clearer. But she remains always in another realm from us.

PRELUDE

As audience enters, a cozy armchair visible downstage in a pool of light, darkness surrounding it.

A clock heard ticking in the dark.

Lights to black.

Hold.

When the lights come back, EMILY STILSON, *a woman well into her seventies, is sitting in the armchair reading a book. Some distance away, a floor lamp glows dimly. On the other side of her chair, also some distance away, a small table with a clock. The chair, the lamp, and the table with the clock all sit isolated in narrow pools of light, darkness between and around them.*

The clock seems to be ticking a trifle louder than normal.

MRS. STILSON, *enjoying her book and the pleasant evening, reads on serenely.*

And then she looks up.

The lamp disappears into the darkness.

But she turns back to her book as if nothing odd has happened; resumes reading.

And then, a moment later, she looks up again, an expression of slight perplexity on her face. For no discernible reason, she turns toward the clock.

The clock and the table it is sitting on dis-

appear into the darkness.

She turns front. Stares out into space.

Then she turns back to her book. Resumes reading. But the reading seems an effort; her mind is on other things.

The clock skips a beat.

Only after the clock has resumed its normal rhythm does she look up. It is as if the skipped beat has only just then registered. For the first time, she displays what one might call concern.

And then the clock stops again. This time the interval lasts longer.

The book slips out of MRS. STILSON's *hands; she stares out in terror.*

Blackout.

Noise.

_____

The moment of a stroke, even a relatively minor one, and its immediate aftermath, are an experience in chaos. Nothing at all makes sense. Nothing except perhaps this overwhelming disorientation will be remembered by the victim. The stroke usually happens suddenly. It is a catastrophe.

It is my intention that the audience recognize that some real event is occurring; that real information is being received by the victim, but that it is coming in too scrambled and too fast to be properly decoded. Systems overload.

And so this section must not seem like utter

"noise," though certainly it must be more noisy than intelligible. I do not believe there is any way to be true to this material if it is not finally "composed" in rehearsal, on stage, by "feel." Theoretically, any sound or image herein described can occur anywhere in this section. The victim cannot process. Her familiar world has been rearranged. The puzzle is in pieces. All at once, and with no time to prepare, she has been picked up and dropped into another realm.

In order that this section may be put together in rehearsal (there being no one true "final order" to the images and sounds she perceives), I have divided this section into three discrete parts with the understanding that in performance these parts will blend together to form one cohesive whole.

The first group consists of the visual images MRS. STILSON *perceives.*

The second group consists of those sounds emanating outside herself. Since these sounds are all filtered by her mind, and since her mind has been drastically altered, the question of whether we in the audience are hearing what is actually occurring or only hearing what she believes is occurring is unanswerable.

The third group contains MRS. STILSON'S *words: the words she thinks and the words she speaks. Since we are perceiving the world through* MRS. STILSON'S *senses, there is no sure way for us to know whether she is actually saying any of these words aloud.*

Since the experience we are exploring is not one of logic but its opposite, there is no logical reason for these groupings to occur in the order in which I have presented them. These are but components, building blocks, and can therefore be repeated, spliced, reversed, filtered, speeded up or slowed down. What should determine their final sequence and juxtaposition, tempi, intensity, is the "musical" sense of this section as a whole; it must pulse and build. An explosion quite literally is occurring in her brain, or rather, a series of explosions:

the victim's mind, her sense of time and place, her sense of self, all are being shattered if not annihilated. Fortunately, finally, she will pass out. Were her head a pinball game it would register TILT—*game over—stop. Silence. And resume again. Only now the victim is in yet another realm. The Catastrophe section is the journey or the fall into this strange and dreadful realm.*

In the world into which MRS. STILSON *has been so violently and suddenly transposed, time and place are without definition. The distance from her old familiar world is immense. For all she knows, she could as well be on another planet.*

In this new world, she moves from one space or thought or concept to another without willing or sometimes even knowing it. Indeed, when she moves in this maze-like place, it is as if the world around her and not she were doing all the moving. To her, there is nothing any more that is commonplace or predictable. Nothing is as it was. Everything comes as a surprise. Something has relieved her of command. Something beyond her comprehension has her in its grip.

In the staging of this play, the sense should therefore be conveyed of physical and emotional separation (by the use, for example, of the dark transparent screens through which her surrounding world can be only dimly and partly seen, or by alteration of external sound) and of total immersion in strangeness.

Because our focus is on MRS. STILSON'S *inner self, it is important that she exhibit no particular overt physical disabilities. Furthermore, we should never see her in a wheelchair, even though, were we able to observe her through the doctors' eyes, a wheelchair is probably what she would, more often than not, be in.*

One further note: because MRS. STILSON *now processes information at a different rate from us, there is no reason that what we see going on around her has to be the visual equivalent of what we hear.*

CATASTROPHE

IMAGES   SOUNDS OUTSIDE HERSELF

(SOUNDS live or on tape,
altered or unadorned)

Of wind.

Mostly, it is whiteness.
Dazzling, blinding.

Of someone breathing with
effort, unevenly.

Of something ripping, like a
sheet.
Of something flapping, the
sound suggestive of an old
screen door perhaps, or a sheet
or sail in the wind. It is a rapid
fibrillation. And it is used
mostly to mark transitions. It
can seem ominous or not.

Occasionally, there are brief
rhombs of color, explosions of
color, the color red being
dominant.

Of a woman's scream (though
this sound should be altered by
filters so it resembles other
things, such as sirens).

The mirrors, of course, reflect
infinitely. Sense of endless
space, endless corridors.

Of random noises recorded in a
busy city hospital, then altered
so as to be only minimally
recognizable.

Of a car's engine at full speed.

Nothing seen that is not a
fragment. Every aspect of her
world has been shattered.

Of a siren (altered to resemble a
woman screaming).
Of an airplane coming closer,
thundering overhead, then
zooming off into silence.

MRS. STILSON'S VOICE.

(VOICE live or on tape, altered
or unadorned)

Utter isolation.

Oh my God oh my God oh my
God—

—trees clouds houses mostly
planes flashing past, images
without words, utter disarray
disbelief, never seen this kind of
thing before!

Where am I? How'd I get here?

My leg (What's my leg?) feels
wet arms . . . wet too, belly
same chin nose everything
(Where are they taking me?)
something sticky (What has
happened to my plane?) feel
something sticky.

Doors! Too many doors!

Must have . . . fallen cannot
. . . move at all sky . . .
(Gliding!) dark cannot . . . talk
(Feel as if I'm gliding!).

Yes, feels cool, nice . . . Yes,
this is the life all right!

IMAGES	SOUNDS OUTSIDE HERSELF
In this vast whiteness, like apparitions, partial glimpses of doctors and nurses can be seen. They appear and disappear like a pulse. They are never in one place for long. The mirrors multiply their incomprehensibility.	Of random crowd noises, the crowd greatly agitated. In the crowd, people can be heard calling for help, a doctor, an ambulance. But all the sounds are garbled. Of people whispering. Of many people asking questions simultaneously, no question comprehensible.
Sometimes the dark panels are opaque, sometimes transparent. Always, they convey a sense of layers, multiplicity, separation. Sense constantly of doors opening, closing, opening, closing.	Of doors opening, closing, opening, closing. Of someone breathing oxygen through a mask.
Fragments of hospital equipment appear out of nowhere and disappear just as suddenly. Glimpse always too brief to enable us to identify what this equipment is, or what its purpose.	VOICES (*garbled*). Just relax. / No one's going to hurt you. / Can you hear us? / Be careful! / You're hurting her! / No, we're not. / Don't lift her, leave her where she is! / Someone call an ambulance! / I don't think she can hear.
	MALE VOICE. Have you any idea—
MRS. STILSON'S *movements seem random. She is a person wandering through space, lost.*	OTHER VOICES (*garbled*). Do you know your name? / Do you know where you are? / What year is this? / If I say the tiger has been killed by the lion, which animal is dead?
	A hospital paging system heard.
	MRS. STILSON'S VOICE
	My plane! What has happened to my plane!

Help . . .

*—all around faces of which
nothing known no sense ever all
wiped out blank like ice I think
saw it once flying over
something some place all was
white sky and sea clouds ice
almost crashed couldn't tell
where I was heading right side
up topsy-turvy under over I was
flying actually if I can I do yes
do recall was upside down can
you believe it almost scraped
my head on the ice caps
couldn't tell which way was up
wasn't even dizzy strange things
happen to me that they do!*

*What's my name? I don't know
my name!*

*Where's my arm? I don't have
an arm!*

What's an arm?

IMAGES.

Finally, MRS. STILSON *is led by
attendants downstage, to a
chair. Then left alone.*

SOUNDS OUTSIDE HERSELF.

Equipment being moved
through stone corridors, vast
vaulting space. Endless
echoing.

MRS. STILSON'S VOICE.

*AB-ABC-ABC123DE451212
what? 123—12345678972357
better yes no problem I'm okay
soon be out soon be over storm
. . . will pass I'm sure. Always
has.*

AWAKENING

*In performance, the end of the CATASTRO-
PHE section should blend, without interrup-
tion, into the beginning of this.*

———

MRS. STILSON *downstage on a chair in a pool
of light, darkness all around her. In the distance behind her, muffled sounds of a hospital.*

*Vague images of doctors, nurses attending to
someone we cannot see. One of the doctors
calls* MRS. STILSON'S *name. Downstage,* MRS.
STILSON *shows no trace of recognition. The
doctor calls her name again. Again no response. One of the doctors says, "It's possible
she may hear us but be unable to respond."*

One of the nurses tries calling out her name. Still no response. The doctor leaves. The remaining doctors and nurses fade into the darkness.

Only MRS. STILSON *can be seen.*

Pause.

———

MRS. STILSON. Still . . . sun moon too or . . . three times happened maybe globbidged rubbidged uff and firded-forded me to nothing there try again *(We hear a window being raised somewhere behind her)* window! up and heard *(sounds of birds)* known them know I know them once upon a birds! that's it better getting better soon be out of this.

(pause)

Out of . . . what?

(pause)

Dark . . . space vast of . . . in I am or so it seems feels no real clues to speak of. *(behind her, brief image of a doctor passing)* Something tells me I am not alone. Once! Lost it. No here back thanks work fast now, yes empty vast reach of space desert think they call it I'll come back to that anyhow down I . . . something what *(brief image of a nurse)* it's SOMETHING ELSE IS ENTERING MY!—no wait got it crashing OH MY GOD! CRASHING! deadstick dead-of-night thought the stars were airport lights upside down was I what a way to land glad no one there to see it, anyhow tubbish blaxed and vinkled I commenshed to uh-oh where's it gone to somewhere flubbished what? with *(brief images of hospital staff on the move)* images are SOMETHING ODD IS! . . . yes, then there I thank you crawling sands and knees still can feel it hear the wind all alone somehow wasn't scared why a mystery, vast dark track of space, we've all got to die that I know, anyhow then day came light came with it so with this you'd think you'd hope just hold on they will find me I am . . . still intact.

(Pause)

In here.

(Long silence.)

Seem to be the word removed.

(Long silence.)

How long have I been here? . . . And wrapped in dark.

(Pause)

Can remember nothing.

(Outside sounds begin to impinge; same for images. In the distance, an attendant dimly seen pushing a floor polisher. Its noise resembles an animal's growl.

(trying hard to be cheery). No, definitely I am not alone!

(The sound of the polisher grows louder, seems more bestial, voracious, it overwhelms everything. Explosion! She gasps.

(Rapidly and in panic, sense of great commotion behind her. A crisis has occurred) There I go there I go hallway now it's screaming crowded pokes me then the coolbreeze needle scent of sweetness can see palms flowers flummers couldn't fix the leaking sprouting everywhere to save me help me CUTS UP THROUGH to something movement I am something moving without movement!

(Sound of a woman's muffled scream from behind her. The scream grows louder.)

(with delight) What a strange adventure I am having!

(Lights to black on everything. In the dark, a pause. When her voice is heard again, it is heard first from all the speakers. Her voice sounds groggy, slurred. No longer any sense of panic discernible. A few moments after her voice is heard, the lights come up slowly on her. Soon, only she is speaking; the voice from the speakers has disappeared.)

Hapst aporkshop fleetish yes of course it's yes the good ol' times when we would mollis I mean collis all around still what my son's name is cannot for the life of me yet face gleams smiles as he tells them what I did but what his name is cannot see it pleasant anyway yes palms now ocean sea breeze wafting floating up and lifting holding weightless and goes swoooop-ing down with me least I . . . think it's me.

(Sound of something flapping rapidly open and closed, open and closed. Sound of wind. Lights change into a cool and airy blue. Sense of weightlessness, serenity. In another realm now.)

Yes, out there walking not holding even danger ever-present how I loved it love it still no doubt will again hear them cheering wisht or waltz away to some place like Rumania . . .

(The wind disappears.)

Nothing . . .

(The serene blue light begins to fade away. Some place else now that she is going.)

Of course beyond that yet 1, 2 came before the yeast rose bubbled and MY CHUTE DIDN'T OPEN PROPERLY! Still for a girl did wonders getting down and it was Charles! no Charlie, who is Charlie? see him smiling as they tell him what I—

(Outside world begins to impinge. Lights are changing, growing brighter, something odd is

happening. Sense of imminence. She notices.)

(Breathless with excitement). Stop hold cut stop wait stop come-out-break-out light can see it ready heart can yes can feel it pounding something underway here light is getting brighter lids I think the word is that's it lifting of their own but slowly knew I should be patient should be what? wait hold on steady now it's spreading no no question something underway here spreading brighter rising lifting light almost yes can almost there a little more now yes can almost see this . . . place I'm . . . in and . . .

(Look of horror)

Oh my God! Now I understand! THEY'VE GOT ME!

(For first time doctors, nurses, hospital equipment all clearly visible behind her. All are gathered around someone we cannot see. From the way they are all bending over, we surmise this person we cannot see is lying in a bed. Lights drop on MRS. STILSON, *Downstage.)*

NURSE *(talking to the person upstage we cannot see).* Mrs. Stilson, can you open up your eyes?

(Pause)

MRS. STILSON *(separated from her questioners by great distance).* Don't know how.

DOCTOR. Mrs. Stilson, you just opened up your eyes. We saw you. Can you open them again?

(No response)

Mrs. Stilson . . .?

MRS. STILSON *(proudly, triumphantly).* My name then—Mrs. Stilson!

VOICE ON P.A. SYSTEM. Mrs. Howard, call on three! Mrs. Howard . . .!

MRS. STILSON. My name then—Mrs. Howard?

(Lights fade to black on hospital staff. Sound of wind, sense of time passing. Lights come up on MRS. STILSON. *The wind disappears.)*

The room that I am in is large, square. What does large mean?

(pause)

The way I'm turned I can see a window. When I'm on my back the window isn't there.

DOCTOR *(in the distance, at best only dimly seen).* Mrs. Stilson, can you hear me?

MRS. STILSON. Yes.

SECOND DOCTOR. Mrs. Stilson, can you hear me?

MRS. STILSON. Yes! I said yes! What's wrong with you?

FIRST DOCTOR. Mrs. Stilson, CAN YOU HEAR ME!

MRS. STILSON. Don't believe this—I've been put in with the deaf!

SECOND DOCTOR. Mrs. Stilson, if you can hear us, nod your head.

MRS. STILSON. All right, fine, that's how you want to play it—there!

(She nods.)

(The doctors exchange glances.)

FIRST DOCTOR. Mrs. Stilson, if you can hear us, *nod your head!*

MRS. STILSON. Oh my God, this is grotesque!

(Cacophony of sounds heard from all around, both live and from the speakers. Images suggesting sensation of assault as well. Implication of all these sounds and images is that MRS. STILSON *is being moved through the hospital for purposes of examination, perhaps even torture. The information we receive comes in too fast and distorted for rational comprehension. The realm she is in is terrifying. Fortunately, she is not in it long. As long as she is, however, the sense should be conveyed that her world moves around her more than she through it.)*

WHAT WE HEAR (THE COMPONENTS). Are we moving you too fast? / Mustlian pottid or blastigrate, no not that way this, that's fletchit gottit careful now. / Now put your nose here on this line, would you? That's it, thank you, well done, well done. / How are the wickets today? / *(sound of a cough)* / Now close your— / Is my finger going up or— / Can you feel this? / Can you feel this? / Name something that grows on trees. / Who fixes teeth? / What room do you cook in? / What year is this? / How long have you been here? / Are we being too rippled shotgun? / Would you like a cup of tea? / What is Jim short for? / Point to your shoulder. / No, your shoulder. / What do you do with a book? / Don't worry, the water's warm. We're holding you, don't worry. In we go, that's a girl!

(And then, as suddenly as the assault began, it is over. Once again, MRS. STILSON *all alone on stage, darkness all around her, no sense of walls or furniture. Utter isolation.)*

MRS. STILSON *(trying hard to keep smiling).* Yes, all in all I'd say while things could be better could be worse, far worse, how? Not quite sure. Just a sense I have. The sort of sense that only great experience can mallees or rake, plake I mean, flake . . . Drake! That's it.

(She stares into space. Silence. In the distance behind her, two doctors appear.)

FIRST DOCTOR. Mrs. Stilson, who was the

first President of the United States?

MRS. STILSON. Washington.

(pause)

SECOND DOCTOR *(speaking more slowly than the first doctor did; perhaps she simply didn't hear the question)*. Mrs. Stilson, who was the first President of the United States?

MRS. STILSON. Washington!

SECOND DOCTOR *(to first)*. I don't think she hears herself.

FIRST DOCTOR. No, I don't think she hears herself.

(The two doctors emerge from the shadows, approach MRS. STILSON. *She looks up in terror. This should be the first time that the woman on stage has been directly faced or confronted by the hospital staff. Her inner and outer worlds are beginning to come together.)*

FIRST DOCTOR. Mrs. Stilson, makey your naming powers?

MRS. STILSON. What?

SECOND DOCTOR. Canju spokeme?

MRS. STILSON. Can I what?

FIRST DOCTOR. Can do peeperear?

MRS. STILSON. Don't believe what's going on!

SECOND DOCTOR. Ahwill.

FIRST DOCTOR. Pollycadjis:

SECOND DOCTOR. Sewyladda?

FIRST DOCTOR *(with a nod)*. Hm-hm.

(exit doctors)

MRS. STILSON *(alone again)*. How it came to pass that I was captured! *(She ponders)* Hard to say really. I'll come back to that.

(pause)

The room that I've been put in this time is quite small, square, what does square mean? . . . Means . . .

(Sense of time passing. The lights shift. The space she is in begins to change its shape.)

Of course morning comes I think . . . *(She ponders)* Yes, and night of course comes . . . *(ponders more)* Though sometimes . . .

*(*MRS. STILSON *some place else now. And she is aware of it.)*

Yes, the way the walls choose to move around me . . . Yes, I've noticed that, I'm no fool!

(A nurse appears carrying a dazzling bouquet of flowers. This bouquet is the first real color we have seen.)

NURSE. Good morning! Look what somebody's just sent you! *(She sets them on a table)* Wish I had as many admirers as you.

(exit nurse, smiling warmly)

*(*MRS. STILSON'S *eyes are drawn to the flowers. And something about them apparently ren-ders it impossible for her to shift her gaze away. Something about these flowers has her in their thrall.*

What it is is their color.

It is as if she has never experienced color before. And the experience is so overwhelming, both physiologically and psychologically, that her brain cannot process all the information. Her circuitry is overloaded. It is too much sensory input for her to handle. An explosion is imminent. If something does not intervene to divert her attention, MRS. STILSON *will very likely faint, perhaps even suffer a seizure.*

A narrow beam of light, growing steadily in intensity, falls upon the bouquet of flowers, causing their colors to take on an intensity themselves that they otherwise would lack. At the same time, a single musical tone is heard, volume increasing.

A nurse enters the room.)

NURSE. May I get you something?

MRS. STILSON *(abstracted, eyes remaining on the flowers)*. Yes, a sweater.

NURSE. Yes, of course. Think we have one here. *(The nurse opens a drawer, takes out a pillow, hands the pillow to* MRS. STILSON*)* Here.

MRS. STILSON *accepts the pillow unquestioningly, eyes never leaving the flowers. She lays the pillow on her lap, promptly forgets about it. The musical tone and the beam of light continue relentlessly toward their peak. The nurse, oblivious of any crisis, exits. The single tone and the beam of light crest together. Silence follows. The beam disappears. The flowers seem normal. The lights around* MRS. STILSON *return to the way they were before the gift of flowers was brought in.)*

MRS. STILSON *(shaken)*. This is not a hospital of course, and I know it! What it is is a farmhouse made up to look like a hospital. Why? I'll come back to that.

(Enter another nurse)

NURSE. Hi! Haven't seen you in a while. Have you missed me?

MRS. STILSON *(no hint of recognition visible)*. What?

NURSE *(warmly)*. They say you didn't touch your dinner. Would you like some pudding?

MRS. STILSON. No.

NURSE. Good, I'll go get you some.

(exit nurse, very cheerfully)

MRS. STILSON. Yes no question they have got me I've been what that word was captured is it? No it's—Yes, it's captured how? Near as it can figure. I was in my prane and crashed, not unusual, still in all not too common. Neither is it very grub. Plexit rather or I'd say propopic. Well that's that, jungdaball! Anyhow to resume, what I had for lunch? That's not it, good books I have read, good what, done what? Whaaaaat? Do the busy here! Get inside this, rubbidge all around let the vontul do some yes off or it of above semilacrum pwooosh! what with noddygobbit nip-n-crashing inside outside witsit watchit funnel vortex sucking into backlash watchit get-out caught-in spinning ring-grab grobbit help woooosh! cannot stoppit on its own has me where it wants *(And suddenly she is in another realm. Lights transformed into weightless blue. Sense of ease and serenity)* Plane! See it thanks, okay, onto back we were and here it is. Slow down easy now. Captured. After crashing, that is what we said or was about to, think it so, cannot tell for sure, slow it slow it, okay here we go . . . *(speaking slower now)* captured after crashing by the enemy and brought here to this farm masquerading as a hospital. Why? For I would say offhand information. Of what sort though hard to tell. For example, questions such as can I raise my fingers, what's an overcoat, how many nickels in a rhyme, questions such as these. To what use can they be to the enemy? Hard to tell from here. Nonetheless, I would say must be certain information I possess that they want well I won't give it I'll escape! Strange things happen to me that they do! Good thing I'm all right! Must be in Rumania. Just a hunch of course. *(The serene blue light starts to fade)* Ssssh, someone's coming.

(A nurse has entered. The nurse guides MRS. STILSON *to a doctor. The blue light is gone. The nurse leaves. The space* MRS. STILSON *now is in appears much more "real" and less fragmentary than what we have so far been observing. We see* MRS. STILSON *here as others see her.)*

DOCTOR. Mrs. Stilson, if you don't mind, I'd like to ask you some questions. Some will be easy, some will be hard. Is that all right?

MRS. STILSON. Oh yes I'd say oh well yes that's the twither of it.

DOCTOR. Good. Okay. Where were you born?

MRS. STILSON. Never. Not at all. Here the match wundles up you know and drats flames fires I keep careful always—

DOCTOR. Right . . . *(speaking very slowly, precise enunciation)* Where were you born?

MRS. STILSON. Well now well now that's a good thing knowing yushof course wouldn't

call it such as I did andinjurations or aplovia could it? No I wouldn't think so. Next?
(pause)
DOCTOR. Mrs. Stilson, are there seven days in a week?
MRS. STILSON. . . . Seven . . . yes.
DOCTOR. Are there five days in a week?
(pause)
MRS. STILSON *(after much pondering)*. No.
DOCTOR. Can a stone float on water?
(long pause)
MRS. STILSON. No.
DOCTOR. Mrs. Stilson, can you cough?
MRS. STILSON. Somewhat.
DOCTOR. Well, would you show me how you cough?
MRS. STILSON. Well now well now not so easy what you cromplie is to put these bushes open and
DOCTOR. No no, Mrs. Stilson, I'm sorry— I would like to hear you cough.
MRS. STILSON. Well I'm not bort you know with plajits or we'd see it wencherday she brings its pillow with the fistils-opening I'd say outward always outward never stopping it.
(long silence)
DOCTOR. Mrs. Stilson, I have some objects here. *(He takes a comb, a toothbrush, a pack of matches, and a key from his pocket, sets them down where she can see)* Could you point to the object you would use for cleaning your teeth?
(Very long silence. Finally she picks up the comb and shows it to him. Then she puts it down. Waits.)
Mrs. Stilson, here, take this object in your hand. *(He hands her the toothbrush)* Do you know what this object is called?
MRS. STILSON *(with great difficulty)*. Tooooooooovvvv . . . bbbrum?
DOCTOR. Very good. Now put it down.
She puts it down.)
Now, pretend you have it in your hand. Show me what you'd do with it.
(She does nothing.)
What does one do with an object such as that, Mrs. Stilson?
(No response.)
Mrs. Stilson, what is the name of the object you are looking at?
MRS. STILSON. Well it's . . . wombly and not at all . . . rigged or tuned like we might twunter or toring to work the clambness out of it or—
DOCTOR. Pick it up.
MRS. STILSON *(as soon as she's picked it up)*.

Tooovebram, tooove-britch bratch brush bridge, two-bridge.

DOCTOR. Show me what you do with it.

(For several moments she does nothing. Then she puts it to her lips, holds it there motionless.) Very good. Thank you.

(She sighs heavily, puts it down. The doctor gathers up his objects, leaves. Once again MRS. STILSON *all alone. She stares into space. Then her voice is heard coming from all around. She herself does not speak.*

HER VOICE. Dark now again out the window on my side lying here all alone . . .

(very long silence)

MRS. STILSON. Yesterday my children came to see me.

(pause)

Or at least, I was told they were my children. Never saw them before in my life.

(She stares out, motionless. No expression. Then after a while she looks around. Studies the dark for clues.)

Time has become peculiar.

(And she continues this scrutiny of the dark. But if this activity stems from curiosity, it is a mild curiosity at most. No longer does she convey or probably even experience the extreme, disoriented dread we saw earlier when she first arrived in this new realm. Her sense of urgency is gone. Indeed, were we able to observe MRS. STILSON *constantly, we would inevitably conclude that her curiosity is now only minimally purposeful; that, in fact, more likely her investigations are the actions, possibly merely the reflex actions, of someone with little or nothing else to do. This is not to deny that she is desperately trying to piece her shattered world together. Undoubtedly, it is the dominant motif in her mind. But it is a motif*

        MRS. STILSON *(her words overpowering his).*

I don't trust him, don't trust anyone. Must get word out, send a message where I am. Like a wall between me and others. No one ever gets it right even though I tell them right. They are playing tricks on me, two sides, both not my friends, goes in goes out too fast too fast hurts do the busy I'm all right I talk right why acting all these others like I don't, what's he marking, what's he writing?

(Exit doctor and nurse)

MRS. STILSON. I am doing well of course!

probably more absent from her consciousness than present, and the quest it inspires is intermittent at best. Her mental abilities have not only been severely altered, they have been diminished: That is the terrible fact one cannot deny. And then suddenly she is agitated.)

Mother! . . . didn't say as she usually . . .

(pause)

And I thought late enough or early rather first light coming so when didn't move I poked her then with shoving but she didn't even eyes or giggle when I tickled.

(pause)

What it was was not a trick as I at first had—

(pause)

Well I couldn't figure, he had never lied, tried to get her hold me couldn't it was useless. Then his face was, I had never known a face could . . . It was like a mask then like sirens it was bursting open it was him then I too joining it was useless. Can still feel what it was like when she held me.

(pause)

So then well I was on my own. He was all destroyed, had I think they say no strength for this.

(Then she's silent. No expression. Stares into space. Enter a doctor and a nurse.)

DOCTOR *(warmly).* Hello, Mrs. Stilson.

(He comes over next to her. We cannot tell if she notices him or not. The nurse, chart in hand, stands a slight distance away.)

Your're looking much, much better. *(He smiles and sits down next to her. He watches her for several moments, searching for signs of recognition)*

Mrs. Stilson, do you know why you're here?

MRS. STILSON. Well now well now . . .

(She gives it up. Silence.)

DOCTOR. You have had an accident—

DOCTOR *(To all intents and purposes, what he says is lost).* At home. Not in an airplane. It's called a stroke. This means that your brain has been injured and brain tissue destroyed, though we are not certain of the cause. You could get better, and you're certainly making progress. But it's still too soon to give any sort of exact prognosis. *(He studies her. Then he rises and marks something on his clipboard)*

(pause, secretive tone) They still pretend they do not understand me. I believe they may

be mad.

(pause)

No they're not mad, I am mad. Today I heard it. Everything I speak is wronged. SOMETHING HAS BEEN DONE TO ME!

DOCTOR *(barely visible in the distance).* Mrs. Stilson, can you repeat this phrase: "We live across the street from the school."

(She ponders.)

MRS. STILSON. "Malacats on the forturay are the kesterfats of the romancers."

(Look of horror comes across her face; the doctor vanishes. Through the screens, upstage, we see a nurse bringing on a tray of food.)

NURSE *(brightly).* Okay ups-a-girl, ups-a-baby, dinnertime! Open wide now, mustn't go dribble-dribble—at's-a-way!

(MRS. STILSON screams, swings her arms in fury. In the distance, upstage, the tray of food goes flying.)

MRS. STILSON *(screaming).* Out! Get out! Take this shit away, I don't want it! Someone get me out of here!

NURSE *(while MRS. STILSON continues shouting).* Help, someone, come quick! She's talking! Good as you or me! It's a miracle! Help! Somebody! Come quick!

While MRS. STILSON continues to scream and flail her arms, nurses and doctors rush on upstage and surround the patient we never see. And although MRS. STILSON continues to scream coherently, in fact she isn't any better, no miracle has occurred. Her ability to articulate with apparent normalcy has been brought on by extreme agitation and in no way implies that she could produce these sounds again "if she only wanted"; will power has nothing to do with what we hear. Her language, as it must, soon slips back into jargon. She continues to flail her arms. In the background, we can see a nurse preparing a hypodermic.

MRS. STILSON *(struggling).* —flubdgy please no-mommy-callming holdmeplease to slee-EEEEP SHOOOOP shop shnoper CRROOOOOCK SNANNNNG wuduitcoldly should I gobbin flutter truly HELP ME yessisnofun, snofun, wishes awhin dahd killminsilf if . . . could *(in the distance, we see the needle given)* OW! . . . would I but . . . *(She's becoming drowsy)* . . . awful to me him as well moas of all no cantduit . . . jusscantduit . . .

(Head drops. Into sleep she goes. Exit doctors, nurses. Sound of a gentle wind is heard. Lights fade to black on MRS. STILSON. Dark-

ness everywhere; the sound of the wind fades away. Silence. Lights up on Amy, downstage right. Then lights up on MRS. STILSON staring into space.)

AMY. Mrs. Stilson?

(MRS. STILSON turns toward the sound, sees AMY.)

You have had what's called a stroke.

(Change of lights and panels open. Sense of terrible enclosure gone. Birds heard. We are outside now. AMY puts a shawl around MRS. STILSON's shoulders.)

AMY. Are you sure that will be enough?

MRS. STILSON. Oh yes . . . thhhankyou.

(She tucks the shawl around herself. Then AMY guides her through the panels as if through corridors; no rush, slow gentle stroll. They emerge other side of stage. Warm light. AMY takes in the view. MRS. STILSON appears indifferent.)

AMY. Nice to be outside, isn't it? . . . Nice view.

MRS. STILSON *(still with indifference).* Yes indeed.

(There are two chairs nearby, and they sit. Silence for a time.)

AMY. Are you feeling any better today?

(But she gets no response. Then, a moment later, MRS. STILSON turns to AMY; it is as if AMY's question has not even been heard.)

MRS. STILSON. The thing is . . .

(But the statement trails off into nothingness. She stares out, no expression.)

AMY. Yes? What?

(Long silence)

MRS. STILSON. I can't make it do it like it used to.

AMY. Yes, I know. That's because of the accident.

MRS. STILSON *(seemingly oblivious of AMY's words).* The words, they go in sometimes then out they go, I can't stop them here inside or make maybe globbidge to the tubberway or—

AMY. Emily. Emily!

MRS. STILSON *(shaken out of herself).* . . . What?

AMY. Did you hear what you just said?

MRS. STILSON. . . . Why?

AMY *(speaking slowly).* You must listen to what you're saying.

MRS. STILSON. Did I . . . do . . .

AMY *(nodding, smiling; clearly no reproach intended).* Slow down. Listen to what you're saying.

(silence)

MRS. STILSON *(slower).* The thing is . . .

doing all this busy in here gets, you know with the talking it's like . . . sometimes when I hear here [*She touches her head*] . . . but when I start to . . . kind more what kind of voice should . . . it's like pfffft! *(She makes a gesture with her hand of something flying away.)*

AMY *(smiling)*. Yes, I know. It's hard to find the words for what you're thinking of.

MRS. STILSON. Well yes.

(long pause)

And then these people, they keep waiting . . . And I see they're smiling and . . . they keep . . . waiting . . . *(Faint smile, helpless gesture. She stares off. Long silence.)*

AMY. Emily.

*(*MRS. STILSON *looks up.)*

Can you remember anything about your life . . . before the accident?

MRS. STILSON. Not sometimes, some days it goes better if I see a thing or smell . . . it . . . remembers me back, you see? And I see things that maybe they were me and maybe they were just some things you know that happens in the night when you . . . *(struggling visibly)* have your things closed, eyes.

AMY. A dream you mean.

MRS. STILSON *(with relief)*. Yes. So I don't know for sure.

(pause)

If it was really me.

(long silence)

AMY. Your son is bringing a picture of you when you were younger. We thought you might like that.

(No visible response. Long silence.)

You used to fly, didn't you?

MRS. STILSON *(brightly)*. Oh yes indeed! Very much! I walked . . . out . . .

(Pause. Softly, proudly.) I walked out on wings. *(Lights fade on* AMY. MRS. STILSON *alone again.)*

Sitting here on my bed I can close my eyes shut out all that I can't do with, hearing my own talking, others, names that used to well just be there when I wanted now all somewhere else. No control. Close my eyes then, go to—

(Sound of something flapping rapidly. A fibrillation. Lights become blue. Sense of weightlessness, serenity.)

Here I go. No one talks here. Images coming I seem feel it feels better this way here is how it goes: this time I am still in the middle Stilson in the middle going out walking out wind feels good hold the wires feel the hum down below far there they are now we turn it bank it now we spin! Looks more bad than really is, still

needs good balance and those nerves and that thing that courage thing don't fall off! . . . And now I'm out . . . and back and . . . *(with surprise)* there's the window.

(Lights have returned to normal. She is back where she started. AMY *enters.)*

AMY. Hello, Emily.

MRS. STILSON. Oh, Amy! . . . Didn't hear what you was . . . coming here to . . . Oh!

AMY. What is it?

MRS. STILSON. Something . . . wet.

AMY. Do you know what it is?

MRS. STILSON. Don't . . . can't say find it word.

AMY. Try. You can find it.

MRS. STILSON. Wet . . . thing, many, both sides yes.

AMY. Can you name them? What they are? You do know what they are.

(pause)

MRS. STILSON. . . . . Tears?

AMY. That's right, very good. Those are tears. And do you know what that means?

MRS. STILSON. . . . . Sad?

AMY. Yes, right, well done, it means . . . that you are sad.

EXPLORATIONS

Stage dark.

In the dark, a piano heard: someone fooling around on the keyboard, brief halting snatches of old songs emerging as the product; would constitute a medley were the segments only longer, more cohesive. As it is, suspicion aroused that what we hear is all the pianist can remember.

Sound of general laughter, hubbub.

Lights rise.

What we see is a rec room, in some places clearly, in others not (the room being observed partly through the dark scrim panels).

Upstage right, an upright piano, players and friends gathered round. Doctors, therapists, nurses, attendants, patients, visitors certainly are not all seen, but those we do see come from such a group. We are in the rec room of a rehabilitation center. Some patients in wheelchairs.

The room itself has bright comfortable chairs, perhaps a card table, magazine rack, certainly a TV set. Someone now turns on the TV.

What emerges is the sound of Ella Fitzgerald in live performance. She sings scat: mellow, upbeat.

The patients and staff persuade the pianist to cease. Ella's riffs of scat cast something like a spell.

MRS. STILSON wanders through the space.

The rec room, it should be stressed, shows more detail and color than any space we've so far seen. Perhaps a vase of flowers helps to signal that MRS. STILSON's world is becoming fuller, more integrated.

Movements too seem normal, same for conversations that go on during all of this, though too softly for us to comprehend.

The music of course sets the tone. All who listen are in its thrall.

New time sense here, a languor almost. The dread MRS. STILSON felt has been replaced by an acknowledgment of her condition, though not an understanding.

In this time before she speaks, and in fact during, we observe the life of the rec room behind and around her. This is not a hospital any more, and a kind of normalcy prevails.

The sense should be conveyed of corridors leading to and from this room.

Then the music and the rec room sounds grow dim; MRS. STILSON comes forward, lost in the drifts of a thought.

———

MRS. STILSON (relaxed, mellow). Wonder . . . what's inside of it . . .

(pause)

I mean, how does it work? What's inside that . . . makes it work?

(Long pause. She ponders.)

I mean when you . . . think about it all . . .
(pause)

And when you think that it could . . . ever have been . . . possible to . . . be another way . . .

(She ponders. But it's hard for her to keep in mind what she's been thinking of, and she has to fight the noise of the rec room, its intrusive presence. Like a novice juggler, MRS. STILSON is unable to keep outside images and inner thoughts going simultaneously. When she's with her thoughts, the outside world fades away. When the outside world is with her, her thoughts fade away. But she fights her way through it, and keeps the thought in mind. The rec room, whose noise has just increased, grows quiet.)

Maybe . . . if somehow I could— (She searches for the words that match her concept)—get inside . . .

(pause. Sounds of the rec room pulse louder. She fights against it. The rec room sounds diminish.)

Prob'ly . . . very dark inside . . . (She ponders; tries to picture what she's thinking) Yes . . . twisting kind of place I bet . . . (ponders more) With lots of . . . (She searches for the proper word; finds it) . . . passageways that . . . lead to . . . (Again, she searches for the word. The outside world rushes in.)

PATIENT IN A WHEELCHAIR (only barely audible). My foot feels sour.

(An attendant puts a lap rug over the patient's limbs. Then the rec room, once again, fades away.)

MRS. STILSON (Fighting on). . . . lead to . . . something . . . Door! Yes . . . closed off now I . . . guess possib . . . ly for good I mean . . . forever, what does that mean? (She ponders)

ATTENDANT. Would you like some candy?

MRS. STILSON. No.

ATTENDANT. Billy made it.

MRS. STILSON. No!

(The attendant moves back into the shadows.)
Where was I? (She looks around) Why can't they just . . . let me . . . be when I'm . . .

(Lights start to change. Her world suddenly in flux. The rec room fades from view. Sounds of birds heard, dimly at first. Aware of the change as it is occurring) . . . okay. Slipping out of . . . it and . . . (MRS. STILSON in a different place.) Outside now! How . . . did I do that?

AMY (emerging from the shadows). Do you like this new place better?

MRS. STILSON. Oh well oh well yes, much, all . . . nice flowers here, people seem . . . more like me. Thank you. (AMY moves back toward the shadows.)
And then I see it happen once again . . .
(AMY gone from sight.)
Amy kisses me. Puts her—what thing is it, arm! yes, arm, puts her arm around my . . .
(pause) . . . shoulder, turns her head away so I can't . . . (pause) Well, it knows what she's doing. May not get much better even though I'm here. No, I know that. I know that. No real need for her to . . .
(long pause) Then she kisses me again. (Pause) Walks away . . . (Pause)
(Lights change again, world again in flux. Noises of the building's interior can be heard like a babel, only fleetingly coherent. The rec room seen dissolving.)

MRS. STILSON. Where am I?

(She begins to wander through a maze of passageways. The mirrors multiply her image, create a sense of endlessness. Note. The following blocks of sound, which accompany her expedition, are meant to blend and overlap in performance and, to that end, can be used in any order and combined in any way desired, except for the last five blocks, numbers 12–16, which must be performed in their given sequence and in a way that is comprehensible. The sounds themselves may be live or prerecorded; those which are pre-recorded should emanate from all parts of the theater and in no predictable pattern. The effect should be exhilarating and disorienting. An adventure. With terrifying aspects to be sure. But the sense of mystery and adventure must never be so overwhelmed by the terror that it is either lost altogether or submerged to the point of insignificance. MRS. STILSON *may be frightened here, but the fear does not prevent her from exploring. She wanders through the labyrinth of dark panels as if they were so many doors, each door leading into yet another realm.)*

BLOCK 1. It was but a few years later that Fritsch and Hitzig stimulated the cortex of a dog with an electric current. Here at last was dramatic and indisputable evidence that—

BLOCK 2. Would you like me to change the channel?

BLOCK 3. . . . presented, I would say, essentially similar conclusions on the behavioral correlates of each cerebral convolution.

BLOCK 4 *(being the deep male voice, speaking slowly, enunciating carefully, that one hears on the speech-therapy machine known as "The Language Master").* Mother led Bud to the bed.

BLOCK 5. . . . In the laboratory then, through electrical stimulation of neural centers or excisions of areas of the brain, scientists acquired information about the organization of mental activities in the monkey, the dog, the cat, and the rat. The discovery of certain peculiar clinical pictures, reminiscent of bizarre human syndromes, proved of special interest.

BLOCK 6. Can you tell me what this object's called?

BLOCK 7. *Ella's riffs of scat, as if we were still in the rec room after all.*

BLOCK 8. One has only to glance through the writings of this period to sense the heightened excitement attendant upon these discoveries!

BLOCK 9. Possibly some diaschisis, which would of course help account for the apparent

mirroring. And then, of course, we must not overlook the fact that she's left-handed.

BLOCK 10. Of course, you understand, these theories may all be wrong! *(Sound of laughter from an audience)* Any other questions? Yes, over there, in the corner.

BLOCK 11. Mrs. Stilson, this is Dr. Rogans. Dr. Rogans, this is Emily Stilson.

BLOCK 12. MALE VOICE. —definite possibility I would say of a tiny subclinical infarct in Penfield's area. Yes? FEMALE VOICE. Are you sure there is a Penfield's area? MALE VOICE. No. *(laughter from his audience)* MALE VOICE AGAIN *(itself on the verge of laughter).* But *something* is wrong with her! *(raucous laughter from his audience)*

(Note. Emerging out of the laughter in Block 12, a single musical TONE. This tone increases in intensity. It should carry through Block 16 and into MRS. STILSON'S *emergence from the maze of panels, helping to propel her into the realm and the memory to which this expedition has been leading.)*

BLOCK 13. The controversy, of course, is that some feel it's language without thought, and others, thought without language . . .

BLOCK 14. What it is, of course, is the symbol system. Their symbol system's shot. They can't make analogies.

BLOCK 15. You see, it's all so unpredictable. There are no fixed posts, no clear boundaries. The victim, you could say, has been cut adrift . . .

BLOCK 16. Ah, now you're really flying blind there!

(MRS. STILSON emerges from the maze of corridors. Sound perhaps of wind, or bells. Lights blue, sense again of weightlessness, airiness.)

MRS STILSON *(in awe and ecstasy).* As I see it now, the plane was flying BACKWARDS! Really, wind that strong, didn't know it could be! Yet the sky was clear, not a cloud, crystal blue, gorgeous, angels could've lived in sky like that . . . I think the cyclone must've blown in on the Andes from the sea . . . *(Blue light fades. Wind gone, bells gone, musical tone is gone.) (coming out of it)* Yes . . . *(She looks around; gets her bearings)* Yes, no question, this . . . place better. *(And now she's landed)* All these people just . . . like me, I guess.

(She takes in where she is, seems slightly stunned to be back where she started. Sense of wonderment apparent. An attendant approaches.)

ATTENDANT. Mrs. Stilson?

MRS. STILSON *(startled)*. Oh!

ATTENDANT. Sorry to—

MRS. STILSON. Is it . . . ?

ATTENDANT. Yes.

MRS. STILSON. Did I . . . ?

ATTENDANT. No, no need to worry. Here, I'll take you. *(The* ATTENDANT *guides* MRS. STILSON *to a therapy room, though, in fact, more likely (on the stage) the room assembles around her. In the room are* AMY, BILLY *(a man in his middle thirties),* MRS. TIMMINS *(elderly, in a wheelchair), and* MR. BROWNSTEIN *(also elderly and in a wheelchair. The* ATTENDANT *leaves.)*

AMY. Well! Now that we're all here on this lovely afternoon, I thought that maybe—

BILLY. She looks really good.

AMY. What?

BILLY. This new lady here, can't remember what her name is, no bother, anyhow, she looks really nice all dressed like this, an' I jus' wanna extent a nice welcome here on behalf o' all of us. *(The other patients mumble their assent.)*

AMY. Well, that is very nice, Billy, very nice. Can any of the rest of you remember this woman's name?

BILLY. I seen her I think when it is, yesterday, how's that?

AMY. Very good, that's right, you met her for the first time yesterday. Now, can any of you remember her name?

BILLY. Dolores

AMY *(laughing slightly)*. No, not Dolores.

MR. BROWNSTEIN. She vas, I caught sight ya know, jussaminute, flahtied or vhat, vhere, midda *(He hums a note)*—

AMY. Music.

MR. BROWNSTEIN. Yeah right goodgirlie right she vas lissning, I caught slight, saw her vooding bockstond tipping-n-topping de foot vas jussnow like dis. *(He starts to stamp his foot)*

AMY. Mrs. Stilson, were you inside listening to some music just now?

MRS. STILSON. Well . . . *(pause; very fast)* Well now I was yes in the what in-the-in-the where the—

AMY *(cheerfully)*. Sssssllllow dowwwwn.

(The other patients laugh; MRS. TIMMINS *softly echoes the phrase "slow down.")* *(speaking very slowly)* Listen to yourself talking.

MRS. STILSON *(speaking slowly)*. Well yes, I was . . . listening and it was it was going in . . . good I think, I'd say, very good yes I liked it very nice it made it very nice inside.

AMY. Well, good.

MRS. TIMMINS. Applawdgia!

AMY. Ah, Mrs. Timmins! You heard the music, too?

MRS. TIMMINS *(with a laugh)*. Ohshorrrrrrn. Yosssssso, TV.

AMY. Well, good for you! Anyway, I'd like you all to know that this new person in our group is named Mrs. Stilson.

MR. BROWNSTEIN. Sssssstaa-illlllsssim.

AMY. Right! Well done, Mr. Brownstein!

MR. BROWNSTEIN *(laughing proudly)*. It's vurktiddiDINGobitch!

AMY. That's right it's working, I told you it would.

BILLY. Hey! Wait, hold on here—jus' remembered!

AMY. What's that, Billy?

BILLY. You've been holdin' out pay up where is it?

AMY. Where . . . is what?

BILLY. Where is for all what I did all that time labor which you—don't kid me, I see you grinning back there ate up *(He makes munching sounds)* so where is it, where's the loot?

AMY. For the cheesecake.

BILLY. That's right you know it for the cheesecape, own recipe, extra-special, pay up.

AMY *(to* MRS. STILSON*)*. Billy is a terrific cook.

MRS. STILSON *(delighted)*. Oh!

BILLY. Well used t' be, not now much what they say, anyhow, hah-hah! see? look, laughing, giggles, tries t' hide it, she knows she knows, scoundrel, thief, can't sleep nights can you, people give their arms whatnots recipe like that one is. Cheapskate. Come on fork over hand it over, don't be chief.

AMY. . . . What?

BILLY. Don't be chief. *(pause)* You know, when someone don' pay, you say he's chief.

AMY *(warmly, nearly laughing)*. Billy, you're not listening.

BILLY. Okay not the word not the right word what's the word? I'll take any help you can give me. *(He laughs)*

AMY. Cheap.

BILLY. That's it that's the word that's what you are, from now on I'm gonna sell my recipes somewhere else.

AMY. Billy, say cheap.

(He sighs mightily.)

BILLY. . . . Chief. *(Her expression tells him everything.)* Not right okay, try again this thing we can, what's its, lessee okay here we go CHARF! Nope. Not right. Ya know really, this could take all day.

AMY. Well then, the sooner you do it, the sooner we can go on to what I've planned.

BILLY. You've got somethin' planned? You've never got somethin' planned.

AMY. I've *always* got something planned.

BILLY. Oh come on don' gimme that, you're jus' tryin' to impress this new lady, really nice new lady, Mrs. . . .

AMY. Stilson.

BILLY. Yeah her, you're jus' tryin'—what's that word again?

AMY. Cheap.

BILLY. Cheap right okay lessee now—

AMY. Billy! You just said it!

BILLY. Did I? Good. Then maybe we can go on to somethin' else, such as when you're gonna fork over for the cheesecake, I could be a rich man now.

AMY. Billy, I never made the cheesecake.

BILLY. I'll bet you've gone sold the recipe to all the stores the whatnot everywhere fancy bigdeal places made a fortune, gonna retire any day t' your farm in New Jersey.

AMY. I don't have a farm in New Jersey, *you* have a farm in New Jersey!

BILLY. Oh? Then what were you doin' on my farm then?

AMY. I wasn't on your farm, Billy, I've been here! (BILLY *starts arguing about something incomprehensible and seemingly unrelated to farm life, the argument consisting mostly of the recitation of a convoluted string of numbers;* AMY *cuts him short before he goes too far astray*) Billy, cheap, say cheap! (*long silence*)

BILLY (*simply and without effort*). Cheap. (AMY *cheers*) (*overjoyed*) Cheap!—Cheap-cheap-cheap-cheap-cheap!

MR. BROWNSTEIN. I vas hoping you could polsya and git vid mustard all dis out of dis you gottit right good I say hutchit and congratulupsy!

AMY. Congratu*lations*.

MR. BROWNSTEIN. Yeah right dassit good-girlie, phhhhew! fin'lly!

(*Lights fade to black all around* MRS. STIL-SON. *Nothing seen but her. Silence for a time.*)

MRS. STILSON. What it was . . . how I heard it how I said it not the same, you would think so but it's not. Sometimes . . . well it just goes in so fast, in-and-out all the sounds. I know they mean—(*pause*) I mean I know they're . . . well like with me, helping, as their at their in their best way knowing how I guess they practice all the time so I'd say must be good or even better, helps me get the dark out just by going you know sssslowww and thinking smiling . . . it's not easy. (*pause*) Sometimes . . . how can . . . well it's just I think these death things, end it, stuff like sort of may be better not to listen anything no more at all or trying even talking cause what good's it, I'm so far away! Well it's crazy I don't mean it I don't think, still it's just like clouds that you can't push through. Still you do it, still you try to. I can't hear things same as others say them. (*pause*) So the death thing, it comes in, I don't ask it, it just comes in, plays around in there, I can't get it out till it's ready, goes out on its own. Same I guess for coming. I don't open up the door.

(*Silence. Lights up on a chair, small table. On the table, a small cassette recorder.* MRS. STILSON *goes to the chair. Sits. Stares at the recorder. A few moments later,* BILLY *and a* DOCTOR *enter.*)

BILLY. Oh, I'm sorry, I didn't know you was in . . . here or . . .

MRS STILSON. Dr. Freedman said I could . . . use room and his . . . this . . . (*She gestures toward the recorder*)

DOCTOR. No problem, we'll use another room. (*He smiles. Exit* BILLY *and* DOCTOR.)

(MRS. STILSON *turns back to the machine. Stares at it. Then she reaches out, presses a button.*)

DOCTOR'S VOICE (*from cassette recorder*). All right, essentially, a stroke occurs when there's a stoppage . . . When blood flow ceases in one part of the brain . . . And that brain can no longer get oxygen . . . And subsequently dies. Okay? Now, depending upon which part of the brain is affected by the stroke, you'll see differences in symptoms. Now what you've had is a left cerebral infarction. Oh, by the way, you're doing much, much better. We were very worried when you first arrived . . .

(*Silence. She clicks off the recording machine. Does nothing, stares at nothing. Then she reaches out and pushes the rewind button. The machine rewinds to start of tape. Stops automatically. She stares at the machine. Deep breath. Reaches out again. Presses the playback button.*)

DOCTOR'S VOICE. All right, essentially, a stroke occurs when there's a stoppage . . . When blood flow ceases in one part of the brain . . . And that brain can no long—

(*She shuts it off. Stares into space. Silence.*)

MRS. STILSON *with* AMY *sitting next to her on another chair.*

MRS. STILSON *(still staring into space)*. "Memory" . . . *(pause)*

AMY. Yes, come on, "memory" . . . *(no response)* Anything. *(still no response)* *(warmly)* Oh, come on, I bet there are lots of things you can talk about . . . You've been going out a lot lately . . . With your son . . . With your niece . . . *(pause)* What about Rhinebeck? Tell me about Rhinebeck. *(pause)*

MRS. STILSON. Oh . . . Saturday . . . *(She ponders)* On . . . Sunday my . . . son . . . *(ponders again)* On Saturday my son . . . took me to see them out at Rhinebeck.

AMY. See what?

MRS. STILSON. What I used to . . . fly in.

AMY. Can you think of the word?

MRS. STILSON. . . . What word?

AMY. For what you used to fly in. *(long pause)*

MRS. STILSON. Planes!

AMY. Very good!

MRS. STILSON. Old . . . planes.

AMY. That is very good. Really!

MRS. STILSON. I sat . . . inside one of them. He said it was like the kind I used to . . . fly in and walk . . . out on wings in. I couldn't believe I could have ever done this. *(pause)* But he said I did, I had. He was very . . . proud. *(pause)* Then . . .I saw my hand was pushing on this . . . stick . . . Then my hand was . . . pulling. Well I hadn't you know asked my hand to do this, it just went and did it on its own. So I said okay Emily, if this is how it wants to do it you just sit back here and watch . . . But . . . my head, it was really . . . hurting bad. And I was up here both . . . sides, you know . . .

AMY. Crying.

MRS. STILSON *(with effort)*. Yeah. *(long pause)* And then all at once—it remembered everything! *(long pause)* But now it doesn't. *(silence)*

(Faint sound of wind. Hint of bells. The screens open. We are outside. Sense of distance, openness. All feeling of constraint is gone. AMY *helps* MRS. STILSON *into an overcoat;* AMY *is in an overcoat already.)*

AMY. Are you sure you'll be warm enough?

MRS. STILSON. Oh yes . . .

(And they start to walk—a leisurely stroll through a park or meadow, sense of whiteness everywhere. They head toward a bench with snow on its slats. The sound of wind grows stronger. Faint sound of an airplane overhead, the sound quickly disappearing.)

MRS. STILSON. This is winter, isn't it?

AMY. Yes.

MRS. STILSON. That was just a guess, you know.

AMY *(with a warm, easy laugh)*. Well, it was a good one, keep it up! (MRS. STILSON *laughs.* AMY *stops by the bench.)* Do you know what this is called?

MRS. STILSON. Bench!

AMY. Very good! No, I mean what's on top of it. *(no response)* What I'm brushing off . . . *(still no response)* What's falling from the sky . . . *(long silence)*

MRS. STILSON. Where do you get names from?

AMY. I? From in here, same as you.

MRS. STILSON. Do you know how you do it?

AMY. No.

MRS. STILSON. Then how am I supposed . . . to learn?

AMY *(softly)*. I don't really know.

MRS. STILSON *stares at* AMY. *Then she points at her and laughs. At first,* AMY *doesn't understand. Then she does. And then both of them are laughing.)*

MRS. STILSON. Look. You see? *(She scoops some snow off the bench)* If I pick this . . . stuff up in my hand, then . . . I know its name. I didn't have to pick it up to know . . . what it *was*.

AMY. No . . .

MRS. STILSON. But to find its name . . . *(She stares at what is in her hand)* I had to pick it up.

AMY. What's its name?

MRS. STILSON. Snow. It's really nuts, isn't it!

AMY. It's peculiar! *(They laugh. Then, laughter gone, they sit; stare out. Silence for a time.)*

MRS. STILSON. A strange thing happened to me . . . *(pause)* I think last night.

AMY. Can you remember it?

MRS. STILSON. Perfectly.

AMY. Ah!

MRS. STILSON. I think it may have been . . . you know, when you sleep . . .

AMY. A dream.

MRS. STILSON. Yes, one of those, but I'm not . . . sure that it was . . . that. *(Pause. Then she notices the snow in her hand.)* Is it all right if I . . . eat this?

AMY. Yes! We used to make a ball of it, then pour maple syrup on top. Did you ever do that?

MRS. STILSON. I don't know. *(pause)* No, I remember—I did! *(She tastes the snow. Smiles. After a time, the smile vanishes. She turns back to* AMY.*)* Who was that man yesterday?

AMY. What man?

MRS. STILSON. In our group. He seemed all right.

AMY. Oh, that was last week.

MRS. STILSON. I thought for sure he was all right! I thought he was maybe, you know, a doctor.

AMY. Yes, I know.

MRS. STILSON *(searching her memory).* And you asked him to show you where his . . . hand was.

AMY. And he knew.

MRS. STILSON. That's right, he raised his hand, he knew. So I thought, why is Amy joking? *(She ponders.)* Then you asked him . . . *(She tries to remember)* . . . where . . . *(She turns to* AMY*)*

AMY. His elbow was.

MRS. STILSON. Yes! And he . . . *(She struggles to find the word)*

AMY *(helping).* Pointed—

MRS. STILSON *(at the same time).* Pointed to . . . *(But the struggle's getting harder)*

AMY. The corner of the room.

MRS. STILSON. Yes. *(pause.) (softly)* That was very . . . scary.

AMY. Yes. (MRS. STILSON *stares into space. Silence).* What is it that happened to you last night?

MRS. STILSON. Oh yes! Well, this . . . *person* . . . came into my room. I couldn't tell if it was a man or woman or . . . young or old. I was in my bed and it came. Didn't seem to have to walk just . . . came over to my . . . bed and . . . smiled at where I was. *(pause)* And then it said . . . *(in a whisper)* "Emily . . . we're glad you changed your mind." *(pause)* And then . . . it turned and left.

AMY. Was it a doctor? (MRS. STILSON *shakes her head*) One of the staff? (MRS. STILSON *shakes her head*) How do you know?

MRS. STILSON. I just know. *(pause.)* Then . . . I left my body.

AMY. *What?*

MRS. STILSON *(with great excitement).* I was on the . . . what's the name over me—

AMY. Ceiling?

MRS. STILSON. Yes! I was floating like a . . .

AMY. Cloud? (MRS. STILSON *shakes her head.)* Bird?

MRS. STILSON. Yes, up there at the—*(She searches for the word; finds it)*—ceiling, and I looked down and I was still there in my bed! Wasn't even scared, which you'd think I would be . . . And I thought, wow! this is the life

isn't it? *(Sound of wind. Lights begin to change.* AMY *recedes into the darkness.)* It comes now without my asking . . . Amy is still beside me but I am somewhere else. I'm not scared. It has taken me, and it's clear again. Something is about to happen. *(pause.* AMY *now completely gone.* MRS. STILSON *in a narrow spot of light, darkness all around.)* I am in a plane, a Curtiss Jenny, and it's night. Winter. Snow is falling. Feel the tremble of the wings! How I used to walk out on them! Could I have really done— . . . Yes. What I'd do, I'd strap myself with a tether to the stays, couldn't see the tether from below, then out I'd climb! Oh my, but it was wonderful! I could feel the wind! shut my eyes, all alone—FEEL THE SOARING! *(The wind grows stronger. Then the wind dies away. Silence. She notices the change.)*

MRS. STILSON. But this is in another time. Where I've been also . . . It is night and no one else is in the plane. Is it . . . remembering? *(pause)* No . . . No, I'm simply there again! *(pause)* And I'm lost . . . I am lost, completely lost, have to get to . . . somewhere, Omaha I think. The radio is out, or rather for some reason picks up only Bucharest. Clouds all around, no stars only snow, don't possess a clue to where I am, flying blind, soon be out of gas . . . And then the clouds open up a bit, just a bit, and lights appear below, faint, a hint, like torches. Down I drop! heart pounding with relief, with joy, hoping for a landing place, I'll take anything—a field, a street, and down I drop! No place to land . . . It's a town but the smallest—one tiny street is all, three street lamps, no one on the street, all deserted . . . just a street and some faint light in the middle of darkness. Nothing. Still, down I go! Maybe I can find a name on a railroad station, find out where I am! . . . But I see nothing I can read . . . So I begin to circle, though I know I'm wasting fuel and I'll crash if I keep this up! But somehow, I just can't tear myself away! Though I know I should pull back on the stick, get the nose up, head north into darkness— Omaha must be north! But no, I keep circling this one small silly street in this one small town . . . I'm scared to leave it, that's what, as if I guess once away from it I'll be inside something empty, black, and endless . . . *(pause)* So I keep circling—madness!—but I love it, what I see below! And I just can't bring myself to give it up, it's that simple—just can't bring myself to give it up! *(pause)* Then I know I have to. It's a luxury I can't afford. Fuel is running low, almost gone, may be too late anyway, so— *(pause)* I pull the nose up, kick the rudder, bank, and head out into darkness all in terror! GOD, BUT IT TAKES EFFORT! JUST DON'T WANT TO DO IT! . . . But I do. *(pause) (suddenly calm)* Actually, odd thing, once I did, broke free, got into the dark, found I wasn't even scared . . . Or was I? *(Slight laugh)* Can't remember . . . Wonder where that town was . . . ? *(pause)* Got to Omaha all right. *(pause)* Was it Omaha . . . ? *(pause)* Yes, I think so . . . Yes, Topeka, that was it! *(pause)* God, but it was wonderful! *(slight laugh)* Awful scary sometimes, though!

(AMY seen in the distance.)

AMY. Emily! Emily, are you all right!

(Sudden, sharp, terrifying flapping sound. MRS. STILSON gasps. AMY disappears.)

MRS. STILSON *(rapidly)*. Around! There here spins saw it rumple chumps and jumps outgoes inside up and . . . takes it, gives it, okay . . . *(Pause. Easier)* Touch her for me, would you? *(Pause. Even easier)* Oh my, yes, and here it goes then out . . . there I think on . . . wings? Yes . . . *(Pause. Softly, faint smile)* Thank you. *(No trace of terror.) (Music. Hint of bells. Lights to black. Silence.)*

The Elephant Man

Bernard Pomerance

First presented by Richmond Crinkley at The Booth Theatre in New York City, on April 22, 1979, with the following cast:

(*in order of appearance*)

FREDERICK TREVES BELGIAN POLICEMAN	Kevin Conway
CARR GOMM CONDUCTOR	Richard Clarke
ROSS BISHOP WALSHAM HOW SNORK	I. M. Hobson
JOHN MERRICK	Philip Anglim
PINHEAD MANAGER LONDON POLICEMAN WILL EARL LORD JOHN	John Neville-Andrews
PINHEAD MISS SANDWICH COUNTESS PRINCESS ALEXANDRA	Cordis Heard
MRS. KENDAL PINHEAD	Carole Shelley
ORDERLY	Dennis Creaghan
CELLIST	Davis Heiss

Directed by Jack Hofsiss
Scenery by David Jennings
Costumes by Julie Weiss
Lighting by Beverly Emmons

TIME: 1884–1890.
PLACE: London. One scene is in Belgium.

The Elephant Man by Bernard Pomerance was originally produced in 1977 by the Foco Novo at the Hampstead Theatre Club in London. Philip Anglim, the gifted actor who played the part of John Merrick both on and Off Broadway, discovered the play in London and brought it to Richmond Crinkley, the head of the American National Theatre and Academy (ANTA) and of the Vivian Beaumont Theatre. Anglim was not merely responsible for its Broadway production; he raised most of the money to have the play produced by ANTA at St. Peter's Church in New York, on January 14, 1979. Then Anglim and Crinkley brought it to Broadway where it opened at the Booth Theatre on April 19, 1979. *The Elephant Man* is based on the life of Joseph (John) Merrick who suffered from neurofibromatosis, a disease that enlarged his head and right arm to grotesque proportions and covered his body in fibrous tissue. The play is based on the last four years of his life in London Hospital (1886–1890), where he was cared for by Dr. Frederick Treves.

Merrick was born in Leicester, England, to working-class parents. His mother was a Baptist school teacher, and his father was a truck driver. Although he was deformed at birth, the alarming aspects of his disease did not manifest themselves until he was five. As he grew, a painful hip disease rendered him lame, after which he could not walk without the aid of a cane. Tumors then grew all over his body giving it an elephantlike appearance. Only his mother cared for him, and when he was twelve she died of pneumonia. His father married the landlady and Merrick's troubles worsened; taunted by his stepmother's children and removed from school, he was put to labor in a cigar factory. Next he lost the use of his right hand, and to avoid punishment he ran away into the streets where the authorities condemned him to life in a workhouse. Merrick was then persuaded to make his livelihood by exhibiting himself as a freak in carnival sideshows. Through a series of unscrupulous managers and unfortunate occurrences, most of the money he earned was lost to him. Eventually Dr. Treves, a surgeon at London Hospital, found Merrick and placed him under the protectorship of the hospital. Dr. Treves and the hospital's director, Carr Gomm, raised enough money to maintain Merrick at the hospital for life—a life that was to be tragically brief.

Dr. Frederick Treves was born in Dorchester and was educated by the poet William Barnes, who instilled in him a lifelong love of words. In his book, *The Memoirs of Frederick Treves* (1923), he uses this training to write passionately and eloquently of John Merrick: "I supposed Merrick was imbecile and had been imbecile from birth. . . . It was not until I came to know that Merrick was highly intelligent, that he possessed an acute sensibility and worse than all— a romantic imagination, that I realized the overwhelming tragedy of his life."

When Treves realized he could do nothing to improve Merrick's physical condition, he decided to make Merrick's life as normal as possible. "To ensure Merrick's recovery . . . to bring him . . . to life once more, it was necessary that he should make the acquaintance of men and women who would treat him as a normal and intelligent young man, and not as a monster of deformity. Women I felt to be more important. . . . Merrick had an admiration of women . . . that attained almost to adoration . . . they were not real women but the products of his imagination."

Merrick thrived at London Hospital. Beneath his monstrous exterior lived a piercing intelligence and wit and a lively spirit. He entertained an elite circle of admirers that included Princess Alexandra, the Prince of Wales and the celebrated actress Madge Kendall. He also became a voracious reader. Treves states, "I think he had been taught when he was in the hospital with his diseased hip . . . the Bible and Prayer Book he knew intimately . . . the delight of his life was a romance, especially a love romance. These tales were very real to him, as real as any narrative in the Bible . . . in his outlook upon the world he was a child, yet a child with some of the tempestuous feelings of a man. He was an elemental being so primitive that he might have spent the twenty-three years of his life immersed in a cave."

Merrick always remained fond of his mother's memory. He was never without the small locket that carried her likeness; her love and care for him are believed to be the only factors that spared him the emotional crippling so often accompanying physical deformity. He never complained or spoke unkindly of those who had mistreated him. John Merrick died at the age of twenty-eight, falling victim to his desire to be like other people. According to Dr. Treves, "He had often said that he wished he could lie down to sleep like other people. I think this last night he must have with some determination made the experiment. The pillow was soft . . . " Merrick was found dead by asphyxiation, his neck broken by his heavy head in an attempt to lie flat on his bed.

Playwright Bernard Pomerance was born in Brooklyn, New York, and raised in Great Neck, New York. He received his education at the University of Chicago. He has lived and worked in London since 1969. At the time he was an aspiring novelist and his arrival coincided with the explosion in London of left-wing fringe theatre groups that seem to fill every backroom pub and cellar in the West End. He gravitated to this milieu with growing awareness that his writing found better expression in dramatic rather than narrative form. "It's true that I didn't write plays before I came to London. I had been working in narrative form, but I realized all my notes were coming out as dialogue. . . . It was a good period for people to experiment with new kinds of techniques and material. . . ."

He went into partnership with Roland Rees and together they formed the Foco Novo group. Rees subsequently directed all of Pomerance's work. With regard to *The Elephant Man*, Pomerance states, "I'm still not sure what I saw in it then. I find it hard to express myself outside the play. Perhaps the fact of his [Merrick's] being rejected by one society but accepted by another . . ." Regarding theatre and his role in it, "I don't think there is a kind of theatre that I have a particular interest in. I am more interested in content. So much of what is called theatre is antiquated and boring . . . I think the answer is that it is some form of social memory. It serves to bring back points that are too volatile, too dangerous to be lived every day—the skeletons in the closet. . . . The most important element in theatre is the audience's imagination. The audience is people. What is in them is in me. . . . My function is to remind them that this too is true, though our consciousness may deny it. My interest in the audience is to bring them a common thing and, if only temporarily, they . . . then become a community, a unity."

The Elephant Man won the New York Drama Critic's Circle award, three Drama Desk awards, three Obie awards, four Outer Circle Critic's awards, the Drama Guild award, a Theatre World award and three Tony awards, including Best Play of 1979.

Bernard Pomerance's other works include *High in Vietnam, Hot Damn,* about U.S. urban guerillas; *Foco Novo,* concerned with the military dictatorship in Brazil; *Hospital: Thanksgiving Before Detroit,* about American G.I.'s; *Someone Else Is Still Someone,* portraying the manners and convictions of the middle class and *Quantrill in Lawrence* about the guerilla leader Quantrill in Lawrence, Kansas, 1863.

AUTHOR'S NOTE

The Elephant Man was suggested by the life of John Merrick, known as The Elephant Man. It is recounted by Sir Frederick Treves in *The Elephant Man and Other Reminiscences,* Cassell and Co. Ltd., 1923. This account is reprinted in *The Elephant Man, A Study in Human Dignity,* by Ashley Montagu, Ballantine Books, 1973, to whom much credit is due for reviving contemporary interest in the story. My own knowledge of it came via my brother Michael, who told me the story, provided me with Xeroxes of Treves' memoirs until I came on my own copy, and sent me the Montagu book. In Montagu's book are included photographs of Merrick as well as of Merrick's model of St. Phillip's Church. Merrick's bones are still at London Hospital.

I believe the building of the church model constitutes some kind of central metaphor, and the groping toward conditions where it can be built and the building of it are the action of the play. It does not, and should not, however, dominate the play visually, as I originally believed.

Merrick's face was so deformed he could not express any emotion at all. His speech was very difficult to understand without practice. Any attempt to reproduce his appearance and his speech naturalistically—*if* it were possible—would seem to me not only counterproductive, but, the more remarkably successful, the more distracting from the play. For how he appeared, let slide projections suffice.

If the pinheaded women are two actresses, then the play, in a pinch, can be performed with seven players, five men, two women.

SCENE ONE

HE WILL HAVE 100 GUINEA
FEES BEFORE HE'S FORTY

The London Hospital, Whitechapel Rd. Enter GOMM, *enter* TREVES.

———

TREVES. Mr. Carr Gomm? Frederick Treves. Your new lecturer in anatomy.

GOMM. Age thirty-one. Books on Scrofula and Applied Surgical Anatomy—I'm happy to see you rising, Mr. Treves. I like to see merit credited, and your industry, accomplishment, and skill all do you credit. Ignore the squalor of Whitechapel, the general dinginess, neglect and poverty without, and you will find a continual medical richesse in the London Hospital. We study and treat the widest range of diseases and disorders, and are certainly the greatest institution of our kind in the world. The Empire provides unparalleled opportunities for our studies, as places cruel to life are the most revealing scientifically. Add to our reputation by going further, and that'll satisfy. You've bought a house?

TREVES. On Wimpole Street.

GOMM. Good. Keep at it, Treves. You'll have an FRS and 100 guinea fees before you're forty. You'll find it is an excellent consolation prize.

TREVES. Consolation? I don't know what you mean.

GOMM. I know you don't. You will. *(exits)*

TREVES. A happy childhood in Dorset. A scientist in an age of science. In an English age, an Englishman. A teacher and a doctor at the London. Two books published by my thirty-first year. A house. A wife who loves me, and my god, 100 guinea fees before I'm forty. Consolation for what? As of the year AD 1884, I, Freddie Treves, have excessive blessings. Or so it seems to me.

BLACKOUT

SCENE TWO

ART IS AS NOTHING TO NATURE

Whitechapel Rd. A storefront. A large advertisement of a creature with an elephant's head. ROSS, *his manager.*

———

ROSS. Tuppence only, step in and see: This side of the grave, John Merrick has no hope nor expectation of relief. In every sense his situation is desperate. His physical agony is exceeded only by his mental anguish, a despised creature without consolation. Tuppence only, step in and see! To live with his physical hideousness, incapacitating deformities and unremitting pain is trial enough, but to be exposed to the cruelly lacerating expressions of horror and disgust by all who behold him—is even more difficult to bear. Tuppence only, step in and see! For in order to survive, Merrick forces himself to suffer these humiliations, I repeat, humiliations, in order to survive, thus he exposes himself to crowds who pay to gape and yawp at this freak of nature, the Elephant Man.

Enter TREVES *who looks at the advertisement.*

ROSS. See Mother Nature uncorseted and in malignant rage! Tuppence.

TREVES. This sign's absurd. Half-elephant, half-man is not possible. Is he foreign?

ROSS. Right, from Leicester. But nothing to fear.

TREVES. I'm at the London across the road. I would be curious to see him if there is some genuine disorder. If he is a mass of papier-maché and paint however—

ROSS. Then pay me nothing. Enter, sir. Merrick, stand up. Ya bloody donkey, up, up.

(They go in, then emerge. TREVES *pays.)*

TREVES. I must examine him further at the hospital. Here is my card. I'm Treves. I will have a cab pick him up and return him. My card will gain him admittance.

ROSS. Five bob he's yours for the day.

TREVES. I wish to examine him in the interests of science, you see.

ROSS. Sir, I'm Ross. I look out for him, get him his living. Found him in Leicester workhouse. His own ma put him there age of three. Couldn't bear the sight, well you can see why. We—he and I—are in business. He is our capital, see. Go to a bank. Go anywhere. Want to borrow capital, you pay interest. Scientists even. He's good value though. You won't find another like him.

TREVES. Fair enough. *(He pays.)*

ROSS. Right. Out here, Merrick. Ya bloody donkey, out!

(Lights fade out.)

SCENE THREE

WHO HAS SEEN THE LIKE
OF THIS?

TREVES *lectures.* MERRICK *contorts himself to approximate projected slides of the real Merrick.*

———

TREVES. The most striking feature about him was his enormous head. Its circumference was about that of a man's waist. From the brow there projected a huge bony mass like a loaf, while from the back of his head hung a bag of spongy fungous-looking skin, the surface of which was comparable to brown cauliflower. On the top of the skull were a few long lank hairs. The osseous growth on the forehead, at this stage about the size of a tangerine, almost occluded one eye. From the upper jaw there projected another mass of bone. It protruded from the mouth like a pink stump, turning the upper lip inside out, and making the mouth a wide slobbering aperture. The nose was merely a lump of flesh, only recognizable as a nose from its position. The deformities rendered the face utterly incapable of the expression of any emotion whatsoever. The back was horrible because from it hung, as far down as the middle of the thigh, huge sacklike masses of flesh covered by the same loathsome cauliflower stain. The right arm was of enormous size and shapeless. It suggested but was not elephantiasis, and was overgrown also with pendant masses of the same cauliflower-like skin. The right hand was large and clumsy—a fin or paddle rather than a hand. No distinction existed between the palm and back, the thumb was like a radish, the fingers like thick tuberous roots. As a limb it was useless. The other arm was remarkable by contrast. It was not only normal, but was moreover a delicately shaped limb covered with a fine skin and provided with a beautiful hand which any woman might have envied. From the chest hung a bag of the same repulsive flesh. It was like a dewlap suspended from the neck of a lizard. The lower limbs had the characters of the deformed arm. They were unwieldy, dropsical-looking, and grossly misshapen. There arose from the fungous skin growths a very sickening stench which was hard to tolerate. To add a further burden to his trouble, the wretched man when a boy developed hip disease which left him permanently lame, so that he could only walk with a stick.

(to MERRICK*)* Please. *(*MERRICK *walks.)* He was thus denied all means of escape from his tormentors.

VOICE. Mr. Treves, you have shown a profound and unknown disorder to us. You have said when he leaves here it is for his exhibition again. I do not think it ought to be permitted. It is a disgrace. It is a pity and a disgrace. It is an indecency in fact. It may be a danger in ways we do not know. Something ought to be done about it.

TREVES. I am a doctor. What would you have me do?

VOICE. Well, I know what to do. *I* know.

(Silence. A policeman enters as lights fade out.)

SCENE FOUR

THIS INDECENCY MAY NOT
CONTINUE

Music. A fair. PINHEADS *huddling together, holding a portrait of Leopold, King of the Congo. Enter* MAN.

———

MAN. Now, my pinheaded darlings, your attention please. Every freak in Brussels Fair is doing something to celebrate Leopold's fifty year as King of the Congo. Him. Our King. Our Empire. *(They begin reciting.)* No, don't recite yet, you morons. I'll say when. And when you do, get it *right*. You don't, it's back to the asylum. Know what that means, don't you? They'll cut your heads. They'll spoon out your little brains, replace 'em in the dachshund they were nicked from. *Cut you*. Yeah. Be back with customers. Come see the Queens of the Congo! *(exits)*

(Enter MERRICK, ROSS.)

MERRICK. Cosmos? Cosmos?

ROSS. Congo. Land of darkness. Hoho! *(sees* PINS*)* Look at them, lad. It's freer on the continent. Loads of indecency here, no one minds. You won't get coppers sent round to roust you out like London. Reckon in Brussels here's our fortune. You have a little tête-à-tête with this lot while I see the coppers about our license to exhibit. Be right back. *(exits)*

MERRICK. I come from England.

PINS. Allo!

MERRICK. At home they chased us. Out of London. Police. Someone complained. They beat me. You have no trouble? No?

PINS. Allo! Allo!

MERRICK. Hello. In Belgium we make money. I look forward to it. Happiness, I mean. You pay your police? How is it done?

PINS. Allo! Allo!

MERRICK. We do a show together sometime? Yes? I have saved forty-eight pounds. Two shillings. Nine pence. English money. Ross takes care of it.

PINS. Allo! Allo!

MERRICK. Little vocabulary problem, eh? Poor things. Looks like they put your noses to the grindstone and forgot to take them away.

(MAN enters)

MAN. They're coming.

(People enter to see the girls' act.) Now.

PINS *(dancing and singing)*
> We are the Queens of the Congo,
> The Beautiful Belgian Empire
> Our niggers are bigger
> Our miners are finer
> Empire, Empire, Congo and power
> Civilizuzu's finest hour
> Admire, perspire, desire, acquire
> Or we'll set you on fire!

MAN. You cretins! Sorry, they're not ready yet. Out please.

(people exit)

Get those words right, girls! Or you know what.

(MAN exits. PINS weep.)

MERRICK. Don't cry. You sang nicely. Don't cry. There there.

(Enter ROSS in grip of two POLICEMEN.)

ROSS. I was promised a permit. I lined a tour up on that!

POLICEMEN. This is a brutal, indecent, and immoral display. It is a public indecency, and it is forbidden here.

ROSS. What about them with their perfect cone heads?

POLICEMEN. They are ours.

ROSS. Competition's good for business. Where's your spirit of competition?

POLICEMEN. Right here. *(smacks MERRICK)*

ROSS. Don't do that, you'll kill him!

POLICEMEN. Be better off dead. Indecent bastard.

MERRICK. Don't cry girls. Doesn't hurt.

PINS. Indecent, indecent, indecent, indecent!!

(POLICEMEN escort MERRICK and ROSS out, i.e., forward. Blackout except spot on MERRICK and ROSS.)

MERRICK. Ostend will always mean bad memories. Won't it, Ross?

ROSS. I've decided. I'm sending you back,

lad. You're a flop. No, you're a liability. You ain't the moneymaker I figured, so that's it.

MERRICK. Alone?

ROSS. Here's a few bob, have a nosh. I'm keeping the rest. For my trouble. I deserve it, I reckon. Invested enough with you. Pick up your stink if I stick around. Stink of failure. Stink of lost years. Just stink, stink, stink, stink, stink.

(enter CONDUCTOR)

CONDUCTOR. This the one?

ROSS. Just see him to Liverpool St. Station safe, will you? Here's for your trouble.

MERRICK. Robbed.

CONDUCTOR. What's he say?

ROSS. Just makes sounds. Fella's an imbecile.

MERRICK. Robbed.

ROSS. Bon voyage, Johnny. His name is Johnny. He knows his name, that's all, though.

CONDUCTOR. Don't follow him, Johnny. Johnny, come on boat now. Conductor find Johnny place out of sight. Johnny! Johnny! Don't struggle, Johnny. Johnny come on.

MERRICK. Robbed! Robbed!

(Fadeout on struggle)

SCENE FIVE

POLICE SIDE WITH IMBECILE
AGAINST THE CROWD

Darkness. Uproar, shouts.

———

VOICE. Liverpool St. Station!

(Enter MERRICK, CONDUCTOR, POLICEMAN.)

POLICEMAN. We're safe in here. I barred the door.

CONDUCTOR. They wanted to rip him to pieces. I've never seen anything like it. It was like being Gordon at bleedin' Khartoum.

POLICEMAN. Got somewhere to go in London, lad? Can't stay here.

CONDUCTOR. He's an imbecile. He don't understand. Search him.

POLICEMAN. Got any money?

MERRICK. Robbed.

POLICEMAN. What's that?

CONDUCTOR. He just makes sounds. Frightened sounds is all he makes. Go through his coat.

MERRICK. Je-sus.

POLICEMAN. Don't let me go through your coat, I'll turn you over to that lot! Oh, I was joking, don't upset yourself.

MERRICK. Joke? Joke?

POLICEMAN. Sure, croak, croak, croak, croak.

MERRICK. Je-sus.

POLICEMAN. Got a card here. You Johnny Merrick? What's this old card here, Johnny? Someone give you a card?

CONDUCTOR. What's it say?

POLICEMAN. Says Mr. Frederick Treves, Lecturer in Anatomy, the London Hospital.

CONDUCTOR. I'll go see if I can find him, it's not far. *(exits)*

POLICEMAN. What's he do, lecture you on your anatomy? People who think right don't look like that then, do they? Yeah, glung glung, glung, glung.

MERRICK. Jesus. Jesus.

POLICEMAN. Sure, Treves, Treves, Treves, Treves. .

(Blackout, then lights go up as CONDUCTOR *leads* TREVES *in.)*

TREVES. What is going on here? Look at that mob, have you no sense of decency. I am Frederick Treves. This is my card.

POLICEMAN. This poor wretch here had it. Arrived from Ostend.

TREVES. Good Lord, Merrick? John Merrick? What has happened to you?

MERRICK. Help me!

(Fadeout)

SCENE SIX

EVEN ON THE NIGER AND
CEYLON, NOT THIS

The London Hospital. MERRICK *in bathtub.* TREVES *outside. Enter* MISS SANDWICH.

———

TREVES. You are? Miss Sandwich?

SANDWICH. Sandwich. Yes.

TREVES. You have had experience in missionary hospitals in the Niger.

SANDWICH. And Ceylon.

TREVES. I may assume you've seen—

SANDWICH. The tropics. Oh those diseases. The many and the awful scourges our Lord sends, yes, sir.

TREVES. I need the help of an experienced nurse, you see.

SANDWICH. Someone to bring him food, take care of the room. Yes, I understand. But it is somehow difficult.

TREVES. Well, I have been let down so far.

He really is—that is, the regular sisters—well, it is not part of their job and they will not do it. Be ordinarily kind to Mr. Merrick. Without—well—panicking. He is quite beyond ugly. You understand that? His appearance has terrified them.

SANDWICH. The photographs show a terrible disease.

TREVES. It is a disorder, not a disease; it is in no way contagious though we don't in fact know what it is. I have found however that there is a deep superstition in those I've tried, they actually believe he somehow brought it on himself, this thing, and of course it is not that at all.

SANDWICH. I am not one who believes it is ourselves who attain grace or bring chastisement to us, sir.

TREVES. Miss Sandwich, I am hoping not.

SANDWICH. Let me put your mind to rest. Care for lepers in the East, and you have cared, Mr. Treves. In Africa, I have seen dreadful scourges quite unknown to our more civilized climes. What at home could be worse than a miserable and afflicted rotting black?

TREVES. I imagine.

SANDWICH. Appearances do not daunt me.

TREVES. It is really that that has sent me outside the confines of the London seeking help.

SANDWICH. "I look unto the hills whence cometh my help." I understand: I think I will be satisfactory.

(Enter PORTER *with tray.)*

PORTER. His lunch. *(exits)* .

TREVES. Perhaps you would be so kind as to accompany me this time. I will introduce you.

SANDWICH. Allow me to carry the tray.

TREVES. I will this time. You are ready.

SANDWICH. I am.

TREVES. He is bathing to be rid of his odor.

(They enter to MERRICK.*)*

John, this is Miss Sandwich. She—

SANDWICH. I—*(unable to control herself)* Oh my good God in heaven. *(bolts room)*

TREVES *(puts* MERRICK'*s lunch down).* I am sorry. I thought—

MERRICK. Thank you for saving the lunch this time.

TREVES. Excuse me.

(exits to MISS SANDWICH*)*

You have let me down, you know. I did everything to warn you and still you let me down.

SANDWICH. You didn't say.

TREVES. But I—

SANDWICH. Didn't! You said—just words!

TREVES. But the photographs.

SANDWICH. Just pictures. No one will do this. I am sorry.

(exits)

TREVES. Yes. Well. This is not helping him.
(Fadeout)

SCENE SEVEN

THE ENGLISH PUBLIC WILL PAY
FOR HIM TO BE LIKE US

The London Hospital. MERRICK *in a bathtub reading.* TREVES, BISHOP HOW *in foreground.*

BISHOP. With what fortitude he bears his cross! It is remarkable. He has made the acquaintance of religion and knows sections of the Bible by heart. Once I'd grasped his speech, it became clear he'd certainly had religious instruction at one time.

TREVES. I believe it was in the workhouse, Dr. How.

BISHOP. They are awfully good about that sometimes. The psalms he loves, and the book of Job perplexes him, he says, for he cannot see that a just God must cause suffering, as he puts it, merely then to be merciful. Yet that Christ will save him he does not doubt, so he is not resentful.

(enter GOMM)

GOMM. Christ had better; be damned if we can.

BISHOP. Ahem. In any case Dr. Treves, he has a religious nature, further instruction would uplift him and I'd be pleased to provide it. I plan to speak of him from the pulpit this week.

GOMM. I see our visiting bather has flushed the busy Bishop How from his cruciform lair.

BISHOP. Speak with Merrick, sir. I have spoken to him of Mercy and Justice. There's a true Christian in the rough.

GOMM. This makes my news seem banal, yet yes: Frederick, the response to my letter to the *Times* about Merrick has been staggering. The English public has been so generous that Merrick may be supported for life without a penny spent from Hospital funds.

TREVES. But that is excellent.

BISHOP. God bless the English public.

GOMM. Especially for not dismembering him at Liverpool St. Station. Freddie, the London's no home for incurables, this is quite irregular,

but for you I permit it—though god knows what you'll do.

BISHOP. God does know, sir, and Darwin does not.

GOMM. He'd better, sir; he deformed him.

BISHOP. I had apprehensions coming here. I find it most fortunate Merrick is in the hands of Dr. Treves, a Christian, sir.

GOMM. Freddie is a good man and a brilliant doctor, and that is fortunate indeed.

TREVES. I couldn't have raised the funds though, Doctor.

BISHOP. Don't let me keep you longer from your duties, Mr. Treves. Yet, Mr. Gomm, consider: is it science, sir, that motivates us when we transport English rule of law to India or Ireland? When good British churchmen leave hearth and home for missionary hardship in Africa, is it science that bears them away? Sir it is not. It is Christian duty. It is the obligation to bring our light and benefices to benighted man. That motivates us, even as it motivates Treves toward Merrick, sir, to bring salvation where none is. Gordon was a Christian, sir, and died at Khartoum for it. Not for science, sir.

GOMM. You're telling me, not for science.

BISHOP. Mr. Treves, I'll visit Merrick weekly if I may.

TREVES. You will be welcome, sir, I am certain.

BISHOP. Then good day, sirs. *(exits)*

GOMM. Well, Jesus my boy, now we have the money, what do you plan for Merrick?

TREVES. Normality as far as is possible.

GOMM. So he will be like us? Ah. *(smiles)*

TREVES. Is something wrong, Mr. Gomm? With us?

(Fadeout)

SCENE EIGHT

MERCY AND JUSTICE ELUDE
OUR MINDS AND ACTIONS

MERRICK *in bath.* TREVES, GOMM.

MERRICK. How long is as long as I like?

TREVES. You may stay for life. The funds exist.

MERRICK. Been reading this. About homes for the blind. Wouldn't mind going to one when I have to move.

TREVES. But you do not have to move; and

you're not blind.

MERRICK. I would prefer it where no one stared at me.

GOMM. No one will bother you here.

TREVES. Certainly not. I've given instructions.

(PORTER and SNORK peek in.)

PORTER. What'd I tell you?

SNORK. Gawd almighty. Oh. Mr. Treves. Mr. Gomm.

TREVES. You were told not to do this. I don't understand. You must not lurk about. Surely you have work.

PORTER. Yes, sir.

TREVES. Well, it is infuriating. When you are told a thing, you must listen. I won't have you gaping in on my patients. Kindly remember that.

PORTER. Isn't a patient, sir, is he?

TREVES. Do not let me find you here again.

PORTER. Didn't know you were here, sir. We'll be off now.

GOMM. No, no, Will. Mr. Treves was precisely saying no one would intrude when you intruded.

TREVES. He is warned now. Merrick does not like it.

GOMM. He was warned before. On what penalty, Will?

PORTER. That you'd sack me, sir.

GOMM. You are sacked, Will. You, his friend, you work here?

SNORK. Just started last week, sir.

GOMM. Well, I hope the point is taken now.

PORTER. Mr. Gomm—I ain't truly sacked, am I?

GOMM. Will, yes. Truly sacked. You will never be more truly sacked.

PORTER. It's not me. My wife ain't well. My sister has got to take care of our kids, and of her. Well.

GOMM. Think of them first next time.

PORTER. It ain't as if I interfered with his medicine.

GOMM. That is exactly what it is. You may go.

PORTER. Just keeping him to look at in private. That's all. Isn't it?

(SNORK and PORTER exit.)

GOMM. There are priorities, Frederick. The first is discipline. Smooth is the passage to the tight ship's master. Merrick, you are safe from prying now.

TREVES. Have we nothing to say, John?

MERRICK. If all that'd stared at me'd been sacked—there'd be whole towns out of work.

TREVES. I meant, "Thank you, sir."

MERRICK. "Thank you sir."

TREVES. We always do say please and thank you, don't we?

MERRICK. Yes, sir. Thank you.

TREVES. If we want to properly be like others.

MERRICK. Yes, sir, I want to.

TREVES. Then it is for our own good, is it not?

MERRICK. Yes, sir. Thank you, Mr. Gomm.

GOMM. Sir, you are welcome. *(exits)*

TREVES. You are happy here, are you not, John?

MERRICK. Yes.

TREVES. The baths have rid you of the odor, have they not?

MERRICK. First chance I had to bathe regularly.

TREVES. And three meals a day delivered to your room?

MERRICK. Yes, sir.

TREVES. This is your Promised Land, is it not? A roof. Food. Protection. Care. Is it not?

MERRICK. Right, Mr. Treves.

TREVES. I will bet you don't know what to call this.

MERRICK. No, sir, I don't know.

TREVES. You call it, Home.

MERRICK. Never had a home before.

TREVES. You have one now. Say it. John: Home.

MERRICK. Home.

TREVES. No, no, really say it. I have a home. This is my. Go on.

MERRICK. I have a home. This is my home. This is my home. I have a home. As long as I like?

TREVES. That is what home is.

MERRICK. That is what is home.

TREVES. If I abide by the rules, I will be happy.

MERRICK. Yes, sir.

TREVES. Don't be shy.

MERRICK. If I abide by the rules I will be happy.

TREVES. Very good. Why?

MERRICK. Why what?

TREVES. Will you be happy?

MERRICK. Because it is my home?

TREVES. No, no. Why do rules make you happy?

MERRICK. I don't know.

TREVES. Of course you do.

MERRICK. No, I really don't.

TREVES. Why does anything make you happy?

MERRICK. Like what? Like what?

TREVES. Don't be upset. Rules make us happy because they are for our own good.

MERRICK. Okay.

TREVES. Don't be shy, John. You can say it.

MERRICK. This is my home?

TREVES. No. About rules making us happy.

MERRICK. They make us happy because they are for our own good.

TREVES. Excellent. Now: I am submitting a follow-up paper on you to the London Pathological Society. It would help if you told me what you recall about your first years, John. To fill in gaps.

MERRICK. To fill in gaps. The workhouse where they put me. They beat you there like a drum. Boom boom: scrape the floor white. Shine the pan, boom boom. It never ends. The floor is always dirty. The pan is always tarnished. There is nothing you can do about it. You are always attacked anyway. Boom boom. Boom boom. Boom boom. Will the children go to the workhouse?

TREVES. What children?

MERRICK. The children. The man he sacked.

TREVES. Of necessity Will will find other employment. You don't want crowds staring at you, do you?

MERRICK. No.

TREVES. In your own home you do not have to have crowds staring at you. Or anyone. Do you? In your home?

MERRICK. No.

TREVES. Then Mr. Gomm was merciful. You yourself are proof. Is it not so? *(pause)* Well? Is it not so?

MERRICK. If your mercy is so cruel, what do you have for justice?

TREVES. I am sorry. It is just the way things are.

MERRICK. Boom boom. Boom boom. Boom boom.

(Fadeout)

SCENE NINE

MOST IMPORTANT ARE WOMEN

MERRICK *asleep, head on knees.* TREVES, MRS. KENDAL *foreground.*

———

TREVES. You have seen photographs of John Merrick, Mrs. Kendal. You are acquainted with his appearance.

MRS. KENDAL. He reminds me of an audience I played Cleopatra for in Brighton once. All huge grim head and grimace and utterly unable to clap.

TREVES. Well. My aim's to lead him to as normal a life as possible. His terror of us all comes from having been held at arm's length from society. I am determined that shall end. For example, he loves to meet people and converse. I am determined he shall. For example, he had never seen the inside of any normal home before. I had him to mine, and what a reward, Mrs. Kendal; his astonishment, his joy at the most ordinary things. Most critical I feel, however, are women. I will explain. They have always shown the greatest fear and loathing of him. While he adores them of course.

MRS. KENDAL. Ah. He is intelligent.

TREVES. I am convinced they are the key to retrieving him from his exclusion. Though, I must warn you, women are not quite real to him—more creatures of his imagination.

MRS. KENDAL. Then he is already like other men, Mr. Treves.

TREVES. So I thought, an actress could help. I mean, unlike most women, you won't give in, you are trained to hide your true feelings and assume others.

MRS. KENDAL. You mean unlike most women I am famous for it, that is really all.

TREVES. Well. In any case. If you could enter the room and smile and wish him good morning. And when you leave, shake his hand, the left one is usable, and really quite beautiful, and say, "I am very pleased to have made your acquaintance, Mr. Merrick."

MRS. KENDAL. Shall we try it? Left hand out please. *(suddenly radiant)* I am *very* pleased to have made your acquaintance Mr. Merrick. I am very *pleased* to have made your acquaintance Mr. Merrick. I am very pleased to have made your *acquaintance* Mr. Merrick. I *am* very pleased to have made *your* acquaintance Mr. Merrick. Yes. That one.

TREVES. By god, they are all splendid. Merrick will be so pleased. It will be the day he becomes a man like other men.

MRS. KENDAL. Speaking of that, Mr. Treves.

TREVES. Frederick, please.

MRS. KENDAL. Freddie, may I commit an indiscretion?

TREVES. Yes?

MRS. KENDAL. I could not but help noticing from the photographs that—well—of the un-afflicted parts—ah, how shall I put it? *(Points to photograph.)*

TREVES. Oh. I see! I quite. Understand. No, no, no, it is quite normal.

MRS. KENDAL. I thought as much.

TREVES. Medically speaking, uhm, you see the papillomatous extrusions which disfigure him, uhm, seem to correspond quite regularly to the osseous deformities, that is, excuse me, there is a link between the bone disorder and the skin growths, though for the life of me I have not discovered what it is or why it is, but in any case this—part—it would be therefore unlikely to be afflicted because well, that is, well, there's no bone in it. None at all. I mean.

MRS. KENDAL. Well. Learn a little every day don't we?

TREVES. I am horribly embarrassed.

MRS. KENDAL. Are you? Then he must be lonely indeed.

(Fadeout)

SCENE TEN

WHEN THE ILLUSION ENDS HE
MUST KILL HIMSELF

MERRICK *sketching. Enter* TREVES, MRS. KENDAL.

TREVES. He is making sketches for a model of St. Phillip's church. He wants someday to make a model, you see. John, my boy, this is Mrs. Kendal. She would very much like to make your acquaintance.

MRS. KENDAL. Good morning Mr. Merrick.

TREVES. I will see to a few matters. I will be back soon.

(Exits.)

MERRICK. I planned so many things to say. I forget them. You are so beautiful.

MRS. KENDAL. How charming, Mr. Merrick.

MERRICK. Well. Really that was what I planned to say. That I forgot what I planned to say. I couldn't think of anything else I was so excited.

MRS. KENDAL. Real charm is always planned, don't you think?

MERRICK. Well. I do not know why I look like this, Mrs. Kendal. My mother was so beautiful. She was knocked down by an elephant in a circus while she was pregnant. Something must have happened, don't you think?

MRS. KENDAL. It may well have.

MERRICK. It may well have. But sometimes I think my head is so big because it is so full of dreams. Because it is. Do you know what happens when dreams cannot get out?

MRS. KENDAL. Why, no.

MERRICK. I don't either. Something must. *(silence)* Well. You are a famous actress.

MRS. KENDAL. I am not unknown.

MERRICK. You must display yourself for your living then. Like I did.

MRS. KENDAL. That is not myself, Mr. Merrick. That is an illusion. This is myself.

MERRICK. This is myself too.

MRS. KENDAL. Frederick says you like to read. So: books.

MERRICK. I am reading *Romeo and Juliet* now.

MRS. KENDAL. Ah. Juliet. What a love story. I adore love stories.

MERRICK. I like love stories best too. If I had been Romeo, guess what.

MRS. KENDAL. What?

MERRICK. I would not have held the mirror to her breath.

MRS. KENDAL. You mean the scene where Juliet appears to be dead and he holds a mirror to her breath and sees—

MERRICK. Nothing. How does it feel when he kills himself because he just sees nothing?

MRS. KENDAL. Well. My experience as Juliet has been—particularly with an actor I will not name—that while I'm laying there dead dead dead, and he is lamenting excessively, I get to thinking that if this slab of ham does not part from the hamhock of his life toute suite, I am going to scream, pop off the tomb, and plunge a dagger into his scene-stealing heart. Romeos are very undependable.

MERRICK. Because he does not care for Juliet.

MRS. KENDAL. Not care?

MERRICK. Does he take her pulse? Does he get a doctor? Does he make sure? No. He kills himself. The illusion fools him because he does not care for her. He only cares about himself. If I had been Romeo, we would have got away.

MRS. KENDAL. But then there would be no play, Mr. Merrick.

MERRICK. If he did not love her, why should there be a play? Looking in a mirror and seeing nothing. That is not love. It was all an illusion. When the illusion ended he had to kill himself.

MRS. KENDAL. Why. That is extraordinary.

MERRICK. Before I spoke with people, I did not think of all these things because there was no one to bother to think them for. Now things just come out of my mouth which are true.

(TREVES enters.)

TREVES. You are famous, John. We are in the papers. Look. They have written up my report to the Pathological Society. Look—it is a kind of apotheosis for you.

MRS. KENDAL. Frederick, I feel Mr. Merrick would benefit by even more company than you provide; in fact by being acquainted with the best, and they with him. I shall make it my task if you'll permit. As you know, I am a friend of nearly everyone, and I do pretty well as I please and what pleases me is this task, I think.

TREVES. By god, Mrs. Kendal, you are splendid.

MRS. KENDAL. Mr. Merrick I must go now. I should like to return if I may. And so that we may without delay teach you about society, I would like to bring my good friend Dorothy Lady Neville. She would be most pleased if she could meet you. Let me tell her yes?

(MERRICK nods yes.)

Then until next time. I'm sure your church model will surprise us all. Mr. Merrick, it has been a very great pleasure to make your acquaintance.

TREVES. John. Your hand. 'She wishes to shake your hand.

MERRICK. Thank you for coming.

MRS. KENDAL. But it was my pleasure. Thank you. *(exits, accompanied by TREVES)*

TREVES. What a wonderful success. Do you know he's never shook a woman's hand before?

(As lights fade MERRICK sobs soundlessly, uncontrollably.)

SCENE ELEVEN

HE DOES IT WITH JUST
ONE HAND

Music. MERRICK *working on model of St. Phillip's church. Enter* DUCHESS. *At side* TREVES *ticks off a gift list.*

———

MERRICK. Your grace.

DUCHESS. How nicely the model is coming along, Mr. Merrick. I've come to say Happy Christmas, and that I hope you will enjoy this ring and remember your friend by it.

MERRICK. Your grace, thank you.

DUCHESS. I am very pleased to have made your acquaintance. *(exits)*

(enter COUNTESS*)*

COUNTESS. Please accept these silver-backed brushes and comb for Christmas, Mr. Merrick.

MERRICK. With many thanks, Countess.

COUNTESS. I am very pleased to have made your acquaintance. *(exits)*

(enter LORD JOHN*)*

LORD JOHN. Here's the silver-topped walking stick, Merrick. Make you a regular Piccadilly exquisite. Keep up the good work. Self-help is the best help. Example to us all.

MERRICK. Thank you, Lord John.

LORD JOHN. Very pleased to have made your acquaintance. *(exits)*

(Enter TREVES *and* PRINCESS ALEXANDRA.*)*

TREVES. Her Royal Highness Princess Alexandra.

PRINCESS. The happiest of Christmases, Mr. Merrick.

TREVES. Her Royal Highness has brought you a signed photograph of herself.

MERRICK. I am honored, your Royal Highness. It is the treasure of my possessions. I have written to His Royal Highness the Prince of Wales to thank him for the pheasants and woodcock he sent.

PRINCESS. You are a credit to Mr. Treves, Mr. Merrick. Mr. Treves, you are a credit to medicine, to England, and to Christendom. I am so very pleased to have made your acquaintance.

(PRINCESS, TREVES exit. Enter MRS. KENDAL.*)*

MRS. KENDAL. Good news, John. Bertie says we may use the Royal Box whenever I like. Mrs. Keppel says it gives a unique perspective. And for Christmas, ivory-handled razors and toothbrush.

(enter TREVES*)*

TREVES. And a cigarette case, my boy, full of cigarettes!

MERRICK. Thank you. Very much.

MRS. KENDAL. Look Freddie, look. The model of St. Phillip's.

TREVES. It is remarkable, I know.

MERRICK. And I do it with just one hand, they all say.

MRS. KENDAL. You are an artist, John Merrick, an artist.

MERRICK. I did not begin to build at first. Not till I saw what St. Phillip's really was. It is not stone and steel and glass; it is an imitation of grace flying up and up from the mud. So I make my imitation of an imitation. But even in that is heaven to me, Mrs. Kendal.

TREVES. That thought's got a good line, John. Plato believed this was all a world of illusion and that artists made illusions of illusions of heaven.

MERRICK. You mean we are all just copies? Of originals?

TREVES. That's it.

MERRICK. Who made the copies?

TREVES. God. The Demi-urge.

MERRICK *(goes back to work)*. He should have used both hands shouldn't he?

(Music. Puts another piece on St. Phillip's. Fadeout.)

SCENE TWELVE

WHO DOES HE REMIND
YOU OF?

TREVES, MRS. KENDAL.

———

TREVES. Why all those toilet articles, tell me? He is much too deformed to use any of them.

MRS. KENDAL. Props of course. To make himself. As I make me.

TREVES. You? You think of yourself.

MRS. KENDAL. Well. He is gentle, almost feminine. Cheerful, honest within limits, a serious artist in his way. He is almost like me.

(Enter BISHOP HOW)

BISHOP. He is religious and devout. He knows salvation must radiate to us or all is lost, which it's certainly not.

(enter GOMM)

GOMM. He seems practical, like me. He has seen enough of daily evil to be thankful for small goods that come his way. He knows what side his bread is buttered on, and counts his blessings for it. Like me.

(enter DUCHESS)

DUCHESS. I can speak with him of anything. For I know he is discreet. Like me.

(All exit except TREVES.)

TREVES. How odd. I think him curious, compassionate, concerned about the world, well, rather like myself, Freddie Treves, 1889 AD.

(enter MRS. KENDAL)

MRS. KENDAL. Of course he is rather odd. And hurt. And helpless not to show the struggling. And so am I.

(enter GOMM)

GOMM. He knows I use him to raise money for the London, I am certain. He understands I would be derelict if I didn't. He is wary of any promise, yet he fits in well. Like me.

(enter BISHOP HOW)

BISHOP. I as a seminarist had many of the same doubts. Struggled as he does. And hope they may be overcome.

(enter PRINCESS ALEXANDRA)

PRINCESS. When my husband His Royal Highness Edward Prince of Wales asked Dr. Treves to be his personal surgeon, he said, "Dear Freddie, if you can put up with the Elephant bloke, you can surely put up with me."

(All exit, except TREVES. Enter LORD JOHN.)

LORD JOHN. See him out of fashion, Freddie. As he sees me. Social contacts critical. Oh— by the way—ignore the bloody papers; all lies. *(exits)*

TREVES. Merrick visibly worse than 86–87. That, as he rises higher in the consolations of society, he gets visibly more grotesque is proof definitive he is like me. Like his condition, which I make no sense of, I make no sense of mine.

(Spot on MERRICK placing another piece on St. Phillip's. Fadeout.)

SCENE THIRTEEN

ANXIETIES OF THE SWAMP

MERRICK, *in spot, strains to listen:* TREVES, LORD JOHN *outside.*

———

TREVES. But the papers are saying you broke the contracts. They are saying you've lost the money.

LORD JOHN. Freddie, if I were such a scoundrel, how would I dare face investors like yourself. Broken contracts! I never considered them actual contracts—just preliminary things, get the old deal under way. An actual contract's something between gentlemen; and this attack on me shows they are no gentlemen. Now I'm only here to say the company remains a terribly attractive proposition. Don't you think? To recapitalize—if you could spare another—ah.

(enter GOMM)

Mr. Gomm. How good to see you. Just remarking how splendidly Merrick thrives here, thanks to you and Freddie.

GOMM. Lord John. Allow me: I must take Frederick from you. Keep him at work. It's in his contract. Wouldn't want him breaking it. Sort of thing makes the world fly apart, isn't it?

LORD JOHN. Yes. Well. Of course, mmm.

GOMM. Sorry to hear you're so pressed. Expect we'll see less of you around the London now?

LORD JOHN. Of course, I, actually—ah! Overdue actually. Appointment in the City. Freddie. Mr. Gomm. *(exits)*

TREVES. He plain fooled me. He was kind to Merrick.

GOMM. You have risen fast and easily, my boy. You've forgot how to protect yourself. Break now.

TREVES. It does not seem right somehow.

GOMM. The man's a moral swamp. Is that not clear yet? Is he attractive? Deceit often is. Friendly? Swindlers can be. Another loan? Not another cent. It may be your money, Freddie; but I will not tolerate laboring like a navvy that the London should represent honest charitable and compassionate science, and have titled swindlers mucking up the pitch. He has succeeded in destroying himself so rabidly, you ought not doubt an instant it was his real aim all along. He broke the contracts, gambled the money away, lied, and like an infant in his mess, gurgles and wants to do it again. Never mind details, don't want to know. Break and be glad. Don't hesitate. Today. One-man moral swamp. Don't be sucked in.

(enter MRS. KENDAL)

MRS. KENDAL. Have you seen the papers?

TREVES. Yes.

GOMM. Yes, yes. A great pity. Freddie: today. *(exits)*

MRS. KENDAL. Freddie?

TREVES. He has used us. I shall be all right. Come.

(MRS. KENDAL, TREVES enter to MERRICK) John: I shall not be able to stay this visit. I must, well, unravel a few things. Nurse Ireland and Snork are—?

MERRICK. Friendly and respectful, Frederick.

TREVES. I'll look in in a few days.

MERRICK. Did I do something wrong?

MRS. KENDAL. No.

TREVES. This is a hospital. Not a marketplace. Don't forget it, ever. Sorry. Not you. Me. *(exits)*

MRS. KENDAL. Well. Shall we weave today? Don't you think weaving might be fun? So many things are fun. Most men really can't enjoy them. Their loss, isn't it? I like little activities which engage me; there's something ancient in it, I don't know. Before all this. Would you like to try? John?

MERRICK. Frederick said I may stay here for life.

MRS. KENDAL. And so you shall.

MERRICK. If he is in trouble?

MRS. KENDAL. Frederick is your protector, John.

MERRICK. If he is in trouble? *(He picks up small photograph.)*

MRS. KENDAL. Who is that? Ah, is it not your mother? She is pretty, isn't she?

MERRICK. Will Frederick keep his word with me, his contract, Mrs. Kendal? If he is in trouble.

MRS. KENDAL. What? Contract? Did you say?

MERRICK. And will you?

MRS. KENDAL. I? What? Will I?

(MERRICK silent. Puts another piece on model. Fadeout.)

SCENE FOURTEEN

ART IS PERMITTED BUT NATURE
FORBIDDEN

Rain. MERRICK *working.* MRS. KENDAL.

————

MERRICK. The Prince has a mistress. *(silence)* The Irishman had one. Everyone seems to. Or a wife. Some have both. I have concluded I need a mistress. It is bad enough not to sleep like others.

MRS. KENDAL. Sitting up, you mean. Couldn't be very restful.

MERRICK. I have to. Too heavy to lay down. My head. But to sleep alone; that is worst of all.

MRS. KENDAL. The artist expresses his love through his works. That is civilization.

MERRICK. Are you very shocked?

MRS. KENDAL. Why should I be?

MERRICK. Others would be.

MRS. KENDAL. I am not others.

MERRICK. I suppose it is hopeless.

MRS. KENDAL. Nothing is hopeless. However it is unlikely.

MERRICK. I thought you might have a few ideas.

MRS. KENDAL. I can guess who has ideas here.

MERRICK. You don't know something. I have never even seen a naked woman.

MRS. KENDAL. Surely in all the fairs you worked.

MERRICK. I mean a real woman.

MRS. KENDAL. Is one more real than another?

MERRICK. I mean like the ones in the theater. The opera.

MRS. KENDAL. Surely you can't mean they are more real.

MERRICK. In the audience. A woman not worn out early. Not deformed by awful life. A lady. Someone kept up. Respectful of herself. You don't know what fairgrounds are like, Mrs. Kendal.

MRS. KENDAL. You mean someone like Princess Alexandra?

MERRICK. Not so old.

MRS. KENDAL. Ah. Like Dorothy.

MERRICK. She does not look happy. No.

MRS. KENDAL. Lady Ellen?

MERRICK. Too thin.

MRS. KENDAL. Then who?

MERRICK. Certain women. They have a kind of ripeness. They seem to stop at a perfect point.

MRS. KENDAL. My dear she doesn't exist.

MERRICK. That is probably why I never saw her.

MRS. KENDAL. What would your friend Bishop How say of all this I wonder?

MERRICK. He says I should put these things out of my mind.

MRS. KENDAL. Is that the best he can suggest?

MERRICK. I put them out of my mind. They reappeared, snap.

MRS. KENDAL. What about Frederick?

MERRICK. He would be appalled if I told him.

MRS. KENDAL. I am flattered. Too little trust has maimed my life. But that is another story.

MERRICK. What a rain. Are we going to read this afternoon?

MRS. KENDAL. Yes. Some women are lucky to look well, that is all. It is a rather arbitrary gift; it has no really good use, though it has uses, I will say that. Anyway it does not signify very much.

MERRICK. To me it does.

MRS. KENDAL. Well. You are mistaken.

MERRICK. What are we going to read?

MRS. KENDAL. Trust is very important you know. I trust you.

MERRICK. Thank you very much. I have a book of Thomas Hardy's here. He is a friend of Frederick's. Shall we read that?

MRS. KENDAL. Turn around a moment. Don't look.

MERRICK. Is this a game?

MRS. KENDAL. I would not call it a game. A surprise. *(She begins undressing.)*

MERRICK. What kind of a surprise?

MRS. KENDAL. I saw photographs of you. Before I met you. You didn't know that, did you?

MERRICK. The ones from the first time, in '84? No, I didn't.

MRS. KENDAL. I felt it was—unjust. I don't know why. I cannot say my sense of justice is my most highly developed characteristic. You may turn around again. Well. A little funny, isn't it?

MERRICK. It is the most beautiful sight I have seen. Ever.

MRS. KENDAL. If you tell anyone, I shall not see you again, we shall not read, we shall not talk, we shall do nothing. Wait. *(undoes her hair)* There. No illusions. Now. Well? What is there to say? "I am extremely pleased to have made your acquaintance?"

(enter TREVES)

TREVES. For God's sakes. What is going on here? What is going on?

MRS. KENDAL. For a moment, Paradise, Freddie. *(She begins dressing.)*

TREVES. But—have you no sense of decency? Woman, dress yourself quickly.

(Silence. MERRICK goes to put another piece on St. Phillip's.)

Are you not ashamed? Do you know what you are? Don't you know what is forbidden?

(Fadeout)

SCENE FIFTEEN

INGRATITUDE

ROSS *in* MERRICK'*s room.*

———

ROSS. I come actually to ask your forgiveness.

MERRICK. I found a good home, Ross. I forgave you.

ROSS. I was hoping we could work out a deal. Something new maybe.

MERRICK. No.

ROSS. See, I was counting on it. That you were kindhearted. Like myself. Some things don't change. Got to put your money on the things that don't, I figure. I figure from what I read about you, you don't change. Dukes, Ladies coming to see you. Ask myself why? Figure it's same as always was. Makes 'em feel good about themselves by comparison. Them things don't change. There but for the grace of. So I figure you're selling the same service as always. To better clientele. Difference now is you ain't charging for it.

MERRICK. You make me sound like a whore.

ROSS. You are. I am. They are. Most are. No disgrace, John. Disgrace is to be a stupid whore. Give it for free. Not capitalize on the interest in you. Not to have a manager then is stupid.

MERRICK. You see this church. I am building it. The people who visit are friends. Not clients. I am not a dog walking on its hind legs.

ROSS. I was thinking. Charge these people. Pleasure of the Elephant Man's company. Something. Right spirit is everything. Do it in the right spirit, they'd pay happily. I'd take ten percent. I'd be okay with ten percent.

MERRICK. Bad luck's made you daft.

ROSS. I helped you, John. Discovered you. Was that daft? No. Only daftness was being at a goldmine without a shovel. Without proper connections. Like Treves has. What's daft? Ross sows, Treves harvests? It's not fair, is it John? When you think about it. I do think about it. Because I'm old. Got something in my throat. You may have noticed. Something in my lung here too. Something in my belly I guess too. I'm not a heap of health, am I? But I'd do well with ten percent. I don't need more than ten percent. Ten percent'd give me a future slightly better'n a cobblestone. This lot would pay, if you charged in the right spirit. I don't ask much.

MERRICK. They're the cream, Ross. They know it. Man like you tries to make them pay, they'll walk away.

ROSS. I'm talking about doing it in the right spirit.

MERRICK. They are my friends. I'd lose everything. For you. Ross, you lived your life. You robbed me of forty-eight pounds, nine shillings, tuppence. You left me to die. Be satisfied Ross. You've had enough. You kept me like an animal in darkness. You come back and want to rob me again. Will you not be satisfied? Now I am a man like others, you want me to return?

ROSS. Had a woman yet?

MERRICK. Is that what makes a man?

ROSS. In my time it'd do for a start.

MERRICK. Not what makes this one. Yet I am like others.

ROSS. Then I'm condemned. I got no energy to try nothing new. I may as well go to the dosshouse straight. Die there anyway. Between filthy dosshouse rags. Nothing in the belly but acid. I don't like pain, John. The future gives pain sense. Without a future— (*pauses*) Five percent? John?

MERRICK. I'm sorry, Ross. It's just the way things are.

ROSS. By god. Then I am lost.

(*Fadeout*)

SCENE SIXTEEN

NO RELIABLE GENERAL ANESTHETIC HAS APPEARED YET

TREVES, *reading, makes notes.* MERRICK *works.*

_____

MERRICK. Frederick—do you believe in heaven? Hell? What about Christ? What about God? I believe in heaven. The Bible promises in heaven the crooked shall be made straight.

TREVES. So did the rack, my boy. So do we all.

MERRICK. You don't believe?

TREVES. I will settle for a reliable general anesthetic at this point. Actually, though—I had a patient once. A woman. Operated on her for—a woman's thing. Used ether to anesthetize. Tricky stuff. Didn't come out of it. Pulse stopped, no vital signs, absolutely moribund. Just a big white dead mackerel. Five minutes later, she fretted back to existence, like a lost explorer with a great scoop of the undiscovered.

MERRICK. She saw heaven?

TREVES. Well. I quote her: it was neither heavenly nor hellish. Rather like perambulating in a London fog. People drifted by, but no one spoke. London, mind you. Hell's probably the provinces. She was shocked it wasn't more exotic. But allowed as how had she stayed, and got used to the familiar, so to speak, it did have hints of becoming a kind of bliss. She fled.

MERRICK. If you do not believe—why did you send Mrs. Kendal away?

TREVES. Don't forget. It saved you once. My interference. You know well enough—it was not proper.

MERRICK. How can you tell? If you do not believe?

TREVES. There are still standards we abide by.

MERRICK. They make us happy because they are for our own good.

TREVES. Well. Not always.

MERRICK. Oh.

TREVES. Look, if you are angry, just say so.

MERRICK. Whose standards are they?

TREVES. I am not in the mood for this chipping away at the edges, John.

MERRICK. That do not always make us happy because they are not always for our own good?

TREVES. Everyone's. Well. Mine. Everyone's.

MERRICK. That woman's, that Juliet?

TREVES. Juliet?

MERRICK. Who died, then came back.

TREVES. Oh. I see. Yes. Her standards too.

MERRICK. So.

TREVES. So what?

MERRICK. Did you see her? Naked?

TREVES. When I was operating. Of course—

MERRICK. Oh.

TREVES. Oh what?

MERRICK. Is it okay to see them naked if you cut them up afterwards?

TREVES. Good Lord. I'm a surgeon. That is science.

MERRICK. She died. Mrs. Kendal didn't.

TREVES. Well, she came back too.

MERRICK. And Mrs. Kendal didn't. If you mean that.

TREVES. I am trying to read about anesthetics. There is simply no comparison.

MERRICK. Oh.

TREVES. Science is a different thing. This woman came to me to be. I mean, it is not, well, love, you know.

MERRICK. Is that why you're looking for an anesthetic.

TREVES. It would be a boon to surgery.

MERRICK. Because you don't love them.

TREVES. Love's got nothing to do with surgery.

MERRICK. Do you lose many patients?

TREVES. I—some.

MERRICK. Oh.

TREVES. Oh what? What does it matter? Don't you see? If I love, if any surgeon loves her or any patient or not, what does it matter? And what conceivable difference to you?

MERRICK. Because it is your standards we abide by.

TREVES. For God's sakes. If you are angry, just say it. I won't turn you out. Say it: I am angry. Go on. I am angry. I am angry! I am angry!

MERRICK. I believe in heaven.

TREVES. And it is not okay. If they undress if you cut them up. As you put it. Make me sound like Jack the, Jack the Ripper.

MERRICK. No. You worry about anesthetics.

TREVES. Are you having me on?

MERRICK. You are merciful. I myself am proof. Is it not so? (pauses) Well? Is it not so?

TREVES. Well. I. About Mrs. Kendal—perhaps I was wrong. I, these days that is, I seem to. Lose my head. Taking too much on perhaps. I do not know—what is in me these days.

MERRICK. Will she come back? Mrs. Kendal?

TREVES. I will talk to her again.

MERRICK. But—will she?

TREVES. No. I don't think so.

MERRICK. Oh.

TREVES. There are other things involved. Very. That is. Other things.

MERRICK. Well. Other things. I want to walk now. Think. Other things. (Begins to exit. Pauses.) Why? Why won't she?

(Silence. MERRICK exits.)

TREVES. Because I don't want her here when you die. (He slumps in chair.)

(Fadeout)

SCENE SEVENTEEN

CRUELTY IS AS NOTHING TO
KINDNESS

TREVES asleep in chair dreams the following: MERRICK and GOMM dressed as ROSS in foreground.

———

MERRICK. If he is merely papier-mâché and paint, a swindler and a fake—

GOMM. No, no, a genuine Dorset dreamer in a moral swamp. Look—he has so forgot how to protect himself he's gone to sleep.

MERRICK. I must examine him. I would not keep him for long, Mr. Gomm.

GOMM. It would be an inconvenience, Mr. Merrick. He is a mainstay of our institution.

MERRICK. Exactly that brought him to my attention. I am Merrick. Here is my card. I am with the mutations cross the road.

GOMM. Frederick, stand up. You must understand. He is very very valuable. We have invested a great deal in him. He is personal surgeon to the Prince of Wales.

MERRICK. But I only wish to examine him. I had not of course dreamed of changing him.

GOMM. But he is a gentleman and a good man.

MERRICK. Therefore exemplary for study as a cruel or deviant one would not be.

GOMM. Oh very well. Have him back for breakfast time or you feed him. Frederick, stand up. Up you bloody donkey, up!

(TREVES, still asleep, stands up. Fadeout.)

SCENE EIGHTEEN

WE ARE DEALING WITH
AN EPIDEMIC

TREVES *asleep.* MERRICK *at lectern.*

———

MERRICK. The most striking feature about him, note, is the terrifyingly normal head. This allowed him to lie down normally, and therefore to dream in the exclusive personal manner, without the weight of others' dreams accumulating to break his neck. From the brow projected a normal vision of benevolent enlightenment, what we believe to be a kind of self-mesmerized state. The mouth, deformed by satisfaction at being at the hub of the best of existent worlds, was rendered therefore utterly incapable of self-critical speech, thus of the ability to change. The heart showed signs of worry at this unchanging yet untenable state. The back was horribly stiff from being kept against a wall to face the discontent of a world ordered for his convenience. The surgeon's hands were well-developed and strong, capable of the most delicate carvings-up, for others' own good. Due also to the normal head, the right arm was of enormous power; but, so incapable of the distinction between the assertion of authority and the charitable act of giving, that it was often to be found disgustingly beating others—for their own good. The left arm was slighter and fairer, and may be seen in typical position, hand covering the genitals which were treated as a sullen colony in constant need of restriction, governance, punishment. For their own good. To add a further burden to his trouble, the wretched man when a boy developed a disabling spiritual duality, therefore was unable to feel what others feel, nor reach harmony with them. Please. *(*TREVES *shrugs.)* He would thus be denied all means of escape from those he had tormented.

*(*PINS *enter.)*

FIRST PIN. Mr. Merrick. You have shown a profound and unknown disorder to us. You have said when he leaves here, it is for his prior life again. I do not think it ought to be permitted. It is a disgrace. It is a pity and a disgrace. It is an indecency in fact. It may be a danger in ways we do not know. Something ought to be done about it.

MERRICK. We hope in twenty years we will understand enough to put an end to this affliction.

FIRST PIN. Twenty years! Sir, that is unacceptable!

MERRICK. Had we caught it early, it might have been different. But his condition has already spread both East and West. The truth is, I am afraid, we are dealing with an epidemic.

MERRICK *puts another piece on St. Phillip's.* PINS *exit.* TREVES *starts awake. Fadeout.*

SCENE NINETEEN

THEY CANNOT MAKE OUT
WHAT HE IS SAYING

MERRICK, BISHOP HOW *in background.* BISHOP *gestures,* MERRICK *on knees.* TREVES *foreground. Enter* GOMM.

———

GOMM. Still beavering away for Christ?

TREVES. Yes.

GOMM. I got your report. He doesn't know, does he?

TREVES. The Bishop?

GOMM. I meant Merrick.

TREVES. No.

GOMM. I shall be sorry when he dies.

TREVES. It will not be unexpected anyway.

GOMM. He's brought the hospital quite a lot of good repute. Quite a lot of contributions too, for that matter. In fact, I like him; never regretted letting him stay on. Though I didn't imagine he'd last this long.

TREVES. His heart won't sustain him much longer. It may even give out when he gets off his bloody knees with that bloody man.

GOMM. What is it, Freddie? What has gone sour for you?

TREVES. It is just—it is the overarc of things, quite inescapable that as he's achieved greater and greater normality, his condition's edged him closer to the grave. So—a parable of growing up? To become more normal is to die? More accepted to worsen? He—it is just a mockery of everything we live by.

GOMM. Sorry, Freddie. Didn't catch that one.

TREVES. Nothing has gone sour. I do not know.

GOMM. Cheer up, man. You are knighted. Your clients will be kings. Nothing succeeds my boy like success. *(exits)*

*(*BISHOP *comes from* MERRICK's *room.)*

BISHOP. I find my sessions with him utterly moving, Mr. Treves. He struggles so. I suggested he might like to be confirmed; he leaped at it like a man lost in a desert to an oasis.

TREVES. He is very excited to do what others do if he thinks it is what others do.

BISHOP. Do you cast doubt, sir, on his faith?

TREVES. No, sir, I do not. Yet he makes all of us think he is deeply like ourselves. And yet we're not like each other. I conclude that we have polished him like a mirror, and shout hallelujah when he reflects us to the inch. I have grown sorry for it.

BISHOP. I cannot make out what you're saying. Is something troubling you, Mr. Treves?

TREVES. Corsets. How about corsets? Here is a pamphlet I've written due mostly to the grotesque ailments I've seen caused by corsets. Fashion overrules me, of course. My patients do not unstrap themselves of corsets. Some cannot—you know, I have so little time in the week, I spend Sundays in the poor-wards; to keep up with work. Work being twenty-year-old women who look an abused fifty with worn-outedness; young men with appalling industrial conditions I turn out as soon as possible to return to their labors. Happily most of my patients are not poor. They are middle class. They overeat and drink so grossly, they destroy nature in themselves and all around them so fervidly, they will not last. Higher up, sir, above this middle class, I confront these same—deformities—bulged out by unlimited resources and the ruthlessness of privilege into the most scandalous dissipation yoked to the grossest ignorance and constraint. I counsel against it where I can. I am ignored of course. Then, what, sir, could be troubling me? I am an extremely successful Englishman in a successful and respected England which informs me daily by the way it lives that it wants to, die. I am in despair in fact. Science, observation, practice, deduction, having led me to these conclusions, can no longer serve as consolation. I apparently see things others don't.

BISHOP. I do wish I understood you better, sir. But as for consolation, there is in Christ's church consolation.

TREVES. I am sure we were not born for mere consolation.

BISHOP. But look at Mr. Merrick's happy example.

TREVES. Oh yes. You'd like my garden too. My dog, my wife, my daughter, pruned, cropped, pollarded and somewhat stupefied. Very happy examples, all of them. Well. Is it all we know how to finally do with—whatever? Nature? Is it? Rob it? No, not really, not nature I mean. Ourselves really. Myself really.

Robbed, that is. You do see of course, can't figure out, really, what else to do with them. Can we? *(laughs)*

BISHOP. It is not exactly clear, sir.

TREVES. I am an awfully good gardener. Is that clear? By god I take such good care of anything, anything you, we, are convinced—are you not convinced, him I mean, is not very dangerously human? I mean how could he be? After what we've given him? What you like, sir, is that he is so grateful for patrons, so greedy to be patronized, and no demands, no rights, no hopes; past perverted, present false, future nil. What better could you ask? He puts up with all of it. Of course I do mean taken when I say given, as in what, what, what we have given him, but. You knew that. I'll bet. Because. I. I. I. I—

BISHOP. Do you mean Charity? I cannot tell what you are saying.

TREVES. Help me. *(weeps)*

(BISHOP consoles him)

MERRICK *(rises, puts last piece on St. Phillip's)*. It is done.

Fadeout.

SCENE TWENTY

THE WEIGHT OF DREAMS

MERRICK *alone, looking at model. Enter* SNORK *with lunch.* _____

SNORK. Lunch, Mr. Merrick. I'll set it up. Maybe you'd like a walk after lunch. April's doing wonders for the gardens.

(A funeral procession passes slowly by.)
My mate Will, his sister died yesterday. Twenty-eight she was. Imagine that. Wife was sick, his sister nursed her. Was a real bloom that girl. Now wife okay, sister just ups and dies. It's all so—what's that word? Forgot it. It means chance-y. Well. Forgot it. Chance-y'll do. Have a good lunch. *(exits)*

(MERRICK eats a little, breathes on model, polishes it, goes to bed, arms on knees, head on arms, the position in which he must sleep.)

MERRICK. Chancey? *(sleeps)*

Enter PINHEADS *singing.*

PINS.
> We are the Queens of the Cosmos
> Beautiful darkness' empire
> Darkness darkness, light's true flower,
> Here is eternity's finest hour
> Sleep like others you learn to admire

Be like your mother, be like your sire.

They straighten MERRICK *out to normal sleep position. His head tilts over too far. His arms fly up clawing the air. He dies. As light fades,* SNORK *enters.*

SNORK. I remember it, Mr. Merrick. The word is "arbitrary." Arbitrary. It's all so— oh. Hey! Hey! The Elephant Man is dead!

(Fadeout)

SCENE TWENTY-ONE

FINAL REPORT TO THE INVESTORS

GOMM *reading,* TREVES *listening.*

———

GOMM. "To the Editor of the *Times*. Sir; In November, 1886, you were kind enough to insert in the *Times* a letter from me drawing attention to the case of Joseph Merrick—"

TREVES. John. John Merrick.

GOMM. Well. "—known as the Elephant Man. It was one of singular and exceptional misfortune" et cetera et cetera " . . . debarred from earning his livelihood in any other way than being exhibited to the gaze of the curious. This having been rightly interfered with by the police . . . " et cetera et cetera, "with great difficulty he succeeded somehow or other in getting to the door of the London Hospital where through the kindness of one of our surgeons he was sheltered for a time." And then . . . and then . . . ah. "While deterred by common humanity from evicting him again into the open street, I wrote to you and from that moment all difficulty vanished; the sympathy of many was aroused, and although no other fitting refuge was offered, a sufficient sum was placed at my disposal, apart from the funds of the hospital, to maintain him for what did not promise to be a prolonged life. As—"

TREVES. I forgot. The coroner said it was death by asphyxiation. The weight of the head crushed the windpipe.

GOMM. Well. I go on to say about how he spent his time here, that all attempted to alleviate his misery, that he was visited by the highest in the land et cetera, et cetera, that in general he joined our lives as best he could, and: "In spite of all this indulgence, he was quiet and unassuming, grateful for all that was done for him, and conformed readily to the restrictions which were necessary." Will that do so far, do you think?

TREVES. Should think it would.

GOMM. Wouldn't add anything else, would you?

TREVES. Well. He was highly intelligent. He had an acute sensibility; and worst for him, a romantic imagination. No, no. Never mind. I am really not certain of any of it. *(exits)*

GOMM. "I have given these details thinking that those who sent money to use for his support would like to know how their charity was used. Last Friday afternoon, though apparently in his usual health, he quietly passed away in his sleep. I have left in my hands a small balance of the money for his support, and this I now propose, after paying certain gratuities, to hand over to the general funds of the hospital. This course I believe will be consonant with the wishes of the contributors.

"It was the courtesy of the *Times* in inserting my letter in 1886 that procured for this afflicted man a comfortable protection during the last years of a previously wretched existence, and I desire to take this opportunity of thankfully acknowledging it.

"I am sir, your obedient servant,

F. C. Carr Gomm

"House Committee Room, London Hospital."

15 April 1890.

*(*TREVES *reenters.)*

TREVES. I did think of one small thing.

GOMM. It's too late, I'm afraid. It is done. *(smiles)*

(Hold before fadeout)

Crimes of the Heart

Beth Henley

FOR LEN, C. C. AND KAY.

First presented by Warner Theatre Productions, Inc., Claire Nichtern, Mary Lea Johnson, Martin Richards, and Francine Le-Frak at the John Golden Theatre on November 4, 1981, with the following cast:

(*in order of appearance*)

LENNY MAGRATH	Lizbeth Mackay
CHICK BOYLE	Sharon Ullrick
DOC PORTER	Raymond Baker
MEG MAGRATH	Mary Beth Hurt
BABE BOTRELLE	Mia Dillon
BARNETTE LLOYD	Peter MacNicol

Directed by Melvin Bernhardt
Scenery by John Lee Beatty
Costumes by Patricia McGourty
Lighting by Dennis Parichy

PLACE: The setting of the entire play is the kitchen in the MaGrath sister's house in Hazlehurst, Mississippi, a small Southern town. The old-fashioned kitchen is unusually spacious, but there is a lived-in, cluttered look about it. There are four different entrances and exits to the kitchen: the back door, the door leading to the dining room and the front of the house, a door leading to the downstairs bedroom, and a staircase leading to the upstairs room. There is a table near the center of the room, and a cot has been set up in one of the corners.

TIME: In the fall, five years after Hurricane Camille.

Not very often does a Broadway play open that has already won the Pulitzer Prize. Beth Henley's tragicomedy of three flamboyant southern sisters, each beset by her own peculiar troubles and all full of eccentric charm, was greeted by universal, enthusiastic acclaim. Its heart, wit and zany passion carried all before it.

One of four sisters, Beth Henley was born and raised in Jackson, Mississippi. Her mother was involved in the local theatre, and as a child she enjoyed reading the plays that her mother brought home. She remembers reading Albee's *Who's Afraid of Virginia Woolf?* when she was in the sixth grade: "They were doing it at the New State Theatre and children were banned from seeing it. And I remember thinking, this isn't so tough, I can take this. 'Course I'm sure I didn't understand one word I was reading."

Henley studied drama at Southern Methodist University in Dallas, where she wrote her first play, *Am I Blue,* for a sophomore playwriting class. After college she moved to Los Angeles and embarked on a less than successful career as an actress. "You never could hardly get an *audition,*" she recalls. She wrote a screenplay that she couldn't get produced, then tried her hand at a play, figuring that she could produce it herself on a shoe-string, if she had to. The play was *Crimes of the Heart.* Through a friend, it ultimately reached the Actors Theatre in Louisville, where it was co-winner of the 1979 Great American Play Contest. Prior to coming to New York, it had three other resident theatre productions in addition to Louisville: California Actors Theatre in Los Gatos, Loretto-Hilton Repertory Theatre in St. Louis, and Center Stage in Baltimore.

Winning the Pulitzer came as a real surprise. "I really hadn't even gotten to the stage in my career where I was *dreaming* about winning . . . it was like winning the *Nobel.* It was so from left field for me."

Crimes of the Heart is set five years after Hurricane Camille, in the town of Hazlehurst, Mississippi, where Henley's grandparents lived. The homespun humor pokes fun at southern ways and is often outrageously coincidental. People don't quite behave like this, and yet, there is enough basic truth behind the improbabilities to make them even more funny through the contrast. Almost everything could have happened, if not quite at the same time.

Henley's second play, *The Miss Firecracker Contest,* has also had regional theatre productions, while her third, *The Wake of Jamey Foster,* had a brief Broadway run. While she would like to act from time to time (one summer, in Los Angeles, she played a young bag lady in a radical farce called *No Scratch*), she is committed to her writing. "I just hope I can keep doing it for my living," she says. "That's my main concern."

ACT ONE

The lights go up on the empty kitchen. It is late afternoon. LENNY MAGRATH, *a thirty-year-old woman with a round figure and face, enters from the back door carrying a white suitcase, a saxophone case, and a brown paper sack. She sets the suitcase and the sax case down and takes the brown sack to the kitchen table. After glancing quickly at the door, she gets the cookie jar from the kitchen counter, a box of matches from the stove, and then brings both objects back to the kitchen table. Excitedly, she reaches into the brown sack and pulls out a package of birthday candles. She quickly opens the package and removes a candle. She tries to stick the candle onto a cookie—it falls off. She sticks the candle in again, but the cookie is too hard and it crumbles. Frantically, she gets a second cookie from the jar. She strikes a match, lights the candle, and begins dripping wax onto the cookie. Just as she is beginning to smile we hear* CHICK'S *voice from offstage.*

_____

CHICK'S VOICE. Lenny! Oh, Lenny! *(*LENNY *quickly blows out the candle and stuffs the cookie and candle into her dress pocket.* CHICK, *twenty-nine, enters from the back door. She is a brightly dressed matron with yellow hair and shiny red lips.)*

CHICK. Hi! I saw your car pull up.

LENNY. Hi.

CHICK. Well, did you see today's paper? *(*LENNY *nods.)* It's just too awful! It's just way too awful! How I'm gonna continue holding my head up high in this community, I do not know. Did you remember to pick up those pantyhose for me?

LENNY. They're in the sack.

CHICK. Well, thank goodness, at least I'm not gonna have to go into town wearing holes in my stockings. *(She gets the package, tears it open, and proceeds to take off one pair of stockings and put on another throughout the following scene. There should be something slightly grotesque about this woman changing her stockings in the kitchen.)*

LENNY. Did Uncle Watson call?

CHICK. Yes, Daddy has called me twice already. He said Babe's ready to come home. We've got to get right over and pick her up before they change their simple minds.

LENNY *(hesitantly)*. Oh, I know, of course, it's just—

CHICK. What?

LENNY. Well, I was hoping Meg would call.

CHICK. Meg?

LENNY. Yes, I sent her a telegram: about Babe, and—

CHICK. A telegram?! Couldn't you just phone her up?

LENNY. Well, no, 'cause her phone's . . . out of order.

CHICK. Out of order?

LENNY. Disconnected. I don't know what.

CHICK. Well, that sounds like Meg. My, these are snug. Are you sure you bought my right size?

LENNY *(looking at the box)*. Size extra-petite.

CHICK. Well, they're skimping on the nylon material. *(struggling to pull up the stockings)* That's all there is to it. Skimping on the nylon. *(She finishes one leg and starts the other.)* Now, just what all did you say in this "telegram" to Meg?

LENNY. I don't recall exactly. I, well, I just told her to come on home.

CHICK. To come on home! Why, Lenora Josephine, have you lost your only brain, or what?

LENNY *(nervously, as she begins to pick up the mess of dirty stockings and plastic wrappings)*. But Babe wants Meg home. She asked me to call her.

CHICK. I'm not talking about what Babe wants.

LENNY. Well, what then?

CHICK. Listen, Lenora, I think it's pretty accurate to assume that after this morning's paper, Babe's gonna be incurring some mighty negative publicity around this town. And Meg's appearance isn't gonna help out a bit.

LENNY. What's wrong with Meg?

CHICK. She had a loose reputation in high school.

LENNY *(weakly)*. She was popular.

CHICK. She was known all over Copiah County as cheap Christmas trash, and that was the least of it. There was that whole sordid affair with Doc Porter, leaving him a cripple.

LENNY. A cripple—he's got a limp. Just kind of, barely a limp.

CHICK. Well, his mother was going to keep *me* out of the Ladies' Social League because of it.

LENNY. What?

CHICK. That's right. I never told you, but I had to go plead with that mean old woman and convinced her that I was just as appalled with what Meg had done as she was, and that I was only a first cousin anyway and I could hardly be blamed for all the skeletons in the Ma-

Graths' closet. It was humiliating. I tell you, she even brought up your mother's death. And that poor cat.

LENNY. Oh! Oh! Oh, please, Chick! I'm sorry. But you're in the Ladies' League now.

CHICK. Yes. That's true, I am. But frankly, if Mrs. Porter hadn't developed that tumor in her bladder, I wouldn't be in the club today, much less a committee head. *(as she brushes her hair)* Anyway, you be a sweet potato and wait right here for Meg to call, so's you can convince her not to come back home. It would make things a whole lot easier on everybody. Don't you think it really would?

LENNY. Probably.

CHICK. Good, then suit yourself. How's my hair?

LENNY. Fine.

CHICK. Not pooching out in the back, is it?

LENNY. No.

CHICK *(cleaning the hair from her brush).* All right then, I'm on my way. I've got Annie May over there keeping an eye on Peekay and Buck Jr., but I don't trust her with them for long periods of time. *(dropping the ball of hair onto the floor).* Her mind is like a loose sieve. Honestly it is. *(as she puts the brush back into her purse)* Oh! Oh! Oh! I almost forgot. Here's a present for you. Happy birthday to Lenny, from the Buck Boyles! *(She takes a wrapped package from her bag and hands it to LENNY.)*

LENNY. Why, thank you, Chick. It's so nice to have you remember my birthday every year like you do.

CHICK *(modestly).* Oh, Well, now, that's just the way I am, I suppose. That's just the way I was brought up to be. Well, why don't you go on and open up the present?

LENNY. All right. *(She starts to unwrap the gift.)*

CHICK. It's a box of candy—assorted crèmes.

LENNY. Candy—that's always a nice gift.

CHICK. And you have a sweet tooth, don't you?

LENNY. I guess.

CHICK. Well, I'm glad you like it.

LENNY. I do.

CHICK. Oh, speaking of which, remember that little polk-a-dot dress you got Peekay for her fifth birthday last month?

LENNY. The red-and-white one?

CHICK. Yes; well, the first time I put it in the washing machine, I mean the very first time, it fell all to pieces. Those little polka dots just dropped right off in the water.

LENNY *(crushed).* Oh, no. Well, I'll get something else for her, then—a little toy.

CHICK. Oh, no, no, no, no, no! We wouldn't hear of it! I just wanted to let you know so you wouldn't go and waste any more of your hard-earned money on that make of dress. Those inexpensive brands just don't hold up. I'm sorry, but not in these modern washing machines.

DOC PORTER'S VOICE. Hello! Hello, Lenny!

CHICK *(taking over).* Oh, look, it's Doc Porter! Come on in Doc! Please come right on in!

(DOC PORTER enters through the back door. He is carrying a large sack of pecans. DOC is an attractively worn man with a slight limp that adds rather than detracts from his quiet seductive quality. He is thirty years old, but appears slightly older.)

CHICK. Well, how are you doing? How in the world are you doing?

DOC. Just fine, Chick.

CHICK. And how are you liking it now that you're back in Hazlehurst?

DOC. Oh, I'm finding it somewhat enjoyable.

CHICK. Somewhat! Only somewhat! Will you listen to him! What a silly, silly, silly man! Well, I'm on my way. I've got some people waiting on me. *(whispering to DOC)* It's Babe. I'm on my way to pick her up.

DOC. Oh.

CHICK. Well, goodbye! Farewell and goodbye!

LENNY. 'Bye.

(Chick exits.)

DOC. Hello.

LENNY. Hi. I guess you heard about the thing with Babe.

DOC. Yeah.

LENNY. It was in the newspaper.

DOC. Uh huh.

LENNY. What a mess.

DOC. Yeah.

LENNY. Well, come on and sit down. I'll heat us up some coffee.

DOC. That's okay. I can only stay a minute. I have to pick up Scott; he's at the dentist.

LENNY. Oh; well, I'll heat some up for myself. I'm kinda thirsty for a cup of hot coffee. *(She puts the coffeepot on the burner.)*

DOC. Lenny—

LENNY. What?

DOC *(not able to go on).* Ah . . .

LENNY. Yes?

DOC. Here, some pecans for you. *(He hands her the sack.)*

LENNY. Why, thank you, Doc. I love pecans.

DOC. My wife and Scott picked them up around the yard.

LENNY. Well, I can use them to make a pie.

A pecan pie.

DOC. Yeah. Look, Lenny, I've got some bad news for you.

LENNY. What?

DOC. Well, you know, you've been keeping Billy Boy out on our farm; he's been grazing out there.

LENNY. Yes—

DOC. Well, last night, Billy Boy died.

LENNY. He died?

DOC. Yeah. I'm sorry to tell you when you've got all this on you, but I thought you'd want to know.

LENNY. Well, yeah. I do. He died?

DOC. Uh huh. He was struck by lightning.

LENNY. Struck by lightning? In that storm yesterday?

DOC. That's what we think.

LENNY. Gosh, struck by lightning. I've had Billy Boy so long. You know. Ever since I was ten years old.

DOC. Yeah. He was a mighty old horse.

LENNY *(stung)*. Mighty old.

DOC. Almost twenty years old.

LENNY. That's right, twenty years. 'Cause; ah, I'm thirty years old today. Did you know that?

DOC. No, Lenny, I didn't know. Happy birthday.

LENNY. Thanks. *(She begins to cry.)*

DOC. Oh, come on now, Lenny. Come on. Hey, hey, now. You know I can't stand it when you MaGrath women start to cry. You know it just gets me.

LENNY. Oh ho! Sure! You mean when Meg cries! Meg's the one you could never stand to watch cry! Not me! I could fill up a pig's trough!

DOC. Now, Lenny . . . stop it. Come on. Jesus!

LENNY. Okay! Okay! I don't know what's wrong with me. I don't mean to make a scene. I've been on this crying jag. *(She blows her nose.)* All this stuff with Babe, and Old Grand-daddy's gotten worse in the hospital, and I can't get in touch with Meg.

DOC. You tried calling Meggy?

LENNY. Yes.

DOC. Is she coming home?

LENNY. Who knows. She hasn't called me. That's what I'm waiting here for—hoping she'll call.

DOC. She still living in California?

LENNY. Yes; in Hollywood.

DOC. Well, give me a call if she gets in. I'd like to see her.

LENNY. Oh, you would, huh?

DOC. Yeah, Lenny, sad to say, but I would.

LENNY. It is sad. It's very sad indeed.

(They stare at each other, then look away. There is a moment of tense silence.)

DOC. Hey, Jell-O Face, your coffee's boiling.

LENNY *(going to check)*. Oh, it is? Thanks. *(after she checks the pot)* Look, you'd better go on and pick Scott up. You don't want him to have to wait for you.

DOC. Yeah, you're right. Poor kid. It's his first time at the dentist.

LENNY. Poor thing.

DOC. Well, 'bye. I'm sorry to have to tell you about your horse.

LENNY. Oh, I know. Tell Joan thanks for picking up the pecans.

DOC. I will. *(He starts to leave.)*

LENNY. Oh, how's the baby?

DOC. She's fine. Real pretty. She, ah, holds your finger in her hand; like this.

LENNY. Oh, that's cute.

DOC. Yeah. 'Bye, Lenny.

LENNY. 'Bye.

(DOC exits. LENNY stares after him for a moment, then goes and sits back down at the kitchen table. She reaches into her pocket and pulls out a somewhat crumbled cookie and a wax candle. She lights the candle again, lets the wax drip onto the cookie, then sticks the candle on top of the cookie. She begins to sing the "Happy Birthday" song to herself. At the end of the song she pauses, silently makes a wish, and blows out the candle. She waits a moment, then relights the candle, and repeats her actions, only this time making a different wish at the end of the song. She starts to repeat the procedure for the third time, as the phone rings. She goes to answer it.)

LENNY. Hello . . . Oh, hello, Lucille, how's Zackery? . . . Oh, no! . . . Oh, I'm so sorry. Of course, it must be grueling for you . . . Yes, I understand. Your only brother . . . No, she's not here yet. Chick just went to pick her up . . . Oh, now, Lucille, she's still his wife, I'm sure she'll be interested . . . Well, you can just tell me the information and I'll relate it all to her . . . Uh hum, his liver's saved. Oh, that's good news! . . . Well, of course, when you look at it like that . . . Breathing stabilized . . . Damage to the spinal column, not yet determined . . . Okay . . . Yes, Lucille, I've got it all down . . . Uh huh, I'll give her that message. 'Bye, 'bye.

(LENNY drops the pencil and paper. She sighs deeply, wipes her cheeks with the back of her hand, and goes to the stove to pour herself a cup of coffee. After a few moments,

the front door is heard slamming. LENNY *starts. A whistle is heard, then* MEG'*s voice.)*

MEG'S VOICE. I'm home! *(She whistles the family whistle.)* Anybody home?

LENNY. Meg? Meg!

*(*MEG, *twenty-seven, enters from the dining room. She has sad, magic eyes and wears a hat. She carries a worn-out suitcase.)*

MEG *(dropping her suitcase, running to hug* LENNY*).* Lenny—

LENNY. Well, Meg! Why, Meg! Oh, Meggy! Why didn't you call? Did you fly in? You didn't take a cab, did you? Why didn't you give us a call?

MEG *(overlapping).* Oh, Lenny! Why, Lenny! Dear Lenny! *(Then she looks at* LENNY'*s face.)* My God, we're getting so old! Oh, I called, for heaven's sake. Of course, I called!

LENNY. Well, I never talked to you—

MEG. Well, I know! I let the phone ring right off the hook!

LENNY. Well, as a matter of fact, I was out most of the morning seeing to Babe—

MEG. Now, just what's all this business about Babe? How could you send me such a telegram about Babe? And Zackery! You say somebody's shot Zackery?

LENNY. Yes, they have.

MEG. Well, good Lord! Is he dead?

LENNY. No. But he's in the hospital. He was shot in his stomach.

MEG. In his stomach! How awful! Do they know who shot him? *(*LENNY *nods.)* Well, who? Who was it? Who? Who?

LENNY. Babe! They're all saying Babe shot him! They took her to jail! And they're saying she shot him! They're all saying it! It's horrible! It's awful!

MEG *(overlapping).* Jail! Good Lord, jail! Well, who? Who's saying it? Who?

LENNY. Everyone! The policemen, the sheriff, Zackery, even Babe's saying it! Even Babe herself!

MEG. Well, for God's sake. For God's sake.

LENNY *(overlapping as she falls apart).* It's horrible! It's horrible! It's just horrible!

MEG. Now calm down, Lenny. Just calm down. Would you like a Coke? Here, I'll get you some Coke. *(She gets a Coke from the refrigerator. She opens it and downs a large swig.)* Why? Why did she shoot him? Why? *(She hands the Coke bottle to* LENNY.*)*

LENNY. I talked to her this morning and I asked her that very question. I said, "Babe, why would you shoot Zackery? He was your own husband. Why would you shoot him?" And do you know what she said? *(*MEG *shakes*

her head.*)* She said, " 'Cause I didn't like his looks. I just didn't like his looks."

MEG *(after a pause).* Well, I don't like his looks.

LENNY. But you didn't shoot him! You wouldn't shoot a person 'cause you didn't like their looks! You wouldn't do that! Oh, I hate to say this—I do hate to say this—but I believe Babe is ill. I mean in-her-head ill.

MEG. Oh, now, Lenny, don't you say that! There're plenty of good sane reasons to shoot another person, and I'm sure that Babe had one. Now, what we've got to do is get her the best lawyer in town. Do you have any ideas on who's the best lawyer in town?

LENNY. Well, Zackery is, of course; but he's been shot!

MEG. Well, count him out! Just count him and his whole firm out!

LENNY. Anyway, you don't have to worry, she's already got her lawyer.

MEG. She does? Who?

LENNY. Barnette Lloyd. Annie Lloyd's boy. He just opened his office here in town. And Uncle Watson said we'd be doing Annie a favor by hiring him up.

MEG. Doing Annie a favor? Doing Annie a favor! Well, what about Babe? Have you thought about Babe? Do we want to do her a favor of thirty or forty years in jail? Have you thought about that?

LENNY. Now, don't snap at me! Just don't snap at me! I try to do what's right! All this responsibility keeps falling on my shoulders, and I try to do what's right!

MEG. Well, boo hoo, hoo, hoo! And how in the hell could you send me such a telegram about Babe!

LENNY. Well, if you had a phone, or if you didn't live way out there in Hollywood and not even come home for Christmas, maybe I wouldn't have to pay all that money to send you a telegram!

MEG *(overlapping).* BABE'S IN TERRIBLE TROUBLE—STOP! ZACKERY'S BEEN SHOT—STOP! COME HOME IMMEDIATELY—STOP! STOP! STOP!

LENNY. And what was that you said about how old we're getting? When you looked at my face, you said, "My God, we're getting so old!" But you didn't mean we—you meant me! Didn't you? I'm thirty years old today and my face is getting all pinched up and my hair is falling out in the comb.

MEG. Why, Lenny! It's your birthday, October 23. How could I forget. Happy birthday!

LENNY. Well, it's not. I'm thirty years old

and Billy Boy died last night. He was struck by lightning. He was struck dead.

MEG *(reaching for a cigarette)*. Struck dead. Oh, what a mess. What a mess. Are you really thirty? Then I must be twenty-seven and Babe is twenty-four. My God, we're getting so old.

(They are silent for several moments as MEG *drags off her cigarette and* LENNY *drinks her Coke.)*

MEG. What's the cot doing in the kitchen?

LENNY. Well, I rolled it out when Old Granddaddy got sick. So I could be close and hear him at night if he needed something.

MEG *(glancing toward the door leading to the downstairs bedroom)*. Is Old Granddaddy here?

LENNY. Why, no. Old Granddaddy's at the hospital.

MEG. Again?

LENNY. Meg!

MEG. What?

LENNY. I wrote you all about it. He's been in the hospital over three months straight.

MEG. He has?

LENNY. Don't you remember? I wrote you about all those blood vessels popping in his brain?

MEG. Popping—

LENNY. And how he was so anxious to hear from you and to find out about your singing career. I wrote it all to you. How they have to feed him through those tubes now. Didn't you get my letters?

MEG. Oh, I don't know, Lenny. I guess I did. To tell you the truth, sometimes I kinda don't read your letters.

LENNY. What?

MEG. I'm sorry. I used to read them. It's just, since Christmas reading them gives me these slicing pains right here in my chest.

LENNY. I see. I see. Is that why you didn't use that money Old Granddaddy sent you to come home Christmas; because you hate us so much? We never did all that much to make you hate us. We didn't!

MEG. Oh, Lenny! Do you think I'd be getting slicing pains in my chest if I didn't care about you? If I hated you? Honestly, now, do you think I would?

LENNY. No.

MEG. Okay, then. Let's drop it. I'm sorry I didn't read your letters. Okay?

LENNY. Okay.

MEG. Anyway, we've got this whole thing with Babe to deal with. The first thing is to get her a good lawyer and get her out of jail.

LENNY. Well, she's out of jail.

MEG. She is?

LENNY. That young lawyer, he's gotten her out.

MEG. Oh, he has?

LENNY. Yes, on bail. Uncle Watson's put is up. Chick's bringing her back right now— she's driving her home.

MEG. Oh; well, that's a relief.

LENNY. Yes, and they're due home any minute now; so we can just wait right here for 'em.

MEG. Well, good. That's good. *(as she leans against the counter:)* So, Babe shot Zackery Botrelle, the richest and most powerful man in all of Hazlehurst, slap in the gut. It's hard to believe.

LENNY. It cerrtainly is. Little Babe—shooting off a gun.

MEG. Little Babe.

LENNY. She was always the prettiest and most perfect of the three of us. Old Granddaddy used to call her his Dancing Sugar Plum. Why, remember how proud and happy he was the day she married Zackery.

MEG. Yes, I remember. It was his finest hour.

LENNY. He remarked how Babe was gonna skyrocket right to the heights of Hazlehurst society. And how Zackery was just the right man for her whether she knew it now or not.

MEG. Oh, Lordy, Lordy. And what does Old Granddaddy say now?

LENNY. Well, I haven't had the courage to tell him all about this as yet. I thought maybe tonight we could go to visit him at the hospital, and you could talk to him and . . .

MEG. Yeah; well, we'll see. We'll see. Do we have anything to drink around here—to the tune of straight bourbon?

LENNY. No. There's no liquor.

MEG. Hell. *(She gets a Coke from the refrigerator and opens it.)*

LENNY. Then you *will* go with me to see Old Granddaddy at the hospital tonight?

MEG. Of course. *(She goes to her purse and gets out a bottle of Empirin. She takes out a tablet and puts it on her tongue.)* Brother, I know he's gonna go on about my singing career. Just like he always does.

LENNY. Well, how is your career going?

MEG. It's not.

LENNY. Why, aren't you still singing at that club down on Malibu beach?

MEG. No. Not since Christmas.

LENNY. Well, then, are you singing someplace new?

MEG. No, I'm not singing. I'm not singing at all.

LENNY. Oh. Well, what do you do then?

MEG. What I do is I pay cold-storage bills for a dog-food company. That's what I do.

LENNY *(trying to be helpful)*. Gosh, don't you think it'd be a good idea to stay in the show business field?

MEG. Oh, maybe.

LENNY. Like Old Granddaddy says, "With your talent, all you need is exposure. Then you can make your own breaks!" Did you hear his suggestion about getting your foot put in one of those blocks of cement they've got out there? He thinks that's real important.

MEG. Yeah. I think I've heard that. And I'll probably hear it again when I go to visit him at the hospital tonight; so let's just drop it. Okay? *(She notices the sack of pecans.)* What's this? Pecans? Great, I love pecans! *(She takes out two pecans and tries to open them by cracking them together.)* Come on . . . Crack, you demons! Crack!

LENNY. We have a nutcracker!

MEG *(trying with her teeth)*. Ah, where's the sport in a nutcracker? Where's the challenge?

LENNY *(getting the nutcracker)*. It's over here in the utensil drawer.

(As LENNY *gets the nutcracker,* MEG *opens the pecan by stepping on it with her shoe.)*

MEG. There! Open! *(She picks up the crumbled pecan and eats it.)* Mmmm, delicious. Delicious. Where'd you get the fresh pecans?

LENNY. Oh . . . I don't know.

MEG. They sure are tasty.

LENNY. Doc Porter brought them over.

MEG. Doc. What's Doc doing here in town?

LENNY. Well, his father died a couple of months ago. Now he's back home seeing to his property.

MEG. Gosh, the last I heard of Doc, he was up in the East painting the walls of houses to earn a living. *(amused)* Heard he was living with some Yankee woman who made clay pots.

LENNY. Joan.

MEG. What?

LENNY. Her name's Joan. She came down here with him. That's one of her pots. Doc's married to her.

MEG. Married—

LENNY. Uh huh.

MEG. Doc married a Yankee?

LENNY. That's right; and they've got two kids.

MEG. Kids—

LENNY. A boy and a girl.

MEG. God. Then his kids must be half Yankee.

LENNY. I suppose.

MEG. God. That really gets me. I don't know why, but somehow that really gets me.

LENNY. I don't know why it should.

MEG. And what a stupid-looking pot! Who'd buy it, anyway?

LENNY. Wait—I think that's them. Yeah, that's Chick's car! Oh, there's Babe! Hello, Babe! They're home, Meg! They're home.

(Meg hides.)

BABE'S VOICE. Lenny! I'm home! I'm free!

*(*BABE, *twenty-four, enters exuberantly. She has an angelic face and fierce, volatile eyes. She carries a pink pocketbook.)*

BABE. I'm home!

*(*MEG *jumps out of hiding.)*

BABE. Oh, Meg—Look, it's Meg! *(running to hug her)* Meg! When did you get home?

MEG. Just now!

BABE. Well, it's so good to see you! I'm so glad you're home! I'm so relieved.

*(*CHICK *enters.)*

MEG. Why, Chick; hello.

CHICK. Hello, Cousin Margaret. What brings you back to Hazlehurst?

MEG. Oh, I came on home . . . *(turning to* BABE*)* I came on home to see about Babe.

BABE *(running to hug* MEG*)*. Oh, Meg—

MEG. How are things with you, Babe?

CHICK. Well, they are dismal, if you want my opinion. She is refusing to cooperate with her lawyer, that nice-looking young Lloyd boy. She won't tell any of us why she committed this heinous crime, except to say that she didn't like Zackery's looks—

BABE. Oh, look, Lenny brought my suitcase from home! And my saxophone! Thank you! *(She runs over to the cot and gets out her saxophone.)*

CHICK. Now, that young lawyer is coming over here this afternoon, and when he gets here he expects to get some concrete answers! That's what he expects! No more of this nonsense and stubbornness from you, Rebecca MaGrath, or they'll put you in jail and throw away the key!

BABE *(overlapping to* MEG*)*. Meg, come look at my new saxophone. I went to Jackson and bought it used. Feel it. It's so heavy.

MEG *(overlapping* CHICK*)*. It's beautiful.

(The room goes silent.)

CHICK. Isn't that right, won't they throw away the key?

LENNY. Well, honestly, I don't know about that—

CHICK. They will! And leave you there to rot. So, Rebecca, what are you going to tell Mr. Lloyd about shooting Zackery when he gets here? What are your reasons going to be?

BABE (*glaring*). That I didn't like his looks! I just didn't like his stinking looks! And I don't like yours much, either, Chick the Stick! So just leave me alone! I mean it! Leave me alone! Oooh! (*She exits up the stairs.*)

(*There is a long moment of silence.*)

CHICK. Well, I was only trying to warn her that she's going to have to help herself. It's just that she doesn't understand how serious the situation is. Does she? She doesn't have the vaguest idea. Does she, now?

LENNY. Well, it's true, she does seem a little confused.

CHICK. And that's putting it mildly, Lenny honey. That's putting it mighty mild. So, Margaret, how's your singing career going? We keep looking for your picture in the movie magazines. (MEG *moves to light a cigarette.*) You know, you shouldn't smoke. It causes cancer. Cancer of the lungs. They say each cigarette is just a little stick of cancer. A little death stick.

MEG. That's what I like about it, Chick—taking a drag off of death. (*She takes a long, deep drag.*) Mmm! Gives me a sense of controlling my own destiny. What power! What exhilaration! Want a drag?

LENNY (*trying to break the tension*). Ah, Zackery's liver's been saved! His sister called up and said his liver was saved. Isn't that good news?

MEG. Well, yes, that's fine news. Mighty fine news. Why, I've been told that the liver's a powerful important bodily organ. I believe it's used to absorb all of our excess bile.

LENNY. Yes—well—it's been saved.

(*The phone rings.* LENNY *gets it.*)

MEG. So! Did you hear all that good news about the liver, Little Chicken?

CHICK. I heard it. And don't you call me Chicken! (MEG *clucks like a chicken.*) I've told you a hundred times if I've told you once not to call me Chicken. You cannot call me Chicken.

LENNY. . . . Oh, no! . . . Of course, we'll be right over! 'Bye! (*She hangs up the phone.*) That was Annie May—Peekay and Buck Jr. have eaten paint!

CHICK. Oh, no! Are they all right? They're not sick? They're not sick, are they?

LENNY. I don't know. I don't know. Come on. We've got to run on next door.

CHICK (*overlapping*). Oh, God! Oh, please! Please let them be all right! Don't let them die! Please, don't let them die!

(CHICK *runs off howling, with* LENNY *following after.* MEG *sits alone, finishing her cig-*

arette. After a moment, BABE'*s voice is heard.*)

BABE'S VOICE. Pst—Psst!

(MEG *looks around.* BABE *comes tiptoeing down the stairs.*)

Has she gone?

MEG. She's gone. Peekay and Buck Jr. just ate their paints.

BABE. What idiots.

MEG. Yeah.

BABE. You know, Chick's hated us ever since we had to move here from Vicksburg to live with Old Grandmama and Old Granddaddy.

MEG. She's an idiot.

BABE. Yeah. Do you know what she told me this morning while I was still behind bars and couldn't get away?

MEG. What?

BABE. She told me how embarrassing it was for her all those years ago, you know, when Mama—

MEG. Yeah, down in the cellar.

BABE. She said our mama had shamed the entire family, and we were known notoriously all through Hazlehurst. (*about to cry*) Then she went on to say how I would now be getting just as much bad publicity, and humiliating her and the family all over again.

MEG. Ah, forget it, Babe. Just forget it.

BABE. I told her, "Mama got national coverage! National!" And if Zackery wasn't a senator from Copiah County, I probably wouldn't even be getting statewide.

MEG. Of course you wouldn't.

BABE (*after a pause*). Gosh, sometimes I wonder . . .

MEG. What?

BABE. Why she did it. Why Mama hung herself.

MEG. I don't know. She had a bad day. A real bad day. You know how it feels on a real bad day.

BABE. And that old yellow cat. It was sad about that old cat.

MEG. Yeah.

BABE. I bet if Daddy hadn't of left us, they'd still be alive.

MEG. Oh, I don't know.

BABE. 'Cause it was after he left that she started spending whole days just sitting there and smoking on the back porch steps. She'd sling her ashes down onto the different bugs and ants that'd be passing by.

MEG. Yeah. Well, I'm glad he left.

BABE. That old yellow cat'd stay back there with her. I thought if she felt something for anyone it woulda been that old cat. Guess I musta been mistaken.

MEG. God, he was a bastard. Really, with his white teeth. Daddy was such a bastard.

BABE. Was he? I don't remember.

(MEG blows out a mouthful of smoke.)

BABE *(after a moment, uneasily)*. I think I'm gonna make some lemonade. You want some?

MEG. Sure. *(BABE cuts lemons, dumps sugar, stirs ice cubes, etc., throughout the following exchange.)* Babe. Why won't you talk? Why won't you tell anyone about shooting Zackery?

BABE. Oooh—

MEG. Why not? You must have had a good reason. Didn't you?

BABE. I guess I did.

MEG. Well, what was it?

BABE. I . . . I can't say.

MEG. Why not? *(pause)* Babe, why not? You can tell me.

BABE. 'Cause . . . I'm sort of . . . protecting someone.

MEG. Protecting someone? Oh, Babe, then you really didn't shoot him! I knew you couldn't have done it! I knew it!

BABE. No, I shot him. I shot him all right. I meant to kill him. I was aiming for his heart, but I guess my hands were shaking and I— just got him in the stomach.

MEG *(collapsing)*. I see.

BABE *(stirring the lemonade)*. So I'm guilty. And I'm just gonna have to take my punishment and go on to jail.

MEG. Oh, Babe—

BABE. Don't worry, Meg, jail's gonna be a relief to me. I can learn to play my new saxophone. I won't have to live with Zackery anymore. And I won't have his snoopy old sister, Lucille, coming over and pushing me around. Jail will be a relief. Here's your lemonade.

MEG. Thanks.

BABE. It taste okay?

MEG. Perfect.

BABE. I like a lot of sugar in mine. I'm gonna add some more sugar.

(BABE goes to add more sugar to her lemonade as LENNY bursts through the back door in a state of excitement and confusion.)

LENNY. Well, it looks like the paint is primarily on their arms and faces, but Chick wants me to drive them all over to Dr. Winn's just to make sure. *(She grabs her car keys from the counter, and as she does so, she notices the mess of lemons and sugar.)* Oh, now, Babe, try not to make a mess here; and be careful with this sharp knife. Honestly, all that sugar's gonna get you sick. Well, 'bye, 'bye. I'll be back as soon as I can.

MEG. 'Bye, Lenny.

BABE. 'Bye. *(LENNY exits.)* Boy, I don't know what's happening to Lenny.

MEG. What do you mean?

BABE. "Don't make a mess; don't make yourself sick; don't cut yourself with that sharp knife." She's turning into Old Grandmama.

MEG. You think so?

BABE. More and more. Do you know she's taken to wearing Old Grandmama's torn sunhat and her green garden gloves?

MEG. Those old lime-green ones?

BABE. Yeah; she works out in the garden wearing the lime-green gloves of a dead woman. Imagine wearing those gloves on your hands.

MEG. Poor Lenny. She needs some love in her life. All she does is work out at that brick yard and take care of Old Granddaddy.

BABE. Yeah. But she's so shy with men.

MEG *(biting into an apple)*. Probably because of that *shrunken* ovary she has.

BABE *(slinging ice cubes)*. Yeah, that *deformed* ovary.

MEG. Old Granddaddy's the one who's made her feel self-conscious about it. It's his fault. The old fool.

BABE. It's so sad.

MEG. God—you know what?

BABE. What?

MEG. I bet Lenny's never even slept with a man. Just think, thirty years old and never even had it once.

BABE *(slyly)*. Oh, I don't know. Maybe she's . . . had it once.

MEG. She has?

BABE. Maybe. I think so.

MEG. When? When?

BABE. Well . . . maybe I shouldn't say—

MEG. Babe!

BABE *(rapidly telling the story)*. All right, then. It was after Old Granddaddy went back to the hospital this second time. Lenny was really in a state of deep depression, I could tell that she was. Then one day she calls me up and asks me to come over and to bring along my Polaroid camera. Well, when I arrive she's waiting for me out there in the sun parlor wearing her powder-blue Sunday dress and this old curled-up wig. She confided that she was gonna try sending in her picture to one of those lonely-hearts clubs.

MEG. Oh, my God.

BABE. Lonely Hearts of the South. She'd seen their ad in a magazine.

MEG. Jesus.

BABE. Anyway, I take some snapshots and she sends them on in to the club, and about two weeks later she receives in the mail this whole load of pictures of available men, most of 'em fairly odd-looking. But of course she doesn't call any of 'em up 'cause she's real shy. But one of 'em, this Charlie Hill from Memphis, Tennessee, he calls her.

MEG. He does?

BABE. Yeah. And time goes on and she says he's real funny on the phone, so they decide to get together to meet.

MEG. Yeah?

BABE. Well, he drives down here to Hazlehurst 'bout three or four different times and has supper with her; then one weekend she goes up to Memphis to visit him, and I think that is where it happened.

MEG. What makes you think so?

BABE. Well, when I went to pick her up from the bus depot, she ran off the bus and threw her arms around me and started crying and sobbing as though she'd like to never stop. I asked her, I said, "Lenny, what's the matter?" And she said, "I've done it, Babe! Honey, I have done it!"

MEG (whispering). And you think she meant that she'd done it?

BABE (whispering back, slyly). I think so.

MEG. Well, goddamn!

(They laugh.)

BABE. But she didn't say anything else about it. She just went on to tell me about the boot factory where Charlie worked and what a nice city Memphis was.

MEG. So, what happened to this Charlie?

BABE. Well, he came to Hazlehurst just one more time. Lenny took him over to meet Old Granddaddy at the hospital, and after that they broke it off.

MEG. 'Cause of Old Granddaddy?

BABE. Well, she said it was on account of her missing ovary. That Charlie didn't want to marry her on account of it.

MEG. Ah, how mean. How hateful.

BABE. Oh, it was. He seemed like such a nice man, too—kinda chubby, with red hair and freckles, always telling these funny jokes.

MEG. Hmmm, that just doesn't seem right. Something about that doesn't seem exactly right. (She paces about the kitchen and comes across the box of candy LENNY got for her birthday.) Oh, God. "Happy birthday to Lenny, from the Buck Boyles."

BABE. Oh, no! Today's Lenny's birthday!

MEG. That's right.

BABE. I forgot all about it!

MEG. I know. I did, too.

BABE. Gosh, we'll have to order up a big

cake for her. She always loves to make those wishes on her birthday cake.

MEG. Yeah, let's get her a big cake! A huge one! (suddenly noticing the plastic wrapper on the candy box) Oh, God, that Chick's so cheap!

BABE. What do you mean?

MEG. This plastic has poinsettias on it!

BABE (running to see). Oh, let me see—(She looks at the package with disgust.) Boy, oh, boy! I'm calling that bakery and ordering the very largest size cake they have! That jumbo deluxe!

MEG. Good!

BABE. Why, I imagine they can make one up to be about—this big. (She demonstrates.)

MEG. Oh, at least; at least that big. Why, maybe it'll even be this big. (She makes a very, very, very large-size cake.)

BABE. You think it could be that big?

MEG. Sure!

BABE (after a moment, getting the idea). Or, or what if it were this big? (She maps out a cake that covers the room.) What if we get the cake and it's this big? (She gulps down a fistful of cake.) Gulp! Gulp! Gulp! Tasty treat!

MEG. Hmmm—I'll have me some more! Give me some more of that birthday cake!

(Suddenly there is a loud knock at the door.)

BARNETTE'S VOICE. Hello . . . Hello! May I come in?

BABE (to MEG, in a whisper, as she takes cover). Who's that?

MEG. I don't know.

BARNETTE'S VOICE (He is still knocking). Hello! Hello, Mrs. Botrelle!

BABE. Oh, shoot! It's that lawyer. I don't want to see him.

MEG. Oh, Babe, come on. You've got to see him sometime.

BABE. No, I don't. (She starts up the stairs.) Just tell him I died. I'm going upstairs.

MEG. Oh, Babe! Will you come back here!

BABE (as she exits). You talk to him, please, Meg. Please! I just don't want to see him—

MEG. Babe—Babe! Oh, shit . . . Ah, come on in! Door's open!

(BARNETTE LLOYD, twenty-six, enters carrying a briefcase. He is a slender, intelligent young man with an almost fanatical intensity that he subdues by sheer will.)

BARNETTE. How do you do. I'm Barnette Lloyd.

MEG. Pleased to meet you. I'm Meg MaGrath, Babe's older sister.

BARNETTE. Yes, I know. You're the singer.

MEG. Well, yes . . .

BARNETTE. I came to hear you five different

times when you were singing at that club in Biloxi. Greeny's I believe was the name of it.

MEG. Yes, Greeny's.

BARNETTE. You were very good. There was something sad and moving about how you sang those songs. It was like you had some sort of vision. Some special sort of vision.

MEG. Well, thank you. You're very kind. Now . . . about Babe's case—

BARNETTE. Yes?

MEG. We've just got to win it.

BARNETTE. I intend to.

MEG. Of course. But, ah . . . *(She looks at him.)* Ah, you know, you're very young.

BARNETTE. Yes. I am. I'm young.

MEG. It's just, I'm concerned, Mr. Lloyd—

BARNETTE. Barnette. Please.

MEG. Barnette; that, ah, just maybe we need someone with, well, with more experience. Someone totally familiar with all the ins and outs and the this and thats of the legal dealings and such. As that.

BARNETTE. Ah, you have reservations.

MEG *(relieved)*. Reservations. Yes, I have . . . reservations.

BARNETTE. Well, possibly it would help you to know that I graduated first in my class from Ole Miss Law School. I also spent three different summers taking advanced courses in criminal law at Harvard Law School. I made A's in all the given courses. I was fascinated!

MEG. I'm sure.

BARNETTE. And even now, I've just completed one year working with Jackson's top criminal law firm, Manchester and Wayne. I was invaluable to them. Indispensable. They offered to double my percentage if I'd stay on; but I refused. I wanted to return to Hazlehurst and open my own office. The reason being, and this is a key point, that I have a personal vendetta to settle with one Zackery F. Botrelle.

MEG. A personal vendetta?

BARNETTE. Yes, ma'am. You are correct. Indeed, I do.

MEG. Hmmm. A personal vendetta . . . I think I like that. So you have some sort of a personal vendetta to settle with Zackery?

BARNETTE. Precisely. Just between the two of us, I not only intend to keep that sorry s.o.b. from ever being reelected to the state senate by exposing his shady, criminal dealings; but I also intend to decimate his personal credibility by exposing him as a bully, a brute, and a red-neck thug!

MEG. Well; I can see that you're—fanatical about this.

BARNETTE. Yes, I am. I'm sorry if I seem outspoken. But for some reason I feel I can talk to you . . . those songs you sang. Excuse me; I feel like a jackass.

MEG. It's all right. Relax. Relax, Barnette. Let me think this out a minute. *(She takes out a cigarette. He lights it for her.)* Now just exactly how do you intend to get Babe off? You know, keep her out of jail.

BARNETTE. It seems to me that we can get her off with a plea of self-defense, or possibly we could go with innocent by reason of temporary insanity. But basically I intend to prove that Zackery Botrelle brutalized and tormented this poor woman to such an extent that she had no recourse but to defend herself in the only way she knew how!

MEG. I like that!

BARNETTE. Then, of course, I'm hoping this will break the ice and we'll be able to go on to prove that the man's a total criminal, as well as an abusive bully and contemptible slob!

MEG. That sounds good! To me that sounds very good!

BARNETTE. It's just our basic game plan.

MEG. But now, how are you going to prove all this about Babe being brutalized? We don't want anyone perjured. I mean to commit perjury.

BARNETTE. Perjury? According to my sources, the'll be no need for perjury.

MEG. You mean it's the truth?

BARNETTE. This is a small town, Miss MaGrath. The word gets out.

MEG. It's really the truth?

BARNETTE *(opening his briefcase)*. Just look at this. It's a photostatic copy of Mrs. Botrelle's medical chart over the past four years. Take a good look at it, if you want your blood to boil!

MEG *(looking over the chart)*. What! What! This is maddening. This is madness! Did he do this to her? I'll kill him; I will—I'll fry his blood! Did he do this?

BARNETTE *(alarmed)*. To tell you the truth, I can't say for certain what was accidental and what was not. That's why I need to talk with Mrs. Botrelle. That's why it's very important that I see her!

MEG *(her eyes are wild, as she shoves him toward the door)*. Well, look, I've got to see her first. I've got to talk to her first. What I'll do is I'll give you a call. Maybe you can come back over later on—

BARNETTE. Well, then, here's my card—

MEG. Okay. Goodbye.

BARNETTE. 'Bye!

MEG. Oh, wait! Wait! There's one problem

with you.

BARNETTE. What?

MEG. What if you get so fanatically obsessed with this vendetta thing that you forget about Babe? You forget about her and sell her down the river just to get at Zackery. What about that?

BARNETTE. I—wouldn't do that.

MEG. You wouldn't?

BARNETTE. No.

MEG. Why not?

BARNETTE. Because I'm—I'm fond of her.

MEG. What do you mean you're fond of her?

BARNETTE. Well, she . . . she sold me a pound cake at a bazaar once. And I'm fond of her.

MEG. All right; I believe you. Goodbye.

BARNETTE. Goodbye. *(He exits.)*

MEG. Babe! Babe, come down hcrc! Babe! *(BABE comes hurrying down the stairs.)*

BABE. What? What is it? I called about the cake—

MEG. What did Zackery do to you?

BABE. They can't have it for today.

MEG. Did he hurt you? Did he? Did he do that?

BABE. Oh, Meg, please—

MEG. Did he? Goddamnit, Babe—

BABE. Yes, he did.

MEG. Why? Why?

BABE. I don't know! He started hating me, 'cause I couldn't laugh at his jokes. I just started finding it impossible to laugh at his jokes the way I used to. And then the sound of his voice got to where it tired me out awful bad to hear it. I'd fall asleep just listening to him at the dinner table. He'd say, "Hand me some of that gravy!" Or, "This roast beef is too damn bloody." And suddenly I'd be out cold like a light.

MEG. Oh, Babe. Babe, this is very important. I want you to sit down here and tell me what all happened right before you shot Zackery. That's right, just sit down and tell me.

BABE *(after a pause)*. I told you, I can't tell you on account of I'm protecting someone.

MEG. But, Babe, you've just got to talk to someone about all this. You just do.

BABE. Why?

MEG. Because it's a human need. To talk about our lives. It's an important human need.

BABE. Oh. Well, I do feel like I want to talk to someone. I do.

MEG. Then talk to me; please.

BABE *(making a decision)*. All right. *(After thinking a minute)* I don't know where to start.

MEG. Just start at the beginning. Just there at the beginning.

BABE *(after a moment)*. Well, do you remember Willie Jay? *(Meg shakes her head.)* Cora's youngest boy?

MEG. Oh, yeah, that little kid we used to pay a nickel to, to run down to the drugstore and bring us back a cherry Coke.

BABE. Right. Well, Cora irons at my place on Wednesdays now, and she just happened to mention that Willie Jay'd picked up this old stray dog and that he'd gotten real fond of him. But now they couldn't afford to feed him anymore. So she was gonna have to tell Willie Jay to set him loose in the woods.

MEG *(trying to be patient)*. Uh huh.

BABE. Well, I said I liked dogs, and if he wanted to bring the dog over here, I'd take care of him. You see, I was alone by myself inost of the time 'cause the senate was in session and Zackery was up in Jackson.

MEG. Uh huh. *(She reaches for LENNY's box of birthday candy. She takes little nibbles out of each piece throughout the rest of the scene.)*

BABE. So the next day, Willie Jay brings over this skinny old dog with these little crossed eyes. Well, I asked Willie Jay what his name was, and he said they called him Dog. Well, I liked the name, so I thought I'd keep it.

MEG *(getting up)*. Uh huh. I'm listening. I'm just gonna get me a glass of cold water. Do you want one?

BABE. Okay.

MEG. So you kept the name—Dog.

BABE. Yeah. Anyway, when Willie Jay was leaving he gave Dog a hug and said, "Goodbye, Dog. You're a fine old dog." Well, I felt something for him, so I told Willie Jay he could come back and visit with Dog any time he wanted, and his face just kinda lit right up.

MEG *(offering the candy)*. Candy—

BABE. No, thanks. Anyhow, time goes on and Willie Jay keeps coming over and over. And we talk about Dog and how fat he's getting, and then, well, you know, things start up.

MEG. No, I don't know. What things start up?

BABE. Well, things start up. Like sex. Like that.

MEG. Babe, wait a minute—Willie Jay's a boy. A small boy, about this tall. He's about this tall!

BABE. No! Oh, no! He's taller now! He's fifteen now. When you knew him he was only about seven or eight.

MEG. But even so—fifteen. And he's a black boy; a colored boy; a Negro.

BABE *(flustered)*. Well, I realize that, Meg. Why do you think I'm so worried about his getting public exposure? I don't want to ruin his reputation!

MEG. I'm amazed, Babe. I'm really completely amazed. I didn't even know you were a liberal.

BABE. Well, I'm not! I'm not a liberal! I'm a democratic! I was just lonely! I was so lonely. And he was good. Oh, he was so, so good. I'd never had it that good. We'd always go out into the garage and—

MEG. It's okay. I've got the picture; I've got the picture! Now, let's just get back to the story. To yesterday, when you shot Zackery.

BABE. All right, then. Let's see . . . Willie Jay was over. And it was after we'd—

MEG. Yeah! Yeah.

BABE. And we were just standing around on the back porch playing with Dog. Well, suddenly Zackery comes from around the side of the house. And he startled me 'cause he's supposed to be away at the office, and there he is coming from round the side of the house. Anyway, he says to Willie Jay, "Hey, boy, what are you doing back here?" And I say, "He's not doing anything. You just go on home, Willie Jay! You just run right on home." Well, before he can move, Zackery comes up and knocks him once right across the face and then shoves him down the porch steps, causing him to skin up his elbow real bad on that hard concrete. Then he says, "Don't you ever come around here again, or I'll have them cut out your gizzard!" Well, Willie Jay starts crying— these tears come streaming down his face— then he gets up real quick and runs away, with Dog following off after him. After that, I don't remember much too clearly; let's see . . . I went on into the living room, and I went right up to the davenport and opened the drawer where we keep the burglar gun . . . I took it out. Then I—I brought it up to my ear. That's right. I put it right inside my ear. Why, I was gonna shoot off my own head! That's what I was gonna do. Then I heard the back door slamming and suddenly, for some reason, I thought about Mama . . . how she'd hung herself. And here I was about ready to shoot myself. Then I realized—that's right, I realized how I didn't want to kill myself! And she— she probably didn't want to kill herself. She wanted to kill him, and I wanted to kill him, too. I wanted to kill Zackery, not myself. 'Cause I—I wanted to live! So I waited for him to come on into the living room. Then I held out the gun, and I pulled the trigger, aiming for his heart but getting him in the stomach. *(after a pause)* It's funny that I really did that.

MEG. It's a good thing that you did. It's a damn good thing that you did.

BABE. It was.

MEG. Please, Babe, talk to Barnette Lloyd. Just talk to him and see if he can help.

BABE. But how about Willie Jay?

MEG *(starting toward the phone)*. Oh, he'll be all right. You just talk to that lawyer like you did to me. *(Looking at the number on the card, she begins dialing.)* See, 'cause he's gonna be on your side.

BABE. No! Stop, Meg, stop! Don't call him up! Please don't call him up! You can't! It's too awful. *(She runs over and jerks the bottom half of the phone away from MEG.)*

(MEG stands, holding the receiver.)

MEG. Babe!

(BABE slams her half of the phone into the refrigerator.)

BABE. I just can't tell some stranger all about my personal life. I just can't.

MEG. Well, hell, Babe; you're the one who said you wanted to live.

BABE. That's right. I did. *(She takes the phone out of the refrigerator and hands it to MEG.)* Here's the other part of the phone. *(She moves to sit at the kitchen table.)*

(MEG takes the phone back to the counter.)

BABE *(as she fishes a piece of lemon out of her glass and begins sucking on it)*. Meg.

MEG. What?

BABE. I called the bakery. They're gonna have Lenny's cake ready first thing tomorrow morning. That's the earliest they can get it.

MEG. All right.

BABE. I told them to write on it, *Happy Birthday, Lenny—A Day Late*. That sound okay?

MEG *(at the phone)*. It sounds nice.

BABE. I ordered up the very largest size cake they have. I told them chocolate cake with white icing and red trim. Think she'll like that?

MEG *(dialing the phone)*. Yeah, I'm sure she will. She'll like it.

BABE. I'm hoping.

CURTAIN

ACT TWO

The lights go up on the kitchen. It is evening of the same day. MEG's *suitcase has been moved upstairs.* BABE's *saxophone has been taken out of the case and put together.* BABE *and* BAR-

NETTE *are sitting at the kitchen table.* BAR-
NETTE *is writing and rechecking notes with
explosive intensity.* BABE, *who has changed
into a casual shift, sits eating a bowl of oatmeal, slowly.*

———

BARNETTE *(to himself).* Mmm huh! Yes! I
see, I see! Well, we can work on that! And of
course, this is mere conjecture! Difficult, if
not impossible, to prove. Ha! Yes. Yes, indeed. Indeed—

BABE. Sure you don't want any oatmeal?

BARNETTE. What? Oh, no. No, thank you.
Let's see; ah, where were we?

BABE. I just shot Zackery.

BARNETTE *(looking at his notes).* Right.
Correct. You've just pulled the trigger.

BABE. Tell me, do you think Willie Jay can
stay out of all this?

BARNETTE. Believe me, it is in our interest
to keep him as far out of this as possible.

BABE. Good.

BARNETTE *(throughout the following,* BAR-
NETTE *stays glued to* BABE'*s every word).* All
right, you've just shot one Zackery Botrelle,
as a result of his continual physical and mental
abuse—what happens now?

BABE. Well, after I shot him, I put the gun
down on the piano bench, and then I went out
into the kitchen and made another pitcher of
lemonade.

BARNETTE. Lemonade?

BABE. Yes, I was dying of thirst. My mouth
was just as dry as a bone.

BARNETTE. So in order to quench this raging
thirst that was choking you dry and preventing
any possibility of you uttering intelligible
sounds or phrases, you went out to the kitchen
and made up a pitcher of lemonade?

BABE. Right. I made it just the way I like
it, with lots of sugar and lots of lemon—about
ten lemons in all. Then I added two trays of
ice and stirred it up with my wooden stirring
spoon.

BARNETTE. Then what?

BABE. Then I drank three glasses, one right
after the other. They were large glasses—about
this tall. Then suddenly my stomach kind of
swole all up. I guess what caused it was all
that sour lemon.

BARNETTE. Could be.

BABE. Then what I did was . . . I wiped my
mouth off with the back of my hand, like this
. . . *(She demonstrates.)*

BARNETTE. Hmmm.

BABE. I did it to clear off all those little beads

of water that had settled there.

BARNETTE. I see.

BABE. Then I called out to Zackery. I said,
"Zackery, I've made some lemonade. Can you
use a glass?"

BARNETTE. Did he answer? Did you hear an
answer?

BABE. No. He didn't answer.

BARNETTE. So what'd you do?

BABE. I poured him a glass anyway and took
it out to him.

BARNETTE. You took it out to the living
room?

BABE. I did. And there he was, lying on the
rug. He was looking up at me trying to speak
words. I said, "What? . . . Lemonade? . . .
You don't want it? Would you like a Coke
instead?" Then I got the idea—he was telling
me to call on the phone for medical help. So
I got on the phone and called up the hospital.
I gave my name and address, and I told them
my husband was shot and he was lying on the
rug and there was plenty of blood. *(She pauses
a minute, as* BARNETTE *works frantically on
his notes.)* I guess that's gonna look kinda bad.

BARNETTE. What?

BABE. Me fixing that lemonade before I called
the hospital.

BARNETTE. Well, not . . . necessarily.

BABE. I tell you, I think the reason I made
up the lemonade, I mean besides the fact that
my mouth was bone dry, was that I was afraid
to call the authorities. I was afraid. I—I really
think I was afraid they would see that I had
tried to shoot Zackery, in fact, that I *had* shot
him, and they would accuse me of possible
murder and send me away to jail.

BARNETTE. Well, that's understandable.

BABE. I think so. I mean, in fact, that's what
did happen. That's what is happening—'cause
here I am just about ready to go right off to
the Parchment Prison Farm. Yes, here I am
just practically on the brink of utter doom.
Why, I feel so all alone.

BARNETTE. Now, now, look—Why, there's
no reason for you to get yourself so all upset
and worried. Please don't. Please. *(They look
at each other for a moment.)* You just keep
filling in as much detailed information as you
can about those incidents on the medical reports. That's all you need to think about. Don't
you worry, Mrs. Botrelle, we're going to have
a solid defense.

BABE. Please don't call me Mrs. Botrelle.

BARNETTE. All right.

BABE. My name's Becky. People in the family call me Babe, but my real name's Becky.

BARNETTE. All right, Becky.

(BARNETTE and BABE stare at each other for a long moment.)

BABE. Are you sure you didn't go to Hazlehurst High?

BARNETTE. No, I went away to a boarding school.

BABE. Gosh, you sure do look familiar. You sure do.

BARNETTE. Well, I—I doubt you'll remember, but I did meet you once.

BABE. You did? When?

BARNETTE. At the Christmas bazaar, year before last. You were selling cakes and cookies and . . . candy.

BABE. Oh, yes! You bought the orange pound cake!

BARNETTE. Right.

BABE. Of course, and then we talked for a while. We talked about the Christmas angel.

BARNETTE. You do remember.

BABE. I remember it very well. You were even thinner then than you are now.

BARNETTE. Well, I'm surprised. I'm certainly . . . surprised.

(The phone rings.)

BABE *(as she goes to answer the phone).* This is quite a coincidence! Don't you think it is? Why, it's almost a fluke. *(She answers the phone.)* Hello . . . Oh, hello, Lucille . . . Oh, he is? . . . Oh, he does? . . . Okay. Oh, Lucille, wait! Has Dog come back to the house? . . . Oh, I see . . . Okay. Okay. *(after a brief pause)* Hello, Zackery? How are you doing? . . . Uh huh . . . uh huh . . . Oh, I'm sorry . . . Please don't scream . . . Uh huh . . . uh huh . . . You want what? . . . No, I can't come up there now . . . Well, for one thing, I don't even have the car. Lenny and Meg are up at the hospital right now, visiting with Old Granddaddy . . . What? . . . Oh, really? . . . Oh, really? . . . Well, I've got me a lawyer that's over here right now, and he's building me up a solid defense! . . . Wait just a minute, I'll see. *(to BARNETTE).* He wants to talk to you. He says he's got some blackening evidence that's gonna convict me of attempting to murder him in the first degree!

BARNETTE *(disgustedly).* Oh, bluff! He's bluffing! Here hand me the phone. *(He takes the phone and becomes suddenly cool and suave.)* Hello, this is Mr. Barnette Lloyd speaking. I'm Mrs. . . . ah, Becky's attorney . . . Why, certainly, Mr. Botrelle, I'd be more than glad to check out any pertinent information that you may have . . . Fine, then I'll be right on over. Goodbye. *(He hangs up the phone.)*

BABE. What did he say?

BARNETTE. He wants me to come see him at the hospital this evening. Says he's got some sort of evidence. Sounds highly suspect to me.

BABE. Oooh! Didn't you just hate his voice? Doesn't he have the most awful voice? I just hate—I can't bear to hear it!

BARNETTE. Well, now—now, wait. Wait just a minute.

BABE. What?

BARNETTE. I have a solution. From now on, I'll handle all communications between you two. You can simply refuse to speak with him.

BABE. All right—I will. I'll do that.

BARNETTE *(starting to pack his briefcase).* Well, I'd better get over there and see just what he's got up his sleeve.

BABE *(after a pause).* Barnette.

BARNETTE. Yes?

BABE. What's the personal vendetta about? You know, the one you have to settle with Zackery.

BARNETTE. Oh, it's—it's complicated. It's a very complicated matter.

BABE. I see.

BARNETTE. The major thing he did was to ruin my father's life. He took away his job, his home, his health, his respectability. I don't like to talk about it.

BABE. I'm sorry. I just wanted to say—I hope you win it. I hope you win your vendetta.

BARNETTE. Thank you.

BABE. I think it's an important thing that a person could win a lifelong vendetta.

BARNETTE. Yes. Well, I'd better be going.

BABE. All right. Let me know what happens.

BARNETTE. I will. I'll get back to you right away.

BABE. Thanks.

BARNETTE. Goodbye, Becky.

BABE. Goodbye, Barnette.

(BARNETTE exits. BABE looks around the room for a moment, then goes over to her white suitcase and opens it up. She takes out her pink hair curlers and a brush. She begins brushing her hair.)

BABE. Goodbye, Becky. Goodbye, Barnette. Goodbye, Becky. Oooh.

(LENNY enters. She is fuming. BABE is rolling her hair throughout most of the following scene.)

BABE. Lenny, hi!

LENNY. Hi.

BABE. Where's Meg?

LENNY. Oh, she had to go by the store and pick some things up. I don't know what.

BABE. Well, how's Old Granddaddy?

LENNY *(as she picks up* BABE*'s bowl of oatmeal).* He's fine. Wonderful! Never been better!

BABE. Lenny, what's wrong? What's the matter?

LENNY. It's Meg! I could just wring her neck! I could just wring it!

BABE. Why? Wha'd she do?

LENNY. She lied! She sat in that hospital room and shamelessly lied to Old Granddaddy. She went on and on telling such untrue stories and lies.

BABE. Well, what? What did she say?

LENNY. Well, for one thing, she said she was gonna have an RCA record coming out with her picture on the cover, eating pineapples under a palm tree.

BABE. Well, gosh, Lenny, maybe she is! Don't you think she really is?

LENNY. Babe, she sat here this very afternoon and told me how all that she's done this whole year is work as a clerk for a dog-food company.

BABE. Oh, shoot. I'm disappointed.

LENNY. And then she goes on to say that she'll be appearing on the Johnny Carson show in two weeks' time. Two weeks' time! Why, Old Granddaddy's got a TV set right in his room. Imagine what a letdown it's gonna be.

BABE. Why, mercy me.

LENNY *(slamming the coffeepot on).* Oh, and she told him the reason she didn't use the money he sent her to come home Christmas was that she was right in the middle of making a huge multimillion-dollar motion picture and was just under too much pressure.

BABE. My word!

LENNY. The movie's coming out this spring. It's called, *Singing in a Shoe Factory.* But she only has a small leading role—not a large leading role.

BABE *(laughing).* For heaven's sake—

LENNY. I'm sizzling. Oh, I just can't help it! I'm sizzling!

BABE. Sometimes Meg does such strange things.

LENNY *(slowly, as she picks up the opened box of birthday candy).* Who ate this candy?

BABE *(hesitantly).* Meg.

LENNY. My one birthday present, and look what she does! Why, she's taken one little bite out of each piece and then just put it back in! Ooh! That's just like her! That is just like her!

BABE. Lenny, please—

LENNY. I can't help it! It gets me mad! It gets me upset! Why, Meg's always run wild—she started smoking and drinking when she was

fourteen years old; she never made good grades—never made her own bed! But somehow she always seemed to get what she wanted. She's the one who got singing and dancing lessons, and a store-bought dress to wear to her senior prom. Why, do you remember how Meg always got to wear twelve jingle bells on her petticoats, while we were only allowed to wear three apiece? Why?! Why should Old Grandmama let her sew twelve golden jingle bells on her petticoats and us only three!

BABE *(who has heard all this before).* I don't know! Maybe she didn't jingle them as much!

LENNY. I can't help it! It gets me mad! I resent it. I do.

BABE. Oh, don't resent Meg. Things have been hard for Meg. After all, she was the one who found Mama.

LENNY. Oh, I know; she's the one who found Mama. But that's always been the excuse.

BABE. But I tell you, Lenny, after it happened, Meg started doing all sorts of these strange things.

LENNY. She did? Like what?

BABE. Like things I never even wanted to tell you about.

LENNY. What sort of things?

BABE. Well, for instance, back when we used to go over to the library, Meg would spend all her time reading and looking through this old black book called *Diseases of the Skin.* It was full of the most sickening pictures you've ever seen. Things like rotting-away noses and eyeballs drooping off down the sides of people's faces, and scabs and sores and eaten-away places all over all parts of people's bodies.

LENNY *(trying to pour her coffee).* Babe, please! That's enough.

BABE. Anyway, she'd spend hours and hours just forcing herself to look through this book. Why, it was the same way she'd force herself to look at the poster of crippled children stuck up in the window at Dixieland Drugs. You know, that one where they want you to give a dime. Meg would stand there and stare at their eyes and look at the braces on their little crippled-up legs—then she'd purposely go and spend her dime on a double-scoop ice-cream cone and eat it all down. She'd say to me, "See, I can stand it. I can stand it. Just look how I'm gonna be able to stand it."

LENNY. That's awful.

BABE. She said she was afraid of being a weak person. I guess 'cause she cried in bed every night for such a long time.

LENNY. Goodness mercy. *(after a pause)* Well, I suppose you'd have to be a pretty hard person to be able to do what she did to Doc Porter.

BABE *(exasperated)*. Oh, shoot! It wasn't Meg's fault that hurricane wiped Biloxi away. I never understood why people were blaming all that on Meg—just because that roof fell in and crunched Doc's leg. It wasn't her fault.

LENNY. Well, it was Meg who refused to evacuate. Jim Craig and some of Doc's other friends were all down there, and they kept trying to get everyone to evacuate. But Meg refused. She wanted to stay on because she thought a hurricane would be—oh, I don't know—a lot of fun. Then everyone says she baited Doc into staying there with her. She said she'd marry him if he'd stay.

BABE *(taken aback by this new information)*. Well, he has a mind of his own. He could have gone.

LENNY. But he didn't. 'Cause . . . 'cause he loved her. And then, after the roof caved in and they got Doc to the high school gym, Meg just left. She just left him there to leave for California—'cause of her career, she says. I think it was a shameful thing to do. It took almost a year for his leg to heal, and after that he gave up his medical career altogether. He said he was tired of hospitals. It's such a sad thing. Everyone always knew he was gonna be a doctor. We've called him Doc for years.

BABE. I don't know. I guess I don't have any room to talk; 'cause I just don't know. *(pause)* Gosh, you look so tired.

LENNY. I feel tired.

BABE. They say women need a lot of iron . . . so they won't feel tired.

LENNY. What's got iron in it? Liver?

BABE. Yeah, liver's got it. And vitamin pills.

(After a moment, MEG enters. She carries a bottle of bourbon that is already minus a few slugs, and a newspaper. She is wearing black boots, a dark dress, and a hat. The room goes silent.)

MEG. Hello.

BABE *(fooling with her hair)*. Hi, Meg.

(LENNY quietly sips her coffee.)

MEG *(handing the newspaper to BABE)*. Here's your paper.

BABE. Thanks. *(She opens it.)* Oh, here it is, right on the front page.

(MEG lights a cigarette.)

BABE. Where're the scissors, Lenny?

LENNY. Look in there in the ribbon drawer.

BABE. Okay. *(She gets the scissors and glue out of the drawer and slowly begins cutting out the newspaper article.)*

MEG *(after a few moments, filled only with the snipping of scissors)*. All right—I lied! I lied! I couldn't help it . . . these stories just came pouring out of my mouth! When I saw how tired and sick Old Granddaddy'd gotten—they just flew out! All I wanted was to see him smiling and happy. I just wasn't going to sit there and look at him all miserable and sick and sad! I just wasn't!

BABE. Oh, Meg, he is sick, isn't he—

MEG. Why, he's gotten all white and milky—he's almost evaporated!

LENNY *(gasping and turning to MEG)*. But still you shouldn't have lied! It just was wrong for you to tell such lies—

MEG. Well, I know that! Don't you think I know that? I hate myself when I lie for that old man. I do. I feel so weak. And then I have to go and do at least three or four things that I know he'd despise just to get even with that miserable, old, bossy man!

LENNY. Oh, Meg, please don't talk so about Old Granddaddy! It sounds so ungrateful. Why, he went out of his way to make a home for us, to treat us like we were his very own children. All he ever wanted was the best for us. That's all he ever wanted.

MEG. Well, I guess it was; but sometimes I wonder what we wanted.

BABE *(taking the newspaper article and glue over to her suitcase)*. Well, one thing I wanted was a team of white horses to ride Mama's coffin to her grave. That's one thing I wanted.

(LENNY and MEG exchange looks.)

BABE. Lenny, did you remember to pack my photo album?

LENNY. It's down there at the bottom, under all that night stuff.

BABE. Oh, I found it.

LENNY. Really, Babe, I don't understand why you have to put in the articles that are about the unhappy things in your life. Why would you want to remember them?

BABE *(pasting the article in)*. I don't know. I just like to keep an accurate record, I suppose. There. *(She begins flipping through the book.)* Look, here's a picture of me when I got married.

MEG. Let's see. *(They all look at the photo album.)*

LENNY. My word, you look about twelve years old.

BABE. I was just eighteen.

MEG. You're smiling, Babe. Were you happy then?

BABE *(laughing)*. Well, I was drunk on champagne punch. I remember that! *(They turn the page.)*

LENNY. Oh, there's Meg singing at Greeny's!

BABE. Oooh, I wish you were still singing at Greeny's! I wish you were!

LENNY. You're so beautiful!

BABE. Yes, you are. You're beautiful.

MEG. Oh, stop! I'm not—

LENNY. Look, Meg's starting to cry.

BABE. Oh, Meg—

MEG. I'm not—

BABE. Quick, better turn the page; we don't want Meg crying—(She flips the pages.)

LENNY. Why, it's Daddy.

MEG. Where'd you get that picture, Babe? I thought she burned them all.

BABE. Ah, I just found it around.

LENNY. What does it say here? What's that inscription?

BABE. It says "Jimmy—clowning at the beach—1952."

LENNY. Well, will you look at that smile.

MEG. Jesus, those white teeth—turn the page, will you; we can't do any worse than this!

(They turn the page. The room goes silent.)

BABE. It's Mama and the cat.

LENNY. Oh, turn the page—

BABE. That old yellow cat. You know, I bet if she hadn't of hung that old cat along with her, she wouldn't have gotten all that national coverage.

MEG (after a moment, hopelessly). Why are we talking about this?

LENNY. Meg's right. It was so sad. It was awfully sad. I remember how we all three just sat up on that bed the day of the service all dressed up in our black velveteen suits crying the whole morning long.

BABE. We used up one whole big box of Kleenexes.

MEG. And then Old Granddaddy came in and said he was gonna take us out to breakfast. Remember, he told us not to cry anymore 'cause he was gonna take us out to get banana splits for breakfast.

BABE. That's right—banana splits for breakfast!

MEG. Why, Lenny was fourteen years old, and he thought that would make it all better—

BABE. Oh, I remember he said for us to eat all we wanted. I think I ate about five! He kept shoving them down us!

MEG. God, we were so sick!

LENNY. Oh, we were!

MEG (laughing). Lenny's face turned green—

LENNY. I was just as sick as a dog!

BABE. Old Grandmama was furious!

LENNY. Oh, she was!

MEG. The thing about Old Granddaddy is, he keeps trying to make us happy, and we end up getting stomachaches and turning green and throwing up in the flower arrangements.

BABE. Oh, that was me! I threw up in the flowers! Oh, no! How embarrassing!

LENNY (laughing). Oh, Babe—

BABE (hugging her sisters). Oh, Lenny! Oh, Meg!

MEG. Oh, Babe! Oh, Lenny! It's so good to be home!

LENNY. Hey, I have an idea—

BABE. What?

LENNY. Let's play cards!!

BABE. Oh, let's do!

MEG. All right!

LENNY. Oh, good! It'll be just like when we used to sit around the table playing hearts all night long.

BABE. I know! (getting up). I'll fix us up some popcorn and hot chocolate—

MEG (getting up). Here, let me get out that old black popcorn pot.

LENNY (getting up). Oh, yes! Now, let's see, I think I have a deck of cards around here somewhere.

BABE. Gosh, I hope I remember all the rules—Are hearts good or bad?

MEG. Bad, I think. Aren't they, Lenny?

LENNY. That's right. Hearts are bad, but the Black Sister is the worst of all—

MEG. Oh, that's right! And the Black Sister is the Queen of Spades.

BABE (figuring it out). And spades are the black cards that aren't the puppy dog feet?

MEG (thinking a moment). Right. And she counts a lot of points.

BABE. And points are bad?

MEG. Right. Here, I'll get some paper so we can keep score.

(The phone rings.)

LENNY. Oh, here they are!

MEG. I'll get it—

LENNY. Why, look at these cards! They're years old!

BABE. Oh, let me see!

MEG. Hello . . . No, this is Meg MaGrath . . . Doc. How are you? . . . Well, good . . . You're where? . . . Well, sure. Come on over . . . Sure I'm sure . . . Yeah, come right on over . . . All right. 'Bye. (She hangs up.) That was Doc Porter. He's down the street at Al's Grill. He's gonna come on over.

LENNY. He is?

MEG. He said he wanted to come see me.

LENNY. Oh. (after a pause) Well, do you still want to play?

MEG. No, I don't think so.

LENNY. All right. (She starts to shuffle the

cards, as MEG *brushes her hair.)* You know, it's really not much fun playing hearts with only two people.

MEG. I'm sorry; maybe after Doc leaves I'll join you.

LENNY. I know; maybe Doc'll want to play. Then we can have a game of bridge.

MEG. I don't think so. Doc never liked cards. Maybe we'll just go out somewhere.

LENNY *(putting down the cards. Babe picks them up).* Meg—

MEG. What?

LENNY. Well, Doc's married now.

MEG. I know. You told me.

LENNY. Oh. Well, as long as you know that. *(pause)* As long as you know that.

MEG *(still primping).* Yes, I know. She made the pot.

BABE. How many cards do I deal out?

LENNY *(leaving the table).* Excuse me.

BABE. All of 'em, or what?

LENNY. Ah, Meg, could I—could I ask you something?

*(*BABE *proceeds to deal out all the cards.)*

MEG. What?

LENNY. I just wanted to ask you—

MEG. What?

(Unable to go on with what she really wants to say, LENNY *runs and picks up the box of candy.)*

LENNY. Well, just why did you take one little bite out of each piece of candy in this box and then just put it back in?

MEG. Oh. Well, I was looking for the ones with nuts.

LENNY. The ones with nuts.

MEG. Yeah.

LENNY. But there are none with nuts. It's a box of assorted crèmes—all it has in it are crèmes!

MEG. Oh.

LENNY. Why couldn't you just read on the box? It says right here, *Assorted Crèmes,* not nuts! Besides, this was a birthday present to me! My one and only birthday present; my only one!

MEG. I'm sorry. I'll get you another box.

LENNY. I don't want another box. That's not the point!

MEG. What is the point?

LENNY. I don't know; it's—it's—You have no respect for other people's property! You just take whatever you want. You just take it! Why, remember how you had layers and layers of jingle bells sewed onto your petticoats while Babe and I only had three apiece?!

MEG. Oh, God! She's starting up about those stupid jingle bells!

LENNY. Well, it's an example! A specific example of how you always got what you wanted!

MEG. Oh, come on, Lenny, you're just upset because Doc called.

LENNY. Who said anything about Doc? Do you think I'm upset about Doc? Why, I've long since given up worrying about you and all your men.

MEG *(turning in anger).* Look, I know I've had too many men. Believe me, I've had way too many men. But it's not my fault you haven't had any—or maybe just that one from Memphis.

LENNY *(stopping).* What one from Memphis?

MEG *(slowly).* The one Babe told me about. From the—club.

LENNY. Babe!

BABE. Meg!

LENNY. How could you! I asked you not to tell anyone! I'm so ashamed! How could you? Who else have you told? Did you tell anyone else?

BABE *(overlapping, to Meg).* Why'd you have to open your big mouth?

MEG *(overlapping).* How am I supposed to know? You never said not to tell!

BABE. Can't you use your head just for once? *(to* LENNY*)* No, I never told anyone else. Somehow it just slipped out to Meg. Really, it just flew out of my mouth—

LENNY. What do you two have—wings on your tongues?

BABE. I'm sorry, Lenny. Really sorry.

LENNY. I'll just never, never, never be able to trust you again—

MEG *(furiously coming to* BABE*'s defense).* Oh, for heaven's sake, Lenny, we were just worried about you! We wanted to find a way to make you happy!

LENNY. Happy! Happy! I'll never be happy!

MEG. Well, not if you keep living your life as Old Granddaddy's nursemaid—

BABE. Meg, shut up!

MEG. I can't help it! I just know that the reason you stopped seeing this man from Memphis was because of Old Granddaddy.

LENNY. What—Babe didn't tell you the rest of the story—

MEG. Oh, she said it was something about your shrunken ovary.

BABE. Meg!

LENNY. Babe!

BABE. I just mentioned it!

MEG. But I don't believe a word of that story!

LENNY. Oh, I don't care what you believe!

It's so easy for you—you always have men falling in love with you! But I have this underdeveloped ovary and I can't have children and my hair is falling out in the comb—so what man can love me? What man's gonna love me?

MEG. A lot of men!

BABE. Yeah, a lot! A whole lot!

MEG. Old Granddaddy's the only one who seems to think otherwise.

LENNY. 'Cause he doesn't want to see me hurt! He doesn't want to see me rejected and humiliated.

MEG. Oh, come on now, Lenny, don't be so pathetic! God, you make me angry when you just stand there looking so pathetic! Just tell me, did you really ask the man from Memphis? Did you actually ask that man from Memphis all about it?

LENNY (breaking apart). No, I didn't. I didn't. Because I just didn't want him not to want me—

MEG. Lenny—

LENNY (furious). Don't talk to me anymore! Don't talk to me! I think I'm gonna vomit—I just hope all this doesn't cause me to vomit! (She exits up the stirs sobbing.)

MEG. See! See! She didn't even ask him about her stupid ovary! She just broke it all off 'cause of Old Granddaddy! What a jackass fool!

BABE. Oh, Meg, shut up! Why do you have to make Lenny cry? I just hate it when you make Lenny cry! (She runs up the stairs.) Lenny! Oh, Lenny—

(MEG gives a long sigh and goes to get a cigarette and a drink.)

MEG. I feel like hell. (She sits in despair, smoking and drinking bourbon. There is a knock at the back door. She starts. She brushes her hair out of her face and goes to answer the door. It is DOC.)

DOC. Hello, Meggy.

MEG. Well, Doc. Well, it's Doc.

DOC (after a pause). You're home, Meggy.

MEG. Yeah, I've come home. I've come on home to see about Babe.

DOC. And how's Babe?

MEG. Oh, fine. Well, fair. She's fair.

(DOC nods.)

MEG. Hey, do you want a drink?

DOC. Whatcha got?

MEG. Bourbon.

DOC. Oh, don't tell me Lenny's stocking bourbon.

MEG. Well, no. I've been to the store. (She gets him a glass and pours them each a drink.

They click glasses.)

MEG. So, how's your wife?

DOC. She's fine.

MEG. I hear ya got two kids.

DOC. Yeah. Yeah, I got two kids.

MEG. A boy and a girl.

DOC. That's right, Meggy, a boy and a girl.

MEG. That's what you always said you wanted, wasn't it? A boy and a girl.

DOC. Is that what I said?

MEG. I don't know. I thought it's what you said.

(They finish their drinks in silence.)

DOC. Whose cot?

MEG. Lenny's. She's taken to sleeping in the kitchen.

DOC. Ah. Where is Lenny?

MEG. She's in the upstairs room. I made her cry. Babe's up there seeing to her.

DOC. How'd you make her cry?

MEG. I don't know. Eating her birthday candy; talking on about her boyfriend from Memphis. I don't know. I'm upset about it. She's got a lot on her. Why can't I keep my mouth shut?

DOC. I don't know, Meggy. Maybe it's because you don't want to.

MEG. Maybe.

(They smile at each other. MEG pours each of them another drink.)

DOC. Well, it's been a long time.

MEG. It has been a long time.

DOC. Let's see—when was the last time we saw each other?

MEG. I can't quite recall.

DOC. Wasn't it in Biloxi?

MEG. Ah, Biloxi. I believe so.

DOC. And wasn't there a—a hurricane going on at the time?

MEG. Was there?

DOC. Yes, there was; one hell of a hurricane. Camille, I believe they called it. Hurricane Camille.

MEG. Yes, now I remember. It was a beautiful hurricane.

DOC. We had a time down there. We had quite a time. Drinking vodka, eating oysters on the half shell, dancing all night long. And the wind was blowing.

MEG. Oh, God, was it blowing.

DOC. Goddamn, was it blowing.

MEG. There never has been such a wind blowing.

DOC. Oh, God, Meggy. Oh, God.

MEG. I know, Doc. It was my fault to leave you. I was crazy. I thought I was choking. I felt choked!

DOC. I felt like a fool.

MEG. No.

DOC. I just kept on wondering why.

MEG. I don't know why . . . 'Cause I didn't want to care. I don't know. I did care, though. I did.

DOC *(after a pause)*. Ah, hell—*(He pours them both another drink.)* Are you still singing those sad songs?

MEG. No.

DOC. Why not?

MEG. I don't know, Doc. Things got worse for me. After a while, I just couldn't sing anymore. I tell you, I had one hell of a time over Christmas.

DOC. What do you mean?

MEG. I went nuts. I went insane. Ended up in L.A. County Hospital. Psychiatric ward.

DOC. Hell. Ah, hell, Meggy. What happened?

MEG. I don't really know. I couldn't sing anymore, so I lost my job. And I had a bad toothache. I had this incredibly painful toothache. For days I had it, but I wouldn't do anything about it. I just stayed inside my apartment. All I could do was sit around in chairs, chewing on my fingers. Then one afternoon I ran screaming out of the apartment with all my money and jewelry and valuables, and tried to stuff it all into one of those March of Dimes collection boxes. That was when they nabbed me. Sad story. Meg goes mad.

(DOC stares at her for a long moment. He pours them both another drink.)

DOC *(after quite a pause)*. There's a moon out.

MEG. Is there?

DOC. Wanna go take a ride in my truck and look out at the moon?

MEG. I don't know, Doc. I don't wanna start up. It'll be too hard if we start up.

DOC. Who says we're gonna start up? We're just gonna look at the moon. For one night just you and me are gonna go for a ride in the country and look out at the moon.

MEG. One night?

DOC. Right.

MEG. Look out at the moon?

DOC. You got it.

MEG. Well . . . all right. *(She gets up.)*

DOC. Better take your coat. *(He helps her into her coat.)* And the bottle—*(He takes the bottle.* MEG *picks up the glasses.)* Forget the glasses—

MEG *(laughing)*. Yeah—forget the glasses. Forget the goddamn glasses.

(MEG shuts off the kitchen lights, leaving the kitchen with only a dim light over the kitchen sink. MEG *and* DOC *leave. After a moment,* BABE *comes down the stairs in her slip.)*

BABE. Meg—Meg? *(She stands for a moment in the moonlight wearing only a slip. She sees her saxophone, then moves to pick it up. She plays a few shrieking notes. There is a loud knock on the back door.)*

BARNETTE'S VOICE. Becky! Becky, is that you?

(BABE puts down the saxophone.)

BABE. Just a minute. I'm coming. *(She puts a raincoat on over her slip and goes to answer the door.)* Hello, Barnette. Come on in.

(BARNETTE comes in. He is troubled but is making a great effort to hide the fact.)

BARNETTE. Thank you.

BABE. What is it?

BARNETTE. I've, ah, I've just come from seeing Zackery at the hospital.

BABE. Oh?

BARNETTE. It seems . . . Well, it seems his sister, Lucille, was somewhat suspicious.

BABE. Suspicious.

BARNETTE. About you?

BABE. Me?

BARNETTE. She hired a private detective: he took these pictures. *(He hands BABE a small envelope containing several photographs.* BABE *opens the envelope and begins looking at the pictures in stunned silence.)* They were taken about two weeks ago. It seems she wasn't going to show them to Botrelle straightaway. She, ah, wanted to wait till the time was right. *(The phone rings one and a half times.* BARNETTE *glances uneasily toward the phone.)* Becky? *(The phone stops ringing.)*

BABE *(looking up at BARNETTE, slowly)*. These are pictures of Willie Jay and me . . . out in the garage.

BARNETTE *(looking away)*. I know.

BABE. You looked at these pictures?

BARNETTE. Yes—I—well . . . professionally, I looked at them.

BABE. Oh, mercy. Oh, mercy! We can burn them, can't we? Quick, we can burn them—

BARNETTE. It won't do any good. They have the negatives.

BABE *(holding the pictures, as she bangs herself hopelessly into the stove, table, cabinets, etc.)*. Oh, no; oh, no; oh, no! Oh, no—

BARNETTE. There—there, now———there—

LENNY'S VOICE. Babe? Are you all right? Babe—

BABE *(hiding the pictures)*. What? I'm all right. Go on back to bed.

(BABE hides the pictures as LENNY comes down the stairs. She is wearing a coat and

wiping white night cream off of her face with a washrag.)

LENNY. What's the matter? What's going on down here?

BABE. Nothing! *(then as she begins dancing ballet style around the room).* We're—we're just dancing. We were just dancing around down here. *(signaling to* BARNETTE *to dance.)*

LENNY. Well, you'd better get your shoes on, 'cause we've got—

BABE. All right, I will! That's a good idea! *(She goes to get her shoes.)* Now, you go on back to bed. It's pretty late and—

LENNY. Babe, will you listen a minute—

BABE *(holding up her shoes).* I'm putting 'em on—

LENNY. That was the hospital that just called. We've got to get over there. Old Granddaddy's had himself another stroke.

BABE. Oh. All right. My shoes are on. *(She stands.)*

(They all look at each other as the lights black out.)

CURTAIN

ACT THREE

The lights go up on the empty kitchen. It is the following morning. After a few moments, BABE *enters from the back door. She is carrying her hair curlers in her hands. She lies down on the cot. A few moments later,* LENNY *enters. She is tired and weary.* CHICK's *voice is heard.*

———

CHICK's VOICE. Lenny! Oh, Lenny!

(LENNY turns to the door. CHICK *enters energetically.)*

CHICK. Well . . . how is he?

LENNY. He's stabilized; they say for now his functions are all stabilized.

CHICK. Well, is he still in the coma?

LENNY. Uh huh.

CHICK. Hmmm. So do they think he's gonna be . . . passing on?

LENNY. He may be. He doesn't look so good. They said they'd phone us if there were any sudden changes.

CHICK. Well, it seems to me we'd better get busy phoning on the phone ourselves. *(Removing a list from her pocket)* Now, I've made out this list of all the people we need to notify about Old Granddaddy's predicament. I'll phone half, if you'll phone half.

LENNY. But—what would we say?

CHICK. Just tell them the facts: that Old Granddaddy's got himself in a coma, and it could be he doesn't have long for this world.

LENNY. I—I don't know. I don't feel like phoning.

CHICK. Why, Lenora, I'm surprised; how can you be this way? I went to all the trouble of making up the list. And I offered to phone half of the people on it, even though I'm only one-fourth of the granddaughters. I mean, I just get tired of doing more than my fair share, when people like Meg can suddenly just disappear to where they can't even be reached in case of emergency!

LENNY. All right; give me the list. I'll phone half.

CHICK. Well, don't do it just to suit me.

LENNY *(wearily tearing the list in half).* I'll phone these here.

CHICK *(taking her half of the list).* Fine then. Suit yourself. Oh, wait—let me call Sally Bell. I need to talk to her, anyway.

LENNY. All right.

CHICK. So you add Great-uncle Spark Dude to your list.

LENNY. Okay.

CHICK. Fine. Well, I've got to get on back home and see to the kids. It is gonna be an uphill struggle till I can find someone to replace that good-for-nothing Annie May Jenkins. Well, you let me know if you hear any more.

LENNY. All right.

CHICK. Goodbye, Rebecca. I said goodbye. *(BABE blows her sax.* CHICK *starts to exit in a flurry, then pauses to add)* And you really ought to try to get that phoning done before twelve noon. *(She exits.)*

LENNY *(after a long pause).* Babe, I feel bad. I feel real bad.

BABE. Why, Lenny?

LENNY. Because yesterday I—I wished it.

BABE. You wished what?

LENNY. I wished that Old Granddaddy would be put out of his pain. I wished it on one of my birthday candles. I did. And now he's in this coma, and they say he's feeling no pain.

BABE. Well, when did you have a cake yesterday? I don't remember you having any cake.

LENNY. Well, I didn't . . . have a cake. But I just blew out the candles, anyway.

BABE. Oh. Well, those birthday wishes don't count, unless you have a cake.

LENNY. They don't?

BABE. No. A lot of times they don't even count when you do have a cake. It just depends.

LENNY. Depends on what?

BABE. On how deep your wish is, I suppose.

LENNY. Still, I just wish I hadn't of wished it. Gosh, I wonder when Meg's coming home.

BABE. Should be soon.

LENNY. I just wish we wouldn't fight all the time. I don't like it when we do.

BABE. Me, neither.

LENNY. I guess it hurts my feelings, a little, the way Old Granddaddy's always put so much stock in Meg and all her singing talent. I think I've been, well, envious of her 'cause I can't seem to do too much.

BABE. Why, sure you can.

LENNY. I can?

BABE. Sure. You just have to put your mind to it, that's all. It's like how I went out and bought that saxophone, just hoping I'd be able to attend music school and start up my own career. I just went out and did it. Just on hope. Of course, now it looks like . . . Well, it just doesn't look like things are gonna work out for me. But I know they would for you.

LENNY. Well, they'll work out for you, too.

BABE. I doubt it.

LENNY. Listen, I heard up at the hospital that Zackery's already in fair condition. They say soon he'll probably be able to walk and everything.

BABE. Yeah. And life sure can be miserable.

LENNY. Well, I know, 'cause—day before yesterday, Billy Boy was struck down by lightning.

BABE. He was?

LENNY (nearing sobs). Yeah. He was struck dead.

BABE (crushed). Life sure can be miserable.

(They sit together for several moments in morbid silence. MEG is heard singing a loud happy song. She suddenly enters through the dining room door. She is exuberant! Her hair is a mess, and the heel of one shoe has broken off. She is laughing radiantly and limping as she sings into the broken heel.)

MEG (spotting her sisters). Good morning! Good morning! Oh, it's a wonderful morning! I tell you, I am surprised I feel this good. I should feel like hell. By all accounts, I should feel like utter hell! (She is looking for the glue.) Where's that glue? This damn heel has broken off my shoe. La, la, la, la, la! Ah, here it is! Now, let me just get these shoes off. Zip, zip, zip, zip, zip! Well, what's wrong with you two? My God, you look like doom!

(BABE and LENNY stare helplessly at MEG.)

MEG. Oh, I know, you're mad at me 'cause I stayed out all night long. Well, I did.

LENNY. No, we're—we're not mad at you.

We're just . . . depressed. (She starts to sob.)

MEG. Oh, Lenny, listen to me, now; everything's all right with Doc. I mean, nothing happened. Well, actually a lot did happen, but it didn't come to anything. Not because of me, I'm afraid. (smearing glue on her heel) I mean, I was out there thinking, What will I say when he begs me to run away with him? Will I have pity on his wife and those two half-Yankee children? I mean, can I sacrifice their happiness for mine? Yes! Oh, Yes! Yes, I can! But . . . he didn't ask me. He didn't even want to ask me. I could tell by this certain look in his eyes that he didn't even want to ask me. Why aren't I miserable! Why aren't I morbid! I should be humiliated! Devastated! Maybe these feelings are coming—I don't know. But for now it was . . . just such fun. I'm happy. I realized I could care about someone. I could want someone. And I sang! I sang all night long! I sang right up into the trees! But not for Old Granddaddy. None of it was to please Old Granddaddy!

(LENNY and BABE look at each other.)

BABE. Ah, Meg—

MEG. What—

BABE. Well, it's just—It's . . .

LENNY. It's about Old Granddaddy—

MEG. Oh, I know; I know. I told him all those stupid lies. Well, I'm gonna go right over there this morning and tell him the truth. I mean every horrible thing. I don't care if he wants to hear it or not. He's just gonna have to take me like I am. And if he can't take it, if it sends him into a coma, that's just too damn bad!

(BABE and LENNY look at each other. BABE cracks a smile. LENNY cracks a smile.)

BABE. You're too late—Ha, ha, ha!

(They both break up laughing.)

LENNY. Oh, stop! Please! Ha, ha, ha!

MEG. What is it? What's so funny?

BABE (still laughing). It's not—It's not funny!

LENNY (still laughing). No, it's not! It's not a bit funny!

MEG. Well, what is it, then? What?

BABE (trying to calm down). Well, it's just—it's just—

MEG. What?

BABE. Well, Old Granddaddy—he—he's in a coma!

(BABE and LENNY break up again.)

MEG. He's what?

BABE (shrieking). In a coma!

MEG. My God! That's not funny!

BABE (calming down). I know. I know. For some reason, it just struck us as funny.

LENNY. I'm sorry. It's—it's not funny. It's sad. It's very sad. We've been up all night long.

BABE. We're really tired.

MEG. Well, my God. How is he? Is he gonna live?

(BABE and LENNY look at each other.)

BABE. They don't think so!

(They both break up again.)

LENNY. Oh, I don't know why we're laughing like this. We're just sick! We're just awful!

BABE. We are—we're awful!

LENNY *(as she collects herself)*. Oh, good; now I feel bad. Now I feel like crying. I do; I feel like crying.

BABE. Me, too. Me, too.

MEG. Well, you've gotten me depressed!

LENNY. I'm sorry. I'm sorry. It, ah, happened last night. He had another stroke.

(They laugh again.)

MEG. I see.

LENNY. But he's stabilized now. *(She chokes up once more.)*

MEG. That's good. You two okay?

(BABE and LENNY nod.)

MEG. You look like you need some rest.

(BABE and LENNY nod again.)

MEG *(going on, about her heel)*. I hope that'll stay. *(She puts the top back on the glue. A realization.)* Oh, of course, now I won't be able to tell him the truth about all those lies I told. I mean, finally I get my wits about me, and he conks out. It's just like him. Babe, can I wear your slippers till this glue dries?

BABE. Sure.

LENNY *(after a pause)*. Things sure are gonna be different around here . . . when Old Grand-daddy dies. Well, not for you two really, but for me.

MEG. It'll work out.

BABE *(depressed)*. Yeah. It'll work out.

LENNY. I hope so. I'm just afraid of being here all by myself. All alone.

MEG. Well, you don't have to be alone. Maybe Babe'll move back in here.

(LENNY looks at BABE hopefully.)

BABE. No, I don't think I'll be living here.

MEG *(realizing her mistake)*. Well, anyway, you're your own woman. Invite some people over. Have some parties. Go out with strange men.

LENNY. I don't know any strange men.

MEG. Well . . . you know that Charlie.

LENNY *(shaking her head)*. Not anymore.

MEG. Why not?

LENNY *(breaking down)*. I told him we should never see each other again.

MEG. Well, if you told him, you can just untell him.

LENNY. Oh, no, I couldn't. I'd feel like a fool.

MEG. Oh, that's not a good enough reason! All people in love feel like fools. Don't they, Babe?

BABE. Sure.

MEG. Look, why don't you give him a call right now? See how things stand.

LENNY. Oh, no! I'd be too scared—

MEG. But what harm could it possibly do? I mean, it's not gonna make things any worse than this never seeing him again, at all, forever.

LENNY. I suppose that's true—

MEG. Of course it is; so call him up! Take a chance, will you? Just take some sort of chance!

LENNY. You think I should?

MEG. Of course! You've got to try—You do!

(LENNY looks over at BABE.)

BABE. You do, Lenny—I think you do.

LENNY. Really? Really, really?

MEG. Yes! Yes!

BABE. You should!

LENNY. All right. I will! I will!

MEG. Oh, good!

BABE. Good!

LENNY. I'll call him right now, while I've got my confidence up!

MEG. Have you got the number?

LENNY. Uh huh. But, ah, I think I wanna call him upstairs. It'll be more private.

MEG. Ah, good idea.

LENNY. I'm just gonna go on and call him up and see what happens—*(She has started up the stairs.)* Wish me good luck!

MEG. Good luck!

BABE. Good luck, Lenny!

LENNY. Thanks.

(LENNY gets almost out of sight when the phone rings. She stops; MEG picks up the phone.)

MEG. Hello? *(then, in a whisper)* Oh, thank you very much . . . Yes, I will. 'Bye, 'bye.

LENNY. Who was it?

MEG. Wrong number. They wanted Weed's Body Shop.

LENNY. Oh. Well, I'll be right back down in a minute. *(She exits.)*

MEG *(after a moment, whispering to BABE)*. That was the bakery; Lenny's cake is ready!

BABE *(who has become increasingly depressed)*. Oh.

MEG. I think I'll sneak on down to the corner and pick it up. *(She starts to leave.)*

BABE. Meg—

MEG. What?

BABE. Nothing.

MEG. You okay?

(BABE *shakes her head.*)

MEG. What is it?

BABE. It's just—

MEG. What?

(BABE *gets the envelope containing the photographs.*)

BABE. Here. Take a look.

MEG *(taking the envelope).* What is it?

BABE. It's some evidence Zackery's collected against me. Looks like my goose is cooked.

(MEG *opens the envelope and looks at the photographs.*)

MEG. My God, it's—it's you and . . . is *that* Willie Jay?

BABE. Yah.

MEG. Well, he certainly *has* grown. You were right about that. My, oh, my.

BABE. Please don't tell Lenny. She'd hate me.

MEG. I won't. I won't tell Lenny. *(putting the pictures back into the envelope)* What are you gonna do?

BABE. What can I do?

(*There is a knock on the door.* BABE *grabs the envelope and hides it.*)

MEG. Who is it?

BARNETTE'S VOICE. It's Barnette Lloyd.

MEG. Oh. Come on in, Barnette.

(BARNETTE *enters. His eyes are ablaze with excitement.*)

BARNETTE *(as he paces around the room).* Well, good morning! *(shaking* MEG's *hand)* Good morning, Miss MaGrath. *(touching* BABE *on the shoulder)* Becky. *(moving away)* What I meant to say is, How are you doing this morning?

MEG. Ah—fine. Fine.

BARNETTE. Good. Good. I—I just had time to drop by for a minute.

MEG. Oh.

BARNETTE. So, ah, how's your granddad doing?

MEG. Well, not very, ah—ah, he's in this coma. *(She breaks up laughing.)*

BARNETTE. I see . . . I see. *(to* BABE*)* Actually, the primary reason I came by was to pick up that—envelope. I left it here last night in all the confusion. *(pause)* You, ah, still do have it?

(BABE *hands him the envelope.*)

BARNETTE. Yes. *(taking the envelope)* That's the one. I'm sure it'll be much better off in my office safe. *(He puts the envelope into his coat pocket.)*

MEG. I'm sure it will.

BARNETTE. Beg your pardon?

BABE. It's all right. I showed her the pictures.

BARNETTE. Ah; I see.

MEG. So what's going to happen now, Barnette? What are those pictures gonna mean?

BARNETTE *(after pacing a moment).* Hmmm. May I speak frankly and openly?

BABE. Uh huh.

MEG. Please do—

BARNETTE. Well, I tell you now, at first glance, I admit those pictures had me considerably perturbed and upset. Perturbed to the point that I spent most of last night going over certain suspect papers and reports that had fallen into my hands—rather recklessly.

BABE. What papers do you mean?

BARNETTE. Papers that, pending word from three varied and unbiased experts, could prove graft, fraud, forgery, as well as a history of unethical behavior.

MEG. You mean about Zackery?

BARNETTE. Exactly. You see, I now intend to make this matter just as sticky and gritty for one Z. Botrelle as it is for us. Why, with the amount of scandal I'll dig up, Botrelle will be forced to settle this affair on our own terms!

MEG. Oh, Babe! Did you hear that?

BABE. Yes! Oh, yes! So you've won it! You've won your lifelong vendetta!

BARNETTE. Well . . . well, now of course it's problematic in that, well, in that we won't be able to expose him openly in the courts. That was the original game plan.

BABE. But why not? Why?

BARNETTE. Well, it's only that if, well, if a jury were to—to get, say, a glance at these, ah, photographs, well . . . well, possibly . . .

BABE. We could be sunk.

BARNETTE. In a sense. But! On the other hand, if a newspaper were to get a hold of our little item, Mr. Zackery Botrelle could find himself boiling in some awfully hot water. So what I'm looking for, very simply, is—a deal.

BABE. A deal?

MEG. Thank you, Barnette. It's a sunny day, Babe. *(realizing she is in the way)* Ooh, where's that broken shoe? *(She grabs her boots and runs upstairs.)*

BABE. So, you're having to give up your vendetta?

BARNETTE. Well, in a way. For the time. It, ah, seems to me you shouldn't always let your life be ruled by such things as, ah, personal vendettas. *(looking at* BABE *with meaning)* Other things can be important.

BABE. I don't know, I don't exactly know. How 'bout Willie Jay? Will he be all right?

BARNETTE. Yes, it's all been taken care of. He'll be leaving incognito on the midnight bus—heading north.

BABE. North.

BARNETTE. I'm sorry, it seemed the only . . . way.

(BARNETTE *moves to her; she moves away.*)

BABE. Look, you'd better be getting on back to your work.

BARNETE *(awkwardly).* Right—'cause I— I've got those important calls out. *(full of hope for her)* They'll be pouring in directly. *(He starts to leave, then says to her with love)* We'll talk.

MEG *(reappearing in her boots).* Oh, Barnette—

BARNETTE. Yes?

MEG. Could you give me a ride just down to the corner? I need to stop at Helen's Bakery.

BARNETTE. Be glad to.

MEG. Thanks. Listen, Babe, I'll be right back with the cake. We're gonna have the best celebration! Now, ah, if Lenny asks where I've gone, just say I'm . . . Just say, I've gone out back to, ah, pick up some pawpaws! Okay?

BABE. Okay.

MEG. Fine; I'll be back in a bit. Goodbye.

BABE. 'Bye.

BARNETTE. Goodbye, Becky.

BABE. Goodbye, Barnette. Take care.

(MEG *and* BARNETTE *exit.* BABE *sits staring ahead, in a stage of deep despair.*)

BABE. Goodbye, Becky. Goodbye, Barnette. Goodbye, Becky. *(She stops when* LENNY *comes down the stairs in a fluster.)*

LENNY. Oh! Oh! Oh! I'm so ashamed! I'm such a coward! I'm such a yellow-bellied chicken! I'm so ashamed! Where's Meg?

BABE *(suddenly bright).* She's, ah—gone out back—to pick up some pawpaws.

LENNY. Oh. Well, at least I don't have to face her! I just couldn't do it! I couldn't make the call! My heart was pounding like a hammer. Pound! Pound! Pound! Why I looked down and I could actually see my blouse moving back and forth! Oh, Babe, you look so disappointed. Are you?

BABE *(despondently).* Uh huh.

LENNY. Oh, no! I've disappointed Babe! I can't stand it! I've gone and disappointed my little sister, Babe! Oh, no! I feel like howling like a dog!

CHICK'S VOICE. Oooh, Lenny! *(She enters dramatically, dripping with sympathy.)* Well,

I just don't know what to say! I'm so sorry! I am so sorry for you! And for little Babe here, too. I mean, to have such a sister as that!

LENNY. What do you mean?

CHICK. Oh, you don't need to pretend with me. I saw it all from over there in my own back yard; I saw Meg stumbling out of Doc Porter's pickup truck, not fifteen minutes ago. And her looking such a disgusting mess. You must be so ashamed! You must just want to die! Why, I always said that girl was nothing but cheap Christmas trash!

LENNY. Don't talk that way about Meg.

CHICK. Oh, come on now, Lenny honey, I know exactly how you feel about Meg. Why, Meg's a low-class tramp and you need not have one more blessed thing to do with her and her disgusting behavior.

LENNY. I said, don't you ever talk that way about my sister Meg again.

CHICK. Well, my goodness gracious, Lenora, don't be such a noodle—it's the truth!

LENNY. I don't care if it's the Ten Commandments. I don't want to hear it in my home. Not ever again.

CHICK. In your home?! Why, I never in all my life—This is my grandfather's home! And you're just living here on his charity; so don't you get high-falutin' with me, Miss Lenora Josephine MaGrath!

LENNY. Get out of here—

CHICK. Don't you tell me to get out! What makes you think you can order me around? Why, I've had just about my fill of you trashy MaGraths and your trashy ways: hanging yourselves in cellars; carrying on with married men; shooting your own husbands!

LENNY. Get out!

CHICK *(to* BABE*).* And don't you think she's not gonna end up at the state prison farm or in some—mental institution. Why, it's a clearcut case of manslaughter with intent to kill!

LENNY. Out! Get out!

CHICK *(running on).* That's what everyone's saying, deliberate intent to kill! And you'll pay for that! Do you hear me? You'll pay!

LENNY *(picking up a broom and threatening* CHICK *with it).* And I'm telling you to get out!

CHICK. You—you put that down this minute—Are you a raving lunatic?

LENNY *(beating* CHICK *with the broom).* I said for you to get out! That means out! And never, never, never come back!

CHICK *(overlapping as she runs around the room).* Oh! Oh! Oh! You're crazy! You're crazy!

LENNY *(chasing* CHICK *out the door).* Do

you hear me, Chick the Stick! This is my home! This is my house! Get out! Out!

CHICK *(overlapping)*. Oh! Oh! Police! Police! You're crazy! Help! Help!

(LENNY chases CHICK out of the house. They are both screaming. The phone rings. BABE goes and picks it up.)

BABE. Hello? . . . Oh, hello, Zackery! . . . Yes, he showed them to me! . . . You're what! . . . What do you mean? . . . What! . . . You can't put me out to Whitfield . . . 'Cause I'm not crazy . . . I'm not! I'm not! . . . She wasn't crazy, either . . . Don't you call my mother crazy! . . . No, you're not! You're not gonna. You're not! *(She slams the phone down and stares wildly ahead.)* He's not. He's not. *(As she walks over to the ribbon drawer)* I'll do it. I will. And he won't . . . *(She opens the drawer, pulls out the rope, becomes terrified, throws the rope back in the drawer, and slams it shut.)*

(LENNY enters from the back door swinging the broom and laughing.)

LENNY. Oh, my! Oh, my! You should have seen us! Why, I chased Chick the Stick right up the mimosa tree. I did! I left her right up there screaming in the tree!

BABE *(laughing; she is insanely delighted)*. Oh, you did!

LENNY. Yes, I did! And I feel so good! I do! I feel good! I feel good!

BABE *(overlapping)*. Good! Good, Lenny! Good for you!

(They dance around the kitchen.)

LENNY *(stopping)*. You know what—

BABE. What?

LENNY. I'm gonna call Charlie! I'm gonna call him up right now!

BABE. You are?

LENNY. Yeah, I feel like I can really do it!

BABE. You do?

LENNY. My courage is up; my heart's in it; the time is right! No more beating around the bush! Let's strike while the iron is hot!

BABE. Right! Right! No more beating around the bush! Strike while the iron is hot!

(LENNY goes to the phone. BABE rushes over to the ribbon drawer. She begins tearing through it.)

LENNY *(with the receiver in her hand)*. I'm calling him up, Babe—I'm really gonna do it!

BABE *(still tearing through the drawer)*. Good! Do it! Good!

LENNY *(as she dials)*. Look. My hands aren't even shaking.

BABE *(pulling out a red rope)*. Don't we have any stronger rope than this?

LENNY. I guess not. All the rope we've got's in that drawer. *(about her hands)* Now they're shaking a little.

(BABE takes the rope and goes up the stairs. LENNY finishes dialing the number. She waits for an answer.)

LENNY. Hello? . . . Hello, Charlie. This is Lenny MaGrath . . . Well, I'm fine. I'm just fine. *(an awkward pause)* I was, ah, just calling to see—how you're getting on . . . Well, good. Good . . . Yes, I know I said that. Now I wish I didn't say it . . . Well, the reason I said that before, about not seeing each other again, was 'cause of me, not you . . . Well, it's just I—I can't have any children. I—have this ovary problem . . . Why, Charlie, what a thing to say! . . . Well, they're not all little snot-nosed pigs! . . . You think they are! . . . Oh, Charlie, stop, stop! You're making me laugh . . . Yes, I guess I was. I can see now that I was . . . You are? . . . Well, I'm dying to see you, too . . . Well, I don't know when, Charlie . . . soon. How about, well, how about tonight? . . . You will? . . . Oh, you will! . . . All right, I'll be here. I'll be right here . . . Goodbye, then, Charlie. Goodbye for now. *(She hangs up the phone in a daze.)* Babe. Oh, Babe! He's coming! He's coming! Babe! Oh, Babe, where are you? Meg! Oh . . . out back—picking up paw-paws. *(as she exits through the back door)* And those paw-paws are just ripe for picking up!

(There is a moment of silence; then a loud, horrible thud is heard coming from upstairs. The telephone begins ringing immediately. It rings five times before BABE comes hurrying down the stairs with a broken piece of rope hanging around her neck. The phone continues to ring.)

BABE *(to the phone)*. Will you shut up! *(She is jerking the rope from around her neck. She grabs a knife to cut it off.)* Cheap! Miserable! I hate you! I hate you! *(She throws the rope violently across the room. The phone stops ringing.)* Thank God. *(She looks at the stove, goes over to it, and turns the gas on. The sound of gas escaping is heard. She sniffs at it.)* Come on. Come on . . . Hurry up . . . I beg of you—hurry up! *(Finally, she feels the oven is ready; she takes a deep breath and opens the oven door to stick her head into it. She spots the rack and furiously jerks it out. Taking another breath, she sticks her head into the oven. She stands for several moments tapping her fingers furiously on top of the stove. She speaks from inside the oven)* Oh, please. Please. *(After a few moments, she reaches for the box of matches with her head still in the oven. She tries to strike a match. It doesn't catch.)* Oh, Mama, please! *(She throws the match away and is getting a second one.)* Mama . . . Mama . . . So that's why you done it! *(In her excitement she starts to get up, bangs her head, and falls back in the oven.)*

(MEG enters from the back door, carrying a birthday cake in a pink box.)

MEG. Babe! *(She throws the box down and runs to pull* BABE'*s head out of the oven.)* Oh, my God! What are you doing? What the hell are you doing?

BABE *(dizzily)*. Nothing. I don't know. Nothing. *(MEG turns off the gas and moves* BABE *to a chair near the open door.)*

MEG. Sit down. Sit down! Will you sit down!

BABE. I'm okay. I'm okay.

MEG. Put your head between your knees and breathe deep!

BABE. Meg—

MEG. Just do it! I'll get you some water. *(She gets some water for* BABE.*)* Here.

BABE. Thanks.

MEG. Are you okay?

BABE. Uh huh.

MEG. Are you sure?

BABE. Yeah, I'm sure. I'm okay.

MEG *(getting a damp rag and pulling it over her own face)*. Well, good. That's good.

BABE. Meg—

MEG. Yes?

BABE. I know why she did it.

MEG. What? Why who did what?

BABE *(with joy)*. Mama. I know why she hung that cat along with her.

MEG. You do?

BABE *(with enlightenment)*. It's 'cause she was afraid of dying all alone.

MEG. Was she?

BABE. She felt so unsure, you know, as to what was coming. It seems the best thing coming up would be a lot of angels and all of them singing. But I imagine they have high, scary voices and little gold pointed fingers that are as sharp as blades and you don't want to meet 'em all alone. You'd be afraid to meet 'em all alone. So it wasn't like what people were saying about her hating that cat. Fact is, she loved that cat. She needed him with her 'cause she felt so all alone.

MEG. Oh, Babe . . . Babe. Why, Babe? Why?

BABE. Why what?

MEG. Why did you stick your head into the oven?!

BABE. I don't know. Meg. I'm having a bad day. It's been a real bad day; those pictures, and Barnette giving up his vendetta; then Willie Jay heading north; and—and Zackery called me up. *(trembling with terror)* He says he's gonna have me classified insane and then send me on out to the Whitfield asylum.

MEG. What! Why, he could never do that!

BABE. Why not?

MEG. 'Cause you're not insane.

BABE. I'm not?

MEG. No! He's trying to bluff you. Don't you see it? Barnette's got him running scared.

BABE. Really?

MEG. Sure. He's scared to death—calling you insane. Ha! Why, you're just as perfectly sane as anyone walking the streets of Hazlehurst, Mississippi.

BABE. I am?

MEG. More so! A lot more so!

BABE. Good!

MEG. But, Babe, we've just got to learn how to get through these real bad days here. I mean, it's getting to be a thing in our family. *(slight pause as she looks at* BABE*)* Come on, now. Look, we've got Lenny's cake right here. I mean, don't you wanna be around to give her her cake, watch her blow out the candles?

BABE *(realizing how much she wants to be here)*. Yeah, I do, I do. 'Cause she always loves to make her birthday wishes on those candles.

MEG. Well, then we'll give her her cake and maybe you won't be so miserable.

BABE. Okay.

MEG. Good. Go on and take it out of the box.

BABE. Okay. *(She takes the cake out of the box. It is a magical moment.)* Gosh, it's a pretty cake.

MEG *(handing her some matches)*. Here now. You can go on and light up the candles.

BABE. All right. *(She starts to light the candles.)* I love to light up candles. And there are so many here. Thirty pink ones in all, plus one green one tó grow on.

MEG *(watching her light the candles)*. They're pretty.

BABE. They are. *(She stops lighting the candles.)* And I'm not like Mama. I'm not so all alone.

MEG. You're not.

BABE *(as she goes back to lighting candles)*. Well, you'd better keep an eye out for Lenny. She's supposed to be surprised.

MEG. All right. Do you know where she's gone?

BABE. Well, she's not here inside—so she

must have gone on outside.

MEG. Oh, well, then I'd better run and find her.

BABE. Okay; 'cause these candles are gonna melt down.

(MEG starts out the door.)

MEG. Wait—there she is coming. Lenny! Oh, Lenny! Come on! Hurry up!

BABE *(overlapping and improvising as she finishes lighting candles)*. Oh, no! No! Well, yes—Yes! No, wait! Wait! Okay! Hurry up!

(LENNY enters. MEG covers LENNY's eyes with her hands.)

LENNY *(terrified)*. What? What is it? What?

MEG and BABE. Surprise! Happy birthday! Happy birthday to Lenny!

LENNY. Oh, no! Oh, me! What a surprise! I could just cry! Oh, look: *Happy birthday, Lenny—A Day Late!* How cute! My! Will you look at all those candles—it's absolutely frightening.

BABE *(a spontaneous thought)*. Oh, no, Lenny, it's good! 'Cause—'cause the more candles you have on your cake, the stronger your wish is.

LENNY. Really?

BABE. Sure!

LENNY. Mercy! *(MEG and BABE start to sing.)*

LENNY *(interrupting the song)*. Oh, but wait! I—can't think of my wish! My body's gone all nervous inside.

MEG. For God's sake, Lenny—Come on!

BABE. The wax is all melting!

LENNY. My mind is just a blank, a total blank!

MEG. Will you please just—

BABE *(overlapping)*. Lenny, hurry! Come on!

LENNY. Okay! Okay! Just go!

(MEG and BABE burst into the "Happy Birthday" song. As it ends, LENNY blows out all the candles on the cake. MEG and BABE applaud loudly.)

MEG. Oh, you made it!

BABE. Hurray!

LENNY. Oh, me! Oh, me! I hope that wish comes true! I hope it does!

BABE. Why? What did you wish for?

LENNY *(as she removes the candles from the cake)*. Why, I can't tell you that.

BABE. Oh, sure you can—

LENNY. Oh, no! Then it won't come true.

BABE. Why, that's just superstition! Of course it will, if you made it deep enough.

MEG. Really? I didn't know that.

LENNY. Well, Babe's the regular expert on birthday wishes.

BABE. It's just I get these feelings. Now, come on and tell us. What was it you wished for?

MEG. Yes, tell us. What was it?

LENNY. Well, I guess it wasn't really a specific wish. This—this vision just sort of came into my mind.

BABE. A vision? What was it of?

LENNY. I don't know exactly. It was something about the three of us smiling and laughing together.

BABE. Well, when was it? Was it far away or near?

LENNY. I'm not sure; but it wasn't forever; it wasn't for every minute. Just this one moment and we were all laughing.

BABE. Then, what were we laughing about?

LENNY. I don't know. Just nothing, I guess.

MEG. Well, that's a nice wish to make.

(LENNY and MEG look at each other a moment.)

MEG. Here, now, I'll get a knife so we can go ahead and cut the cake in celebration of Lenny being born!

BABE. Oh, yes! And give each one of us a rose. A whole rose apiece!

LENNY *(cutting the cake nervously)*. Well, I'll try—I'll try!

MEG *(licking the icing off a candle)*. Mmmm—this icing is delicious! Here, try some!

BABE. Mmmm! It's wonderful! Here, Lenny!

LENNY *(laughing joyously as she licks icing from her fingers and cuts huge pieces of cake that her sisters bite into ravenously)*. Oh, how I do love having birthday cake for breakfast! How I do!

(The sisters freeze for a moment laughing and catching cake. The lights change and frame them in a magical, golden, sparkling glimmer; saxophone music is heard. The lights dim to blackout, and the saxophone continues to play.)

CURTAIN